P9-CQM-080

ENCYCLOPEDIA OF ANTIQUES

Editors	Ian Cameron
	Elizabeth Kingsley-Rowe
Designer	Tom Carter
Researchers	Mimi Errington
	Adriana Davies
	Elisabeth Cameron
Picture researcher	Philippa Lewis
Additional researchers	Carolyn Eardley
	Frances Kennett
	Mary Clark
	Jane Lewis
	Margaret Wiener
	Karen de Groot
	Ada Lynn
Photographers	Angelo Hornak
	Karin Hoddle
Editorial Consultants	Hugo Morley-Fletcher
	Julia Raynsford
	Shirley Bury
	Beresford Hutchinson
	Claude Blair
	Gabriella Gros-Galliner
	Ian Venture
	Phillis Rogers
	Tom Errington
	Michael I. Wilson
	Anthony Radcliffe

In compiling a book covering the whole field of antiques, the editors have drawn on the knowledge and experience of specialists, who are listed here as editorial consultants. A book of this sort has to work to the most rigorous editorial scheme in order to achieve the necessary consistency of treatment. The final content of the book, and any errors which may have crept into it, can therefore be attributed only to the editorial team.

The Encyclopedia Of
ANTIQUES

with Introduction by

SIR JOHN POPE-HENNESSY

Greenwich House
New York

Frontispiece: library by Robert Adam at Kenwood House, London.

This 1982 edition is published by Greenwich House, a division of Arlington House, Inc., distributed by Crown Publishers, Inc. by arrangement with Ottenheimer Publishers, Inc.

The editors wish to thank John Culme for his help with the silver entries. Other contributors and consultants are listed on pI. Photographic credits appear on pp 399 and 400.

First published in Great Britain by William Collins Sons & Co. Ltd.

Previously published in the United States by Random House Inc.

Printed in Spain

Library of Congress Cataloging in Publication Data
Main entry under title:

The Encyclopedia of antiques.

Bibliography: p.
1. Antiques—Dictionaries.
[NK28.E5 1982] 745.1'03'21 82-6227
ISBN 0-517-38197-4 AACR2

h g f e d c b a

INTRODUCTION

Encyclopedias of art are legion. This book is, however, something rather different; it is devoted to the applied arts, and is the first fully efficient Encyclopedia of Antiques. To establish the difference in practical terms, it is sufficient to say that under the first letter of the alphabet the reader will find an excellent entry on John Arnold, the eighteenth century maker of chronometers, but none on Arnolfo di Cambio, while under the second letter the sculptors Boizot and Giovanni Bologna are dealt with in the context respectively of Sèvres biscuit figures and bronze statuettes. This clear focus is maintained through the whole book, and the result is a volume from which information about the applied arts, designers and factories, styles and techniques, can be obtained as effortlessly as information on painters, sculptors and architects from earlier dictionaries.

No one who is in charge of a museum can doubt that there is a place for such a book. Day by day and week by week, the prices fetched at auction by works of applied art are reported in *The Times* and other newspapers, and the result has been a sharp increase in the number of museum visitors requiring information about objects that they own. It is felt, perfectly correctly, that when for the first time in history antiques are in short supply, almost anything may prove to be of interest or significance. And so it may, for the first result of shortage is that taste widens and readjusts, till it embraces artefacts which would not have been considered by earlier collectors or which were made in the recent past. In the present book the definition of the term 'antiques' is necessarily flexible, but the entries relate in the main to a period between the early fifteenth and late nineteenth centuries.

Their scope is factual. They are conceived, that is to say, not as loose-knit critical essays on the topics with which they deal, but as summaries in which the available information is faithfully condensed. The success with which this process of distillation has been achieved can be judged from the entries dealing with the treacherous subject of styles (Biedermeier is a good example), or with the often complex history of the centres of ceramic manufacture, for instance porcelain in Berlin. Time was when the study of these topics, especially of furniture, was no more than approximate, but thanks to years of pertinacious investigation, much of it conducted in museums, what was once a tissue of hypotheses based on received opinion has in many cases been translated into historically demonstrable fact. From this standpoint, the comprehensive, accurate review of the whole field which is supplied in this encyclopedia is very welcome.

This book is addressed primarily to collectors, and for this reason the categories of works of art that are generally available for purchase are dealt with more fully than others which may be of greater value but are less readily procurable. Its merits are the merits of a book written with the help of experienced specialists for the general public, and particularly for those members of the public, and they are very numerous, who buy works of art.

The field it covers is, however, so vast that anyone who is professionally concerned with works of art is likely to find in it information that is useful and relative to his activities.

The main impulsion towards collecting is the simple fact that it is more agreeable to live against a background of antiques, or works which recall the civilised responses of other generations than our own, than in the sparsely furnished rooms that are illustrated in the Sunday colour supplements. Most collectors start in a comparatively modest way. They are casually attracted by this object or that, some piece of silver or faïence, perhaps; they buy it for no other reason than that it gives them pleasure; before long, they find themselves buying other pieces of the same kind; and then, with scarcely the least transition, they move on to works in other media, sometimes of the same date and style, sometimes from a different culture of which they know nothing at all. At this point, they feel the need to adopt a more professional approach to the whole business of collecting. This may take the negative form of fear of being taken in by dealers, who – so their commonsense assures them – are not always as disinterested as they appear, or the positive form of a wish to secure objects which are not just average examples of standard artefacts, but in some respect or other, preferably in that enigmatic attribute that we call quality, can be regarded as exceptional. Once the moment of conversion occurs, quite a number of courses are open to them. There are regular articles in the daily press that they can read, there are magazines to which they can subscribe, and if they are really diligent, they can climb the stairs of the Victoria and Albert Museum and visit its serried study collections.

But even if they do all these things, they may still feel at sea – in the museum because, in addition to the little group of works that they are studying, they will encounter thousands of bewildering objects of which they know nothing at all, and with magazines and occasional articles because they are filled with technical descriptive terms of which some may be ambiguous and others will require to be explained. It is then that they must turn (if they have not in common prudence done so earlier) to the *Encyclopedia of Antiques*. One of the strongest and most constructive human instincts is curiosity. When we wish to praise collectors, we habitually commend their eyes, but the truth is that eyes are not of much avail unless they are directed by an inquisitive intelligence. One of the most important things about this book is that it panders to curiosity. If you walk up Kensington Church Street or along the Portobello Road, and see in some shop window a cup said to have been made at Kelsterbach or at the Hague, it will tell you, exactly but succinctly, what is known about these factories. If you cannot quite remember the dates between which red tôle was made at Pontypool, you will find them here. If you are not absolutely clear as to the meaning of expressions like 'tin enamel glaze' or 'cracked ice ground', here they are elucidated. If you want to know how a '*commode à encoignures*' differs from a '*commode à vantaux*', you have only to look up the two terms in this encyclopedia. And if you read on the front page of *The Times* that some piece of Ju ware has fetched much more money than it should have done, or that a piece of Kamakura lacquer work has been bought for a museum, you have only to look up the entries for Ju ware and Kamakura and lacquer for the mystery to be explained.

The function of encyclopedias is not only to quench curiosity but to provoke it, and working through the entries in this volume, I have found repeatedly that they operate precisely in this way. For every entry which answers some question in one's mind, there is a contiguous entry from which new questions spring. For this reason, I hope that the *Encyclopedia* will not be treated merely as a dictionary, which is pulled out of the shelf only to resolve a state of doubt, but will be looked on rather as a book for casual reading, which can be relied on to enlarge the horizons of everybody who consults it and which will prove a continuing source of pleasure and enlightenment.

JOHN POPE-HENNESSY

ABOUT THIS BOOK

Any single volume encyclopedia has to work within clearly defined limits if it is to be an effective work of reference. This book has a firm end date for its coverage: 1875, which restricts it to antiques in the strict sense of objects more than a hundred years old. The starting date is necessarily vaguer, corresponding roughly to the beginning of the Renaissance in Europe. However, it did not seem justifiable to extend this criterion outside Europe. Earlier Islamic products are dealt with as they are relevant to styles and techniques used later in Europe. The treatment of the Far East appeared to require extending back many centuries to the archaic cultures.

Subject limitations have been more rigorously imposed in order to concentrate the coverage on the more important categories of antiques. Thus we have excluded painters except where their designs appear on, say, ceramics or tapestries, architects except where they have influenced furniture styles, and sculptors except where their work has appeared as small bronzes or ceramic figures. We have not attempted to deal with anything involving paper and print, again except where it affects antiques: there is no coverage of maps and prints, old books and fine bindings, or printed ephemera. Other specific exclusions are coins and medals, dolls and children's play-things, needlework, militaria, and ethnographica. The general criterion for inclusion has been that an object or class of objects must have been intended to have some aesthetic appeal – there is thus little coverage of primitive domestic equipment and none at all in the area of industrial archaeology. Key examples from museums are covered, but otherwise the choice of entries has been slanted towards collectable antiques.

Within the chosen limits, our aim has been to compress the maximum amount of information into the available space, using a highly condensed style to avoid relying on abbreviations. We have carefully removed any expressions of personal tastes and opinions, always keeping it in mind that the users of an encyclopedia will be looking for facts, and that any dilution of the factual content would be a fault in a book of this sort. The alphabetical structure has been chosen to make the facts easily accessible. Rather than embedding them in long articles, we have split up the book into a large number of usually brief entries, providing cross-references for alternative names and spellings. Except for biographical entries, which are listed under surnames, all article headings are given in their usual word order, i.e. 'soft-paste porcelain' not 'porcelain, soft-paste', and 'English silver' not 'silver, English'.

Our aim has been to make the book valuable to as wide a readership as possible. However, we have not avoided technical terminology as the attempt is likely to result in inadequate paraphrases which would dismay the more knowledgeable reader. Instead, all the terms we have used which are not standard English are defined in the book. These definitions are simply there for anyone who needs them. They are not cross-referenced and are assumed in the other entries.

Cross references are indicated by asterisks, which are used in most articles only where following the reference through will provide the reader with further information that is specifically about the subject he has initially looked up. In addition, asterisks are used to mark all mentions of people who have entries in the book. In the most general articles, such as national entries, cross-reference asterisks are used more liberally to give an indication of the range of more specific related entries. In captions, asterisks are used to show entries elsewhere in the book that are represented in the illustrations.

The entries themselves present very compact summaries of the information available. This has meant shearing away a mass of subtleties and qualifications, and trying to concentrate on the more typical examples. Therefore generalizations should not be read as categorical. The statement that something is round or square should not be taken to imply that it is never, say, triangular or hexagonal. The principle applies particularly to materials – many objects were made in a wide range of materials, not all of which will necessarily be mentioned. If an item is described as being silver or glass, this should not be taken as a statement that it was not made in ceramics – indeed, the large number of silver shapes imitated in ceramics makes it very likely that it was.

Apart from the main alphabetical sequence of entries, the book contains sections of maps and marks as well as a bibliography. The maps indicate most of the centres of production mentioned in the main text; the boundaries shown are modern ones. No brief appendix can give an adequately detailed selection of silver and ceramic marks; rather than make a pretence of balanced coverage, we have chosen to limit ourselves to the date letter systems of the four surviving British assay offices and to the ceramic marks which require illustration to supplement the descriptions in the text. The bibliography is arranged under alphabetical headings in the same way as the main text. Only books in English are mentioned – many of the books listed have bibliographies giving the main works in other languages. Books which are still useful have been included even if they are long out of print, as they will be obtainable through libraries.

MAPS

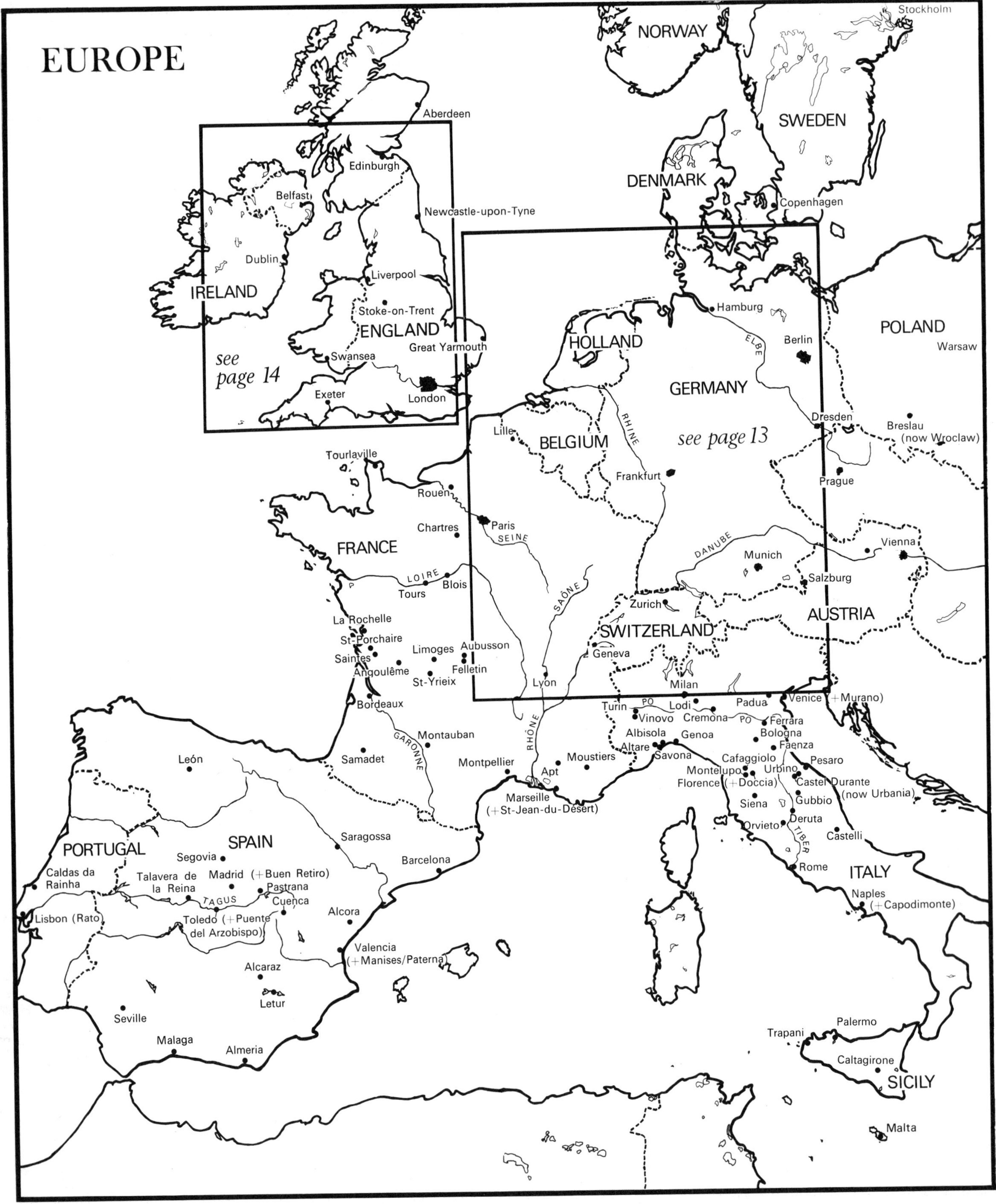
EUROPE
NORWAY
Stockholm
SWEDEN
Aberdeen
Edinburgh
DENMARK
Copenhagen
Belfast
Newcastle-upon-Tyne
Dublin
Liverpool
IRELAND
Stoke-on-Trent
ENGLAND
Great Yarmouth
see page 14
Swansea
Exeter
London
Hamburg
ELBE
Berlin
POLAND
Warsaw
HOLLAND
GERMANY
Dresden
Breslau (now Wroclaw)
Lille
BELGIUM
RHINE
see page 13
Frankfurt
Prague
Tourlaville
Rouen
Paris
SEINE
Chartres
FRANCE
DANUBE
Munich
Vienna
LOIRE
Tours
Blois
Salzburg
SAÔNE
Zurich
AUSTRIA
La Rochelle
SWITZERLAND
St-Porchaire
Saintes
Limoges
Aubusson
Geneva
Angoulême
Felletin
St-Yrieix
Lyon
Milan
Bordeaux
Turin
PO
Lodi
Padua
Venice (+Murano)
Vinovo
Cremona
Ferrara
Albisola
Genoa
Bologna
Montauban
GARONNE
RHÔNE
Altare
Faenza
León
Samadet
Montpellier
Moustiers
Savona
Cafaggiolo
Pesaro
Apt
Montelupo
Urbino
Florence (+Doccia)
Castel Durante (now Urbania)
Marseille (+St-Jean-du-Désert)
Siena
Gubbio
Deruta
Orvieto
Castelli
PORTUGAL
SPAIN
Saragossa
TIBER
Segovia
Barcelona
Rome
ITALY
Caldas da Rainha
Talavera de la Reina
Madrid (+Buen Retiro)
Pastrana
TAGUS
Cuenca
Naples (+Capodimonte)
Lisbon (Rato)
Toledo (+Puente del Arzobispo)
Alcora
Valencia (+Manises/Paterna)
Alcaraz
Letur
Seville
Palermo
Trapani
Malaga
Almeria
Caltagirone
SICILY
Malta

NORTHERN EUROPE
Rendsburg
Kiel
Petersdorf
Stralsund
Kellinghusen
Hamburg
Jever
ELBE
Leeuwarden
Bolsward
HOLLAND
Lesum
Haarlem
Amsterdam
Weesp
The Hague
Delft
Utrecht
Rotterdam
GERMANY
Berlin
Plaue
Potsdam
Zerbst
RHINE
Antwerp
Oudenaarde
Brussels
Lille
Tournai
Enghien
St-Amand-les-Eaux
Douai
Arras
BELGIUM
Raeren
Cologne
Siegburg
Iserlohn
Cassel
Munden
Fürstenberg
Halle
Hubertusburg
Wallendorf
Meissen
Dresden
Gotha
Erfurt
Ilmenau
Limbach
Gera
Freiburg
Höhr/Grenzhausen
Fulda
Groszbreitenbach
Hanau
Höchst
Frankfurt (+Flörsheim/Kelsterbach)
Bayreuth
Kreussen
Würzburg
Frankenthal
Beauvais
Sinceny
St-Gobain
Creil
Chantilly
Reims
Paris
Mennecy
FRANCE
Ottweiler
Pfalz-Zweibrücken
St-Louis
Mosbach
Crailsheim
Ansbach
Nuremberg
Durlach
Ellwangen
Oettingen-Schrattenhofen
Ludwigsburg
Nancy
Lunéville
St-Clément
Baccarat
Niderviller
Strasbourg
SEINE
Fontainebleau
Troyes
Bellegarde
Auxerre
Schramberg
DANUBE
Augsburg
Göggingen
Passau
Munich (+Nymphenburg)
Salzburg
Beaucourt
Zurich
Winterthur
La Chaux-de-Fonds
Neuchâtel
Fleurier
AUSTRIA
SWITZERLAND
Nevers
LOIRE
RHÔNE
Nyon
ITALY
Lyon
Milan
Bassano (Angarano/Le Nove)

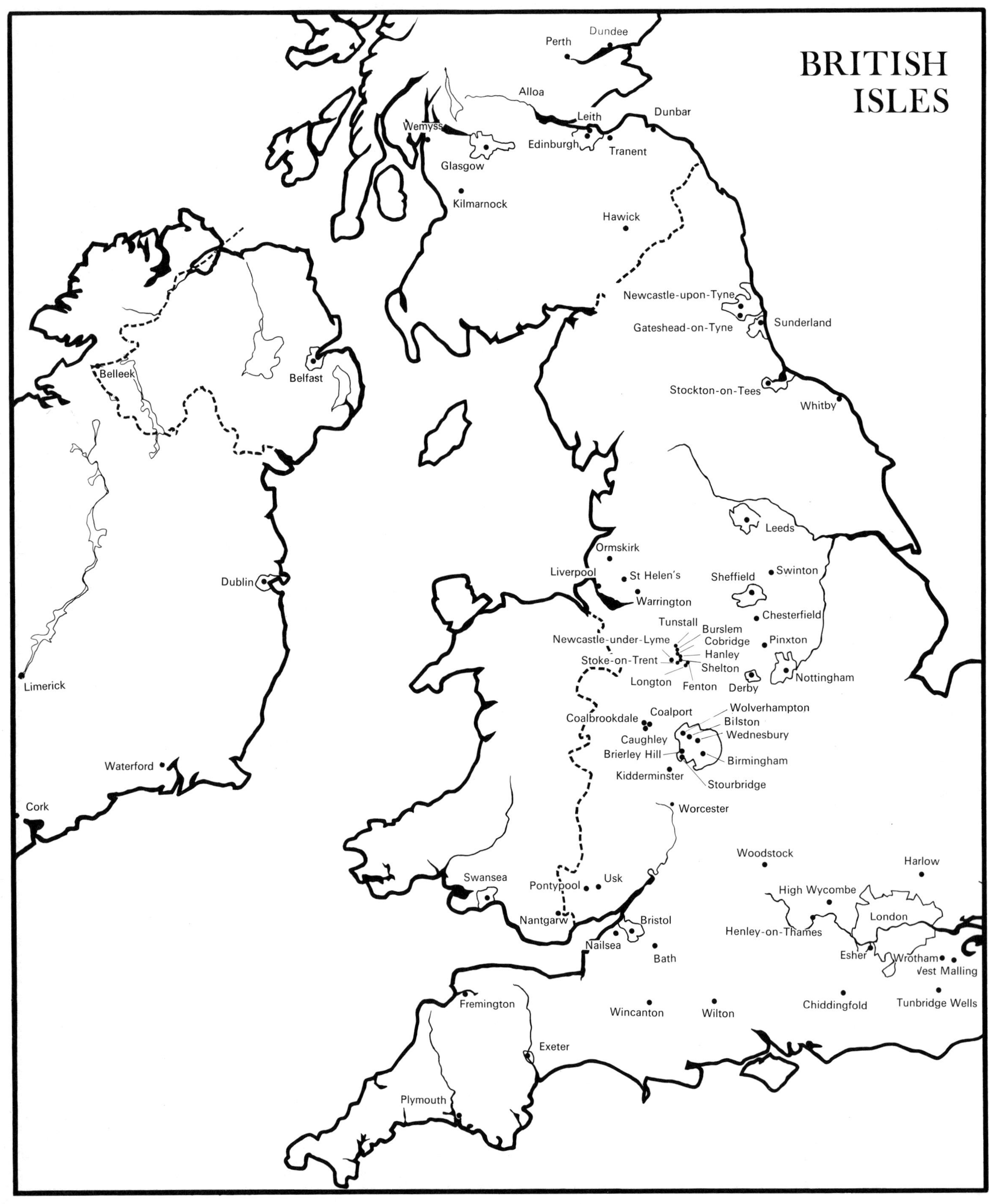
BRITISH ISLES
Perth
Dundee
Alloa
Leith
Dunbar
Wemyss
Edinburgh
Tranent
Glasgow
Kilmarnock
Hawick
Newcastle-upon-Tyne
Sunderland
Gateshead-on-Tyne
Belleek
Belfast
Stockton-on-Tees
Whitby
Leeds
Ormskirk
Liverpool
St Helen's
Sheffield
Swinton
Dublin
Warrington
Chesterfield
Tunstall
Burslem
Newcastle-under-Lyme
Cobridge
Pinxton
Hanley
Stoke-on-Trent
Shelton
Limerick
Longton
Fenton
Derby
Nottingham
Coalport
Wolverhampton
Coalbrookdale
Bilston
Caughley
Wednesbury
Brierley Hill
Birmingham
Waterford
Kidderminster
Stourbridge
Cork
Worcester
Woodstock
Harlow
Swansea
Usk
Pontypool
High Wycombe
London
Nantgarw
Bristol
Henley-on-Thames
Nailsea
Esher
Bath
Wrotham
Vest Malling
Fremington
Wincanton
Wilton
Chiddingfold
Tunbridge Wells
Exeter
Plymouth

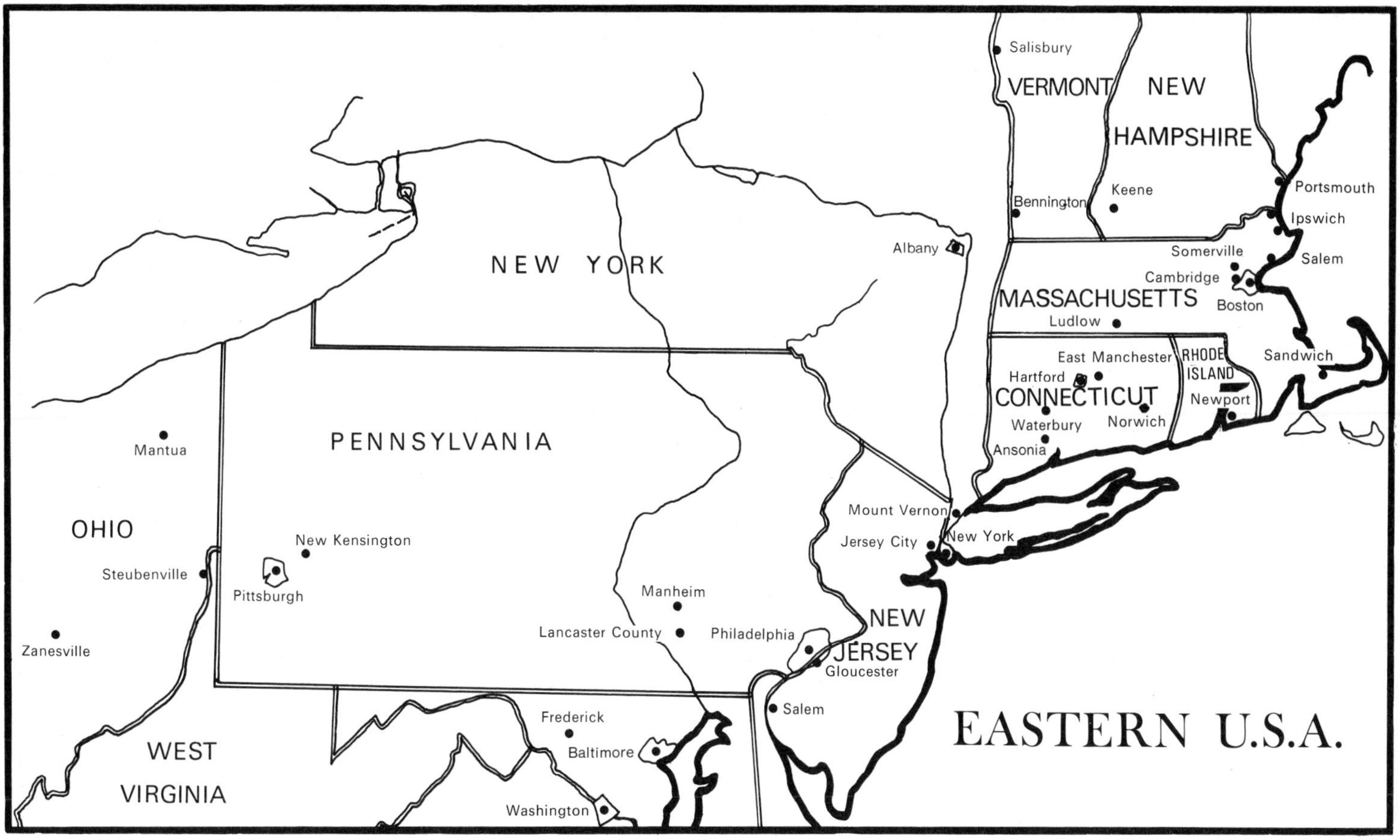

EASTERN U.S.A.

Salisbury
VERMONT
NEW HAMPSHIRE
Portsmouth
Bennington
Keene
Ipswich
Somerville
Salem
Albany
NEW YORK
Cambridge
MASSACHUSETTS
Boston
Ludlow
East Manchester
RHODE ISLAND
Sandwich
Hartford
CONNECTICUT
Newport
Waterbury
Norwich
Ansonia
Mantua
PENNSYLVANIA
OHIO
Mount Vernon
New Kensington
Jersey City
New York
Steubenville
Pittsburgh
Manheim
NEW JERSEY
Zanesville
Lancaster County
Philadelphia
Gloucester
Salem
Frederick
WEST VIRGINIA
Baltimore
Washington

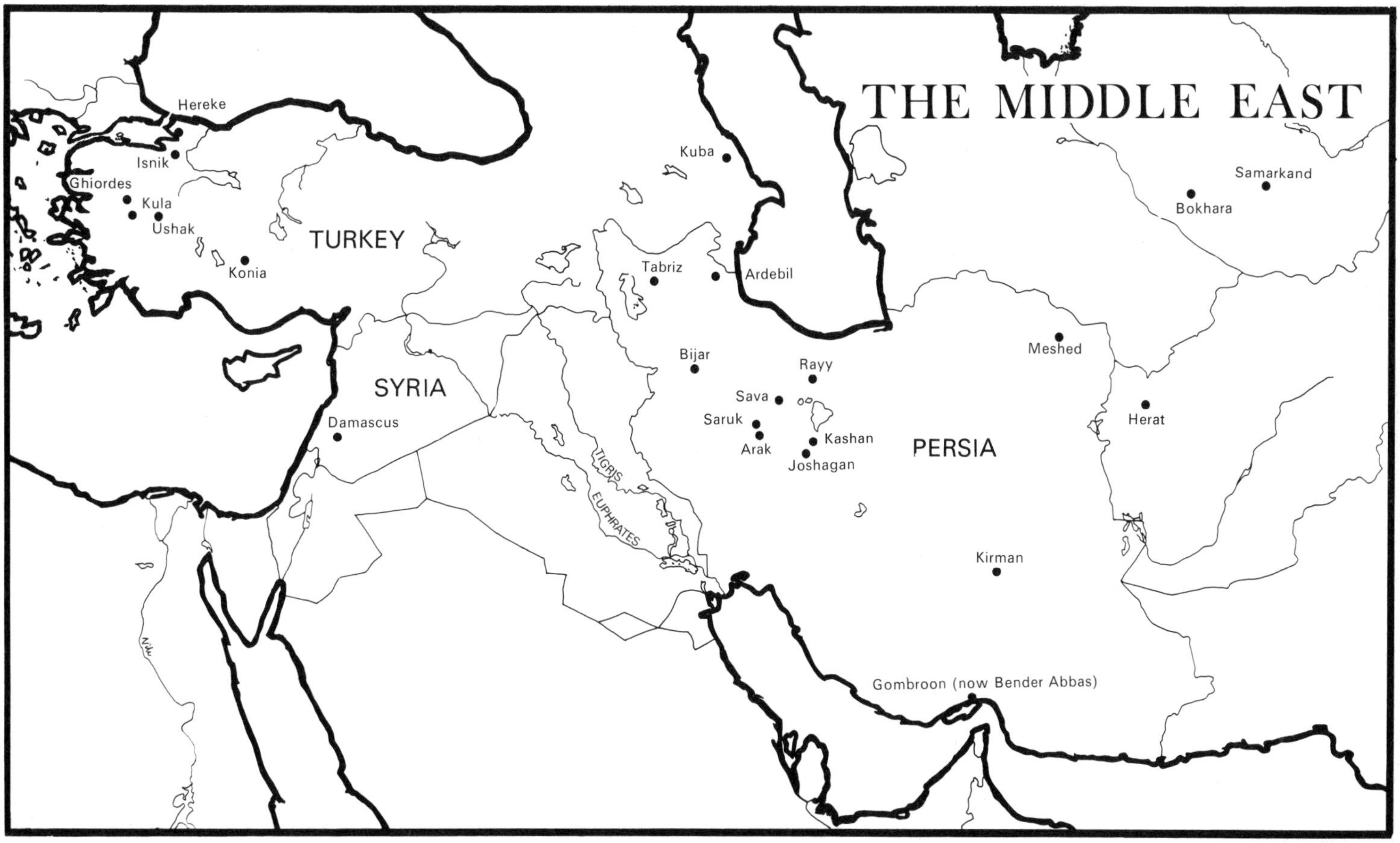

THE MIDDLE EAST

Hereke
Kuba
Samarkand
Isnik
Bokhara
Ghiordes
Kula
Ushak
TURKEY
Tabriz
Ardebil
Konia
Meshed
Bijar
Rayy
SYRIA
Sava
Saruk
Herat
Damascus
Kashan
Arak
PERSIA
Joshagan
TIGRIS
EUPHRATES
Kirman
Nile
Gombroon (now Bender Abbas)

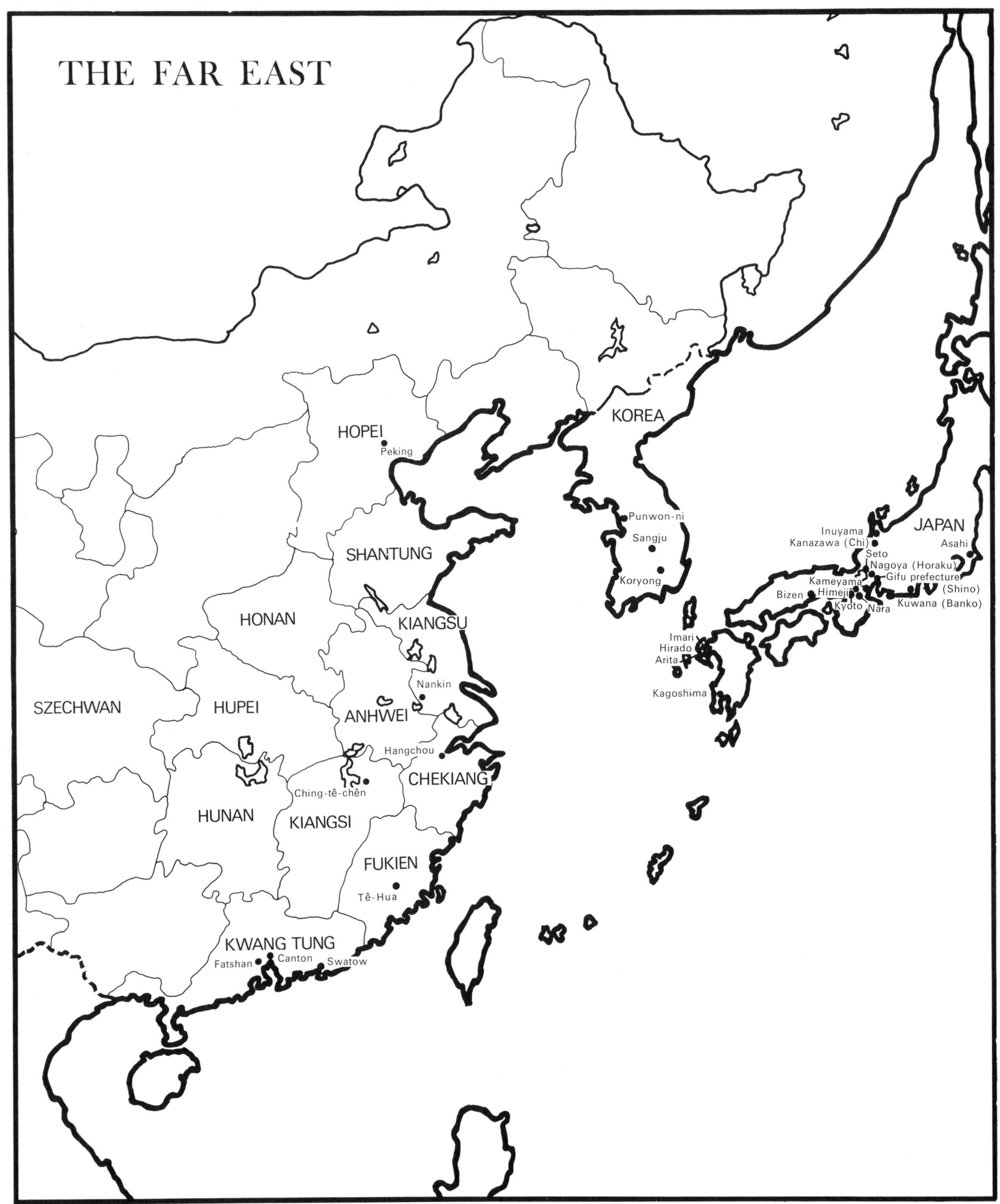
THE FAR EAST
HOPEI
Peking
KOREA
SHANTUNG
HONAN
KIANGSU
SZECHWAN
HUPEI
ANHWEI
Nankin
Hangchou
CHEKIANG
Ching-tê-chên
HUNAN
KIANGSI
FUKIEN
Tê-Hua
KWANG TUNG
Fatshan
Canton
Swatow
Punwon-ni
Sangju
Koryong
Imari
Hirado
Arita
Kagoshima
JAPAN
Inuyama
Kanazawa (Chi)
Seto
Asahi
Nagoya (Horaku)
Gifu prefecture
(Shino)
Kameyama
Bizen
Himeji
Kyoto
Nara
Kuwana (Banko)

A to Z ENCYCLOPEDIA

abacus. Arithmetical calculating device long known in Far East (perhaps introduced from ancient Rome via silk trade), also widely used until present day in some European countries, e.g. Russia and Poland. Outer framework of wood, ivory, etc. supports wires or rods with sliding beads, each row representing column of appropriate mathematical notation, e.g. (in decimal system) units, tens, hundreds.

a barbottina. Ceramic decoration, partly in applied relief, reminiscent of beaten metal. On 16th century Italian (e.g. Venetian) maiolica.

Abbotsford style. Late 19th century name given to imitation furniture made in 1820s and 1830s in Gothic, Tudor, Stuart, and Jacobean styles, featuring architectural details (cusps and buttresses), materials (black oak, velvet coverings), and motifs and designs (bulbous carving on legs, spiral twists on verticals, high backs on chairs). Named after Abbotsford, Sir Walter Scott's home, reflecting influence of contemporary neo-Gothic literature (e.g. Scott's) on design and furnishing.

Absolon, William (fl 1784–1815). English enameller, gilder, and glass dealer. Worked independently in Great Yarmouth, Norfolk. Painted clear, blue, and opaque glass in gilt and enamel colours. Specialized in cream jugs. Some work initialled. Work in clear glass mainly simple mementoes of Great Yarmouth. From 1790, decorated cream-coloured earthenware and porcelain bought from J. *Wedgwood, J. *Turner, *Shorthose & Co, *Leeds Pottery, etc. Painted *botanical flowers, monograms, shields, landscapes; also star patterns and flower-sprig decoration with simple inscriptions. Mark: Absolon Yar$^{m.}$ painted; also painted arrow said to be his mark.

Abtsbessingen (Thuringia). German faience factory founded *c*1739. Products decorated in high-temperature colours include blue-and-white tureens in style influenced by Dorotheenthal, pyramids of modelled flowers, Schwarzburg arms, and yellow boxes shaped like pug dogs. Painted coats of arms enclosed in *Laub-und-Bandelwerk.* Some *muffle colours used. In 1750s, painted vases with S-shaped handles. Painters included J. P. *Dannhöfer (no mark; work indistinguishable from that painted at Bayreuth). Sometimes marked with two-pronged fork of Schwarzburg and painter's initials.

acacia leaf. Ceramic decoration: motif resembling stylized leaf of acacia. Found on Hispano-Moresque ware made at Manises from 1427 to late 15th century. Often combined with pattern of trailing vine leaves and round-petalled flowers, either in bands around *albarello* or in concentric circles on dish.

acanthus motif. Stylized representation of leaf of *Acanthus spinosus* used as ornament in Greek and Roman architecture and metalwork. Used extensively on furniture and in interior decoration. Popular on 17th century silver; usually embossed on base of two-handled cups, beakers, etc.; also acanthus-shaped finials. Revived on neo-classical silver of late 18th and early 19th centuries.

Acier, Michel-Victor (1736–95). French porcelain modeller. Appointed joint *Modellmeister* with J. J. *Kändler at Meissen (1764) in attempt to revive Saxon strength against Sèvres competition. Stayed until 1781. Exponent of neo-classical style. Responsible for numerous models of children, shepherdesses, etc., besides more famous groups, e.g. The Happy Parents (1775); also for introducing *lacework on figures, and biscuit forms.

Abtsbessingen faience. Vase; yellow ground with three reserve panels painted in blue and white, mid 18th century. Height $13\frac{1}{2}$*in.*

acorn clock. American shelf clock in form of acorn, made mid 19th century by J. C. *Brown; base sometimes decorated with local views. Possibly derived from French *lyre clock. *See* Connecticut clocks.

acorn or **York flagon.** Pewter flagon made in first half of 18th century in Yorkshire region. Short, wide, swelling base rises to tapering cylindrical body resembling acorn in shape, with domed cover and finial.

acorn-knop spoon. 14th and 15th century form with acorn-shaped finial. Made in silver (including a few of later date). Also in English pewter; a few examples in brass.

acorn motif. Finial or other decoration in shape of acorn.

Act of Parliament, tavern, or **coaching clock.** Large English wall clock with prominent dial, round or shaped, *c*30in. diameter. Weight-driven, usually non-striking. Dial and case frequently lacquered or painted; sometimes dial is painted white and case made of mahogany. Form in existence from early 18th century. Incorrectly named after Act of 1797–98, when government taxed clocks and timepieces; most examples found in coaching inns and assembly rooms.

Acts of the Apostles tapestry. Early 16th century tapestry. 10 panels, most *c*42×15ft; wool and silk with gold and silver. Original commissioned 1515 by Pope Leo X; woven 1515–19 in Brussels by P. *van Aelst, supervised by J. *van Orley, from cartoons by *Raphaël. Design inaugurated new tapestry style; dramatic pictorial compositions applying Italian Renaissance canons of space and perspective, monumentality and mass, to tapestry; disregard for older considerations of textile composition. Several sets woven in Brussels during 16th and early 17th centuries, notably by J. *Raes. Charles I of England acquired most cartoons in 1623; seven-piece set reproduced *c*1630 at Mortlake tapestry works, with new border, probably by F. *Cleyn. Series copied several times during century. Cartoons remain in possession of British Crown.

Adam and Eve chargers. *See* blue-dash chargers.

Adam, Charles (fl mid 18th century). French sculptor who financed manufacture of soft-paste porcelain at Vincennes from 1745. Factory obtained royal privilege; traded under Adam's name until his retirement, *c*1752.

Adam, Robert (1728–92). Architect and designer; son of leading Scottish Palladian architect, William Adam (1688–1748). Often worked with younger brother James. From 1754, travelled in France and Italy; with French neo-classical architect Charles-Louis Clérisseau, made detailed drawings of Diocletian's Palace at Spalato (now Split, Yugoslavia). Practised as architect in London from 1759. until *c*1768, mainly completed or remodelled existing houses, working on exteriors and interiors, notably Harewood, Yorkshire, Osterley Park and Syon House, near London, and Luton Hoo, Bedfordshire. Major architectural venture, with brothers, was The Adelphi, area of houses between The Strand and River Thames (started 1768; largely demolished 1936).

Design extended from architecture to details of interior decoration, emphasizing unity of conception (e.g. carpets woven to accord with ceiling designs). Thus influenced style in all fields. His designs executed by, e.g. M. *Boulton in ormolu, *Moorfields carpet factory (for e.g. Osterley Park), and *Carron Company in cast iron.

Adam style. Main British expression of neo-classicism through work of R. *Adam and others. Style derived from English Palladian architecture of, e.g. W. *Kent, from French and Italian neo-classicism, from archaeological finds in Italy, Greece, etc. (*see* Etruscan style), and from Italian *Cinquecento* decoration. R. Adam's furniture style may be divided into four phases: early (1762–64), transitional (1765–68), mature (1769–77), and late (1778–92).

Early work typified by square, somewhat heavy, architectural pieces, decorated with carved wooden classical motifs, sphinx, urn, acanthus, etc.; effect is of applied rather than integrated ornament.

In transitional phase, metal and plaster replaced wood for carved and moulded decoration, giving lightness to work; many pieces were white painted, gilt, or mahogany. Motifs of unifying type, e.g. *guilloches,* scrollwork and fretwork, floral and husk festoons, characteristically light-

Act of Parliament clock. English, George III; japanned oak case with gilded decoration and numerals; front decorated with tinted engraving. Eight-day movement.

ened and adapted. Transitional case furniture rectangular, often with baluster legs.

Mature work often has semi-circular design and tapering legs; also favours pairs of front legs at each end of case pieces. Mature decoration delicate, with widely spaced ornamental features, joined by festoons and swags. Adam mirrors, at first fairly heavy, then more restrained, have still lighter frames by mature phase; often divided into three longitudinal sections with partitions of fine filigree work laid over glass (often with female sphinx at top of partitions). Coloured medallions first appeared on furniture at end of transitional phase. Pastel colours used on mature pieces; brightly coloured panels on those in *Etruscan style, often also with square tapering legs and block feet, reminiscent of early phase, but lighter.

By 1778, Adam techniques and designs adopted by other cabinet makers; fewer rich clients (due to economic stringencies imposed by American War of Independence); his own inventiveness declined.

Adams family. Staffordshire potters, working late 18th and early 19th century, descended from William Adams of Burslem (d 1617).

William (1745–1805). Pupil of J. *Wedgwood; established Greengates pottery, Tunstall, *c*1768, made deep-blue jasper ware and cream-coloured earthenware, notably blue transfer-printed tableware. Pottery run from 1800 by son Benjamin. Marks: Adams & Co (1769–1800: cream-coloured earthenware); ADAMS & CO (1779–*c*1790: jasper ware); ADAMS (1787–1805: general); all impressed.

William (1748–1831). Potter at Brick House, Burslem, and at Cobridge. No mark.

William (1772–1829). Maker at Cliff Bank works, Stoke-on-Trent, of blue transfer-printed ware (much exported to America), ironstone, and bone china. Firm inherited by sons. Marks include ADAMS WARRANTED STAFFORDSHIRE, clockwise around an eagle (1804–40); ADAMS (from *c*1809); WA & S (from 1829); all impressed. Exported wares marked with blue-printed eagle over scroll bearing title of view.

Adams, George (1704–73). English instrument-maker, set up workshop in 1735; maker to George III. Produced mathematical instruments of high quality, air-pumps, etc., and complicated microscopes with interchangeable lenses and adjustable supports. Succeeded by son, also George (1750–95).

Adam style. Dining Room at Osterley Park, Middlesex; room and furniture to designs by Robert Adam, 1761–80.

Ador, Jean-Pierre (fl 1770–85). French goldsmith working in St Petersburg, Russia. Made oval, circular, or oblong snuff-boxes decoration included enamelling, chased borders, and miniatures.

Aelmis, Jan (1714–after 1788). Dutch potter; owner of The Flowerpot factory, Rotterdam. Supplied Delft tiles for Amalienburg hunting pavilion at Nymphenburg (completed 1734), and for tiled rooms in Augustusberg Palace and Falkenlust hunting pavilion at Brühl, near Cologne. *Illustration at* tile pictures.

Affenkapelle (German, 'monkey band'). Series of over 20 porcelain figures of monkeys playing musical instruments, and conductor; also singers. Introduced at Meissen under J. J. *Kändler (*c*1750–60); may have satirized players of Dresden court orchestra, although *singeries* originated in France. Widely copied by many European factories from late 18th century.

Affleck, Thomas (d 1795). British-born cabinet maker; worked in Philadelphia, Pennsylvania, from 1763. Followed contemporary English styles, developing individual interpretation of T. *Chippendale's designs.

Afghan carpets. Very tough *Turkoman carpets made by tribes on Turkestan–Afghanistan border. Thick, coarsely-knotted pile on undyed foundation with long, fringed ends. Field design very large guls, diagonally quartered in blue and green with stylized leaf or tree motifs. Ground infilled with stylized animals or star clusters in contrasting colours. Colouring usually rich and sombre. Narrowest bordered of Turkoman carpets.

agate. Transparent or translucent gem with lustre of wax; variety of *chalcedony; colours in parallel strips or bands, or blended in clouds, often with strange markings. Used particularly in Renaissance Europe for range of luxury articles mounted in gold, silver, or silver-gilt, e.g. handles of knives, forks, etc., seals, standing cups, ewers and basins, etc. Used in jewellery (often as *cameo material) in classical period, Renaissance, and 19th century.

agate ware. Earthenware made in Stafford-

*Agate ware. Left: salt-glaze agate cat decorated in brown and white with blue splash decoration. Centre: lead-glazed teapot by T. *Whieldon with crabstock spout and handle, height $5\frac{1}{4}$in. Right: cream jug with lion mask and paw feet, also Whieldon lead-glaze, height $3\frac{1}{2}$in. c1745–50.*

shire from mid 18th century, covered with coloured slips or glazes to resemble natural stone (sometimes used to include *solid agate). Makers include T. *Whieldon, J. *Wedgwood.

Aghkand (Kurdistan). *Sgraffiato* earthenware, produced with green, brown, and yellow colours separated by incised outlines of design. Name given to ware made in 11th and 12th century Persia; later produced in Egypt, Syria, and Byzantine territories.

agitable lamp. Brass oil-lamp, invented during 1780s in Birmingham. Popular in America, where used with whale-oil, until superseded in mid 19th century by paraffin lamp. So-called because of air-tight oil reservoir.

Agricola, Georgius (1490–1555). German doctor and mineralogist, acknowledged as 'father of mineralogy'. Wrote treatise on mining and mineralogy, *De Re Metallica*. Volume 12, published in Basel (1556), deals with glass and contains descriptions of different manufacturing techniques.

aide mémoire. In 18th century, ivory leaves bound in book-form for note-taking; 19th century version had paper leaves. *See tablette, carnet de bal.*

aigrette. Head ornament with jewels mounted in feather shape (usually symmetrical); size varied. Perhaps first used as male ornament in Middle Ages. In use in Britain and Europe, predominantly by women, from late 16th century; popular in early 17th century Britain, decorated with gems, pearls, enamel, and sometimes with real feathers. Again fashionable in France during reign of Louis XV (1715–74); stems sometimes made to vibrate when head moved, displaying brilliance of stones (often diamonds).

air twist. Stem decoration in English glasses, mainly *c*1745–*c*1770, containing single or multiple spirals of air. Can be produced by introducing tears into metal, then drawing out and twisting; more usually produced by shaping metal in grooved, cylindrical mould, then coating with molten glass which traps air in grooves, then also drawing out and twisting. *See* mercury twist.

à jet d'eau. French ceramic decoration. Fountain with trellis-work above, sometimes faint landscape behind; painted in underglaze blue on porcelain made at Chantilly. Introduced in 1760s.

Aka Oribe. *See* Oribe ware.

Akerman, John (fl 18th century). English glass seller. Operated in London, 1719–85. First seller to advertize diamond-cut flint glass (1719). Employed English cutters and at least one German. Sold ceramics and plain and cut glass in London and provinces. Held Mastership of Glass Sellers' Company (1740–48).

alabaster. Semi-transparent gypsum, usually whitish in colour and resembling marble. Used from antiquity, and particularly in late 18th century for ornamental vases, clock cases, etc., mounted in gilt-bronze.

à la brindille. *See* Chantilly sprig.

à la corne. French ceramic decoration: cornucopia spilling over with flowers, surrounded by birds and insects; painted in blue, and, rarely, polychrome high-temperature colours on faience at Rouen in mid 18th century.

alafia (Arabic, 'blessing'). Ceramic decoration of stylized Arabic lettering included in decoration of Hispano-Moresque ware, e.g. in Valencia from 15th century. Often appears as repeating design, e.g. in band around body of *albarello*. Motif sometimes resembles two inverted Vs, the lower with loop at point; also seen in more rounded form resembling scroll.

alarm or **alarum.** Part of clock or watch mechanism giving audible warning, usually by ringing bell at predetermined time; set off by *going train. In early clocks, alarm mechanism sometimes separate and detachable. Other, rare, systems include devices to light candles or to let off miniature cannons.

Alarm. On German clock, c1720. Bell rings and candle is lighted by means of small charge of gunpowder ignited by self-acting flintlock mechanism.
Alarm device. English, c1840, to be used in conjunction with a pocket watch. Small weight descends during night and trips catch, releasing bell.

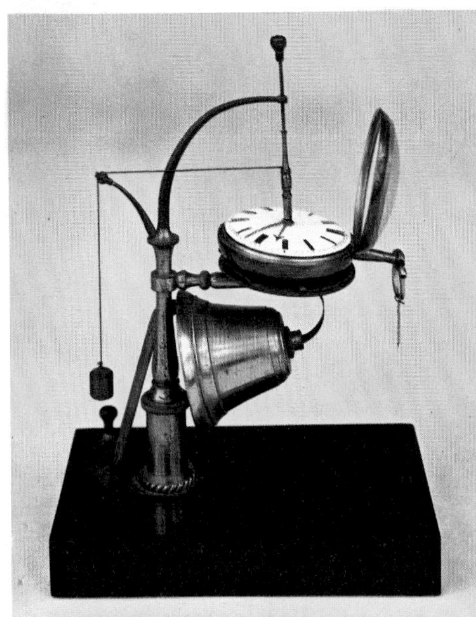

Albany couch. *See* reading seat.

Albany slip. Dark brown clay found near Albany, New York. Used from early 19th century to line salt-glazed stoneware vessels. Sometimes also incorporated in glaze.

albarello. Near-cylindrical tin-glazed earthenware drug pot, waisted for ease of handling. Made in Near East from 14th century; introduced into Italy from Spain. Copied in Dutch Delft and English delftware. *Illustration also at* Deruta maiolica.

Albertolli, Giacomo (1742–1839). Italian ornament designer. Pioneer of neo-classical style in Italy.

Albisola (Liguria), Italy. Maiolica manufactured in 17th and 18th centuries; makers include *Conrade family. Products difficult to distinguish from those of Savona and Genoa.

Alcaraz carpets. Spanish carpets with coarsely Spanish-knotted woollen pile on undyed woollen foundation, woven in Alcaraz from 15th century. Earliest carpets in sombre colours, dark browns, yellows, blue, and green, usually with red ground. Patterns largely geometrical; field divided into oblong or square compartments dominated by large star-ornamented octagons. Borders with chain of rosettes; extra border often added at top and bottom of rug with animal or human figures. By mid 15th century, growing importance of Turkish carpets in Europe brought change in style: Turkish designs adopted, palmettes replaced star motifs. From late 15th century, Gothic patterns, influenced by Spanish and Italian velvet designs, appeared, e.g. ogees with palmettes in lattice of interlacing green ribbons on red ground. Kufic border. From early 16th century until mid 17th century, Alcaraz major carpet production and manufacturing centre in Spain, with large trade to rest of Europe. Patterns designed to suit growing export market; most popular 16th century pattern wreaths infilled with arab-

Albarelli. *Spanish. Left: *Talavera pottery decorated with arms of El Escorial monastery and yellow and blue sponged decoration, late 16th century. Centre: Catalan pottery, decorated with scene running around pot, c1700. Right: Talavera pottery, heavy, with plain thick glaze, 15th century.*

esque motif; artichoke patterns, dragon and phoenix borders. In 17th century, field patterns copy Ushak models, particularly *Holbeins and *Lottos; borders Spanish, with detached leaf forms in candelabra system derived from fleur-de-lis. Production continued for some time, but largely superseded in importance by Cuenca after 1649.

Alcora (near Valencia). Spanish faience factory, established *c*1726 by 9th Count of Aranda. Faience made until after 1785, decorated by J. *Olerys until 1737 in styles of A. *Tempesta and J. *Berain, resembles that of Moustiers. Products include pharmaceutical ware and table centrepieces; also dishes painted with religious and mythological scenes. Decoration usually in polychrome, rarely in blue monochrome; designs, repeated at Moustiers from 1739, include **décor à guirlandes*, *potato flower, and grotesques, painted in polychrome, green or yellow monochrome, and, occasionally from *c*1749, copper lustre. Later table services, vases, etc., in rococo style; figures and portrait busts include historical, mythological, and allegorical subjects. Experiments made in porcelain manufacture from 1751; yellowish porcelain paste made from *c*1775, decorated with sprigs of flowers, Pompeian scrolls, and landscapes with figures. Cream-coloured earthenware figures and tableware, also imitations of jasper ware, made until 1798. Mark, until at least 1784, A, incised or printed in brown, black, or gold; in early 19th century, Fab^{co} de Aranda A, within circle, printed in red.

ale glasses. English drinking glasses with long, narrow bowl (*c*3–4oz capacity), popular 1703–1805, though examples are known from *c*1670. Early 18th century stems plain, moulded, facet cut, air or opaque twist. From *c*1740, bowls engraved with hop bloom and ears of barley. Enamelled motifs usually of *Beilby period. Late 18th century bowls straight-sided and conical, with vertical fluting at base. Stem plain or knopped. In 19th century, similar to champagne flutes with plain foot. *See* dwarf ale, yard-of-ale. *Illustration at* flute.

ale-measure. *See* measure.

à l'épi. *See* Chantilly sprig.

ale warmer. Pan for preparing mulled ale over open fire, made from 18th century in England. Usually copper, sometimes with iron handles. Early types boot or shoe shaped, superseded by conical shape ('donkey's ear') late 18th century. Many made in both shapes in 19th century; few earlier examples survive.

Alhambra vase. Large Hispano-Moresque vase with two wing handles. Decorated in gold lustre and pale blue, with arabesques, foliage, and gazelles; 4ft3in. high. Discovered at Alhambra Palace, Granada, Spain; made late 14th century, supposedly at Granada, but similar vases made at Palermo, Sicily, and Malaga, perhaps in different periods.

alicate or **spur motif.** Ceramic decoration of stylized spur shapes repeated to form band. Used on Hispano-Moresque ware made e.g. in Valencia from early 15th century.

alla porcellana. Contemporary description of Italian maiolica decoration in style of 15th and early 16th century Chinese porcelain. Motifs, painted in blue on white background include flowers, sprays, leaves, and vines, trailing or festooned from border, initially surrounding oriental subjects, e.g. junks, pagodas, silkworms. Used at Faenza in late 15th and early 16th centuries; continued at Cafaggiolo and Montelupo throughout 16th century.

Allen, Robert (1744–1835). English porcelain painter. At *Lowestoft factory from 1757; manager of factory from 1780. After its closure, worked independently; enamelled porcelain made, e.g. at Rockingham and in China.

Allgood, Thomas (d 1716). British japanner who developed lacquer used at *Pontypool. Obtained black colour by mixing raw linseed oil, asphaltums, thinning, etc., to imitate effect of Japanese lacquered goods. Descendants established rival factory at Usk, Monmouthshire, in 1763 which continued until 1862.

Allison, Michael (fl *c*1800–45). Cabinet maker in New York City. Pieces in American Federal-style, similar to D. *Phyfe's.

alloy. Composition metal, e.g. *brass, *bronze, *pewter, made by fusing two or more elementary metals. Also, base metal added to precious metal to give toughness and malleability.

Allwine, Lawrence (fl *c*1786). American chair maker, who specialized in *Windsor chairs, often painted or gilded. Invented 'Allwine Gloss', a fast-drying varnish.

almirah. Anglo-Indian term for movable wardrobe or cupboard.

almond design. *See* boteh motif.

almorrata. Spanish rose-water sprinkler with wide neck and four small spouts from shoulder. Catalan form dating from 14th century, showing strong Islamic influence. Popular in 17th century with *façon de Venise* decoration, e.g. *latticinio* threads, embossed prunts below spouts, and pinched, trailed glass round rim. *cf Kuttrolf.*

alms dish. Broad-rimmed plate (diameter 9in. or more) for ecclesiastical use, made in silver, pewter, brass, etc., throughout Europe from Middle Ages, though part of furnishings of English parish churches only after Reformation. No English silver examples earlier than 17th century survive. Most important date from *c*1660–*c*1700; plain, with coat of arms or inscription on rim; most elaborate forms mainly intended for royal or private chapels, or for cathedral use, with all-over embossed ornament. Some elaborate pieces produced in 18th and early 19th centuries, although collecting plates, modelled on form of dinner plates, were coming into use. With Tractarian movement of 1830s and 1840s came revival of alms dish, generally designed in Gothic style inspired by A. W. N. *Pugin. Pewter examples usually plain and similar to secular dishes; sometimes decorated with central boss and/or fluting, rarely enamelled; made until 19th century. Brass examples plain or with embossed decoration (biblical scenes, etc.) common, particularly in southern Germany, after late 15th century.

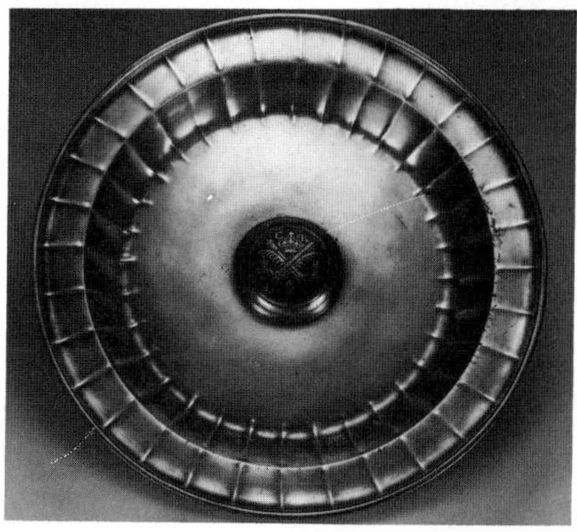

Alms dish. Pewter, enamelled with arms and monogram of Charles I. English, 1626. Diameter 14¾in.

Styles of engraved and other ornament vary with period.

Alpujarra rugs. Small, brightly-coloured Spanish peasant rugs with coarse, weft-loop pile on linen foundation, woven from 18th century in Alpujarra, Pyrenees. Attractive crudely-drawn designs in up to six strong colours. Favourite motifs include animals, birds, plants (especially tree of life); borders with vine scrolls, stars, rearing lions, pomegranates. Flourishing export trade in 19th century, particularly to America.

Altai rugs. *See* Pazyryk carpets.

altar clock. Italian wooden-case clock of mid 17th to mid 18th centuries, built in shape of altar; also produced in southern Germany, where name originated. Little known in England, but version by E. *East, *c*1665.

altar cruet. Vessel for water and wine used in celebration of Mass from Middle Ages or earlier. Usually made in pairs, often with letters A (*aqua*) and V (*vinum*) engraved or enamelled on covers. Also in pairs with one cruet plain silver, other gilt; alternatively cruets distinguished by one having e.g. gilt stopper or vine scroll round body. Medieval examples resemble small jug with ovoid body, or bellied tankard with spout, often mounted on oval or boat-shaped stand. Earliest examples ivory, crystal, or silver; in Middle Ages generally silver, silver-gilt, or latten. Also in pewter from 14th century, shaped as small bottle (burette); most surviving examples of European origin.

Altare (Liguria). Italian glass making centre founded in early Middle Ages by French immigrants; documentary evidence of glass manufacture in 1282. Attracted fugitive glass workers from Venice. Altarist styles indistinguishable from Venetian. Glassmakers' Guild constitution, *L'Università dell'arte vitrea* (1495), encouraged craftsmen to work abroad, spreading **façon de Venise* throughout Europe, notably in France (Nevers) and Flanders.

altar vase. Silver vessel for flowers placed on altar. Few known to have been made specifically for this purpose. Uncommon before mid 17th century, even in Spain. Made in large quantities, mainly in Gothic and baroque styles in 19th century.

amalgam. Metal dissolved in mercury by various methods. *See* fire-gilding.

Amati family (fl 16th and 17th centuries). Italian family of violin makers working in Cremona; also produced violas and cellos. First famous member, Andrea Amati (*c*1505–80); greatest was his grandson, Nicolò (1596–1684). A. *Stradivari was a pupil.

amatory jewellery. Brooches and other jewellery with amatory motifs and/or inscriptions used at least from early Middle Ages in Britain and Europe. In 16th century betrothal rings sometimes had heart-shaped bezels set with gems or with miniature portrait. *Posy rings and brooches probably made from Middle Ages, reaching greatest popularity in 16th and 17th centuries. From mid 18th century *regard rings and brooches made. Rings with gem-set bezels in shape of heart, bow and quiver, etc., also made. Some *hair jewellery also used as love token. Love brooches became particularly popular in England in mid 19th century, reaching height of fashion in late 1880s when Queen Victoria relaxed mourning. These often in thin silver and gold, machine-stamped, and cut in variety of shapes. Types included flower shapes, hearts, hands, knots, anchors, letters, names, etc. Various shapes also used for bezels of rings, sometimes engraved around outside with word or motto.

*Amatory jewellery. English and French, 19th century, with heart and love-knot motifs. *Regard brooches, top left and top right, with initials of stones spelling Regard (top left).*
Right:
Ambulante. *Louis XVI, satinwood with one drawer banded in purpleheart; ormolu gallery. Width 26in.*

ambassadorial plate. Custom of ambassador being assigned plate for ceremonial and domestic use while representing monarch at a foreign court probably dates from 16th century England. At first, loan of royal plate from jewel house was made. By 18th century, ambassadors and other high-ranking government officials were assigned a specified number of ounces of plate, e.g. 1000, and commissioned a silversmith to produce the pieces, which were engraved with royal insignia. Before 1688, it was theoretically incumbent upon ambassadors to return plate to jewel house unless they could plead extra expense or other extenuating circumstance; system grew increasingly lax from early 18th century until after 1815, when it ended and ambassadors often retained the plate.

amber. Fossilized resin of tree *Pinus succanifer* (extinct today); name derived from Arabic *anbar* (originally meaning ambergris, substance produced in intestines of whale). Resin found in nodules, rods, drops, etc.; ranges in colour from pale yellow to brown. Blue amber exists but is very rare. In use from ancient times as gem material (e.g. by Greeks and Romans); can be carved easily. Early use for beads for necklaces, earrings, etc. From late 14th century in Britain and Europe widely used in *rosaries. From late 18th century set in *parures*. Largest amber producing area of world is Baltic coast.

amber gilding (in ceramics). *See* gilding.

ambry. *See* aumbry.

ambulante. Portable serving table, introduced during Louis XV period.

Amelung, John Frederick (fl *c*1784–95). German-born glass maker. In America from 1784; set up *New Bremen Glass Manufactory near Frederick, Maryland. Specialized in luxury and domestic glassware using non-lead glass. Overestimated demand and in 1795 went bankrupt.

Amen glasses. *See* Jacobite glass.

American ceramics. Lead-glazed earthenware made chiefly by individual potters for local use includes *redware, made in colonies from late 17th century. *Pennsylvania German pottery decorated with slip includes *tulip ware. Manufacture flourished in New England, New York, and Pennsylvania, began to move westward in 1780s. Early examples of stoneware made by *Duché family, and in New York by W. *Crolius and J. *Remmey. Many potters making lead-glazed earthenware changed to production of stoneware in late 18th century because of injurious effects of working with lead. Successful factories established from late 1830s include potteries of J. *Norton and C. W. *Fenton at *Bennington. Production of cream-coloured earthenware in second half of 19th century developed in Ohio and New Jersey. First serious attempt to manufacture porcelain, by *Bonnin and Morris, failed financially. W. E. *Tucker supplied home market with first large-scale production in 1830s.

American clocks. Tall (i.e. long-case) clocks produced by *c*1690, notably in Pennsylvania. First makers include A. *Cottey. Early clocks followed English style: flat-topped hood, with no decoration on trunk (possibly result of Quaker influence). Metal dial, *c*10½in. square, sometimes with attachments, such as calendar, or phases of moon. From *c*1725, examples with break-arch dial, domed top, and finials; *c*1740 with break-arch hood. Distinctive feature is *'whale's-tail' decoration on hood; introduced from *c*1790 by makers including T. *Harland, A. and S. *Willard. Movements brass or often wood, owing to scarcity of metal; thirty-hour, or eight-day. *Dwarf-tall clocks also made in early 19th century. Typically American weight-driven wooden shelf clocks, produced in large quantities from *c*1800; probably introduced by Willard family. First type was *Massachusetts shelf clock; others are *lighthouse, and shelf-*lyre clocks. Many with *kidney dial. Numerous kinds of *Connecticut shelf clock: e.g. *box-case, *pillar-and-scroll (introduced by E. *Terry), looking-glass, and ogee. Different

versions include *acorn, *beehive, and *steeple clocks. Variety of wall clocks: e.g. *wag-on-wall, *coffin, *banjo, *lyre, and *girandole. Also *New Hampshire mirror clock; examples by B. *Morrill, J. *Collins, etc. Clock making by individual craftsmen until end of 18th century, when large-scale production, pioneered by Harland, began to develop. Clock producing factories include *Ansonia Clock Company. *See also* New York clocks.

American Colonial style. General term for American styles of furniture (and architecture) dating from first settlements (early 17th century) until 1789, when Federal government was established. *See* Chippendale style, Georgian style, Jacobean style, Pennsylvania-Dutch style, Pilgrim furniture, Queen Anne style, Restoration style, Salem furniture, Shaker furniture, William and Mary style.

American Directoire style. Furniture style prevalent in America *c*1805–15, reflecting classical Greek and Roman influence, e.g. in chairs modelled on *klismos, and settees with ends scrolling outwards. *See* Phyfe style.

American eagle flask. Produced in America *c*1813–30. Blown in full-size two-piece moulds usually with masonic emblem one side and eagle on reverse copied from American seal or coins.

American Empire style. Furniture style prevalent in America *c*1810–30, influenced by French *Empire style, featuring ornamental columns, animal feet, etc. Own characteristic motifs also developed, including cornucopias, fruit, flowers, stars, and, particularly, American eagle. Mahogany was much used.

American Federal style. General term for

Above:
American Colonial style. Mid 18th century bedroom at Shirley Plantation, Virginia. Furnished with chest of drawers, fourposter bed (posts carved with sheaves of rice), three-sided cot, and clothes press.
*American eagle flask. Made by T. W. Dyott at *Dyottville Glass Works; blue glass with portrait of George Washington on reverse. Pint capacity. c1833.*

Below:
*American Federal style. Ground-floor drawing room of Gardner-Pingree House, Salem, Massachusetts, designed by S. *McIntire, 1804.*
American Federal style. Armchair, 1805, attributed to John and Hugh Findlay of Baltimore. Medallion on top rail shows Bolton, home of Englishman, George Grundy, who established himself in Baltimore in 1795.

American furniture styles dating from the establishment of Federal government (1789) until 1830; marks the end of work considered 'antique' in America. *See* American Directoire style, American Empire style, Hepplewhite style, Sheraton style.

American furniture. *See* American Colonial style, American Directoire style, American Empire style, American Federal style.

American glass. First glasshouse established by English settlers at Jamestown, Virginia, in 1608. Other early glasshouses set up in Massachusetts, New Amsterdam, and Pennsylvania. These factories used coarse green, blue, or terracotta glass for production of flasks, window glass, and beads for trading with Indians. No factories survived for long; most glassware in 17th century America was imported. First successful factory founded by C. *Wistar in 1739. In 18th century, fine glass produced by *Manheim Glass House; work European in style but moulded by new *blown-three-mould technique, with distinctive *lacy design. In 1820s, mechanical pressing revolutionized production methods; by mid 19th century three-quarters of American glass production pressed ware, but free-blown glass still made, e.g. *violin flasks. Fine paperweights produced, notably by *New England and *Boston companies, 1850–80.

American Porcelain Manufacturing Company. Established at Gloucester, New Jersey, making soft-paste porcelain (1854–57). Became Gloucester China Company and sold undecorated tableware until closure in 1860.

American Pottery Company. Established 1833 as development of existing company in Jersey City, New Jersey; traded as American Pottery Manufacturing Company. Produced buff or cream-coloured earthenware. First transfer-printing by English methods in America introduced before 1840. Traded, 1840–45, as American Pottery Company, then sold; became Jersey City Pottery Company, making only white earthenware until company dissolved in 1854. Later reorganized as Rouse & Turner until 1892. Marks include AM. POTTERY/MANUFG Co/ JERSEY CITY, printed in flag (1833–40); AMERICAN/POTTERY CO/JERSEY CITY, within circle. After 1845, only white earthenware sold for decoration marked, with British royal coat of arms and R & T.

American glass. Milk pitcher by Gillinder & Sons of Philadelphia. Pattern called Westward Ho, frosted with acid. c1875. Height $7\frac{3}{4}$*in.*

American silver. Chief centres of silver production in 17th century, Boston and New York. Boston largely inhabited by English settlers and produced English influenced silver. One of earliest Boston silversmiths, J. *Hull, appointed mint master 1652. Initially objects brought over from England copied, e.g. spoons, tankards, two-handled cups, dishes, salts, etc. In colonies, as in England, silver plate represented social standing as well as wealth easily convertible to currency. New York was settled by Dutch and, though it passed under English rule in 1674, did not abandon former traditions: Dutch main language until mid 18th century. Much silver produced for burghers of New World in Dutch styles: coin tankards, beakers, canns, two-handled cups, etc. Many Huguenots came to New York in late 17th century bringing with them French-style cut-card work, helmet ewer shape, acanthus motif, etc. By late 17th century, production of silver had begun in Philadelphia; by 18th century, also in Baltimore. Early 18th century marked increased production of domestic silver. Queen Anne style silver popular *c*1715–50. Use of engraved arms for ornament and identification borrowed from English silver. Tea and coffee services, punch bowls, chafing dishes, tea caddies, salvers, etc., as well as various types of drinking vessel (including American style *porringer) and spoons made. English domestic silver made in rococo style *c*1750–85. Forks still quite rare; followed spoon fashion. After Independence, America still culturally dependent on England. So-called Federal style silver used English neo-classical motifs. Spoon remained most popular article of American silver; whereas larger items generally commissioned, spoons probably permanently stocked by silversmiths. Uniquely American is *coffin-end spoon. 19th century silver, like English counterpart, larger and of heavier gauge; featured Roman and Egyptian ornament. Many urn-shaped presentation pieces made, e.g. two-handled cups, etc.

Much American church plate consists of secular objects bequeathed to churches. Most popular type of communion cup, beaker, introduced by Dutch to New York. In early 18th century Queen Anne donated to leading Episcopal churches altar sets containing communion cups and paten-covers, patens, flagons, and alms dishes. These probably not only influenced production of local church plate, but also introduced Queen Anne style silver to America.

No system of assaying and hallmarking existed in America, except in Maryland (from 1814). Silversmiths initially used *Sterling Standard, or announced that they did, but *coin silver, of varying standards, also used. Many goods marked with a device and initials. From *c*1725, silversmiths often used full surname preceded by initial enclosed in triangle. After 1850, letter D, C, or term Coin, or Pure Coin stamped on silver to indicate that item had been made from dollars or other silver coins. After 1860, term, Sterling, used nationally as silver mark.

American snuff-boxes. Gold and silver boxes made in 18th century; rarely marked, making identification difficult. Surviving gold boxes are of *'Freedom' type. Chief makers: C. *Le Roux, S. *Johnson. Silver boxes commoner; silver and silver-plated boxes also imported from England and set with local hardstones and shells. Oval boxes with loose covers decorated with engraved arms on lids made until 1730. By 1770 oval boxes based on English models made with hinged lids, engraved with monograms and border design; silver-mounted boxes of native shell or tortoise-shell were also popular. Prominent silversmiths who made or sold boxes: J. *Coney, J. *Hurd, and P. *van Dyck.

American watches. Mainly produced after 1850. Makers reported working in early 19th century (e.g. T. *Harland in Norwich, Connecticut soon after 1800) probably imported movements or parts for assembly from England. First entirely American watches made by H. and J. *Pitkin in Hartford, Connecticut, 1837, but company ceased in 1845 through growing competition from Swiss; output of under 1000 watches. Modern watch industry in U.S. pioneered e.g. by E. *Howard in Boston, *c*1850; eight-day watch with machine-made parts produced 1850.

amethyst. *See* quartz.

amorini (Italian, 'cupids'). Winged cupids or cherubs; of classical origin, Renaissance decorative motif. Also used on furniture, and as ornament applied or embossed on late 17th and mid 18th century silver (including toilet services).

amphora. Ancient Greek and Roman two-handled storage jar or vase, with circular foot, ovoid body and narrow neck flaring slightly at

*Amphora. Chinese, *T'ang dynasty, white stoneware with colourless glaze.*

Amstel. Porcelain coffee-pot painted with two Dutch landscapes, mid 18th century.

rim. Term also used for Egyptian glass vessel with pointed base ending in button or small disc foot, designed to rest on wood or metal stand. Shape adopted in Europe for neo-classical silver hollow-ware, etc., also used as decorative motif. Form used in ceramics of Chinese T'ang dynasty, usually with white glaze; handles often in form of dragons, rising above rim. Copied in Ming period. *See also* *Alhambra vase.

ampulla. Small, circular flask, usually with two handles, for consecrated oil or holy water, often bought as souvenir by pilgrims in Middle Ages; earlier examples are known. Made in Europe, especially France and Italy; often decorated with biblical scenes or inscriptions in relief. Made in pewter, brass, etc. *See* chrismatory.

Amstel. Dutch porcelain factories. *Oude Loosdrecht factory transferred to Oude Amstel in 1784. Sold by auction (1799); moved to Nieuwer Amstel in 1809; factory closed in 1820.

Amsterdam clock. *See* Dutch clocks.

Anatolian animal carpets. Very large Turkish carpets woven in western Anatolia during 13th and 14th centuries. Design: simple rows of identical stylized striding quadrupeds or stylized birds on either side of plant. Red and blue predominate.

Anatolian carpets. *See* Anatolian animal carpets, Bergama, Ghiordes, graveyard, Kula, 'Lotto', Medjid, Megri, Melas, Mudjur, Smyrna, and Ushak carpets.

anchor escapement. *See* escapement.

andirons. Outside pair in set of six fireplace irons. Originally supporters of logs in hearth, used from Roman times; by 17th century, purely ornamental. Made in pairs: two front feet rise to decorative stem with finial; one long foot on which logs rest extends horizontally to back of hearth. Medieval examples of wrought iron with Gothic decoration; by 16th century cast iron used with Renaissance ornament and bronze, brass, silver, or silver-gilt enrichments (cast and applied figures, etc.); also made entirely of bronze. From *c*1580, some examples bore enamelled ornament. Feet normally scroll-shaped. Commonwealth style plainer, with simple decorative device, e.g. coat of arms. From 1660s again ornate, cast or wrought iron, facings of copper, brass, bronze, steel, highly polished. Late 17th century styles show Huguenot and Dutch influence. Early 18th century brought wider use of coal, necessitating use of grates, which gradually replaced andirons; those still made were often of steel or gilt bronze. *See also* creepers, fire-dogs, spit-dogs.

Andreoli, Maestro Giorgio (d *c*1553). Italian maiolica potter and painter, born in Lombardy. In 1498, with brother, became citizen of Gubbio, where established workshop. Applied lustre decoration to maiolica made there and at Urbino, Castel Durante, etc. Marks (1518–41) include monograms of GA or MG, sometimes with cross incorporated; also MG on each side of orb with cross; often with date; painted in lustre.

Andries or **Andriesz,** Guido (fl early 16th century). Italian potter, believed identical with Guido Da Savino of Castel Durante, mentioned by C. *Piccolpasso as moving to *Antwerp. Made tin-glazed ware in Antwerp from 1512. Sons (d 1570s) also potters; one admitted to Guild of St Luke, Antwerp, in 1552 and owned pottery in Middelburg, Holland, from 1564. Another, Frans, recorded as working at Seville in 1561. Son or grandson, Jasper Andries, worked as delftware potter in England, at Norwich, *c*1567.

Angarano, near Bassano (Veneto). Italian maiolica made at *Manardi workshop from 17th century until *c*1740. Cream-coloured earthenware also made. Products include figures and groups. Porcelain believed to have been made 1777–80 with help of workers from Le Nove.

angel pattern. Ceramic decoration: angel with outstretched wings holding scroll which bears inscription. Usually found on English delftware made in London, *c*1660 to end of 17th century. Scallop shell below scroll, introduced in late 17th century, attributed to Lambeth.

Angers Tapestry (1376–79). Only surviving major 14th century French tapestry. Seven hangings (total size, 468×18ft) depict Visions of Apocalypse. Scenes in light tones; backgrounds red and blue chequer pattern, plain, or with foliage and geometrical figures. Commissioned by Louis I, Duke of Anjou, and woven in Paris by N. *Bataille from cartoons by Hennequin.

angle chair. *See* corner chair.

Angoulême (Charente). French faience factory, established in 1748; lasted until late 19th century. Products, sometimes marked ANGOULEME, include vases, holy water stoups, and large animal figures; style influenced by Rouen and Nevers.

Angoulême sprig. *See* barbeau sprig.

an hua (Chinese, 'secret decoration'). Originated in *Ming period, found on porcelain of *Ching-tê-chên. Design incised in paste with thin tool; only visible when piece held up to light (*cf* Yung Lo and Te Hua.) Early pieces decorated with archaic characters.

anima. *See* core.

animal carpets. 16th and 17th century court carpets woven in north-west Persia. Field of numerous floral motifs and wild animals, usually those of royal hunt. Double scroll borders.

animal clock. Automaton table clock, made in Augsburg and other German towns during 16th and 17th centuries. Animal figure, e.g. lion, elephant, or griffon, moves as clock ticks or

Animal clock. Gilded metal lion sitting on engraved plate with dials for hours and quarters, made in Germany by Johann Oth Halleicher, c1670. Three-train movement; lion's eyes move with balance wheel; mouth opens to show tongue at the hour. Two bells mounted in ebony plinth. Height 9½in.

Les Animaliers. *Bronze figure of camel by Delabrierre, signed and dated 1849. Height $11\frac{1}{2}$in.*

strikes. Base (containing movement) of wood or metal, with metal figure.

animal style. Style of decoration common to most nomadic peoples of Central Asia and southern Siberian Steppes, originating *c*1500 B.C. (For Chinese animal style, *see* Ordos style, Huai style.)

Animaliers, les. 19th century school of French sculptors specializing in animal sculpture. Most distinguished was A-L. *Barye; later animaliers included A-N. *Cain, E. *Frémiet, and P-J. *Mène.

Annagelb. *See* J. Riedel.

Annagrün. *See* J. Riedel.

annealing. Means of softening, and relieving internal stresses (resulting in cracking and deterioration) in metal and glass. Material is heated, then cooled, usually slowly and uniformly. Improvements in annealing technique in late 18th century removed many defects found in earlier glass. Some metal-work processes, e.g. raising, wire-work, require repeated annealing to prevent metal from becoming brittle.

Ansbach (Bavaria). German factory producing faience *c*1715–1804, notably in 1730s. Characterized by blue painting, further decorated with red enamel and gilding in Japanese Imari style; also copied **famille verte*. Colours include translucent bottle-green, yellow, red-brown, and manganese purple. Secret of green, and special glaze to raise enamels, lost by 1768. No factory marks used. Master painter often signed pieces with date and town; before 1769, On occurs, probably for Onolzbach (alternative name for Ansbach); after 1769, AP used, probably Ansbach Popp (owner). Initials of various painters also appear as marks.

Hard-paste porcelain made with Passau clay at faience factory, from 1758, by workers from Meissen and Berlin porcelain factories. Changed hands 1806; closed 1860. *c*1767–85, factory premises established in neighbouring castle. Decoration includes crimson or purple monochrome landscape medallions framed with gilt rococo borders; also figure painting in style of J-A. *Watteau, on tableware. Coffee and chocolate pots have female mask at base of spout. Figure modelling ascribed to J. F. *Kändler includes *commedia dell'arte* characters, peasants, and grotesque Chinese figures outlined in red. Marks (all underglaze blue): A over Brandenburg shield (1758–62); A with or without eagle (1762–1860); sometimes on figures, Brandenburg shield impressed (after 1762).

Ansbach porcelain. Group of man and girl fishing from boat, beside lighthouse or tower. c1770. Height $6\frac{1}{4}$in.

Ansonia Clock Company. American factory in Ansonia, Connecticut, 1851–78. Produced wall and shelf clocks in *Connecticut style. Then in New York City, 1879–*c*1930.

anthemion or **honeysuckle motif.** Stylized flower or leaf design in radiating pattern resembling honeysuckle flower. Origin in Greek and Roman architecture. Used extensively on furniture and in interior decoration. Common on late 18th and early 19th century silver flat and hollow ware in neo-classical style.

Antikzierat (German, 'antique decoration'). Moulded design of fluting and reeding introduced on tableware at *Berlin porcelain factory in 1767.

antimony. Element with hardening properties sometimes used in pewter or similar alloys, e.g. *Britannia metal, *Ashberry metal.

Antonibon, Giovanni Battista (fl 1728–41), son Pasquale (fl 1738–73) and grandson Giovanni Battista II (fl from 1762). Italian potters and porcelain makers. In 1728, Giovanni Battista opened factory at *Le Nove. Succeeded *c*1740 by Pasquale, who experimented with manufacture of porcelain from 1752. Giovanni Battista II, manager from 1762. Porcelain production, started 1762, interrupted by illness of Pasquale (1763–65). In 1773, Pasquale ennobled; retired. Maiolica factory leased to G. M. *Baccin. Porcelain manufacture discontinued until 1781, when factory leased.

Antwerp. First centre of tin-glazed earthenware manufacture in Low Countries. In early 16th century, maiolica made by Italian settlers, including G. *Andries. Large ceremonial bowls in style of Patanazzi workshop attributed to Antwerp; wide rims; grotesque ornament in brown, outlined in purple.

Antwerp style. Ceramic decoration, inspired by Italian, mainly Venetian, painting of maiolica, found on tin-glazed ware (including tiles) made at Antwerp in mid 16th century. Characterized by spiral scrolls, strapwork, and *ferronneries*. Painted in blue outline, with ground of brownish-orange, and touches of green and yellow.

Antwerp tapestry. Antwerp Flemish tapestry-weaving centre from 15th century, and major distribution centre (for Flemish tapestries) until mid 17th century. In 16th century, fine *verdures*, and numerous floral borders designed and woven for Brussels and Oudenaarde tapestries. Production reached peak in 17th century, with influx of Protestant refugees from other Flemish weaving centres. Popular subjects: History of Jacob, History of Troy, History of Achilles, landscapes, and *grotesques.

Antwerp tapestry. Huntsman with his dogs, c1700. 17ft3in.×13ft2in.

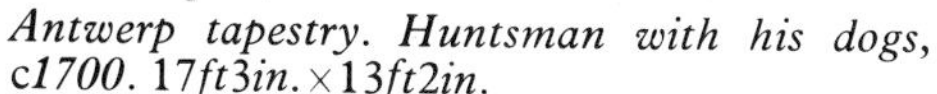

Apostle spoons. English. Left: Charles I spoon with gilt figure of St Jude with St Esprit nimbus; dated 1640, maker's mark, EI. Centre: James I spoon, surmounted by figure of apostle, without emblem; pierced ray nimbus; c1630, maker's mark, RC with mullet above and dotted circle below. Right: James I spoon, surmounted by gilt figure of St Paul with St Esprit nimbus; 1618; maker's mark, IF with mullet below.

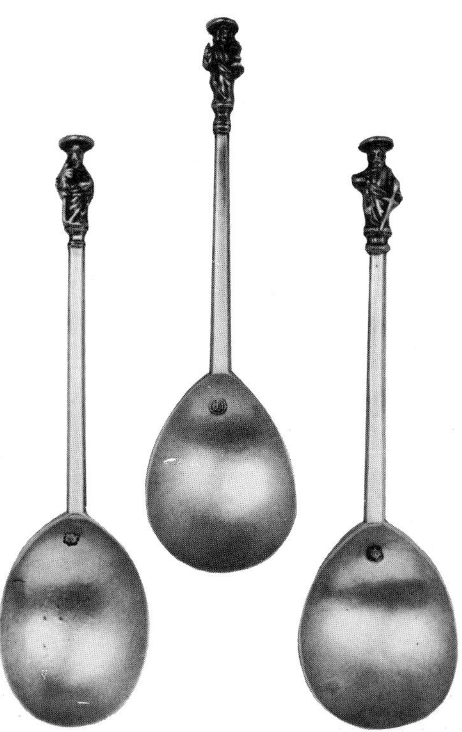

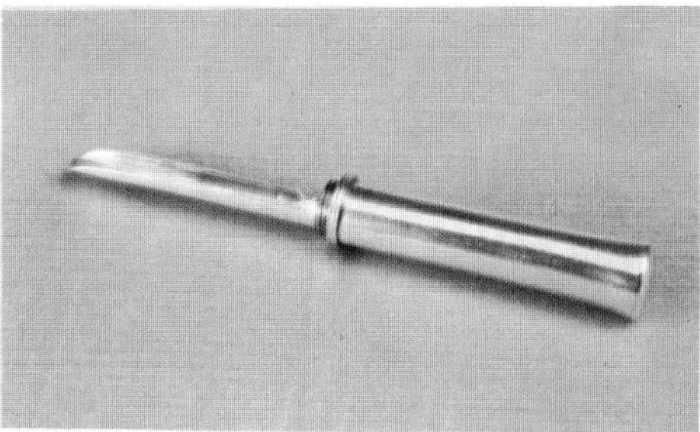

Apple corer. George III, made in 1808.

Ao Oribe. *See* Oribe ware.

Apocalypse Tapestry. *See* Angers Tapestry.

apostle glasses. **Humpen* with enamelled decoration portraying religious figures. Mainly 17th century, Bohemian and German.

apostle spoons. Silver—less often pewter or brass—spoons made from 15th to 17th centuries in Britain and Europe. Made in sets of 13, with knops formed as figures of Christ and 12 apostles. Complete sets, fully hall-marked, of same year and maker extremely rare. Each apostle depicted with own emblem (e.g. Peter with key, Andrew with cross) held in right hand. Emblems often cast separately and may have broken off. Style revived in 19th century England; used for mass-produced coffee spoons. *See* christening spoon.

apothecary jar. *See* drug-pot.

apple corer. Silver utensil, usually with cylindrical handle and scoop blade crescent-shaped in cross-section; sometimes with spice compartment in handle. Earliest examples date from late 17th century; majority date from late 18th and early 19th centuries. In some later ones, blade can be unscrewed to fit inside handle.

*Apple-green crackled glaze bottle. *Ch'ien Lung period. Height 7in.*

apple green. Chinese glaze colour found on porcelain of Ch'ing period; derived from iron oxide. Emerald green enamel, applied over white or grey crackled glaze. Also trade name for ground colour introduced at Worcester, *c*1770, resembling colour introduced at Sèvres in 1756. Thought to be colour advertized on introduction at Worcester as pea green.

applied ornament or **appliqué.** Ornament separately shaped and worked, then fixed to object. In metalwork, includes *cut-card and cast decoration; also gives added strength. Applied relief ornament used on ceramics e.g. *Hafnerware,* German stoneware and Staffordshire earthenware.

Aprey (Haute-Marne). French faience factory established in 1744. At first produced faience with decoration in high-temperature colours resembling Strasbourg in style. In 1760, enamel painting introduced by P. *Pidoux; colours include thick purplish-crimson. From 1766, large bold flower decoration gradually replaced by small, neat bouquets; rococo shapes. F. *Ollivier, director 1769–72. 1770s decoration includes bird painting by J. *Jarry and A. *Mege; also panels with *chinoiserie* designs on reserves in striped grounds. Sometimes ground has decoration painted in enamel, or scratched through tin glaze. In 1780s, products more commonplace, relying on flower decoration and *chinoiseries.* Production lapsed during French Revolution; re-opened by J-M. *Ollivier, director 1806–32. Work marked with monogram

AP or AR, rarely APREY or aprey, with initials of painter in enamel colours; most common before 1772.

apron or **skirting board.** On furniture, piece of wood, often ornamented, beneath frieze-rails of stands and tables, and under seat-rails of chairs.

Apt (Vaucluse), France. Centre of earthenware manufacture from early 18th century to present; several potteries in existence from 1728. Early ware has buff body and thick yellow glaze subject to crazing. *Ecuelles*, ewers and basins modelled after silver shapes with low relief decoration, e.g. of scrollwork and cupids. By 1780s, yellowish cream-coloured earthenware produced with marbled slip decoration, and leaves, flowers, and scrolls applied in light-coloured clay. Pieces include figures, vases, and *écuelles*; occasionally marked by individual potteries.

aquafortis. Old name for nitric acid; used in *leaching. *See* electro-plating.

aquamanile. Ewer or water bottle, for hand-washing, often in animal or human form (e.g. mounted knight). Made from metal (usually bronze) by lost-wax process, throughout Europe from 13th to 16th centuries; 13th and 14th century English examples occur in lead-glazed pottery. Replaced by simpler jug-shaped ewer.

Aquamanile. *Brass cast in form of standing lion; handle, a long-bodied monster with triple tail. Flemish, 13th century. Height 11½in.*

a quartieri. Italian maiolica decoration of 16th century: rim or whole surface of plate divided into six or eight panels radiating from centre.

arabesque or **Shah Abbas carpets.** 17th century court carpets, woven in central Persia during reign of Shah Abbas (1586–1628), attributed to Isfahan. Field has richly-coloured pattern of cloud-bands, large, naturalistic palmettes and blossoms, usually on claret or dark rose ground. Borders with alternating palmettes and peony or lotus blossoms, linked by vine scroll, usually on green ground. Exported, and copied extensively (particularly in Caucasus, until mid 19th century). Also, any carpet with dominant arabesque pattern, particularly Turkish *Lotto carpets.

arabesques or **rabeschi.** Widely used pattern, of Roman origin, usually symmetrical, consisting of interlaced branches, leaves, scrollwork, etc., sometimes also containing stylized flower, fruit, or animal forms. Common motif in carpets and tapestries and in medieval Islamic art and decoration; occurs on *Hispano-Moresque pottery. Use on 16th century Italian maiolica especially associated with Venice and Genoa. Found on wares inspired by Hispano-Moresque until 19th century. (*Illustrations at* Faenza, Moustiers). Found as pierced, embossed, etc., ornament on 16th and early 18th century silver and revived in England *c*1830–60.

Arabic numerals (on clocks and watches). *See* numerals.

Arak carpets. *See* Mahal carpets.

Arazzeria Medici. *See* Florentine tapestry.

arbor (in clocks and watches). Any axle or revolving spindle in mechanism. Normally made of steel.

arbour groups. Porcelain figures modelled periodically in Germany at Meissen, Höchst, and elsewhere from 1750s onwards. Central characters backed by elaborate, formalized, rococo arbour, sometimes scrolled and decorated with applied coloured flowers. P. *Reinicke among originators. 19th century versions abound. Figures of lovers sitting in alcove or leafy arbour made in Staffordshire salt-glaze or Whieldon ware in mid 18th century England.

arcaded minute ring. Arrangement of numerals to show minutes on dial of watch in series of 12 arches outside hour circle; commonly used in Holland in 18th century, but also in Geneva.

arcading. Decoration in form of arch or arches on furniture backs or panels; often found on late 16th and 17th century furniture.

arcanist. Workman claiming knowledge of secret (arcanum) of porcelain making, and other processes, e.g. faience making, particularly in 18th century.

Archambo, Peter the Elder (d 1767) and the Younger (fl mid 18th century). English silversmiths of Huguenot descent working in London; Peter the Elder received freedom from Butchers' Company in 1720. Made some domestic silver in rococo style. Mark, registered in 1720, AR crowned; in 1739, PA in script. Son, Peter the Younger, was apprenticed to him and to P. *de Lamerie in 1738; granted freedom in 1747–48; mark, registered 1749–50 with another of father's apprentices, Peter Meure, PA with P above and M below. *Illustration at* egg-frame.

arch-back Windsor. Late 18th and early 19th century Windsor chair made in New England. Arching back-rail bends toward front of chair, forming arms.

architect's table. Form of desk or *artist's table, incorporating drawing-board and drawers for art materials.

architectural case. Clock case with portico top based on lines of classical architecture; triangular pediment, supported by capitals and columns each side. Used in early long-case clocks, until *c*1700; makers include E. *East and A. *Fromanteel. English bracket and wall clocks of this type also produced, notably *c*1660–*c*1675.

*Architectural case on table clock by A. *Fromanteel. English, c1663. Ebony case with cast and chased gilt metal mounts. Bells inside cupola for half-hour striking.*

archlute. *See* lute.

Ardebil carpet. Persian court carpet made 1540, probably in north-west Persia for mosque at Ardebil. Field design, 16-point golden star medallion surrounded by intricate floral system on indigo field. Main border alternates red cartouches and green multifoils. In Victoria & Albert Museum, London.

Ardebil shrine. Originally housed large collection of oriental ceramics formed by Shah Abbas the Great, presented (1611) to shrine of Shaikh Safi, near Caspian Sea. Incised marking of all items with Shah's seal provides valuable evidence for dating or attribution. Remnants of collection, mostly blue-and-white porcelain, now in Tehran, Persia.

Ardus (Tarn-et-Garonne). French faience factory established *c*1739. Until *c*1752, high-temperature blue decoration followed **style Berain*, copied from faience made at Moustiers, with portraits in addition to usual motifs. Reddish body covered by glaze with tendency to craze. Later products inspired by Nevers, decorated in high-temperature polychrome and sometimes, from 1770s, enamel. From 1780, *faïence fine* made. Factory closed in 1876.

Arfe family (fl 16th century). Castilian silversmiths celebrated for elaborate church plate. Founder of family, Enrique (d 1545), came from Harff in the German Rhineland (hence name Enrique de Arfe) and trained in Cologne. Executed church plate of architectural type in Gothic style, e.g. huge **custodia* for cathedral of Toledo, Spain. Grandson, Juan, published several books of designs for secular and church plate; worked in Renaissance style; like grandfather and father, Antonio, emphasized architectural ornament.

Ardebil carpet. Persian, 1540. Knotted woollen pile on silk warp. Inscription at bottom reads: 'I have no refuge in the world other than thy threshold. There is no place of protection for my head other than this door. The work of the slave of the threshold Maqsud of Kashan in the year 946.' 17ft6in. · 34ft.

Argand lamp or **quinquet.** Oil lamp, invented *c*1782 in Geneva by Aimé Argand; has glass tube supplying air to flame, tubular wick, and glass chimney above; up to six wicks fed from central oil reservoir. Manufactured in England by *Boulton & Watt of Birmingham, in France by Quinquet; also elsewhere. Adjustable burner developed by *c*1810.

argentine, argentan, German or **nickel silver.** Alloy of nickel, copper, and zinc; of Chinese origin. Analyzed by a Scottish chemist in early 1820s; his findings encouraged firm of Johnson Matthey to import nickel from Germany (hence name, German silver) in order to manufacture the alloy a few years later in London. S. *Roberts patented its use in 1830 as interpolated layer between copper and silver in Sheffield plate; nickel alloy being nearer in colour and tone to silver would show less in wear. First called 'argentan' in 1836. Used as base for Sheffield plate in last days of industry (*c*1836–*c*1860), and for electro-plating.

argyle or **gravy warmer.** Silver or Sheffield plate vessel for serving gravy. Body sometimes

Argyle. Silver. Made in Edinburgh, 1799; maker's mark, M & F. Height 8in.

*Arita ware. One of pair of dragon vases, Japanese, late 17th century. Dragon holds conch shell; coloured in *Kakiemon enamels. Height 7in.*

modelled on shapes of tea and coffee pots; spout generally at right-angle to handle with lining for hot water or socket to take hot iron. Used in Britain from mid 18th century; allegedly named after inventor, a Duke of Argyll.

Arita (Hizen). Semi-legendary Japanese figure, Shonzui, introduced art of porcelain manufacture in early 16th century. Wares found there possibly of Korean origin, but main stylistic and technical influence came from China. Polychrome enamel decoration introduced on porcelain in 17th century, imitating Chinese Ming period porcelain. Also, celadon porcelain produced, mainly in 18th century.

ark. Chest with sloping top; peculiar to the north of England. Originally made of hewn oak, and pegged; in 19th century, a flour or meal chest.

Arlaud, Jacques-Antoine (1688–1743). Swiss-born miniaturist. In France, worked for jeweller in Dijon, then in Paris, where gained patronage of Duc d'Orléans. Visited London (1721); painted Princess of Wales. Miniatures in gouache on vellum or card. Painted portraits and historical subjects.

Arlaud, Louis-Aimé (b 1752). Miniaturist, grand nephew of J-A. *Arlaud. Painter at court of Louis XVI. Exhibited at Royal Academy, London, 1792. Miniatures in enamel or water-colour, sometimes on ivory.

Armada chest. Wrought-iron coffer with complicated locking mechanism and strengthening

Armada chest. Iron with wrought handles and false lock plate; keyhole is on the top concealed by hinged flap. Mid 17th century.

wrought-iron bands. Made in southern Germany (chiefly Nuremberg) from late 16th to late 18th century. Sizes vary from a few inches to c6ft long. Many bore painted designs, but few survive in original condition; elaborate engraving often found on lock-plate. Name probably derives from 19th century belief that such coffers were found in wrecks of ships from Spanish Armada.

armadio. Large Italian rectangular movable

Armoire. *Walnut, with shaped, arched cresting; two panelled doors with chamfered angles; engraved brass handles. Dutch, mid 18th century.*

John R. Arnold. Movement of Pocket *chronometer c1805, showing balance and detent. Original helical spring replaced by spiral.

cupboard, similar in form and purpose to *armoire. Dates from 15th century.

Armenian bole. *See* sealing-wax red.

Armenian dragon rugs. Long, narrow Caucasian carpets with woollen foundation and longish Turkish-knotted pile, woven possibly from 16th century. Stylized dragon-like creatures appear within ascending lattice of lozenge panels, sometimes alternating with very large palmettes. Design in bold primary colours on red, blue, or dark brown ground. Main border very narrow with stylized vine-scroll or calyx-and-leaf ornament. From 17th century, widely copied, with dragons reduced to angular S-forms or floral motifs.

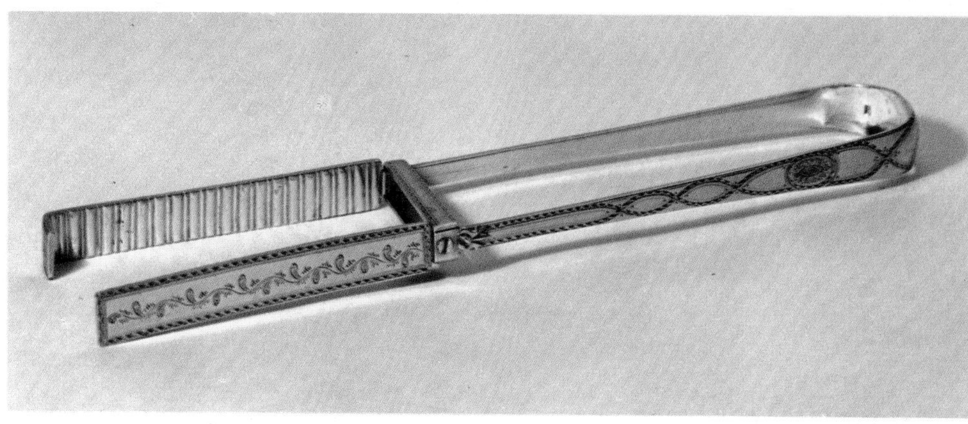

Asparagus tongs. Silver, George III, made by George Smith, c1790. Ribbed blades; outside decorated with bright-cut engraving.

armillary sphere. Early astronomical instrument representing universe, formed from concentric rings or hoops, usually of bronze, showing main celestial features, e.g. equator, tropics, orbits of sun and moon, etc. Devised in 2nd century A.D. by Ptolemy, and made to end of 16th century showing earth at centre of universe. Later models based on Copernican system, with sun at centre of universe, made for comparative demonstration purposes.

armoire. Large cupboard or wardrobe with one or two doors, originating in late 16th century France.

armorial porcelain. Coats of arms painted on table services, e.g. Chinese porcelain made for export from 16th century. Articles manufactured at Imperial kilns of *Ching-tê-chên; often sent to Canton for decoration. Complete dinner, breakfast, or dessert services, including oil, vinegar, pepper, and mustard containers (even egg cups) all with coats of arms or crests. Widely distributed in most European countries. Coats of arms also painted on porcelain table services, particularly in 18th century Germany, e.g. *Sulkowski service.

Arnold, John (1736–99). English clock and watch maker, noted for work on *chronometers. Developed chronometer *escapement, mainly for marine chronometers, but also in precision watches (pocket chronometers). Concerned with exact timekeeping; used helical, or spiral, balance spring, and made tiny ring-watch purchased in 1764 by King George III. Made regulators for Royal Observatory, Greenwich. Leading partner of firm Arnold & Son (with John Roger Arnold), 1787–99.

Arras (Pas-de-Calais). French soft-paste porcelain factory established in 1770. Made tablewares painted in blue or crimson monochrome with flowers, *chinoiseries*, or coats of arms; also occasionally polychrome flower decoration. Marks include AR painted in underglaze blue, or purple or crimson enamel, and AA in underglaze blue.

Arras tapestry. Flemish town of Arras among oldest European high-warp loom tapestry-weaving centres. Industry developed from mid 14th century under patronage of Philip the Bold of Burgundy (1342–1404). Design and style similar to contemporary Paris tapestries. After Paris fell to English (1418), Arras became continental centre for tapestry artists, weavers, and merchants, under patronage of Charles the Bold. Tapestries beautifully woven from quality wool, often with gold and silver. Functioned as portable signs of wealth and power; given as royal gifts to courts, princes, and ecclesiastics throughout Europe. Superior quality led to adoption of term *arras* for all fine high-warp loom tapestries. Style influenced strongly by book illumination: dense compositions of figures in episodic tales drawn from range of medieval literature, particularly chivalric and religious. Main products, enormous hangings used as partitions or 'woven walls'; also numerous panels and furniture covers. After death of Charles the Bold (1437), industry declined; finally collapsed after city taken by Louis XI, and Flemish tapestry centre shifted first to Tournai, then Brussels.

arris. Angle where two plane or curved surfaces meet forming sharp edges; emphasized in neo-classical silver.

arrow-back Windsor. Windsor chair, popular in 19th century America. Flat arrow-shaped back-supports; arms also flat. Back rectangular; arms attached to outside back verticals.

arrow spindle (in furniture). Thin rod with pointed terminal resembling arrow-head.

Arte Vetraria (Italian, 'Art of Glass'). Standard work on glass making, written by Antonio Neri, published in Florence 1612 and 1661, in Venice 1663 and 1678. Translated into English by Dr Merret (1662), into Latin and published in Amsterdam (1668), into German by J. *Kunckel (1679), and into French (1752).

artificial porcelain. *See* soft-paste porcelain.

artist's table. 18th century form with many variations, but incorporating leaves and adjustable top. Some have pillar bases; others supported on four legs, resembling writing table.

artwork. *See* Bantam work.

Asahi (Japanese, 'morning sun'). Japanese pottery centre, active in early Edo period; name evokes glaze colour found in most pieces. Mainly produced tea vessels, prized for beauty of shape and colour, resembling Korean *Karatsu ware. Translucent blue-green glaze covers coarse brown body. Potteries still active in same tradition, but finest work in second half of 17th century.

Ashberry metal. Pewter-like alloy containing c25% antimony and zinc; used for buttons, buckles, forks, spoons, etc. Named after inventor, P. Ashberry (fl late 18th, early 19th centuries).

Ash, Gilbert (1717–85). American joiner and cabinet maker, possibly trained in Philadelphia. Worked in New York City; noted for chairs in style of T. *Chippendale.

Askew, Richard (fl late 18th century). English porcelain painter, at Chelsea; designs include figure subjects on vases. 1772–95, worked at Derby; painted figures in style of F. *Boucher and cupids *en camaïeu.*

asparagus tongs. Silver or Sheffield plate servers for asparagus; used in Britain from 17th century, though earliest surviving examples 18th century. Two 18th century types: earlier is scissor-like implement with corrugated ridges on inside of one or both arms; later examples have pierced arms. Other type resembles *sugar tongs, with pierced, flat grips, and often with guide bracket.

assay. Testing purity of gold or silver (traditionally toughened by alloying with base metals), or pewter, etc., by *touchstone, *cupellation, or chemical means. Standards of purity set by individual governments and implemented by assay offices or institutions, e.g. Pewterer's Company from Middle Ages; vary throughout world. *See* hallmarking, Sterling Standard. Assay or test-piece also name given to piece submitted as sample of work by craftsman registering with guild.

Astbury, John (1688–1743). Potter at Shelton, Staffordshire; maker of *Astbury ware from *c*1730. Credited with manufacture (from *c*1735) of figure jugs in form of fiddlers and midshipmen. Employed as apprentices R. *Wood I and T. *Whieldon. Traditionally associated with improvement of earthenware body by addition of ground flints and white Devonshire clay.

Astbury ware. English lead-glazed earthenware associated with J. *Astbury and contemporaries, made *c*1740–*c*1770, e.g. in Staffordshire and Yorkshire. Designs stamped on pads of cream-coloured clay applied to red or brown body; covered with thick, honey-coloured

Astbury-Whieldon wares. Coffee-pots, both c1755–60, lead-glazed earthenware with applied decoration; glazed in green, brown, and yellow. Height of left-hand pot 8¾in.

glaze. Occasionally, dark reliefs stamped on pale body. Used for domestic ware and figures, including horsemen, soldiers, and musicians.

Astbury-Whieldon ware. Mid 18th century Staffordshire earthenware with stamped decoration on contrasting coloured clay in manner of *Astbury ware, covered by lead glaze stained with metallic oxides, as used by T. *Whieldon.

aster pattern. Ceramic decoration; round-headed pointed-petalled flower shape, with symmetrically-paired leaves found on Chinese porcelain of Ming and Ch'ing periods. Derived from lotus flower.

astragal. Architectural term for small moulding, semi-circular in cross-section; found round top or bottom of column. Often enriched with beading. Much used in late 18th century neo-classical silver.

astrolabe. Instrument for astronomical calculation and finding altitude of sun, stars, or terrestrial objects, current from cA.D.500, or earlier, to mid 17th century. Introduced to Europe in Middle Ages from Islam. Three essential parts are flat disc (mater) with ring for suspension, degree scale engraved on rim and face hollowed to accept plate (tympanum), interchangeable for different latitudes, engraved with lines representing tropics, meridians, etc., and pierced plate (rete) forming map of constellations and fixed stars. Sighting bar (alidade) pivoted at centre of disc. All normally of bronze or brass, sometimes elaborately decorated. Can be used to find time by measuring altitude of sun or fixed star (after turning rete to correspond with observed position), for astrological purposes, or for measuring heights in surveying. Type used at sea (mariner's astrolabe) simpler, with heavy brass plate, cut away in parts to reduce wind resistance; graduated at rim and with alidade for sighting. Superseded by more accurate instruments and finally by *sextant.

astronomical dial. Dial on clock or watch showing movement of planets, stars and other celestial bodies including sun and moon, also ordinary mean time. Large public clocks made from 14th century, domestic examples from 16th century.

asymmetrical knot. *See* Persian knot.

athénienne. Form of basin on tripod stand, devised in 1773. Basin could be used uncovered as plant-stand or wash-basin; covered, as perfume-burner.

Astrolabe. Engraved rete for 23 fixed stars; mater contains three plates for latitudes of 1) Meknes and Fez, 2) Marrakesh and Sala and Tripoli, 3) Cairo and Sijil Masa. North African, 18th century. Diameter 4½in.

Atterbury & Company. Glass house founded 1859 as White House Works in Pittsburgh, Pennsylvania, by T. Atterbury. Produced blown and pressed tableware.

Aubusson carpets. From second half of 18th century, tapestry-weave carpets woven at Aubusson manufactory in France on high-warp looms. Design and style follow *Savonnerie models. With decline of fashion for tapestry hangings, production concentrated on carpet-weaving. Peak period, early 19th century. Carpets less expensive than Savonnerie, reaching wider market throughout Europe, also America. Name, Aubusson, adopted for any carpet based on original from Aubusson manufactory.

Aubusson tapestry. Aubusson French tapestry-weaving area from late 15th century. By 1637, *c*2000 weavers active, producing hangings, furniture covers and carpets (*see* Aubusson carpets). Royal Manufactory of Aubusson established 1665 by Colbert. Throughout century largely neglected, with moderate production of mediocre hangings, mainly depicting landscapes, and furniture coverings. Under artistic direction of J. de Mons (1731–55), productivity and stature increased, until became one of great French manufactories; specialized in low-warp loom work. Identification, when present: Aubusson (or initials MRD or MRDA) and weaver's initial woven in border; and blue selvage cord. In 18th century, produced mainly furniture covers and small panels, also some larger hangings. Subjects include decorative landscapes with distant

Astronomical dial. German, made in Augsburg in late 17th century. Dials for solar and lunar time, phase and age of moon; astrolabe shows positions of selected stars. Water-gilded tabernacle case on moulded ebony base with drawer for keys. Height 1ft7in.

views of châteaux, gardens, and trees, luxuriant foliage, flowers, birds, animals, and small figures; also pastoral scenes, with central composition surrounded by picture-frame border, ornamented with festoons and swags of flowers and draperies. From *c*1750, produced mainly tapestries woven from modified cartoons by Beauvais and Gobelins designers, particularly J-B. *Oudry, F. *Boucher, and J-B. Huet. Distinguishing characteristics: duller and coarser; subjects more complex and confused with addition of figures, or damasked wall hung with painting or decorative objects. After Revolution, manufactory maintained steady high-quality production, especially reproductions of finest 17th and early 18th century Gobelins tapestries.

au carquois. French ceramic decoration, incorporating quiver of arrows and torch, painted in high-temperature colours on faience at Rouen in mid 18th century.

Aufenwerth, Johann (d 1728). Earliest known

Aubusson. Tapestry, woven in wool and silk, from Draperies Rouges *series; name refers to border motif. Central panel illustrates different country pursuits. Louis XVI.* 9ft3*in.* × 7*ft*4*in.*

German porcelain *Hausmaler*. Director of Augsburg studio (*c*1715–28), helped by daughter, S. *Hosenestel. Decorated white porcelain from Meissen and China with *chinoiseries* in iron-red, purple, and gold, sometimes with gold and silver silhouetted figures. Occasionally used mark IAW or JAW over Augsburg.

Augsburg clocks. Clocks made in Augsburg (Germany), notably during 16th and early 17th centuries. Many types produced. Elaborate *automaton and *animal clocks: with wooden or metal bases and metal figures; also *nef and other novelty clocks. Ornate *tabernacle clocks, with many dials containing astronomical information (reproductions made in late 19th century). *Monstrance and *crucifix clocks. Frequent use of revolving dial on all types.

Auguste, Henri (1759–1816). French silversmith working in Paris; son of R-J. *Auguste whom he succeeded as court goldsmith to Louis XVI; master in 1785. Made grandiose dinner services until outbreak of Revolution (1789). Best works in Empire style, many for Napoleon I, e.g. ewer and basin used at coronation, and table centrepiece given as coronation gift by city of Paris to Napoleon. In 1809, caught trying to smuggle 97 cases of silver out of France, bankrupted. Died in Port-au-Prince, Haiti. Mark (before Revolution): a fleur-de-lis crowned, two pellets, HA, and a crossed palm branch.

Auguste, Robert-Joseph (*c*1736–1805). French jeweller and silversmith working in Paris; pupil of F-T. *Germain; master in 1757. Favourite goldsmith at court of Louis XVI; together with crown jeweller, Ange-Joseph Aubert, made gold crown, chalice, and regalia for coronation in 1774 (since disappeared). Best known for domestic silver in rococo and neo-classical styles. Made dinner services for Catherine II (the Great) of Russia, Joseph I of Portugal, and many other royal and aristocratic patrons. Son H. *Auguste succeeded to his official appointment; made supplier and manager of Paris mint in 1788. Mark: a fleur-de-lis crowned, two pellets, RJA, and a palm branch.

Augustin, Jean-Baptiste-Jacques (1759–1832). French miniaturist; exhibited 1791–1831. Work characterized by strong, pure colours and high finish. Court painter to Napoleon. Chief miniature painter to Louis XVIII.

Augustus Rex mark. AR monogram mark in underglaze blue used *c*1725–30 on Meissen porcelain commissioned by *Augustus the Strong as gift or as addition to his collection. 19th century forgeries common.

Augustus the Strong (1670–1733). Succeeded brother, Elector of Saxony, as Frederick Augustus I (1694); crowned King of Poland (Augustus II) in 1697, later deposed (1704) and recovered crown in 1709. Employed J. F. *Böttger, first as alchemist, then to experiment

Augsburg table clock. Made by Johannes Martin (1642–1720). Hexagonal form, case of gilt metal. 30-hour movement with alarm mechanism; verge escapement with balance.

with E. W. *von Tschirnhaus in production of porcelain. In 1710, established Saxon porcelain manufacture, which operated in Albrechtsburg fortress and Meissen. In 1717, bought Japanese Palace (originally called Dutch Palace) at Dresden to house collection of porcelain. Commissioned and inspired much work from factory for personal use or as gifts (*see* Augustus Rex mark).

Augustus III. King of Poland. Succeeded father, Augustus II (the Strong) in Electorate of Saxony as Frederick Augustus II (1733–63), and continued patronage of Meissen porcelain factory. Portrait modelled on vase by J. J. *Kändler (1741–42).

Auliczec, Dominicus (1734–1804). Bohemian sculptor, architect, and porcelain modeller. Studied in Vienna, Paris, London, Rome. Worked at Nymphenburg (1764–97); last 20 years as manager. Figures in Louis XVI style, e.g. Roman gods and goddesses; also animals. Famous for garden statues in Nymphenburg park.

aumbry or **ambry.** Early form of doored cupboard; originally, as almery, a receptacle for left-over food to be offered as alms. By 15th century, a safe. Versions with pierced doors for ventilation used to store food. *See armoire.*

auricular motif. Decoration based on forms from human anatomy, particularly of the ear. First appeared in early 17th century Holland; use on furniture spread to England through the Low Countries and Germany. *See* Dutch grotesque style.

Austin, Jesse (1806–79). English pottery decorator. Apprenticed to J. *Davenport as engraver of copperplates for transfer-printing. Designer and copperplate engraver in Burslem, 1826–40. Employed by F. and R. *Pratt; decorated vitreous earthenware pot-lids with underglaze

Aumbry. Henry VIII, oak with chip-carved border to top; two doors and six pierced panels of Gothic tracery. Height 3ft10in.

Austrian clocks. Chiming bracket clock, c1780, presented to Queen Charlotte by Louis XVI. Mahogany case mounted with silver and ormolu. Engraved dial with cherub spandrels; arch contains Meissen plaque, mother-of-pearl strike/not strike and chime/not chime dials. Height 2ft8½in.

engravings; pictures broken down into component colours for reproduction by transfer from stippled copperplates. Bear series (including Bears at School, Performing Bears, Bear-hunting, Bear Pit) for lids of pots containing bear grease.

Austrian clocks. Followed general European styles, until discovery of pendulum (1657). From *c*1680, pendulum bracket clocks on English lines introduced. English influence predominant, *c*1680–*c*1780: metal cresting, brass dials (on long-case clocks); bracket clocks based on English design, combined with Austrian baroque decoration. French influence marked during 19th century: ormolu decoration, attaining fine quality in late examples; many carriage clocks produced; long-case clocks, based on French provincial models. From mid 18th century, characteristic Austrian form for mantel clocks was **Stockuhr*. Bracket clocks in national style, composed of English and French elements, produced from *c*1740; case ebony, with ormolu mounts; inverted bell-top. From *c*1780, form of regulator clock introduced, later known as *Vienna regulator. After *c*1800, wide range of styles, e.g. 'Gothic ruin', with elaborate ormolu mounts, simulating design of English landscape garden, and *Zappler clock.

Austrian snuff-boxes. Based on French styles. Few gold boxes marked; identification based on external evidence, e.g. subjects of portraits.

Aventurine glass. Flask, Venetian, 18th century.

Some porcelain boxes made by Vienna Porcelain Factory *c*1725–35: various shapes; decorated with gaming motifs, e.g. playing cards, chessboards.

autograph (in bronzes). Bronze made, or at least finished, by artist who made model.

automata. Mechanically-animated figures before 18th century made in gilded brass; product of horological industry, often set in watches and clocks. Animals were favourite subjects, though soldiers and figures playing musical instruments or dancing also common. Made in England by J. *Cox from 1760. Writer-automaton made by P. *Jacquet-Droz in Switzerland *c*1772; son Henri-Louis combined music-making mechanism with automaton to produce life-size lady playing organ *c*1784. *'Singing-bird' box invented by Jacquet-Droz firm particularly successful. Animated scenes set in lids of snuff-boxes also popular. Life-size birds in cages with musical mechanism made from *c*1790; with cylinder-and-comb musical box from *c*1830. Dancing dolls with musical boxes set in motion by penny-in-slot made from 1830; monkeys in red tunics from 1850 in Vienna.

automaton clock or **watch.** Clock or watch with animated figures or objects, set in motion by going or striking train.

Avelli, Francesco Xanto (fl 1530–42). Italian maiolica painter at Urbino; studied in Ferrara and Faenza. Used strong, vivid colours, heavily outlined, to paint classical subjects, and scenes from contemporary literature and everyday life, often inspired by engravings.

aventurine or **venturine** (in furniture). Sparkling lacquered surface, achieved by adding powdered gold or gold alloy wire, or silver particles to surface during lacquering. Resembles aventurine glass.

aventurine glass. Glass with inclusion of metallic flakes of copper or gold; decorative technique dating from antiquity and revived during ensuing centuries, particularly in 17th century Venice (e.g. at Miotti Glass House). Brown opaque glass was favoured for this technique. Chinese aventurine called 'gold star glass' (*see* Chinese glass).

Awata. Japanese kiln site near Kyoto. In 18th century continued tradition of potters *Kenzan and *Ninsei. Utensils for tea ceremony painted in enamel colours.

Axminster carpets. Sturdy, good quality English carpets woven at Axminster Carpet Manufactory, Devon; founded 1755 by T. *Whitty and run by Whitty family. Thick-textured, Turkish-knotted woollen pile with *c*35 knots per sq in.; until 1770, warp coarse hemp or linen, later white wool; weft, hemp or linen. Designs woven from full-size colour cartoons, distinguished by fine colours and delicate shading, show Savonnerie influence. Mainly elaborate, meticulously drawn floral patterns or loose copies of *Ushak carpets. Most important commissions, carpets for Carlton House (*c*1790) and three great carpets for State rooms at Brighton Pavilion, woven 1810–20 from designs by Inigo Jones. Also numerous exports, particularly to America. Unable to recover from effects of 1828 fire, factory closed 1835; looms and orders taken over by Wilton Carpet Manufactory, but name Axminster retained.

Axson, William, Jr (d 1800). Woodworker and furniture maker in Charleston, South Carolina. Partner of S. *Townsend.

baby-walker, baby cage, go-cart, or **going-cart.** Open frame designed to support child in standing position while he learns to walk. Consists of two rings (smaller one above larger), connected by several turned rods. Lower ring is attached to castors. Dates from 16th century.

Baccarat. Glasshouse of Ste-Anne established by Bishop of Metz at Baccarat, France, in 1764 to produce table and window glass; unsuccessful; taken over in 1818 by M. d'Artigues, owner of Vonèche glassworks producing lead crystal glass. In 1822, factory changed hands again and became La Compagnie des Cristalleries de Baccarat, incorporating glasshouse at Trelon in 1828. Under direction of Jean-Baptiste Toussaint (1822–58), high quality lead crystal glass produced and experiments with colour encouraged, e.g. *cristal dichroïde*, a green or yellow crystal glass similar to *Annagrün* and *Annagelb*. 1850–70, opal glass in milk or pastel colours made in decorative, often classical forms (term *opaline first used at Baccarat). In 1832, acquisition, in association with *Cristallerie de Saint Louis, of Cristallerie du Creusot, specializing in *sulphides, led to manufacture from 1846 of Baccarat paperweights. Majority of *millefiori* glass; other groups are overlay weights and bouquet weights; rarer animal weights include caterpillars, snakes, ducks, and butterflies. Large and miniature weights also made. Many signed B, followed by date and occasionally craftsman's initials. From 1818, fine cut crystal table glass produced in rich and dignified style; also coloured ornamental glass and variety of moulded glass, often in four-piece moulds with name Baccarat impressed on inside. In late 19th century, pressed glass in imitation of cut crystal produced. Factory still flourishes. *Illustrations at* paperweight, French glass, *millefiori*.

Bacchus, George, and Sons. 19th century glass house in Birmingham, England. Produced cut, engraved, and coloured table glass. Well known for fine *cameo glass.

Baccin, Giovan Maria (fl 1773–1803). Italian potter and maiolica painter. Worked at Cozzi factory. Leased maiolica factory of P. *Antonibon, 1773–1803. In 1784, began production of cream-coloured earthenware, marking this (*c*1784) G.M.B.*.

Bachelier, Jean-Jacques (1727–1805). French porcelain maker. Worked at Vincennes porcelain factory from 1748; artistic director at Vincennes and Sèvres, 1751–93. In early 1750s introduced biscuit porcelain as medium for figure modelling. Regarded as responsible for high quality of production in first 40 years of porcelain manufacture at Vincennes and Sèvres.

bachelor chest. Modern description of small,

Baby-walker. Charles II, walnut, with wooden castors and turned struts. Hinged circular opening. Height 1ft6in.

Bachelor chest. Queen Anne, walnut. Folding rectangular top supported by slides either side of top drawer. Four graduated drawers, cross-banded and moulded; bracket feet. Width 2ft7in.

low chest of drawers made from early 18th century, with folding flap for use as table.

backgammon table. Table with top designed as backgammon board. Developed in 17th century France and England.

back-plate. One of pair of plates containing watch or clock movement; sometimes engraved with decorative motifs, or maker's name.

back screen. Mid 19th century device, often of cane-work, attached to back of dining-room chair to shield occupant with back to fire from the heat.

back-staff or **Davis's quadrant.** Development of *cross-staff for measuring altitude of sun; invented by English maker, John Davis, in 1594. Staff carries graduated arc on either side. Observer stands with back to sun, sights horizon through eye vane on one arc and slit on fixed vane at end of staff, then moves vane on second arc until shadow coincides with slit. Sum of angles on both arcs gives altitude. Construction usually of wood with ebony or ivory scales, later replaced by brass or steel.

back stool. Stool with back attached. Developed in late 16th century, common by mid 17th century; evolved into *single chair.

Baddeley, William (fl *c*1790–*c*1825). Established pottery at Eastwood, near Hanley, Staffordshire (*c*1802–22). Made lightweight *Egyptian black, teapots often have swan finial. Also produced blue-and-white transfer-printed ware. Mark: EASTWOOD, impressed (on teapots, at base of spout).

badge. Pewter or lead badges bought by pilgrims (or 'palmers', from custom of returning with palm branch or leaf from Holy Land) from churches and shrines throughout Europe from 12th to 16th centuries. Worn on hat or chest as sign of accomplished aim and, on return from journey, displayed in house as amulet; believed to have miraculous properties. Bore effigy or emblem of saint, or inscription. Custom grew in France of wearing badges to honour local saints or Virgin Mary. Churches derived substantial revenue from sale of badges; bishops often demanded fee for granting licence to sell.

Beggars' badges, in pewter, brass, and later zinc, issued to genuinely needy throughout Europe from Middle Ages until at least 1800 in some countries; these granted right to beg in streets and pass freely through city gates (porters or keepers on gates also wore badge of office). Other badges worn to proclaim political allegiance. Most examples were designed to be worn on hat, sleeve, or chest; alternatively as pendant to hang round neck. Many 19th century fakes made (*see* Billies and Charlies). *See also enseigne.*

Badlam, Stephen (1751–1815). Massachusetts cabinet and looking-glass maker. Worked in neo-classical style.

Baerdt, Claes Fransen (*c*1628–after 1691). Dutch silversmith working in Bolsward, Friesland; master in 1654. Made mainly domestic silver; specialized in relief decoration, embossed flowers, tiny insects, marine life, also battle scenes. Few surviving pieces include brandy bowls, dishes, salts, and candlesticks. Mark: a crescent between three stars, or work signed, C. Baerdt fec.

bagpipe. Wind instrument characterized by reed-pipe (or pipes) and bag air reservoir guaranteeing continuous air supply to pipes. One of most ancient instruments; origin obscure; possibly introduced to Europe from Middle East. In general use in Britain and Europe from Middle Ages. Chanter or reed-pipe with holes (usually eight) produces melody and one or more additional pipes, referred to as drones, produce a single note. Pipes attached to bag, traditionally made of goat, sheep, or kid skin, by wooden stocks often ornamented with carving (e.g. head of goat, etc.). Instrument is mouth or bellows-blown, through blow-pipe; in 16th century bellows adopted in Ireland and France; held under and worked by left arm of player. Traditional shepherd's instrument in Asia, North Africa, Britain, and Europe. Small bellows-blown *musette* popular among French aristocracy during 17th and 18th centuries.

bahut. Medieval French movable chest with curved top and studded leather cover.

bail handle. Simple, metal semi-circular handle.

Baillon, Jean-Baptiste (d *c*1770). French clock and watch maker. Clock maker to Queen Marie Leczinska (wife of Louis XV), 1751; later to Marie Antoinette. Maker of gold enamel watches (*c*1750–*c*1760); travelling clocks, and mantel clocks, including elephant clock, with black lacquered base, and gilt-bronze decoration.

Baily, Edward Hodges (1788–1867). English sculptor and silver designer; pupil of J. *Flaxman. Worked as modeller for *Rundell, Bridge & Rundell from 1815; became chief modeller (1826). Left in early 1830s to work for P. *Storr and his partner John Mortimer. Designed domestic and presentation silver in style of Flaxman and in naturalistic style popular in Britain in first half of 19th century.

Bain, Alexander (*c*1811–77). Scottish scientist and clockmaker; main work *c*1838–58. Invented type of *electric clock in 1843, with current obtained from metal plates buried in ground. Most designed as long-case clocks, some with shorter cases for wall-mounting.

Bakewell & Co. Glasshouse founded 1808 in Pittsburgh, Pennsylvania. Probably first in America to produce flint-glass on commercially successful basis. Produced bottles, flint, cut and engraved tableware, and pressed glass. Closed 1882 during Depression.

Bakewell, Robert (fl 1708–18). English worker in *wrought iron at Derby. Greatest work considered to be garden pavilion ('Birdcage') at Melbourne Hall, Derbyshire.

baking-iron or **dough-grate.** Long-handled iron stand for small iron oven or cooking-pot, which could be placed in centre of open fire. Used from 16th to 18th century.

Baku carpets. East Caucasian carpets with low, Turkish-knotted pile and flabby texture, woven near Baku. Brown woollen foundation with white edges and ends, cut at bottom only, knotted or braided. Muted colours with many blues and yellows in pattern on indigo or black ground. Early field design, two vertical rows of yellow stepped polygons on turquoise ground; later all-over pattern of coloured botehs surrounding pale blue central medallion. Main border has many diagonal coloured bands.

balance (in *escapement of watches and certain clocks). Oscillating wheel (or rarely, as in J. *Harrison's chronometers 1–3, weighted bar) forming basic timekeeping element; developed from *foliot. Early forms crude and erratic; balance spring, applied independently by R. *Hooke and C. *Huygens *c*1675, increased accuracy, as did more sophisticated escapements and methods of *compensation for temperature change. Balance spring generally flat spiral, but different forms devised by A-L. *Breguet and others to obtain *isochronism, e.g. overcoils, with outermost coil curving in towards centre over body of spring, and helical springs, used in marine chronometers.

Ball, William (fl mid 18th century). English potter or potters. Associated with manufacture of porcelain at *Limehouse and mentioned in contemporary tax records as living in same area (1747). Possibly identical with 'china maker' of same name listed in Liverpool Directory (1766–69). Credited with porcelain made from *c*1755 in Ranleigh Street, Liverpool; first dated

Bakewell & Co. Sugar bowl and cover, probably by this company, c*1815–35. Free-blown, with cut decoration. Height 8½in.*

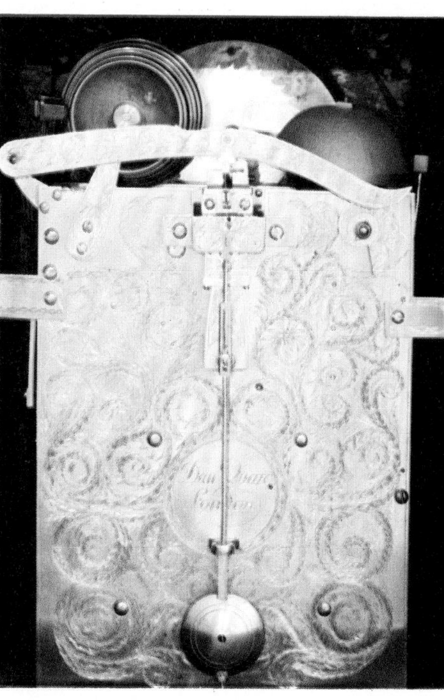

Far left:
*Backgammon table. *Sheraton style; maplewood with ebony inlay. Two halves of table-top draw back to reveal backgammon board in well.*
Left:
*Backplate to bracket clock by D. *Quare, c1720. Finely engraved and signed with Quare's name and London in central medallion. Date wheel and bell can be seen at top; in front of the backplate is lentil bob pendulum. Ebony case.*

example inscribed 1756. Products transfer-printed in polychrome, with enamel over-painting, recall some decoration at Longton Hall. Bright underglaze painting characterized by *sticky blue, covered with soft, brilliant glaze. Shapes and oriental patterns resemble those of Bow; mugs, cornucopia wall pockets and flat wares notable. Other products include goat and bee jugs, tall, covered vases, candlesticks, pickle trays, and toys. Porcelain formula early instance of inclusion of soapstone. Rare examples inscribed in underglaze blue, e.g. with M.:.B or a cross. *Illustration at* Liverpool porcelain.

Ball, William (d 1884). Potter at Sunderland, County Durham. Established Deptford Pottery in 1857. Decorated earthenware produced at Deptford or bought in white from other potters, with transfer-printing and with painting in pink lustre, markedly orange-tinted (*Sunderland ware). Figures include lions. Ware usually unmarked.

ball-and-bar thumbpiece. Thumbpiece on pewter tankards in which straight bar from handle to centre of lid is surmounted at handle end by ball. Used in Scotland, late 18th and early 19th centuries.

ball-and-claw foot. Foot composed of talons or paw holding ball. Of Oriental origin. Found on silver vessels mainly of early 18th century. In furniture, commonly found on cabriole leg, particularly *c*1710–60.

ball-and-wedge thumbpiece. Thumbpiece on English 16th and 17th century pewter vessels in which ball surmounts thick end of wedge.

ball clock, rolling ball clock, or **Congreve clock.** Clock in which ball, instead of balance or pendulum, is used to unlock escapement or train. First invented by N. *Grollier de Servière in 17th century. Best known form developed by W. *Congreve in 1808, with pediment-shaped top containing three dials supported above escapement, which is pivoted 'table' with grooves along which ball rolls alternately from side-to-side, reversing angle of table as each 'journey' is completed.

ballet figures. First modelled in porcelain at Ludwigsburg, *c*1760–65, possibly by J. *Louis, when famous contemporary dance theorist resident at Ducal Palace. Series also modelled by F. C. *Link at Frankenthal.

Ball clock. Brass, with Congreve escapement. Designed by G. H. Bell of Winchester, early 19th century.

ball foot. Spherical foot found on 17th century silver vessels and on mainly large pieces of late 17th and early 18th century furniture.

Ballin, Claude I (*c*1615–78). French silversmith working in Paris; apprenticed to father; master in 1637. Royal goldsmith to Louis XIV. Works on large scale: massive silver vessels, andirons, chandeliers, furniture, etc. All secular works melted down by royal decree in 1689; church plate (at outbreak of Revolution) in 1789. Work for crown well-documented; one of creators of baroque style. In 1676 appointed director of Paris mint.

Ballin, Claude II (1661–1754). French silversmith working in Paris; studied under uncle, Claude Ballin I; master in 1688; given apartments in Louvre in 1703. Royal goldsmith to Louis XV; supplied regalia for coronation (1722). Most work melted down in 1789, but some commissions for foreign royalty have survived, including dinner service for Queen of Spain (Elizabeth Farnese), basin for Elector Maximilian II Emmanuel of Bavaria, and table centrepiece. Worked mainly in baroque style, though rococo style well-established in France before death. Mark: a fleur-de-lis crowned, two pellets, CB, and a ring.

ball knop. Ball-shaped finial on some English pewter spoons in 13th and 14th centuries.

balloon-back. *Loop-back chair back which narrows toward seat. Common 19th century form. *See* buckle-back, Montgolfier back. *Illustration at* Pennsylvania Dutch.

balloon clock. English clock made from mid 18th century until *c*1810; shape resembles hot air balloon. Possibly derived from French bracket clock. Reproductions made during Victorian period. French versions, following interest in ballooning, produced in mid 19th century, with pillars on each side of clock case, and ormolu mounts.

Baltimore monument flasks. 19th century American flasks (purple, blue, amber, yellow, or puce), depicting monument erected to commemorate Battle of North Point (1815). Blown in full-size, two-piece moulds.

Baluchi, Belouchi, or **Belouchestan carpets.** Durable, wool or wool and goat-hair carpets woven by Baluchi tribe in area north-east of Persia and west of Afghanistan. Often classified as Turkoman carpets; structure and design similar, but greater Persian and Chinese influence in patterns. Limited palette with dark blue or blue-black, plum-red, brown, and natural dominating geometric design, usually on camel ground, infilled with numerous stylized floral and tree motifs (particularly single angular tree), or stylized birds and animals. Numerous prayer rugs with mihrab pattern of single, large geometric tree with long, horizontal branches, or of narrow central tree surrounded by large botehs; small, rectangular arch; borders with lozenges, stars, rosettes, and angular stem-scrolls.

baluster. Column with elliptical or pear-shaped bulge at base. Common shape for furniture parts, bodies of tankards and other vessels, stems of candlesticks, goblets, etc.,

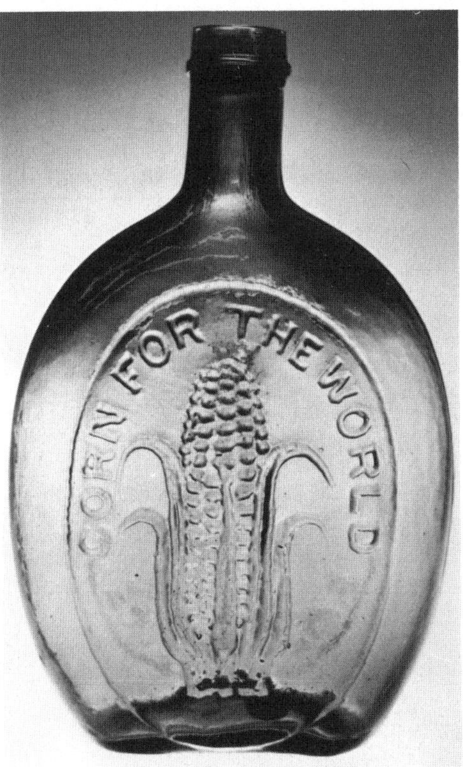

Baltimore Glass Works. Reverse of Washington Monument flask in amber glass, inscribed 'Corn for the World', c1848. Quart capacity.

pillars in watch movements, and *knops, particularly in 16th to mid 18th centuries. Also used in furniture for any small column in series supporting rail, usually turned, but occurring in various ornamental shapes.

baluster and spindle back. *Windsor chair-back with central pierced splat and spindles on either side.

baluster knop. Baluster-shaped knop on some 16th century pewter and brass spoons.

baluster measure. *See* measure.

baluster stem. Earliest form of English wine-glass stem; solid glass with baluster or knop in various shapes, sometimes with tear. Made mainly *c*1685–*c*1725. Early versions normally combined with folded foot. Accompanying bowl shape initially straight-sided, later bell-shaped, both with solid base set on stem with, at most, rudimentary collar.

balustroid stem. Stem form in English glasses; lighter version of *baluster stem on smaller, lighter glasses, made *c*1725–*c*1760. Varying bowl shapes; solid base less pronounced than in baluster-stemmed varieties; late examples with bowl sometimes engraved, moulded, or fluted. Feet folded or plain, both with high conical kick.

Balzac, Edmé Pierre (d after 1781). French silversmith working in Paris; master in 1739 and appointed goldsmith to court of Louis XV. Best known for domestic silver in rococo style. Filled many royal commissions for dinner services. In

*Banjo clock. By A. *Willard, made in Boston, 1808.*

1749, relinquished royal appointment to brother, Jean-François. Mark: a fleur-de-lis crowned, two pellets, EPB, and a cinquefoil.

bamboo furniture. Furniture of Chinese inspiration, using *bamboo turning; chairs often have caned seats. Late 19th century furniture made from genuine bamboo is less sturdy than earlier imitation bamboo pieces.

bamboo turning. Imitation bamboo made of turned beech or ash wood painted to resemble bamboo. Used to make furniture in England and America in late 18th and early 19th century.

Bandelwerk. *See Laub-und-Bandelwerk.*

bandy leg. *See* cabriole leg.

banister-back. American chair back with upright splats (some ornamented) or split spindles. Dates from early 18th century; pierced balusters used late 18th century.

Banko ware. Japanese pottery made near Kuwana, Mie Prefecture, in Edo period. Output includes *raku, *Shino, *Oribe, and imitations of Ming porcelain and early Japanese *Karatsu pieces. Also produced *Kyo-yaki ware, copying western designs, e.g. those of Delft. Very popular in Japan, in 18th century. Examples of rustic character, include wine ewers in thick stoneware, often covered in cream-coloured glaze, with bright red, green, or indigo-purple designs; Chinese-style landscapes, sometimes combined with western-inspired borders.

banjo clock. American wall clock in shape of banjo. Variation of French lyre clock made *c*1802–60, introduced by *Willard family. Pendulum, round face, painted glass panels, and rectangular base.

bannock rack. Silver rack for oatmeal bannocks, resembling outsize *toast rack. Most surviving examples are Scottish from late 18th century; rare.

banquette. French upholstered bench, often with eight legs. Sometimes with ends, and used as window seat.

Bantam work or **artwork** or **Coromandel lacquer.** Incised lacquer-work found on late 17th century Dutch and English furniture. Named after Bantam, province of Dutch Java trading with Orient. Design was cut into ground of black lacquer, sometimes coloured with gold scattering.

baptismal basin. Silver basin used in holy baptism; resembles secular rose-water basin. Ornamented with religious figures and scenes. Uncommon in Europe, because most churches had baptismal font. *See* laver and basin.

barbeau, cornflower, or **Angoulême sprig.** Porcelain decoration of cornflower sprigs, one of later patterns introduced at Chantilly in mid 18th century. Usually painted in underglaze blue; also in blue, purple, brown, or crimson enamel. Frequently used at factory owned by Duc d'Angoulême in Paris. Also copied, e.g. at Niderviller, and in England at Derby, Lowestoft, Pinxton, and Worcester in 18th and 19th centuries.

Barbedienne, Ferdinand (fl mid 19th century). French founder; established foundry for small bronzes in Paris, 1838, in partnership with Achille Collas, inventor of mechanical reducing machine. Also produced furniture and art objects of all kinds.

Barberini workshop. Tapestry manufactory established *c*1633 in Rome by Cardinal Barberini with Jacopo della Riviera as art director, supervizing French and Flemish weavers. Important subjects: History of Constantine, from designs by Pietro da Cortona; *Putti* at Play, designed by Giovanni da Udine, modified by Romanelli; Mysteries of Life and Death of Christ, designed by Romanelli and da Cortona. After death of Pope Urban VIII (uncle of founder) in 1644, production ceased; revived in 1660 and continued until death of Barberini (1679).

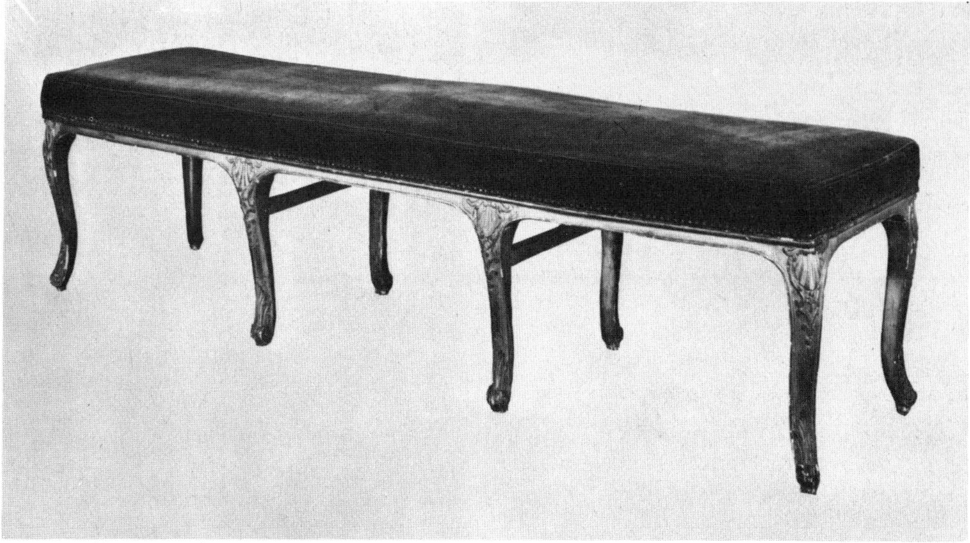

Banquette. *Louis XV. Gilt-wood; eight carved cabriole legs. Length 6ft5in.*

Barber's bowl. *English pewter, late 17th century; maker's mark, I H within shield.*

barber's bowl, basin or **dish,** or **shaving dish.** Bowl or dish with piece cut from rim for placing against neck. Used, probably from late 15th century by barber-surgeon, who dressed hair, shaved, drew teeth, and let blood. 16th and 17th century brass or pewter bowls often graduated and with single handle (*cf* bleeding bowl). Deep bowls with wide, flat rims made in Dutch Delft and English delftware in 17th and early 18th centuries; decorated in blue or polychrome, often with tools of barber's, sometimes also surgeon's trade. Oval or circular dishes in silver or pewter from late 17th and 18th centuries sometimes accompanied by jug and soap box; also made in Sheffield plate.

barber's chair. 19th century corner chair with adjustable head-rest attached above yoke rail; evolved from *shaving chair. By mid 19th century, some models had adjustable swivel seat.

barber's clock. Late 19th century American clock with dial and rotation of hands reversed: reads normally when seen in mirror, e.g. of barber's shop.

Barbin, François and son Jean-Baptiste (both d 1765). French potters. François managed porcelain factory under patronage of Duc de Villeroy in Paris from establishment in 1734; in 1748, factory moved to Mennecy. In 1751, joined by Jean-Baptiste in management. François thought also to have made faience.

Barcheston tapestries. *See* Sheldon Tapestry Works.

barding needle. Early larding needle; long pointed silver spike with looped handle attached to spike by half-crescent. In use in Britain from late 17th century, but earliest surviving examples early 18th century. (From bard, 'slice of bacon used to cover fowl'.)

bargueño. *See vargueño.*

barilla. Maritime plant (*Salsola soda*), grown near Alicante, Spain, and elsewhere. Dried plants burnt to produce impure soda, used as alkali in Renaissance glass making. Widely exported in 16th century to Mediterranean countries and England.

barley-sugar twist. Form of spiral turning giving appearance of two strands twisted together. *Illustration at vargueño.*

Barlow or **Booth,** Edward (1636–1716). English cleric and horologist. Invented rack-striking mechanism for clocks, 1676; also repeating watch, *c*1686; form of cylinder *escapement, *c*1695.

Barnard, Edward & Sons. Firm of London silversmiths; continuation of *Emes & Barnard.

In 1828 Edward Barnard took sons Edward the Younger, John, and William into partnership; joint mark in 1829: initial B with EE above and JW below. Firm was continued by sons after father's retirement (by 1846); initial B now with EJ above & W below; mark registered 1846. In 1851, mark changed to EB&JB, as Edward the Younger and William left firm. *Illustration at* wine coaster.

Barnes, Zachariah (1743–1820). Potter at Liverpool, Lancashire. Made delftware in silver-inspired shapes, painted with thick, dark blue. Supplied white tiles for transfer-printing by J. *Sadler and G. *Green. Made heavily-potted porcelain printed in smudged, dark underglaze blue; body has yellowish translucency in transmitted light; glaze flawed with black specks. Products include large teapots with pointed finials, and sparrow-beaked cream jugs with rounded lips. Credited with jug dated 1779, with *Heinzelman border.

barometer. Instrument for measuring pressure of atmosphere; based on experiments of Torricelli (1643), Pascal (1647), and others. Basis is glass tube containing liquid, usually mercury, closed at top and with reservoir or short U-shaped arm at foot. Height of column of liquid varies with atmospheric pressure. Named barometer by Robert Boyle in 1663. R. *Hooke devised form with revolving pointer to indicate reading. Many 19th century instruments made on same principle.

Usual form of mercury barometer from late 17th century remained direct-reading type with scale of ivory, etc., mounted beside tube, often in glass-fronted wooden case. Accuracy improved after *c*1756 by boiling mercury to remove water and impurities. Many makers added methods for setting basic level of liquid, perfected by French scientist Fortin (*c*1810), who also enclosed glass tube in brass frame.

*Barometers. English. Left: mahogany, carved in *Chippendale style, mid 18th century. Centre: mahogany, also carved in Chippendale style, with shell motifs; brass plate with thermometer. Right: burr-yew c1720, made by John Halifax of Barnsley.*

Baroque pearl: 16th century German pendant in form of fabulous bird. Gold and enamel setting with rubies. Height 3¾in.

baroque pearl. Irregularly shaped pearl; usually abnormally large. Feature of ornate jewellery, especially in 16th century (e.g. pendants, earrings) with shape of pearl often incorporated as part of body of fabulous monster, bird, human being, etc. *See* Canning Jewel.

baroque style. Flamboyant, heavy, decorative rectilinear style derived from 17th century Italian architecture. Carved, often gilt, baroque motifs including *amorini,* flowers, fruit, helmets, horns and other musical instruments, expressive masks, shields, etc., were symmetrically applied to large architectural pieces of furniture, silver vessels, etc. Style prevalent in Europe and England in late 17th and early 18th centuries, and, in more restrained form, in America *c*1700–50.

In German ceramics, found expression in Bayreuth faience and in work of J. F. *Metzsch; also in Meissen and Vienna porcelain, *c*1720–60. Faience and porcelain painting characterized by *Laub-und-Bandelwerk* decoration. Modelling typified by porcelain figures of J. J. *Kändler and J. G. *Kirchner, although these later showed traces of rococo style.

Barre, Alfred (fl mid 19th century). French romantic sculptor. Made many bronze portrait statuettes and medallions.

barrel (in clocks and watches). Metal drum containing driving spring. Outer end of spring attached to barrel, inner to spindle, or barrel arbor, passing through centre of barrel. In high quality movements, difference in spring's power as it unwinds equalized by use of *fusee. Barrel which drives train directly, without fusee, termed going barrel. Alternatively, in weight-driven clocks, barrel is drum on which cord is wound.

barrel chair. In England, round-backed easy-chair, based on French *gondole.* In America, upholstered high-backed chair with round seat and no arms. Also chair with round seat and incurving back, with sides sloping towards front of chair. Based on shape of barrel (or actually made from barrel, cut at angle to give back line, and with inset seat), overstuffed and upholstered. Dates from *c*1850 in America.

barrel organ. Mechanical portable organ probably used in Britain and Europe from late 17th century. Usually consisted of two or more rows of organ pipes in cabinet set above bellows; pipes controlled by pinned or stapled horizontal cylinder (barrel) rotated by hand crank, which also operated bellows. From early 18th century, more elaborate examples made for drawing-room use. Wooden cylinder could have up to 10 popular tunes, each requiring complete revolution of cylinder; spare cylinders (three to five) stored in cabinet of instrument. Commonly used in English churches in late 18th, early 19th centuries. Also popular at this time in France, where many 'improvements' made to mechanism. *cf* hurdy-gurdy.

Barr, Flight & Barr. *See* Worcester.

Barr, Martin (d 1813) and sons, Martin Junior and George (fl early 19th century). English porcelain manufacturers; partners in Warmstry House factory, *Worcester, Martin from *c*1793, Martin Junior from 1807, and George from 1813.

Bartmannkrug. *See bellarmine.*

Barye, Antoine-Louis (1796–1875). French romantic sculptor and painter. Apprenticed as goldsmith; made gold models of animals. Exhibited bronzes from 1831; set up own business in 1838. Chiefly known for small bronze groups of animals, but also produced bronzes with mythological and historical subjects. Most important member of *les *Animaliers.* Earlier bronzes usually produced by lost-wax method, cast either by himself or H. *Gonon. Later productions sand-cast.

basaltes. *See* black basalt.

bas d'armoire (French, 'low chest'). Low architectural piece of case furniture, dating from 18th century. Two or three doors enclose cupboards and drawers. May have marble top. Some designed to fit between windows, thus also called *entre-deux.*

base metals. All metals other than gold, silver, platinum, and their alloys. Main base metals are copper, iron, lead, tin, zinc, and their alloys which include brass, bronze, and pewter and secondary or more modern inventions, e.g. Britannia metal, paktong, pinchbeck. Different properties of metals determine treatment and functions. Hammering and casting are shaping methods in use over many centuries; rolling, drawing into wires, spinning, stamping, are more recent processes. Chief functions according to suitability are as follows:

For flatware and vessels for eating and drinking: pewter, which does not impart taste, is sufficiently hard and durable and of good appearance.

For cooking-vessels and general domestic utensils: copper, brass. Interiors of food containers tinned due to fear of poisoning and because metallic taste is imparted. Reasonably cheap, malleable, and hard-wearing. Bronze used for stronger pieces.

For tough, fire-resistant interior and exterior fittings or objects: iron, for qualities of strength, durability, and very high melting-point. Steel used where exceptional strength, hardness, or sharpness required.

For other exterior fittings and garden ornaments: lead, which is non-corrosive and water-resistant.

For finely-detailed cast ornamental work and strongest utensils: bronze, due to great toughness and exceptional fluidity in molten state.

basin-stand or **wash-stand.** Pedestal, tripod, or cabinet stand designed to carry wash-basin. Simple tripod or stool-like examples date from Middle Ages. By 18th century, common in Europe and America. Often made to fit in corner, with bowed door in front and flaps extending upwards from sides to protect wall from water splashes. By 19th century had become larger, heavier unit, usually with marble top, and drawers in front, sometimes with cupboard space below for chamber pot.

Baskerville, John (1706–75). English manufacturer of *japanned metal ware in Birmingham from 1738. Invented rolling and grinding machine for iron, 1742. Japanned ware competed with products of J. *Taylor and *Pontypool factory. Thought to be first japanner to employ polychrome painting as decoration; mahogany, black, or tortoiseshell grounds. From 1757, renowned typographer and printer.

basket. Gold, silver-gilt, silver, Sheffield plate, or electro-plate serving container for bread, cake, or fruit, probably made from 16th century. Late 16th century British example survives. In early 18th century, basket was generally oval, with solid walls and two D-shaped handles. *c*1730 fixed central handle appeared, soon followed by swing handle. In mid 17th century, rare examples shaped like giant cockle-shells, but commonly circular or oval with simulated basket-work weave piercing, engraving, or chasing. Feet cast or with pierced foot-mount. Late 18th and early 19th century examples often constructed entirely of silver or Sheffield plate wire, ornamented with applied chased floral motifs. Many late 18th and 19th century baskets machine-made. Miniature baskets for sweetmeats and as fittings for épergnes made from 18th century.

basket chair. Chair of woven cane or wicker work. Craft ancient, but rose to great popularity in 19th century (by *c*1875, term referred to cane-work only). 19th century models include round-seated single chairs and lounge chairs with extending foot-rests.

basket-top. Open metal top, with handle, above case of *bracket clock; introduced in late 17th century. Shape similar to domed-top; elaborately pierced design allows bell to be clearly heard.

bas-relief. *See* relief.

basse-taille enamelling. Design engraved or engine-turned on metal and covered with one or more coats of translucent enamel to give intaglio effect. Developed in Pisa, Italy, in 13th century for decoration of silver plate.

Left:
Basin stand. American, probably from New England, c1770–80; mahogany with brass handles. Height when closed 2ft11in.
Below:
Baskets. For sweetmeats. Pair made in London, 1776, by Charles Chesterman; decorated with tea-drinking putti, *and windmills; blue *glass liners. Height including handles 5¾in.*
Basse-taille *enamelling. Cornflower border to French gold box, Paris, 1749. Carnations are in raised enamel. Width 3in.*

basting spoon. *See* serving spoon.

Bataille, Nicolas (*c*1330–1400). Parisian high-warp loom tapestry master-weaver. From 1370, royal tradesman to Louis I, Duke of Anjou, for whom he wove so-called *Angers Tapestry.

Batavian ware. Chinese export porcelain, chiefly plates and vases, of Ch'ing period, named after Dutch East India Company trading station in Java, through which freighted. Coffee-brown iron glaze, with *famille rose* panels. Characterized by lack of true Chinese taste, though not made to European specifications. *cf* Nankin ware.

batch or **mixture.** Raw materials for glass making before firing in furnace.

Bateman family. English silversmiths. On retirement of H. *Bateman (1790), sons Peter and Jonathan registered joint mark, PB above IB, but silver thus marked rare because Jonathan died in 1791. Widow, Ann, registered mark with brother-in-law: PB above AB. In 1800, Ann's son, William, joined firm; mark: PB above AB above WB. Ann retired in 1805 and Peter in 1815 leaving William sole owner. Succeeded (1839) by son, also William. Threaded edge ornament common on Peter and Ann pieces. William the Elder worked in ornate Victorian styles.

Bateman, Hester (1709–94). English silversmith working in London; took over husband's business on his death in 1760. Much of early work commissioned by other silversmiths, thus her mark usually overstruck by theirs. First produced mainly flatware (spoons predominate); later made range of domestic objects. Forms simple; beaded decoration. Also made some civic and church silver, snuff-boxes, seals, etc. For wine labels preferred crescent shape with feathered or bright-cut border or wide-mouthed goblet surrounded by festoons. Retired in 1790. Sons Peter and Jonathan, the widow of Jonathan, Ann, and grandson William continued production until after 1815. Mark (registered 1761): HB, in script; similar marks used until 1787.

Batenin, Sergei (d 1814) and sons Peter (d by 1829) and Filipp (d 1832). Russian porcelain manufacturers. Sergei established porcelain factory at St Petersburg in 1812. Succeeded by sons. Specialized in vases and tea sets decorated with flowers or portraits, or as souvenirs of St Petersburg. No figures known to have been produced. Factory believed closed by fire in 1839. Marks, always in paste, often covered by glaze, include SB in Cyrillic characters, single letter B, or SFMB.

Bath border. *See* pie-crust border.

Bath chair. Chair on three wheels, popular in English spas; invented in Bath, Somerset, by James Heath *c*1750. Long steering handle attached to small front wheel, swivelled to allow chair to be pulled from front or, with passenger steering, pushed from back.

Bath metal. Alloy of copper and zinc used from late 18th century for small items, e.g. buttons, boxes, etc.

Bayreuth porcelain. Coffee-pot, late 18th century.

bat printing. Method of transfer-printing pottery, first used in Staffordshire *c*1777. Flexible sheet (bat) of glue or gelatine used to transfer pattern in oil from copper engraving to glazed ware; colour then dusted on and fired. Used until *c*1890.

Battersea, London. Enamelling factory at York House (1753–56). Made enamel snuff-boxes, plaques, wine labels, watch cases, and toothpick cases, blanks for which probably came from *Birmingham. Managed by inventor of transfer-printing, J. *Brooks. Used white enamel ground with transfer-prints of neo-classical or religious subjects, scenes from *The Ladies Amusement*, portraits, or sketches by J-A. *Watteau. Paint applied thinly over print. Chief engraver S-F. *Ravenet. Boxes had gilt-metal mounts. Porcelain said to have been transfer-printed with engravings, e.g. by R. *Hancock. Some early porcelain boxes made at Chelsea have enamelled lids made at Battersea.

battery metal. *See* latten.

Baudesson, Daniel (fl 1733–67). French Huguenot goldsmith and box maker who worked in Berlin and made boxes there for Frederick II. *See* Berlin school.

Baudoin, Pierre-Antoine (1723–69). French painter and miniaturist; son-in-law and pupil of F. *Boucher. Painted erotic scenes in gouache; also portrait miniatures. Elected to *Académie Royale des Beaux-arts* in 1763.

Baumhauer, Joseph (d 1772). German-born cabinet maker, in Paris from youth. Became *ébéniste privilégié* to Louis XV *c*1767, working in marquetry and lacquer. Stamp: 'Joseph' between fleurs-de-lis; son, Gaspard Joseph (1747–72), used same stamp.

Baxter, Thomas (1782–1821). English porcelain painter; worked for father, outside decorator, in London; signed pieces exist dated 1802, 1808, and 1809. At Worcester from 1814 as instructor and outside painter. At Swansea, 1816–18, then returned to Worcester. Painted landscapes, flowers, figure subjects, and, notably, shells and feathers.

bayonet joint. Joint for securing cover of silver vessel to body, e.g. caster. Two lugs or projections soldered to rim of cover lock with notches in upper rim of body; when cover twisted, lugs grip moulding on body rim.

Bayreuth (Bavaria). German faience factory founded 1714 by J. C. *Ripp. Produced brown glazed pieces with intricate silver or gold baroque patterns fired on, also with facets cut in style of J. F. *Böttger; 'misty' blue faience, and plain white faience resembling porcelain, used for armorial dinner services with painted strapwork and scrolled borders. Most productive period 1728–44; painters active included J. P. *Dannhöfer and A. F. *von Löwenfinck. After 1744, more utility ware produced, and painting limited to blue. In early 19th century creamware introduced. No regular marks before 1728; from 1728–44 BK in blue, sometimes above painter's initials. Hard-paste porcelain possibly made successfully by 1767. In 19th century, hard-paste porcelain, stoneware, and creamware manufactured. Some products impressed with counterfeit Wedgwood mark.

Bayreuth Hausmalerei. Independent decoration of porcelain and faience done mainly by J. F. *Metzsch and his workshop *c*1735–*c*1751. Usual subjects include polychrome landscapes framed with baroque cartouches and sprays of flowers; other motifs are masks, music sheets, trellis and scale borders. At first painted mainly on small porcelain pieces from Meissen and Vienna; encouraged manufacture of hard-paste porcelain at Bayreuth. Mark FM or Metzsch, over Bayreuth. Also painted on faience. J. P. *Dannhöfer may have been associate, responsible for *chinoiseries* and figure painting.

Bay State Glass Company. Founded 1853 in Cambridge, Massachusetts. Produced plain, moulded, cut and engraved flint glass, lamp chimneys, and mirrors. Closed *c*1877.

bead-and-reel moulding. Classical moulding semi-circular in cross section with alternating beads and reels (oblong cylindrical forms).

bead moulding (in silver). Moulding resembling string of beads; common on 18th century silver.

beads and marbles. Beads among earliest glass objects; like metal and stone counterparts, valued for magical, decorative, and barter value. Beads found in Egypt, dating from *c*4000 B.C., have coloured glazing over stone or clay base. Glass beads developed from 2nd millennium B.C. After *c*1000 B.C., 'eye' beads particularly popular: simple form has spot of coloured glass impressed into matrix of opaque glass; ringed form has small rings of glass, usually white, impressed into mainly blue matrix; inlaid coil form has thick thread of coloured glass, or several twisted threads, impressed into clear matrix; and stratified form has drop of coloured glass pressed into matrix with other bits of glass superimposed on it. Such beads widely made throughout glass-making world, also more sophisticated forms, e.g. mosaic beads, and beads shaped like human or animal heads.

Venetians developed bead making on highly organized, commercial basis. From 13th century, makers divided into specialized groups: *margaritai*, made small, pearl-like beads; *paternostreri*, made rosary beads; and *perlai*, made large, blown beads. *Margaritai* and *perlai* also made marbles, mainly for children's games. Apart from large, blown variety, beads made from a glass rod with small hole bored through centre; rod broken into small sections, mixed with sand and charcoal and placed in iron container, then rotated in furnace until sections became completely round. After cooling, beads shaken in a bag to remove sand and charcoal, and finally polished. Marbles made in same way, but from a solid glass rod, prepared by same method as for **latticinio* or *filigree glass. Venetian beads widely exported; in 16th and 17th centuries much used by explorers for barter (some South American Indians still wear beads taken over by Spanish conquistadors). Throughout 19th century, popular for embroidery, for curtains (bugle beads) and for jewellery, particularly those known as Roman pearls: pearl-like form made by introducing iridescent paste made from certain fish scales into spheres of thin glass. Marbles at height of popularity in 1860s and 1870s; fine quality examples fairly rare.

beaker. Stemless cylindrical drinking vessel of ancient origin, sometimes with sides tapering slightly towards base. Made in various materials, earliest include wood, glass and ceramics. Glass examples, plain or coloured, may have engraved or enamelled decoration (tall cylindrical German and Bohemian form is **Humpen*). Silver, silver-gilt, or gold beakers made in Britain at least from 11th century. Some surviving late medieval pieces have projecting foot and/or cover and engraved or embossed ornament. In 17th century taper more pronounced, lip slightly flared, decoration engraved foliated scrollwork. Dutch and German late 17th century beakers are squatter, embossed all over in floral patterns with moulded rim and three pomegranate feet. Few made in 18th century except in Scandinavia (apart from those in travelling sets); replaced by glass vessels for table use. Occasionally found in Sheffield plate. German beakers engraved with biblical scenes used as chalices in Lutheran churches from early 18th century. In general, English beakers less elaborate than those from other European countries.

Beale, Mary (1632–97) and son Charles (b 1660). English miniaturists. Mary, pupil of Sir Peter Lely, painted copies of many of his works. Extensive clientele for portraits and portrait miniatures; worked in oils and crayons. With husband, Charles, interested in chemistry; experimented with pigments. Son, Charles, worked in oils and watercolours; also drawings in red chalk. Miniatures exist dated 1679–88. Abandoned painting in 1689 because of poor eyesight.

Beakers. Left to right: 1) Hungarian parcel-gilt beaker with engraved decoration, 1657. 2) English, 1686. 3) German, made at Hanau, c1665, maker's mark GM. 4) English, by Richard Crossley, with bright-cut cartouche enclosing a crest, made in London, 1803. 5) c1820 by Hamilton & Co of Calcutta.

bear jug. English pottery jug moulded in form of a bear hugging a dog, to represent bear-baiting; detachable bear's head used as cup. Made in white Staffordshire salt-glaze; also in brown stoneware, e.g. at Nottingham and Derby in 18th century. Enamelled examples made in Staffordshire and Yorkshire during late 18th and early 19th centuries.

Beatty & Sons, Alexander J. Glasshouse founded *c*1850 in Steubenville, Ohio, by A. Beatty. Produced blown and pressed tableware. Noted for goblets and tumblers.

Beauvais carpets. *Savonnerie-style knotted carpets made at Beauvais 1780–90, and for several years under Napoleon I. Production stopped when high-warp looms transferred to Gobelins in 1819.

Beauvais tapestry. Beauvais French tapestry-weaving centre from mid 16th century. Royal Manufactory established (1664) by Colbert, under direction of Parisian tapestry-weaver and merchant, Louis Hinard. Trademark: B and fleur-de-lis. Quantities of generally mediocre low-warp loom tapestries produced in first 20 years. Favourite subjects, *verdures* and landscapes; also figure tapestries, including Children Playing, History of Psyche, and Village Festivals. Under direction of P. *Béhagle

*Beauvais tapestry panel. Toilet of Psyche, from cartoon by F. *Boucher; silk on woollen warp. Mid 18th century. 9ft11in. 15ft6in.*

(1684–1704), quality improved; productivity and popularity rivalled Gobelins. Brief decline at turn of century. Best period 1726–80, under artistic directors J-B. *Oudry, F. *Boucher and J. du Mons, when finest tapestries made in decorative baroque style. Borders became increasingly important, with elaborate imitations of carved gilt frames often dwarfing central landscape, pastoral, or exotic compositions. Increasing concentration on furniture covers and small panels. Last great wall hangings woven late 18th century at Beauvais. Most popular subjects: four-piece Four Ages, designed by François Casanova; 10-piece Pastorals in Blue Draperies and Arabesques, designed by J-B. Huet; and three-piece Conquest of Indies, after La Vallée Poussin. After Revolution, production revived in early 19th century under State ownership. High-warp looms transferred to Gobelins in 1819; thereafter manufactory specialized in furniture covers, using modified designs of older popular subjects.

Becerril family (fl 16th century). Spanish silversmiths working in Cuenca; made primarily elaborate church plate, e.g. *custodias*, crosses, chalices, patens, etc. Three members of family, Alonso, Francisco, Cristobal, worked (1528–74) on huge *custodia* for cathedral of Cuenca (destroyed by French in 1808).

Becker, Johann Albrecht (fl late 18th and early 19th centuries). Saxon glass engraver. Worked mainly in rococo style. At Nøstetangen glass house in Norway, 1767–73; then own workshop in Bragernes, 1773–1807.

bed. From early times considered important piece of furniture. In Gothic period distinguished for hangings more than woodwork. Richly carved four-poster beds developed during 16th century. Beds became increasingly elaborate in baroque period. Generally conceived in simpler form in 18th century, when framework was sometimes left revealed. *See* boat bed, bureau bedstead, day bed, dome bed, four-poster bed, *lit à l'anglaise, lit à la dauphine, lit à la duchesse, lit à la turque,* low-post bed, sofa bed, table bedstead, tester, truckle bed, trundle bed.

bedside cupboard. *See* night table.

bedside table. Table used beside bed, with shelf or shelves beneath top, sometimes bookshelves above. Introduced *c*1870 in France.

bedstead. Frame which holds bed-clothes, mattress, etc. Developed as independent piece of furniture (rather than architectural, built-in object) by 1500. Metal framework for bed introduced mid 19th century. Made of cast brass, later brass tubes; also cast iron, often covered with brass or japanned, sometimes with brass finials and ornament.

bed steps. Set of steps for access to high beds in 18th century England and America. Some of open construction; others closed, providing storage space for chamber pot.

bed table. Legged tray, dating from 18th century and intended for use by invalids. Legs folding, solid, or screw-on; some 19th century models have adjustable tray on pillar support.

*Bedside table. French, Louis XV. Kingwood parquetry in manner of M. *Criaerd; detachable* vernis Martin *book rest, three drawers in serpentine front, one drawer at back. Pierced ormolu *sabot feet. Height 2ft5in.*

Isabella Beetham. Silhouette, c1790, of unknown lady. Painted on glass.

bed-warmer. *See* warming pan.

beefeater flagon. Mid 17th century English pewter flagon with broad, spreading base and flat-topped cover similar in shape to hat worn by 'beefeaters' at Tower of London.

beehive clock. American shelf clock, in form of pointed arch, with rounded sides. Manufactured in Connecticut from *c*1847.

beer jug. *See* jug.

Beetham, Mrs Isabella (b 1750). English silhouettist. In 1773 married impoverished actor, Edward Beetham. First portraits cut from black paper (examples exist from 1774). Opened studio in Cornhill, London, and began painting portraits on card. Took lessons from miniaturist J. *Smart. Perfected technique of painting on underside of convex glass, with backing of card or plaster; used varying densities, with profile in black, but hair and costume details in thinner pigment. Often used glasses with border patterns in white or gold. Husband visited Venice (1784–85) to investigate gilding technique. He became successful inventor and businessman; took out patent for washing machine. On husband's death (1809), she sold washing machine business and retired.

'beetle and poker' hands (on watches). *See* hands.

beggar's badge. *See* badge.

Béhagle, Philippe (d 1704). Flemish tapestry master-weaver; emigrated to France; at Tournai until 1684. Artistic director of Beauvais manufactory (1684–1704) where responsible for establishing school of design, for improved quality, new designs, and first period of popularity. Successful subjects under his direction included Conquests of Louis XIV; eight-piece Acts of the Apostles; eight-piece Metamorphoses of Ovid; and Grotesques, after designs by J. *Berain. After his death, manufactory directed until 1711 by widow, and son, also Philippe; among several new subjects introduced at that period were Chinese Hangings.

Beilby, William (1740–1819) and sister Mary (1749–97). English glass enamellers. Worked in Newcastle-upon-Tyne for local glasshouses *c*1672. Decorated ale glasses and small wine glasses in monochrome white with naturalistic motifs, rustic, and classical scenes; drinking glasses in colours with landscape subjects and rococo scrollwork; goblets and decanters in white and colours for elaborate heraldic work. Pieces occasionally signed with butterfly and family, but never individual, name. Impossible to distinguish between their work; rose motif attributed to Mary. *Illustration at* enamelled glass, bumping glass.

John Belter. Love seat in laminated rosewood. New York, 1855.

Beinglas (German, 'bone glass') or **milk and water glass.** Semi-opaque white glass produced in Bohemia and Thuringia from mid 17th century. Resembles **Milchglas,* but obtained by adding bone-ash to other ingredients. Popular basis for enamelled decoration.

bekerschroef. *See* wine glass stand.

Belfast Glass Company. Founded in 1781 in Belfast, Ireland, by Bristol glass maker, Benjamin Edwards. Employed English craftsmen trained in Bristol. Produced enamelled, cut, and plain wine glasses, plain tableware, cruets, salts, and lustres. Noted for cut and plain tapering decanters with two or three triangular neck rings. Seal: B. Edwards, Belfast. Closed *c*1829.

bell. Hollow metal body with clapper, or tongue, emitting musical note when rung; used in churches, monasteries, etc. to announce prayer-time. Portable bells were made for domestic use (*see* table-bell); also light, simple type used by shepherds, farmers, etc., hung round neck of animal to indicate whereabouts. Early iron or bronze church bells varied in shape from long and narrow to roughly cubic; the (now) standard flaring shape in bronze, found to be strongest and most resonant, was universally adopted in Europe by *c*1500. Damaged or unwanted old bells were often melted down to make new. Casting is done in clay moulds, using bronze alloy specifically developed for the purpose, known as *bell-metal. Inscriptions are relief-cast in moulds. *Illustrations at* Chinese bronzes, table bell.

bell and baluster turning. Turning on legs, with bell-shaped portion above, baluster-shape below. Common on stands and tables of late 17th and early 18th centuries.

bellarmine, Bartmannkrug (German, 'bearded man jug'), or **greybeard.** Sturdy, round-bellied stoneware jug produced in Cologne during 16th century. Neck decorated with grotesque, bearded mask, likened to unpopular Cardinal Bellarmine (hence name). Some examples bear single relief medallion; others richly decorated with oak, rose, or vine leaves in relief. Possibly copied in England by J. *Dwight.

Belleek. Porcelain factory established in 1857 on island in River Erne, County Fermanagh. *Parian porcelain often thinly potted with nacreous glaze, used for vases in naturalistic shell forms, busts, and tableware; noted for high quality. Also made ironstone and painted or transfer-printed earthenware, often gilded.

Bellegarde tapestry. Bellegarde developed as French tapestry-weaving centre in 17th century. Fine *verdures* woven, often mistaken for contemporary Aubusson work.

Bellevue (Meurthe-et-Moselle). French faience factory, established *c*1755. From 1771, named *Manufacture Royale.* Figures and groups made in chalky biscuit earthenware from moulds by P-L. *Cyfflé. Tableware made in faience and cream-coloured earthenware (*faïence fine*); sometimes decorated with black or dark brown monochrome. Large garden-figures made in painted terracotta. Faience and biscuit figures in 18th century marked Bellvue ban de Toul, incised on edge of base. Tableware marked Bellvue, impressed. Production of copies of Cyfflé figures continues.

bell-flower motif. Stylized floral decoration, painted, inlaid, or carved; the bell-shaped flower has three or five petals. Often used on early American furniture.

bellied tankard. 16th century British silver drinking vessel with bulbous body, short neck, and domed cover hinged to top of S-scrolled handle. Modified form of style became fashionable again in early 18th century, probably under Huguenot influence; then with baluster-shaped body, its greatest width occurring just above boldly moulded foot, and often with double-scroll handle.

Belli, Valerio (*c*1468–1546). Italian goldsmith and crystal cutter working in Vicenza and Rome; also cut dies for coins and medals. Executed papal commissions for secular and church silver. Work includes crystal caskets and cups with silver or gold mounts; crystal, enamel, and silver-gilt cross.

Belli, Vincenzo (1710–87). Italian silversmith working in Rome. Trained in Turin; in 1741 became master in Rome. In 1765 elected Fourth Consul of Guild and in 1779 chamberlain (refused honour). Produced domestic and church silver in extreme rococo style. Employed *c*20 assistants in workshop. Family continued business until *c*1850.

bell-metal. Form of bronze, used for casting bells and occasionally domestic objects, e.g. some cooking-vessels, mortars. *Illustration at* skillet.

bell-pull. 19th century ornamental handle attached to silk cord or embroidered fabric strap hanging on wall of principal rooms; when pulled, system of wires caused bell to ring in servants' hall. Later cordless type was handle attached directly to wall 3–4ft from floor; usually bronze, cast or stamped as e.g. stylized flower or leaf, sometimes gilt.

bell salt. Silver, silver-gilt, or pewter salt in narrow bell-shape, used mainly in 16th and early 17th century England; silver examples usually in three sections: two for salt, third, upper, pierced to serve as spice or pepper caster. Plain or simply chased with strapwork and flowers. Sometimes with three or four ball feet.

bell-top. Top part of *bracket clock, outline in shape of hand-bell. Widely made in England in late 17th century, by most leading makers. *See* inverted bell-top.

Belouchestan carpets. *See* Baluchi carpets.

Belter or **Beltier,** John H. (fl *c*1840–60). German-born cabinet maker, who worked in New York City. Furniture distinguished by heavily-carved frames, floral motifs and arabesque lines. Devised form of lamination with layered rosewood or walnut, and patented machine for cutting arabesques on chair-backs.

*Bellarmine. *Rhineland stoneware; impressed with face and coat of arms. Height 8½in.*

Bell salt. Jacobean, maker's mark TS monogram, dated 1607.

bench. Backless long seat; sometimes attached to wall. Alternatively, a work table.

bench table. Bench with arms and hinged back which, when lowered, rests flat on arms, forming table.

Benckgraff, Johann (1708–53). German arcanist. Apprenticed at Vienna. Worked at Künersberg (1747–49), Nymphenburg (1748), and Höchst (1750–53), where learned or stole secret of porcelain kiln construction. Co-founder (1752) of *Wegeley's factory, Berlin; manager at Fürstenberg in 1753.

bended-back. Chair back with flat *baluster-shaped splat, curved to fit human back.

bends (in furniture). Upward curving sections attached to legs on rocking chair to allow rocking motion.

Beneman or **Benneman,** Jean Guillaume (fl 1784–1804). *Ebéniste* born and trained in Germany; worked in Paris, becoming *maître-ébéniste* in 1785. From 1784 employed by Louis XVI, and subsequently received commissions under Directoire and Consulate. Collaborated with leading contemporary craftsmen. Stamp: G. BENEMAN.

bénitier. Holy-water stoup, of lead, pewter, or ceramics, in form attachable to wall, or to stand on table. Few surviving examples earlier than 17th century. Portable type (for carrying around church) dates from 14th century.

Bennington. Flint-enamel water cooler in shape of temple with apostle between each pillar; c1853. Lyman Fenton & Co. Height 1ft11½in.

Bennett, E. & W. Pottery established in 1846 inBaltimore, Maryland. Made relief-decorated Rockingham ware, e.g. teapot with scene of 'Rebekah at the Well'. Also produced jugs in hard green or blue stoneware, with e.g. fish in relief, or with moulded features, e.g. hand-shaped handle. Traded after 1856 as E. Bennett.

Bennington, Vermont. Two potteries flourished in mid 19th century. First established 1783 by John *Norton; largely made stoneware until closure in 1894. Mark, when found, normally name and Bennington, Vt. C. W. *Fenton started second factory in 1847, at first on same premises, moving 1848. Produced white earthenware for domestic use, and, from 1849, *flint enamel ware vases and jugs with applied relief decoration; also blue-and-white porcelain, and figures in *parian ware. Animal figures and Toby jugs usually have Rockingham glaze. In 1850s, made Staffordshire-style jugs and rarely *scroddled ware. Traded as United States Pottery Co from c1853 until closure in 1858. Only c20% of wares marked; marks include Norton & Fenton, Bennington Vt (1847–48, porcelain and parian ware), Lyman Fenton & Co, Bennington Vt (1849–58, flint enamel and Rockingham ware), United States Pottery on ribbon (1852–58, porcelain and parian ware).

Benood, William (fl mid 17th century). English tapestry master-weaver; worked at Mortlake tapestry works mid 17th century, then established Lambeth workshop with brother, John. Excellent tapestries produced, often copies of earlier Mortlake works, including Vulcan and Venus, and The Horses.

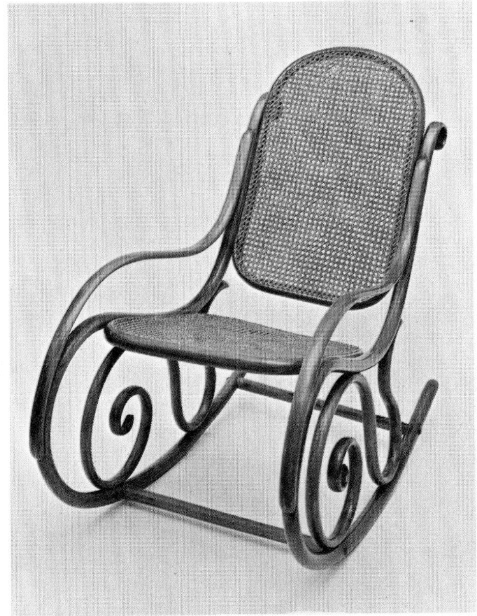

*Bentwood furniture. Rocking chair with cane seat, made at M. *Thonet's factory, Vienna, c1860.*

Bentley, Thomas (1730–80). Liverpool merchant, partner of J. *Wedgwood I from 1768, in charge of London showrooms. Supervised enamelling workshop.

bentwood furniture. Has components permanently steam-bent. Technique ancient. M. *Thonet applied scientific principles in bending to obtain greatest strength from shapes. Mass-produced from mid 19th century. Common throughout Europe and America.

Berain, Jean (c1639–1711). French designer, engraver, and draughtsman. Official court designer to Louis XIV from 1674. Developed **style Berain* and published designs which strongly influenced production of silver, furniture (especially by A-C. *Boulle), tapestries, etc., in Europe and Britain. Arabesques, *singeries*, fantastic figures, scrollwork, festoons, foliate ornament, birds, canopies, etc., characterize his style. Followed as court designer by son, Jean II (1674–1728).

Bergama carpets. Turkish-knotted carpets made almost exclusively by nomads in western and southern Anatolia and sent to town of Bergama for sale. Woollen warp and weft, sometimes with addition of goat-hair; fairly deep soft pile of good quality lustrous wool. Many examples may be identified by use of red weft threads, producing effect of red stripes on back; also by shape, characteristically almost square. Mainly used as prayer rugs. Linked by affinity of design to 16th, 17th, and 18th century rugs known by other names (e.g. Holbein, Transylvanian) but almost certainly made in Bergama area; these are of geometrical design, and also show some resemblance to carpets from parts of Caucasus, e.g. Kazak. Dominant motif in quite large numbers of Bergama carpets is large central rectangle; at sides are small octagons and four-sided figures decorated with eight-pointed star or stylized flower motif. Designs vary widely, but certain motifs betray common origin, e.g. eight-pointed star, often enclosed in octagon or circle. Octagons and squares frequently outlined in particularly brilliant blue. Predominant colours of motifs: pale turquoise, white, and orange.

bergère. French armchair with upholstered sides, back, and seat, made from c1725. Later, upholstery replaced by cane; loose cushions on seat.

bergère en confessionnal or **fauteuil en confessionnal** (French, 'confessional chair'). High-backed *wing chair, dating from Louis XV period; more common in Louis XVI style.

Berg, Magnus (1666–1739). Norwegian ivory carver; worked in various European cities; settled in Copenhagen. Carved ivory cups to be silver-mounted; also ivory panels set into tankards.

Beringer, David (fl mid 18th century). German instrument-maker, worked in Nuremberg and later Augsburg. Made complicated sundials, many of cube form, wooden with printed paper scales, adjustable for use in various latitudes. *Illustration at* sundial.

Berkeley Castle Service. Silver dinner service made (1735–58) by J. *Roettiers in French rococo style; probably for Augustus, 5th Earl of Berkeley. 168 pieces include dinner dishes, meat dishes or platters of various sizes, tureens, candlesticks, cruets, casters, flatware, etc. (Re-

*Bergama rug. Turkish, mid 17th century. Red field with white vase at each end; black-stemmed flowers in blue, yellow and white; black *spandrels with yellow arabesques. Main border with white lozenge medallions. 5ft6in × 3ft10in.*

mained at Berkeley Castle until 1960, when purchased by S. Stavros Niarchos.)

Berlin, Germany. Faience made at four factories established during 17th and 18th centuries, earliest in 1678. Reddish body shows through rather thin glaze; work of three of factories hard to distinguish; seldom marked. Style influenced by Delft and Isnik pottery. Fourth factory (founded 1699) produced more easily identifiable work, including tankards, sometimes decorated with Prussian eagle, panels, and painted columns, and sprayed with purple or blue ground; polychrome vases have pale blue or olive ground painted with ships, sometimes with border of coiled scrolls or spirals. Work often marked with initial F.

Porcelain made at *Wegely's factory from

Bergère. *French, Louis XV. One of a pair by J-J. Pothier; grey-painted and gilt-wood moulded frames.*

1752. Berlin Porcelain Factory founded 1761; E. H. *Reichard art director up to 1764. Purchased by Frederick the Great in 1763 (after his withdrawal of support from Wegely's factory in 1757), and known as Royal factory until 1918. Many Meissen workmen moved to Berlin during Seven Years' War, including painters K. W. *Bohme, J. B. *Borman, and K. J. *Klipfel; also figure modellers, W. C. *Meyer, and F. E. *Meyer (figures characterized by small heads) who worked in style of J. J. *Kändler. Strongly-coloured tableware and vases produced in large quantities (1763–86) particularly for court. Style of painting on decorative wares initially features flowers and fruit; Bohme and Borman specialized in landscapes. *Gotzkowsky pattern used on tableware. **Neuzierat* pattern introduced 1763, appears on yellow 'Potsdam' service: **Antikzierat* pattern first used 1767. Utility porcelain painted in underglaze blue after certain Meissen flower patterns (notably modified *Zwiebelmuster*) produced periodically from 1763. In 1770 addition of kaolin led to colder body colour; styles began to show neo-classical influence, but full impact delayed until death of Frederick in 1786. Thereafter standard of porcelain decoration declined; surfaces painted to imitate marble, lapis lazuli, etc.

Figures modelled by F. E. and W. C. Meyer (1761–85) initially had three-footed rococo base, later square or oval plinth or lightly-coloured grassy mound, and finally neo-classical pedestal. Painting of figures at first in restrained colours with sections unpainted; some flower sprigs on dresses; later pale colours applied in flat washes. Neo-classical styles followed with frequent use of biscuit. J. G. *Schadow employed in late 18th century. In 19th century, produced *lithophanes. Marks, all in underglaze blue unless otherwise stated: 1761–63 or later, G.; 1763–1810, sceptres of various shapes and proportions; 1832 onwards, KPM (Royal Porcelain Manufacture) under orb printed in red; 1837–44, KPM under sceptre, printed, also impressed, on plaques, lithophanes; 1870 to present, sceptre printed.

Berlin iron jewellery. Finely cast iron jewellery made by Prussian Royal Iron Foundry probably initially in Silesia and from *c*1804 in Berlin. Became fashionable in 1813–15 during Prussian war of independence against French when women were asked to give up jewels to finance campaign and received cast iron jewellery inscribed *Gold gab ich für Eisen 1813* (I gave gold for iron), and similar mottoes. Early jewellery is neo-classical in style; oval or circular medallions with portraits or classical subjects in low relief linked together to form necklaces, bracelets, brooches, etc. Open-work medallions also used. Later made in revived Gothic style (e.g. foliage, tracery, etc.). During French occupation (1806) models removed from foundry, and factory set up in Paris. Berlin-inspired iron jewellery probably also made in Netherlands. Remained popular after mid 19th century.

Berlin school. Artists and craftsmen invited to work in Berlin by Frederick II in mid 18th century. Produced hardstone boxes (mainly chrysoprase) decorated in *Reliefmosaik* technique and gold boxes with diamond thumbpieces and *en plein* enamelled decoration.

Berlin tapestry. Main tapestry production in 18th century Berlin stemmed from workshop established 1699 by French émigrés, J. Barraban and brother-in-law P. Mercier. Designs influenced by Beauvais, particularly grotesques and *chinoiseries*. Works include History of the Great Elector, Grotesque Inventions, and Scenes from *Commedia dell'Arte*.

Berovieri family. Notable 15th century Venetian glass makers. Re-invention of enamelling and gilding technique practised by Islamic craftsmen attributed to Angelo Berovieri. Characteristic example of work is marriage cup in Correr Museum, Venice; made *c*1440 of transparent blue glass, enamelled with medallion heads of man, women, and procession of horsemen and women. Son, Marino, head of *fioleri* (makers of vessels and window glass) in 1468; daughter, Marietta, married apprentice, who founded Ballerini glasshouse with dowry.

berrettino. Italian pottery. Tin-glaze stained lavender grey with cobalt. On maiolica made at Faenza from late 15th century. Used as ground for stylized painting, e.g. of trophies, grotesques, fruit, and flowers, in colour with opaque white and blue predominating.

Berthoud, Ferdinand (1727–1807). Swiss-born maker of clocks, watches and chronometers, living in Paris. Worked with J. & P. *LeRoy, 1745. Noted for extensive research on timekeeping, *c*1766. Published many works, including *Essai sur l'Horlogerie*, 1763.

Beshir carpets. *See* Ersari carpets.

Besnier, Nicolas (d 1754). French silversmith working in Paris; master in 1714. Royal goldsmith to Louis XV (1723). Produced mainly domestic silver; surviving work includes toilet service for the Spanish Infanta, fiancée of Louis XV. Became director of Beauvais tapestry works (1734), after which probably little time spent on silver production. Mark: a fleur-de-lis crowned, NB, two pellets, and a star.

betrothal plate. *See* marriage plate.

Better Nine. *See* Britannia Standard.

Bettisi, Leonardo or **Don Pino** (d *c*1589). Italian maiolica potter and painter at Faenza. Among early painters in *compendiario* style. Credited with mark Do Pî.

Betts, Thomas (d 1767). English glass cutter and merchant. In *c*1730, opened shop in London employing English and European engravers. Supplied fine tableware, e.g. cruets, wine glasses, stoppered decanters, champagne quart decanters, carafes, water glasses.

betty lamp. *See* crusie.

Beutmuller, Hans (d 1622). German goldsmith working in Nuremberg; master in 1588. Prolific maker of standing cups, some in revived Gothic style popular in late 16th century Nuremberg.

Beyer, Johann Christian Wilhelm (1725–1806). German architect, painter, sculptor. Studied in Dresden, Paris, and Rome. Court sculptor at Stuttgart soon after 1759; porcelain modeller at Ludwigsburg (1761–67). Work includes musicians, Cupid and Psyche, Three Graces, Fisherman, and Bacchantes; also scent-bottles in shape of hunter and huntress. Designs combining elements of rococo and neo-classical styles, probably influenced contemporary, J. *Louis. From 1768, court sculptor at Vienna; executed large marble statues.

bezel. Wire or thin strip of metal sprung in and soldered to rim of cover of vessel, or inside shutting edge of box or casket. In clocks and watches, grooved frame in which glass is set; also similar frame not containing glass. In jewellery, upper part of ring, usually holding stone; various shapes.

bianchi di Faenza. *See faïence blanche.*

bianco sopra bianco. Ceramic decoration: white enamel painted on white or slightly tinted tin-enamel glaze. Found on 16th century Italian maiolica, and faience made e.g. at Nevers in 17th century and Marieburg in 18th century. In English delftware associated particularly with Bristol; also used at Lambeth and Liverpool. Designs include pineapple motif with two groups of three pineapples on opposite sides of border, separated by flowers. At Rörstrand, in mid 18th century, used in basketwork design as ground pattern.

bible box. Portable oak box with hinged lid, usually intended to hold family bible. Often has carved decoration on front. Occasional examples with sloping lid, allowing box, set on stand or suitable table, to be used as lectern. Made during 17th century. *cf* desk box.

bibliothèque. Large French bookcase; form based upon *commode. Doors glazed or with grilles. Dates from reign of Louis XVI.

bibliothèque basse (French, 'low bookcase').

Bibliothèque. *Louis XV. Marquetry; one drawer within frieze has ormolu lockplate and key.*

*Bible box. Pine and oak, from Lyme County, New Hampshire. Carving similar to *Hadley chests. c1670. Length 26in.*

Above:
Berlin porcelain. Coffee-pot, c1790–1800. Painted and gilded.

Berlin iron jewellery. Necklace of ironwork cameos and mesh linked with gold settings, c1800. Bracelet and cross, c1870, in later, heavier style.

Right:
*Berlin school. Both 1755–60. Leftè enamel snuff-box in form of riding boot; heel holds snuff shaker. Right: enamel snuff-box, A. *Fromery's workshop.*

*Biedermeier glass. Left to right: 1) Amber beaker with engraved decoration, c1845. 2) Beaker and plate in blue glass with silvered decoration, c1845. 3) Goblet, probably by F. *Egermann, ruby bowl; amber flash panel with engraved hunting scene, c1830. 4)* *Ranftbecher, *turquoise glass, c1815–20 with gilt and silver decoration; height 5in.*

Low, rectangular case piece with grille or glazed doors protecting book shelves. Popular in 18th century.

Bickley, Benjamin (d 1776). English toy maker and enameller whose factory in *Bilston lasted from 1748 to his death.

bidet. Stool with basin-like metal or ceramic container set into top. Variations include models with attached back, and chest-shaped bidets for travelling. Dates from 18th century France.

Bidjar or **Bidshar carpets.** *See* Bijar carpets.

Biedermeier style. German-based decorative style which spread throughout Europe and to England *c*1815–60: emerged as reaction against ornate 18th century styles. Most apparent in furniture, reflecting modified Sheraton, Regency, Directoire, and particularly Empire styles. Early pieces generally rectilinear, undecorated, and simple; towards middle of period, curves used more in chair backs, legs, etc. Scroll forms popular after *c*1840, on bases, legs, etc., often with upper terminal animal head (sometimes gilt). Dark mahogany much used, also ash, birch, and cherry. Upholstered pieces characteristically padded with horse-hair and covered with velvet. Designed for comfort rather than ostentation; popular with prosperous bourgeoisie. Glass followed furniture, with simpler, functional (though still decorative) forms favoured, e.g. straight-sided beakers. *See* Mohn, G. S., *Ranftbecher*.

Biennais, Martin-Guillaume (1764–1843). French silversmith working in Paris. In 1789 established himself as *tabletier*: maker of table games, cane handles, cases for **nécessaires de voyage* (which he supplied for some of officers involved in Italian and Egyptian campaigns). Official goldsmith to Napoleon; supplied him with domestic plate, church plate for marriage in 1810, for birth of son in 1811, and military decorations and insignia. Exponent of Empire style. Filled commissions for Russian imperial family. Headed workshop employing *c*600 workmen. Keen businessman, but not craftsman; probably left design to staff of draughtsmen. Retired in 1819. Mark: B, two pellets, and a monkey, in a lozenge.

Biffin or **Biffen,** Sarah (1784–1850). English miniaturist. Born without arms and legs. Learned to manipulate pencil and brush with mouth. In 1812, travelled around England demonstrating ability. Also went to Brussels and perhaps elsewhere in Europe. Awarded medal by Society of Arts in 1821.

biggin. English late 18th and 19th century silver or Sheffield plate coffee-pot with cylindrical body, short lip spout, and built-in strainer to filter coffee grounds, Named after inventor, George Biggin.

Biggin. By William Eaton. London, 1821. Height 12*in.*

Bijar, Bidjar, or **Bidshar carpets.** Very solid, lustrous, Kurdistan carpets with extremely heavy Turkish knotted woollen pile on cotton or woollen foundation; woven from 18th century. Bold designs in strong blues, lime-green, and tomato-red. Patterns include herati, stylized medallions with corner pieces on monochrome grounds, palmette lattices, and stylized adaptations of earlier *Isfahan designs.

bilbao or **bilboa.** Mirror with marble (and sometimes wooden) frame. Imported into America from Bilbao, Spain, in late 18th century.

Biller, Johann Jacob II (d 1777). German silversmith working in Augsburg; master in 1745. Family prominent silversmiths throughout 18th century; made range of domestic plate (including wine coolers, wine fountains, centrepieces, toilet services, etc.) as well as some silver furniture in French styles. Mark: II over B, with star above.

*Bijar carpet. 18th century. Turquoise field with *palmettes and lily-filled diamonds in red, dark blue and green, joined by narrow red branches of carnations; deep pile.* 13*ft* × 4*ft* 5*in.*

Billies and Charlies. Medallions and badges of cock's metal and lead, all with 12th century dates, impressed with king's heads, knights, and saints. Each approximately 4*in.*

billet. *See* thumbpiece.

billet moulding. Norman moulding of short cylinders or squares at regular intervals.

Billies and Charlies. Mid 19th century faked medieval amulets, figures, seals, etc. Usually in poor quality pewter ('cock-metal') with relief decoration. Large numbers produced by William Smith and Charles Eaton of Tower Hill, London, who claimed to have found them by digging in the Thames river-bed. Sometimes betrayed by 11th to 14th century dates in Arabic, rather than Roman, numerals.

Billingsley, William (1758–1828). English porcelain maker and enameller; apprentice at Derby from 1774. In 1795, established porcelain factory at Pinxton, Derby; left in 1799, and worked as independent porcelain decorator. 1808–13, employed at Worcester. In 1813, raised finance to start porcelain manufacture at *Nantgarw; in 1814, sought help from Board of Trade, and business transferred to *Cambrian Pottery, Swansea. Resumed production, 1817–19, at Nantgarw; then worked at Coalport factory. Painted naturalistic flowers, especially roses, on white ground; developed method of applying paint and wiping off colour for highlights. *Illustration at* Pinxton.

Bilston, Staffordshire. Produced large quantity of enamel products in 18th and early 19th centuries, probably including boxes and scent bottles in animal and other *fantasy shapes copied from Meissen and Chelsea porcelain. More durable than porcelain originals, but liable to chipping. Largest factory established 1748 by B. *Bickley. *See* South Staffordshire enamel. *Illustration at* English enamel.

Bimann, Dominik (1800–57). Bohemian glass engraver, often using stained and *cameo glass. Worked during winters in Prague; in summer followed clients to spa at Franzenstad, eventually settling there. Subjects particularly portraits and landscapes.

Birch, William Russell (fl late 18th century). English enamel painter. Exhibited at Royal Academy 1775–94. Emigrated to Philadelphia in 1794. Work includes miniature of George Washington, used as subject for engraving.

bird-beaked or **sparrow-beaked jug.** Pear-shaped English porcelain jug with loop or simple scrolled handle and small, beak-shaped pouring lip. Made, e.g. at Bow, Worcester, and Lowestoft, in late 18th century. Body normally plain; occasionally ribbed or fluted.

Bird cage. Mahogany with turned balusters and fretted panels at front door. Dutch, c1750. Height 1ft9in.

*Biscuit-box. Barrel-shaped, with cover, made by Henri Polonceau, Montreal, c1815. Decorated with four reeded bands, repeated on lid which rises to ball finial; plain *swing handle.*

birdcage. Cage for song-bird; fashionable mainly in Italy and France from Renaissance, and throughout Europe from early 18th century. Made of wood, wickerwork, brass or copper wire, etc.; form varied according to fashionable style of period. Often important and highly ornamental feature of room. Mechanical song-birds in cages also made.

birdcage or **squirrel.** Hinged construction on tables, allowing top to revolve, or tip vertically when not in use. Composed of two squares of wood, joined by turned pegs. Upper square hinged to underside of table top. Shaft on pedestal head passes through central hole in lower square allowing top to rotate. Found on English and American tables, particularly during 18th century.

birdcage frame. *See* posted frame.

bird carpets. *See* white Ushak carpets.

birds in branches or **birds in a tree.** Pattern transfer-printed on Worcester and Caughley porcelain from *c*1776. Usually three, sometimes two, birds in branches of tree set in hilly landscape.

bird organ or **serinette.** Miniature *barrel organ for teaching birds to sing; used in Britain and Europe from late 17th century. French name, *serinette*, derived from original use for teaching canary (*serin domestique*) to sing.

bird tureens. Rococo style tureens made in pottery or porcelain in shape of domestic and game birds: duck, chicken, partridge, etc. Made in tin-glazed earthenware, e.g. at Delft, Strasbourg, and in porcelain, e.g. at Meissen from 1740s. In England, made from *c*1750, apparently first at Chelsea. At Bow, from 1756, copies made of Meissen partridge tureens. Original models of pigeons made at Derby and Worcester.

Birmingham. Centre of English metal industry from 16th century, supplying raw materials and finished goods in iron, steel, copper, brass, to Britain and Europe. Production was at its peak from 1760s throughout 19th century. Much manufacturing was carried out under system whereby fully equipped workshops were hired out to workers who made their goods there, selling them at end of week to merchants; materials and rental for following week were bought from proceeds.

Birmingham enamels. Produced from late 1740s; large export trade. Also made blanks and mounts for use elsewhere. Early works decorated with pastoral scenes painted in style of e.g. J-A. *Watteau and F. *Boucher. After 1756, copperplates from Battersea factory probably used but Birmingham enamels differ from Battersea by thickness of paint applied over transfer-print. Notable for boxes; less successful with household utensils including tea-caddies, canisters, candlesticks, beakers, and urns. Decoration as in *South Staffordshire enamels. Quality declined after 1780. From 1790 patch-boxes with *memento mori* motif and souvenir boxes inscribed 'A trifle from . . .' produced in quantity. Makers included J. *Taylor.

biscuit. Earthenware or porcelain which has been fired but not glazed.

biscuit-box. Dutch silver rectangular or circular box used from late 18th century as biscuit container. Body of box usually plain, except for engraved border; beading common around rim of tight-fitting lid where it meets body. Very popular with English electro-plate manufacturers of late 19th century.

biscuit porcelain. Unglazed porcelain introduced at Vincennes before 1753 by J-J.

*Biscuit porcelain. *Sèvres, 1760. The Leaning Satyr, original model by E-M. *Falconet.*

*Bachelier as medium for figures and groups, often modelled in soft-paste porcelain after F. *Boucher, e.g. by E-M. *Falconet and J-B. *de Fernex. Biscuit figures produced by many porcelain factories in late 18th century. First English biscuit figures made at Derby; many early examples modelled by J-J. Spängler in 1790s. Used to make plaques with relief portraits or coats of arms, framed with modelled flower wreaths, at Bristol in 1770s; also vases. In 19th century, produced as *parian ware. *Illustration at* temple clock.

bishop bowls. Faience bowls in shape of bishop's mitre, intended to hold bishop (kind of punch). Made at several Scandinavian centres, e.g. Copenhagen, Herrebøe, and, in Germany, at Kiel, Schleswig, and Rendsburg, 1720s to 1770s.

bismuth or **tin-glass.** Metallic hardening agent sometimes added to pewter.

Bizen, near Okayama. Japanese stoneware manufactured from 13th century (notably late 16th to early 17th centuries). Brick-red body without glaze, made into simple, strong shapes, sometimes with delicate linear patterns achieved by covering vessel in brine-dampened straw before firing. Production continued in later Edo period, also glazed ware introduced, mostly blue or white monochrome. From 18th and early 19th centuries, incense-burners and decorative figures in naturalistic style produced, very popular in West.

Blaataarn. *See* Copenhagen.

blackamoor. *See guéridon.*

black basalt or **basaltes.** Hard, unglazed, black stoneware, developed from *Egyptian black, by J. *Wedgwood at Brick House, Burslem in 1760s. Made from native clay, ironstone, ochre, and manganese. Hard and fine-grained; suitable for polishing on lathe, or engine-turning. Used for vases, busts, and moulded relief tablets; also tea ware. Six black basalt vases thrown by Wedgwood himself to celebrate opening day of Etruria factory in 1769. Marks: W&B, Wedgwood & Bentley, or Wedgwood & Bentley, Etruria, and WEDGWOOD (impressed) from 1769 to present day. Other makers include: W. *Baddeley, *Herculaneum pottery, *Leeds pottery, E. *Mayer, J. *Spode, and *Copeland.

Black Forest clocks. Clocks produced by peasant craftsmen in Black Forest, southern Germany, from *c*1640; first models foliot clocks, made entirely of wood, with single hand on dial. *c*1730–*c*1740, pendulum and striking mechanism incorporated; first pendulums short, hung in front of dial; often known as 'cow's tails'. Many wall clocks, with bells initially of glass, then metal; large wooden dial-plate, top in shape of arch, and painted floral decoration. Known in England as Dutch (corruption of *Deutsch*) clocks, in France as Swiss clocks. *Cuckoo clock invented mid 18th century. Other products include *quail, *picture-frame, and **Schottenuhren* clocks. Also, from mid 19th century, automaton and musical clocks, decorated in baroque manner, and *trumpeter clock. Export trade throughout Europe by *c*1800; from mid 19th century, mass-production first by cottage industry methods, then by true factories such as *Junghans.

*Black basalt. J. *Wedgwood. Hedgehog bulb pot, c1800, *engine-turned mug, c1775, and boat-shaped condiment set, c1785.*

black-jack. 17th century British leather jug of tankard shape, often with silver mounts. Capacities from one quart to a gallon or more.

Black Koryo ware. Korean ceramics of Koryo period made, notably, in late 12th and 13th centuries. Iron-black varieties coated with iron-based slip or pigment. Decoration incised, and sometimes inlaid with white clay. Covering of translucent celadon glaze produces lustrous blue-black finish, with green bloom. Bowls, gourd-shaped vases, and water pots chiefly produced. Second type has black glaze, without decoration, giving matt opaque finish.

blackmetal. Alloy of 60 parts tin and 40 parts lead; crude form of pewter, used for some tavern mugs, etc., from 14th century. Fear of lead-poisoning made metal unpopular.

black monochrome. *See Schwarzlot.*

Blanket chest. Queen Anne period. Walnut. On stand with cabriole legs; brass lock-plate and carrying handles.

Bleeding bowls. American, 18th century bleeding bowls (porringers). Left: by Joseph M. Moulton of Newburyport, Massachusetts, c1765. Diameter 5¼in. Right: by John Brevoort of New York, dated 1738.

Block-front desk. Mahogany. Example has lid also blocked. American, c1770. Height 3ft8in.

black Ting. *See* Ting-chou ware.

blanc-de-chine. In France, Chinese white porcelain made at Tê Hua for export, notably to Europe from 15th to 18th centuries.

blanket chest. Chest with one or two drawers under box with hinged top. In colonial American version, box section had hinged façade imitating two drawer fronts.

Blaublümchenmuster (German, 'blue flower pattern'). Ceramic decoration: delicate, oriental blue and white flowers introduced *c*1732 at Meissen and imitated by other German porcelain factories, also notably at Copenhagen, where production continues.

bleeding-bowl or **dish, cupping-dish, blood porringer.** Shallow, circular vessel with single, flat, pierced handle, used in blood-letting; found in silver, pewter and delftware (e.g. Bristol, Lambeth) 17th to 19th centuries; sometimes marked in gradations. In America, also used as *porringer. *cf* barber's bowl.

bleu céleste. French ceramics. Brilliant turquoise enamel ground colour developed in 1752 by J. *Hellot at Vincennes. Later used at Worcester.

bleu de roi. Intense royal blue overglaze enamel introduced at Sèvres by 1760, replacing **gros bleu*. Used at Worcester in broad stripes with gold flowers, late 18th century; also at Derby for vases with reliefs picked out in gilding and bands of colour, in Chelsea-Derby period. Also used as ground colour on gold enamelled *en plein*.

bleus de Nevers or **bleu persan.** Faience with coloured grounds introduced at Nevers in 1630s. Usually blue ground, decorated with birds and flowers painted in opaque white, or yellow, orange, and white; rarely, designs in white painted on orange-yellow ground with details added in other colours. Oriental style in designs led to classification as *décor persan*. Invention traditionally attributed to P. *Custode.

bleu turc. French ceramic decoration: high temperature greyish-blue ground colour introduced at Sèvres in 1770s.

blind caster. *Caster with cover left unpierced; probably used for dry mustard.

blind Earl pattern. Spray of rose leaves and buds in low relief, derived from Meissen motif, used at *Worcester to decorate porcelain plates from *c*1760. Later named after Earl of Coventry, who became blind in 1780.

blind man's watch. Indicates time through sense of touch, having raised studs on dial, or separate pointer moved by finger until it coincides with hour hand, as in A-L. *Breguet's **montre à tact*. Additional device introduced in some repeating watches, perhaps by G. *Graham, is 'pulse piece' through which repeater blows can be felt.

blinking-eye clock. Type of *animal clock with eyes of automaton figure connected to mechanism. Originally south German, from 16th century, but similar examples made in United States during 19th century.

block front. American façade design in furniture. Block composed of concave or convex panel section within proportionally larger longitudinal area. Panel often surmounted by applied stylized convex or concave shell. Used on case pieces, often in groups of three panels. Associated with *Newport school.

Blois enamel. Enamel painting technique, used in decoration of watch cases, developed *c*1630, by J. *Toutin. Centred in Blois, France during 17th and 18th centuries; later in Geneva. Technique used e.g. by *Huaud family. Miniature paintings depict flowers, figures, or scenes; very vivid colours until *c*1650. Before *c*1675, work rarely signed.

Blondeau (fl mid 18th century). French modeller of porcelain figures at Vincennes. Work includes series of eight glazed *Enfants d'après Boucher* (1752-53), and groups of animals (1752-76).

blood-porringer. *See* bleeding bowl.

Bloor, Robert (fl early 19th century). English potter. Clerk to W. *Duesbury; from 1811, owner of Derby porcelain factory until became insane in 1826. Products sometimes marked BLOOR DERBY between two concentric circles surrounding crown (printed in red); ware in style inspired by Sèvres marked with crown over B inside two entwined Ls of Sèvres (blue enamel).

blower. 18th century device for fanning fire embers; wood or brass box encloses a fan turned from outside by handle. Metal tube directs air at fire.

blowhole. Hole in metal object to allow escape of hot air during casting or soldering processes. Sometimes found in handle, base of body etc. *See* whistle tankard.

blowing-tube. Long, narrow cylinder of brass or copper; draught created by blowing down tube helped to start or revive open fire in 18th and 19th centuries.

blown-three-mould. American glassware blown in three sectional mould *c*1815-35. Characterized e.g. by baroque or geometrical motifs.

blue-and-white transfer-printed ware. Porcelain and earthenware transfer-printed in underglaze blue, developed in late 18th century England. First earthenware printed by T. *Turner. First patterns derived from Chinese designs; later landscapes and scenes with buildings or figures, some taken from books of engravings. Borders often defined by narrow bands and geometrical motifs. Makers include J. *Davenport, *Herculaneum Pottery, the *Adams family, *Coalport, *Leeds Pottery, T. *Minton, J. and W. *Ridgway, *Rockingham, John *Rogers, J. *Spode I and II, J. *Turner, E. *Wood.

blue-dash chargers. Large, ornamental English delftware dishes made *c*1640 to early 18th century, mainly in London. Foot-rims undercut for hanging with string; sometimes pierced. Rims usually decorated with hatched blue lines; later decoration sponged, particularly at Bristol. Reverse lead-glazed until *c*1690, then usually tin-glazed. Bold designs: stylized portraits of Charles I and II, James II, William III, and

Blue-dash charger. Tin-glazed earthenware. Lambeth, mid 17th century.

equestrian figures in armour (royal portrait chargers); scenes depicting fall of Man (Adam and Eve chargers); in late 17th century, formal flower arrangements recalling Isnik pottery of 16th century (tulip chargers); also oak-leaf patterns (oak-leaf chargers). Colours include grey, orange, yellow, green, purple, and turquoise, with blue predominating. *Illustration also at* charger.

blue flower pattern. *See* *Blaublümchenmuster.*

blue john. Crystalline fluorspar mined in small quantities at Castleton, Derbyshire; also known as Derbyshire spar. Discovered by Romans; mine reopened in late 18th century. Highly prized for yellow, blue, and purple colouring. Used ornamentally, particularly in vases, etc., and mounted in gilt-bronze by M. *Boulton. Shown at Great Exhibition, 1851. Name derived from French *bleu-jaune,* 'blue-yellow'. *Illustration also at cassolette.*

boat bed, gondola bed, or **lit en bateau.** Low, heavy bed with head- and foot-boards of elongated S-shape, giving bed boat-like outline from the side. Originated in France during Empire period; adopted in America (as *sleigh bed) and Britain.

Blue john. *Garniture *of urn and pair of candlesticks. English, late 18th century; silver mounted, with candlestick tops and plinths of marble.*

Boat bed. French, Charles X period, amboyna wood. Curved ends capped with swan's necks and heads in gilt metal.
Bobbin turning. On back and arms of English 16th century armchair.

bobbin salt. *See* salt.

bobbin turning. Bobbin-shaped decorative turning on furniture members. Swellings more elongated than in *spool turning.

bocage. Modelled foliage and flowers forming background of porcelain and earthenware figures; made in Germany from *c*1740 and England from *c*1760; leaves often like hawthorn, arranged in groups of five or six, with brightly painted flower at centre of each group. Feature of figures and groups modelled in style of J. *Walton.

boccaro, bucaro, or **buccaro.** Originally, perfumed red earthenware made in Central and South America, brought to Europe by Portuguese. Later, applied to Yi-hsing stoneware.

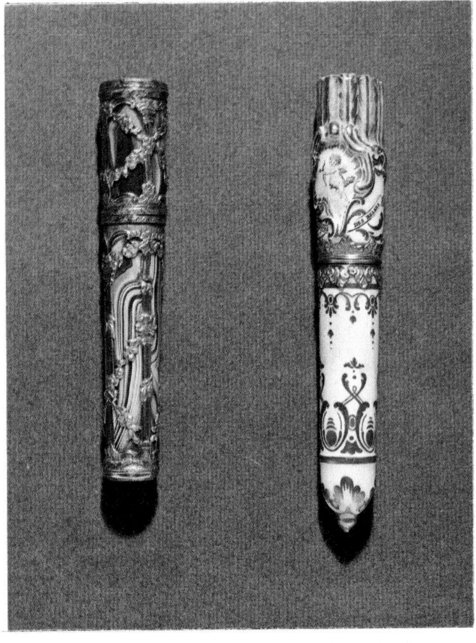

Above:
*Bocage supporting two *Worcester porcelain figures of Dr *Wall period: sportsman carrying gun; companion figure, girl holding powder flask. Height 7½in.*
*Bodkin cases. English, 1770–80. Left: pink agate mounted in gold *cage-work. Right: *Chelsea porcelain case in form of quiver, gold mounted.*

bodkin case. Small 18th century English enamel or porcelain case for bodkins (small pointed instruments with large eye used to draw tape through hem or loop) and needles; decoration as on snuff-boxes.

Boelen, Jacob (1657–1729). Dutch-born American silversmith working in New York. Work shows Dutch influence; includes beakers, coin tankards (with corkscrew thumbpiece, bands of stamped foliate ornament at base, and coins set in lid), also spout and dram cups. Mark: barred IB in a shield.

Bogaert, Johannes (1626–*c*1677). Dutch silversmith working in Amsterdam; son of T. *Bogaert. Works ornamented in *Dutch grotesque style. Made domestic and church plate. Surviving work includes many oval dishes, *tazze,* ewers, monstrances, ciboria, chalices.

Bogaert, Thomas (*c*1597–1653). Dutch silversmith working in Utrecht, possibly apprenticed to A. *van Vianen; master in 1622; alderman of guild 1635; dean in 1640. Specialized in church plate: beakers, pyxes, chalices, ciboria, incense-boats, etc. Few known domestic wares include embossed salts inspired by A. *van Vianen. Son, J. *Bogaert, continued business. Mark: TB, signed.

Bogle, John (*c*1746–1803). British miniaturist, working first in Glasgow and Edinburgh, then in London. Exhibited miniatures 1769–92. Used soft colouring and minute stippling, particularly in rendering hair, which gives woolly effect when viewed through lens.

Bohemian glass. *See* German and Bohemian glass.

Bohme, Carl or Karl Wilhelm (1720–89, or 1795). German porcelain painter; worked at Meissen (1736–61); chief painter at Berlin from 1761 until death. Known for figure painting and especially monochrome landscapes.

bois durci. Wood-based compound used for simulated ebony carvings, patented in France by F. C. Lepage. Sawdust, water, and blood combined by heat treatment, then die-stamped into decorative shapes such as medallions, rosettes, or heads. Popular in France and England, *c*1850–1900.

Boit, Charles (1662–1727). Enamel painter, born in Stockholm; father French. Initially jeweller. In England, drawing master, then enamel painter, first notable one in England. Commissioned by Queen Anne to produce large (24×18in.) enamel portrait group, left unfinished at her death. Went to France; worked for court. In 1700, worked in Düsseldorf, Germany; also in Vienna. Painted enamel portrait miniatures, copies of paintings, and large groups. C. F. *Zincke was his pupil.

boîte à mouches. *See* patch-box.

boîte à portrait. *See* portrait box.

boîte à rouge. *See* rouge box.

Boizot, Louis Simon (1743–1809). French sculptor; head of modelling department at Sèvres (1774–1802). After his appointment, some figures made in hard-paste porcelain. Work includes *Baigneuse* (26in. high, 1774), coronation group of Louis XVI (*l'Autel Royale,* 1775), Zephyr and Flora, and equestrian portrait of Frederick the Great (1781).

Bokhara, Bakhara, or **Bukhara carpets.** Trade name given to Turkoman rugs woven by *Salor, Saryq, and *Tekke tribes. Bokhara was trade centre; carpets not woven there. Name most frequently applied to Tekke rugs.

Bologna maiolica. 16th century dish. *Sgraffiato *decoration of youth and maiden; leaf border.*

Boleyn Cup. Silver-gilt covered standing cup traditionally said to have belonged to Anne Boleyn and to have been given by Elizabeth I, her daughter, to her physician Dr Master, grantee of lands of Cirencester Abbey. V-shaped bowl decorated with gadrooning, with similar ornament on foot and cover. Probably based on German design by H. *Brosamer. Falcon finial is badge of Boleyn family. Bears London hallmark for 1535; property of Cirencester Church, Gloucestershire.

Bologna (Emilia), Italy. Lead-glazed *sgraffiato* earthenware, usually bowls and dishes, made in late 15th and early 16th centuries; red clay exposed in designs scratched through white slip, under transparent glaze, either yellowish or coloured with patches of brown or green. Decoration includes coats of arms, portraits, or animals, with borders of stylized foliage, sometimes dotted by roulette. Maiolica manufacture mentioned in work of C. *Piccolpasso; in 16th and 18th centuries, maiolica influenced by styles of Faenza. Cream-coloured earthenware factory established in late 18th century. Much ware sold in white; also transfer-printed or painted in blue.

Bologna, Giovanni or **Boulogne,** Jean (1529–1608). Flemish sculptor who settled in Italy from *c*1555. He spread mannerist style through Europe, largely because patrons, Medici family, sent bronzes as diplomatic gifts. Many replicas of his pieces made in highly industrialized workshop.

Bolsover, Thomas. *See* Boulsover, Thomas.

bombé. Vertical surface in convex curve, e.g. bow front and/or sides on furniture, including commodes, chests, and desks. Also similar shape in snuff-boxes and in late 18th and early 19th century silver and Sheffield plate teapots, tureens, etc. *Illustration at* bureau.

bonbonnière. *See* sweetmeat box.

bone ash. Calcined and ground bones, proposed in Germany in 1649 as ingredient of porcelain; commonly used as flux in glass, e.g. *Beinglas,* in proportion up to *c*5%. Use in soft-paste porcelain patented by T. *Frye (1749); used at Bow (from 1750), Chelsea (*c*1755), Lowestoft (1758), and Derby (1770). With ingredients of hard-paste porcelain forms English standard *bone china, introduced *c*1800 by J. *Spode II. Addition gives stability during firing. Presence in ceramics identifiable by test for phosphate: warming with ammonium molybdate in nitric acid gives yellow precipitate. Also contained, possibly as whitening agent, in some cream-coloured earthenware.

bone china. Hard-paste porcelain modified with addition of up to *c*40% *bone ash. Standard English porcelain since 1800 – proportions attributed to J. *Spode II.

Bone, Henry (1755–1834), sons Henry Pierce (1779–1855) and Robert Trewick (1790–1840). English enamel painters. Henry initially decorated porcelain at Plymouth and then Bristol, painting landscapes and flowers. In London from *c*1780 as decorator of watch cases, buttons, and brooches, and enamel painter, becoming most successful of his period. Associate of the Royal Academy, 1801; member in 1811. Enamel painter to George III, George IV, and William IV. Portrait miniatures in enamel or rarely on ivory. Also enamel copies of old master paintings and of 85 portraits of illustrious Englishmen. Henry Pierce painted portraits in oil, 1799–1833, then enamel painter to Queen Adelaide and Queen Victoria. Robert Trewick exhibited classical and sacred pictures, 1813–38; also painted enamel miniatures.

bonheur du jour or **cheveret.** Lady's small, light writing desk with central drawer in

Bonheur du jour. **Sheraton style. Mahogany with satinwood panels, cross-banding and stringing; writing flap folds out over front drawer. Late 18th century. Height 3ft4in.*

front and tiered shelves and cupboards at back. May have shelf between legs. First made in France *c*1760.

bonnet-scroll pediment. *See* swan-neck pediment.

Bonnin and Morris. Porcelain factory established in Philadelphia, Pennsylvania in 1769, probably using soft-paste porcelain formula with bone ash, as at Bow. Rare examples exist, painted in blue, in style influenced by English factories, e.g. Bow. Factory closed 1772. Mark: small P.

Bonsach, Baard Gandolphi (d 1701). Norwegian-born silversmith working in Copenhagen. Domestic silver (e.g. beakers, brandy bowls) characterized by granulated ornament.

Bontemps, Georges (1799–1884). Director of Choisy-le-Roi glasshouse in France, 1823–48. Experiments with shape and colour influenced fine 19th century paperweights. Produced opal, filigree, and *millefiori* glass. Left France 1848 to work for *Chance Bros in England. Wrote *Guide du Verrier,* published Paris, 1868.

booge or **bouge.** Curved area of plate between rim and base.

bookbinding (in silver). Book cover of precious metal, ivory, enamel, etc., for sacred work, e.g. gospel, epistle, common during Middle Ages. Often set with gems; metal engraved or embossed with ornamental motifs, sacred symbols, or religious scenes. From 14th century, Gothic architectural motifs used as ornament. From 16th century, bindings of sacred books more often wood or leather with silver or copper mounts. In 17th century England, books sometimes covered with velvet or embroidered work, with engraved and pierced silver mounts; such covers are rare, because Reformed churches rejected ostentation of Roman Catholic church. Bindings in precious materials reappeared during 19th century Gothic revival.

bookcase or **bibliothèque.** Shelved structure with glazed or grill-work doors, used for holding books. Free-standing style dates from 17th

Book-binding. Silver. Pierced and engraved with sphinxes, mermaids, animals, insects, and birds; central engraved medallion with Return of the Prodigal Son; two clasps. Dutch, 1624. Height $3\frac{1}{2}$*in.*

*Bookcase. English, mid 18th century. Mahogany. After design from T. *Chippendale's 'Director'; moulded and broken pediment, carved Gothic arched glazing bars. Height 9ft2in.*

Boscobel Oak snuff-box. Lid with inset oak panel upon which, in silver, is scene of Charles II hiding in oak tree. English, c1700. Length $3\frac{3}{4}$*in.*

Right:

Bottles. English wine bottles. Left to right: 1) Dark green glass bottle, stamped Thomas Carlyon, 1708. 2) Round-ended wine bottle, pale brown glass, c1630. 3) Late 17th century sack bottle of opaque glass. 4) Wine bottle, c1630, pale blue glass.

Boston rocker. Maple and pine, painted black and stencilled with flowers and leaves; bowed back. 1832.

Johann Friedrich Böttger. Porcelain coffee-pot, with applied reliefs of flowers and birds, some in polychrome. c1720.

century; early forms were built-in. 18th century bookcases tended to be large architectural pieces with two glazed doors or *breakfront design. Towards end of century, smaller models made, sometimes incorporating small shelves for curios.

bookstand. Stand on four short legs, with two or more book shelves. Often in mahogany or satinwood; may have castor feet. Made from late 18th to end of 19th century.

boot-heel. Style of lower handle terminal on pewter tankards, etc., particularly in late 17th century, supposedly resembling contemporary boot-heel.

Booth, Edward. *See* Barlow, Edward.

Booth, Enoch (fl mid 18th century). Master potter at Tunstall, Staffordshire, maker of *scratch-blue and creamware. Credited with invention *c*1740 of liquid glaze for creamware, in which both lead ore and flints ground in water to avoid injury to workers from dust. Marked salt-glaze wares Enoch Booth or EB with date.

booze bottle. American whisky bottles, made in 1860 by Whitney Glass Works for Edward G. Booz of Philadelphia, Pennsylvania.

Bordeaux (Gironde), France. Faience made *c*1708–82 with help of workmen from Montpellier; products include pharmaceutical and domestic ware, also wall fountains, cisterns, etc. Decoration includes **style Berain*, grotesques, potato flower, and **décor à guirlandes*. Hard-paste porcelain made 1781–90 with clay from Saint-Yrieix. Marks include VV in gold (1781–87), and BORDEAUX around monogram of V and A, stencilled in red (1787–90). Cream-coloured earthenware made 1834–45; mainly transfer-printed.

Borelly, Boselli, or **Boselly,** Jacques (fl late 18th century). French maker of faience at Marseilles; *c*1780 moved workshop to Savona. Produced wares with high-temperature or enamel decoration.

Boreman, Zachariah (1738–1810). Porcelain painter at Chelsea (until 1783) and Derby (1784–95). Early work includes landscapes in Sèvres styles on large vases with claret ground. Later, painted Derbyshire dale landscapes in black or brown monochrome with coloured washes. Thought to have worked as outside enameller in London after leaving Derby.

Borghese urn. Silver form derived from classical Roman urn with thistle-shaped body and two loop handles belonging to Borghese family. Sometimes used for Louis XIV style wine fountains; also wine coolers, coffee urns, etc. Also decorative motif.

Borman, Johan Balthazar (1725–84). German porcelain painter, worked at Meissen and Berlin (1763–79); known for landscapes, figures, and battle scenes.

Borough, John. *See* Burrough, John.

boscages tapestry. **Verdure* tapestry design. Field with stylized or relatively realistic large foliage; borders have pillars with grotesque or caryatid-like figures, or broad floral bands with vases and birds.

Boscobel oak box. Type of oak and silver snuff-box commemorating legend of Charles II hiding from searchers in an oak in Boscobel Wood after Battle of Worcester (1651). Scene depicted in engraved and cut silver on lids of oval or rectangular boxes.

Bos, Cornelis (b 1510). Flemish engraver and silver designer working in Antwerp. Studied in Rome; returned to Netherlands in 1540s and published designs for decorative panels. Influenced by Italian mannerist styles. Used strapwork to enclose contorted satyrs, animals, etc. Influenced *Dutch grotesque style, developed by *van Vianen family.

Boselli or **Boselly,** Jacques. *See* Borelly, Jacques.

boss. Decorative knob or stud on metal or wooden object, e.g. at centre of shield or ornament.

Bossierer or **Poussierer** (German, 'repairers'). German craftsmen who re-assembled porcelain figure sections after firing. *See* repairers.

boss up. Forming of hollow-ware by beating sheet metal from the back into rough approximation of desired shape.

Boston rocker. American rocking chair made in and near Boston, Massachusetts; combines features of Sheraton *fancy chair with *rod-back Windsor. Has spindle-back, shaped yoke-rail, ogee-curved arms; seat curves up toward back, scrolls downward in front. Painted, with gilt decoration. Dates from early 19th century.

Boston & Sandwich Glass Company. American glasshouse established 1825 at Cape Cod, Massachusetts by D. *Jarves, to produce fine quality lead-glass, hand cut or blown-three-mould. Pressed glass was developed *c*1828 and factory noted for fine *lacy glass made up to 1850 in clear or coloured glass. Credited with first pressed drinking glass, but majority of early pieces of simpler shape, e.g. *cup-plates, for which over 500 patterns have been recorded. Pressed ware usually marked B & S Glass Co. Sandwich (*see* Sandwich glass). Opaline glass produced from *c*1830. 1850–80 paperweights made by Nicholas Lutz, formerly of Cristallerie de St Louis. Floral bouquets or miniature fruit on *latticinio* base popular motifs. 1850–70, Bohemian-style cameo and cut ruby-stained glass also produced. Factory closed in 1888 during Depression.

botanical flowers. Naturalistic flowers, inspired by **deutsche Blumen*, painted on porcelain at Chelsea (1750–56), on creamware by *Absolon, L. W. *Dillwyn, and T. *Pardoe. Notable examples with botanical names inscribed on back of porcelain pieces attributed to W. *Pegg. *Illustration at* Hans Sloane plates.

boteh (Arabic, 'leaf'), **buta, cone, almond, pine, pear,** or **palm top motif.** Most extensively used leaf motif on oriental carpets. Simple leaf with crested top, stylized in numerous ways. When very small, sometimes humorously called flea motif.

Bott, Thomas John (1829–70). English porcelain painter and designer at *Worcester. From early 1850s specialized in white enamel decoration on dark coloured ground, reproducing effect of 16th century *Limoges painted enamels.

Bottengruber, Ignaz (fl *c*1720–*c*1736). German porcelain *Hausmaler* and book illustrator. Worked at Breslau and Vienna. Chose unusual hunting, military, and bacchanalian subjects. Painted in violet-purple or iron-red monochrome on cups, saucers, and tea-bottles (1728). These scenes later surrounded by polychrome flowers, scrolls, and *putti*, under influence of C. I. *du Paquier in Vienna (*c*1730). Work sometimes marked with elaborate signature, or monogram IB.

Böttger, Johann Friedrich (1682–1719). German alchemist from Saxony. First European to manufacture hard-paste porcelain (1708), after seizure (1710) by *Augustus the Strong, who ordered him to make gold; as no gold was produced, ordered by King to collaborate (1706–08) with E. W. *von Tschirnhaus in search for porcelain arcanum. In July 1708, joint efforts produced first white unglazed **Böttgerporzellan*; glaze mastered in March 1709, after von Tschirnhaus's death. Some glazed and biscuit bowls, decorated with applied leaves, shown at Leipzig Fair (1710). Director of Meissen factory from establishment in 1710. Experiments at Meissen resulted in development of satisfactory enamels and gilding technique. Earlier discovery, *red stoneware, was also being produced commercially. Key workmen left to set up first rival factory at Vienna (notably S. *Stölzel and C. C. *Hunger). Released in 1715, but ill-health and alcohol precipitated early death. *Illustration at* red stoneware.

Böttger lustre. Pale, purplish mother-of-pearl lustre first made in Europe by J. F. *Böttger from gold, at Meissen porcelain factory. Used in 1720s by J. G. *Herold, in painting of cartouches.

Böttgerporzellan (German, 'Böttger's porcelain'). First European hard-paste porcelain. Made by J. F. *Böttger and E. W. *von Tschirnhaus at Meissen, Germany, in 1708. Typically, body is smoky or yellowish-white and glaze has minute bubbles. Variety of useful and decorative wares made at new *Meissen porcelain factory from 1710. Greatest accomplishments are perhaps sets of unpainted pieces with double walls, outer pierced in oriental lattice fashion (reticulated ware). Chinese shapes inspired many coffee and tea pots, etc. Contemporary silver styles also influential. Decorated either with applied moulded or modelled relief work; by painting in gold or silver (now blackened); by enamelling with small range of 'dry-looking' colours, devised by Böttger; or with *Böttger lustre. Some small figures produced *c*1715, perhaps by G. *Fritzsche. Mark: monogram of two Ks on shield (rare).

bottle. From Roman times, blown or blown-moulded bottles produced in quantities, corresponding in size and shape to metal and clay counterparts. English bottles from *c*1650 had distinctive form; made of dark green or brown *bottle glass, some examples had impressed medallion or glass seal applied to base of body or shoulder bearing date, initials, arms, or other device indicating owner or maker. Shaft and globe form, popular throughout 17th century, has bulbous body, long neck, ringed $c\frac{1}{2}$in. below mouth, and deep kick in base; from *c*1680, neck became shorter and body broader. Early 18th century bottles taller, with slightly curved or perpendicular sides, square shoulders, and neck ring immediately below the mouth. From *c*1830 straight-sided cylinder bottles became common, following custom of stacking wine bottles on sides in a bin. Earliest type, made in clay moulds, bulged slightly at base; by 1750, single metal moulds used and bulge disappeared. Machine-moulded bottles date from *c*1840. In America, bottles, usually of dark olive-green or amber glass, main product of most 18th and early 19th century glasshouses. Most common form was free-blown, chestnut-shaped *Ludlow bottle. Swirl bottles pattern-moulded with vertical ribs (swirling usually to right) popular in Mid-West; made in blue, green, aquamarine, yellow, and amber, either with spherical body, long neck and collared mouth, or short, cylindrical or rounded body, sloping shoulders, short neck, and collared mouth. Pocket flask bottles also popular throughout period in various shapes and designs (*see* flasks). Cylindrical bottles made in 19th century (mainly imported from Europe in 18th century). In late 19th century, fully automatic bottle-making machine patented by M. J. Owens of Toledo, Ohio.

bottle case. Wooden box designed to hold square bottles. Might be veneered and could stand e.g. on sideboard. Dates from 18th century. *cf* cellaret.

bottle glass. Glass containing no lead. Aquamarine, green, olive, or amber colouring caused by impurities in *batch. Early bottle glass known as 'black glass'.

bottle-jack, roasting-jack. Cylindrical clockwork device in brass or copper hanging from mantelpiece or *Dutch oven; twists and untwists with weight of meat hanging from it, to give even cooking. Invented in 1760s, improved (by J. Linwood) in 1790s.

bottle labels or **tickets.** *See* wine labels.

bottle turning (in furniture). Decorative turning, originally Dutch, found on late 17th century English and American furniture.

Boucher, François (1703–70). French court painter in rococo style. In Italy (1727–37), influenced by Tiepolo. Under patronage of Madame de Pompadour from 1740; chief painter to Louis XV from 1765. Figures, notably children, after Boucher, painted on faience and on porcelain in Germany (e.g. at Berlin and Meissen) and France (at Chantilly, Mennecy, Vincennes, and Sèvres); also at Copenhagen, Tournai, etc. Modelled e.g. by E-M. *Falconet. Boucher was artistic director of *Beauvais tapestry manufactory 1736–55. Paintings and cartoons sustained manufactory, and style had profound influence on tapestry design and technique. Huge palette with subtle tonal modulations (up to 1000 hues) led to introduction of interlocking wefts and necessitated very fine texture with 20–40 warps to 1in. Compositions: decorative, romantic and pastoral scenes. Wide range of subjects include 14-piece *Fêtes Italiennes*, five-piece History of Psyche, nine-piece *Amours des Dieux*, and sketches for highly successful six-piece Chinese Hangings. *Illustration at* Beauvais tapestry.

*Bougie box. Made by W. *Fountain in 1809. Engraved with royal coat of arms; reeded borders and reeded loop handles; chained extinguisher and slip-off cover. Height $3\frac{3}{4}$in.*

Boulle-work. Table top, veneered on oak with première-partie *(central panel) and* *contre-partie *(scrollwork surround) marquetry of brass and tortoiseshell. Design depicts cage of birds surrounded by* *singeries. *French, mid 18th century.*

bougie or **taper box.** Small silver or Sheffield plate drum-shaped container with handle for wound taper; circular funnel in centre top through which taper end projects. Conical extinguisher generally attached by chain. Sometimes made with pierced body and glass liner. From late 18th century in Britain.

bouillotte table. Round-topped French card table; usually has marble top surrounded by metal gallery, pair of drawers and slides in frieze. Four cylindrical, downward-tapering legs ending in sabot feet. Designed for card game, *bouillotte*. Dates from Louis XVI period.

Boulle, André-Charles (1642–1732). French; *ébéniste* to Louis XIV (from 1672); made furniture for royal palaces, especially Versailles. Perfected form of brass and tortoiseshell marquetry (subsequently called *Boulle work) and made much use of elaborate ormolu mounts.

Boulle or **Buhl work.** Marquetry of tortoiseshell and brass (or other metals), originating in

Italy, perfected by A-C. *Boulle. Designs achieved by glueing sheet of tortoiseshell to one of brass, cutting shape of design through both, separating the two pieces, and inlaying each in its opposite background. Inlaying brass shape in shell ground called *première-partie* work, the reverse, *contre-partie*. Both may appear on same piece of furniture, or separately, on matching pair of objects. Tortoiseshell inlay may be backed or painted, and panels of **pietra dura* included on object. Boulle work popular with *ébénistes* during 18th century; found e.g. on clock cases. G. *Jensen and P. *Langlois among British exponents of technique. *Illustrations at* A. Weisweiler, *bureau plat*, Louis XIV style.

Boulsover or **Bolsover,** Thomas (1704–88). English silversmith who invented Sheffield plate, 1742. Produced buttons and boxes. Boxes were circular with lift-off lids; hand-worked all over in relief with foliage and scroll-work, classical scenes, or portraits.

Boulton, Matthew (1728–1809). English manufacturer of silver and Sheffield plate, working in Birmingham. Took over father's button and buckle business (1759); between 1759 and 1766 built large factory at Soho, near Birmingham. Soho Manufactory had large number of workshops turning out buckles, snuff-boxes, sword hilts, etc. From *c*1762 concentrated on Sheffield plate; largest producer in Britain (*c*1775–1800). From *c*1765 also made domestic silver. *c*1762, took as partner John Fothergill; latter had European contacts which broadened area of trade; partnership continued until Fothergill's death (1783). Instead of filling individual commissions, Boulton supplied items from stock. In 1768, began production of ormolu objects (vases, candlesticks, clock cases) and mounts (for marble, blue john, and Wedgwood pieces). Adopted Adam style which lent itself to mass-production; parts of objects often machine stamped, then assembled by workers. Most wares designed by his staff, though some designs obtained from R. *Adam and other designers (both architects and artists). Visited Catherine the Great in Russia, where introduced techniques of steel faceting to Russian furniture manufacture. Petitioned Parliament for assay office in Birmingham; granted in 1773. Formed successful partnership (1773) with James Watt for development and sale of steam engine. 1781–1809, traded as Matthew Boulton & Plate Co.; 1809–34 son traded as M. R. Boulton; in 1843 firm became Soho Plate Co. Mark (on Sheffield plate): two suns. *Illustrations at* cruet-stand, cut-steel jewellery, *guilloche* ornament, pounce-box, urn clock.

Matthew Boulton. One of set of four combined incense-burners and candelabra, in ormolu, after design by James Stuart. Chased bowl-shaped container with pierced cover (incense-burner) supporting scrolling candle-branches, classical tripod headed with female busts; white marble bases. Height 2ft3in.

bouquetière. Early Venetian glass bowl with wide, flared mouth and wavy-edged brim. Mounted on stem and foot. Decorated with moulded fluting, applied ribbing, and *mascarons. Form revived in 18th and early 19th century France.

Bouquet, David (d 1665). French watch maker, working in London. Joined Blacksmiths' Company, 1628; founding member of Clockmakers' Company, 1631. Maker of *Puritan watch, *c*1640.

Bourg-la-Reine (Seine), France. Site of faience and porcelain factory founded 1772 by J. *Jullien and S. *Jacques, who transferred porcelain manufacture from Mennecy in 1773. Work hard to distinguish from Mennecy unless marked (BR, incised, 1773–*c*1780).

bow. Metal ring attached to pendant of watch, into which chain or fob is inserted. Various shapes; e.g. oval, circular, and 'stirrup'.

bow-back or **sack-back Windsor.** Windsor chair, popular in America *c* mid 18th century. Arms continuous, curving horizontally around back of chair. Back of arm-piece surmounted by inverted U-shaped bow. Seat U-shaped. H-shaped stretcher often has bulb-and-ring turning.

Bowen, John (fl mid 18th century). Painter of delftware at Bristol from 1734; employers included J. *Flower. Blue and white decoration on tiles, etc.: figures, landscapes, views across river of building backed by mountains, accurately detailed ships.

Bowes Cup. Ornate silver-gilt covered *standing cup ($19\frac{3}{4}$in. high) made for Lord Mayor of London, Sir Martin Bowes, and used by Queen Elizabeth I at coronation. Has crystal bowl and cut crystals set in stem and cover. Largest and most magnificent of 16th century standing cups with thistle-shaped bowl. Bears London hallmark for 1554–55; property of Goldsmiths' Company.

Bowes, Sir Jerome (d 1616). English soldier turned entrepreneur. Bought G. *Verzelini's monopoly and Broad Street Glass House in 1592. When granted 12 years renewal in 1596, was first glass manufacturer to pay monarch for monopoly to make and import all *façon de Venise* glass. Bad relations with workmen lowered standards set by Verzelini.

bow front. Outward-curving front on furniture. Found particularly on 18th century commodes, drawers, sideboards, and tables.

bowl (in Chinese ceramics). Found in various forms; most common, small rice bowl with curved or straight-flaring sides. Shallower bowls used for soup; deep bowls with lids, like jars, used as tea bowls, covered for infusion of tea instead of using teapot. Size and finish of foot distinctive feature helping to identify period, group, etc. Variations include *bubble-bowl, *brinjal bowls, *conical bowl.

bowl (in silver, etc.). *See* bleeding bowl, brandy bowl, bratina, broth bowl, charka, *écuelle*, mazer, monteith, pot-pourri bowl, punch bowl, quaich, sugar bowl.

Bow Porcelain Manufactory. Soft-paste porcelain factory founded *c*1748 at Bow, London, by partners including T. *Frye. *Bone ash added to paste from 1749. Many figures produced: some modelled after Meissen; others, of topical interest, include Kitty Clive as The Fine Lady, General Wolfe, and the Marquis of Granby. Early figures press-moulded and left white or painted sparingly; until *c*1760 with mound bases. Later figures rest on pedestals with four scroll feet packed out in purple. Large output of blue-and-white porcelain, often with mauve-tinted blue. Domestic ware often enamelled in Kakiemon style; also with *botanical flowers in soft colours including pinkish-purple and light blue. Mugs commonly bell-shaped with lower terminal of handle heart-shaped. Transfer-printing occasionally occurs in black or brick red. After *c*1760, deterioration in quality of modelling and painting. Factory closed 1776; moulds taken by W. *Duesbury for use at Derby. Marks include incised planet symbols (on soft-paste porcelain

Bow Porcelain Manufactory. Left: cream jug with famille rose *decoration, c1755, unmarked; height $2\frac{3}{4}$in. Centre: figure of Winter, one of set of Four Seasons, c1760–65, unmarked; height $6\frac{3}{4}$in. Right: basket, shape derived from silverware and decorated in underglaze blue, 1750–55; diameter 5in.*

before *c*1750); figure repairers' marks, 1750–70, include T° of Tebo, impressed. Blue-and-white ware marked with B, script G, or planet symbols in underglaze blue. Marks on later figures include anchor and dagger in red, underglaze blue letters, dots, or crescent, which can be confused with Worcester mark. *Illustration also at* knife and fork handles.

box bedstead. Bed with high panelling at both ends and along one side. Open side has curtains on rails which can be drawn for privacy; flat *tester. English derivative of medieval enclosed bed; made until *c*1850.

box-case clock. American shelf clock in shape of box, with wooden movement; patented by E. *Terry, 1816.

box chair. High-backed panelled Gothic chair, with arms and box base. Hinged seat forms top of box.

boxes. *See* bodkin case, cagework box, candle box, casket, counter box, *étui*, 'freedom' box, Freemasonic box, musical box, *nécessaire*, nutmeg grater, patch-box, pomander, portrait box, rouge box, snuff-box, souvenir box, spice box, sweetmeat box, tobacco box, and vinaigrette.

box on box. *See* Massachusetts shelf clock.

box settle. *Settle with seat top forming lid of box base. Medieval form.

box stretcher. *Stretcher composed of four rails; two join front legs to corresponding back legs, third joins the front legs, and a fourth the back legs, thus forming box-like square or rectangle.

braced-back. Windsor chair-back support formed by two spindles running from shelf-like rear extension of chair seat up to yoke-rail.

bracelet. Ornament for arm or wrist made in variety of materials (gold, silver, base metals, wood, etc. according to fashion or occasionally age and rank of wearer). In use from ancient times; in Egypt arm bracelets (plain or enamelled metal) worn by kings and women; hoop, spiral shapes common. Spiral snake form popular during Roman era and again in 15th and 16th centuries, some surviving 16th century examples made from meshwork of chains or linked scrolls, decorated with medallions, gems, pearls, etc. In modern times bracelets did not become general in Britain and Europe until 17th century; worn by women. Might consist of linked pieces in decorative forms (floral, arabesque, etc.) set with precious stones, pearls; sometimes enamelled (usually black and white). Common 18th century forms included diamonds (or pastes) set in openwork ornamental frame sometimes with enamelled medallion clasp. 18th and 19th century bracelets often part of *parure*. In early 19th century bracelets of pearls, gems, linked cameos, etc., sometimes worn over gloves. Many early and mid 19th century bracelets inspired by classical styles (made available by archeological discoveries), e.g. Etruscan, Roman, Greek, Assyrian. Decline in use of diamonds; enamel decoration and granulation revived.

bracket. Right-angled wall-fitting acting as support for e.g. shelf, pot-hook, lamp, or (on external wall) lantern, or inn or shop sign. Made from Middle Ages of wrought iron or brass in plain or scrolling forms, or highly elaborate designs. 18th century type (also known as console), made less often in metal than in gilt wood, used to support clock, vase, ornament, etc. Exterior sign-brackets were of wrought iron, often ornate, sometimes echoing subject of sign.

Bracket. Wrought-iron sign bracket. Flemish, 18th century. Length 3ft6in.

bracket clock. Spring-driven clock to stand on table, shelf, or fixed bracket on wall. Introduced after invention of pendulum, 1657. English makers include W. *Clement, T. *Tompion, and J. *Knibb. Styles followed those of long-case clocks. *c*1660–*c*1700, mainly architectural; later with *domed-top, *basket-top, etc., according to current style. Early English examples, under Dutch influence, frequently engraved with tulips on dial and back-plate. *French versions known as mantel clocks, *horloges de cheminée,* but often include wall brackets of same material as clock case.

Bracket clock, with original supporting bracket. Mahogany case and bracket and painted dial. c1800, by Handley & Moore.

bracket foot. Shaped square foot, usually on case furniture, cut away to resemble, in profile from both sides, a bracket. Much used from early 18th to mid 19th century. *Illustration at* chest of drawers.

Bradburn or **Bradbourne,** John (fl *c*1764–77). English; cabinet-maker to George III; specialized in carving. Many commissions to royal household (1765–75).

Bradbury, Thomas (1763–1838). English manufacturer of Sheffield plate working in Sheffield. Apprenticed to Matthew Fenton & Co in 1777; partnership with Thomas Watson & Co in 1795, firm known as Watson and Bradbury (mark: TW & Co). In 1832 firm became Thomas Bradbury and Sons (mark: TB & S). Grandson, Joseph (1825–77), remained with firm until decline of Sheffield plate. Thereafter, firm made silver and electro-plated wares.

Brameld, John (1741–1819) and sons, William (1772–1813), Thomas (1787–1850), George Frederic (1782–1853), and John Wager (1797–1851). Potters at Swinton, Yorkshire. Worked at Swinton Pottery, later *Rockingham pottery and porcelain factory. John, working partner by 1786, brought sons into business at first as apprentices. After his retirement (1813), Thomas director of factory; after closure, probably worked in flint mill (1842–44). George Frederic, corresponding clerk, then agent for factory in St Petersburg. John Wager worked as traveller for firm; also painter – work includes enamelled panels of first *Rhinoceros Vase. After closure of firm, worked as potter in London.

Brandenburg porcelain. German copies of J. F. *Böttger's red stoneware made at Plaue-on-Havel, Brandenburg, 1713–30. Examples include octagonal boxes, and polished jugs with relief decoration and gilding. Distinguishable from originals by greater thickness and weight of body. No marks identified with certainty.

brander. Gridiron, used for cooking and known in various forms from Middle Ages; especially type with pierced iron plate and rigid semi-circular handle, by which suspended from pot-hook, used mainly in Scotland for making brander bannocks (oatmeal cakes).

Brandt, Reynier (1707–after 1784). Dutch silversmith working in Amsterdam. Speciality pierced-work in French rococo and neo-classical styles. Made domestic and church plate; work includes bread baskets, salvers, soap-boxes, baptismal basins, etc. Mark: RB, signed.

brandy bowl. Dutch silver oval bowl with two handles from which raisins steeped in brandy were eaten at family occasions in 17th and 18th

Brass. Inkstand: inkpot, sand box, and candle-holder. Dutch, late 18th century. Length 5½in.

centuries. Early handles shaped like human head, etc., later, more common handles flat and chased. Bowl either left undecorated or chased and embossed. Made mainly in Friesland, often silver-gilt. Many later versions of traditional style produced from 19th century.

brandy warmer. *See* saucepan.

brass. Alloy made from copper and calamine; pure zinc replaced calamine in 18th century. Strong, malleable metal which can be hammered (*see* latten), rolled, drawn into wire, stamped, or cast (though unsuitable for delicate cast-work or fine details). Can be brightly polished, but tarnishes. Earliest surviving brass objects are Roman (vessels, brooches, rings). From Middle Ages used throughout Europe for domestic and plainer ecclesiastical utensils; main centres of production were Flanders and Germany. Commercial production began in England in late 16th century; range of wares widely increased to include lamps, chandeliers, domestic vessels, etc. In 17th century, many small items (e.g. spoons) were tinned and burnished to resemble silver. Main producers: *Dockwra's Copper Company, *Bristol Brass Wire Company; *Birmingham took lead in second half of 18th century. By this time process of extracting pure zinc from calamine was known, and Emerson's patent (1780) used zinc in brass for first time on large scale. 'New brass' considered of better colour than old; also found more suitable for casting, giving sharper detail. Some objects were gilt.

In 19th century, after many technical improvements and introduction of stamping, wares included inkstands, watch-stands, letter-racks, picture-frames, *door furniture, etc. Varnish was frequently applied to prevent tarnishing; to give appearance of gold a colouring agent (gamboge, saffron, *dragon's blood) was added.

Little brass was produced in America before 19th century; until then, goods mainly imported ready-made.

Proportions of copper and zinc vary; brass-type alloys, developed for different purposes, include *Bath metal, *Dutch metal, *patent metal, *pinchbeck, *prince's metal, *tombac.

bratina. Russian drinking vessel of gold or silver. Squat bellied body has foot-ring and slightly narrower lip-band generally inscribed in niello engraving or chasing; sometimes with pointed dome cover. In use from Middle Ages to 17th century; peasants used wooden versions.

brazier. Portable stove made from medieval

Brazier. English, 1685; maker's mark, IS with pillar between letters. Movable pierced base-lining and pierced sides, three decorated stays holding grid. Height 4¾in.

times in Eastern countries and probably also in Europe; earliest surviving European examples known from late Middle Ages. Usual form is three or four legged iron stand fitted with copper bowl with pierced lid to contain burning charcoal; used to heat rooms or to keep kettles, etc., warm. Low-standing Spanish type dating from 17th century has wide wooden rim and copper bowl, sometimes with pierced domed cover; used as foot-warmer. *See also* chafing-dish.

bread basket. *See* basket.

break-arch or **broken arch.** Arch-shaped top of long-case or bracket clock, when semi-circle of arch is broken at each side by 'step' or ridge. Also dial-opening in same form, with line of arch broken just above dial-plate. Extra space created by arch may contain calendar, subsidiary dial, spandrel ornaments, etc. First example of long-case clock, with break-arch top and dial, made by T. *Tompion, 1695; on bracket clock by D. *Quare, *c*1720. Style in use throughout 18th century.

breakfast service. Silver, silver-gilt, or Sheffield plate service including pots for coffee, chocolate, and tea, cream-jug, sugar bowl, spoons, egg-cups, tea-caddies, etc., decorated *en suite*. In use from 19th century.

breakfast table. Small table incorporating two

*Breakfast table. Oval *snap table, with three rows of cross-banding. Shown in vertical position. English, early 19th century.*

*Breakfast service. Empire style, made in Paris by Boden, 1809–19. Silver-gilt. Comprising two dishes, knife, fork, spoon, cut glass salt, covered jam pot and spoon, and *chafing dish with ivory handle.*

hinged flaps which, opened, increase size of surface. Alternatively *snap table.

breakfront. Piece of furniture, e.g. bookcase, in which central vertical section projects slightly in front of side sections. Popular in England during late 18th century.

Brede pottery. Slipware formerly thought to come from Brede, Sussex, now ascribed to Bethersden, Kent. Late 18th to early 19th century. Decoration includes foliage, trees, stars, and inscriptions, inlaid in clay, either white in red or red in white.

Breguet, Abraham-Louis (1747–1823). Swiss-born watch maker, working in Paris. Exiled during French Revolution, from 1791 in Switzerland and England; returned to France in 1795. Began career in Paris, *c*1762; probably worked for F. *Berthoud. Known work produced from 1782; signed *Breguet à Paris* until 1791. Made *subscription watches, **montres à tact*, many self-winding watches, and **tourbillons*. Watch cases often very thin, with gold or silver dials. Developed *secret signature to discourage faking of work. Used cylinder, lever, and spring detent *escapement; introduced *parachute device in watches from *c*1793. Went into partnership with son, Louis-Antoine, *c*1807; work subsequently signed Breguet et Fils. Appointed *Horloger de la Marine*, 1815. *Illustrations at montre à tact*, travelling clock.

Breguet overcoil. Balance spring of complex form devised by A-L. *Breguet. *See* balance, isochronism.

*Abraham-Louis Breguet. *Subscription watch no. 2267,* c*1800. Enamel dial, silver case with gold bezels; cylinder escapement with 'parachute' shock absorber for balance bearings. Dial has signature scratched very finely below figure 12.*

breloque. Tiny gold or enamel ornament; for hanging on chatelaine.

Breslau Hausmalerei. **Hausmalerei* produced mainly by I. *Bottengruber and associates (*c*1720–*c*1740); style of decoration influenced Vienna porcelain factory where unpainted pieces obtained. Some pieces inscribed with names, possibly of pupils or patrons.

Brewer, John (1764–1815). British artist and porcelain painter, brother of R. *Brewer. Work includes landscapes and birds on porcelain made at Derby.

Brewer, Robert (d 1857). British artist, drawing teacher, and porcelain painter. Nautical subjects on porcelain made at Derby thought to be his work; also painted porcelain made at Coalport and Worcester.

Brewster chair. 17th century American spindle arm chair with two rows of spindles in back, between seat and stretchers, and between arms and rush seat. Named after William Brewster, a founder of Massachusetts Bay Colony. *cf* Carver chair.

Briati, Guiseppe (1686–1772). Murano glass maker. After working in Bohemia for three years, specialized in Bohemian style. Established glassworks in Venice in 1739. Noted for mirrors and *latticinio* glass.

brick. Delftware brick shape made mainly in mid 18th century England. Top pierced, usually with central large hole and rows of small holes, for use as flower holder, or possibly inkstand with provision for holding pens. Made at Lambeth, Bristol, and Liverpool. *c*6in. long, though larger specimens exist. Decoration normally blue and white *chinoiserie* scenes or flowers; polychrome decoration used at Bristol.

Brewster chair. Early 17th century, made in America, possibly by John Alden. Height 3ft10in.

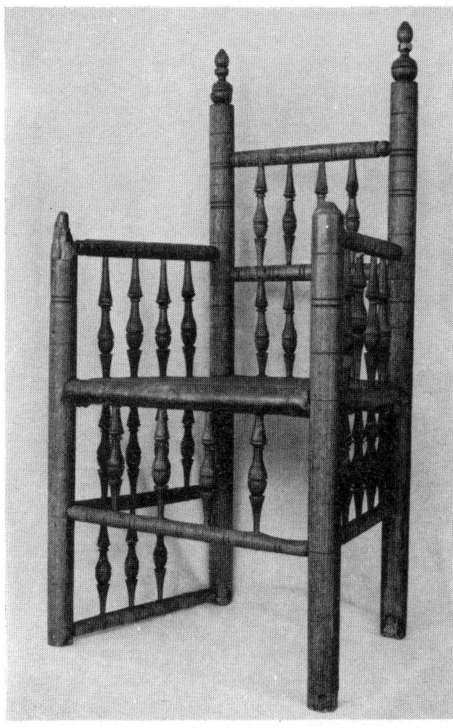

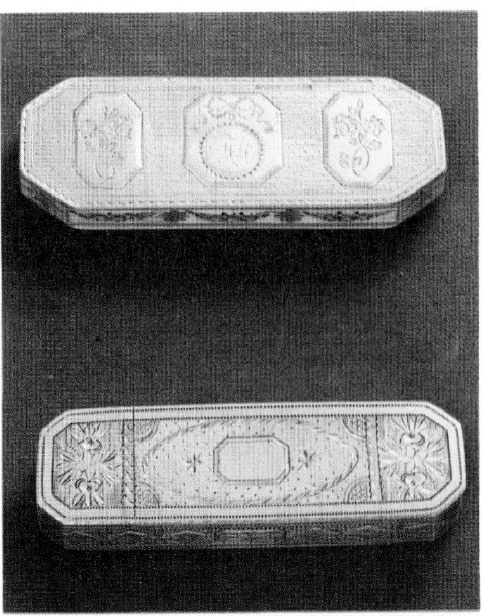

Bright-cut engraving. Silver toothpick case, made in Birmingham by Samuel Pemberton, 1791. Length 3½in.

bridal cup. Ceremonial silver cup or mazer used by bride and bridegroom for toasting after religious ceremony, in pre-Reformation England.

bridge cock. *See* cock.

Brierley Hill. English glasshouse founded *c*1779 in Stourbridge by Richard Honeybourne. Noted for glass cutting and intaglio work.

bright-cut engraving. Faceted engraving in which double edge of graver removes sliver of silver and burnishes cut. Developed in late 18th century in Birmingham. Used to ornament silver and Sheffield plate wares, including flatware.

brilliant cut. Form of diamond cutting perfected by Vincenzo Peruzzi in late 17th century Venice. Cut made full use of high refractive index of diamond. In perfect example 58 facets, 33 above and 25 below girdle of stone. Method generally adopted by 18th century. Term 'brilliant' used to refer to stone cut in this way.

brin. Decorated part of fan-stick between rivet and leaf. *See* Pompadour fan.

brinjal bowls. Chinese porcelain bowls and, rarely, plates, made during reign of K'ang Hsi; name derived from same root as 'aubergine' of characteristic glaze colour. Incised decoration of formal flower sprays, coloured leaf-green, yellow, and greenish-white over dark manganese-purple glaze. Sometimes imitates dappled effect of *T'ang ware. Red and blue enamels also used; designs drawn with brownish-black outline.

briolette. Drop-shaped, faceted gemstone; variant of *rose cut.

Briot, François (1550–*c*1616). Huguenot medallist and pewterer working in Lorraine; fled *c*1580 to Mömpelgard (Montbéliard) in Württemberg, Germany; appointed engraver to Count (later Duke) Friedrich of Württemberg in 1585. Created new category of display pewter, **Edelzinn*. Masterpiece is *Temperantia dish and ewer (1585–90); other pieces include another dish and ewer, a bowl, and a salt. Work much copied, particularly in Nuremberg.

brisé fan. Fan without leaf, consisting of overlapping sticks of ivory or mother of pearl riveted at one end and held together by a ribbon threaded through slots at broad end. At first imported from Orient; produced in France from *c*1700. Lacquered *brisé* fans, called **vernis Martin* fans, popular in France in mid 18th century.

Bristol Brass Wire Company. Founded 1702 at Baptist Mills, Bristol; employed Dutch and German workmen. Used copper ore from Cornwall, calamine from Mendip Hills; well placed for coal supplies and water-power, also main export centre. Supplied raw material for Birmingham brass industry; produced pins, small domestic articles, toys, kitchen utensils. Exported brass to Africa and elsewhere. Expanded in early 18th century; absorbed smaller companies (probably including *Dockwra's), and acquired warehouses in London, still in operation.

Bristol delftware. Tin-glazed earthenware made in and near Bristol from mid 17th century until 1770s; first factory established at Brislington by potters from *Southwark. Distinguished by hard, bluish surface of glaze. *Bricks, shoes, and domestic wares made. Earliest pieces include blue and white posset pots painted with figures. Chargers made from *c*1650; colours used often include strong red; edge decoration and foliage of trees sometimes applied with sponge. Designs inspired by K'ang Hsi porcelain, in blue and, in early 18th century, blue, green, and red. High-sided punchbowls painted with foliage patterns and panels containing flowers or Chinese figures. In mid 18th century, figure scenes and landscapes painted in blue.

Bristol delftware. Posset cup and cover. c1720, painted with stylized flowers in red, blue, and green. Height 10in.

*Bristol glass. Set of three decanters, 1822, with gilded wine labels; faceted ball stoppers bearing initial letter of decanter: R, B, or H. Electroplated *tantalus with rings for holding stoppers.*

Bianco sopra bianco decoration from *c*1755 on borders surrounding landscapes attributed to J. *Flower. Punchbowls and plates decorated with ships made for their captains, *c*1750–*c*1770. Commemorative plates and bowls sometimes have election inscriptions and date.

Bristol glass. Bristol important English glass making centre in 18th century. Noted for *opaque white glass resembling porcelain, enamelled with motifs such as birds, flowers, scrollwork, and Chinese figures. Objects made include jars, vases, bottles, mugs, cruets, candlesticks, and tea-caddies. M. *Edkins among leading enamellers. Bristol also noted for rich blue glass, often gilded, e.g. decanters, toilet bottles, finger bowls, and dishes (*see* I. Jacobs). High quality flint-glass, cut and engraved, also produced.

Bristol or **West Country measure.** English bulbous measure; bulbous at base, narrowing towards everted top. Made of pewter from *c*1750–*c*1830; in bronze or tin-lined copper in 18th century (rare) and throughout 19th; much reproduced in 20th century. Made chiefly in Bristol area for local distilleries.

Bristol porcelain. English ceramics. Soapstone porcelain manufactured 1749–52 at B. *Lund's factory in Lowdin's glasshouse, hence formerly known as Lowdin's Bristol. Hard-paste porcelain produced from 1770 at factory initially owned by W. *Cookworthy and managed by R. *Champion, owner from 1773 until closure in 1781. Early wares hard to separate from *Plymouth; body has less tendency to distortion in firing. Glaze very hard; enamel colours include leaf-green and deep red. Elaborate figures and groups in styles of Sèvres, first with scrolled bases, as at Plymouth, then with mounds coloured brown and green; subjects include Seasons, and Elements. Large vases, usually hexagonal, with applied flowers; some by *Tebo; painters include *Soqui and H. *Bone. Also biscuit porcelain models of birds' nests and bouquets; biscuit decorative plaques. Table services, often with arms or initials, in Sèvres style with e.g. ribbons, festoons, and grey *en camaïeu* portrait busts. Simpler *cottage china made. Marks: alchemist's sign for tin (as at Plymouth, used before 1773); copy of Meissen crossed swords; cross in blue enamel or gold and B in blue usual on tableware. *Illustration at* underglaze blue.

Bristol porcelain. Teapot produced at R. Champion's factory, decorated with polychrome chinoiserie pattern; ogee-shaped handle; characteristic border on lid and rim of pot, marked with overglaze cross. Height 5½in.

Britannia, High or **New Standard,** or **Better Nine.** Standard of purity of silver plate compulsory in Britain from 1697 to 1720 (and optional thereafter); 928 parts pure per 1000 (11oz10dwt per pound Troy). Instituted to prevent melting down of coinage for domestic ware. Silver hallmarked with Britannia seated and lion's head erased. *See* Sterling Standard.

Britannia metal. Alloy of tin, antimony, and copper first made *c*1770, known as white, or hard metal, and used as cheap substitute for Sheffield plate. Largely superseded pewter. Main producers were Jessop & Handcock, and J. *Dixon, both of Sheffield. In 1842, patent granted to R. F. Sturges for composition and name, Britannia metal. Products usually shaped by spinning, an easier and cheaper process than casting (latter method essential for pewter manufacture, which thus dropped from favour from late 18th century). Used instead of copper in *electro-plating. In early 1850s, E.P.B.M. accepted mark for electro-plated Britannia metal. Not entirely successful; use discontinued.

broad-rimmed pewter ware. Category of English pewter plates and dishes with unusually wide rims, made early 17th century to *c*1675; some have central boss, otherwise plain.

broad glass. Window and mirror glass made by technique developed in 12th century Lorraine. Cylinder of glass blown, opened, and flattened. Smoother surface than *crown glass, but duller.

Introduced into England from Venice by Sir R. *Mansell in 1623. Method improved by *Chance Bros., in 1830, by opening cylinder with diamond instead of shears. In later 19th century process mechanized.

Broadwood, John (1732–1812). English piano maker working in London. Became partner and son-in-law of B. *Shudi and succeeded to harpsichord manufacturing firm. Much improved J. C. *Zumpe's square piano (*c*1772). In 1783, patented soft pedal; in early 19th century, experimented with metal supports for wooden piano frame. *Illustration at* pianoforte.

brocade or **Imari pattern.** Japanese porcelain design featuring chrysanthemums, birds, formal discs, and vases of flowers, painted in red, blue, and gold; originally exported to Europe from *Imari harbour. Style imitated on faience at Ansbach (1730–40), on porcelain at Meissen (*c*1725–30), and in England at Chelsea, Derby, and Worcester (late 18th and early 19th centuries).

Brocot escapement. *See* escapement.

Brocot suspension. Means of regulating pendulum clock from front of dial. Small winding square projects through dial; can be turned to adjust two curb pieces up or down pendulum suspension spring, thus altering effective length of pendulum and its time of vibration.

Brogden, John (fl 1846–80). English silversmith and jeweller working in London. Specialized in archaeological jewellery (inspired by Etruscans, Assyrians, Egyptians, etc.) with filigree or granulated decoration from *c*1860. Exhibited at London Exhibitions of 1851 (with partner James Henderson Watherston) and 1862; also at Paris in 1867.

broken-arch. *See* break-arch.

broken handle (in pewter). Similar to *double-curved handle, with lower curve an S-shape, giving appearance of a break where two curves join. Found on pewter tankards from late 18th and 19th centuries.

Brongniart, Alexandre (1770–1847). French geologist; appointed director of Sèvres porcelain factory by Napoleon Bonaparte in 1800. Soon after appointment abandoned manufacture of soft-paste porcelain because of high cost. In 1844 published researches, *Traité des arts céramiques*. Collaborated in establishment of Sèvres museum.

bronze. Dense, hard alloy of copper and tin, often with additional ingredients (e.g. lead, zinc); known from before 2500 B.C. Used originally for weapons and utensils, later for large and small statuary and decorative objects, also for utensils where particular strength or durability required, e.g. buckets, basins, lamps. Rarely shaped by any method other than casting, for which especially suitable due to great fluidity in molten state, slightness of contraction on cooling and solidifying, ease with which finishing process of chiselling may be carried out, and retention of sharp details.

bronze doré (French, 'gilt bronze'). *See* ormolu.

bronze patination (in oriental antiquities). Corrosion occurring in bronze, caused by oxidization either from burial or long exposure to atmosphere. Most common are red copper oxide, white powdery lead oxide, blue and green carbonates, and azurite and malachite encrustations. Patina highly prized by collectors is melon skin or water patina: very smooth, pale green, even colour formed under dry, stable conditions. Most patinations are protective, apart from extremely destructive cuprous chloride. Bronze disease indicated by pale, powdery green spots.

Bronzino, Angiolo (1503–73). Florentine mannerist painter. Designed many tapestries, particularly for newly established Arazzeria Medici (*see* Florentine tapestry). Monumental compositions include allegorical door hangings, Flora and Justice, History of Joseph, and Apotheosis of the House of Medici.

brooch. Ornamental clasp or dress-fastening. Earliest safety-pin type (*fibula*) in use at least from 1000 B.C. During Dark Ages disc or saucer, S-shaped, and ring types made in gold, silver, and base metals and ornamented with gems and enamel. Metal pierced, moulded, engraved, with filigree or granulation. Use continued during Middle Ages. Ring brooch (round, pentagonal, lobed, wheel-shaped, etc.) often carried amatory inscription in Gothic script, or stylized *repoussé* animals and flowers. Larger examples also made in various geometrical forms. Ornament included gems, pearls, filigree and enamel. Fashion for jewelled brooches endured through 15th and 16th centuries, often with realistic human or animal figures, and use of natural shapes of gems and pearls. Ship brooches common in late 16th century England with rise as maritime power. In 17th century gemstones largely replaced enamel as decoration, often in floral and scrolling designs. Late 17th century *sévigné* brooch, in form of ribbon-bow (named after Mme de Sévigné), remained in fashion throughout 18th century, sometimes with pendant attached to bow; **girandole* brooches also worn from shoulders. From 1760s floral types widely used, initially stylized, later naturalistic, with sprays of flowers and ribbons.

Memorial brooches popular from 17th century in Britain, sometimes including miniature, lock of hair, initials of deceased, etc. Many 19th century designs influenced by Gothic revival and archaeological discoveries. *See* amatory jewellery, Berlin iron jewellery, hair jewellery, jet jewellery, mourning jewellery.

Brooks, Hervey (fl early 19th century). American potter at Goshen, Connecticut, from 1820s. Made red earthenware for domestic use. Some pieces dated.

Brooks, John (*c*1710–after 1756). Irish designer and engraver: invented transfer-printing which revolutionized English enamel manufacture. Attempted unsuccessfully to patent transfer-printing method for enamels and ceramics in Birmingham (1751) and London (1753). Managed Battersea Factory until its bankruptcy in 1756.

Brookshaw, George (fl *c*1783). English cabinet maker, specializing in commodes. Received commissions from George, Prince of Wales; made pieces for Carlton House, 1783–86.

Brosamer, Hans (fl *c*1520–*c*1552). German silver designer; worked in Nuremberg, and Fulda (1536–50). Published designs for standing cups, e.g. ostrich egg, coconut, gourd, double cup, highly influential.

broth bowl. Now usually identified as shallow silver bowl with small moulded foot, sometimes with two handles, and slightly domed cover ornamented with bud-shaped handle, snake coiled to form ring, etc. Otherwise little ornamentation except sometimes engraved arms. *c*5in. diameter. Made in England and Ireland in late 17th and early 18th centuries.

Brouwer, Justus (d 1775) and son, Hugo (fl mid to late 18th century). Dutch potters at Delft, owners of factories, The Porcelain Axe (1739–88) and The Three Porcelain Bottles (1760–77). Justus decorated e.g. octagonal bowls in K'ang Hsi style, signed JB; also made *peacock plates. Work of Hugo includes sauceboats with lids in form of soles, and prawn finials; also jugs, vases, flowerpots, and figures; marked with initials HB.

Brown, Jonathan Clark (1807–72). American clock maker in business at Bristol, Connecticut, 1831–55. Produced acorn clocks (*c*1847–50), some depicting own house.

brown mouth and iron foot. Chinese term for feature of southern *Kuan ceramic wares. Glaze poured over vessel ran down, covering mouth less thickly than body; underlying dark body (due to high iron content of clay) visible at rim and at base.

brown ware. *See* Rockingham ware.

Bruges tapestry. Corporation of tapestry weavers chartered in Bruges 1302. Early tapestries mainly religious subjects. Important distribution centre for Flemish tapestries from mid 15th century. From late 15th century, Bruges school of painting main influence on Flemish tapestry design before *Raphaël. Greatest activity in 16th century. High-loom weavers incorporated 1506. From 1544, mark: weaver's spindle and gothic B crowned. Much emigration from mid 16th century caused decline. Little activity in 17th century.

Bruguier, Charles Abraham (1788–1862). Swiss maker of 'singing-bird' boxes in Geneva. Rivalled Frères *Rochat in quality; song of bird longer than in Rochat boxes. After his death, business continued by family.

Brunetto, Thomaz (fl mid to late 18th century). Italian-born potter. In 1767, established faience factory at *Rato, Portugal.

Brunswick (Germany). Original faience factory founded 1707 by Duke Anton Ulrich. Blue-and-white wares in Delft style produced (1710–49), marked with monogram VH. E. H. *Reichard co-director (1749–56); work marked B & R or R & B. All pieces compulsorily marked with ducal B after 1781. In latter half of 18th century, products included figures, tureens shaped like fruit and birds, baskets with pierced decoration, and neo-classical vases decorated in muffle colours. Tin-glazed ground typically dull and uneven. Another factory, opened 1747, made figures of peasants, negroes, pedlars, etc.,

*Brush-rest. *Celadon, *Yüan dynasty. Three angular pinnacles with floral meander between line borders to upper part which is decorated with 'pearls' issuing from cloud scrolls. Height 5in.*

vases decorated with Delft-style landscapes, bird-and-flower motifs, or strapwork. Mark: crossed Cs, usually in manganese purple.

brush-rest. Chinese ceramic holder for glaze decorator's or calligrapher's brushes. Often shaped like round pill-box, with perforations in lid; handle ends vertical. Other examples, on which brushes rest horizontally, represent miniature range of hills.

Brussa carpets. Finely-knotted Turkish silk carpets with brightly-coloured open, floral designs woven in Brussa, centre of silk production until 18th century.

Brussels carpet. *See* moquette carpet.

Brussels tapestry. Brussels centre of Flemish tapestry-weaving from 14th century. Earliest high-warp loom tapestries woven in small workshops. From late 15th century, under patronage of Hapsburgs, developed as main European tapestry-weaving centre. Works prized for fine compositions, technical and colour perfection, and good quality materials (wool, silk, gold, and silver). From late 15th century types include *mille-fleurs* and figure tapestries with religious and chivalric subjects. Also, low-warp looms introduced, increasing production and lowering costs without reducing quality. Brussels tapestries unrivalled; widely exported, and determined 16th and early 17th century European tapestry designs and styles. Early 16th century designs influenced by 15th century Flemish painting: increasingly decorative Gothic-style compositions, with conventionalized figures, bordered by intricately twined leaves, flowers, and fruit. Major designer J. *van Roome; master-weavers include P. *van Aelst, P. *de Pannemaker.

From 1519, after weaving of *Acts of the Apostles tapestry completed, Italian school of painting dictated tapestry design. Cartoons or sketches by G. *Romano, J. *van Orley, Michiel Coxcie, and Giovanni da Udine. Chief weaver, W. de Pannemaker. Trade marks from 1528: red shield between two Bs (Brussels and Brabant), and weaver's mark. From mid 16th century, subjects mainly hunting, religious or mythological scenes and *verdures*. Also first *grotesques. Horizon raised, figures cover whole field; colours often sombre. Borders increasingly important, ornamented with festoons of fruit, armorial scrolls, trellis-work, and bunches of flowers. By end of century, religious persecution and political upheavals forced many master-weavers to emigrate; subsequently became instrumental in developing French, Italian, German, and English tapestry centres. Technique and design deteriorated in Brussels, but remained most important centre. Hunting and pastoral compositions fashionable, also allegorical scenes. In 17th century, design revolutionized by *Rubens, who worked in oils, as well as tempera, then enlarged sketches to full-scale cartoons. Return to monumental style. Figures concentrate attention on foreground; high horizon. Border and centrepiece more closely aligned, lower margin often omitted; sidepieces indicated by pillars supporting superstructure. Rubens's followers, particularly J. *Jordaens, main designers. With decline of industry, tapestry quality also deteriorated. Designs eventually replaced by landscapes, especially rustic scenes of D. *Teniers. Principal 17th century weavers: J. *Raes, François van Cotthem, C. and J. *Geubels, F. and J-F. *van der Hecke, and Albert Auwercx. From mid 17th century, Brussels followed lead of great French manufactories, particularly the Gobelins. By 1700, only nine master-weavers: A. Auwercx, J. *de Vos, F. *van der Hecke, Jacques and Gaspard van den Borght, Jerome le Clerk, Guillaume Potter, H. *Reydams, and later U. *Leyniers. Though industry contracted, many fine tapestries executed. Few new designs, most follow older Flemish or Gobelins designs. Distinguishable from French by colours: soft, brown-green tints for backgrounds and trees, warm soft colours for main pattern with only touches of intense colour. Especially effective treatment of light. Early 18th century borders have arrangement of military accoutrements; by 1750, narrow borders. Industry collapsed with outbreak of French Revolution.

Brustolon, Andrea (b 1622). Italian sculptor and furniture maker. In Venice 1684–96 where specialized in chairs, *guéridons*, vase stands, mirror and picture frames. Noted for elaborate carving motifs including arabesques, *putti*,

Andrea Brustolon. Italian 17th century chair in manner of Brustolon, gilt-wood.

Brussels tapestry. The Banquet of the Gods, c1720. 17ft×11ft.

floral and foliate designs, acanthus, classical subjects, figures, etc.

Bryce, McKee & Company. Glasshouse founded 1850 in Pittsburgh, Pennsylvania by J. and F. McKee and J. Bryce. Produced mainly flint table glass and lamps.

bryony leaf decoration (in ceramics). Tangle of leaves and flowers like those of white bryony. Occurs on Hispano-Moresque pottery made in Valencia by mid 15th century.

bubble bowl. Chinese ceramic shape found from Sung period: small bowl with finely-trimmed foot, and swelling, curved body, narrowing to lipless neck.

bucaro or **buccaro.** *See boccaro.*

Buchwald, Johann (fl 1748–1780s). Ceramic repairer and wandering arcanist. Worked at Höchst and Fulda in 1748, at Holitsch in 1754, Stralsund (*c*1755–57), Rörstrand (1757), and Marieberg (1758). At Eckernforde from 1765, with daughter and son-in-law, both faience painters; probably introduced bright enamel painting and increased use of relief decoration; also produced some figures. At Kiel, by 1768, decorated trays, wall-fountains, bishop bowls, and large ornamental pieces with enamel colours, e.g. pinkish-purple, blue, and bright yellow. Moved, still with family, elsewhere in Germany until 1785.

buckle. Fastening for belt etc., often decorative and reflecting contemporary sculptural influences. Used e.g. in ancient Rome; from early Middle Ages in Britain and Europe, worn by wealthy women. From early 14th century, some made in gilt metal with inscriptions and niello ornament. Gothic tracery decoration popular in 15th and 16th centuries. Buckles for shoes fashionable in late 17th and 18th centuries; also worn at waist and to fasten bands of velvet at throat and wrists. Made in variety of materials, e.g. gold, gilt-metal, silver set with diamonds, pastes, marcasites, etc. *Cut or faceted steel buckles popular in late 18th century in Britain and France. Made in variety of shapes (e.g. oval, circular, rectangular) but square type most popular. *Illustration at* cut steel jewellery.

buckle-back. Chair back; variation of *balloon-back. Transverse rail, sometimes ornamented, joins sides of back frame.

bud-and-wedge thumbpiece. Thumbpiece shaped as opening bud, resting on thick end of wedge (with thin end at centre of lid); on English pewter vessels *c*1680–1740.

bud thumbpiece. Thumbpiece shaped as one or two bursting buds growing from a single stem; on late 17th and early 18th century English pewter vessels.

Buen Retiro (Madrid). Spanish porcelain factory established in 1759, when Charles III transferred *Capodimonte factory to Madrid on accession to Spanish throne. Early products indistinguishable from Capodimonte. Porcelain room, completed 1765 in palace of Aranjuez, constructed after that at Portici. G. *Gricci, director from 1764, modelled figures and groups in rococo style. Other products include holy water stoups, mirror frames, chandeliers, ewers, and basins. Paste, when not made with materials imported from Italy, yellowish and heavy. Porcelain room in neo-classical style completed at royal palace in Madrid, possibly under directorship of C. *Schepers (1770–83). Better quality paste thought to have been used under directorship of C. *Gricci (1784–95). Factory closed in 1812.

Buen Retiro porcelain. Roman on horseback, c1765. Figure and battle scenes around plinth decorated with polychrome and gilding. Height 18in.

buffet. Used since Middle Ages for displaying china, glass, silver, plate, etc. In 16th and 17th century England, synonymous with *court cupboard. In 18th century, term embraced a set of recessed wall shelves; a cabinet with doored, enclosed lower section; and a small room next to dining-room used for storing china, glass, silver, etc. (more often called butler's pantry). Towards end of 18th century, *sideboard replaced buffet in dining-room.

Buggin bowls. Pair of *Ravenscroft bowls of *crizzled lead-glass made for wedding of Butler Buggin (1676). Engraved in diamond-point with family coat of arms, scrollwork, flowers, etc. One in Victoria & Albert Museum, London, other in Corning Museum of Glass, Corning, New York.

Buhl work. *See* Boulle work.

Bukhara carpets. *See* Bokhara carpets.

bulb or **melon bulb** In furniture, decorative turned enlargement on legs and vertical supports of tables, cupboards, beds, etc. Bulbous shape, sometimes with carved decoration and gadrooning, used on 16th and 17th century English furniture. *See* cup and cover motif.

Buffet. Charles I. Carved oak with strapwork panels along frieze, base, drawers, and divisions between each moulded cupboard door. Free-standing large baluster columns on upper section. Height 5ft.

Bullet teapot. Engraved around lid with scrolls; ebony handle. Swiss, made in Geneva, c1725.

bulbous tavern measure. *See* Bristol measure.

bullet teapot. Early 18th century silver teapot with spherical or sometimes polygonal body; lid cut out of upper part of body; foot-ring. Design of handle, spout, and foot-ring varied. In Scotland, made with foot and stem: revived in mid 19th century.

bull's eye. Central boss attached to *pontil in manufacture of *crown glass.

bumping or **firing glasses.** English drinking glasses with conical or bucket-shaped bowl, short stem and thickened foot (to withstand hammering on table during toasts). Most examples plain, sometimes engraved with Masonic or Jacobite emblems. Popular in 18th century.

bun cover. Shallow, domed lid found on early 17th century pewter flagons.

bun foot. *Ball foot, somewhat flattened at top and bottom. Dates from mid 17th century. *Illustration at kas.*

*Bumping glass. Enamelled by *Beilby family with Masonic coat of arms and insignia. 1765. Height 3in.*

Buquoy, Georg Franz Longueval, Count von (1781–1851). Owner of glass factory at Gratzen, south Bohemia, which introduced sealing-wax red hyalith glass (1803), imitating J. *Wedgwood's *rosso antico,* and black hyalith (1817) to look like Wedgwood's Egyptian black.

bureau. Desk, distinguished by sloping flap front (with exception of **bureau plat*); drawers in base. Flap hinged at base, rests on *lopers when open, folds up at angle when closed. Dates from late 17th century England and France. In America, term also describes bedroom chest of drawers. *See* bureau bedstead, bureau bookcase, bureau dressing table.

bureau à cylindre. *See* roll-top desk.

bureau bedstead. 18th century folding bed which fitted into a bureau-shaped case.

bureau bookcase or **secretary bookcase.** Piece of furniture in two sections. Upper section, set of (usually adjustable) bookshelves enclosed by doors, glazed in later examples. Lower section, bureau with sloping fall-front concealing pigeon-holes, drawers, etc., and long drawers beneath. Made from mid 18th century, mainly in England. *cf* secretary cabinet.

bureau clock. French desk clock, produced 1800–15 by makers including A-L. *Breguet, A. *Janvier. Silver or gilt case; moon hands. Engine-turned decoration.

bureau dressing table or **bureau toilette.** 18th century writing and dressing table. Bureau bottom with cabriole legs, and slant top surmounted by mirror.

bureau en pupitre (French, 'pupil's desk'). Louis XVI desk, tall enough to allow user to

*Bureau. South German, c1750. Inlaid with marquetry and parquetry. Moulded and scrolled cornice with gilt-wood finial; sides are *bombé and drawers in base are *serpentine; scrolled feet. Height 7ft2in.*

stand. Some models mechanically adjustable to sitting or standing heights.

bureau plat (French, 'flat writing desk'). Large table with two or three drawers beneath. May have slides above drawers to provide extra working surface. *Illustration also at* Dubois, J.

bureau table. Writing table with kneehole recess, dating from 18th century. Has drawers in pedestal supports and central front frieze drawer.

Bureau plat. *Rectangular top containing three drawers; cabriole legs with satyr's masks mounted above knee, and scrolled feet, both in ormolu. Veneered with ebony and Boulle marquetry of engraved brass on tortoiseshell. French, early 18th century. Length 6ft3in.*

bureau toilette: *See* bureau dressing table.

burette. *See* altar-cruet.

Burghley Nef. Late medieval French ceremonial salt in form of ship, hull formed from nautilus shell mounted in silver, parcel-gilt and supported on back of mermaid with upraised torso and tail. Deck has tiny cast figures of Tristan and Yseult playing chess. Hallmarked in Paris; maker Pierre le Flamand; in Victoria & Albert Museum, London.

Burgi, Jost (1552–1632). Swiss-born scientist, mathematician, and clock maker, working in Cassel (Germany) and Prague. Appointed clock maker to Rudolph II in 1602. Inventor of cross-beat escapement, and *remontoire.* Made rock-crystal clock, *c*1615, and *celestial globes, used by astronomers.

burgomaster chair. Dutch chair, popular early

Burgomaster chair, satinwood with cane-work plaques and seat; 18th century. Dutch, probably made in Dutch East Indies.

18th century. Has round, cane seat; curving back composed of three panels (often filled with pierced carving); and usually six equidistant cabriole legs with three stretchers (each connecting leg to diametrically opposite number) forming wheel-spoke pattern. Carving may reflect oriental influence.

burin. *See* graver.

burl. *See* burr.

Burnham, Benjamin (fl *c*1769). Furniture maker of Hartford, Connecticut. Made *block-front furniture, particularly desks and chests.

burning-on. Process of joining two pieces of pewter or lead by pouring molten metal over them until they fuse.

burnishing. Method of smoothing and polishing metal surface by friction with agate, bloodstone, silica, or steel.

burr or **burl.** Diseased growth on certain trees, such as ash, elm, maple, oak, walnut, and yew, yielding wood particularly suitable for veneering because of unusual but attractive grain.

Burt family. John (*c*1692–1745), American silversmith working in Boston, Massachusetts; probably apprenticed to J. *Coney. Surviving work includes several pieces now owned by Harvard University (e.g. pair of candlesticks, 1724) tankards, casters, salt cellars, chafing dishes, sugar bowl, and salver. Sons, Benjamin, Samuel, and William, continued in trade. Marks: IB crowned with pellet in shield; I BURT in cartouche; or name in two lines in oval.

Burrough or **Borough,** John (1662–*c*1690). London cabinet maker, in partnership with William Farmborough. Cabinet makers to Charles II, and William and Mary.

Benjamin Burt. Pepper and salt casters, made in Boston, Massachusetts 1750–75. Height 5⅛in.

Busch, Christian Daniel (d 1790). German arcanist, colour-chemist, painter, and potter. At Meissen until 1745. Escaped with porcelain secret to Vienna (1745–48). Worked at Neudeck, Nymphenburg (1748), Künersberg (1749), Bayreuth (1748–50). At Vincennes (1754) and Sèvres (1764), experimented with hard-paste porcelain formula. At Kelsterbach (1761–64); returned to Meissen, 1765–90.

Bustelli, Franz Anton (1723–63). Celebrated Swiss-born modeller of porcelain figures. *Modellmeister* at Nymphenburg 1754–63. His slim, lively figures are renowned for capturing essential rococo spirit. Subjects include vivid interpretations of usual contemporary themes, e.g. street vendors and, notably, *commedia dell'arte* figures. Used restrained colours or left figures unpainted. Bases regular: flat, oval, or polygonal. *Illustration at* Nymphenburg.

buta motif. *See* boteh motif.

butler's desk. American cupboard with back-curving ends and several storage areas with doors, incorporating writing area in centre front, where horizontally rectangular section, hinged at base, drops down to form writing surface and reveal drawers and storage space for writing materials. Three frieze drawers. Dates from 18th century.

butler's sideboard. American sideboard with glass-fronted china cupboard mounted at back of top, and drawers below. Central drawer-front often hinged at base; when open, forms writing surface and reveals compartments for writing materials. Intended for butler's use, when doing household accounts. Also called *Salem secretary. Dates from 18th century.

butler's tray or **standing tray.** Tray, usually rectangular, occasionally oval or kidney-shaped, with gallery pierced for hand-holds at each end. Usually mahogany, but some examples papier mâché. Used from early 18th century by butler for serving drinks and removing empty glasses. Called 'standing tray' when on *voider stand.

Butler's tray. Oak. Tray separate from stand, which folds. English, mid 19th century.

*Butter dish. Silver. Stand and cover, made in London, 1841, by C. and G. *Fox. Dish, stand, and domed cover all pierced with foliate scrolls within applied moulded borders; green glass liners. Flower finial by E. *Barnard & Sons. Diameter 8½in.*

butter dish. Silver containers for butter uncommon in 18th century, but small silver scallop-shaped dishes with glass liners, and sometimes ball feet, made from *c*1725 in Britain, may have been butter dishes. Most 18th century examples Irish; shallow pierced bowl with glass liner and cover, sometimes feet. Also, glass bowl with silver saucer and cover. Sometimes found with cow finial. Type in vogue in early 19th century usually has stand, dish of silver or glass, and cover; other examples are straight-sided, oval, with cover and knob finial, four feet, and handle at each end. Tub shape also popular. Also made in Sheffield plate and electro-plate.

Butterfield, Michael (1635–1724). English instrument-maker, working in France from *c*1677. Made surveying instruments etc., but mainly noted for type of portable *sundial, usually of engraved silver. Characteristic examples have gnomon in shape of bird, and compass set in octagonal, rarely oval, dial plate. 'Butterfield' dials also produced by other makers.

butterfly table. American drop-leaf table with outward-slanting legs. 'Butterfly' refers to shape of brackets which support raised leaves. Dates from early 18th century.

butter knife. Small silver knife with scimitar-shaped blade; dates from late 18th century in Britain. Handle sometimes ivory or mother-of-pearl.

buttons. Glass, gold, and earthenware buttons used by ancient Egyptians, Greeks, and Persians but decorative rather than functional. In use in 13th century Paris which had buttonmakers' guild. Widespread in 17th century Europe but still chiefly decorative; mainly fabric decorated with needlework. In 18th century many elaborate buttons produced in France of gold, silver, precious jewels, ivory, or **passementerie*. Gold and jewelled buttons in floral or conventional shapes (round, octagonal); jewels also used as borders around other materials. Paste used to simulate precious stones. Metal buttons popular in England from *c*1700, moulded or stamped from copper, silver, pewter, and brass;

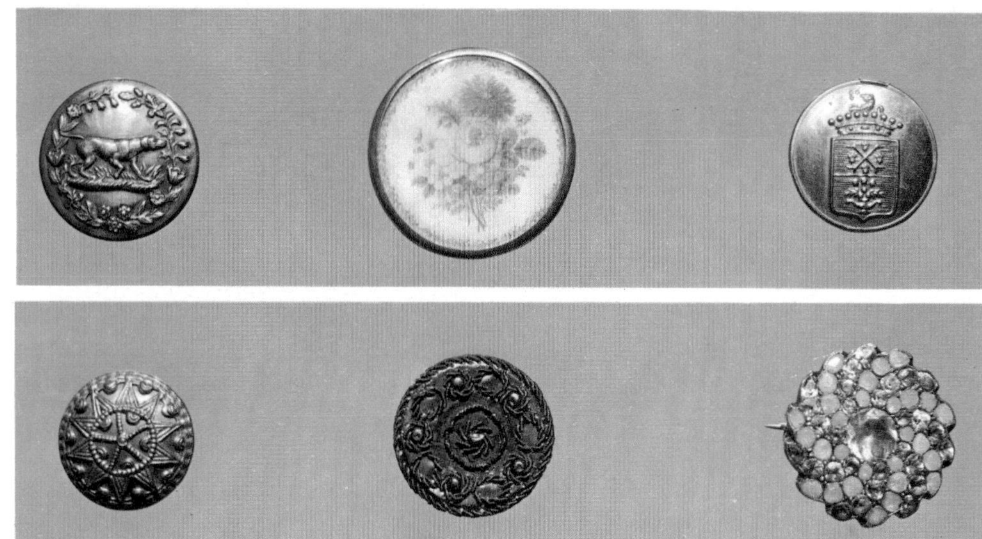

Buttons. Top row, left to right: 1) Stamped brass sporting button with traces of enamel decoration, c1825–50. 2) One of numbered set, c1770, painted in watercolour on parchment with brass rim and backing. 3) Silver livery button, European, c1800. Bottom row, left to right: 1) Gilt metal with bone and cat-gut back, mid 18th century. 2) Silver and purple foil with silver 'lace', c1760. 3) Opaline and plain pastes set in silver, c1800 (converted into brooch).

could be inset with ivory, tortoiseshell, Wedgwood jasper ware medallions, and jewels. Cut-steel buttons popularized by M. *Boulton in England. Later in century came enamel and porcelain buttons painted in manner of F. *Boucher, J-A. *Watteau, and contemporaries. Sold in elaborately-boxed sets of 5 to 35, identical or with different scenes in same mount. Painted buttons mounted under convex glass with metal rims. *Habitat and *rebus buttons popular in France after 1750. Metal buttons made in America, from *c*1750, of copper, silver, brass, and steel, with chased, engraved, or engine-turned geometrical designs, notably by C. *Wistar. More complicated design found on series of *Washington inaugural buttons.

19th century buttons generally half size of 18th century ones; less elaborate, mass-produced. Gilt buttons made in Birmingham, England, from 1790; finest 1830–50 with hand-chased designs, flowers, fruit, grain, etc. In Europe and America *c*1820–50 brass or silver sporting, hunt club, and livery buttons made in sets of 5 to 18 with game-birds, dogs, horses, and other hunt motifs on them. From 1850, machine-produced fabric buttons common. Cloth-covered button with metal shank patented in Birmingham before 1825 by B. *Sanders. From 1840s glass buttons made in factories throughout Europe; difficult to date, as no identifying marks. Jet buttons popularized by Queen Victoria in 1861; imitated in black glass. Porcelain buttons hand-painted or with transfer-printed designs current throughout Europe from 1859. Shell or 'pearl' buttons machine-made *c*1850.

Bux, Buchs, or **Bochs,** Johann Baptist (b 1711). German wine merchant; obtained privilege to found Schrezheim faience factory (1752). Employed L-V. *Gerverot. Also produced hard-paste porcelain.

B.V.R.B. *See* van Risenburgh, Bernard.

Byerley, Thomas (d 1810). Staffordshire potter, son of J. *Wedgwood I's sister. Managed Wedgwood's London showrooms after death of T. *Bentley (1780). Managed Etruria factory from retirement of J. *Wedgwood II (1795). Relieved of job (1804), returned to manage London showrooms until death.

cabaret, déjeuner, or **tête à tête.** Porcelain service comprising tea or coffee pot, sugar bowl, jug, cups, saucers, and tray, made by many European factories in 18th century.

cabinet. Box-like structure, with door or doors at front; usually fitted with small interior drawers, and used to store valuables. Possibly derived from chest; in Renaissance Europe rested on stand and often lavishly decorated. Cabinet-on-stand popular in 17th century; often decorated in lacquer-work or marquetry. From 18th century, cabinets on bases containing drawers; from *c*1750, some examples have glazed doors. *See* china cabinet, *serre bijoux, vargueño.*

cabinet maker. Term used from 17th century to denote furniture maker specializing in veneered case pieces. *See ébéniste, menuisier.*

cable moulding. *See* rope moulding.

cabochon. Gem stone cut in curved shape and polished; not faceted. Cabochon cutting practised from Roman times.

cabochon motif (in furniture). Decorative shape reminiscent of cabochon gem: round or oval, polished, but unfaceted. Used in conjunction with strapwork decoration *c*1500–1700; also on rococo pieces, sometimes surrounded by decorative carving. Often on knee of cabriole leg.

cabriole or **bandy leg** (in furniture). Based on stylized hind leg of animal; often terminating in *paw or *mask foot. Much used in Europe in late 17th and 18th centuries.

Cabinet-on-stand. Lacquer cabinet in red, black, and gold, with raised decoration; inside are 13 drawers. Contemporary gilt-wood stand. English, c1690. Height of cabinet, 3ft.

cabriolet fan. French fan made from *c*1755. Leaf divided into two or three strips with spaces between, sometimes with painting of cabriolet carriage on whose wheels the fan was modelled. *Illustration at* fan.

cachemire. Style of reeded Dutch Delft bowls and, especially, vases made in early 18th century, e.g. at The Metal Pot factory; rich floral decoration, often polychrome, in Chinese style.

Cadaval toilet set. Silver toilet service commissioned from four French silversmiths, including A. *Loir III, by Don Jaime, 3rd Duke of Cadaval, Portugal; pieces bear his arms and Paris hallmarks for 1738–39. Service includes mirror, ewer and basin, candlesticks, two large and three small boxes, covered pots, brushes and combs, etc.

caddinet. *See cadenas.*

caddy. *See* tea-caddy.

caddy spoon. Silver spoon made in Britain from late 18th century. Short stem; bowl in various shapes (e.g. shell, leaf). Used for

Caddy spoons. English. Top: left, made 1793 by Richard Crossley; centre, made 1810 by Joseph Taylor; right, made 1845 by George Unite. Bottom: both by unknown makers c1795.

*Cafaggiolo maiolica. Dish with *lustre glaze, c1510, decorated with arms of Cesi impaling Bellnormi.*

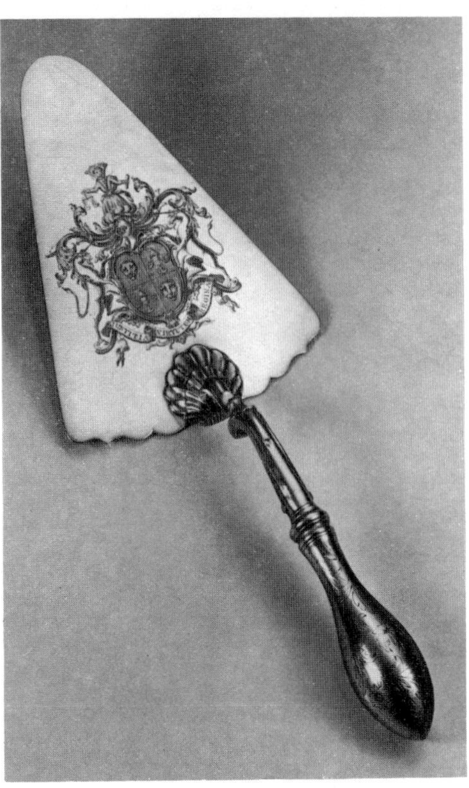

Cake slice. English, silver gilt, 1751. Maker's mark BC. Engraved with coat of arms of Goldsmiths' Company.

Calcedonio *vase. Italian, made by Salviati of Venice, exhibited at 1862 Exhibition, London. Mounted in ormolu. Height* $13\frac{1}{2}$*in.*

transferring tea leaves from caddy to teapot. Some made in Sheffield plate.

cadenas. French ceremonial silver platter or salver for royalty, dating from 14th century; held napkin or dish. Various shapes, generally with feet; box-like section at one end for knife, fork, spoon, salt, and other condiments; has lock to guard against poisoning. Engraved royal insignia. English version known as caddinet; two examples used at coronation of William and Mary (1689) survive in Victoria & Albert Museum.

Cadogan teapots. Tall, narrow earthenware pots decorated with foliage in relief, made at *Rockingham, 1806–42. Spout and handle have trail of foliage joined to them from body of pot. Filled through tube which extends from hole in base to within $\frac{1}{2}$in. of inside of top, preventing spillage when pot is righted. Presumably intended as hot water pots; unsuitable for brewing tea. Height $3\frac{1}{2}$in. to over 7in. Usually covered with characteristic brown Rockingham glaze; decoration sometimes picked out in gold; many unmarked.

caduceus mark. Meissen porcelain mark used intermittently from 1722 to early 1730s. First painted mark, in underglaze blue; vertical stroke and spiral resemble Mercury's rod.

Cafaggiolo (near Florence, Italy). Early centre of Tuscan maiolica. Under patronage of Pier-Francesco de' Medici, workshop established *c*1506 by *Fattorini family. Colours including dark brownish-red, dark blue, and shades of yellow used in *istoriato* painting of allegorical and religious subjects on plates, sometimes bordered by grotesques. Famous dish, dated *c*1510, shows maiolica painter with his subjects, an engaged couple. In mid 16th century, imitations made of imported Chinese porcelain. Production continued until late 16th century.

café au lait glaze, or **t'zŭ chin.** Chinese glaze colour varying from dark brown to beige or yellow gold. Developed at *Ching-tê-chên porcelain factory during reign of K'ang Hsi, under direction of *Tsang Ying-hsüan. Obtained by firing glaze with some iron content at high temperature. Sometimes found on outside of plates, with inside decorated in underglaze cobalt-blue. Often called Nankin yellow in 18th century, because found on *Nankin porcelain. Copied at Meissen (*dead leaf brown).

Caffiéri, Jacques (1678–1755). French *fondeur-ciseleur* and engraver, working in rococo style. From 1736 received commissions from Crown (Louis XV). Stamp: CAFFIERI. Also, with son Philippe (1714–74) designed and made clock-cases, including *elephant clock.

cage-work (in silver). Pierced and sometimes chased sleeve enclosing inner, plain section of object. Technique probably of German origin, used in Britain in late 17th century for bodies of two-handled cups, beakers, tankards, etc. *Illustration at* étui, bodkin case.

cage-work box or **tabatière à cage.** Snuff-box consisting of plaques of various materials set in a metal frame.

caille, quail, or **partridge pattern.** European ceramic decoration in **décor coréen* style used at Chantilly (1725–40). Comprises foliage, rocks, and pair of quails. Used in 18th century on porcelain from Meissen, Bow, Chelsea, and Worcester; also on delftware.

caillouté. French ceramic decoration. Diaper pattern of oval shapes connected by network of small circles, giving pebbled effect. Painted over ground colours. Introduced at Sèvres in mid 18th century. Copied at Worcester.

Cain, Auguste-Nicolas (1822–94). French sculptor; one of *les *Animaliers*. Pupil of F. *Rude.

Cairene carpets. *See* Turkish Court Manufactory carpets.

cairngorm. Yellow or brown variety of *quartz; name derived from Cairngorms, range of mountains in Scotland. Most important stone in Scottish jewellery.

Cairo carpets. *See* Mamluk carpets.

cake basket. *See* basket.

cake-slice. Silver utensil with large, flat, engraved and pierced blade (oval, triangular, etc.) and handle resembling that of knife or flatware stem. In use from mid 18th century to serve cake, pie, etc. *cf* fish-slice.

cake-tongs. Silver implement similar to *sugar-tongs but larger; used from 18th century for serving cake. *cf* asparagus-tongs.

Calamelli, Virgilio or Virgiliotto (d before 1570). Italian maiolica potter and painter at Faenza. Made fluted dishes, decorated *a quartieri* with stylized leaves in yellow and blue; also plates decorated in *compendiario* style. Signed examples exist.

calamine. Ore (*lapis calaminaris*) from which zinc is extracted. Method of extraction not generally known in Europe until 18th century; before then, calamine as such was used, e.g. in making brass.

calcedonio or **Schmelzglas.** Glass imitating precious and semi-precious stones, e.g. onyx, agate, chalcedony. Popular in Venice during 15th and 16th centuries. Made in 19th century England and Bohemia.

Caldas da Rainha (Portugal). Several potteries existed, notably one established 1853, imitating work of B. *Palissy. Mark: M. MAFRA with anchor above CALDAS/PORTUGAL, impressed.

Caldwell, James (1760–1838). English potter. Partner of E. *Wood (1790–1819). Produced cream-coloured earthenware, including figures. Marks: WOOD & CALDWELL, or W & C.

calendar. Indication on clock or watch of day, month or year. Used in public clocks at Norwich Priory (1325) and St Alban's Abbey (1336) in England and at Padua, Italy (1364). These examples also gave astronomical information. Used on domestic clocks from 16th century.

Callegari or **Caligari,** Filippo Antonio (fl mid to late 18th century). Italian maiolica painter at Lodi. Established workshop with A. *Casali at Pesaro in 1763. Later established own workshop. Marks: initials F.A.C. above P; or Callegar Pesaro.

Callot, Jacques or **Il Calotto** (*c*1592–1635). French painter, etcher, and engraver. In 1607, apprenticed to goldsmith. Worked in Rome and, from 1611, in Florence at court of Duke Cosimo III. From 1621, worked chiefly in Nancy. Celebrated for etchings of pageants, crowd and battle scenes, and grotesque figures. Work includes series of etchings, *Les Grandes Misères de la Guerre* (1633). Paintings after Callot's own designs appear on faience of Sinceny or Rouen, Moustiers, and Alcora; also on maiolica made e.g. at Savona in 18th century. *See* Callot figures.

Calendar clock. By Charles Oudin, Paris, c1815. Shows time, day of week, day of month, age and phase of moon. Height 1ft8in.

Callot figures. Grotesque figures of dwarfs after J. *Callot, made at Meissen, Höchst, and Vienna in 17th century. Also at Mennecy in 18th century and at Chelsea and Derby. Most taken from book of engravings in style of Callot, published in 18th century.

Caltagirone (Sicily). Maiolica made from 17th century includes drug-pots and vases. Decorated e.g. with flowers.

calyx. Decorative feature in form of whorl of sepals or leaves encircling flower bud.

Cambrian Pottery Works. Pottery established *c*1767 at Swansea, Glamorganshire, to make domestic earthenware and stoneware; traded as Cambrian Pottery from 1790. Made cream-coloured earthenware, and pearlware transfer-printed in black, brown, or blue. In 1802, acquired by L. W. *Dillwyn; produced pearlware enamelled with naturalistic flowers, fruit, birds, insects, and shells, with inscription identifying species. Also earthenware Toby jugs and biscuit figures. Soft-paste porcelain made (1814–17) by W. *Billingsley; soapstone added to formula in effort to reduce cost of manufacture by strengthening paste. In 1817, factory let by Dillwyn; traded as Bevington and Roby or Bevington, Roby and Co.; produced earthenware, pearlware, and bone china. Again under Dillwyn in 1824, with his son as manager; made domestic earthenware, pearlware, and stoneware. From mid 19th century also made terracotta vases decorated with black enamel, and black basalt figures

*Cambrian Pottery. Shell-shaped dish, c1805, painted with ruff by William Weston-Young; initials RJR gilded by T. *Pardoe. On base, inscribed ruff, impressed Swansea and large C; diameter 8in. Mug with moulded rim and base, dated 1831 and inscribed Elizth. Jane Hodge Legoe; typical chocolate edging and freely painted flowers; height 3in. Lobed desert plate, border painted by Pardoe, c1808; diameter 7in.*

Cambrian porcelain. Left: cabinet cup and saucer, early 19th century, decorated and gilded in London; height of cup 3¼in. Right: cup and saucer, early 19th century; moulded with ozier or basket-weave pattern and fluting, locally decorated with sepia flowers and banding; height of cup 2½in.

and vases. Factory closed in 1870. Marks include CAMBRIAN (impressed or painted in gold or red, until 1802), DILLWYN SWANSEA (impressed on pottery, 1802–17, 1824–50), IMPROVED STONEWARE DILLWYN & CO surrounded by leaves, painted. Porcelain marked SWANSEA impressed or stencilled in red, sometimes with trident, or two crossed tridents. *Illustration also at* transfer-printing.

cameo. Gem, hardstone, or shell cut to leave design in relief; also glass and paste similarly cut or moulded. Gem-cutting in ancient world mainly in *intaglio style for seals until Hellenistic period (from *c*350 B.C.) when decorative relief-cutting became common. Agate and sardonyx much used for contrast between successive coloured layers. Engraved stones first used as jewellery in form of seals mounted in rings, later embodied in pendants, medallions, bracelets, and earrings. Cameos widespread in Roman era, inspired by Greek examples. Art revived during Italian Renaissance, main centres Florence, Rome, and Venice, and (in late 16th century) Milan. Subjects included portraits and mythological scenes. Circular and oval cameos mounted in gold frames with enamel or engraved ornament. Frames gradually elaborated to overshadow cameo. Again revived in late 18th century neo-classical period. Shell

Cameos. Four varieties of mid-Victorian cameos: shell (top left), onyx (top right), both set in gold; glass (bottom left), set in gilt metal, and lava (bottom right), set in silver.

cameos carved in Naples and Rome exported to Britain and other parts of Europe; used for bracelets, necklaces, belts, diadems, etc., framed in gold and linked by small chains or strings of pearls. Remained fashionable throughout 19th century. *See* J. Tassie, Wedgwood jewellery.

cameo, cased or **overlay glass.** Ornamental glass of two or more coloured layers in which glass surrounding decoration carved or cut away, leaving pattern in deep relief. Technique developed by Romans. Most famous example of Roman cameo glass is *Portland Vase. Popular in 18th century China, particularly for snuff bottles (*see* Chinese glass). Technique revived in 19th century England by J. *Northwood; extremely popular in mid century. Also used in German and Bohemian glass in 19th century; Bohemian technique of flashing with clear glass adopted in England in 1850s.

Campaign chair. Seat and back leather; front and back stretchers hinged for folding. Spanish, 17th century.

Canabas. Table à rafraîchir. *Louis XV, mahogany. Stamped Canabas, pseudonym of Joseph Gengenbach. Width 23in.*

cameo incrustation. *See* sulphides.

camicia. *See* investment.

campaign furniture. Case furniture, often teak, with recessed handles and protective brass corners. Designed to be easily dismantled, for use by officers (on campaign) during 18th and 19th centuries.

Campbell, Robert (fl *c*1774–94). British upholsterer and cabinet maker. Possibly worked for H. *Holland at Carlton House; received commissions from George, Prince of Wales.

Canabas or **Gengenbach,** Joseph (1715–97). French *ébéniste,* at first employed by P. *Migeon and J-F. *Oeben. Became *maître-ébéniste* in 1766. Stamp: J. CANABAS.

canapé. 18th century *settee or wide chair, with arms at both ends and high back.

canapé à confidante. *Canapé* with corner seats attached at outer side of each arm. Dates from 18th century France.

candelabrum. Branched form of *candlestick; made in same materials and with similar base and stem designs. Term also occasionally applied to *chandelier. Two or more curved branches radiate from central stem, which is surmounted by finial. In use in Europe from Middle Ages; surviving examples date from 17th century. From mid 18th century, pieces such as vases, figures, or simple decorative shapes in porcelain, marble or blue john, were mounted in ormolu and fitted with sockets for candles. Decorative branched candelabra also made in glass from 18th century; evolved from plain to heavily ornamented, with pendant lustres, crescents, stars, and other motifs. 19th century style typified by fringe of long pendant drops round socket. *See* lamp.

candle board. Retractable ledge or shelf under table top, used to hold candle.

candle-box. Rectangular or cylindrical box, usually lidded, attached to wall and used to store candles. Made from Middle Ages to 19th century. Metal examples from 18th century sometimes japanned.

candle sconce. *See* sconce.

candle slide. Retractable sliding shelf for candlestick, incorporated above or level with working surface of bureau or writing table.

candle-snuffers. *See* snuffers.

candle stand or **torchère.** Stand composed of pillar support with tripod base, surmounted by small table-top; used for candlestick or

Canapé. *Carved birch frame painted white and gilded; square back banded with husk pattern; tapering, fluted legs; upholstered in *Beauvais tapestry. French, late 18th century, by G. *Jacob. Width 5ft9in.*

Candlesticks. *Made in London. In chronological order (left to right): 1) 1685. 2) 1708, by Joseph Bird. 3) 1748, by William Grundy; height 9$\frac{5}{8}$in. 4) 1819, by Samuel Whitford.*

Right:

Candelabrum. English, c1790. Base ormolu and blue gilded glass. Height 21in.

*Candlestand. French, Régence. Gilt-wood, triple support with double *scrolled legs and foliated decoration. Height 2ft11in.*

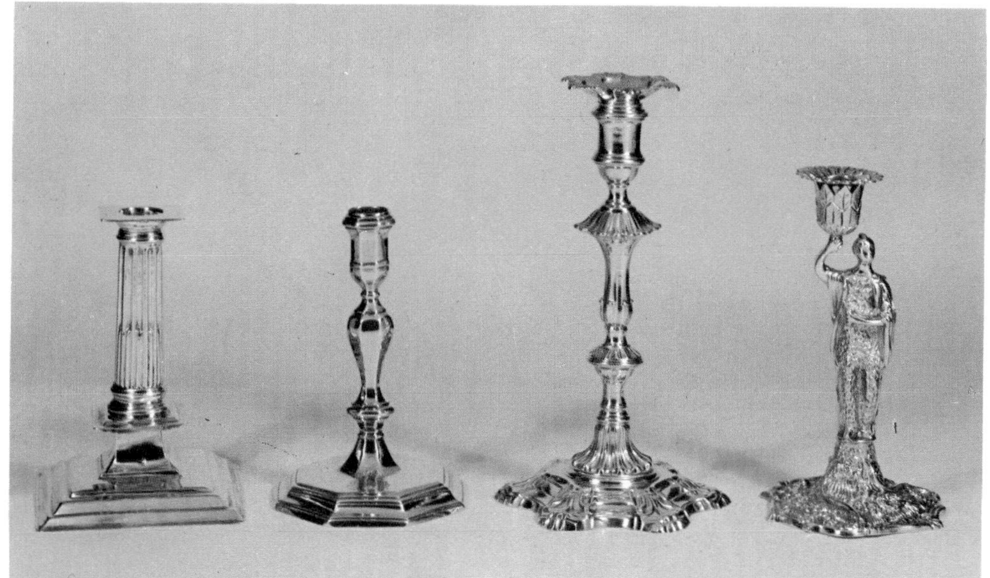

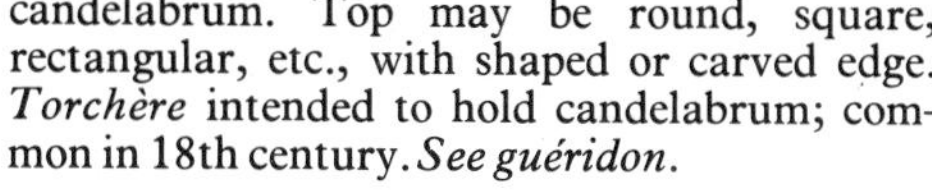

candelabrum. Top may be round, square, rectangular, etc., with shaped or carved edge. *Torchère* intended to hold candelabrum; common in 18th century. *See guéridon.*

candlestick. Made throughout Europe from 10th century or earlier, for ecclesiastical and domestic use. Earliest type *pricket, on plain, ridged or knopped stem, and flat (later spool or trumpet-shaped) base with halfway *greasepan. Baluster stem evolved by mid 16th century in England, remaining most popular shape. By 17th century socket superseded pricket almost entirely, and by late 17th century greasepan vanished to be replaced by enlarged socket rim, usually removable. Silver, silver-gilt, gold, pewter, and brass most popular metals; brass-casting techniques improved in 1690s to give noticeably finer texture; pewter fell from favour after mid 18th century. From 17th century some candlesticks incorporated small sliding rod in stem which adjusted height of candle or ejected stump; bases square or octagonal, plain, moulded, sometimes engraved. *Chamber candlesticks much used.

In early 18th century, general outline of base still square, but rounded corners and lobed edges normal; examples in precious metal had chased ornament, and from *c*1730, were made in rococo style with ornate, moulded, grotesque masks, foliage and scrollwork. From mid 18th century, detachable nozzle used for candlesticks in classical column form (Corinthian column common); square base ornamented with floral swags. In England these were die-stamped in thin sheet silver or Sheffield plate, soldered together, and loaded, e.g. with resin. In base metals, plain baluster stems persisted until end of 18th century when silver designs were followed and neo-classical urn shapes, etc., became popular. Gun-metal sometimes used from 18th century; pewter used again from *c*1800 but declined in popularity after *c*1860. Candlesticks with telescopic stems produced in Sheffield plate from *c*1790; cloth lining inside stem ensured metal parts did not come into contact. 19th century silver candlesticks again cast; massive and ornate. Human figure stems with upraised arm holding candle made in 17th century and revived in early 19th century; rather rare.

Glass candlesticks of ungainly shape, with hollow knopped stem and pedestal foot first made in 17th century. Towards end of century, design improved, tending to follow metal counterparts with solid, knopped baluster stem and wide, domed foot, plain or moulded. Silesian stem with domed foot, ribbed to match socket, appeared in early 18th century. After *c*1740, examples more delicately balanced; stems generally match contemporary wine glasses, although domed foot usual throughout century. Cut-glass candlesticks first advertized 1742; scalloped sockets and feet popular, with shallow diamond-cutting on stem. Towards end of 18th century, Adam influence apparent in fluted column stems and square cut, terraced feet. Irish glasshouses often specialized in cut-glass candlesticks, characterized by square, heavy foot, scalloped edges, and removable socket. From mid 18th to mid 19th centuries, *Bristol produced opaque-white examples, either enamelled or surface painted (latter wears badly). Many candlesticks also made in ceramics, roughly following metal forms.

C and S scrolls. Scrolls based on letters C and S, common 18th century ornamental motif.

cane-coloured stoneware or **caneware.** Buff, fine-textured stoneware developed in Staffordshire during late 1770s by addition of Cornish stone to local clay. Began to supersede red stoneware *c*1780. Used by J. *Wedgwood for ornamental and domestic ware; sprigged decoration, often fern leaves in tan or green; brilliant blue or green enamel painting, later also red. Teapots, hot water jugs, and bulb pots modelled to imitate bamboo. Makers include J. *Turner, J. *Spode, S. *Hollins.

cane-work. Strips of cane from rattan palm (East Indies) interwoven to form mesh; used to fill seat, back, and arm-frames of chairs, day-beds, settees, etc.; also in head and foot boards of beds. Popular in England during 17th century and in America and Europe in late 17th and early 18th centuries. Popularity revived in England, particularly for use with lacquered furniture, from *c*1750; also used during 19th century. *See* Sheraton style, fancy chair.

canister. *See* tea-caddy.

canister clock. Early cylindrical table clock, made in 16th century. *See* drum clock.

cann. Late 17th and 18th century American silver drinking vessel modelled on English *mug. Earliest type had tapering cylindrical body, moulded rim, rat-tail handle, and with or without short, moulded foot. From *c*1730 had bellied body. Makers include J. *Hurd and P. *Revere.

cannetille. 19th century jewellery consisting of units of coiled gold wire (e.g. pyramids, rosettes, beads) produced in large quantity and then assembled; sometimes combined with gems. Popular in England and France. Named after twisted metal thread (*cannetille*) used in embroidery.

*Canework backs. On English walnut chairs. Charles II period. Pierced and carved backs and front stretchers; *spirally turned uprights and back stretchers; *squab cushions.*

*Canopic jar. J. *Wedgwood, c1790; *rosso antico with black decoration.*

Canning Jewel. *Pendant in form of merman; torso, *baroque pearl, mounted in enamelled gold and set with pearls, rubies and diamonds. Probably made in late 16th century Italy; one of finest Renaissance jewels. Said to have been given by member of Medici family to Indian Emperor; purchased in India by Lord Canning in late 1850s. Now in Victoria & Albert Museum, London.

canopy. Raised covering over altar, bed, throne, etc. On beds, supported either by bedposts, or by wall or ceiling fixtures.

Canton enamel. Tray, painted in imitation of porcelain. Chinese, late 18th century.
Capodimonte. Porcelain teapot, c1750, marked with fleur-de-lis in underglaze blue.
Bottom:
Caqueteuse. Oak with elaborate carving; turned arms and front legs. Scottish, 16th century.

canopic jar. Pottery urn, in ancient Egypt to hold viscera of embalmed bodies; also adopted by Etruscans. Copies made by J. *Wedgwood.

cántaro (Spanish, 'pitcher'). Glass vessel for wine or water. Spherical or ovoid body on high, spreading foot, with two spouts rising from opposite sides of shoulder: one slender, for pouring, other wider, for filling. Topped by ring-shaped handles with flower or hen finial. Made in many parts of Spain from 17th century, often with *façon de Venise latticinio* decoration.

canteen, nécessaire de voyage or **travelling set.** Decorative leather case containing eating utensils, in use from late 17th century. Varies in size from small leather case with personal spoon, knife, fork, beaker, etc., to late 18th and early 19th century cumbersome fitted wooden boxes, containing articles for table use, toilet use, and writing implements. Most famous French maker, M-G. *Biennais, who supplied *nécessaires de voyage* for Napoleon and his Empress as well as many French army officers. Rarely found complete in original container.

Canterbury. Late 18th century English table-side stand with three transverse divisions to hold cutlery, and curved end for plates. Also, stand for holding music books and sheet music, from early 19th century.

Canton enamels. Chinese enamel work, derived from technique of painting enamels on copper without use of *cloisons* (*see* Chinese *cloisonné* enamel) developed in Europe at Limoges in 16th century. In reign of Emperor K'ang Hsi, French missionaries brought examples to China for copying. Early work exclusively for European orders: winepots, teapots, etc., decorated at main port of shipment, Canton, in same manner as ceramics (*see* armorial or Jesuit porcelains). *Illustration at* Chinese snuff bottles.

Cape Cod Glass Works. Founded 1858 in Sandwich, Massachusetts, by *D. Jarves when he left *Boston and Sandwich Glass Company. Produced lamps and tableware, mainly of pressed and cut glass. Closed 1869.

Cape plates or **Kaapsche schotels.** Dutch imitations of imported Chinese ceremonial plates in Wan-Li style, made at Delft from *c*1675. Decorated in purplish-blue with outlines in black or dark blue. Central octagonal medallion encloses landscape with bird, animal, or vase of flowers in foreground; border has Wan-Li symbols alternating with e.g. flowers or birds in small frames. Many made by potters including L. *Cleffius, L. *van Eenhoorn, J. W. and R. *Hoppesteyn.

Capodimonte (Naples). Italian porcelain factory established in 1743 by Charles III of Bourbon. Soft-paste formula made by G. *Schepers. G. *Gricci chief modeller. Products include stick-handles, tableware, and *garnitures de cheminée.* Snuff-boxes *c*1743 in shape of sea-shells decorated with marine animals moulded in relief and painted or gilded; portraits or mythological scenes inside lids. *c*1745–47, snuff-boxes painted with *chinoiseries.* Painting characterized by stippling, or fine lines; clouds often in violet or pale red; colours include red, brown, and shades of green. Porcelain room in royal villa at Portici furnished 1757–59. In 1759, factory transferred to *Buen Retiro. Mark, when used is fleur-de-lis impressed or painted in underglaze blue. *Illustration at* Italian ceramics.

capstan salt. *See* spool salt.

caquetoire, caqueteuse (French, from *caqueter,* 'to chatter'). Woman's portable chair with arms, high narrow back, and trapeziform seat, widening at front, designed to accommodate wide skirts. Dates from 16th century France; introduced to England late 16th century.

Carabagh carpets. *See* Karabagh carpets.

carafe. Glass water or wine container, bottle shaped, conical, or globular and without stopper. Made in cut or plain glass, often decorated with trailing and vertical ribbing. Popular in 18th century.

*Canterbury. For music. Satinwood, in *Sheraton style. Top lifts; drawers below slatted divisions. English, late 18th century. Width 1ft8in.*

carat. Measure of weight for precious stones: $3\frac{1}{6}$ grains. Also measure of fineness of gold based on 24 units, e.g. 20 carat gold is 20 parts pure gold, four parts alloy.

carbuncle. *See* garnet.

Carcher, Jan and Nicholaus. *See* Karcher, J. and N.

card-cut ornament (on furniture). Chinese

*Card table. Early *American Federal style, attributed to C–H. *Lannuier; satinwood and kingwood, parcel-gilt. Edges inlaid with brass stars; supported by two spirally fluted baluster legs, and carved and gilded winged caryatid. Height 2ft7in.*

Carillon clock. By Nicholas Vallin, dated 1598, made in London. Iron mechanism with case partly iron, partly brass. 13 bells strike tunes of differing lengths on quarter, half, three-quarter and hour. Height 1ft11in.

lattice decoration carved in low relief. Used on *Chinese Chippendale pieces. *See* Chippendale style.

card case. Small box for visiting cards (generally contains six) used in Britain from *c*1800. Earliest examples in silver usually decorated with chased foliage and flowers or architectural subjects which are embossed in high relief (e.g. Windsor Castle, Abbotsford, etc.); mainly made in Birmingham. Also made of wood, mother-of-pearl, papier mâché, ivory. N. *Mills one of chief Birmingham makers.

cardinal's hat. Pewter dish with broad rim and deep well, known from 15th century.

card table. Table designed specifically for card games; became popular in Europe and America during 18th century. Usually has folding top, supported when open by *swing leg or (increasingly from early 18th century) *concertina support. Top has dished areas for candlesticks and money or chips; playing area covered with baize, velvet, or other fabric. Some circular models, e.g., **bouillotte* table, *commerce table.

carillon. Series of bells, rung either mechanically or manually. Mechanical form used in clocks from about 14th century.

Carlin, Martin (d 1785). French. *Maître-ébéniste* from 1766 working in Louis XVI style. Pieces had simple lines and were often inlaid with Sèvres plaques, marble mosaic, or panels of Japanese lacquer. Noted for elegant proportions and fine quality. *Illustration also at* Sèvres. Stamp: M. CARLIN.

Carlton House desk or **table.** Writing table with several levels of drawers and storage areas at back and sides of work surface; may have frieze of drawers beneath top. Named after Carlton House (now demolished; residence of Prince Regent, later George IV), but no known examples from there.

*Carlton House desk. English, Regency. Mahogany with pierced metal gallery; leather writing surface; legs on *castors.*

carnet de bal. Leaf of ivory in decorative case used in 18th and 19th centuries. Unlike **tablette* could be removed from case so that names of dancing partners could be inscribed in lead pencil and removed with damp cloth. Cases gold, enamel or ivory often inscribed and/or decorated with miniatures.

Carolean style. *See* Restoration style.

Caron, Pierre Augustin (1732–99). French watch maker and dramatist. As Beaumarchais, author of play, *Le Barbier de Seville.* Clock maker to Louis XV, 1755; made small ring watch for Mme de Pompadour.

carpet. Usually a knotted or woven floor covering; until 19th century, term denoted any cover of thick fabric, especially woollen, e.g. for table, bed, etc.

Carrack or **k'raak porcelain.** Chinese export porcelain captured in Portuguese carrack, Catherina, and taken to Amsterdam in 1603. Decorated boldly in underglaze blue, with floral sprays, or fruits placed simply in panels or borders. Style influenced early 17th century Delft.

Carré, Jean (d 1572). Lorraine glass maker. In England from 1549; employed Lorraine glass makers in Surrey (*see* Wealden glass). In *c*1567,

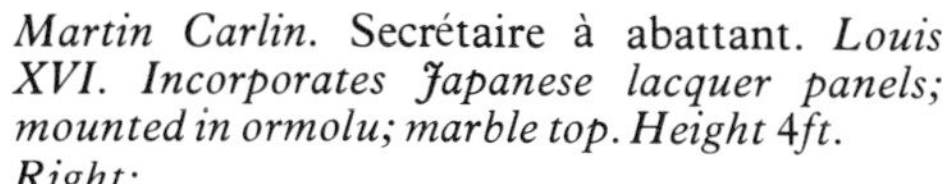

Martin Carlin. Secrétaire à abattant. *Louis XVI. Incorporates Japanese lacquer panels; mounted in ormolu; marble top. Height* 4*ft.*
Right:
Carnet de bal. *Louis XVI. Gold and blue enamel, cameo and diamonds. Inscribed with* *Souvenir, *and, on reverse,* D'Amitié.

Carriage clocks. Both c1870. Left: French clock with repeater, plain brass case, inscribed on dial, Charles Frodsham and Co., Paris, by whom it was sold. Height $6\frac{1}{4}$*in. Right: English clock with engraved dial. Height* $4\frac{1}{4}$*in.*

moved to *Crutched Friars, London. Imported Venetians to make *façon de Venise* crystal glass.

carriage clock. French travelling clock produced in 18th century; probably derived from **pendule d'officier,* pioneered by A-L. *Breguet. Rectangular case, *c*3–12in. high, with carrying handle. Well-finished movement, often with alarm, striking, or repeating mechanism; calendar work in some examples. Case usually brass, plain, or decorated with engraving, enamelling, or filigree work. Also made from *c*1820 in England, America, and Austria.

carriage-warmer. *See* brazier, foot-warmer.

Carriera, Rosalba (1675–1757). Italian portrait painter and miniaturist. Pioneered use of pastels. First known for miniatures on ivory, *fondelli,* e.g. for use on snuff-boxes. Worked in Venice; painted royalty and notables visiting city. Many paintings bought by Augustus the Strong for collection in Dresden. Visited Paris (1721–22); elected to *Académie Royale des Beaux-arts;* painted 36 portraits including Louis XV as child. Equally triumphant visit to Vienna (1730). Noted for delicacy of work and freshness of colour. Eyesight failed *c*1750; portraits in crayons before blindness total. Younger sister,

Albert Carrier-Belleuse. Gilt bronze medieval figure, c1870. Signed and numbered 888. Bears founders stamp, H. Pigard. Width 17*in.*

Cartel clock. Louis XV, with rococo ormolu case; white enamel dial signed Amy Dentan à Paris.

Giovanna (d 1737), assisted with backgrounds and draperies.

Carrier-Belleuse, Albert (1824–87). French sculptor; pupil of David d'Angers; first exhibited at Salon in 1851, and regularly thereafter. Produced many small bronzes. Well-known works include *La Bacchante, Le Messie,* and *Salve Regina* group.

Carron Company. Scottish ironworks founded in 18th century at Carron, Stirlingshire. Experimented with, and improved casting techniques. Produced many decorative objects in cast iron designed by R. and J. *Adam in late 18th century.

cartel clock. Form of French wall clock, dating from *c*1750. Highly ornamental case, worked in wood with **vernis Martin* decoration, or in gilt bronze. Motifs include wings, laurel leaves, cupids, and representations of themes such as triumph of love over time. Also made in England, Holland, and Scandinavia.

cartilaginous style. *See* Dutch grotesque style.

cartonnier or **serre papier.** French storage unit for desk papers, composed of several small compartments. Placed either at one end of writing table, or on cupboard base. May have bronze ornament, figure, or clock on top. Dates from 18th century.

cartoon. Detailed, full-scale preparatory drawing or painting for tapestry, fresco, painting, mosaic-work, etc. In tapestry, design woven from cartoon prepared by workshop's designer, or, for many important commissions, by painter of standing, e.g. *Raphaël, F. *Boucher. Design first traced in outline on warp threads. With *high-warp loom, cartoon normally placed behind weaver on wall or easel and constantly referred to; as weaver worked from behind tapestry, mirror might be placed in front to assist him. With *low-warp loom, cartoon normally cut into sections and placed beneath horizontal warp; design produced in reverse, so cartoons prepared for low-warp loom often recognizable. Preliminary sketches, enlarged for cartoon, known as *petits patrons* (small patterns).

cartouche. Ornamental device with curved or rolled edges, suggesting partly opened scroll or volute of Ionic capital. Used as surround to space (oval, lozenge-shaped etc.) for inscriptions, coats of arms, or emblems, and as border ornament.

cartouche dial. Enamel plaques attached to dial-plate of clock or watch, usually carrying blue or black numerals on white ground and sometimes maker's name. Mainly on French pieces *c*1680–1740, but often copied later.

Carver chair. American 17th century spindle arm chair. One row of spindles in back. Named for John Carver, a founder of Massachusetts Bay colony. *cf* Brewster chair.

carving or **German fork.** Two-pronged silver carving fork used in Europe from 16th century. Prongs sometimes of steel. In 17th and 18th centuries often part of *travelling service.

caryatid. Female figure used as supporting column; derived from Greek architecture. Used in Britain and Europe from Renaissance e.g. for handles, stems, and supports.

Casali, Antonio (fl mid to late 18th century). Italian maiolica painter at Lodi. With F. *Callegari, established workshop at Pesaro in 1763. Mark: CC Pesaro, with date and painter's signature. Decorated tin-glazed ware with enamel in imitation of porcelain, particularly Chinese. Also used high-temperature colours for miniature painting. Later established workshop alone.

Casa Pirota. Italian maiolica workshop at Faenza. From early 16th century, made plates with *istoriato* painting, geometrical motifs, or grotesques on blue enamel ground. Marked with rebus of fire bomb: circle divided into quadrants, one containing small circle; sometimes with flames.

case bottles. Set of glass bottles specially designed to fit box or case. Popular in late 18th century England. Included large wine and spirit bottles (*see* tantalus), small, cut scent bottles, and rectangular, cut toilet bottles.

cased glass. *See* cameo glass.

casket. Box, usually with complicated locking mechanism, for safe-keeping of jewellery or money. Used from early times; most surviving examples date from Middle Ages onwards. Types include cabinets of ebony, mother-of-pearl, lapis lazuli, rock-crystal, enamel, etc., with extensive gold, silver, or silver-gilt mounts and fittings; small, brass-mounted ivory chests from Sicily. 15th century iron, or iron-bound wooden type made throughout Europe had filigree decoration of rosettes, trellis-work, etc., and iron rings for fastening to belt or saddle when travelling. Style with arched lid originated in France; later examples had etched ornament or damascening (latter also appeared on Milanese caskets). 16th century decoration was less elaborate. Many caskets made in Nuremberg and Augsburg were of sheet-iron etched with sporting, rustic, or allegorical subjects and mounted in gilt brass (*cf* Armada chest). Miniature caskets (*c*4in high) produced by Michael and Conrad Mann of Nuremberg in early 17th century were highly elaborate, of gilt brass with silver or enamel enrichments and engraved decoration. Caskets were not commonly made in iron or steel in 17th and 18th centuries, though some ornate examples exist in cut steel.

*Caskets. Above, iron, showing complex *locking mechanism on back of lid. German, 16th century. Below, English silver. With gilt-bronze frame, finials, and cherub feet. Silver panels embossed with strapwork.* c*1640. Height* $9\frac{1}{2}$*in.*

cassapanca. Italian long wooden seat with chest base; shape derived from combination of wall bench and chest. Possibly first made in 15th century Florence.

Cassel (Hesse-Nassau). German faience factory, flourished *c*1680–*c*1788. Produced mainly blue-and-white wares, under Delft influence. Mark used *c*1725–*c*1750: HL (Hessel-Land). Hard-paste porcelain produced (1766–88). Somewhat smoky and imperfect. Made functional blue-and-white wares; also examples enamelled in Kakiemon style identified; occasionally, figures. Marks: HC, or two-tailed lion rampant of Hesse, both in underglaze blue. Cream-coloured earthenware made in Wedgwood style (1771–1862); mark: lion, impressed.

casserole. 18th and 19th century European stewpot in silver, etc. Plain cylindrical bowl had flat base and usually straight handle (often of wood) and heavy cover with finial; generally had its own stand. Sometimes found with two handles.

cassolette. Metal (usually gilt-bronze) vase with pierced lid for burning perfume pastilles, made in France from 17th century, copied to small extent elsewhere in Europe. Made in England by M. *Boulton. 18th century examples often have cover which reverses to form candlestick. Sometimes incorporates spirit-lamp.

cassone. Italian dowry chest with carved, gilt, inlaid, or painted decoration. Painted front and side panels less common after 16th century.

cast brass. *See* brass.

Castel Durante (Marche), Italy. Near Urbino; renamed Urbania in 1635. Unidentified maiolica produced before early 16th century; manufacture described by C *Piccolpasso. In early 16th century *Zoan Maria developed style of painting with demons, cupids, and later masks and grotesques, accompanied by foliage and *trophies. N. *Pellipario, thought to be native of Castel Durante, continued style with grotesques, but made important contribution to development of *istoriato* painting; work includes *Correr service, one for Isabella d'Este, and two with unidentified coats of arms.

Cassolettes. *George III, of *blue john mounted in ormolu; plinth decorated with lion masks and swags of laurel, base with two bands of* guilloche *pattern. Height* 12*in.*

Cassone. *Walnut carved with classical figures and* putti; *banding, and base and top of chest consists of grotesque heads; lion supports. North Italian, early 16th century.*
Castel Durante. *Armorial saucer dish painted in* *istoriato *style with The Judgement of Paris, after Raphaël; school of N.* *Pellipario, *c1530.*

Castellani, Fortunato Pio (1793–1856). Italian goldsmith and jeweller working in Rome; in 1814 joined father's workshop. From early 1820s imitated jewellery excavated from ancient Roman tombs. Discovered method of imitating *granulation. Also used filigree to produce jewellery in revived Etruscan style. Retired in 1851 and succeeded by sons Alessandro (1824–83) and Augusto (1829–1914) who shared his interest in archaeological jewellery. Castellani workshop jewellery marked with crossed capital Cs.

Castelli (Abruzzi), Italy. Maiolica tiles made from 16th century; also vases and dishes decorated in *compendiario* style. In mid 17th and early 18th centuries, noted for *istoriato* decoration by *Grue and *Gentile families. Potteries of area survived until 19th century.

caster. Silver or pewter container for sugar, pepper, or other condiments, in use from early 17th century, or possibly before. Earliest form cylindrical with gadrooned or moulded base and pierced dome cover for casting (sprinkling). Cover surmounted by decorative knob and attached by *bayonet joint. Made in sets of three, largest up to *c*9in. high. After 1700, with vase or pear shaped body and moulded foot; piercing of cover elaborate, e.g. arabesque and floral designs. Pull-off cover common. From mid 18th century casters assume baluster or elongated pear shape; cover wavy rather than simply curved in contour. One of fittings in *cruet frame. *Illustration also* at F. Garthorne.

casting or **founding.** Method of shaping metal by pouring it, in molten state, into moulds and allowing it to cool. Used for most metals (copper unsuitable, owing to emission of gases and formation of bubbles when heated). Articles of all kinds produced by this process: bells and large hollow-ware in clay moulds; smaller hollow-ware and simple pieces by *sand-casting method; sophisticated pieces with sharp relief decoration (e.g. **Edelzinn*) in bronze moulds; more complicated pieces by *lost-wax process.

Castelli. *Maiolica plate, one of set of four, c1680. All painted with different hunting scenes and with borders of arabesques. Diameter 11¼in.*

Casting. *Silver mace in form of crowned maiden (part of arms of Mercers' Company). English, made by Edward Pinfold in 1679. Cast in one solid piece. Height 11in.*
Caster. *Set of three octagonal casters by D.* *Willaume, *1735. Baluster outline and moulded borders; covers pierced and engraved. Heights 6¾in. and 8¾in.*

cast iron. *See* iron.

castor. Roller or wheel attached to foot or under corners of piece of furniture. Increasingly common from 17th century; during 18th and 19th centuries, incorporated into design of piece. At first made of wood or leather, in 18th century of brass; some earthenware examples from second half 19th century. *Illustration at* Carlton House desk.

cat. *See* plate-warmer.

cathedral clock. Clocks in cases formed as Gothic cathedrals, often highly ornate, popular in France *c*1840–70. Usually stylized, not representing particular buildings. Influenced development of *skeleton clocks in England in mid 19th century, sometimes made with frames in elaborate architectural forms, e.g. of York Minster.

Catherine wheel pattern. *See* Queen Charlotte pattern.

Caucasian carpets. *See* Armenian dragon rugs, Baku, chichi, Dagestan, Gendje, Hatchli, Karabah, Karagashli, Kazak, Kuba, Mogan, Perepedil, Seichur, Shirvan, sileh, sumak, and Talish carpets, verneh rugs.

caudle-cup. One or two handled cup for drinking caudle (hot, sweet, spiced drink often given to invalids), made in silver, pewter, and ceramics in 17th and 18th centuries throughout Europe and America. Posset (warm milk curdled with wine or ale) was drunk from similar vessel, called posset pot or cup. Body is straight-sided or baluster-shaped with flared mouth; domed lid with finial. Sometimes has stand with central depression. Embossed decoration common. *Illustration also at* J. Dummer.

Cathedral clock. French, mid 19th century, in form of Gothic cathedral. Dial formed as rose window above west door. Two-train movement, gong striking hour and half-hour. Gilt metal. Height 2ft8in.

Caughley, near Broseley, Shropshire. Pottery established soon after 1750. T. *Turner, proprietor from 1772, introduced manufacture of soaprock porcelain similar to Worcester product but generally whiter in appearance, and warm brown by transmitted light; decoration commonly printed or painted in blue of steelier tone than used at Worcester. In 1775, advertized association of R. *Hancock with factory; examples of Hancock's engravings with Caughley marks exist. First transfer-printing of earthenware in underglaze blue in 1780. Polychrome decoration with Chinese figures and flowers, sometimes red and blue, resembles Lowestoft and Worcester; possibly executed by independent decorators. Blue-and-white ware gilded by outside decorators in London. From *c*1780, some copies of later products of Chantilly factory, e.g. plates with borders of moulded basket work; decoration includes Chantilly sprig; hunting horn mark occasionally copied. In 1790, factory bought by J. *Rose; made ware to be glazed and painted at Coalport. Closed in 1814. Marks include letters C, S, or Sx, SALOPIAN, or mock Chinese numerals.

Caudle cup. Ogee curved bowl embossed with daffodils, tulips, stag, and boar; flattened dome cover with plain flanged edge, grotesque head finial; scrolled handles. English, c*1660; maker's mark AC with star below shield. Height 8⅛in.*

cauldron. Earliest type of cooking-vessel, known in bronze from *c*500 B.C. From 16th century, made of cast iron. Usual form is pot-bellied, three-legged, with one or two handles on sides or single swing-handle. Often known as kettle; small size also called crock.

cauliflower ware. English green and yellow lead-glazed earthenware, e.g. teapots in form of cauliflowers or various kinds of fruit, supplied in biscuit by W. *Greatbatch for glazing by J. *Wedgwood, 1760–*c*1766. Also made by other contemporary potters, including T. *Whieldon. Salt-glaze teapots made in form of cabbages by W. *Littler, and porcelain cauliflower ware made e.g. at Chelsea, Worcester, and Longton Hall.

caulking or **corking.** Top edge of hollow-ware hammered down to thicken it after object has been raised over stake or anvil. *See* raising.

causeuse. *See* love seat.

Caussy, Paul (d 1731). French maker of faience at Rouen from 1707. Credited with introduction of yellow-ochre ground colour appearing on some Rouen faience in 1720s and 1730s.

cavetto moulding. Concave moulding, a quarter circle in cross-section.

Caxton chair. *Side chair commonly made in High Wycombe, Buckinghamshire, from *c*1850–1900. Usually has back uprights sloping and central back-slat, cane seat. Stretcher and front legs turned. Etymology uncertain.

celadon. Pottery or porcelain; greyish body covered with translucent feldspathic glaze in varying shades of green, dependent on amount of iron (1–3%) present. Yüeh ware made in southern China *c*6th century. *Lung-ch'üan celadon made from early Sung dynasty (960–1279) until 17th century has jade-like quality. Relief decoration, when left free of glaze, turns brown in firing. Celadon with spots of iron colour (*tobi seiji) made by Japanese. Celadon

*Caughley porcelain. Leaf-shaped pickle dish, 1785–90, transfer-printed with fisherman pattern, used only at Caughley; marked Sx. Coffee pot from *toy service, 1780–85. Height 3¼in. Marked S. Asparagus server, printed with fisherman pattern, 1785–90, marked Sx.*

Cellaret on stand. Oval, George III, mahogany. Rising top encloses fitted and lined interior; square legs and castors. Width 2ft.

glaze also used at *Ching-tê-chên on white porcelain and at *Kwang-tung on stoneware. *Northern celadon has greyish-brown stoneware body and olive-green glaze. Lung-ch'üan ware inspired e.g. *Korean, *Japanese and *Sawankalok celadon; also imitations made in earthenware in Persia and Egypt. *Illustrations at* brush-rest, iron-brown spots, Lung-ch'üan, Yüeh.

celery glass. Tall glass vessel for sticks of celery; has cylindrical body flaring at rim, short stem, and low foot. Usually engraved. Popular in 18th century England and America. *Illustration at* New England Glass Co.

celestial globe clock. 16th century clock combined with revolving globe, sometimes used by astronomers for demonstration; spring-driven. Makers include J. *Burgi.

cellaret, garde du vin, or **sarcophagus.** Deep box-like container for holding wine bottles, dating from 18th century; either free-standing or incorporated in sideboard. Hepplewhite term, *garde du vin*; Sheraton term, sarcophagus.

cellaret sideboard. *Sideboard incorporating *cellaret in top, possibly also with glass-washing basin or plate drawer. Dates from 18th century.

Cellini, Benvenuto (1500–71). Italian goldsmith, sculptor, and medallist. Worked in Rome from 1519–39; visited France in 1537 and 1540; retired to Florence in 1545. Reputation as best Renaissance goldsmith based on own writings and those of contemporaries, and on surviving work in gold, *Cellini salt. Writings inspired later goldsmiths.

Cellini salt. Ceremonial gold salt made by B. *Cellini; commissioned by Cardinal Ippolito d'Este but completed for François I of France in 1543. Reclining naked male and female figures representing sea and earth respectively hold containers for salt and pepper. In Kunsthistorisches Museum, Vienna.

cello. *See* violin family.

censer or **thurible.** Metal container for hot charcoal on which incense is burned in church. Earliest type, open brazier; spherical form with two interlocking sections (upper pierced to allow smoke to escape); used from *c*9th century. Bottom half hangs from three chains attached to disc permitting vessel to be swung; cover lifts by pulling on chain attached to top of cover and going through centre of disc. From *c*1200, cover of architectural form, e.g. Gothic tower. Most are made of bronze, silver, or silver-plated copper. Post-Medieval examples tended to follow current fashions in ornament, but 19th century Gothic revival brought return to earlier forms. *See* incense boat.

centrepiece. *See* épergne.

centre-seconds hand or **sweep seconds hand.** Long hand on clock or watch, indicating seconds; concentric with hour and minute hands, but extending full radius of dial.

centre table. Table, usually circular, designed to be free-standing. Elaborately decorated examples date from 15th century Italy, becoming increasingly popular in 16th. Restoration and William and Mary centre tables often of gate-leg form, in oak or walnut. Mahogany often used from *c*1750 in England and America. Very popular table in 19th century. Marble-topped examples common in Directoire and Empire periods.

centre wheel. Wheel in clock or watch movement normally driving minute hand.

ceramics. Materials made with dried clay, hardened by heating (firing) to over *c*500°C, causing irreversible chemical change: on cooling, no longer softened by water. At very high temperatures, difficult to achieve in kiln, clay will fuse (vitrify) to glassy, non-porous substance. *Earthenware, made from pottery clay fired at 800°–900°C, below temperature of vitrification, is opaque and slightly porous unless glazed. *Stoneware, also made from pottery clay, is fired to 1200°–1400°C, which produces partial vitrification without collapse; non-porous and usually opaque. *Porcelain is vitrified, non-porous, and translucent unless heavily potted; composed of refractory clays with temperature of vitrification lowered by addition of ground glass or fusible rock; on firing at 1200°–1400°C, fusible material melts, sealing pores in clay which holds shape.

*Centre table. French, *Empire style. Mahogany with three heavily-mounted ormolu feet; variegated marble top.*

ceremonial flagon (German). *See* guild flagon.

certosina. Inlay of ivory, metal, bone, or mother-of-pearl in dark wood ground. Designs usually geometrical. Technique possibly Mohammedan; used in Italy from 15th century and in Moorish furniture.

Chaffers, Richard (1731–65). Liverpool potter. In 1751, employed at Worcester; also worked for J. *Wedgwood. Established factory at Shaw's Brow, Liverpool; much blue-and-white delftware exported to America. From *c*1756, assisted by R. *Podmore, made high quality porcelain using Worcester formula, chiefly transfer-printed in blue, also with polychrome enamelled *chinoiserie* decoration. Blue-and-white ware has simple diaper borders, often formed of trellis-work. Succeeded by P. *Christian, partner from 1755. *Illustration at* Liverpool porcelain.

chafing-dish. Circular or shaped metal container, generally with long turned wood handle attached to side, for hot charcoal; bowl has pierced ornament and rests on cast supports. Some early and mid 18th century British and American examples in silver; Dutch equivalents made of copper or brass. In use from 17th century to keep silver or pewter dishes hot. Sometimes called brazier. *cf* pipe-lighter. *Illustration at* breakfast service.

Chaillot, la Savonnerie de. *See* Savonnerie carpets.

chair. Single seat, with back, and with or without arms. *See* back stool, barber's chair, barrel chair, Bath chair, *bergère,* Boston rocker, box chair, Brewster chair, burgomaster chair, Carver chair, Caxton chair, chair table, *chaise à la capucine, chaise en cul de four,* corner chair, Cromwellian chair, Dutch chair, easy chair, elbow chair, fancy chair, farthingale chair, *fauteuil, fauteuil à la reine,* fly chair, French chair, Glastonbury chair, hall chair, Harvard chair, Hitchcock chair, hunting chair, Martha Washington chair, Mendlesham chair, monastic chair, Nelson chair, nursing chair, Oxford chair, parlour chair, porter chair, *prie dieu,* Quaker chair, reading chair, rocking chair, rout furniture, Salem rocker, sample chair, sedan chair, shaving chair, side chair, Windsor chair, wing chair, X-frame chair.

chair (in glass). Glass blower's seat with flat-topped arms on which *pontil rotated and *paraison shaped. Also collective name for team of glass makers.

chair-back settee. *See* settee.

Chaise-longue. *English, Regency, c1815; beech-wood simulating rosewood, gilded.*
Left:
Chair-table. Dutch, c1645, oak. Back swivels on pins to form table; drawer under seat.

chair-back settle. *See* chair-table.

chair-back thumbpiece. Thumbpiece on pewter tankards in which top curves slightly backwards over handle. Common 18th century style in most European countries.

chair-table, chair back settle, monk's bench, or **table-chair.** Dual-purpose chair and table, dating from 15th century. Armchair has tall or round back, hinged to back of chair arms. Chair-back swings forward, rests on chair arms to form table top.

chaise à la capucine. Simple French provincial wooden side chair or armchair, with open back; rush or straw seat. Originated in French monasteries; in general use after *c*1650.

chaise or **coach clock** (or watch). *See* coach clock.

chaise or **fauteuil en cul de four.** French side chair or armchair with back curved in shape of stylized horse-shoe, arched at top, sloping outwards at base. Dates from Louis XV period; popular in Louis XVI style.

chaise longue. Narrow day bed resembling *bergère* with seat extended towards foot. Length might be made up of two or three separate sections (*see duchesse*).

Ch'ai ware. Chinese Imperial porcelain made in reign (954–59) of Shih Tsung. Known only from later literary references; described as 'blue as the sky, as clear as a mirror, as thin as paper, as resonant as a musical stone'. Items doubtfully attributed. Succeeding Imperial ware was *Ting.

chalcedony. Cryptocrystalline variety of *quartz (microscopically fine quartz crystals bonded by *opal). Most common types are cornelian (orange-red), chrysoprase (apple-green), *agate and onyx (banded variety), *jasper, bloodstone (dark green with scattered spots of red jasper), sardonyx (brown and white, black and white, orange-brown), etc. Agate, onyx, sardonyx, and jasper often used as material for *cameos; in use primarily in classical period, Renaissance, and 19th century. Found in various regions, e.g. Brazil, Madagascar, Uruguay. Term sometimes incorrectly used to refer to bluish variety of quartz.

chalice. Ecclesiastical gold, silver-gilt, or, sometimes, pewter vessel used for sacramental wine from earliest times. Normally accompanied by *paten to hold wafers or bread. Some early chalices also produced in bronze and copper. Custom was to bury with priest or bishop the chalice he received at consecration; early examples (e.g. 8th or 9th century) buried for this reason, or to avoid pillage, may still be discovered. By 13th century, pewter or lead copy commonly substituted, by the Reformation wax copy used. Many larger chalices used in western Europe until 12th century made with handles, which were absent in later versions; standard chalice form of bowl, stem, and spreading foot (to prevent overturning) evolved. Forms and decoration were subject to changes of fashion: in 12th century, probably in France, knop added to stem to make chalice easier to lift; this has remained standard feature. In 14th century, crucifix or sacred monogram normally engraved or applied to foot of chalice to indicate front to priest; also, circular foot often replaced by incurved hexagonal foot (so that chalice could be laid on side on paten to drain at end of Mass, after cleansing). During 15th and early 16th century, additional embellishments introduced. Ornament varies; more elaborate examples found in Europe than in Britain. From 12th century, some chalices made with plain inner cup and ornamental (pierced, filigree, gem-set, etc.) outer cup; knop commonly enriched with piercing, engraving, or gems, etc.; bowl sometimes set into ornamental calyx. In early 16th century, inscriptions around top of bowl became common in England. Most parishes from 12th century owned two silver chalices; monasteries and large churches had 6–10. After Reformation, many English chalices converted into *communion cups. Medieval chalice form revived in 19th century by A. W. N. *Pugin and other adherents of Gothic revival.

chalkware. Ornaments made in plaster of Paris, imitating more expensive pottery and porcelain figures of 18th and 19th centuries in America; thought to have been imported from Europe before first manufacture in United States (advertised in 1768). Figures of animals, birds, and contemporary personalities, as well as modelled fruit, slip-moulded in plaster of Paris, then coated inside with heavier plaster to add weight; lamps in form of cottages also occur. Early figures painted in oils; later watercolours used; never glazed.

chamber candlestick or **chamberstick.** Candleholder of silver, Sheffield plate, or brass with carrying handle (scroll, loop, etc.), short moulded socket attached to broad greasepan serving as base, in bowl form with square or round outline, or flat with octagonal, square or circular shape, often decoratively engraved. Sometimes with feet and/or conical extinguisher fitting on handle or stem. Made from 16th century, though earliest survivors are late 17th century. Also with long, straight handle, resembling small frying-pan. Cylindrical glass shade fitting into pierced gallery at base of stem added to some chamber candlesticks from early 19th century. Also made in Britannia metal and electro-plate.

Chalkware. Pennsylvania, early 19th century. Left: girl on a rooster. Right: angel; base decorated with candle smoke. Height 8½in. Both hand painted.

Chamber candlestick with extinguisher and scissors. English silver, made by Richard Sibley, 1815.

Chamber clock. Probably Swiss, c1600; iron movement with original verge and balance escapement; strikes the hours. Gothic case. Height 15in.

chamber clock or **Gothic clock.** Late 15th and 16th century domestic iron clock, made in Germany. Sometimes with top in form of pointed arch. In 17th and 18th century England, *lantern clock.

chamber horse. Exercize chair, with flexible leather seat, resembling upright concertina, with open arms and vertical handle each side extending above arms. When uprights are pushed to and fro by user, seat rises and falls, giving sensation of sitting astride a moving horse. Dates from late 18th century.

Chamberlain, Robert (fl late 18th and early 19th centuries). Painter at *Worcester Porcelain Factory; in 1783, opened rival factory in Worcester, at first as decorating workshop. Made porcelain from 1792. Naturalistic decoration on lavishly painted and gilded wares; also Japan patterns. In 1840, factory amalgamated with Worcester Porcelain Factory (Flight, Barr & Barr).

chamber organ. Small positive (non-portable) organ resembling large cupboard, usually with single keyboard (manual) and varying number of *stops. Used in British and European homes from 17th to mid 19th century. Case and pipes often lavishly ornamented with carving, gilding, painting, etc.

chamberstick. *See* chamber candlestick.

chamfer-top case. On some *bracket clocks after 1800. Shape resembles low pitched roof of building, often with step at base; may have gadrooned or reeded decoration and finial at apex.

Champion, Richard (1743–91). English porcelain manufacturer, owner of porcelain factory in *Bristol. Worked with W. *Cookworthy in *Plymouth from 1760s. In 1772, granted licence by Cookworthy to make porcelain; patent assigned to him in 1774. Lost exclusive right to use of Cornish minerals when extension of patent opposed by Staffordshire potters, including J. *Wedgwood, in 1775. Sold rights to *New Hall Company in 1781. Whig politician; Deputy Paymaster General of the Forces under Edmund Burke. In 1784, emigrated to farm in South Carolina.

champlevé enamelling. Inlay enamelling with design scooped out of metal field. After firing, enamel polished level with top of field metal. Technique of enamelling developed by Greeks, Etruscans, and Celts *c*6th to 3rd centuries B.C. Used at Limoges from 12th century. Effect similar to **cloisonné* enamelling. *Illustration at* German watches.

Chance Bros. Glass House. Founded 1825 by W. and R. L. Chance in Birmingham, Warwickshire. Employed English and European workmen. Produced glass shades. Improved techniques for making plain and coloured *sheet glass, optical glass, and lighthouse glass, for which still main manufacturer.

chandelier. Branched, hanging candle-holder known in Europe from Middle Ages. Early examples of pricket type made in wood and brass for churches; later, designs in brass and silver became more elaborate. 17th century Dutch examples, much copied elsewhere in Europe, had central baluster or vase-shaped column or globe of burnished brass, and up to 36 branches and sockets. Some in wrought-iron, which was also used to make *suspension rods which sometimes replaced chains for hanging chandelier from ceiling. Glass chandeliers made in Venice and in Bohemia probably by late 17th century; metal supporting base, usually bronze, decorated with rock-crystal or, in Venetian specimens, coloured, opalescent glass moulded into foliate, floral, and other naturalistic shapes. Originator of Venetian chandelier said to be Guiseppe Briati (1686–1772). Bohemian examples simpler. Introduced into early 18th century England. Earliest form simple, with plain glass arms, candle-sockets, and grease pans; central shaft covered with shallow-cut glass spheres. By mid 18th century, all over shallow-cutting popular and cut pendants introduced; from then, elaborate cutting and decoration increased rapidly. Throughout 18th century, gilt bronze examples made in prevailing styles. By late 18th century, Adam influence apparent in Grecian urn shape of shaft, emphasized by small swags of pendant drops wired together to form chains. In early 19th century chandeliers, shaft disappears beneath elaborate swags of pendants; curved branches replaced by short arms attached to metal rings round base of shaft. After gas lighting was introduced in mid 19th century, gasoliers made in many styles using brass, bronze and glass. Term also applied to *candelabrum and *lustre.

Chandelier. English, c1725. Faceted central core; six candle arms made in single piece, (characteristic of earliest examples). Small size, height 2ft5in.

Ch'ang-ch'ing. *See* Yü-yao.

Chang family. Noted Chinese potters of Sung period. Elder brother, Shêng-i, famous for *Ko ware, with pronounced crackle; younger, Shêng-erh, made finer-formed smooth-glazed objects, regarded as contributing to high reputation of *Lung-ch'üan ware throughout world. Supposedly both worked at *Kuan kiln site.

Ch'ang-sha. Important Chinese kiln site in Hunan province, active from late T'ang to early Sung periods. Produced mainly celadons, closely resembling *Yüeh ware, with many variations in decoration: brown or green mottling, painting, appliqué, etc. Objects usually brittle, with glaze damaged by flaking. Often classed as *Yo-chou ware.

Chantilly (Seine-et-Oise). Porcelain factory founded in 1725 by Louis-Henri de Bourbon, Prince de Condé. Patent granted in 1735. Soft-paste porcelain made from formula used at Saint-Cloud; sometimes covered with tin-glaze. Early decoration, until *c*1740, inspired by Chinese and Japanese porcelain, particularly in Kakiemon style (**décor coréen*). Products include teapots and sweetmeat boxes in melon shape, and octagonal cups and saucers inspired by Japanese forms; also pear-shaped jugs and drug-pots derived from forms of French faience and silver. Finial in shape of two or three fully opened flowers characteristic. Figures influenced by Meissen, in style adapted from oriental, include Chinese people and *magots*. Decoration, from *c*1740, includes naturalistic flowers painted or modelled in relief; later, table services painted *en camaïeu* in blue. From *c*1750, porcelain covered with creamy-yellow lead-glaze. Products influenced by Vincennes include vases and *cachepots* decorated with rococo foliage and scrollwork. Flower painting in manner of Meissen and Sèvres gave way to simple, delicate patterns, e.g. *à l'épi, à la brindille* (*Chantilly sprig), and *à jet d'eau*, usually in underglaze blue, sometimes blue enamel, crimson, manganese-purple, or brown, found on table services (1755–80). In 1770s, more formal decoration appears on tableware made for use in châteaux. Polychrome pieces often edged in brown or yellow. Proportion of output marked with hunting horn in red, rarely black or gold, enamel, and from *c*1750 in underglaze blue or crimson. Same mark, incised or raised, on white figures. Chantilly, written in blue, occasionally seen on late productions with painting in underglaze blue. Marks of individual workmen also appear. *Illustration at* knife and fork handles.

Chantilly sprig. Ceramic decoration: delicate, sketchy pattern of flower sprays, twigs, grasses, or ears of corn (*à la brindille* or *à l'épi*). Often painted in underglaze blue, more rarely in blue, crimson, purple, or brown enamel, on porcelain at Chantilly (1755–80). Copied on porcelain at Arras, Mennecy, Tournai, and, in England, at Caughley, Derby, and Worcester; also occasionally on faience.

Chapelle, Jacques (fl mid 18th century). French potter and chemist. Worked at several French potteries. From *c*1749 at Sceaux,

Chantilly. Porcelain cup decorated in Kakiemon style, and leaf dish; both c*1740.*

Right, above:
*Charger. English, tin-glazed earthenware *blue-dash charger, made in London* c*1640–45; painted with the Expulsion of Adam and Eve from the Garden of Eden. Diameter* $10\frac{1}{4}$*in.*
Centre:
A. Charles. Silhouette, c*1790, of unknown lady. Painted on card.* $2\frac{1}{2}$*in ×* $3\frac{1}{2}$*in.*
Below:
Chatelaine and watch. Gold and enamel. Chatelaine has space for four other objects. London, 1781.

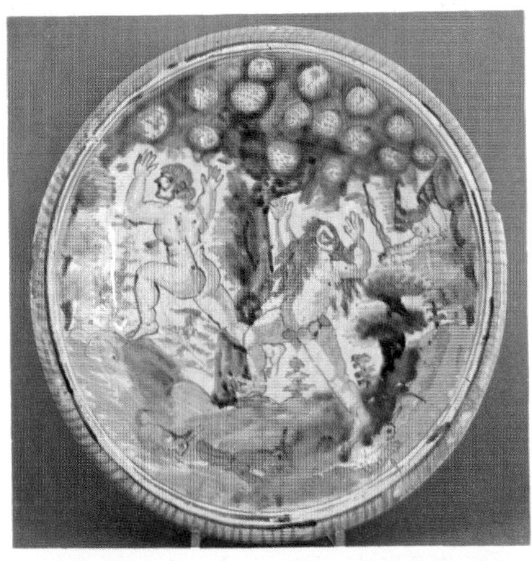

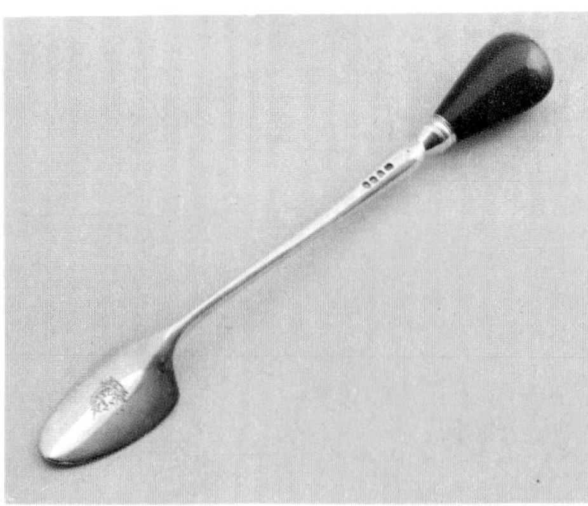

Cheese scoop. Made in London, 1792, by Smith & Fearn. Crest on back; turned mahogany handle.

Chelsea. Porcelain candelabrum, one of pair; scrolled rococo base, gilded and enamelled decoration. Gold anchor period.

Chelsea. Porcelain teapot, c*1755, decorated with bison by J. *O'Neale.*

initially to make soft-paste porcelain, but prevented by Sèvres monopoly; made **faïence japonnée*. Proprietor of factory from 1759. Retired 1763, renting factory to J. *Jullien and S. *Jacques; sold it in 1772.

Chapin, Aaron (1753–1838). Cabinet maker who worked in East Windsor and Hartford, Connecticut; cousin of E. *Chapin. Style simple and light, influenced by T. *Chippendale. Pieces often in cherry.

Chapin, Eliphalet (1741– after 1807). American furniture maker, who worked in Philadelphia, Pennsylvania, and in Connecticut. Many case pieces (including clock cases), usually in cherry wood, showing *Philadelphia Chippendale influence.

chapnet. *See* salt.

chapter ring. Ring on dial of clock, upon which numerals or strokes, marking time-division, are painted or engraved.

charge mark. Mark struck on unfinished French gold and silver before piece was tested and counter-marked by wardens of guild. Instituted in 1672, as result of tax on gold and silver introduced by Louis XIV to discourage conversion of silver of kingdom to plate, and as source of revenue. In towns with mint, mint letter used (until Revolution). In Paris, charge mark at first only struck on large pieces. *cf* discharge mark.

charger. Very large dish, used from Middle Ages for serving food, e.g. for carrying meat to the table, or as ornament. *See* blue-dash charger, meat dish, venison dish.

charka. Small 17th century Russian drinking vessel with shallow, circular bowl, and single, flat handle. Used for drinking brandy and other spirits. Made of rock-crystal or other semi-precious stones mounted in gold, or of silver with niello ornament. Sometimes has three tiny ball feet.

Charles, A. (fl late 18th century). English silhouettist. Worked in The Strand, London; very prolific – claimed to have taken over 11,600 profiles by 1792. Work often signed: by Charles, R.A., although not member of the Royal Academy.

Charlier, Jacques (1720–79). French miniaturist. Court painter under Louis XV. Said to have been pupil of F. *Boucher, whose works he copied.

char pot. Shallow cylindrical jar in English delftware made notably at Liverpool in 18th century. Painted with large fish; possibly contained preserved char (fish related to trout).

chasing. Surface modelling of metal with punch and hammer. Chaser uses hundreds of differently-shaped punches. Widely used in conjunction with other decorative techniques; frequently used to finish cast piece. *See* flat-chasing, matting, *repoussé*.

chatelaine. Hooked ornament worn at waist by men and women in 18th century Europe; elaborate chain panels supported watch, crank key, fob seal, *étui*, and other trinkets decorated *en suite*. Made of gold, gilt-metal, and in England, *c*1780, of pinchbeck. Most elaborate after 1750; out of fashion by 1800.

Chatsworth Toilet Service. 22-piece toilet service made by Paris silversmiths (including P. *Prévost) 1670–71. In 1677, became property of William of Orange (later William III of England) and Mary II of England on their marriage. Their arms were added to most of pieces, which are ornamented with all-over *repoussé* foliage. Now in collection of Duke of Devonshire.

Chaudor carpets. *See* Chodor carpets.

cheese scoop. Silver utensil with solid handle (silver or ivory) and crescent-shaped scoop blade. Larger than *marrow scoop. Used in Britain from late 18th century. Some examples from *c*1800 have ejecting rod for removing cheese from blade.

Chelsea. London factory making soft-paste porcelain by 1745, date of *goat-and-bee jugs, earliest known English porcelain. Factory periods until 1769 known by most common marks.

Triangle (until *c*1750) period wares often unmarked; incised triangle sometimes appears (examples also exist with Chelsea and date 1745), very rarely crown and trident in underglaze blue. Body milky, very translucent, like opaque glass, often with black specks; flecks and pin holes of greater translucency visible by transmitted light; glaze soft. Shapes from silver, with relief moulding, e.g. salts in form of crayfish, tea wares of overlapping acanthus or strawberry leaves. Other wares with applied reliefs of e.g. prunus blossoms inspired by *blanc-de-Chine* porcelain, sometimes with small floral sprays, painted in Meissen style, and insects concealing flaws in body. Also fluted dishes with rock bases and applied relief of shells and coral. Rare figures include teapot in shape of fat Chinaman, and group of lovers. *Girl-in-a-swing family possibly by Chelsea workmen at rival factory.

Overlapping raised anchor and red anchor periods correspond with management of factory by N. *Sprimont. Marks are anchor in two circles in applied relief, sometimes picked out in red (*c*1750–52), and anchor in red, or sometimes enamel or underglaze blue, or purple enamel (1752–56); often placed very inconspicuously. Body less glassy than triangle wares, stronger; greenish by transmitted light, with circles of greater translucency (moons) caused by concentrations of frit in body. Glaze slightly opaque, with black specks on raised anchor wares. From *c*1755, up to 40% of bone ash added to body. Foot-rims frequently ground level; exposed paste very smooth. Some decoration by outside painters, notably W. *Duesbury. Collection of Meissen borrowed for copying (1751); influence visible e.g. in harbour scenes and *indianische Blumen*; Kakiemon (including *caille* pattern) and Imari styles possibly taken from Meissen versions. Wide range of enamel colours but sparse honey gilding. Purple or crimson monochrome used for painting landscapes and figures; underglaze blue very rare. *Botanical flowers appear on *Hans Sloane plates. Fable paintings, usually illustrating Aesop, in colour or monochrome, e.g. by J. *O'Neale. Rococo style moulding after Meissen; silver shapes include vessels with applied flowers and twig handles; many tureens and boxes in wide range of vegetable, fruit, and animal shapes. Figures include oriental *blanc-de-chine* adaptations, Meissen-influenced birds with naturalistic colouring, *chinoiseries*, subjects after F. *Boucher, *commedia dell'arte* characters, classical and allegorical figures (e.g. by J. *Willems), and dwarfs after engravings of J. *Callot. *Toys, made from *c*1754, e.g. needle cases, and most frequently seals, usually modelled in form of figures, often with inscription in approximate French; scent bottles modelled initially on silver shapes or Chinese ceramic forms, Kuan Yin and Pu-Tai ho shang. Many different figure models made in early 1750s, such as girl seated on green marble plinth picking grapes, man with arms around woman against rose-tree. Bottles (1755–58) made in animal and bird shapes; also monks and nuns; bases gilt-rimmed, painted on underside with spray of flowers. Earlier models continued (1758–63) but with bases washed with green; lavish gilding.

In gold anchor period (1758–69), Sprimont proprietor. Meissen influence progressively replaced by Sèvres; rococo style prevalent. New ground colours, from 1759–60, include turquoise (from **bleu céleste*), crimson or claret (from somewhat different **rose Pompadour*), and *pea green; *mazarine blue in use from *c*1755. Much gilding by mercury process, sometimes used as ground colour for paintings. Products include elaborate table services and *garnitures de cheminée*. Simpler wares have black painting with green wash, some possibly from J. *Giles's studio. Painters include R. *Askew, J. *Donaldson, and Z. *Boreman. Gold anchor figures richly coloured and gilded, on rococo scrolled bases, often with elaborate *bocages*. Modellers include Willems and N-F. *Gauron, both from Tournai. Factory acquired by Duesbury and J. *Heath in 1770; used mainly to make tableware in style of *Derby until closure in 1784. *Illustrations at* bodkin case, goat-and-bee jug, Hans Sloane plates, knife and fork handles, scent bottle.

Chelsea-Derby. *See* Derby.

chenets. French term for *andirons, *creepers, and *firedogs.

chêng. Ancient Chinese bronze bell made during Shang and early Chou dynasties. In form similar to *chung, but without nipple decoration. Oval in section with wide mouth. Short, hollow handle for mounting on wooden pole, open end up. *cf* tui.

Cheng Ho. *See* Kuan ware.

Ch'êng Hua (1464–87). Chinese emperor, Ming dynasty. Reign noted for continuation of excellent porcelain work at *Ching-tê-chên factories. Five-colour enamel decoration (*wu ts'ai) main development. Best examples, 'chicken-cups', so-called after decorative motif. Blue-and-white ware has thinner, weaker cobalt-blue underglaze than earlier *Hsüan Tê items. Eggshell-thin bodies, thick glazes, characteristic. Much copied in later periods; earlier originals rare.

Cheng Tê (1506–21). Chinese Emperor of Ming dynasty. Came to throne when a child.

*Chest of drawers. English, William and Mary period. Walnut with drawers banded in contrasting wood; *bracket feet (probably later) and axe-drop handles.*

Blue-and-white porcelain decorated with inscriptions, e.g. from Koran, in Islamic script, reflecting influence of Moslem eunuchs who held power for most of reign. Most pieces, e.g. desk objects, brush-rests, boxes, ink-slabs, believed to be for Chinese rather than for export to Middle East. *Cobalt-blue colour clear, with slight green tinge. Pieces bear Emperor's *nien hao. Other products: blue-and-white bowls, ewers, *lei jars with dragon motif and four-character nien hao. Particularly notable *san ts'ai work, green dragons pursuing pearls, on bright yellow background, with incised effect round edge of colours like *Chinese *cloisonné* work. Overglaze *famille verte* became more common, a few pieces bearing nien hao; yellow monochromes also noteworthy.

chenille Axminster. Method of carpet manufacture called 'patent Axminster' introduced 1839 by James Templeton of Glasgow, Scotland; inspired by chenille fur then being used as curtain material. Invention revolutionized industry; allowed limitless number of colours and diversity of design in pieces ranging from cheap reversible rugs to rich pile carpets.

Ch'ên-tzŭ-shan (Chekiang). Chinese ceramic kiln site near Shang-lin Hu; active in Six Dynasties and T'ang periods. Produced high-quality celadon pieces, e.g. ewers, bowls, basins, engraved or incised under glaze with waves, lotus petals, and dragons.

cherub spoon. 17th century British and European silver spoon with knop representing cherub's head and neck.

chest. Used for storage. Earliest examples possibly made from hollowed out tree trunk; generally, rectangular or square, with hinged lid. Common in 16th and 17th centuries until superseded by *chest of drawers. *See* Armada chest, bachelor chest, blanket chest, *cassone*, Connecticut chest, Danzig chest, dowry chest, Hadley chest, lobby chest, mule chest, Nonsuch chest, Wellington chest.

Chesterfield brown ware. Salt-glazed stoneware made in area of Chesterfield, Derbyshire from mid 18th century. Puzzle jugs decorated with simple incised patterns or with figures and designs in relief; usually 7-8in. high. 1820-90, jugs decorated with hunting scenes or game subjects in relief; handles usually modelled in form of greyhounds; beak spouts, sometimes with mask below. Spirit flasks made from *c*1832 have tops modelled as busts of contemporary statesmen and politicians.

chestnut-roaster. Small, long-handled, pierced brass box with hinged lid for roasting chestnuts over open fire. English, 19th century.

chestnut-urn or **server.** 18th and 19th century urn-shaped container of Dutch origin for serving roast chestnuts. Made of silver or japanned metal; also Britannia metal until *c*1820, later of copper alloy.

chest of drawers. Piece of storage furniture with entire interior composed of drawer space, and façade of drawer fronts; developed in latter part of 17th century, but uncommon until 18th. *See* commode, tallboy.

chest-on-chest. *See* tallboy.

cheval, horse or **swing glass.** Long mirror, suspended between two columns resting on trestle-like feet; named after pulley mechanism (horse) used to adjust mirror angle. Small models on tables and chests date from mid 18th century; full-length examples from late 18th century.

Cheval glass. English, Regency period. Frame in bamboo turning.

cheval or **horse screen.** Fire or draught screen, with fabric-filled panel suspended between two vertical supports on trestle feet. Panel set in grooves and adjustable vertically. William and Mary style cheval screen has ornate pierced cresting. Late 17th century English examples based on European models; rarely, if ever, made in America.

cheveret. *See bonheur du jour.*

chia. Ancient Chinese bronze ritual vessel produced only during Shang dynasty; based on neolithic pottery prototype. Wine cup, mounted on three splayed legs, with handle, and capped with two pillars on lip, but with no spout (*cf* chüeh). Four-legged versions exist, but are rare.

Chia Ching (1521-66). Chinese emperor, Ming dynasty. Period marked by deterioration in quality of porcelain made at *Ching-tê-chên. Underglaze cobalt-blue noted for rich, dark brilliance. Taoism, dominant religion of reign, reflected in designs: emblems of immortality, e.g. pine or peach tree, deer, crane, and eight *'immortals'. Monochrome pieces (especially with tomato-coloured *iron-red enamel glaze), and gilt over-decoration important. New technique: bold painting with three enamel colours (chiefly yellow, purple, green), on biscuit (*see* san ts'ai). Items widely exported to West. *Illustration at* san ts'ai.

Chi-an or **Kian ware.** Chinese pottery produced near or at Chi-chou kiln site, Kiangsi province, in late T'ang and early Sung periods. Light grey body, sometimes with wash of dark slip, in imitation of Chien ware; covered with lustrous *temmoku glaze. Distinctive controlled glaze techniques, e.g. leaf placed on glaze before firing, producing vivid textured design. All-over underglaze patterning common: birds or flowers; palm-trunk or snake-skin effect. Some celadon ware, with dark green glaze, also produced.

Chiao-t'an (Chinese, 'altar of heaven'). Kiln site at Hang-chou in Chekiang province, discovered in 1929. Official factory for *Southern Sung Imperial court. Produced types of *Kuan ware; porcelain body, normally grey, varying from light to near black, with iron content of clay. Glaze colours: light brown to bluish-green or grey. Very finely potted; glaze applied in repeated layers until thicker than body. Luminous opacity caused by high lime content of glaze; invariably found with dense crackle. Best examples noted for jade, gem, or metallic feel. Forms: desk objects, e.g. small vases, brush-holders, bowls, incense burners, with square or fluted sections. Factories continued into Yüan, possibly even Ming times, although not under Imperial direction. *Illustration at* Hangchou.

Chia-pi-ts'un (Hopei). Largely unexplored kiln site near Tz'u-chou, active in Sui period. Produced early celadons, similar to *Yüeh ware, but in simpler form: thickly potted, roughly made, archaic forms, at times imitating bronze metal-work.

Chicaneau family. French makers of soft-paste porcelain at Saint-Cloud. Berthe Coudray (d *c*1722), widow of faience potter Pierre Chicaneau (d 1678) improved manufacturing process for soft-paste porcelain discovered by husband. In 1679, married to H-C. *Trou; continued in business with son, Pierre Chicaneau II (d 1707 or 1710), as manager. Widow of Pierre II established independent factory (1722) in premises of Saint-Cloud shop in Paris; this factory leased to cousin, Louis-Dominique-François Chicaneau; rejoined with Saint-Cloud under proprietorship of Henri *Trou II, *c*1742.

chichi carpets. *Very low pile, velvety *Kuba carpets woven by Chechen tribe. Medallion field with tiny hooked, stepped polygons, usually on indigo or medium blue ground. Main borders have flowers alternating with diagonal bands.

Chi-chou ware. Chinese ceramics named after important T'ang kiln site in Kiangsi province. White porcellanous ware; few surviving pieces. Sung *temmoku bowls, e.g. *Chi-an ware; and white-glazed items with incised decoration (*cf* Ting) also produced.

chicken-head spout. Decorative form found on early Chinese pottery of Han and T'ang periods. Especially noted on Yüeh ware, e.g. ewers. Produced at Chiu-yen and Tê-ch'ing kilns. One of several motifs adapted from bronze wares of same period.

chicken skin. White kid used for fan leaves in Europe from mid 17th century.

chien. Ancient Chinese ritual bronze shape: deep bowl, with grooved neck, and animal-mask handles (*see* t'ao-t'ieh), bearing hanging rings. Dates from *c*5th century B.C. Precise use uncertain, but possibly used as water vessel for ceremonial ablutions.

Ch'ien Lung (1736–95). Chinese Emperor of Ch'ing dynasty. Ceramics of his reign include, notably, imitation of other materials, e.g. bamboo, tarnished silver, carved jade. Archaistic copies of earlier periods, made notably of *Hsüan Tê pieces. **Famille rose* style predominated in enamel painting used even in monochrome; increasing European influence on style and technique. Brocaded surfaces (e.g. **kinrande chawan*) also popular. Blue painting went out of fashion, except for decoration of soft-paste porcelain. Monochrome and polychrome ware of Yung Chêng's reign further developed. *See* armorial porcelain, Nankin porcelain, Ku Yüeh Hsüan ware. *Illustrations at* apple-green, Kwang-tung, ox-blood, screen, Shou Lao.

*Chicken-head spout. On late 14th century stoneware ewer with brown-black glaze, probably from *Te-ch'ing kilns.*

Chien ware. Chinese pottery of Sung period, originally manufactured at Chien-an, Fukien province. Dark-brown stoneware body, with brownish-black *temmoku glaze, stopping short of foot and collecting in thick, treacly drops. Deep, straight-sided bowls typical. Glazes frequently imitated in other provinces. *See* Ting, T'zŭ-chou, Chi-chou, and Chi-an.

chiffonier. In England, open-shelved case piece, shaped like **commode à l'anglaise*, with front enclosed by metal-work frame. Designed to display books or china. Dates from 19th century.

chiffonnier. Tall, many-drawered **commode* designed for storing ladies' lightweight garments. Popular in Louis XV and XVI periods. *cf semainier.*

chih. Ancient Chinese ritual bronze vessel, of Shang and early Chou periods. Wine cup, generally with S-curved sides, sometimes with domed cover (especially more ornate examples). Stands on ring foot.

Chiffonier. *Louis XV, tulipwood and marquetry with shaped brass border to tabletop. Stamped Nicholas *Petit. Height 2ft3in.*

Ch'i-lin. *See* Kylin.

chime. Sound made when clock strikes hour, or hour-divisions on more than one bell, with different notes. Examples of chimes are ting-tang, and Cambridge or Westminster chime. *See* striking systems.

chimney-crane. Hinged wrought-iron mechanism of pulleys, swivels, ratchets, etc., attached to back wall of fireplace for suspending pot, kettle, etc., over fire; height and position adjustable. Also known as cobrell, cottrell, jib-crook, trammel, sway or swey (Scottish).

chimney glass. Mirror designed to fit chimney breast above fire-place; popular in 18th century. Early shape horizontal, becoming square, and then vertical. In early 18th century, made in three pieces, occasionally with fourth painted mirror. Popular subjects: landscapes, flowers, sporting scenes, and *chinoiserie* motifs. Gilt or wooden frames follow contemporary fashion in furniture.

chimney ornaments. Produced in Birmingham and elsewhere; highly popular from first half of 19th century. Best known are bronze and Britannia metal copies of the Marly horses by G. Cousteau (1677–1746), generally found in pairs. Other bronze, pewter, and Britannia metal ornaments include figures of Apollo, Mercury, Cupid, etc., and animals, birds and romanticized human figures, e.g. shepherdesses. Similar figures, were made of stamped brass and stood on wide bases. *cf garniture de cheminée.*

china. In 18th century England, many kinds of white porcelain, especially with blue painting in Chinese style. Came to denote translucent porcelain in 19th century. Now, often has restricted meaning of *bone china.

Chimney ornaments. Bronze by Alfred Stevens. c1855; design executed by Hode of Sheffield. Height 15in.

china cabinet or **case.** Case piece with glass-fronted upper section containing shelves for displaying china. Often surmounts chest of drawers, although bottom section may have doors in front enclosing storage space. Less common in America than Europe. Dates from 18th century.

china clay. *See* kaolin.

china stone. In crushed form, component of *hard-paste porcelain and bone china; equivalent of *petuntse discovered in Cornwall by W. *Cookworthy before 1758. Forms 20–30% of body of English bone china.

Chinese blue-and-white. *See* Chinese porcelain.

Chinese bronzes. Bronze alloy used in China contains 12–20% tin, often up to 20% lead, and remainder copper and impurities. Art of bronze casting probably pre-dates Shang dynasty; exact origin unknown. Earliest archaeological sites found to date are near Anyang, last Shang capital in northern Honan province. Sites yielding bronzes date from 15th century B.C. Earliest objects, weapons, chariot fittings, and ritual vessels used in sacrifice, show complete mastery of casting from clay moulds (*see* chia, chih, chüeh, fang-i, ku, kuang, tsun, yu). Up to 10th century B.C., decoration consisted of t'ao-t'ieh masks, cicada blades, whorl circles, thunder-cloud spirals, and interlocked Ts. Vessel forms probably derived from pottery prototypes. Decoration from 10th century B.C. through Han dynasty flatter, and monster motif used less except on handles. Designs more abstract with introduction of S-shaped, knotted, and spiral patterns covering entire surface. Forms of vessel more closely allied to contemporary ceramic shapes. During Chou dynasty, certain Shang forms disappeared; new shapes, *tou and *i, introduced. From 5th century B.C., Huai style emerged and openwork and inlay techniques introduced (*see* Ordos style, animal style). Small bronze objects, e.g. brooches, buckles, hooks, and harness trappings made, showing influence of western art through cultures of Steppe peoples. In late Chou period, humans depicted naturalistically for first time. Gilt bronzes first appeared; and inlaid work using gold, silver, and turquoise reached high standard by 3rd century B.C. Inscriptions widely used from late Shang period: recorded name of person for whom object made, and extolled his ancestors. *See* Chinese mirrors.

*Chinese bronzes. Bell of *chung form. Western Chou dynasty. Oval in section, with three pierced beak-shaped projections. Height 1ft4½in.*

Chinese carpets. Despite existence of highly developed Chinese textile art from antiquity, and documented use of carpets from 1122 B.C. (at court), no evidence of carpet-weaving in China before 17th century (needs of court supplied by eastern Turkestan imports). Industry developed under patronage of Emperor K'ang Hsi and grandson Ch'ien Lung. Floor and *pillar carpets woven primarily for court use; coarse Persian-knotted shaggy pile of good quality wool and coarse foundation with several wefts inserted between rows of knots. Designs employ range of Chinese symbolic motifs in pictorial composition framed by border. Palette limited, with large one-colour areas of blue or yellow with red or black. No deep colour except blue; patterns use much (Imperial) yellow. Carpets exported to West from 1850; new designs often westernized. Many rugs woven in silk to western notions of Chinese patterns.

Chinese celadon. High-fired, porcellanous *celadon ware with distinctive feldspathic green glaze. *Northern celadon olive or brownish-green, fired in oxidizing atmosphere; other prominent Sung celadons tend to blue-green, due to prevalence of reducing atmosphere in firing. Earliest type, Han dynasty *Yüeh. T'ang wares of similar class: *Grey, *Yo-chou, *Shou-chou, *Hung-chou, *Chi-an. Sung celadons considered finest: *Kuan, *Ko, *Ju. Production of *Lung-ch'üan, best-known variety, continued in Yüan and Ming periods. Copies of all celadons made in Ming and Ch'ing eras. *Illustrations at* brush-rest, iron-brown spots, Lung ch'üan, Yüeh.

Chinese carpet. c1870. 12ft4in.×9ft7in.

Chinese Chippendale style. *See* Chippendale style.

Chinese clocks. Timekeeping in China by *water clocks, *fire clocks etc., until introduction of mechanical clocks from Europe from 17th century; these often treated as toys, hence popularity of decorated cases, musical movements and centre-seconds hands. Chinese craftsmen made copies of European originals, usually of lower quality, reproducing all details including maker's signature.

Chinese cloisonné enamel. Earliest examples probably date from Yüan or Ming dynasties, when art was introduced from West. Byzantines used plates of gold, but Chinese worked on copper base. Partitions (*cloisons*) made by soldering on copper wire strips. Enamel powders then added inside *cloisons* and fired. After firing, rough surfaces polished, and exposed copper gilded. Fine Ming and K'ang Hsi examples, based on archaic forms, decorated in brilliant colours. Ch'ien Lung pieces tend to weaker forms and shallower colouring, but greater technical perfection. *See* Canton enamels.

Chinese duplex. *See* Chinese watch.

Chinese export porcelain. Early instance of export trade in Chinese ceramics is T'ang dynasty pottery found in Middle East. Sung celadons exported, mostly to East Indies, Japan, and south-east Asia. (Later, from 16th to early 17th century, *Swatow ware also popular there.) Most exported ware was blue-and-white porcelain, which first appears in Yüan period. Many examples found in *Ardebil Shrine collection, Tehran. Earliest European traders in China, in 16th and 17th centuries, Portuguese: first blue-and-white wares made exclusively for export trade for Portuguese market (*cf* Carrack porcelain). *Batavian ware named after Dutch East India Company's base in Indonesia, from which exported. Wares of late 16th and early 17th centuries almost entirely blue-and-white, of inferior quality to Imperial wares. Also in 16th century, *wu ts'ai and *san ts'ai armorial porcelain decorated with coloured enamel appeared, notably from reign of *Chia Ch'ing. Many examples from late 17th and early 18th centuries, especially *famille verte* or *famille rose* work, in purer Chinese taste, while *Mandarin or *Jesuit porcelain styles show strong European influence. **Blanc-de-chine* also exported; some examples painted on arrival in Europe. Many pieces also mounted in ormolu or silver in West, from 16th to 18th centuries. Western pieces sometimes sent to China for exact copying, e.g. *Oriental Lowestoft. In later periods, imitation of European styles became extensive at factories of Ching-tê-chên, both for Imperial and export wares. In late 18th and 19th centuries, quality deteriorated while Ch'ing dynasty shaken by political events. Effects of mass production and European imperialism in the East lessened interest in 'exotic' wares, and export declined.

Chinese glass. Earliest specimens of Chinese glass, dating from Han dynasty, mainly found

*China cabinet. Lacquered mahogany, probably by T. *Chippendale in Chinese style; pagoda-roofed top hung at corners with imitation bells, and supported on twisted columns. English, c1755. Height 4ft10in.*

Chinese clock. Table clock c1820. Enamel dial with centre-seconds hand; mechanism copied from contemporary English work, and bears spurious signature.

Chinese cloisonné enamel. Pair of quails and a duck. Ch'ien Lung period.

Chinese export porcelain. Dish, mid 18th century, depicting whale hunt; flag on ship is Batavian; fishermen probably from Zaan in northern Holland. Diameter 8in.

in tombs. Glass probably used as cheap substitute for jade in ritual objects, and carved in same manner. Pieces include jewellery, e.g. armlets, beads, and animal-shaped pendants, objects carved in insect shapes, particularly cicada, and flat discs with central hole (*pi). Blue or green glass used, generally containing barium (exclusive to Chinese glass). Little development until Ch'ing dynasty, as most glassware from intervening period imported, e.g. Islamic glass. Glass blowing probably introduced by 17th century Jesuits. In 1680 Emperor K'ang Hsi established glasshouse in Peking, producing blown glass vessels; most subject to *crizzling. Glass produced shows influence of *façon de Venise* (*latticinio* decoration and applied gadrooning); also Dutch-style diamond-engraving; few examples survive. Chinese glass makers soon reverted to moulded glassware, usually heavy, with an oily texture, decorated with lapidary carving or cutting. Reign of Yung Chêng produced fine opaque-white glass vases painted in softly coloured enamels. Under Ch'ien Lung most glassware imitated precious and semi-precious stones, e.g. onyx, chalcedony, jade, and rock-crystal; also lacquer or tortoiseshell, marble-like glass and aventurine glass, known as gold star glass. Wide variety of colours includes red, blue, and yellow. Cameo glass common, usually with several layers. Snuff bottles, rarely over 3in. high, made in all varieties, notably in opaque-white glass, delicately enamelled, occasionally inside as well as outside.

Chinese Imari. *See* Imari porcelain.

Chinese ivory. Earliest known examples date from Shang dynasty, found in excavations at Anyang (*cf* Chinese bronzes), e.g. small dragons, and tortoises. Most objects for ritual use. In Chou period, greater variety of purpose found: decoration of furniture, armrests, combs, etc., with angular geometric designs. Up to 6th century B.C., bone and walrus tusk used, later ivory imported from Siam, Burma, India, or Africa. Art continued through T'ang and Sung dynasties. Most pieces now found, dating from Ming dynasty onwards, depict deities, scholars, farmers, beggars, etc. In 1680, Emperor K'ang Hsi established ivory workshop employing Cantonese workers famous for skill, e.g. in carving 3–21 concentric openwork balls from single block. Canton ivory work usually delicate, complex, and left in natural colour; products of Peking school sometimes stained, etched, or lacquered. In Ch'ing dynasty, ivories became more varied: writing table objects, fans, toilet boxes, picture-frames, chess and other board-game sets, etc., besides screens or inlay work in furniture. Carving of human figures continued, but subject matter expanded to include female images e.g. *Kuan Yin. Ch'ing pieces appear technically perfect, but are less imaginative (*cf* ceramics of Ming and Ch'ing dynasties).

Chinese jade. Name given in West to hard-stones, nephrite and jadeite. Similar in appearance, with wide range of colour. Both very hard and do not mark when scratched with metal. Neither stone native to China. Nephrite probably imported from Central Asia (eastern Siberia) in neolithic era, but jade, from Burma, not until 18th century A.D.

In Shang dynasty, nephrite was probably cut using bamboo and stone tools on abrasive of quartz sand. Earliest jades form three categories, i.e. ritual objects, including *pi, *tsung, *kuei; weapons, including arrowheads and knives; and ornaments, including small figures in the round, and flat pendant plaques in

Chinese jade. Pi. Late Chou dynasty; both sides carved in relief with grain pattern (ku wên); raised borders around rim. Diameter 5⅝in.

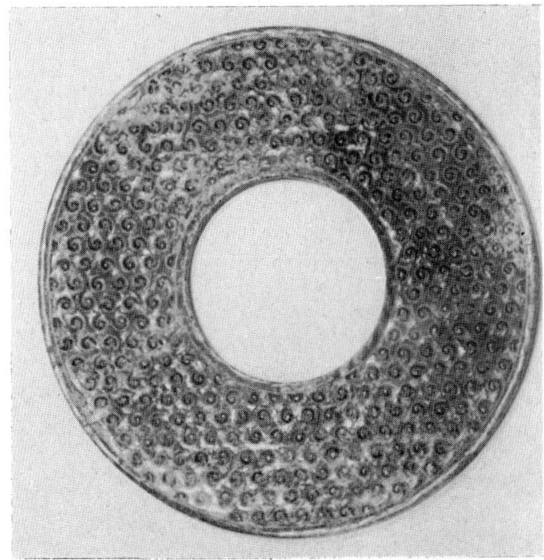

form of serpent, dragon, fish, bird, or cicada. During Chou dynasty, bronze tools probably used against abrasive of crushed garnets, allowing more detail, e.g. open work. Design similar to contemporary bronze decoration. Possibly use of corundum as abrasive, and iron tools, enabled Han dynasty jade workers to produce amulets and decorative pieces nearly perfect in form. Tradition carried through T'ang, Sung and Ming dynasties, when jade vessels similar to archaic bronze forms produced, e.g. vases, cups, seals, and dishes. Finest Ch'ing dynasty examples made in reign of Ch'ien Lung; mountains carved from jade boulders with high relief landscapes; bowls, flowers and panels for screens.

Forms known as mutton fat jade (pure white nephrite), spinach jade (dark green nephrite with black flecks, from Siberia), and chicken bone (white nephrite fired to dead matt tone).

Chinese lacquer. Resinous sap of lac tree (*Rhus vernicifera*) which may be coloured, then applied in thin layers to surface being treated. When dry, extremely hard and resistant to salt and acid. Origin in China obscure, but found as inlay on some Shang dynasty bronze vessels, as glue, and as protection for wood. During Chou dynasty, used as decorating and painting medium on wooden boxes, weapons, and pottery, and reached peak of technical achievement by Han Dynasty when, with silk, lacquer wares main Chinese export to western Asia. Predominant pigments used were iron sulphate (black), cinnabar (red), white lead (white), chromium (green), cadmium (yellow). By Tang dynasty, three techniques developed: lacquer carving; lacquer inlaid with mother-of-pearl (*lac burgauté*); also process known as dry lacquer and modelled over wooden armature, removed once lacquer was dry. Objects decorated with lacquer during Ming and Ch'ing dynasties include screens, tables, chairs, boxes, trays, and vases; however, as technical skill increased, pieces lost original simplicity.

Chinese lacquer. Screen, reign of Ch'ien Lung (1736–95). Height 5ft8in.

Chinese-market clocks. Clocks made specially for export to China by English makers in late 18th century. Design highly ornate, frequently incorporating special effects; examples with revolving glass bars to create impression of cascading water, or with two lotus flowers, one opening as the other closes, at the hours. Dials often include centre-seconds hand.

Chinese mirrors. Made of bronze with high tin content from 5th century B.C. to 10th century A.D. Usually circular. One surface highly polished, other decorated in relief. Earliest examples decorated with Huai style motifs. 4th century B.C. decoration T-shaped, resembling character Shou: mountain. In 2nd century B.C., TLV and cosmic types. TLV named after decoration resembling initials. Cosmic type decorated with complicated symbolism, including 12 Branches (zodiac symbols), Animals of Four Quarters: Tortoise and Snake, The North; Green Dragon, The East; Scarlet Bird, The South; White Tiger, The West. Sometimes included TLV motif. Cosmic mirrors often inscribed with Taoist exhortations. By T'ang dynasty, design mainly decorative, with gold and silver inlay and lobed and foliate rims.

Chinese market clock. English gilt-metal and enamel mantel clock, c*1770, attributed to J. *Cox, and said to have been looted from Royal Palace at Peking during Boxer risings.*

Chinese porcelain. *Kaolin and *petuntse both found in abundance near *Ching-tê-chên in central Kiangsi, centre of industry from 14th century A.D. Porcelain paste covered with thin, feldspathic glaze, fired at *c*1300–1500°C, produces tough, thin, semi-opaque body, with brilliant, luminous colour, unique in porcelain. Technique first developed in *T'ang period, in Yüan and Ming dynasties. Blue-and-white porcelain, made with underglaze *cobalt-blue, foremost type produced for following 600 years (*see* Chinese export porcelain), but *copper-red glaze work also popular. In *Ming dynasty, both Imperial and private kilns flourished at Ching-tê-chên. *Nien hao (reign marks) introduced at this time; those of Emperors *Hsüan Tê, *Ch'êng Hua, *Chia Ching, *Wan Li and *T'ien Chi important. Chief developments of Ming dynasty: three-colour and five-colour enamelled porcelains; gold-leaf decoration used; and increase in export porcelain. *Mei p'ing, or baluster shaped vases, massive jars (e.g. *tsun), ewers, and plates common shapes. Decorative elements include dragons, *Three Friends, phoenixes, scrolls of lilies, lotus blossom, poppies, chrysanthemums, and floral sprays. In 16th century, Taoist motifs, e.g. *Immortals, introduced. By reign of Wan Li, local clay materials becoming exhausted, and porcelain began to vary in quality. In following *Ch'ing

Chinese watches. Left: anonymous, 19th century, eight-day movement, white enamel dial with steel hands and centre-seconds hand; border bezel and pendant set with half pearls. Diameter $2\frac{1}{2}$in. Centre: gold and enamel single case watch by William Ilbery, no. 6267, early 19th century. Right: anonymous, c1800, white enamel dial with pierced blued-steel hands and second hand; gold and enamel single case bordered with half pearls.

Ch'ing dynasty. Blue-and-white porcelain jar with cap cover. Four upright panels with rockery and plants; on shoulders ju-i shaped lappets with foliage scrolls and ju-i heads between; lotus flower on cover. Height 8in.

dynasty, Emperor *K'ang Hsi rebuilt (1681) Imperial factory at Ching-tê-chên. First new director-general, *Tsang Ying-hsüan, developed many new glazes and polychrome enamels (*see famille verte*). Later *Nien Hsi-Yao and *T'ang Ying supervised remarkable copies of earlier *Sung period wares. Important *nien hao*: *K'ang Hsi, *Chia Ching, Ch'ien Lung, and Yung Chêng. *Soft-paste porcelain also used, mostly for small objects, e.g. *snuff bottles. Influence from western art noticeable in paintings of 18th century porcelain, with landscapes, figures, birds, and use of shading or perspective. *Ku Yüeh Hsüan wares date from this period. (Porcelain for palace use, made in Imperial factories, finer in execution and decorative technique than export porcelain from private, commercial kilns.) Late *Ch'ing ware decorated with *famille verte* and other colours, deteriorating into gaudy and artificial shades. Imitations of chiselled gold, embossed silver, carved jade, **cloisonné* work popular. Foreign pieces, e.g. Dutch Delft ware, Limoges enamels, and Imari from Japan sources of inspiration. In 19th century, industry declined through lack of Imperial encouragement, and political disruption.

Chinese watch, Chinese duplex watch, or **Fleurier watch.** Watch made in Switzerland from late 18th century for Chinese market. Sometimes sold in pairs. Circular shape, diameter 2–6in.; case silver, gilt-metal, or gold. Richly ornamented, painted, and engraved; pearls used as decoration on frame and pendant; sometimes worked into pictorial design. Some examples represent figures in Swiss national costume. Produced in Geneva or cantons of Vaud and Jura, for Geneva dealers; active industry in Fleurier, Neuchâtel, from *c*1825. Watch known as Chinese duplex, after form of duplex escapement, invented *c*1830; large centre-seconds hand on dial. Musical watches of this type also manufactured for export.

Ch'ing dynasty (1644–1912). Chinese period beginning with invasion of Manchus, supplanting Ming dynasty. Rulers showed enthusiasm for absorbing Chinese tradition of culture, and patronage of arts: e.g. *K'ang Hsi and *Ch'ien Lung. Towards end of period, self-conscious formalism and perfection in techniques, e.g. ceramics, lacquer-work, jade, etc., produced ornate work lacking freshness of colour or simplicity of form. Increase in export trade through East India Companies also led to lowering of standards at home, and to eclectic approach to art styles, e.g. borrowing of designs from European painting and ceramics. *See* Chinese export porcelain; *famille verte, famille rose*; Chinese jade; Chinese lacquer-work.

Ching-pai or **Ying-ch'ing ware.** Chinese pottery of Sung period, manufactured in Kiangsi and Hopei provinces. Thin, translucent, pale buff body, with sugary texture when broken. Pale blue glaze covers carved decoration of foliage, spiral scrollwork, dragons, or waves. Conical-shaped bowls common (occasionally with copper rim sheaths). Some *mei p'ing vases, and stem cups. Continued in Yüan period: predecessor of blue-and-white porcelain of Yüan and Ming eras. *cf* Shu-fu.

Ching-tê-chên or **Kingtechen Imperial kilns.** Chinese ceramic factory established by Emperor *Hung Wu in 1369 at site in central Kiangsi, famous for pottery production since early *Sung period. Made porcelain exclusively for palace use, *Shu-fu earliest type. Factories expanded in 1681. Imperial porcelain, notably blue-and-white, produced in large quantities in *Ming and *Ch'ing periods; widely exported. *See* Tsang Ying-hsüan, Lang T'ing-chi, Yung Chêng.

chinoiseries. Western adaptation of Chinese shapes and motifs used on furniture, silver, ceramics etc. Mid to late 17th century interest in Orient fostered by East India Companies' introduction into Europe of e.g. porcelain, lacquer-work, and by new travel books on the East. Fashion revived during rococo period in mid 18th century. Characteristics of style are pagoda shapes, fretwork and Chinese-type finials; motifs include figures of mandarins, coolies, and pagods; birds, butterflies, landscapes, river scenes, etc.

In furniture, *chinoiseries* extensively used with lacquer-work, influenced by publication of A Treatise on Japanning and Varnishing by Stalker and Parker, 1688, which gave designs and motifs in Chinese style. Such motifs also engraved on silver porringers, tankards, toilet services, etc., of mid 17th century and painted on contemporary Delft and early porcelain (at Vienna and by I. *Preissler, J. *Aufenwerth, and B. *Seuter). Polychrome *chinoiseries*, often within elaborate cartouches, painted at Meissen by J. G. *Herold in 1720s. *Chinoiserie* designs frequent on Dutch Delft and on faience made e.g. at Rouen and Sinceny.

From *c*1740, Chinese forms and motifs

Ch'ing-pai. Bottle of soft bluish glaze; shoulder applied, with carved feng with streaming tail; probably Yüan dynasty.

Chinoiserie. *Chair after design by W. *Chambers. Bamboo with turned ivory finials. Late 18th or early 19th century.*

returned to popularity; many further designs circulated. Furniture was often in pagoda shapes with dragon finials; much carved fretwork and other oriental or quasi-oriental characteristics, including painting or lacquering and gilding. Embossed or engraved *chinoiseries* reappeared on rococo style silver teapots, tea kettles, caddies, etc.; silver épergnes made in pagoda shape. In ceramics, *chinoiseries* painted in gilt on dark grounds at Sèvres; also notably on porcelain at Bristol; transfer-printed on Caughley and Lowestoft porcelain. *Chinoiserie* figures made e.g. at Meissen, Höchst, and Frankenthal; also at Chantilly, Mennecy, and Saint-Cloud.

Chinese style enjoyed short revival in England during Regency, e.g. in fittings for Brighton Pavilion.

Chiodo family. Italian maiolica potters at Savona in late 17th and early 18th centuries. Painted animals and plants in sketchy style with bright colours, often light blue; influenced by late Ming porcelain. Mark: trumpet with triangular pennant.

chip carving. Incised decoration based upon geometric forms. Found on chests from 13th century.

Chippendale border. *See* pie-crust border.

Chippendale style. Furniture style in England *c*1754–80, in America *c*1760–85, based on T. *Chippendale's The Gentleman and Cabinet-Maker's Director (1754, 1755, 1762) containing designs for a wide range of furniture. Style basically rococo, with elements of Chinese, Gothic, and neo-classical design. Designs in The Director originally considered exclusively Chippendale's, and furniture in that idiom from his workshop alone; however, H. *Copland and M. *Lock since established as responsible for some designs; also, many so-called Chippendale pieces designed and made by other cabinet makers, including W. *Ince and J. Mayhew, W. *Vile and J. *Cobb, G. *Grendey, and W. *Hallett. Rococo elements in Chippendale's designs reflect Louis XV influence, e.g. undulating line of seat rails and chair backs, and carving, gilding, and chair-back motifs (particularly ribbon back). Unlike French rococo furniture, bronze mounts seldom appear in Chippendale rococo (although used on late pieces with neo-classical elements). *Chinoiseries* incorporated in rococo designs include fretwork (pierced, or card-cut and applied on solid ground), lacquer-work, and pagoda-shaped roofs on case furniture and testers. Pieces featuring such motifs known as 'Chinese Chippendale'. In other designs, Gothic cusps and arches, cluster columns, and tracery occur. Generally, carving is predominant form of decoration. Brass bail handles characteristic, also light cabriole legs with whorl feet and straight legs of square section.

From 1760s, R. *Adam's neo-classicism began to influence Chippendale's work: pieces finished in satinwood veneer and marquetry. In later work (*c*1775), some painted decoration also used. Common upholstery fabrics include leather, brocade, and tapestry. *Illustrations at* barometer, china cabinet, corner chair, kettle base, pier glass, shelves, spinet.

Chippendale, Thomas the Elder (1718–79). English cabinet maker, whose workshop produced some of finest quality furniture in rococo and neo-classical styles. Published The Gentleman and Cabinet-Maker's Director (1754, 1755 and with additional plates, 1762), which was first important published book of furniture designs, with widespread influence. Partner of James Rannie *c*1753–66, then from 1771 with Thomas Haig as Chippendale, Haig & Co.

Chippendale, Thomas the Younger (1749–1822). English, son of T. *Chippendale the Elder. Upholsterer and cabinet maker to Duke of Gloucester. After father's death, partner of Thomas Haig until 1822.

chiselled steel. Small steel articles with chiselled decoration fashionable from 16th to 18th centuries. Mounts for swords and fire-arms, scissors, snuff-boxes, thimbles, tweezers, decorated with floral and mythical subjects in Brescia, Italy; chatelaines, *étuis*, shuttles, and snuff-boxes also made in Paris. Similar work done in Germany, Russia (*Tula), and England (*Woodstock).

chitarrone. *See* lute.

Ch'iung-lai. Chinese ceramics kiln site, in Szechwan province, active in Six Dynasties period. Thought chiefly to have made *Yüeh-type ware. Few examples known.

Chiu-yen (Chinese, 'nine rocks'). Ancient kiln site in Chekiang province, discovered in 1936. Important from Han to Six Dynasties. Typical are chicken-head spouts, animal masks, and bizarre forms, e.g. frogs, toads, lions, bears, monkeys. Ancient name for nearby Shao-hsing hsien, Yüeh-chou, leads to term *Yueh, used

Chocolate pot. Wooden handle and lidded spout; finial on lid can be removed for stirring chocolate. Silver. By J. Clifton, 1709; stand by William Gamble, London 1718. Height 9¼in.

for ware produced here and at many sites in Chekiang and Fukien provinces. Products featured concave base with brown haloes where piece rested on lumps of clay during firing. Celadon glaze sometimes putty-coloured. Most surviving objects funerary ware (*see* ming ch'i).

chocolate-pot. Silver pouring vessel indistinguishable from *coffee-pot except in versions with hinged or sliding finial on top of cover to permit insertion of rod for stirring contents. Hot chocolate at height of popularity in England and France *c*1675–*c*1725. Rarely made in Sheffield plate.

Chodor or **Chaudor carpets.** Turkoman carpets of Chodor tribe, with distinctive chestnut or violet-brown ground. Rows of diamond-shaped guls in contrasting colours form diagonal colour bands within zig-zag lattice broken by tiny geometrical figures. Also all-over flower-head pattern.

Chodowiecki, Daniel (1726–1801). Polish enamel painter, etcher, and book illustrator, working in Berlin. Copied engravings and painted enamel snuff-boxes. Painted miniatures from 1745. Became chief artistic adviser to Frederick II. *See* Berlin school.

chopin. Scottish measure of 4 Scots gills (1½ Imperial pints); also pewter measure of this capacity, made from 17th century.

chopnet or **chopnut.** *See* salt.

Chou dynasty (*c*1027–221 B.C.). Chinese period under domination of Chou people, probably originally vassals of Shang régime. Period divides into two. Western Chou had capital at Chang-an (*c*1027–771 B.C.); no cultural change, merely development from Shang. Eastern Chou: capital moved to Lo-yang; period of expansion known as The Spring and Autumn Annals (771–481 B.C.); appearance of philosophers, Confucius and Lao Tzu (Taoism). Period of decline known as The Warring States (481–221 B.C.). Ming ch'i pottery funerary wares probably introduced, replacing human sacrifice in religious ceremonies. *See* Chinese bronzes, Chinese jade, Huai style, Ordos style.

Chou dynasty. Vase, unglazed with mat markings.

Chrismatory. Pewter, early 17th century. Height 4in.

Christening mug. By William Bainbridge, 1698. Decorated with fluting and matting which strengthened thin silver fashionable at this time.

chrismatory. Container, usually as set of three small flasks (ampullae) for holy oil; in use from early times. Earliest surviving examples of ampullae, *c*1290, belong to cathedral of Ratisbon (now Regensburg, Bavaria). Only wealthiest churches and abbeys owned silver or silver-gilt examples; most were brass or pewter. Enamel ornament common.

christening cup. Small silver *mug or covered cup given as christening gift, mainly in 19th century Britain and America. Copied older styles; ornament normally embossed or engraved. Name or initials of child, date of birth, etc., engraved on body.

christening goblet. Silver goblet, usually with chased and/or embossed ornament, favoured as christening gift by British royalty in 19th century. Sometimes accompanied by knife, fork, and spoon.

christening spoon. Silver spoon given by godparent to child at christening; single *apostle spoon with knop in form of apostle whose name child bears, or set of apostle spoons, may have been given in Britain from 16th to mid 17th century; sometimes inscribed. Other knop spoons with pricked or engraved initials and/or dates may also have served this purpose.

Christian, Philip (fl mid 18th century). Porcelain maker at Shaw's Brow, Liverpool; associate and successor to R. *Chaffers. Products include large porcelain vases in Chinese style, tortoiseshell glazed earthenware in round and octagonal forms, and fine tableware.

chronometer. Exact timekeeper: usually, as marine chronometer, timepiece with spring detent *escapement. Originally developed in 18th century to keep accurate time at sea for establishing longitude; pioneered by work of J. *Harrison. Later developed by makers including the *Arnolds, T. *Earnshaw and E. J. *Dent in England and A-L. *Breguet in France. Variation by Dent chronometer of only 0·54 seconds in 12 months recorded during trials at Greenwich (1829). Marine chronometers in drum-shaped brass case suspended in gimbals in wooden box, with one, two, or eight day movements, often with up-and-down indicator hand on dial to show state of winding. Box usually mahogany with observation glass covered by lid. Other features of movement may include *tourbillon (in pocket chronometers) and special forms of *compensation.

chronometer escapement or **spring detent escapement.** *See* escapement.

chronoscope. *See* wandering-hour watch.

Ch'u-chou ware. Chinese ceramic wares produced in southern Sung, Ming, and Ch'ing periods, near Hangchow. Kilns once thought to have moved from *Lung-ch'üan at beginning of Ming era to this site (near *Li-shui) causing change of descriptive term for later pieces of Lung-ch'üan group; in fact manufacture spread over wide area, including this site, in Ming period.

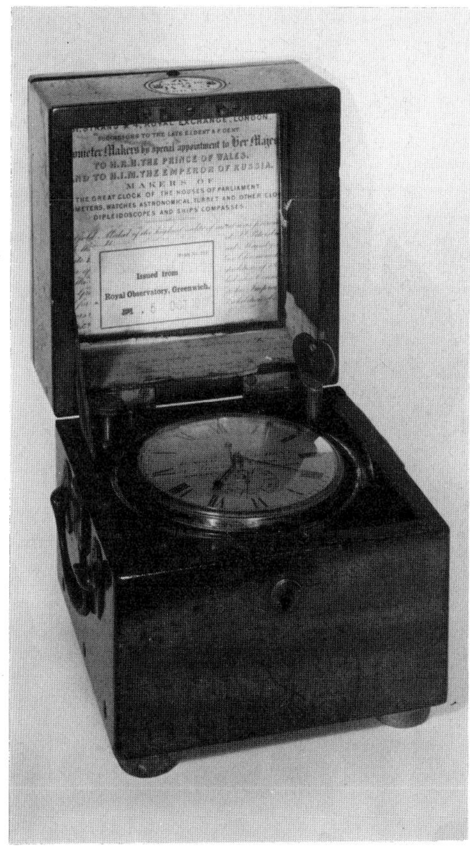

Chronometer. Made by Arnold & Dent, c1830; movement on gimbals in brass-bound case; mahogany box. Length $5\frac{1}{2}$in.

chüeh (in jade). *See* pi.

chüeh. Ancient Chinese ritual bronze vessel produced during Shang and early Chou dynasties: wine cup on three splayed, pointed legs, handle to one side, standing over one leg,

Chüeh. Wine vessel; tapering tripod legs of triangular section; centre decorated with frieze of t'ao t'ieh masks. Shang dynasty. Height $8\frac{1}{4}$in.

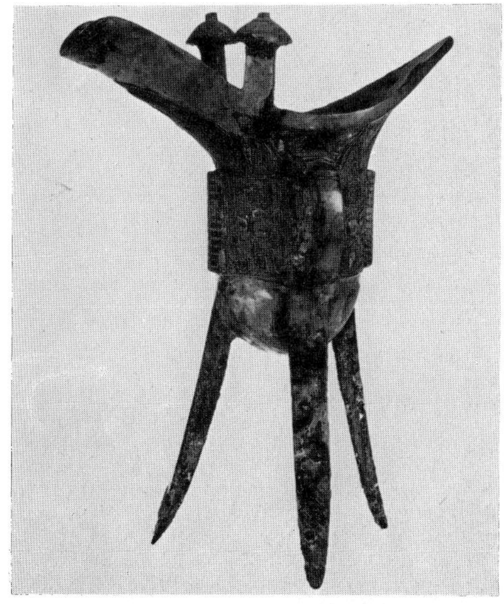

and usually bearing bovine mask. At right angle to handle, lip extends on one side into wide, rounded channel spout, and on other rises to a point. On both sides of vessel, where body joins spout, two short columns rise, surmounted by caps, domed and sometimes decorated with spiral pattern (*cf* chia). Rarer chiao lacks columns over mouth, and has pointed ends to both spout pieces. Derived from neolithic ceramic form, and possibly originally from ox-horn or gourd vessel (*see* ku).

chufti knot. *See* jufti knot.

chung. Ancient Chinese bronze bell without clapper, made from 9th century B.C. Shape wider at base than top; top flat and elliptical in section. Decorated with nipple design in rows. Hung mouth down by handle, often made of two beasts confronting each other. *cf* chêng, tui.

Ch'ün-shan (Kiangsu). Chinese ceramic kiln site near I-hsing. Active during Six Dynasties; mainly produced *Yüeh celadon. Fragments of ewers, bowls, basins discovered, with incised or impressed motifs: waves, lotus petals, dragons, phoenixes, or other birds.

Chün ware. Chinese pottery named after kilns founded in Sung period at Chün Chou (now Jü Hsien), Honan province. Opalescent blue, thick-glazed ware mostly with purple or crimson *flambé according to degree of oxidation of copper in glaze. Style continued into Ming period. Buff stoneware body, left bare at foot; base usually unglazed; notably numbered flower pots and bulb bowls, deep purple outside, pale lavender inside, with Chinese numeral (1–10) incised under base: significance uncertain. Sometimes fine *crackle glaze instead of *flambé*, or network of grooves or wandering lines. Green ware with denser glaze than celadon also manufactured, notably small objects (e.g. water pots, table boxes, shallow foliate dishes) with design features in common with Northern celadon ware.

*Chün ware. Above: bottle, *Sung dynasty, greyish white porcellanous ware burnt brown on unglazed edge of base; height 11½in. Below: bulb bowl or flower pot stand, Sung dynasty; oblong quatrefoil shape on four cloud scroll feet; incised numeral chiu (9) on base and ring of spur marks; length 6¾in.*

church fan. 18th century English fan printed with Biblical scenes and/or quotations; carried by churchgoers.

Churrigueresque style. Spanish baroque style based on 17th and 18th century architecture, named after José Churriguera (d 1725), leading exponent of style. Furniture with elaborate carving and spiral turning, gilding, floral inlay, and painted mythological and biblical scenes.

Churrigueresque style. Spanish folding table in light walnut, 17th century, with original irons supporting legs.

ciborium. Gold or silver-gilt covered cup; used in churches from 13th century, initially to expose consecrated wafer or carry it in procession (superseded by *monstrance), later to hold wafers for consecration. Bowl of cup larger than that of *chalice; domed or hemispherical cover is surmounted by a cross (in 17th and 18th centuries, sometimes by a pelican). Ornament similar to that of chalice. Not used by Reformed churches, (except by Anglo-Catholics from late 19th century). *Illustration also at* Spanish silver.

Ciborium. French, c1500, made at Perpignan. Hexagonal turret form in Gothic style, with Virgin and child finial and lion couchant feet of slightly later date. Height 13in.

cider glass. English drinking glass, similar to ale glass, but engraved with apple blossom or trees. Usually flute-shaped; opaque-twist stem with central knop, mounted on high, spreading foot. Popular from mid 18th century. *Illustration at* flute.

cider pitcher. Round-bellied jug with lid and decorative thumbpiece. Pierced backing to spout prevents sediment escaping. Made in pewter in 1–3 pint sizes, from late 18th to mid 19th century.

cigar box. Rectangular silver or Sheffield plate box with close-fitting, air-tight lid, used for cigars in Britain, Germany, and Holland from early 19th century. German and Dutch examples often have embossed or die-stamped genre scenes.

cigogne. *See décor Coréen.*

cimaise, cymaise, cimarre, or **cymarre.** 14th–16th century pewter flagon for wine to be offered to visiting royalty or dignitary, chiefly in France and Belgium. One handle at side for pouring; carried by a swing handle, attached to top by loops.

Cinquecento (Italian, '16th century'). Refers particularly to Italian art and literature of high *Renaissance period.

Cipriani, Giovanni Battista (1727–85). Florentine decorative painter and draughtsman. In England from 1755, was early promulgator of neo-classical style, reflected in his decorative and historical painting. *Illustration at* urn clock.

cire-perdue. *See* lost-wax process.

Cistercian wares. English pottery made in 16th and 17th centuries, commonly found on abbey sites; hard red earthenware body covered with brilliant brownish-black glaze, occasionally decorated with applied circles of white clay or trails of white slip showing yellow through

Clair de lune. *Waterpot, *K'ang Hsi; engraved with three archaic style dragon scroll medallions. Height* 4½*in.*

glaze. Vessels include tygs, cups, and tall cylindrical mugs.

cittern. Wire-stringed musical instrument in use in Britain and Europe from Middle Ages; early form known as *citole* until early 16th century. Played with *plectrum until late 16th century, when finger-plucking adopted. Body is squat pear-shape; back flat; depth of body originally tapered towards neck. Number of strings (paired) varied throughout history; fretted; central sound-hole usually covered with *rose. Size also varied. Extremely popular from late 16th century in Britain and Europe; commonly found in barber's shop for entertaining patrons. In 18th century, form known as English guitar popular among amateurs; disappeared in 19th century. Body usually wooden; body and head often elaborately ornamented with carving, inlay, painting, etc.

clair de lune. Very pale bluish glaze, used (rarely) on Chinese porcelain in K'ang Hsi period (1662–1722); examples of high quality made (1726–36) under *Nien Hsi-yao in reign of Yung Chêng.

clap table. *See* console table.

claret jug. 18th and 19th century British jug, of silver or silver gilt or with glass body and generally extensive silver or silver-gilt mounts; some early 19th century examples stoppered, after *c*1830 hinged cover common. Frosted or coloured glass popular; mounts often ornamented with cast or embossed grape and vine motifs. Variety of body shapes, e.g. ovoid, pear-shaped.

classical revival. *See* neo-classical style.

Clauce or **Gloss,** Isaak Jakob (1728–1803). German miniature painter, working at Meissen porcelain factory (c1753). At *Wegely's factory, Berlin (1754–55). Credited with enamel snuff-box and some porcelain at Berlin porcelain factory, continuing after 1763. Rarely signed work.

clavichord. Stringed keyboard musical instrument of rectangular box shape (up to 4ft2in. long, 12in. wide); keyboard on long front side (*cf* spinet); metal strings (two per note) run parallel to keyboard from hitch pins on player's left to tuning pins on right. Sound produced, when key depressed, by small piece of metal (tangent) set up on rear portion of key which strikes and vibrates string from below; sound dampened (muted) by contact of string between tangent and hitch pin with felt strip. Origin of clavichord uncertain; probably existed from mid 14th century. Extremely popular in France until end of 17th century and in Germany, until late 18th century; less popular in Britain (replaced by spinet) or Italy. From mid 18th century, commonly supplied with separate stand or legs of screw type. Wooden case often elaborately ornamented with inlay, carving, painting, etc.

claw foot. Foot shaped like talon; of oriental origin. Commonly used on 18th century silver vessels.

claw or **tripod table.** Occasional table, with top square, rectangular, round, etc., mounted on column with tripod base. Top may be hinged to fall vertically when not in use, as with *snap table. Dates from 18th century; made in Britain, Europe, and America.

Clay, Henry. English developer of type of papier mâché, patented 1772. Worked in Birmingham; made boxes, tea-caddies, trays, and furniture. Boxes lacquered black and painted with pastorals, classical scenes, or contemporary English portraits.

Clayton, David (fl early 18th century). English silversmith working in London; specialized in miniature silver (e.g. beakers, tankards, tea services, warming pans, etc.). Mark in 1697, C enclosing L; in 1720, DC.

Cleffius, Lambert (d 1691). Dutch potter; maker of red earthenware teapots in Delft from 1678. Owner of The Metal Pot factory until death. Shareholder in The Peacock factory. In 1684, member of trade delegation sent to revive trade in England. Also made blue-and-white Delft ware, including wigstand, and covered bowl with compartments for spices or tea, initialled LC.

Claret jug and stand. Frosted glass jug with applied pierced and chased fruiting vines; handle in form of vine branch; hinged lids with crown terminals. English, made by John S. Hunt, 1844. Height 14*in.*

Clement Augustus service. Armorial service decorated by C. F. *Herold (1735) with *chinoiseries.* Made at Meissen for Clement Augustus, Archbishop Elector of Cologne. A later service made 1741 with painted hunting scenes in *saxe ombré*, and gilded pilgrim shells in applied relief; marked with monogram CA, crowned, enclosed in ribbon, and cross of Grand Master of Teutonic Knights.

Clement, William (member Clockmakers' Company, 1677). English clock maker; pioneered use of anchor escapement. Maker of long-case and lantern clocks; turret clocks dated 1670 and 1671.

clepsydra. Form of *water clock, used in antiquity.

Clerici, Felice (fl mid and late 18th century). Italian maiolica potter. Worked in Milan from 1745; owner of maiolica factory. Copied Japanese vases in Imari style. Decoration includes *chinoiseries*, pastoral scenes, and *commedia dell'arte* figures. Marks include 4 over Greek letter omega with C or FC, below Milano.

Clérissy, Joseph (1649–85). French faience maker. From 1677, director of faience factory at Saint-Jean-du-Désert, near Marseille. Products influenced by Nevers and Moustiers include large dishes, ewers, and vases, painted in blue, usually with outlines in purple. Subjects include Chinese figures, shepherds, and biblical subjects. Rarely decoration includes thin polychrome washes in addition to blue painting. Some later pieces in **style Berain*; example dated 1718. Signed work sometimes marked: *a St Jean du desert.*

Clérissy, Pierre (1651–1728). French faience maker, brother of J. *Clérissy. Son of earthenware potter at Moustiers. Established faience factory there, *c*1679. Director until 1728. Made finely-potted faience with brilliant glaze, decorated in blue. Hunting scenes, biblical, or mythological subjects (e.g. Labours of Hercules), painted in centre panels of large dishes; borders sometimes incorporate masks, with tracery of flowers and foliage. Later style, from *c*1710, in manner of J. *Berain, and influenced by Rouen or Nevers. Succeeded by son Antoine (1673–1743), partner from 1710, and grandson Pierre II (1704–94), director from 1736, who was made baron and retired in 1774, selling factory to owner of rival pottery in Moustiers. Some signed pieces marked: *chez Clerissy a Moustiers.*

Clews, James and Ralph (fl *c*1814–37). Potters at Cobridge, Staffordshire; made black basalt with brittle body, high gloss, and engine-turned decoration. Mark: CLEWS. By 1817, acquired pottery at Cobridge; produced fine transfer-printed earthenware, much exported to America. Designs include series of American views, Zoological Garden views, Don Quixote, Aesop's Fables, and Doctor Syntax series; also The Landing of Lafayette (1824). After closure of pottery in 1834, James Clews started pottery at Troy, Indiana; returned in 1836 after failure.

Cleyn, Francis (d 1658). Danish court painter

Clichy vase. Blue and white spiral opaque glass, c1860. Height 9½in.

to King Christian IV. In England, court painter to James I. From 1624, chief artistic designer at *Mortlake tapestry works. Designs include seven-piece Hero and Leander; Royal Horses.

Clichy. Glass works founded 1837 in Billancourt, Paris; made cheap glassware for export. Moved (1844) to Clichy-la-Garenne. Specialized in cameo, filigree, and *millefiori* glass; also coloured and painted opal glass. Only French glasshouse represented at 1851 Great Exhibition in London. Noted for brightly coloured paperweights, particularly swirl patterned, often signed with C and incorporating rose in design. Merged with Sèvres glassworks in 1875. *See* paperweights.

clobbering. Addition of enamel decoration to blue-and-white porcelain, usually Chinese. Pieces from Worcester, Chelsea, and Lowestoft clobbered in London *c*1825–50; also Meissen blue-and-white porcelain enamelled by F. J. *Ferner in mid 18th century.

clock. Originally, mechanical timekeeper with striking mechanism, now refers to many devices for time measurement not designed to be worn (*see* watch). In Europe mechanical clocks began to replace *water clocks, *sundials, etc., in late 13th century, probably first in Italy, but were confined to churches, monasteries, etc. Appearance of domestic clock in 15th century led to development of national styles. Timekeeping was erratic before use of pendulum and balance spring, *c*1675, followed by attainment of high accuracy in *chronometers and *precision clocks.

Outside Europe mechanical clocks were late

Clock case. Meissen porcelain, c1750, on separate stand. Gilded borders, relief figures and applied flowers. Height approximately 20in.

Clock watch. French, made by Jean Baptiste Duboule c1660. Strikes hours; fitted with alarm. Silver case and protective outer leather case with silver pin-work decoration.

introduction, e.g. *Japanese clocks, wide use being made of devices such as water clocks and *fire clocks. *See* domestic clock, American, Dutch, English, French, German, and Italian clocks.

clock cases. In porcelain, speciality of Sèvres factory. Clocks set in columns or vase-shaped cases. Example made by P-P. *Thomire for Marie-Antoinette, constructed of porcelain and marble with gilt mount, dates from 1780s, when most made; rare examples date from mid 18th century. Made at Meissen by G. *Fritzche (*c*1727) and by J. J. *Kändler (in 1740s); also at Vienna in *Du Paquier period and in 18th century Chinese *famille rose.* Also made for B. *Vulliamy in Derby porcelain from *c*1780; clocks and barometers supported by allegorical biscuit figures with marble and ormolu settings. Faience clock cases made in eastern France, e.g. Strasbourg, in mid 18th century.

clock cases (in wood). Not in common use before late 17th century: wooden cases later became general for *long-case and *bracket clocks. Earliest, in English clocks, of oak with ebony or other veneers (e.g. mulberry used by T. *Tompion) or pearwood stained to simulate ebony. Olive wood also used before 1700 veneered with stars, etc. formed of ebony and boxwood. *c*1690–*c*1760, plain burr walnut popular, followed *c*1740 by Spanish and Cuban mahogany, then *c*1755 by Honduras mahogany or bay wood. Cheaper clocks still cased in oak sometimes inlaid with walnut, box and holly, or from *c*1775 in softwood.

clock dials. Earliest public clocks often without dial, used for striking only; dials, where fitted, may be of complex calendar or astronomical type. Form of dial on domestic clocks varies with local systems of *time measurement, some showing 24 hours or with adjustable scales. Single hour hand general until late 17th century (retained in some English examples, particularly alarm clocks, to *c*1830). Alternative arrangement with fixed hand and revolving dial used on e.g. German automaton, animal, and crucifix clocks from Augsburg mainly in 16th century, revived in France in late 18th and 19th centuries. Dials for single-hand clocks have ring with quarter-hour divisions within main chapter-ring; half-hours often marked with fleur-de-lis ornament etc. After introduction of minute hand, minute numerals added outside hour markings (normally at 5-minute intervals, rarely at each minute); quarter-hour ring little used after mid 18th century.

Dials on English long-case and bracket clocks typically square or rectangular in early examples, with applied circular chapter-ring; plain solid silver plate and ring, *c*1660; brass plate with thin silver plate applied, engraved all over, *c*1665 or with matted centre and corner *spandrels, *c*1670; silvered brass plate from *c*1675. Spandrels more elaborate from *c*1685, with size of dial increased from 8in. to 12in. or more. *Break-arch form introduced *c*1710, common from 1730; with brass dial plate and brass ornaments, often gilded, silvered, or lacquered. Plain silvered and engraved dials used for *precision clocks from c1730, for domestic clocks from *c*1770. White painted dials on sheet iron base introduced *c*1775 for low cost and legibility; used generally since. *See* hands, numerals.

clock lamp. Tall metal table lamp with glass oil container marked with hours to show time as level drops. Wick holder protrudes from side. Made from *c*1730.

Clockmakers' Company of London. Professional trade guild for clock makers, founded in 1631 under charter granted by Charles I. (Previously clock makers belonged to other guilds, notably Blacksmiths'.)

clock-watch. Pocket watch striking every hour automatically. May also repeat hours and quarters at will. Sometimes large watch, e.g. *sedan clock. *Illustration also at* German watch.

Clodion, or **Michel,** Claude (1738–1814). French sculptor. Made terracotta pastoral figures and groups. Worked in Rome, 1762–71. Employed to make and adapt models for Sèvres biscuit porcelain; work includes figure of Montesquieu dated 1783. Believed also to have made models for use at Niderviller in 1795. After Revolution, worked in monumental neoclassical style. Many forgeries of his terracotta figures made in 19th century; also copies in bronze with forged signature, Clodion.

cloisonné enamelling. Application of enamel to small metal partitions or enclosures soldered on to field to form design. Technique developed in 10th century Byzantium. Gold used as base. Effect similar to *champlevé* enamelling. *Illustration also at* Chinese *cloisonné* enamel.

close chair. Single chair or armchair with hinged seat concealing metal or ceramic basin (chamberpot without handle). Conceals view of basin from outside, or lower part of seat may be completely boxed in. Dates from 16th century; popular in 18th century.

close cupboard. 17th century term describing cupboard with enclosed shelves and doors at front.

close nailing. Sturdy fastening of heavy fabric, such as leather covering on chest, trunk, or furniture. Fabric secured by round-headed brass nails hammered close together around edge.

closed knot. *See* Turkish knot.

close or **necessary stool,** or **night commode.** Stool with hinged seat concealing, when closed, a metal or ceramic basin. Stool may have wide apron, concealing basin from outside, or completely enclosed sides. Common from 17th to early 19th century. Kept in dressing-room, or in bedroom, where it might be concealed in night cupboard.

close-plating. Process known from Middle Ages by which steel or iron given silver coating. Object dipped in flux, usually sal ammoniac, then in molten tin. Silver foil placed on surface; hot soldering iron passed over melts tin which acts as solder. Used for small objects requiring plating, e.g. knife blades, skewers, buckles, etc. Sir E. *Thomason experimented with process in 1810 in Birmingham. Precursor of Sheffield or fused plate.

closing-ring. *See* door-furniture.

clothes horse. *See* towel horse.

Cloisonné *enamelling. Russian silver baluster-shaped tea pot, late 19th century. Brightly coloured enamels. Height 6in.*

clothes press. *Press cupboard for storing clothes. Lower section usually with drawers; upper section has doors concealing either shelves, sliding trays, or hanging space. Common in 17th and 18th centuries; synonymous with *wardrobe in 18th century.

cloud band or **pattern.** Motif in carpet design, occurring in border or ground pattern; derived from chi motif, Chinese symbol of immortality, represented by variously-shaped cloud or bands of clouds. Extensively used, e.g. on Chinese, Caucasian, and particularly Persian carpets from Saffavid dynasty (1501–1736).

Clouet, Jean (*c*1485–*c*1540) and son François (*c*1520–72). French painters. Jean, of Flemish origin, at court of François I; painted miniatures, some in illuminated manuscripts; work combined Flemish and Italian Renaissance influences. François court painter to François I, Henri II, François II, Charles IX, and Henri III.

clous d'or. Gold or silver nail points used in **piqué*.

cloven foot. *See* hoof foot.

club or **Dutch foot** (in furniture). Chair and table foot resembling rounded disc, widening and turning slightly outwards at bottom. May rest on round, flat base. Much used in 18th century, sometimes on cabriole leg. 'Dutch foot' American term.

Clothes-press. George II, mahogany. Two panelled doors enclose oak trays supported by runners in doors when they are drawn out; drawers in base. Height 4ft 1in.

clustered column. In architecture, decorative or supporting column composed of four or more small columns joined together; dates from Middle Ages. In furniture, three or more thin columns joined at intervals, as decoration or to form legs on tables and chairs; from mid 18th century.

Coalport. Group of three campana shaped vases, c1815. Chinoiserie *decoration.*
Right:
*Coaster. Silver-gilt, made by E. *Barnard & Sons, 1843–44. Sides cast, pierced and chased; wooden base. Diameter 6in.*

coach or **chaise clock** (or watch). Large 18th century pocket watch used in travelling. Metal case, sometimes gold, with enamelling; others silver, or base metal covered with leather, etc.

coach horn. *See* post horn.

coaching clock. *See* Act of Parliament clock.

coaching glass. Small, footless, English drinking glass dating from late 18th and early 19th centuries. Short, thick, cut stem, usually ending in heavy knop. Used at wayside inns.

coal box. *See* coal scuttle.

Coalbrookdale Company (Shropshire). Iron works begun 1709 by A. Darby. Experimented widely using pit-coal; improved casting techniques. By 19th century, making wide variety of objects, e.g. gates, railings, garden furniture, door-knockers, hall tables, hat-and-coat stands, wall-plaques. Wrought iron also produced.

Coalport or **Coalbrookdale.** Porcelain factory established by J. *Rose and partners at Coalport, Shropshire, *c*1796. Earliest porcelain impossible to separate from Caughley; decoration mainly printed or painted in underglaze blue on ware sometimes made at Caughley, probably using Caughley marks. Also made porcelain to *Nantgarw formula. Leadless feldspathic glaze introduced in 1820. Domestic porcelain (1820–50) sparingly decorated, usually with flowers, or with moulded patterns and light-coloured gilding. Flowers sometimes painted over printed outlines in pink or purple. Ornamental ware (1820–30) has much moulded flower decoration in *revived rococo style; predominant colours pink and green. From 1840s, products inspired by Sèvres style; ground colours imitate Sèvres. Also made flat porcelain plaques with naturalistic painting of fruit and flowers. Marks, usually in underglaze blue, include: CD as initials or monogram on soft-paste porcelain from *c*1796; CDale, Coalport, or Coalbrookdale (*c*1815–*c*1825); large circular marks commemorating Society of Arts gold medal for leadless glaze in 1820, with words Coalport Felt Spar Porcelain in garland; several marks worded J or John Rose & Co, Coalport or Coalbrookdale Porcelain (*c*1825–*c*1850). Also CBD monogram (1851–61), and SCN in loops of tangled line (1861–75). Marks usually in underglaze blue.

coal-scuttle. Introduced early 18th century with wider domestic use of coal. Few examples known until mid 19th century when helmet or scoop types made in copper with brass handles, copper, or zinc. Coal-vases smaller, highly ornamental, made of japanned metal in, e.g. Gothic or Italianate styles. The Purdonium, box-type coal container (devised by a Mr Purdon), usually of japanned metal, often with back-painted glass panel in lid and slot for shovel.

coaster, bottle or **decanter stand** or **slider.** Circular silver, Sheffield plate and/or wooden stand with raised rim or gallery for coasting (i.e. sliding) wine bottle or decanter on polished table top after tablecloth has been removed at end of meal. In use from late 18th century in Britain; earliest entirely silver with concave base. Later with hardwood base. With rollers or, from *c*1755, green baize underside to protect table surface; silver boss often found at centre for crest, etc. Shallow rings cut round inside centre of base to prevent decanter from sticking. Decoration (generally around rim of gallery) cast, embossed, pierced, or engraved on silver and Sheffield plate examples. Made in pairs or multiples of two. Boat or figure eight-shaped examples made to hold two bottles. *See* wine wagon.

cobalt-blue. Cobalt oxide used as high temperature colour in Chinese ceramics notably in decoration of porcelain; perfected at *Ching-tê-chên, Yüan period. Finest oxide, 'Mohammedan blue', imported from Near East from 15th century; prized for intensity of colour. By late Ming period, native Chinese ores (duller because of manganese content) used.

Cobb, John (fl 1749–78). English partner of W. *Vile in Vile & Cobb, 1750–65, cabinet makers and upholsterers to George III. Continued business after Vile's death until 1778.

Cochin, Charles-Nicolas (b 1717). French engraver and archaeologist under patronage of Mme de Pompadour. Criticized elaborate Louis XV style; argued for simplicity and return to classical line.

cock. Bracket in clock or watch movement. In early watches all wheels pivot in front and back plates of movement except balance, which is supported at one end by balance cock, often finely pierced or engraved, fixed to back plate. European watches have bridge cock spanning balance and supported at both ends. Use of cocks for other wheels in movement spread after *c*1675, although old style persisted longer in England. J-A. *Lépine introduced movement with no back plate but bars to support all wheels of train, 1770; style called Lépine calibre.

cock beading (in furniture). Moulding resembling string of small, finely-carved beads, usually applied to edges of drawer-front. Dates from *c*1750.

cock-fighting chair. *See* reading chair.

cock-metal. Alloy of lead with small quantity of copper, used for soldering and for crudest cast wares, e.g. *tokens, *Billies and Charlies.

Cockpit Hill, Derby. Site of earthenware factory, *c*1750–79; proprietors included J. *Heath. Work usually unsigned, although some signed pieces of transfer-printed creamware exist. Also produced colour-glazed earthenware and salt-glaze. Creamware teapot with transfer print in black signed *c*1765 by T. *Radford, 'Radford sculpsit, DERBY Pot Works'; transfer-printed wares also engraved and marked by R. *Holdship, Derby, with anchor.

coconut cup. 15th and 16th century ceremonial *standing cup. Bowl made of coconut shell; stem and base of silver or silver-gilt. Stem designs

Coach watch. Two-train watch with alarm and repeat, verge escapement, pierced cock foot, silver dial, Dutch-style arcaded minute ring, alarm rose in centre, pierced gilt hands. Shown with outer case of silver covered with black fish-skin. Made by Cabrier of London c1775. Diameter of dial 3in.

Left:
Coconut cup and cover. Repoussé *silver mounts. Dutch, made in Wageningen, 1656. Height to top of finial* 17*in.*
Below:
*Cockpit Hill. Creamware teapot, mid 18th century; with *crabstock spout and handle.*

include vase-shape, pedestal, or baluster, and standing figures. Mainly English and German. In 17th century some coconut cups in *porringer form, usually without stems and sometimes raised on ball feet or spreading rim foot, with or without covers, made in Hull, Yorkshire, and Dublin. Fashion revived during mid 18th century; mount resembles *goblet; nut often carved with figures or geometric designs.

coffee-can. Cylindrical coffee-cup without foot-ring, produced in porcelain e.g. at Sèvres and *Derby (in Crown Derby period).

coffee-mill. Mechanism evolved in early 18th century Europe for grinding coffee beans (previously used whole). Outer, box-like case was of wood, brass, or japanned metal; small tray beneath received ground coffee, replaced in 1740s by a drawer. Basic design survived well into 20th century, with mirror variations.

coffee-pot. Coffee became fashionable in mid 17th century Britain and Europe. Earliest silver containers were of cylindrical shape tapering towards top; peaked dome lid had baluster finial; straight spout and handle were on opposite sides of body. Others until early 18th century had handle set at right angle to spout. Curved spout introduced in late 17th century. Coffee-pots do not appear in any great number until after *c*1700. *c*1700–30 cylinder shape, plain or octagonal, common with lower part of body rounded into base; domed lid with mouldings. After 1730, often made with pear-shaped body, moulded foot, cast and chased ornament. *c*1740–65 baluster or elongated pear shape common. Urn-shaped coffee-pot on rounded or square plinth base made in 1770s. From late 18th century shapes varied; most earlier styles revived. Made in Sheffield plate from *c*1760.

coffee urn. Silver or Sheffield plate coffee container with spigot and tap at base of body instead of spout; one or two handles (usually two, loop, harp-shaped, lion mask and ring, etc.); on feet or stand. Sometimes in shape of *Borghese urn. In use from mid 18th century in Britain and Europe; most popular in Netherlands where extremely large examples were made. From mid 1780s made of Sheffield plate. Less common than *tea urn.

coffer. Medieval metal or metal-bound wooden strong-box in shape of small chest.

coffered panel. Panel with main surface deeply-recessed from frame. *cf* sunken panel.

coffin clock. American wall clock, in form of coffin, encasing banjo-shaped movement. Made late 18th century.

coffin-end or **coffin-handle spoon.** 19th cen-

*Coffer. Oak, panels of carved *linen-fold decoration, unusual in being placed horizontally. Inside, box for candles. English, early 16th century.*
Coffin-end spoons. American. Two tablespoons by John and Peter Targee of New York City, c1811; salt-spoon by Tunis du Bois, who worked in New York 1797–99. Length $3\frac{3}{4}$in.

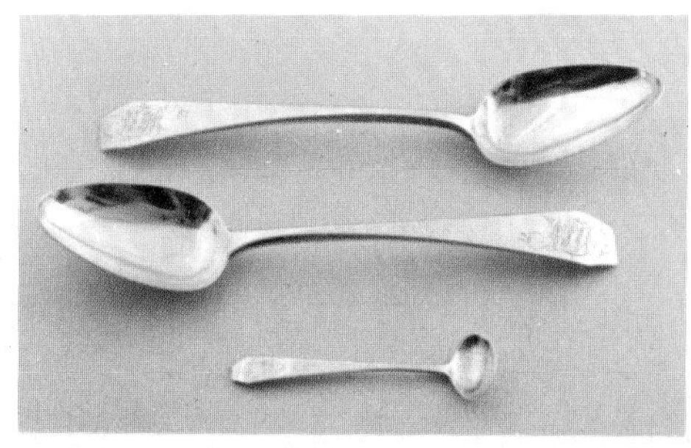

tury American silver spoon with square-ended stem clipped at corners to resemble coffin; either plain or decorated, with bright-cut reserve for monogram. Pattern was also used for other flatware. Resulted from mania in New York and New England for funeral display.

Cogswell, John (fl *c*1760–1818). Cabinet maker in Boston, Massachusetts. Pieces rococo with much carving.

Coignet, Michel (1544–1623). Flemish mathematician and instrument-maker working in Antwerp. Produced astronomical and surveying devices.

coin. English 18th century term for *corner cupboard (from French *coin*, 'corner').

coin cabinet. *See* medal cabinet.

coin glass. Wine glass, goblet, or tankard with coin enclosed in hollow knop. Popular from mid 17th century; probably originated in Murano. Common Jacobite and Hanoverian drinking glass.

coin silver. Silver alloy used in America for coinage since mid 17th century; initially *Sterling Standard, lowered to 90% silver, 10% copper in 19th century. Coins commonly melted down by silversmiths as source of silver.

coin tankard. Silver tankard with coin or coins set in lid; sometimes whole surface covered with coins. Probably originated in Germany in 17th century; also made in Scandinavia and America.

coin weights. First recorded in 15th century, widely produced by specialist makers from mid 17th century; made mainly for merchants, to check coins for forgery or clipping. Set of weights often contained in leather-covered box with small pair of scales, each weight stamped with representation of appropriate coin. Sometimes small additional weights measure deficiency of coin.

cold gilding (in ceramics). *See* gilding.

cold-hammering. *See* forging.

cold painting. Unfired painting on glass or ceramics, usually in oil or lacquer colours. Easily worn away unless protected by layer of varnish, foil, or glass, as with 18th century **verre églomisé*. Popular in 17th and 18th century Germany, where known as *Kalte Malerei.*

cold-working. Working cold metal. Objects hammered out of thin sheet of gold or silver (made by casting, rolling, or hammering), without heating.

Cole, James Ferguson (1799–1880). English watch maker noted for precision workmanship in style similar to A-L. *Breguet; made many fine watches with lever *escapement.

Cole, Thomas. English clock maker, brother of J. F. *Cole; produced high-grade spring-driven mantel clocks, etc., *c*1840–*c*1865.

Collaert, Hans (fl 16th century). Designer

College cup. English, 1616. Maker's mark, SO with mullet in shaped shield. Engraved with arms of Thomas, Earl of Arundel. Height 8½in.

and copperplate engraver working in Antwerp. Published *Monilium Bullarum in aurumque icones* (1581) which included designs for jewelled pendants, mainly showing human figures riding sea-monsters and other grotesque beasts, e.g. pear-shaped pendant owned by Elizabeth I (1592), 'a fishe called a bull of the sea', carrying kneeling man; set with diamonds, rubies, and suspended from three small chains similarly set. Also noted for engravings of architectural pendants using lines of square-cut stones.

college or **ox-eye cup.** 17th and 18th century English silver drinking vessel, often with low foot, pear-shaped body, and two ring handles attached to neck; most in possession of Oxford colleges. Usually 17th century; 18th century examples rare.

Collins, James (1802–44). American clock maker. Made *New Hampshire mirror clocks.

Collis, George Richmond (fl mid 19th century). English silver and Sheffield plate retailer working in Birmingham; took over Sir E. *Thomason's firm in 1835. In 1842 acquired several models from *Rundell, Bridge & Rundell sale which he put into production (including Storr coaster of 1814). Domestic plate shown at 1851 Great Exhibition characterized by naturalistic plant ornament.

cologne bottle. Moulded panelled bottle of two main types, either in wide range of colours and sizes, or mainly clear or aquamarine-coloured. Made in blown-three-mould, often elaborately shaped and decorated. Produced in America from mid 19th century.

Cologne, Germany. First centre of *Rhineland stoneware production to achieve artistic importance; active *c*1520–*c*1600. Produced greyish stoneware with brown mottled glaze, sometimes called *tigerware in England. Most familiar are the globular *bellarmine jugs.

Colonial style. *See* American Colonial style.

coloured glass. Early Egyptian glass makers attempting to imitate precious stones in glass became highly skilled in producing fine colours. Initially finely-ground coloured stones used, e.g. malachite and lapis lazuli for green and blue, but experiments produced wider range of colours from other minerals: green and blue (copper); green or yellow (iron); dark and light blue (cobalt); amethyst and purple (manganese). Colour varies according to degree of oxidation and to composition of *metal. From 18th dynasty, fine red *blood glass also produced from copper. Multicoloured vessels produced in *mosaic and **millefiori* glass. Apart from ruby-red glass developed by J. *Kunckel in late 17th century Bohemia, using gold chloride, few changes in range of colours took place from antiquity until early 19th century, when increased technical knowledge allowed production of new colour effects. *Illustration at* decanter.

coloured grounds. *See* ground colours.

colour twist. Style of stem used in English glasses, *c*1755–*c*1775; made in same way as *opaque twist, but using coloured glass canes; often in combination with opaque or air twists. *Illustration at* English wine glasses.

Columbia flasks. American flasks blown in full-size two-piece mould, bearing bust of Columbia (oldest personification of United States). Usually have American eagle on reverse. Made 1815–70.

columbine cup. 16th century German silver drinking vessel with body shaped like columbine

Cologne stoneware. Tankard with black body; applied decoration of dancing peasants; metal mounts. 17th century. Height 9¼in.

Left, top to bottom
Columbia flask. Light yellow-green glass. Pint capacity. c*1820–40.*
Comb-back armchair. American 18th century with seven spindles; vase-turned arms.
Combed slip decoration. Large earthenware mug, made in Staffordshire, c*1710.*

flower; pedestal stem; engraved and embossed ornament. *See* master cup.

column clock. French mantel clock, introduced *c*1780. Marble case consists of two side-columns, with portico-top; clock hangs between columns. Supports are caryatids, or in some versions, bronze figures. Also with large musical box as base.

column Ladik carpets. *See* Ladik carpets.

comb. Made in wood, bone, horn, ivory, metal, etc. from ancient times. From early 19th century, popular in Britain and Europe as hair ornament. Many of gold ornamented with cameos, gems, pearls, coral or amber beads, etc. Sometimes with interchangeable ornamental mounts. In Germany, Italy, and Switzerland some combs set with red or green *pastes.

comb-back Windsor. Type of Windsor chair popular in America *c*1760. Typically, has arms of single piece curving horizontally around back of chair. Spindles surmounted by shaped yoke-rail rise from back of arm-piece to form 'comb'. H-stretcher with bulbous decoration.

comb base. *See* Nabeshima ware.

combed, feathered, or **marbled slip decoration.** Contrasting colours of slip worked into pattern with brush or stick, in manner of marbling paper. In some cases, feathered designs made by drawing point across differently coloured lines of slip. Used from 16th century, most often in late 17th and early 18th centuries.

comfit box. *See* sweetmeat box.

comfit glass. Small *sweetmeat glass with short stem or none, used for comfits or dry sweetmeats, e.g. chocolate, caraway seeds, nuts. Mainly 18th century English and Irish.

commedia dell'arte. Characters from Italian *commedia dell'arte* often taken as subject for figures and groups in European porcelain from early 18th century, and for decoration on porcelain, etc. Among rare stoneware figures made in early years of Meissen factory; made in porcelain there by 1720s; important series of characters modelled by J. J. *Kändler in 1730s and by P. *Reinicke (1743–44) provided inspiration for many other porcelain factories, e.g. Mennecy (by 1750), Bow (in 1750s), Chelsea (red anchor period), and Longton Hall (1754–57). Other series include 16 figures made by F. A. *Bustelli at Nymphenburg in late 1750s. Also among earliest figures made at Capodimonte by G. *Gricci (1743–45); at Doccia beside leaf-shaped bowls on shell bases, *c*1750, and slightly later on square marbled bases; also made at Cozzi factory, *c*1770. *Illustration at* Meissen.

commerce table. *Card table with oval top resting on X-frame base; introduced second half 18th century, when bartering card game, commerce, very popular. Made into 19th century.

commode. French low chest of drawers. Dates from 17th century, very popular in 18th. *See commode à encoignures, commode à la régence, commode à vantaux, commode en console.*

commode à encoignures. *Commode with quarter-circular cupboard at each end, derived from combination of simple commode and pair of *encoignures* (*see* corner cupboard). End cupboards usually have one door, occasionally two. Frieze drawers above central section and ends. Dates from Louis XVI period.

*Commode. French, mid 18th century, probably by C. *Cressent. Double bowed and bombé front and splayed bombé sides. Two pairs of drawers in front on either side of* *espagnolette *head; rococo mounts of dragons, shells, sprays, cartouches, and scrolls on top of kingwood veneer. Length* 5*ft*10*in.*

Commode à la régence. *Louis XV, attributed to P. Hache of Grenoble; mulberry wood with geometrical inlay of walnut; *splayed feet.*

commode à l'anglaise or **commode-dessert.** **Commode à encoignures* with curving end sections as open shelves rather than cupboards. Shelves have gallery. Examples often veneered mahogany or ebony with bronze mounts. Dates from Louis XVI period.

commode à la régence or **en tombeau.** French, 18th century chest of drawers originally distinguished by three drawers in base (top drawer often divided into two narrow ones) and short legs. May have serpentine front. Later, lightened form has two main drawers under narrow top drawer or frieze of drawers, and longer legs. Sometimes with side cupboards.

commode à vantaux. French *commode with doors concealing drawer fronts. Dates from 18th century.

commode-desserte. *See commode à l'anglaise.*

commode en console. French chest with one frieze drawer, on high legs, designed to be placed beneath wall mirror. Dates from 18th century; popular Louis XV piece. *cf* console table.

commode en tombeau. *See commode à la régence.*

Commonwealth or **Puritan tankard.** British silver tankard with cylindrical body, wide skirt foot; *stepped lid with projecting point on surrounding flange opposite handle; kidney-shaped thumbpiece. Holds one pint. Dates from Commonwealth (1649–60).

common white. *See* salt-glaze ware.

communion cup. Usually silver, occasionally pewter, vessel for consecrated wine used by Reformed churches in communion service. In England, melting of chalices and re-making them in shapes of contemporary wine cups or goblets began during reign of Edward VI (1547–53). In 1559, Elizabeth I decreed use of covered wine cup by laity (indicating break with ritual of Rome and link with lay usage). Most popular form was based on contemporary drinking cups in domestic use. It had beaker-shaped bowl, spool-shaped stem with central moulding, and stepped, moulded base. Baluster stem also common. Cover was slightly domed

*Communion cup and *paten. English, 1570, in typical post-Reformation style; maker's mark, SH interlaced. Parcel-gilt engraved with band of foliage. Height 6¾in. without paten.*

with flat knob serving as foot when used as *paten. Older paten sometimes used, with centre cut out and knob added. Pious inscriptions around upper part of bowl common. Top of knob often engraved with date of manufacture.

In Scotland and Holland, beaker was most popular communion cup. Often engraved with sacred subjects (e.g. Last Supper, figures of Faith, Hope, and Charity), or arms of donors. In America, besides beaker and English-style goblet, ordinary secular drinking vessels were used, e.g. two-handled cups, canns.

compass or **pin-cushion seat.** Upholstered chair-seat, with raised, dome-like centre. Dates from Queen Anne period, when often used on *bended-back chairs.

compendiario style. Maiolica decoration characterized by simple designs, sketchily painted in limited colour range, e.g. of cobalt-blue, orange, and yellow, contrasting with large expanse of white tin-glaze; emphasis on form rather than decoration. Developed at Faenza *c*1540; quickly adopted all over Italy, then in rest of Europe. Wares with decoration in *compendiario* style often known as *bianchi di Faenza* (**faïence blanche*).

compensation (in clocks and watches). Means of maintaining accuracy despite changes of temperature. Change of 1°C causes loss or gain of *c*11 seconds per 24 hours in uncompensated movement. In watches, methods of compensation applied to *balance, often by forming rim of wheel from a layer each of steel and brass: as temperature increases, brass expands more than steel, bending rim of wheel inwards, reducing effective diameter and compensating for changes in behaviour of balance spring. Auxiliary compensation devices found in e.g. marine *chronometers for greater accuracy; rarely, mercury used as temperature-sensitive element. In clocks, temperature changes cause length of *pendulum to vary: compensation devices aim to keep centre of gravity constant by using 'grid-iron' of brass and steel rods (introduced by J. *Harrison), concentric tubes of steel and zinc (as in Westminster clock), or containers of mercury (used by G. *Graham).

complicated work. Mechanisms in clock or watch other than those connected with striking and timekeeping. Examples include calendar, repeating, or astronomical work.

Complin, George (fl late 18th century). Porcelain painter; work includes fruit and birds painted at Derby before 1795.

comport. Large glass stand or salver with round, flat top on heavy stem, mounted on flared foot. Used to hold sets of jelly or syllabub glasses, and designed to match. Popular in 18th century England in cut flint-glass. From *c*1840, pressed examples common. Brief vogue in 1850s for silvered comports, with added cutting, enamelling, and gilding.

Commonwealth or **Puritan style.** Simple, plain, style, which flourished in England under Protectorate of Oliver Cromwell (1649–60), reflecting needs and tastes of commoner rather than aristocracy. Heavy oak furniture characteristic, with basically straight lines and emphasis on practicality; lacks decoration apart from turning on legs, arms, vertical supports, and stretchers. Popularity of dual-purpose pieces, e.g. *settle-table, *chair-table, revived. Chair-backs and seats were often covered with close-nailed leather. Many gate-leg tables were made.

companion figure. *See* dummy-board figure.

Comtoise clock. French regional long-case or lantern clock, made in Franche-Comté, early 18th century to *c*1900. (Also called Morbier clock, after main producing town.) Noted for large, highly ornate pendulum bob, in form of elongated violin; *repoussé* decoration around dial. Often with inverted crown-wheel escapement and vertical rack-striking mechanism. Clock strikes on the hour, and again at two minutes past. Marked with name of dealer, rather than maker. Found also in Belgium and Switzerland.

concertina construction. Supporting structure for table with folding top (e.g. card table), consisting of hinged horizontal support and two legs for flaps. When not in use, concertina support folds under stationary section of table top. Dates from early 18th century.

cone device. *See* boteh motif.

Coney, John (1665–1722). American silversmith working in Boston, Massachusetts; probably apprenticed to J. *Dummer. Earliest known work is two-handled covered cup presented to First Parish Church in Concord. Probably engraved plate for first American bank notes. Made mainly domestic silver; much survives, including candlesticks, tea and coffee pots, casters, salvers, inkstands, sugar or sweetmeat boxes, etc. Also made earliest examples of

John Coney. Bowl, made in Boston, Massachusetts, on collet foot; engraved with Riddell coat of arms.

American snuff-boxes, two known are oval with loose covers and arms of Jeffries and Wentworth families on lids. Style English-inspired; some objects in Queen Anne style. Marks include IC, with a fleur-de-lis below in shield (early period); shield with a rabbit and initials (after *c*1700); also two smaller marks with initials.

confidante, sociable, or **tête-à-tête.** 19th century seat; shape generally follows line of horizontal serpentine back-rail, with a seat in each curve of the 'S', allowing occupants to sit facing each other. Variations include model based on elongated 'S' (with a table built into middle of piece), and four-seated design, based on two *confidantes* interlocking at right angles.

Congreve clock. *See* ball clock.

Congreve, William (Comptroller, Woolwich laboratory, 1808–23). English scientist and clock maker; invented rolling *ball clock, 1808.

conical bowl. Chinese pottery form, dating from early Sung period; common shape for wine or tea vessels. Shallow, wide-brimmed, with straight, flaring sides; usually without handles.

conical pendulum. Introduced in clocks by J. Bodeker (1587). Top attached to last wheel of clock train, bob at bottom revolves in circular path. Frequency of rotation increases as bob moves outward and upward; counteracted by attached vane moving in glycerine or other viscous fluid. Used chiefly in clocks driving astronomical telescopes, where normal pendulum and escapement cause jerking in motion, but also found in French mantel clocks *c*1840.

Connecticut chest. American rectangular blanket or storage chest, produced mainly in Connecticut. Usually oak, with three vertical rectangular panels in front, over one or two drawers in base: decoration on panels, commonly carved or painted sunflower motif (central panel), and tulip motif (outer panels). Round applied bosses on drawers; split balusters on *stiles, which extend to form short legs. Dates from 17th century.

Connecticut shelf clock. Large variety of American shelf clocks produced in Connecticut from *c*1816. Examples include *pillar and scroll, *looking-glass, *transition, *ogee, and *steeple.

*Connecticut chest. 17th century. Oak, decorated with *split turning.*

*Console table. To design by W. *Kent. Carved and gilded wood; scrolled legs decorated with scalework acanthus leaves and guilloche patterns. Marble top. English, early 18th century.*

Many makers, e.g. S. *Thomas, *Ansonia Clock Company.

Connelly, Henry (1770–1826). American cabinet maker; worked with E. *Haines in Philadelphia, Pennsylvania. Style neo-classical.

Conrade, Courrade, or **Corrado family:** Domenico (d after 1638), Baptiste (d between 1613 and 1618), and Augustin. Italian-born potters, brothers, regarded as founders of faience industry at Nevers. Granted 30-year privilege for manufacture of faience in 1603. Work followed Italian maiolica style, difficult to distinguish from products of Italian potters at Lyon.

console or **clap table.** Architectural side table, often with *bracket support (instead of legs) attaching it to wall. Usually semi-circular, contoured, or rectangular. Often has marble top and matching mirror. Dates from 17th century.

Constitution mirror. American term for mirror distinguished by carved gilt eagle cresting. Frame often parcel gilt. Made from early 18th century.

consular case. Watch case with very wide bezels meeting at centre, so that body of watch cannot be seen. Makers include J. *Arnold and T. *Earnshaw; French form derived from *oignon* watch.

conversion (in clocks and watches). Substitution of part of movement, especially *escapement; mainly where verge type has been altered to later, more accurate anchor (in clocks) or lever (in watches). Other watch escapements, e.g. duplex and chronometer, sometimes changed to lever for greater robustness and easier maintenance. Conversion often involves deliberate removal of other parts, e.g. repeating work, when new components take up more space.

convex mirror. Circular mirror with convex surface. Frame, often gilt, may be decorated with small balls; carved cresting common, especially with central eagle, also carved ornament at base of frame. Earlier examples often have candle sconces at sides or base. Dates from 18th century France; introduced to England and America *c*1800.

Cookworthy, William (1705–80). Quaker apothecary in Plymouth, Devon; first maker of hard-paste porcelain in England. Possibly devised formula for soapstone porcelain introduced at B. *Lund's Bristol factory in 1749. Discovered china clay and fusible rock in Cornwall before 1758. In 1760s, experimented with R. *Champion to make true porcelain; in 1768, obtained patent and opened porcelain factory in *Plymouth with partners including Champion. Transferred manufacture to *Bristol, *c*1770. Retired in 1772.

Cooper, Alexander (1605–60). English miniaturist. Pupil of J. *Hoskins and P. *Oliver. Much work in Europe including series in Berlin (1632–33) of the Elector Palatine, Frederick V, and family. In Sweden, 1647–57 (apart from 1655–56, in Denmark), portrait painter to Queen Christina, then to Charles X. Worked mainly in watercolours; also in enamel.

Cooper, Samuel (1609–72). English miniaturist. Pupil of uncle, J. *Hoskins, with elder

Samuel Cooper. Portrait of Inigo Jones, c1630.

brother, A. *Cooper. Travelled in Europe; lived in France and Holland. Most celebrated miniaturist of period, mentioned by John Aubrey, John Evelyn; friend of Samuel Pepys. Appointed limner to Charles II. Most work painted from life. Work characterized by broad, strong brush strokes and sobriety of colour.

Copeland, William Taylor (fl 19th century). Staffordshire potter; succeeded father as partner in Spode factory (1826), with T. *Garrett (1833–47); firm then W. T. Copeland, late Spode, and from 1867, W. W. Copeland & Sons. Marketed figures in parian ware from 1842; commissioned artists to model copies of marble sculpture. Introduced ground colours, e.g. *Sardinian green, cyclamen, and vermilion. Manufactured panels, e.g. of bone china, as decorative inserts for furniture, often painted with flowers (notably convolvulus), or figures. Also made first English porcelain inlaid with jewels. Marks include COPELAND AND GARRETT clockwise in circle around or below crown (printed in blue), and from 1847 Copeland late Spode (impressed or printed in blue), COPELAND with crown (impressed), COPELAND with crown and garlands (printed in green or blue), and Copeland Stone China (printed in blue). Lord Mayor of London in 1835; Conservative M.P. for Stoke-on-Trent (1837–65). Helped in formation of North Staffordshire Railway, 1846. *Illustration at* parian ware.

Copenhagen, Denmark. Støre Kongensgade factory established in 1722 to produce faience, under privilege allowing monopoly and preventing import of any blue painted ware. Products usually painted in blue, sometimes with speckled manganese-purple background, e.g. on tiles and tankards. Decoration normally derived from that of Delft and Nuremberg, but *c*1750 rococo styles adopted. Products include bishop bowls and table-tops. Factory closed in 1769, after losing last of several lawsuits in defence of privilege, renewed in 1752.

Blaataarn (Blue Tower) factory opened in 1738 under patronage of King Christian IV, to make faience for architectural use. Stoves, tiles, and ornamental ware, often with relief decoration, made at first by workers from Germany. Rarely, gilding or enamel colours used. On closure of business (1754), factory transferred to Kastrup, Copenhagen, by court builder, primarily to produce architectural faience. Privilege granted in 1755 for manufacture of faience other than that covered by Støre Kongensgade monopoly. Produced domestic and ornamental ware, including figures and groups, frequently large. In late 18th century, manufacture of cream-coloured earthenware superseded faience production. Factory at Østerbro established 1760s, making faience with decoration in blue and/or manganese-purple (sometimes with gilding) forced to cease production after six years, because Støre Kongensgade claimed infringement of monopoly.

Soft-paste porcelain made by L. *Fournier in 1760s. Flower-painting on tableware usually reminiscent of Mennecy; rare figures include bust of King Frederik V. Mark: F5, in gold, or blue enamel. King stopped production in 1765, as too costly, though mark C7 (King Christian VII succeeded in 1766) occurs in one case. Royal Copenhagen Porcelain Manufactory (Den Kongelige Porcelainsfabrik Copenhagen)

Copenhagen. Porcelain figure group of couple with two dogs, c*1780. Height 6in.*

established in 1775, with help of German workmen, e.g. A. C. *Luplau (from 1776) who formulated paste and glaze. Company, in which Queen Juliane Marie held large share, gained support of King in 1779 and began trading as royal factory. White, translucent paste developed by 1780, used to make table and ornamental ware, toys, furniture, plaques, etc. Style much influenced by Meissen. Early work includes *Flora Danica service. In 1867, factory sold, but retained right to fly royal flag, and use mark (adopted 1775) of three wavy lines, painted in blue.

coperta. Clear lead-glaze sometimes applied over tin-glaze of Italian maiolica before firing, to give glossier finish. Described in C. *Piccolpasso's account of maiolica manufacture at Castel Durante in mid 16th century. *See kwaart.*

Copland, Henry (fl 1752). English designer in rococo and neo-classical styles. In collaboration with M. *Lock, 1752–68, published A New Book of Ornaments, Chimneys, Tables etc. (1752), A New Drawing Book of Ornament (1754), and A New Book of Ornaments (1786), and also worked on T. *Chippendale's The Gentleman and Cabinet-Maker's Director.

Copley, John Singleton (1737–1815). American painter and miniaturist. Produced miniatures on ivory from *c*1762. Some miniatures in oils on copper. After 1774, in Italy, then England. Later work includes large historical paintings.

copper. Moderately hard, reddish metal, probably the first known to man. Found in many parts of the world, particularly Far East, Egypt, central Europe, Greece, Germany, Belgium, England, and Wales. Most important use from early times was alloying with tin to make bronze; later, with calamine, to make brass; also many other alloys, including *paktong, *pinchbeck, *Britannia metal, *speculum, and *fine pewter. *c*1742, fused with silver to make *Sheffield plate which became highly popular silver substitute, but largely superseded in 1850s by electro-plating process. Pure copper unsuitable for casting; in contact with air, acids, salts, fats, etc., corrodes or produces poisonous oxides. Cooking utensils therefore hammered, wrought, and lined with tin by various processes over the centuries; by 18th century, many other items of kitchen equipment were treated in this way, e.g. buckets, jugs, salt cellars, bread-bins, etc., and a few display items, e.g. wine coolers. Copper coffee and tea pots also made, particularly in Europe. Copper reacted well to gilding; gilt-copper widely used in the Middle Ages (until mid 16th century), particularly in European monasteries and churches for all decorative pieces and as substitute for gold; enamelled copper similarly used from 11th to 13th centuries.

copper blank. Object cut from thin sheet of copper, shaped by hand or die-stamped, for finishing in enamel.

copper-red decoration. Ceramic technique invented by Korean potters during late 12th century A.D.; also found on some later Chinese or Japanese ceramics. Originated because cobalt-blue, main decorative oxide on mainland, difficult to obtain, and at times restricted (e.g. 15th century) to use on ware for nobility. Speciality of official Punwon factories, near Seoul. Clear red colour very difficult to achieve, as oxidation in firing produces green colour, and insufficient heat causes running or blotching. Lotus flowers, bamboo, or birds appear in strong red on white porcelain under clear glaze. Used throughout Yi period. Later, sometimes combined with cobalt-blue. In rare cases, used as monochrome colour. Technique developed in China under Yüan dynasty at *Ching-tê-chên: copper oxide applied under white glaze. Perfected under Emperor *Hsüan Tê. Quite frequently overfired to produce grey colour. *Illustration at* stem cup.

coqueret. In European watches before introduction of jewelling from England, polished teel end plate on balance *cock, reducing iction of top balance pivot.

coquillage (French, from *coquille,* 'shell-fish'). Decorative shell shapes, popular design on rococo furniture, etc.

coral. Hard skeletons of various marine organisms chiefly consisting of calcium carbonate. Red or precious coral found in Mediterranean Sea used from ancient times as personal ornament and for decoration. Coral branches hung round children's necks by Romans to protect them from danger; also thought to have medicinal virtues. Viewed as charm during Middle Ages when it was often used for rosary beads (sometimes carved). In 16th and 17th centuries used for pendants. In early 19th century France used for decorating combs and other articles. Extremely popular in England *c*1845–65. Worn as necklace, tiara, etc. in natural or branch form or carved to form crosses, roses, hands, cameos, etc. Coral rattles and teething rings given to babies. Much coral jewellery made in Naples and Genoa and exported to other parts of Europe. Coral cameos carved in Italy and mounted e.g. in France and Britain.

cordial glass. Before 1740s, similar to wine glass but smaller and thicker with funnel or bell shaped bowl. Stems then became longer with short, squat, or trumpet bowls. From mid 18th century more graceful and ornate.

core or **anima** (in bronzes). In *lost-wax

Cork Glass Company. Left: decanter c1810 with typical moulded base and shallow cut decoration. Right: decanter made by Waterloo Company, Cork, c1810.

process of hollow casting, central element of clay, etc., around which metal is poured. After cooling, it may be chipped out or left inside finished object.

Corinthian column. Classical Greek column with bell-shaped upper part or capital adorned with rows of acanthus and other foliage. Shape employed for some neo-classical style silver *candlesticks.

Cork Glass Company. Founded 1793 in Cork, Ireland. Employed English glass blowers, mainly from Stourbridge, to produce plain glassware and black bottles. Became noted for mould-blown hollow glassware and finely cut flint-glass of unusual clarity and brilliance. Pieces marked Cork Glass Co. date from *c*1812. Ownership changed frequently. Factory closed 1818.

corking. *See* caulking.

corkscrew. Implement for removing bottle corks; generally consists of cross-bar and screw; mount or handle sometimes silver, but screw usually steel. Various shapes and sizes used in Britain, Europe, and America from late 17th century, when corks adopted as bottle stoppers; some types patented.

corkscrew thumbpiece. Twisted thumbpiece of Dutch origin much used in America, particularly on tankards made in New York 18th century.

corner, angle, desk, roundabout or **writing chair.** Chair with concave yoke-rail continuing to form arms (yoke-rail may be higher than arm level); seat frame horizontally convex at front, extending beyond arms. One leg at each side, at back, and at centre front. Cane back

*Corner chair. *Chippendale style, English, mid 18th century; carved mahogany with *vase splats.*

and seat common in 18th century. May be used as desk chair (*fauteuil de bureau*), because position of arms allows user to draw chair close to desk. Dates from 18th century.

corner cupboard or **encoigneur.** Free-standing cupboard designed to fit into corner of room; solid or glazed door or doors form flat or *bombé* front. Popular by 18th century when often made in pairs with marble top and matching set of shelves to go above. Few

*Corner cupboard. Veneered on oak with tulip wood, lozenge-shaped marquetry, mounted with ormolu trophies, gladiatorial masks, swags etc.; marble top. French, late 18th century, by G. *Joubert. Height 3ft.*

examples today found with original set of shelves.

cornflower sprig. *See barbeau* sprig.

cornucopia or **horn of plenty.** In ceramic decoration, motif of goat's horn overflowing with fruit, vegetables, or flowers, symbolic of abundance; appears from Renaissance period. Feature of rococo style *décor *à la corne.* Frequently modelled as flower holder; examples include vases in parian ware made at Bennington, porcelain made at Worcester in mid 18th century, and salt-glaze in Staffordshire.

cornucopia flasks. American glass flasks blown in full-size two-piece moulds, mainly pint and half-pint sizes. Bear intaglio devices of urn of fruit or cornucopia. Made 1815–40.

Coromandel lacquer. *See* bantam work.

Corrado family. *See* Conrade family.

Correr service. Italian maiolica service, with *istoriato* decoration, early work of N. *Pellipario, dated *c*1515. 17 plates preserved in Correr Museum, Venice.

Coster, Salomon (d 1659). Dutch clock and watch maker; maker of first pendulum clock for C. *Huygens (1657).

costrel. *See* pilgrim bottle.

Cosway, Richard (1742–1821). English miniaturist. Exhibited portrait miniatures from 1760. Elected Royal Academician in 1771. Patronized by Prince Regent from 1785; very fashionable and flamboyantly wealthy until illness stopped work (1806). Miniatures on ivory, rarely enamel. Work characterized by blue sky backrounds flecked with white clouds. Wife Mary (d 1838) also artist.

Coteau, Jean (*c*1739–after 1812). French enamel painter who worked at Sèvres, 1780–84. Developed method of translucent enamelling

Richard Cosway. Portrait of unknown lady.

Samuel Cotes. Portrait of Mrs Yates, the actress. Signed and dated 1776.

using **paillons* to decorate snuff-boxes, etc., in Louis XVI style.

Cotes, Samuel (1734–1818). English enamel painter. Exhibited portrait enamels at Royal Academy, 1769–89. Also painted miniatures on ivory and portraits in pastel.

cottage china. Porcelain tableware with decoration restricted to polychrome flower sprigs and garlands; no gilding. Made by R. *Champion in Bristol; later made at New Hall.

cottage clock. Small, inexpensive mantel clock (*c*7in. high), produced in 19th century England. Wooden case, with verge watch movement. Name also describes American clock of same period: small version of *Connecticut shelf clock (less than 12in. high). Makers include S. *Thomas.

cottages. English earthenware or porcelain modelled in shape of cottages, adapted for use as night lamps, money boxes, storage jars, and, particularly, pastille burners, from 17th century. Makers include T. *Whieldon, Rockingham, Coalport, Minton, and Spode. Models of houses where murders committed made in earthenware from 1830s, notably by S. *Smith, *c*1850.

Cotterill, Edmund (1795–1858). English sculptor and silver designer trained at Academy schools. In *c*1833, joined R. *Garrard the Younger, as head of design section. Designed many pieces for royal collections and presentation pieces, particularly racing trophies, e.g. Ascot Cup (1842), Queen's Cup for Ascot (1848). Exponent of naturalistic style popular in first half of 19th century; trophies generally realistic figure groups, e.g. battle incident, Mexican lassoing wild horse, Arab horsemen at oasis.

Cottey, Abel (1655–1711). English-born clock maker; emigrated to America, setting up business in Philadelphia, 1682. Possibly first American clock maker; produced tall clocks, with eight-day brass movements.

cotton-stalk painter. Unknown porcelain decorator working at Derby, *c*1760. Painted flower sprays inspired by Meissen, with extremely fine stalks, often including red flower with some petals in outline only, on costume and base of figures.

cottrell. *See* chimney-crane.

couch. Like low-backed sofa but with only one end. Later, alternative name for *settee or *sofa.

counter box. Circular silver box approximately $1\frac{1}{4}$in. long by $1\frac{1}{2}$in. in diameter containing 20–37 thin silver discs. Box and discs decorated with engraved portraits or scenes. May have been used as gaming counters or for mathematical calculations in 17th century England, France, and Holland.

count wheel. *See* striking mechanism.

Courrade family. *See* Conrade family.

Courtauld, Augustin II (*c*1686–1751). Huguenot silversmith working in London; apprenticed to S. *Pantin in 1701. Work includes range of domestic ware. Salt of 1730 presented to Corporation of London. Son S. *Courtauld continued in trade. Marks (registered 1708): three lobes enclosing CO with fleur-de-lis above, with variant in Gothic letters.

Court cupboard. English, James I period. Oak with three tiers; drawer under top; middle shelf lifts to form box.

*Cow creamer. George III, made in 1768 by J. *Schuppe.*

Third mark was registered in 1729: trefoil enclosing AC with larger fleur-de-lis above in irregular lobed shield, and variant in 1739, with fleur-de-lis below.

Courtauld, Samuel (1720–65). Huguenot silversmith working in London; apprenticed to father A. *Courtauld II in 1734. Took over father's business (*c*1746). Made range of domestic silver in rococo style. Marks: SC with sun above in three-lobed shield; SC in rectangle. Business continued until 1780 by wife Louisa (mark: LC in lozenge) in partnership with George Cowles (1768–77) and then with her son, Samuel II (joint mark: LC above SC).

court cupboard. Low, two or three storeyed stand (up to *c*4ft high) with open shelves on plain back, and bulbous front supports; used from 16th century to display pewter, silver, etc. Most surviving examples oak, also sometimes walnut; many include central enclosed cupboard with canted sides. Largely replaced from early 18th century by more sophisticated cupboards, sideboards, etc.

Courtenay, Hercules (fl *c*1762). English-born carver and gilder; worked in Philadelphia for B. *Randolph in Chippendale style.

Cousinet, Ambroise-Nicolas (d 1788). French silversmith working in Paris; master in 1745. Made domestic silver in rococo style. Table centrepiece (made 1757–58) consists of 16 silver-gilt statuettes (Chinese man and woman, French man and woman, etc.) for Portuguese Duke of Aveiro. Mark: fleur-de-lis crowned, two pellets, ANC, and serpent.

Cousinet, Henry-Nicolas (d 1768). French silversmith working in Paris; master in 1724; brother of A-N. *Cousinet. Made domestic silver in rococo style. Mark: a fleur-de-lis crowned, two pellets, HNC, and a stirrup.

couvert. French gold, silver, or silver-gilt place setting: dish or plate, spoon, fork, and knife.

couvre-feu. *See* curfew.

cow creamer. Silver or ceramic cream jug in form of cow. Tail, looped over back, serves as handle; mouth as spout. Oval opening in back covered by lid, often with full relief decoration of fly or bee and sometimes small flowers. Made in early 18th century Dutch Delft; silver versions notably by J. *Schuppe, *c*1753–73; also made in traditional style in 19th and 20th century Holland. In English earthenware, made mid 18th to mid 19th centuries in Staffordshire, and in 19th century, usually with lustre decoration, in Sunderland.

cowhorn-and-spur stretcher. Chair stretcher composed of horizontal bent stick with ends attached to front legs, and curve joined to back legs at an angle by two short straight spindles.

cow's tail pendulum. Pendulum swinging in front of clock dial, usually German or Austrian. *See* Black Forest clocks. *Illustration at* plate clock.

Cox, James (fl 1760–90). English maker of automata working in London. Made birds in

James Cox. Combined musical box and clock, mid 18th century. Tinted agate panels held within gold repoussé *cagework and set with pastes and jewels. Height approximately 15in.*

cages, animated figures dancing or playing musical instruments. East India Company presented his work to local officials and rulers. Produced works on commission for Chinese and Russian courts. In 1790 established works in Canton, China. *Illustration also at* Chinese-market clocks.

Coypel, Charles-Antoine (1694–1752). French historical painter, grandson of N. *Coypel; designer at Gobelins tapestry manufactory. Major work, designs for popular 28-piece Story of Don Quixote. Motifs in small pictures, surrounded by ornamented, curving gilt frames; richly-decorated ground. All within complementary border.

Coypel, Noël (1628–1707). French painter; collaborated on decoration of palace of Versailles; designer at *Gobelins tapestry manufactory, where works include eight-panel adaptations of 16th century Triumph of the Gods and eight panels of History of Moses.

Cozzi, Geminiano (fl 1764–1812). Italian porcelain maker, previously banker. In 1765, granted 20-year monopoly of porcelain manufacture in Venice; for a time, employed workmen from Le Nove. From 1769, also made maiolica. Porcelain paste resembles that of Le Nove; used to make tableware and figures. Mark: anchor thickly sketched in iron-red, found usually on tableware and rarely on figures.

crabstock. Handles, spouts, and occasionally finials, moulded in form of knotted branch, found on teapots and other vessels e.g. in salt-glaze, unglazed red stoneware, and creamware made in Staffordshire, Leeds, Liverpool, and Derby, *c*1745–*c*1770. Also found on cream jugs made at Vincennes and Sèvres (1750–65). *Illustration at* Cockpit Hill.

Crace & Son (fl late 18th and 19th centuries). London firm of interior decorators and manufacturers. Imported Chinese goods, including furniture, from late 18th century. Frederick Crace (1779–1859) worked at Royal Pavilion, Brighton, where responsible for *chinoiserie* decoration. John G. Crace worked from 1840s on neo-Gothic designs for furnishing schemes, wallpapers, and textiles, many in collaboration with A. W. N. *Pugin. Exhibited furniture, etc. in Gothic style in Medieval Hall at Great Exhibition of 1851 in London.

cracked ice ground. On *Bristol delftware from *c*1770: pattern resembling cracked ice, painted in blue as background to other decoration. Derived from Chinese porcelain of K'ang Hsi period.

crackle, cracquelure. Ceramic decoration produced by addition to glaze of substance, e.g. pegmatite, which makes it contract more rapidly than body after firing and produces mesh of fine cracks (*cf* *crazing.) Deliberately used on Chinese celadon and porcelain from Sung period, e.g. Lung-ch'üan, Kuan, and Ko wares. *Illustrations at* apple green, Kuan ware.

cradle. Baby's bed, with high sides; either rests on *bends, or is suspended between vertical supports or from horizontal bar, allowing it to rock gently to and fro. Dates from Middle Ages or earlier.

Crailsheim (Württemberg). German faience factory, flourished *c*1749–*c*1810. No mark used consistently, but some tankards painted with hunting scenes have been identified by factory name and W (initial of owner).

crane's-neck bottle. Shape found in pottery of *Koryo period. Round body, with long narrow tube neck, comparable with bamboo rod stuck in gourd. Typical of predominant 'growing' shapes of period, e.g. gourds, flower-blooms, pods.

crazing. Network of fine cracks in ceramic glaze where glaze has contracted more than body in cooling. Some glazes, e.g. tin-enamel, liable to craze if subjected to rapid changes of temperature. Crazing sometimes intentionally produced as *crackle decoration.

Cream jugs. English silver. Left to right: 1) George III, 1794. 2) George II, made in 1799 by Alexander Field. 3) Helmet-shaped jug by Charles Hougham, 1790. 4) George III, made in 1814 by Alice and George Burrows.

cream or **milk jug.** Silver or Sheffield plate container for milk or cream introduced as part of British and European tea service in early 18th century; not regarded as essential until later. Early shapes sometimes reflect those of ewers. Pyriform, shell-shaped, helmet-shaped and oval examples existed from early 18th century; all with either circular foot or three or four cast feet. From *c* 1740 jugs in shape of sauce-boats made. Broad-shaped jugs soon followed, often elaborately decorated in rococo style. Vase-shape predominated in 1780s and *c*1800 low jugs with bulging body on four ball feet made *en suite* with tea service in England. Helmet shape was revived *c*1800 but made with flat base and no foot. *See* cow creamer, goat-and-bee jug.

creamware, cream-coloured earthenware, or **cream-coloured ware.** Low-fired earthenware containing white Devon clay and ground calcined flints, developed in Staffordshire, 1720–40. At first had deep cream body, with yellowish glaze produced by dusting of galena before single firing; often decorated with small stamped motifs. Powdered metallic oxides, sometimes dusted on before firing, ran in glaze; technique developed into *tortoiseshell ware. To avoid injury to potters, patents taken out (1726–32) for grinding flints under water; dusting with powdered galena gradually replaced by use of liquid glaze, said to have been invented *c*1740 by E. *Booth and applied to biscuit before firing. Much creamware made concurrently with salt-glaze ware and decorated with enamel by same potters, e.g. T. *Whieldon, and in same centres, e.g. Leeds, Liverpool, and Derby. J. *Wedgwood, working in 1760s called perfected creamware Queensware and introduced *pearlware, 1779. Creamware produced

*Creamware. Teapot, Staffordshire, c1765; decorated with print and coloured by W. *Greatbach.*

Credence table. Oak, table top shown folded. English, 17th century.

Credenza. *Walnut, architectural design with fluted pilasters and *dentil moulding beneath rectangular top. Italian, 17th century. Width 2ft4in.*

in Paris from 1760; began generally to supersede other forms of tableware, including *tin-glazed earthenware and *salt-glaze. *Illustrations also at* Cockpit Hill, Leeds.

credence. Medieval table holding consecrated communion bread and wine. By late 16th century used by laity as small side table. Became display-piece for plate and eventually developed into *buffet.

credenza. Italian *sideboard with two or three doors separated by panels or columns. Frieze between doors and top has drawers above door areas, decorative carving over dividing sections. Three-door examples uncommon after end of 15th century.

creepers. Smallest and inside pair of set of six fireplace irons (*cf* andirons, firedogs) usually simple, low, scroll-footed, wrought or cast-iron objects which took main weight of logs.

Creil (Oise). French factory established 1794 for production of *faïence fine,* mainly decorated in Paris with transfer-printing in black enamel. In early 18th century, united with factory at Montereau. Production continued until 1895. Mark: CREIL, impressed; printed initials of decorators include monograms AS (red) and SCL (black).

Crespin, Paul (1694–1770). Huguenot silversmith working in London; family settled in England *c* 1687; received freedom in 1721. Made range of domestic silver; earliest work in Régence style, later rococo. Patronized by British and European aristocracy: in 1724 made silver bath (since disappeared) for John V of Portugal; supplied plate to Russian royal family (1726); in 1730s and 1740s patronized by Dukes of Devonshire and Portland. Latterly, produced many pierced baskets and dishes; retired *c*1759. Marks: CR with a star below; PC (1739); CR in script (1740).

Cressent, Charles (1685–1768). French *ébéniste* and *fondeur-ciseleur.* Studied under A-C. *Boulle. Cabinet maker to the Regent, Philippe, duc d'Orléans; became sculptor to Louis XV sometime after 1746. Furniture characterized by high-quality ormolu mounts. Prosecuted several times for casting and gilding mounts himself, ignoring guild regulations. Stamp: C. CRESSENT; used only on late work. *Illustration at commode.*

cresset. Iron basket for fuel, attached to long rod; used as firelighter or lantern.

crest. Figure or *device placed on wreath or coronet and appearing above shield and helmet in coats of arms. *See* heraldic engraving.

crest or **cresting.** Free-standing pierced ornament in wood or metal above clock case.

cresting. In furniture, carved ornament on top of *yoke-rail of chair, head-board or foot-board of bed, along back rail of settee, day bed, etc; also on top of picture or mirror frame. In silver, feature of Gothic style. Found on standing cups and salts. Also device above shield and helmet on coat of arms.

crest-rail. *See* yoke-rail.

Criaerd, Mathieu (b 1689). French *ébéniste* of Flemish descent; became *maître-ébéniste* in 1738. Worked for J-F. *Oeben. Known particularly for *commodes* decorated in lacquer work and marquetry.

cri or **cri de l'étain.** Crackling sound (French, 'cry') emitted by tin, or tin content in good quality pewter, when object bent backwards and forwards.

cricket. Simple low wooden footstool common in England and America from 17th century.

cricket table. 17th century small simple three-legged table.

crimping. Creating wavy effect on body or rim of glass vessel. Popular in *façon de Venise* and American glass.

crinoline groups. *See* J. J. Kändler.

Cripps, William (d after 1767). English silversmith working in London; apprenticed to D. *Willaume the Younger, 1730–31; granted freedom in 1738. Made mainly domestic silver, some in rococo style. Mark (in 1738): WC in wavy shield; retired (or died) in 1767 when son, Mark, entered his mark from same address. *Illustration at* race cup.

cris de Paris (French, 'street cries of Paris'). Group of Meissen porcelain figures of Parisian artisans modelled 1742–44, includes Bird Seller (1742), Sower (1744), Gardeners (1746); after drawings of street vendors by French sculptor Edmé Bouchardon (1698–1762). Second series modelled by J. J. *Kändler and P. *Reinicke (1753–55) includes Peepshowman, Lemonade Seller and *c*20 other subjects.

Cristallerie de St Louis. French glasshouse founded in 1767 under royal patronage. First producer in France of English-type lead crystal. From 1782, established on commercial basis. Specialized in coloured glass from 1839; vessels such as vases, jugs, and scent bottles distinguished by bright colouring and graceful design, frequently gilded and mounted in gilt-bronze. Throughout 19th century, main producer of fine glass tableware in France. Also noted for *paperweights, made mainly from 1847–49, signed SL, often with flattened dome. Made finest snake weights, though floral and fruit motifs frequently used, all characterized by soft colouring.

cristallo. *See* crystal glass.

cristallo ceramie. *See* sulphides.

Cristofori, Bartolommeo (1655–1731). Italian inventor of *pianoforte, *c*1709; worked in Florence. Two of his intruments survive; one, dated 1720, now in Metropolitan Museum of Modern Art, New York; other, dated 1726, in Leipzig.

crizzled glass. Condition usually created by faulty proportioning of ingredients or uneven heating (mainly in pre-18th century glass), causing sour surface smell and fine cracks in glass, which eventually disintegrates. *Illustration at* G. Ravenscroft.

crock. *See* cauldron.

croft. Writing cabinet, with oval drop-leaf top. 12 shallow drawers behind door in base. Invented by the Revd Sir Herbert Croft, Bt (1751–1816).

Crolius, William (b 1700). German-born potter of stoneware in America, brother-in-law of J. *Remmey. In New York from 1718; produced jugs, jars, and dishes; succeeded by family until 1887.

Cromwellian chair. Modern term for oak armchair or side chair, with seat and upper section of back upholstered in leather, fastened with round-headed brass nails. Arms may be leather-covered, or plain wood with ball-shaped turnings (also found on front section of box stretcher and front legs). Seat square; back slightly rectangular. Made in mid 17th century England and much reproduced from mid 19th century.

Cromwellian clock. Name sometimes incorrectly used for *lantern clock.

cross. Earliest type of cross used in Christian worship was processional cross mounted on tall staff; 9th century Spanish examples survive. By 11th century, head of processional cross sometimes removed and placed on altar, but altar crosses not generally used until 17th and 18th centuries; then formed part of set with two or more candlesticks; foot, stem, etc., in style of latter. (Crosses not allowed on Church of England altars until 19th century Tractarian movement.) Only wealthiest churches or abbeys had silver crosses; most examples base metal. Widely used type of processional cross from 13th century was of wood covered with embossed silver or copper plaques; enamel ornament also common. Ends of arms generally had stylized flowers, sacred symbols, figures of evangelists, etc. In Europe, filigree crosses were also made (filigree work covers entire surface), often further embellished with enamel. Many 15th and 16th century Spanish processional crosses survive; usually silver-gilt, with realistic figure of Christ and translucent enamel ornament.

Cross worn as personal ornament or devotional symbol in Britain and all other parts of Europe from early Middle Ages, made from enamelled or gem-set gold, coral, etc., and sometimes containing receptacle for relic. Tau cross (resembling Greek letter T), of pre-Christian origin, and similar ancient Egyptian 'ankh' (life) symbol with loop above crossbar, used as shapes for pendants in 16th century England and Denmark, subsequently common in Spain together with normal Latin cross. Spanish types large, worn on long chain, and made in various materials decorated with precious stones, rock-crystal, filigree, etc. Cross pendants again fashionable in 19th century England during Gothic revival; also Maltese cross based on eight-pointed badge of knights of Malta. Some examples in white chalcedony with coloured gold and turquoises. *See* rosary.

cross-banding. Decorative use of thin cross-grained strips of veneer on furniture or panelling. *Illustration at poudreuse.*

cross-beat escapement. *See* escapement.

Crosse, Richard (1742–1810). English enamel painter. Also painted miniatures in watercolours and portraits in oils. Deaf and dumb, very prolific, painted *c*100 miniatures in 1777 alone. Appointed enamel painter to George III in 1790. Noted for small full-length portraits. Invariably used greenish-blue tint for shading features, and often on hair and background. Many of his colours have faded.

cross-hatching. Creation of shade or tone on silver surface with sets of engraved parallel lines crossing each other. *See* heraldic engraving.

cross-staff or **Jacob's staff.** Early instrument for measuring altitudes in astronomy, navigation, and surveying; probably invented *c*1300. Graduated wood or ivory staff, 3–4ft long, carries sliding cross-piece. Observer places end of staff against cheek and moves cross-piece until lower end coincides with horizon, upper end with sun or object to be measured. Angle of altitude read from scale. Developed into *back-staff in late 16th century, but still in use until mid 18th century.

cross watch. *See* form watch.

crouchware. Drab grey or brownish salt-glazed stoneware, traditionally described as antecedent of white Staffordshire salt-glaze; believed to date from before 1714. Staffordshire grey stoneware decorated with white reliefs, sometimes called crouchware, made later, *c*1740.

crowned C or **C-poinçon.** Excise mark occurring on French ormolu between 5 March 1745 and 4 February 1749.

crown glass. Window glass produced by opening blown paraison, transferring it to pontil and rotating it in front of furnace opening with frequent re-heating. Centrifugal force produces large, circular pane of glass with 'bull's eye' mark in centre from pontil. Technique probably dates from antiquity though attributed to 12th century Normans, who introduced technique to England. Also called Normandy process. In foreign literature, 'crown glass' denotes English flint-glass.

crown wheel. Escape wheel of verge *escapement.

crozier. Bishop's staff of office, with curved end resembling shepherd's crook. Probably used from 5th century; by 7th century, at consecration bishop received crozier which was often buried with him. Early French examples of carved ivory; also made of precious metals, ornamented with enamel and gems. Figure, e.g. Madonna and child, saint, etc., often set in volute of handle. Very elaborate Gothic examples exist with node shaped like a Gothic church below volute; also elaborately modelled architectural motifs and figures set in niches. Many Spanish croziers of this period survive in silver-gilt.

crucifix clock. *Pillar clock, in form of Christ on the cross, made in Augsburg, Germany from early 17th century. Gilt metal crucifix; automaton figures on base. Revolving globe at top, with hour band indicating time. Many surviving examples are 19th century copies.

Crucifix clock. German, gilt copper, 17th century. Brass ball on top of cross rotates to show time.

*Cruet frame. Tray with gadrooned borders; reeded frame containing cut-glass bottles for oil, vinegar, mustard, and salt. Made by M. *Boulton, 1808. Height 7½in.*

cruet frame or **stand** or **oil and vinegar stand.** Silver or Sheffield plate frame to hold cruets and sometimes casters; made from 18th century. Simplest with open-work frame of two silver rings following shape of cruets, flat base, and lateral handle. Some raised on four moulded feet. In late 18th century boat-shaped stands with handles at ends and stands with piercedwork sides both common. Central handle, a vertical rod terminating in large oval loop, sometimes replaced lateral handle. Glass cruets had matching silver caps and mounts. *See* Warwick frame.

cruets. Small glass bottles for vinegar and oil. Introduced to England from Venice in 17th century. Made by G. *Ravenscroft in flint-glass with nipt diamond waies decoration. Up to mid 18th century, mallet shaped, later with swelling body tapering at foot and neck; by late 18th century, with pedestal foot. From *c*1776, cylindrical body with tapering neck found; from *c*1778, urn-shaped bottle on spreading foot, usually of cut glass. *Cruet frames, mainly silver, introduced early 18th century. Enamelled opaque-white cruets made at *Bristol from 1750s, usually with wooden cover and ivory finial; M. *Edkins specialized in enamelling gold-mounted examples with birds, foliage, and scrollwork. *cf* altar-cruet.

Crunden, John (1740–*c*1828). English architect, noted for designs in Joyner and Cabinetmaker's Darling or Pocket Directory (1765) and in collaboration with J. H. Morris, The Carpenter's Companion for Chinese Railings and Gates (1765), containing fretwork and latticework designs.

cruisie or **betty lamp.** Simple oil-lamp; evolved from round clay dish in 16th century or earlier to oval iron or latten type with handle or hanging-bracket and pointed end for wick. Late 17th century 'double crusie' has pan beneath for drips of oil; by 1700 wick-holder design improved and drip-pan unnecessary. Room for two or more wicks. From mid 18th century, made of brass or copper; improved design includes spreading hollow foot, weighted with sand, and hinged cover.

Crutched Friars Glass House. Founded *c*1567 by J. *Carré who employed first Lorraine then Venetian glass blowers to produce *façon de Venise* glass. Taken over by G. *Verzelini in 1572. Produced presentation goblets of soda-lime glass, many with hollow blown baluster stems, engraved by A. *de Lysle; also functional table glass. Factory burnt down in 1575, probably by rivals.

crystal. *See* rock-crystal.

crystal glass. 15th century Venetians, attempting to reproduce clarity and brilliance of rock-crystal, developed clear soda-glass (*cristallo*) decolourized with manganese; had to be thinly blown to avoid slight grey or brown tinge. *c*1680, Bohemiansused clear soda-lime glass particularly suited to deep cutting and engraving, having a rather hard refractive quality; clearer, less brittle glass not subject to crizzling introduced probably by J. *Kunckel at Potsdam by 1714. In late 17th century England, G. *Ravenscroft made fine crystal, *lead glass, first using calcined flints ground to fine powder for silica, with lead oxide as flux, but flint shortly replaced by sand. English crystal still often referred to as flint-glass. Will not blow as thinly as Venetian *cristallo,* but has finer brilliance and refractive quality than any other glass. From late 17th century, glasshouses established at home and abroad for manufacture of fine tableware and ornamental glass, particularly in Holland and Scandinavia (*Nøstetangen). Term *cristal* first used in France with founding of Manufacture Royale des Cristaux de la Reine in 1780, to produce fine glass *à l'anglaise*.

crystal watch. *See* rock-crystal watch.

C-scroll (in silver). Decorative motif in form of letter C. Also handle, especially on tankards, mugs, ewers, two-handled cups, etc., from 16th century.

Cucci, Domenico (*c*1635–*c*1705). Italian cabinet maker, sculptor, goldsmith. Brought to Gobelins, Paris, to work for Louis XIV; naturalized French in 1664. Specialized in making elaborate ebony cabinets, with lavish use of bronze, tortoise-shell, mosaic, and lapis lazuli.

cuckoo clock. Development of *Black Forest clock, *c*1730, with striking mechanism actuating wooden cuckoo from behind trap-door; simulated bird-call sounded on two small organ pipes. Early examples with short pendulum in front of dial, although *foliot still used until 1760. Brass wheels introduced in late 18th century, but still mounted on turned wooden arbors, with brass pivot holes set in wooden plates; all-brass movements from mid 19th century. Few survive from before 1840.

Cucumber slicer. Silver plate, c*1810. Adjustable blade with ivory handle; baluster stem and gadrooned base. Height 7¼in.*

Cuenca *technique on two southern Spanish tiles, mid 16th century.*

cucumber slicer. Utensil made in silver in late 18th century, more often in Sheffield plate in early 19th century Britain; rare. Cucumber fixed inside horizontal cylinder with handle at one end, on stand; when handle is wound, cucumber moves forward and slicing blade revolves.

cuenca. Ceramic technique for controlling glaze on tiles, developed at Toledo and Seville, Spain in early 16th century. Patterns deeply impressed in soft clay, forming sunken areas which held coloured glazes and prevented mixing during firing. *cf cuerda seca.*

Cuenca carpets. Spanish carpets woven in Cuenca from 15th century; peak production in 17th and 18th centuries, when also major centre for European carpet trade. Early patterns similar to those of *Alcaraz, especially wreath motifs and *Holbein or *Lotto types. From mid 17th century, used Turkish knot for woollen pile on goat-hair foundation, with undyed warp and dyed weft. After brief period of decline in early 18th century, industry revived under patronage of Charles III, with foundation of royal state factory (Fabrica Real) and school for knotting. Carpets follow English and French models, with particularly fine copies of *Savonnerie and *Aubusson carpets woven until 19th century.

cuerda seca (Spanish, 'dry cord'). Ceramic technique invented by early Islamic potters to prevent mingling of different coloured glazes or enamels during firing. Outlines of pattern drawn in manganese-purple mixed with grease which burned away in firing but acted as barrier between colours. Used in northern Africa from 11th century, Persia from 14th century, and Spain from *c*1500 (on tiles). At Valencia in 14th century used in decoration of vases and dishes.

Cufic script. *See* Kufic script.

Cuerda seca *technique on four southern Spanish earthenware tiles. Late 14th century.*

cullet. Broken glass added to *batch to promote fusion and improve quality of *metal. Also economic use of glasshouse waste. During period of *Glass Excise Act, cullet cheaper than new ingredients. In manufacture of lead glass, constituted 25–50% of ingredients. Also used to form *frit in early manufacture of soft-paste porcelain.

Cummings, Thomas Sier (1804–94). English-born American miniaturist and portrait painter. Teachers included H. *Inman. Worked in oils and watercolours. Son, Thomas Augustus Jr. (1823–59) also portrait painter and miniaturist.

cup. Vessel, for drinking or display, usually footed and with one or two handles, made throughout Europe from Middle Ages. Display piece generally of precious metals but examples of 15th century cup-and-cover survive in gilt copper. Plain pewter cups on flared foot, with plain or scrolled handles, common in 19th century. *See* Boleyn Cup, Bowes Cup, bridal cup, caudle cup, chalice, christening cup, ciborium, coconut cup, college cup, columbine cup, communion cup, double cup, dram cup, feeding cup, font-shaped cup, globe cup, gourd cup, guild cup, hanap, Jack-in-the-Cellar, *Jungfrauenbecher*, King John's Cup, loving cup, Magdalen cup, Marston Cup, master cup, melon cup, Myddleton Cup, nautilus cup, obelisk cup, ostrich-egg cup, ox-eye cup, pineapple cup, porringer, posset cup, puzzle cup, race cup, *Riesenpokal*, seal cup, spout cup, standing cup, steeple cup, stirrup-cup, *tazza*, teacup, thistle cup, two-handled cup, wager cup, wassail bowl, welcome cup, windmill cup, wine cup.

cup-and-cover motif. Turned *bulb, shaped to resemble oval cup-and-cover. Common on 16th and 17th century English furniture.

cupboard. In Middle Ages, open-shelved structure used to hold and display cups and drinking vessels. Enclosed section with doors introduced *c*1550. In 17th century evolved into large piece of wall furniture; lower section enclosed, with doors at front, and surmounted by series of recessed shelves; some examples completely enclosed, with doors to both top and bottom sections. *See* almirah, *armoire*, aumbry, corner cupboard, court cupboard, *kas*, livery cupboard, night table, Welsh dresser.

cupboard plate. *See* sideboard plate.

cupellation. Assaying of gold or silver in a cupel (small, circular vessel of bone ash formed in mould). For silver, scraping from object weighed, wrapped in pure lead foil, and heated. Base metal oxidizes or is absorbed in bone ash of cupel leaving pellet of pure silver for weighing. For gold, scraping wrapped in pure lead and silver foil. Silver removed from pellet of gold and silver by hot nitric acid, leaving pure gold to be weighed. Process in use from 15th century.

cupid's bow (in furniture). Yoke-rail or cresting curved to resemble bow-frame. Used *c*1750.

cupped top. Semi-circular indentation at mid-point of yoke-rail on upholstered chair back, designed to accommodate sitter's pigtail. Georgian.

cupping-dish. *See* bleeding-bowl.

Curfew. Probably English, brass with repoussé *heads within wreaths and floral ornament; mid 17th century. Height* 16*in.*

Curtain holders. Mid 19th century English bead-work.

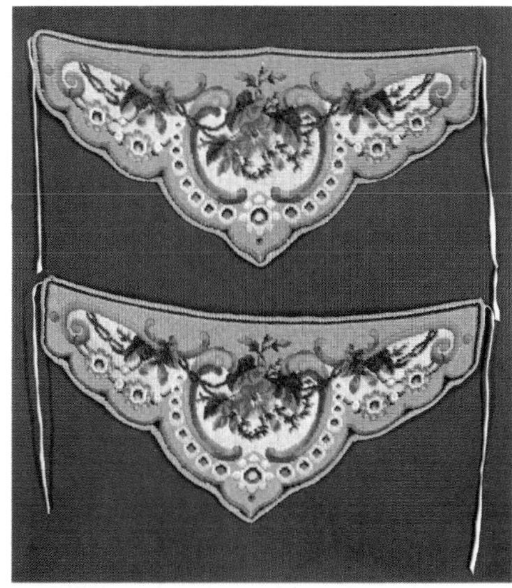

cup plate. Small glass plate (diameter $2\frac{1}{2}$–$4\frac{1}{2}$in.), with circular depression in centre for holding cup when pouring tea into saucer to cool. Popular *c*1827–50 in Europe and, in lacy pressed glass, in America.

cup salt. Salt with wide bowl, on stem and moulded foot, made in pewter throughout second half of 18th century.

curfew or **couvre-feu.** Quarter-spherical hearth cover, first of forged iron, later of brass or copper with embossed ornament. Plain strap handle runs from top to bottom, joined at both ends. Used at night on *down hearth, to reduce fire risk, during 16th and 17th centuries.

curricule. Armchair similar in shape to seat of open carriage. *Sheraton design.

curtain-holder or **hold-back.** Usually gilt-brass, decorative wall-fitting to hold drawn-back curtains in place at sides of window; sometimes U-shape at right-angle to window; or short steel rod with gilt embellishment. Made in pairs, introduced mid 18th century, popular throughout 19th.

Curtis, Lemuel (1790–1857). American clock maker, from Massachusetts; apprenticed to Willard family. Designer of *girandole clock, and maker of varied types of wall clock. *Illustration at* girandole clock.

curule chair. *See* X-frame chair.

curule frame (in furniture). *See* X-frame.

cusp-back. 19th century chair back derived from waisted *balloon-back. Continuous back frame has cusps at top.

cuspidor. *See* spittoon.

Custode, Pierre (d 1656). One of family of French potters working at The Ostrich faience factory, Nevers, established on expiry of privilege granted to *Conrade family, *c*1633. Traditionally credited with introduction of **bleus de Nevers*. Factory continued until late 18th century.

custodia. Huge gold or silver-gilt *monstrance in architectural form; central tower surrounded by gables, flying buttresses, pinnacles, small statuettes, or religious figures, etc. Most common in 15th and 16th century Spain; also made in France, Netherlands, Germany, and Poland.

cut-card work. Gold or silver applied ornament; design cut out of thin sheet and soldered to object; often also pierced and/or engraved. Much used from mid 17th to early 18th centuries, e.g. foliate ornament applied as calyx or border round body of vessel. *See* Huguenot silver.

cut glass. Glass decorated by cutting and polishing to bring out refracting qualities. Wheel cutting first practised successfully by Romans. Technique died out in Europe, apart from 12th century *Hedwig glasses, until revived in 17th century by C. *Lehmann. Became highly developed in Germany and Bohemia, typical is work of G. *Spiller. English glass makers in 18th century, e.g. J. *Akerman, employed German glass cutters to train native apprentices. New *lead glass particularly suited to cutting and fine work produced until *Glass Excise Act (1745) restricted use of metal, popularizing shallow cutting, e.g. *fluting. Dia-

Cut-card work around base of bowl of Queen Anne two-handled cup, made by John Leach, London, 1702. Moulded, stepped foot; applied with cast grotesque handles.

Cut glass. Comport. English, dated c1830 because of hobnail cut of glass.

Cut steel. Shoe *buckle, English, c1785, with Wedgwood *jasper ware plaques. Probably from workshop of M. *Boulton.

mond patterns cut in deep relief common from early 19th century. Free trade granted to Ireland (1780), where fine cut glass produced until development of mechanically pressed glass. *See* glass cutting.

cut or **faceted steel.** Decorative facet-cut steel fashionable in 18th and early 19th centuries. Used at *Tula factory for large and small objects; at *Woodstock and by M. *Boulton for buttons, buckles, jewellery, sword-hilts. *See* chiselled steel.

cut or **sliced fruit painter.** Unknown painter, perhaps J. *Giles or member of his workshop. Decorated plates from Worcester, Chelsea, and, less often, Bow, with sprays of leaves and fruit, e.g. cherries, plums, and cut apples, as well as exotic birds or naturalistic insects (cut-fruit-and-insects pattern), sometimes on claret or turquoise ground.

cut steel jewellery. Buckles, necklaces, bracelets, etc. made of *cut steel especially in France and England from 17th century. In late 18th and early 19th centuries, used as cheaper and more durable alternative to *marcasite. Sometimes used as setting for *Wedgwood jewellery.

Cyfflé, Paul-Louis (1724–1806). Belgian-born sculptor and ceramic modeller. From 1741, worked as goldsmith in Paris. Modelled figures in material resembling biscuit porcelain and in pipeclay, both sold as **terre de Lorraine*; worked at Lunéville (*c*1752), Saint-Clément, and Bellevue. Established factory at Lunéville (1766–80). Many figures dated 1772–80 made from his moulds at Niderviller. Established factory in Flanders. Models, taken from every-day life, include Stocking-mender, Cobbler, Boy Sweep, and Children with a Dead Bird. Some figures copied in porcelain at *Vinovo, and in Staffordshire earthenware, e.g. by R. *Wood. Biscuit porcelain made at Lunéville marked TERRE DE LORRAINE in rectangle over C, CYFFLE A LUNEVILLE and TDL, all impressed.

cylinder escapement. *See* escapement.

cylinder-top desk. *See* roll-top desk.

cymaise or **cymarre.** *See* cimaise.

cyma recta. Moulding with convex curve below, concave above.

cyma reversa. *Ogee moulding; double continuous curve in cross-section, concave below, convex above.

Daffinger, Moritz Michael (b 1790). Austrian miniaturist. Studied under F. H. *Füger. Work includes portraits of members of court at Vienna.

Dagestan or **Daghestan carpets.** Stiff north Caucasian carpets with extremely tight weave, woollen foundation, and medium-length Turkish-knotted pile. Fringed ends woven into honeycomb design. Mainly prayer rugs with all-over mihrab pattern of stylized trellis or individual flowers on light, often white, ground. Numerous borders. Also some long runners with trellis or stepped pattern of star-like forms.

Jules Dalou. Bronze figure of peasant woman, c1875, signed. Base inscribed Merby and S. Susses Frères Edte Paris cire perdue, and with founder's stamp. Height 4in.

Dalou, Jules (1838-1902). French sculptor of naturalistic school. Many sculptures of allegorical groups, common people, and peasants (reflecting influence of J-F. Millet). In London 1871–79. Well-known works include *Triomphe de la République* (Place de la Nation, Paris), and memorial to Delacroix (Luxembourg Gardens, Paris). Many small bronzes from his clay sketches made after his death by founder Hébrard.

damascening. True damascening is process of inlaying metal body with contrasting metal strips; fine channels are cut in iron, bronze, or brass body and gold, silver, or copper wires inserted, hammered flush with the surface, and burnished. Developed originally in Near East (Damascus). Usual European method ('counterfeit' or 'false' damascening) was hatching of entire surface of object with fine lines to give 'tooth'. Design was then outlined with brass stylus and gold or silver applied with chasing tool. Damascening first practised in Europe at Milan, Italy, *c*1550–1600, particularly on sword-blades and furniture mounts; adopted elsewhere in 17th century; largely died out by 18th century.

Damascus carpets. Inaccurate term for Islamic carpets with Turkish-knotted pile and Mamluk designs. Name also erroneously given to *Mamluk carpets, before discovery of Cairo origin.

Damascus ware. *See* Isnik.

Dameral (fl early 19th century). French neo-classical silversmith, and founder. Bronze statuettes of Empress Marie-Louise (signed *Dameral coelavit*) and Napoleon I, now in Wallace Collection, London.

Daniel, Joseph (d 1806) and Daniel (*c*1760–1806). English jewellers, engravers, and miniaturists; brothers, working at Bath, Somerset. Impossible to distinguish between their work. Used crayons or oils; also made pictures in hair. Daniel exhibited miniature of a 'Jew Rabbi' at Society of Artists, 1783. No signed work.

Dannhäuser, Leopold (d 1786). Porcelain modeller at Vienna (*c*1762–86). Best known for figures of courtiers, artisans, and 'crinoline groups' which typify Austrian rococo porcelain.

Dannhöfer, Joseph Philip (1712–90). German ceramic artist; painted faience and porcelain. Famous for baroque style *chinoiseries,* and especially landscapes. Developed styles at Vienna, influence spread to Bayreuth (1737–44), Abtsbessingen (1744–47), Höchst (1747–51), and Ludwigsburg (1762). Probably also worked at Fulda and Hanau and as *Hausmaler.*

Danske pot. *See* tankard.

Danzig chest. Spruce chest imported into Britain and western Europe from Poland during 16th and early 17th centuries.

Darley, Matthew (*c*1750–78). English designer, engraver, and caricaturist. Design books include A New Book of Chinese, Gothic and Modern Chairs (1750) and A New Book of Chinese Design (1754). The Ornamental Architect or Young Artist's Instructor (1770). Engraved many plates for T. *Chippendale.

da Savino, Guido. *See* Andries, Guido.

date letter (in ceramics). *See* Sèvres, Wedgwood date letters, Worcester.

date letter (in gold and silver). Letter of alphabet stamped on gold or silver pieces at assay office indicating year of stamping (not necessarily year of manufacture) and identity of assay-master. Served as guarantee of standard of fineness of article. Different letter used in alphabetical sequence for each year (not necessarily a calendar year). System was first used in France from 1461; 23 letters were employed (J, U, and W excluded). Used in London from 1478; 20 letters used (J, V, W, X, Y, and Z excluded). Each assay-office could have its own cycle. In England, form of letter and shield surrounding it varied to differentiate between cycles; this practice was not regularly followed in France. *See* national entries, e.g. English gold and silver.

Dattel, Heinrich. *See* Taddel.

davenport. Late 18th and 19th century English desk with drawers at side; writing area is slanted or sliding top, often over storage space and additional drawers at rear. Also large American settee dating from 19th century, many examples including bed which is extended mechanically.

Davenport, John (*c*1766–1848). Staffordshire potter. *c*1793, took over pottery at Longport (established 1773); produced blue transfer-printed earthenware until retirement in 1830, when sons took over firm. Maker of flint-glass from *c*1800, and of domestic ironstone china from 1805. Porcelain made from *c*1820; body varies from greyish to translucent white, often painted with naturalistic flowers and fruit in style of Derby. Toby jugs in brightly enamelled cream-coloured earthenware. Marks: impressed anchor or Davenport over anchor (until 1887), DAVENPORT LONGPORT impressed, or DAVENPORT in curved ribbon over anchor.

Davenport. Walnut. Sloping front has fitted interior; four drawers to one side. English, Victorian. Width 4ft8in.

John Davenport. Jardinière *in Chinese style, c1820.*

Davidson & Company. Founded 1867 as Teams Glass Works, at Gateshead-on-Tyne, Durham, by George Davidson to produce glass chimneys for lamps. By 1877, also making wine glasses and small bottles. Warehouse destroyed by fire in 1880. Rebuilt (1881) as Davidson & Company. By 1886 had established large export trade to Australia as well as home market in jugs, dishes, compotes, salad bowls, salvers, butter dishes, sweetmeat glasses, and water sets.

Day-bed. Carved, painted and gilded walnut frame with original Genoa velvet upholstery. English, c1695. Length 5ft.

Davis's quadrant. *See* back-staff.

day-bed or **lit de repos.** Usually a narrow bed, with head and/or foot piece and possibly back, giving it general appearance of settee. Introduced into England from Italy in 16th century. Early models have solid, outward-canted ends; but by turn of 17th century, had only head-piece. Basically, until early Georgian era had no back-piece, and loose cushions on seat. Early examples often distinguished by scrolled legs; William and Mary style has tapered legs; in Queen Anne period, cabriole legs. The **duchesse brisée* became popular in England *c*1780, and continued in use into 19th century. In America from mid 17th century, day-bed followed English models, although Sheraton and Hepplewhite styles not generally copied. In 19th century classical couch, with outward-scrolling ends, popular. In France, day-bed (*lit de repos*) dates from early 17th century, becoming more generally used during Louis XIV period. In Louis XV period, many examples have caned seats. *Duchesse* became popular Louis XVI style, used during 19th century as also were neo-classical examples made during Directoire and Empire periods.

deacon's mark. Mark of deacon of guild struck on Scottish gold and silver from 1457 as guarantee of standard of fineness. Abolished 1681 and replaced by assay-master's mark (usually initials), replaced in turn by thistle in 1759.

dead-beat escapement. *See* escapement.

dead leaf brown or **Kapuzinerbraun** (German, 'Capuchin brown'). Glaze coloured with iron; originated in China and used at Meissen under J. G. *Herold from *c*1720. Used first on reverse of tablewares with upper surfaces painted in underglaze blue on white. Later used throughout 18th century on functional pieces.

Debaufre, Peter and Jacob (fl *c*1700). French watch makers working in London. First applied *jewelling to watches, *c*1704. Peter developed type of verge *escapement with two escape wheels, used in modified form in *Ormskirk watches and some carriage clocks.

de Bettignies, Maximilien-Joseph (d 1865) and brother Henri (fl early 19th century). Members of French family of potters and porcelain makers who managed soft-paste porcelain factory at Tournai and faience factory at Saint-Amand-les-Eaux. In 1818, Henri bought Tournai factory from brother; continued production, succeeded by sons, until 1850. Maximilien-Joseph re-established manufacture of soft-paste porcelain (previously made by J-B-J. *Fauquez, 1771–78) at Saint-Amand-les-Eaux, producing forgeries of Sèvres porcelain; also made earthenware. Succeeded by son.

de Caluwe, Jacobus (d 1730). Dutch potter; maker of red stoneware teapots, 1701–11, in premises of The Pole factory, Delft, bought from van Eenhoorn family. Also recorded in 1713 as teapot maker. Work decorated with prunus blossom in relief against ground of intersecting dotted lines cut with toothed wheel. Mark: IACOBUS .D. CALUWE in oval around running deer.

decanter. In 17th century, *bottles used for decanting wine, but clear, flint-glass decanters became popular after introduction of binning in 18th century, also because more suitable for finely laid table. By late 17th century, some flint-glass decanters similar to shaft and globe bottles made; also have high kick, but looped handle, spout lip, and rim for tying cork. G. *Ravenscroft made a few flint-glass bottle-decanters decorated with *nipt diamond waies. Rare examples made 1725–50 have wider mouth and no handle. In early 18th century heavy based, mallet decanters popular, usually six or eight sided, occasionally cruciform, with

Decanters. Green glass. Gilded labels with stoppers bearing initials for brandy or rum. English, late 18th century.

Decimal dial on silver pocket watch by Chastenet of Limoges, c1800. Enamel dial indicates 10 hours and 100 minutes, smaller dial indicates duodecimal time.

Right:

Décor bois. **Niderviller teapot* c*1770; tin-glazed earthenware with scene* *en camaïeu, *signed J. Deutsch.*

*Paul de Lamerie. Basket, made in London, 1739. Pierced and engraved; with feet in form of grotesque heads; *swing handle. Length 1ft2in.*

Delft. Plate, marked with R for De Roos (The Rose), illustrating Jacob's Dream, from bible; Chinese-influenced border pattern. Early 18th century.

tall neck and rim for tying cork. Stoppers came into general use *c*1750. Ovoid, broad or narrow shouldered decanters made *c*1750–1800; from *c*1755, often decorated with engraved labels depicting contents, naturalistic motifs, and occasionally Jacobite emblems. Independent enamellers in London, Bristol, Birmingham, and Newcastle also worked on decanters, e.g. J. *Giles and *Beilby family. Bristol produced fine blue glass examples with gilded labels (*see* I. *Jacobs, M. *Edkins). From *c*1750, decanters made in cut glass, either with shallow diamond motifs or geometric patterns. In late 18th century, barrel shape with vertically cut lines and incised rings common. Deeply cut, broad, heavy decanters with cut, raised neck rings made particularly in Ireland until mid 19th century. Sets of three or four square, cut glass decanters popular from late 18th century, when heavily cut mallet form also revived. From early 19th century, decanters with cylindrical body cut in deep relief common. In later 19th century some earlier forms revived, but glass whiter and clearer and often pressed. From *c*1870, reaction against mass-produced, machine pressed cut glass wares encouraged some firms, e.g. *Whitefriars, to produce graceful, free-blown decanters with simple, cut or engraved decoration. Claret decanters have glass or, more often, silver, handles. *See* stoppers, ship's decanters.

deception table. Table designed to resemble *Pembroke table, but with concealed storage space large enough to hold chamber pot or other items. Dates from late 18th century.

decimal dial. Dial of clock or watch divided into ten instead of twelve hours. Made in post-Revolution France, 1789–99.

Deckelpokal. Covered goblet made in Germany and Austria; fine examples produced in 18th century Bohemian glass. *Illustration at* engraved glass.

deck watch. Large watch with precision movement, mounted in wooden case: used for checking performance of ship's *chronometer with time obtained from observations of sun or stars taken on deck.

decolourizing (in glass). Substances added to batch to improve clarity and counteract colouring effect of impurities, particularly iron in silica which gives green tint. Main decolourizer is manganese dioxide, once known as 'glassmakers' soap'. Principle of decolourizing known in antiquity, rediscovered by 16th century Venetians. *See* crystal glass.

de Comans, Marc (fl 1600–34). Brussels tapestry master-weaver. With F. *de la Planche, contracted 1607 by Henri IV of France to establish first low-warp loom tapestry workshop in Paris. Manufactory started in or near Hôtel des Gobelins (former residence of prominent Gobelins family), making tapestries modelled on contemporary Flemish styles and designs. Soon most successful in France, and rivalling Brussels and Oudenaarde. Formed basis of *Gobelins tapestry manufactory, and remained major low-warp loom workshop of latter.

décor à guirlandes. Ceramic decoration developed in 1730s at Alcora and in 1740s at Moustiers, associated with J. *Olerys. Border pattern with flowers in festoons hanging from edge of vessel. Often includes portrait medallions and central decoration of figure subjects with garlands of flowers.

decorative clocks. Decoration was major feature of clocks made before improvement in timekeeping performance in late 17th century. Table clocks of *tabernacle and other German types were highly elaborate, often with engraving on gilt-brass case and striking hammers in grotesque animal form. English *lantern clocks were decorated with pierced frets in floral, heraldic, or dolphin motifs. In 18th century English clock cases were restrained except those for export to *Turkish market. French clocks from Louis XIV period often combined high-quality movement with richly ornamented case of ormolu, etc., followed by rococo style with use of horn, shell, *vernis Martin*, and porcelain. Dials also mounted on animal figures (e.g. *elephant clocks) or in branches of tree with porcelain flowers.

décor aux cinq bouquets. Ceramic decoration of five flower sprays arranged on centre and rim of porcelain plates made at Tournai from mid 18th century. Painted in blue, sometimes with outlines in gold. Variation, *décor ronda,* has bouquet at centre, sometimes flies and birds flying on rim.

décor bois. Ceramic *trompe l'oeil* decoration representing engraving printed in monochrome red, black, or grey, of landscapes (sometimes with figures) after e.g. J-A. *Watteau or F. *Boucher, attached to grained wood. On faience made at Niderviller from *c*1770; imitated on porcelain made e.g. in Paris, Brussels, Tournai, and Le Nove. Occasionally found on German porcelain made at Frankenthal, Gera, Nymphenburg and Vienna; also on Chinese *famille rose* wares.

décor coréen. French ceramic decoration, characteristic of Chantilly porcelain (1725–40); derived from Kakiemon style, possibly inspired by Meissen versions, though treatment uses black outlines and brilliant flat colours, e.g. blue, yellow, and turquoise-green. Designs include ripe pomegranate (*grenade*), squirrel (*écureuil*) and banded hedge (*haie fleurie*), wheatsheaf (*gerbe*), quail or partridge (**caille*) and stork (*cigogne*). Usually found on vessels in Japanese-inspired shapes.

décor persan. *See bleus de Nevers.*

décor ronda. *See décor aux cinq bouquets.*

de Fernex, Jean-Baptiste (*c*1729–83). French sculptor and modeller at Vincennes (*c*1753–56). Work in biscuit porcelain modelled after F. *Boucher includes Little Stonemason.

de Gault, Jacques-Joseph (1735–*c*1812). French miniaturist who began as painter at Sèvres porcelain factory (1758–60). His *grisaille* miniatures of neo-classical scenes (bacchanalia, myths, allegory) were mounted on gold boxes. Dated works appeared from 1771–95.

déjeuner. *See* cabaret.

de Koningh, Gilles and Hendrik (fl 18th century). Dutch ceramic painters. Worked at The Double Jug factory, Delft. From 1735, held factory as trustees for ward. Flowerpots initialled GDK and HDK, dated 1721, have medallions decorated with animals, birds, and flowers, in green, red, purple, and gold; blue borders with golden arabesques in Imari style.

de Lamerie, Paul (1688–1751). Dutch Huguenot silversmith; family settled in Westminster, London, *c*1691. Apprenticed to P. *Platel (1703); appointed goldsmith to George I (1716); admitted to Livery of Goldsmiths' Company (1717) where also served as warden (1743, 1747). Originally made domestic silver in Huguenot style; by 1730s, was producing cast and embossed plate in rococo style. Work varies from flatware to giant wine cisterns. Kept large stock of wrought silver, indicating that much work not commissioned. Registered first mark in 1712: LA with crown and star above and fleur-de-lis below; 1732 Sterling Standard mark similar, but with initials PL; 1739 mark: PL, in script, with a large crown above and dot below. *Illustrations at* dessert plate, rat-tail spoon, tea caddy.

Delanois, Louis (1731–92). French; became *maître-menuisier* in 1761; patrons included Mme du Barry, the Prince de Condé, and Stanislas II of Poland. Stamp: L. DELANOIS.

Delapierre, Michel II (d after 1785). French silversmith working in Paris; master in 1737. Made mainly domestic plate in rococo style; some ornate church plate. Mark: a fleur-de-lis crowned, two pellets, MDLP, and a stone.

de la Planche, François or **van der Planken,** Frans (d 1635). Low-warp loom tapestry master-weaver from Brussels. Commissioned 1607 by Henry IV to establish first low-warp loom royal tapestry workshop in Paris with M. *de Comans.

Delatour, Alexandre (1780–1853) and son Edouard (1816–63). Belgian miniaturists. Alexandre exhibited at Paris Salon, 1804–10. Noted for portrait of lady, believed to be Mme Récamier.

Delaunay, Nicolas or **de Launay,** Nicolas (d 1727). French silversmith and medallist working in Paris; master in 1672. Produced domestic plate for Louis XIV (1680–1715) and Louis XV (1724–27). Works included nefs, *cadenas,* dishes, salt-cellars, etc. Little work survives, though the designs for some pieces exist. Surviving pieces include silver-gilt ewer with leopard handle, and mirror belonging to toilet service for Spanish Infanta, fiancée of Louis XV (rest of service by N. *Besnier). Director (1696) of Paris mint. Mark: a fleur-de-lis crowned, two pellets, and NDL below.

Delaune, Étienne (*c*1520–after 1590). French goldsmith, medallist, jeweller and engraver working in Paris and Strasbourg. Designs for jewellery in Renaissance mannerist style (masks, strapwork, mythological figures, etc.) circulated throughout Europe. Designs include pendants, bracelets, enamelled backs of pendants. Some designs now in Ashmolean Museum, Oxford.

Delft, near Rotterdam. Dutch tin-glazed earthenware, called Delft, manufactured from early 17th century. Originated from attempt to reproduce Chinese porcelain (imported by Dutch East India Company from 1602). In period of development, designs from maiolica of 16th century Netherlands and Flanders combined with those of Wan Li porcelain, e.g. plates with central panel containing pious inscription or Virgin and Child enclosed by panelled border of Wan Li symbols. Manufacture gradually centred in Delft where explosion of boatload of gunpowder in 1654 necessitated redevelopment; decline in brewery trade made available premises suitable for potteries. Potters had been admitted to *Guild of Saint Luke from 1613.

Earliest pieces, decorated in underglaze blue, closely imitated Chinese porcelain; **kwaart* used to reproduce brilliant surface. By mid 17th century, individual Delft style began to develop, with Dutch elements added to oriental decoration, and growing influence of contemporary oil-painting, as in work of F. *van Frijtom, who painted landscapes on Delft plaques from 1658. Biblical subjects and seascapes also became popular. Decoration in Chinese style, e.g. by A. *Keyser, also developed, influenced by K'ang Hsi porcelain, imported from 1660s. *Trek introduced *c*1675. Factories noted for blue painting include The *Greek A, The *Metal Pot, The *Double Jug, and The *Rose. Polychrome painting in high-temperature colours, usually in oriental style, developed *c*1700, particularly by L. *van Eenhoorn and H. J. *Peridon. Outside decorators of period include J. T. *Godtling. The Rose factory developed characteristic style with painting in blue, red, green, and brown spread freely over object, not confined in panels. Polychrome painting on black (**delft noir*) and other dark grounds possibly derived from lacquer ware or perhaps K'ang Hsi *famille noire*; produced e.g. by L. *van Dalen.

Enamel colours introduced in 18th century, used particularly for reproductions and adaptations of Imari porcelain; also *famille verte.* Polychrome decoration in Dutch styles includes jars and dishes with heraldic devices or figures, and naturalistic tile pictures of flower arrangements in pots. Bird figures, cow creamers, and model shoes made in 18th century; also allegorical figures and dwarfs after Meissen. Other moulded ware includes tulip vases in pagoda shape, and finger vases.

Growth of Meissen and Sèvres, with increasing availability of porcelain and introduction of cream-coloured earthenware, contributed to decline in Delft production. Only tin-glaze pottery now surviving in Delft, The *Porcelain Bottle, began production of cream-coloured ware in 18th century. J. *Turner, Herculaneum, and Leeds potteries exported cream-coloured ware for decoration in Holland; agent of J. *Wedgwood I sold creamware in Amsterdam.

Tin-glazed earthenware associated with Delft also made, e.g. at Amsterdam, Dordrecht, Gouda, Haarlem, and Rotterdam. Only about one in eight of factories devoted to production of *tiles and simple dishes was in Delft. Attribution to specific makers difficult on pieces made before 1764, date of order regulating marks.

Red earthenware teapots in imitation of Yihsing stoneware made at Delft 1672–*c*1731, first advertized by L. *Cleffius. Hardest body, most resembling stoneware, made by A. *de Milde. Decoration includes applied sprigs of prunus blossom; sometimes other plant forms, e.g. pomegranates, painted in polychrome; diamond-shaped panels with dotted outlines and silver mounts found on pots made by J. *de Caluwe. *See* (in order of foundation) Porcelain Plate, Peacock, Two Little Ships, Young Moor's Head, Three Golden Ash-barrels, Porcelain Axe, White Star, Three Porcelain Bottles, Heart, Fortune, Old Moor's Head.

Delftfield Pottery. Glasgow delftware factory established in 1748. Also produced white stoneware (from 1766), cream-coloured earthenware (from 1770), and black basalt (from *c*1785). Bone china introduced by 1800 includes brown-glazed tea ware, and tableware with matt black enamel and brightly painted flowers. Closed in 1810.

delft noir. Delft ware with polychrome decoration on black ground, dated 1670–1740. Early examples have tin-glaze stained black, with painting in green and yellow, resembling decoration of Chinese lacquer. Later examples, made e.g. by P. A. *Kocks, have polychrome flower painting in blue, red, yellow, and greyish-green, on white tin-glazed surface; black ground colour then applied, leaving narrow white border around flower pattern.

delftware. *See* English delftware.

Della Robbia, Luca (*c*1399–1482) and nephew Andrea (1435–1525). Italian sculptors working in Florence. Ceramic work consists of terracotta reliefs covered with coloured tin-glazes, notably wreathed borders of naturalistic foliage and fruit. Succeeded by Andrea's sons, Giovanni (1469–*c*1529) and Girolamo (1488–1566).

Delorme, Adrien (d after 1783). French *ébéniste,* brother of J-L-F. *Delorme. Became *maître-ébéniste* in 1748. Made and sold furniture until 1783; specializing in marquetry, although early pieces included lacquer work. Stamp: DELORME.

Delorme, Jean-Louis-Faizelot (fl 1763–80). French *ébéniste,* brother of A. *Delorme; became *maître-ébéniste* in 1763. Inherited father's business, which specialized in lacquered furniture, in 1768; worked there until 1780. Stamp: J. L. F. DELORME.

de Lysle, Anthony (fl 16th century). Probably came from France: independent pewter and glass engraver. Only known glass engraver and gilder in England in late 16th century. Engraved in diamond-point and gilded for G. *Verzelini and Sir Jerome *Bowes. *Illustration at* G. Verzelini.

de Maecht, Philippe. 17th century Flemish tapestry master-weaver worked in M. *de Comans's workshop, Paris; then head-weaver at *Mortlake tapsstry works in England.

de Mailly, Charles Jacques (1740–1817). French enamel painter who specialized in floral arrangements and allegorical scenes *en grisaille* set in gold boxes.

Demay or **de May,** Stephen. English tapestry master-weaver, active from 1700. Numerous tapestries woven for nobility, including Acts of the Apostles, Hero and Leander (after design by F. *Cleyn), and The Months.

de Melter, Jean (d 1698). Tapestry master-weaver from Brussels. Established high-warp loom manufactory in *Lille, France, 1617. Subjects include religious scenes after *Rubens; and *'Teniers' tapestries. Workshop continued by son-in-law, Guillaume Wernier.

Demetrius, Daniel. *See* Momma, Jacob.

demi-commode (French, 'half-commode'). Type of commode, but narrow enough to resemble movable table with one or more drawers beneath top. Often designed *en suite* with *pier glass; may be highly decorated with inlay, veneer, bronze mounts, etc. Dates from 18th century.

Demigot, Victor (d 1743). Italian low-warp tapestry master-weaver. 1710–15, principal weaver at *Papal workshop; 1715–31 at Florentine tapestry manufactory; from 1731, director of Turin manufactory.

de Milde, Ary (1634–1708). Dutch potter; member of Guild of St Luke from 1658. Manager of The Greek A factory, Delft, until 1665. In 1671, with Martinus Gouda, partner in The Roman factory. From 1672, manufactured red earthenware teapots in Delft. Said to have been consulted in development of German red stoneware. Owned The Crowned Teapot factory; succeeded by daughter, manager until 1724. Marks include oval medallion enclosing ARY DE MILDE around leaping fox; also crowned teapot, embossed with DE MILDE.

de Nehou, Louis-Lucas (fl 17th century). French mirror maker. Specialized in new process developed in 17th century France of making plate-glass mirrors – molten glass poured into iron frame, rolled, ground, and polished. Founded factory in Tourlaville, Normandy, in 1688 under patronage of Louis XIV. In 1693 established Manufacture Royale des Grandes Glaces at St Gobain, Picardy. Amalgamated (1695) with factory in Paris. Known as 'St Gobain', this factory still flourishes.

Dennis, Thomas (fl late 17th century). Joiner in Ipswich, Massachusetts. Pieces in oak; several examples of New England furniture considered his work.

Denon, Baron Dominique-Vivant (1747–1825). French engraver; director-general of French museums under Napoleon I, whom he accompanied on Egyptian campaigns; gathered material for *Voyage dans la basse et la haute Egypte* (1802), two-volume study of Egyptian art and design. This popularized Egyptian motifs (including lotus flower, lily, papyrus, reed, sphinx) common in Directoire furniture decoration.

Dent, Edward John (1790–1853). English maker of clocks, watches, and chronometers. Established own business in London, 1840, after partnership with J. R. Arnold. Awarded commission for Westminster clock ('Big Ben'), eventually carried out by stepson, Frederick.

dentil motif. Ornamental moulding in classical architecture, consisting of sequence of identical square or rectangular tooth-like blocks, equally spaced. Used extensively on furniture. *Illustration at credenza.*

de Pannemaker, Pieter or Pierre. Early 16th century tapestry master-weaver in Brussels. Commissions for Marguerite of Austria, Governess of Netherlands, François I of France, and Emperor Charles V.

Derby. English ceramics. Soft-paste porcelain possibly made from *c*1745. Oldest surviving examples three cream jugs of low quality marked Derby or D 1750. Early porcelain by A. *Planché probably fired at *Cockpit Hill; some *dry-edge figures possibly by him. In 1756, new porcelain factory erected by partnership including W. *Duesbury, J. *Heath, and Planché; Duesbury soon sole proprietor. From 1756, auctions of wares advertized with slogan 'Derby

Derby. Ice-pail, c1785, marked with crowned D in blue; decorated in French style. Complete with covers and liners.

*Derby porcelain. *Patch family figure of Britannia, c1765. Height* 13*in.*

or the second Dresden'. Before 1770, wares almost always unmarked; occasionally with imitation of Chelsea anchor; one figure marked WD-Co. Figures *c*1756–60 are *pale family; *c*1760–70, *patch family, formerly ascribed to Chelsea or Bow, although colours include characteristic *dirty turquoise. Useful wares less common; also have unglazed patches caused by pads of clay supporting objects during glaze firing. Dirty turquoise used for edging; polychrome decoration, e.g. by *cotton stalk and *moth painters. Also some Kakiemon-style decoration. Occasional black overglaze transfer-printing probably by R. *Holdship; blue and white painted wares also unusual.

In 1770, Duesbury and Heath bought Chelsea factory and ran it with Derby (Chelsea-Derby or Derby-Chelsea period). Body of Chelsea bone ash formula; glaze rather thick but clear, with tendency to craze. Figures influenced by Sèvres, e.g. copies of models by E-M. *Falconet, and subjects after F. *Boucher. Colours pale, notably yellowish-green on bases; pink flesh tones; rich chocolate brown added to palette; clear blue replaces dirty turquoise; costumes sometimes decorated with *indianische Blumen*. Biscuit figures made from 1771 include many from engravings after A. *Kauffmann paintings; some figures possibly by M. *Kean; others after P-L. *Cyfflé. Three groups, 1770–*c*1773, of George III and family after painting by J. Zoffany. *Toys, previously produced at Chelsea, continued. Vases and decorative wares in styles from Chelsea, but claret ground colour brownish, and *mazarine blue replaced by *Derby blue. Painters included R. *Askew and Z. *Boreman. Tablewares in neo-classical style decorated with festoons, urns, classical figures, etc.; cupids in monochrome, or grey and pink, painted by Askew. Rodney jugs commemorating Admiral Rodney's victory over French in West Indies (1782) have spout modelled in form of Admiral's head. Bankruptcy of Heath and competition from cream-coloured earthenware possible factors leading to closure of Chelsea in 1784.

In subsequent Crown Derby period, Duesbury's son William II appointed Kean as partner and manager. On his death, Kean sole proprietor; married William II's widow (1798); firm traded as Duesbury and Kean until 1811. Traditions of Chelsea-Derby continued. Painters included Askew, possibly as outside decorator, Boreman, F. *Duvivier, and flower painters W. *Billingsley and W. *Pegg. Coffee cans, cylindrical cups without foot-ring (shape derived from Sèvres) often decorated with nautical scenes by R. *Brewer. Ground colours include pale red, pink, and canary yellow. Biscuit figures continued.

In 1811, Kean separated from wife and left Derby; factory sold to R. *Bloor. In Bloor period, much poor-quality bone china transfer-printed, often in *Japan patterns. Painters included T. *Steele, M. *Webster, and G. *Robertson. Porcelain plaques and pictures painted by J. *Haslem. After Bloor became mad, factory continued under managers until closure in 1848; moulds sold to *Copeland factory. Other porcelain companies continued production in Derby until present day.

Marks painted in colour or gold include: D combined with anchor (Chelsea-Derby); crowned D (Derby 1780–84); crowned anchor (1770–80); D or DK or DUESBURY/DERBY, all crowned and with crossed batons and six dots (1784–1810). In Bloor period, crown surrounded by BLOOR DERBY between two circles, or crown over ribbon with DERBY, both printed in red. *Illustrations at trembleuse,* urn clock.

Derby blue or **Smith's blue.** Ceramic colour: blue enamel based on Sèvres **bleu de roi*, used in Chelsea-Derby period.

De Re Metallica. Treatise on glass making by G. *Agricola, published in Basel, 1556. Gives detailed information on metals, melting pots, furnaces, and tools used in 16th century glass making.

*Deruta maiolica. *Drug-pots. Left: ewer with globular body, inscribed Oxizacara 1502. Centre:* albarello, *glazed only on outside, and painted with mythological scene. Right: similar to left-hand pot, but inscribed Oximel/Simrece 1501.*

Deruta (Umbria), Italy. Maiolica made from late 14th century; decoration influenced by contemporary Umbrian painting. Period of greatest importance began in late 15th century. *c*1500–*c*1520, dishes, plates, and drug-pots painted, e.g. with figures in blue, brownish-orange, and yellow, sometimes with purple and green; plates and dishes characterized by reverse pattern of striped petals. Rarely, figure subjects have flesh tints rendered in buff clay, with tin-glaze removed, covered by *coperta*. Lustre painting introduced *c*1500; golden lustre with mother-of-pearl sheen used until 1560s, ruby lustre until 1515. Polychrome dishes, often with lustre decoration, produced 1515–40; bust or figure drawn at centre; borders usually composed of panels with scales alternating with leaves and other motifs. Designs sometimes occur in relief.

desk. *See* writing desk.

desk and bookcase. T. *Chippendale's term for *bureau bookcase.

desk box. Portable box, with top sloping forward, hinged at back, and with lock. Of size suitable to rest on table top when in use; may have carved ornamentation at sides. Dates from 16th century.

desk chair. *See* corner chair.

desk seal. *See* seal.

Desoches (fl late 18th century). French sculptor and porcelain modeller at Fürstenberg, Germany (1769–74). Specialized in neo-classical biscuit portrait busts on glazed pedestals.

Desprez, father and son (fl late 18th, early 19th centuries). French glass makers of Rue des Récollets du Temple factory in Paris. Experimented with *sulphides in late 18th century, using porcelain and glass paste. By early 19th century were enclosing cameo portraits of royalty and other prominent people in crystal glass plaques, framed to be hung. Many sulphides impressed with name, Desprez, D.P., or with whole or part of factory address.

dessert basket. *See* basket.

dessert service. At first, separate sets of dishes in gold, silver, or silver-gilt for dessert course. Sets of knives, forks, spoons, baskets, small dishes, etc., for dessert uncommon before late 18th century. In early 18th century, standard size silver knives with matching forks made for dessert use; size decreased in mid century. Blades of dessert knives elaborately engraved or chased, from early 19th century. Green-tinted ivory or mother-of-pearl hafts common in mid 19th century for silver or electro-plated dessert knives and forks.

detent escapement. *See* escapement.

de Troy, Jean-François (1679–1752). One of most brilliant 18th century French painters; created numerous cartoon designs for Gobelins, including seven-piece History of Esther, and seven-piece History of Jason.

deutsche Blumen, German or **Strasbourg flowers.** Naturalistic flowers painted either singly or in loose bunches on European faience and porcelain, often after botanical plates. Anemones, peonies, and roses painted in red, purple, blue, and green on porcelain at Vienna from *c*1730. At Meissen, flowers with insects, e.g. ants, butterflies, painted by J. G. *Klinger on porcelain from 1730s, or carefully shaded in grey enamel from 1740s (*fleurs fines*). Widely copied e.g. on faience at Strasbourg and Niderviller in mid 18th century, and on porcelain at Vincennes, Sèvres, and Chantilly. Inspired English *botanical flowers. Distinct from stylized **indianische Blumen. Illustration at* Vienna porcelain.

device (in silver). Emblematic figure or design, particularly one identified with a particular person (e.g. maker's mark of silversmith) or a family (e.g. coat of arms).

de Vos, Josse (fl 1705–25). Tapestry master-weaver in Brussels. Numerous historical subjects woven for English Crown and private clients. Also copies of Gobelins designs. Works include Amours of Venus and Adonis, Four Continents, and History of Alexander (after design by C. *Lebrun).

Dextra, Jan Theunis (fl late 18th century). Dutch potter at Delft. Owner of The Greek A factory, 1758–64. Work based on European forms, with Chinese blue decoration; also produced polychrome animal figures. Factory mark, registered in 1758, A with D below, or initials ITD (reserved for 'best products', presumably own work).

diadem. Head ornament derived from band of metal, or wreath of leaves or flowers worn round head by ancient Greeks. In early 19th century, during Napoleonic era, Greek style diadems (plain band or garland) studded with gems, pearls, cameos, etc. fashionable.

*Dessert service. Plate by P. *de Lamerie, 1724.*

dial clock or **English dial.** English wall clock, entire front consisting of round dial. Early examples *c*1770 had silvered brass dials with engraved numerals. After 1800 dials usually painted white with black Roman numerals: some before 1860 of convex form. Commonly used in offices and schools. *See also* drop-dial.

diamond. Crystallized carbon; hardest of all natural substances. Usually found in octahedral shape; can be split along planes running parallel to four faces of octahedron. Takes high polish. High reflectivity and refractive index produce characteristic lustre and colour (fire). Usually colourless (white or blue-white); sometimes tinged with yellow, brown, etc. Mines in India probably worked from 3000 B.C.; exhausted in 18th century. In early 18th century deposits found in Brazil became principal source until major discovery of diamonds in South Africa in 1866.

With improved method of cutting, diamond became most important gem in early 17th century. Since used for whole range of jewellery and imitated in *paste, cut steel, etc. *See* brilliant cut, point cut, rose cut, table cut.

diamond-point engraving (on porcelain). Technique similar to glass engraving used on porcelain by mid 18th century *Hausmaler*, E. A. O. *von dem Busch.

diamond-point engraving (in glass). *See* engraved glass.

diamond-point spoon. Spoon with diamond or pyramid-shaped knop; made in silver probably from late 14th to late 15th century; knop sometimes silver-gilt. Also in brass and pewter, 14th to 16th century. *Illustration at* knop.

diaper. Pattern of repeated small geometrical shapes, e.g. lozenges or squares, sometimes enclosing dots. On furniture in carving, marquetry, gesso decoration, etc. Often engraved on medieval silver and revived on English silver during 1720s and 1730s. In ceramics used as ground pattern on oriental porcelain, often in underglaze blue. In early 18th century Europe, commonly found in association with baroque motifs. At Sèvres, applied in gilt or enamel over ground colours; technique developed in mid 18th century to soften effect of colours.

die. Block or stamp engraved with design, used to impress ornament on sheet silver or other metal.

die-stamping. *See* stamping.

diet. Metal scraped from gold or silver article for assaying.

Dietrich, Christian Wilhelm Ernst (1712–74). German child prodigy, painter, etcher, art-director at Meissen porcelain factory (1764–70). Established 'academic school' for porcelain painters, treating porcelain primarily as medium for painting.

Dillwyn, Lewis Weston (1778–1855). Welsh porcelain manufacturer, naturalist, and botanical writer. Operated *Cambrian Pottery at Swansea from 1802, except 1817–24, when factory let. Authorized by Board of Trade to investigate claim of W. *Billingsley for state subsidy to manufacture soft-paste porcelain. In 1824, joined in business by son, as manager. Retired in 1852.

Dinanderie or **Mosan brass.** Discovery of calamine led to production of brassware in Meuse valley in and around Dinant, near Liège, Belgium. Brass used with great success for domestic objects normally of bronze; production grew until, in 1466, Dinant captured by Philippe le Bon, causing departure of brassfounders to other regions or countries. Objects include candlesticks, drinking and cooking vessels, aquamaniles, and ecclesiastical objects.

Dinglinger, Johann Melchior (1664–1731). German goldsmith working in Dresden; appointed court jeweller (1698) to *Augustus the Strong, for whom worked exclusively; surviving pieces mainly in Green Vaults, Dresden, Germany. First major work (1701), coffee set perched on silver-gilt pyramidal stand, included enamelled gold cups, dishes, sugar basins, crystal flasks, ivory statuettes, and, at apex, coffee-pot with dragon spout and serpent handle; cups and saucers painted to simulate porcelain. Other projects: fantasy centrepieces based on a theme, e.g. The Court at Delhi on the Birthday of Great Mogul Aureng-Zeb (132 modelled figures of men and animals, vases, cups, etc. made *c*1700–08), and the Apis altar (Egyptian fantasy); historical details derived from engravings in travel and archaeological books. Worked in gold, silver, silver-gilt, enamel, precious and semi-precious stones, etc. Continued tradition of other great European goldsmiths, B. *Cellini and W. *Jamnitzer.

dinner service. Silver, silver gilt, or gold eating utensils employed by royalty and aristocracy from 16th century in Britain and Europe. 18th century services include meat and fish dishes, dinner dishes, entrée dishes, tureens, sauce boats, dessert dishes, baskets, etc. Services belonging to nobility and royalty also had épergnes, candlesticks, candelabra, salvers, etc. Few royal services survive. *See* Berkeley Castle Service, Orloff Service.

Directoire style. Stool, c1810, by Jacob D. R. Meslée from the Château de Saint-Cloud; carved and gilt-wood legs in form of crossed sabres. Original embroidered silk covers and cushion.

dipped enamels. *Copper blanks dipped in liquid, milky enamel before decoration.

diptych dial. *See* sundial.

Directoire style. Transitional French furniture style combining elements of *Louis XVI and *Empire styles, popular *c*1790–*c*1804. Still featured neo-classical forms and ornament, but lines simpler; closer to classical prototypes, e.g. in sofa with outward-scrolling ends, *klismos, and tripod candlesticks. Some examples with Revolutionary symbols, e.g. clasped hands, tricolor rosettes, Phrygian cap of liberty. In American Directoire furniture, indigenous ornament used. Towards end of period, Egyptian motifs (e.g. sphinx, lotus flower, palm leaf, papyrus leaf, etc.) became popular, after Napoleon's Egyptian campaigns and publication of D-V. *Denon's *Voyage dans la basse et la haute Egypte* (1802).

dirty turquoise. Ceramic colour: turquoise tending to become drab and brownish if overfired. Used on Derby porcelain, *c*1758–70 on figures and as edging of dishes.

Disbrowe, Nicholas (*c*1612–83). English-born furniture maker who worked in Hartford, Connecticut. Made *Hadley and possibly *Connecticut chests; also other oak furniture.

disc-end spoon. Silver spoon; flat stem decorated with engraved acanthus foliage and disc terminal. Face of terminal sometimes engraved with skull: face and back of stem with motto 'live to die' or 'die to live'. Made in 16th and 17th century Scotland and northern England. Few American examples. Thought to have originated in Scandinavia.

discharge mark. Mark struck on finished silver by French *tax-farmer (after 1681), indicating that duty on piece had been paid. Generally depicted animals, birds, human heads, etc.; varied in size depending on piece. *cf* charge mark.

dish. Shallow, usually circular or oval vessel of wood, metal, or porcelain with central depression and flat rim. Silver dishes used by Romans; gold and silver dishes by later European kings and nobles. Made in variety of sizes for individual use as dinner plate or larger serving dish, e.g. meat dish or charger. All-over embossed ornament or completely plain except for ornamental border (waved, gadrooned, moulded, etc.) and/or engraved arms.

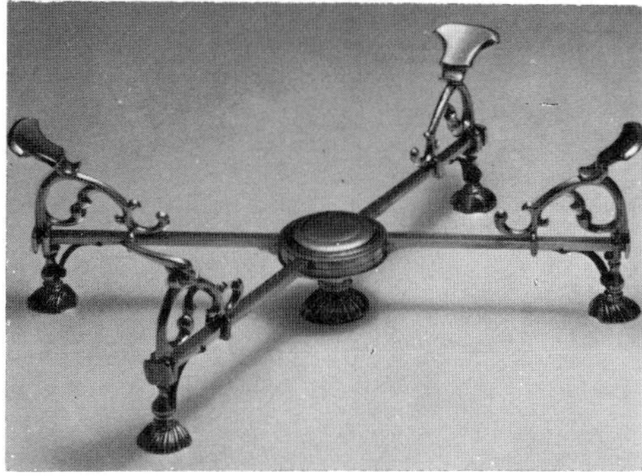

*Dish cross. Made by R. *Innes, London, 1751. Arms extend to* c12*in.*

dish cover. 18th and 19th century domed or bell-shaped silver or Sheffield plate cover to keep food warm. Generally with decorative handle at top; some, especially early examples, elaborately decorated, but most plain except for engraved coat of arms. Commonly made in sets including various sizes.

dish cross. British silver or Sheffield plate utensil for supporting hot dishes or bowls to prevent heat from damaging table top; same purpose as Irish *dish-ring. Consists of two bars with feet at each end joined by circular connecting ring at middle; bars usually with sliding socket to allow extension. Spirit lamp can be placed beneath central ring. Made from mid 18th to early 19th century.

dished dial. Round, convex dial made of metal, sometimes used on *Massachusetts shelf clocks.

dished or **saddle seat.** Chair seat set beneath level of seat rails; cushion inserted within rims of rails. Often found on 17th century chairs. Saddle seat is American term.

dish-ring. Irish hollow, spool-shaped silver support (*c*3–4in. high and *c*7–8½in. in diameter) for hot dishes or bowls. Usually has upper and lower rings of plain silver; between them, concave section with chased, embossed, and pierced design. In use from mid 18th to early 19th century. Also made of Sheffield plate; probably for Irish market, since never very popular in England. Sometimes incorrectly called 'potato ring'. *See* dish cross.

dish-strainer. *See* mazarine.

Dixon, James (fl early and mid 19th century). English manufacturer of Britannia metal ware; founded firm in Sheffield in about 1806. Firm became Dixon & Son in 1830, when also produced Sheffield plate and silver-plated Britannia metal ware. From *c*1833 (as James Dixon & Sons) also produced silver wares. In 1848, bought licence from *Elkington & Co; began production of electro-plate with Britannia metal as base. Firm continued by sons, and is still in existence.

Dixon, Nicholas (fl *c*1660–*c*1708). English miniaturist. Pupil of Sir Peter Lely. Succeeded S. *Cooper as king's limner. Produced large miniature copies of old master paintings; also watercolours of nymphs and satyrs. Portraits include Duke and Duchess of Marlborough, Samuel Pepys.

Djoushegan carpets. *See* Joshagan carpets.

djufti knot. *See* jufti knot.

Doccia (near Florence). Italian porcelain factory established in 1735 by Marchese Carlo Ginori (d 1757); obtained privilege for porcelain manufacture in Tuscany (1740); porcelain marketed from 1746. Hybrid hard-paste porcelain subject to firecracks, greyish in tone until tin oxide added (*c*1770); by 1800 translucent white paste developed. Glaze has marked greenish tinge. Low relief decoration moulded on tableware and vases; by late 18th century, large relief plaques modelled after contemporary paintings and bronzes. Figures, both white and enamelled (colours include characteristic iron-red), often covered with tin-glaze, include *commedia dell'arte* characters, mythological and religious groups, and pastoral subjects. Factory remained under control of Ginori family until 1896; then traded as Richard-Ginori until present day. Marks include star from Ginori arms, used from late 18th century in blue, red, or gold, sometimes impressed in double triangle form (1792–1800); in mid 19th century GI, GIN, or GINORI impressed.

Dockwra's Copper Company. Founded 1694 near Esher, Surrey. Smelted copper, produced brass; made pins and other finished articles. By 1697, produced half England's copper output. Probably absorbed by *Bristol Brass Wire Company in early 18th century.

dog of Fo. Chinese ceramic figure; combines features of dog and lion, commonly made in porcelain or pottery as guardian for Buddhist temples. Mythological attributes, e.g. flames pouring from mouth, often found. Produced in all periods, from T'ang. Smaller examples, occur later, e.g. in Ming porcelain, for room decoration, sometimes in pairs.

dog-nose spoon. *See* wavy-end spoon.

Doccia porcelain. *Commedia dell'arte *figures, Harlequin (left) and Columbine. Both* c1760.

Dole cupboard. Oak and ash. English, 17th century. Approximately 4ft long.

dole cupboard. *Livery cupboard used in churches to hold bread to be given to poor. Had pierced doors; carving and workmanship often less fine than on domestic livery cupboards. Used mainly in 16th century.

Domanek, Anton Matthias (1713–79). Austrian silversmith working in Vienna; master in 1736. Executed work for Empress Maria Theresa, including gold toilet service of *c*1750. Made domestic silver in French rococo style. Mark: DOMANEK.

dome. *See* hood.

dome bed. 18th century term for bed with domed canopy to which bed curtains attached.

domed tankard. *See* tankard.

domed-top. Top part of bracket clock, outline in shape of dome, matching wood of clockcase and surmounted by handle. Used in England from *c*1670; also on long-case clocks, sometimes topped by metal ornament.

domestic clock. Timekeeper for household or personal use, originally simple scaled-down version of medieval *turret clock. First noted in general use in late 15th century, in form of weight-driven iron chamber clock of Gothic shape, often with hour striking and alarum. In England developed into characteristic *lantern clock.

Donaldson, John (1737–1801). English miniaturist, said to have decorated porcelain at Chelsea. Elaborate figure-painting on porcelain made at Worcester bears his initial; vases sent to him in London for decoration.

Don Pino. *See* Bettisi, Leonardo.

door furniture. Earliest door-knockers were plain, heavy, and purely functional, of iron cast or wrought in ring, lyre, or hammer shapes. Handles (closing rings) were plain or twisted rings, sometimes incorporating human or animal heads, similar to designs for knockers. Little change over centuries, but became lighter, and sometimes made of brass. Regarded as ornamental accessories in late 18th century. Neo-classical designs included urns, lions' masks, rams' heads, etc., in minute detail, particularly on interior doors; finger-plates, escutcheon-plates, and handles on these were made *en suite* in gilt bronze. Door-stops (originally door-porters) were made from 18th century or earlier in iron cast in figure or half-bell form; more expensive brass examples in more sophisticated styles; most have long handles. Hinges evolved from plain, short, iron straps to 16th century 'butterfly' type, and a strong, long-strapped style, often highly ornamental. 16th century 'cockspur' or 'cockshead' hinge is elaborate H-shape. Hinges in brass and iron became smaller and plainer until late 18th century when made in delicate designs to harmonize with other fittings.

door-stop (in glass). Ovoid door-stop of bottle glass (3–6in. high) enclosing bubble decoration, usually plant(s) or fountain(s); flat base and pontil mark. Sometimes called bottle-green paperweight. Made from late 18th century to fairly recent times.

Doppelfrieskrug (German, 'double frieze jug'). Large, round-bellied *Rhineland stoneware jugs produced *c*1560–90 at Raeren, Germany, by workshop of J. *Emens. Decorated with medallions or intricate friezes in relief, sometimes set in Gothic arches.

Dorotheenthal (Thuringia). German faience factory founded *c*1710 by Augusta, daughter of Duke of Brunswick. Products include picture-panels of religious subjects, notably in 1720s. Vessels and figures characterized by brightness of high-temperature colours. Most pieces decorated with **Laub-und-Bandelwerk.* Mark AB sometimes used in monogram with painter's mark.

dotaku. *See* Japanese metal-work.

Double beaker. Made in Edinburgh, 1815, maker's mark, M and R; two ends of barrel fit together to make height of $6\frac{1}{2}$in.

*Double and triple decker clocks. Triple decker, made c1838 by Dyer Wadsworth and Co., Augusta, Georgia; case open to show *wagon spring movement.*

Douai (Nord). French *faïence fine* factory established in 1781 by potters from Staffordshire. Fretted open-work decoration in style of cream-coloured earthenware made at Leeds. Factory closed in 1820. Marks include Douai, impressed, and names of proprietors.

double basket top. Metal top above bracket clock consisting of single *basket-top, topped by second basket; introduced *c*1700.

double beakers. Silver beakers fitting together to form barrel. Made in Britain mainly in late 18th century, though one 16th century example is known.

double-bottom case (in watches). Style with inner 'dome' in one piece: bezel must be opened and movement swung out on hinge to give access to back.

double-C back. Mid 19th century variation on *balloon-back chair-back. Inside edge of back frame shaped to resemble two Cs, facing each other.

double chest. *See* tallboy.

double cup. German silver drinking vessel: two matching cups each with pedestal foot, the smaller, when inverted, fits as lid to larger. Initially of wood, then silver from late 15th century to mid 17th century. 16th and 17th century examples covered with large bosses; generally with cut or twisted wire-work ornament simulating thorns or leafage in Gothic manner.

double-curved handle. Roughly S-shaped curve surmounting smaller reversed C-shape curve; found on pewter tankards in late 18th and 19th centuries.

double and **triple deckers.** American shelf clocks made from *c*1830; often with side columns. Clock divided into two or three 'decks' or sections; dial on upper part, with panel or panels below containing decorative scenes, portraits, or sometimes advertisements. Makers include E. *Terry.

double-domed tankard. *See* tankard.

double gourd vase. Chinese ceramic shape, mostly occurring in later Ming or Ch'ing times. Double-curved vase; round, waisted shape, topped with slim neck. Early examples moulded in horizontal sections; 18th century copies moulded vertically. Foot-rims of early vases formed integrally; later added separately.

Double Jug, The (De Dobbelde Schenckan). Delft factory (1661–1777) owned by V. and L. *Victorson, 1688–1735. K'ang Hsi decoration, often white on blue background, alternating with flourishes in blue on white.

*Double gourd vase. Transitional period, decorated in underglaze blue with *Immortals in pairs, supported on scrolling clouds reserved on ground of *Shou characters. Upper bulb decorated with continuous chrysanthemum scroll. Height 7½in.*

double volute thumbpiece. Thumbpiece on English pewter vessels *c*1730–*c*1810, similar to volutes on Ionic column.

dough-grate. *See* baking-iron.

Doulton Pottery. London stoneware factory established at Vauxhall in 1818; later transferred to Lambeth. First specialized in commercial and industrial stoneware. Later made domestic and ornamental articles including mugs, tankards, jugs, and vases in stoneware, terracotta, and earthenware. Production continues. Mark DOULTON LAMBETH sometimes with name of artist and nature of ware, e.g. faience.

douters or **out-quenchers.** Scissor-like instrument with arms ending in flat discs for extinguishing candle flame. In silver, brass, or iron, from 15th or 16th centuries, though earliest surviving silver examples are late 17th century; often made *en suite* with *snuffers.

dower or **dowry chest.** General term for any chest suitable for storing linen and other items of bride's dowry.

down hearth. Early form of fireplace with slab of iron or stone on which logs, supported by *andirons, etc., were burnt.

drageoire. *See* sweetmeat box.

dragon's blood. Red, resinous substance obtained from dragon tree (*Dracaena draco*), indigenous in Canary Islands; also from *Calamus draco*, found in Sumatra, Borneo, etc.; used for colouring varnishes applied to metals, particularly brass.

*Drawing instruments. For mathematics. Brass, early 18th century. Made and signed by M. *Butterfield, Aux Armes d'Angleterre, Quai des Morfonds, Paris. Original leather and wood case, length 6¼in.*

Dower chest. Painted pine, made in Jonestown, Pennsylvania, by Christian Seltzer, dated 1784.

Drais, Pierre-François (fl 1763–88). French goldsmith whose boxes were in neo-classical style. Miniatures by J-J. *de Gault mounted in lids. Signed initials P.F.D. and heart device.

dram cup. Small silver cup of *standing or *two-handled cup shape used in 17th century Britain and America.

draught screen. *See* screen.

drawback mark. Incised mark of Britannia used in England on export plate from 1 December 1784 to 24 July 1785 to indicate repayment of duty charged on assaying of piece. Discontinued, because mark damaged pieces and also because of delay caused to export trade.

drawing instruments. Generally made in sets including ruler, pencil-holder, pens, compasses, etc. Cases often of engraved metal. Silver and gold sets made for presentation. Graphite first used for pencil 'lead' *c*1565. Many complex instruments produced for specialist purposes, including pantograph – framework of jointed rods for enlarging or reducing drawings – invented in Germany in 1603.

draw-leaf table. Extending table with top in

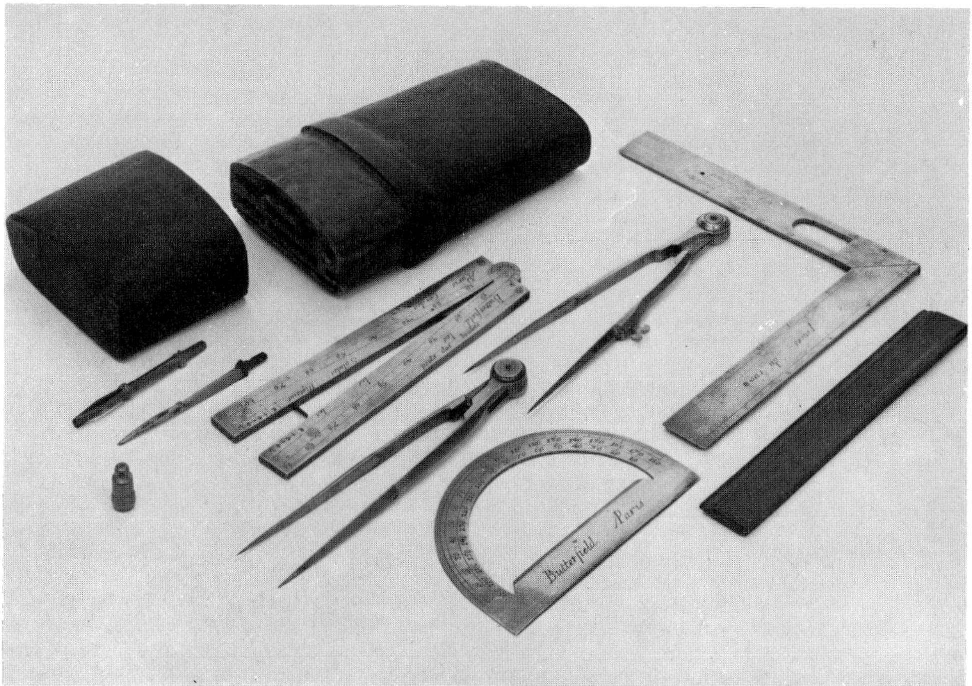

Draw-leaf table. Oak, rectangular triple plank top; baluster legs, fluted, and with guilloche *capitals. 17th century. Length 7ft4in.*
Dresser. English. Oak, early 18th century, back of upper part slightly later; below are three drawers and shelf. Width 5ft4in.

Dressing table. Maple and sycamore; transitional style between William and Mary and Queen Anne. American, made in New Hampshire, 1740.

*Drinking horn. Victorian silver-mounted horn, with gilt interior by G. *Fox, 1873.*

three sections; the outer leaves slide on runners beneath centre section when table is closed. Dates from 16th century.

drawplate. Implement with holes of decreasing size used in wire-making. Wire drawn through series of holes to reduce it to narrower gauge. *See* wire-work.

dredger. Large *caster.

Drentwett family (fl 16th to 18th centuries). German silversmiths working in Augsburg. Balduin Drentwett (1545–1627) first of family of craftsmen; seven members active in 18th century, producing domestic silver in French and English styles: Philipp Jacob (d 1702 or 1712, mark: PID); Emmanuel (1681–1753, mark: ED); Johann Christoph (d 1763, mark: ICD); Jacob Philipp (d 1754, mark: IPD); Gottlieb Christian (1723–54, mark: GCD), Abraham IV (*c*1709–85, mark: AD); and Christian II (*c*1728–1801, mark: CD).

Dresden, Germany. Faience factory founded 1708 by J. F. *Böttger, a year before he set up Meissen porcelain factory. Best-known examples (*c*1710–*c*1718: unmarked) include set of egg-shaped drug-pots for court pharmacy at Dresden decorated with arms of Saxony and Poland; also Kuan Yin and *commedia dell'arte* figures. Mark, DH used 1768–84.

Dresden china. *See* Meissen porcelain factory.

dresser. In medieval Europe, an open cupboard (very similar to *court cupboard) for display of plate. Some examples heavily carved and with hangings. Later examples have closed back. 17th century French dresser (*dressoir*) in form of table (sometimes with frieze drawers), surmounted by horizontally rectangular cupboard with doors. Evolved into high-backed cupboard with narrow, open shelves; wooden galleries at front of shelves secured displayed plate. By end of 17th century, English dresser was long table with frieze drawers beneath top, turned front legs, plain back legs (square in section), sometimes with stretcher at floor level. Made into 18th century, when dressers began to have high

back with rows of open shelves and enclosed cupboard space beneath. Sideboards, side tables, and buffets took place of dresser. *See* Welsh dresser.

dressing box. Small box with sectioned interior and hinged lid intended for jewellery and other accessories. Mirror attached to underside of lid. Dates from 17th century.

dressing chest, dresser, or **dressing commode.** Low chest of drawers, may have mirror attached. Chippendale dressing chest has four drawers, top one with compartments for toilet articles. Top may be hinged with mirror on underside. Sometimes with knee-hole front.

dressing glass. *See* toilet mirror.

dressing or **toilet table.** Table designed to hold toilet articles; used while dressing. Drawer space and mirrors ingeniously incorporated in design. Form dates from 17th century; increased in popularity in 18th century, when mirror was added. In 19th century, mirror in three panels fixed to top.

drinking-horn. Ceremonial drinking vessel of ancient origin made of ox or buffalo horn with silver ornamental bands and cover surmounted by finial; sometimes also with feet. Made in England, Germany, and Holland, until 16th century. Later examples have engraved and cast ornament in Gothic style.

drip-pan. *See* greasepan.

drop dial clock. Form of *dial clock with extra section of case below dial, containing pendulum. Made in England, United States, and Germany from *c*1800.

drop or **fall front.** On desk or English bureau; hinged flap, when lowered is supported beneath by sliding rails or brackets to form writing surface.

drop-leaf, fall-leaf, or **flap table.** Table with one or two hinged outer leaves which hang down when not in use. When raised, leaves supported by slides, rudders, or hinged supports which swing out under them. *See* butterfly table, gate-leg table, swing-leg table.

dropped bottom. Bulge or sag in bottom of rounded body of vessel such as caster, tea or coffee pot, tea-caddy, etc. Common in mid 18th century rococo examples.

drug-pots, pharmacy jars, or **apothecary jars.** Ceramic vessels in shapes derived from Middle East via Spain; intended to hold medicaments. Forms include **albarello* or more flared vase shape, usually with handles, for storing dry medicines. Globular jar with spout, or bottle with narrow neck used for liquids. Sometimes lidded, or provided with groove around top for securing parchment cover with string. Among most frequent vessels made in tin-glazed earthen-ware, notably at Alcora, Delft, Faenza, and Lambeth.

drum clock. Common form of early table clock, especially in early 16th century. Precursor of square and hexagonal table clock. Oldest surviving spring-driven clock, with early use of *fusee, is drum shaped, made by Jacob the Czech for Sigismund I of Poland and dated 1525. Iron movement typically of skeleton form with balance, case frequently of gilt-brass with silver chapter ring. Striking mechanism not

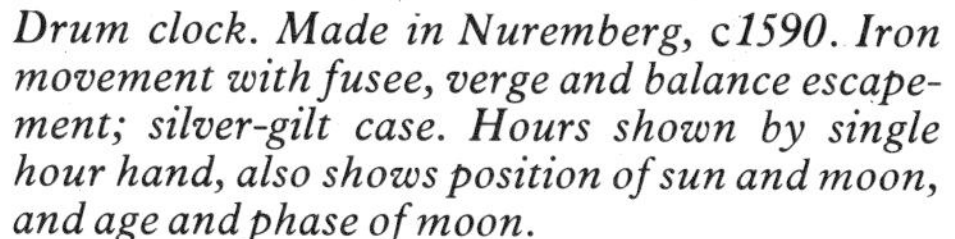

Drum clock. Made in Nuremberg, c1590. Iron movement with fusee, verge and balance escapement; silver-gilt case. Hours shown by single hour hand, also shows position of sun and moon, and age and phase of moon.
Drum watch. With alarm. Made in Germany, c1580. Gilt-metal case pierced to emit sound of bell; pendant for wearing around neck; iron movement with open mainsprings.

Dublin delftware. Hors d'oeuvre dish. c1760. Diameter 9in.

usual, but where present, bell placed between plates of movement, or above case, covered with ornamental fret and with small dial above; in later examples bell is in cover hinged to bottom of case. Early types may have separate alarm mechanism, positioned on legs over clock case when required. Alternatively, French wall clock fitted into brass drum-shaped case, produced late 19th century with French movement.

drum-head clock. Clock with circular dial and case, set on raised stand. English movement. Made for use in offices and public institutions *c*1790 onwards. Design popular in Scotland, particularly for long-case clocks.

drum table. Round *library table with central columnar support on three or four outward-curving legs. Drawers or bookshelves in deep frieze. Usually mahogany, often with leather top. Dates from late 18th century.

drum watch. 16th century German watch in drum-shaped case, with cover.

dry-edge figures. English slip-cast figures in soft-paste porcelain containing no bone ash; made at Derby (1750–55). Characterized by unglazed dry edge around base; funnel-shaped hole commonly found in underside of base. Models include five groups of Chinese figures representing The Senses; *putti* and adult figures in two series of Seasons; also gods and goddesses, and figures with animals, probably after Italian marble or bronze originals. Some thought to have been modelled by A. *Planché. Colours, when used, possibly enamelled by W. *Duesbury in London; include red, blue, pink, and dull yellow, with purple sometimes used for fur and hair.

dry sink. Common 19th century American kitchen cabinet, with hinged top opening to reveal metal-lined sink, or area divided into sink and shallower storage area. Usually has enclosed cupboards below.

Dublin delftware. Tin-glazed earthenware made in Dublin *c*1730–*c*1771. Many pieces painted in bright blue or purple monochrome with delicate scrollwork borders. Sometimes marked Dublin, or with a harp. Other wares difficult to distinguish from Liverpool or Bristol.

Dubois, Abraham (fl *c*1777–1807). American silversmith working in Philadelphia, Pennsylvania. Made domestic silver in neo-classical style, e.g. tea service made *c*1785–95 now at Yale University Art Gallery, New Haven, Connecticut.

Dubois, Gilles (b 1713). French potter and painter. Worked at Chantilly (1731–38), then with brother, Robert *Dubois, experimented in manufacture of porcelain at Vincennes (1738–41). Later worked in Paris (at Rue de la Roquette), and at Sceaux in 1752.

Dubois, Jacques (*c*1693–1763). French. Became *maître-ébéniste* in 1742. Lacquered work exported from Paris throughout France and

Abraham du Bois. Vase-shaped coffee pot with beaded rims, square base, and curved, beaded spout; waisted cover with wooden pineapple finial. Made in Philadelphia, c1770. Coat of arms engraved later.

Jacques Dubois. Louis XV ormolu-mounted Chinese lacquer *bureau plat, *stamped I. Dubois. Height 2ft8in.*

abroad. Business carried on by widow with son, R. *Dubois. Stamp: I DUBOIS.

Dubois, Réné (1737–99). French *ébéniste*, who continued business of father, J. *Dubois. Became *maître-ébéniste* in 1755, *ébéniste* to Marie Antoinette in 1779. Pieces typify French neo-classical style, often including lacquer-work and intricate fittings. Used father's stamp: I. DUBOIS. *Illustration at secrétaire en armoire.*

Dubois, Robert (b 1709). French potter and arcanist. Said to have worked at Saint-Cloud; at Chantilly (1725–38). Went with brother, G. *Dubois, to Vincennes in 1738 to experiment in making porcelain; unsuccessful – discharged 1741. Director of porcelain factory at Tournai in 1753.

Jacques-Androuet du Cerceau. French walnut cabinet decorated in manner of J-A. du Cerceau; the small panels are inlaid with black and white marble.

du Cerceau, Jacques-Androuet the Elder (*c*1570–85). French architect, engraver, and designer. Studied in Rome in 1540s; at court of Henri II, *c*1558–80. His furniture designs are architectural and elegant, reflecting Italian Renaissance influence.

Duchesse. *Louis XV. Gilt-wood, in manner of Tilliard. Arched cresting on back with central cabochon. Length 5ft10in.*

Duchesse brisée. *Louis XV, waxed beechwood. Length 4ft2in.*

Duché family (fl 17th and 18th centuries). Antoine Duché, potter of Huguenot origin at Philadelphia, Pennsylvania from 1692; four sons, all potters of stoneware, include James, owner of pottery at Charlestown, Massachusetts. Andrew (b 1709), a Quaker, settled in Savannah, Georgia; probably discovered *unaker and brought first samples to England (1744). On return to America, possibly experimented with porcelain making, but only specimens of doubtful attribution exist.

duchesse. French day-bed resembling elongated armchair, with concave back and arms in gondola form; bottom end often of similar shape. When made up of separate chair-like sections, with stool between (or of two chairs, one with extended seat) known as *duchesse brisée. cf chaise longue.*

Ducrollay, Jean (1709-after 1761). French goldsmith; master in 1734. Specialized in boxes, e.g. with sculptured four-colour gold borders, enamelled decoration, lacquer panels, and/or portrait miniatures. Signed initials J.D. and heart device.

ductility. Property of metal allowing it to be drawn into fine wire.

Duesbury, William (1725–86). English ceramic painter. In London (1751–53), independently enamelled porcelain e.g. of Bow, Chelsea, Derby, and probably Longton Hall. Work-book, preserved and published, also refers to salt-glaze figures of swans enamelled in red, turquoise, and purple. Held controlling interest in porcelain factories at *Derby (1756–86), Bow (1763), and Chelsea (1770–84); succeeded at Derby by son, William (d 1797).

Duguay or **Duguet,** Jacques (1700–49). French silversmith working in Paris; master in 1726. Made domestic silver in rococo style. Mark: crowned fleur-de-lis, JD, and two pellets (after 1733, shell added). Son, Joseph-Pierre-Jacques, continued in trade.

du Halde, Jean Baptiste (1674–1743). French Jesuit missionary at court of Chinese emperor K'ang Hsi whose book, *Description géographique, historique, etc., de la Chine* (Paris 1735), was important in developing interest in oriental art. Translated into English as *General History of China* (1736).

dulcimer. Musical instrument in shape of shallow closed box (rectangular, triangular, or trapezoidal), on which metal wires are strung; sound produced by striking strings with small wooden hammers. Number of strings (paired) varied (e.g. in late 16th and early 17th centuries, 12 or 13 pairs). Origin uncertain; possibly introduced to Spain in 12th century from Middle East. In 14th century Spain, known as *dulcema*; in 15th century France as *dulce melos* or *doucemelle*; and *c*1475 in England as dulcimer. In decline by 16th century. In late 17th century larger version made, known as *pantaleon* (after maker, Pantaleon Hebenstreit); popularity revived, but displaced by pianoforte in mid 19th century. Played on lap of sitting player; carried suspended from neck or, later, provided with stand or four legs.

dumb waiter. Portable table, usually with two or three round surfaces of diminishing size

Dumb waiter. Mahogany, with three tiers. English, 18th century.

(largest at bottom), on central column support with tripod or four-footed base. Held plates, cutlery and other dining equipment when not on table; dates from mid 18th century in England and Europe. In America, lift or elevator for carrying food from kitchen to pantry above; dates from 19th century.

Dummer, Jeremiah (1645–1718). American silversmith working in Boston; apprenticed to J. *Hull. Surviving works include tankards with

Antoine-Sébastien Durand. Double salt. Louis XV, parcel gilt. Paris, 1762. Length 5in.

*Jeremiah Dummer. *Caudle cup, c1692, made in Boston, Massachusetts. Marked I D on the side. Height 3⅛in.*

François Dumont. Miniature of Louis-Antoine de St Just, signed. Diameter 2⅝in.

fluted or gadrooned borders on lids, standing cups, beakers, candlesticks, bleeding bowls, and spoons (slipped-stem type). Also made one of three surviving American standing salts. Mark: ID with a fleur-de-lis in a heart.

dummy-board figure or **companion figure.** Life-sized figure of man, woman, or child, realistically painted in contemporary, exotic, or mythological dress. Cut out of flat board. Stood upright with prop; placed near, and with back to, wall. Fashion, introduced to Britain from Netherlands *c*1620, lasted until 1700 or later. *Illustration at* Jacobean furniture.

Dumont, François (1751–1831). French miniaturist. In Paris from *c*1770, painted on mother-of-pearl and ivory for buttons. Elected to Académie Royale des Beaux-arts in 1787; exhibited miniatures at Paris salon until 1824. Married daughter of A. *Vestier (1789). *Illustration at* French snuff-boxes.

Dunlap, Samuel, II (1751–1830). New Hampshire joiner who made furniture and panelling; fourth generation of furniture-making family. Usually worked in maple; often used deeply-carved shell motif.

du Paquier, Claudius Innocentius (d 1751). Dutch-born founder and director of *Vienna porcelain factory (1719–44). Made some of rarest and most coveted European hard-paste porcelain tableware, but never achieved financial success. *Illustration at* ollio pot.

Duplessis, Claude-Thomas (d 1774). French goldsmith at court of Louis XV. Supervisor of forms at Vincennes (1745–*c*1755); also modelled decoration. Associated with early ornamental vase with flared, scalloped rim and scroll-shaped handles (1750). Continued to design bronze mounts for Sèvres porcelain until death.

Duplessis, Jean-Claude-Thomas (d 1783). French sculptor, son of C-T. *Duplessis. From 1761, modelled figures made in biscuit porcelain at Sèvres.

duplex escapement. *See* escapement.

Dupont, Pierre (d 1644). French carpet-weaver; established first European manufactory of Turkish-knotted pile carpets at Louvre workshop, Paris in 1604, commissioned by Henry IV. With former pupil, S. *Lourdet, established Savonnerie workshop, also under royal patronage, in 1627. After dispute with Lourdet, returned to Louvre workshop. Published carpet-making treatise, *De la Stramouraie.*

Durand, Antoine-Sébastien (d after 1785). French silversmith working in Paris; master in 1740. Made domestic silver in rococo style ornamented with plant forms, clouds, children, etc. (Also, commissions for Joseph I of Portugal.) Most interesting pieces include several pairs of mustard barrels on wheelbarrows pushed by cherubs; ewer with handle in form of boyish satyr, and basin shaped like shaving dish; and elaborate dish cover with realistic still-life of fish. Mark: fleur-de-lis crowned, two pellets, ASD, and heart.

Samuel Dunlap II. Highboy attributed to him. Maple, made in Salisbury, New Hampshire, c1775–90. Fan motif carved under cornice and at base.

Durantino or **Fontana,** Guido (d 1576). Italian maiolica painter, son of N. *Pellipario; established workshop in Urbino, *c*1520. Painting resembles work of father. Credited with service made in 1535 for Anne de Montmorency, Constable of France; also plate made *c*1530, painted in blue, green, yellow, orange, manganese-purple, grey, black, and white, with scene of Circe and Glaucus. Another plate from 1530–35 depicts Death of Cleopatra. Succeeded by son O. *Fontana.

Durlach (Baden). German faience factory established 1722. Most productive and distinctive period from late 18th to early 19th century. Produced small pear-shaped jugs, and coffee-pots painted with rustic figures inscribed with dedication, and initials of recipient (in black letters); vine-leaf borders and dragons' heads common motifs. Early identification only by painter's initials; Durlach, impressed on bases after 1818.

dust board. Thin sheet of wood inserted between drawers to keep contents dust free.

dust cap. Mainly on English watches with movement hinged to case, protective cover of gilt-brass or rarely silver, *c*1715–*c*1890.

Dutch ceramics. Maiolica made in early 16th century by Italian settlers; decorative styles developed, differing from Italian, include **ferronnerie*. *Delft became famous for manufacture of tin-glazed earthenware in 17th century. Hard-paste porcelain made at *The Hague from 1776; manufacture started at *Weesp (1764), transferred to *Oude Loosdrecht, and later, *Amstel.

Dutch chair. In America, 18th century *bended-back chair. In England, synonym for *corner chair.

Dutch clocks. Bracket and long-case clocks made in Holland, particularly after inventions of C. *Huygens, though less widely than in England. Strong Dutch influence on late 17th century English clock case design and use of inlay followed immigration of many Dutch makers. Holland developed own *striking system known as double striking (called Dutch striking in England).

Regional varieties include Zaandam clocks, made in area north-west of Amsterdam, *c*1670 to mid 18th century; weight driven, usually with pear-shaped weights, and counterweights in form of apples; hooded, curvilinear case enclosing pendulum and posted frame movement with pillars normally of spiral twist shape. Chapter ring and spandrels mounted on velvet-covered dial plate, with hour hand only or with subsidiary dial carrying quarter hour divisions. Thirty-hour movements with striking train behind going train, and locking-plate striking mechanism; arbors of characteristically Dutch decorative turned form; verge escapement with vertical escape wheel; alarm sometimes present.

Highly decorative clocks from Friesland, in north-west Holland, first appeared in early 18th

Dutch clocks. Staartklok, *1790–1820; half-hour striking movement with centre sweep hand, and moon phases.*

century; lantern movement with verge escapement similar to Zaandam clocks; iron back plate, side doors of glass, and iron dial often with painted floral pattern and landscape above. In early examples, hour hand only; sometimes also date indicator and phases of moon dial. Dial ornaments of gilded lead; upper one conceals bell. Weights suspended by chain with twisted figure-of-eight links, alarm weights cone-shaped. Case has wooden back flanked by pierced wooden ornaments, generally mermaids, and canopy with cast lead decorations and finials. Sometimes known as *stoelklok* because of small stool on bracket under movement. *Staartklok* also mid 18th century Friesian development; movement has anchor escapement mounted in hood like that of long-case clock; dial often with calendar and automata; pendulum swings in flat wall-mounted case widened at base with window showing bob; chain-hung weights fall in front of pendulum case. Both forms found in miniature with short pendulum for use on shipboard (*schippertjeklok*). Amsterdam clock more finely executed form of *staartklok*: movement has trains mounted side by side with locking plate or rack striking; weights hung by ropes; oak case, often with walnut veneer.

*Dutch furniture. Mid 18th century marquetry *secretary cabinet; shaped cornice with central carved cartouche of basket of flowers; arched panel doors; bombé front containing three graduated long drawers. Height 8ft.*

Dutch Colonial style. Simple baroque style made in America by Dutch settlers in colony of New Amsterdam (later southern New York State) in 17th and 18th centuries. Similar to *Pennsylvania Dutch furniture; characterized by large, architectural pieces (e.g. **kas*), with prominent mouldings, elaborate turning, and brightly painted decoration, often floral.

Dutch furniture. Indigenous Dutch style emerged in Holland *c*1650 with baroque features including highly ornate carving and turning, and floral marquetry. Pieces large and imposing. Some French baroque influence was introduced by immigrant Huguenot craftsmen after the Revocation of the Edict of Nantes (1685). Lacquered furniture also became popular during the 17th century, imitating Chinese lacquer-work imported by Dutch trading companies. From 18th century Dutch furniture styles became increasingly derivative, assimilating features from Queen Anne, Georgian, Louis XV, and Louis XVI styles. *See* D. Marot, Burgomaster chair, bended-back chair, *kas*.

Dutch glass. Little evidence of Dutch glass making before 16th century, though examples similar to German **Waldglas* imported to England in 15th century. In mid 16th century, glass makers from Venice and Altare had established glasshouses. *Waldglas* and *potash glass (using *barilla imported from Spain) made until late 16th century, though Venetian styling predominated, particularly in large goblets and elaborately blown ships (often used as wine containers), and use of *mascarons* on *Humpen*. By early 17th century, Venetian *cristallo* had replaced *Waldglas* at most glasshouses, particularly in those set up during cultural revival following Dutch independence from Spain in 1609. Throughout 17th century, *façon de Venise* *winged glasses, long-necked bulbous bottles, large *Römers,* and native flute glasses in plain or *latticinio* glass all popular.

Dutch glass. Goblet, mid 17th century. Funnel bowl decorated with trailing and spiked gadrooning; stem has hollow, moulded knop.

Dutch glass noted for fine engraved decoration. Earliest examples are late 16th century, but best work is mainly 17th century, by often amateur diamond-point engravers, notably A. R. *Visscher, who popularized calligraphic designs. Stipple engraving on glass, almost exclusive to Holland, executed e.g. by F. *Greenwood and D. *Wolff in 18th century; subjects include portraits, still-lifes, copies of contemporary paintings, allegorical and armorial motifs. Large amount of German-style wheel engraving in early 18th century, mainly by German craftsmen, e.g. J. *Sang. 18th century Dutch engraving outstripped home glass production, mainly through lack of fuel for furnaces; much glass imported, particularly English lead glass which provided ideal medium for engraving.

Dutch gold and silver. Little medieval Dutch plate survives. Most important group of surviving 15th and 16th century plate consists of drinking vessels. Earliest type are *drinking horns, but *standing cups, *beakers, *tankards (rare), *goblets, and **tazze* made later, many based on German engraved designs. In late 16th century, many natural materials mounted as cups, e.g. *coconut, *nautilus shell, often with figure stems derived from Italian mannerist style. Dutch silver reached peak in period 1600–50 with development of *Dutch grotesque style, initiated by *van Vianen family; ornament mainly chased and embossed. Vessels so ornamented include various drinking vessels, as well as *rose-water ewers and basins, *salts, *candlesticks, *dishes, etc. Uniquely Dutch vessels of period include *brandy bowls, *wine glass stands, *marriage caskets, *windmill cups. Domestic silver decorated with engraved or embossed botanical motifs, particularly the tulip, often with matting as background, found c1650–90. With rise of wealthy merchant class in late 17th century, demand for table silver as evidence of prosperity increased. Styles derived from Huguenots, e.g. D. *Marot, who became architect and decorator to William of Orange (later William III of England). In early 18th century, English influence also felt (possibly because of royal link); but predominant influence in 18th and 19th centuries, French. Full range of rococo table silver made, though more reminiscent of Dutch grotesque style.

Little medieval church plate survives. In 17th century, Antwerp influenced production of Catholic plate because of shortages caused by religious wars, but most important item of post-Reformation Dutch church plate was beaker (used as *communion cup). Some examples have secular ornament (interlaced bands of arabesques, foliage, etc.), others engraved with sacred figures or scenes, e.g. Last Supper, figures of Faith, Hope, and Charity.

Maker's mark used from 14th century; in 15th century, guilds given right to set standard of fineness for gold and silver. Marks in early 16th century included *town mark (usually city arms), *date letter, and *maker's mark. In 1633, 'Republic of Seven Provinces' established, each province having own regulations. Centres of production included Amsterdam, The Hague, Haarlem, Rotterdam, Utrecht, and Friesland. In 1789, after French conquest, guilds abolished, and French provincial marks used, until Netherlands freed from French rule (1814) when new marks introduced.

Dutch gold (gold substitute). *See* Dutch metal.

Dutch grotesque, auricular, cartilaginous, lobate, or **oleaginous style.** Ornamental style developed by Dutch silversmiths in first half of 17th century; characterized by fluid, curving forms (thought to resemble ear-lobe or cartilage, etc.) and grotesque figures (human or animal), dolphins, masks, etc. Variation on mannerist style developed by *van Vianen family. Style spread to Britain and Europe (C. *van Vianen worked for Charles I and Charles II of England). Silver so ornamented includes *tazze,* ewers and basins, salts, etc. Motifs always embossed. Other prominent Dutch silversmiths working in this style were T. *Bogaert and J. *Lutma the Elder and Younger.

Dutch metal or **Dutch gold.** *Pinchbeck hammered into thin leaves and used as cheap substitute for gold leaf from 18th century on e.g. papier mâché wares. Unless varnished, green discolouration occurs.

Dutch oven. Sheet-iron or brass open-fronted oven, on three or four legs, placed before open fire for roasting meat. Curved sides and hood reflect heat on to joint, which hangs from hook in hood. Used from 16th century.

Dutch striking. *See* striking systems.

Dutch watches. Makers in Holland followed English and French styles throughout 17th and 18th centuries, with some local variation, but favouring general European practice with bridge *cock for balance. Early movements often have engraved border to back plate and large balance with square for winding passing inside rim of balance and through cock. Silver *pair-case watches with bridge cocks, sometimes called 'Dutch fakes', probably had imported movements and were cased in Holland. Many examples carry names of London makers but Dutch origin is shown by presence of *arcaded minute ring, the movements often being of inferior quality.

duty-dodging. Attempt to avoid payment of sixpence per ounce levied on British plate made 1719–58. Silversmiths sent small piece of silver for assay then incorporated hallmarked section in much heavier object. Marks were usually built into base as false bottom between body and foot of coffee-pot, teapot, etc., so are difficult to detect.

duty mark. Mark struck on gold or silver indicating that tax or duty had been paid. Sovereign's head was used in Britain 1784–1890; in France, *charge and *discharge marks.

Duvivier, Fidèle (fl late 18th century). Porcelain painter at Chelsea (1764–69), and Derby (1769–73). Later, outside decorator for Worcester, Derby, Pinxton, and New Hall porcelain factories. In 1775, worked at Sceaux faience factory. Work, occasionally signed, includes cup and saucer made *c*1800 painted with wolf and crane, and mug with elaborate figure painting, probably made at Caughley. Cousin of H-J. *Duvivier.

Duvivier, Henri-Joseph (1740–71). Belgian porcelain painter, born in Tournai. Thought to have studied in England; worked at Chelsea. Chief decorator at Tournai factory (1763–71); responsible for painting in Sèvres style. Credited with exotic birds in predominantly reddish-brown setting of rocks, usually against white ground; also with crimson monochrome figures in landscape with castle, and cupids.

dwarf ale. English drinking glass, similar to *ale glass but stemless, or with knop between foot and bowl. In late 17th century, knop pinched and foot folded or plain. Early 18th century bowl sometimes wrythen. Spiral swirling popular from 1720. Late 18th century examples occasionally have domed square or hexagonal foot.

dwarf bookcase. 19th century term for low bookcase (of dado height), sometimes with glass doors.

dwarf-tall clock, small-tall clock, or **grandmother clock.** American clock; smaller version of *tall clock; *c*4ft or less. Produced early 19th century; makers include B. *Morrill.

Dwight, John (1637–1703). London potter, previously ecclesiastical lawyer. Granted patent

*Dutch grotesque style. Detail from candle sconce by A. *van Vianen, 1622.*

John Dwight. Salt-glaze stoneware mug made at Fulham, c*1680. Rim mounted in silver.*

by Charles II to make stoneware (1671); established factory at Fulham. In 1676–77, contracted to supply the Glass Sellers' Company with bottles similar to German *bellarmines, often bearing tavern devices. Used thin, greyish-white slightly translucent stoneware for small mugs with rounded bodies and cylindrical, horizontally reeded necks; also figures including mythological characters, portraits, and, notably, Dwight's dead daughter, Lydia. In 1693–94, sued other makers of stoneware, including J. P. and D. *Elers, for infringement of patent.

dwt. *See* pennyweight.

Dyottville Glass Works. American glasshouse established at Kensington, Pennsylvania, in 1771 as Kensington Glass Works. Bought by Dr T. W. Dyott in 1831. Produced pictorial and historical flasks, also vials, bottles and some flint-glass tableware. Dyott went bankrupt in 1838 but glassworks continued, adding coloured glass to range in 1840s.

eagle bracket or **table.** Console or side table; top supported by eagle with outspread wings. Dates from early 18th century.

eared cup. *See* porringer.

Earnshaw, Thomas (1749–1829). English watch and clock maker working in London, originally as finisher of verge and cylinder watches. Taught himself *jewelling and making cylinder *escapements. Set up in business; perfected spring detent escapement for marine chronometers and made first effective *compensation balance. With work of J. *Arnold, Earnshaw's improvements made marine chronometer commercially viable. Early examples smaller than Arnold's, *c*3in. diameter, and highly finished; later movements left without polishing or decoration ('in the grey'). Also made pocket chronometers, many with movement screwed into case, and some clocks, including regulator for Archbishop of Armagh. Business continued by son and grandson, also christened Thomas.

earring. Ornament hung from hook or ring through lobe of ear, usually in matched pair. Used from antiquity; often with talismanic significance; made in many materials. Worn by both sexes in Orient, generally by women only in West. Typical ancient Egyptian form, disc and pendant chain; in Assyria knob or pendant attached to rigid ring. Gold earrings ornamented with filigree, granulation, etc., in disc, palmette, or other shapes worn in Greece; in Roman period usually in plain gold; sometimes set with pearls or gems. Few examples survive from Dark Ages in Europe; not much used in Middle Ages. Widely worn in 16th century Europe. Usual form drop-shaped pearl or gem in gold mount; more elaborate types with three pendant pearls on gem-set mount. Single earring worn by gallants in 16th and early 17th centuries. From mid 17th century set with various faceted gems, mounts silver, or gold where visible; shapes often floral. Bow shape with pendant drops popular in late 17th century. Use of lavish gem-setting increased in 18th century, with diamonds, emeralds, rubies, topazes, etc., and paste. **Girandole* was elaboration of traditional drop form. 19th century designs eclectic; influenced by Gothic revival, archaeological research, etc. Egyptian, Greek, Etruscan, styles fashionable at different periods of 19th century, also various materials including iron, pinchbeck, coral, jet. *See* Berlin iron jewellery, hair jewellery, jet jewellery, mourning jewellery. *Illustration at girandole.*

Eagle table. English, mid 18th century; carved and gilded wooden eagle supporting marble table top.

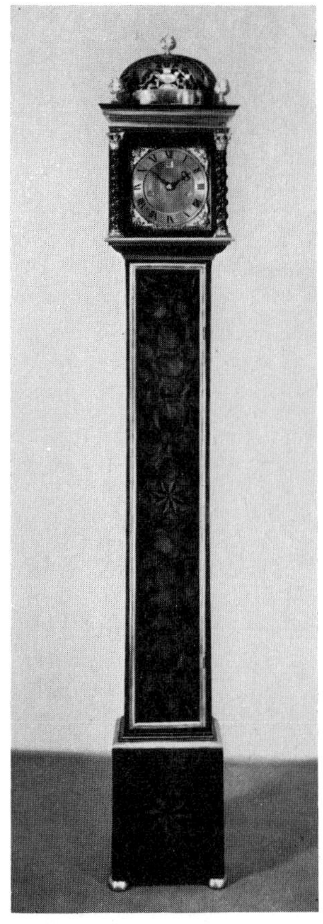

*Johann Friedrich Eberlein. Candelabrum, Meissen, 1750. Figure of Diogenes with barrel, against *rococo background. Height* c12*in.*
Left:
*Edward East. Small *long-case clock,* c*1670, height 5ft8in. Eight-day striking movement. Case veneered with olivewood oyster pieces.*

earthenware. Pottery in which clay fired only until particles begin to fuse together. Result is permeable; usually covered with lead or tin glaze. Primitive method of decoration with clay slip under lead glaze (**sgraffiato*) and *slipware reached high development in e.g. *Staffordshire slipware, **Hafnerware,* or isolated case of *Saint-Porchaire ware. Hard red earthenware made in Delft from late 17th century imitated Chinese Yi-hsing stoneware. *Cream-coloured earthenware often fired at higher temperature to point of resonance and higher level of vitrification.

East, Edward (*c*1610–*c*1693). English clock and watch maker. Served apprenticeship as goldsmith; founding member, Clockmakers' Company. Clockmaker to Charles I and Charles II. Among first makers of *night clocks in England. Other, lesser makers of this name also recorded. *Illustration also at* night clock.

East India flowers. *See indianische Blumen.*

Eastlake, Charles Lock (1836–1906). English furniture designer and architect. Promulgator of modern English Gothic style, known as *Eastlake style, exemplified in illustrations in Hints of Household Taste, Upholstery, and Other Details (1868), popular in Britain and America.

Eastlake style. Interpretation by C. L. *Eastlake of medieval British furniture styles, popular in Britain and America *c*1870–80. He advocated use of oak, with peg joinery, simple rectangular designs, prominent hinges; condemned curves in design and use of French polish or other varnish on wood. Cupboard and bookcase backs in Eastlake style may be constructed of narrow vertical or diagonal boards of unequal width, imitating medieval hewn wood. Despite intended simplicity, many pieces have elaborate carved decoration.

easy chair. Upholstered *wing chair, popular in Europe, Britain, and America from late 17th or early 18th century. Also, general term for upholstered chair designed for comfort.

ébauche. Watch movement, often incomplete, requiring addition of escapement, jewels, etc.; especially used to describe early factory-made movements supplied to individual makers for finishing and casing.

ébéniste (French, 'worker in ebony'). From mid 17th to end of 18th century, furniture maker who employed technique of veneering, as opposed to **menuisier*, who used turned or carved ornament.

Eberlein, Johann Friedrich (d 1749). German porcelain modeller at Meissen (1735–49). Close collaborator with J. J. *Kändler. Work includes The Three Graces, a large proportion of the *swan service, and a series of deities and virtues on high pedestals. *Illustration also at* Meissen.

ebonizing. Staining of wood or metal to resemble ebony. Technique used from 17th century.

echinus. Classical moulding, one quarter circle in cross-section; often enriched with *egg-and-dart.

Eckernförde (Schleswig). German faience factory founded 1765. Products include tableware with flowers and outlines of shell-mouldings painted in strong blue; large trays and table tops; tureens in animal or vegetable shapes. Marks: E, or Eckernförde, with painters and date.

écuelle. Shallow, two-handled, lidded bowl used in France and Germany particularly for giving nourishment to women at childbirth (known in Germany as *Wöchnerinschüssel,* 'midwife's bowl'). Made late 17th to mid 18th centuries, usually in silver (with flat pierced handles) or porcelain, occasionally pewter. Silver examples sometimes have salver or stand; rarely made in England and America.

écureuil. *See décor coréen.*

Edelzinn (German, 'noble pewter'). Late 16th and 17th century display pewter with relief decoration, cast in copper moulds and minutely worked with treatment of sculptural detail usually reserved for precious metals. Ewers, dishes, jugs made in this way e.g. by F. *Briot, Kaspar Enderlein and others in *Nuremberg and elsewhere.

edges, side cords, or **selvage.** Weft threads at sides of carpet, looped around outermost warp threads and reinforced by overcasting with wool, silk, or cotton thread.

Edkins, Michael (1734–1811). Independent English glass and delftware enameller in Bristol. Initially painted ornaments, plates, dishes, and Flemish tiles. Some early pieces (*c*1760) marked MEB (including initial for wife, Betty). 1762–87, specialized in enamelling and gilding opaque-white and blue glass. Work unsigned. Opaque-white glass enamelled with *chinoiserie* motifs, particularly perched birds and bunches of flowers; blue glass decorated with gilded borders. Subjects included tea-canisters, vases, and cruets. *Illustration at* opaque-white glass.

Edmands & Co. Pottery established 1850 at Charlestown, Massachusetts. Manufactured domestic stoneware until 1868.

Edo period (1615–1868). Japanese period, succeeding Momoyama, named after newly established capital, Edo (now Tokyo). Noted for peace, prosperity, and general flourishing of arts, especially ceramics. Work greatly influenced by Korean *Yi wares. *Seto and *Karatsu potteries active; *Raku work appears in Kyoto. Arita established as pottery centre, with production of first Japanese porcelain. Some overglaze enamel painting in style of Chinese Ming period. Ivory (e.g. *netsuke and *inro) and lacquer work both flourished but metal-work declined. Towards end of period, trade with outside world, especially West, increased.

Edouart, Augustin (1789–1861). French-born silhouettist, in England from 1814. Silhouettist from 1826; work usually full-length figures, always cut from black paper folded double to produce profile and duplicate in one process. Sitters included Sir Walter Scott and exiled Charles X of France and family. In America, 1839–49, cut profiles of Henry Wadsworth Longfellow, Benjamin Franklin, and three presidents. Published book, A Treatise on Silhouette Likenesses, 1835.

Edwards, John (1671–1746). English-born silversmith working in Boston, Massachusetts; probably apprenticed to J. *Dummer. With partner, John Allen, made one of three surviving American standing salts (now at Yale University). Surviving works include salvers, beakers, flagon, standing cup. Sons, Samuel and Thomas, and grandson, Joseph, continued in trade. Own mark unproven; joint mark: IE and IA in quatrefoil.

Egermann, Friedrich (1777–1864). Bohemian glass maker; developed form of coloured glass called *lithyalin, and others, at factory in Blottendorf. *Illustrations at* Biedermeier glass, hyalith.

egg-and-dart or **egg-and-tongue moulding.** Of classical origin; *ovolo moulding alternating with arrowhead or tongue-like motif. Much used as ornament on late 16th, early 17th, and 19th century silver. Stamped in low relief on feet, covers, etc., of hollow-ware or cast and applied. Common on furniture from early 16th century.

egg boiler. Silver, silver-gilt, Sheffield plate or electro-plated vessel (oval, hemispherical, or cylindrical); earlier types sometimes with open-work feet, two handles on sides, flat lid with two

Ecuelle *and cover. Made in Rome by Giovanni Bouchard,* c*1720.*

Augustin Edouart. Silhouette of Cramsie family of Ballymoney, County Antrim. Cut paper on pen, ink, and watercolour background. Signed and dated 1838. Size 14*in.* × 20*in.*

*Egg boiler. Silver. By J. *Emes, 1802. Boiler has two-sectioned hinged cover inside which is holder for four eggs; on top is sand timer on swivel; raffia-covered handles; stand fitted with spirit lamp on four paw supports. Height* 13*in.*

*Egg frame. Made in London, 1740, by P. *Archambo; egg cups engraved with arms of George Booth, 2nd Earl of Warrington.*

hinged flaps, and central column handle terminating in oval loop; occasionally with egg-timer mounted on column. Spirit lamp fitted between feet. Wire-work frame inside body held four to six eggs. Generally made *en suite* with egg-cups and spoons. Used in Britain from late 18th century. Electro-plated versions usually simpler, without egg-cups.

egg cruet. *See* egg frame.

egg-cup. In 18th century silver, shaped like hour-glass. By 1800 inverted bell-shaped cup supported on decorative foot most common form. Also made in Sheffield plate. Often part of *egg frame. *Illustration at* travelling set.

egg frame or **cruet.** Silver, silver-gilt, or Sheffield plate frame or cruet to hold varied number of egg-cups and sometimes spoons. Used from late 17th century, though earliest surviving examples from early 18th century. In 19th century Britain some made in novelty shapes, e.g. hen sitting on basket. Later made in electro-plate.

eggshell. In Chinese ceramics, porcelain characterized by extreme thinness of body. Achieved by paring, trimming, scraping, or smoothing firm, partly dried surface of vessel before firing.

egg-spoon. Small silver spoon resembling teaspoon in use from late 17th century. Later common in ivory or horn as sulphur content of eggs tarnishes silver. *Illustration at* travelling set.

Egyptian black. Unglazed stoneware, stained black throughout body, produced in Staffordshire, *c*1720–*c*1890. Until mid 1760s, coloured with iron oxide, basis from which J. *Wedgwood developed black basalt. From 1760s, improved quality, stained with manganese dioxide. Frequently used for tea ware; much exported.

Egyptian carpets. Egyptian textiles among earliest made; *kelims from 1400 B.C. discovered in tomb of Thotmes IV, and by 3rd or 4th century A.D., weft-loop carpets exported to furnish wealthy Roman homes. Oldest surviving knotted-pile fragments from *Fostat (9th to 11th centuries). From 12th to 14th centuries, mainly *Spanish imported carpets used at Egyptian court. During Mamluk period (1400–1517) productive court carpet industry developed in Cairo under royal patronage; exported to courts throughout Near East, probably also Europe, via Venice and Spain. After Ottoman occupation of Cairo in 1517, flourishing industry produced carpets modelled on those of *Turkish Court Manufactory, and *Ushak. In 17th century, designs copied contemporary *Persian court carpet models, particularly floral *Isfahans. By 18th century, competition from other countries caused decline, and major Cairo manufactories closed. However, Cairo remained important distribution centre for oriental carpets until late 19th century.

Ehrenreich, Johan Ludwig Eberhard (1722–1803). German-born pottery proprietor, previously court dentist to Frederick I of Sweden. Established Marieberg factory (1758); produced faience, although porcelain privilege granted in 1759. In 1766 left because of financial failure. Worked at Stralsund (1766–70) and Königsberg (from 1772).

Eisenrotmalerei. *See* red monochrome

elbow chair. In 17th century, armchairs as opposed to single chairs in dining-room set.

electric clock. In 19th century, clock using electricity to replace spring or weight as motive power, with pendulum as timekeeper. First system invented by A. *Bain in 1843.

electro-gilding. Silver object immersed in gold-plating bath activated by electric current; gold particles deposited on silver surface. Process discovered early 19th century, but not widely used until 1840s.

electro-plating. Silver coating deposited by electrolysis on base metal, e.g. Britannia metal, copper, or nickel alloy. Silver anode and object to be plated immersed in electrolytic solution; current passed through. Silver particles transfer from anode to object, which acts as cathode. Process patented in Birmingham in 1840 by G. R. *Elkington. Pure silver used in electro-plating makes possible simple test to determine whether vessel is Sheffield plate or electro-plate: former (in which Sterling Standard silver used) turns blue when dipped in dilute nitric acid; electro-plate does not change.

Production of large range of electro-plated domestic articles begun in England by *Elkington & Co. and firms they licensed (e.g. J. *Dixon & Sons). By 1851 (time of Great Exhibition in London), electro-plated wares (although derided by official jury) tacitly approved; by 1862 electro-plating had largely replaced alternative methods of plating. Earliest electro-plated articles were first cast in nickel alloy, Britannia metal, etc.; later pieces were spun and stamped. Electro-plating became extremely successful; whereas early pieces copied silver styles, from *c*1860 electro-plated wares were in forefront of design. Many firms produced same designs in both electro-plate and silver. In mid 19th century, electro-plate wares modelled on natural plant forms or with plant ornament. Sheffield became centre of production of electro-plated knives, forks, and spoons.

Electro-plate. Pie-dish, cover and stand, with detachable liner, English, c1875; base stamped G. R. Collis & Co., 130, Regent Street. Width 9½*in.*

electrotyping. Model or copy of object formed by deposition of thin layer of copper, bronze or other metal on original model by electrolysis. Improved process patented in 1843 by *Elkington & Co. in Birmingham. Insects, leaves, etc., preserved by metal coating. Encouraged contemporary interest in naturalistic design. Firm of Smith & Nicholson, founded by B. *Smith the Younger, showed dessert plates electrotyped from vine-leaves at the Great Exhibition (1851). Process also used to copy antique metal-work.

electrum. Term used in antiquity for alloy of gold with *c*25% silver ('green gold'); occasionally used in Middle Ages for *brass.

elephant clock. French mantel clock, produced in mid 18th century. Round clock case (often with figure on top), mounted on back of elephant. (Base sometimes contains musical

Elers brothers. Red stoneware mug, silver mounted, c1690. Applied relief decoration of sprigs in imitation of Chinese prunus blossom.

box.) Example by J-B. *Baillon. Elephant figures notably by J. and P. *Caffiéri. Also made with other animals, e.g. bull or lion, as supporting figures. Rococo style, generally in solid bronze, although porcelain elephants found in some examples.

Elers, John Philip (1644–1738) and David (1656–1742). Makers of English stoneware; originally silversmiths from Danzig, trading in Cheapside, London *c*1686. Established pottery at Vauxhall, London (1690), then at Bradwell Wood, Staffordshire (*c*1695–*c*1698). J. P. Elers thought to have moved to Dublin, as seller of glass and china. Among those sued by J. *Dwight in 1693–94. Made some salt-glazed wares and unglazed red stoneware imitating Yi-hsing stoneware and using silver shapes. Teapots, tea bottles, jugs, mugs, beakers, cups, and saucers engine-turned and decorated with finely-moulded sprigs of flowers, leaves, and other motifs in relief, notable for delicacy and good finish, occasionally gilded or enamelled. Also made black stoneware, similar to later black basalt of J. *Wedgwood. Wares usually unmarked; stag within circle and imitation Chinese characters occur, all impressed.

Elfe, Thomas (fl 1747–75). Cabinet maker in Charleston, South Carolina. Made case pieces with heavy carving.

Elizabethan furniture. Mainly simple, functional beds, chairs, tables, chests, settles, etc., usually in oak (though finest pieces occasionally walnut), dating from *c*1560. Carved decoration most common, at first using medieval cusps, arches, and grotesques, later including motifs largely derived from Italian Renaissance style, e.g. strap-work, medallions containing profiles, scrolls, and arabesques. Bulbous swellings *bulb and *cup-and-cover) on table, bed, and cupboard legs Flemish in origin. Inlaid decoration also used, often in floral, geometric, or architectural designs (*see* Nonsuch chest). Split balusters applied to case furniture façades. Characteristic pieces of Elizabethan furniture include *court cupboards, *low-poster beds (sometimes with head-board), beds with inlaid tester and drapery, simple day-beds, long tables with fixed tops (replacing trestle), *joint and three-legged stools, *settles and *settle tables, and, less common, chairs, e.g. *Glastonbury, *wainscot. *Illustrations at* food cupboard, four-poster bed, Nonsuch chest, *tazza*.

Elkington, George Richards (1801–65). English manufacturer of electro-plate in Birmingham. Trained as gilt toy and spectacle-maker, worked first in partnership with George Richards (uncle), later with Henry Elkington (cousin), building large factory in Birmingham. In 1836 took out first of many patents for new methods of gilding and plating. Decisive patent (1840, jointly with Henry) covered electro-plating process, giving control over its exploitation, followed by patents in other countries. Manufacture of silver and various materials was added when firm was successfully established, becoming largest producers in England. *See also* Elkington & Co. *Illustration at* wine funnel.

Elkington & Co. Firm manufacturing mainly electro-plated wares; founded (1829–36) by G. R. and H. *Elkington in Birmingham. In 1842, Josiah Mason became third partner. Electro-plate marked E & Co., in a shield, and EM & Co., in three separate shields with firm's own date letter sequence. Henry died in 1852; Mason left firm *c*1859, but initials not omitted from mark until 1864. Firm produced wide range of domestic articles, earliest copying contemporary silver styles; later employed French sculptors and designers, e.g. P. E. *Jeannest (1853–57) and L. *Morel-Ladeuil (1859–88). Prices of electro-plate set quite high to overcome snobbish prejudice against it. Also successfully challenged *Garrard's and *Hunt & Roskell in production of silver presentation and display pieces. Used *electrotype process to make replicas in silver of natural objects and early masterpieces. Death of founders did not affect prosperity of firm.

Ellicott, John (1706–72). English inventor and clock maker. Worked on pendulum, and cylinder escapement. Clockmaker to George III; Fellow of Royal Society, 1738. Devised form of *compensation pendulum, 1753. Son of John Ellicott the Elder (*c*1687–1733).

Elliott, John, Senior (fl *c*1753–76) and John, Junior (fl 1776–1809). English mirror maker, in Philadelphia, Pennsylvania from 1753; John Jr took over business in 1776. Known for fretwork, Philadelphia Chippendale style, and architectural mirrors.

Ellwangen or **Utzmemmingen** (Württemberg). Small German porcelain factory involving arcanist J. J. *Ringler, founded *c*1758. Products believed to be functional wares and some figures; none identified with certainty. Possible mark: bishop's mitre bearing cross in underglaze blue.

émail en résille sur verre. Type of *enamelling on glass or rock-crystal practised in early 17th century France, probably also in Germany. Design (usually arabesques, scrolls, flowers, etc.) engraved on surface of glass or crystal; cavities lined with gold foil and then filled with enamel of low melting point. Used for jewellery, miniatures, and watch cases, etc. Practice declined quickly because of difficulties of medium (e.g. problem of fusing enamel without cracking or melting glass).

*John Ellicott II. Table clock, mid 18th century; walnut case with silver-gilt mounts probably designed and executed by G. M. *Moser.*

ember-tongs. *See* smokers' tongs.

embossing. Design in relief produced by hammering reverse side of metal which is supported on pliable bed of pitch, wax, or softwood. If object is hollow-ware, *snarling iron used. Much used to ornament 17th century silver in Dutch grotesque style and mid 18th century rococo silver. *See repoussé.*

embryo shell thumbpiece. Thumbpiece of rough cockleshell shape on Scottish pewter vessels of late 18th and early 19th centuries.

Emens, Jan (fl 1566–94). Most famous member of *Mennicken family of potters making Rhineland stoneware at Raeren, Germany, during 16th century. Known for intricate relief decoration on **Doppelfrieskrüge*; also introduced use of clear blue lead-glaze in panels on stoneware, a technique later developed in *Westerwald. Mark: IE.

emerald. Bright green variety of beryl (silicate of aluminium beryllium) with hexagonal crystal (aquamarine is bluish-green variety). Colour due to traces of chromic oxide. Soft in comparison with other gems; often flawed and containing inclusions. Refractive powers low therefore has little 'fire'. Mined in Egypt from *c*2000 B.C.; these mines lost until rediscovery by Frédéric Cailliaud in 1818. After classical period, emeralds not used until Spanish conquest of South America. From 16th century Spaniards brought back vast quantities to Europe. Used to ornament ecclesiastical plate, jewellery, etc. In 1558 emeralds discovered in Colombia near Bogotá. In early 19th century discovered in Russian Urals.

Emery, Josiah (*c*1725–1797). Swiss-born watch maker working in London. Developed lever escapement for watches after invention by T. *Mudge, using it in about 30 watches, 1782–*c*1795. Used dial adapted from regulator clock, with two subsidiary dials marking hours and seconds. Also made high-quality watches with other escapements.

Emes, John (d 1808). English silversmith working in London; not a freeman of Goldsmiths' Company. In 1796 became partner of established silversmith, Henry Chawner. Mark (with Chawner): HC above IE; in 1798 registered own mark, JE. On retirement of Chawner (probably 1798) Edward Barnard became chief journeyman and, on death of Emes, became partner of latter's wife, Rebecca. Mark of Emes & Barnard registered in 1808: RE above EB. On Rebecca's death (1828), firm became Edward *Barnard & Sons. *Illustrations at* egg boiler, wax jack, wine labels.

Empire style. Furniture style popular in France *c*1804–30, and America *c*1810–30. Typified by severe, formal treatment of classical forms and designs; principal tenets summarized by C. *Percier and P. *Fontaine in *Recueil des décorations intérieures* (1812). Furniture rectilinear, with uncluttered ornament or flat bronze appliqués; motifs include amphorae, chimeras, crowns surmounted by Napoleonic N, festoons, flowers, laurel sprigs, lions, lyres, palm leaves, sphinxes, swags, swans, tridents, and wreaths. Monopodia common supports; columns popular as façade decoration. Woods included ebony, elm, maple, and, particularly, mahogany. *See* American Empire style. *Illustration also at* centre table.

*Empire style. Candelabra by P-P. *Thomire, c1800; bronze and ormolu.*

enamel blanks. Copper boxes, plaques, watch-backs, etc., covered in white enamel. Stock-piled until needed and then painted in current style.

enamel. Glass, melted with metallic oxides as colouring agents, powdered and fused to surface of metal (most successfully gold or copper), ceramics, or glassware. Used in ancient Egypt and Assyria, and in classical antiquity; by Celts, and notably by Byzantine craftsmen. Earliest method applied to metal is *champlevé* enamelling: metal ground is cut away to leave troughs in which enamel paste is laid, then heated and fused; *cloisonné* technique developed in Byzantium and introduced from there to Cologne, Germany, in late 10th century, uses thin metal strips laid edgewise on base to form cells for enamel, modified in *plique-à-jour* form, mainly in Russia and Scandinavia, in which base is removed, leaving translucent enamel 'windows'. *Basse-taille* enamelling first produced in Pisa, Italy at end of 13th century; enamel is laid over ground engraved in low relief. Craft of enamelling centred at Limoges, France, through Middle Ages; painted enamel on metal (developed in Venice) used from 15th century, often applied in several successive layers; technique of white painting on dark ground (*en grisaille*), giving light-and-shade effect, common in 16th

*Enamels. Left to right: 1) *Staffordshire enamel scent flagon, 1770–75. 2) *Battersea enamel snuff box, c1750. 3) Staffordshire enamel étui, painted after portrait by Joshua Reynolds of Lady Fenhoulet, 1770–75. 4) *Bilston enamel patch-box, c1770.*
Below:
*Enamelled glass by *Beilby family. Left to right: 1) Wine glass by William Beilby; funnel bowl decorated with fruiting vine, opaque twist stem; 1765; height $6\frac{1}{4}$in. 2) Beaker, 1768; height $4\frac{1}{2}$in. 3) Tumbler inscribed And the Coal Trade, referring to Newcastle's glass and coal trade, 1765; height $3\frac{3}{4}$in. 4) Wine glass, waisted bell bowl enamelled with obelisk, opaque twist stem, 1770. Height c7in.*

century. Enamel objects produced in England at *Battersea, in *Birmingham and *South Staffordshire. Enamel widely used on watch-cases, etc.; *see* Blois, Geneva enamel, Huaud family. Far Eastern techniques derived from Europe, *see* Canton enamels, Chinese *cloisonné* enamel.

Enamel on glass and ceramics applied as paste after initial production of article, then re-fired to fuse with surface; used notably on *Islamic glassware, e.g. hanging mosque lamps, in 13th and 14th centuries, and on contemporary Persian earthenware; also found on Chinese ceramics ascribed to 13th century, not fully developed until reign of Ch'êng Hua (1465–87); combination with underglaze decoration in *tou ts'ai method made wide colour range possible. Employed on 15th century Venetian glass, often combined with gilding, e.g. by *Berovieri family and 16th-18th century German and Bohemian enamellers including I. *Preissler, J. *Schaper. Armorial motifs common in 16th century; by 17th century, glasses and goblets, e.g. **Reichsadlerhumpen, *Hofkellerei* glasses, decorated with motifs including coats of arms, trade symbols, family groups, and religious subjects. Revived in Germany in 19th century by various artists (transparent enamelling carried out by *Mohn family and A. *Kothgasser). Process introduced to English glass in late 17th century, reached peak in work by W. and M. *Beilby in 18th century. Popular decoration at Bristol for opaque-white and blue glassware, notably by M. *Edkins; used by J. *Giles in London (though principally known for gilding). English 19th century enamelled glass typically rather heavy and ornate, with floral and landscape motifs and exaggerated copies of Islamic work. Chinese ceramic enamelling techniques applied directly to biscuit porcelain in late 17th and early 18th centuries in *famille verte* and (from *c*1720) *famille rose* palettes. In Europe first introduced on pottery at Kreussen, probably derived from glass enamelling; European porcelain enamelled from establishment of Meissen factory. Also used on faience, particularly at Strasbourg from mid 18th century, often in imitation of porcelain. Enamel colours in ceramics sometimes described as low-temperature or overglaze colours.

en camaïeu. Ceramic decoration imitating cameos painted in monochrome of varying intensity on porcelain e.g. of late 18th century Sèvres, Bristol, and Derby. Subjects usually portraits or figures, notably *putti*; characteristic of late rococo style; executed **en grisaille*. Also feature of neo-classical decoration. *Illustration at décor bois.*

encoigneur. *See* corner cupboard.

en cuvette (French, 'basin-shaped'). 18th century term describing porcelain or hollowed-out hardstone boxes.

endive or **seaweed marquetry.** Sinuous, ornate marquetry, with scrolls and arabesques resembling seaweed or endive (chicory) leaves. Italian form, popular in late 17th century England.

end-stone. Cap of diamond or ruby over bearing in clock or watch movement to take lengthwise thrust of pivot.

Enghalskrug (German, 'narrow-necked jug'). Round-bellied, narrow-necked jug, normally produced in faience, sometimes with pewter lid. Common in Germany during 17th and 18th centuries.

Enghien tapestry. Flemish tapestry-weaving centre at Enghien from 14th century. Peak period first half of 16th century with numerous fine quality *verdures*, particularly *boscages*; also historical and religious subjects. From mid 16th century, decline followed emigration of some of best weavers. Revived in 17th century, but activity ceased *c*1685. Design and style follow Brussels tapestry models.

engine-turning. Machine-engraving applied to wide variety of materials, developed in 1760s. Used initially in France to decorate gold work; in England on ceramics. Designs engraved on surface of dry, unfired pot as it is rotated on a lathe. Used by D. and J. P. *Elers and by J. *Wedgwood from 1760s for decoration of red or cane-coloured stoneware, black basalt and jasper dip. Patterns include chevrons, chequers, fluting; also irregular basket-work produced by *rose-engine. *Illustration at* black basalt.

Englehart, George (1752–1829). English miniaturist. Pupil of Sir Joshua Reynolds, whose works he copied in miniature. From 1775 to retirement in 1813, painted 4853 miniatures; exhibited at Royal Academy until 1812. Miniature painter to George III from 1790, succeeding J. *Meyer; many portraits of king and royal family.

Englehart, John Cox Dillman (*c*1783–1862). English miniaturist. Nephew and pupil of G. *Englehart. Exhibited at Royal Academy 1801–28. Used hotter, darker colours than uncle. Most notable miniature is of Richard Brinsley Sheridan.

English baluster measure. *See* measure.

English carpets. *See* Axminster, Exeter, Fulham, Kidderminster, Moorfields, needlework, and Wilton carpets.

Endive marquetry. On case of 17th century English long-case clock.
*English carpet. Hand tufted oval carpet, woven in style of R. *Adam, c1780, probably made at *Axminster. 17ft7in.+12ft9in.*

English ceramics. Lead-glazed earthenware of 14th and 15th centuries made into domestic ware, following metal forms. Jugs elaborately decorated until mid 15th century, became more uniform with development of mass-production. Improvement in firing technique by 16th century made possible manufacture of smooth red earthenware in variety of forms, including for first time, cups, plates, and dishes; often covered with brown glaze. *Cistercian pottery, made in Midlands, and *Tudor green ware in South are examples of increasing range of production. Tin-glazed earthenware made from mid 16th century, beginning with *Malling jugs; manufacture of *English delftware lasted until 18th century, at centres including *Bristol, *Lambeth, *Liverpool, and *Wincanton; also *Glasgow and *Dublin. In 17th century, lead-glazed slipware made throughout England, e.g. in south-east (*Metropolitan and *Wrotham slipware) and notably by *Toft family and R. *Simpson in Staffordshire. In late 17th century, stoneware developed by J. *Dwight, and D. and J. P. *Elers; in early 18th century also made at *Nottingham, and by mid century salt-glaze ware made by many potters, e.g. T. *Whieldon, W. *Littler and R. *Wood I. Staffordshire developed, in 18th century, into main centre of English pottery industry, evolving techniques which foreshadowed Industrial Revolution, e.g. division of labour, use of labour-saving machinery, and standardization of methods and materials. Among many potters producing e.g. cream-coloured earthenware, tortoiseshell, agate, and salt-glazed ware were J. *Astbury, T. *Heath, Wood family, H. *Palmer, J. *Turner, and S. *Hollins. Contribution to industrialization of Staffordshire pottery made by J. *Wedgwood I; work includes refinement of cream-coloured earthenware, marketed as *creamware and later *pearlware, and decorative stoneware, e.g. *black basalt and *jasper ware. *Transfer-printing, developed in 18th century, e.g. by Z. *Barnes, J. *Sadler and G. *Green, R. *Hancock, and T. *Turner, provided quick method of decorating cream-coloured earthenware, which was generally to replace tin-glazed earthenware in Europe by late 18th century (also used on porcelain). Important pottery centres outside Staffordshire include Leeds and Liverpool; some cream-coloured earthenware from *Leeds pottery transfer-printed at workshop of J. *Robinson and D. *Rhodes. Lustreware produced from early 19th century, notably at *Sunderland. *Stone and *ironstone china introduced in 19th century Staffordshire.

Soft-paste porcelain made from mid 18th century at *Chelsea, *Derby, *Longton Hall, and, later, *Nantgarw, and Swansea (*Cambrian Pottery Works). Use of *bone ash in soft-paste porcelain, patented by T. *Frye (1749), adopted at *Bow (from 1750), Chelsea (*c*1755), *Lowestoft (1758), and Derby (1770). Formula for hard-paste porcelain containing bone ash attributed to J. *Spode II (1800) provided basis of standard English *bone china. Soapstone porcelain made at *Bristol, *Worcester, *Caughley, and *Liverpool. Hard-paste made at *Plymouth, Bristol, and *New Hall from formula discovered by W. *Cookworthy, developed in experiments with R. *Champion.

English ceramics. Copper lustre jug made in Staffordshire. Printed with scene of mother playing with child, and painted; c1830.

English clocks. Earliest clocks of large iron construction with *foliot-controlled verge *escapement for monastic or church use, e.g. at Salisbury Cathedral, made *c*1386; originally had striking mechanism and no dial, later fitted with complex astronomical dials and automaton figures, e.g. at Exeter and Wells. Many makers probably blacksmiths but three Dutch clock makers recorded working in England in 1386. Domestic clock first mentioned in 1469; house clocks followed style of German Gothic chamber clock through 16th century, with characteristic *lantern clock developing by *c*1620. Table clocks were made in European styles by B. *Newsam and others in late 16th century.

*Long-case and *bracket clocks evolved after introduction of pendulum *c*1675 by makers including A. *Fromanteel and T. *Tompion. Period from *c*1660 to *c*1750 marked English supremacy in clock making, resulting from technical improvements such as rack *striking, *repeating mechanisms, and improved forms of escapement. Accuracy of timekeeping was paramount, inspired by work on *chronometer by J. *Harrison, J. *Arnold, T. *Earnshaw. Principal clock makers include T. *Tompion, D. *Quare, G. *Graham, T. *Mudge, J. *Knibb, and E. *East. English industry hampered by brief imposition of tax on clocks and watches in 1797. Long-case clocks declined after 1750, but many were still made in provincial areas. After 1800 many makers, including firm of *Vulliamy, followed styles of French clocks of Louis XVI and Directoire periods, also producing carriage clocks. Decline of industry during 19th century caused by makers' refusal to produce cheap clocks to compete with imports, and reluctance to follow changes in style.

English delftware. Tin-glazed earthenware made in England from late 16th to late 18th centuries; first known examples *Malling jugs. Early ware, *English maiolica in Italian tradition; then, influenced by workmen from Holland, closely followed Dutch Delft in style, though with harder body; second lead glaze (**kwaart*) used *c*1690–*c*1740, but with less brilliant effect. High temperature colours used almost exclusively. In early 17th century, ware painted in blue after Wan-Li porcelain; later Ming porcelain copied at *Lambeth in late 17th century. Polychrome *chinoiserie* decoration introduced in early 18th century; also landscapes in Dutch style and copies of Dutch engravings. *Bianco sopra bianco* decoration of leaves and pine-cones on borders introduced in 1740s; used at *Bristol, *Lambeth, and *Liverpool. Punchbowls painted with hunting scenes and seascapes. *Bricks, chiefly blue and white, made in mid 18th century. Transfer-printed tiles made in Liverpool from 1750s; tiles with landscapes made in Bristol from 1760s. In 1770s, tin-glazed ware largely succeeded by creamware. English delftware also made at *Wincanton, *Glasgow, *Dublin, and at Wednesbury, Staffordshire.

English dial. *See* dial clock.

English embroidered carpets. *See* English needlework carpets.

English furniture. *See* Elizabethan style, Jacobean style, Commonwealth style, Restoration style, William and Mary style, Queen Anne style, Palladian style, Chippendale style, Adam style, Hepplewhite style, Sheraton style, Regency style, Victorian style.

English glass. Early English *Wealden glass was produced in wooded areas of southern England; first recorded glass maker, *Laurence Vitrearius, worked in Chiddingfold, Surrey, *c*1226. Glass makers from Lorraine, headed by J. Carré, and from Italy, notably G. *Verzelini, began to arrive in mid 16th century to produce window glass and *façon de Venise* soda glass. Settled initially in London and the Weald, but as fuel supplies ran short, moved to other areas, establishing *Stourbridge and *Newcastle-upon-Tyne as important glass making centres. 17th century glass making was controlled by monopolists, mainly businessmen; most enterprising was R. *Mansell, who controlled 20 glass houses throughout England, producing window glass, bottles, domestic ware, *façon de Venise* drinking glasses, and tableware. Later glass making controlled by Glass Sellers' Company, founded 1635 and reconstituted 1664 after Restoration. The Company financed G. *Ravenscroft's experiments to find a clear crystal glass stronger than Venetian soda glass, using English materials; resulting flint-glass, perfected in 1675, revolutionized English glass making. By 1695, 47 glasshouses producing flint-glass, greatly valued for exceptional brilliance and durability. Large quantities exported, particularly to Scandinavia and Holland for engraving. In 18th century, *façon de Venise* replaced by English style, particularly in drinking glasses with baluster, tear, air-twist, and enamel twist stems. Cutting and engraving introduced by German immigrants. Engraving was used particularly for commemorative glasses, a speciality of Newcastle; fine enamelling by M. *Edkins at Bristol and the *Beilbys at Newcastle. *Bristol, Stourbridge, and Newcastle each produced distinctive glass. *Glass Excise Act of 1745 influenced style of flint-glass, encouraging manufacture of smaller, lighter, vessels with shallow cutting, often using rococo motifs. By late 18th century many glass makers had moved to Ireland; Anglo-Irish glass, heavier and more elaborately cut than in England. *Nailsea decorative bottle glass, not subject to high taxation, became popular. In early 19th century, A. *Pellatt developed *sulphides; *millefiori* glass used for paperweights, doorknobs, and ink-wells. From 1833, pressed glass introduced; used to make tableware with open lace or basket-like work, and imitating cut glass. Renewed activity after repeal of Excise Acts in

1845. Much English glass shown at 1851 Great Exhibition was clear cut-crystal tableware and chandeliers, also wide variety of coloured and elaborately decorated ornamental glass. From mid 19th century, popularity of hand-blown and cut-glass declined with increased production of pressed wares. Ancient techniques were revived, e.g. *cameo cutting in work of J. *Northwood.

English gold and silver. Little medieval plate survives. Conventional view that Wars of Roses destroyed much of baronial plate not proved conclusively, but Reformation, Civil War, and period of Commonwealth (1649–60) certainly resulted in destruction of most early secular and religious plate still in existence then. Much domestic plate from 14th to early 17th centuries of ceremonial or display nature, was saved because it belonged to colleges, guilds, etc. Most popular item, as in northern European countries, drinking vessel. Only five drinking horns survive, but larger numbers of mazers, standing cups, tankards, mugs, beakers, goblets, etc. Besides silver-gilt cups, other materials, e.g. coconut and ostrich eggs mounted as cups. Most important item of English plate of the period, the ceremonial standing salt, survives in numerous forms (unlike in Europe). Other surviving domestic items: spoons, candlesticks, dishes, perfume-burners, rose-water ewers and basins, jugs, flagons, etc. Largest extant collection of Tudor and Jacobean plate in Russia in the Kremlin (*see* Kremlin silver) testifying to 16th and early 17th century practice of giving lavish presents of plate to royalty, civic authorities, churches, etc. Until *c*1650, chief stylistic influence on English silver, German *pattern books; succeeded by Dutch examples until late 17th century, when influence of French design, via *Huguenot silversmiths, paramount.

Vast quantities of domestic silver made from Restoration era: aristocracy wanted to replace lost plate, and rising merchant class wanted visible means of displaying new-found wealth. Functional wares began to outnumber display pieces; range of vessels for drinking, eating, and lighting produced. Introduction of new beverages – tea, coffee, cocoa, and punch – in late 17th century resulted in production of vessels for serving and consuming them. Private plate usually plain silver; corporation or royal plate more commonly gilt. Besides Dutch ornament (e.g. embossed floral motifs on plain or matt ground), engraved *chinoiserie* motifs used *c*1660–85 on tea-caddies and teapots, toilet services, etc. Silver furniture, a taste Charles II probably acquired in France during exile, continued to be made until beginning of Queen Anne's reign (1702), although little survives.

In 18th century England, silver used by upper middle classes, but in Europe, use largely restricted to royalty and nobility. Queen Anne style silver characterized by simplicity of form and ornament, but enhanced by mouldings, faceting, and use of cut-card work. Simplicity possibly based on practical consideration: cost of silver increased as result of institution of *Britannia Standard. By 1730, French rococo style established in England; notable exponent, P. *de Lamerie, London silversmith of Huguenot descent. Lavish table silver produced, but soon superseded by neo-classical Adam style which lent itself to mass-production; adopted by new Sheffield plate concerns in Sheffield and Birmingham. Largest and perhaps most important manufacturer of Sheffield plate (later, silver), M. *Boulton.

English silver. Muffin dish by Peter Podie, 1798. Engraving around top of dish, on cover, and on urn finial.

English silver. Left: knife and two-pronged fork, made in Sheffield, c1780. Right: later version made in Sheffield, 1835, by Atkin & Oxley, with four-pronged fork.

Early 19th century silver characterized by massiveness, with Roman and Egyptian motifs dominant. Royal goldsmiths, *Rundell, Bridge & Rundell, employed distinguished artists; other firms followed. Many presentation pieces made, e.g. race cups and trophies, épergnes, etc., with figure groups representing symbolic virtues, scenes of battle, the hunt, etc. During the Regency, a revival of rococo silver occurred; also of Gothic motifs, later used by A. W. N. *Pugin for church plate. Simultaneously silver in stylized natural forms and with floral ornament produced. Development of *electro-typing encouraged naturalistic style: dishes, cups, etc. made in leaf and flower forms. Production of *electro-plated ware began in 1840s; by 1860, produced in larger quantities than silver, replacing *Sheffield plate. Design developments also led by manufacturers of electro-plate, e.g. *Elkington & Co.

Most medieval English church plate melted down in 16th century, after dissolution of monasteries in 1530s. Surviving pre-Reformation plate mainly chalices and patens, a few pyxes, altar cruets, reliquaries, chrismatories, croziers, etc. Communion cup replaced chalice in Church of England worship, and secular flagon adopted for sacramental wine. Paten in salver form adopted; alms dish also introduced. Roman church plate continued to be used by recusants who commissioned pieces; in late 17th century, some pieces made by Huguenot silversmiths.

London silversmiths had guild from 12th century. In 1300 hallmarking instituted: leopard's head punch used on gold and silver. In 1363, maker's mark or device introduced; date letter system in 1478. In 1544, *Sterling mark adopted. Duty mark: sovereign's head in profile (1784–1890). Statute of 1423 created assay offices in York, Newcastle, Lincoln, Norwich, Bristol, Salisbury, and Coventry (no evidence that last ever functioned), with hallmarking systems based on that of London. In 1773, offices opened in Birmingham and Sheffield. Attribution of London makers' marks before 1697 conjectural. Fire in assay office in 1681 destroyed parchment strips on which makers signed names (marks struck on brass plates attached to these survived). In 1697, following institution of Britannia Standard, makers had to register new marks (first two initials of surname). Large plate-workers' register for 1758–83 and small plate-workers' register for 1739–58 also missing.

English maiolica. Polychrome tin-glazed earthenware made in late 16th and early 17th century England; usually considered as *English delftware. Much early *Lambeth delftware, including early blue-dash chargers and pharmaceutical ware, in styles derived from Italian, but by 1700, Dutch stylistic influence began to overcome Italian maiolica tradition in tin-enamelled ware.

English needlework or **embroidered carpets.** English carpets, embroidered in wool on linen or canvas, popular from 15th century as floor covering or, more often, as table, cupboard, or window covering. Usually worked in tent-stitch. Most woven in homes of wealthy: fashionable occupation for ladies. Fine examples survive from 16th and 17th centuries. With establishment of knotted-carpet manufactories in 17th century, popularity declined. Revived again in early 18th century, with renewed interest in all types of embroidery. Design nearly always closely packed mass of realistically drawn flowers and leaves in natural colours. Grounds often black. Border stripes often with simple ribbon pattern. Popularity finally declined with development of machine-made carpets.

English pewter. *See* fine pewter.

English snuff-boxes. 18th and 19th century snuff-boxes most numerous in silver and enamel, but also made in gold, lacquer, ivory, tortoiseshell, horn, and base metals. Little known about box makers; gold boxes rarely signed; silver ones hallmarked but continual use has made some marks indecipherable. Gold boxes *c*1714–60 were mainly oval, chased with classical decoration, and after 1720 frequently with miniatures on lids. Rectangular boxes popular 1760–1815, though other shapes made. French influence evident in enamel decoration and *four-colour gold relief designs. *c*1800 engine-turned decoration replaced enamelling. Silver boxes mainly oval with gilded interiors, and typically with engraved arms, ciphers, or monograms. After 1750, silver often combined with tortoiseshell, mother-of-pearl, and agate; many boxes in *fantasy shapes. 19th century Birmingham centre of silver and gold box production. Boxes oblong with slightly in-turned wall and panels of engine-turning. After 1830, silver boxes ornamented with views of buildings in light relief. Silver-plated snuff-boxes made 1755–60 in Sheffield.

Manufacture of enamel snuff-boxes in *Birmingham, *South Staffordshire, and *Battersea from 1750. Various sizes and shapes; mountings gilded copper or alloys like pinchbeck. Lacquered metal boxes probably made in *Pontypool and Birmingham, from 1738; few lacquer, brass, copper, or steel boxes have survived. Tortoiseshell boxes with silver *piqué* decoration date from early 18th century; difficult to determine country of origin.

English tapestries. *See* W. Benood, Mortlake tapestry works, Sheldon Tapestry Works, Soho Tapestry works.

English watches. None recorded before 1590, then style followed German and French practice until appearance of characteristic English *Puritan watch. High reputation of English makers founded in 17th century by e.g. T. *Tompion, D. *Quare: introduction of *balance spring *c*1675 brought more attention to movement of watch, less to decoration of case. Technical improvements in 18th century associated with work of G. *Graham, J. *Harrison, J. *Arnold, and T. *Earnshaw culminated in invention of lever *escapement by T. *Mudge, *c*1765, and led to evolution of typical English style of movement which lasted through 19th century. Full-plate type has complete circular top-plate carrying balance cock; three-quarter-plate type has section cut away with balance cock sunk level with plate; half-plate type has larger section cut away with cock for fourth wheel as well as balance and escapement. During 19th century English makers lost leading position in world markets because of reluctance to adopt mechanized production methods.

English wine glasses. Before invention of lead glass, most wine glasses imported, particularly from Venice. From *c*1690, stemmed wine glasses produced in quantity with many stylistic variations. Early glasses (before *c*1730) usually have *folded foot. Stem styles include *air twist, *baluster, *balustroid, *colour twist, *faceted, *hollow, *incised, *mercury twist, *moulded pedestal, *opaque twist. Twists made in two pieces up to *c*1745; later three-piece manufacture allowed more complex twist patterns in stems.

engraved glass. Engraving on glass is executed with wheel or diamond-point. Wheel engraving technique similar to that for cut glass. Practised in ancient Alexandria and Rome; revived in 17th and 18th century Germany (e.g. by C. *Lehmann and G. and H. *Schwanhardt) and England, particularly as result of development of crystal glass. Widely practised in 18th century Germany together with relief and intaglio cutting (*Hochschnitt* and *Tiefschnitt*). *Potsdam was important centre for engraved work. Ruby-red and opaque-white *cameo glass pieces popular in early 19th century. In England finest engraving produced in 18th century, when commemorative glasses (e.g. *Jacobite glasses) and flowered glasses (e.g. *ale glasses) popular.

In diamond-point engraving, surface of glass scratched with sharp splinter of diamond. Diamond-point favoured by 16th century Venetians; more suitable than cutting for decoration of thin soda-glass. Technique practised in Austria at Innsbruck and *Hall-in-the-Tyrol, and especially in Holland, where calligraphic glasses of A. R. *Visscher and W. *van Heemskirk are outstanding 17th century examples; *stippling revived, particularly by F. *Greenwood and D. *Wolff in 18th century.

Engraved Glass. Covered goblet made at court glasshouse in Innsbruck, Austria (1570–91). Diamond engraved smoky grey glass; hollow stem with lion mask knop. c1580.

engraving. Tracing of ornamental pattern or inscription in metal with *graver, which removes fine threads of metal. Probably oldest technique of decorating metal. From 16th century, *pattern books of engraved designs circulated among British and European silversmiths; included scenes and motifs, coats of arms, mottoes, etc. *See* bright-cut engraving, feather-edge, heraldic engraving, engine-turning.

en grisaille. Technique of grey monochrome painting representing objects in relief and giving appearance of depth. Developed by Limoges enamellers in 16th century with white enamel laid on darker ground. Style frequently used in painted mural decoration, furniture, porcelain, etc., in late 18th century.

en plein enamelling. Application of enamel directly to whole surface of object rather than on panels.

enseigne or **hat badge.** Brooch worn on hat; derived from *badge (usually cast base metal) worn by pilgrim from early Middle Ages in

*English wine glasses 18th century. Left to right: 1) Baluster stem with triple cushion knop containing tear, 1720. 2) Triple knop stem with beaded and tear drop knops, 1750. 3) Plain columnar stem, hollow blown, result of *Glass Excise Act, 1745. 4) Mercury twist stem: spiral mercurial central ribbon surrounded by eight-ply air twist ribbon, 1755. 5) Incised twist stem, 1755. 6) Colour twist stem: multi-ply air twist intertwined with royal blue colour, 1765. 7) Colour twist stem: multi-ply opaque twist ribbon edged with red and green intertwined with single opaque thread, 1770. 8) Faceted stem with centre knop, 1780.*

Europe. In 16th century developed into expensive jewel, usually gold ornamented with enamel and gems. Sometimes featured classical scene in low relief. Loops attached for sewing on garment.

entablature. On clock cases in style of classical architecture: parts at top of columns, supporting cornice or pediment.

entre-deux. *See bas d'armoire.*

entrée dish. Covered serving dish made in Britain in silver or Sheffield plate from *c*1760, probably modelled on chafing dish. Shapes include oval, round, and octagonal; cover shaped like dish but slightly smaller to fit over rim within outer border of dish. Cover generally with detachable handle to allow use as serving dish. Generally unornamented except for gadrooned border. *c*1800 stand, resembling dish, generally of Sheffield plate, with spirit lamp or hot iron for keeping food hot introduced.

E-Oribe ware. *See* Oribe ware.

Epargnie. Table centrepiece (*épergne) made by German porcelain factories for aristocratic households from mid 18th to mid 19th century; sometimes has separate detachable figures. Replaced sugar decorations previously made by confectioners.

E.P.B.M. Electro-plated Britannia metal; mark found on such objects from 1850s.

épergne (French, *épargner*, 'to save'). Intended to save guest trouble of passing dishes at table. Elaborate silver or Sheffield plate table centrepiece with various fittings including bread and cake baskets, fruit and sweetmeat dishes; condiment containers hung from branches; also sometimes candle sockets to allow use as candelabrum. Used in Britain and Europe from *c*1730. Some mid 18th century in rococo style; sometimes with three branches radiating from moulded four-footed stem; others modelled on Chinese pagodas. Neo-classical épergnes often pierced or wire-work. 19th century examples more massive with cut glass dishes and baskets; also made in glass with decoration of coloured threads of spun glass. *cf Epargnie.*

Ersari carpet. 18th century; 12*ft*6*in.*×6*ft.*

Epergne. Silver-gilt, made in London, 1747. Reeded frame standing on paw feet holds oval cut-glass bowl; four branches hold smaller oval bowls.

Ephraim pot. *See* tankard.

episcopal ring. Ring given to bishop at consecration. In use before 7th century A.D. Probably did not differ from signet (seal) rings worn by laity. Many contained antique (therefore pagan) engraved gems and Christian inscriptions were usually added (sometimes in niello). At end of 12th century Innocent III ordered episcopal rings to be made of pure gold and mounted with plain gem (probably to counteract use of pagan carved gems), but rule was not strictly kept. Custom that ring be returned to royal treasurer also not adhered to strictly; many rings have been found in coffins of bishops.

E.P.N.S. Electro-plated nickel silver.

equation clock. Clock with dial to show difference between mean time and solar time. True midday as shown by sundial varies through year from 16 minutes 18 seconds before noon mean time to 14 minutes 28 seconds after. Mean and solar time coincide on four occasions each year.

Érard, Sébastien (1752–1831). French harp and piano maker working in Paris, and London, where workshop established (1786). One of creators of modern harp; also furthered development of piano. Patented improved single-action harp (1792); also patented double-action harp (1810) with Greek-style column and scrollwork ornament. Succeeded by nephew, Pierre, who patented 'Gothic' harp (1836).

Erfurt (Thuringia). German faience factory, flourished 1717–*c*1792. Owned by pewter manufacturing family. Many cylindrical tankards produced with pewter mounts; also *Enghalskrüge* and figures. Factory mark (rare) small, rough wheel similar to *Höchst. Decoration in bright high-temperature colours. Subjects include landscapes with flowers, *chinoiseries*, flowers, and animals. Painters' marks common.

Ersari carpets. Heavy, loose-woven Turkoman rugs woven by Ersari tribe near River Oxus (on Russian-Afghan border). Numerous designs incorporating motifs from neighbouring tribes, Persia, Caucasus, and China. Most common pattern, stepped guls within broad, stylized floral lattice. Blues, yellows, and browns dominate pattern. Lightish red or indigo ground. Strong yellow outlining field and border motifs. Sometimes known as Beshir carpets on American market.

escapement (in clocks and watches). Device controlling rate of unwinding of train, and movement of hands; gives energy, or 'impulse' to *pendulum or *balance. All forms have 'escape wheel' allowed to rotate tooth by tooth as pendulum or balance swings. Earliest form, verge escapement, used on early clocks, and on watches until mid 19th century: escape wheel (with teeth standing up from rim, hence also called crown wheel), mounted at right angle to balance staff or verge on which are two pallets (small flat projections) meeting teeth on opposite sides of wheel. After introduction of pendulum, R. *Hooke and others devised anchor, or recoil, escapement, used widely in long-case clocks: escape wheel teeth are like those of saw, pallets are at ends of anchor-shaped bar and intercept teeth before pendulum reaches end of swing, thus making wheel turn back slightly or recoil; when pendulum starts to swing back, one tooth escapes, passing on impulse to pallet. Recoil also very pronounced in cross-beat escapement devised by J. *Burgi, in which two interconnected pallets drove independent balances. Later recoil type was J. *Harrison's 'grasshopper', driving either balance or pendulum and avoiding friction between escape wheel teeth and pallets. G. *Graham modified anchor to form recoil-less 'dead beat' escapement: pallet faces are curved, stopping tooth without forcing it back, and may be jewelled. Other modifications of similar type were made by many British and European makers; T. *Mudge used system of independently mounted pallets to interfere less with free motion of pendulum. Pin pallet or Brocot escapement found on small French clocks (often mounted visibly in front of dial) uses same principle as dead beat, with jewelled pins as pallets. Other clock escapements include pin wheel (invented *c*1753) and three or four legged gravity escapement, used mainly in turret clocks, e.g. Westminster clock ('Big Ben'), rarely in other *precision clocks. In gravity types, clock train lifts two weighted arms which, in falling back, give impulse to pendulum rod.

For watches, E. *Barlow and W. Houghton patented cylinder escapement in 1695, later perfected by Graham (sometimes called horizontal – first type to have balance and escape wheel in same plane): escape wheel teeth pass in and out of slotted hollow cylinder, often of ruby, on balance staff. Cylinder watches made by J. *Arnold and A-L. *Breguet, and throughout 18th and 19th centuries, particularly by French and Swiss makers. Similar escapement is *virgule*, used in some early 18th century French watches. Major innovation made by Mudge with invention of lever escapement in *c*1765: escape wheel and pallets arranged rather as in dead beat clock escapement, but pallets are attached to pivoted lever, one end meshing with roller and pin on balance staff; as balance swings, pin moves lever and pallets from side to side receiving impulse at same time. Pallets and pin usually jewelled. This escapement, with minor variations, since used very generally; Swiss form often has lever at right-angle to pallets instead of English in-line layout. In duplex escapement, patented 1782 but probably invented earlier, escape wheel has two sets of teeth, one set projecting outwards and released one-by-one by ruby roller on balance staff, other set projecting upwards from face of wheel to give impulse to pallet attached to staff. Frequently used in good quality watches in 19th century; variation to accommodate centre second hand used in *Chinese watches.

Marine chronometers normally fitted with spring detent escapement originated by P. *LeRoy and perfected *c*1780 by T. *Earnshaw and J. *Arnold: escape wheel teeth locked by jewelled stone mounted on thin steel strip (detent). Projection on balance staff acts against gold spring on detent, releasing escape wheel which gives impulse to balance via second projection on balance staff. On return swing, gold spring is designed to allow first projection to pass without moving detent. In foreign chronometers, detent is often pivoted and kept in position by miniature hairspring.

Other types of escapement include many rare and curious forms.

escutcheon-plate. Metal plate fitted round keyhole for protection and ornament, usually of cast brass. Mid and late 18th century examples elaborate, gilt bronze. Later designs simpler, set flush with surface of door or drawer.

espagnolette. Bust, female, used ornamentally on vertical supports of furniture. Common on 18th century French furniture. *Illustration at commode.*

Essex, William (1784–1869). English enamel painter. Exhibited at Royal Academy, 1818–64. Appointed enamel painter to Queen Victoria in 1839. Work includes landscapes, classical subjects, and animals, e.g. dogs painted in enamel on gold. Portraits include Napoleon I after J-B-J. *Augustin, and Duke of Wellington after Sir Thomas Lawrence; also painted portrait enamels from life.

étagère. *See* whatnot.

etching. Formation of incised pattern on metal or glass by action of acid. Surface is coated with resisting layer of wax, varnish, etc.; design is drawn through coating with fine steel point, exposing surface to acid. Depth of line controlled by length of application of acid. Effect is similar to engraving, with fine greyish lines. Technique probably first developed to decorate armour in 15th century; extensively used on copper plates for printing from 16th century and applied to glass *c*1670 by H. *Schwanhardt. Rarely found as ornament before 19th century, then common feature on glass and silver.

Etruscan or **Pompeian style.** Late 18th century decorative style in furniture distinguished by use of colours (terracotta, black, white) and motifs (classical figures, acanthus, urns, etc.) related to late classical Greek red and black vases (thought in 18th century to be Etruscan) unearthed e.g. at Herculaneum and Pompeii. Used first in France (from *c*1760) in Louis XVI furniture; then extensively by R. *Adam in England.

étui. Small case made from precious metal, leather, tortoiseshell, porcelain and many other materials. Contains personal articles such as knife, spoon, and fork, later sewing and drawing implements, etc. In use at least from early 17th century; in 18th century, usually of cylindrical form (4–6in. long) hung from chatelaine.

Eulenkrug. *See* owl jug.

European lacquer or **japan.** Resinous substances dissolved in alcohol and coloured by the addition of dyes in attempt to imitate Japanese lacquer. Applied to article in numerous coats, each permitted to dry and polished before the next is added. In France, Martin brothers developed **vernis Martin* in early 18th century. T. *Allgood developed lacquer used at Pontypool factory, Wales. *See* japanned metal.

ewer. Large pouring vessel, originally with lid, in gold, silver-gilt, silver, bronze, or pewter; made in Europe and Britain, probably from 13th century. Earliest surviving silver examples, from 16th century, have round or octagonal body on circular foot, and lid raised by thumbpiece attached to top of handle. In 17th century, ewers lavishly decorated, e.g. with embossed and chased foliage and masks, or cast relief ornament and fluting; bronze examples sometimes inlaid with silver, gilded, or *damascened. Main forms: vase shape, with tall narrow neck and small spout, bulbous body, and handle in shape of scroll or grotesque human figure; straight-sided goblet with scroll handle and curved spout; and helmet shape. From early 18th century, made mainly for ceremonial use. *See* aquamanile, hawksbill, helmet ewer, ravensbill, rosewater ewer and basin.

Exeter carpets. Among earliest English carpets, with coarse Turkish-knotted woollen pile on woollen warp, and woollen or linen weft. Woven 1755–59 at C. *Passavant's manufactory in Exeter, Devon. Weavers mainly ex-Savonnerie workmen, formerly employed by P. *Parisot. Ponderous, elaborate designs based on *Savonnerie patterns with rococo scrolls, foliate motifs, and flowers. Carpets signed Exon and dated.

extinguisher. Metal (usually brass) conical cap, with long handle, for extinguishing candles; often ecclesiastical. Also made *en suite* with *chamber candlesticks.

Ewer. Louis XV, made in Paris, 1766, by Pierre-Joseph Wattiaux.

William Essex. Portrait of Queen Victoria. Enamel, signed and dated 1858.

European lacquer. On English bureau bookcase. c1730.

*Faenza. Maiolica plate, c1575, marked F in circle. Painted with wide border of *arabesques; in centre, man playing lute. Diameter 9½in.*

*Étui. Top, left to right: 1) French, engraved gold, 1725. 2) English, lapis lazuli mounted in gold, 1755. 3) English, incorporating telescope at one end, jasper in *cagework mount, 1755. Bottom right: French Directoire, malachite, 1795. Bottom left: German, gold set with agate cameos, 1725.*

Right:
Façon de Venise. *Wine glass from Low Countries, late 17th century. Octagonal funnel bowl; stem, interwoven coil of colour twist glass with pincered wings. Height 6½in.*

extension table. Table which can be enlarged by addition of leaves. Frame extends horizontally, usually by winding detachable handle, creating opening in centre between leaves; extra leaves slotted into gap. Dates from early Georgian period. *See* draw-leaf table.

Fabeltiere decoration. Subjects for painting on porcelain tableware or decorative pieces taken from Aesop's fables. First found on Meissen wares painted by A. F. *von Löwenfinck *c*1730. Also, notably, used at Chelsea in mid 18th century, and later in 18th century at Niderviller.

faceted steel. *See* cut steel.

faceted stem. Stem form in English glasses; cut into facets, commonly diamond-shaped or hexagonal. Style increasingly fashionable from 1750s; predominant in late 18th and early 19th centuries. Bowl usually simple ovoid or funnel shape, with faceting on base. Feet plain, less often domed; cutting on underside of plain feet from 1780s. *Illustration at* English wineglasses.

Facio, Nicholas (b 1664). Swiss-born scientist and inventor of *jewelling for watches; in England worked with makers P. and J. *Debaufre with whom he was granted patent in 1704, later rescinded.

façon de Venise. Venetian-style glassware made outside Venice by, or under influence of, Italian craftsmen who, by late 16th century, had set up glasshouses in France, Spain, Portugal, Bohemia, Germany, England, and Scandinavia. Influence of *façon de Venise* remained predominant in European glass throughout 16th and 17th centuries. Each glasshouse retained characteristic aspects of Venetian styles, while developing distinct local variations.

Faenza (Emilia), Italy. Gave name to *faience. Green and purple ware produced in late 14th and early 15th centuries. Oak-leaf jars decorated in blue, green, and manganese-purple in late 15th century; large range of maiolica, including drug-pots, decorated, e.g. with bird, portrait, or label of contents and plant motifs. Service made between 1476 and 1490 for King Matthias Corvinus of Hungary. Pavement of hexagonal tiles, 1487, for Church of San Petronio at Bologna decorated in **stile severo* with many patterns commonly used at Faenza: animals, birds, grotesques, Gothic floral motifs, peacock feathers, and palmettes, in blue, yellow, orange, green, and purple. Jars decorated with palmettes, made from 1490s, have figures and portraits in style of Deruta. *Berrettino* ground introduced in late 15th century; later much used. In early 16th century, *istoriato* decoration on plates with borders of masks, grotesques, trailing vines, palmettes, and fruit, developed, e.g. at *Casa Pirota, set style until *c*1530. Painting of period created by limited number of artists including *Maestro Benedetto, and B. *Manara (in 1530s). Reverse of dishes usually decorated, either with elaborate foliage, or with simple concentric bands, often in yellow. *Compendiario* style introduced in mid 16th century, e.g. by V. *Calamelli and later L. *Bettisi.

Dishes decorated with gadroons or open-work borders painted with coats of arms, soldiers, or single *putti*. Much white ware (*bianchi di Faenza* or **faïence blanche*) exported. Moulded dishes made in 16th and 17th centuries often painted with grotesques.

fa hua. *See* san ts'ai stoneware.

faience. Tin-glazed earthenware in imitation of Chinese porcelain (e.g. 17th century Dutch *Delft ware), and in later styles developed, e.g. in France (initially at Rouen in late 17th century) and Germany (at Nuremberg, Abtsbessingen, etc. in early 18th century). Distinct from tin-glazed earthenware decorated in maiolica tradition.

faïence blanche or **bianchi di Faenza.** Tin-glazed earthenware for everyday use, with simple paintings of one or two figures in *compendiario* style, or coat of arms, sometimes with sparse border decoration, introduced at Faenza in mid 16th century. Low cost of production encouraged imitation throughout Italy. Introduced in France by potters from Faenza. Vessels decorated with French heraldic devices attributed to Lyon and Nevers. Great quantities also made in Belgium, Holland, and central Europe; production continued until mid 19th century. In 18th century France, included **faïences parlantes*.

faïence fine. White or *cream-coloured earthenware of English type, usually lead-glazed, produced in France by 1768 at Chantilly and Lunéville; afterwards throughout Europe.

faïence japonnée. High quality French faience painted with enamel colours in styles of oriental porcelain; introduced *c*1750 by J. *Chapelle at Sceaux.

faïences parlantes or **faïence populaire.** Class of **faïence blanche* made as simple ornaments, with satirical or humorous inscriptions, in 18th century France, notably at Nevers. Includes *faïences patronymiques*, picturing patron saints, to commemorate births, weddings, etc. Revolutionary emblems and mottoes found on *faïences patriotiques*.

fairings. Porcelain souvenirs made in Germany (*c*1850–90) after English designs, for sale at country fairs. Heavy body and simple form, lightly gilded, high-temperature polychrome colours; *c*4in. high. Subjects, often amusing or risqué references to marriage, include: Last in bed to put out the light. Some inspired by popular songs. Produced cheaply and in great quantities; very popular in England, but not in France or Germany.

Famille rose. *Vase and cover with lion knop. Yung Chêng period. Decorated with rock, flowering magnolia, prunus and peony; also gilded. Height* $35\frac{1}{2}$*in.*

Famille verte. *Enamelled vase. K'ang Hsi period. Design of birds and flowering plants. Height* c19*in.*

Fairings. Left: English Neutrality, 1870. Attending the Sick and Wounded, which refers to the Franco-Prussian war. Centre: Free and Independent Elector, referring to bribery in politics. Right: Beware of a Collision; c*1870.*

Falconet, Etienne-Maurice (1716–91). French sculptor. Head of modelling department at Sèvres (1757–66). Work in biscuit porcelain includes groups of children (*La Loterie* and *La Lanterne Magique*), and Leda, all after F. *Boucher; also Cupid (1758), *La Baigneuse* (1758), *Le Sabot Cassé* (1760), Psyche (1761), Pygmalion and Galatea (1763), *Le Baiser Donné* and *Le Baiser Rendu* (both 1765). In Russia (1766–68), made bronze statue of Peter the Great. *Illustration at* biscuit porcelain.

faldstool. Wooden or iron X-frame folding stool, with cushion on top; often has brass knob at each corner. Originally used as seat and prayer stool in churches; dates from Middle Ages.

fall front. *See* drop front.

fall-leaf table. *See* drop-leaf table.

false knot. *See* jufti knot.

famille rose. Ceramic decoration: palette of opaque enamels used on 18th century Chinese porcelain of Ch'ing period. Predominant rose-pink, derived from gold chloride and tin, discovered in Europe, 1650. Greens, blues, and yellows also appear; opaque white used for shading. Colours, known in China as yang ts'ai ('foreign colours') or juan ts'ai ('soft colours'), introduced by traders. Both Imperial and export wares manufactured at Ching-tê-chên, but latter decorated at Canton (export centre), often with European-inspired motifs. High quality *famille rose* decoration characteristic of reign of Yung Chêng; European influence increased during reign of Ch'ien Lung. *Illustrations also at* Ku Yüeh Hsüan, Shou Lao.

familles jaune and **noire.** *See famille verte.*

famille verte. Chinese ceramic decoration; enamel colours used over white glaze, on Chinese porcelain of Ch'ing period. Name derived from distinctive green predominant in

Famille noire. *Vase with baluster body, painted with two five-clawed dragons, one grasping pearl, other pursuing pearl. K'ang Hsi period. Height* 17*in.*

designs. Based on Ming period *wu ts'ai painting, but with enamel-blue replacing underglaze cobalt-blue. Colour derived from manganese, leaves lustre or halo on surrounding glaze, recognized as sign of authenticity, though subject to wear and chipping; often repainted later. Best examples from reign of *K'ang Hsi: dishes with floral sprays, scenes of agriculture, scattered flowers, or human figures. Similar works of same period with black colour predominating, covered with transparent greenish glaze of iridescent sheen known as *famille noire*. High cost of production limited number of examples produced. Yellow soft-toned enamel also used with brownish-black outlines, to depict flowers, dragons, and landscapes (e.g. with birds on rocks) known as *famille jaune*. In early 18th century, *famille rose* replaced *familles verte, jaune*, and *noire*, on all but cheapest export wares.

fan. Two types: rigid or screen fan and folding fan. Rigid fan has long handle with bat-shaped *leaf of feathers, parchment, or fabric; used by ancient Egyptians, Assyrians, and later Indians and Chinese, and in Renaissance Europe. Folding fan of Chinese Ming dynasty origin brought to Europe in 15th century by Portuguese traders. This has sticks of ivory held together at one end by rivet or pin; pleated leaf mounted on sticks to permit opening and closing. Mid 17th century European folding fans made with entire leaf painted with classical or mythological scenes; sticks of carved ivory or ivory with silver *piqué* decoration; leaf of paper, leather, or white kid. **Brisé* fans introduced from Orient early 18th century. Copied in France centre of European fan trade: ivory field near rivet painted with *chinoiseries*, main field with pastoral scenes; examples covered with clear lacquer known as **vernis Martin* fans. Eighteenth century fans rarely signed. From *c*1740 fans larger, scenes after F. *Boucher in blue and pink in middle of leaf surrounded by elaborate scrollwork. Sticks narrower in Louis XVI period, like wheel spokes and often individually decorated. Front of leaf painted with three related scenes; *guards carved with urns and other neo-classical motifs. From 1770, gilt thread, brass sequins, and netting used for decoration. From *c*1775, souvenir fans with Roman scenes painted over whole leaf produced in Italy. Manufacture of fans with printed leaves in England from *c*1725; mass-produced from engraved plate – often poor in design and colour; printed with advertizing from 1750. 1790–1825 fans painted with figures in neo-classical dress. From 1860, very large fans popular with wide sticks but narrow leaf. Many 19th century fans painted with 18th century scenes; sticks therefore important for period identification. *See* cabriolet, church, marriage, medallion, mourning, Pompadour, puzzle, and quizzing fans.

fan-back. Chair back incorporating fan-shaped decoration, dating from 18th century. Also, *Windsor chair back with spindles splaying out from base, popular in America *c*1760.

fancy-back spoon. Silver spoon with back of bowl ornamented with embossed, chased, etc., motifs. Particularly popular from *c*1740 to end of 18th century in Britain. Motifs include shells, scrolls, spray or basket of flowers, political or commemorative motifs, etc.

fancy chair. Common open-back, painted, American side chair, based on *Sheraton models, popular *c*1800–50. Often black, green, gilt, white, etc., with gilt and painted decoration (often with floral motif), particularly on yoke-rail, back slat, and front of seat-rail. Has rush or cane seat, turned front legs. *See* Hitchcock chair.

Fans. Both French. Top: battoir *type,* c*1770, hand-painted with allegorical scene of wedding of Louis XVI and Marie Antoinette; sticks are tortoiseshell decorated with piqué. Bottom:* cabriolet *type,* c*1755, with hand-painted ivory sticks.*

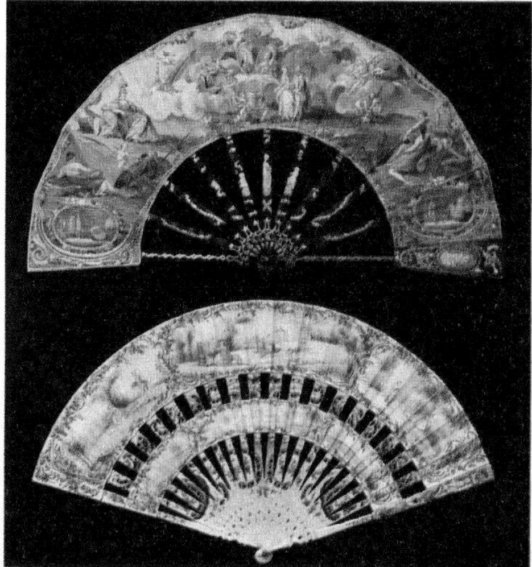

*Fan-back. Elbow chair, American, late 18th century. Painted wood; arm supports and legs have vase and ring turnings; *knuckle arms.*

fang i. Chinese ritual bronze shape of late Shang period; possibly wine container, but exact use uncertain. Apparently important piece: high level of craftsmanship and rich decoration employed. Looks like small house, with roof-shaped lid, surmounted by a little knob also shaped like a roof. Earlier examples have straight sides, leaning slightly outwards; later pieces bulge in shallow curve.

fantasy box. Snuff-box in unusual shape, e.g. animal, item of clothing, or furniture.

farmhouse clock. Form of tall, standing clock, with curved case-lines, made in Sweden and Finland, late 18th and early 19th centuries. Movement similar to English long-case clock; case-style French in origin. Influence on American clocks.

Farsibaff carpets. *See* Meshed carpets.

farthingale chair. Upholstered chair with wide seat, probably for women wearing farthingales. Made late 16th and 17th centuries.

Fatshan Chun. *See* Kwang-tung (Canton) stoneware.

Fattorini, Pietro (d 1507), brother Stefano, and son Jacopo (both fl early 16th century). Italian maiolica painters from Montelupo, working in Cafaggiolo district from late 15th century; established workshop *c*1506. Jacopo thought to be painter of several *istoriato* dishes; one depicts Judith, and servant on horseback holding severed head, against dark blue background, with grass in foreground painted in spidery tufts, signed Jacopo in Chaffagguolo. Succeeded by family, possibly until end of 16th century.

Fauteuil. *Louis XVI, carved gilt-wood.*

Fauquez, Jean-Baptiste-Joseph (1742–1804). One of Belgian-born family of potters at Saint-Amand-les-Eaux; made faience with delicate white floral decoration on pearl-grey glaze. In 1771, introduced soft-paste porcelain in styles of Tournai and Chantilly, made until 1778 – marked with SA and crossed, curving lines, painted in blue. Obtained privilege (1785) for manufacture of hard-paste porcelain at Valenciennes. Marked with monogram of FLV in blue.

fauteuil (French, 'armchair'). Open-sided armchair with back, seat, and often arms upholstered. Dates from 18th century, when it occupied fixed position in formal room setting. Popular mid 19th century in England and America.

fauteuil à la reine (French, 'queen's armchair'). Throne-like architectural armchair with flat back and carved frame, dating from Louis XV period; popular in late 18th century.

fauteuil en cabriolet. French armchair of light, graceful shape, with cane back and seat, or upholstered arms, back, and seat. Distinguished by concave back. Popular Louis XV style.

fauteuil en confessional. *See bergère en confessional.*

fauteuil en cul de four. *See chaise en cul de four.*

Favre-Bulle, Frédéric-Louis (1770–1849). Swiss watch maker from region of Neuchâtel; made duplex watches.

Fazackerley colours. English ceramics. Palette with full range of high-temperature colours – blue, green, red, yellow, and purple – used on *Liverpool delftware. Two mugs reputedly made for a Thomas Fazackerley and wife. Colours also used on bowls, and on painted tiles with sailors and girls. Patterns include flowers with purple-veined petals and leaves. *Illustration at* Liverpool delftware.

feather banding. *See* herring-bone banding.

feather-edge. Engraved ornament of fine, oblique lines on edge of silver. Used to decorate flatware from *c*1760–90. Related to *bright-cut engraving.

feathered slip decoration. *See* combed slip decoration.

feeding cup. *See* spout cup.

Feilner or **Feylner,** Simon (d 1798). German porcelain painter and modeller. Working at Höchst (*c*1750); produced *commedia dell'arte* figures; *Modellmeister* (1753–68) at Fürstenberg, director at Frankenthal (1775–98). Also modelled scent bottles in fruit shapes.

Fell, Thomas (fl 19th century). English potter. In 1817, established St Peter's Pottery at Newcastle-upon-Tyne, Northumberland, trading as Thomas Fell & Co. Produced creamware and white earthenware, sometimes transfer-printed. Company failed in 1890. Marks include FELL NEWCASTLE, FELL, and F with anchor, all impressed; also T.F. & Co, printed.

Felletin tapestry. French tapestry-weaving centre, active from 16th century. Peak production in 17th century when numerous Flemish and French Gobelins-trained workers employed. Designs and subjects modelled on tapestries of larger manufactories, e.g. Gobelins and Aubusson. Distinguished by deep colour, simple technique, and coarse texture. Identified by brown selvage thread woven into border (though often omitted or replaced by more prestigious Aubusson mark). Received title of Royal Manufactory 1727, also grants of pictures and services of Aubusson artists. Highly productive until decline during years of Revolution. Most important type, landscape design with foreground of large trees with parakeets, ponds with waterfowl; in background, château and wood. Also numerous simplified copies of Gobelins and Aubusson designs.

fender or **fend-iron.** Metal frame round hearth to hold back burning embers. With *grate, formed new style of fireplace which evolved in early 18th century due to widespread use of coal instead of wood. Originally, long strips of rolled iron balanced on edge by curved ends; by late 18th century developed with grate into ornamental object of pierced steel or brass, bowed, straight, or serpentine in shape.

Fenton, Christopher Webber (fl mid 19th century). American potter at *Bennington. Worked at Norton pottery from 1837, became partner (1843–47). Established own pottery in premises of Norton works; developed glaze for *flint enamel ware. In 1853, formed United States Pottery Company, which closed in 1858.

Ferahan, Fereghan, or **Ferrahan carpets.** Firm-textured, west Persian carpets woven in Ferahan (near Arak) from late 18th century. Short, finely Persian-knotted wool pile on cotton or cotton and wool foundation. Mainly with herati pattern in blues, reds, and greens on blue or dark red ground. Main border with herati motif in characteristic celadon green. Corrosive dye produces pattern relief effect.

Ferahan pattern. *See* herati pattern.

Ferguson, James (1710–78). Scottish miniaturist, astronomer mechanician and amateur clock maker. Studied astronomy in Edinburgh and London, supporting himself by producing precisely drawn miniatures in plumbago or Indian ink. Mechanical works include 3-wheel clock movement, tidal dial, and *orreries.

Fernández, Juan (fl 1560s and 1570s). Spanish maiolica painter; work includes blue and white tiles (1570–72) and pharmaceutical ware for monastery of Escorial Palace, Madrid. Credited with polychrome tile panel of crucifixion made *c*1570 at Talavera de la Reina.

Ferner, F. J. (fl mid 18th century). Bohemian *Hausmaler*. Decorated much defective blue-and-white Meissen porcelain rather crudely in gold, or red and other enamels. Marks: Ferner inve, F. J. Ferner pinxit.

Ferrahan carpets. *See* Ferahan carpets.

Ferrara tapestry. Manufactory established in Ferrara, Italy, in 1536 by Ercole II d'Este under direction of master-weavers J. and N. *Karcher and J. *Rost. Works include Metamorphoses, from models by Battista Dosso, and History of Hercules. After departure of N. Karcher to Mantua (1539) and Rost to Florence (1546), manufactory continued by J. Karcher and later by son Luigio. Numerous hangings woven; subjects include landscapes, mythological and historical scenes, similar to contemporary *Brussels tapestries, but much lighter and airier. Manufactory closed after death of L. Karcher in 1580.

Ferretti, Antonio (fl early and mid 18th century). One of family of Italian maiolica potters working at Lodi in 18th century. Decorated products with rococo motifs, e.g. bunches of flowers.

Ferrière, François (1752–1839). Miniaturist, said to be Swiss-born. In England from youth; exhibited at Royal Academy, 1793–1822. Portraits in pastel, oil, and watercolour mixed with much gum to give effect like oil painting. Appointed portrait painter to Dowager Empress of Russia, 1819. Subjects include Lord Nelson and Captain Masterman Hardy.

ferronneries. Ceramic decoration based on designs used in wrought-iron work. Found on *Antwerp style maiolica of 16th century; possibly Hispano-Moresque in origin. In 17th and early 18th centuries on faience e.g. of Rouen, Moustiers, and Strasbourg.

festoon or **swag.** Pendant garland of flowers and, sometimes, fruit. Common ornamental motif of Renaissance, later characteristic e.g. of **style Berain*. Occurs as painted or moulded ceramic decoration, as in *décor à guirlandes* on faience at Alcora and Moustiers. Used on 16th century silver, and neo-classical silver of late 18th and early 19th centuries; embossed, cast applied ornament, etc.

Fiat glasses. *See* Jacobite glass.

Fictoor or **Fitoorsz,** Louwijs (fl late 17th and early 18th centuries). Dutch potter at Delft; at The Double Jug factory 1687–*c*1714. Associated with vases decorated in **cachemire* style.

fiddle-back. Chair back with violin-shaped central splat. Common early 18th century design.

fiddle pattern. 18th and 19th century British and European silver flatware stem pattern; broad, flat stem end resembling shape of violin or fiddle narrowing until immediately above bowl where it forms shoulders. Stem left plain, engraved with arms, or ornamented with *threaded edge, *thread and shell pattern, etc. Style first in use in France in mid 18th century; in use in Britain from late 18th century.

Field, John (1771–1841). English silhouettist. From 1800, assistant to J. *Miers; also exhibited landscapes at Royal Academy. Later, partner with Miers's son William until 1831. Established own studio; appointed profilist to Queen Adelaide. Profiles embellished with gold or bronze paint; usually bust-length. Also miniature profiles on ivory, incorporated into jewellery.

Fiddle pattern. Variations: Left, fiddle pattern, c1810. Centre: fiddle and thread, c1850. Right: fiddle and shell, c1819.

Filigree. Decoration in gold wire on 6th century Viking gold collar from Sweden.

Field, Robert (1769–1819). English-born miniaturist, in United States from 1794. Painted miniatures in Boston, New York, Washington, and Philadelphia; work finely executed in pastel shades, with soft brush strokes. In 1816, moved to Jamaica.

filigree. Lace-like ornament made from very fine gold or silver wire. In use from antiquity for jewellery. Also open-work panels set into baskets, boxes, cups, etc., or forming complete object. Much used in late 17th century Europe. Birmingham important centre for filigree manufacture in 18th and early 19th centuries, but also imported to Britain from India and Malta in 19th century.

filigree glass. Technique using interwoven threads of white, clear, or coloured glass; first used by Romans. Glass threads wound round mould and fused to form vessel. 16th century Venetians used similar technique, but glass free-blown to give delicate tracery effect (*see latticinio*). Popularity spread throughout Europe with *façon de Venise*.

fillet. Narrow flat band separating two types of moulding or flutes of column.

fine or **English pewter.** Alloy of tin and copper, laid down by London Pewterers' Company (1348 charter) as metal to be used for best quality wares, e.g. platters, chargers, and all squared or ribbed pieces. Proportions of metal not defined, but copper was to be added to the tin 'as much as of its own nature it will take'. Later established as approximate proportion of 112 lb tin to 26 lb copper. Plates, etc., had to be hammered for added hardness. By 18th century, fine pewter usually contained 112 lb tin to 6 or 7 lb antimony.

finger bowl. Small glass bowl for rinsing fingers at dining table. Usually clear flint-glass; some blue, purple, red, or green. Many made in Bristol glasshouses. Finest heavy cut glass. Popular in England from *c*1760. Many blown examples from 19th century Ireland.

Finger plate. Brass, one of set of four; early 19th century.

Fireback. Cast iron. Dutch, 17th century. Height 2ft8in.

finger-plate. Metal or ceramic ornamental plaque fixed to door to protect it from finger marks. *See* door furniture.

finger vase. Flower vase with five tubular holders arranged in fan shape. Made in 17th century Dutch Delft; in late 18th century copied in cream-coloured earthenware, e.g. in Staffordshire; described in Leeds catalogue as quintal flower horn. Example in Vienna porcelain, 1721.

finial. Ornamental knob, projection or terminating feature of general application and varied form, including acorn, ball, flower, pineapple, vase, etc. and many more elaborate forms (particularly on glassware, e.g. *winged glasses). *See also* knop.

fireback. Cast-iron panel at back of fireplace to radiate heat, to protect wall, and for decoration. Made from 15th century, when wide and low and impressed with any ornamental shape; by mid 17th century tall and narrower to suit new chimneys. From early 18th century, made in one piece with grate. 17th century ornamental devices were figures, mythical or biblical scenes, fleurs-de-lis, Tudor rose, domestic animals, etc.; coats of arms, monograms, stylized floral motifs, and scrolls. Also known as fireplate, iron chimney, reredos.

fire clock. Time-measuring device used mainly in Far East, with passage of hours marked by burning of sticks of incense, as used in Japanese geisha houses; or powdered incense laid in channel cut in block of stone or wood. Also found in Europe in form of candle, or oil-lamp reservoir marked with hour divisions.

Firedogs. Cast iron with brass finials; front two feet cast in form of scaly human legs and feet. English, c1685.
Fire-irons. Left: early 19th century steel fire-irons with brass finials. Right: Adam style steel fire-irons.

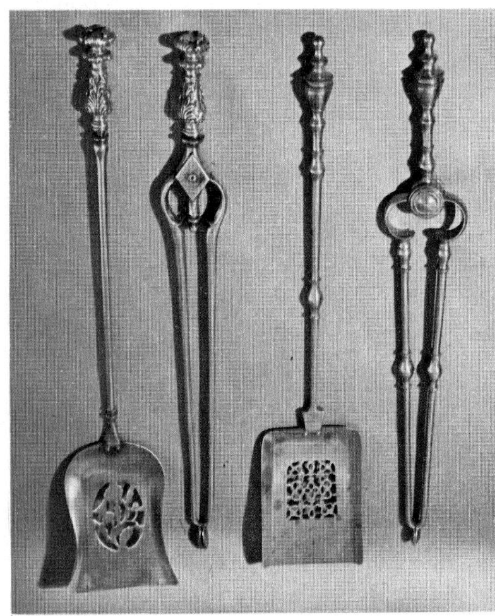

firedogs. Irons made in pairs to stand between *andirons and *creepers. Originally cast in shape of seated hounds, later in 16th century in form of human head or bust or animal head, then in similar form to andirons on smaller scale. *Illustration also at* ormolu.

fire-fork. Wrought-iron implement for rearranging burning logs, with two prongs and long handle. Replaced by poker and tongs in 18th century.

fire-gilding. *See* gilding.

fire-guard. Wrought-iron frame enclosing wire mesh, placed before fire to stop jumping sparks and cinders. Frame slightly raised on small feet. Known from 17th century. Polished brass top-rail replaced wrought-iron in 18th century.

firehouse Windsor. American type of *low-back Windsor chair, but with box stretcher and legs less splayed than 18th century prototype. Dates from mid 19th century.

fire-irons. Set including shovel, tongs, and poker. In 18th century of burnished iron or steel, larger than modern equivalents. Costly examples have handle decoration of copper or brass; most sophisticated have gilt-bronze ornament to match grate and fender. Twisted-shank type became popular in 1790s. Brass sets made in Europe and England from mid 19th century often include brush for sweeping hearth. *See* fire-fork.

*Fish slice. Made in London by P. *Storr, 1831. Blade pierced with scrolls and mullets; engraved with whale chasing fish; handle formed as dolphin intertwined with coral strand. Length 14in.*

fire mark. Stain on silver caused by oxidation of copper with which silver is alloyed during *annealing process. Removed by polishing with abrasive or placing piece in acid bath to dissolve copper oxide.

fireplace furniture. Early *down hearth was furnished with *fireback, *andirons, *firedogs, *creepers or *spit-dogs, *fire-fork, and occasionally a *fire-guard. *Grate and *fender were introduced early 18th century; with these *fire-irons, *blowing-tube, bellows, and *coal-scuttle were used.

fireplate. *See* fireback.

fire screen. *See* screen.

firing glasses. *See* bumping glasses.

fish knife. Silver knife with blunt, shaped blade resembling contemporary *fish slice; haft sometimes of ivory or mother-of-pearl. In use in Britain and Europe from early 19th century. After *c*1850 in Britain mainly electro-plated.

Fishley family. Potters at Fremington, North Devon in 18th and 19th centuries. Made domestic earthenware, also watchstands and ornamental ware including bust of John Wesley and agate ware figures, notably cat with slip decoration. Harvest jugs with rolled handles have *sgraffiato* decoration.

fish servers. British silver utensils for serving fish in use from *c*1790. Several types made: *fish slice with additional small blade fitted over larger and operating on spring (pressure on lever above the handle raises small blade for gripping); alternatively, matching fish slice and large fork, or large knife and fork.

fish slice. Utensil with wide, flat, engraved, or pierced silver or electro-plate blade (triangular, oval, etc.) and silver or ivory handle; dates from mid 18th century in Britain and Europe. In 19th century designed *en suite* with table silver, handle pattern matching spoon and fork stems; also blade less symmetrical. Few made in Sheffield plate.

fishtail. Lower handle terminal on pewter tankards from *c*1710–*c*1750; name derives from shape.

Fitoorsz, Louwijs. *See* Fictoor, Louwijs.

Fitzhugh border. Chinese ceramic decoration; found mostly on export porcelain of Ch'ing dynasty. Rim of plate, dish, or jar covered with trellis-work, enriched with butterflies, flowers, or key fret, and sometimes repeated at centre of design, enclosing fruits. Resembles transfer-printing in its precision. Found as border on 'willow pattern' plates. Mostly executed in underglaze cobalt-blue (*cf* Nankin porcelain); found also in iron-red and green.

Five Dynasties (907–59 A.D.). Chinese period noted for quality of ceramics. Important kiln sites, Tê-ch'ing and Chiu-yen. Work characterized by grey body, which turns dark red when exposed in firing, and high-splayed foot rim. Carved or incised decoration includes palmettes, lotus petals, leaf friezes, waves, or dragons. Glaze is blue or greenish-grey. Marks transition from strong T'ang period shapes imitating bronze, to smooth, fine lines of following Sung period (to which pieces are often attributed).

flagon. Large vessel for serving wine, made throughout Europe and Britain from 16th century or earlier. Silver and silver-gilt examples mainly for ceremonial use. After Reformation in England, also used for Communion wine (since laity allowed to participate, large quantities of wine needed); earliest surviving silver example dated 1572. Generally made in pairs. Originally of *pilgrim bottle form; by 17th century, resembled tall, cylindrical tankard with moulded foot.

Earliest known English pewter examples date from late 16th century, but rare until early 17th century, when Church sanctioned use of pewter flagons for Communion. Shapes approximately followed silver; early form, tall, plain tapering cylinder on wider base, with simple curved handle, plain *bun or *muffin cover and heavy *chairback thumbpiece. By mid 17th century, base spread further, to give more stability; cover of *beefeater type. Other styles appeared with addition of knops, more detailed mouldings at

Flagon. One of pair from church of St Petrock, Exeter, Devonshire. Made in London, dated 1692.

Flambé glaze. On Kwang-tung stoneware bottle of Ch'ien Lung period.

base and neck, and styles of lid, thumbpiece, etc., roughly following *tankard. Few with spouts before mid 18th century.

Pewter flagons also in domestic use from *c*1700; kept on sideboard to replenish diners' cups with wine or ale. Comparatively few silver flagons made, except for ecclesiastical use, after

Flask. For holding spirits; oval in section; screw-on cap chained to ring on flask. Made in Edinburgh by Alexander Kincaid, c1715. Height 5in.

17th century. Continental styles more ornate, usually engraved; German flagons sometimes have small feet; particularly elaborate. Scottish and Irish flagons roughly followed English styles with regional variations: many Scottish examples have inverted saucer-like lids and bands of moulded decoration; some Irish examples have very large, curving handles. *See* acorn flagon, Guild flagon, cimaise, Jan Steen flagon, livery pot, sideboard plate.

flambé glaze. Chinese ceramic glaze first used successfully on Sung *Chün ware; splashes of brilliant red or purple on blue ground caused by oxidation of copper in iron-based glaze. Technique copied on Kwang-tung stoneware, streaked with red, purple, brown, or greyish-green. Examples based on copper-red glaze, made in Ch'ing period from reign of K'ang Hsi, have glassy appearance. Copies made in late 19th century Europe.

flame carving. Carved flame-shapes, realistic or stylized, used on finials, particularly in 18th century America.

Flanders chest. 15th and 16th century heavily carved chest made in Low Countries; imported into Britain.

flap table. *See* drop-leaf table.

flask. Narrow-necked vessel, usually for storing liquids or for use when travelling. Found in earthenware, leather, silver, and occasionally pewter, e.g. group of highly elaborate screw-topped examples made in 17th century Nuremberg. *See* pilgrim bottle.

flat-back figures. Earthenware figures made, notably in Staffordshire, also in Scotland, from mid 19th century. Press-moulded and decorated with underglaze colours or enamel and gilding; intended for viewing from one side only, e.g. as chimney ornaments. Makers include S. *Smith.

flat-chasing. Linear surface decoration of silver in low relief; no metal removed. Surface supported on bed of soft wood, pitch, or wax during hammering to prevent buckling. Result sometimes similar to engraving but distinguished by impressions on back; engraving leaves no such mark. Much used in late 17th century; e.g. *chinoiserie* ornament flat-chased on ginger jars, beakers, toilet services, tea-caddies, etc.

flat hammering. Silver ingot reduced to sheet-form by using hammers of various weights. From mid 18th century, sheet silver commonly produced by mechanical rolling mill.

flat-iron or **sad-iron** (American). Implement used from 15th century or earlier for pressing clothes, etc., after heating by various methods. Usually of cast iron; made in variety of shapes, most common being plain block with simple handle, heated by placing on end against firebars. Charcoal iron has hollow body, in which embers are placed, with smoke outlets. 'Box' iron has hollow body and hinged back through which is inserted iron block, previously heated till red-hot in fire. Particularly narrow, rounded examples were used by tailors for pressing, e.g. inside sleeves.

Flatman, Thomas (1635–88). English poet and miniaturist. Miniatures, painted from 1661, show influence of S. *Cooper. Subjects include Charles II and self-portraits.

flat-top, on long-case clocks, introduced in late 17th century England. Sometimes ornamented at front, and sides, by carved wood cresting.

flatware. Generic term for silver, gold, and Sheffield plate objects of flattened form, e.g. dishes, saucers, salvers, etc. In antique trade and silver manufacturing, term refers to spoons, forks, slices, etc., forming part of service.

Flaxman, John (1755–1826). English sculptor, draughtsman and designer in neo-classical

*John Flaxman. Vase designed by Flaxman for J. *Wedgwood, c1780, in *jasper ware.*

style. Worked at studio of father, a cast maker, before entering Royal Academy Schools in 1770. Employed from 1775 by J. *Wedgwood; modelled *jasper ware reliefs and figures, including Triton candleholders and chessmen. In Rome, 1787–94. Elected to Royal Academy in 1800. Designed silver for P. *Rundell (later *Rundell, Bridge & Rundell). Major works for Rundell include *Trafalgar vase (1805) and *Shield of Achilles (1818). Designed some domestic silver as well as presentation pieces.

Fleming, William (fl late 17th and early 18th centuries). English silversmith working in London; apprenticed 1687–88; granted freedom in 1694. Produced domestic silver. Mark (in 1697): FL crowned. *Illustration at* sugar bowl.

Flemish tapestries. *See* Antwerp, Arras, Bruges, Brussels, Enghien, Oudenaarde, and Tournai tapestries.

fleur de solanée. *See* potato flower.

Fleurier watch. *See* Chinese watch.

fleurs des Indes. *See indianische Blumen.*

fleurs fines. *See deutsche Blumen.*

fliegender Kinder (German, 'flying children'). Winged figures of children resembling **amorini*, painted on ornamental German porcelain (e.g. at Berlin factory *c*1770). Inspired by work of F. *Boucher.

Flight, Thomas (fl late 18th century) and sons John (d 1791) and Joseph (fl late 18th century). English porcelain manufacturers. Thomas, previously London agent for *Worcester porcelain bought Warmstry House Factory for £3000 in 1783. John managed factory until death; then Joseph manager until 1793, when M. *Barr taken into partnership.

Flight & Barr and **Flight, Barr & Barr.** *See* Worcester.

flint enamel ware. American pottery glazed by process patented by C. W. *Fenton at Bennington, Vermont, in 1849. Powdered metal oxides, e.g. copper and cobalt, sprinkled on unfired *Rockingham glaze, fused with glaze to form streaks of brilliant green, orange-yellow, and blue on brown.

flint-glass. Developed by G. *Ravenscroft in experiments from 1673. Form of crystal glass using calcined and ground flints as source of silica. Particularly suitable for cutting and engraving. Initial tendency to crizzling remedied by adding red lead, producing *lead glass (1676).

flintporslin. Swedish *cream-coloured earthenware introduced in 1770s at Marieberg and Rörstrand.

flirt. *See* striking mechanism.

floor clock. In America, *long-case clock.

floral carpets. Central Persian court carpets with diaper or ascending patterns of leaves, palmettes, and other blossoms on stem lattices; cloud bands often infilling ground. Later palmettes and blossoms dominate; stems disappear. Also, any carpets adopting similar pattern.

Flora Danica service. Banquet service made at Copenhagen porcelain factory *c*1789–1802; originally intended for Catherine the Great of Russia. Painted with named plants from G. C. Oeder's Flora of Denmark (started 1761). Border pattern includes acanthus leaf motif. Preserved in Rosenborg Castle, Copenhagen.

Florence (Tuscany), Italy. Produced *green and purple ware in 15th century; probably centre of development of **stile severo* (*c*1425–*c*1450) in maiolica. Oak-leaf jars made 1425–55. Border of curling leaves characteristic of dishes (introduced *c*1450) decorated in blue, yellow, green, and manganese-purple, e.g. with portraits or animals. *Albarelli* (1460–70) painted with vine leaves derived from Hispano-Moresque ware, in blue and manganese-purple. Other maiolica in Florence area made at *Cafaggiolo and *Montelupo. *Medici porcelain made 1575–87.

Florentine tapestry. Florence major *Italian tapestry-weaving centre. Manufactory, Arazzeria Medici, established 1546 by Cosimo I. Until political disruption at end of century, great quantity of tapestries produced. Finest works in early years, under master-weavers N. *Karcher and J. *Rost. Cartoons by Florentine mannerist painters, particularly Salviati, A. *Bronzino and Alessandro Allori. Mainly figure tapestries; subjects include mythological, historical, biblical, and allegorical scenes. Industry revived early 17th century and flourished 1630–47 under direction of Parisian master-weaver P. *Lefebvre. Few new designs, most copy work of 16th century Italian masters, particularly *Raphaël. Quality deteriorated with increased output in late 17th century, woven by decreasing number of weavers. In early 18th century, many door hangings, landscape tapestries, and small religious hangings produced. Manufactory closed 1737 (after death of last Medici duke, Giovanni Gastone) and director and some weavers moved to *Naples.

Flörsheim (Hesse). German faience factory founded 1765. Sold to Carthusian monks (1773); later let. Finally sold (1797) to firm which continued production into 20th century. Majority of 18th century pieces painted in high-temperature polychrome or blue; some enamel painting. Marks, before 1781, usually FH in monogram. Initials MIW impressed on creamware produced 1781–93.

flow blue. In America, *transfer-printing in underglaze blue with lines blurred in fusion of glaze. Technically a fault, but sought by many collectors.

Flower, Joseph (fl 1743–85). Owner of pottery in Bristol, 1743–85. Painted tin-enamelled earthenware in delicate style resembling engravings. Credited with first examples of *bianco sopra bianco* decoration made at Bristol. Employees included J. *Bowen. Products sold at shop in Bristol.

flower table or **stand.** Four-legged table or pedestal stand designed to hold flower container. Both date from late 17th century. Originally about 2ft high, taller and more elaborate after *c*1750; later designed to hold several containers. Dual purpose examples have metal-lined flower container concealed below removable wooden table top. Fore-runner of **jardinière*.

flowers (modelled in porcelain). Relief moulded flowers occur on Meissen tableware, e.g. coffee-pot of *c*1720; in 1740s, more naturalistic flower modelling developed on tableware and particularly ornamental ware, e.g. on trellis setting of arbour group, or standing in rococo vase. Bouquets of separate blooms on wire stems fashionable from late 1740s, modelled in soft-paste, notably at Vincennes and Buen Retiro (after 1775). Modelled flowers frequently used as finials, or in clusters as handles on ornamental and table ware in rococo style. Characteristic also of revived rococo style in 19th century, e.g. at Coalport in 1820s and 1830s.

flute. Tubular wind instrument, with or without mouthpiece; two basic types, end-blown (e.g. *recorder), and side or cross-blown transverse flute: term flute commonly used only to refer to latter. Usually has six finger-holes. Used from antiquity; still found in both primitive and developed forms. Made of various materials including bone, bamboo, wood, clay, glass, metal, etc. By 12th century, cross or transverse flute established in western Europe. Used chiefly as military instrument in Switzerland and Germany in late Middle Ages in combination with drum, when known as fife. Introduced to England in 16th century as German flute; commonly made of box-wood; has cylindrical tube with six finger-holes (equidistant) and one end plugged. Family of flutes in existence by 16th century: bass in C, tenor in G, and soprano in D (forerunner of modern concert flute). In late 17th century bore or hole altered to inverted conical, holes arranged in two groups of three, and additional hole with key added. Bore of flute and keying varied (particularly in France) until modern form established *c*1831–32 by Munich flute maker, Theobald Boehm (1794–1881).

flute (in glass). Tall, slender drinking glass with

*Flute. English flute glasses. Left: *ale glass, bowl engraved with hops and barley, 1760; height 7¾in. Centre: champagne glass, bowl engraved in manner of J. *Giles with urns and paterae, 1780; height 6¼in. Right: *cider glass, bowl gilded with band of apples and flowers, 1770; height 7½in.*

deep conical bowl attached to foot by knop. Popular during 17th and 18th centuries. Probably of Dutch origin.

flûte à bec. *See* recorder.

fluting. Ornamentation with shallow parallel grooves of semi-circular cross-section, usually vertical, sometimes oblique or curved. Used on silver, particularly on bodies of late 17th and early 18th century two-handled cups, monteiths, tankards, ewers etc. (sometimes alternating with *gadrooning), and on late 18th century English neo-classical pieces. Cut on glassware as border or body pattern e.g. on bowls of 18th century wine glasses (also on stems from *c*1750) and Regency *flutes. Carved (sometimes painted) as decoration on furniture from 16th century.

flux. Substance used in melting processes in glass, porcelain, and metal manufacture to reduce melting-point, promote fusion, and prevent formation of oxides. Many substances used include potash, soda, and borax.

fly. *See* striking mechanism.

fly chair. In early 19th century, chair of light structure.

fob. Small pocket in waistband of breeches for watch, seal, etc.

fob-chain. For attaching watch to clothing; used from late 17th century; developed in 19th century to standard form also carrying watch key and seal, named 'Albert' after example presented to Prince Consort by Birmingham jewellers in 1845. Elaborate chatelaines for ladies often made with decoration to match watch case.

fob seal. *See* seal.

Fogelberg, Andrew (fl 1770–93). Swedish silversmith, established in London by *c*1770. P. *Storr apprenticed to him *c*1785. Made range of domestic silver in neo-classical style, featuring in particular applied medallions (some modelled on work of J. *Tassie). Registered mark in 1780 with partner Stephen Gilbert: AF above SG. Retired probably in 1793, when Storr took over premises from him.

folded foot. Foot of glass vessel, e.g. wine glass, strengthened by folding edge inwards underneath. Developed in Venice; typical feature of *façon de Venise*. Also found on English wine glasses of late 17th and early 18th centuries.

foliate ornament. Leaf-shaped ornament, engraved and cast-applied to much early 16th century silver hollow-ware. In 17th century, embossed as primary decoration on silver in *Dutch grotesque style. Also in late 17th and early 18th century *cut-card work around base of body of hollow-ware. *See* Huguenot silver.

foliot. Timekeeping element in earliest clocks: metal bar pivoted at centre, swinging back and forward at roughly constant intervals, but controlled only by own inertia. Attempts at regulation made by adjusting small weights at ends of bar. Replaced by *balance and *pendulum. *Illustration at* stackfreed.

fond écaille. French ceramic decoration. High-temperature tortoiseshell ground colour. Introduced at Sèvres in 1775 for use on hard-paste porcelain. Often painted with gilt or silvered designs.

fondelli. Miniatures on ivory so-called by R. *Carriera who devised technique *c*1705.

fondeur-ciseleur. French: maker of bronze or gilt-copper mounts for furniture. Technique of Greco-Roman origin; in 18th century France, *fondeurs-ciseleurs* worked closely with **ébénistes*.

fondi d'oro. Glass enclosing gold-leaf decoration. Roman origin; made mainly between 1st and 4th centuries. Main motifs Christian and Jewish symbols, games, classical mythology. Revived in 16th century Venice. Also in 18th century in Bohemia as **Zwischengoldglas*, and in France as **verre églomisé*.

fondporzellan. *See ground colours.*

Fontaine, Pierre-François-Léonard (1762–1853). French architect; with C. *Percier, established French Empire style under patronage of Napoleon I. Architect to Napoleon, Louis XVIII, and Louis Philippe; engaged on principal architectural works in Paris during these reigns.

Fontainebleau workshop. First French royal tapestry manufactory established at Fontainebleau *c*1535 by François I, with Flemish, Italian, and French weavers. Under Italian artistic director, Baroque compositions adapted from pictures and decorations of palace gallery. Production continued into reign of Henri IV (reigned 1589–1610).

Fontana, Guido. *See* Durantino, Guido.

Fontana, Orazio (d 1751). Italian maiolica painter, son of G. *Durantino. Worked at Urbino from 1542; owned workshop from 1565. Painted landscapes with many figures in bright polychrome; examples include plates with scenes from Roman history, and arms of Urbino at top left, dated 1565–70.

font-shaped cup. 16th century British and European covered *standing cup in silver or silver-gilt with shallow cylindrical bowl, trumpet stem, and moulded foot; cover slightly domed with flat-topped finial. Few covers survive.

footman. Wrought-iron or brass four-legged *trivet with pierced and engraved ornament and larger pierced hole in top for lifting. Made after 1750.

foot-ring. Protective rim in variety of shapes and sizes attached to base of vessel, also serving as ornament. In silver, found on some tankards, two-handled cups, etc. Also occurs in ceramics and early glass.

foot-warmer or **carriage-warmer.** 17th-19th century brass or copper receptacle for charcoal embers (later for hot water) often in wooden box case; pierced lid allowed heat to escape and kept embers alight. Used in the house, or in carriages when travelling; a brass carrying-handle was usual. Often elaborately ornamented with embossed work, engraved dates, names, etc. Made throughout Europe. Dutch 17th century examples resemble foot-stools. Scandinavian examples are known in carved wood with metal lining. *cf* brazier.

Foot-warmer. English, oak; carved inscription; lid pierced; twisted iron handle. Height c18 *in.*

forging. Earliest method of working iron by hammering, usually when red hot, occasionally when cold (cold-hammering).

fork. Pronged eating or serving utensil with stem. Two-pronged gold or silver forks used in Middle Ages for eating fruit or sweetmeats; large iron two-pronged forks for serving meat, made from 15th century; silver forks with two to four prongs for eating from 15th century in Italy. Use spread to France, Holland, and finally England in late 16th century, when also of gilt copper. Usually designed to accompany spoons; early examples have flat stem of *Puritan or *trefid type. Three-pronged fork known from late 17th century and four-pronged examples became established after mid 18th century. Some designed as set with knives; handles of various materials, including ivory, amber, tortoiseshell, silver filigree, etc. 18th century British fork sometimes has steel prongs and stamped silver handle weighted with resinous substance; pistol butt handle shape matched that of knife. 18th century fork normally larger than earlier examples. Custom of large fork for main course and smaller one for dessert not common until end of 18th century. *See* carving fork, dessert service French fork.

fork handles (in ceramics). *See* knife and fork handles.

form box. *See* fantasy box.

form watch. Watch made in non-standard shape, e.g. book, crucifix, skull, animal, or flower, particularly tulip. Popular in 17th

Form watches. Above: crucifix shaped. Movement signed by C. Tinelly à Aix, c1630; embossed gold case with outer protective case. Below: tulip-shaped. Made in Amsterdam by Daniel van Pilcom, c1640.

century. Revived in late 18th century in forms including lyres, mandolins, baskets of flowers, or fruit; again in late 19th century by Swiss makers. *Illustrations also at* German watches, skull watch.

Forster, Thomas (b *c*1677). English plumbago miniaturist, working in early 18th century. Drawings in very hard, highly sharpened pencil on vellum, occasionally with grey wash, carefully executed and highly finished.

Fortune ('t Fortuyn). Delft factory (1661–1791), property of *Mesch family, 1661–1724, except 1691–94 when owned by D. *Hofdyck and partner. H. J. *Peridon thought to have been employed *c*1692. Wares mass-produced in mid to late 18th century.

Fostat carpets. Oldest surviving fragments of Egyptian knotted-pile carpets, discovered in remains of Fostat (old Cairo), date from 9th to 11th centuries. Knots formed by primitive *weft-loop technique. Pile largely wool, with cotton for white pattern elements; foundation linen. Geometrical designs with finely stepped diamond lozenges, hexagons, eight-pointed stars, and stylized flowers; or Kufic inscriptions on solid ground. Limited palette; chief colours rust or wine-red, green, white, light-blue, olive, and brown tones.

Fourposter bed. Elizabethan. Carved oak, back with elaborate ornament of caryatids and profile heads set within lozenges, which are repeated underneath tester, and inlaid with Tudor roses and pansies. Height 6ft8in.

François I style. Dresser in walnut, c1545. Height 8ft6in.

Foster, Edward (1762–1867). English silhouettist. Retired from military career in 1805. Appointed miniature painter to the royal family at Windsor. By 1811, working as silhouettist, mainly in The Strand, London and in native town of Derby. Took likenesses with device allegedly of own invention. Work of variable quality. Painted on card, typically in red with bronzing; also used blue, brown, or black. Signed work Foster Pinxt. Lived to 104.

Foucher, Blaise (d 1662). French watch maker and enamel painter, from Blois. Decorated cases with mythological scenes.

founding. *See* casting.

Fountain, William (fl late 18th century). English silversmith working in London; granted freedom in 1785. Prolific maker of domestic silver. Mark in 1791, with Daniel Pontifex, WF above DP; in 1794 registered own mark, WF, and in 1798, WF in script.

Fouquay, Nicolas (1686–1742). French faience maker. Bought faience factory of L. *Poterat at Rouen in 1720. Made painted busts of Apollo and The Seasons, each 7ft 4in. high with faience pedestal.

four-colour or **quatre-couleur gold.** Gold with colour changed by admixture of other metals. Basic colours: white gold, containing more silver than gold; green, alloyed with silver; red, with copper; blue, with arsenic or steel filings. Developed mainly in Paris *c*1750–75; used for watch cases, snuff-boxes, and other objects of vertu; after 1760 restricted to panels and borders. *Illustration at* French snuff-boxes.

Fournier, Louis (fl 1746–66). French modeller and porcelain maker. Worked at Vincennes (1747–49); figures include naiad (1747). Also at Chantilly (1752–56). Made soft-paste porcelain from 1759 in Copenhagen.

fourposter. Bed with tall posts rising from corners and sometimes supporting canopy or tester. Originally called a posted or post bed; dates from 16th century.

Fox, Charles (d *c*1838). English silversmith working in London; founded firm which continued in production until 1890s. Entered mark, CF, in 1804. Son, Charles Thomas, took over business *c*1838; first registered mark (also CF) in 1822. Fox family produced silver for retailers, e.g. *Lambert & Rawlings. Silver exhibited at Great Exhibition (1851) characterized by advanced styling and decorative use of exotic plant forms. *Illustrations at* butter dish, mustard pot.

fox-head cup. *See* stirrup-cup.

Fragonard, Jean-Honoré (1732–1806). French painter, pupil of F. *Boucher. Travelled in Italy; influenced by Tiepolo. First exhibited historical subjects, then more intimate pictures, tending to eroticism after death of friend P-A. *Baudoin. Also painted landscapes and miniatures. Wife, Marie-Anne, *née* Gérard (1745–1823), was successful miniaturist whose work is difficult to separate from husband's.

France, Edward (fl 1768–86). English cabinet maker and upholsterer, partner in France & Beckwith. Received commissions from households of George III and George IV.

Francis Gardner Porcelain Factory. Russian factory established in 1766 at Verbilki, near Moscow by F. *Gardner under privileges granted by Peter the Great. Employed German and Swiss craftsmen to teach native workers.

Produced good quality off-white porcelain. Tableware includes services for imperial Orders, intended for use on feast days of their patron saints; commissioned by Catherine the Great, 1777–83. Entire service, including knife and fork handles, draped with ribbon and badge of particular Order; some pieces also with star. Figures made from *c*1770, at first in Meissen style; from early 19th century, coloured and biscuit figures represented Russian workers and their trades; erotic figures also made. Colours both underglaze and enamel, often on same figures; bases round or rectangular with gilt line in early 19th century; from 1860s, rococo scrolled, or coloured in imitation of earth. Faience also made; during 1847–53, production exceeded that of porcelain. From 1829, factory traded as Gardner Brothers; name continued until 1917, although factory sold to owners of Kuznetzov factory in 1892. Marks include G Roman or Cyrillic character) in underglaze blue or puce enamel until 1891; in early 19th century, Gardner in Roman or Cyrillic characters, black enamel or impressed; from 1829, St George and Dragon of Moscow, with Cyrillic inscription indicating 'of the Brothers Gardner', printed initially in red, later also in green or violet.

François Ier style. Early French Renaissance furniture style, coinciding roughly with reign of François Ier (1515–47). Furniture was not yet plentiful, and mainly rectangular in shape, decorated with Gothic motifs (linen-fold panelling, tracery, etc.) or Italian Renaissance motifs (medallions, Romayne work, fruit, flowers, fabulous beasts, etc.). Carving, at times elaborate, was main decoration. Oak or walnut was used, with iron mounts. François Ier pieces include heavily-ornamented cabinets, X-frame chairs, high-backed panelled chairs with box base, plate cupboards, cushioned stools, trestle tables.

Frankenthal (Palatinate). German hard-paste porcelain factory, flourished 1755–99. Products of first 20 years highly regarded. Founded by P-A. *Hannong with support from local prince, Elector Carl Theodor; later directed by twin sons, C-F-P. Hannong (until 1757), and J-A. Hannong (1759–62), then purchased by Elector. Produced fine-grained, milk-white paste with opaque glaze from Passau clay. Figures distinguished by subtle enamel colours. Early, simply-dressed examples by J. W. *Lanze (1755–61); later series, more fashionably dressed, attributed to J. F. *Lück (1758–64), with possible influence of G. F. *Riedel. F. C. *Linck modelled ballet figures, busts, allegorical, and neo-classical subjects (1762–66). K. G. *Lück *Modellmeister* from 1766. Subjects include hunting figures, family groups, dancers, beggars, and statues of Elector; figures among last examples characterized by green base with gold rococo edges and intricately striped, spotted, and flower-sprigged costume. S. *Feilner, next appointment, left few models. J. P. *Melchior *Modellmeister* 1779–93; produced groups of children, official portrait reliefs, and busts.

Table and decorative wares of high quality feature elaborate original subjects, and versions of Meissen themes; artists include J. B. *Magnus. Designs include gilt-striped grounds, trellis and chintz patterns, with crimson and green in combination.

French wars of 1794–95 forced closure, and moulds removed to Nymphenburg (where earthenware and porcelain copies later made). Marks: PH and PHF impressed (1755–56); remainder in blue; chequered quartering from Palatine arms (1756); Palatine lion rampant (1756–59); monogram of J-A H (1759–62); CT, with or without Electoral crown (1762–88); also used at modern *Nymphenburg factory; monogram of VR (von Recum, last director, 1795–99).

*Frankenthal. Group of dancers with two dogs, c1770–80; modelled by J. F. *Lück. Height 7¾in.*

Frankfurt faience. Vase, c1680, with blue-and-white chinoiserie *decoration.*

Frankfurt, Germany. Faience factory founded 1666. Products at first imitated Chinese styles and, like Delft (from which they are hard to distinguish), have **kwaart* applied over blue and white painting. Designs on plates echo late Ming porcelain, with detailed plants, trees, birds, and Chinese figures. Best-known domestic wares are large, nine-lobed, plated vases and narrow-necked ewers with rope-like handles. Jugs painted in purple or decorated with armorial bearings. J. K. *Ripp (mark: KR), best known artist, painted in Chinese style, using mainly blue and red. Numerous Frankfurt pieces towards end of 17th century painted by *Hausmaler*. Factory mark, F, fairly common on jugs and dishes. Pieces rarely dated, sometimes signed by painters.

Freedom box. Engraved with arms of Dublin and of Sir John Stanley. c1710, unmarked.

'freedom' box. British or American gold or silver box similar in size to snuff-box used in 18th and 19th centuries for conferring freedom of city. Lid engraved with arms of city.

Freemason box. British silver or silver-gilt snuff-box engraved with masonic emblems; made from late 18th century.

Frémiet, Emmanuel (1824–1910). French sculptor; originally known as one of *les *Animaliers,* later famous for statue of Joan of Arc (Place des Pyramides, Paris). Nephew and student of F. *Rude. Collection of sculptures on theme of French army commissioned by Napoleon III.

French carpets. Knotted oriental carpets and Spanish carpets introduced into France from 15th century; used mainly as covers for beds and tables. Small French workshops operated producing Turkish-design carpets. From early 17th century carpet industry developed under royal patronage. First royal workshop established by Henry IV at *Louvre under direction of P. *Dupont. *Savonnerie workshop established 1626. Embargo placed on import of Eastern carpets in 1627 and French industry expanded rapidly. Earliest designs adaptations of eastern floral patterns, Turkish-knotted and worked in bold colours. In 1662, due to Louis XIV's encouragement of decorative arts, Savonnerie manufactory purchased and incorporated into newly formed Manufacture Royale des Meubles de la Couronne (the *Gobelins). Individual Savonnerie style developed and copied at other manufactories, particularly *Aubusson and *Beauvais. Exported throughout Europe, and, following mass emigration of Huguenot weavers (after Revocation of Edict of Nantes, 1685), technique and designs adopted by manufactories in England, Spain, and Italy. During 18th and early 19th centuries, Savonnerie and Aubusson styles served as models for carpet manufactories in other countries.

French ceramics. Lead-glazed earthenware possibly made from 9th century; until 14th century, attribution very difficult. By late 15th century, pottery decorated with slip, or stamped reliefs, and splashes of colour in glaze, made in many provincial centres. Relief-decorated ware made by B. *Palissy from mid 16th century. Renaissance-style ornament in contrasting coloured clay found on *Saint Porchaire ware made *c*1530–70. Important pottery centre developed at *Apt in 18th century. Lead-glazed tile pavements made from 12th century, largely superseded in 16th century by tin-glazed tiles; stoneware made 16th-18th century often used for tiles with moulded relief.

Tin-glazed earthenware made in 16th century e.g. at *Rouen, *Lyon, and *Nevers, in style of Italian maiolica. In 17th century, **bleus de Nevers* developed alongside faience decorated in maiolica colours. Faience of late 17th century dominated by blue decoration of Rouen; style followed by manufacturers e.g. in *Paris, *Saint-Cloud, *Saint-Amand-les-Eaux, and *Strasbourg. Polychrome decoration at Rouen in 18th century influenced faience of *Sinceny and *Samadet. Decoration developed at *Moustiers in 18th century copied e.g. at *Ardus, *Bordeaux, *Limoges, Lyon, and *Montpellier. Enamel decoration introduced on faience made at Strasbourg in mid 18th century inspired by painting of porcelain; followed at *Aprey, *Marseille, Moustiers, *Niderviller, Rouen, and *Sceaux, largely superseding painting in high-temperature colours.

Soft-paste porcelain said to have been made *c*1673 by L. *Poterat, and made in late 17th century at Saint-Cloud by *Chicanneau family. *Chantilly, *Mennecy, and *Vincennes also producers by mid 18th century. Monopoly granted to *Sèvres effectively prevented manufacture of porcelain by other factories until 1766; porcelain then required to bear registered mark. After lifting of restrictions, factories including *Lunéville, Marseille, Niderviller, Strasbourg, and Paris firms began to make hard-paste porcelain. Important factor in production of hard-paste, discovery of kaolin deposits at Saint-Yrieix, near Limoges. French artists largely responsible for manufacture of soft-paste porcelain in existing faience factory at *Tournai, from mid 18th century.

French chair. Term introduced in England and America *c*1750 to describe elbow chair with upholstered seat, back, and arms. Often in rococo style, with cabriole legs, carved decoration.

French clocks. Many table clocks produced in 16th century; *hexagonal shape predominant. First pendulum clocks (after 1657) showed Dutch influence, notably of S. *Coster. Subsequently, national style developed in **pendule religieuse*; later model was **tête de poupée*. Design and decoration became increasingly elaborate. Typical Louis XIV form evolved by *c*1680: mantel clock with slightly curved sides; arched top, surmounted by large sculpted figure, other, seated, figures on either side of base, which has ornamental head of Louis XIV at centre. Circular metal dial plate, gilt *repoussé*, with hour numerals inscribed on white enamel plaques. Case decoration in ormolu, or *Boulle work. *Pedestal clock, made e.g. by I. *Thuret, etc. During Régence (1715–23), symmetry was replaced by curved, wavy, asymmetrical decoration; case waisted at sides; gilt bronze figures; made e.g. by J. *LeRoy.

Many Louis XV types. Characteristic form is bronze, rococo mantel clock, with abstract motifs, based on foliage, flowers or shells; introduced by C. *Cressent, J-A. *Meissonier, etc. Also examples with sculpted figures (e.g. by F. *Berthoud), and models with porcelain elements, e.g. clock-face set in bronze tree decorated with porcelain blossoms, or with porcelain figures of animals or birds at base. Other varieties include animal or *elephant clocks; many *cartel clocks; wall-bracket clocks, decorated with horn and **vernis Martin*; **régulateurs* (or tall clocks). Cases generally signed after 1750. Makers include J-B. *Baillon, J. and P. *LeRoy.

Prolific clock making during Louis XVI period. Revival of straight lines, and influence of classical architecture. Many mantel clocks; **pendule cage*, *lyre clock, etc. Also *urn clocks, often of gilt-bronze, with horizontal ring dial, and head of snake – symbolizing eternity – pointing at time; *temple clocks; **pendules d'officier* and other travelling clocks. Musical clocks include *column clocks, others with mechanical organs. Some made in Neuchâtel, decorated in Paris. Co-operation between artists and clock makers always close, especially so under Louis XVI. Considerable use of white marble, for whole or part of case; ornamental porcelain figures manufactured at Sèvres. Development of dial design. Makers include A. *Janvier and P-A. *Caron.

In Revolutionary era, *decimal dial introduced. During Directoire period plain clocks made with neo-classical influence. Under Napoleon I, mantel clocks characterized by marble and bronze cases, with figures; various forms, including Roman chariot. Ancient Greek and Egyptian decorative motifs used. Models supported by four columns, standing on base, with short gridiron pendulum hanging between columns. *Bureau clocks by A-L. *Breguet, etc., who also devised **pendule sympathique*. Regulator clocks, with complicated astronomical work, by A. *Janvier and other makers.

After *c*1830 Gothic style fashionable; also automaton, and *picture-frame clocks. Outside Paris, less sophisticated styles, e.g. *Comtoise clock. Typical national product is *carriage clock. Factory production developed in France during 19th century, accompanied by increased export.

French clock. Pedestal clock. Case veneered on oak with Boulle marquetry; mounted with ormolu figures representing Love Triumphing over Time. Ormolu dial with figures on white enamel plaques in blue; inscribed Thuret, who made movement. Height 4ft4in.

French foot. Splayed *bracket foot; used on case furniture, particularly in late 18th century.

French fork. Silver fork with three or four short curved prongs and curved stem; late form in evolution of fork. Made from late 17th century.

French furniture. *See* François Ier style, Henri II style, Louis XIII style, Louis XIV style, Louis XV style, Louis XVI style, Directoire style, Empire style, Louis Philippe style, Second Empire style.

French glass. Early French **verre de fougère* produced in wooded areas of Lorraine, Normandy, and Poitou from Roman times (*cf*

*French glass. Decanter, c1790; fluted neck and base; faceted lozenge stopper. Engraved with festoons, flowers, and cornucopia; enriched with fired gilding. Height 13in. Tumbler, *Baccarat, c1848; sides cut with flutes and bands of narrow prisms; decorated with enamelled plaque of butterfly; height 3⅝in.*

Waldglas). Between 12th and 16th centuries French glass makers chiefly noted for fine stained glass, and clear *crown and *broad window glass, for home market and export. French window glass makers often settled abroad, particularly in England from 13th century. 13th century Lorraine glass makers used broad glass process for crude mirrors. Plate glass process (invented by Bernard Perrot and developed by L-L. *de Nehou) laid foundation for prestige of 18th century French mirrors. *Nevers famous for small glass figures and toys in 17th and 18th centuries, but France lagged behind rest of Europe in manufacture of fine table glass. Some crystal glass made in Lorraine area, but most fine glass imported from Bohemia, England, and Germany. In 1760, the Académie des Sciences offered prize for improving crystal glass, which resulted in establishment of *Baccarat (1765), *Cristallerie de Saint Louis (1767), and Manufacture Royale des Cristaux de la Reine (1780). English-style cut glass of good quality made, but French glass did not achieve distinction in own right until 19th century, with emphasis on new techniques and original use of colour. **Pâte-de-verre* technique revived for making glass panels, later for moulding bowls and vases; *opaline glass widely produced; and, *c*1830–70, Baccarat, Saint Louis and *Clichy produced fine paperweights and *sulphides. *Latticinio, millefiori,* overlay, and cameo glass used for these and other decorative pieces. Fine cut crystal tableware, plain and coloured, produced throughout 19th century.

…ch gold and silver. Production of plate domestic and ecclesiastical use in France probably greater than elsewhere in Europe, but very little survives. Wars of 14th and 15th centuries seriously depleted medieval plate. In 1689 and 1709, Louis XIV melted down royal and aristocratic silver to pay war expenses. During French Revolution, 18th century silver melted down for economic reasons, and destroyed because of association with monarchy.

Styles created by French silversmiths affected silver production throughout Britain and Europe. Early 16th century silver ornament, Gothic; by 1550, influence of Italian Renaissance mannerist style gaining ground. In late 17th century, baroque style of Louis XIV period superseded Germanic and Netherlandish styles, aided by forced emigration of many *Huguenot silversmiths. *Silver furniture of court and nobility no longer survives, but well documented in inventories, designs, and paintings, as are ceremonial vessels associated with French monarchy, e.g. nef and *cadenas.* Much functional and display table silver made, e.g. flatware, goblets, dishes, casters, *écuelles,* candlesticks, rose-water ewers and basins, wine cisterns and fountains, *pots-à-oille,* etc.; again, few pieces survive. Early 18th century silver enriched with engraved and applied ornament derived from designs of D. *Marot and J. *Berain. Rococo style (inspired e.g. by J-A. *Meissonier) used on silver and silver-gilt dinner services made *c*1730–70 for French and foreign royalty and aristocracy. T. and F-T. *Germain among most important makers of period. Neoclassical domestic silver produced in late 18th and early 19th centuries, followed by Egyptian and Roman motifs associated with Napoleonic Empire style. **Nécessaires de voyage,* used by soldiers on campaign and travelling noblemen made in Empire period, particularly by M-G. *Biennais.

Few existing examples of church plate include medieval portable altars, reliquaries, crosses, chalices, and patens, found in cathedral treasuries. Altar sets in baroque style, consisting of cross, two candlesticks, chalice and paten, ciborium, monstrance, pyx, etc., commonly made in 17th and 18th centuries.

Silversmiths' guild founded in Paris in 13th century. First marks, 1275, guild marks; maker's mark consisted of town symbol (e.g. crowned fleur-de-lis for Paris) and silversmith's device (after 1540, initials). *Date letter introduced in 1461 as further safeguard; made compulsory in 1506. In 1672, *charge mark added; from 1681, *discharge mark also. Revolution caused breakdown in hallmarking system. Guild system abolished in 1791, though allowed to continue until 1797. State took control of assaying of silver and gold and new marks registered: standard marks (varying forms of Gallic cock numbered to indicate standard worked), guarantee marks (on large pieces, two heads, for Paris and departments), and maker's marks.

French lamp. *See* Sinumbra lamp.

French plating. Pure silver foil is heated and applied to base metal article; then burnished down until metals fuse. Process discovered in France *c*1715, used for domestic wares; precursor of Sheffield plate (in Britain, process used to repair blemishes on Sheffield plate wares). A thin coating of silver applied to pre-shaped vessels does not adhere readily, therefore method proved impractical for large-scale production of plated wares, and was not widely used.

French polish. Furniture finish obtained by first rubbing down surface with mixture of plaster of Paris and methylated spirits or Russian tallow, cleaning and scraping surface, then applying repeated coats of oil and dilute varnish. Technique dates from end of 18th century.

French provincial style. Furniture with features specific to past or present provincial regions of France. Often simplified versions of Parisian forms, made of solid, local woods, seldom upholstered (if seat furniture), and with decoration varying from area to area.

Early 17th century Flemish and Dutch furniture imported into France; characteristic turning and carved decoration (e.g. animals, flowers, grotesques, and strapwork) appear in provincial pieces, particularly in Burgundy region (*see* H. Sambin, Henri II style). Geometric carved decoration also popular. *Armoires* and high cupboards popular Louis XIII style provincial pieces, made into 18th century. Louis XIV style had little impact outside Paris and major cities, save in chair design, but following Louis XV style widely adopted: furniture simply made with rococo curves but little or no surface decoration; *commodes* particularly common. Louis XVI style not popular with provincial cabinet-makers, except in Burgundy (elaborately decorated mahogany furniture) and Paris environs (modified neo-classical chairs). Neither Directoire nor Empire style significant in provincial design.

Provincial styles with individual characteristics:

Alsace. Many pieces decorated with marquetry veneer of various coloured woods, and colourful painting; German influence particularly noticeable in low-backed Tyrolean chair (with pierced decoration on chair back, and splayed legs) and in prevalence of Biedermeier style. Also, some Empire-influenced pieces.

Auvergne. Simple furniture, e.g. Louis XIII *armoires*; Louis XV pieces with geometrically ornamented mouldings.

Basque region. Simple, well-made, and well-proportioned furniture, often decorated with all-over low-relief carving (motifs include animals, geometric forms, figures).

Brittany. Much oak furniture often decorated with low-relief carving; large, heavy, and rectilinear, with weighty moulding, and turning.

Burgundy. Furniture tended to reflect current Parisian styles more than other regions, because of close political ties; noted for high-relief carving on architectural pieces. (Bresse provincial furniture similar.)

Champagne. Simple line and decoration characteristic, with very little, if any, carved ornament.

Flanders. 17th century Dutch influence apparent, particularly in use of floral marquetry, although by 18th century, simplified versions of Louis XIV, XV, and XVI pieces also made.

Gascony. Louis XIII *armoires* and cupboards with doors on lower section surmounted by recessed shelves popular; typical are mouldings ornately carved in high-relief, also diamond or star shaped carved geometrical design.

Lorraine. Furniture characterized by simple Louis XV shapes, some with ingenious mouldings; also more ornate pieces in Louis XVI style, sometimes with floral marquetry.

French snuff-boxes. Left: *vernis Martin *snuff-box, Paris, 1761, decorated with gold piqué and painting. Right: blonde tortoiseshell *portrait box with miniature of unknown lady by F. *Dumont, mounted in gold and enamel. Top: oval snuff-box in *four-colour gold, Paris, 1768. Bottom: enamel portrait box, mounted in gold, Paris, 1785.*

Normandy. Furniture reflects affluence of area; well-proportioned graceful pieces with carved decoration and pierced steel locks and hinges; besides oak and other local woods, mahogany and ebony also used.

Poitou. Many Louis XIII case pieces produced, often with richly-carved geometrical decoration, as well as *commodes* and *buffets*; also, simplified Louis XVI forms.

Provençal. Noted for good integration of carved decoration with shape; panelled furniture decorated with various mouldings characterized by use of steel buttress hinges and pierced keyhole covers; Louis XV style adopted.

Saintonge. Furniture noted for good proportion and line; Louis XV shapes popular, particularly for chairs.

Illustrations at reading stand, stool.

French snuff-boxes. Greatest number of boxes are gold, made in 18th century; demand *c*1740 such that certain goldsmiths made only boxes. After 1750 oblong, circular, and oval shapes most common, with miniatures, enamelled floral patterns, or scenes enamelled *en plein*. All-gold boxes ornamented by four-colour gold worked in relief. These techniques used by J. *Ducrollay, J. *George, and P. F. *Drais. *c*1768 engine-turning perfected and engraved boxes covered with translucent enamel made. Range of enamel colours used in 1770s; in 1780s midnight blue and purple dominated. Common engine-turned pattern was horizontally-lined background broken at regular intervals by depressed circles, stars, or rosettes. Silver boxes little in demand in Paris; made in style of gold boxes, often gilded or decorated with four-colour gold. Revolution drastically reduced luxury trades; boxes depicting revolutionary themes made in other materials.

Porcelain boxes made at Saint-Cloud *c*1723–50, small, shell-shaped, or circular, painted with *chinoiseries*. Porcelain high-heeled shoe box made at Chantilly, 1740–50. Mennecy boxes moulded in basket-weave pattern and painted with floral sprays; shapes made: high-heeled shoe (from 1775), commodes, trunks, baskets, etc. Snuff-boxes of Vincennes and Sèvres porcelain rare. **Vernis Martin* boxes popular 1744–64; like porcelain boxes had gold mounts; crimson and dark green backgrounds painted with French pastoral and genre scenes. From *c*1700 tortoiseshell boxes made with *piqué point* or *posé* decoration. J. *Berain designs used. Until Revolution, boxes clearly marked with master, farmer-general, and year marks; precisely identifiable, unlike other European boxes.

French tapestry. France among first European countries to develop high-warp loom tapestry. From 13th century, secular industry developed under royal and noble patronage with centre in *Paris. 14th century peak period. Due to prolonged upheaval of Hundred Years' War, industry shifted to Flemish tapestry centres. 15th century style highly decorative: minutely ornamented *mille-fleurs* tapestries; later, works in Flemish-style. Most tapestries imported from Flanders. French weaving continued on modest scale (possibly by itinerant weavers) under individual noble or clerical patronage; subjects mainly from church or provincial history. With growing stability, wealth and power of France in 16th century, industry revived. By mid 16th century, centres in Paris, *Tours, Troyes, Limoges, Beauvais, Rouen, and *Fontainebleau. During reign of Henri IV, emphasis on luxury production. Religious tolerance helped industry; Flemish weavers encouraged to settle in France; attempts made to compete with great Flemish centres, particularly Brussels; productivity increased with introduction of first low-warp looms. Royal tapestry workshop system began, with Paris main centre; high-loom workshops at the *Hôpital de la Trinité and the *Louvre, and first Parisian low-warp loom workshop started by M. *de Comans and F. *de la Planche at the *Gobelins. Other centres: Amiens, *Aubusson, *Beauvais, *Bellegarde, *Felletin, Lille, Nancy, Reims and Tours. Small manufactories followed designs of Paris workshops, mainly influenced by Flemish models. From 1607, embargo imposed on import of Flemish tapestries. During reign of Louis XIV, under directing force of Colbert (Minister of Fine Arts), French decorative arts unrivalled and styles dictated European tastes. In 1662, all royal workshops in Paris incorporated into state-owned Manufacture Royale des Meubles de la Couronne, or, the *Gobelins, under artistic direction of C. *Lebrun. Soon followed by establishment of royal manufactories of Beauvais and Aubusson. Tapestries important part of developing French court style, serving as wall and door hangings, curtains and pelments, *entre-fenêtres,* and furniture covers. Designs created by artistic élite, with emphasis on 'woven painting' tapestry as decorative element. Subjects in grand historical style include mythological scenes, religious subjects, contemporary history, *'Teniers', and **verdures*. After death of Colbert, temporary decline, financial difficulties. Revival in 18th century, under influence of F. *Boucher and J-B. *Oudry; designs by C-A. *Coypel. Decorative function stressed. Compositions smaller, moving towards exact imitations of paintings. Motifs arranged in small 'pictures', framed by elaborately ornamented, simulated carved gilt frame borders, with curves and rococo ornament. Subjects largely exotic: visions of East and Far East, pastorals, and landscapes. Developing fashion for wall-paper encouraged concentration on smaller furniture covers and tapestry carpets. By late 18th century, woven pictures stale and lifeless. From reign of Louis XVI, allegorical and mythological themes fashionable, closely reproducing paintings (e.g. by J-L. David). Ornament refined and reduced. Revolution temporarily closed manufactories. In 19th century, tapestry had diminishing role in interior decoration. Few large tapestries woven, those mainly modelled on older designs.

French watches. Early development closely followed *German watches: *spherical form *c*1550; oval with domed cover and elongated octagon common in late 16th century. French watch making industry centred at Blois until *c*1650, with emphasis in fine case decoration (*see* Blois enamel). Little further development until *c*1720 when efforts were made to revive industry and stop importation of watches; impetus given in 18th century by work of J. *LeRoy and J-A. *Lépine. Finest examples produced by A-L. *Breguet in Paris from *c*1762. French makers adopted methods of mechanization from Switzerland in early 19th century as in *Japy factory. Widespread interchange of movements and parts between France and Switzerland often makes identification difficult.

Frères Rochat. *See* Rochat, Frères.

fret (in clocks). Pierced metal plate, originally to cover balance wheel in *lantern clock; later, of wood or metal, pierced section in various clock cases to allow sound of striking to escape.

fret (in stringed musical instruments). Division of finger-board to simplify stopping strings; usually gut loops, or wood, metal, etc., ridges.

Friendly Society emblems. 18th and 19th centuries; from west of England; used by Friendly Societies on annual walks.

fret pattern. *See* key pattern.

fretted. In clavichords, refers to one string being used to produce two or more notes. Also, stringed instrument having *frets.

fretwork. Interlocking geometrical designs, cut from thin wood and used ornamentally on furniture, with or without backing. *Illustrations at* bureau bookcase, kettle stand.

Friendly Society emblem or **pole-head.** Cast, pierced, or stamped brass plate, found in great variety of shapes, with socket for attaching to end of wooden pole; carried on parade by members of Friendly Societies (formed as mutual aid associations from early 18th century; in 19th century, over 5000 existed all over England). Each society had own emblem; many depict common interest or indicate name of inn where meetings were held. Most brass examples from west of England or Midlands.

Friesian carving. Wheel-form scratch-carved designs, used on early American Colonial furniture, e.g. Pennsylvania-Dutch pieces.

Friesland clock. *See* Dutch clock.

Friesian teapot. Silver teapot with pear-shaped, broad-bellied body, and small plain foot; may have ebony finial and/or handle. Ornate embossed and chased strap and scroll work ornament against punched background; body often divided into two parts, each ornamented in slightly different manner. Popular in early and mid 18th century in Friesland, where style was developed by G. and J. *van der Lely; copied in Amsterdam and Haarlem.

frieze. In furniture, decorative band at top of piece of case furniture, or below projecting surface of table, desk, etc., often containing drawers. In silver, ornamental band of relief engraving around rim, body or foot of silver object.

Frisard, Jacob (1753–1812). Swiss watch maker who made movements of 'singing-bird' boxes in Geneva; worked for a time in London.

frit. Mixture of raw materials and *cullet, first melted to remove impurities, then ground to powder form ready for reheating in manufacture of glass and soft-paste porcelain.

Fritzsche, Georg (fl 1720–*c*1730). German porcelain *repairer and modeller. Worked at Meissen porcelain factory from *c*1712 under J. F. Böttger; some grotesque dwarf figures and chess pieces ascribed to him. Under J. G. *Herold, probably modelled numerous rather primitive folk figures (Poles, Dutchmen, etc.), animals, and moulded decoration for vases and clock cases.

frog mug. English earthenware mug containing realistically modelled frog which is revealed as liquid is drunk. Most made in 18th and 19th centuries; frequently decorated with copper lustre at *Sunderland.

'Frog' service. Dinner service completed in 1774 by J. *Wedgwood for Catherine the Great. 952 pieces hand-painted in sepia with named English landscapes and buildings. Named after heraldic device of Empress's palace, *La Grenouillère.* Each piece has small green frog transfer-printed in border design. Service preserved in Leningrad.

Fromanteel family. Clockmakers of Dutch extraction, working mainly in England. Ahasuerus (apprenticed 1654, d 1685) introduced pendulum-controlled long-case clocks in London, 1658. Example in British Museum has architectural case and short bob pendulum. Also made bracket clocks. Several other makers of same name recorded in late 17th century. John Fromanteel (member of Clockmakers' Company 1663–80), known to have made long-case and bracket clocks, worked with S. *Coster in Holland, 1657–58. *Illustration at* architectural case.

Froment-Meurice, François-Desiré (1802–55). French goldsmith and jewellery designer. Pioneered Gothic revival in France, also designed jewels in Renaissance, Moorish, Byzantine, etc., styles. Though trained craftsman, employed sculptors to model many of his pieces. Works shown at Great Exhibition in London (1851) influenced English jewellery design. Succeeded by wife and later by son Emile (1837–1913) who continued production of Renaissance-inspired jewellery.

Fromery, Alexander. 18th century enamel box maker from Berlin. Chief producer of enamel wares in Europe before 1750. Mastered technique of raised gilding, sometimes covered with translucent enamel. Made boxes mounted in silver, with gilded or silver relief work on white ground. Output declined after 1770 with growing popularity of hardstone, porcelain, and less expensive English enamel wares. May have initiated C. C. *Hunger and J. G. *Herold from Meissen, some of whose gilding is similar.

frosting (in silver). Creation of textured surface on silver articles by first heating object then dipping it in hot, dilute sulphuric acid. Film of pure silver left on surface. Common silver ornament in 19th century, particularly after 1840.

Frothingham, Benjamin (fl *c*1756–1809). Cabinet maker in Charlestown, Massachusetts. Pieces in modified *Chippendale style. Block fronts on bookcases, desks, and chests.

fruit fork. Small, two-pronged gold or silver fork used in Britain (rarely) and the rest of Europe from Middle Ages for serving and eating fresh and preserved fruit. Late 17th century German examples have wide prongs with knife edges.

Frye, Thomas (1710–62). Dublin-born mezzotint engraver. Took out patents for manufacture of porcelain in 1744 using *unaker and in 1749 using *bone-ash. Manager at *Bow Porcelain Manufactory, London, until 1759.

fuddling cup. Vessel consisting of number of cups joined together, usually by hollow handles, so that to empty one cup, it was necessary to drink contents of all. Examples in English delftware from late 17th century; many made in slip-decorated earthenware in 18th century Staffordshire.

Fueter, Daniel Christian (fl 1753–76). Swiss-born silversmith who registered mark in London before moving to New York. Made domestic

*Fuddling cups. Tin-glazed earthenware, *Lambeth, c1790.*

Daniel Christian Fueter. Teapot made in New York, 1754–69. Pear-shaped form with high-domed lid terminating in acorn knop; mahogany handle. Height 8in.

silver in rococo style. Surviving works include medal (1760) presented to leading North American Indian chiefs loyal to Britain in conquest of French Canada during Seven Years' War; child's gold whistle, with teething coral and bells; bread baskets; salvers; milk jugs; etc. Son Lewis Fueter continued in New York after father returned to Switzerland. Mark: DCF in oval.

Füger, Friedrich Heinrich (1751–1818). German painter. Studied in Leipzig and Vienna; lived in Rome, 1776–83. In 1783 became vice-director of academy in Vienna. Influenced by baroque and English portraiture. Painted miniatures until 1789, when eyesight began to fail.

Fujiwara period (898–1185). Japanese period when contact with China was discontinued: high-quality painting and literature and some excellent lacquer-work produced, but art of ceramics declined noticeably. Often included in *Heian period, 794–1185.

Fulda (Hesse). German faience factory: flourished *c*1741–*c*1758. A. F. *von Löwenfinck used *muffle colours and gold in Chinese style, e.g. on vases and tureens, usually signed. Underglaze painting in blue, with manganese-purple outlines. J. C. *Ripp may have been master potter in 1742. Marks include arms of Fulda, initials of von Löwenfinck (F v L), FD, and FD over BS. Seven Years' War ended production abruptly in 1758.

Hard-paste factory established 1764 with help of arcanist N. *Paul. Many remarkable figures produced in first 10–15 years, notably shepherds, *commedia dell'arte* characters, fashionably bewigged men and women, all simply and delicately modelled, painted in fresh colours. Some may have been modelled by L. *Russinger. Early tableware skilfully decorated in Meissen style, often in iron-red monochrome. Marks: '+' (on figures, 1765–80), and FF (Fürstlich Fuldaisch) in monogram (1765–88), all in underglaze blue.

Fulham carpet manufactory. English knotted-carpet weaving workshop established in Fulham in 1750 by P. *Parisot. With patronage of Duke of Cumberland from 1753, manufactory expanded under direction of two ex-

Fulda. Pair of porcelain figures, c1770.
Right:
Fürstenberg. Porcelain group, probably depicting Charity, with two putti *on elaborate rococo base of* rocaille *and lattice-work; c1755.*

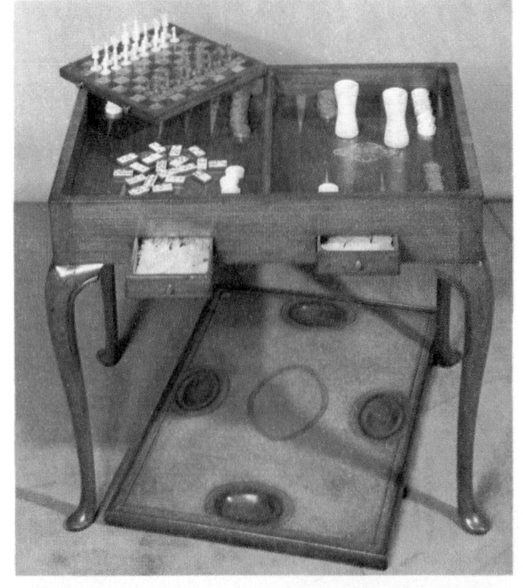

Right:
Garden carpet (detail). Persian, late 18th century. Probably woven in Kurdistan; broad stream running full length down centre interrupted by islands with branches of white blossom on red ground. Sides have flower border medallions.
Games table. Walnut, with cabriole legs and pad feet. Solid top reverses to leather-lined games table with counter wells. Internal well patterned with marquetry for backgammon. Two drawers for counters on one side; on other, side for chess and cribbage. English, c1710. Height 2ft4in.
*Francis Garthorne. Set of three Charles II *casters of lighthouse type with cable banding at bases and at junction of body and lid. Bayonet-fitted covers pierced with cinquefoils and fleur-de-lis; topped with cut-card work and baluster finials. *Trefid mustard spoon. All made 1680–85.*

Savonnerie Huguenot master-weavers, and numerous ex-Savonnerie workers. Fine quality carpets woven, modelled on Savonnerie and Turkish designs. Also tapestries copying Gobelins models. Exorbitant prices charged forced closure of manufactory in 1755.

Fulham carpets. First large Turkish-knotted English carpets, woven 1750–55 in London workshop of P. *Parisot (in Paddington until 1753, then Fulham). By 1753, manufactory employed nearly 100 workers including many ex-Savonnerie Huguenots, under direction of two ex-Savonnerie master-weavers. Carpets with good quality, coarsely-knotted woollen pile, woollen warp, and hemp or flax weft. Savonnerie designs. Exorbitant prices limited market and forced closure of manufactory in 1755, when equipment bought by C. *Passavant.

funerary wares. *See* ming-ch'i.

Fürstenberg (Brunswick). German porcelain factory founded 1747; first successful hard-paste porcelain made after arrival of arcanist, J. *Benckgraff, in 1753. Early tablewares and vases have moulded rococo patterns, which hide imperfections in body. Enamels used after 1768 include dark purple and green, brown, and yellow; painting influenced first by Meissen, later Berlin. S. *Feilner modelled *commedia dell'arte* figures, mythological subjects and, notably, miners (*c*1755). By 1770s, modellers included J. C. *Rombrich, A. C. *Luplau, *Desoches, and P. *Hendler, and pieces lacked originality. L-V. *Gerverot, manager 1795–1814, introduced neo-classical style with use of black basalt, and probably promoted manufacture of blue *jasper ware after Wedgwood. Factory continued to mid 20th century. Marks: F (in blue), since 1755; biscuit busts sometimes bear impressed horse; modern mark sometimes includes A. a. M. (aus alten Modell, 'from an old model').

fused plate. *See* Sheffield plate.

fusee. Spirally grooved cone-shaped pulley in clock or watch train to equalize uneven force of spring as it unwinds; connected to barrel by gut or fine flat chain; often contains small spring to supply *maintaining power. In use before 1485. Earliest recorded signed and dated example by Jacob the Czech of Prague, 1525.

fusee chain. Replaced gut as link between mainspring of clock or watch and *fusee from *c*1600; universal in watches by 1675. Formed from flat metal links fitting in squared grooves on fusee; size of links decreased with growing skill of makers. In clocks, presence of fusee chain often indicates product of superior quality, unless deliberately altered from gut, etc.

Gabri ware. Islamic *sgraffiato* earthenware. Designs, formed when dark clay of body exposed by large areas of pale slip being cut away, include Kufic script, animals, or human figures against background of scrolls. Glaze stained green or brown. Produced from 11th century in Kurdistan; at one time believed associated with Zoroastrian fire-worshippers (Gabri).

gadrooning. Ornamental relief pattern used on furniture, glass, silver, etc., often as border. In form of repeated parallel flutes or lobes, at right angles or slanting from edge of object. In furniture, used on mouldings or turned sections during Italian Renaissance, in England in late 16th, late 17th, and second half of 18th centuries, in America during 18th century, and elsewhere. In metalwork, hammered or cast as border ornament from 16th century on cups, dishes, candlesticks, etc. In glass, formed from small *gather applied to surface of vessel and tooled into shape; a feature of *façon de Venise* glassware. Particularly popular in English glass and in 18th century American blown-moulded glass.

gadroons. Ceramic decoration. Loops or curved shapes filled with small, repeating motifs, e.g. asterisks painted on circular reserves in ground colour, little flowers, or network of lines with tiny circles. Patterns often repeat in threes on flat or curved surfaces, sometimes as background to heraldic device. Found on Hispano-Moresque ware made at Manises in late 15th century; popular in early 16th century. Also, moulded edge similar to gadrooning in silver, e.g. on Worcester tableware *c*1770.

gaffer. Master glass blower; head of team of glass makers or *chair.

Gaines, John (fl 1724–43). American cabinet maker from Ipswich, Massachusetts; worked in Portsmouth, New Hampshire, 1724–43. Style combines characteristics of William and Mary and Queen Anne styles, e.g. chairs featuring straight back and violin-shaped splat.

Galanterien (German, 'trinkets'). Scent bottles, snuff-boxes, sweet dishes, etc., in form of fruits, figures, animals. In porcelain, originated at Meissen, under J. J. *Kändler, and inspired *Chelsea toys. Also *étuis, nécessaires, carnets de bal*, patch-boxes, etc.

gallery. Ornamental railing or parapet around edge of table, shelf, tray, etc.; derived from architecture. Pierced or cast gallery found around foot or stem of *standing cups in Gothic style. On *chamber candlestick, pierced rim around stem to hold glass shade. Pierced gallery frequently found on large late 18th and 19th century trays in silver and Sheffield plate.

gallipot or **galleypot.** In 16th century, English tin-glazed earthenware; word possibly derived from Dutch, referring to pottery brought in galleys from Italy and Spain.

games table. Table equipped for particular game or games. In England, made from 16th century with compartments for dice. By 18th century, made with folding or removable top; design often incorporated several gaming boards, and drawers or compartments for counters, chessmen, etc. Especially popular in 18th century England and France. *cf* card table.

garde du vin. *See* cellaret.

garden carpets. Brilliantly-coloured 16th and 17th century court carpets of wool and silk, made in north-west Persia. Design copies layout of formal garden, symbol of Paradise. Based on 7th century *Spring of Chosroes Carpet.

Gardner, Francis (d 1796). English-born manufacturer of porcelain in Russia; financier in Moscow before establishing *Francis Gardner Porcelain Factory outside city, at Verbilki, in 1766. Succeeded by son, Frantz Frantsevich (d 1799), and grandsons, Frantz and Alexander.

garnet. Family of gemstones made up of crystalline silicate compounds. Name derived from Latin *granatum* ('pomegranate') because of resemblance of crystals to seeds. Most common type used in jewellery is deep red almandine (carbuncle) commonly obtained from Bohemia. Much used in 19th century when *rose cut.

garnish. Set of pewter vessels: 12 platters, 12 bowls or cups, and 12 'saucers' or small plates. Alternatively *sideboard plate in general.

garniture de cheminée. Set of five, sometimes seven, vases for decoration of mantelpiece, made in China for export during late 17th and 18th centuries. Usually consists of three covered baluster-shaped vases and pair of trumpet-shaped beakers. Imitations made in Dutch Delft; also in porcelain at Meissen. Decoration of later examples made at Sèvres lacks Chinese influence.

Garrard & Co. London silver retailers and jewellers. Robert Garrard the Younger (1793–1881) took control of firm (with his younger brother) on death of R. *Garrard in 1818. Succeeded *Rundell, Bridge & Rundell as goldsmiths to Queen Victoria in *c*1840. Royal commissions included race prizes, christening cups, and centrepieces designed by Prince Consort. Also patronized by Russian imperial family, including Czar. With *Hunt & Roskell, chief suppliers of presentation silver (race cups and trophies, centrepieces, etc.). In 1833, E. *Cotterill joined firm as head of design section. Chief source of income, elaborate plate (dinner services, tea services, etc.). *See* E. and J. Wakelin.

Garrard, Robert the Elder (d 1818). English silver retailer working in London; apprenticed to hardwareman. In 1792 went into partnership with silversmith E. *Wakelin; in 1802, on Wakelin's death, gained complete control of firm. Sons inherited business, *Garrard & Co., on his death.

Garrett, Thomas (1785–1865). Staffordshire potter. Principal traveller for J. *Spode II. Partner in firm with W. T. *Copeland (1833–47), trading as Copeland & Garrett.

Garthorne, Francis (fl late 17th to early 18th centuries). English silversmith working in London; received freedom from Girdlers' Company before 1694 (earliest extant records). G. *Garthorne apprenticed to an F. Garthorne in 1669, but probably not same man (possibly father). Worked in Huguenot style. Executed commissions for William III and Queen Anne. Mark: G enclosing A in a shaped shield.

Garthorne, George (fl late 17th–early 18th centuries). English silversmith working in London; apprenticed to Thomas Payne and F. *Garthorne (presumably a relation) in 1669; obtained freedom in 1680. Work influenced by Huguenot silversmiths. Filled commissions for William III and Queen Anne, also aristocracy. Work ranges from casters and cruet frames to chandeliers. Marks: (probably) GG above a pellet, and Britannia mark (registered in 1697); GA crowned with a crescent below, in a shield.

Gate-leg table. Charles II. Walnut and ash; bobbin-turned legs and stretchers. Height 3ft3in.

gate-leg table. Table with one or two hinged leaves; gate-shaped frame swings out under raised leaf to make extra leg. Single gate-leg table called tuckaway table in America. Dates from end of 16th century. *cf* swing-leg table.

Gates, William (fl *c*1777–83). Cabinet maker to George III 1777–83; worked in London. Noted for pieces decorated with marquetry. Partner of B. *Goodison the Younger in 1783.

gather. Blob of unformed, molten glass taken from melting pot on end of blow-pipe.

Gaudreau or **Gaudreaux,** Antoine Robert (*c*1680–1751). French, *ébéniste* to Louis XV from 1726. Received commissions from the court and Mme de Pompadour. Collaborated with the two elder *Slodtz brothers on medal cabinet for Louis XV. No stamp; stamping regulations not yet introduced.

gaudy Dutch. American term for white earthenware plates and teaware made in Staffordshire for American, particularly Pennsylvania German, market, *c*1810–*c*1830. Brightly coloured decoration usually in blue, yellow, green, and red.

Gaudy Dutch. Plate, exported from Staffordshire to America, early 19th century.

gaudy Welsh. American term for translucent teaware made in Swansea area for American market, *c*1830–*c*1845. Decorated with flower patterns, often picked out with copper lustre or gilding.

Gauron, Nicolas-François (b 1736). French modeller and faience maker. By 1750, apprenticed to uncle, silversmith and watch maker in London. Employed as modeller at Mennecy from 1753; work includes signed, dated figure of River God (1754) in white glazed porcelain, mounted on clock. Worked at Tournai (1758–64); credited with *pietà* (repeated at Chelsea) and allegorical group with Bishop of Liège (1764). Later modelled figures made in hard-paste porcelain in Holland, at Weesp and Oude Loosdrecht. Worked at Brussels in 1766. Made faience at Liège; factory sold *c*1770. Modelled figures at Chelsea in 1773.

Gechter, Jean-François-Théodore (1796–1844). French romantic sculptor; exhibited at Salon 1827–44. Known for works such as The Battle of Aboukir (low-relief for Arc de Triomphe), and The Rhine and the Rhone (Place de la Concorde), both in Paris. Earliest of *Les *Animaliers*; his small bronzes, produced in limited quantities, are very rare.

Gemini, Thomas (d 1562). Flemish scientific instrument-maker, emigrated to England and set up workshop for producing instruments and maps. Introduced art of engraving on copper to England. Noted for type of *astrolabe.

Gemma Frisius (1508–54). Flemish astronomer and instrument-maker. Influential in early development of scientific instruments for surveying, etc.; introduced circumferentor: graduated disc for measuring angles, with compass in centre. Products of workshop inglude fine *armillary spheres and *globes.

Gendje carpets. South Caucasian carpets woven by Armenians in Gendje from 18th century. Structure and design similar to *Kazak carpets, but edges often bound in two or more colours, patterns smaller and more varied, colours paler. Fields usually divided into diagonal bands of botehs and/or flowers. Borders use star or calyx-and-leaf motifs.

Geneva enamel. Enamel painting based on technique developed in *Blois; centred in Geneva from *c*1700. Used for decoration of watches; painters include *Huaud brothers.

Gengenbach, Joseph. *See* Canabas.

Genoa (Liguria), Italy. Maiolica manufacture recorded in mid 16th century by C. *Piccolpasso. Tile panels with religious subjects thought to have been made in 1530s, but later ware indistinguishable from *Savona and *Albisola products. In 17th century, maiolica painted with Chinese motifs in blue. Manufacture continued until late 18th century.

Gentile family. Italian maiolica potters at Castelli from late 17th century. Bernardino painted panel of crucifixion dated 1670, also landscapes and mythological subjects with horses. Son, Carmine (*c*1678–1763), said to be pupil of C. A. *Grue. Grandsons, Giacomo (1717–65) and Bernardino II (1727–1813), also painted in style of Grue.

*Georgian style. Bureau bookcase. English, mid Georgian. Mahogany. Upper part of architectural design with broken pediment; rococo cartouche; frieze of blind *fretwork. Pierced brass handles and lock plates, ogee feet. Height 8ft8in.*

George, Jean (d 1765). French box maker characterized by extreme inventiveness. Made boxes in *fantasy shapes, e.g. hip-bath. Used Sèvres porcelain plaques, four-colour gold in relief designs, or miniatures. Signed initials J.G. and mullet.

Georgian style. Term broadly describing furniture, etc., made in Britain and America from beginning of reign of George I (1714) to end of reign of George IV (1830). *See* Chippendale style, Adam style, Hepplewhite style, Sheraton style, Regency style.

Gera (Thuringia). Small German porcelain factory founded 1779; in 1780, run by two members of *Greiner family and operated in conjunction with *Volkstedt factory until 1782. Products mainly copies of functional Meissen wares, include some decorative presentation sets, with views of town, etc. Marks: G, or Gera; either sometimes occurs with Meissen crossed swords.

gerbe. *See décor coréen.*

Germain, François-Thomas (1726–91). French silversmith working in Paris; in 1748 succeeded father, T. *Germain, as royal goldsmith and sculptor. Domestic and church commissions for European royalty. Employed 60–80 workmen; probably designed, and directed workshop. More of his work than of father's survives; little difference in style (rococo) and quality. Declared bankrupt (1765) and dismissed from royal post; died in obscurity. Mark: a fleur-de-lis crowned, two pellets, FTG, and a fleece.

Germain, Nicolas (d 1787). Faience maker at *Holitsch, Hungary, from 1746; by 1773, described as master potter.

Germain, Pierre II, Le Romain (1716–83). French silversmith working in Paris; from 1736 pupil of N. *Besnier; master in 1744. Had workshop in Louvre galleries from 1748–50. In 1748, published book of rococo silver designs, *Eléments d'Orfèvrerie*; designs less elaborate than those of J-A. *Meissonier. No relation to T. and F-T. *Germain. Little work survives. Collaborated on several royal toilet services. Mark: PG and fleur-de-lis crowned, two pellets, PG, and a seed.

Germain, Thomas (1673–1748). French silversmith working in Paris; master in 1720; father also in trade (goldsmith to Louis XIV). Studied in Rome from *c*1687; returned to France *c*1706. Early commissions mainly for ecclesiastical silver (monstrances, crucifixes, candlesticks). With C. *Ballin II and N. *Besnier, appointed court goldsmith to Louis XV (1723). For coronation, made large monstrance for king to present to Reims Cathedral (destroyed 1790). His workshop made domestic silver in rococo style for European royalty. Son, F-T. *Germain, continued in trade. Marks: (1720) a fleur-de-lis crowned, two pellets, TG, and a fleece; (1733) new mark without fleece.

German ceramics. *Cologne, and *Rhineland in general, early centres for production of pottery, often fired to hardness of stoneware. Salt-glazed stoneware made from mid 16th century at Cologne, *Raeren, *Siegburg and *Westerwald; enamelled decoration developed at *Kreussen in 17th century. **Hafnerware*, made from 15th century, include tiles and domestic utensils, often with coloured glazes, especially green. Tin-glazed panels used in large earthenware stoves in 16th century; *owl jugs made from *c*1540.

Faience industry developed in late 17th century, in competition with blue-and-white porcelain imported from China, e.g. at *Berlin, *Brunswick, *Frankfurt, and *Hanau. Undecorated faience bought from factories and painted by **Hausmaler*, mainly in Nuremberg (e.g. J. *Schaper); also at Augsburg (e.g. B. *Seuter). Baroque style decoration in high-temperature colours used at factories in Nuremberg, *Bayreuth, *Abtsbessingen, and at *Dorotheenthal, near Anstadt; also at *Ansbach, which also produced copies of Chinese painting. By mid 18th century, influence of porcelain generally felt; enamel painting used e.g. at *Fulda, *Höchst, and *Künersberg; full enamel palette introduced by German painters under P-A. *Hannong in *Strasbourg (1750). From late 18th century, cream-coloured earthenware made by many factories, some of which, like *Kiel and *Rendsburg, were already producers of faience. Rare examples of manufacture of soft-paste porcelain include that in early years of *Volkstedt factory.

Existence in Germany of many independent and competitive princedoms provided suitable environment for development of arts. Many aristocrats, notably *Augustus the Strong, Elector of Saxony, attracted, in late 17th and early 18th century, to imported oriental or *Batavian porcelain, and keen to produce hard-paste porcelain themselves. Relative peace prevailed between states until 1756, and craft tradition already established in towns. After discovery of *red stoneware and hard-paste porcelain by J. F. *Böttger and W. *von Tschirnhaus in 1708–09, careful security precautions surrounded production in *Meissen factory; isolated breach of ten-year monopoly was establishment of *Vienna porcelain factory in 1719, with help of Meissen workmen. However, secret held from potential German competitors, who continued to make and decorate faience, until set-backs of Seven Years' War (1756–63). Meissen factory consistently marked products from 1723. *Hausmaler* worked on porcelain, notably at Augsburg, and possibly in Dresden itself; undecorated stock from Meissen painted outside factory. Some factory painters appear also to have worked outside. By 1758, eight princedoms had set up own factories, *Höchst, that of W. K. *Wegely at Berlin, *Fürstenberg, *Nymphenburg, *Frankenthal, *Ludwigsburg, and *Ansbach. Another 12 minor factories established in addition to royal factory of Frederick the Great at Berlin; *Gotha and *Kloster-Veilsdorf noted for high quality of manufacture. Mobility of *arcanists, modellers, painters, etc., sometimes makes attribution difficult.

German clocks. During Middle Ages, German makers followed pattern of iron, weight-driven turret, and Gothic chamber clocks, but by early 16th century developed distinctive style of spring-driven clock. Industry was based first in Augsburg and Nuremberg, but latter turned mainly to production of *German watches. Early examples may have dials conforming to local systems of time measurement, e.g. with sections adjustable for differing lengths of night and day. Augsburg noted for *drum and other forms of table clocks, with steel movement and brass-gilt case, then, e.g. *animal, *crucifix, and *nef clocks; also elaborate forms with astronomical dials and automata. From *c*1570, standard domestic clock was of *tabernacle type, continuing to mid 17th century. Thirty Years' War (1618–48) brought decline in German industry and lead was taken over by French and English makers. Importance regained by 1700, particularly in production of spring-driven table clocks; large numbers of popular domestic clocks produced from *c*1820, especially in Black Forest.

German flowers. *See deutsche Blumen.*

German fork. *See* carving fork.

German and Bohemian glass. Early German **Waldglas* produced in forest regions from Middle Ages. From 15th century, wooded areas of Bohemia, Silesia, and Hesse, as well as Saxony and Thuringia, supported glasshouses producing typically German forms, e.g. **Igel*, **Kuttrolf* and **Maigelein*, and in 17th century, **Krautstrunk* and **Römer*. Popularity of *Waldglas* largely undermined in 16th century by influence of Venetian glass, of which large quantities imported; also Venetian glass workers employed in some forest glasshouses, e.g. at Hall-in-the-Tyrol (Austria), Nuremberg, and Cassel. With revival of glass engraving technique in 17th century (initiated by C. *Lehmann) and development of *soda-lime glass (*c*1680), engraved decoration reached peak of popularity. Notable exponents: *Schwanhardt family, F. *Gondelach, and M. *Winter; all used diamond-point and wheel engraving techniques (e.g. **Hochschnitt* and **Tiefschnitt*). Glass engraving centres in late 17th and early 18th centuries included Petersdorf, Berlin, *Potsdam, and Dresden. In 1670s, J. *Kunckel, experimenting with coloured glass, used gold chloride to produce outstanding ruby-red. In 18th century, **Zwischengoldglas* technique popular; inspired tumblers of J. J. *Mildner. Enamel decoration in opaque colours reached peak in 16th and 17th centuries, e.g. on **Humpen*, **Halloren* glasses, **Stangengläser*, and **Passgläser*. **Schwarzlot painting*, as seen in work of J. *Schaper and I. *Preissler, also popular, particularly in 17th century Nuremberg. Painting in coloured transparent enamels began with work of G. S. and S. *Mohn of Dresden in early 19th century; technique further developed by A. *Kothgasser. Also in first half of 19th century, with *Biedermeier style predominant, significant advances made in coloured glass, e.g. discovery of *lithyalin and *hyalith glass, and colours *Annagrün* and *Annagelb* by J. *Riedel. Coloured decoration also achieved by use of flashed colour (*see* *cameo glass), with contrasting colour beneath revealed by cutting. Engraved portraits in glass (e.g. by D. *Bimann) fashionable by mid 19th century.

German and Bohemian glass. Red flash body, engraved with the Crystal Palace; inscribed 'Interior view of the building in Hyde Park'. Bohemian, 1851.

German gold and silver. Little secular silver from Middle Ages survives. Chief centres of European plate production in 16th century, German cities of Nuremberg and Augsburg; most important wares, numerous drinking vessels in varying styles and sizes. Many silver examples, fewer gold, survive. Cups popular gift among princes, guilds, nobility, etc. Earliest type, drinking horn, with gold or silver mounts. *Double cup, predominantly German vessel, made from late 15th century. In 16th and 17th centuries, inventiveness of German standing cups supreme in Europe. Outstanding maker, W. *Jamnitzer. Types include **Riesenpokal*, *columbine cup, *globe cup, *nautilus cup, *ostrich-egg cup, *coconut cup, **Jungfrauenbecher*, cups in animal shapes, etc. Ornament influenced by Italian mannerist style. Beakers and tankards also popular drinking vessels. Former made from 16th to 18th centuries; early examples on animal or human figure feet. *Nesting beakers also popular. Tankard development parallel to that of English tankard, although crystal or glass tankard in filigree frame predominantly 16th century German form. Lid often set with coin in 17th and 18th centuries (*see* coin tankard). *Tazze* also made.

Early 17th century domestic silver influenced by *Dutch grotesque style; from late 17th century, French influence dominant, although some northern German centres influenced by English and Scandinavian silver styles in 18th century. Table silver produced in large quantities in 18th century Augsburg, Berlin, Hamburg, Munich, and Nuremberg. Establishment of *Meissen porcelain factory in 1710 resulted in decline of prestige of German silver in 18th century; wars also affected production (e.g. Seven Years' War, 1756–63). French rococo style popular *c*1740–80, but more crudely applied in Germany and over-elaborate. Neo-classical forms uncommon.

Much church plate from late Middle Ages to 17th century survives in Rhineland churches. Often shows Italian influence. Cologne, important religious centre, one of chief centres of production.

Until rise of Prussia in late 19th century, Germany was conglomeration of small states within Holy Roman Empire. Each state had own hallmarking system based on stamps of principal towns. Standards varied from state to state, depending on ruler or local guild. Austria and France periodically conquered parts of German territory and imposed own systems (system of hallmarking for whole country established 1884).

German silver. Tankard by Daniel Mylius, made in Danzig, c1700. Silver-gilt, decorated with *repoussé *work scenes.*

*German snuff-boxes. Top left: gold box set with multi-coloured agates by *Johann Christian Neuber, Dresden, c1780. Top right: double-ended rock-crystal box in barrel form, gold mounted, 1780. Bottom left: rock-crystal box in form of shoe carved with grotesque head, gold mounted, 1780. Bottom right: *Meissen circular box, gold mounted, c1755.*

German half-post. Technique for making bottles and flasks using two gathers (or posts) of glass; particularly associated with early American flasks, e.g. *Pitkin flask. Method introduced to America by European glass blowers in early 18th century. First gather re-dipped in *metal and half covered before being blown into part-sized mould.

German silver. *See* argentine.

German snuff-boxes. Predominantly in hardstone or porcelain and rarely signed. Boxes carved from local stones of *quartz family, *lapis lazuli, etc., with silver or gold mounts, made in quantity after 1720. Boxes *c*1730–45 circular, shell, or basket-shaped with mythological or oriental scenes in ivory or mother-of-pearl appliqué on lids. Hardstone lids decorated in relief common in Berlin until 1760. *c*1775–1800 **Zellenmosaïk* boxes made in Dresden by H. *Taddel and his pupil J. C. *Neuber. Gold boxes made from *c*1750 based on French models.

Snuff-boxes in Meissen porcelain with gold or silver mounts made 1735–65. Based on gold, silver, and hardstone models but with higher sides to accommodate painted decoration. Painted scenes enclosed in medallions on solid-coloured grounds. *Chinoiseries*, landscapes, and shipping scenes executed by Meissen painters J. G. *Heintze and C. F. *Herold. *Fantasy boxes made in barrel, basket, and animal shapes after 1755. Meissen supremacy challenged from 1767 by Kelsterbach, Ludwigsburg, Nymphenburg, and Berlin. Many boxes painted by *Hausmaler*. Production of enamel boxes centred at *Fromery factory in Berlin. Enamel blanks made cheaply and sent out to be painted by *Hausmaler* who also probably worked on porcelain. By 1770 production of porcelain boxes outstripped that of enamel ones.

German tapestry. Germany among first European countries to develop tapestry-weaving. Medieval tapestry hangings of monumental size commissioned by local churches and feudal princes and executed in small monastery or convent workshops. Subjects allegorical or biblical. In 14th century, with decreasing demand for large hangings, workshops concentrated on production of small panels, altar frontals, and dossals, pew covers and cushions, etc. Subjects almost exclusively religious, with Gothic design and style strongly influenced by book illumination. From 15th century, use in homes increased; secular themes included rustic tapestries, scenes of everyday life, fables, and popular allegories with doll-like figures of warriors, fabulous creatures, and scrolling vegetation. Central scenes sometimes enclosed in cartouche with proverbial text. From late 16th century, influx of Protestant master-weavers from Spanish Netherlands, brought new techniques and more sophisticated styles. Prolific period in 17th and 18th centuries, with small workshops flourishing briefly in most principalities. Lacked continuing patronage of powerful monarchy, so industry did not develop as elsewhere.

German watches. Left: single case verge watch made by Martin Gerdts in Hamburg, c1675, with gilt-metal dial around which is silvered date ring; single hour hand; finely enamelled case (shown) with Biblical scenes; diameter 1¾in. Centre: **clock watch, c1575–1600 with maker's mark, C. P.; mainly steel movement between circular brass plates; silver dial with* champlevé *enamel decoration; single brass hour hand; pierced and engraved metal single case; diameter 4⅜in. right: form watch by Johann Sigmund of Nuremberg, 17th century.*

Ghiordes. Prayer rug, c1720, Turkish. Size 5ft×4ft1in.

In 17th century, manufactories mainly copied popular Flemish works. Most important centre, *Munich. From late 17th century, dominating influence was French, with numerous workshops established or directed by Huguenot refugees. Copies of *Beauvais tapestries especially popular, particularly grotesques from designs of J. *Berrain, *chinoiseries*, and burlesques. Most important 18th century manufactories in Munich and *Berlin. Small workshops also continued production of furniture covers and minor hangings following earlier folk tradition.

German watches. Developed from portable *table clocks, probably by P. *Henlein of Nuremberg, first known watch maker. Earliest form is *spherical watch, followed in late 16th century by drum shape, then octagon and other forms; movement at first of iron with *foliot balance and verge *escapement, *stackfreed, and often striking work with case pierced to emit sound of bell; brass introduced for plates and wheels from *c*1580. Dial has Roman numerals I–XII, sometimes with Arabic 13–24 below to conform with 24-hour 'Italian' system then used in central Europe, and knobs for feeling time in the dark. German watch making declined because of Thirty Years' War (1618–48); partially recovered in late 18th century, notably in work of Philipp Han (1730–90), maker of many fine examples, usually with *calendar and *repeating mechanisms.

Gerrits, Jarich (fl 1628–67). Dutch silversmith working in Leeuwarden, Friesland; master in 1628; assayer several times. Works include domestic and church pieces: dishes, *tazze*, chalices, etc., with chased and embossed ornament. Adopted name Lely, or van der Lely *c*1651; mark: a lily. Family continued in trade. *See* G. and J. *van der Lely.

Gerverot, Louis-Victor (1747–1829). French potter, painter, and arcanist. Porcelain painter at Sèvres (1764–65) and Niderviller; worked at many German faience factories, including Fulda, Ludwigsburg, Ansbach, Höchst, and Schrezheim (1773–75). Arcanist at Oude Loosdrecht soon after factory's transfer from Weesp. In 1786, visited English factories of J. *Wedgwood, and J. *Turner; started manufacture of cream-coloured earthenware in Cologne (1788–92). Director at Fürstenberg, 1795–1814.

gesso. Plaster-like compound of size and whiting, used as ground for gilding, painting, and incised work, applied to carved surfaces before gilding.

Geubels, Franz or François (fl 1540–90). Prominent tapestry master-weaver in Brussels. Subjects include The Seven Virtues, The Months, and Triumphs of the Gods. After death, manufactory continued by widow, Catherine van Ende Geubels, and brother, Jacques, until 1629.

Geyger, Johann Casper (d 1780). German master potter and porcelain modeller. Founder of *Würzburg porcelain factory (1775). Group of porcelain figures (*c*1775) on uniform white pedestals sometimes attributed to him.

Gesso. Moulded and gilded to form top of Queen Anne table.

Ghiordes carpets. Highly-prized, smooth-textured west Anatolian prayer rugs with very short, finely Turkish-knotted pile, woven in Ghiordes from early 17th century. Widely exported, strongly influencing carpet design and structure elsewhere. Stylized floral and leaf motifs; recognizable flowers, especially carnations, lining narrow mihrab field and on broad spandrels, panels (above and/or below mihrab), and wide borders. Grounds red, deep blue, natural, or green with red, yellow, blue, and pale green dominating pattern. 17th century design: mihrab usually light-coloured with hanging lamp and two pillars supporting curved arch; spandrels with scroll motif; ornamented panel above or below mihrab. Broad main border with floral motif on light ground. Design from 18th century: short mihrab, often with stylized flowers at bottom; unsupported, steeply angled arch; dissimilar panels, above and below mihrab, ornamented with angular flowers and leaves or with stylized cloud-band scroll. Main border: detached flowers, particularly gigantic carnations; stylized floral scrolls; or sub-divided into narrow stripes with tiny detached blossoms and buds. Also, *graveyard carpets, double-ended prayer rugs similar to Kulas, kis-Ghiordes carpets, and all-over pattern carpets.

Ghiordes knot. *See* Turkish knot.

Giardini, Giovanni (1646–1721). Italian silversmith working in Rome; from 1665, in workshop supplying plate for Vatican and Cardinal Barberini; master in 1675; in partnership with Marco Ciucci from 1676–80. In 1686, elected Fourth Consul of Corporation of Goldsmiths and Silversmiths; chamberlain of organization in 1692, 1703, 1716. In 1689, commissioned to make silver mask for Queen Christina's lying-in-state. Most work destroyed during Napoleonic wars; surviving pieces include large dish, reliquary, papal mace, crucifixes, candlesticks, etc. Book of engraved designs for silver published in 1714. Worked with gold, silver, base metals, hardstones, etc.

Gibbons, Grinling (1648–1721). Master carver to Charles II; received commissions from George I. Carving in high relief, mainly in lime or pear wood; common motifs include *amorini*, swags and wreaths of fruit and flowers, musical instruments, birds, etc. Worked for Christopher Wren on churches, country houses, and palaces.

Gibbon Salt. Ornate silver ceremonial *standing salt presented to Goldsmiths' Company in 1632 by Samuel Gibbon. In form of temple with four Ionic columns surrounding a crystal column; encloses figure of Neptune above which rests salt-bowl. Bears London hallmark for 1576. Earliest known British standing salt of architectural design.

gilding. Ornamental gold coating on glass, ceramics, metals, furniture, etc., used from antiquity to cover whole articles, or in conjunction with other forms of decoration, e.g. painting, enamelling. Methods of application include:

Cold gilding or water gilding; gold leaf applied with size or on gesso surface; produces impermanent surface liable to wear. (*Illustration at* astronomical clock.)

Lacquer gilding: ground gold leaf, mixed with lacquer and painted on surface; result also impermanent.

Oil gilding: gold leaf fixed with mixture of linseed oil, gum arabic, and mastic; drying may be accelerated by gentle heating in oven; result more durable, but produces matt surface.

Fire gilding: powdered gold and mercury painted on surface and fired to evaporate mercury; commonly used on metals; largely superseded, especially on silver, by *electrogilding. Mercury gilding applied to ceramics and glass, *c*1785.

Honey gilding: gold leaf, ground with honey or other flux, painted on ceramics or glass and fired at low temperature. Produces surface hard enough to be tooled or chased.

Amber gilding: on ceramics from early 1760s, gold leaf fixed with varnish prepared from crushed amber and fired at low temperature.

Liquid gold: method used on Meissen porcelain by 1830, and in England from *c*1855, based on power of oils containing sulphur to dissolve gold. Achieves thin film of metal resembling lustre painting; also used on glass.

Giles, James (1718–after 1780). English glass and porcelain painter. Established independent enamelling workshop at Kentish Town, London; by 1760, advertizing Worcester porcelain painted in any pattern. From 1771, decorated porcelain made at Bow, Worcester, and Frankenthal for sale at Cockspur Street, Westminster. In 1777, received financial help from W. *Duesbury, who finally took over premises and stock. Decoration include painting of birds on porcelain made at Plymouth, Worcester, and Longton Hall; also cut fruit and probably landscapes painted in green and black on Chinese and Worcester porcelain. May have employed J. H. *O'Neale. *Illustrations at* flute, scale pattern.

gilim or **ghilim carpets.** *See* kelim carpets.

Gillingham, James (fl *c*1760–75). Cabinet maker in Philadelphia, Pennsylvania. Worked in *Philadelphia Chippendale style.

Gillow's. English furniture making firm, active in 18th and 19th centuries. Founded by Robert Gillow (1703–73), and headed by members of family until 1830. Furniture, noted for quality of workmanship, made in Lancaster and sold in London, where branch opened in 1761. Stamp: Gillow's, Lancaster.

gilt-bronze. *See* ormolu.

gilt buttons. Brass buttons washed with gold; made in Birmingham, England, from 1790. *See gilding.*

gimmel flask. Dual glass flask made by fusing two individually blown bottles, with spouts in opposite directions. Used for oil and vinegar. Made from 17th century.

ginger jar or **hawthorn ginger jar.** Chinese ceramics; covered porcelain jar with wide mouth and ovoid body, slightly elongated towards base. Often decorated with Prunus blossom. Associated with hawthorn through confusion with Prunus blossom in decoration of examples from Ming and Ch'ing dynasties. Thought to have been filled with sweetmeats, ginger, etc., as gift for Chinese New Year, and returned when empty. Term ginger jar also applied to large silver or silver-gilt display vessel based on Chinese porcelain model; piece of 17th century *sideboard plate, 13–15in. high; chased with foliage, fruit, masks, or *chinoiseries*. Cover with foliage finial and decorated with swags. Generally in pairs; sometimes on stand. Rare after 1700.

Giovanni Maria. *See* Zoan Maria.

girandole. Form of earring, pendant, brooch, etc., resembling chandelier. Pearl or gem drops (usually three) suspended from symmetrical horizontal spray or bow attached to single stone or cluster.

girandole (in furniture). Ornate candle *sconce; asymmetrical and often heavily carved and gilded; may have mirror back-plate. In England from late 17th century.

girandole clock. American wall clock, resembling *banjo clock in shape, but with circular base. Designed by L. *Curtis, *c*1818.

girl-in-a-swing family. Class of soft-paste porcelain figures and groups, also scent bottles and some tableware, made *c*1750, possibly by Chelsea workmen. At one time thought to be experimental products of Chelsea factory. Porcelain body sometimes with greyish or greenish tint resembles that of *Chelsea triangle period. Slip-cast models include Girl in a Swing, Hound, Hercules and Omphale, and Britannia Mourning the Death of Frederick, Prince of Wales (1751). Usually left in white; decoration, when used, mainly sprigs of flowers on dress and base. *Illustration at* sweetmeat box.

Left:
Girandole earrings. Late 18th century English. Rose-cut diamonds in silver setting.
*Girandole clock. American, by L. *Curtis, early 19th century. Gilt-wood with painted decoration. Thermometer in neck of clock. Height 3ft3in.*

Giuliano, Carlo (d *c*1912). Italian goldsmith and jeweller working in London. Probably sponsored by London jeweller, Robert Phillips; opened business in Piccadilly in late 1860s. Produced work in Renaissance, classical, and 'archaeological' (Etruscan etc.) styles. Noted for enamelling technique; used polished, not faceted, gems consistent with period of his designs. Usually signed work with initials C & AG. Sons, Federico and Fernando took over father's business in 1890s. *Illustration at* jewellery.

Glasgow delft. Tin-glazed earthenware made from 1748 at *Delftfield Pottery. Decoration in blue monochrome, or full range of high-temperature colours with preponderance of yellow; often speckled black background. Much exported to America.

glass. Product of fusing silica with carbonates of sodium (soda) or potassium (potash) and sometimes calcium (lime). This cools to a rigid state without crystallizing; can be classified as a supercooled liquid. Usually transparent, but may be opacified, e.g. with bone ash or lead oxide (*opaque-white glass); *coloured glass results either from impurities in *metal or from addition of metal oxides. Glass becomes plastic when heated and can be manipulated by blowing, moulding, drawing, trailing, etc. Unlike ceramics, can be melted and remodelled repeatedly. Made from ancient times; European forms of glass dating from Middle Ages include **Waldglas* and **verre de fougère,* both using plant ash as source of alkali (basically potash); **barilla* was used e.g. in 16th century Venice as source of soda and lime. Use of lead oxide (red lead) as component of glass introduced by G. *Ravenscroft in 1675 in *lead glass. From 19th century, forms of glass with other components made.

*Glass. Egyptian. Left: *amphora of opaque glass decorated with bands of yellow and turquoise, 4th–3rd century* B.C.*; height* $2\frac{3}{4}$*in. Right: palm bowl decorated with wheel cutting on inside, 3rd–1st century* B.C. *Height* $3\frac{1}{2}$*in.*

Glass. Roman. Left: cinerary urn, 1st to 2nd century; height $8\frac{1}{2}$*in. Centre: three pieces of burial glassware, 1st to 4th century. Right: jug, 1st to 2nd century; height* 10*in.*

glass blowing. Process invented in Syria in 1st century A.D., developed by Roman glass makers between 1st and 3rd centuries; technique has remained basically unchanged. *Gather of molten glass collected at end of the blow-pipe by footmaker (first member of *chair), who forms metal into hollow, pear-shaped bulb or *paraison, by blowing through pipe and using *marver, checking size with calipers. In manufacture of stemmed drinking glasses and vases, servitor (second member of chair) adds small blobs of metal which can be drawn out to form stem and shaped to form foot or base. *Pontil then attached to foot; blow-pipe detached from mouth of vessel by tapping along line made by moistened metal tool, e.g. file. Rough rim trimmed with shears, then smoothed by reheating. *Gaffer completes formation of vessel by rotating pontil on long arms of his chair, adjusting diameter and edge with tongs. These can also be used to make trails of glass for decoration, e.g. 17th century *nipt diamond waies. Trails of clear or coloured glass may added e.g. to make *mereses, and small blobs to form *prunts. Plasticity of glass during shaping is maintained by frequent reheating in small furnace (glory-hole). On completion, pontil is broken off, leaving mark which, since *c*1780, has been polished smooth. Vessel is then put in *annealing oven.

glass-bottomed tankard. *See* tankard.

glass cutting. Method of glass decoration: design sketched with water-resistant paint; glass then held against revolving iron wheel fed by sand and water for rough cutting. Pattern completed and smoothed by sandstone or copper wheels of varying sizes fed with water. Resulting dull surface polished by wooden wheel fed with fine abrasive; finally, brushed with putty powder (tin oxide) to produce distinctive lustre.

Glass Excise Acts. Levy initially imposed 1745–46 by English Parliament on materials used for making flint-glass, to raise money for French wars. Tax rigidly enforced; increased in 1777 and 1787. Had important effect on development of English glass, because economical use of flint-glass dictated style and decoration. Heavy, traditional forms abandoned in favour of smaller, lighter, thinly blown vessels (particularly noticeable in drinking glasses). Shallow cutting, rococo enamelling, and engraving popular (e.g. work of W. *Beilby, M. *Edkins), handles often dispensed with (e.g. jelly glasses). Bottle glass used more for domestic ware, often mottled to increase attractiveness (*see* Nailsea glass). Encouraged migration of English glass makers to Ireland, where Acts did not apply, particularly when free trade granted (1780). In 1825, Irish glass also taxed. Acts repealed in 1845.

glass liner. Inner section or lining of gold or silver vessel, to protect it from corrosive contents, or merely for ornament. From late 18th century, glass liners (e.g. Bristol blue glass, flint or frosted glass) commonly used for salt cellars, sugar bowls, mustard pots, silver baskets, etc. *See* claret jug. *Illustrations at* mustard pot, sweetmeat basket.

Glastonbury chair. Oak and ash; two bishops' mitres carved on top-rail; on the back, a stag (a heraldic device). English, late 16th century.

Glastonbury chair. Folding oak chair with X-frame base, solid back (sometimes with carved decoration), and seat; arms are shaped diagonals running from upper corners of back to front corners of seat. Possibly named after 16th century Abbot of Glastonbury.

glaze. Vitreous coating fused to pottery or porcelain, providing impervious surface for porous bodies as well as decorative effect. Normally consists of flux, e.g. lead, borax, soda, or potash, sometimes mixed with silica in sand, quartz, or flint. Alkaline glaze used in ancient Egypt, containing silica and soda or potash, cannot be used successfully on body which does not contain high proportions of same elements, but makes possible brilliant turquoise colour. *Lead glaze, known from *c*1700 B.C., provides impervious surface for earthenware; also applied to soft-paste porcelain. *Tin glaze, made opaque by addition of tin oxide to basic lead glaze, used (*c*1000–*c*600 B.C.) in Babylon and developed in Mesopotamia in 8th century B.C., is characteristic of *maiolica, *Delft (sometimes given, in addition, brilliant surface of lead glaze, **coperta*, or **kwaart*), and *faience. *Salt-glaze evolved in Germany, in late 14th or early 15th century, applied to stoneware there and e.g. in England. Stoneware in China (1155–255 B.C., Chou dynasty) had been glazed with feldspar, mixed with wood ash, which fuses into glassy surface layer during firing; such glaze, fired at high temperature, sometimes described as *couverte*. *Smear glaze sometimes intentionally applied, e.g. to *parian ware, occurs at any time when glaze material present in firing of unglazed ware.

Globes. Pair of table globes, English, c1750, diameter of each 12in. Left: celestial globe inscribed New Celestial Globe by L. Cushee. Horizon scale marked with signs of zodiac and figures, zodiacal scale, days, months, points of compass, amplitude and azimuth scales. Right: terrestial globe inscribed A New Globe of the Earth, laid down according to the latest observations by Leonard Cushee.

globe. Spherical model of Earth (terrestrial) or of apparent sphere of sky and constellations (celestial). Celestial globes made in 3rd century B.C. or before, mainly ornamental, also used in China in early centuries A.D. Mentioned in European writings in 10th century; produced in engraved bronze by Islamic astronomers in Middle Ages. Popular in Europe in 16th century, made in copper-gilt or painted wood, often supported on base. Terrestrial globe by Crates of Mallus (d 145 B.C.) with world divided in four quarters, probably origin of orb as insignia of royalty. 15th century globes, e.g. Nuremberg Globe made by Martin Behaim in 1492, based on maps by Ptolemy of Alexandria (d 195 B.C.). Discoveries of Columbus and Vasco da Gama created new interest and greater accuracy. Production simplified by use of segments or gores of paper on base e.g. of papier mâché (1507). Globes produced in workshop of *Gemma Frisius, probably under supervision of cartographer Mercator, of fine quality. From 17th century, globes made in sizes from pocket type of *c*2in. diameter (often in case of leather, etc.) to examples of 15ft diameter in elaborate frames and stands.

globe cup. 16th century German covered *standing cup with body and lid forming globe. Stem baluster-shaped or human figure supporting globe on shoulders. Globe generally engraved with contemporary information about earth or heavens.

globe inkstand. Silver, silver-gilt, or Sheffield plate globe containing inkpot, sandbox, etc., supported on four feet or baluster stem with moulded foot. Revolving cover. Made in late 18th and early 19th centuries in Britain.

Globe watch. French, c1560, by Jacques de la Garde. Strikes the hour; gilt-metal case engraved with map of world and pierced to release sound; 24-hour chapter ring calibrated I–XII twice. Height 3⅛in.

globe watch or **clock.** Spherical watch or clock with map of world engraved on case. Originally made in France *c*1550, probably as centre of *armillary sphere showing planets; also produced in mid 17th century Germany.

gnomon. *See* sundial.

goat-and-bee jugs. Earliest examples of soft-paste porcelain made at Chelsea factory from mid 18th century. Cream jugs with lower part of body in form of two reclining goats; twig handle; usually with bee in applied relief below lip. Form copied from silver. Sometimes painted in polychrome enamel. Marked Chelsea 1745 with triangle, incised, or with triangle alone. Made in same period as several pieces which closely resemble silverware of N. *Sprimont, although derived from work of other silversmiths. Many contemporary examples made in silver. Forgeries exist, cast in silver from porcelain jugs.

*Goat-and-bee jug. *Chelsea porcelain, with incised triangle mark, 1745.*

Gobelins. Name of family of cloth-dyers in Faubourg Saint Marcel, Paris, from mid 15th to late 16th centuries. In 1607, Flemish weavers, led by M. *de Comans and F. *de la Planche, set up tapestry looms in surrounding area under patronage of Henri IV. Gobelins buildings bought by state in 1662 under supervision of Colbert and extended to become *Manufacture Royale des Meubles de la Couronne,* instituted 1667, housing high and low-warp tapestry looms, also premises for cabinet makers, goldsmiths, etc. Factory contained five tapestry workshops employing *c*250 men excluding apprentices, with C. *Lebrun as director. Production continued successfully for 28 years with output of 19 sets of high-warp and 34 sets of low-warp tapestries of high quality. Style followed existing traditions with classical, architectural, and landscape subjects taken from cartoons by Lebrun and others, and from paintings by earlier artists including *Raphaël. Contemporary themes include famous set of 14 hangings, History of the King, depicting supremacy of Louis XIV, and Royal Palaces; other examples illustrate Months, Elements, Children in a Garden, etc. Series of Indians and Animals of the Indies, or Indian Hangings, inspired by natural history paintings presented to Louis XIV by Prince of Nassau.

Gobelins factory closed in 1694 through national financial crisis, but re-opened in 1697 with continuation of History of the King, and many repetitions of old designs. New designs, e.g. Triumphs of the Gods (rewoven throughout 18th century), and Grotesque Months, by Claude Audran the Younger, retained features of grand style of 17th century, but Story of Don Quixote, begun in 1714 from cartoons by

Gobelins tapestry. Wool and silk, from series of Indian Hangings, from cartoon by Albert Eckhout. 1689.

Charles Coypel, show development of less monumental, more ornamental manner compatible with architecture and furniture of 18th century. Subjects bordered by simulated gilt mouldings, on ornate ground, surrounded by woven representation of elaborate frame. J-B. *Oudry, director of Beauvais factory, appointed as inspecter at Gobelins in 1733, produced designs in naturalistic style for Hunts of Louis XV. Other successful subjects were Story of Esther and Story of Jason by Jean-François de Troy, and new version of Indian Hangings (1738). Success of F. *Boucher in painting cartoons for Beauvais led to appointment as inspector at Gobelins (1755) after death of Oudry. Many decorative tapestries from Boucher's designs include historical and mythological subjects, often sets with matching panels as, chair-coverings etc. From this period tapestry largely reproduced painting; many portraits produced, e.g. of Louis XV, the Dauphin (later Louis XVI), and Empress Maria Theresa.

After accession of Louis XVI (1774), style restrained with mainly historical subjects, e.g. History of Henri IV, and History of France; also designs based on classical motifs. Factory taken under control of Directoire after Revolution; many works showing royalist emblems destroyed in 1793; others burnt to retrieve gold and silver thread used in manufacture. Revolutionary themes and scenes of classical heroism produced until establishment of Empire in 1804, then copies of paintings illustrating military triumphs of Napoleon, e.g. J-L. David's Napoleon Crossing the Alps. Factory remained in existence into 20th century, with continued output of tapestry reproductions of paintings. Carpet production at Gobelins introduced after closure of *Savonnerie workshop in 1825.

Goblet. English, 1657; maker's mark, GS with two dots above and crozier between in a shaped shield. Trumpet-shaped stem with band of matting in the middle. Bowl chased with pomegranate design. Height $3\frac{3}{4}$*in.*

goblet or **wine cup.** Silver, silver-gilt, or gold stemmed drinking vessel for individual rather than for ceremonial use like *standing cup. Made mainly from mid 16th to end of 17th century. Various bowl and stem shapes, e.g. spherical, cylindrical bowls and/or baluster, spool-shaped stems. In 17th century usually with conical bowl, baluster stem, and slightly concave conical foot. Either left plain or with all-over chased ornament (foliate scrolls, grapes, etc.). Largely superseded by *two-handled cup. Some examples with bell-shaped bowl (usually plain but sometimes with semi-fluted, bright-cut, or engraved ornament) made from mid 18th century in England. *See* christening cup.

go-cart or **going-cart.** *See* baby-walker.

goddard. *See* tankard.

goddard foot. *Bracket foot sloping outwards, beyond vertical edge of object. Named after J. *Goddard, used particularly by him and *Newport school.

Goddard, John, I (1723–85). Cabinet and chair maker at Newport, Rhode Island. Apprenticed to J. *Townsend; one of *Newport school. Worked in mahogany, using block front design.

Godtling, Jeremias Theunison (fl late 17th century). Dutch pottery decorator. Worked independently; then, by 1668, in factory at The Hague. Used secret technique to fix enamel colours, including red and gold, before invention of muffle kiln. In early 1690s, contracted by R. *Hoppesteyn to make and fire gilded Delft ware.

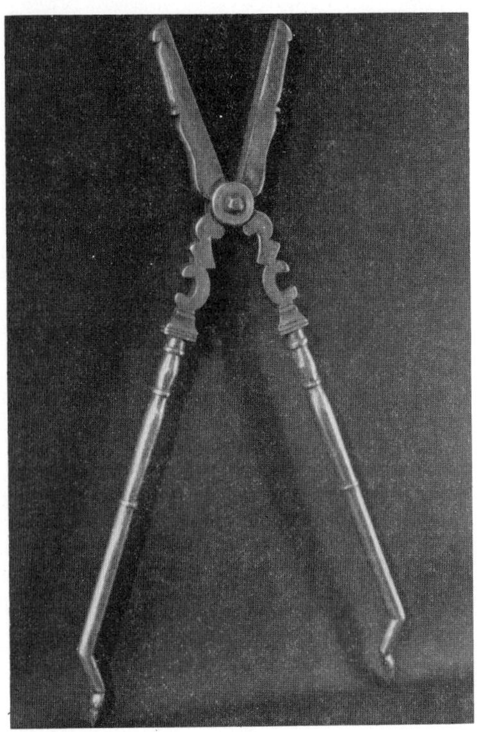

Goffering iron. English, mid 17th century. Length approximately 16*in.*

goffering iron. Iron implement used in 16th and 17th centuries for crimping fashionable neck ruff; material pressed between heated upper convex blade and lower, concave blade. Another type is single iron rod (on stand), over which material is stretched and pulled. (Name derives from French *gaufre,* 'honeycomb', which finished work resembles.)

Göggingen (Bavaria). German faience factory founded 1748. Produced wide variety of wares, e.g. wall tiles and figures; noted for thin, light body. Rococo moulded plates and narrow-necked jugs common, painted in blue or high-temperature colours in Chinese and European styles. Ceased production after three years. Usual factory mark: Göggingen, in full or contracted.

going barrel. *See* barrel.

gold. Precious metal, bright yellow in colour; one of earliest metals used, may be worked in unrefined state. Alluvial gold, eroded from rock, is found in soil of river-beds; reef gold is embedded in quartz or other rock in veins with various metals including silver, copper, lead, etc., extracted usually by washing with chemicals. Gold has highest density, *malleability, and *ductility of decorative metals. Highly resistant to action of solvents; also resists corrosion. In pure state resists oxidation after *annealing. Usually alloyed with other metals because of softness. Deposits are world-wide, used from ancient times for religious objects, personal adornment, coinage, royal use, etc. In Europe from collapse of Roman Empire to Middle Ages, church main focus of culture, and gold used primarily for ecclesiastical plate. Discovery of New World increased amount of gold in European treasuries and resulted in augmented production of gold objects for display, ceremonial, and domestic use, limited, however, to royal and noble households and church.

gold anchor period. *See* Chelsea.

gold Chinese style. German ceramic decoration. Chinese figures, birds, and flowers, silhouetted in gold on white ground. Style characteristic of porcelain *Hausmalerei* by e.g. J. *Aufenwerth and workshop of B. *Seuter at Augsburg (*c*1730–40).

golden rose. *See* papal rose.

gold ground. European porcelain decoration for vases and tableware fashionable, notably at Vienna, Berlin, and Sèvres porcelain factories, *c*1800–25; large expanses of body gilded to simulate metal. At Meissen, *c*1745, sometimes used with reserve panels (e.g. on coffee cups and saucers).

Goldsmiths' Company or **Worshipful Company of Goldsmiths.** Guild of goldsmiths existed in London before 1180. In 1327, charter granted by Edward III confirmed powers it exercized over goldsmiths and silversmiths. In 1462 it obtained right to search out and *assay gold and silver throughout kingdom. In 1675, Company ordered all plate-workers to register, though already usual from mid 15th century for apprentices to register names at Goldsmiths' Hall. Completion of apprenticeship (seven years) usually meant granting of freedom.

Gombroon ware. Translucent white Persian earthenware with pierced decoration, e.g. on walls of vase or bowl, or on rim of plate. Clear glaze fills perforations; pattern resembles scattered grains of rice: sometimes called rice grain or grain of rice decoration. Painted decoration, often in black or blue (or both), on unpierced part of object. Vases, jars, bowls, plates, and ewers made in Persia from 12th century. Fashionable in India and Europe in 17th and 18th centuries. Chinese imitations made in 18th century. Named after English East India Company's trading station, Gombroon (now Bender Abbas) on Persian Gulf.

Gondelach, Franz (1663-after 1716). German glass engraver in baroque style; used both **Hochschnitt* and **Tiefschnitt* techniques – usually combined – mainly on Potsdam style glasses. Pupil of G. *Spiller; worked at glass-house of Landgrave Carl in Hesse-Cassel. In 1695, named glass cutter to Emperor Leopold I. Subjects include portraits, monograms, and armorial pieces.

gondola bed. *See* boat bed.

gong. Metal, usually bronze, disc which sounds when struck with stick. Eastern origin: used outside temples to announce prayer time. Used from 19th century in England to summon diners at meal times. Usually slung from wooden frame. In clocks and watches, flat resonant coil of wire sometimes used instead of bell for striking, originally to save space. Said to have been introduced by A-L. *Breguet *c*1800; popular in late 19th century clocks.

Gonon, Honoré (fl early 19th century). French founder; made many superb casts for A-L. *Barye. Continued to cast by lost-wax process despite increasing use of sand-casting. Work of exceptional quality.

*Benjamin Goodison. Side table, c1730, carved and gilded pine with marble top. Height 2ft*11*in.*

Goodison, Benjamin (fl 1727–67). English cabinet maker, working in London; supplied furniture to George II. Work noted for excellence of craftsmanship and design. Favourite motifs include facing acanthus scrolls with central shell, plume, or crown.

goose-neck pediment. *See* swan-neck pediment.

Gostelowe, Jonathan (1744–95). Cabinet maker in Philadelphia, Pennsylvania; noted for pieces in *Philadelphia Chippendale style.

Gotha (Thuringia). Small German porcelain factory founded *c*1757. Limited production

Gothic revival. Chair, English, c1830; gilt beechwood with contemporary upholstery.

Gothic style furniture. Carved oak chest, c1450. Carved panels at base added later. Front decorated with five panels of intricate Gothic tracery divided by crocketed buttresses; back has linenfold panelling. Width 6ft7in.

before 1772, when cream-coloured earthenware in neo-classical style distinctly resembled that of other Thuringian factories. In 1770s and 1780s forms and painting inspired by Fürstenberg, as were biscuit vases, busts, and figures in 1790s. Marks: before 1783, R in underglaze blue or impressed; 1783–1805, R—g (Rotberg, founder); 1805–30, Gotha, or G, in underglaze or enamel blue; after 1830, cockerel on mountain peak enclosed by buckled belt bearing inscription Gotha (impressed).

Gothic clock. *See* chamber clock.

Gothic floral style. Characteristic decoration of Italian maiolica, particularly from Faenza and Tuscany from mid 15th to early 16th centuries. Predominant motif, scrolled foliage (accompanied e.g. by bands of decoration, *San Bernardino rays, or lettering), framed panel with portrait, figure, animal, or heraldic device, treated in stylized manner.

Gothic revival or **neo-Gothic style.** Decorative style based on *Gothic forms and motifs (cluster columns, cusping, tracery, pointed arches). Mainly literary Georgian revival (*see* H. Walpole), inspired some *Chippendale style furniture. Sir Walter Scott's novels encouraged development of Regency Gothic (*see* Abbotsford style). A. W. N. *Pugin leading figure in Gothic revival.

Gothic style. Form and ornament of Gothic architecture reflected in furniture, etc.; style lasted from mid 12th century to early 16th century in Europe and Britain. Furniture simple and utilitarian, with straight lines and vertical emphasis. Carving most common form of decoration, although some gilding and painting used. Ornamental motifs include pointed arches, fabulous birds and animals, fleurs-de-lis, grotesque figures, leaf and vine designs, linen-fold panels, strapwork, and open tracery. Pieces included benches, box chairs, chests, stools, and tables.

Gotzkowsky pattern or **erhabene Blumen.** German ceramic decoration: circle of flowers in well of plate, with bouquets on rim, moulded in low relief, on porcelain made at Meissen from 1744. Named after financier, Johan Gotzkowsky (b 1710), and copied from 1761 at factory established by him in Berlin. Also imitated at Chelsea.

gouache. Watercolour paint with white added to produce opacity. Lightens in colour during drying. Cracks if applied thickly, but gives effect similar to oil paint and is less viscous, so easier to work. Used widely in miniatures on vellum and ivory.

gouge carving. Repetitive pattern of flutes or concave areas carved with gouge. Used particularly on flat surfaces of 16th and 17th century case furniture.

gourd cup. 16th and 17th century British and European *standing cup with gourd-shaped bowl and cover (large sphere set on small) and stem in form of plant stalk or tree trunk (sometimes set round with figures of woodmen). First made in Germany.

gout stool. Footstool with top either raked or adjustable, allowing user to rest gouty foot comfortably. Dates from 18th century.

Gouthière, Pierre (1732–*c*1813). French *fondeur-ciseleur*; became master gilder in 1758. Work characterized by contrasts of burnished and matt areas and of various degrees of depth in chasing. Made mounts for J-H. *Riesener until *c*1768. Employed at court from *c*1769; worked on jewel cabinet for Dauphine, Marie Antoinette. Known works rare.

Govaers, Daniel (d 1737). French court goldsmith and box maker from 1725. Supplied boxes for *corbeille de mariage* or marriage gift of Queen Maria Leczinska, and boxes with miniature portraits by J-B. *Massé for Louis XV. Bankrupted 1735; fled Paris 1736. Signed initials D.G, mullet, and Gouers à Paris.

Goya y Lucientes, Francisco José de (1746–1828). Spanish court painter. In 1776, in Madrid, commissioned to paint cartoons for royal tapestry manufactory (*Santa Barbara). Completed *c*45 cartoons (1776–91), depicting Spanish life.

grace cup. Term loosely used to refer to ceremonial *standing cup (silver, silver-gilt, etc.) passed round after grace is said. In use in

*Pierre Gouthière. Perfume-burner in form of fluted *jasper bowl supported on tripod of ormolu, richly decorated with scrolls, satyr's masks and vine swags; within this is a serpent coiled spirally down to jasper base. Height 19in.*

Grace cup. English, 1619, silver-gilt; maker's mark, RP. Octagonal bowl on baluster stem, embossed and chased with pomegranates and acanthus foliage. Height $7\frac{1}{8}$in.

Britain probably from late Middle Ages. Early surviving example is Warden's Grace Cup of New College, Oxford, made *c*1480.

Graham, George (*c*1673–1751). English clock and watch maker; apprenticed 1688, admitted to Clockmakers' Company 1695, later became master. Worked with T. *Tompion; some clocks survive signed Tompion & Graham. After Tompion's death carried on business, then moved to own premises in Fleet Street, London. Member of Council of Royal Society (1722). Modified Tompion's early form of cylinder *escapement and in 1715 perfected dead beat escapement for clocks. Experimented widely with *compensation methods, introducing mercury compensated pendulum in 1726. Made over 170 clocks of various types, and nearly 3000 watches. Early Graham verge watches have pierced foot to *cock, soon abandoned for plain type with engraved foot; work much forged but identifiable by signature and number on back plate, on pillar plate under dial, and on underside of cock. Made about 400 repeating watches, always smaller than his other forms, and scientific instruments.

grain of rice decoration. *See* Gombroon ware.

Grainger, Lee & Co. English porcelain factory, established in 1801 at Worcester by Thomas Grainger, artist from *Chamberlain works; traded as Grainger & Wood until 1812, then as Grainger, Lee & Co. Until 1815, decorated bone china bought in white e.g. from Coalport. Soft-paste porcelain produced 1815–20, then bone china. Products include tableware with flowers, birds, and butterflies. In 1829, licensed to

*Grainger, Lee & Company. Mid 19th century plate transfer-printed with *willow pattern.*

manufacture *lithophanes. From 1839, traded as G. Grainger & Co.; made inexpensive vitrified ware marked from *c*1850 as semi-porcelain. Also produced parian ware and, from *c*1840, figures with lacework. Absorbed by Royal Worcester Porcelain Company in 1889. Marks include George Grainger, Royal China Works Worcester, painted in script; GRAINGER LEE & CO WORCESTER; and ROYAL CHINA WORKS ENGLAND around shield containing G & CO ESTABLISHED 1801.

graining (in furniture). Painting surface of object to produce effect of hardwood grain. Origin of technique unknown, but more common from 18th century.

grande sonnerie. *See* striking systems.

grandfather clock. *See* long-case clock.

*Grape-scissors. English, George III period. Silver-gilt, together in original case with two pairs of *nutcrackers.*

grand feu. *See* high-temperature colours.

grandmother clock. *See* dwarf-tall clock.

granite ware (in English and American ceramics). Strong, moderately hard, white earthenware containing feldspar. Made in England from late 1850s, e.g. by J. *Davenport's firm. Much exported to America, India, Australia, etc. Used as ships' tableware because of strength. Alternatively, cream-coloured earthenware sprayed with liquid lead-glaze in mottled blue or grey, imitating natural granite; developed in late 18th century by J. *Wedgwood. Other makers include *Neale & Co and, in early 19th century, E. *Wood.

Granja de San Ildefonso, La. Spanish glass house founded in 1728 near royal palace outside Segovia. Employed Bohemian craftsmen and specialized in large mirrors; received patronage of Philip V in 1738. Also made Catalan style vessels, particularly in blue and *latticinio* glass. Wheel engraving introduced *c*1750; fire gilding in late 18th century. Due to foreign influences, output not typically Spanish. Characterized by cutting and engraving in German style, as well as gaily coloured enamelling. Main subjects formal flowers, landscapes, and baroque motifs. Factory sold in 1829 and standard declined. *Illustration at* Spanish glass.

granulation. Metal decoration in which small grains of gold or silver are joined to metal surface without solder; technique originating in classical times, mainly used in decorating jewellery in 19th century.

grape scissors. Silver fruit scissors used in Britain, probably from late 18th century. Earliest examples have ring handles and straight blades of sewing scissors. Later, handles decorated with vine leaves; blades cross-over (as in pruning shears). Sometimes included in dessert service.

grasshopper escapement. *See* escapement.

Grassi, Anton (1755–1807). Austrian porcelain modeller. Apprenticed to J. C. W. *Beyer; leading modeller at Vienna 1778–1807. Adopted academic forms after visit to Italy in 1792.

grate. Metal, basket-like, portable framework of bars to contain fire. Replaced *down hearth in

Grate. Basket shaped, silvered brass with applied brass acanthus leaves; bun feet. English, late 18th century.

early 18th century to accommodate coal, and to allow current of air to circulate. Early examples made of iron, becoming more ornamental towards mid 18th century, often with enrichments of polished steel, later brass. By *c*1780, grates were highly ornate, made in fashionable metals (*paktong, or burnished steel) to neo-classical designs; these were superseded in 19th century by elaborate cast-iron grates, frequently with brass mounts or finials.

Gravant, François (d 1765). French arcanist; worked with G. and Robert *Dubois at Chantilly; went with them to Sèvres and took over experiments to find porcelain formula after their dismissal. Successfully manufactured soft-paste porcelain in 1745, and supervised production of paste until death; succeeded by son.

graver or **burin.** Sharp cutting and gouging tool used by engraver.

graveyard, mazarlik, or **turbelik carpets.** Turkish prayer rugs reserved for burial ceremonies; woven in Kula, Ladik, Ghiordes, and Kirshehir. Mihrab has horizontal or vertical repeat of distinctive 'graveyard motif': small stylized house flanked by two angular trees.

gravity clock. Type deriving power from its own weight in falling or rolling. *See* hanging clock, inclined plane clock, rack clock.

gravy-boat. *See* sauce-boat.

gravy warmer. *See* argyle.

greasepan or **drip-pan.** On early pricket candlesticks, small curved pan round stem to catch drips of grease from burning candle. Retained after introduction of socket-type candlestick, until superseded in late 17th century by enlarged socket rim.

Greatbatch or **Greatbach,** William (1735–1813). Modeller and potter in Staffordshire; established pottery at Lower Lane and later at Lane Delph, Fenton. Worked as modeller for T. *Whieldon; left 1759 to manufacture earthenware. Vessels in cauliflower, melon, and pineapple shapes, and pear and apple teapots supplied in biscuit to J. *Wedgwood for lead-glazing; also for Wedgwood modelled relief designs of figures and landscapes used on salt-glaze and green glazed earthenware. Produced some cream-coloured earthenware with black or red transfer-printing painted over in enamel. Mark: Greatbatch and date (*c*1778). *Illustration at* creamware.

Greek A, The (De Grieksche A). Delft factory (1658 to after 1818), founded by W. *van Eenhoorn; son, Samuel, manager from 1674. Sold, 1687, to A *Kocks, succeeded by family in 1701. Commissioned between 1689 and 1694 to produce tile tables and ornamental ware for dairy at Hampton Court Palace. Peak production, 1701–22, through success of work in Imari style, speciality of factory. J. T. *Dextra owner 1758–65.

Greek fret. *See* key pattern.

green and purple ware. Italian maiolica, decorated in Gothic style, with manganese-purple outlines filled in with copper green, made in or near Florence from *c*1400; examples also discovered at Orvieto. Heraldic device, portrait, or animal, painted in panel against background of foliage. Colours echo palette of earliest maiolica, made notably in northern Italy from 13th century; decoration in these colours continued in Italy throughout 15th century, and in Spain, particularly in Aragon, well into 16th century.

green Chün ware. Chinese celadon ware of Sung period, manufactured in Honan province. Similar to *Chün in form, but with rich grey-green glaze, often finely crazed and discoloured at edges. Certain features, e.g. shaping of foot, echo *northern celadon ware; thus items represent possible link between two main products of period. Copied at Ching-tê-chên in 18th century.

Green, Guy (fl 1756–99). Transfer-printer of English ceramics. From 1763, partner with J. *Sadler in Printed Ware Manufactory at Liverpool; then sole proprietor. In late 1770s, for J. *Wedgwood, printed tableware in outline, then coloured it with pea-green enamel. *Illustration at* J. Sadler.

green Watteau service. German ceramics. 17 porcelain table services made at Meissen factory (*c*1738–40) as gift for daughter of Augustus III of Poland on her marriage to King Charles IV of Naples (later Charles III of Spain). Leaf-green monochrome pastoral scenes underpainted in black (after J-A. *Watteau) appear on every piece. Two further green Watteau services made in 1745: one for Augustus III, decorated with panels of unpainted flowers in low relief alternating with green monochrome scenes; other for Empress Elizabeth of Russia, featuring battle scenes as well as pastoral idylls.

Greenwood, Frans (1680–1761). Dutch glass engraver of English descent. Born in Rotterdam, moved to Dordrecht in 1726. Popularized *stippling with diamond-point on imported English lead glass. Earliest work in linear form, mainly *commedia dell'arte* figures (after J. *Callot). From *c*1720, engraved entirely by stippling. Main subjects floral and fruit motifs, classical themes, and copies of contemporary paintings. Worked largely on drinking glasses and goblets. Signed examples 1722–55.

Greiner family. Founders of several small porcelain factories in Thuringia, central Germany in 18th century. Gotthelf Greiner, co-founder of *Wallendorf (1764), also founded *Limbach (1772), *Grozbreitenbach (1782), and *Ilmenau (1786). In 1797, his five sons acquired *Kloster-Veilsdorf; other kinsmen, J. G. W. and J. A. Greiner, painters at *Volkstedt, and took over *Gera in 1780; succeeded by W. H. Greiner at Volkstedt (1799) as part-owner.

grenade. *See décor coréen.*

Grendey, Giles (1693–1780). English cabinet maker working in London. Known for japanned and mahogany furniture in simple style; exported some work.

grès. *See* stoneware.

grès de Flandres. *See* Rhineland stoneware.

greybeard jug. *See* bellarmine.

grey ware. Chinese celadon manufactured in T'ang and Sung periods in Chekiang province. Resembles *Yüeh, but has lighter grey porcellanous body. Vases often made with loops on shoulder near neck; round bodies divided into panels, usually five. Glaze colour varies from blue or greyish-green tone to off-white.

Gribelin, Simon (1661–1731). Huguenot artist and engraver in London from *c*1680; in 1686, became member of Clockmakers' Company. First published book of designs (1697), A Book of Ornaments useful to Jewellers, Watchmakers & all other Artists. Second book (1700) more general: A Book of Ornaments useful to all Artists. Designs copied by British decorators of plate. Specific pieces attributable to him owing to survival in British Museum of his book of prints *Livre d'Estampes de Sim. Gribelin, fait Relié à Londres* 1722, which contains proofs of some of his engraved silverwork.

Gricci, Giuseppe or José (d 1770). Porcelain modeller. Worked as chief modeller at *Capodimonte factory (1743–59). Made moulds for cane-handles and snuff-boxes in form of shells; also shell-shaped ewers and basins. Figures (1743–56), typically with small heads, include characters from *commedia dell'arte,* religious subjects, and groups of country people. Moved with factory to *Buen Retiro in 1759–60 as chief modeller; acted as director from *c*1764. Modelled boys, often playing with animals, or representing Seasons or Continents; also country folk in rococo style. Sons Carlos (d 1795) and Felipe (d 1803) acting directors at Buen Retiro from 1783. Under Carlos, factory produced figures inspired by Meissen in glassy white porcelain.

gridiron pendulum. *See* compensation.

Grilley, Henry, Samuel, and Silas (fl from 1790). American founders of pewter button factory in Waterbury, Connecticut. Buttons small and round with iron shanks; moulded with designs such as star, sunray, and flowers. Produced brass buttons from early 19th century.

Grollier de Servière, Nicolas (1593–1686). French clock maker and inventor from Lyon. Designer of unusual clocks, including *ball clock.

gros bleu. Dark blue ground colour applied under glaze on soft-paste porcelain of Vincennes and Sèvres, *c*1744–*c*1760. Frequently imitated, notably at Chelsea (*mazarine blue), *Longton Hall, and *Worcester.

Groszbreitenbach (Thuringia). German porcelain factory founded *c*1778, acquired 1782 by G. Greiner. Initial wares mainly underglaze blue; some modelling and enamelling by artists employed also at other factories of *Greiner family. Production continued to mid 20th century. Mark: trefoil (as *Limbach).

grotesque. Ornamental style derived from decorations in Roman 'grottoes', rediscovered *c*1500 and since identified as remains of Nero's palace; initiated by *Raphaël in paintings for Vatican *loggie* (*cf* mannerist style). Characteristic elements human, half-human, and animal figures with entwined foliage and arabesques. Found in 16th century as decoration on maiolica from *Urbino and centres throughout Italy, and on other tin-glazed ware with Italian influence. Used as chased, engraved, embossed, or applied cast ornament on silver from 16th century. Grotesque tapestries widely produced in 17th century, e.g. at *Beauvais (after J. *Berain) and again in 18th century, e.g. at *Gobelins. *See* Dutch grotesque style, *style Berain*.

Groth, Albret (fl 1706–17). Norwegian silversmith working in Christiania, now Oslo. Produced domestic silver in French and English styles.

ground colours or **fondporzellan.** Ceramic decoration: background colour achieved either by use of coloured body (e.g. jasper ware) or by coating of colour (e.g. jasper dip, clay slip, glaze, high-temperature colour, or enamel). Coloured glazes used in 12th and 13th centuries in Middle East, e.g. in *minai and *lajvardina wares. Tin-glaze tinted with cobalt, e.g. under lustre painting in Islamic countries from 13th century and, rarely, in Hispano-Moresque ware of 15th century; *berrettino* glaze introduced at Faenza in late 15th century. Dark grounds used at Delft, at Nevers from *c*1675, and later at Lambeth, Rouen, and Saint-Omer. Ground colours with reserved decoration on porcelain derived from oriental styles; used at Meissen from 1720s, known as *fondporzellan*. Wide range of ground colours introduced at *Sèvres in mid 18th century; attempts at reproducing them made at *Chelsea and *Worcester.

Grue, Carlo Antonio (1655–1723). Italian maiolica painter; member of *Grue family in Castelli; decorated plates, jars, and tiles with religious subjects, grotesques, seascapes, landscapes, and ruined buildings, taken from paintings of 16th and 17th centuries. Borders of cherubs, with flowers and architectural motifs. Work characterized by delicacy of colours, including pale yellow and green, sometimes with gilding.

Grue family. Italian maiolica potters at Castelli from early 17th century. Francesco painted dishes and panels dating from 1640s and 1650s. Succeeded by son C. A. *Grue, and grandsons: Francesco Antonio (1686–1746), doctor of philosophy and medicine, and landscape painter, also at Naples; Anastasio (1691–1743), also landscape painter; Aurelio (1699–1744), painter of animals and pastoral scenes with background of scrolls and foliage; Liberio or Liborio (1702–76) painter of figures and landscapes, mainly on large pieces. Saverio (1731–99), son of Francesco Antonio, painted figures, sometimes in enamel colours. Many pieces signed by individual painters, who also include Niccolò Tommaso (1726–81) and Francesco Saverio (1720–55).

gryphon's egg. *See* ostrich-egg cup.

guards (in fan). The outer sticks; generally more elaborately decorated than others.

guard stripes. Narrow borders on either side of main carpet border.

Guarneri family (fl 17th and 18th centuries). Italian family of violin makers working in Cremona. Most notable member, Giuseppe Guarneri (1698–1744). Also made violas and cellos.

Gubbio (Umbria), Italy. Pottery centre from Middle Ages, noted for gold and ruby lustre decoration introduced at workshop of G. *Andreoli. Moulded decoration often used on vases and dishes to display sheen of metallic lustre. Reverse of plates normally decorated with flowers, scrolls, concentric bands of decoration, or gadroons. Wares sent to Gubbio for lustre-decoration include plate painted with Presentation of the Virgin at the Temple by N. *Pellipario, marked 1532 MG (i.e. Maestro Giorgio) fini de maiolica. From mid 16th century, backgrounds often tinted grey or blue; white highlights used in decoration.

guéridon. French candlestand. In 17th and early 18th centuries tall pedestal on tripod base, the support baluster-shaped or in form of negro figure holding tray above head (probably named from French equivalent of 'blackamoor'). Materials include ormolu, carved and gilded wood, less commonly silver or silver-gilt. Alternatively, small round table for candelabrum or candlestick.

guéridon table. Small French circular table, based on column and tripod *guéridon*; sometimes has smaller, circular tier above main top. First made during 18th century.

Guérin, Jean-Urbain (1760–1836). French miniaturist. Studied under J-L. David with J-B. *Isabey. Portraits include Louis XVI, Marie Antoinette, General Kléber, deputies, generals, and Empress Josephine in court dress.

Guidobono, Gian Antonio or Giovanni (1605–85) and sons Bartolommeo (1657–1709) and Domenico (1670–1746). Italian maiolica painters, owners of workshop at Savona producing pharmaceutical ware, and large dishes with moulded rims, painted in *compendiario* style with sea gods, nymphs, and *putti*. Jugs, mugs, and vases also have relief decoration in style of contemporary beaten metal-work. Thought to have marked work with sketch of lighthouse.

guild cup. Tall-stemmed ceremonial drinking-vessel, in gold, silver, pewter, or other metal, elaborately ornamented, with ornate lid surmounted by crest or emblem of guild as finial. Medieval English version sometimes called *hanap. Known in Germany as *Zunftbecher* (examples up to 24in. high); particularly popular in 17th and 18th centuries.

guild flagon. Made in Germany from late 15th century for serving wine or beer at guild banquets. Large (up to 30in. tall), and richly ornamented with engraved figures or inscriptions. Polygonal, cylindrical, or conical in shape.

Guild of Saint Luke. Dutch painters' craft guild, founded 1611; makers of tin-glazed earthenware admitted, although other potters at first excluded. Regulations prevented anyone other than master potter or painter from managing factory. However, owners permitted to hire guild members as pottery directors if not themselves qualified. Records of Guild show slow rise in membership from average of one new maker of tin-glazed ware admitted per year (1613–50), to two per year (1651–60), then nine in 1661, reflecting sharp rise in Delft trade in mid 17th century. Number of factories rose from *c*10 (1650) to 28 (1670).

Guilloche *ornament banding rim of *slop basin made by *Boulton & Fothergill, c1780. Bowl with applied festoons of *husk ornament and classical medallions. Height 4in.*

Guillibaud, Jean-Baptiste (d 1739) and widow. Faience makers at Rouen, 1720–*c*1750. Credited with copies in underglaze colours of Chinese porcelain with *famille rose* and *famille verte* decoration. Several pieces signed or initialled GB or GAR (i.e. *Guillibaud à Rouen*).

guilloche. Ornament of interlaced ribbon-like bands (two or more), sometimes enclosing circles or rosettes. Applied by various techniques (chasing, embossing, etc.) on 16th and late 18th century silver. Many watch-cases *c*1790–1820 were decorated with transparent enamel laid over *guilloché* or engine-turned ground. Similar ornament is common feature of neo-classical furniture, and as painted, moulded, or incised pattern on ceramics of same period.

guinea hole or **pit.** *See* money dish.

guitar. Stringed musical instrument of *lute type with *fretted finger-board, played by plucking strings with fingers or *plectrum. Guitar has waisted body (less pronounced in early examples), top and bottom ends rounded, flat back (slightly rounded in older forms), long neck, flat peg disc, rear turning pegs, and large, circular sound-hole with ornamental *rose (until 18th century). Form and stringing modified over centuries; early instrument double-strung (four or five pairs of strings) became single-strung in early 18th century (usually six strings). Traditionally Spanish instrument; modern guitar descendant of 13th century Spanish *guitarra latina*, or gittern. In late 16th century, popularity spread to Italy, and then to rest of Europe and Britain; known as Spanish guitar. Another Spanish type, *vihuela*, used primarily by aristocracy. By mid 18th century popular amateur instrument in Britain and Europe. Body usually wooden; many examples highly ornate, with mother-of-pearl and ivory inlay.

Guild cup. German, pewter, inscribed 'This is the loving cup of the Masons' Guild.' 1609.

gul (Arabic, 'rose' or 'flower') or **elephant's foot.** Octagonal or diamond-shaped medallion forming decorative device on Turkoman carpets. Also, any such motif on oriental carpets.

Gumley, John (fl *c*1694–1729). English looking-glass maker, and cabinet maker to George I. Partner of J. *Moore (1714–26) and of W. Turing (*c*1720–29).

gun-metal. Type of bronze developed for use in making gun-barrels, occasionally extended to other objects, e.g. domestic hollow-ware.

Gutenbrunn. *See* Pfalz-Zweibrücken.

Guitar. Left: 17th century French guitar, made in Paris. Right: early 19th century French lyre-guitar, neo-classical variation designed as drawing-room instrument.

Habaner ware. Tin-glazed earthenware made from late 16th century in Moravia and border districts of Hungary by German-speaking Anabaptist sect, the Habaner. Earliest dated example made 1598. Decoration includes flowers, leaves, and scrollwork, but never human or animal figures because religion forbade their representation. In late 17th century, birds and architectural motifs introduced as sect gradually broke up.

Habermel, Erasmus (d 1606). Scientific instrument-maker; worked in Prague. Produced drawing instruments and surveying devices of fine construction, usually in gilt copper. Patrons included German Emperor Rudolph II.

habitat button. French late 18th century button incorporating insects, grasses, flowers, stones, etc., arranged under convex glass and mounted in metal frame.

Habrecht, Isaac (fl late 16th century). German clock maker of Swiss origin; made astronomical clock for Strasbourg Cathedral, 1571–74, and smaller version traditionally for Pope Sixtus V. This clock, now in British Museum, is *c*5ft tall, of three-storey architectural form, with two dials showing hours and quarters, and third, rotating once a year, indicating month, day of month, Dominical letter, phase and age of moon; also feast days and signs of Zodiac. Top storey has four tiers of automaton figures and *carillon striking. Movement is of iron, with trains for going, hour-striking, quarter-striking, and music. Similar clock, some years later, is in Rosenborg Castle, Denmark.

Hackwood, William (d 1839). Assistant modeller at Etruria factory of J. *Wedgwood,

Isaac Habrecht. Monumental clock. Strasbourg, 1589. Cock on finial crows on the hour; figure of Death strikes the hour after tune has played; below the figures revolve and strike bell on the quarter. Copper-gilt with silver figures. Height 5ft2in.

Hadley chest. Oak and pine, c1700; tulip and leaf carving in flat relief; initials I P for Joanna Porter, for whom it was made.

1769–82; then head of modelling until 1832. Responsible for much finely modelled jasper ware in low-relief, notably portrait medallions.

Hadley chest. American dowry chest with lid-topped chest section surmounting one or two drawers; decoration includes tulip motif. Made in towns along Connecticut River in Connecticut and Massachusetts Bay colonies around Hadley, Massachusetts, *c*1675–1740. Rare.

Hafner (German, 'potter' or 'stovemaker'). Medieval or Renaissance German potter, originally specializing in manufacture of earthenware stove tiles (**Hafnerware*) for local sale.

Hafnerware. (German, 'potter's ware'). Originally mainly stove tiles (made by **Hafner*) from Middle Ages in Central Europe, Austria, Germany, and Switzerland. Romans probably introduced manufacture of earthenware stoves; surviving examples not normally dated earlier than 15th century. Early tiles have relief decoration, covered with green lead glaze. By late 15th century, yellow and brown added, with use of clear glaze over white clay, or tin-glaze, to provide white, when needed in design. In 16th century, *Hafner* working throughout Germany, Austria, and Switzerland; made stoves with figures and other motifs modelled separately and applied in addition to usual relief decoration; designs, usually religious or historical, often taken from engravings. Much use of white, in form of applied clay, or tin-glaze. 16th century products include jugs and dishes, tomb slabs, wall fountains. Salzburg, and particularly Nuremberg, important centres. From late 16th century, lead-glazed, relief-decorated tiles accompanied by tin-glazed panels painted, notably, in blue and yellow on white ground.

Hague, The. *See* The Hague.

haie fleurie. *See décor coréen.*

Haines, Ephraim (fl *c*1805–35). Cabinet maker in Philadelphia, Pennsylvania. Pieces in neo-classical style; made many chairs.

hair jewellery. In 17th century England, lock of hair sometimes set under faceted crystal medallion on silk background or gold slide, with initials in gold wire as memorial to dead. Worn on black ribbon at neck or wrist. From late 17th century mourning rings adapted to hold lock of hair; ornamented with black and white enamel, pearl borders, etc. Hair *mourning jewellery temporarily out of fashion *c*1720 but revived in mid century. Brooches and lockets made with central medallion (covered with crystal) filled with plaited hair; more elaborate examples had pictures often painted in sepia on ivory with bits of hair mixed into paint; subjects usually funereal, e.g. tomb, willows, weeping widow. Less morbid examples given as sentimental gifts. Picture sometimes coloured to resemble miniature. *c*1770, hair jewellery became fashionable in Britain and France and remained so until 1850s. In England popularity continued throughout 19th century. Hair plaiting and preparation businesses established in France and England to meet demand; horse hair often added to human hair to give it firmer finish. Gold wire thread and small pearls sometimes included. In 1840s and 1850s, lengths of hair braided to form bracelets, earrings, etc. In mid century, French jeweller, *Lemonnier, removed funereal association from hair jewellery by fanciful treatment in flower brooches etc. *c*1880, fashion declined; hair concealed in glass box at back of brooch, or locket.

hair spring. *Balance spring.

hakeme. *See* Punch'ŏng ware.

halb-Fayence. Earthenware covered with clear lead glaze over white slip. Similar effect to *faience. Applied to functional wares produced by German faience factories during 17th and 18th centuries. *cf mezza-maiolica.*

Hales, Stephen (1677–1761). English instrument-maker mainly noted for form of planetarium demonstrating orbits of planets round sun, driven by hand or clockwork mechanism.

half clock. *See* Massachusetts shelf clock.

half-hunter watch or **Napoleon watch.** Development of *hunter watch with aperture in front to show hands when cover is closed: traditionally invented by Napoleon Bonaparte, who cut hole in cover of his watch for convenience.

half-quarter repeater. *Repeating clock or watch which sounds a further stroke at or after middle of every quarter hour.

half-tester. Bed with *tester, attached to head-board, which extends over upper half of bed.

Hall, Peter Adolph (1739–93). Swedish-born miniaturist. From 1760, in Paris; painter to Louis XV; member of *Académie Royale des Beaux-arts* from 1769. Worked in oils and pastels. Ivory panels were mounted on gold boxes.

hall bench. *See* hall seat.

hall chair. Wooden side chair, placed in front hall. Often mahogany, with carved or ornamented back, sometimes incorporating family coat of arms. Dates from 18th century.

Hall chair. George II. Fruitwood, with painted eagle crest on back; one of a pair.

hall clock. In America, *long-case clock. Term also used in England, *c*1900.

Hallett or **Hallet,** William (1707–81). Eminent English cabinet maker, working in Chinese style. Received commissions from Duke of Chandos and other nobility. Possibly associated with W. *Vile and J. *Cobb.

Hall-in-the-Tyrol. Austrian glasshouse founded 1534 at Hall, near Innsbruck. Produced *façon de Venise* bowls, glasses, vases, and *tazze* in blue, green, and colourless glass, characterized by diamond-engraving and unfired lacquer-painting and gilding (often very similar to G. *Verzelini's glassware made at Crutched Friars Glasshouse). The **Reichsadlerhumpen* and **Stangengläser* display more hybrid style. In late 16th century, came under patronage of Archduke Ferdinand. Given to Franciscan order in 1635. Ceased production *c*1640.

hallmark or **poinçon** (French, 'punch' or 'stamp'). Symbol or device struck at assay office on gold or silver indicating that article conformed to legal standards of fineness set up by monarch, local guilds, government, etc. Can vary with each assay office. Term 'hallmark' means literally mark applied at Goldsmiths' Hall (London assay office since 1300). *See* charge mark, date letter, deacon's mark, discharge mark, drawback mark, duty mark, maker's mark, merchant's mark, month mark, province mark, Sterling mark, town mark.

hallmarking. System used for identification, and to guarantee, for buyer's protection, certified amount of pure gold or silver in finished article; necessary because precious metals must be alloyed with base metals for hardness and ease of working. Marks scratched or struck on gold or silver from ancient times; widely used

*Hall seat. George II. Mahogany, possibly designed by M. *Darly. Gothic carving and arched outline. Width 4ft3in.*

by Romans and Byzantines, but by Middle Ages practice had lapsed. France first European country to institute assay process, stamping wares with mark guaranteeing standard of fineness; England quickly followed. Philip II of France set standard of silver in 1275, and called for stamping of city mark. In 1300, leopard's head used as London city mark. Master's mark, first instituted at Montpellier, France, in 1355 (1363 in London), also indicated adherence to standard of fineness. Date letters introduced in France (1461) and England (1478) as additional safeguard. Rules applied with varying rigidity according to country. In general, hallmarking systems of France and England are not only oldest, but most consistent. *See* national entries, e.g. English gold and silver.

Halloren glasses. *Humpen made in Halle-an-der-Saale, Saxony, for members of salt-worker's guild. Enamelled with views of town, and processions. Popular in late 17th century; earliest known example, 1679.

hall seat or **bench.** Wooden seat with back and arms; usually ornate, e.g. back pierced, or carved with coat of arms of owner. Designed to be placed in hall. Dates from early 18th century. 19th century examples often in neo-classical or Elizabethan style.

hall or **hat stand.** Piece of wooden or metal hall furniture for holding coats, hats, umbrellas. May be tree-like structure with numerous pegs projecting from top of pole set in base incorporating metal tray to catch water from wet umbrellas. Circular support attached to pole holds umbrellas vertical, point downwards. Other models designed to stand against wall, may include shelf and mirror. Dates from early 19th century.

Hamadan carpets. West Persian village carpets woven around Hamadan from 19th century. Long goat or camel hair pile with coarse Turkish-knotting. Foundation usually cotton. Distinctive Hamadan weave has single thick weft thread woven between rows of knots; alternate warp threads raised, giving carpet's reverse side ribbed texture. Designs are simple, rectilinear; ground either unornamented in two tones of natural camel, or with overall small *boteh pattern. Broad camel-coloured band surrounding cartouche border. Chief colour camel, with dark blues, strong madders, and yellows in pattern. Numerous modern types, often of runner form.

William Hamlet Senior. Silhouette of naval officer. Painted on convex glass with details of uniform églomisé. *c1800.*

Han dynasty. Gilt bronze figure of bear. Gilt worn off in places. Length 5⅝in.

Hamburg, Germany. Faience factory flourished *c*1625–*c*1670. Form and decoration in contemporary Spanish styles, possibly because of trade connections. Products include dishes, and large pear-shaped jugs with spreading feet. Glaze subject to crazing. Mark: painter's initials only.

Hamlet, William (fl late 18th century). English silhouettist, working mainly in Bath, Somerset. Painted many full-length and equestrian profiles on glass, frequently with gold leaf enrichment. Subjects included George III. Also worked on card and ivory. Work has been mistakenly ascribed to son, William (1779–1815).

hammer-head thumbpiece. Thumbpiece on English pewter vessels from late 16th to end of 17th centuries: shaped like hammer-head surmounting, and at right-angles to, wedge.

Han dynasty (206 B.C.–A.D. 220). Chinese period following unification of China under Shih Huang Ti (221–206 B.C.). Era of intellectual freedom, expansion, and wealth. Trade with Roman Empire. Introduction of Buddhism; large stone sculptures and green glazed pottery wares often based on previous bronze forms. *See* Chinese jade, Ordos style, Chinese lacquer, hill jar, ming-ch'i. *Illustrations also at* hill-jar, hu, proto-porcelain.

hanap. English medieval term for *standing cup.

Hanau (Hesse). German faience factory founded in 1661 by religious refugees from Netherlands; continued, with many changes of ownership until 1806. Influenced first by Delft ware in Chinese style, e.g. double gourd-shaped vases; European motifs soon accompanied Chinese decoration. Jugs have spirally fluted bodies, long horizontally reeded necks, twisted rope-like handles, and often pewter mounts; in 18th century, often found with plain body and narrower neck and foot. *Vögelesdekor* often used. Plates in lobed and fluted shapes painted with shields, coats of arms, landscapes, or biblical scenes. From *c*1750, decoration both in high temperature colours and enamel. Cream-coloured earthenware produced from 1797. Until 1740, faience often marked with incised crescent; later, HVA or Hanau. Cream-coloured earthenware marked with crescent and small H.

Hancock, Joseph (*c*1711–91). English cutler working in Sheffield: became master cutler *c*1763. Earliest producer of wide range of Sheffield plate articles, including saucepans, coffee-pots, candlesticks, spoons, forks, tea urns. Turned to manufacture of rolled sheet metal for other makers, *c*1765.

Hancock, Robert (1730–1817). English engraver; thought to have been pupil of J. *Brooks at Battersea. Some engravings by him on Battersea enamels. Pioneer in transfer-printing porcelain, at first with overglaze enamels; engravings later printed in underglaze blue. Possibly worked at Bow, *c*1756. By 1757, introduced transfer-printing to Worcester; work includes portraits of Frederick the Great for use on mugs, and engraving, The Tea Party; shareholder in factory, 1772–74. In 1775, engravings used for transfer-printing at Caughley. Initials appear with anchor of R. *Holdship on transfer-printed porcelain made at Worcester. *Illustration at* transfer-printing.

hand-bell. *See* table bell.

handle-back. Chair back with opening in yoke-rail allowing chair to be carried easily. Term used *c*1850.

hands. On clocks, earliest style, *c*1550–*c*1675, simple black steel hour hand pinned to central arbor, usually with long tail projecting on opposite side for setting alarum dial (where present), which revolves with hand. Hand ends in arrowhead design; in evolution of hand, barbs of arrow gradually extended and curved away from shaft, eventually forming two complete circles in figure-of-eight pattern from which spade hand evolved in late 17th century. 18th century hands became more elaborate, often pierced and gilt on bracket clocks.

Minute hands, when introduced, of plain pointer form, often with small S-shaped section of shaft near centre. Use of wider *chapter-ring, c1700, accompanied by shorter hour hand, and most makers abandoned spade shape for decorated form. Early long-case clocks followed similar style; in early 18th century, use of anchor *escapement and long pendulum made seconds hand practicable; at first finely formed wihout tail and with narrow seconds dial; later becoming heavier.

Seconds hands used with tails from c1710, with hour and minute hands lighter in form; followed, c1770, by serpentine hands with arrowhead ends. Gilt hands, often pierced, found with painted dials from c1775. On French clocks, distinct style evolved by Louis XVI period, with hour and minute hands elaborately decorated, often of gilt-brass with lattice-work designs. Subsequently plain steel hands usual.

Watches, c1550–c1675, normally fitted with black steel hands, well shaped and finished, with long tails; other forms rarely found, e.g. of enamelled animal and bird shape. Minute and seconds hands unusual before introduction of balance spring, c1675; minute hand general by 1700. Beetle and poker style common in 18th century, with hour hand roughly resembling stag beetle, and minute hand straight. Hour hand also sometimes found with other elegant designs. Steel hands mostly 'blued' from early 18th century; gold hands used with white enamel dials. In France and Switzerland pierced shapes occur from c1750, but A-L. *Breguet favoured plain steel form and retained use of hour hand alone on *subscription watches. On watches, hands are set by fitting winding key to central square spindle carrying minute hand or (on *keyless types) by pressing push-piece to engage winding button with hands.

Hang-chou celadons. Chinese ceramics: *Kuan ware with greyish-white body, supposedly manufactured in Sung dynasty, in or near capital, Hang-chou (Chekiang province). Bluish or greyish green glaze applied in many layers with crackled effect resembling jade. Kiln site unidentified: name applied to any item too crackled or otherwise untypical (e.g. in shape) of *Lung-ch'üan celadon.

*Hang-chou ware. *Incense burner with greenish-grey crackle glaze. Found on the site of, and therefore probably made at, the *Chiao-t'an factory; Sung dynasty. Diameter 3½in.*

Hanging ball timepiece. Made in Augsburg, c1675, by Jacobus Mayr.

hanging clock. Clock suspended by chain, etc., wound round barrel: its own weight supplies power to movement. Weak spring rewinds chain when clock is lifted.

hanging shelves. *See* shelves.

hanging wall clock. *See* wall clock.

haniwa. Japanese ceramics: funerary ware (*cf* ming ch'i) figures dating from Tomb Mound Age (300–600). Originally hollow unglazed cylinders of reddish earthenware pierced with decoration, placed on tumuli; later, clay figures of men, women, horses, boats, miniature houses, are found.

Hannong family. Paul-Antoine Hannong (1700–60) established *Frankenthal porcelain factory 1755 (owner), having been forced by protectors of Vincennes monopoly to abandon porcelain production at *Strasbourg. Son, Charles-François-Paul (1732–57), director of Frankenthal factory, 1755–57. Joseph-Adam, also son, director at Frankenthal (1759–62) and Strasbourg (1762–81).

Hanoverian pattern. 18th century silver flatware pattern: tapering rib runs down front of stem from flat, rounded, slightly up-turned stem-end. Mainly produced c1710 to c1775, roughly corresponding to reign of Hanoverian monarchs in Britain.

Hanseatic bowl. 12th or 13th century brass, bronze, or copper basin for washing in; used with ewer, possibly of *aquamanile type. Round, with horizontal rim; inside decorated with engraved biblical or mythological scenes, also allegorical, philosophical, or moralizing themes. Made around Hanseatic League area of northern Germany.

Hanseatic Tankard. Pot-bellied, pewter drinking-vessel, dug up on North Sea coast bordering Hanseatic League area; believed to date from 14th century.

Hans Sloane plates. English porcelain plates made at Chelsea from 1755; painted with botanical specimens (Sir Hans Sloane's plants), butterflies, and caterpillars. Some designs from engravings of G. D. Ehret (d 1770, at Chelsea). Associated with Sir Hans Sloane, plant collector and founder of Chelsea Botanical Gardens, although he had died in 1753.

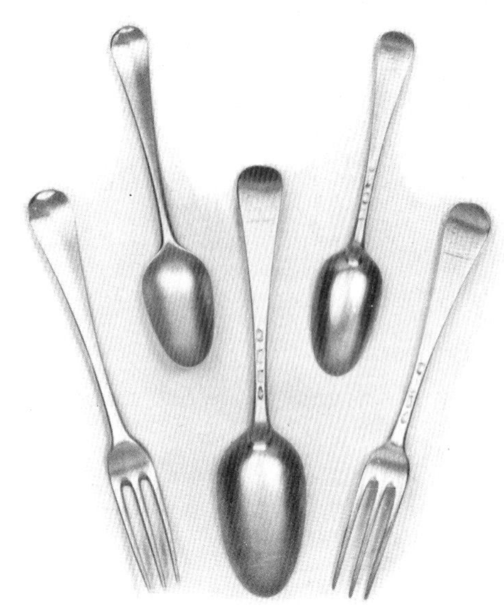

Hanoverian pattern. Table silver. Terminals engraved with contemporary crests; made by Isaac Callard, 1739–43.

Hanukkah lamp. Made in Frankfurt, c1760 by Rödger Herrfurt; embossed backpieces. Height c12in.

Hanukkah lamp. Brass or copper candelabrum with eight branches in single row, for oil lamps or candles, used at Jewish eight-day feast of Hanukkah.

Harache, Pierre (fl late 17th to early 18th centuries). Huguenot silversmith who probably arrived in London c1681; received freedom 1682 (first Huguenot to do so). Made range of domestic plate; patronized by aristocracy and royalty (William III, Queen Anne). S. *Pantin

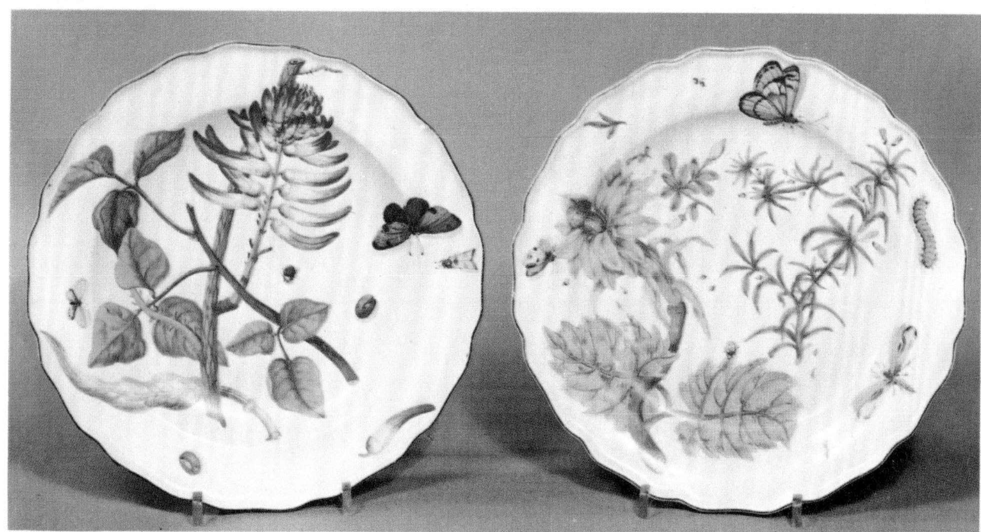

*Hans Sloane plates. *Chelsea porcelain, both with red anchor marks. Left, marked no. 8. Right: specimen of* Corallodendron, *flowers, leaves, and seeds, marked np. 34. Diameter of both 9½in.*

apprenticed to him; also son, Pierre, who continued in trade. Mark (1697): HA below two crosses with a crown above.

harbour scenes. Ceramic decoration introduced by J. G. *Herold at Meissen *c*1726. Groups of Turkish and Chinese traders in harbour setting, with bales on quayside, painted in polychrome enclosed by cartouches. Usually on teaware or vases in 1730s, notably by J. G. Herold, C. F. *Herold, B. G. Häuer, and J. G. *Heintze. Copied at Chelsea in 1751. Service made at Meissen painted in Berlin by J. B. *Bormann with Dutch harbour scenes, *c*1763.

Hardman, Iliffe & Co. Firm of button-makers in Birmingham; in 1837, formed subsidiary partnership with G. R. *Elkington to exploit patent for gilding metal. John Hardman the Younger, in association with A. W. N. *Pugin, founded additional firm (John Hardman & Co.) in 1838, to produce ecclesiastical plate and church furnishings in Gothic style. Pugin was firm's designer until his death (1852), when succeeded by pupil and son-in-law, John Hardman Powell.

hard metal. *See* Britannia metal.

hard-paste or **true porcelain.** *Porcelain made of clay mixed with fusible rock, fired at *c*1300°–1400°C. Chinese porcelain made from *kaolin and *petuntse. Glazed with powdered feldspathic rock and flux, e.g. lime and potash, dusted on and fused in single firing of body. Made in China from *c*9th century in primitive form, but type which reached West dates from Yüan dynasty. Secret of manufacture discovered *c*1708 by J. F. *Böttger, leading to production of Meissen porcelain; by mid 18th century hard-paste made also in e.g. France (at Strasbourg in 1750s, using kaolin imported from Germany), Italy, and Russia. First English hard-paste made by W. *Cookworthy, patented 1768. In America, first successful commercial porcelain manufacture by W. E. *Tucker, *c*1825.

hardstone. Stone used in jewellery or for decorative purposes, e.g. varieties of *quartz. *See pietra dura.*

hare's fur glaze. Chinese ceramics; dark brown glaze, streaked or mottled to resemble hare's fur. Found on stoneware tea bowls made in Sung dynasty, e.g. at Fukien, Honan, and Kiangsü.

Harland, Thomas (1735–1807). English-born watch and clock maker. Emigrated to America, 1773, setting up business in Norwich, Connecticut. Maker of many tall clocks characteristically with *'whale's-tail' hood. Developed methods of mass-production from 1791.

harlequin table. Late 18th century variation of *Pembroke table; combined breakfast and writing table. Concealed nest of drawers for writing materials may be mechanically raised from table interior when needed. (Name derived from obscure definition of harlequin, 'to conjure away'.)

harness furniture. *See* horse-brass.

harp. Ancient musical instrument consisting of series of strings stretched over open frame; played by plucking with fingers. Earliest known type was arched harp, semi-circular form used by Sumerians from *c*3000 B.C., and Egyptians from *c*2600 B.C.; also popular with Romans and Greeks. Earliest post-classical example known is six-stringed harp found in Sutton Hoo burial-ship, in Suffolk, dating from 7th century. Became extremely popular in Ireland from *c*11th century; triangular shape with pillar connecting curved neck and resonator (body) of harp; vary in size and number of strings. Medieval European harps probably based on Irish form. Slender Gothic harp, which evolved in mid 15th century with almost straight pillar, was used until 18th century; strings increased regularly. Double harp with two rows of strings common in 16th and 17th centuries; tuned diatonically. *Welsh harp common in 17th century. Single-action pedal harp appeared in early 18th century (said to have been invented in 1720 by Bavarian maker, Simon Hochbrucker); by use of pedals, any string could be shortened, altering pitch by semitone. Double-action pedal harp, invented by S. *Erard, *c*1810, used throughout Britain and Europe; two pedals could be depressed to variable degree, altering in pitch by tone or semitone. Harps usually elaborately ornamented with carving (scrolls, figures), gilding, etc., using contemporary motifs.

*Hare's fur glaze. Bowl, *temmoku, Sung dynasty.*

harp-lyre or **harpo-lyre.** Stringed instrument with guitar body and three fretted necks; plucked. 21 strings: right-hand neck has seven chromatic bass strings; middle neck, six strings tuned as ordinary guitar; and left-hand neck, eight gut treble strings. Strings pass over one or three soundholes; have common bridge. Patented in 1829 by Jean-François Salomon of Besancon, France.

harpsichord family. Group of stringed keyboard instruments including virginal, spinet, and harpsichord proper. Earliest form is virginal (often referred to as pair of virginals); oblong box for placing on table (sometimes has four-legged frame); number of strings varied but only one string per note; strings parallel to keyboard. Used from early 15th century; superseded in late 17th century by spinet and harpsichord. Spinet used

Harpsichord. Two manuals; keyboard has ivory naturals with boxwood mouldings and ebony accidentals. Walnut case with engraved brass hinges. By Thomas Blasser, 1744. Length 8ft1in.

*Harpsichord family. Spinet. By Baker Harris of London, 1766. Contemporary mahogany stand in *Chippendale style, with carved cabriole legs.*

from 16th century; very early example made in Italy in 1503. Like virginal, has one string per note, but is wing-shaped or triangular; strings at 45° angle to keyboard. Strings plucked by quills set in uprights ('jacks'). Most elaborate member of family is harpsichord; early surviving example made in Rome in 1521 by Geronimo di Bologna. Wing-shaped body, like spinet, but much larger; long straight side on player's left and keyboard on shorter side (*cf* clavichord). Two to four strings per note; metal strings at right angle to keyboard. Often has two manuals (keyboards), sometimes three. Also found with pedal keyboard. Harpsichord industry well-established in Italy from 16th century; cases and sound-boards made of thin cypress, with ornamental mouldings, inlaid ivory, etc. Rival centre of production at this time was *Ruckers family's workshop in Antwerp; instruments usually have two manuals (Italian examples, one); cases elaborately decorated with paintings. French 16th century examples based on Italian models; few survive. Production revived in 18th century, based on Antwerp models. In England, mainly produced in latter half of 18th century by B. *Shudi and J. Kirckman. In 18th century Germany produced by Hieronymus Hass and son, Johann, and Grabner family. Superseded in 19th century by pianoforte. Wooden cases of harpsichord group often lavishly decorated with carving, inlay, painting, etc. *Rose soundholes sometimes present.

Harrington, Sarah (fl from 1775). British silhouettist. In 1775, patented machine for taking profiles and reducing them (combination of camera obscura and pentagrapher, a primitive pantograph). Profiles usually cut from centre of white paper (hollow cut); aperture backed with black card or silk. Also cut profiles from black paper, and painted on silk or satin.

Harrison, John (1693–1776). English horologist; trained as carpenter but soon turned to clock making, e.g. made long-case clock in 1714, invented gridiron *compensation in 1725. Devoted most of life to development of accurate marine timekeeper for determining longitude at sea. First example, No 1, made with financial help from G. *Graham, embodied gridiron compensation applied to double bar balance, complex escapement known as 'grasshopper', and *maintaining power; tested 1736. No 2, built 1737–39 with improvements including *remontoire, never tested at sea. No 3 with further refinements, e.g. roller-bearings, built 1740–57. No 4 with similar mechanism but in form of large watch, qualified for award of £20,000 from Board of Longitude in voyages to Jamaica (1761) and Barbados (1764), with error of less than 0·1 second per day, but Harrison was paid prize only after intervention of George III. Duplicate of No 4 made by L. Kendall, taken on Captain Cook's second voyage, now with Harrison's Nos 1–4 in National Maritime Museum, Greenwich.

Hartl, Johann Paul Rupert (1715–92). German porcelain chemist, possibly modeller, son of repairer. Factory manager at Nymphenburg (1754–61). No work identified with certainty.

Hartley Greens & Co. *See* Leeds.

Hartmann, Georg (1489–1564). German priest and mathematician. Designed complicated sundials; also made instruments, including astrolabes.

Harvard chair. Three-legged chair, made entirely of turned parts. American, 17th century.

harvester. *See* haystack.

harvest jugs. English *sgraffiato* earthenware jugs with various motifs, e.g. ships, compasses, heraldic animals, deer, flowers, and birds, scratched through white slip. Often stained or mottled green with copper oxide; clay coiled at base of handle. Made by *Fishley family and other North Devon potters from late 17th century to *c*1900, commemorating harvest.

hash spoon. *See* serving spoon.

Haslem, John (d 1808). English miniaturist and porcelain painter. Painted portraits and figures on porcelain plaques and pictures at Derby until 1848. Wrote history of factory, published 1876. Also worked as painter on enamel.

hastener. Semi-circular metal plate attachable to *spit for reflecting heat from fire on to meat. *cf* Dutch oven.

haster. High cupboard with open, metal-lined back, which faces fire, thus keeping plates in cupboard warm. Dates from 18th century.

hat badge. *See* badge, *enseigne*.

hatching. Creation of shade or tone on silver surface with engraved parallel lines (*see* cross-hatching, heraldic engraving). Similer technique used in painting, and applied to miniatures, etc.

Hatchlie, Hatchlu, or **Katchlie rugs.** Small, post-Crusades Turkoman or Caucasian prayer rugs. Large cross divides field into quarters decorated with numerous small candle-holders.

hat stand. *See* hall stand.

Häuer or **Hoyer,** Bonaventura Gottlieb (1710–82). One of leading *Meissen porcelain painters (1724–82). Specialized in landscapes and armorial decoration. Occasionally signed pieces BGH Ping.

Haupt, George (1741–84). Swedish cabinet maker; worked in Paris, probably with Simon Deben, and in London (1768–69) before returning to Sweden.

Hausmaler (German, 'home painter'). Independent painter of glass, faience, porcelain, and enamel wares. *See Hausmalerei.*

Harvest jug. Earthenware, made in North Devon, dated 1741; covered with cream slip and *sgraffiato *decoration.*

Hatchlie carpet (detail). Turkoman, 19th century, showing central ground of candlesticks.

Heart-back chair. Mahogany with inlay of eagle and shell at centre and base of splats. Late 18th century.

Johann Martin Heinrici. Gold mounted lapis lazuli box decorated in lac burgauté *technique. Length 2½in.*

Hausmalerei (German, 'work of **Hausmaler*'). Independent decoration of faience, and porcelain, glass, and enamel objects in Germany, Austria and Bohemia. Early *Hausmaler* flourished late 17th century, enamelling glass, silver, and copper, then painting faience, and, later, porcelain. Earliest centres from which undecorated faience was obtained, Frankfurt, Hanau, and Nuremberg (where J. *Schaper active). Polychrome palette first used on faience in painting of intricate biblical scenes at Nuremberg *c*1675 (marked with monogram, AH). Numbers rose with growth of faience production. Some *Hausmaler* were factory employees who obtained unpainted pieces dishonestly; others, like J. F. *Metzsch at Bayreuth, purchased out-dated porcelain pieces from Meissen and Vienna before they were manufactured locally. Quality of decoration varies widely. Important *Hausmaler* include J. *Aufenwerth, I. *Bottengruber, S. *Hosenestel, D. *Preissler, I. *Preissler, B. *Seuter, and E. A. O. *von dem Busch. After 1730 most faience decoration was applied in factories, although signed pieces, probably painted independently by artists such as J. P. *Dannhöfer and A. F. *von Löwenfinck, have been identified. After 1728, in some states, heavy theoretical penalties limited *Hausmaler*, whose flourishing workshops threatened business of new porcelain factories. However, Meissen released numerous undecorated pieces (1735–45). Demand for *Hausmalerei* subsided in 18th century, but revived briefly in Empire period, when souvenir ceramics were in vogue.

haute-lisse loom. *See* high-warp loom.

hawksbill. Large, early 17th century type of *ewer.

hawthorn ginger jar. *See* ginger jar.

haystack or **harvester.** 19th century Irish pewter measure with cylindrical base diminishing from lower handle-joint to narrow neck, and wide, flaring brim.

heaped and piled effect. *See* Hsüan Tê

Heart, The ('t Hart). Delft factory (1661–after 1762) managed by *Mesch family until 1745. J. *van der Laan employed.

heart-back. Hepplewhite variation of *shield-back chair, with heart-shaped outline incorporated in rim of back.

hearth furniture. *See* fire-place furniture.

heart pattern. Dutch ceramic decoration: heart-shaped medallion surrounding painting, e.g. of flowers, on Delft ware vessels from *c*1725; later mainly on plates.

Heath, John (fl mid and late 18th century). English banker and pottery manufacturer. With brother Christopher among partners in Cockpit Hill pottery, Derby, *c*1751–79. Partner with W. *Duesbury in porcelain factories at Derby from 1756 and Chelsea from 1770. Bankrupted 1780.

Heath, Thomas (fl mid 18th century). Potter at Shelton, Staffordshire, credited by J. *Wedgwood with addition of ground flints to stoneware body to produce white *salt-glaze (development also attributed to J. *Astbury).

heddle. In weaving, assembly of leashes and rod; when lifted, rod raises appropriate warp threads so that weft may be inserted.

Hedwig glasses. Small group of beakers named after Hedwig, patron saint of Silesia and Poland (d 1243), said to have owned one. 3–5in. high, of thick, transparent glass, with greyish-green or yellow tinge. Deeply cut in stylized high relief; main motifs heraldic, or animals, e.g. lion, eagle, or griffin. Origin thought to be Egypt or Byzantium, though recent discoveries suggest 12th century Kiev, Russia.

Heian (794–1185). Japanese period, when nation remained peaceful; Chinese influence in arts became less pronounced. Imported Chinese art forms, e.g. lacquer-work, progressively naturalized. Fine inlaid pieces, with gold, silver, or mother-of-pearl. Buddhism provided impetus for art forms, notably sculpture in wood, lacquer, and metal-work. Few objects survive, except for mirrors. In ceramics, increasingly Japanese character developed in motifs and shapes; domestic stone-ware most notable product. Followed by Kamakura period.

Heinrici, Johann Martin (1711–86). German porcelain painter, working at Meissen (1741–56). Specialized in miniature portraits; signed examples exist. At Frankenthal (1756–63) as *Hausmaler*; original work includes snuff-boxes and *Galanterien* decorated with gold, mother-of-pearl and shell inlay, and black lacquer. Returned to Meissen 1764.

Heintze, Johann Georg (fl 1720–49). German porcelain painter at Meissen under J. G. *Herold. Specialized in European landscape medallions of harbour scenes, small figures, etc., set against elaborate, symmetrical gilt-patterned ground (1740). Occasionally signed pieces. Imprisoned 1749 for activities as *Hausmaler*. Subsequently worked at Prague, Vienna, and Berlin (no work after 1749 identified with certainty).

Heinzelman border. Porcelain decoration in blue, surrounding rim of jug, inscribed Frederick Heinzelman, Liverpool, and attributed to Z. *Barnes. Band of blue with joined white hexagons, each enclosing blue and white flower shape. Border used with flower decoration, e.g. convolvulus.

Helchis, Helkis, or **Helchs,** Jacobus (*c*1700–50). Porcelain painter, born in Trieste, Italy; worked in Vienna, either at factory, or as *Hausmaler* *c*1725–47. Known for *Schwartzlot* painting. Subjects include cupids and masks, *putti*, flowers. Occasionally added touches of yellow and pink to monochromes. Style resembles that of D. and I. *Preissler, and

I. *Bottengruber. Known marks: Jacobus Helchs fecit, and IH (1725).

Hele, Peter. *See* Henlein, Peter.

Hellot, Jean (1685–1766). Porcelain decorator and colour chemist at Vincennes and Sèvres, 1745–66. Developed underglaze and enamel ground colours including **bleu céleste,* **jaune jonquille,* and *pea green.

helmet ewer. Vessel shaped like deep, circular, inverted helmet with curved pouring lip and wide foot. Made in silver, silver-gilt, and gold in late 17th and 18th centuries, with scroll or harp-shaped handle; form adopted by French Huguenot silversmiths and widely used (*see* rosewater ewer and basin). Also made in French faience from early 18th century, notably at Rouen and Moustiers. Decoration usually in blue, *style Berain* or elaborate *lambrequins. Illustration at* G. Ravenscroft.

Heming, Thomas (fl *c*1740–82). English silversmith working in London. Appointed royal goldsmith to George III (1760). Prepared regalia and plate for coronation and supplied domestic plate for next 20 years. In 1764 received order for Communion plate for Anglican churches in America (chalices, patens, etc.); plain, in contrast with secular work in rococo style. Made almost identical toilet services for Princess Caroline Matilda (1766) and Williams-Wynn family (1768). Probably retired in 1773; son, George, and partner, W. Chawner, completed order for two dinner services for Catherine the Great of Russia. Marks: TH (registered 1745); TH crowned (*c*1770).

Hendler, Philipp (fl late 18th century). German porcelain modeller. Worked at Meissen (until 1769) and Vienna; also at Fürstenberg (*c*1780–85), where some neo-classical models, including Metamorphosis of Dryope (1782), and a Venus (1785) are attributed to him.

Henlein or **Hele,** Peter (*c*1479–1542). German watch maker from *Nuremberg; master lock-smith, 1509. First reported maker of pocket watches, *c*1510–*c*1520.

Hennell family. Family of silver craftsmen working in London (over 30 marks registered at Goldsmiths' Hall). David (1712–85) granted freedom in 1735, and set up business in following year. Mark: DH, in Gothic and Roman script. Son, Robert (1741–1811), granted freedom in 1763 and joined father in business; joint mark: DH with R above, H below (two versions). When David retired (1772), Robert registered own mark RH (four versions). In 1795 Robert's son David (b 1767) registered mark with father: RH above DH. With second son, Samuel (1778–1837), another mark registered 1802: RH, DH, SH (in two sizes). David retired in 1802, leaving father and Samuel in possession; mark: RH above SH. Samuel left in sole possession of firm in 1811 on death of father; 1814–16, in partnership with John Terry. Samuel died 1837.

Second family firm founded by David's grandson, Robert (b 1769), whose father, John, also trained as silversmith, but had never practised trade. Robert received freedom (1785) after serving apprenticeship with uncle, Robert, and an engraver. Probably worked only as engraver until 1808, when formed silversmithing partnership with H. Nutting (joint mark: two versions of HN above RH); partnership lasted only a year; in 1809, Robert registered first of own marks: RH. Retired 1833; succeeded by son Robert (1794–1868), whose own son, also Robert (*c*1826–92) was apprenticed (to father) and in turn took over business. *Illustrations at* mustard pot, sauceboat, sugar nippers.

Henri II style. Includes two contrasting mid French Renaissance furniture styles (from Paris and Burgundy regions) both identified with reign of Henri II (1547–89). In Paris region, Italian Renaissance influence was stronger than in preceding François I style; architectural forms replaced simple, Gothic rectangular style in furniture, and severe classical simplicity and proportion was introduced, with slim columns, architectural mouldings, and lighter treatment of carved decoration. Other style centred around Burgundy; characterized by rich, ornate carving and exaggerated mouldings, particularly suited to large pieces of furniture, e.g. *armoires;* H. *Sambin was a leading exponent. During period, walnut replaced oak as main wood; rich fabrics and draperies important in furnishing. Characteristic pieces in both styles include testers, draped and built-in beds, heavily-carved chests, refectory tables.

*Henri II style. Walnut cabinet in manner of J. *Goujon. Broken *swan-neck pediment with figure of seraph in architectural niche. Central figure below is Ceres; cupboard doors either side carved with allegorical oval medallions. Upper section supported by male and female winged caryatids with goat feet. Height 6ft8in.*

Henri II ware. *See* Saint-Porchaire. 19th century copies of Saint-Porchaire, e.g. by C. *Toft, referred to as Henri II ware.

Henzey family. Important glass making family in England from 1568, when Thomas and Balthazar de Henezel came from Lorraine to Weald of southern England, under contract to J. *Carré to make window glass. With other Lorrainers, e.g. Tyzack and Tittery families, descendants (known as Hennese, Hennesy, Henzeym, Henzie, Henzell, or Ensell) moved to other glass making areas, particularly Stourbridge and Newcastle-upon-Tyne. In 17th century Newcastle, under licence to Sir R. *Mansell, helped to establish glasshouses, to make window glass. In 18th century, W. Henzell & Co, and Henzell & Co, specialized in producing bottles. In Stourbridge, Joshua Henzey, also under licence to Mansell, established two glasshouses to produce window glass, and a bottle factory. George Ensell founded Red House Glass Works (1776), specializing in fine German-style cut glass. Frederick Stuart, a former apprentice, acquired works in 1881; firm now known as Stuart & Sons Ltd. Family also connected with *Brierly Hill Glass Works and Wordsley Glass Works, both noted from 18th century for fine cut glass. *See* Lorraine glass makers.

Hepplewhite, George (d 1786). English cabinet maker and designer. Known for designs published posthumously in The Cabinet-Maker and Upholsterer's Guide (1788, 1789, 1794). Designs inspired light, elegant furniture fashionable in late 18th century.

Hepplewhite style. Furniture style popular in England *c*1780–95; in America, *c*1785–1800; based on drawings in G. *Hepplewhite's The Cabinet-Maker and Upholsterer's Guide.

Herculaneum Pottery. Plate, with pierced and basketwork rim; enamelled with two figures in landscape. Early 19th century.

Hepplewhite style. Poudreuse. *Late 18th century. Satinwood with *cross-banding around every edge and two plaques of burr-wood inset at either side of mirror.*

Influenced by Adam and Louis XVI styles, also by work of T. *Chippendale and, later, T. *Sheraton. Peak of neo-classical development in English furniture.

Pieces usually rectilinear, elegantly proportioned; curves introduced in seat rails, chair and sofa backs, tracery on glazed doors, etc. Legs often turned, or square in section and tapered, sometimes with reeded and fluted surfaces. Cabriole legs shown mainly in the 1788 and 1789 Guides. Chair and settee backs frequently shield-shaped or oval, enclosing open-work designs; others square-backed (mainly in 1794 Guide). Chairs seldom have stretchers. Beds usually draped, or with testers; emphasis on hangings. Slim bedposts taper upwards; often reeded. The **confidante* and **duchesse brisée* reflect Louis XVI style. *Pier, *card, and *Pembroke tables, also pedestal furniture (desks, sideboards, library tables, etc.) common. Wardrobes began to replace tallboys in popularity. Much work in mahogany and satinwood e.g. carved, or with marquetry in rare woods, stringing, or inlay (sometimes in panels and ovals). Painting, lacquering, and gilding also used. Neo-classical decorative motifs on Hepplewhite furniture include acanthus, husk, lyre, swags, wheat, and wreaths; neither animal nor human figures appear. Upholstered pieces padded and covered with linen, leather, tapestry, or figured and painted satins and silks. *Illustration also at* sideboard.

heraldic engraving. Heraldic ornament (usually coats of arms) popular on gold and silver plate from Middle Ages; executed in enamels. Practice continued until 16th century, when engraved coats of arms became popular. Silversmith often left blank escutcheon to be filled in with coat of arms by engraver. Simple line engraving normally used; from *c*1600, *hatching also used in Europe to obtain effect of depth; uncommon in England until end of 17th century. Heraldic engraving became particularly popular in England; development can be traced in style of shield and secondary ornament. From *c*1635, square-topped shield surrounded by laurel wreath popular; also with added helmet and crest and plumed mantling. In mid 17th century, basically square shield used, with flat or three-pointed top. Ornament varied, e.g. palm leaves crossed and knotted below shield, feathered ornament. Generally even number of plumes, arranged to fall towards or away from shield. Embossed, scrolled cartouche appeared briefly in late 17th century for coat of arms. In early 18th century, shield circular, oval, or shaped cartouche, surrounded by foliate ornament and scrollwork, later by swags, grotesque masks, etc. In rococo period, shield became irregular, as did scrollwork. Late 18th century shield has three-pointed top and tapers to V, with festooning ornament or two palm branches. At end of 18th century, shield again square with flat top and sides splayed out at angle below top. 19th century coats of arms similar to preceding two, but more florid. Manufacturers of Sheffield plate developed method of applying silver shield to article so that copper would not show through when coat of arms was engraved. Heraldic engraving unreliable indication of age of piece; coat of arms could be engraved on earlier piece (with blank shield), or old coat of arms could be erased and new one engraved (detectable by weakening of silver at that point). Engraving of initials of owner on plate also common practice. English styles much copied in America.

Herat carpets. Large east Persian carpets woven in Herat. Peak production in 16th and 17th centuries with numerous floral court carpets; many exported to India and via India to Europe. Deep wine-red, moss-green, and yellow dominate characteristic floral design, so-called herati motif. 16th century pattern has superimposed spiral stem lattices with lanceolate, curved leaves, palmettes, and cloud bands; animals or birds often infill field. In 17th century, reduced scale, with simplified herati motif; widely copied. Also, from mid 18th century, durable carpets with central medallion and herati pattern on dark blue or white ground.

herati or **Ferahan pattern.** Floral motif on Persian carpets. Four curved, serrated leaves separate rosettes or palmettes within angular trellises. *Illustration at* Mogul carpet.

Herculaneum Pottery, Liverpool, Lancashire. Opened in 1796. Produced cream-coloured earthenware, transfer-printed in underglaze blue and black enamel, sometimes with added colour, notably on jugs decorated with ships. Pearlware jugs sometimes have black lines and transfer-printing or relief decoration with underglaze colours. Also produced buff stoneware, and black basalt including black vases with white stoneware plinths. Some porcelain made from early 19th century. Closed in 1841. Marks include HERCULANEUM, sometimes on garter, with crown, printed (until 1833), HERCULANEUM, impressed or printed in blue (1822–71), and liver bird, impressed or printed from *c*1825.

Hereke carpets. Good quality west Turkish woollen or silk carpets woven at Hereke court manufactory from 1844. No original style; designs based on 16th and 17th century Persian and Turkish court carpets.

Heriz carpets. Very tough, west Persian medallion pattern carpets with coarse, Turkish-

Hereke carpet. Woven in silk. 19th century. 6ft1in.×4ft5in.
Heriz carpet. Persian, silk, c1850. 4ft9in.×3ft1in.

knotted woollen pile, woven in Heriz. Design has large, angular central medallion with palmette pendants along vertical axis, corner-pieces repeating medallion pattern, and stylized floral background. Design in reds, blues, pale green, and browns on characteristic rust-red ground. Borders often use double stem scroll and palmettes.

Herold, Christian Friedrich. German porcelain painter, probably related to J. G. *Herold. Began as enamel painter at Fromery workshop, Berlin. Key painter at Meissen factory 1725–77. Specialized first in harbour scenes in panels reserved from delicate ground colours (e.g. sea-green, *c*1735). Painted battle and genre scenes on snuff-boxes. Identified work includes signed snuff-boxes, tankard, cup and saucer. Signatures *Herold invt,* or *Herold fec* might be his.

Herold or **Höroldt,** Johann Gregorius (1696–1775). German court painter; also designed tapestries; as porcelain painter, apprenticed (1719) at Vienna porcelain factory. Art director at *Meissen (1720–65); reorganized factory after death of J. F. *Böttger, improving whiteness of porcelain body. Also promoted Chinese and Japanese designs, *chinoiseries,* and European landscapes (1722 onwards). Extended range of enamels, introducing enamel ground colours (1726–27), notably pale blue, deep lilac, pale violet, purple, apple-green, sea-green, *dead-leaf brown, and yellow. Introduced *harbour scenes (1730); **deutsche Blumen,* and naturalistic birds (*c*1737). Rare examples of work include presentation pieces and snuff-boxes. Isolated signatures, and mark H in double circle, ascribed to him, but most identification speculative. Keen competition with J. J. *Kändler, contemporary *Modellmeister*. Influence declined after *c*1760.

Herrebøe. Norwegian faience factory established by 1758. Products, including wall fountains, wash basins, trays, tureens, bishop bowls, and other tableware, usually painted in underglaze blue or manganese-purple, although rare polychrome examples exist; occasionally turquoise ground colour used. Rococo motifs, sometimes modelled in relief, include foliage, scrollwork, shells, and naturalistic flowers. Factory changed hands in 1762; continued to operate until 1772. Sold in 1778. Marks, rarely used, include HB monogram, HERREBÖE FABRIQE or, more frequently, numbers.

Herrengrund cups. 17th and 18th century display goblets made in Herrengrund, Germany, from local copper. Often elaborately moulded and gilded, set with precious stones, or enamelled.

Herrera style. Spanish style of architecture and furniture, during late 16th century, named after Juan de Herrera (*c*1530–97), architect to Philip II. Reaction against elaborate *Plateresque style apparent in classical simplicity of form and line, lack of all but simplest surface decoration, and influence of Italian architects, e.g. Palladio. Herrera beds have characteristic architectural head-board decorated with rows of arcading, possibly also ivory inlay, and religious bronze on top. Superseded by *Churrigueresque style in 17th century.

herring-bone or **feather banding.** Decorative use of thin diagonally-grained strips of veneer on furniture or panelling. Strips set side by side, with angle of grain alternating from row to row to resemble feather or herring-bone design.

Heuglin, Johann Erhard II (*c*1672–1757). German silversmith working in Augsburg; master in 1717. Designed and made domestic silver; favourite motif, human bust in medallion. Mark: IE above H. *Illustration also at* pattern book.

hexagonal table clock. Spring-driven six-sided table clock, produced mainly in Germany and France. German development of *drum clock, with dial on top; bun feet, sometimes claw form; made from late 16th until 18th century. In France, clocks in form of upright hexagon produced, notably during 16th century.

hibachi. *See* Japanese metal-work.

Hickes, Richard. *See* Hyckes, R.

high-boy. American tall chest, resembling chest of drawers set on *low-boy. Often of Cuban mahogany, or with veneered or lacquered surface; commonly with cabriole legs. May be made to match low-boy. Popular from end of 17th century and throughout 18th. Fine examples from Philadelphia, Pennsylvania, and Rhode Island; also produced in other parts of New England. *cf* tallboy.

High-boy. Mahogany, made in Philadelphia, Pennsylvania, c*1760–75. Height 8ft 1in.*

high-post bed. *Fourposter with posts ending in finials, without tester. Popular in America *c*1800–50.

High Standard. *See* Britannia Standard.

high-temperature, underglaze, or **grand feu colours.** Metallic pigments applied to raw glaze and fixed in firing of glaze. Usually oxides mixed with flux and substance such as flint to prevent running and blurring under glaze. Range of colours restricted to those which withstand high temperature (usually 1200–1400°C): blue (cobalt), purple or brown (manganese), green (copper), yellow (antimony), brick-red (iron).

Hillebrand, Friedrich (d 1608). German silversmith working in Nuremberg; master in 1580. Made numerous ornate standing cups; favoured nautilus shell with silver or silver-gilt mount.

Hill, John (fl late 18th, early 19th centuries). English glass manufacturer from established glass making family in Stourbridge, Worcestershire. Because of *Glass Excise Act, went to Ireland, *c*1783, where employed by *Penrose brothers to establish Waterford Glass Works. According to contemporary records, took with him 'the best set of workmen he could get in the county of Worcester'. Factory achieved worldwide reputation for high quality glassware under his directorship (three years).

Hilliard, Lawrence (1581–*c*1647). English miniaturist and goldsmith, son of N. *Hilliard and successor as limner to James I. Miniatures in style of father, but weaker.

Hilliard, Nicholas (d 1619). English goldsmith and miniaturist, first native miniaturist of note. Limner to Elizabeth I and James I; also designed and engraved second Great Seal of Elizabeth I; possibly executed jewels and medals. Painted on prepared parchment. Visited France 1577–78; work related to French court painting as well as to H. *Holbein. Miniatures usually three-quarter face with no dark shading; carmines have usually faded. Early work varied in shape; later predominantly elliptical. Work includes various portraits of Elizabeth I, of self, and family; also Queen Anne of Denmark and half- and full-length miniatures, e.g. man leaning against a tree, with rose-bushes.

hill jar. Pottery and bronze shape typical of Han dynasty. In pottery, takes form of cylindrical jar, often glazed green, on three feet, with conical lid moulded to form mountains. Animals are sometimes depicted in relief on stylized landscape. In bronze, shape may be stimilar, or in form of *tou. In both cases, hill lid is pierced for use as censer. Origin obscure, but possibly derived from Taoist Shou Shan hills where Hsi Wang Mu, Queen Mother of the West, guards peaches of immortality.

Himeji. Japanese kiln site in Harima province; manufactured celadon and blue-and-white porcelain in 19th century.

hinge. *See* door-furniture.

hip. *See* knee.

hipped leg. Cabriole chair leg with top extending above level of seat rail.

Herrera style. Late 16th century Spanish rustic table. Walnut, with deep moulded drawers and heavily turned legs.

Hirado (Hizen). Japanese porcelain made for princes of Hirado at Mikawachi. Pottery formerly produced in same area, but porcelain dates from 1712. Finest wares made during princes' patronage, 1751–1843. Never marked. Delicate, fine-grained, pure white paste, painted in miniature style with figures, e.g. boys playing, and landscapes, in soft, violet-toned blue. Deeper shade of blue used as ground colour. Some relief decoration, or separate figures and small objects, modelled in the round. Sometimes, celadon-glazed porcelain produced.

Hispano–Moresque ware. Tin-glazed earthenware produced by potters in Spain, *c*1200–*c*1800, using techniques developed under Islamic rule. Early work includes bowls, dishes, pitchers, and storage jars decorated with predominantly Moorish designs, made at Malaga. Usually painted with foliage, Kufic script, and sometimes animals, e.g. deer, in blue, finished with lustre, often pale straw colour or, in 17th century, copper. Examples include *Alhambra vase. **Cuerda seca* technique used in 11th and 12th centuries to control glazes, chiefly on dishes made in Valencia. From late 15th century, pottery decorated in underglaze colours without lustre decoration at *Talavera de la Reina. Soon after end of Moorish rule in Andalusia (1487), main production of lustre ware moved to Valencia area, notably *Manises, where **mudéjar* style developed. Rise of Catholicism in Spain and removal of Moslem prohibition on use of precious metal encouraged replacement of lustre ware with metal, glass, and porcelain. However, lustre ware manufacture continued at Manises in 17th century for export, e.g. to England.

Hitchcock, Lambert (1795–1825). American cabinet maker, best known for *Hitchcock chairs. Born in Cheshire, Connecticut; estab-

Above:
Johann Erhard Heuglin II. Pair of footed salvers, made in Augsburg, c1720. Border patterned with guilloches *and engraving of animals, vases of foliage, and floral trellis-work; four applied vignettes of* putti *in landscapes on each salver.*

Hilliard family. Left: portrait of young man with black doublet and embroidered shirt, by Lawrence Hilliard, c1620. Right: portrait of young man in bed jacket, by Nicholas Hilliard, c1585.
Below:
*Hill jar. *Han dynasty; red earthenware and brown glaze. Moulded lid possibly represents Taoist Shou Shan hills.*

Hispano-Moresque pottery. Left: tazza with gadrooned decoration from Teruel or Majorca, mid 16th century; diameter 10in. Centre: jug with all over lustre glaze, 15th century. Right: plate, probably Catalan, late 15th century.

Hitchcock chair. American, c1820, marked Hitchcockville. Stencilled metallic fruit and leaf decoration; gilded striping and arrows pointing downwards on back posts; rush seats.

lished business in Berkhampstead, Connecticut, where adjacent area became known as Hitchcockville. Firm first called L. Hitchcock; after 1829, became partnership of Hitchcock, Alford & Co; from 1843 (when Hitchcock left business), called Alford & Co.

Hitchcock chair. Open-back American side chair with rush, cane, or wooden seat. Back has turned yoke-rail, widening at centre; central slat (sometimes shaped), often with narrower slat below. Back legs and uprights made from continuous single pieces, flat in front; front legs turned. Painted black, with gilt stencilled or painted decoration, usually with fruit or floral motif. First made by L. *Hitchcock (*c*1825–45); 1826–43, firm's name and Warranted, printed under seat. Also made by other firms and cabinet makers.

high-warp, vertical, or **haute-lisse loom.** Tapestry-loom on which warp threads stretched between two vertically aligned rollers, then divided by hand (with batten) into sets of odd and even threads through which weft threads pass to form pattern. Tapestry-weaver stands behind loom, facing reverse side of work. As pattern worked, finished portion winds round bottom roller and unwoven warps unwind from top roller. High-warp loom employed exclusively for great tapestries woven from 13th to late 15th centuries. Replaced by more efficient *low-warp looms, first used in Brussels, later throughout Europe. In 17th and 18th centuries, Gobelins Manufactory alone valued high-warp loom tapestries above low-warp loom works.

historical china. In America, cream-coloured eathenware imported from England in late 18th and early 19th centuries; transfer-printed with American views, portraits of contemporary personalities, and historical events, such as Landing of Lafayette (1824) and opening of Erie Canal. Made in Staffordshire, e.g. by *Adams family, J. and R. *Clews, E. *Mayer, J. and W. *Ridgway, and E. *Wood. Other examples include *Liverpool jugs.

ho. Ancient Chinese ritual bronze vessel, of late Shang and Chou periods. Three-lobed body (*cf* li), tapering to column feet, covered with domed lid, and bearing bold, tubular spout. Used probably as wine serving vessel. *cf* ting.

Hoadley, Silas (1786–1870). American clock maker, from Connecticut. Worked with E. *Terry. Made tall clocks in pine cases with 30-hour wooden movement. Also shelf clocks, including *pillar and scroll.

Hochschnitt (German, 'high cut'). High relief engraving on glass; technique perfected by 18th century German engravers, particularly in Bohemia. Usually employed in conjunction with **Tiefschnitt*. Most notable *Hochschnitt* engraver, F. *Gondelach.

Höchst (Hesse). German factory founded 1746 for production of faience under patronage of Elector of Mayence (Mainz) by A. F. *von Löwenfinck, who introduced enamel-painting and employed painters including J. P. *Dannhöfer. *c*1746–*c*1756, produced vases painted with landscapes, sometimes in black, with rococo painted frames, or *deutsche Blumen*. Small tureens moulded with rococo scrollwork, painted in yellow, light blue, and crimson, similar to examples from Strasbourg. Figures, bird-groups, and tureens, e.g. in form of game birds or boar's heads, sometimes painted by J. *Zeschinger. Marks: six-spoked wheel of Mayence, generally with painter's initials, including D (possibly Dannhöfer). Zeschinger used surname, or Z.

Porcelain made from *c*1750 by J. *Benckgraff and J. J. *Ringler. Paste initially rather coarse; later milk-white, and fine, like that of Frankenthal. Best period, *c*1750–75. Closed down 1798. Employed, e.g. Zeschinger (painter), S. *Feilner (modeller), and G. F. *Riedel (designer). Figures (except later biscuit models) and later tableware, generally marked. Modern reproductions of figures sometimes detectable by high gloss or heaviness of form. Groups include Freemasons, Minuet Dancers, etc. (*c*1755). L. *Russinger, *Modellmeister* 1762–66, introduced Louis XVI style; naturalistic grassy mounds replaced rococo bases of figures. J. P. *Melchior, *Modellmeister* 1767–79, noted for many figures of children, a Venus, a bust of Goethe, and creamy biscuit busts in neo-classical style (*c*1715). Tablewares *c*1750–65 recall Meissen and Frankenthal in rococo forms and painting style. *Teniers subjects delicately executed (*c*1765–80); typical colours include egg-yolk yellow, bright blue, and clear red. During last period (*c*1780–99) mainly functional wares produced, sometimes with dull blue ground and elaborately gilded decoration. Marks: several versions of six-spoked wheel motif from Mayence arms in red or purple enamel (1750–62) or in underglaze blue (1762–96); also impressed wheel (*c*1760–65).

Höchst. Pair of porcelain figures of quarrelling children, c1770. Height c6in.

Höckel, Jacob Melchior. German porcelain painter, modeller, arcanist. Worked at Höchst (1767) and Pfalz-Zweibrücken (1767–75). At Kelsterbach, after 1789; work may have included copy of a Meissen Pierrot.

Hofdyck, Dammas (d 1726). Dutch potter at Delft. Joint owner (1691–94) of Fortune factory. Managed The Rose factory, 1694–1712. Specialized in religious subjects, painted in blue. Owned The White Star factory from 1705.

Hoffmeister of Vienna (fl early 19th century). One of many Bohemian glass enamellers imitating style of S. and G. S. *Mohn and A. *Kothgasser. Decorated several similar enamelled beakers with cog-wheel-cut base. Signed name in full.

Hofkellerei glasses (German, 'Court cellar glasses'). **Humpen*, usually bearing enamelled arms of local Court brewers; most made in Saxony during 16th and 17th centuries.

Hogarth glasses. Short English drinking glasses with rudimentary stem and thick foot, similar to *bumping glass. Name derives from paintings by W. *Hogarth in which they appear (e.g. The Rake's Progress).

Hogarth, William (1697–1764). English painter and engraver working in London; apprenticed to goldsmith in 1712. Possibly engraved for P. *de Lamerie *c*1718–*c*1735; engravers' work generally unsigned, therefore difficult to attribute pieces to him with certainty. *See* Walpole Salver.

Ho Ho Erh Hsien. Chinese ceramics. Ragged boys, Buddhist twin merry spirits of Union and Harmony; often depicted with one carrying broom, other, small box. Made as figures or used in decoration of stoneware and porcelain.

'Holbein' carpets. 16th and 17th century Turkish carpets woven around Ushak; name from depiction in paintings of H. *Holbein the

Younger. Ground either solid in red, green, or blue, or checker-board in red and green, or red and blue. Alternating repeat pattern of octagons with interlaced outline and lozenges with arabesque outlines; field filled in with small star rosettes. Stylized Kufic script borders.

Holbein, Hans the Younger (*c*1498–1543). German artist. Worked for father in Augsburg, then in Switzerland as painter, also making wood blocks for printer. First visit to England in 1526; patronized by Sir Thomas More. Lived in England from 1532 to death, working for Henry VIII as court painter, and designing costumes, silverware and jewellery. Small, round oil portraits. English miniatures, painted against blue ground on parchment or card and roughly circular. Few authenticated miniatures surviving include Henry VIII and his later queens. Designed table fountain given by king to Anne Boleyn in 1534 (only drawings survive); and rock-crystal and enamelled gold covered bowl (in Munich Schatzkammer). *Boleyn Cup, though in Holbein's style, probably not designed by him.

hold-back. *See* curtain-holder.

Holdship, Richard (fl mid 18th century). Engraver and part-proprietor, with brother of original porcelain works at *Worcester, 1751–59; previously glover. With R. *Hancock, transfer-printed porcelain with black enamel or underglaze blue. Work difficult to distinguish from that of Hancock. In 1750s, transfer-printed cream-coloured earthenware made at Cockpit Hill. Later printed porcelain in manner of Worcester at Derby. Mark: anchor, thought to be rebus of name; initials RH likely to be those of Hancock.

Holitsch. Hungarian faience factory established in 1743 by Francis of Lorraine, consort of Empress Maria Theresa; under imperial patronage until 1827. N. *Germain employed from 1746, and J. *Buchwald from 1754. Products, at first inspired by Strasbourg styles, usually painted in enamel colours, include butter dishes and tureens, e.g. in form of birds or vegetables. Animals, birds, flowers, and architectural motifs of *Habaner ware influenced decoration. Also produced maiolica, decorated with high-temperature colours, resembling products of Castelli. From 1786, lead-glazed cream-coloured earthenware made in English style. Marks: monogram of HF, and HOLICS, HOLITSCH (impressed), or rarely HOLITSH on cream-coloured earthenware.

Holland, Henry (1745–1806). English architect and interior designer; partner of Lancelot 'Capability' Brown (1715–83). Patrons included Prince Regent (later George IV). Style influenced by R. *Adam and contemporary French designers.

Hollins, Samuel (1748–1820). Potter at Shelton, Staffordshire; made coloured stoneware, e.g. in red, green, maroon, in style of J. *Wedgwood, also cream-coloured earthenware. In 1796, Mayor of Hanley and Shelton. From 1781, partner in New Hall China Manufactory. Mark, impressed: S. HOLLINS.

hollow-casting. Production of hollow metal objects by various methods including *lost-wax process.

hollow stem. Rare form of stem in English wineglasses; simple hollow cylinder sealed at ends by joining foot and bowl. Made *c*1740–*c*1750. *Illustration at* English wine glasses.

hollow-ware. Generic term for gold, silver, Sheffield plate or electro-plate vessels (cups, bowls, tankards, etc.) shaped by *raising with block, hammer, and *stake, *casting, *stamping, *spinning, etc.; also widely applied to vessels in cheaper materials e.g. pewter and earthenware.

holy-water bucket. Bucket or vase shaped vessel with swing handle and separate sprinkler used for holy water; sprinkler, pierced sphere with baluster-shaped handle. Silver examples found in wealthier churches and abbeys from 14th century; more common in base metal. Ornament often engraved or embossed. A. W. N. *Pugin was first to design examples in revived Gothic manner in 19th century.

holy-water stoup. Container for holy water consisting of back plate, usually embossed with sacred scene, and stoup resembling bowl of cup. Rare in silver; generally base metal or ceramic.

Hone, Nathaniel (1718–84) and son Horace (1755–1825). Nathaniel, Dublin-born, exhibited ivory miniatures and enamels in London. Most miniatures small; often fitted into bracelets. Horace exhibited at Royal Academy 1772–1822; appointed miniature painter to Prince of Wales in 1795, and painted larger miniatures, usually on ivory.

Holy-water stoup. Silver, repoussé *chased and gilded. Central panel depicts Baptism of Christ. French, mid 18th century. Unusually small, approximately 9in. high.*

*Honey-pot. Silver. In form of a skep; ring handle, *reed-and-tie border. By P. *Storr, 1798*

honey gilding (in ceramics). *See* gilding.

honey-pot. Silver or Sheffield plate honey container shaped like bee-skep; top of hive forms lid, with bee or ring finial; alternatively whole hive covered glass container on matching silver dish. Also made of glass, with silver mounts and dish. Used in Britain from late 18th century. P. *Storr one of first makers.

honeysuckle motif. *See* anthemion motif.

hood or **dome.** Arched top found on high pieces of case furniture.

hood. In long-case clocks, top part of case above trunk, encasing dial and movement. Removable to expose movement. Before *c*1700, rising, slide-up, or lift-up hood employed to give access for winding, hood moved upwards along groove at back, released by *spoon locking mechanism. As taller clocks were made, pull-forward hoods, with glass doors, introduced. Earliest hoods square, later made according to current style, e.g. *domed-top, or *break-arch.

hooded clock. Wall clock, resembling bracket clock, or hood of long-case clock, sometimes with weights hanging below; wooden case. Made in England *c*1660–*c*1675; makers include *Knibb brothers. Also produced in Holland, Austria, and Black Forest of Germany.

hoof or **cloven foot,** or **pied de biche** (in furniture). Foot in shape of hoof or cloven hoof. Of archaic origin; often used on early form of cabriole leg.

hookah. *See* narghili.

Hooke, Robert (1635–1703). English scientist, mathematician, and inventor. Fellow of Royal Society from 1663. Possibly invented anchor *escapement for clocks, *c*1676. From *c*1658, made experiments on balance springs for watches; in collaboration with T. *Tompion, produced first English balance spring watches.

Experimented with optics of e.g. *microscope and *telescope.

Hoolart, G. H. (*c*1716–72). Dutch artist and glass engraver, thought to be related to F. *Greenwood whose wife had same maiden name. Used stippling technique. Work characterized by use of areas of plain glass for deep shadows. Signed work GHH.

Hope, Thomas (1769–1831). English architect, influenced by work of C. *Percier. Helped to establish Empire style in England; published Household Furniture and Interior Decoration (1807), adapting classical principles and showing wide use of Egyptian forms in furniture and decoration.

Hôpital de la Trinité workshops. French royal tapestry workshops established in Paris in 1551. Low-warp loom tapestries woven until 1650. *See* Paris tapestry.

Hoppesteyn, Jacob Wemmerson (d 1671) and Rochus (1661–92). Dutch potters at Delft. Jacob master potter from 1660. Partner (1657–68) in The Porcelain Axe factory. Owner from 1664 of The Young Moor's Head factory. Work, initialled IW, possibly by employees, includes religious and mythological scenes; also mountain landscapes. Succeeded by widow (d 1686), who also used IW mark; manager with her second husband until 1679. Son, Rochus, master potter from 1680, manager with mother until her death, then sole owner. Developed technique of polychrome enamel decoration before invention of muffle kiln; used for painting in Chinese style; colours include violet, blue, red, green, and gold. Factory sold in 1692 to L. *van Dalen, who continued some decoration in same style. Mark, attributed to Rochus, moor's head with monogram RHS.

Horchhaimer, Nikolaus (fl mid to late 16th century). Master pewterer in Nuremberg. Specialized in display pieces with figure decoration cast in low relief in technique known as 'woodcut style', achieved by etching, rather than engraving, design in mould. Bowls, dishes, etc., made by this technique decorated with religious or mythological subjects.

Horenbout, Hornebolt, or **Hornebond,** Gerard (1498–*c*1540), son Lucas or Luke (d 1544) and daughter Suzanne or Susanna (d 1545). Flemish-born painters and miniaturists. Gerard English court painter during reigns of Henry VIII, Edward VI, and Mary; children accompanied him to England. Lucas painted miniatures of Henry VIII and Jane Seymour; perhaps taught miniature painting to H. *Holbein the Younger. Suzanne painted portraits.

horizontal or **cylinder escapement.** *See* escapement.

horizontal loom. *See* low-warp loom.

horloge de cheminée. *See* bracket clock.

horloge de parquet. *See régulateur.*

horn. Lip-vibrated wind instrument; earliest type of animal horn (curved, conical, end-blown tube); later produced in various metals. In use from ancient times. 14th century French inventories list *hunting horns. Coiled metal musical horn of *post horn or hunting horn type, probably originated in 16th century Europe. Developments of horn in 17th century France resulted in modern orchestral or French horn, with funnel-shaped mouthpiece, cylindrical mouthpiece end, $1\frac{1}{2}$–$2\frac{1}{2}$ coils, and wide bell. All were natural horns, i.e. valveless, and restricted to notes of harmonic series. Valves (applied to brass instruments to alter tube length to lower or raise pitch) introduced *c*1815 in Germany; patented 1818 by Heinrich Stölzel and Friedrich Blühmel in Berlin. At first two employed; third one introduced *c*1830.

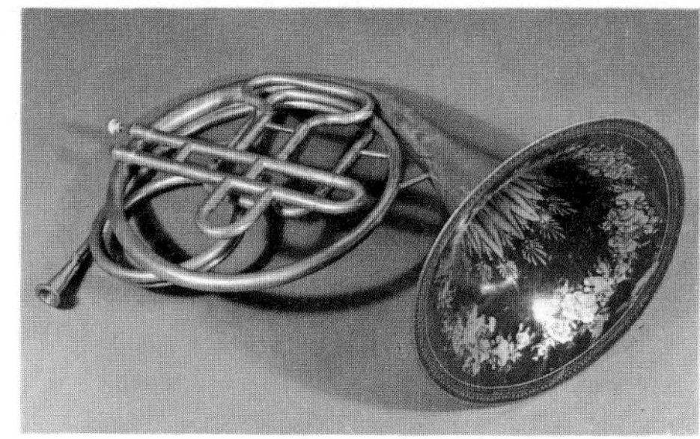

Horn. French horn, made by Charles Pace, London, early 19th century; painted decoration inside bell.

Horn, Johann Christoph (b 1698). German painter of faience at Dresden factory *c*1718, then painted porcelain at Meissen (*c*1720–60). Influenced by style of J. G. *Herold.

horn case. Painted watch case, covered with transparent horn; sometimes has floral or leaf design. Used on English and Swiss watches, mid 18th to early 19th centuries.

horned head-dress knop. Knop in form of female bust with horned head-dress; found on late 15th century pewter and latten spoons.

Hornemann, Christian (1765–1844). Swedish-born miniaturist. Lived in Germany and Italy, 1787–1803. In 1804, appointed court miniaturist in Denmark. Also noted for pastels.

Hornick, Erasmus (d 1583). Flemish goldsmith and designer working in Germany, first in Augsburg, then Nuremberg (1559–66). In 1582 appointed royal goldsmith to Emperor Rudolph II. Published series of pattern books: first set in 1562, two further sets in 1565; designs for jewellery, scent bottles, vases, ewers and basins, flagons, etc. included. Used Renaissance motifs, e.g. strapwork, masks, arabesques. Later work, after 1565, in *mannerist style. Very influential. No signed pieces survive.

horn of plenty. *See* cornucopia.

Höroldt, Johann Gregorius. *See* Herold, Johann Gregorius.

horology. Science and technique of time measurement based on construction of artificial devices, including sundials, sand-glasses, clocks and watches.

horse-brass. Flat or convex, usually circular, brass plates with pierced, engraved, or stamped decoration, intended for attaching to horse's harness. Custom thought to have ancient oriental origin, but did not reach England until 19th century. Examples from before 1860 rare. Numerous designs made e.g. to ward off evil, advertize occupation of owner, bring good luck, etc.; include crescent moon, sun, heart, bird, animal, anchor, barrel, flowers, etc. *Rumblers also worn.

horse figures. Chinese ceramics. Found in pottery and porcelain from T'ang period; early ming-ch'i examples in striking naturalistic poses. Favourite Taoist design element for pottery from *c*4th century B.C.; eight horses of Emperor Mu Wang figure in Chou dynasty legend. In Buddhism (from 1st century A.D.), one of seven Gems or Paraphernalia of Universal Sovereign, found as motifs on porcelain and stoneware. White horse (pai ma) which brought scriptures from India frequently depicted.

horse glass. *See* cheval glass.

horse screen. *See* cheval screen.

horseshoe-shaped furniture. *See* kidney-shaped furniture.

hoseki zogan. *See* zogan.

Hosenestel, Sabina (*c*1700–*c*1750). German porcelain *Hausmaler* from Augsburg. Worked with father J. *Aufenwerth until his death (1728), thereafter directed flourishing studio. No mark.

Hoskins, John (d 1664). English miniaturist, uncle and teacher of A. and S. *Cooper. Painted on parchment stuck on card. Colouring typically subdued. Miniatures before 1632 with blue or brown background, occasionally with red curtain or landscape. Late work under influence of A. van Dyck, with freer, more vigorous brushwork. Son, with same name, probably also miniaturist who worked with him.

hot water plate or **stand.** Circular or oval shallow covered pan of Sheffield plate with two handles (generally of ring type) and hinged trap at lip for filling with hot water; put under dishes to keep them warm. Also made to hold hot iron bar instead of water. Most popular during early 19th century, appearing *en suite* with silver entrée dishes; most often of oblong or shaped oblong form.

Houdon, Jean-Antoine (1741–1828). French sculptor; work copied in porcelain at Derby and notably Sèvres, and in Staffordshire cream-coloured earthenware, includes bust of Voltaire dated 1781.

hound sejant mark. Mark of unidentified English silversmith; flourished in London *c*1640–66; outstanding craftsman of Commonwealth period. Specialized in church plate in revived Gothic style for Royalist private chapels, when prayer-book services banned from parish churches. Some work not hall-marked, obviously due to his association with Royalists. Secular plate includes two-handled cups, dram cups, and flagons.

hour-glass. *See* sand-glass.

hour-glass salt. British silver or silver-gilt *standing salt of hour-glass shape; cover generally shaped like one half of hour-glass. Used in late 15th and early 16th centuries.

hour-glass seat. Circular upholstered seat with round base and pinched waist, like hour-glass. Sometimes made in straw for use in garden or summer-house. Common in mid 19th century.

house mark. Stamp of ownership on some pewter wares. *See* pewter marks.

Howard, Edward (1813–1904). American clock and watch manufacturer; apprenticed to A. *Willard, *c*1830. Pioneered large-scale watch production in America, from *c*1850. Maker of tower and wall clocks. Produced first *banjo clock in 1842: shapes include the figure 8; rounded sides at base, and wooden bezels are typical.

Höyer, Cornelius (1741–1804). Scandinavian miniaturist. Studied in Paris; influenced by R. *Carriera. Worked in Stockholm from 1783; died in Copenhagen. Works include several portraits of German royalty.

H-shaped stretcher. *Stretcher with a rail running from front to back leg on each side of object; another rail joins these half-way along.

Hsiang-yin (Hunan). Chinese kiln site active in late T'ang, early Sung period; manufactured wide variety of wares with brown, yellow, and green celadon glazes. Some similar to Yüeh and Yo-chou wares. Few pieces definitely identified.

Hsiao-pai-shih (Chekiang). Ancient Chinese kiln site near Yin or Ning-po, active in Six Dynasties or T'ang periods. Recently but briefly excavated, revealing fine specimens of early *Yüeh ware. Other newly-found sites where similar remains have been unearthed are Hsia-pi-shan and T'an-t'ou, near Ying-chia; Hsia-p'u-hsi, near Shao-hsing; and Hsu-shan, near Wên-chou.

hsien. Ancient Chinese ritual bronze cooking vessel; form originated in neolithic era. Bowl, with handles, mounted on *li shape (i.e. three-lobed body with tripod feet). Some pieces have partition with perforations at waist as if intended as steamer for cooking sacrificial food. Made through Shang, Chou, and until Han period, when bottom half of vessel had been omitted. Pottery versions, made in two separate pieces, also survived into Han era.

Hsin-yang (southern Honan). Chinese ceramics. Kiln site producing light grey, porcellanous body with semi-transparent, light olive glaze in late Han period; similar to Six Dynasties Yüeh ware. Provides evidence of early manufacture of celadon-type ware, 1st to 2nd century A.D.

Hsiu-nei-ssu ware. Chinese Imperial celadon made in southern Sung capital, Hang-chou, immediately after court's flight from North China. Kilns probably started in palace precincts (name means 'official office concerned with inspection and furnishing of palaces'). Kilns at some time transferred to Chiao-t'an. Credited in Japan with white-body and pale blue glaze; in West, such ware identified as superior *Lung-ch'üan. Pieces of undisputed attribution resemble *Kuan and *Ko; carefully finished; have dark body covered with crackled glaze, foot rim unglazed.

Hsüan Tê (1426–35). Chinese emperor, Ming dynasty; encouraged production of blue-and-white porcelain at *Ching-tê-chên. Work in his reign characterized by black blobs where brushwork left thick deposit of blue colouring, known as 'heaped and piled' effect; also by precision of decoration. Both features occur in later periods. Underglaze *copper-red perfected; vitrified coloured enamels introduced. Massive examples include *mei p'ing vases, jars, and bottles; delicate bowls, stem cups, small vases also produced. *Nien hao used; some unmarked items also attributed. *Illustration at* stem cup.

Hsü Ching (1091–1153). Chinese scholar, calligrapher, and artist; visited Korea *c*1123. Work, 'Illustrated Account of Kao-li' (i.e. Korea), describes periods and manufacture of Korean ceramics, and includes description of tea ceremony and its utensils. Contributes evidence for identification of *Korean celadon forms.

hu. Ancient Chinese ritual bronze vessel; general term, denoting wide variety of vase forms, mostly tall-shouldered with handles set near mouth. Shang period bronzes have pear-shaped body, with short vertically-positioned tubular handles for slotting rope through. Heavier, big-bellied type appeared *c*900 B.C., continuing until 7th century. In late 6th and 5th centuries B.C., modelled animal ring handles or feet added, also openwork carved lips. From 4th to 2nd centuries, B.C., flat flask shape, pien hu or *ch'ü, also found (*cf* pilgrim flask).

Huai-nan shih. *See* Shou-chou ware.

Huai style. Named after late Bronze Age objects found in area of Huai River, but term given to northern Chinese decorative style, 600–200 B.C. Influenced by nomadic *animal style. Motifs include rope pattern, hook and volute pattern, and lozenge designs. *T'ao-t'ieh mask became full face animal head. Generally objects richly decorated for private rather than religious use. *cf* Ordos style.

*Hu. Bronze vessel. *Han dynasty; inlaid with copper and gold.*

huan. Chinese archaic jade shape, possibly ritualistic. Similar to *pi, but with circular hole about half total diameter.

Huang-shan-shan (Chekiang). Chinese kiln site; early pieces of fine T'ang period Yüeh ware recently discovered.

Huang-yen. *See* Yü-yao.

Huaud family. Enamellers and miniaturists; Pierre the Elder (fl *c*1640), sons (who studied under J. *Petitot the Elder), Pierre (1647–*c*1698), Jean-Pierre (1655–1723), Aimé (1657–1729). Elder Pierre worked in Geneva, younger Pierre was painter to Elector of Brandenburg from 1691; Jean-Pierre and Aimé (known as 'Frères Huaud') worked at Prussian court in Berlin from 1686, returning to Geneva in 1700. Noted for watch cases in brightly coloured enamels, many with portraits or landscapes, and other works including medallion painted on gold with copy of C. *Lebrun's Alexander in the Tent of Darius.

Hubertusburg (Saxony). German faience factory founded 1770 by J. S. F. *Tännich. Rare products include vases painted in muffle-colours; mark: Hubertusburg T. Suffered from proximity to Meissen. Factory eventually presented to Count C. *Marcolini, who promoted manufacture of cream-coloured earthenware influenced by work of Leeds Pottery; also by Wedgwood factory, using mark Wedgwood, impressed. Other marks include KSSTF (i.e. *Königliche Sächsische Steingut-Fabrik*), with H or Hubertusburg impressed.

Huguenot silver. Persecution of French Protestants (Huguenots) in late 17th century by Louis XIV led them to seek asylum in Britain and other countries. In 1681, Charles II of England granted 'Letters of Denization' allowing Huguenot craftsmen to settle freely and practise their trades. In 1682, P. *Harache became first Huguenot to receive freedom from Goldsmiths' Company. Revocation of Edict of Nantes (which had given religious freedom) in 1685 caused wave of emigration. Huguenot silversmiths brought French styles which superseded influence of Dutch pattern books throughout Britain and Europe. Besides specific forms, e.g. helmet ewer and two-handled cup, Huguenots introduced far-reaching changes in silver ornament. Innovations included *cut-card work for formal borders (acanthus leaves, diapers, ribbons, straps, etc.), flutes and gadroons, and S-scroll and harp-shaped handles. Work was characterized by fine detailing and high quality; Huguenots at first opposed by local silversmiths (in England, petitions were made to King and Goldsmiths' Company), but later accepted and their designs adopted. Among successful Huguenot silversmiths working in London were D. *Willaume, P. *Platel (first generation of immigrants), and S. *Pantin, A. *Courtauld, P. *de Lamerie, D. *Tanqueray, and P. *Crespin (second generation). Influence in Britain continued until mid 18th century. English silversmiths who worked in Huguenot style include G. and F. *Garthorne, B. *Pyne, and A. *Nelme.

Hull, John (1624–83). English-born silversmith; family settled (1634) in Boston, Massachusetts, where he was apprenticed to half-brother (silversmith). In 1652, appointed to coin new money (shillings and sixpences) in Sterling Standard; received one coin for every 20 minted. Few surviving pieces with his mark, or joint mark with partner, R. Sanderson (IH above RS), include caudle cup, dram cup and beaker. In 1659, took J. *Dummer as apprentice.

Humpen. Tall, cylindrical German drinking glass or beaker, often extremely large, particularly popular in 17th century. Bohemia notable centre of production. *Humpen* usually enamelled in bright opaque colours; favoured subjects include coats of arms, and historical, biblical, allegorical, etc. scenes, often painted between borders of white or multicoloured dots. Made into 18th century, but standards of design and execution declined. *See Kurfürstenhumpen, Reichsadlerhumpen, Ochsenkopf* glasses, *Willkomm* glasses.

Humphry, Ozias (1742–1810). English miniaturist. Worked in London from 1764; miniature bought by George III in 1766 led to royal commissions. 1773–77, in Italy, initially with George Romney. In India, 1785–88, painted miniatures of native princes. Copied in miniature long series of family portraits for Duke of Dorset. Failing eyesight led to taking up crayon painting. Member of Royal Academy from 1791; appointed painter in crayons to George III in 1792; abandoned painting in 1797.

Hung-chou ware. Chinese celadon of late T'ang, early Sung periods, manufactured in Kiangsi province. Bowls, dishes, with carved lotus decoration at inside centre, under light olive green glaze, traditionally identified from literary source, Tea Classic, by Lu Yü. Attribution unproved.

Hunger, Christoph Conrad (fl *c*1710–*c*1750). Saxon porcelain painter and arcanist; noted for relief gilding and enamel painting. Gilder at Meissen (*c*1715); helped C. I. *du Paquier in establishment of Vienna factory (1719). Later worked in Venice, Copenhagen, and St Petersburg, where he claimed successful manufacture of hard-paste porcelain.

Hunt & Roskell. English firm of silversmiths; succeeded *Mortimer & Hunt in 1844. Partners: J. S. Hunt, J. Hunt, and R. Roskell. Mark, until death of elder Hunt in 1865, ISH crowned; afterwards IH over RR crowned. Many designs based on those of *Rundell, Bridge & Rundell (may have purchased models from sales after dissolution of firm). In Great Exhibition of 1851 displayed works based on designs of J. *Flaxman and E. H. *Baily from early 19th century, e.g. large trophies, candelabra, vases, etc. Greatest success was Titan vase made by A. *Vechte, with embossed and chased figures in violent action.

hunter watch. Watch with front lid entirely covering glass and dial; opened by pressing push-piece. *See* half-hunter watch.

hunting board. American sideboard or long table used for serving drinks to hunters. Designs vary, but all tall enough for hunters to remain standing. Table with frieze, but no drawers, called hunting sideboard, has cupboards and drawers. Dates from 18th century.

hunting chair. Overstuffed armchair with bare mahogany legs, and concealed framepiece extending beyond seat; cushion from chair-back placed on extended frame to form foot-rest. Made during 19th century.

hunting horn. Earliest examples made of animal horn used by Romans. Earliest surviving European examples used in France from 16th century; of brass or copper and circular, permitting greater range of notes; large; carried around head or arm. In England from 17th century small, usually straight horn used for fox-hunting, *c*19½in. long; in 19th century, reduced to *c*9in. long.

hunting scenes. Found in decoration of maiolica, e.g. at *Castelli and Talavera de la Reina in mid 17th century. Hunting scenes after engravings by A. *Tempesta painted on faience of Nevers in mid 17th century, and Moustiers in late 17th and early 18th centuries; also at Perrin factory, Marseille. Meissen hunting figures and groups frequently made in 1740s, e.g. by P. *Reinicke and J. F. *Eberlein; popular theme at other porcelain factories, including Frankenthal, where table decoration of stag hunt modelled by K. C. *Lück (1770), Nymphenburg, and Vienna, and in work of *Hausmaler*, e.g. I. *Bottengruber, J. *Helchis, F. F. *Mayer, and I. *Preissler; also on faience at Nuremberg. Outside Germany, hunting scenes appeared on porcelain made at *Vezzi factory, Capodimonte, Oude Loosdrecht, and Worcester.

Hurd, Jacob (*c*1702–58). American silversmith working in Boston, Massachusetts. Many pieces of domestic silver survive, e.g. gold snuff-box, tea kettle and stand, two-handled cups, tea and coffee pots, tankards, braziers, etc. Sons, Nathaniel and Benjamin, continued in trade. Marks: I HURD in cartouche, HURD in oval.

hurdy-gurdy. Stringed musical instrument with mechanical bow used in Britain and Europe from 11th century; known as *organistrum.* Large, fiddle-shaped body with three strings; ornamental peg-box (carved figures, etc.). Played by turning with right-hand crank handle operating rosined wooden wheel (at lower end of body) which vibrates strings, while playing with left hand a row of finger-keys (resembling piano keys) set parallel to strings. Commonly used in churches until 13th century, when lost favour. Became smaller, and adopted as folk instrument; various names used (e.g. *symphonie, chifonie, vielle,* etc. in France; hurdy-gurdy English 18th century term). Number of strings varied. Revived in France as popular instrument in 18th century with two melody strings (*chanterelles*), four drones (one-note strings) and 10–12 keys. Made in guitar, lute or fiddle form in late 18th century, some built with miniature organ in body. In 19th century used by street musicians and beggars. Wooden case often lavishly ornamented with carving, inlay, etc. *cf* barrel organ.

husk ornament. Stylized representation of corn husk used as decorative motif in baroque and neo-classical silver and furniture of late 18th and early 19th centuries. Festoons of husks in repeating or diminishing pattern embossed, cast, etc., on silver hollow-ware, or as e.g. carved ornament on furniture. *Illustration at guilloche* ornament.

*Jacob Hurd. *Kitchen pepper made in Boston, Massachusetts 1725–50; octagonal form with removable lid.*

Hurdy-gurdy. French, 18th century, with ivory inlay and handle.

hutch (from French *huche,* 'chest'). Originally a chest or box; in 16th and 17th centuries, a simple chest with one or two doors in front, on legs. Intended for general storage if doors solid, for larder if doors or sides pierced. Most primitive examples probably for storing grain.

Huygens, Christian (1629–95). Dutch scientist, astronomer and clock maker; studied in Leyden and Breda. Worked in Paris, 1665–81. Invented pendulum clock in 1657. Developed balance spring for watch in 1675. Published writings include *Horologium Oscillatorium,* The Hague, 1658.

hyalith glass. Varicoloured, opaque glass imitating precious stones, developed from early 19th century in Bohemia. Colours include black,

*Hyalith glass. Mug from factory of F. *Egermann, c1830. Height 4½in.*

introduced *c*1820 (often used to imitate Chinese lacquer-work or Wedgwood *black basalt pieces), brick-red, ruby, green, deep amethyst, etc.

Hyckes or **Hickes,** Richard (fl mid 17th century). Among first English high-warp loom tapestry master-weavers. Trained in Holland, active in England mid 16th to early 17th centuries. Commissioned *c*1650 by patron, W. Sheldon, to establish and direct *Sheldon Tapestry Works at Barcheston, Warwickshire. In London at Great Wardrobe, 1584–88. From 1588 at Barcheston with son, Francis. After Sheldon's death, Hyckes family continued tapestry production.

hydrostatic balance. Instrument for finding density of materials by weighing in air, then water. First described by Galileo in 1586.

i. Ancient Chinese ritual bronze shape; earliest examples date from 8th century B.C. Resembles a lidded sauce-boat; like *kuang, but much larger; origin uncertain, since two centuries separate two shapes, but possibly used as water vessel for ceremonial ablutions. *cf* p'an.

ibrik (Arabic, 'water-pitcher'). Widely used prayer rug motif. Stylized representation of water-pitcher used by Moslems for washing hands before prayer. When no water available, washing motions performed after rubbing hands on prayer rug's ibrik.

ice bucket or **pail.** *See* wine cooler.

ice glass. Clear glass with frost-like surface achieved by dipping warm glass in cold water or rotating in powdered glass before reheating. Technique developed in 16th century Venice. Used for decorating vessels of clear glass throughout Europe as *façon de Venise* spread.

Ido tea bowls. Korean pottery rice-bowls taken to Japan in 16th century, named after one of Buddhist Tea Masters by whom preserved in temples. Flawed body, with irregular cracked glaze, characteristic of Korean affection for rough, strong objects; imperfections thought to enhance natural beauty. Most bowls have deep foot, small spur marks inside. Imitated by later Japanese potters.

Igel (German, 'hedgehog'). Small **Waldglas* beaker covered with spiky *prunts. Dates from 15th century.

Il Calotto. *See* Callot, Jacques.

Ilmenau (Thuringia). Small German porcelain factory, founded 1777. Many early pieces unmarked; trefoil mark possibly used, 1788–92, by Gotthelf *Greiner. Mark i, used haphazardly after 1792. Noted (1792–1808) for medallions imitating blue Wedgwood jasper ware.

Imari (Arita). Japanese seaport serving Arita province, through which large quantities of porcelain exported in 17th and 18th centuries, mainly by Dutch East India Company. Associated with porcelain decorated with crowded, sometimes confused, patterns of chrysanthemum heads or other flowers, scrollwork, panelling, or figures mostly painted in blackish underglaze blue. Paste often cloudy in colour; coarser than contemporary *Kakiemon pieces. Early examples sometimes known as 'old Imari'; later decoration predominantly in red; also green, blue, yellow, purple, black, with gold and silver. European forms appearing in later work include spirit bottles, and western motifs, ships, figures, landscapes, etc., occur in decoration. Mounts in ormolu or silver sometimes added in Europe. Imari ware copied extensively at Chinese factories, e.g. by *Tang Ying at Ching-tê-chên. Japanese dishes and plates have unique spur mark on base. Also imitated widely in West, at *Delft, *Meissen, and *Worcester in 17th and 18th centuries. In 19th century, work declined in standard, with gaudy colours and over-elaborate designs. Marked with adaptations of Chinese *nien hao, or Japanese characters of good omen, e.g. fuku (good luck) or ju (long life).

Imari porcelain. Early 19th century. Beaker with low bowl and wide flaring mouth; figures and blossoms modelled in relief. Dragons around the body. Height 27½in.

Imperial porcelain factory, Moscow. Nicholas I period plate from the Hermitage, decorated with Russian imperial eagle. Inscription in Russian: Nicholas, Emperor and Autocrat of all the Russias. Burnished gold ground with enamelled foliage and rosettes. Diameter 8½in.

Imari pattern. *See* brocade pattern.

immortals. Chinese ceramic decoration derived from Taoist belief in attainment of immortality. Figures often depicted in group of eight accompanying founder of faith, Lao Tzŭ. Traditionally, each holds emblematic object: fan (revives dead); sword (slays evil); pilgrim's gourd (patronage of astrologers and musicians); pair of castanets (patronage of actors); basket of flowers (patronage of gardeners); drum (patronage of scholars, artists, calligraphers); flute (patronage of music); and lotus flower (genius of housewifery; only female figure). *Illustration at* double gourd vase.

impasto. Underglaze blue paint, thickly applied, standing out slightly from background. Found on 15th century Tuscan maiolica; characteristic in decoration of *oak-leaf jars.

Imperial Porcelain Factory, Saint Petersburg, Russia. Established at instigation of Empress Elizabeth in 1744; attempts made, e.g. by C. C. *Hunger and D *Vinogradoff, to produce hard-paste porcelain. Regular manufacture started *c*1758 by J. G. Muller. After accession of Catherine the Great (1762), ware decorated with dark ground colours, painting *en camaïeu*, rich scrollwork, and gilding in imitation of French, German, and Viennese porcelain. Biscuit and enamelled figures of Austrian workers made in late 18th century. Mark usually monogram and emblem of reigning monarch.

*Imperial yellow. *Ming dynasty bowl. Reign of Hung Chih (1488–1505).*

Imperial yellow. Chinese ceramics: glaze colour used on porcelain; yellow derived from iron with small addition of antimony, usually dark with brownish tinge. Introduced in Ming dynasty. Best examples date from reign of K'ang Hsi, Ch'ing period; sometimes used in monochrome decoration.

incense boat. Boat-shaped container for incense, usually with hinged lid; foot sometimes resembles that of chalice. Used to replenish *censer. Made of bronze, silver, silver-plated copper, shell, etc.

incense burner. Chinese ceramic form; occurs from Han dynasty; originally in modified *ting shape. Small versions used for holding joss-sticks. Vessels with pierced covers also found, some carved to represent small hills (*see* hilljar). Later porcelain versions often included tableware: intricately made pierced and enamelled balls, little boxes, flower-shapes, ornate gilded vases with lids. Symbol for incense-burner found as mark on Ming and Ch'ing pieces. *Illustration at* Hang-chou.

Ince, William (fl 1759–1803). English cabinet maker, partner of John Mayhew; co-author with Mayhew of Universal System of Household Furniture, 1759. Designs in rococo and neo-classical styles. *Illustration at* overmantel.

incised decoration (in ceramics). Designs scratched in firm clay before firing, sometimes by use of roulette with which small repeating motifs, dots, dashes, etc., can be cut along line, e.g. on red earthenware teapots of J. *de Caluwe. Characteristic of Nottingham ware. *cf sgraffiato.*

incised stem. Stem form in English wine glasses; spiral pattern incised on surface. Less popular than *air twists; surviving examples, *c*1750–65, have simple bowls and usually plain feet. *Illustration at* English wineglasses.

inclined plane clock. Drum-shaped clock invented in late 17th century. Movement powered by clock's own action in rolling down slope; hour hand kept in same position by counterweight, dial attached to case revolves around it.

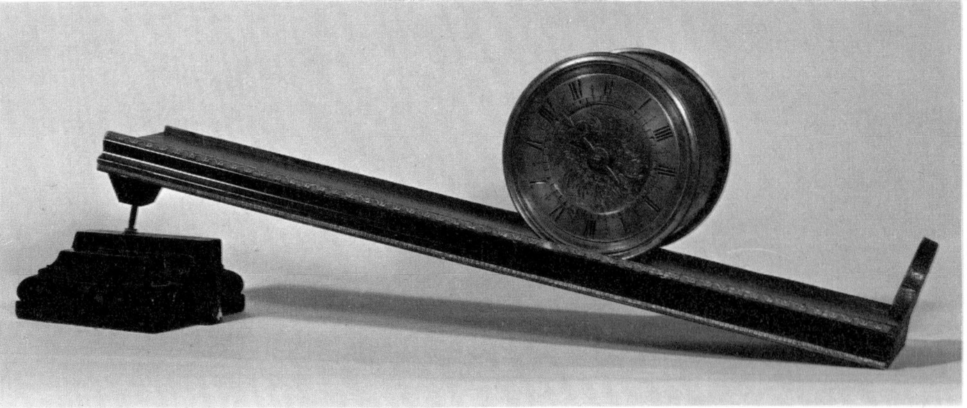

Inclined plane clock. Probably French, late 17th century. Each day timepiece is placed at top of slope, and rolls down, thus providing its own motive power. Single hand showing hours and quarters.

India or **Indian.** In 16th and 17th century England, often used to describe goods from Japan, China, and East Indies, i.e. imported by East India companies, or styles derived from them.

indianische Blumen, India flowers, East India flowers, or **fleurs des Indes.** Formal flowers derived from Kakiemon and *famille verte* styles, used as decoration on Meissen porcelain from 1720s. Painted in polychrome with iron-red predominating; also in monochrome, sometimes pink or purple. Imitated by many factories, notably Strasbourg, and in England by Derby until 1780s.

Indian jail carpets. Extremely tough north Indian carpets woven in prison workshops (particularly Agra and Jaipur) in early 19th century. Industry developed to meet demands of burgeoning European and American markets cheaply. Designs copied 16th and 17th century Persian models. Quality of early rugs very good, later deteriorated.

Indo-Isfahan carpets. Fine quality 19th century north Indian carpets woven mainly for European market. Structure and design meticulously copied 16th and 17th century *Isfahan carpets. Also name sometimes given to Mogul carpets copying contemporary Isfahan designs.

Indianische Blumen. *With animals and insects on pair of *Meissen coral-ground vases. Marked AR in underglaze blue. Height 18½in.*

Indo-Persian Mogul carpets. *See* Mogul carpets.

ingrain carpets. Reversible tapestry-weave carpets, usually in two contrasting colours. Weaving technique makes identical pattern elements appear in one colour on one side, and in another on reverse. Woven e.g. at Kidderminster, Worcestershire, from 1825; later, in America.

inkstand or **standish.** Tray or box-like container for writing implements including inkpot, sand and/or pouncebox, wafer box, sealing wax,

Inkstand. James I, silver-gilt. Top chased with foliate scrolls and stylized flowers on matted ground; four bracket feet, each a double open C-scroll. Width 6¼in.

*Inkstand. Rare French silver example, made in Avignon, c1670. Includes box for pens, inkpot, and *sand caster. Length c6½in.*

Inros. Japanese. Left: three-case inro, dark brown ground decorated in gold and black takamakie raised lacquer with beetle and leaves; early 19th century, signed Koma Kyuhaku. Centre: four-case inro of tsuishu (carved red lacquer), depicting figures in a landscape, with ojime (bead) and netsuke en suite; *18th century, unsigned. Right: three-case black lacquer inro, decorated with tethered horse and performing monkey in gold and coloured takamakie with mother-of-pearl details; late 18th century, unsigned.*

Intarsia. Panel, one of set of four representing Morning, Noon, Afternoon, and Night. Inlaid with variety of woods; faces and other details in engraved ivory. North Italian, 18th century. Height 19*in.*

taper-stick, hand bell, and quill pens. In use from 16th century; earliest surviving examples 17th century. Containers either fitted into box or rested on tray. Box or tray and fittings of silver, gold, Sheffield plate, or base metals. Cut glass containers set in pierced silver or Sheffield plate sockets in use from *c*1760. *See* globe inkstand, Treasury inkstand.

inkwell or **inkpot.** Made as fitting for inkstand, or as separate ink container. Former type, dating from 17th century or earlier, is plain, cylindrical pot made of silver, pewter, or lead, often with hole in centre of cover for dipping quill, also with lining of horn. Later shapes include hexagon, baluster, and vase, which evolved from round form, illustrated in medieval manuscripts, first into broad-based well (base later became tray, forming early type of inkstand) then into late 17th century capstan or loggerhead type, with solid, stable base tapering to narrower neck. This remained most popular type; usually made with removable china well. Glass ink bottles first used in England mid 18th century. Usually made in pairs in colourless, transparent glass with flat, polished sides, set in wood or metal stand. In first half of 19th century, glass makers in Stourbridge, Worcestershire produced stoppered bottles with *millefiori* pattern in stopper and base of bottle. Also made in plain and cut glass, often with silver or Sheffield plate mounts, with ornament *en suite* with other fittings.

inlaid ware. *See* zogan.

inlaying. Decorative technique in which pieces of wood, ivory, metals, mother-of-pearl, etc., contrasting in colour with ground material, are fitted into chiselled-out areas of ground, forming patterns or pictures. Used on furniture in 15th century Italy. During 16th century appeared in France, Holland, and Germany; in England by end of century (popular Elizabethan ornament, as on Nonsuch chests). *See* mar[illegible]ry, damascening, Boulle-work.

Inman, Henry (1801–1846). American portrait painter and miniaturist working in Philadelphia, Pennsylvania. Studied under J. W. *Jarvis. Noted for miniature watercolour portraits.

inn sign. *See* sign.

inro (Japanese, 'seal container'). 15th century Japanese used small box to carry seal for signature of documents, and pigment. Same container gradually became used to carry aromatic herbs or medicines, in separate compartments. Boxes *c*3–4in. wide, 4–5in. long, ½in. thick. Attached by cord to sash, and held in place by *netsuke. Finest examples made from 16th to 18th centuries in lacquer, decorated with gold or silver in delicate, elaborate patterns: birds, flowers, blossom, dragons, or clouds.

inro watch. Japanese timekeeper mounted in small rectangular case, developed from *inro, and hung from belt. Dial has adjustable hour divisions to conform with system of *Japanese time measurement, and often appears next to visible balance wheel. Supporting cord passes through bead (ojime) and carries *netsuke ornament at end.

intaglio. Decorative technique originally applied to gemstones and glass in antiquity; design cut into surface, as opposed to *cameo work (cutting away background). Revived on Bohemian 17th and 18th century glass with shallow incisions; deep cutting practised in Bohemia and France in late 18th and 19th centuries, with rococo motifs popular. Also applied to ceramics, where mould is incised to produce relief ornament on surface of article. Similar incised decoration used on silver and other metal-work. *See Tiefschnitt.*

intarsia. Type of pictorial or geometric inlay, associated with Italian work; often in materials other than wood (ivory, tortoiseshell, metals). Technique based on eastern ivory inlay. First recorded Italian use in 13th century Siena.

integral hinge. Hinge of pin running through tiny metal cylinders soldered alternately along edge of box and lid. In use in Europe from *c*1730. Ensured close fitting lid necessary in snuff-boxes; since hinge did not stand out from box, provided unbroken surface for decoration.

Inuyama ware. Japanese ceramics of late Edo

period, manufactured at castle of Inuyama, Owari province. Potters used mark of *Kenzan. Enamel painted decoration characterized by maple foliage, cherries, or bright floral patterns, in red and green.

inverted bell-top case. Form of clock case in which curvature of more usual bell-top is reversed, i.e. lower section is concave, upper convex.

investment, camicia, or **waste mould.** In casting by *lost-wax process: the clay, plaster of Paris, or sand covering placed on top of wax layer surrounding *core. Investment thickly applied, leaving hole at top to allow melted wax to escape, also for pouring in metal. Used only once: broken off when metal has hardened.

iridescence. Surface lustre caused naturally in ancient glass by long exposure to damp soil or air; produced artificially by application of metallic lustre in late 19th century glass.

Irish baluster measure. *See* noggin.

Irish carpets. Knotted carpets introduced to Ireland through trade with Spain in 14th century. Sir Robert Rothe attempted unsuccessfully to start local carpet and tapestry trade in 1530, using Flemish weavers. After Revocation of Edict of Nantes (1685), French Savonnerie weavers among Huguenots settling in Ireland, and small industry developed, using mainly Savonnerie designs. Only major Irish manufactory established *c*1790 making *moquette carpets with elaborate Savonnerie-influenced designs. Motifs include acanthus foliage and scrolls, human figures, and fruit baskets. Rich, almost garish colours.

Irish glass. Boat-shaped bowl on square foot, with cut decoration, c*1790. Length* 13*in.*

Irish glass. Frenchman known as William the Glassmaker was working in Dublin in 1258; other glass makers recorded during 14th and 15th centuries; all produced window glass and coarse domestic wares. In 1639, use of wood for glass furnaces forbidden; as coal in short supply, very little glass making carried out until 1690, when Philip Roche of the Round Glasshouse in Dublin began production of G. *Ravenscroft's flint-glass. Firm operated until 1759, producing glass wares in English style including wine glasses, decanters, jugs, and dessert glasses. Glass making seriously affected by export ban in 1745, although Royal Dublin Society helped local glasshouses with financial grants. When free trade granted in 1780, industry boomed, as Ireland exempt from *Glass Excise Acts; craftsmen came from England, e.g. J. *Hill, who helped to establish *Waterford Glass Works. In Anglo-Irish period, 1780–1825, Irish glass differs from contemporary English work mainly in being thicker and more deeply cut, as in salad bowls produced by most glasshouses. In 1776, *Belfast Glass Company established and during 1780s several glasshouses set up in Cork, notably Cork Glass Company and Waterloo Glasshouse Company. Products included cut lustres, chandeliers, candlesticks, and dessert glasses. Decanters usually have triple neck rings, mushroom stoppers, and heavy cutting. Vesicas (pointed oval designs) are characteristic cut patterns; some articles are embossed on the base with *Cork Glass Co, or, Waterloo Co Work. Dublin glasshouses specialized in chandeliers, bowls, decanters, and épergnes. Glass making declined with extension of Glass Excise Act to Ireland (1825).

Irish gold and silver. Gold and silver ornaments produced in Ireland from prehistoric times; jewellery survives from *c*1600 B.C. Christianity introduced in 6th century A.D. Much church plate made: chalices, croziers, processional crosses, reliquaries, and bookbindings. Earliest surviving chalices 8th century. Norman conquest in 12th century and religious persecution in 15th and 16th centuries disrupted tradition of silver making. Surviving silver mainly church plate of 16th and 17th centuries.

Iron-brown spots on Lung-ch'uan celadon bottle; Yuan dynasty. Height $10\frac{3}{4}$*in.*

Domestic silver in English styles (usually 5–10 years behind) exists from 17th century; wares generally of heavier gauge than English counterparts. Native forms began to develop after *c*1730. Helmet-shaped cream jugs and sauce-boats on three feet or single central foot made (mainly Irish development). *Dish-rings, specifically Irish form, made from mid 18th century. Flat-chased rococo scrollwork combined with birds (particularly swan) widespread ornament on all domestic silver. Return of absentee landlords *c*1765–80 resulted in increased production of dinner plate. Bright-cut engraving popular in late 18th century, particularly on flatware with pointed handles. Parliamentary union with England in 1800 curbed development of Irish silver by reducing prosperity of country. So-called 'famine silver' of 1840s, distinguished by extremely heavy gauge, provided form of investment for few unaffected by widespread depression.

Silversmiths' guild existed in Dublin from 12th century. In 1637 Dublin Goldsmiths' Company established by charter of Charles I, and Sterling standard made compulsory. Crowned harp, maker's initials, and date letter (introduced 1638) employed. In 1730, figure of Hibernia added as *duty mark; replaced by king's head in 1807, Hibernia becoming Dublin town mark. Cork, Galway, and Limerick silversmiths assayed own wares; practice illegal: official assay office in Dublin. 18th century Irish hallmarking very lax; many pieces 'modernized', illegal practice after hallmarking. From 1770, stricter system began with use of date letter X.

Irish measure. *See* measure, haystack, noggin.

iron. Hard, strong, ductile metal suitable for interior and exterior use; most widely used of all metals for architectural, ecclesiastical, and domestic purposes. Known from 3500 B.C., but rarely used except for simple forged items, e.g. tools and weapons, until early Middle Ages when *wrought iron methods were developed. Casting on a large scale feasible in Europe only from 15th century; very high melting-point of iron not attainable until introduction of improved furnaces and water-powered bellows. Process remained unsatisfactory for decorative pieces, owing to considerable contraction of iron when cooling, causing ornament to be ill-defined or blurred; use restricted to items such as stoves and firebacks (made by *sand-casting method). Large ironworks set up in 18th century (e.g. *Coalbrookdale, *Carron) experimented widely and achieved many technical advances. In 19th century, technique (improved by Samuel Lucas of Sheffield) for producing cheap, malleable cast iron, enabled still sharper detailing to be achieved; stamping could also be used. Many domestic and decorative items (fenders, grates, wall-plaques, door furniture, candlesticks, figurines, jewellery) made in this way. Rolling and tinning processes improved in early 18th century, permitting large-scale production of *tin-plated iron kitchen utensils; *japanned metal fashionable from mid 18th century. Enamelled iron widely used for kitchen utensils from *c*1850. *See* steel.

iron-brown spots. Chinese ceramics. Spots of iron oxide applied over green celadon glaze before firing, spread to produce blots, sometimes with metallic sheen. Limited use during Yüeh, Six Dynasties, Sung, and Yüan periods.

iron chimney. *See* fireback.

iron clock. Domestic clock, made of iron, in Middle Ages; small version of turret clock; weight-driven, sometimes with alarm. Type survived in Europe and Japan until mid 18th century.

iron-red decoration. Korean ceramic technique, imitating Chinese *Tzu-chou ware imported in quantity. Used experimentally in 12th century; developed and popular by mid 13th century. Used on *punch'ŏng ware, produced mainly at Keryongsan kilns. At end of 16th century, occurs on white or grey stoneware, and porcelain, sometimes in combination with cobalt-blue. Commonly used because of local difficulty in obtaining cobalt oxide.

ironstone china. English ceramic body said to contain iron slag, patented 1813 by C. J. *Mason. Strength allowed use for, e.g. large vases, fireplaces; much tableware produced. Made by many other potters in England and United States.

Isabey, Jean-Baptiste (1767–1855). French miniaturist. Pupil of J-L. David. Court painter to Marie Antoinette, Napoleon I, Louis XVIII, Charles X, and Louis Philippe. Painted on vellum, card, or ivory, usually oval. Until *c*1800, favoured dark gouache background on ivory miniatures. Later used sky backgrounds, or characteristic white draperies on female portraits. Many portraits of Bonaparte family; also painted Madame Récamier, and Duke of Wellington on snuff-box.

Jean-Baptiste Isabey. Miniature of Napoleon, signed and dated 1815. Diameter 1⅞in.
Right:
Isfahan carpet. Tree of Life pattern. c1870. 7ft2in.×4ft5in.

Iserlohn boxes. Copper or brass tobacco-boxes produced 1760–1800 at Iserlohn, West Germany. Long, oval shape, lid engraved, chased, or embossed with military or rustic scenes or motifs, or portrait of Ferdinand II.

Isfahan or **Ispahan carpets.** Sumptuous, meticulously executed late 16th and 17th century east Persian court carpets of wool, or wool and silk, woven in Isfahan (capital of Safavid empire 1598–1722). Designs developed from earlier Court carpets, but more elaborate and worked in greater range of colours. Most important types, *vase, *Polish, and *arabesque carpets, all copied extensively elsewhere. Also elaborately ornamented prayer rugs, often with Kufic borders. Industry collapsed mid 17th century; revived in mid 19th century, when traditional designs used for short-pile, woollen carpets with ivory or blue grounds.

Islamic glass. After fall of Roman Empire, glass making declined in West but flourished in Middle East under Islamic rule: Turkestan, Armenia, Mesopotamia, Persia, Syria, Arabia, Egypt, and most of Spain. Early glass difficult to date or place: glass makers and their work travelled widely, particularly to Court of Caliphs of Baghdad. Excavations at Samarra (Iraq), where Court moved in 9th century, reveal wide range of techniques and styles. Simple goblets and vessels made of thick, coloured glass cut in relief in manner of semi-precious stones. Stylized animals and arabesque foliage frequent motifs. Glass decorated with lustre-painting also found; technique probably allied to contemporary lustre-painting on ceramics, and involving application of design in pigment which on firing forms lustrous, metallic film. Such glassware reached peak in 12th century Egypt. From 9th to 12th centuries, Islamic craftsmen excelled in engraved and cut cameo glass; main centres were Damascus, Tyre, Antioch, and Cairo. Vessels decorated all over with intricate, stylistic patterns, including animal motifs, hearts, palmettes, and spirals. Of uncertain origin, but cut in typically Islamic

Islamic glass. Syrian mosque lamp, mid 14th century. Enamelled glass, with dedication to Shibl-abdaula, Kafur ar-Rumi, Treasurer to Mamluk Sultan of Egypt, as-Salih Ismail.

*Islamic glass. Persian. Left: sprinkler bottle of *mould-blown glass, two applied rings on neck, 10th–12th century; height* 10*in. Centre: jug with tooled swan-neck handle, 10th–12th century; height* $5\frac{3}{4}$*in. Right: ewer, 6th–8th century; height* 10*in.*

fashion, are *Hedwig glasses, generally transparent but tinged brown because of impurities. Enamelling and gilding particularly associated with Islamic glass. Thick white, gold, and turquoise enamel on transparent vessels incorporating bead-like drops produced in Raqqa, Syria, *c*1171–1259. Aleppo noted during 13th century for rich white, blue, and red colouring and broader, more elaborate style, depicting figures, animals, flowers, trees, and Mamluk crests, surrounded by arabesque patterns. From *c*1250, Damascus famous for exquisitely enamelled small figures, birds, animals, fish, and elaborately scrolled borders. From late 13th century, Chinese influence apparent in Islamic work, particularly Persian, in use of naturalistic plant forms, e.g. lotuses, peonies, and vines. Finest examples of enamelled Islamic glass are late 13th and early 14th century mosque lamps, designed to contain oil lamp, and suspended from ceiling by chains attached to three or six loops round body; made in Damascus, Aleppo, and in Egypt; usually decorated with arms of reigning sultan, flattering Arabic inscriptions, and texts from Koran; background normally filled with floral pattern. Damascus fell to Tamerlane in 1402; glass making industry declined because of Mongol invasions.

Islamic pottery. In Mesopotamia from 9th century, lead-glazed earthenware decorated with splashes of underglaze colour, sometimes with *sgraffiato* decoration. Tin-glazed earthenware painted with underglaze blue, green, or yellow, in patterns of flowers or Kufic inscriptions; sometimes lustre decoration used, e.g. on tiles and domestic ware. Unglazed buff pottery – bowls, jars, and vases – decorated with applied or moulded relief and incised patterns, e.g. of animals, birds, and geometrical designs. Slipware made in Persia and Afghanistan decorated with Kufic script in underglaze brown, red, or purple over white slip. Lustre ware decorated e.g. with birds, animals, or figures made in Egyptian Fatimid dynasty (969–1171). *Sgraffiato* pottery made in Persia has simple designs incised through white slip before glazing; also includes *Gabri and *Aghkand ware. In 12th and 13th centuries, majority of *Seljuq ware made at Rayy and Kashan under rule of Turks, who had overrun eastern Mediterranean area in mid 11th century. Lustre ware possibly made at Gurgan in early 13th century, until Mongol invasion. Bowls, jars, and *albarelli* painted with panels of underglaze blue and black made in Syria and Egypt under rule of Mamluks who controlled area from mid 13th to late 15th century, allowing refugee potters from Persia and Mesopotamia to work, e.g. at Damascus. In 15th century, imported Chinese Ming porcelain copied in Syria and Persia, e.g. at Meshed and Kirman, where underglaze blue-and-white ware made until 19th century. Ottoman–Turkish pottery made at *Isnik from late 15th century to *c*1700, then at Kutahia in 18th and 19th centuries. Attempted porcelain manufacture in 19th century Turkey abandoned because of high cost. Under Safavid rule, from 1499, lustre painting reintroduced and e.g. *Kubachi and *Gombroon ware made. Many vessels with coloured glazes inspired by Chinese celadon produced from 16th to 18th centuries; most apparently made at Kirman. In 19th century, imported European wares superseded local pottery.

Isnik (Anatolia). Pottery made 1490–*c*1700, once divided into three classes attributed to Kutahia, Damascus, and Rhodes (Rhodian ware). Products include dishes, footed bowls, jars, jugs, lamps, boxes, and tiles, made in buff clay, characterized by painting in rich colours on white clay slip, covered with brilliant, clear glaze. Early decoration in blue, or blue and

Isnik. Kutahia ewer, decorated in underglaze blue. Mid 17th century.

turquoise, shows influence of imported Ming porcelain combined with arabesques and Kufic inscriptions. From *c*1525, designs mainly of naturalistic flowers, e.g. tulips, carnations, and other plant forms. *Sealing-wax red added to palette, *c*1555; decoration still includes flowers, often with borders of scrolls and arabesques. In 17th century, quality of ware declined; manufacture ceased by 1800. *Illustration also at* sealing-wax red.

isochronism. In horology, the ability of a pendulum or balance to maintain oscillations whose frequency remains constant though the length of the arc of swing may vary. *See* balance.

Ispahan carpets. *See* Isfahan carpets.

istoriato. Italian maiolica decoration: narrative painting of historical, religious, classical, or mythological subjects, normally covering whole surface of plate or dish. Introduced at Faenza in early 16th century; very soon adopted at Castel Durante and Urbino. Particularly associated with N. *Pellipario. *Illustrations at* Castel Durante, Siena.

Italian ceramics. Lead-glazed earthenware made e.g. at *Bologna in 15th and 16th centuries. *Maiolica production reached peak in early 16th century, although painting on tin-glaze known probably from 11th century. Lustre decoration used at *Deruta and *Gubbio. In 17th century, styles influenced by ware imported from French factories, Delft, and Far East. First known European porcelain made in Florence (*Medici porcelain). Later also made at *Doccia, *Le Nove, *Naples, *Venice, and *Vinovo. Manufacture of soft-paste porcelain established by Charles III at Capodimonte, near Naples, transferred to *Buen Retiro on his accession to Spanish throne.

Italian clocks. Mechanical clocks probably originated in Italy during 12th century for regulation of monastery life. First types merely sounded alarm at set intervals, then struck single blow at each hour. Clocks striking number of hours introduced *c*1325; large public clocks and domestic forms, all weight-driven with verge *escapement and *foliot or wheel

*Italian ceramics. Part of tea and coffee service, *Capodimonte factory, c1755, painted and gilded.*

*Italian clock. *Night clock signed Petrus Thomas Campanus, Inventor, Rome, 1683. Hour numerals travel from left to right, indicating minutes; light behind allows time to be seen in dark.*

*balance, in general use by mid 14th century. Astronomer, Giovanni Dondi, completed elaborate clock with astronomical dials c1364. 24-hour system of *time-measurement (Italian hours) used in Italy and other parts of Europe, but gradually superseded from early 15th century by 12-hour system. Italian clock making declined in late Middle Ages, when German industry took lead. Spring-driven table clocks produced in early 16th century follow style of Augsburg makers; 17th century weight-driven wall clocks resemble English *lantern clocks, some with six-hour dial. *Night clocks and *altar clocks made in mid 17th century.

Italian gold and silver. Before unification in 19th century, independent princely states each had centre of plate production, fostered by wealthy nobles and/or church. Much secular plate lost as result of wars, notably during Napoleon's Italian campaign in late 18th century; virtually all gold and silver in great collections sent to Paris and melted down, e.g. that of Medici family in Florence.

Renaissance in Italy was age of great goldsmiths, e.g. B. *Cellini, working in Florence and Paris in 16th century. Though few works survive, designs (and those of foreign copyists) demonstrate exuberant and extravagant treatment of classical motifs. Imaginative reconstruction of Roman forms by Italian goldsmiths produced so-called mannerist style, with elaborate, all-over ornament, carried to various European courts by travelling designer-goldsmiths. Domestic wares became ceremonial or display pieces through elaborate ornamentation, e.g. *Cellini Salt, rose-water ewers and basins, etc. A number of vases, cups, goblets, ewers, flasks, etc., in mannerist style, made of semi-precious stones (jasper, rock-crystal, lapis lazuli, etc.) with gold, silver, or silver-gilt mounts have survived; speciality of Florentine silversmiths, who mounted antique Roman vessels in precious metal for Lorenzo de' Medici in 15th century. Small amount of surviving table silver generally ornate. Large-scale 18th century producers, e.g. Vincenzo *Belli, inspired by French rococo.

Much Italian gold and silver church plate survives. Popes commissioned most famous goldsmiths of day to make *papal roses and swords for yearly presentation. Styles of religious plate lavish and extravagant, but generally slow to change; Gothic, Renaissance, and baroque motifs regularly used.

Regulations regarding gold and silver standards existed in some states from c13th century. Town and master's marks came into general use c15th century. Marks varied with each state; in Rome, date-letter system also used. In early 19th century, French hallmarking introduced. Under mainly Austrian control, after 1815, chief cities again set up own assay offices. In 1872, following unification, national system of hallmarking introduced.

Italian maiolica. *See* Italo-Moresque ware, maiolica.

Italian tapestry. From 14th or 15th century, tapestries popular in Italy as hangings and coverings in churches and wealthy homes. Many Flemish tapestries imported, mainly through Venice; Flemish and French weavers, employed to care for them, established small high-warp loom weaving colonies. Major manufactories established in 16th century at *Ferrara and *Florence. Italian artists had near monopoly of European tapestry design, with cartoons by *Raphaël, Salviati, A. *Bronzino, G. *Romano, Alessandro Allori, and Battista Dosso. Italian tapestries similar to contemporary Flemish designs, but airier and lighter. Principal weavers included J. and N. *Karcher and J. *Rost. 17th century output considerable, particularly from Florence and newly established Barberini manufactory in Rome. Most successful designs by Pietro da Cortona. Last period of great activity, 18th century, with workshops flourishing in Florence, *Naples, *Turin, and *Venice; also *Papal Workshops in Rome. Tapestries follow French style.

Italo-Moresque ware. Italian maiolica of 15th century; decoration derived from Hispano-Moresque ware imported from Valencia, via Majorca. Painted in blue; also polychrome, notably in Tuscany; extra colour replaced lustre tints of Spanish products.

Iusupov, Prince Nicolai Borisovich (1751–1831). Russian aristocrat and artistic patron. 1792–1802, director of Imperial Porcelain Factory. In 1814, established factory on own estate at Arkhangelskoë, where porcelain bought in white, e.g. from Sèvres and from Popov factory, decorated, never for sale but as gifts for friends, relatives, and members of Imperial family. Porcelain usually signed Arkhangel'skoe or Archengelski in gold. Factory closed in 1831.

Ives, Joseph (1782–1862). American clock maker from Connecticut; also worked in New York, 1825–30. Inventor of *wagon-spring clock. Made *long-case clocks first with wooden movements, then with brass; noted for development of rolled brass. Designer of wall *mirror clock, c1818–19.

ivory (as ground for miniatures). Introduced in early 18th century by R. *Carriera; miniatures on ivory termed *fondelli*. Probably derived from generally oval lids on ivory snuff-boxes then fashionable in Venice.

ivory dial. *See* sundial.

ivy leaf. *See* vine leaf decoration.

Iwaibe ware. *See* Sué ware.

jack or **jacquemart.** Automaton figure which strikes bell on clock sounding hours or quarters; used on turret and domestic clocks in Middle Ages. Term also used for repeating watch, known as 'jacquemart' watch, on which puppet figures appear to strike bells. Made in early 19th century France and Switzerland.

'Jackfield' ware. Lead-glazed earthenware, sometimes called 'shining black'. Coloured almost black by addition of iron and manganese

Jackfield pottery. Lidded beaker, ewer painted with flowers, cream jug, and cup and saucer. 18th century.

to clay and glaze; applied vine leaves and grapes picked out with oil-gilding. Made by T. *Whieldon and contemporaries in same shapes as variegated and colour-glazed wares. 'Jackfield' antedates establishment of Jackfield factory, Shropshire (c1750) which produced red earthenware, with brown-tinted glaze often decorated with paint or gilding and dated c1770.

Jack-in-the-cellar. 17th century Dutch and German silver trick cup with short, hollow column in centre of bowl. Figure of small child, contained in column, shoots up as drinker tilts cup.

Jacob-Desmalter, François-Honoré-Georges (1770–1814). French *ébéniste,* son of G. *Jacob. Worked with brothers in father's business, then collaborated with father. Many commissions from Napoleon included refurnishing imperial palaces. Worked mainly in Empire style.

Jacob, Georges (1739–1814). French. Became *maître-ébéniste* in 1765. Earliest works in Louis XV style. Contributed to the birth of French neo-classicism, particularly in chairs. Although an *ébéniste,* also known for carving on furniture. Received commissions from Marie Antoinette. Made suite of mahogany furniture for Jean-Louis David's studio, using classical Etruscan and Greco-Roman motifs, which influenced later furniture (in Directoire, Empire and Restoration styles). Also shows English influence, particularly in chair backs. Stamp: G. JACOB with fleur-de-lis or lozenge (1765–96); JACOB FRERES RUE MESLEE during collaboration with sons (1796–1803); JACOB D.R. MESLEE (1809–13) during collaboration with F. H. G. *Jacob-Desmalter. *Illustration at canapé.*

Jacobean furniture. Prevalent style in England and American colonies during first half of 17th century, spanning reigns of James I (1603–25) and Charles I (1625–49) although term sometimes limited to former.

Popular pieces of furniture include oak tester bed; day-bed; gate-leg, side, and assorted occasional tables; inlaid chests; Farthingale, wainscot, and X-frame chairs; trestle benches; settles; and joined stools. Oak was main wood. Shape and decoration of furniture varied little from *Elizabethan examples; Jacobean ornament more restrained, with smaller bulbs on legs, and less opulent carving. Decoration notably geometrically-ornamented panels, strapwork, and other low carving; also inlaid geometrical and floral patterns (showing Moorish influence) in ivory, mother-of-pearl, and wood. Upholstered chairs and stools more common than in 16th century.

Jacobite glass. English goblets and wine glasses commemorating Old Pretender, James Stuart (1688–1766), Young Pretender, Prince Charles Edward (1720–88) and Jacobite rebellions of 1715 and 1745. Early glass was of fine quality and proportion, with air-twist, knopped, and colour twist stems. After 1745, glasses lighter (*see* Glass Excise Act); plain, panelled, and tear stems common. All were diamond-point or wheel engraved with Jacobite emblems. Principal motif, rose, usually with six petals, sometimes seven or eight, representing English crown, and one or two buds representing Pretenders. Other groups, all fairly rare, include Amen glasses

Jacobean furniture. Dummy board figure. Maidservant with broom, oil paint on wood. Height 5ft1in.

Jacobite glass. Left: wine glass, drawn trumpet bowl engraved with roses and buds, 1745. Height $6\frac{3}{4}$in. Centre: Amen glass, drawn trumpet bowl engraved in diamond point with J R 8 (James VIII of Scotland) Jacobite hymn and inscription to His Royal Highness Prince Henry, Duke of Albany, 1725; height $7\frac{1}{2}$in. Right: wine glass, trumpet bowl engraved with open rose, bud, oak leaf, and Fiat, 1750; height 7in.

(engraved with two or four verses of Jacobite anthem, ending with 'Amen'), most dating from 1740s; portrait glasses, usually bearing likeness of Charles Edward, occasionally with Latin or English inscription; *Fiat* glasses (engraved with word *Fiat*, 'let it be done'), originally associated with Cycle Club (founded 1710), but becoming popular slogan on many glasses after 1745; and those engraved with Jacobite emblems, e.g. stricken or burgeoning oak, oak leaf, star, bee, butterfly, forget-me-not (probably mourning symbol for Old Pretender, after death in 1766), jay, Jacob's ladder foliage, carnation, daffodil, fritillary, Prince of Wales plumes, and thistle; often include Latin or English inscription, e.g. *Redeat* ('may he return'), *Revivescit* ('he grows strong again'), or A Health to J-ms. Jacobite glasses are prized for historical and sentimental associations, and rarity.

Jacobs, Isaac (fl 1771–1806). English glass maker; partner of father, Lazarus (d 1796), at glass house in Temple Street, Bristol. Established Non-Such Flint Glass Manufactory in Bristol; appointed glass maker to George III. Produced wide range of coloured glassware. Specialized in dark blue (Bristol blue) decorated with gilding, particularly key pattern. Pieces such as fine finger bowls, wine-coolers, and decanters bear signature, I. Jacobs Bristol, written in gold on base.

Jacobs, Lazarus (d 1796). English glass maker. Established glass house in Temple Street, Bristol, c1771, which he managed with son, I. *Jacobs. Specialized in dark blue glassware with gilding. Employed M. *Edkins 1786–87 for rococo style gilding and labelling decanters.

Jacob's staff. *See* cross-staff.

jacquemart. *See* jack.

Jacques, Symphorien (d 1798). French potter and painter. With J. *Jullien, operated factories at Sceaux (1763–72), Mennecy (1765–73), and Bourg-la-Reine (from 1772). Joined c1790 by son, Charles-Symphorien.

Jacquet-Droz, Henri-Louis (1752–91). Swiss maker of musical clocks and watches, and automata; worked with father P. *Jacquet-Droz and J-F. *Leschot. Made life-size automata of lady organ-player and small boy drawing. Worked in Geneva and Paris.

Jacquet-Droz, Pierre (1721–90). Swiss maker of automata and musical clocks and watches at La Chaux-de-Fonds. c1772 made writer automaton. Developed 'singing-bird' box in association with J-F. *Leschot.

Jamnitzer, Wenzel (1508–85). Austrian silversmith; born in Vienna, worked in Nuremberg. In 1543, appointed coin and seal die-cutter to city; in 1552 master of city mint. In 1556 became member of Great Council of city and in 1573 of smaller council, governing body of Nuremberg. Served four Hapsburg emperors. He and brother, Alberich, made solid silver casts of snails, worms, weeds, etc., which were used to ornament vessels. Earliest surviving work, centrepiece with female figure, on base covered with plants, small animals, and insects, holding bowl with vase in centre above her head. Published book on perspective (1568). Sons, Abraham and Hans, continued to work in 'rustic' manner.

Jans, or **Jansens,** Jan (d 1691). Flemish tapestry master-weaver. Moved to Paris 1654. From 1662, director of largest Gobelins workshop, manufacturing finest quality high-warp loom tapestries. Son, Jean (d 1731), among best high-loom master-weavers at Gobelins.

Jan Steen flagon or **jug.** Dutch pewter flagon, with baluster-shaped body, domed cover, and long, straight, square-sectioned spout (also with lid) joined to lower part of body; made in 16th and 17th centuries. Appears in paintings by Jan Steen (1626–79).

Janvier, Antide (1751–1835). French scientist, mathematician, and clock maker. Worked on *astronomical clocks. First model produced in 1773; presented to Louis XV. Clock maker to Louis XVI and Louis XVIII. In 1806, made clock based on *decimal time. Maker of mantel and regulator clocks. Published writings include *Étrennes chronométriques,* 1810.

japan. *See* European lacquer.

Japanese celadon. Earliest celadon found in country, imported from China in 10th and 11th centuries. In 12th century, Korean celadon imported, also *zogan ware from *c*13th century. Potters of Owari province learned secret of celadon glaze from Chinese in Heian period; produced *Owari seiji. Glazes at first derived from natural wood ash. Early *Seto ware first true celadon made, although often yellowish through oxidation during firing. Improved later, in Muromachi period, when glaze contained more feldspar. Under influence of *Lung-ch'üan, *Ch'ing pai, and *Koryo decoration, designs incised, carved, impressed, or applied willow, chrysanthemum, etc. Later potteries concentrated on white, black, or other glazes, making celadon only in small quantities. Celadon glaze sometimes applied to white porcelain in style of Chinese work of Ch'ing period, notably for Prince *Nabeshima, or in Kakiemon style. *Arita area produced some excellent celadon wares intermittently in 17th century. A. *Mokubei specialized in celadon, as did kilns at *Kameyama, *Hirado, *Kutani, *Sanda, and *Himeji. Recent copies easily confused with genuine pieces; *Tobi seiji and Lung-ch'üan among types most often copied. Incense burners made in tripod form, or with carved animals on lid.

Japanese clock. Weight-driven iron movement, c1770. Dial calibrated with striking mechanism according to Japanese time system. Double verge and foliot escapement allowing clock to keep two time rates depending on lengths of night and daylight hours.

Japanese clocks. Clocks first introduced into Japan by European missionaries and traders in 16th century. In early 17th century, indigenous type developed lasting virtually unchanged, with uncontrolled *foliot balance, until system of *Japanese time measurement abandoned in 1873. Conservatism of craftsmen during 250 years of production makes dating difficult; signed or dated examples rare. Earliest type has movement similar to English *lantern clock with locking plate striking mechanism, single hour hand, and dial plate carrying movable hour markers adjusted for day and night hours of varying length; development of this has fixed hand or indicator and rotating dial plate. Hour markers have pins projecting behind to set off striker, thus obtaining striking at unequal intervals. Locking plate calibrated for Japanese system. In late 17th century, two separate escapements fitted with going train automatically geared to one for day and other for night: both foliots have movable weights to adjust for differing hour lengths. Movement mounted in frame of lantern clock form with weight drive from early 17th century; side doors, usually of silvered copper, often engraved, surmounted by bell originally of deep round-topped shape, later shallow and flat-topped; this type continued throughout period. Portable spring-driven clocks introduced *c*1830 in cases similar to English bracket clocks but smaller and lighter, 8–9in. tall with carrying handle; sides glazed; movement has pierced and engraved plates. Also *c*1830, weight-driven pillar clocks introduced on cheap basis for ordinary household use, designed to hang on central pillar of house, height 1–4ft, with glazed case around movement at top; single foliot, balance wheel or, rarely, pendulum. Dial consists of numerals mounted vertically on trunk, indicated by pointer fixed to weight as it travels downwards.

Japanese lacquer. Lacquer introduced from China *c*6th century (*see* Chinese lacquer). Earliest work, found e.g. in Buddhist temples, probably executed by Chinese craftsmen from mainland. In Heian period, independent Japanese style emerged; early examples rare, e.g. boxes for storing religious texts, or relics. Lacquer-work found on mirrors of period, combined with mother-of-pearl inlay. In Kamakura period, gold-decorated and inlaid pieces made for Shoguns, e.g. writing desk objects, tea ceremony utensils, jewel boxes. From Momoyama period onwards, lacquer-work plentiful and varied in style and use; stronger decorative effects than in earlier periods characteristic, especially those combining different techniques, e.g. saddles with gold and silver relief lacquer emblems on black lacquer; elaborate sword scabbards, picnic sets, chests or boxes of various sizes (*see* inro), and screens. Lacquered ware exported through Portuguese, Dutch, and British East India Company traders successively; in 18th century, panels of lacquer-work incorporated in European furniture, e.g. chests of drawers. European motifs became more frequent in Japanese work: miniature portraits of kings, scholars, military leaders. In first half of 19th century, old prints sometimes used to provide subjects.

Japanese lacquer. Suzuribako (writing-box), unsigned, late 18th century, in gold, silver, and coloured togidashi (flat burnished lacquer) with design of plum trees against setting sun.

Japanese metal-work. Earliest metal-workers, like Chinese, preferred base metals to gold or silver. Copper most common, and alloyed with tin to form bronze (called in Japanese, karakame, 'Chinese metal'). Earliest pieces, apart from primitive tools or weapons, bells (dotaku), date from 1st and 2nd centuries. Also some mirrors, very similar to *Chinese mirrors. Advent of Buddhism (mid 6th century) gave new outlet for work in image making; also, notable openwork aureoles or crowns made in silver or bronze. Reliquaries or small shrines (sharito), also with openwork decoration, and many containers for cult objects produced throughout Heian and Kamakura periods; religious pieces include censers, incense burners, staff-heads for itinerant monks, hand-bells or sceptres for priests, and begging bowls. Gongs and stands made as temple furniture, and lanterns for temple gardens, sometimes of monumental proportions. Among smaller cult objects adopted from Indian Buddhism were wheel, 'divine sword handle' and sceptre.

Secular pieces designed chiefly for tea ceremony, e.g. iron kettles (originated in 15th century); charcoal braziers (hibachi usually cast in bronze, sometimes iron. Flower vases made in bronze as well as pottery. Mirrors, cast in bronze, increasingly Japanese in style up to Heian period; predominant later shape was plain circle, with inner inscribed circle (like a bordered plate shape), and designs in centre extending into frieze area. Typical motifs: flying cranes, fir branches, sparrows, chrysanthemums; landscapes became popular in Kamakura period. Armour devised *c*12th century;

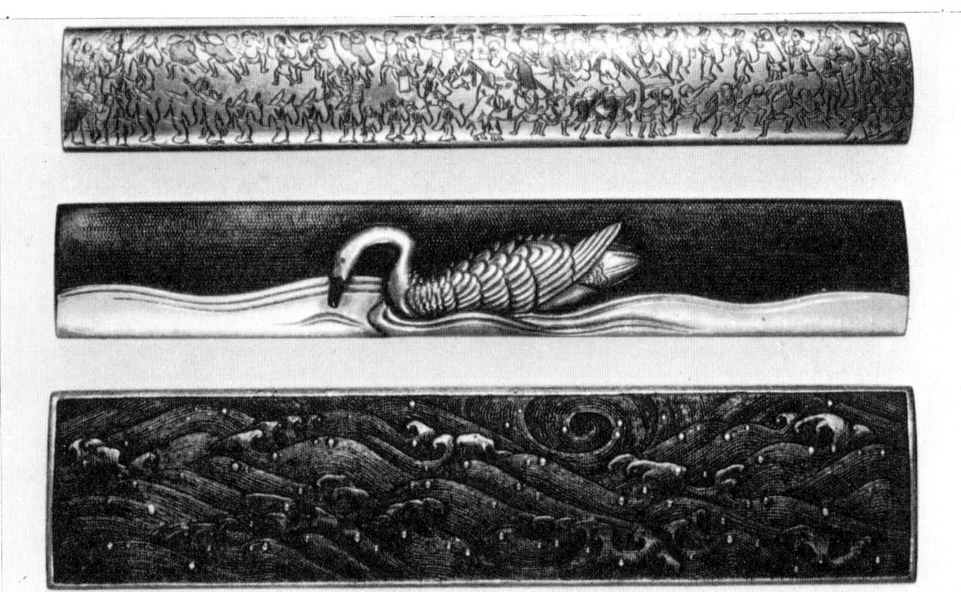

Japanese metal-work. Top: silver, engraved in detail with dancers, musicians, and audience. Centre: shakudo, decorated in gold and silver with swan swimming on still water, signed Yoshioka Inaba No Suke. Bottom: iron, carved in relief with high breaking waves with silver spray drops and rim; signed as above.

Japanese sword-guards. Top left: iron Bamen tsuba, pierced with silhouette of horse; Momoyama period; diameter 3in. Top right: iron Bushu tsuba, pierced and engraved with iris leaves and flowers; middle Edo period. Bottom left: iron Bushu tsuba, carved in relief with waves amongst which is reflected crescent moon applied with gold foil; middle Edo period. Bottom right: iron tsuba pierced and carved with prunus, with details in gold; middle Edo period.

basic shapes changed little during medieval times: suit with metal sections bound together with leather or silk; helmet (often single piece of iron, shaped like fish, dragon, or shell); armbands and gloves of lined metal (sometimes with openwork decoration on metal bands); neck-protecting piece of interlaced iron bands; shin plates; skirt of metal pieces to protect hips and thighs. Horse harness, e.g. bits, and stirrups of inlaid iron, or with openwork decoration. *See* Japanese sword-guards.

Japanese porcelain. Art of making porcelain introduced by Korean potter, who found *kaolin near Arita in 1616. Early styles follow Korean Yi dynasty wares; later work shows influence of Chinese Ming and Ch'ing periods. Products mainly blue-and-white work; *Imari ware notable. Much export to West, by Dutch East India Company. Edo period noted for high quality work of S. *Kakiemon; also *Kutani ware. Examples of *Hirado and *Kyoto wares highly valued.

Japanese pottery. Hand-moulded idols (probably fertility deities), or ritual vessels, made during neolithic Jomon period (*c*5000 B.C.–*c*250 B.C.), with string or rope markings impressed in unglazed clay body. Glazed earthenware introduced in Yayoi period; mortuary ware (*haniwa) found *c*A.D. 300–*c*600. In 5th century, Korean settlers brought new pottery techniques, and *Sué ware, precursor of several important later groups, first found. In Nara period, strong Chinese influence led to development of coloured glazes. Production of Sué-type ware continued; new celadons introduced, e.g. *Owari seiji, and later *Seto. *Toshiro most famous individual potter of Kamakura period, when Chinese influence still important. In Muromachi era, most wares imported from China, and native industry declined. Revival in Momoyama period, when *Shino and *Oribe wares originated; notable products were utensils for tea ceremony. *Raku ware introduced by Kyoto potters at this time. *Karatsu ware shows influence of Korean styling. Minor local kilns, *Bizen and *Tamba, made domestic ware. Japanese porcelain appeared in 17th century, but demand for pottery for daily use continued. In peaceful and prosperous Edo period, kilns flourished all over Japan, but porcelain production now became predominant. Kyoto emerged as centre for industry, replacing Seto, at beginning of 19th century. *Ninsei helped develop *Kyo-yaki ware there, but more famous is disciple, *Kenzan. Many more kilns established at this time, notably *Asahi, and near Kyoto, where *Banko ware made. Most varied and popular types of pottery in western part of country were Karatsu and *Satsuma wares. In central Japan, Seto continued, but towards end of era, porcelain became main type of ware throughout country, and pottery declined further.

Japanese sword-guards. Japanese sword-hilts are wooden, with hollow slit for blade. Slight curve to blade became general *c*A.D. 1000; armoury assumed traditional shapes, unchanging through medieval period. User's hand protected by tsuba, or guard, an iron plate, usually circular, with elongated slit for blade, and slit on each side for sword knife and sword needle. At first, guards manufactured by swordsmiths, later also produced by armourers. Early,

12th century examples noted for fine forging: large, thin discs, with hammered ground and decoration achieved by simple perforations, e.g. silhouettes of pine trees, ferns, gourds, dragonflies, shells, etc. Kamakura style has low relief landscapes; Heianjo has heraldic emblems, flowers, etc. in positive silhouette, leaving very little of original plate. Sword-guards with inlay work found in 16th century. Various masters after 1600, using name of Kaneije, produced guards enriched with inlay of precious metals or bronze. More elaborate designs found from late 16th century, known as mukade or shingen tsuba, where wires of yellow or red copper or silver are woven on to large iron plates, then sometimes studded with silver or bronze nails. Namban sword-guards have beaded decoration, and show influence of Spanish or Italian metal-work. Some enamel work found in 17th and 18th centuries, as well as coloured relief metal-work.

Japanese time measurement. Japan adopted European calendar and timekeeping system in 1873; previously sunrise and sunset divided day and night periods of varying length through year, official time of each changing twice monthly. Night and day each subdivided into six 'hours' of differing duration, requiring clocks having either variable dial divisions or escapement with rate changed at sunrise and sunset. 'Hours' are struck in sequence 9, 8, 7, 6, 5, 4. *See* striking systems.

Japanese watch. *See* inro watch.

japanische Figuren. German ceramics: oriental figures painted in medallions on porcelain made at Meissen under J. G. *Herold; also used by *Hausmaler* in 1720s and 1730s.

japanned metal ware. Black or tin-plated iron (occasionally copper or other metal) coated with lacquer and decorated in manner of oriental lacquer-work; process developed by T. *Allgood of *Pontypool, *c*1680. Hard, glossy surface withstood heat. On introduction of tin-plated iron (1730), process was improved and domestic articles, e.g. trays, boxes, tea-caddies, produced at Pontypool and *Usk. Similar articles produced on larger scale by J. *Baskerville and others at Birmingham, Bilston, Wolverhampton, and London from mid 18th century. Quality and durability is determined by number of coats of lacquer and stovings; heat-resisting qualities improved in 1770s and output extended to tea and coffee urns, kettles, etc. Japanned wares exported from England to France and Holland in mid 1770s, while similar French product, **tôle peinte*, imported. *Illustrations at* Pontypool, toleware.

Japan patterns. In late 18th century England, designs inspired by oriental styles, sometimes Chinese, but particularly Japanese Imari with foliage and flowers in deep blues with red and gilding. Fashion declined in 1820s; revived later in 19th century. Frequently used on porcelain and earthenware, e.g. by J. *Spode II on bone china, and by R. *Bloor at Derby.

Japy factory. French watch factory, founded *c*1770 in Beaucourt (Jura), by Frédéric Japy (1749–1812). Pioneered use of machine tools in manufacture of **ébauches* (1776). Employed unskilled workers for watch production on large scale. Second factory founded in Baderel in 1810. Business continued by sons and in existence as Japy Frères until recent times.

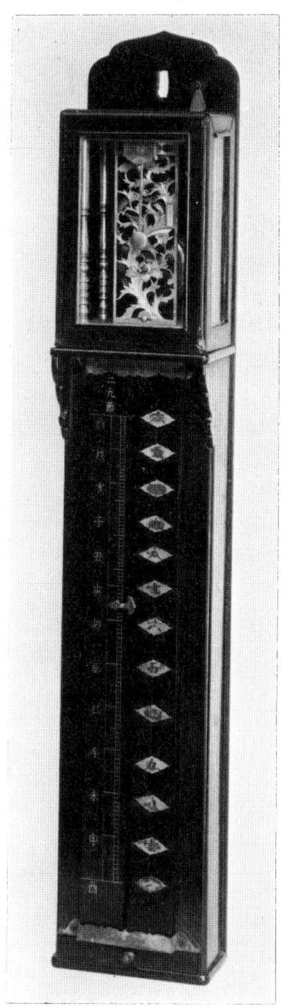

Japanese time measurement. Pillar clock, c1830. Mechanism at top; movement is gravity-driven and travels down case, pointer showing hours as it passes. Scale on left replaced every month; scale on right marks hours which can be adjusted individually; noon is marked at top and bottom; clock must be re-wound exactly when movement reaches bottom.

Japy Factory. Mantel clock in ormolu case with pink-ground porcelain dial and decorative plaques. c1860. Height 1ft9in.

Below:

Jardinière. *Mahogany, one of pair. Trumpet-shaped container carved with overlapping stylized leaves, scrolled monopodium. English, c1820. Height 2ft9in.*

jardinière. Table or stand with metal-lined bowl or tray set in top; used to hold flowers or plants. Popular in 19th century.

Jarry, Jacques (fl late 18th century). French painter of faience at Aprey (1772–81) and at Sceaux in 1784. Noted for enamel painting with fine brushwork of birds.

Jarves, Deming (1790–1869). American glass manufacturer from Boston, Massachusetts. Founder member of *New England Glass Company (1818). Inherited money from father in 1824; founded exceptionally successful *Boston & Sandwich Glass Company. Left in 1858 to found rival *Cape Cod Glass Works. Hoped to be succeeded by son, John, who died in 1863. Lost interest in works, which closed with his death.

Jarvis, John Wesley (1780–1840). English-born American miniaturist in Philadelphia, Pennsylvania from 1785. Apprenticed to engraver before moving to New York (1802) and setting up in partnership as miniaturist and portrait painter. Took H. *Inman as apprentice in 1814.

jasper. Opaque, cryptocrystalline variety of *quartz; colours (usually red, yellow, or brown) produced by presence of iron oxide. Used particularly in Renaissance Europe, for luxury articles; often mounted in gold, silver, or silver-gilt, e.g. drinking vessels, caskets, portable altars, ewers and basins, etc. Again popular in late 18th century for small decorative objects with ormolu mounts e.g. perfume-burners, vases. *Illustration at* P. Gouthière.

jasper ware. English hard stoneware perfected by J. *Wedgwood c1774; still in production. White body stained blue, sage green, lilac, or yellow throughout (solid jasper), or covered with surface colour wash (jasper dip). Detailed relief decoration often sprigged-on in white. Dipped ware could be engine-turned to reveal white body. During peak years (1780–95), useful and decorative wares of high quality produced. Limited edition of 50 copies of *Portland vase produced in 1790. *Illustrations also at* cut steel, J. Flaxman, spy glasses, urn clock.

jaune jonquille. French ceramics. Deep, intense yellow enamel ground colour introduced at Vincennes by J. *Hellot in 1753. *Illustration at* Sèvres (Vincennes).

Jeannest, Pierre Emile (1813–57). French sculptor and designer; came to England c1845; employed by *Minton as ceramic modeller. From c1850, also employed by *Elkington and Co. as designer. Specialized in presentation pieces (race cups, trophies, etc.) in Renaissance and baroque styles; also modelled statuettes and figure groups.

jelly glass. Small, straight-sided, conical glass bowl set directly on foot; made in 18th century England. Later examples more elaborate, often have bell-shaped bowl on high domed foot, with or without knop, and one or two swan-neck or single loop handles.

Jennens and Bettridge. English firm which manufactured papier mâché wares in Birmingham, 1816–64; took over factory of H. *Clay. Produced large range of objects of vertu and household wares including tea-caddies, snuff-boxes, card cases, fire-guards, chairs, etc. Designs in variety of colours on black ground.

Jenny Lind bottle. 19th century American bottle. Usually ovoid with cylindrical neck; blown in full-size, two-piece mould. Depicts Swedish singer who visited America in 1840.

Jensen, Gerreit, or **Johnson,** Garret (fl c1680–1715). Cabinet-maker of Dutch or Flemish origin. Worked for the English court from time of Charles II to end of Queen Anne's reign. Used *Boulle technique of metal and tortoiseshell marquetry.

Jerome, Chauncey (1793–1868). American manufacturer and clock maker in Connecticut. Skilled carpenter; made clock cases with E. *Terry, 1816. Many business undertakings. In 1837–38, organized large-scale production of 30 hour, brass movement clocks in ogee cases; widely imitated until c1914. Worked with U.S. Clock & Brass Co, Chicago, c1866.

Jersey Glass Company. Founded 1824 in New Jersey by glass cutter George Dummer and associates. Produced flint, cut, engraved, and gilded glass and druggists' wares. Improved mechanical pressing techniques, adding pressed, moulded, and plain glass to output. Closed c1862.

Jesuit porcelain. Chinese export porcelain dating from reign of K'ang Hsi; decorated with e.g. nativity, crucifixion, Virgin Mary, and St John. Jesuit missionaries, often attached to Imperial court from 16th century, active in arts and science. Influence of designs imported from Europe (Holland or France), might account for predominance of black monochrome decoration, probably after engravings.

jet. Fossilized wood found in bituminous shale (particularly in cliffs of Yorkshire coastline); takes high polish. Used to make ornaments since Bronze Age; jet beads found in burial sites. Romans made rings of jet. During Middle Ages jet rosary beads and crucifixes common. c1800, Captain Treulett, naval pensioner living in Whitby, Yorkshire, said to have originated process of turning jet beads; instrumental in founding machine-made jet jewellery industry in area. In 1808 John Carter and Robert Jefferson (instructed by Treulett) established first workshop. Demand for jet *mourning jewellery in England increased greatly in first half of 19th century; also exported. Jet earrings, lockets, bracelets, brooches, and necklaces, carved, engraved, set with pearls, etc. Gold, gilded base metal, or gold substitutes, e.g. *pinchbeck, used for mounts. Soft jet from Spain much used in England as cheaper alternative. Imitations in black glass known as French jet.

jet enamel. *See* Worcester.

Jever (Oldenburg). German faience factory founded 1760 by J. S. F. *Tännich, who undertook to make hard-paste porcelain for Prince of Zerbst. Factory lasted 16 years, producing only faience, e.g. table services, figures, and vases. Decoration influenced by Meissen. Mark: Jever, sometimes with painter's initial.

jewelled decoration (in ceramics). Introduced at Sèvres, c1780–84; drops of coloured enamel applied to gold or silver surface. Raised gilding with impressed decoration covered with translucent colours used earlier at Saint-Cloud (1723–38), recalling work of C. C. *Hunger (1715–25), and later enamelled work. In mid 19th century, jewelled porcelain produced at Worcester; blobs of colour incorporated into porcelain and fired with body.

jewellery. Personal ornaments in use from ancient times; made in variety of materials: seeds, bones, teeth, gold, silver, iron, bronze, glass, enamel, etc. Probably worn initially as amulets or talismans and also as sign of status and power. Ancient Egyptians wore elaborate collars of beads, metal, etc., *pendants, scarab rings. In Greece, gold *diadems, *earrings, *bracelets, etc. worn, with *repoussé*, *filigree, or *granulation. Etruscans and Romans wore *brooches, earrings, bracelets, etc. During Dark Ages in Britain and Europe, usual ornament was brooch; all jewellery brightly coloured, set with gem-stones and enamelled. Many pieces buried with owners survive; in 9th century, Charlemagne published decree forbidding burial of personal jewellery with dead. Little subsequent pre-Renaissance jewellery remains. Medieval brooches and rings often with enamelled figures and architectural motifs, set with uncut or *cabochon gems. **Enseigne* with similar ornament introduced.

Renaissance jewellery included pendants and rings. Pearls worn in hair, or as necklaces. Italian lapidaries made cameos (in imitation of classical models) for use as pendants, medallions, etc. Artist-goldsmiths, e.g. B. *Cellini, also designed jewellery. Reverses of objects often richly enamelled, e.g. with strapwork. From late 16th century, gem-stones, particularly diamonds, gradually became more important than setting. Most jewellery broken up for value of gems, or remade with changing fashions.

*Mourning and *hair jewellery developed in 17th century. Invention of *rose cut for diamonds in mid 17th century led to facet-cutting of most stones. Low necklines accentuated by *necklaces, **girandole*-type earrings and brooches. Enamel much used as backing for gem-stones during 17th century, but unfashionable in 18th. *Paste jewellery popular during 18th century; valued for intrinsic beauty, not used as substitute for gems as in 19th century. *Buckles and *chatelaines also worn. From late 18th century, *cameos used in bracelets, necklaces, etc.

19th century jewellery eclectic in form, design, and materials. 18th century styles revived, and elaborate gem-set **parures* made. Realistic botanical jewellery. Archaeological jewellery made e.g. by F. P. *Castellani and C. *Giuliano. In mid 19th century, Gothic revival jewellery designed e.g. by F-D. *Froment-Meurice and A. W. N. *Pugin. 19th century materials included most gem-stones; also iron, *jet, *coral, *pinchbeck, *amber, *cut steel, paste, as well as gold and silver. Later jewellery often machine-made, with consequent decline in quality.

jewelling (in watchmaking). Use of hard gem-stone, usually ruby, to form bearing. Art of piercing jewels patented by N. *Facio, P. and J. *Debaufre in London (1704), but patent successfully opposed by Clockmakers' Company. By 1750, jewelling found in better English watches; not widely used in Europe until 19th century. Jewelled bearings subject to less wear than plain metal pivot holes and require less oil. Jewels also used for part of cylinder, duplex, lever, and chronometer *escapements.

jib-crook. *See* chimney-crane.

J.M.E. or **M.E.** (*juré des menuisiers-ébénistes* or *menuisier-ébéniste*). Stamp used by a committee of *maître-ébénistes* or *menuisiers* after dissolution of their guilds in 1790. Furniture thus stamped had fulfilled the committee's requirements for quality of construction and craftsmanship in decoration.

Johanneum mark. Inventory mark on Meissen porcelain in (or from) *Augustus the Strong's royal collection at Johanneum. Letters and numbers, engraved on base and coloured black, classified Chinese and Meissen porcelain, e.g. W (white Saxon), R (red, or brown Saxon). Forgeries occur.

Johnson, Garret. *See* Jensen, Gerreit.

*Jasper ware. Cups and saucers made at *Wedgwood factory 1785–90.*
Right:
Jesuit porcelain. Chinese, decorated with Ascension of Christ, from European engraving. Mid 18th century. Diameter 8¾in.
*Jewellery. 19th century. Left: gold pendant decorated with enamel by C. *Giuliano. Centre: brooch by F. P. Castellani, gold and enamel with mosaic centre. Right: gold pendant by Castellani set with emerald cameo and pearls. Below: bracelet of ivy leaves in enamel; set with twelve different semi-precious stones. Length 7¼in.*
Right:
Thomas Johnson. Rococo candle-stand, carved and painted wood with ormolu, c1760. Height 5ft2in.

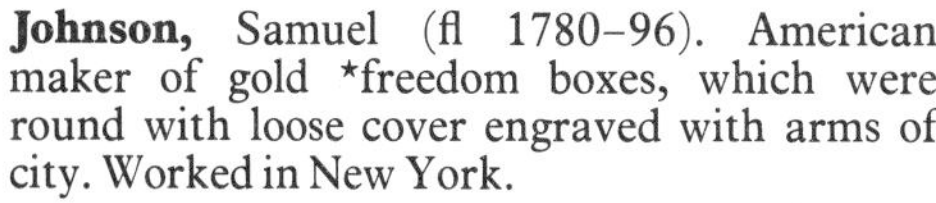

Johnson, Samuel (fl 1780–96). American maker of gold *freedom boxes, which were round with loose cover engraved with arms of city. Worked in New York.

Johnson, Thomas (fl *c*1755–66). English designer and carver working in London; specialized in *girandoles,* candelabra, frames, stands, tables. Published Twelve Girandoles (1755), One Hundred and Fifty New Designs (1756–58). Accomplished wood carver with eccentric style. Motifs include realistic leaf and flower forms, Chinese and classical motifs, dolphins, acanthus, ribbons, and scrolls. Much work in gilt deal.

joined or **panelled furniture.** Furniture made of rectangular panels of wood set into wooden frames, with mortice-and-tenon joints held fast by oak pegs. Dates from 15th century, replacing heavier boarded furniture.

joint stool. Stool of joined construction, height

Joined chair. Henry VIII carved oak chair; carving with Renaissance influence; three-sided back with box seat; carved and panelled lower part.
Left:
Joint stool. Oak with carved panels. English, mid 17th century.

of seat or low table, often with turned legs and box stretcher. Common in 16th and 17th centuries; used into 18th.

Joliffe (fl mid 18th century). Earliest known English silhouettist. Exhibited work at White's Club, London, in 1758. Sitters included Edward, Prince of Wales. Painted on back of flat glass. Profiles three-quarter length, posed beneath draped curtains. Oval black border edged with dots, pierced with circles, and with gilded decoration. Usually with silk backing.

Jones, Henry (d 1695). English clock and watch maker; apprenticed to E. *East, 1654; member Clockmakers' Company, 1663, master, 1691. Made oval watches, long-case and bracket clocks.

Jordaens, Jakob (1593–1678). Flemish painter, student of *Rubens. Numerous cartoons for tapestries included Ulysses, History of Charlemagne, History of Achilles, History of Alexander, Country Life, and Proverbs.

Joshagan, Jushaghan, or **Djoushegan carpets.** Outstanding 16th and 17th century east Persian woollen court carpets made in Joshagan. Two distinctive rectilinear designs commonly found: floral motifs in diamond forms, or diagonal lattice design, with or without central medallion. Still produced, in modified form.

Joubert, François (1743–after 1793). French silversmith working in Paris; master in 1749. Made range of domestic silver in rococo style. Mme Pompadour among aristocratic patrons. Mark: fleur-de-lis crowned, two pellets, FJ, and heart.

Joubert, Gilles, or **Joubert l'aîné** (1689–1775). French. Became *maître-ébéniste* at beginning of Régence period; in 1758 *ébéniste ordinaire du Garde-meuble de la Couronne.* In 1763 followed J-F. *Oeben as *ébéniste* to Louis XV; retired in 1774. Stamp: JOUBERT with a fleur-de-lis on either side. *Illustration at* corner cupboard.

juan ts'ai. *See famille rose.*

jufti (Arabic, 'paired'), djufti, chufti, or **false knot.** Carpet-knot tied in various ways over two pairs of warp threads. Pile produced has half density of usual Persian or Turkish knotted pile.

jug or **pitcher.** Deep vessel for holding water, ale, wine, etc. Generally with handle and pouring lip or spout; sometimes also with cover. Earliest jugs, probably stoneware, pewter, or bronze, date from Middle Ages or earlier. 16th century German stoneware jugs (*tigerware) given silver mounts in Britain. Earliest surviving examples in silver, silver-gilt, or gold also from 16th century. Various body forms include bulbous shape with narrow cylindrical neck, pear shape, mug shaped, and helmet shape; sometimes on pedestal foot or three or four individual feet. Later examples made from sheet brass up to 20th century.

Jullien, Joseph (d 1774). French potter, sculptor, and painter of faience. Chief painter in faience factory of J. *Chapelle at Sceaux. In 1763, with S. *Jacques, rented factory from Chapelle; lease expired 1772. Together also acquired Mennecy porcelain factory on death of J-B. *Barbin (1765) and established faience factory at Bourg-la-Reine (1772), transferring Mennecy porcelain manufacture there in 1773. Succeeded by son, Joseph-Léon.

Ju ware. Bowl with bound copper rim, glaze with faint irregular crackle; glazed base has five oval spur marks. Diameter $6\frac{1}{2}$in.

Jungfrauenbecher. 16th and 17th century German silver marriage cups representing maiden with long skirt and uplifted arms. Small cup on swivel between out-stretched arms; skirt forms larger cup. Bridegroom drank contents of skirt, then turned figure right way up, attempting not to spill contents of swivel cup, to be drunk by bride. Also made in Holland. Average height $c8\frac{1}{2}$in. *See* wager cup. *Illustration at* wager cup.

Junghans factory. German clock factory, established in Schramberg during 1850s. Developed large-scale production of domestic clocks. Firm continues.

Jürgensen, Urban Brunn (1776–1830). Danish watch and chronometer maker. Studied in Paris under F. *Berthoud and A-L. *Breguet, *c*1800; then under J. *Arnold in London. Supplier of chronometers to Danish navy.

Jushaghan carpets. *See* Joshagan carpets.

Jü ware. Chinese ceramics; Imperial stoneware of Sung period, made at Ju-chou (now Lin-ju Hsien), Honan province. Yellowish-buff body covered with smooth, opaque, light greenish-blue glaze, sometimes *crackled; made for use at court. Kilns, established *c*1107, closed when Emperors fled southwards from Chin Tartar invaders in 1127. Connected, and sometimes confused, with *Yüeh ware made contemporaneously in same area.

Kaapsche schotels. *See* Cape plates.

Kaiserteller (German, 'emperor dish'). Large, ornamental pewter dish cast with central image of reigning emperor and medallion border portraits of electors; made in 17th century in Nuremberg.

Kakiemon, Sakaida (1596–1666). Japanese potter in Arita; traditionally credited with introduction of enamel colours in decoration of porcelain, inspired by work of Chinese Ming dynasty. Technique, of which even early examples display great accomplishment, widely adopted; also used on Imari porcelain. Kakiemon and successors produced porcelain of high quality, working as individual craftsmen-potters. Pure white paste, painted with brilliant, clear colours often in asymmetrical patterns. Exotic elements of European design sometimes appear in early work, but Japanese attribute work of highest quality to 5th to 8th generations of Kakiemon's successors (13th potter in line currently at work). Name derived from red fruit of *Diospyros kaki,* Japanese persimmon, popular colour in decoration of this school.

*Kakiemon. Buddhist lion, late 17th century. Typical enamelled colours of turquoise, *iron-red, azure-blue and transparent pale yellow outlined in black.*

Kakiemon style. Japanese ceramic decoration: associated with S. *Kakiemon. Porcelain exported to Europe from Arita in late 17th and early 18th centuries inspired decoration, e.g. at Saint-Cloud (ice pail with lion mask handles, dated 1710–20, has polychrome decoration of birds and plants). Provided stylistic basis for e.g. **décor coréen.* Meticulous copies made at Meissen factory, notably by A. F. *von Löwenfinck and J. E. *Stadler, *c*1730–35. Octagonal bowls, hexagonal covered vases, square saké bottles, often occur, in very white paste; painted with dragons, chrysanthemums, or prunus blossom. Enamel colours include, notably, bright orange-red (*red dragon service), canary yellow, and turquoise. English examples include version of **caille* pattern used at Bow in 1750s. *Illustration at* Arita.

Kalt-Maletei. *See* cold painting.

Kam, Gerrit (d 1705), sons Pieter (d 1705), and David (d 1719). Dutch potters at Delft. Gerrit part-owner of The Three Ash-Barrels factory from 1668. In 1679, became sole owner; transferred factory to Pieter. Owner of The Peacock factory from 1701. Work, characterized by precise imitation of K'ang-hsi porcelain, includes gourd-shaped vases. Pieter painted rich decoration of flower bouquets in geometrical arrangement. David succeeded father at The Peacock; specialized in trailing Chinese flowers and birds, in cream or yellow on background of *bleus de Nevers.*

Kamakura (1185–1333). Japanese period, following Heian; country ruled by numerous war-lords. Buddhist scholarship influential; art forms tended towards realism. Metal-work important, especially armour. Lacquer-work brightly coloured, often dusted with gold, contrasted with mother-of-pearl inlay, etc. Influence of Chinese Sung and Yüan periods considerable, especially in ceramic developments, e.g. porcelain work at *Seto. Followed by Muromachi period.

Kameyama. Japanese kiln near Nagasaki, active 1804–67, manufacturing celadon ware. Private production, set up by prosperous merchant for nearby city market. Blue and white porcelain also produced, imitating work of Chinese Ch'ien Lung era. Chief Dutch source of ware for export in 19th century. Porcelain tends to be thick, and blue colouring poor.

Kandler, Charles Frederick (d *c*1778). German-born silversmith working in London; did not use first name in mark. In 1735 registered marks KA, and FK with a crown above; in 1739, FK in script with a fleur-de-lis above; in 1758, FK in script. Made much domestic silver in rococo and neo-classical styles. In 1735, adopted Britannia standard silver mark of Charles Kandler, thought to be his father, whose surviving work includes wine cooler and tea-kettle and stand in rococo style. (Another Charles Kandler, probably Frederick's son, registered his mark from Frederick's address in 1778.)

Kändler, Johann Friedrich (1734–91). German porcelain arcanist and modeller, apprenticed to uncle, J. J. *Kändler at Meissen. Achieved successful hard-paste porcelain manufacture (1758) at Ansbach faience factory; manager and modeller, 1758–91. At first used lead glaze on figures after Meissen subjects.

Kändler, Johann Joachim (1706–75). Notable German porcelain modeller; apprentice sculptor *c*1723, master by 1730. Worked at Meissen factory (1731–33); *Modellmeister* 1733–75. At first with J. G. *Kirchner, modelled large animals for collection of *Augustus the Strong; work, including pelican, pair of goats, eagle, sheep, leopard, notable for accurate observation of originals; most surviving examples left in white. Animal models produced soon after death of Augustus include teapots in form e.g. of poultry, monkeys, squirrels, with animals' tails as handles; strongly coloured. Later animal models include dogs, notably pugs, and small birds with patches of strong colour. *Sulkowski and *Swan services and **plat de ménage* modelled in 1730s and early 1740s, inspired notably by **commedia dell'arte* characters. Crinoline groups, modelled from *c*1740 characterized by lady in crinoline dress with gentleman and negro servant, e.g. Heart seller. Other figures include beggar musicians with strong colour used in contrast with white of paste. In 1740, appointed head of entire modelling staff, over e.g. J. F. *Eberlein and P. *Reinicke; this year marks replacement of baroque by rococo style. Subsequent figures include series, **Cris de Paris, commedia dell'arte* (also made as scent bottles), woodman and allegorical figures. French influence visible in models after visit to Paris (1749), subjects often pastoral, or domestic; rococo moulding introduced on bases of figures and on scent bottles. From 1749, involvement with modelling probably diminished because of court commitments, and influence of other modellers increased. *Illustration at* Meissen.

K'ang Hsi. Bottle with bulb below lip. Painted in brilliant blue with design of two phoenixes in peony scrolls with stiff plantain leaves on neck. Height 16½in.

K'ang Hsi (1662–1722). Chinese Emperor of Ch'ing dynasty, patron of ceramic art. Rebuilt Imperial factory at *Ch'ing-tê-chên in 1681; instigated revival of porcelain making. Stimulated western interest by welcoming European painters and writers at court; export trade flourished, especially in blue-and-white porcelain. Encouraged imitation of Hsüan Tê and Ch'êng Hua styles; copies difficult to distinguish from originals. Monochrome decoration with e.g. *ox-blood glaze or *mirror-black. Enamelling of e.g. *san ts'ai or *wu ts'ai perfected (*see famille verte*). White wares, sometimes *crackle-glazed, or imitated *Wan-li pierced-work. *Illustrations also at* armorial porcelain, *clair-de-lune, famille noire, famille verte,* peach bloom.

kaolin or **china clay.** White clay produced geologically by action of water on orthoclase feldspar in granitic rocks. Refractory – can be fired at high temperatures without deforming; remains white when fired. Used in hard-paste (true) porcelain, forming 40–50% of body. Also important e.g. in manufacture of paper. Main component is kaolinite, hydrated aluminium silicate, which occurs mixed with various minerals in other clays.

Discovery in China allowed hard-paste porcelain manufacture from *c*9th century. First samples to reach Europe (1712) collected by French Jesuit missionary, François Xavier d'Entrecolles (1662–1741). Earliest deposits found in Europe at Aue (Saxony), used at Meissen, and Passau (Bavaria). Kaolin used at Vienna and Ludwigsburg; in France, discovered at Saint-Yrieix near Limoges. Found in Cornwall by W. *Cookworthy before 1758 and used at Plymouth and Bristol. St Austell area of Cornwall remains among most important sources. Other major deposits in Europe (Italy, Bohemia, Brittany), United States (the Carolinas, Georgia, Florida, Kentucky, Tennessee), Australia, South Africa.

Kapuzinerbraun or **'capuzin' brown.** *See* dead-leaf brown.

Karabah or **Carabagh carpets.** South Caucasian carpets, strongly Persian influenced, with longish Turkish-knotted pile on woollen and cotton foundation; warp ends cut at bottom only. Patterns combine geometrical and floral motifs in strong colours, particularly reddish-purple, on blue-black or black grounds. Borders with rosette and tendril motif. Also, in first half of 19th century pastel-coloured, rose-and-bouquet design carpets woven exclusively for export to Russian nobility; modelled on popular French designs.

Karagashli carpets. Very fine small *Kuba carpets with low, velvety pile and characteristic pattern of rectangular or diamond-shaped palmettes and stylized scrolls in yellow and red. Ground usually pale blue or turquoise.

Karatsu ware. Japanese ceramics, produced in northern Kyushu (Saga prefecture), from 13th to 15th centuries. High-fired, hard pottery, with opaque milk-white or transparent (yellow-green) ash glaze. Developments introduced from north Korea in 16th century include tea-bowls, painted with brown iron oxide under glaze, or with hakeme brushwork (*see* punch'ŏng). Grasses, reeds, wistaria, or simple geometrical patterns, most common decoration. In early Edo period, painted (E-Karatsu) wares, with spirited abstract designs; examples more Korean in style, called Chosen (Japanese for 'Korean') Karatsu, characterized by two-colour decoration. In 18th and 19th centuries, when ware made on industrial scale, quality declined.

Karcher, Jan and Nicholaus (fl mid 16th century). Flemish tapestry master-weavers, brothers, working in Italy. Established Ferrara tapestry manufactory, 1536. Jan remained as director while Nicholaus went to Mantua (1539) then Florence (1546) where, with J. *Rost, he established and directed Arazzeria Medici (*see* Florentine tapestry).

Karrusel watch. *See tourbillon.*

kas or **kasse.** Heavy, often painted, cupboard or wardrobe, originally Dutch. Brought to

Kas. *Oak and ebonized wood; frieze decorated with* amorini *above lions masks; doors with geometrical mouldings; massive *bun feet on front two legs. Dutch, 17th century. Width 5ft9in.*

America by Dutch settlers and made in north-eastern America, mid 17th to end of 18th century.

Kasak carpets. *See* Kazak carpets.

Kashan, Persia. Lustre-decorated tiles made, by 9th century, for decoration of religious and public buildings. In 13th and 14th centuries, tiles rectangular or star-shaped, decorated with intricate designs, often inscriptions picked out in blue. *Laqabi ware made in 12th century.

Kashan carpets. Small, velvet-textured 16th and 17th century central Persian court carpets with short, extremely fine, Persian-knotted silk pile on silk or silk and cotton foundation; woven in Kashan, silk manufacturing centre. Numerous medallion carpets with palmette and arabesque ornamented landscape field; richly-curved, complex central medallion bearing cloud-band cartouches; pendants along vertical axis; corner pieces repeating medallion pattern. Some hunting and animal carpets, particularly shaggy *Polish carpets woven for export in 17th century. Very fine silk prayer rugs woven from 16th century.

Kassel. *See* Cassel.

Kastrup. *See* Copenhagen.

Kauffmann, Angelica (1741–1807). Swiss portraitist and decorative painter, working in England 1766–81; became founder member of Royal Academy. Collaborated with R. *Adam on house decoration. Engravings after her work copied on porcelain made e.g. at Buen Retiro, in late 18th century, and at Vienna in 19th century.

Kazak or **Kasak carpets.** Hard-wearing south-west Caucasian carpets from Kazak area. Long pile, Turkish-knotted, usually on undyed woollen foundation with edges bound in red wool and ends, cut at bottom only, worked into braided fringe. Simple, large-scale field patterns in five to nine clear, basic colours often on red grounds. Motifs include angular medallions, *botehs in diagonal bands, fan-rosettes, hooked lozenges, and latch-hook trellises.

Kashan carpet. Persian, c1870. 6ft3in. × 4ft4in.

Kazak carpet. c1870. 7ft × 5ft9in.

Kean, Michael (fl late 18th and early 19th centuries). Miniature painter; proprietor of Derby porcelain factory from 1795 until retirement in 1811.

Keene Glass Works. Light olive-amber Washington and Jackson portrait flask, c1828–40. Pint capacity.

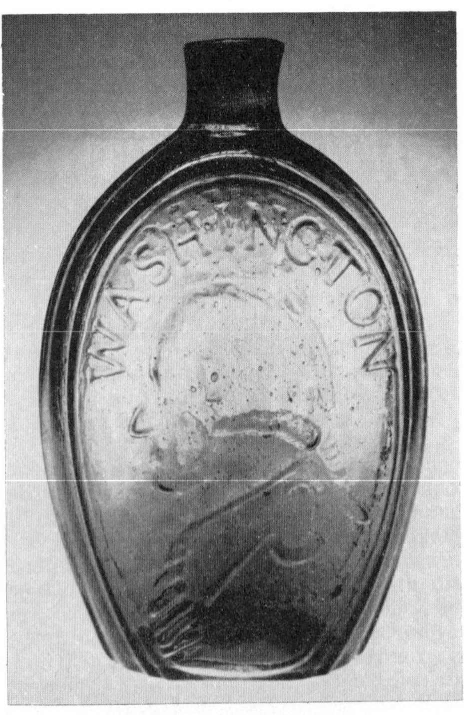

Keene Glass Works. Founded 1815 by Henry Schoolcraft and Timothy Twichell, formerly of Vermont Glass Factory. Ownership changed frequently. Noted for blown-three-mould bottles and flasks in green and flint glass. Closed in 1850.

Keiser, Aelbrecht. *See* Keyser, Aelbrecht.

kelim, kilim, gilim, or **ghilim carpets.** Reversible tapestry-weave carpets woven by particular technique. Weft thread of given colour worked to and fro in own area of pattern; next colour continues pattern from adjacent warp thread, so that no weft threads run across whole width of piece. Resulting slits (between different coloured areas of pattern) reduced to minimum by indenting outlines of design. Older kelims often made of two narrow widths sewn together. Technique much used in Anatolia, Caucasus, and Persia. Finest Anatolian examples, kis kelims, and Persian, *Sehna kelims (woven by Kurds).

Kellinghusen (Holstein), Germany. Several faience factories established, *c*1750–*c*1850, after discovery of local clay deposits. Most work in peasant style. Plates and dishes painted in high-temperature colours with flowers, e.g. tulips and carnations, well into 19th century. KH appears in marks from all factories of area.

Kelsterbach (Hesse-Darmstadt). Faience made at factory established in mid 18th century includes tableware, some painted with blue in style of porcelain. Early faience marked K. Cream-coloured earthenware also made. Hard-

Kelim. Woven in wool. Moldavian district of Rumania. 19th century. 9ft6in. × 6ft.

William Kent. Small gilt-wood console table with Siena marble top supported by female head amongst acanthus scrolls and husk ornament. Height 2ft11in.

Kenzan. Stoneware tea bowl, painted in brown and black over grey glaze. School of Kenzan, 18th century.

paste porcelain produced *c*1761–68, probably at same factory, under direction of C. D. *Busch until 1764. Modelled groups include female cembalo player with *putto* in setting of elaborate moulded scrollwork (*c*1765). Porcelain production lapsed 1768, but resumed briefly in 1798 under J. M. *Höckel; figures moulded in style of F. A. *Bustelli. Mark: HD in monogram, crowned, in underglaze blue; same mark impressed on cream-coloured earthenware.

kende. *See* narghile.

Kent, William (*c*1685–1748). English painter, architect, landscape gardener, and designer; early exponent of Palladian design. Worked closely with Lord Burlington. *Illustration at* console table.

Kenzan (1663–1743). Japanese potter Ogata Shinsho or Ogata Sansei; also screen-painter and artist in lacquer. Worked chiefly at Kyoto potteries, occasionally in *raku, more often in *Awata ware. Noted for boldness of pottery form, with irregular, simple designs. Painted abstract landscape patterns in brown, black, or white slips, impure greens and blues. Calligraphy often appears in free, bold strokes. Many pupils and other potters used his mark (*see* Inuyama ware). Designs influenced development of Japanese ceramics; tea utensils very highly valued. Some pieces attributed to first Kenzan may be work of disciples; attribution to individual potters of school virtually impossible. Tradition still continues at Awata kilns.

*Kettle stands. Mahogany with carved tripods. Those on left and right have pierced *fretwork edges to top. English, mid 18th century.*

Kerman carpets. *See* Kirman carpets.

kettle. Originally denoted cooking pot, especially *cauldron. From late 17th century, spouted *tea kettles made in silver, possibly also copper and brass. Few copper or brass kitchen kettles survive from before *c*1800, those before 1850 are rare.

kettle stand. Small table with round or square top (often with pierced gallery) on central stand with tripod base; designed for tea kettle and burner. Dates from late 17th century England.

kettle-tilter. Pulley system over hearth by which hot, heavy kettle could be tipped.

key (of clock or watch). Earliest clocks wound by turning capstan-like bars on *barrel: use of key fitting square winding spindle evolved at least by appearance of first watches, *c*1550. Pipe fitting over winding square attached direct to small disc (often pierced and engraved until *c*1700), or, from *c*1670, to arm at right-angle with knob at other end (crank key). Some crank keys of folding type for watches.

Tipsy key introduced by A-L. *Breguet has small sphere at top of pipe with sprung ratchet to prevent turning in wrong direction and straining mechanism. Keys for marine chronometers heart-shaped, with cylindrical ratchet.

keyless mechanism. System, patented 1820, of winding watch with ribbed button outside case. Same button used to set hands, either by pulling it outwards on spindle, or on earlier examples by pressing a small push-piece. Keyless mechanisms normally found only in watches with going *barrel.

key pattern, key fret, fret, Greek fret, or **meander ornament.** Repetitive pattern of straight lines, usually at right-angles to each other; derived from classical Greek architecture. Much used as border ornament in neo-classical silver of late 18th and early 19th centuries. Also at German porcelain factories to decorate bases of figures in neo-classical style (e.g. at Fürstenburg, 1782, on low-relief enamelled figures), or as border ornament on tableware, etc. *Illustration at* window seat.

Keyser, Keyzer, or **Keiser,** Aelbrecht (d 1671). Dutch potter; worked at The Two Little Ships factory, Delft; owner from 1642. Produced tiles; also credited with close imitations of Chinese porcelain in blue and polychrome. Monogram AK frequently copied.

khatchlie rugs. *See* hatchlie rugs.

Kian ware. *See* Chi-an ware.

kick. Conical indentation as in modern wine bottles, found in base of most pre-1760 bottles, decanters, bowls, *Humpen,* etc. Raised pontil mark above edge of base, allowing vessel to stand upright.

Kidderminster carpets. Kidderminster, Worcestershire, one of oldest textile-making towns in England. Carpet-weaving practised at least from late 17th century; probably pre-dated Wilton in development of loom-woven carpets. At first, *tapestry-weave carpets a speciality (first manufactory established 1735), but largely superseded by manufacture of *moquette carpets from 1749, in competition with Wilton. From 1750s, steady progress achieved in carpet-weaving: 1000 carpet looms operating by 1807; over 2000 in 1838, producing mainly moquette carpets. Some 'Wilton' pieces also made, more cheaply than in Wilton itself. Jacquard machine, invented by Frenchman Joseph Marie Jacquard in late 18th century, greatly simplified weaving processes; first applied to production of early

Kidney-shaped table. Louis XV, marquetry of various woods. Height 2ft5in.

types of machine-made carpet (*ingrain, moquette, Wilton) at Kidderminster in 1825, and soon used almost universally. Carpet industry in Kidderminster continued to expand throughout 19th century, and flourishes to present day.

kidney dial. Form of dial-opening, found on *Massachusetts shelf clock. Extends below dial itself. Upper part semi-circular, following top line of dial circle, tapering into slightly waisted sides; straight or curved bottom edge. Space under dial decorated with designs, or marked with maker's name, e.g. A. *Willard.

kidney or **horse-shoe shaped furniture.** Kidney shape used for 18th century desks, writing, and work tables, dressing tables, etc. Examples made notably by T. *Chippendale.

Kiel (Holstein). Three attempts made from 1758 to establish manufacture of German faience before factory started by J. S. F. *Tännich in 1763; owned by Duke of Holstein until sold to private company in 1766. Flowers, or landscapes with figures, painted on high-quality tin-glaze, in strong enamel colours, notably green, crimson, and yellow; underglaze blue rarely used. Products include *bishop bowls, wall fountains, plates with lobed or pierced basket-work rims, and *pot pourri* vases. Some work closely resembles that of Strasbourg, e.g. painting of *fleurs fines* (**deutsche Blumen*), through employment of painters from Strasbourg. Under directorship of J. *Buchwald, 1768–71. Factory closed in 1787. Marks usually consist of initials of factory, manager and artist, one over the other, separated by dashes; Kiel sometimes in full.

Cornelius Kierstede. Lidded tankard, made in New York, 1710–40. Applied decoration on handle and above moulding on base. Handle terminating in putto *mask. Height 7½in.*

King's pattern, on knife, fork, dessert and tea spoon, made in 1815.

Kierstede or **Kierstead,** Cornelius (1675–1757). American silversmith working in New York from 1696. Influenced by Dutch styles. Among surviving works are pear-shaped tea kettle, column candlesticks, and tankards. Mark: CK in rectangle or oval.

kilim carpets. *See* kelim carpets.

King John's Cup. Earliest known English covered silver *standing cup (*c*1350); belongs to corporation of King's Lynn, Norfolk. Silver-gilt and enamel, with bell-shaped bowl, baluster stem, and spreading foot. 15in. high.

King's pattern. 19th century British silver flatware pattern. Fiddle stem edged with scroll design; shell in relief on face of stem-end and in reinforcement on back of bowl. Anthemion motif featured in relief on face and back halfway along stem.

Kingtechen. *See* Ching-tê-chên.

kinrande chawan. Chinese porcelain, notably from reign of Chia Ching; coloured glaze (e.g. tomato-red or aubergine) decorated with formal gilded designs of peony, lotus, chrysanthemum, pheasant, crane, peacock, etc. Interiors painted in underglaze blue. Most noteworthy examples of gilding in Ming period. Sometimes bear *nien hao of Yung Lo, even if from Chia Ching era. Highly prized by Japanese who gave ware its name (which means 'gold brocade tea-bowls').

kinuta. *See* Lung-ch'üan ware.

Kirchner, Johann Gottlieb (b 1701). German porcelain modeller. Worked at Meissen 1727–28 and 1730–33. Commissioned by *Augustus III to model large porcelain animals, some over 4ft high, for his collection; helped from 1731 by J. J. *Kändler. Smaller figures include Neptune, which forms part of a table fountain (1728–29), Augustus III (1733), Harlequin, Saints, and, in collaboration with Kändler, *Pietà*.

Kirman, Persia. Celadon wares made in 14th century; by 16th century, monochrome glazes often covered painted or incised decoration. Uneven, bubbly glaze with green tinge characteristic; also very bright, strong blue used without black outlines. From 17th century, pseudo-Chinese character shaped like tassel used as mark, painted in blue. Blue, with tendency to run, painted in either Chinese-inspired or traditional Persian designs; decline in quality noticeable in 18th century. Polychrome decoration has framed panels with painting in bright *tomato-red, and green derived from iron; often black border scratched with white designs.

Kirman or **Kerman carpets.** Very solid, long, narrow south-east Persian court carpets with woollen foundation and finely Persian-knotted pile; woven near Kirman from 16th century. Mainly *vase carpets in 10–15 rich colours, with dominant purple tinge. Patterns of ascending, vertically-linked lozenge systems: rows of richly-drawn palmettes, rosettes, or lilies around vertical axis; individual blossoms decorating multi-coloured, vine-stem lozenges; lattices of lancet leaves and stem-linked blossom groups. Type continued into 19th century, simplified to spiralling vines with flowering, shrub-filled backgrounds.

Also, fine *prayer rugs and, from mid 18th century, finely woven, silky carpets with medium-fine, Persian-knotted woollen pile on cotton foundation. Soft delicately coloured ascending patterns on light grounds. Designs include overall floral and arabesque patterns, double boteh diapers, and vertically striped fields (either plain or with naturalistic birds, trees, and animals).

kis carpets (Arabic, 'bride' or 'girl' carpets). Oriental woven carpets, e.g. *kelims, said to have been made by brides as part of dowry.

Ki Seto. *See* Seto.

kit or **pochette.** Miniature violin used from early 16th century by dancing masters in Britain and Europe; could be carried in pocket (kit, or French, *poche*). Two basic shapes: earlier

Kitchen pepper. Made in Newcastle, c1720, by Francis Batty. Height 3¼in.

pear-shape (15–20in. long) with neck tapering slightly towards end, and later, narrower version of violin (*c*16in. long). Earliest examples had three strings, later three or four; bow *c*15–18in. long. Used in France until late 18th century. Wooden body, sometimes lavishly decorated with carving, inlay, etc.

Kit Cat glasses. Name given to rare early 18th century wine glasses with trumpet bowl and true baluster stem. Name derives from appearance in Sir Godfrey Kneller's painting of Kit-Cat Club, which existed in late 16th and early 17th century to ensure Protestant succession to the British throne.

kitchen pepper or **spice dredger.** Small silver or pewter container with cylindrical tankard-shaped body, scroll handle, spreading moulded foot, and domed pierced cover (sometimes with baluster finial). Also with octagonal body. Used in Britain and America mainly in early 18th century. *Illustration also at* J. Hurd.

kitchen utensils. From 16th century, basic kitchen equipment consisted of iron fireplace furniture (*spit, *spit-jack, *andirons or *spit-dogs, *baking-irons, *pot-hooks, *chimney-crane) and utensils (iron carving and serving knives and forks, brass or bronze *cauldron, bucket, pots, pans, *skillets, mortar with iron or bronze pestle, *ladles, *spoons, *trivets, and *warming-pans). Plates, basins, ewers, mugs and other spoons of pewter. In early 18th century, tinned copper widely used for cooking-vessels made in sets of different sizes, e.g. sauce-pans, pots and pans (for soups, stews, fish, puddings and preserves), frying-pans, flour-boxes, jelly-moulds, etc. New *tin-plated iron used from 1730s for basins, funnels, flour-scoops, etc. Brass bowls and stamped brass vessels appeared at end of century. Tinned steel replaced copper in first half of 19th century for many vessels and utensils, but largely superseded in 1850s by enamelled iron for dishes, basins, etc.

Kleinplastik (German, 'low-relief'). Slight moulded decoration commonly used by German porcelain factories during mid 18th century for elaborate table services (e.g. *green Watteau service), or functional tablewares (e.g. Meissen **Ozier* pattern).

Klingenstedt, Karl Gustav (1657–1734). Latvian-born miniaturist. Worked in Paris, painting small risqué pictures for snuff-boxes. Usually worked *en grisaille,* with flesh tints. Said to have developed technique of painting in indian ink.

Klinger, Johann Gottfried (*c*1701–1781). German porcelain painter and arcanist. Worked at Meissen (1731–46), known particularly for **saxe ombré* flower and butterfly painting (e.g. on signed tankard dated 1742). In 1746 helped to establish porcelain manufacture at Vienna, where worked until death.

Klipfel, Karl Jacob Christian (1725–1802). German porcelain painter; worked at Meissen and Berlin (inspector from 1761); noted for painting of flowers and **Mosaïk* pattern, which he possibly introduced; also for early Berlin relief border designs.

klismos. Classical Greek chair with *sabre legs; front legs curve forwards, back ones, backwards. Back has concave curved yoke-rail attached to verticals. Popular neo-classical form in Europe, England, and America.

Kloster-Veilsdorf (Thuringia). German porcelain factory, founded 1760; N. *Paul arcanist 1766–68. Ornamental and table ware decorated in rococo style with polychrome enamel. Figures produced from *c*1777. Controlled by *Greiner family, 1797–1822. (Still in operation in mid 20th century.) Marks: CV in monogram, sometimes in version imitating Meissen crossed swords (before 1797); Greiner trefoil (1797–1822). *See* Limbach.

kneading trough. Rectangular box with sides slanting outwards towards top, removable flat top, and four legs angled outwards. Trough interior divided into sections for flour and dough; with top in place, becomes table. Medieval origin; made until early 19th century.

knee, hip, or **shoulder** (in furniture). Outward bulge toward top of cabriole leg.

knee-hole (in furniture). Recess at centre front of desk, writing table, dressing table, lowboy, etc., allowing knee space for user. Knee-hole recess often arched or used as central cupboard area. Dates from 17th century.

kneeling chair. *See prie-dieu* chair.

Knibb, John (fl after *c*1650). English clock and watch maker from Oxford; brother of Joseph *Knibb. Made long-case, wall, and bracket clocks.

Knibb, Joseph (d *c*1711). English clock and watch maker, from Oxford. Member of Clock-makers' Company, 1670; worked in London from *c*1677. Maker of lantern, long-case, bracket, and wall clocks. Range includes: *bell-top bracket clock (with less steep sides than customary for this style); *night clock, *c*1670; standard-size long-case clock (*c*6ft4in. high) in oak case with walnut veneer, and typical square-top striking bell, *c*1695; also miniature long-case clock (*c*5ft3in. high), *c*1680. Devised system of Roman *striking mechanism for bracket clocks, and pioneered anchor *escapement and long pendulum.

Joseph Knibb. Table clock. English, c1685. Burr-walnut veneered case with gilt-metal mounts and spandrels. Sound fret above dial.

knife. Until 18th century, host rarely provided knife for each guest: steel, iron or latten table-knives shared; own knife or pair of knives (for meat and bread) sometimes carried at belt or in stocking. Serving-knife with broad, square-ended blade, and iron fork with two long slim prongs, used in carving. After introduction of fork to Europe as eating utensil, knife and fork sets often decorated *en suite*; hafts of gold, silver, silver-gilt, bone, rock, crystal, etc. With spoon, sometimes carried in *étui* or travelling set. In late 17th century, pistol butt haft became popular, earliest examples cast. From 18th century, also made with porcelain hafts (*see* knife and fork handles). From *c*1760 in Sheffield, knives made with stamped silver or Sheffield plate pistol butt hafts weighted with resinous substance; blade end generally rounded. Few stood up to hard use. Knives *en suite* with flatware generally date from late 18th century. Handles of 19th century knives mostly of ivory, bone, etc. From mid 19th century many electro-plated knives made.

knife and **fork handles.** Made in porcelain by mid 18th century, often with pistol butt haft and polychrome floral decoration, or moulded, e.g. in form of figures, at many European factories. Among rare examples of gilding at Saint-Cloud (1725–50); produced at Meissen,

*Knife and fork handles. English and French porcelain. Left to right: 1) Very rare *Bow octagonal-handled fork, 1755–60,* famille rose *colouring. 2) and 3) *Worcester matching knife and fork, blue and white, 1758–60. 4) *Chelsea knife with moulded decoration, raised anchor period, 1750–53. 5) *Saint-Cloud knife with polychrome* chinoiserie *enamelling,* c*1730–40. 6) *Chantilly fork with Kakiemon style decoration,* c*1740.*

*Knops. On British spoons. Left to right: 1) *Diamond-point spoon,* c*1450. 2) *Lion sejant spoon, 1580. 3) *Seal-top spoon with six-sided stem, 1598. 4) *Maidenhead spoon,* c*1612. 5) *Puritan spoon, 1661.*

Chantilly, Mennecy, and Tournai in same period. Made at Chelsea from mid 18th century, at Bow, and by Doccia factory; also imported from China. T. *Whieldon made knife and fork handles in agate ware.

Knife box. Mahogany with elaborate brass mounts; standing on ball and claw feet. Early 18th century.

knife box or **case.** Wooden, shagreen, or metal container for knives. Often shaped like vase; also rectangular with hinged top sloping down towards front; frequently made in pairs. Knives held vertically in slots. Dates from 16th century, but most common in 18th.

knife rest. Dumb-bell-shaped rest (*c*4in. long) for carving knife, made during late 18th and 19th centuries, usually of cut crystal glass, though examples rare. Also made in *millefiori* or filigree glass with coloured twists, mainly red, white, and blue, at Stourbridge.

knife tray. American rectangular tray with high sides, sloping outwards; central divider has brass handle or hand-hold. Used to hold knives. Dates from 19th century.

knop. Small decorative features occurring on articles made in many materials, e.g. in stem of goblet or glass, or as cast finial at end of *spoon handle, etc., sometimes also functional, as handle, or knob on lid. Variety of forms, including acorn, ball, baluster, etc. Particularly elaborate knops occur in stems of 18th century drinking glasses and bowls (*see* merese).

knuckle arm. Arm with carved end, on some Windsor chairs; end curves under and has knuckle-like ridges.

knurl foot. *See* scroll foot.

knurling or **nulling.** Originally (17th century) referred to *gadrooning on metal. Later, particularly in 19th century, much-used zig-zag engraved effect on silver, etc., produced by hand tool or machine.

*Korean celadon. Koryu period; light green celadon glaze with inlaid *mishima decoration. Height* $10\frac{3}{4}$*in.*

Knütgen, Anno (fl *c*1530–*c*1590). Rhineland potter from Siegburg. Produced grey and grey-white stoneware vessels, particularly *Schnellen,* intricately carved with biblical, mythycal, and heraldic subjects, medallions, and floral motifs. Workshop marks include FT (F. Trac), LW, and HH. Sons also worked at Siegburg; moved to Westerwald after 1590.

Kocks, Adriaen or Adrianus (d 1701) and son, Pieter Adriaenson (d 1703). Dutch potters at Delft. Adriaen bought The Greek A factory and managed it with son, who succeeded him. In 1694, bought The Pole factory; transferred stock to The Greek A in 1701. Ware, including vases, at first made in K'ang Hsi style with mark AK. By 1690s, large vases and cisterns made in European forms; tiles, vases, and dairy utensils supplied for palace of William III at Hampton Court. Factory managed by Pieter's widow, also potter, until 1722; from 1700, teapots, ornamental dishes, vases, and *trembleuses* made in **delft noir* with mark PAK.

kohiki. *See* Punch 'ŏng ware.

Köhler, David (d 1725). German potter; worked with J. F. *Böttger at Dresden faience factory and Meissen porcelain factory (*c*1709–25). Discovered first satisfactory underglaze blue for Meissen porcelain in 1719.

Ko-Kutani. *See* Kutani.

Konia, Konya or **Seljuq carpets.** Large 13th and early 14th century central Turkish court carpets woven in Konia. Relatively coarse, Turkish-knotted woollen pile on woollen foundation, often with red weft. Severe, all-over geometrical designs in sombre colours limited to two tones of red, blue, yellow, and green, on red or blue ground. Patterns: diaper of small octagons with simple or hooked outlines; hexagons or stylized animals or birds in lozenge panels; lattices of star-rosette lozenges. Borders usually with very large Kufic script. Also, in 15th century, single prayer rugs and *saphs; from late 16th century, fine *kelims and crude geometrically patterned carpets; from 18th century, peasant prayer rugs with light-coloured speckles on dark ground.

Königsberg (East Prussia). Small German faience factory operating 1772–1811, owned by J. L. E. *Ehrenreich. Faience decorated in blue, notably with flowers; pierced basket-work borders outlined in brilliant blue, reminiscent of work of Stralsund. From 1780, produced lead-glazed earthenware, painted in pale yellow or greyish-blue, with rococo style borders and additional unfired painting in silver, bronze, or gold. In 1788, factory sold to partnership including Ehrenreich's son. Faience marked with monogram of Ehrenreich, impressed, with painted date. Lead-glazed earthenware marked K, impressed. Another factory made stoneware and black basalt in style of Wedgwood; brownish body sometimes covered with marbled glaze. Black basalt medallion exists with portrait of Immanuel Kant. Owners marked products in French, German or English, e.g. 'frères Collin à Königsberg'.

Korean celadon. Hard grey stoneware, burning red where exposed in firing, made in Koryo and Yi periods. Watery, grey-green glaze, more transparent than Chinese celadon glaze; colour varies according to that of body beneath; bluish-green, emerald, grey-green, dove-grey, even yellow found. Glaze often covers foot-rim and base; distinctive rounded foot shape, with spur marks. Important kiln sites at *Sadang-ni, and *Yuch'on-ni. Manufactured from mid 12th century, with revival in late 13th century and sharp deterioration in 14th. Organic forms, e.g. melons, gourds, and petals, typical. Vessels have fine lobing or reeding, graceful handles and spouts; edges are foliate or wavy. Octagonal boxes or dishes common, also kinuta or mei p'ing forms, and pear-shaped bottles; covers, lids, often surmounted by such creatures as lions, ducks, tortoises, phoenixes. Sometimes animal figures carved in the round, e.g. for incense-burner covers. Some designs, especially for head-rests, carved in open-work, or with press-moulded low-relief decoration. *Zogan ware most important in 13th and 14th centuries, often with black and white touches under glaze. Pieces rare, and highly valued, as most come from ransacked tombs; dating of pieces in West is difficult.

Korean pottery. Earliest surviving examples, tomb ware, imitating bronze shapes, resemble Chinese Tang dynasty funerary wares (*Ming ch'i). Hand-modelled pottery of Silla period comparable to Chinese Han dynasty ware. Some ash-grey stoneware. Open-work foot distinctive feature of unglazed pieces. Stoneware body approaching porcelain, with celadon glaze appears in Koryo period. Some *temmoku ware, resembles Chinese Ting. Also notable are *zogan, and painted wares with *iron-red, or copper-red decoration; Black Koryo ware. White porcelain and rarer blue and white highly valued. In Yi period, both porcelain and stoneware made, with fine inlaid decoration (*see* Punch'ŏng ware); imitations of Chinese *T'zu-chou and tea-bowls (e.g. *Ido) also made. After Japanese invasion in 17th century, porcelain, much admired by occupiers, became primary product. In late 18th century, centre of industry, Punwŏn-ni, near Han river; wide variety of objects manufactured until 1883, when no longer officially financed. Closed down in early 20th century.

Kornilov factory. Made porcelain at St Petersburg from 1835. Noted for skill of workmen and artists employed. Designs commissioned from established contemporary artists. Marks: Russian inscription in enamel, 'Of the Brothers Kornilov at St Petersburg', also impressed mark, BRK or BK. From 1884 marked with coat of arms and ribbons over 'In St Petersburg/Of the Brothers Kornilov'.

Koryo (935–1392). Period when Korean Kingdom (Koryo) ruled by Wang dynasty. Country unified, under Buddhist influence. Arts strongly cultivated by monasteries; simple, monumental style of stone sculpture or metalwork, e.g. temple lanterns. Influence of Chinese Sung dynasty increased; high artistic level reached in imitative ceramic forms, notably celadon manufacture. Unique inlaid work (*zogan) developed. Mongol occupation of Korea (1231–1364) resulted in artistic decline.

Ko-Seto. *See* Seto.

Kothgasser, Anton (1769–1851). Austrian painter on porcelain and glass; used transparent enamels and gilding; pupil of G. *Mohn. Subjects include portraits, landscapes, palaces, city scenes, illustrations of proverbs.

Koula carpets. *See* Kula carpets.

kovsch. Russian drinking ladle with boat-shaped body and short flat handle. Made from Middle Ages to end of 17th century in silver, base metal, or wood. Generally made in sets: smaller ones engraved with Imperial eagle and name of owner; larger used only on ceremonial

Kovsh. In form of fabulous bird. Enamelled silver set with cabochon amethysts. Russian, 19th century. Width 6½in.

occasions and passed among guests. After c1650, awarded for services rendered to state. Revived in 19th century, usually for decorative purposes; richly ornamented with enamels.

Ko ware. Chinese pottery of Sung period; noted for intense colour of crackled celadon glaze. Literary sources refer to black glazed objects, but none survive. Generally resembles *Kuan but has more delicate shape. Copied in porcelain at *Ching-tê-chên in Ming period. *Chang family noted makers.

Koyetsu or **Koetsu,** Honami (1558–1637). Japanese potter in Kyoto area. Also famous screen-printer, calligrapher, and artist in lacquer work. Several iron teapots also attributed to him. Produced *raku work, notably tea-bowls, characterized by high quality of workmanship. In 1615, retired to an estate he established for craftsmen.

K'raak porcelain. *See* Carrack porcelain.

krater. Classical Greek vessel with bellied body narrowing at neck, then flaring to wide mouth; vertical handles with inward *volute resembling fern-shoots. Shape used in neo-classical silver hollow-ware (two-handled cups, race cups, jugs, etc.). Also ornamental motif. *See* Trafalgar Vase.

Krautstrunk (German, 'cabbage stalk'). *Waldglas beaker with applied prunts; made in 17th century Germany.

Kremlin Silver. Collection housed in The Kremlin, Moscow, containing treasures of Czars from 14th to early 19th centuries, and of Moscow patriarchs and numerous cathedrals and monasteries. Acquired after October Revolution (1917). Besides Russian domestic and ecclesiastical silver, arms, armour, and regalia, State Museum owns large collection of European silver (dating from 15th to 19th centuries), and largest extant collection of Elizabethan and Jacobean silver, mainly gifts to Czars from English monarchs attempting to secure and maintain trade privileges for merchants, or personal gifts to Czars. Pieces include silver-gilt standing cups, ewers and basins, salts, candlesticks, beakers, perfume-burners, flagons, livery pots, etc. Privileges suspended early in 16th century; after Restoration (mid 17th century) further mission attempted to renew them, but failed. Part of Catherine II's collection of table silver from France and England also in The Kremlin.

Kreussen (Bavaria). Noted for manufacture of stoneware in mid 17th century. Squat tankards with pewter mounts decorated in low relief (e.g. beading, or chain motif); alternatively, incised designs painted over in blue, green, red, yellow, and white enamel, sometimes with gilding. First known European use of enamels to decorate pottery; technique probably taught or executed by Bohemian glass enamellers. Some tankards commemorative; others decorated with e.g. apostles, planets, German Electors, or hunting scenes. Some stoneware made in workshops of *Hafner*. Faience manufactured for c50 years, early to mid 17th century; many shapes derived from contemporary stoneware, e.g. screw-topped vase painted with arms of Saxony in blue, initialled L.S., and dated 1618.

Left, top to bottom:
Krater. Greek, c*450* B.C.
Krautstrunk. *From Germany or Low Countries,* c*1600; later diamond-point engraving on bowl dated 1626.*
Kreussen. Stoneware tankard decorated with twelve apostles in relief; enamel colours. Early 17th century. Silver mounts dated 1682 (later than the stoneware). Height $8\frac{1}{2}$*in.*

Ku. Bronze ritual wine vessel with wide trumpet neck; cast and pierced flared foot. Shang dynasty. Height $10\frac{1}{2}$*in.*

Krüger, Jean Guillaume George (b 1728). English enamel painter who worked in Berlin 1755–68, then in Paris. Designed large hardstone boxes in **Reliefmosaïk*.

ku. Ancient Chinese ritual bronze shape, found in Shang and early Chou periods: wine goblet with wide flaring mouth and elegant, slender body, like a trumpet horn, flaring out again slightly at foot. Possibly derived from cup made of two ox horns, joined at centre (this would account for distinctive band at centre of bronze pieces). Foot section hollow. *cf* tsun.

kuang. Chinese ritual bronze vessel, of *Shang period, shaped like sauce-boat; surmounted by lid, sometimes in stylized representation of an animal. Supposedly used for serving or mixing.

Kuan Ti. Chinese god of war; originally Kuan-yü, general in Sung period, beheaded A.D. 219. Canonized in 12th century; raised by Emperor *Wan-li to rank of Ti, highest in hierarchy, in 1594. Found as motif on porcelain, and as Tê Hua figure. As 'state god', subject to promotion or degradation by emperors of different periods.

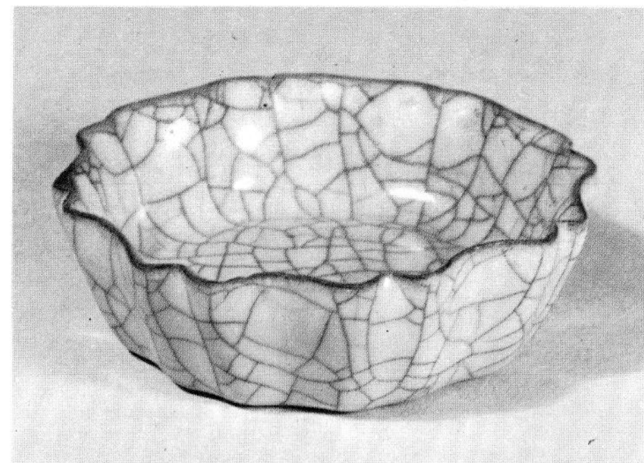

*Kuan ware. Brush-washer; *Sung dynasty; moulded in eight foliate lobes with scalloped rim; thick opaque glaze with black-stained crackle. Diameter $7\frac{3}{4}$in.*

Kuan ware. Chinese ceramics of Sung period; 'official' ware of high quality made for palace use. First made in northern provinces, but transferred to south, mainly Chekiang, after 1127 when court fled from Chin Tartar invaders. Replaced *Ting-chou as Imperial ware. Thinly-potted dark grey stoneware, washed with brown slip; variety of glaze colours, pale green to lavender resembling celadon; characterized by *brown mouth and iron foot; effect of fine crackle heightened by application of brown pigment. Copied in porcelain at *Ching-tê-chên in Ming period.

Kuan Yin. Chinese ceramics: Buddhist figure found notably in Ming porcelain figures made at Tê Hua. Regarded as Goddess of Mercy, to whom childless women prayed; sometimes depicted with baby in arms, like Christian Virgin Mary. Corresponds to Indian sexless Avalokitesvara, the All-Seeing and Compassionate.

Kuba or **Kubistan carpets.** Kuba important carpet weaving and distribution centre in north Caucasus. So-called 'dragon' rugs (*see* Armenian dragon rugs) dating from early 15th century attributed to Kuba or Dagestan area because of exceptionally fine quality wool used. Production of Turkish-knotted carpets reached peak in 18th and 19th centuries. Natural coloured wool used for warp. Kelim at each end characteristically reinforced with pale blue wool or cotton Soumak stitches, though white wool or cotton also used. Low pile of very fine wool feels like silk. Enormous variety of design and colour occurs in carpets from area. Broad mid-blue or deep indigo-blue edge common; also many contain woven date, especially prayer rugs. Types of Kuba carpet include *chichi, *Karagashli, *Perepedil, and *Seichur.

Kubachi ware. Islamic earthenware painted in polychrome under clear glaze with tendency to crazing. Chiefly plates and dishes, dated 15th to 17th century, believed made at Tabriz in north-western Persia; named after Kuba, Daghestan, where early examples found. Decoration includes portraits, figures, and animals, with floral designs or scrollwork, painted in brown, green, yellow, dull red, white, and black. On later examples, decoration becomes simpler; often plant motifs painted in black under turquoise glaze.

Kubistan carpets. *See* Kuba carpets.

Kuei shape. Bronze of 11th to 10th century B.C. *Decorated with frieze of crested birds and with tabbed loop handles. Width $11\frac{1}{2}$in.*

Kudinov factory. Russian porcelain factory founded in 1818 at Lystsovo near Moscow. From 1823 traded as Brothers Kudinov. Porcelain for home market and for export, e.g. to Persia; decorated in bright colours, often with flowers. Factory closed in 1885. Mark usually monogram NK in Cyrillic characters.

kuei. Two entirely distinct ancient Chinese forms. First, ritual bronze vessel, probably used as food serving utensil from Shang dynasty. Deep circular bowl with two loop handles, often with animal-head decoration. Mounted on ring foot. Some examples have covers. Second, ritual jade shape: elongated flat tablet, with pointed top and rectangular base. Used from Shang dynasty, probably as sceptre or badge of office. Possibly derived from neolithic tool. Symbol of Eastern Quarter.

Kufic or **Cufic script.** Used in Islam, at first in parallel with *Naskhi script; later superseded by more cursive Naskhi form for most purposes, but retained for calligraphic and decorative arts. Angular letter-shapes often elongated into foliate motifs, especially in Persia. Found as ornament on early *Islamic pottery; widely used in 9th century, and frequent in Hispano-Moresque style. Common as stylized border decoration on oriental carpets, degenerating to line of broad, abstract forms.

Kugelbecher (German, 'ball beaker'). Silver beaker with ball feet, richly ornamented with embossed leaves, fruit, etc. Made mainly in Nuremberg and Augsburg in late 17th and 18th centuries.

Ku-i (Szechuan). Chinese ceramic kiln site, active during Six Dynasties period; produced early, good examples of Yüeh ware. Other similar sites in same province; Yu huang-kuan, near Hsin-chin, and Liu-li-ch'ang, near Hua-yang.

Kula or **Koula carpets.** West Anatolian prayer rugs woven in Kula from 17th century; similar to Ghiordes carpets. Patterns feature variety of recognizable flowers in subdued colours on apricot-brown, red, or blue grounds. In 17th century examples, mihrab has two floral pillars supporting high arch; spandrels infilled with floral sprays; main border with palmette scroll pattern. In 18th century, pillars reduced to strings of very small, stylized flowers and arches flattened; main border either sub-divided into series of narrow stripes with tiny detached blossoms and buds, or series of identical stylized floral groups with colour-scheme and alignment creating tile-effect. Also graveyard carpets, and Kurmur Jur Kula carpets: double-ended prayer rugs with yellow and blue mihrab; brick-red and yellow border.

Kunckel, Johann (1630–1703). German chemist and glass maker. In 1679, director of Elector of Brandenburg's Potsdam Glass Works. Produced blue, green, and marbled glasses, but best known for gold-chloride based ruby-red glass (1670s), sometimes called 'Kunckel glass'. Published treatise on glass-making, *Ars vitraria experimentalis*, 1679.

Künersberg (Bavaria). German faience factory founded in 1745 by Jacob Küner, Viennese financier, who gave name to factory and town. C. D. *Busch, active 1749. Wares include pear-shaped vases, lobed plates, cylindrical tankards, figures, and plaques. Wide variety of high-temperature colours and enamel colours used. Painting influenced by Rouen and Vienna. Marks: sometimes KB, or full name, in blue with painter's initials.

Kurdistan carpets. *See* Bijar and Sehna carpets.

Kurfürstenhumpen (German, 'Electoral glasses'). *Humpen enamelled with arms of seven Electors; made mainly in 17th century. *cf Reichsadlerhumpen.*

Kurfürstenhumpen. *Painted in enamels with Emperor and seven Electors upon white horses, separated by bands bearing their arms. Bohemian, dated 1625. Height $11\frac{1}{4}$in.*

Kuro-Oribe. *See* Oribe ware.

Kutahia ware. *See* Isnik.

Kutani (Kaga). Place name means 'nine valleys'. Associated with porcelain made from 1644, at factory established by potters returning from kiln-centre of Arita. Kaolin deposits found locally. Early ware, Ko-Kutani ('Old Kutani'), has heavy porcelain paste approaching stoneware in quality, with purplish-black or pale yellow glazes; also green similar to early Imari ware. Decoration includes, notably, bird-and-flowers, peonies-and-butterfly, or lotus-and-heron motifs, and variations of Kakiemon or Arita ware designs boldly painted in red. Kutani or fuku ('happiness') occurs in roughly drawn seal characters. In 18th and 19th centuries, more elaborate designs include thick foliage in red, green, blue, dull yellow, and manganese-purple, imitating enamel work of Chinese reigns of Cheng Hua or Chia Ching. Version of *kinrande chawan work developed, possibly to rival Chinese *famille verte* work for export.

Kuttrolf. German **Waldglas* vessel with numerous twisting necks merging at mouth. 15th century shape of Eastern origin, probably used for controlled pouring or sprinkling, e.g. of rosewater (*cf almorrata*).

Ku Yüeh Hsüan or **Ancient Moon Terrace porcelain.** Chinese enamelled porcelain (origin of name uncertain), first produced in reign of K'ang Hsi under Director General *Ts'ang Ying-hsüan; style adopted from Imperial *cloisonné* bronze work: colours in flat washes applied direct to porcelain body. Colouring materials imported by traders from West. Highly developed, 1720–60. Finest pieces made for palace use. Small objects, e.g. bowls, dishes, vases, wine cups. Delicate painting of flowers, birds, landscapes, rarely figures; some European motifs. Best pieces inscribed with poem in black enamel. Name sometimes also appears on object.

Kuttrolf. *Yellowish-green glass; neck of five separate tubes, twisted and terminating in triangular mouth. German, 17th century. Height* $8\frac{1}{2}$*in.*

*Kylin-shaped vessel in *Ching-pai type porcelain; 14th century or later.*

kwaart. Dutch ceramics. Clear lead glaze applied, after painting over opaque white tin-glaze of Delft ware in 17th and 18th centuries, to give brilliant gloss. Both glazes and high-temperature colours fused in same firing. Equivalent of Italian maiolica **coperta*.

Kwang-tung stoneware. Chinese ceramics, made at Shekwan near Fatshan, Canton (Kwang-tung) province. Kilns active from southern Sung period, under Ming director, *T'ang Ying. Coarse stoneware body, dark brown or grey covered with shining blue, green, white, red, yellow, or green glaze; streaked, mottled, or with *flambé* effect copying *Chün ware. Kilns possibly established by refugee potters from Chün Chou, in late Sung period. White glaze sometimes finely crackled. Large flower pots, ewers, incense-burners, and plates manufactured. Some figures and animals with blue or red glaze (hands and face left in biscuit) also produced. Hsüan Tê and Ch'êng Hua reign marks (*nien hao) found on some objects. *Illustration at flambé* glaze.

kylin (ch'i-lin). Chinese ceramics; composite mythological animal, with deer's hooves, bushy tail, and fierce expression. Thought to be emblem of perfect good. Occurs in decoration from most periods.

kylix. Ancient Greek pottery drinking vessel with wide, shallow bowl; two horizontally placed handles near rim. Early forms with low base; later forms stand on high, stemmed foot.

Kyoto, Japan. Associated with enamelled pottery, originally made in 17th century by *Ninsei. Porcelain made in late 18th and early 19th centuries; colour influenced by **san ts'ai* palette; underglaze blue accompanied by red and green enamel, used in bird or flower designs. Artists include A. *Mokubei. *Awata became centre of production in 18th century.

Kyo-yaki (Japanese, 'ware made at Kyoto'). Japanese ceramics, dating from 17th and 18th centuries. School founded and encouraged by *Ninsei, continued by disciple, *Kenzan. Noted for soft-coloured enamel work, but numerous other types made in area, e.g. *Awata, *Satsuma, and, notably, *raku.

lac. *See* Chinese lacquer.

lacca (Italian, 'lacquer work'). Colourfully-painted furniture produced in 18th century Italy; often has floral or religious motifs. Venetian examples painted with subjects in styles of contemporary painters, e.g. Tiepolo, Guardi, etc.

lacca contraffatta (Italian, 'imitation lacquer'). Cheap furniture lacquer used in 18th century Italy, particularly Venice. Furniture first painted, then decorated with paper cut-outs pasted on to surface, and finally lacquered. Technique particularly used on case furniture and desks.

lace box. Wooden box, sometimes round, often decorated, used to hold lace. Some have *bail handle. Also, work box used to hold lace-making equipment. Dates from 18th century.

lacework. Decoration of porcelain figures, introduced *c*1770 at Meissen by M-V. *Acier. Lace soaked in porcelain slip, arranged round figure. Cotton threads burned away during firing, leaving lace form in porcelain. During 19th century used more elaborately and on larger scale at many European factories.

La Chaux-de-Fonds. One of main centres of Swiss watch industry. *See* Roskopf watch.

lacquer. *See* Chinese lacquer, European lacquer, Japanese lacquer, varnish, *vernis Martin*.

lacquer gilding. *See* gilding.

Lacroix, Roger. *See* Vandercruse-Lacroix, Roger.

lacy glass. Pattern unique to American pressed glass. Small dots in mould produced overall stippled, lacy design. Glittering effect hides dull surface left by contact with mould. Popular 1830–60 for tableware, particularly salts and cup-plates. Speciality of *Boston & Sandwich Glass Company. *Illustration at* pressed glass.

ladder-back or **slat-back.** Chair back composed of horizontal slats. Medieval form, found in country furniture and *Pilgrim furniture; adapted to town furniture in 18th and early 19th centuries. *Illustrations at* Pennsylvania Chippendale, shaker furniture.

Ladies' Amusement or 'Whole Art of Japanning Made Easy'. Book of designs for use on lacquer, enamel, and porcelain ware published *c*1760 in London. Patterns of flowers, insects, sentimental, and fashionable scenes appear reversed to permit direct copying on copper plate. Includes designs by R. *Hancock.

Kutani. Dish decorated with kiku blooms and foliage in overall design; fuku mark on base 17th century. Diameter $15\frac{1}{2}$in.

Ku Yüeh Hsüan style decoration on imperial *famille rose *bowl of Yung Chên period Diameter 5in.*

*Ladik. Column Ladik prayer rug. Oatmeal coloured *mihrab; trellised columns; red end-panel of tulips; blue border of Rhodian lilies. Turkish, late 18th century. 5ft8in.×3ft9in.*

*Lambeth Delftware. Left: *Merryman plate, one of six, c1720. Centre: sack bottle, dated 1649. Right: plate decorated with pattern known as Ann Gomm; this example inscribed instead Mary Johnson, 1793; diameter 9in.*

ladies' watches. Found as distinct form only after *c*1860, when makers first produced small, often decorative watches for ladies' use.

Ladik carpets. Fine-quality south-east Turkish prayer rugs woven in Ladik from 17th century. Peak production in late 17th and early 18th centuries. Short, Turkish-knotted woollen pile on woollen foundation. Designs usually in clear, bright colours, especially red, bright blue, yellow, and pale blue; grounds usually red or blue. 17th century rugs have column Ladik design: two pairs of thin columns supporting triple-arched mihrab; broad spandrel with floral motif; main border with rosette-ornamented cartouches and arabesque scrolls. 18th century rugs adopt tulip Ladik design: distinctive broad panel (above or below mihrab) with row of identical thin-stalked flowers, usually tulips; solid-coloured mihrab with one unsupported, angular stepped arch; spandrel with detached stylized flowers and leaves. In wide main border, stylized rosettes alternate with motif of tulips in fork of stylized leaves. Also graveyard carpets.

ladle. Form of spoon with deep hemispherical or ovoid bowl, plain or shaped, and long stem, used for serving soups, sauces, punch, etc. Surviving examples in silver mainly from early 18th century, though used before then. Size depends on function. Stem designs generally followed those of *spoons. *See* punch ladle.

Lady with the Unicorn tapestries. Set of six *mille-fleurs* tapestries, five portraying chivalric allegories of The Senses. Woven *c*1480–90, probably at Brussels. Red flower-strewn grounds; central blue-green islands with figure of medieval lady, richly clothed and jewelled, at her toilet, and a unicorn. On most panels lion and unicorn support arms of Le Viste family. Renowned for exquisite quality, execution, and rich decorative composition. Now in Metropolitan Museum of Art, New York.

Lafrensen or **Lavrience,** Niclas the Younger (1737–1807). Swedish miniaturist. Miniature painter to Swedish court. Later worked in France. Many of his gouache miniatures used as originals for engravings.

lajvardina ware. *Seljuq pottery with black, red, or white enamel picked out in gold, applied over cobalt-blue or rich turquoise glaze.

Lambert & Rawlings. English firm of silver retailers in London from early 19th century. (Archives of firm's 20th century successor, Harman & Lambert, lost, so little of history known.) Founders were Francis Lambert (d *c*1841) and William Rawlings (d *c*1862). Firm probably took over part of *Rundell, Bridge & Rundell's business in 1842. Produced domestic, church, and display silver. Some plate shown at Great Exhibition, 1851, including gigantic wine flagon (now in Victoria & Albert Museum, London). Extremely successful firm; continued by Lambert's son, George.

Lambeth delftware. Tin-glazed earthenware made at Lambeth, London, from early 17th century to late 18th century. Early examples have soft, sometimes pinkish surface; in 18th century, glaze tends to greenish tint. Many pieces decorated in style derived from Ming porcelain. Early plates thin and well-thrown; from mid 18th century, more heavily potted. Polychrome designs appear in early 18th century, sometimes blending Chinese motifs with European. *Wine bottles have contents identified in blue, with date (1629–72). From same period come candlesticks, vases, and salt cellars in metal forms; also water bottles with concave bases and no foot-rim, narrow-necked *puzzle jugs, and *hors-d'oeuvre* dishes pressed with four or five compartments around central depression. *Blue-dash chargers made from early 17th century. *Merry Man plates show Dutch influence. Pharmacy wares include pill slabs with arms of Apothecaries' Company, and ointment jars. Plates with *bianco sopra bianco* borders, made in mid 18th century, often have daisies and pine-cones alternating with pairs of spiral scrolls. *Illustration also at* fuddling cup.

lamb flagon. 17th century European pewter flagon of baluster form with long spout from base, connected to top of body by strengthening bar.

lambrequin. Scarf or piece of fabric worn over helmet by knight; in coats of arms, usually pendent or floating with one end cut or jagged (*see* heraldic engraving). Also ceramic decoration resembling border pattern of lace, with formal symmetrical motifs arranged, alternately large and small, to form pendant border or central pattern radiating outwards. Basic pattern on Chinese porcelain of K'ang Hsi period, frequently copied. Characteristic of blue-and-white decoration at Rouen in late 17th century.

lamp. Earliest form of artificial lighting, wick floating in clay or metal (copper, bronze) bowl of oil, known from 3000 B.C. Oil lamps developed in various ways, becoming 17th century *crusie and more sophisticated 18th century *Argand and *Sinumbra lamps; also similar *agitable. Carcel lamp of 1798 pumped oil by clockwork; 1836 Moderator operated by spring and piston. Gas introduced for lighting *c*1816, and gradually adopted; oil still remained popular throughout 19th century. Many different shapes and styles of copper, bronze, and brass lamps with glass shades developed. *See* lantern.

lamp-blown glass. Novelty articles made from readily-fusible glass rods or tubes, heated in flame of lamp and manipulated into toys, figures, beads, or jewellery. Produced particularly in France (*Nevers) and Spain from 16th century, though most existing examples outside museums date from early 19th century, when popular throughout Europe. Often very elaborate, e.g. ship with hull and rigging formed with finely drawn threads. In late 19th century, technique practised as entertainment at country fairs. *Illustration at* Nevers.

lamp-bracket. *See* bracket.

Lancaster Glass Works. Founded 1849 in New York by eight glass blowers from Pittsburgh, Pennsylvania. Produced bottles, flasks, flint and green druggists' wares; jugs and bowls with *lily-pad decoration in style of *South Jersey glass. Ownership changed frequently. Closed *c*1900.

landscape dial. Watches with painted landscape decoration on dial popular during late 18th century, chiefly in France but also in England and Holland, especially in early 19th century; often in gold and enamelled cases. Style also common on *Turkish market clocks and watches.

lancet-back. Chair-back enclosing three Gothic arches, set side by side. Popular in England *c*1750.

lancet clock. Type of *bracket clock, with case in shape of pointed arch; introduced in England, *c*1800.

landscape or **lay panel.** Wood panel with horizontal grain.

lange Lyzen or **lange Leisjes.** *See* long Elizas.

Langley, Batty (1696–1751). Pioneer English landscape gardener, architect and furniture designer. Published numerous works including The City and Country Builder's and Workman's Treasury of Design (1740), containing some plates copied from European designers. Later works illustrate many details of Gothic ornament and had considerable influence on country craftsmen.

Langlois, Peter (b 1738). French furniture maker, in England *c*1760–70. Became *maître-ébéniste* in 1774; noted for fine marquetry and ormolu mounts.

Peter Langlois. English commode, painted wood decorated with ormolu and panels of pietra dura. *Mid 18th century.*

Lang yao glaze. *See* ox-blood glaze.

Lannuier, Charles Honoré (fl *c*1805–19). French-born cabinet maker; worked in New York. Pieces show influence of *Directoire style. *Illustration at* card table.

lantern. Partly or wholly enclosed candle-holder, either portable or attached to pole or bracket to illuminate outside gates, doors, etc., or draughty rooms indoors, especially halls. In use before Middle Ages. Earliest surviving form is bronze open-sided cone or cylinder; this developed into square or octagonal shape with sides of thin horn (when popularly known as lanthorn), skin, or bull's eye glass, growing more sophisticated in 18th and 19th centuries.

Lantern. Brass, type known as hall lantern. English, late 18th century.

Lantern clock. English, early 17th century, made by William Selwood of Lothbury; brass case. Height 15½*in.*

lantern clock or **Cromwellian clock.** English weight-driven brass wall clock; development of iron Gothic clock. Introduced to England *c*1620; produced in 17th and early 18th century. First made with balance-wheel escapement, then pendulum, from *c*1670. *Posted frame, backed by iron plate, with brass doors each side. Circular dial at front, with silvered chapter ring, often extending beyond width of frame; alarm dial at centre; usually single hour hand only. Whole clock surmounted by bell (topped by single finial). Bell attached by brackets to tip of four finials above posts of frame. Area between top plate and bell filled by ornamental fretwork; floral or heraldic patterns; many with dolphin motif. Makers include T. *Tompion, Joseph *Knibb. 30-hour movement general, early examples may run for 12 or 15 hours.

lantern pinion. *See* pinion.

Lanze, Johann Wilhelm (fl mid 18th century). German porcelain modeller. *Modellmeister* at Strasbourg *c*1745–54; then at Frankenthal, at least until 1761, where simple, rather stiff early figures in Meissen style have plain mound base; later with purple-edged rococo scrolls.

lapis lazuli. Intense ultramarine-blue mineral mainly composed of lazurite (sodium aluminium silicate with sulphur) and containing golden fleck of pyrite. On furniture, normally used as thin veneer or inlay, sometimes with other stones (*pietra dura*) on e.g. tables and small, ornamental pieces. Used in Renaissance and 17th and 19th centuries for jewellery including bead necklaces and earrings. Found e.g. at Monte Somma, Vesuvius (Italy), Badakshan (Afghanistan), near Lake Baikal (Russia), and Ovalle (Chile). *Illustration at pietra dura.*

lapping. Process of covering copper exposed at edge of Sheffield plate pieces. Earliest method was application of film of tin or silver solder. Later, edge cut with blunt tool so that silver layer extended beyond edge of copper. Technique also used for pierced work. *c*1775, silver wire soldered to edge; method perfected by production of U-shaped wire which fitted perfectly around edge. Decorative border could be added.

laqabi. Islamic pottery decoration: coloured glazes separated by raised or incised lines, used as outlines of design, against white background. Characteristic of class of Seljuq pottery developed from Aghkand ware made in Persia, particularly at Kashan and Rayy, during 12th century.

La Rochelle (Charente-Maritime), France. First successful faience factory established 1752; earlier attempt (1721) failed. Production continued until 1789; early ware influenced by Rouen and Nevers. Later, **deutsche Blumen* painted in enamel colours; products include plates decorated with Chinese figures in red and green, and vases with relief-moulded flowers and foliage. Marked La Rochelle, with date.

latesino. Italian ceramics. Pearly white tin-glaze on maiolica made at Faenza, Lodi, and Venice, in 17th century, e.g. by *Manardi brothers at Angarano.

latten or **battery metal.** Brass made into flat sheets of fine-grained metal by repeated battering with hammers (water or hand-powered), thus making it suitable for production of many domestic utensils, e.g. warming-pans, candlesticks, spoons; also used for monumental brasses. European latten, especially German and Flemish, of finer quality than English, and much imported until late 17th century (although importation prohibited 1660–75). Large-scale battery operations in England began with foundation (1568) under Elizabeth I of Mines Royal. In 1604, Society for the Mineral and Battery Works founded for wider commercial production, including wire, plates, etc. In 1668, bodies amalgamated under governorship of Rupert of Bavaria, and continued with subordinate factories until 1710, when rolling largely superseded battery method; latter retained only for coarser pots and pans. Term often applied to brass in general, in Middle Ages sometimes silvered, probably to deceive buyers.

latticinio or **latticino.** Opaque-white canes embedded in clear or coloured glass. Technique developed in mid 16th century Venice. Canes arranged lining walls of cylindrical pot. By twisting *gather, simple or complicated patterns formed; free-blown, or canes used for applied decoration, e.g. trailing. Popular in Venice until late 18th century. Favourite aspect of *façon de Venise*. Technique used for English wine glass stems, 1755–80. *Illustration at porrón.*

lattimo. Milky-white glass opacified with bone ash, developed by Venetians in early 15th century, though originated in ancient Egypt. During 17th and 18th centuries, made throughout Europe in imitation of porcelain. *cf* Beinglas. *Illustration at* Venetian glass.

Laub-und-Bandelwerk (German, 'leaf-and-strapwork'). Late baroque decoration used widely in Germany during early 18th century on glass, faience, and porcelain. Symmetrical pattern, often in gilt, sometimes framing painted medallion, or as all-over pattern. Popular with *Hausmaler*, D. and I. *Preissler, and I. *Bottengruber, and at Vienna and Meissen porcelain factories.

'Lauche'. Probably German *Hausmaler* in Dresden; decorated porcelain with *chinoiseries* in style of J. G. *Herold (1720s or 1730s), and signed them: *Lauche fecit Dresden.* Painter of this name at Meissen until 1725.

Launay, Nicolas de. *See* Delaunay, Nicolas.

Laurence Vitrearius (Latin, 'the glass maker') 13th century; Norman first recorded glass maker in England. Set up furnace at Chiddingfold, Surrey. In 1240, supplied plain and coloured window glass for Henry III Chapel, Westminster Abbey.

lavabo or **laver.** Brass or bronze vessel, with one or two spouts, hanging on wall above basin; contained water for hand-washing as alternative to *ewer and basin (*see* wall fountain). Also, for ecclesiastical and monastic ritual cleansing. Earliest examples date from *c*1400; continued in use until *c*1800 in various styles, e.g. incorporating animal's head spouts. Particularly common in Germany. In 17th and 18th century Scotland, laver was pewter or silver vessel for carrying baptismal water to font; in form of small spouted flagon with or without lid.

Lavater, John or Johann Caspar (1741–1801). Swiss physiognomist; author of book, *Essays on Physiognomy* (1775–78; English translation 1794), expounding theory of physiognomy as science revealing all human character. Illustrated many profiles and techniques for making them.

lava ware. *See* scroddled ware.

laver. *See* lavabo.

Law, Thomas (1717–75). English cutler working in Sheffield; became master cutler in 1753. Early producer of Sheffield plate. Made candlesticks, etc., and specialized in wares with Sheffield plate mounts, e.g. jasper ware jugs. One of first manufacturers to mark articles (LAW flanked by script letters TL, and variants). Mark registered by his successors in business (in 1784): Thos. Law & Co. and squat vase. Son, John, continued in trade until 1819 although name retained in title, Law, Atkin & Oxley, until 1828. Atkin Bros. of Sheffield was indirect descendant of Law's firm in Victorian times.

Lay, Johann Jakob (fl late 18th century). German potter. Director of Kelsterbach porcelain factory 1767–*c*1768, and 1773–*c*1802.

lay, lea or **ley.** Common pewter; alloy of *c*80% tin to *c*20% lead. Used from Middle Ages until end of 17th century for hollow-ware and rounded forms (e.g. candlesticks), which did not need strength of *fine pewter.

lazy Susan. Early 19th century American revolving circular tray for condiments, etc., fixed to heavy base and placed in centre of dining table.

lea. *See* lay.

leaching. Extraction of silver from ore by dissolving base metals in nitric acid. Process used into 19th century, when modern refining methods introduced.

lead. Soft, malleable, blue-grey metal, in cast or sheet form, used from Roman times for roofing, water-pipes, cisterns, etc.; often tinned. Used later for garden ornaments: statues, urns, vases, *jardinières*. In 1770, hardening process invented by William Storer enabled cast details to be chased to sharper outlines; subsequently much used for interior decorative features, e.g. friezes, rosettes, frames, often in imitation of carved wood, also for small objects, e.g. tobacco boxes. Alloyed with tin to obtain pewter. Sometimes added to bronze to lower melting point.

lead glass or **lead crystal.** The standard form of English crystal glass, introduced by G. *Ravenscroft in 1676; improved *flint glass containing red lead. Use spread to Europe in 1680s.

lead-glaze. Ceramic glaze consisting of silica (such as sand), fused with lead oxide or galena (lead sulphide), known to have been used in Mesopotamia by 17th century B.C. In simplest application, powdered galena dusted on surface of pottery; in firing, fuses with silica in pottery body. Injurious effects of working with dust and lead compounds necessitated e.g. immersion of flints (for silica) in water during grinding, or finally use of liquid glaze, as in development of cream-coloured earthenware. Any iron present in clay gives brown or yellowish stain to glaze in firing. Colour intentionally produced by dusting oxides of copper (green), cobalt (blue), manganese (purple or brown), or manganese with iron (black) on pottery with glaze material, e.g. in *tortoiseshell ware; colours tend to run in fusion of glaze. In 19th century, leadless glaze produced with use of other substances (e.g. borax) as flux.

leaf (in furniture). Hinged, sliding or removable section of table top, providing additional surface area. May be sliding leaf, slipping under centre section of top of *draw-leaf table; flap leaf, hanging vertically at side of *drop-leaf table, supported by gate or swing leg or rudder when raised or removable leaf, slotting into open section at centre of *extension table.

leaf or **mount** (in fan). Paper, kid, or fabric covering of fan.

Lebrun, Charles (1619–90). French designer,

painter, and architect. Became painter to Louis XIV in 1662; director of *Gobelins and *Savonnerie manufactories in 1663. Contributed much to decoration of royal residences. Founder and director of *Académie Royale des Beaux-arts.* Largely responsible for development of mural-style tapestries, using classical and biblical themes in grand style. Numerous designs made into full-scale oil cartoons for Gobelins include Elements, Seasons, Life of Louis XIV, and History of Alexander.

Lecreux, Nicolas (1733–99). Sculptor, modeller of figures at Tournai porcelain factory, Belgium. Noted for delicacy of modelling. Some figures have background of scrollwork and flowered trellis. Sometimes credited with groups of pastoral figures around tree stump decorated with applied flowers, standing on rock base.

Leeds, Yorkshire. The Old Pottery, established *c*1774, traded *c*1770–1820 as Hartley Greens & Co. Good quality cream-coloured earthenware made with greenish-yellow tone and smooth, brilliant glaze. Delicate open-work decoration and twisted handles with moulded flowers and foliage characteristic. In 1770s, transfer-printing at factory in red and black. Much exported by 1780s, and decoration copied in Holland on similar cream-coloured ware. Owners entered into partnership with *Rockingham works, Swinton (1786–1806). Other products include black basalt, red stoneware, tortoiseshell ware, and figures modelled in style of R. *Wood. Lustre decoration from early 19th century includes silver and pink. Work occasionally marked HARTLEY GREENS & C°, or Leeds Pottery, impressed. Factory closed in 1878. Rival pottery established by 1792 made cream-coloured earthenware marked RAINFORTH & Co. Later ware made at factory established in 1888, using old moulds and marks of Leeds Pottery, can be distinguished by very even setting of characters in mark.

*Leeds Pottery. Creamware coffee pot, enamelled in red and black by D. *Rhodes. Handle formed by parallel grooved straps; spout moulded with basket-work. Domed cover has convolvulus knop terminal which matches handle. Mid 18th century. Height 9¾in.*

Caspar Lehmann. Beaker engraved by Lehmann with allegorical figures representing Potestas, Nobilitas and Liberalitas; signed and dated 1605.

*Jean-François Leleu. *Toilet and writing table; table containing a drawer; above this is cupboard concealed by dummy book-backs. Veneered on oak with purple-heart, tulip-wood and other woods; ormolu mounts. Height 3ft7in.*

Lefebvre, le Fèvre, or **Lefèvre,** Jean (d 1700). Parisian high-loom tapestry master-weaver. Son of P. *Lefebvre. From 1669, director of second largest Gobelins Manufactory workshop, at Tuileries, Paris.

Lefebvre, le Fèvre, or **Lefèvre,** Pierre (d 1669). Parisian tapestry master-weaver. Director, 1630–47, of Florentine tapestry manufactory. *Tapissier* to Louis XIV (1647–50), with workshop in Tuileries, Paris. 1650–55, worked on commission in Florence; thereafter in Paris. Succeeded by son, Jean.

Légaré, Gilles (fl mid 17th century). French goldsmith, jeweller and engraver; goldsmith to Louis XIV with workshop in Louvre. Designs in *Livre des Ouvrages d'Orfèvrerie* (1663) focus interest on gems. Used floral settings (rubies, emeralds, diamonds, etc.) for bracelets, necklaces, brooches. Also featured bow-shaped ornament, later called Sévigné after Mme de Sévigné. Also produced silhouette designs for backs of watches, miniature cases, etc.

le Gaugner, Louis Constantin (fl late 18th century). French *ébéniste,* in London from *c*1790. Made furniture decorated in Boulle-work for Prince Regent (later George IV) for Carlton House.

leg rest. Device enabling occupant of chair to rest legs horizontally; vertical, upholstered calf support attached to horizontal base. Also known as 'ease and comfort'. Dates from late 18th century.

Lehman, Benjamin (fl *c*1786). Cabinet and chair maker in Philadelphia, Pennsylvania. Known for price-list of cabinet work published 1786, a record of items available at time.

Lehmann, Caspar (1570–1622). German lapidary; originally gem-cutter to Rudolph II in Prague, but transferred gem engraving techniques to glass. Earliest signed glass piece, a beaker (1605). Granted patent on glass engraving in 1609, transferred on his death to pupil, G. *Schwanhardt.

lei. Ancient Chinese ritual bronze vessel, made from Shang period onwards; general term, denoting various types of wide-necked vase. Commonly have curved sides and two handles, sometimes hanging rings. Early form tall, with narrow mouth and shapely curved shoulder. Some examples square in section, with tall necks, and lids. In late Shang period, bodies more rounded; some have third loop near base for draining dregs of liquid. Shape also found in later Chinese porcelain, sometimes known as *ley vase.

Leithner, Joseph (*c*1750–1800). Austrian porcelain painter, noted for flower painting; at Vienna factory (1770–90); then worked as arcanist and chemist (1791–1800). Invented dark blue glaze (Leithner's blue).

Lelarge, Jean-Baptiste (1734–1802). French *menuisier,* following father and grandfather, both of same name. Became *maître-menuisier* in 1775. Used same I.B. LELARGE stamp as father; worked in neo-classical style.

Leleu, Jean-François (1729–1807). French.

Became *maître-ébéniste* in 1764. Trained under J-F. *Oeben; on Oeben's death, workshop taken over by J-H. *Riesener. Opened own workshop and received commissions from Mme du Barry and Marie Antoinette. Worked in mahogany and with lacquer and marquetry. Stamp: J. F. LELEU or J.F.L.

Lely family. *See* van der Lely.

Lemire. *See* Sauvage, Charles-Gabriel.

Lemonnier (fl mid 19th century). French goldsmith and jeweller; court goldsmith to Napoleon III. Noted for *hair jewellery with sentimental rather than funereal associations. Used hair in ribbon bracelets fastened with forget-me-nots in turquoises and diamonds, necklaces, floral sprays, medallions of leaves and flowers, etc. At Great Exhibition, London (1851), showed jewellery made for Queen Isabella of Spain which featured *pampille* or waterfall setting of floral sprays (stones set on articulated wires). Also designed jewellery for marriage of Napoleon III to Empress Eugénie in 1853 (e.g. *parure* of pearls and rubies).

Lenhendrick, Louis-Joseph (d 1783). French silversmith working in Paris; apprenticed to T. *Germain (1738); master in 1747. Made domestic silver in rococo and neo-classical styles, including some pieces for Imperial Russian dinner services. Mark: fleur-de-lis crowned, two pellets, LL, and a column.

Le Nove, near Bassano (Veneto). Italian maiolica factory established in 1728 by G. B. *Antonibon. Maiolica in rococo style includes plates and dishes with moulded edges, and tureens in form of fish; decorated in high-temperature colours. Rather low-fired hard-paste porcelain, made from 1762, greyish in tone; products include rococo style tableware with relief decoration, and landscapes drawn in green, black, and red. Porcelain production lapsed 1773–81. Some neo-classical shapes used by 1790. Painting includes landscapes and harbour scenes with figures, illustrations of works by Dante, and military subjects. Marks include: Nove and initials GBA; also monogram GBA on early products. Asterisks in red, blue, or gold, standard mark from 1781, but used earlier.

Lens, Bernard (1631–1708), son Bernard (1659–1725), grandson Bernard (1682–1740), great-grandsons Andrew Benjamin and Peter Paul (fl 18th century). English artists. Bernard I Dutch-born enamel painter working in London. Bernard II mezzotint engraver and drawing master. Bernard III prominent miniaturist, limner to George I and George II. Among first miniaturists to use ivory; painted in gouache, using transparent watercolours only on faces. Work includes portraits of Handel, Horace Walpole, Sir Isaac Newton, etc. Two younger sons also miniaturists.

Lépine, Jean-Antoine (1720–1814). French watch maker, apprenticed in Switzerland; in Paris from 1744; maker to Louis XV. Introduced type of watch movement known as Lépine calibre *c*1770, with going *barrel, and separate bars, instead of plate, to support top pivots of train (widely adopted by French and Swiss makers). Associated with Voltaire in starting watch factory at Ferney, near Geneva.

Lequoi. *See* Soqui.

Le Roux, Charles (1689–1745). American silversmith working in New York; probably trained by father, Bartholomew Le Roux (*c*1663–1713). Work shows English and French influence (e.g. use of cut-card ornament). Surviving pieces include salt-cellars, salvers, candlesticks, etc. Made gold *freedom boxes *c*1720–43. Mark: CLR in oval.

LeRoy, Julien (1686–1759). French clock and watch maker, in Paris from 1703. Appointed clock maker to Louis XV in 1739; collaborated with H. *Sully. Work includes tower clocks, astronomical, and equation timepieces. Devised improved mechanism for verge watches, *c*1725. Several other makers with same name.

LeRoy, Pierre (1717–85). French inventor and clock maker, son of J. *LeRoy. Worked on marine chronometer. Devised duplex escapement, and detent escapement for chronometers, *c*1765.

Leschot, Jean-Frédéric (1747-1824). Swiss maker of 'singing-bird' boxes and automata. Associate of Jacquet-Droz firm but did not sign boxes until after death of H-L. *Jacquet-Droz (1791).

Lessore, Emile (1805–76). French-born decorator of pottery and porcelain. Painted porcelain produced at Bourg-la-Reine; worked at Sèvres and independently in France. In England, at Minton (1858) and Wedgwood factories. Returned to France *c*1863, but continued to decorate Wedgwood wares there until death.

Lesum (Hanover). Small German faience factory founded 1755. Products include open-work baskets, tankards painted with a galloping horse, tureens in bird and animal forms in rococo style. Only high-temperature colours used. Early wares marked Vi (owner, J. C. Vielstich), with painter's initials.

Levasseur, Etienne (1721–98). French. Became *maître-ébéniste* in 1767. Was trained with A. C. *Boulle's sons. Among first *ébénistes* to use mahogany, often inlaid with fillets of brass. Also repaired and copied Boulle furniture, and worked in lacquer and wood veneers. Stamp: E. LEVASSEUR.

Levavasseur, Jacques-Nicolas (1715–55), and son, Marie-Thomas-Philémon (1749–93). Members of family of potters working at Rouen from early 18th century. From *c*1770, painted faience in enamel colours to imitate decoration of porcelain. Work includes plates printed with flowers and harbour scenes in manner of Marseille.

lever escapement. *See* escapement.

ley. *See* lay.

Leyniers, Urban (1674–1747). Tapestry master-weaver in Brussels. In partnership with H. *Reydams, 1700–19, when tapestries signed Leyniers-Reydams. From 1719 in partnership, first with brother Daniel (d 1728), then with son, also Daniel (d 1768). Works include six-piece History of Telemachus and many *'Teniers' tapestries.

Ley vase. Decorated in yellow and green enamels on biscuit. Ming, Cheng Tê mark and period, 1506–21. Diameter 5¾in.

Library steps. English, late 18th century, mahogany. When folded, appear to be a cabinet.

ley vase. Shape found in Chinese porcelain of 15th and 16th centuries; high foot; low, bulbous body, surmounted by tall, wide spreading lip of same height as body. Term derived from *lei.

li. Chinese cooking vessel originating in pottery of neolithic cultures, made in both pottery and bronze from Shang period. Body three-lobed, pointed bottoms of lobes forming feet. Has two upright loop handles through which stick could be fitted for lifting. Sometimes has shallow dividing grooves in body. Earliest examples, 14th to 13th centuries B.C.

lia tza or **lotus pod bowl.** Chinese ceramics; made in both pottery and porcelain. Carved under glaze e.g. celadon glaze on exterior of bowl, imitating open lotus flower. Bloom rests above river-mud, as Buddhist emblem of purity; drops of water on petal, symbol of enlightenment. Design used in many similar ways on porcelain, e.g. cups, with incised pattern under slip.

library case. In 18th and early 19th centuries, large bookcase intended for library.

library screen. Fire or draught screen, with square or rectangular fabric-covered panel fixed between two grooved upright supports (similar to *cheval-screen supports). Panel slides upwards in grooves to reveal narrow book-shelves behind. Dates from late 18th century.

library steps. Short ladder or set of steps, usually folding, giving access to higher library

Library table. George III, mahogany. With two reading stands on top, and frieze of drawers which revolves independently of base and top; drawers numbered with ivory plaques. Diameter 4ft5in.

Lily-pad decoration. Aquamarine pitcher, possibly made at Lancaster or Lockport Glass Works in New York, c1840–60. Height $7\frac{1}{8}$in.

shelves. Often ingeniously incorporated in another piece of furniture (chair, table, footstool), and folding out of sight when not in use. Made in 17th century, mainly after *c*1750.

library table. General term for large table suitable for writing or reading in library. Often rectangular, similar to *pedestal-desk in shape; also, circular, e.g. *drum or *rent table. Used mainly from 1725.

lighthouse clock. American shelf clock *c*16in. high, resembling miniature lighthouse; patented by S. *Willard, 1822. Three sections: top part dial with alarm movement, protected by glass dome-shaped lid; circular trunk, widening slightly towards bottom; round, or octagonal base. Copied in Germany.

lilac ground. German porcelain ground colour first devised by J. G. *Herold at Meissen factory *c*1727. Widely used with painted panels on Meissen ornamental and table ware in 18th century, especially late 1730s and early 1740s.

Lille tapestry. Lille active tapestry-weaving centre from 16th to 18th centuries. 16th century products mainly armorial tapestries. Expanded in 17th century with influx of Flemish émigré master-weavers, including F. and A. *Pannemaker from Brussels, and J. *de Melter. From late 17th century, industry prospered.

lily-pad decoration. Used in American glass. Design tooled from applied layer of glass into one of three main shapes: slender stem with bead-like pad; wider stem with small, flattened pad; long, curving stem with flat, ovoid pad. Characteristic decoration of early 19th century *South Jersey glass.

Limbach (Thuringia). German porcelain factory founded 1772 by G. *Greiner and continued by sons. 18th century products mainly functional wares painted in blue or purple. By early 19th century, figures in contemporary flower-sprigged costume, allegorical, and neo-classical groups made; bases either steep grassy mound or rococo-moulded form outlined in distinctive red. Marks: (until 1788) LB in monogram, and crossed Ls with star deliberately resembling Meissen mark: after protest (1788), Greiner trefoil (also probably used at Ilmenau, Kloster-Veilsdorf, and Grosbreitenbach).

lime glass. American substitute for lead glass; cheaper, lighter, and faster cooling. Developed in 1864 by William Leighton, Wheeling Glass Factory, West Virginia. Used for making cut glass tableware.

Limehouse, London. Experiments made in manufacture of porcelain *c*1745–*c*1748. Factory advertized 1747–48; potters named in parish registers, deeds, or tax records include W. *Ball (1747), who may have moved to Liverpool by *c*1755. Work of factory unidentified, but advertizements include ornamental and table ware decorated in underglaze blue. Paste possibly contained soapstone.

lime-soda glass. *See* soda-lime glass.

lime whitening. *See* pickled finish.

limning. Until 18th century, portrait painting in miniature.

Limoges (Haute-Vienne), France. Main centre of European enamel production from 12th to 14th centuries, first with monasteries making enamelled religious objects (reliquaries, plaques, shrines, ciboria, etc.); later lay commercial enterprise made plates, ewers, vases, plaques, etc. *Champlevé* method used with blue ground colour and multicoloured designs. Craft revived in 16th century with development of painted enamel technique. A few families closely guarded craft secrets, among them that of N. *Pénicaud, P. *Reymond, and L. *Limousin. At first, produced vividly coloured plaques with religious scenes, later inspired by Italian Renaissance subjects; miniature portaits also painted. Later in 16th century, fashion for painting religious and classical subjects **en grisaille* developed, e.g. wall-plaques (often with cast brass frames). Production continued to end of 17th century, though in decline. Reproductions made in Paris in mid 19th century.

Saint-Yrieix, near Limoges, known as source of kaolin by 1764. Hard-paste porcelain factory established 1771 using kaolin from Saint-Yrieix; under protection of Comte d'Artois, 1773–77. In 1784, became royal factory, financed by Louis XVI to produce ware for decoration at Sèvres; closed in 1796. Other factories operated in area, first established 1797, producing tableware with creamy-coloured paste, often decorated with flower sprigs. Marks include Cd, incised or painted, or CD with Sèvres mark and painter's initials in blue enamel. Such inscriptions as *Porcelaine de Limoges* sometimes added in red. In late 18th and 19th centuries, other factories opened. Faience made from 1736, largely unidentified. Marked examples include plate with stag hunting scene in blue, green, and purple, and large dish with biblical scene. Tin-glaze tends to craze.

Limoges enamel. Plate, one of set of twelve depicting Months, by P. *Reymond; signed P R and dated 1584. Diameter $7\frac{3}{4}$in.

Limousin, Léonard (*c*1505–*c*1577). French enamel artist, one of family working at Limoges. Mainly produced portraits of royal family and nobility.

linenfold or **parchment panelling.** Decorative carved panelling, supposedly resembling linen with tight pleats or folds, usually vertical. Used on wall panels, chests, doors, etc., from 14th century. Probably of Flemish origin; used in England until early 17th century. *Illustration at* coffer.

linen smoother. Mushroom-shaped glass implement with 5in. long grooved or knopped handle for smoothing linen or rubbing floors. Made in Stourbridge, Worcestershire, from early 18th century; in clear and coloured (bottle) glass.

Link or **Linck,** Franz Conrad (1732–93). German sculptor; porcelain *Modellmeister* at *Frankenthal factory (1762–66). Well-proportioned figures, with applied, moulded detail; somewhat harshly coloured; bases bright green, with scrollwork (sometimes gilded) at sides. Single figures, e.g. Months series, and Oceanus, more highly regarded than groups.

Linnell, John (d 1796). English cabinet maker, furniture designer, and carver. In 1763 took over business of relative William Linnell. Worked in Palladian, rococo, and neo-classical styles.

Linwood, Matthew (1754–1826). English silversmith and box maker working in Birmingham; mark registered 1813. Produced snuff-boxes and vinaigrettes with die-stamped views of buildings or portraits, including series on Admiral Nelson. *Illustrations at* vinaigrette, wine label.

lion (in Chinese ceramics). *See* shih tzŭ.

lion mask. Ornament in shape of lion's head; common e.g. on baroque and neo-classical silver (wine coolers, cisterns, punch bowls, etc.) and on furniture. Sometimes has ring in mouth for use as handle. Also often used at junction of foot with body. *See* mascaron. *Illustration at* soup tureen.

lion-mask handle. Chinese ceramics; found in decoration of early pottery of Han dynasty, e.g. *Yüeh ware, in imitation of bronze vessels. Animal's head applied or carved on neck or shoulder of vessel, sometimes with loop-hole for ring attachment. Form also found in Western ceramic decoration.

lion sejant knop. Knop in form of seated lion, found on some (rare) 15th and 16th century pewter and brass spoons, and on silver examples from early 16th century to *c*1660. *Illustration at* knop.

lion's paw foot (in silver). Foot in shape of lion's paw; sometimes attached to body by lion mask. Used on baroque and neo-classical silver vessels. *Illustration at* soup tureen.

Liotard, Jean-Etienne (1702–90). Swiss miniaturist and pastel painter. Studied in Paris. In 1733, went to Rome, then for five years to Constantinople. On return to Paris, adoption of oriental dress brought notoriety; nicknamed *Le Turc*. Clientele throughout Europe; painted Maria Theresa and Joseph II in Vienna; exhibited at Royal Academy, London (1733–74). Miniatures on ivory or enamel. Ivory often visible against gouache background.

liquid gold. *See* gilding.

Li-shui ware. Chinese celadon made from T'ang period, common in Five Dynasties and early Sung periods. Resembles *northern celadon and *Yüeh wares, with olive or pale green glaze partly wiped away before firing. Heavily built pieces, e.g. funerary urns, vases, and ewers. Carved petal or peony scroll-work often found under glaze. Possibly made at Li-shui near *Lung-ch'üan, site of similar, more important kiln in this period.

lit à la dauphine. French bed with central canopy attached by metal framework to corners of head and foot boards. Dates from 18th century.

lit à la duchesse. French bed, dating from and popular during reign of Louis XV. Low head-board; no posts; tester attached to wall or ceiling extended length of bed.

lit à l'anglaise. Bed resembling settee, having high 'back' (on wall side) and 'sides' (head and foot boards). Originally designed to fit into wall recess; popular during Louis XVI period.

lit à la polonaise. Domed and draped bed, popular Louis XVI style. Head and foot boards of equal height supporting four iron ribs, one rising from each corner to hold central dome. Four curtains, attached to dome, arranged to fall so as to conceal iron framework.

lit à la turque. *See lit de repos.*

lit de repos. French **chaise longue* or *day bed. Forms influenced by fascination with eastern culture in 18th century; *lit à la turque* resembles large sofa or settee, with backpiece and shaped head and foot boards; *sultane* (or *lit de repos a là turque*), usually backless, has outward-scrolling ends of equal height. Both popular from mid 18th century.

lit en bateau. *See* boat bed.

lithophane. Translucent panel of biscuit porcelain with intaglio moulded decoration, visible by transmitted light. Patented in Paris, 1827; rights of manufacture purchased for Germany by Meissen (made 1828). Also made at Berlin until *c*1850, and in England by Grainger, Lee & Co. Designs include portraits, figure groups, and landscapes, often reproductions of known pictures. From 1850s, sometimes tinted by addition of metal oxides to paste. Other manufacturers after expiry of patent include Berlin, Belleek, H. *Minton, W. T. *Copeland.

lithyalin. Opaque Bohemian glass of variegated colour with marbled appearance, developed and patented by F. *Egermann, *c*1828.

Lithyalin glass. Bohemian scent bottle and stopper, c*1830–40.*

*William Littler. Vase in *Littler's blue;* c*1750.*

*Liverpool delftware. Bowl decorated with *Fazackerly pattern.* c*1760. Diameter* 10*in.*

Littler, William (1724–84). Manufacturer of salt-glaze stoneware at Brown Hills, Staffordshire; name associated with *Littler's blue. Manager from *c*1749 of factory making soft-paste porcelain at *Longton Hall. On closure of factory in 1760, moved to West Pans, Musselburgh, near Edinburgh; continued decorating Longton Hall stock, often with heraldic devices of Scottish families.

Littler's blue. White salt-glaze stoneware body dipped in clay slip stained with cobalt before firing. Many pieces painted with flowers in opaque white and black enamel or oil-gilding. Named after W. *Littler, but made by many other English potteries in mid 18th century.

Liu-li-ch'ang. *See* Ku-i.

Liverpool delftware. Tin-enamelled earthenware made at Liverpool, Lancashire, from 1712 until 1770s. Pieces include *bricks, barrel mugs, and jugs. Wall pockets in form of cornucopia often painted with flowers and birds. Much domestic ware exported to America. Punchbowls up to 28in. diameter, often painted with ships and nautical subjects. Covered vases in baluster shape have *chinoiserie* landscapes around whole surface. *Char-pots decorated with fish, and often edged with reddish brown. Some wares decorated in *Fazackerley colours; often flower, foliage, or bird designs, also ships and seascapes. Tiles transfer-printed from 1750s, mainly in black, occasionally red, low-temperature colours. Makers include S. and J. *Pennington, Z. *Barnes, and R. *Chaffers.

Liverpool jugs. Cream-coloured earthenware jugs imported into America in 18th century; transfer-printed at Liverpool with ship or portrait, sometimes both, in black. Late examples printed with American views. Adapted in American silver by P. *Revere; popular in early 19th century. Silver versions have bulging, barrel-shaped body, slightly flared at foot and rim, triangular lip spout, and plain scroll handle.

Liverpool porcelain. Blue-and-white porcelain made by several potters of delftware and cream-coloured earthenware after *c*1750. R.

*Liverpool porcelain. Examples from four of the seven factories. Left to right: 1) *Coffee can by Samuel Gilbody's factory, 1758–60, unmarked; height 2½in. 2) Tea bowl and saucer by R. *Chaffers's factory, unmarked, 1760–65; pattern also at Worcester; diameter of saucer 4½in. 3) Beaker by W. *Reid's factory, unmarked 1755–60; height 4½in. 4) Teapot by W. *Ball's factory, unmarked, 1760–65; with* chinoiserie *pattern in *sticky blue; 4½in.*

Livery pot. Parcel-gilt, Elizabethan, made in 1591, maker's mark H.L. with later inscription, Donavit Guilielmus Smith STP Rector huius Ecclesiae de Tredington, 1638; one of pair. Height 11¾in.

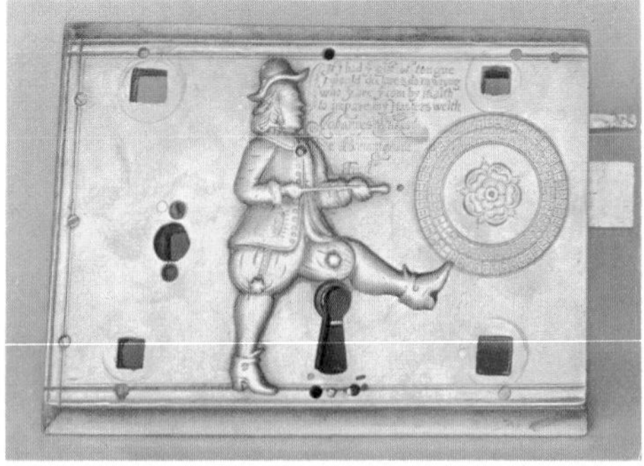

Locks. Above: steel lock in case of pierced and engraved brass, English, late 17th century; signed Walter Bickford. Below: lock of cast and engraved brass, signed Johannes Wilkes de Birmingham fecit, c1680; leg of figure indicates keyhole.

Long-case clock. English, early 18th century, in black lacquer case; movement by Martineau of London.

*Chaffers made soapstone porcelain from c1756 to formula brought from Worcester by R. *Podmore. Porcelain of W. *Ball also included soapstone. Porcelain punchbowls made by S. *Pennington.

livery cupboard. Food cupboard dating from Middle Ages, in use until c1650. Sometimes had pierced doors; also two-tiered open-shelved cupboard, with small enclosed cupboard on upper tier.

livery pot. British silver vessel for serving drink in use from Middle Ages. Earliest surviving examples 16th century; stem similar to *standing cup; baluster-shaped body; scroll handle and cover with thumbpiece attached to top of handle. Also larger examples of cylindrical *tankard shape. From early 17th century, referred to as *flagon.

loading. Use of resin etc. to give weight to hollow centre of object stamped from thin sheet silver or Sheffield plate (e.g. candlestick, knife-handle) or to applied ornamental detail.

lobate style. *See* Dutch grotesque style.

lobby chest. Chest of drawers of about half usual length; often with four drawers (top one divided into two) and sliding writing surface beneath top. Designed to fit into small room or lobby. Dates from late 18th century.

Lock, Matthias (fl c1740–70). English carver, engraver, and furniture designer; among first to rococo style in England. Later adopted neo-classicism. Collaborated with H. *Copland, with whom he engraved plates for T. *Chippendale's The Gentleman and Cabinet-Maker's Director.

lock. Medieval plate-locks for doors, etc., of wrought iron in geometrical or plain designs; worked by heavy key. By 14th century more decorative examples made, e.g. in Gothic style, or with coats of arms enriched with gold-leaf. Latten examples from late 16th century had punched or engraved decoration of flowers and foliate scrolls. From c1740 cases cast with relief designs, and gilt. Mortice lock, introduced in mid 1760s, made *en suite* with back-plate, door knob, and escutcheon-plate (matching dummy escutcheon or knob operated night-lock); all pieces in cast brass, chased and gilt, in neo-classical designs. Locks worked sliding bolt system, until 1784, when Joseph Bramah introduced lock operating on rotating barrel or cylinder system, worked by smaller key. Iron remained in use for cheaper locks (made still cheaper by early 19th century improvements in casting process). L. Yale's cylinder lock introduced 1848. *Illustration at* box.

Livery cupboard. Oak, doors pierced with Gothic designs, iron hinges. English, c1500.

Mathias Lock. Pair of George II painted and gilt-wood candlestands, circular tops with gadrooned borders hung with tassels; S-scrolled tripod legs supporting stand of scrolled acanthus, and trio of male and two female heads. Made c1744. Height 5ft9in.

locket. Small container (oval, circular, heart-shaped, etc.) worn on ribbon or chain around neck or suspended from brooch. Enclosed souvenir, e.g. hair, miniature, or, from c1860, photograph. Those intended for miniatures usually hinged. Common in Britain and Europe from 18th century. Made in variety of materials including gold, silver, pinchbeck, often set with gems. From mid 18th century in England sometimes enclosed lock of hair or hair picture. Extremely popular in 19th century.

locking-plate. *See* striking mechanism.

lock-plate. *See* lock.

Lodi (Lombardy), Italy. Some maiolica made in 18th century. Decoration with high-temperature colours, sometimes in style of Rouen, Moustiers, or Strasbourg. Also produced plain white wares.

Loggan, David (1630–93). Danzig-born engraver and plumbago miniaturist, in England by 1653. Appointed engraver to universities of Oxford (1669) and Cambridge (1690). Plumbago drawings on vellum minutely drawn, with buff tinge on face. Subjects include Oliver Cromwell, Charles II, and Cardinal Mazarin (1659).

Loir, Alexis III (d 1775). French silversmith working in Paris; descended from family of craftsmen (grandfather worked for Louis XIV); master in 1733. Executed several items in *Cadaval Toilet Set. Domestic silver in rococo style. Mark: fleur-de-lis crowned, two pellets, AL, and lamp.

long-case, tall, or **grandfather clock.** Long, narrow clock, standing on floor, introduced in England shortly after invention of pendulum. *Hood at top, with long trunk encasing pendulum and weights, supported by base. First models c6ft6in. high; 8in. square dial, without *spandrel ornaments; classical style, with *architectural (portico) top. Made by A. *Fromanteel and others. Successive styles of hood, included *flat-top, *domed-top, *pagoda-top, etc. Many with *break-arch hood and dial; notable example, *equation clock by T. *Tompion (reaching overall height of 8ft) made for King William III, 1695. Early clock cases

Alexis Loir III. Candlestick. Louis XV period and style.

ebonized; subsequently made in variety of woods, corresponding to furniture styles. Often with aperture in trunk through which pendulum can be seen. After *c*1700, clocks taller (7ft or more) and wider, with 10 or 11in. square dial; concave-shaped moulding beneath hood (replacing earlier convex form). Produced throughout 18th and 19th centuries. Makers included H. *Jones, J. *Knibb, G. *Graham, and D. *Quare, etc. *Precision examples (regulators) made by Graham, J. *Emery, etc.

long Elizas, lange Lyzen, or **lange Leisjes.** Ceramic decoration: tall female figures adapted from those on 18th century blue-and-white Chinese export porcelain. On Dutch Delft and English delftware; also on Worcester porcelain.

Longton Hall (near Newcastle-under-Lyme). First Staffordshire porcelain factory, established by 1751; W. *Littler director. Early products include *snowman figures and moulded tableware; tea and coffee pots often in lobed shape derived from silver, or moulded with raised borders of flowers, foliage, and fruit. Painting in underglaze blue or polychrome. Later, leaf and fruit shapes frequent; painting includes birds and flowers, some by *trembly rose painter. In late 1750s, domestic ware in simpler forms, some transfer-printed by J. *Sadler and G. *Green. Figures enamelled in strong colours, e.g. thick red, and yellow-toned green; scrolled bases often have touches of crimson. Factory closed 1760. Mark, when used, crossed Ls in underglaze blue.

looking-glass clock. Form of Connecticut shelf clock, designed by C. *Jerome, *c*1824; mirror on lower section of clock, below dial.

loop-back or **oval-back Windsor.** Windsor chair popular in late 18th century America. Inverted U-shaped bow attached to seat; arms joined to side of loop. H-shaped stretcher. Oval-back early name.

loo table. Early 19th century card table. Usually round-topped, with pillar support on three or four feet. Used for game, lanterloo.

loper. Retractable wooden sliding support for leaf of table, or slant-front of desk when open.

Lorraine glass makers. Establishment of glass making in England owed mainly to immigrant settlers from Lorraine introduced in late 16th century by J. *Carré with encouragement from Elizabeth I. Prominent among old Lorraine glass making families were *Henzeys, Tyzacks (also known as Tisac, Thisac, Tyzacke), Houx (Hoe, How), and Thiétrys (Tittery, Tyttere). Arrived in 1570s and settled in Weald (*see* Wealden glass), making mainly window glass under Carré's direction. Following disputes with local iron workers, Lorrainers soon dispersed to other wooded areas, particularly in Hampshire, Shropshire, near Stourbridge (Worcestershire), and Newcastle-upon-Tyne (County Durham). Domestic wares also made, e.g. small phials (medicine bottles), long and narrow, four-sided, or cylindrical; ribbed flasks; Bohemian-style beakers with wide, circular foot or encircled by notched thread; tall *façon de Venise* goblets with knopped stems. After development of coal-mining in 17th century under Sir R. *Mansell, immigrants firmly established glass making tradition at *Newcastle and *Stourbridge.

lost-wax or **cire-perdue process.** Oldest and chief method of casting metal objects of complicated design. In hollow-casting, core of clay or plaster roughly carved into shape, covered with layer of wax to thickness of finished object. Wax carved in minute detail, covered with several layers of clay and dried, then heated in oven until wax melts and flows out through channels cut in clay cover. Molten metal poured into mould, replacing wax, and cooled. Mould then cracked open, core broken up and removed; resulting object needs only slight finishing with chisel. In solid-casting, entire core is of wax, producing solid metal object.

Lot. German unit of weight equivalent to $\frac{1}{2}$oz.

'Lotto' carpets. 16th and 17th century Turkish carpets woven around Ushak; depicted in paintings by Lorenzo Lotto. Brilliant yellow interlaced angular arabesques on deep red ground create open pattern of branching forms. Kufic script, cartouche, cloud-band, or scroll borders.

lotus motif. Ancient Egyptian ornament of stylized lotus flower; used on furniture in late 18th and early 19th centuries, and on early 19th century silver.

lotus pod bowl. *See* lia tza.

Louis, Jean-Jacob (1703–72). Chief repairer and modeller at Ludwigsburg porcelain factory (1762–72). Modelled some large birds and traditional rustic groups; most famous are *Venetian fair groups, and satirical group, *Die Hohe Frisur* ('the tall hairstyle'), with hairdressers on step-ladder. Some ballet figures possibly attributable to him. Possibly identical with Belgian born Jean-Jacques Louis, modeller at Tournai (1754), and Jean Louis, modeller or repairer at Sceaux and Strasbourg in mid 18th century.

Louis Philippe style. French furniture style, roughly spanning reign of Louis Philippe (1830–48). Furniture highly derivative, reflecting Gothic, Renaissance, and baroque forms, Louis XIV, and Louis XV styles, but usually in exaggerated manner, with emphasis on curved lines, and heavy ornament. Inset Sèvres plaques used, and bronze mounts on mahogany pieces. Marquetry in light wood also common.

Louis XIII style. French, late Renaissance style in furniture, *c*1600–50. (Louis XIII reigned 1589–1643). Baroque style, showing much Italian Renaissance and Flemish influence, particularly in use of spiral and baluster turning, and motifs such as cherubs, cartouches, floral swags, scrollwork, strapwork, and shields. Other ornament includes carving, gilding, inlaid work, and painting. Commonest wood walnut; also some fine work in ebony, particularly cabinets, carved or decorated with brass and tortoiseshell marquetry. Fabric coverings important feature. *Illustration at* spiral turning.

Louis XIV style. Reign of Louis XIV (1643–1715), marked height of baroque development in French furniture, particularly pieces for court. Style remained heavily derivative, show-

Louis XIV. Bureau mazarin. **Boulle-work, with* contre-partie *top; six bow-fronted drawers between chamfered uprights; curved cross-stretchers. Width 3ft10in.*

Longton Hall porcelain. Figure of Winter, 1758, unmarked. Height 5in. There would also have been coloured versions of this figure. *Leaf dish, 1755, unmarked; painted by the *trembly rose painter. Length 8¼in.*

ing Flemish, Italian, and Spanish baroque influences until Louis assumed power following Cardinal Mazarin's death (1661). Encouraged indigenous French baroque style: furniture became less formal, with cleaner lines and less use of turning, though still richly decorated. Most pieces designed to be placed permanently against wall of room. Furniture basically rectilinear; curves introduced in e.g. scroll supports, and occasional use of cabriole leg with hoof foot. Symmetrical decoration included carving, marquetry, gilding, *Boulle-work, lacquer-work, and *chinoiseries*. Characteristic motifs acanthus, arabesque, C and S scrolls, cartouche, cherub, cupid, diaper, dolphin, flower, leaf, mask, musical instrument, rosette, strap-work, thunderbolt, trident, trophy, and tools (hoe, spade, shovel, etc.). Towards end of reign, furniture became lighter and less ornate (foreshadowing Louis XV, rococo style). *See* A-C. Boulle, D. Cucci, D. Marot, J. Berain. *Illustration also at piqué.*

Louis XV style. French *rococo furniture style associated with reign of Louis XV (1715–74), particularly *c*1720–60. Curved forms predominant (e.g. kidney-shaped tables, cabriole legs, etc.); elaborate marquetry and parquetry; finely-worked bronze mounts. Mahogany began to replace ebony in fine cabinet work; rosewood also used. Pieces occasionally gilt, or painted to harmonize with particular room. Following fashion for smaller rooms, furniture became less grandiose, smaller, and more comfortable, with increased use of upholstery and cushions. Chairs and small tables now free-standing. Silk damask, tapestry, and leather much used for furniture coverings. Decorative motifs included baskets of flowers, laurel branches, palmettes, geometrical designs (in parquetry), *chinoiseries, commedia dell'arte* figures, *singeries,* pastoral, romantic and sporting scenes. Inset porcelain plaques used on small pieces of furniture.

Leading craftsmen include *ébénistes* J. *Baumhauer, A-R. *Caudreaux, J-F. *Leleu, J-H. *Riesener; designers J-A. *Meissonier, and G-M. *Oppenord; *fondeur-ciseleur* J. *Caffiéri. *Illustrations at banquette,* bedside table, *bergère, bibliothèque,* Canabas, cartel clock, *commode à la Régence,* J. Dubois, *duchesse, duchesse brisée,* ewer, kidney-shaped table, ormolu, ottoman, *poudreuse,* reading stand, stool, *vernis Martin.*

Louis XVI style. French furniture style, roughly coinciding with reign of Louis XVI (1774–92), particularly *c*1760–90, when *rococo replaced by *neo-classical (spread e.g. by work of artist Jean-Louis David 1748–1825, leader of neo-classical school of painting). Straight lines and fine mouldings began to replace rococo curves. Classical architectural features (e.g. columns, pediments) adapted and refined. Decorative shapes included acanthus motifs, animal heads, cherubs, diaper motifs, flowers, husks, masks, mythological figures, and Vitruvian scrolls. Some *Boulle marquetry; mahogany pieces sometimes embellished only with bronze mounts or simple inlaid bronze fillets. Mechanical furniture reached height of popularity. Leading cabinet makers included J-G. *Beneman, M. *Carlin, J-F. *Leleu, N. *Petit, J-H. *Riesener, D. *Roentgen, A. *Weisweiler. *Illustrations at ambulante,* Aubusson, M. Carlin, fauteuil, marble clock, D. Roentgen, *semainier.*

Lourdet, Simon. 17th century French carpet-weaver, pupil of P. *Dupont, with whom established *Savonnerie workshop (1627) in Paris. After dispute with Dupont, remained as sole director.

Louvre tapestry workshop. French royal tapestry workshop, established 1608 by Henri IV with rehousing of Marcel Dubourg's and Gérard Laurant's high-warp loom workshop at Louvre Palace, Paris. Works include History of Psyche, from paintings by Michiel Coxcie, and History of Jephtha after Simon Vouet.

Louvre workshop. First French carpet manufactory, established 1604 beneath gallery of Louvre Palace, Paris, by P. *Dupont under patronage of Henry IV. Manufactory directed first by Dupont, then by his son, until 1627, when work transferred to Savonnerie.

love seat, causeuse, or **marquise.** Small sofa, designed to seat two, resembling wide armchair; has deep seat, usually with loose cushion. Dates from 18th century.

loving-cup. Term now used to describe any two-handled cup; originally, probably wedding or anniversary gift to couple. Specifically, two-handled cup with flared foot made in silver or pewter in 18th and 19th centuries, often inscribed with dates and/or initials. Three-handled examples exist. Used also for drinking communal toasts e.g. at guild banquets, *cf* wassail bowl.

low-back Windsor. Early Windsor chair, dating from mid 18th century in America. Curved arms continue horizontally round back of seat to form chair back with cresting at centre. Spindle supports under back and arms, with turned baluster at either end. Has saddle seat and turned splayed legs. Stretcher, set back, has bulbous decoration.

low-boy. American case piece consisting of two-drawer chest mounted on high legs (usually cabriole). Used as bedroom dressing table or dining-room side table. May have matching *high-boy. Also designed with top drawer-front hinged at base; when open, front slides forward to form writing surface, revealing drawers and cubby holes for writing equipment. Popular in

Louis XVI. Console desserte. *Satinwood with kingwood cross-banding and alternate striping on uprights and legs; Carrara marble top and gilt-metal gallery (probably later addition), mirror backing to shelves. Width 2ft.*
Love seat. Louis XVI style; carved and gilded beechwood.

*Low-boy. Walnut, with cabriole legs and *Spanish feet. 1730–40, Pennsylvania from Chester County or Philadelphia.*

Lowestoft porcelain. Left to right: 1) Tea bowl and saucer, unmarked, c1785; diameter of saucer 5in. 2) Cream jug with typical kick handle, unmarked, c1785. Height $3\frac{1}{2}$in. 3) Coffee-pot, c1770, marked with painter's numeral 5. Height $8\frac{1}{2}$in. 4) Tea caddy (lid missing), c1765, marked with painter's numeral 5. Height $3\frac{3}{4}$in.

late 17th and 18th centuries. Fine examples from Rhode Island and Philadelphia, Pennsylvania.

Lowdin's Bristol. *See* Bristol porcelain.

Lowestoft porcelain factory. From 1757, porcelain with high bone-ash content, similar to Bow, manufactured at Lowestoft, Suffolk. Style inspired by Worcester and Chinese models, characterized by pink diaper borders; paintings of figures in gardens often have horizontal dashes of brownish-red indicating ground. Flower painting often combines shades of pink and red. Domestic ware and souvenirs have local views, e.g. of cricket match, painted in naïve style; often with commemorative inscription and date. Blue-and-white porcelain has dark, inky blue underglaze transfer-printing in Worcester style, naïvely executed. R. *Allen manager from 1780 until closure, *c*1800. Marks include Allen Lowestoft. *Illustration also at* transfer-printing.

low-poster bed. Four-poster bed with low posts; has neither *tester nor draperies. Height of posts equal to that of head and foot boards. Examples date from Renaissance Italy and Spain; popular in late 18th and early 19th century America.

low-temperature colours. *See* enamel.

low-warp loom or **horizontal loom.** Tapestry loom on which warp threads stretched on horizontal loom; warp cords moved by *heddles; cartoon beneath loom, reproduced in reverse. Developed in late 15th century Brussels; widely adopted later for Flemish and French tapestries. Loom freed both weaver's hands for insertion of weft threads; technique almost doubled production speed of older *high-warp loom method, without reducing quality, although weaver could not see result of work until completed.

lozenge motif. Decorative diamond-shaped design often used on flat furniture surfaces and as engraved border ornament on silver, particularly in late 16th and early 17th centuries.

Lück, Johann Friedrich (d 1797). German porcelain repairer at Meissen (1741–57); modeller at Höchst (1757–58); modeller at *Frankenthal (1758–64), then returned to Meissen. Figures similar to those of J. W. *Lanze, but have rounder cheeks, are more elaborately finished, and have pierced rococo-scrolled bases and trellis arbours. *Illustration at* Frankenthal.

Lück, Karl Gottlieb (d 1775). German porcelain modeller at *Frankenthal (1756–75). Prolific maker of elaborate figures and groups, distinguished by rather small heads, pink cheeks, and generally strong colours (also on grassy bases similar to those of, F. C. *Link).

Ludlow bottle. 19th century American globular bottle, usually olive-green or amber. Small and medium size often called chestnut bottle. Name derived from association with glassworks in Ludlow, Massachusetts.

Ludwigsburg (Württemberg). German porcelain factory, founded 1758 by J. J. *Ringler, at instigation of Duke Carl Eugen; housed in ducal palace until his death (1793). Paste smoky or brownish-grey, good consistency for figure modelling. G. F. *Riedel chief designer (1759–79); responsible for early allegorical and neo-classical figures, often with rococo trellis background, e.g. Apollo candlestick, rococo-based Months series. J-J. *Louis created *Venetian fair groups (*c*1767); sometimes credited with ballet figures (*c*1760–65). In 1764, J. C. W. *Beyer appointed *Modellmeister*; probably worked earlier on folk types (1760–65). Glazed and biscuit reproductions later made of previous successful models, using square base instead of mound or scrolled base. Tableware decorated after Meissen; distinguishable by mark and body colour. Factory closed 1824. Marks: 1759–93, crossed Cs (for Duke Carl), sometimes with coronet above (similar to *Niderviller); *c*1790–*c*1810, stags' horns from Württemberg arms. (Sometimes also used on modern porcelain from Württemberg, but with WPM added.)

Faience factory began in 1765 under Frau de Becke, widow of A. F. *von Löwenfinck. Work, including vessels with rococo moulding and painting of flowers and fruits, often confused with that of Brunswick because of similarity of marks (crossed Cs) and styles. Production ceased *c*1795. Cream-coloured earthenware manufactured *c*1776–*c*1824, also marked with crossed Cs over ellipse.

lunar work. Part of clock movement actuating dial to indicate age and phase of moon.

Lund, Benjamin (fl mid 18th century). English porcelain manufacturer, previously brass founder. Granted licence to mine soapstone near The Lizard, Cornwall, *c*1748. Partner in factory making soapstone porcelain in Bristol from 1749, to formula possibly devised by W. *Cookworthy. Business, including lease of soapstone mine, bought by R. *Holdship on behalf of *Worcester Porcelain Company in 1752. Known products are cream jugs and sauceboats moulded in silver forms, left in white or with *chinoiserie* painting, either in underglaze blue or polychrome enamel; also rare standing figure of Chinaman, some examples with touches of underglaze manganese-purple (very unusual in English porcelain). Moulds and probably craftsmen went to Worcester; Lund recorded there in 1753. Marks in relief: BRISTOL, or BRISTOLL, sometimes with date 1750. *Illustration at* Worcester.

Lunéville (Lorraine). French faience factory

Ludwigsburg porcelain. Couple dancing; c1770.

*Lung-ch'üan. *Celadon bridal dish, Sung dynasty; moulded with two fish swimming in opposite directions in relief within incised medallion. Diameter 5⅛in.*

established in 1723, closely allied with *Saint-Clément (established 1758). Products include garden ornaments, e.g. large busts, animals (lions, dogs, etc.), painted in high-temperature colours. In early 19th century, made *faïence blanche* with decoration in crimson and green. P-L. *Cyfflé, employed in mid 18th century, established own factory (1766) in Lunéville. Cream-coloured earthenware (*faïence fine*) made by original factory in late 18th century includes tableware and large ornamental pieces. Marks on faience include *Chambrette* (owner) *à Lunéville*, incised (1731–58); K & G (owners) LUNEVILLE, impressed (from 1788); KG with crown between, over Lunéville. Biscuit porcelain marked (1769–77) CYFFLE/A LUNEVILLE, impressed; also TERRE DE LORRAINE or T.D.L. inside rectangle, impressed, with repairer's mark incised.

Lung-ch'üan ware. Chinese ceramics; best-known and most common of classic Sung celadon ware. Manufactured in Chekiang province near capital of Sung court, Hangchou. Light-grey body approaching porcelain, burns yellow when exposed in firing, e.g. on foot ring; thick, hazy glaze, in shades of pale green; sometimes crackled with wide, irregular pattern. Some *iron-brown spotted ware. Typical items; flat dishes, conical bowls, deeper bowls with lotus-petal engraving outside, and wine jars; examples called kinuta, from Japanese term for mallet-shaped, form highly prized. Funeral vases often have modelled decoration of dragons or other animals under-glaze. In Yüan period, dishes, wine jars, etc., made for export to India and Near East; more thickly potted, with much carved and moulded decoration. Export continued in Ming period. *Illustration also at* iron-brown spots.

Luplau, Anton Carl (d 1795). German porcelain modeller, at Fürstenberg (1764–75); best known work, Woman Looking for a Flea. At Copenhagen (1776–95) as arcanist and *Modellmeister*.

lustre. Cut glass pendant, used from 18th

Lustre decoration. In silver on Staffordshire loving cup, c1815–20.

century to decorate chandeliers (instead of rock-crystal). From *c*1850, term also applied to cheap, coloured, vase-like table candelabra.

lustre decoration. Ceramic decoration: thin deposit of metal on surface of pottery, often with iridescent effect; achieved by painting glazed pottery with metallic oxide, then firing in *reducing atmosphere using *muffle kiln to leave film of metal (gold, copper, or platinum). Lustre effects produced in gold, silver, copper, pink, purple, dark red, and rarely yellow. Feature of Islamic pottery from Middle Ages, and of *Hispano-Moresque ware. Red lustre used at *Deruta and *Gubbio from early 16th century. *Böttger lustre used at Meissen until 1730s. English lustre decoration from 19th century, probably first used on Staffordshire salt-glaze. Process developed by J. *Wedgwood on pearlware, sold from 1805 with lustre bands and, usually, enamelled decoration. English lustre includes plain lustre covering whole vessel to give effect of metal, and similar effects with sprigged relief decoration; also bands of lustre to embellish enamel painting or transfer-printing; designs painted or stencilled in lustre, *resist lustre, and mottling. Lustre ware produced at Leeds from early 19th century and in large quantities at *Sunderland in mid 19th century. *Illustrations at* Caffaggiolo, English ceramics, Hispano-Moresque ware, Sunderland.

lustre marks (in ceramics). Initial letters in brownish-red produced by lightly-fired ink or gall written over glaze in porcelain. Some thought to appear on Meissen porcelain decorated by Augsburg *Hausmaler* (*c*1725–40); others probably on pieces painted at factory. Possibly used as identification code for table services, etc.

lute family. Stringed instrument used from antiquity (e.g. Egypt from *c*1500 B.C.); plucked. Probably introduced to Europe in 13th century following Moorish invasions of Spain (name derives from Arabic *al'ud*. Assumed traditional form in 15th century; body shaped like pear halved lengthwise; length of neck varies; head containing peg box generally bent back at sharp angle. Number of strings, usually in pairs, varies with period and country. Unlike members of violin family, does not have bridge; strings stretch almost from end of neck to bottom of body. Frets added in 15th century. Family includes: alto lute (most common type), smaller *mandora, mandore, mandola*, etc., and larger tenor lute (*theorbo*) and bass lute or archlute (*chitarrone*). Most popular in 16th and 17th centuries, though continued to be played long after. Centre of production in 16th century, Bologna, Italy. Among important makers were Germans Hans Frei, Laux Maler, and son, Sigismund. Repeated addition of bass strings to *theorbo* necessitated addition of second pegbox halfway along neck. Lutes made in variety of materials including ivory, ebony, whalebone, and various woods. Often lavishly decorated with inlay, etc.; sometimes with elaborate *rose soundhole.

luting. Attaching separate pieces of clay together with liquid slip, e.g. to join moulded sections or to apply clay decoration to vessel.

Lutma, Joannes the Elder (*c*1585–1669). Dutch silversmith working in Amsterdam. Influenced by A. *van Vianen; further developed *Dutch grotesque style. Most notable chaser of period. Few surviving works include salts, ewers and basins. Son, J. *Lutma the Younger continued in trade.

Lutma, Joannes the Younger (1624–85). Dutch silversmith working in Amsterdam; master in 1643. Made range of domestic silver, with embossed and chased ornament. Skilled in modelling human figures. Work signed with monogram, Joan L.

Lynn or **Norwich glasses.** Fine quality glasses, tumblers, and decanters characterized by horizontal ribbing; often with opaque-white twist stem and folded foot. Made in and near King's Lynn, Norfolk in late 17th and 18th centuries.

Lyon (Rhône). Some of earliest French faience made in Lyon and Nevers, from 1512, initially by Italian settlers. Work later in 16th century resembles contemporary maiolica of Urbino. Some pieces identifiable by French inscriptions on reverse. Decoration often includes steep hill with trees, or water represented by wavy blue lines. Some figure subjects enclosed in medallions and surrounded by grotesques. *Faïence blanche* made from late 16th century. From 1733, style influenced by Moustiers.

lyre-back. Open chair back with pierced splat resembling classical Greek lyre in outline. Introduced by R. *Adam *c*1775. Also occurs in *Hepplewhite, *Sheraton, and *Regency style chairs in England, and in work of D. *Phyfe in America.

lyre clock. Wall or shelf clock first made in late 18th century France; lyre-shaped frames of bronze or bronze-mounted marble often decorated with enamel or *diamanté*. Dial mounted in lower part, gridiron pendulum suspended above to simulate lyre strings; bob connected to escapement, and sometimes forming ring set with paste brilliants surrounding dial. American eight-day form supposedly designed by A.

Lyre clock. White marble and ormolu set with paste jewels. French, mid 18th century.

*Willard Jr, made by Massachusetts firms *c*1820–*c*1840.

lyre-guitar. Type of *guitar invented in France in late 18th century; shaped like classical Greek lyre (harp), following fashionable furniture design. Consisted of square or rectangular flat wooden box resonator, with two arms rising from opposite sides, joined at top by cross-bar. Fretted guitar fingerboard in centre usually with six strings, sometimes nine. May have two *rose soundholes. Extremely popular in Britain and Europe until *c*1830; few made after mid 19th century. Wooden cases often decorated with inlaid ivory, mother-of-pearl, etc.

ma-chia-Kang. *See* Shou-chou ware.

Mackintosh Service. Porcelain table service made at Nantgarw and decorated in London (1817–20); large birds set against distant landscapes, with elaborate border pattern and lavish gilding. *Illustration at* Nantgarw.

Madrid carpets. Madrid important Spanish carpet production centre from 18th century. Royal Manufactory of Madrid, Fabrica Real, established under patronage of Philip V, with Flemish director. Produced fine Savonnerie and Aubusson style carpets. Major commission, carpets for Escorial Palace. Continued in production until 19th century under private ownership.

Maestro Benedetto (fl early 16th century). Italian maiolica potter and painter, son of potter at Faenza. At Siena in early 16th century, made dishes decorated with coats of arms surrounded by e.g. palmettes, interlaced strapwork, and moulded fluting. At Faenza, work includes dish with mark of Casa Pirota (1520), painted with woman untying man from tree, and dishes with religious subjects. Painting said to be characterized by tufted trees and languid attitude of figures.

Maestro Giorgio. *See* Andreoli, Maestro Giorgio.

magazine stand. *See* Canterbury.

Magdalen cup. 16th century English silver or silver-gilt beaker with straight sides widening towards rim; low, moulded foot and domed cover with finial. Body usually embossed with fruit motifs derived from German *pattern books. Name inspired by resemblance to ointment cup held by Mary Magdalen in many medieval and Renaissance paintings.

magnetic compass. Originated either in Far East or Scandinavia; used in late Middle Ages in form of piece of naturally magnetized ore (lodestone) suspended by cord. Stone often held in elaborate mounts of gilt metal, etc. Developed into magnetized iron needle pivoted over calibrated card or dial; incorporated in sundials, surveying instruments, etc., from 16th century. Mariner's compass has bar magnet fixed under revolving card, normally not pivoted, but floating on surface of oil-bath.

Magnetic compass. Inset into base of silver and gilt metal universal equatorial dial by Johann Willebrand of Augsburg, c1748. Pierced and engraved bracket holds plumb-bob. Hinged latitude scale engraved with degrees; also hinged chapter-ring with hour numerals. Original leather box inset with plaque engraved with latitudes of European towns to nearest degree. Diameter of base c2½in.

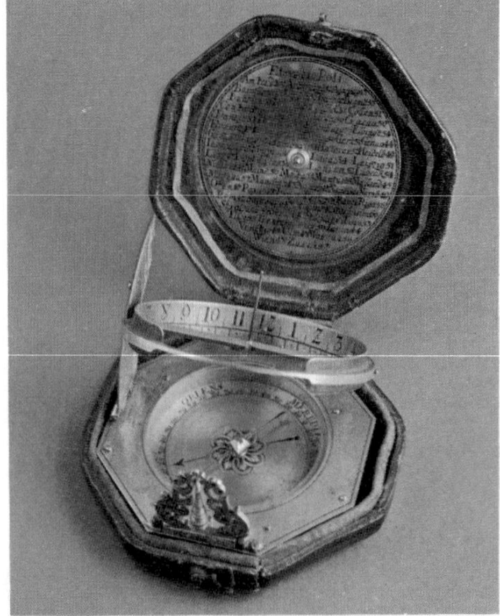

Magnus, Johann Bernard (fl 18th century). German porcelain figure painter at Höchst (1758); painter of decorative ware at Frankenthal (1762–82). Famous for battle scenes on vases. Signed with initials BM.

Magny, Alexis (1712–77). French optical instrument-maker. Produced many types of scientific instrument, but chiefly associated with form of compound *microscope with three lenses and rack-and-pinion focus adjustment; several examples have rococo bronze mounts, probably by J. *Caffiéri.

magot or **pagod.** Figure inspired by *Pu-t'ai Ho-shang. Produced by most early European porcelain makers, e.g. at Meissen, in white porcelain or red stoneware. Examples made at Chantilly *c*1730s closely resemble Chinese originals.

Mahal carpets. Trade term for soft, coarse, west Persian carpets woven in and around Arak (formerly Sultanabad) from 19th century. Turkish or Persian knotted wool pile on cotton foundation. Numerous patterns, including variation of *herati, large-scale flowers scattered on field, and medallions. Strong colours, particularly dark blues and madders.

maidenhead spoon. Silver spoon with knop representing bust of long-haired young woman, perhaps Virgin Mary. Made in Britain and Europe mainly from 14th to mid 17th centuries. *Illustration at* knop.

Maigelein. 15th century German *Waldglas beaker; low, open cup shape, mould-blown, with high *kick, and sometimes simple decoration. One of earliest small drinking vessels.

mail guard's watch. Type of large watch carried on mail coaches in 18th and 19th century England, latterly by railway guards. Set to correct time by official at start of journey, often mounted in locked case.

mainspring. *See* spring.

maintaining power (in clocks and watches). Means of sustaining driving power while main source (either spring or weight) out of action during winding; methods include subsidiary

Maigelein. *Green glass with iridescence. German, 15th century. Diameter 3in.*

springs, brought into play by winding, as in J. *Harrison's system. Bolt and shutter form found in some early long-case clocks. Consists of system of levers, spring-loaded and interconnected: end of one lever normally covers winding hole, but can be moved aside to admit key, thereby winding subsidiary spring. Second lever engages tooth of *centre wheel and drives train while clock is wound. Winding hole closes automatically after short interval. Endless cord system introduced by C. *Huygens and found in many 30-hour long-case clocks, particularly provincial English, automatically maintains power to train during winding.

maiolica. Until 16th century, Spanish pottery with lustre decoration, entering Italy via Majorca; later, all varieties of *tin-glazed earthenware made in Italian manner. Tin-glaze used in Italy from *c*11th century; primitive wares decorated predominantly in brown and green. From 13th to 15th centuries, *green and purple ware made at *Orvieto, *Faenza, and in district of *Florence where **stile severo* developed, adding extra colours to palette, e.g. on **albarelli*. *Italo-Moresque ware derives style from Spanish imports. In 15th and 16th centuries, **alla porcellana* style adopted. In early 16th century, *Fattorini family established workshop at *Cafaggiolo. *Gothic floral style gradually supplanted by *grotesques, *trophies, *arabesques, etc. **Stile bello* developed, often accompanying **istoriato* painting; examples from Faenza, Cafaggiolo, *Castel Durante, and *Urbino; work of N. *Pellipario important. *Deruta and *Gubbio associated with lustre decoration; wares made elsewhere sent for lustre to be added, e.g. by G. *Andreoli. In 16th century, *Siena produced *albarelli* and, notably, dishes by *Maestro Benedetto. *Venetian maiolica reached peak production in mid 16th century, showing influence of Isnik pottery and imported Chinese porcelain; decoration includes **berrettino* glaze. At *Savona, painting often in blue, inspired by oriental styles. *Bianchi di Faenza*, with **compendiario* decoration became popular after mid 16th century (much exported), and relief moulding appeared, particularly at Urbino. *Istoriato* painting revived in 17th century at *Castelli. Fruit and leaf designs painted at *Montelupo. In 18th century, maiolica made in rococo style at *Lodi and *Turin, by e.g. G. G. *Rossetti, also A. *Casali and F. A. *Callegari, later at *Pesaro. At *Milan, work of F. *Clerici and P. *Rubati inspired by oriental styles in mid 18th century. Influence of French faience grew throughout 18th century; particularly noticeable at *Le Nove, Venice (*Cozzi factory), and Faenza.

Although much reduced by spread of cream-coloured earthenware in late 18th century, manufacture of maiolica in Italy continues. Contemporary account of 16th century technique written by C. *Piccolpasso. Vessel, when fired, covered with tin-glaze solution, and dried. At this stage, designs painted on surface with high-temperature colours; best work then given second coat of clear glaze (**coperta*) over colours before firing. Lustre decoration, when applied, requires third firing. *See* Antwerp, Dutch ceramics, English maiolica.

majolica. English earthenware with relief decoration under coloured glaze, introduced by H. *Minton in 1851. Biscuit body usually cane-coloured, dipped in tin-enamel glaze, then

Malachite. Top of early 19th century Russian table; ormolu mounts.

decorated with clear glaze coloured with metallic oxide. Used for large decorative vessels (e.g. umbrella stands, *jardinières*), tableware, tiles, and figures. *Illustration at* H. Minton.

maker's mark. Mark stamped on gold or silver identifying maker. From 14th century, a device (e.g. fish, helmet, grasshopper) employed, later (16th or 17th century) initials and device, or surname, or first two letters of surname, etc., used. Precise practice varied with each country. Indicated adherence to official standard of fineness, since maker of piece could easily be identified and brought to justice. Marks registered at assay offices, e.g. Goldsmith's Hall, London.

Makri carpets. *See* Megri carpets.

malachite. Opaque or slightly translucent bright green veined mineral (hydrous carbonate of copper), taking high polish. Used as thin veneer on base of copper, iron, stone, or marble, for large and small objects, e.g. tables, urns, clock-cases, etc., often in conjunction with gilt-bronze or silver-gilt mounts. Also used architecturally, as in Malachite Hall in Winter Palace, Leningrad, where columns, fireplaces, etc., faced with malachite. Popular in late 19th century Britain.

Malaga (Andalusia), Spain. *Hispano-Moresque ware produced *c*1200 to late 15th century; exported to England by 1303, also to Sicily and Egypt. Products usually small vessels, bowls, dishes, and pitchers, but also e.g. *Alhambra vase. During 15th century, scenes, sometimes with figures, introduced in decoration; late work difficult to distinguish from *Manises.

Malayer carpets. *See* Meleyer carpets.

Malbone, Edward Greene (1777–1807). American miniaturist and portrait painter. Began career as artist at Providence, Rhode Island, in 1794. Travelled around United States painting miniatures. Brief visit to London in 1801.

Malkin, Samuel (1668–1741). Potter at Burslem, Staffordshire. Used moulds with incised decoration to produce dishes for decoration with slip as in **cuenca* technique, e.g. with patterns of leaves, stars, and Adam and Eve. Slight variations in style on dishes initialled SM suggest work of more than one craftsman.

malleability. Property of metal permitting it to be shaped by hammering without cracking.

Malling jugs. Tin-glazed earthenware jugs with silver mounts; among earliest examples of English delftware, made mid 16th century. Glaze splashed with blue, yellow and brown, blue and purple, or blue alone; occasionally coloured deep blue or turquoise throughout. A lead-glazed specimen exists. Examples found at West Malling, Kent.

Maltese clock. Wooden-case clock, *c*24×18in., decorated with carving or gilding, produced by village craft industry in Malta from early 19th century. Weight-driven. Painted dial, with flowers or foliage; single hour hand only on early examples.

Mamluk, Mameluke, Cairo or **Damascus carpets.** Elaborate, geometrical, Egyptian court carpets with finely Persian-knotted wool or wool and silk pile, on wool and silk foundation; woven in Cairo during Mamluk period (1400–1517). Well-balanced designs worked from full-size cartoons. Early rugs in warm red, light green, pale blue, and yellow; later, up to 12 tones used. Dominant central motif of complex, interpenetrating geometrical forms; numerous small stars and polygons or highly stylized plants and floral motifs infilling ground and drawing attention to centre of field. Little distinction between field and border, major and minor pattern elements. Type continued into 17th century, but after 1517 largely replaced by designs based on *Turkish Court Manufactory carpets.

mammy bench or **chair.** American rocking bench with section of seat area convertible into cradle by inserting railing along front of seat. Dates from 19th century.

Manara, Baldassare (d by 1540). Italian maiolica painter at Faenza; decorated dishes and plates dated 1532–39; *istoriato* subjects include horsemen, battle scenes, The Triumph of Time, The Martyrdom of St Cecilia (*c*1535), and unidentified mythological subject with cupids. Blackish-brown outlines and frequent use of

*Mamluk rug. Wine-red field with circular green flower-filled *medallion; blue spandrels; six guard stripes and border of leaves and lotus. 16th century. 8ft3in.×6ft7in.*

Mandoline. Made in Naples by Domenico Vinaccia, 1780. Mother-of-pearl and tortoise-shell inlay.

orange and yellow characteristic; reverse of plate often decorated with concentric bands of yellow and orange, sometimes orange scale-pattern; date may be enclosed in cartouche among foliage and flowers.

Manardi workshop. Italian maiolica workshop established in 1669 by Manardi brothers at Angarano. At first, produced *faïence blanche*; later made plates with trellis-like borders in relief, or with figures and ruined buildings in landscapes painted on *latesino* enamel.

mandarin porcelain. Chinese export ware of 19th century; jars with figure subjects in pink, red, and gold in panels, usually framed in underglaze blue. Inspired similar pieces in English porcelain factories of same period.

mandoline. Stringed musical instrument originating in Europe in early 18th century; plucked, usually with *plectrum. Body resembles *lute, but much deeper, particularly at lower end, and made of narrow ribs. Neck is fretted with four pairs of metal strings, passing over low bridge and attached to flat, rectangular peg disc. In 18th century, made in various Italian towns; stringing and body shape varied locally.

mandoline watch. Watch made in shape of mandoline. French, early 19th century. *See* form watch.

mandora or **mandore.** *See* lute.

Manheim Glass House. Founded by H. W. *Stiegel in 1765 at Manheim, Pennsylvania.

Manheim Glass Works. Two tumblers, free-blown and enamelled, c1770; probably from this glasshouse. Height 4in.

Employed European craftsmen. Produced coarsely-painted bottles and jugs similar to European peasant ware, and high standard of engraved and mould-blown glass. Flint-glass made from blue, green, and amethyst metal with mould-blown pattern incorporating diamond daisy design. Factory closed in 1774. *See* Stiegel glass.

Manicus, Frederick (1740–85). Dutch silver-smith working in Amsterdam. Made domestic silver in French rococo and neo-classical styles. Mark: FM.

Manises (Valencia), Spain. Made lustred *Hispano-Moresque ware from 14th century until *c*1700; main manufacturing centre from late 15th century. Early recapture of Valencia from Moorish rule (1238) allowed development of **mudéjar* style in decoration. Pottery decorated with plants and foliage (e.g. bryony, acacia, or vine leaves), animals (e.g. birds, ungulates, or dogs), and heraldic devices; inscriptions in both Gothic and Kufic script also used. Painting grew slightly more naturalistic. Much ware exported to Italy; coats of arms of Italian families common. Under influence of Renaissance, shapes came to resemble those of metal-work. Relief introduced in decoration; reverse of dishes began to carry designs, e.g. heraldic animals from *c*1430. Mugs, pharmacy ware, and storage jars also produced.

mannerist style. Off-shoot of Renaissance style developed in 16th century by Florentine painters and sculptors. Characterized by fanciful treatment of common Renaissance motifs; scale disregarded and ornament covers whole surface of object. Animal, plant, and architectural motifs combined. Human figures—often erotic—grotesques, marine elements intertwined with scrolls, strapwork, volutes, etc. Primarily court style; Italian craftsmen brought to France in 1530s by François I to decorate Fontainebleau palace further developed style; carried it to other European centres (Antwerp, Augsburg, etc.). Engraved designs in this manner by E. *Hornick, H. *Holbein the Younger, E. *Delaune, W. *Jamnitzer, etc. Plastic treatment of forms suggests later *Dutch grotesque style.

Manises. Ceiling tile with coat of arms of Castille and León surrounded by oak-leaf pattern. 17×13*in.*

Mannheim gold. Silver-like alloy of copper, zinc, and tin, developed in early 18th century.

Männlich, Daniel the Elder (1625–1701). German silversmith working in Berlin from 1650; appointed court goldsmith to Leopold II in 1665. Made ceremonial and domestic silver and gold wares. Mark: DM.

Mansell, Sir Robert (1573–1656). English admiral and financier. Held glass monopoly 1616–49. Reorganized English glass making on sound commercial basis. Successfully converted furnaces from wood to coal. Employed over 4000 craftsmen in factories throughout Britain. Produced green phials, bottles, green table glass, window glass, mirror plates, and *façon de Venise* crystal table glass.

mantel clock. Clock generally placed on mantelpiece. *See* bracket clock, shelf clock.

mantling. Drapery, scrollwork, plumes, etc., frequently appearing behind and around shield in *heraldic engraving.

Mantua and **Kent Glasshouses.** Mantua Glass Works founded in 1821 in Mantua, Ohio by David Ladd. By 1823, had established second glasshouse in Kent, Ohio. Produced bottles, flasks, window glass, plain and flint glasswares and blown-three-mould glass. Closed 1829.

Manwaring, Robert (fl *c*1765). English chair and cabinet-maker; published The Cabinet and Chair-Maker's Real Friend and Companion (1765) and The Chair-Maker's Guide (1766). Designs for Chinese and 'rural' chairs heavily decorated.

marble clock. Heavy mantel clock with case, or part of case, made of marble. Produced in France from late 18th century. Brocot escapement. Term applied to any clock with marble case, even sometimes to clocks in slate or onyx.

marbled slip decoration. *See* combed slip decoration.

marbles. *See* beads.

marbling. In Chinese ceramics, technique dating from T'ang period. Different coloured clays mixed into body, then covered with transparent glaze (*cf* agate ware). General effect imitated in Islamic ceramics, by simpler method: thick slips of contrasting colours applied to plain clay body, combed into wavy pattern (*cf* combed slip decoration).

marbling. Painting surfaces (e.g. of furniture) to imitate marble. Often used in Europe from 17th to late 19th century; technique also adopted later in America.

marcasite. Crystals White of iron pyrites faceted and mounted at first to imitate diamonds. Found throughout world. Widely used in jewellery in England, France, and Switzerland from 18th century. Sometimes set in blue or red glass plaques (in imitation of diamond-set enamels); more usual **pavé* set in silver. From mid 18th century accepted on own merit.

Marcolini, Count Camillo (1739–1814). German aristocrat; favoured courtier of *Augustus

Marble clock. Louis XVI, with ormolu mounts, dial signed De Bon, Paris; arched case surmounted by urn of fruit with swags of fruit and flowers. Height $18\frac{1}{2}$*in.*

III. Minister responsible for Meissen porcelain factory (1774–1814). Under his directorship (Marcolini period), factory regained some of former prosperity, partly by banning imports of rival porcelain, but artistic reputation suffered by sale of many defective wares. Exports to Turkey prospered briefly, but Napoleonic war caused factory's temporary closure in 1813. Mark, crossed swords with star between hilts, in underglaze blue, used at this time.

Marieberg, Sweden. Faience made at factory near Stockholm established (1758) by J. L. E. *Ehrenreich; privilege granted for manufacture of porcelain (1759), but premises damaged by fire. After rebuilding, factory produced finely-potted faience, often left in white when decorated with relief moulding. Painting in brilliant underglaze blue, or bright enamel colours, e.g. crimson or purple; rich green used to decorate tureens, covered jars, and terrace vases. After Ehrenreich's departure (1766), neo-classical style adopted; transfer-printing in black introduced. From 1769, cream-coloured earthenware gradually replaced faience. Factory bought by owners of *Rörstrand in 1782. Mark includes three crowns over line and letters MB; also indicates date, painter, and manager. Soft-paste porcelain made from 1766; styles inspired by Mennecy have spiral moulding and flower painting in soft colours. Figures small, after Meissen and Frankenthal. Body improved by 1772, and hard-paste introduced *c*1777. Produced tableware, including tureens, teapots, bowls, and cabaret sets, in styles largely derived from, e.g. Berlin, Sèvres, and Copenhagen. Marks: MB monogram impressed (until 1769); three crowns over coat of arms in red, with three blue dots (from 1769); three crowns over line and MB in red or three dots in blue.

mark (on silver). *See* hallmark.

marks (in ceramics). Early examples include seals or signatures of maker impressed on Roman pottery, and signatures of Greek painters. Chinese porcelain marks indicate emperor ruling at time of manufacture (*nien hao). Islamic pottery in Chinese style sometimes signed by maker. First consistent factory mark is dome of Florence cathedral, on *Medici porcelain in late 1570s and 1580s. Work felt to be of special importance signed by Hispano-Moresque or maiolica potters; confusion arises here between work of individual artists and their workshops. Consistent marking of products first adopted on porcelain made at Meissen; marks later used at most porcelain factories and by some faience makers. Work of Marieberg and Rörstrand marked with date of manufacture, painter's sign, and sometimes price, as well as mark of factory and manager's initial. Delft makers agreed on regular use of factory marks, in compliance with order of 1764. At e.g. Sèvres, Vienna, and Wedgwood factories, date letters added to mark. Occasionally, in 19th century, manufacture and decoration marked separately, with dates, at e.g. Sèvres and Vienna. However, voluntary nature of marking, and fact that forgeries could be left unmarked, or given adapted mark designed to be mistaken for that of original, while cancelled marks were often entirely removed from undecorated stock sold off cheaply and painted elsewhere, all contribute to making marks alone unreliable grounds for attribution. In 17th and 18th centuries, marks often added by painters and repairers, and at some factories, e.g. Sèvres, Marieberg, and Rörstrand, can be identified with reasonable certainty. Some marks also refer to owners (e.g. *Augustus Rex mark) or dealers.

Marlborough leg. Square leg on furniture, straight or tapering, with larger square foot.

Marot, Daniel (1661–1752). French Protestant architect and designer. After revocation of Edict of Nantes, 1685, fled to Holland, entering service of William of Orange (later William III of England). Employed by William at Hampton Court; in England 1694–98. His baroque designs influenced Dutch and English furniture and silver designers, e.g. J. *van der Lely. Court furnishings included silver-mounted chairs and tables, toilet services, and andirons. None survives.

Daniel Marot. State bed, c*1690, made to his design for First Earl of Melville; pinewood frame covered in crimson velvet and white silk with red braid. Height 15ft2in.*

marquetry. Decorative technique, by which various woods or other materials (ivory, bone,

Marquetry. Detail of English marquetry box, c*1670. Basically walnut, with scorched woods on shading of flowers and staining on green leaves.*

metals, tortoiseshell) are inlaid in sheet of veneer, which is then fixed to surface of furniture. Non-wood inlays used in post-Renaissance Italy; adopted in France where popular with Louis XIV *ébénistes*, such as A-C. *Boulle. Used in England from mid 17th century. *cf* parquetry. *Illustration also at bureau.*

marquise. *See* love seat.

marriage or **wedding casket.** Small silver or silver-mounted casket for rings and gifts of coin to bride; often engraved with wedding scenes. Various shapes; sometimes has ring for wearing on chain. Used mainly in 17th century Holland.

marriage fan. 18th century European fan decorated with nuptial themes and occasionally portraits of couple; given to bride by bridegroom. Costly examples had shagreen cases. Less expensive copies given to bridal party and important guests.

marriage, betrothal, or **pair plate.** Pewter plate, often made in pairs, to commemorate marriage; bears names or initials with date; punched decoration common. Popular from 16th century.

marrow scoop or **spoon.** Silver implement with oval or narrow, elongated bowl and narrow, hollowed-out stem. In use in Britain from late 17th century for scooping marrow out of bones. In early 18th century, made with two grooved channels of different widths instead of spoon bowl. Some made in Sheffield plate. Out of fashion by early 19th century.

Marseille (Bouches-du-Rhône), France. Faience factory established near Marseille at

*Marriage plate (possibly for an anniversary). English pewter, dated 1720. Decorated with *wriggle-work. Diameter 9½in.*

Marrow scoop. Silver, made in 1778 by maker with initials S.A.

Marseille. Faience perfume jar, c1750; flowers modelled in relief and painted; rocaille *base. Height 7¼in.*

Saint-Jean-du-Désert, probably by potters from Nevers; J. *Clérissy and family directors, 1679–1733. Early work influenced by Nevers, Moustiers, or Savona, decorated in blue, often outlined with purple. **Style Berain* appears by 1718 in Marseille and Saint-Jean-du-Désert; also polychrome decoration in style of J. *Olerys. Large fountains have moulded rococo scrollwork and mythological figures; crucifixes and painted or moulded portrait plaques of saints also made. Naturalistic flowers painted in high-temperature colours. From 1750, some blue designs have leaves and details hatched in brick-red. Enamel decoration introduced at *Perrin factory; green and black notable; coloured enamel grounds occur; also painting in gold alone on white ground. Later factories include that of J. *Borelly, *c*1780. Academy of painting and sculpture (established 1753) contributed to high quality of painting, e.g. of naturalistic flowers, still-lifes of fish, and scenes of local life, including fishing and farming.

Marseillemuster. Meissen porcelain relief pattern for plates and dishes devised (*c*1743) by J. J. *Kändler; border of oblong panels framed by raised rococo scrolls, interspaced with dotted trellis-work.

Marsh, William (fl 1775–1810). Cabinet maker to Prince of Wales (later George IV); worked in London; some pieces reflect influence of H. *Holland. Worked with T. *Tatham from 1895.

Marston Cup. English silver standing cup with

Martha Washington chair. Elbow chair in mahogany with balloon back, late 18th century.

plain, wide bowl, trumpet-shaped stem, and moulded base supported on three silver-gilt hounds (unusual feature in cups of mid 15th century). Used as communion cup at Marston Church, Oxfordshire.

Martha Gunn. English pottery. Female version of *Toby jug, representing bathing-machine attendant, seated, wearing voluminous dress, with plume of ostrich feathers in head-dress. Two variations modelled by R. *Wood. Other makers include J. *Walton. *Illustration at* Toby jug.

Martha Washington chair. American upholstered armchair, said to have been type used by Martha Washington at Mount Vernon. High upholstered back, serpentine yoke-rail, open, un-upholstered arms scrolling downwards at ends, and tapering legs, usually joined by plain stretchers. Dates from 18th century.

Martha Washington sewing or **work table.** American work table of type said to have been used by Martha Washington at Mount Vernon. Oval, with enclosed storage space at both ends; top either hinged in one piece, or in three sections, with ends lifting to give access to storage areas. Rows of small drawers beneath top. Dates from 18th century.

Martin, Guillaume (d 1749), Etienne (d 1770), Julien (d 1782), Robert (d 1765). French lacquerers; perfected lacquer named after them, **vernis Martin*. In 1730, Etienne and Guillaume given 20-year monopoly on use of product. Received commissions from Mme de Pompadour and Louis XV; decorated *petits appartements* at Versailles. Did not imitate oriental work; decorative motifs were French – *fêtes champêtres* in manner of F. *Boucher and contemporaries.

marver. Polished iron or marble slab on which *gather of molten glass rolled, i.e. 'marvered'.

C. J. Mason & Co. Ironstone pastille burner, made in Staffordshire c1840.

Mary Gregory glass. Clear or coloured inexpensive glassware, such as jugs, decanters, and tableware, enamelled in opaque white with figures, usually children. During 19th century, quantities made in Bohemia. Named after enameller in Boston & Sandwich Glassworks, Massachusetts, who copied figures on similar glassware.

mascaron. Applied prunt in form of lion mask. Motif on stems of 16th and 17th century Venetian drinking glasses. Lion associated with St Mark, patron saint of Venice. Popular glass decoration during Renaissance period as *façon de Venise* spread. First used in England by G. *Verzelini.

Mashad carpets. *See* Meshed carpets.

Mason, George Miles (1789–1859) and Charles James (1791–1856). Staffordshire potters. Succeeded father, M. *Mason, in pottery at Lane Delph, trading as G. M. & C. J. Mason until 1829, then C. J. Mason & Co. Patent for *ironstone china taken out (1813) in name of C. J. Mason. Some earthenware and ironstone china transfer-printed in blue; patterns include willow pattern, and Chinese dragon, similar to that on Spode porcelain. Also made large vases (*c*5ft high), fireplaces, bed posts, and garden seats in ironstone china. Decoration in styles including Imari and revived rococo. After failure of firm (1848), C. J. worked at Longton (1851–54). Marks include MASONS PATENT IRONSTONE CHINA, impressed or printed in blue.

Mason, Miles (d 1822). Staffordshire potter. Worked on manufacture of porcelain at Liverpool and in Fenton, Staffordshire; later porcelain merchant in London. Established pottery at Lane Delph, making hard bone porcelain in style resembling New Hall; also produced earthenware. Retired in 1813; succeeded by sons, G. M. and C. J. *Mason. Marks include M. Mason or Miles Mason, impressed, sometimes with square seal, outlined with single line.

Miles Mason. Porcelain teapot, fluted and gilded; early 19th century.

Mason, William (1785–1855). Potter at Lane Delph, Staffordshire. Partner of father M. *Mason (1806–11). Made earthenware (1811–24) at Lane Delph; some transfer-printed in blue. Also porcelain dealer in Manchester *c*1815. Rare printed mark: W. Mason.

masonic flasks. American glass flasks blown in full-size, two-piece moulds. Produced widely *c*1815–30. Masonic emblem either on both sides, or on one side with different device, mainly American eagle, on reverse.

Massachusetts shelf clock or **box-on-box** or **half clock.** American shelf clock, made from late 18th century until *c*1825; probably introduced by A. and S. *Willard. Made in two separate parts (upper section sometimes narrower); average height, 30in. Painted tablet, mirror, or panelled door in base (tablet also in upper section on some models). *Kidney dial typical; other styles also used. Examples with broken-arch top; sometimes surmounted by fretwork, with pillars and finials. Later shelf clocks made mainly in Connecticut and New York.

Masonic flask. Made in Pittsburgh, Pennsylvania, c1820–30; light green glass. Pint capacity.

Massachusetts shelf clock. Example of this type with mahogany case; hood decorated with splat and three gilded finials. Made by Nathan Hale of Chelsea, Vermont, c1815. Height 2ft10in.

Massé, Jean-Baptiste (1687–1767). French painter, engraver, and miniaturist. Work includes enamel portraits of Louis XIV set in jewelled boxes.

master cup. *See* masterpiece.

master or **captain glass.** Largest of set of jelly or sweetmeat glasses made to stand on salver of glass or silver. Matches smaller glasses in style and decoration. Popular in mid 18th century America and England. Also refers to tall *bumping glass made as part of set for masonic lodges in late 17th and early 18th centuries. Used only on ceremonial occasions, e.g. election of Master or Grand Master.

masterpiece. Silver or gold object required by guild as qualification for status of master. Practice followed in England in late 16th century and in other European countries but only German masterpieces survive e.g. master cups including 17th century *columbine cups for Goldsmiths' Guild of Nuremberg.

master salt. *See* salt.

Matchbox. French, c1845, with *niello decoration. Length $2\frac{1}{2}$in.

Matting. Around body of flagon made by George Fox, London, 1867; also decorated with flat-chased scrolls and leaves. Height $9\frac{1}{4}$in.

matchbox. Usually made of silver, or occasionally pewter, from late 1830s. Usual form is small oblong case with hinged lid at one end; other end has row of thin parallel ridges for striking match.

matrix. Steel, hardstone, or glass seal intaglio-engraved with device for impressing on wax.

matting (in silver). Textured appearance given to metal surface with punch and hammer. Process dates from 16th century; much used in 17th and 18th centuries as primary ornament on hollow-ware. In early 19th century commonly used as background for cast or chased ornament.

Maximiliansschale. Silver-gilt container perhaps for sweetmeats, consisting of shallow, round bowl with foot-ring. Domed bottom of bowl ornamented with round concave bosses in ring around central medallion with arms of Philip the Fair, son of Emperor Maximilian I and Mary of Burgundy. Probably made in Burgundy at end of 15th century. Property of Historisches Museum, Berne, Switzerland.

Mazarin. Made in London, 1742, by John Le Sage. Length 16in.

Mayer, Franz Ferdinand (fl mid 18th century). enameller, also maker at Hanley from *c*1784 of cane-coloured stoneware, and engine-turned black basalt with close-textured body and bluish tint. Produced vases modelled with flowers in high relief, tea services commemorating victories of Nelson and, from *c*1790, very thinly potted cups. Cream-coloured earthenware includes fluted tea services with blue enamelled stripes, straight-sided teapots, and printed jugs with lion's head spouts. Marks: E.MAYER, or M (1790–1804).

Mayer, Franz Ferdinant (fl mid 18th century). Bohemian porcelain *Hausmaler* from Pressnitz. Either very prolific or head of substantial workshop. Used mainly outdated Meissen tablewares (e.g. plates with raised applied leaves and flowers, 1720s and 1730s). Subjects include *commedia dell'arte* scenes in landscape, mythological subjects, hunting scenes. Borders often feature four sprays of flowers on rich calligraphic scrollwork. Often signed work, Mayer P, Frank Mayr, or F. Mayer. Unsigned work hard to distinguish from that of F. J. *Ferner.

Mayer, Jean-Ghislain-Joseph (fl 1754–1825). Painter of porcelain and faience at *Tournai from 1754; chief painter from 1774. Noted for paintings of birds, after plates in Buffon's *Natural History* (published 1786), in rectangular panels surrounded by plain gilt lines against ground of *bleu de roi.*

Mayhew, John. *See* Ince, William.

Mazarin blue or **powder blue.** Chinese ceramic decoration: shade of glaze derived from cobalt oxide, used for decorating Ch'ing porcelain; deep purple, also known as *gros bleu* (term later used for Sèvres enamel ground colour). In K'ang Hsi period, colour sprayed or blown through gauze-covered bamboo tube on porcelain body before glazing. Slightly mottled effect known as powdered or *soufflé* blue. Both types called Mazarin by French buyers, after Cardinal Mazarin (1602–61). Specimens often mounted in France in ormolu.

mazarine blue. English ceramic ground colour: rich, uneven dark blue imitating Sèvres **gros bleu,* used at Chelsea from *c*1755, but particularly in gold anchor period. Version also adopted at Worcester, *c*1769.

mazarine or **dish-strainer.** 18th century British pierced silver or Sheffield plate dish; fitted into larger dish for serving boiled fish or other food requiring straining.

mazarlik carpets. *See* graveyard carpets.

mazer. 13th to 16th century British and European drinking vessel made of wood (usually maple) with gold, silver, or silver-gilt mounts. Metal band with moulded, chased, or engraved ornament at top of shallow wooden bowl (diameter *c*5–*c*9in.). Silver medallion or 'print' generally riveted to inside bottom of bowl in 14th and early 15th century examples. Occasionally also with cover and/or round foot.

Mazer. Parcel-gilt and maple-wood bowl; made in London, 1501, the earliest recorded marked mazer. Diameter $6\frac{3}{4}$in.

McIntyre, Samuel (1757–1811). American architect, cabinet maker, carver, and designer; worked in Salem, Massachusetts in neo-classical style. Carved motifs include cornucopias, fruit baskets, and grape clusters. Carved for E. and J. *Sanderson and for other Salem cabinet makers. Son, Samuel Field McIntyre, also carver. *Illustrations at* American Federal style, tall-boy.

M.E. *See* J.M.E.

mead glasses. Round-bowled drinking glasses. Early style similar to 15th century **Maigelein*. By 18th century, rummer-shaped with rudimentary stem or none, and cup bowl. Not made after 1760.

meander ornament. *See* key pattern.

measure. Container of stated capacity for ale, spirits, or wine, made of pewter from Middle Ages to 19th century, bronze or tin-lined copper from 18th century. Used in inns to ensure correct quantity of liquid sold, also in still-rooms, breweries, etc. Pewter measures of pottle (half-gallon), quart, and pint referred to in England from 14th century, but earliest surviving examples are from 16th century, in *baluster shape, which remained most common English type (with variation in details, e.g. style of thumbpiece on lidded examples). By 17th century, sizes ranged from gallon to half-gill and included *thirdendale. Crowned hR mark stamped on body or lid is normally assumed to indicate a guaranteed capacity, of standard set by Henry VIII. Later measures bear crowned WR and (rarely) crowned AR marks for William III and Anne, followed by GR and WR marks until 1830s. System appears to have lapsed from then until 1879, when similar crowned VR mark used on tavern mugs. Earthenware pots introduced as measures in 17th century, many bearing imitation of capacity seal, but giving inaccurate measures. Pewterers took steps to resolve situation with only partial success, as 'stone' pots with pewter lids became widely used in 18th century. From *c*1750, *Bristol or West Country measures made in pewter, later copper and bronze.

*Measures. Both pewter. Left: *baluster measure, c1700. Height 3¼in. Right: *tappit hen measure, Scottish, late 17th century.*

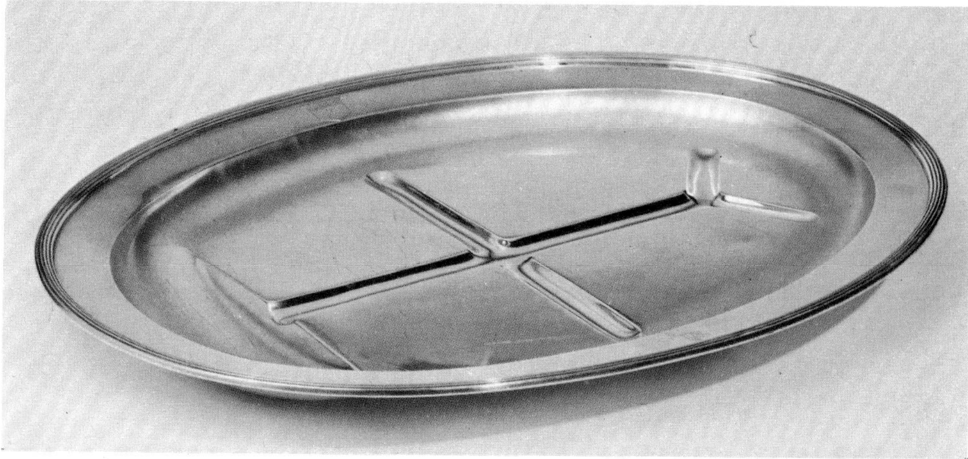

*Meat dish (*Venison dish). English, made in York by H. Prince, 1803. Weight 107oz.*

Scotland produced similar baluster measures with distinctively Scottish thumbpieces, also *pot-bellied measures (*c*1680–*c*1740), *tappit-hens (*c*1669–mid 19th century) and pear-shaped measures (early 19th century to *c*1860). *Thistle-shaped style (*c*1800–*c*1830) unpopular; few survive.

Irish pewter measures include *haystack and *noggin, both 19th century styles.

Dry goods measured in wide cylindrical bronze containers of standard capacity, made in sets normally bearing date and name of town to which they belonged.

meat dish. Large silver dish or platter used in Britain and Europe from Middle Ages for serving meat or fish. Earliest survivors mainly from 17th century. Usually oval; plain, flat border with decorated rim. Generally superseded by porcelain dishes in early 19th century except for ceremonial use. *See* venison dish.

medal cabinet, médaillier, or **coin cabinet.** Chest containing many shallow drawers used to hold and display medals or coins. Dates from 16th century France.

medallion. Oval or circular classical ornament containing portrait head, classical scene, flowers, etc. Used e.g. on Renaissance and neo-classical silver and furniture. In ceramics, small round or elliptical tablet with decorative motif painted or in relief; feature of Renaissance ornament. Later examples include porcelain plaques intended as furniture inlays made at Vincennes and Sèvres; reliefs made in *jasper ware by J. *Wedgwood I. Portrait medallions characteristic of **décor à guirlandes* associated with J. *Olerys in painting on faience.

medallion carpets. Very large, richly-coloured court carpets woven in north-west Persia during 16th and 17th centuries. Design strongly resembles book illumination styles, featuring complex central medallion, often with cartouches and pendants suspended from points, and ornamented corner pieces. Borders with austere, interlocking meanders. Design copied extensively in debased form in 18th, 19th, and 20th centuries.

medallion fan. Mid 18th century European fan; leaf painted with three medallion-shaped scenes; neo-classical decoration.

medallion-Ushak carpets. Very large, vivid-coloured 16th to 18th century *Ushak carpets. Field dominated by red and blue Persian-influenced medallion scheme: central vertical row of decorated, circular medallions with lobed contours; vertical row of ornate, flattened oval medallions with serrated contours on either side. Dark blue ground infilled with yellow blossom-and-vine trellis or three-corner flower diaper. Early rugs have Kufic borders; later ones cloud-band or stem scrolls with palmettes or rosettes. Widely exported and copied.

Medici manufactory. *See* Florentine tapestry.

medicine spoon. 18th and 19th century British silver spoon for administering medicine. Earliest spoons small, short-stemmed, or with different sized bowl at each end. In early 19th century, covered spoon with hinged lid and tubular handle used; sometimes called castor-oil spoon.

Medici porcelain. First known examples of European soft-paste porcelain; made in Florence, 1575–87, under auspices of Grand Duke Francesco I de 'Medici; *c*59 pieces known. Paste, containing sand and frit, rather thickly potted, covered with thick lead-glaze, sometimes liable to craze. Shapes usually resemble contemporary earthenware; some forms, e.g. ewers, inspired by bronze. Decoration, usually in underglaze blue, includes grotesques, coats of arms, flowers and foliage, and landscapes with animals or figures; style usually derived from 16th century Chinese porcelain; also from maiolica made at Urbino and contemporary Isnik pottery. Blue often greyish; sometimes deep blue outlined with

Medicine spoon. Victorian, 1842, by maker with initials E.E.

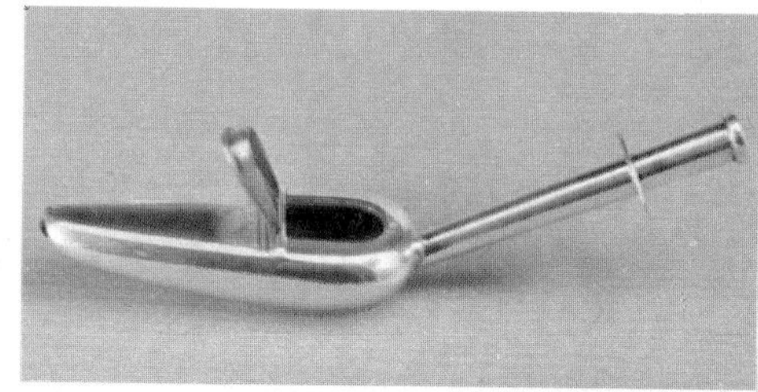

purple. Jug, only example with polychrome decoration, has grotesques in blue, green, and yellow, outlined in purple. Marked (1578–87) with dome of Florence cathedral in underglaze blue.

Medjid or **Mejidieh carpets.** Mid 19th century Turkish carpets named after Sultan Abd el Madyid, woven in Ghiordes, Kula, and Kirshehir. Design, influenced by European rococo, open floral patterns on white ground. Widely exported.

Mege, Antoine (fl late 18th century). French painter of faience at Moustiers, and at Aprey from 1776. Painted birds and landscapes with rococo scrolled borders.

Megri, Rhodes, or **Makri carpets.** Coarse-textured south-west Anatolian prayer rugs woven in Megri (now Fethiye) during 18th and 19th centuries. Usually small, with Turkish-knotted woollen pile on woollen foundation with undyed warp and red weft. Most important colours are blue, orange, yellow, and red. Thin column often bisects central field into two narrow mihrabs with dissimilar geometrically-stylized floral motifs, one always with vertical row of serrated lozenges linked by serrated band. Single mihrab fields often with hanging lamp under arch and candelabra at bottom of mihrab.

mei p'ing (Chinese, 'prunus vase'). Tall, baluster-shaped Chinese vase, narrow at bottom, rising to swelling curve at shoulder. Usually has short, narrow neck. Popular form from 13th to 18th century. Early versions lidded. *Illustration at* Ting-chou ware.

Meissen porcelain factory, Dresden, Germany. Royal Porcelain Manufacture (Königliche Porzellan Manufaktur), established at Meissen in 1710, by *Augustus the Strong, Elector of Saxony, after manufacture of *red stoneware and **Böttgerporzellan*, 1708–09, by J. F. *Böttger and E. W. *von Tschirnhaus. Factory under direction of Böttger until 1719. Early stoneware modelled after original Yi-Hsing ware, or from designs by J. J. Irminger, Saxon court silversmith. Colour varies from orange-red to dark brown, surface polished to high gloss; lower fired examples covered with black glaze. Rare figures usually undecorated, though enamel colours used in one or two cases. Some modelled after Chinese figures, religious subjects taken from sculpture. Production of stoneware seems to have continued until *c*1730.

**Böttgerporzellan* made from 1709, with use of Saxon deposits of kaolin, developed in following years until hard-paste of exceptional whiteness produced. Work includes hexagonal tea-caddies, beakers and cups, bowls and octagonal sugar basins. Gilding frequently used; relief decoration, enamel painting and gilding often occur together. Many figures modelled after those in stoneware; series of **magots* and *Callot figures also produced, often with gilding. Experiments by D. *Köhler in use of underglaze blue for decoration in Chinese manner successful by 1720, when examples exhibited at Leipzig fair, although blue-and-white porcelain never produced in large quantities; surviving examples include vases in double gourd shape. After death of Böttger (1719), factory reorganized; many workmen dismissed, or left voluntarily, despite threats of punishment for desertion.

Meissen. Porcelain figures. Left: Harlequin with a Bird, *commedia dell'arte *figure, modelled by J. F. *Eberlein, c1743; height 5in. Right: Harlequin with a* Passglas, *modelled by J. J. *Kändler, 1741; height 5in.*

J. G. *Herold joined factory in 1720 from Vienna; introduced *chinoiserie* decoration, enclosed by cartouches with strapwork, scrolls and flowers, painted at first in iron-red and gold with small patches of *Böttger lustre; red gradually replaced by pinkish purple. Ground decorated with *indianische Blumen*. Even in early days work divided among several painters. Kakiemon decoration copied on e.g bowls, saké bottles and hexagonal vases, by A. F. *von Löwenfinck and J. E. *Stadtler, as well as Herold. Vases made for personal use of Augustus the Strong, sometimes as gifts, marked with AR (Augustus Rex), now rare on genuine pieces, often forged in 19th century, notably in Dresden. Coloured grounds introduced in 1720s (yellow, green, sea-green, lilac, pink) used with reserve panels painted with *chinoiseries*, *harbour scenes, or river and seascapes (sometimes attributed to J. G. *Heintze). J. G. *Kirchner, after short employment in 1727, returned (1730–33) as modeller. Work includes large animal figures for collection in Japanese Palace; design limited by technical difficulty in firing heavy pieces of porcelain paste; some smaller figures also produced.

J. J. *Kändler appointed modeller in 1731, succeeded Kirchner as chief modeller in 1733; his influence eclipsed that of Herold and decorators in general. At first, modelling of large animals continued, using zoological specimens provided by Augustus the Strong as source material; most left in white. Smaller figures of animals, including birds and hunting groups produced until late 1740s. Human figures notably inspired by *commedia dell'arte*, or by fashionable contemporary courtiers (crinoline groups); other models include beggar musicians. After death of Augustus in 1733, Count H. *von Brühl appointed director; *Swan service and *Plat de ménage commissioned by him in late 1730s follow *Sulkowski service (1735) as examples of tableware modelled in baroque style by Kändler. Some painting of 1730s in styles developed earlier; C. F. *Herold specialised in *chinoiseries* and harbour scenes introduced by J. G. Herold. Armorial tea services possibly painted by B. G. *Häuer, also credited with series depicting Saxon miners. Attribution of painting confused by initial H of Herolds, Haüer, Heintze, J. C. *Horn. **Zwiebelmuster* (*c*1730), **saxe ombré* (1732), etc., introduced in this period; hunting scenes gained in popularity; battle scenes, and landscapes after J-A. *Watteau appear from 1738. Monochrome painting increasingly used. Some modification of shapes; teapots lose pear-shape, straight-sided bowls and tea bowls become shallower and more rounded, tea-caddies more often rectangular and shouldered, sugar basins now frequently cylindrical, and saucers deeper; flower finial often found. Development of **deutsche Blumen* in painting accompanied by modelling of *flowers in porcelain, and shapes based on plant forms, e.g. leaf dishes, tureens in form of vegetables. **Ozier* pattern, at first heavily moulded, becomes lighter, used on lobed or fluted shapes; plates modelled by J. F. *Eberlein often have pierced border, from 1742.

In 1750s, ground colours often broken up by diaper pattern, e.g. scales or chequers; birds, both naturalistic and fanciful become popular in decoration. Figures modelled after engravings include series, Cris de Paris in early 1740s and *c*1752, and *c*1748, miners. With P. *Reinicke, Kändler worked on series of *commedia dell'arte* characters; *c*1744 another series modelled by Reinicke alone, at same time series of Turks also taken from engravings. Figures by Eberlein include series of gods and goddesses, and Seasons. F. E. *Meyer collaborated on series of *chinoiserie* groups, *Les Délices d'Enfance*, after F. *Boucher. Pastoral figures became popular in 1750s; influence of Kändler gradually diminished. *Galanterien* produced throughout 18th century include stick-handles and boxes; many decorated by C. F. Herold, J. M. *Heinrici and J. G. *Wagner. From 1730s, scent bottles often modelled in form of figures. Knife and fork handles have careful miniature painting. Undecorated ware seems to have been available in quantity for about ten years, from *c*1735; though *Hausmaler* had been painting Meissen porcelain from early 1720s. Colours used distinguish work from high-quality decoration of factory; workmen include J. *Aufenwerth, F. J. *Ferner, *Lauche, J. F. *Metzch, I. *Preissler, B. *Seuter. Flower decoration of tableware became more stylized from *c*1745, after *c*1750, painting on ornamental ware often in style of J-A. *Watteau, D. *Teniers or F. *Boucher. Pink or blue monochrome used in imitation of Sèvres, *c*1747–55.

Seven Years' War (1756–63) caused economic difficulty. Frederick the Great commissioned snuff-boxes and some table services; *Mosaïk* border pattern introduced from Berlin. In 1765, C. W. E. *Dietrich became art adviser. M–V. *Acier modeller (1764–99); work includes allegorical groups of children. Products influenced by work of other factories, especially Sèvres.

Under administration of C. *Marcolini, neo-classical style more prominent; copies made of Wedgwood *jasper ware. Biscuit figures modelled in imitation of sculpture. Tableware often decorated in blue *Zwiebelmuster.* In 19th century, models of 18th century adapted to current taste; allegorical figures and crinoline groups often appear; also mirrors, candelabra, vases, etc. heavily encrusted with flowers. Production continues.

First European factory consistently to mark products. Marks include imitation Chinese marks (1720–25), Caduceus mark (from *c*1722), KPF or KPM (Königliche Porzellan Fabrik or Manufaktur), MPM (Meissner Porzellan Manufaktur), all 1723–24. Crossed swords adopted 1724, in blue or black enamel; from then variations occur in underglaze blue. Palace marks include K.H.C., Königliche Hof-Conditorei (Royal pantry or confectionery – K.H.C.W. refers to Warsaw), KHK, court kitchen. Painters' initials and inventory marks also occur. Ware sold undecorated has mark cancelled with scratches. Factory painters who signed work include: Haüer, J. G. and C. F. Herold, C. C. *Hunger, J. J. Kändler, C. D. *Busch and F. J. *Ferner. *Illustrations also at* J. F. Böttger, J. F. Eberlein, German snuff-boxes, red stoneware.

Meissonier, Juste-Aurèle (*c*1693–1750). Italian-born, Paris-based designer, architect, goldsmith, and artist. One of earliest and most influential exponents of flamboyant rococo design, *le genre pittoresque.* Became *Dessinateur du Cabinet* to Louis XV, 1726. Pattern-books, most important survival of his work, include designs for candlesticks, tureens, épergnes, etc.

Mejidieh carpets. *See* Medjid carpets.

Melas or **Milas carpets.** Soft and pliable, small south-west Anatolian prayer rugs woven in Melas from 17th century. Design influenced by *Ushak and *Ghiordes prayer rugs. Broad multi-fold border with stylized floral motifs; long, narrow central field with extremely short mihrab, diamond-shaped arch, and panel above arch often infilled with rows of stylized flowers or leaves on light ground. Rust-red and olive-yellow dominant colours. Also 'striped Melas' carpets: pattern consists almost entirely of concentric borders; central field without niche, reduced to small narrow panel.

Melayer or **Malayer carpets.** Moderate size, north-west Persian carpets with long, coarse to medium Turkish-knotted woollen pile on cotton foundation. Characteristic 19th century all-over

Melas. Prayer rug. Turkish, c1800. 5ft8in.×4ft.
Left:
Juste-Aurèle Meissonier. Three-branched candelabrum from design by Meissonier, c1734; made in Paris by Claude Duvivier.

pattern of zig-zagged diamond medallions on two-tone natural camel grounds, often with small-scale boteh background pattern and broad, camel-coloured edging around border.

Melchior, Johann Peter (1742–1825). German sculptor and porcelain modeller. Part of apprenticeship served in France. Worked at Höchst as *Modellmeister* (1767–79); many models attributed to him by factory records; individual neo-classical style showed French influence. At Frankenthal (1779–93), produced figures of children, distinguished by 'sentimental' treatment; also at *Nymphenburg (1797–1822), where many models made in biscuit.

melon bulb. *See* bulb.

melon cup. 16th and 17th century British and European gold, silver, or silver-gilt *standing cup with melon-shaped bowl and cover (upper part of melon generally forms cover); spiral plant stalk or tree trunk usually forms stem. First made in Germany.

memento mori watch. Style of *form watch produced mainly in England in early 17th century and revived during 19th century. Movement is mounted in silver or occasionally rock-crystal case resembling skull or coffin.

Mendlesham chair. Chair of Windsor type, with turned legs, four back-rails, and solid elm seat (remainder of fruitwood). Made in England from *c*1800.

Mene, Pierre-Jules (1810–70). French sculptor; one of *les *Animaliers.* Pupil of René Compaire; work shown at Salon, 1838–79. Produced many of own bronzes, but many also re-issued by founders such as F. *Barbedienne.

Pierre-Jules Mene. Bronze of an Irish setter, c1840, signed. Height 6in.

Mennecy (Seine-et-Oise). French faience and soft-paste porcelain factory established (1734) in Paris and managed by F. *Barbin; transferred to Mennecy in 1748 because of privilege granted to Vincennes. From 1765, owned by J. *Jullien and S. *Jacques; worked together with *Sceaux factory until 1772. Early porcelain has very brilliant, slightly uneven glaze; decoration, Chinese and Japanese figures, and Kakiemon patterns painted in colours including brown-toned red and green enamel; also *lambrequins* and relief decoration of prunus blossom, left white. Later work in style of Vincennes, although edges were outlined in colours (e.g. characteristic rose-pink) instead of gilt. Tableware sometimes has spiral reeding (e.g. custard cups) or basket-work moulding. Ornamental ware produced, often with daisy-like flowers in applied relief. Figures include orientals, and groups of children after F. *Boucher. Some models by N-F. *Gauron (from *c*1753) or C. and J. *Mô. Dwarfs and *commedia dell'arte* characters also occur. Toys, including snuff-boxes and scent bottles, also knife handles, attributed to Mennecy but usually unmarked.

Mennecy. Porcelain sucrier *and cover decorated with naturalistically painted flowers,* c*1755.*

Factory closed 1773 in favour of new works at *Bourg-la-Reine. Mark: DV in red, black, blue, or incised.

Mennicken family (fl 1566–1646). German stoneware potters and relief modellers working first at Raeren, later at Grenzhausen in Westerwald. J. *Emens noted member of family; others usually included E (Emens) in their marks and omitted M (Mennicken), e.g. GE (1578–85), PE (*c*1585), EE (*c*1585), WE (*c*1600). I. B. Mennicken, leading Raeren potter of late 16th century, first of several to use IM mark.

menuisier. In medieval French, term for carpenter and joiner. In 17th and 18th century France, furniture maker specializing in carved and turned decoration on furniture such as chairs *cf ébéniste.*

merchant's mark. Mark sometimes struck on Dutch silverware, in 18th and 19th centuries, showing name of vendor, usually in full.

mercury gilding. *See* gilding.

mercury twist. Form of *air twist stem with brilliant silvery appearance in twist pattern. Appears in English wine glasses *c*1760. Achieved with glass of high lead content to give greater brilliance and by enlarging and/or flattening twist to corkscrew form. *Illustration at* English wine glasses.

merese or **collar knop.** Flat, disc-shaped *knop or knops in stem of wine glass; useful for covering joins at foot and base of bowl. Appears in most decorative form in typical 17th century Nuremberg goblet.

méridienne. French 18th century day-bed with one or two scrolled ends. May be upholstered and with carved or pierced frame.

Merry Man plates. Octagonal English delftware plates made at Lambeth *c*1680–*c*1740; thickly potted. Each plate bears phrase from poem: 'What is a merry man? / Let him do what he can / To entertain his guests / With wine and merry jests / But if his wife doth frown / All merriment goes down.' Inscriptions, with varied spelling, in blue surrounded by blue decoration including scrolls, garlands, faces, and heraldic animals, on creamy glaze. Similar plates numbered 1–6, each inscribed with one line of verse, sometimes in English, had been made in Delft in early 17th century. *Illustration at* Lambeth delftware.

Mesch or **Mes** family. Dutch potters at Delft. Owned factories, Fortune (1661–1724), The Heart (1661–1706), The Three Wooden Shoes (1670–1840). Produced peacock plates in blue and polychrome, blue, orange, and brown.

Meshed or **Mashed carpets.** Large, purple-rose tinted, east Persian carpets with woollen pile on cotton foundation, broad borders and numerous guard stripes; woven in and around holy city of Meshed. Both Turkish and Persian knots used, often mixed together or combined with native *jufti knots. Carpets using only Turkish knots known as Turkbaffs; those with only Persian knots as Farsibaffs. From late 16th century herati or boteh field patterns with herati borders. From 19th century fine medallion carpets woven in various sizes for export. Pattern has 16-point central star-medallion with pendants on monochrome or richly-flowered ground.

metal. Glass in molten state.

metal mount. *See* mount.

Metal Pot, The (De Metalen Pot). Delft factory (1638–1757) owned by L. *Cleffius, 1666–91, then by L. *van Eenhoorn, 1691–1721, succeeded by widow. Produced *delft noir*, including figures.

metal-spinning. Method of shaping silver and other soft metals, using lathe, worked by treadle from late 18th century, by steam power from *c*1820. Wooden core ('chuck') is carved into shape; the flat metal is rotated at high speed and forced to cover it. Used for small hollow-ware, e.g. teapots, bowls; and for details, e.g. spouts.

metropolitan slipwares. English earthenware vessels of orange red clay with trailed white slip decoration, made in 17th century, mainly near Harlow, Essex. Dishes narrow-rimmed, shallow, 6–15in. diameter, decorated with quatrefoil motifs and herring-bone pattern; drinking vessels or jugs with Puritan inscriptions in slip-trailed capital letters.

Metzsch, Johann Friedrich (d 1766). German porcelain painter, head of decorating workshop and school at Bayreuth (*c*1735–51). Later at Fürstenberg. Signed work includes a decorated Chinese piece, but most unpainted wares came from Meissen, perhaps also Vienna.

Meyer, Christoffel Jansz (fl 17th century). Dutch glass engraver from The Hague. Associated with *hatched technique. Specialized in allegorical subjects on tall flute glasses, usually signed CJM or CFM.

Meyer, Friedrich Elias (1723–85). German porcelain modeller at Meissen (1746–61), *Modellmeister* at Berlin (1761–85). Figures similar to those of J. J. *Kändler, but identified by small heads and long limbs; typical pieces include shepherds and gardeners, mounted on arched, three-footed base (*c*1762). Also made glazed white porcelain reliefs (1765), rococo mirror frames, **Galanterien*, biscuit portrait reliefs and busts of Frederick the Great, also Voltaire, etc. (*c*1780).

Meyer, Jeremiah (1735–89). German-born English miniaturist, pupil of C. F. *Zincke; worked briefly in studio of Sir Joshua Reynolds. Miniaturist to Queen Charlotte; enamel painter to George III. Early work reminiscent of B. *Lens. Among miniaturists who developed use of ivory. *Illustration at* miniatures.

Meyer, Wilhelm Christian (1726–86). German porcelain modeller. Brother of F. E. *Meyer. Style similar, but closer to neo-classical forms. Influenced by French sculptors in Berlin. Mythological and allegorical subjects include Mars and History (unpainted). With brother, modelled (1770–72) large table centrepiece for Catherine the Great.

mezza maiolica. Term formerly applied to earthenware made in Italy from which maiolica derived, although early pottery such as *green and purple ware already contained tin in white glaze. Also applied to *sgraffiato* ware with decoration incised in slip under lead-glaze, made e.g. at *Bologna and *Padua. *cf halb-Fayence.*

Michel, Claude. *See* Clodion.

microscope. Used from early 17th century, first with single lens (simple microscope), usually mounted in frame of wood, ivory, or brass with clip, needle point, etc., for holding object under study. Some late 17th century examples have movable plate with holes of varying size to adjust amount of light passing through lens. Holland main centre of production. From *c*1660, makers experimented with spherical lenses, some only pin-head size (recorded in use by R. *Hooke and C. *Huygens). Instruments with several lenses (compound microscopes) probably first made in Italy *c*1615, with two lenses in wooden mounts at end of cardboard tubes, one sliding inside other. Huygens (*c*1655) and Hooke (*c*1660) made similar types. Early development limited by poor quality of glass and difficulty of polishing lenses. Forms of instrument made after 1700 include those hinged for viewing at different angles, but standard type until *c*1740, devised by Edmund Culpeper, has lower end of larger tube supported by three legs above stage containing object viewed, this mounted on three further legs above base; adjustable mirror to reflect light added in later examples. Tubes often covered in leather or shagreen; legs or pillars of wood, later brass. Modified form has single tripod stand with object stage set half-way between base and lower lens. Maker, John Cuff, introduced type *c*1743 with tube and stage sliding on square vertical pillar and rack-and-pinion focus adjustment. Basis for all further development, with many examples produced from *c*1750, often of elaborate form, e.g. by G. *Adams and A. *Magny. Solar or projection microscope, popular from *c*1740, horizontal, with mirror to reflect sunlight on to object; image cast on screen or wall of room. Lucernal microscope, developed *c*1800, projects image on to ground-glass screen.

Miers, John (1756–1821). English silhouettist, working in Leeds, Yorkshire, from 1781;

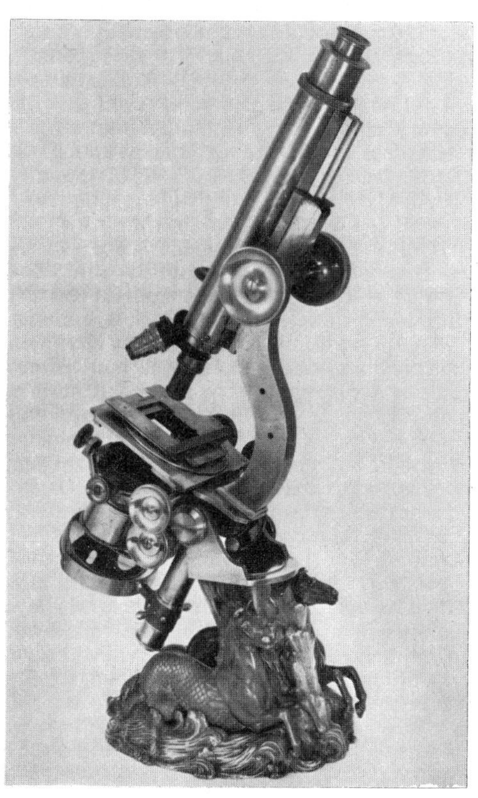

Microscope. Monocular, 19th century, made in Manchester by Aronsberg & Co. Brass on silvered metal and bronze base. Height 2ft2in.

John Miers. Silhouette, c1812, of Cassandra Austen (Jane Austen's sister). Painted on card.

assistants included J. *Thomason. Originated technique of painting on plaster of Paris composition. Silhouettes in black; pigment thinned to diaphanous grey for hair and drapery. From 1783, used reducing instrument to produce miniature profiles on ivory; visited other northern towns. In 1788, started studio as profile painter and jeweller in The Strand, London. Likenesses include Sarah Siddons (1784) and Robert Burns (1786). Succeeded in business by son William and J. *Field.

*Johann Mildner. Two tumblers and *carafe all decorated with gilt and enamelled plaques of the arms of Fügner. Height of carafe 7in.*

Millefiori *canes set into clear glass vase. Made at *Baccarat, c1850: sides and foot also engraved with star patterns. Height 5in.*

Migeon Pierre, II (1701–58). French *ébéniste*, working in Louis XV style. Received royal commissions from 1740; made furniture for toilette of Mme de Pompadour. Used lacquer, marquetry, and veneering. Son, Pierre III, inherited workshop and kept it until 1775, but more interested in selling than making furniture.

Mignot, Daniel (fl late 16th and early 17th centuries). French engraver and jewellery designer working in Paris and Augsburg. Designs published between 1596 and 1616 characterized by symmetrical, formal arrangements of gems against gold ground. Reverse side of jewels (e.g. *aigrette, pendant) ornamented with enamel. Also produced engraved designs for enamelled miniature cases.

mihrab. Prayer niche or arch in mosque to show Moslem worshipper direction of Mecca, which he faces, kneeling. Also occurs as primary motif in *prayer rug, differing in form according to region. *Illustration at* Melas carpets.

Milan (Lombardy), Italy. Maiolica believed made in late 16th century; no examples identified. By 1745, factory established by F. *Clerici; employee, P. *Rubati, started rival factory in 1756. Another factory, established at Santa Cristina in 1770, lasted only five years.

Milas carpets. *See* Melas carpets.

Milchglas or **Porzellanglas.** *Opaque-white glass, made mainly in 18th century Bohemia using tin oxide as opacifying agent. Called *Porcelleinglas* at Potsdam Glass Works.

Mildner, Johann Jacob (1763–1808). Austrian glass maker from Gutenbrunn. Highly successful exponent of **Zwischengoldglas* technique, e.g. tumblers decorated with medallions of gold or silver leaf, sometimes also including wheel or diamond-point engraving.

Miles. *See* Solon, Marc-Louis.

millefiori (Italian, 'thousand flowers'). Canes of coloured glass rods arranged in bundles so that cross section forms pattern; reduced to design in miniature when bundle is heated and drawn out thinly. Slices of *millefiori* canes used in *bead manufacture, and, set out side by side and fused, were moulded into hollow-ware (bowls, etc.). To produce flower pattern, rods of one colour were cased several times in different coloured glass and *marvered on a corrugated slab while still ductile, resulting in star-pattern cross section. Technique of ancient origin, revived in 16th century Venice. Successfully reapplied in 19th century French and English *paperweights. *Illustration also at* Stourbridge glass.

mille-fleurs tapestry. 15th and early 16th century floral tapestry design. Forerunner of **verdure* tapestry. Distinguished by field (often dark blue) strewn with numerous, meticulously drawn tiny flowers, bushes, and flowering shrubs. Some armorial and figure tapestries with scenes of chivalric life. Particular attention given to surface detail, texture of materials, etc. Figures conventionalized. Tapestries once thought work of itinerant weavers in Loire valley; now attributed to Brussels. Best known examples, *Lady with the Unicorn tapestries.

Mills, Nathaniel (fl 1826–50). English silversmith who made boxes and vinaigrettes in Birmingham. Boxes were oblong, decorated with engine-turned panels and views of buildings in high relief.

minai ware. *Seljuq pottery made in Sava, Kashan, and, notably, Rayy, Persia. Biscuit ware painted with pale blue, purple, and green underglaze background to enamel decoration applied over white or blue glaze. Enamel colours include black, brown, red, and white; gilding also used. Hunting scenes, historical, or contemporary figure subjects, and inscriptions feature in decoration.

Mines Royal. *See* latten.

ming-ch'i (Chinese, 'funerary wares'). Term strictly confined to objects made specially for tomb burial. Made from variety of materials including bronze, silver, jade, wood, straw, and pottery. Objects familiar in everyday life buried in tombs to satisfy spirits of dead. Shang and early Chou ming-ch'i consisted of inanimate pieces; for company, dead received human sacrifices and offerings of horses and other livestock. In late Chou times, representations of humans and animals appear in place of live sacrifice, and, by Han dynasty, ming-ch'i almost entirely in form of pottery models: farmyards with animals, homes and pavilions, cooking stones, gaming boards, attendants, acrobats, dancers, and horses. Such objects mainly made of unglazed terracotta, but some examples glazed in basic green or brown. Ming ch'i tradition continued through Six dynasties and Sui periods, reaching climax with opulence of *polychrome wares of T'ang dynasty, including models of foreign warriors and merchants, camels, ferocious tomb guardians, ladies with pet birds, hunters with falcons, and horses from Ferghana. Pieces range in size from a few inches to several feet.

Ming dynasty (1368–1644). Chinese period named after word meaning 'clear' or 'bright'. Important for development of *Ching-tê-chên as production centre of ceramics. Imperial factories founded there in 1369. Porcelain replaced stoneware as main medium: manufacture of Sung celadons and Chün wares discontinued. Blue-and-white porcelain predominant (imported cobalt ores used); some underglaze copper-red and polychrome decoration. Potters believed distortions of shape, imperfections of glazes, aesthetically unimportant: characteristic of work. Ceramic skill evident. Reigns of *Hsüan Tê, *Ch'êng Hua, *Chia Ching, and *Wan-li produced fine work. *Illustrations at* an hua, Imperial yellow, ley vase, Swatow, tou-tsai, wu-ts'ai.

Ming fa-hua. *See* san ts'ai ware.

miniature clocks. Developed in Germany from 1550 in form of tabernacle clock, later many standard types also made in miniature, e.g. lantern, carriage, and some Dutch clocks.

miniature painting or **limning.** Art, predominantly of portraiture, developed in 16th century from traditions of manuscript illumination (e.g. J. and F. *Clouet) and medals. Italian *rametti*, small portraits in oil on metal, produced from *c*1540, derive from easel and panel painting.

In England, visits by H. *Holbein the Younger stimulated fashion for miniatures, already introduced by G. *Horenbout; first notable native artists were N. and L. *Hilliard. Early miniatures in body colour on vellum applied to card. Leading 16th and 17th century British miniaturists included I. *Oliver (who introduced Venetian influences), P. *Oliver, J. *Hoskins, S. and A. *Cooper, M. and C. *Beale. Style of English miniatures in 17th century influenced by visits of Anthony van Dyck. *Plumbago miniatures produced from mid 17th to mid 18th centuries. Enamel painting, developed, e.g. by J. *Toutin, applied to miniatures by J. *Petitot,

*Ming-ch'i. Guardian lion, *Six Dynasties period; grey earthenware painted with red pigment.*

Right:
*Miniatures. English, late 18th and early 19th centuries. Left: unknown young man by W. *Wood, dated 1807. Right: Joanna Plimer, the artist's daughter by A. *Plimer. Top: unknown man by J. *Bogle of Scotland, signed and dated 1793. Bottom: unknown old lady by J. *Meyer.*

*Huaud family, C. *Boit, and C. F. *Zincke. In early 18th century, R. *Carriera introduced ivory as ground for miniatures, probably after Venetian use of ivory for oval snuff-boxes. Enamel and ivory miniatures dominant 18th and 19th century forms, often incorporated in snuff-boxes and other objects of vertu.

Most notable period of French miniatures was 18th century, when main painters included J-A. and L-A. *Arlaud, P-A. *Baudoin, J-H. *Fragonard, P. A. *Hall, J-E. *Liotard, etc. Late 18th and 19th century miniaturists included F. *Dumont, J-B-J. *Augustin, J-B. *Isabey, J-U. *Guérin, and D. *Saint. In Germany and Austria 18th and 19th century miniaturists included F. H. *Füger, D. *Chodowiecki and M. M. *Daffinger; in Scandinavia, C. *Höyer, C. *Hornemann, and A. *Möller. In England, influence of R. Carriera felt through B. *Lens III, who pioneered use of ivory. Among most notable English miniature painters in 18th century, when form most popular, were R. *Cosway, G. *Englehart, O. *Humphry, J. *Meyer, A. *Plimer, and J. *Smart. British enamel painters included W. *Prewitt, R. *Crosse, and H. *Bone (with his family continued to mid 19th century). Among last miniaturists in early 19th century were J. C. D. *Englehart, W. *Essex, W. J. *Newton, and A. *Robertson.

American miniatures widely produced from mid 18th century, e.g. by J. S. *Copley, C. W. and J. *Peale, H. *Inman, J. W. *Jarvis, T. *Sully, and J. *Trumbull; finest American miniaturist possibly the short-lived E. G. *Malbone.

Introduction of daguerreotype led to decline of portrait miniature in mid 19th century.

miniature silver or **silver toys.** Miniature items of domestic plate made in England mainly in late 17th and 18th centuries e.g. by D. *Clayton. Purpose unknown: perhaps samples, fittings for dolls' houses. Well made; reproduce contemporary styles on miniature scale, e.g. tea, coffee, and chocolate services, kettles, candlesticks, cups, mugs, etc. Many silver toys, including furniture and stage-coaches, made in Holland from 18th century; later English examples rare. *See also* toys.

Miniature silver. English, all by George Manjoy. Pair of James II candlesticks, fluted with plain flanges and waxpans, 1686, fully marked; height 1¾in. Centre: Queen Anne two-handled porringer and cover, 1710; no mark on cover; height 1⅜in. Above: James II sconce, repoussé *cartouche backplate, 1685; height 3¼in.*

*Herbert Minton. *Majolica plate, earthenware, designed by A. W. N. *Pugin, c1850. Diameter 13½in.*

Minton, Herbert (1793–1858). Son of T. *Minton; succeeded father in 1836; ran business in partnership, trading as Minton & Boyle. Table services marked M & B with pattern name. From 1841, firm traded as Herbert Minton & Company; from 1845 as Minton & Co. Products mainly inspired by Sèvres *revived rococo style. Figures and groups usually unmarked. *Parian ware made from 1847, *majolica from 1851. Succeeded by partners and sons. *Illustration also at pâte-sur-pâte.*

Minton, Thomas (1765–1836). Staffordshire potter and engraver. Pupil of T. *Turner; employed as engraver by J. *Spode I in London warehouse. By 1793, making blue transfer-printed earthenware. Produced porcelain from *c*1798, including stipple printed designs, monochrome landscapes, and Japan patterns; also used gilding on dark blue ground, and panels of brightly painted flowers. Retired in 1821; firm then run by sons. Present company formed in 1883. No marks on early products. Marks from 1822 include: two elongated Ss crossed over M in blue enamel; M in underglaze blue; FELSPAR PORCELAIN around spiked circular pattern enclosing date and M, printed. From 1842, also with yearly marks impressed.

minute hand. Earliest clocks with separate indicator for minutes date from late 16th century, some with each minute marked on dial; usage became general only from mid 17th century with greater accuracy resulting from introduction of *pendulum and *balance spring. Hour hand still used alone until *c*1780, mainly on clocks by provincial makers, or those used chiefly as alarm clocks.

minute repeater. Repeating clocks or watch sounding strokes for hour, quarters, and minute.

Miotti Glasshouse. Venetian glasshouse established at Murano, Venice, by Miotti family in early 17th century; at first specialized in *aventurine glass, supposedly discovered by accidental addition of copper filings to pot of molten *metal. In 18th century, under direction of Vincenzo Miotti, produced porcelain-like *opaque-white glass, e.g. table service made for Horace Walpole, decorated with Italian views painted in red enamel (1741). Polychrome decoration also popular feature.

Mir carpets. Trade name for early 19th century west Persian carpets with lustrous, longish, Persian-knotted pile. Characteristic, all-over pattern has rows of small botehs, often on madder ground. Border has wavy trellis with blue botehs on natural ground. Turkish knot later used.

mirror. Until 17th century, mirror surface made of polished speculum or bronze; mirror glass backed with amalgam of mercury and tin developed in Venice in mid 16th century; became increasingly common in Europe, Britain, and Colonial America during 17th century. Restoration mirror frames often ornately carved with cherubs, flowers, swags, etc., or decorated with marquetry veneer, lacquer, or needlework. In 18th century, *pier glasses popular; early examples made from more than one piece of glass to achieve required length, but after *c*1750, long, single pieces available. Vertically rectangular mirrors, with paintings above glass area, also date from early 18th century. *See* bilbao, cheval glass, constitution mirror, convex mirror, overmantel mirror, pier glass, toilet mirror.

mirror-black. Black glaze with bluish or brownish tints; colour derived from iron and cobaltiferous manganese ore. Among high-temperature glazes developed for use on Chinese porcelain in K'ang Hsi period. Sometimes overpainted with designs in gold.

mirror clock. Clock with mirror as prominent feature of case, particularly Connecticut looking-glass clock introduced by C. *Jerome to compete with *pillar-and-scroll clock.

Mitchell, John (fl mid 18th century). Staffordshire potter; made salt-glaze at Hill Top, Burslem. *A. Wood block cutter, 1743–50.

Mô, Christophe and Jean or Jean-Baptiste (fl late 18th century). French modellers or repairers, brothers. Worked at Mennecy (Christophe 1761–68, Jean from 1768). Jean worked at Bourg-la-Reine from 1773. Modelled figures. Work by Christophe marked DV MO includes relief portrait of Louis XV, and group of boys with bird cage. Jean's work, marked J. Mo, includes biscuit figure of Boy with Telescope, and glazed and coloured drummer. Mark B R Mo appears on large group of musicians from Bourg-la-Reine.

mocha ware. English pottery decorated with markings of pigment, usually brown, sometimes blue, green, or black, mixed with strong acid infusion of tobacco or hops, in feathery plant forms; named after similarly marked mocha-stone quartz. Decoration applied from 1780s; moved with blow-pipe or trickled over surface; usually accompanied by horizontal bands of light-coloured slip on mugs and jugs. At first in cream-coloured earthenware; later also in pearlware (from *c*1820) and stoneware (from *c*1830). Much produced in Staffordshire and north of

Mocha ware. Jug, probably made in Staffordshire, c1830–40.

England until late 19th century, often for use in taverns.

Modellmeister (German, 'chief modeller'). Highest technical position in porcelain factory; theoretically parallel with **Obermaler*, probably more influential in practice.

Mogan or **Moghan rugs.** South-east Caucasian rugs from Mogan steppe. Closely resembles *Talish carpet in structure, design, and colouring. Distinguishing features include red grounds, stepped border motifs; field patterns of two vertical rows of large, multi-coloured stepped polygons, or all-over repetitive small medallion and blossom-head motif.

Mogul, Mughal, or **Indo-Persian Mogul carpets.** Carpets produced in India at height of Mogul rule (1556–1658). Knotted carpet weaving introduced to India from Persia by Shah Akbar (1556–1605). Royal factory established in Lahore (1580), employing Persian craftsmen; by *c*1600, factories also flourished at Agra, Fathpur, and probably Delhi. Industry supported and encouraged by two succeeding Mogul princes, Jahangir (1605–28) and Shah Jahan (1628–58). Persian-knotted carpets made in finest wool (e.g. from Kashmir), and silk, sometimes with gold and silver brocading. Finest examples rivalled contemporary Persian carpets, though colours less fast. 800–1200 knots to 1in. used, giving lush, velvety texture. Early patterns based entirely on Herat and Kirman models, but recognizably Indian style soon emerged. Mogul flower carpets probably made in Fathpur in reign of Shah Akbar; completely naturalistic, asymmetrical flower patterns contrast sharply with imaginative Persian treatment of same subject. Mogul animal carpets, probably of later date, also wholly naturalistic: landscaped scenes with elephants, leopards, gazelles, etc., full of life and energy; motifs balanced but asymmetrical. Contrast with abstract Persian approach again extremely marked. Wine-red ground (unlike any Persian shade) occurring in Mogul carpets is further distinguishing characteristic.

Mogul prayer rugs generally lighter colour than Persian, with distinctive use of pink, especially for contrast and outline. Weaving technique of best Indian examples (using 702–1258 knots to 1in.) finest employed anywhere. Wool, wool and silk, and silk used, the last sometimes on cotton warp. All-silk rugs probably made in reign of Shah Jahan.

*Mogul carpet. Crimson field woven with large sprays of flowers including carnations, lilies, narcissi, and tulips. Main border with *herati design in crimson. 17th century, from reign of Shah Jahan. 14ft × 6ft7in.*

Mohammedan wares. *See* Cheng Tê.

Mohn, Gottlob Samuel (1789–1825). Son of S. *Mohn. Glass painter in Dresden, Saxony, then in Vienna from 1811. Originally painted stained-glass windows; patronized by Emperor Franz II. Used transparent enamels and yellow stain, e.g. on typically straight-sided **Biedermeier* beakers. Subjects romantic, e.g. ruins, allegories, rustic landscapes, flowers. Many followers.

Mohn, Samuel (1762–1815). Glass painter in Dresden, Saxony from 1809; first painted porcelain and stained-glass windows, then glass. Innovator of transparent, delicate enamels, as opposed to opaque forms. Subjects include silhouettes, views, churches.

Mokubei, Aoki (1767–1833). Japanese artist, connoisseur, devotee of tea ceremony, and potter, making tea-bowls in Korean Ido style, excellent copies of Chinese celadon, and enamel work in san ts'ai colours. Worked in Kyoto; also made blue-and-white porcelain. Pieces usually stamped, Mokubei, between two rings.

Mola, Gaspare (1567–1640). Italian goldsmith and medal engraver. Appointed die-cutter to Ducal mint in Florence (1608); in Modena (1613); and in Duchy of Guastella (1614). In 1625, made engraver of Papal mint. Few works, apart from medals, attributed to him. Only signed piece, large silver-gilt and red jasper plaque commemorating institution of Gregorian calendar. 1599–1604, executed bronze west doors of Pisa cathedral. Also made silver and parcel-gilt parade helmet and shield (now in Museo Nazionale, Florence).

molinet. *See* stirring rod.

Molitor, Bernard (*c*1730–after 1819). German-born *ébéniste*; in Paris from 1773, becoming *maître-ébéniste* in 1787. Commissions from court of Louis XVI and *Garde Meuble Impériale*; worked in neo-classical style. Influenced by A. *Weisweiler. Stamp: B. MOLITOR.

Möller, Andreas (1683–*c*1758). Danish miniaturist, and historical and portrait painter. In Vienna (1724) and England (1728–31). Also in Berlin; work includes oil portraits and miniatures of German royalty.

Momma, Jacob. Joint founder (1649) with Daniel Demetrius of brassworks near Esher, Surrey, for manufacture of wire and other articles using copper imported from Sweden.

Momoyama period (1574–1615). Japanese period noted for gradual revival of ceramic industry, partly caused by invasion of Korea (1592–98), when skilled potters were forced to return to Japan to foster art. Stonewares of this era particularly distinguished, e.g. *Oribe, *Shino, and *Bizen and *Karatsu. *Raku ware invented, largely inspired by importation of Korean pottery pieces highly valued for tea ceremony use, e.g. *Ido tea bowls. Many potters worked in *Arita area, e.g. *Kakiemon, who learnt Chinese art of enamel work from T. *Tokyemon and made earliest attempts at decorated porcelains late in period. *Kyoto also developed as pottery centre; *Koyetsu among notable artists of period. Tradition of fine *Japanese metal-work continued from preceding Muromachi period. Followed by Edo period.

monastic chair. 19th century neo-Gothic chair, resembling medieval single choir stall; made of various pieces of older woodwork and panelling. Example of *Abbotsford style.

Moncrieff's Glass Works. Founded by John Moncrieff at Perth, Scotland, *c*1864 as North British Glass Works. Produced bottles and graduated glasses, later also chemical ware. Firm still flourishes, as John Moncrieff, Ltd.

money dish, guinea hole, or **pit.** Round depression in corner of card table, to hold money and counters.

Monkey Salt. English silver-gilt and crystal

*standing salt; life-like monkey balances crystal hemisphere on head, above which is salt container. Only surviving late medieval English salt in animal shape. Property of New College, Oxford.

monk's bench or **chair.** *See* chair-table.

monk's cap ewer. Chinese ceramic wine vessel surmounted by wavy edged, fluted spout, reminiscent of medieval monk's cap, with peaked front and scalloped side brims, folded flat against crown. Found in Ming and Ch'ing periods. Supposedly of Mongol origin; similar form found in Tibetan metal-work.

monochrome painting. Faience and porcelain decoration popular with 18th century German *Hausmaler* and at factories, before development of full enamel palette. *See Schwarzlot* painting, red monochrome, purple monochrome.

monopodium (in furniture). Classical pedestal support composed of animal's head and single leg. Widely used in early 19th century.

monstrance or **ostensory.** Glass or crystal cylinder set into gold, silver, or silver-gilt structure; used to display Host (consecrated bread or wafer). Feast of Corpus Christi originated in Liège district of Belgium in mid 13th century; practice extended to whole Western Church in 1264 by Pope Urban IV and confirmed by Pope John XXII in 1317; monstrance became general soon after. Various types include cross form, others with cylinder in vertical position with metal mounts (angels, scrolls, wheat-sheaves, etc.) on stem and foot; further examples architectural or sculptural. Reached final form in 15th century: sun type ostensory with glass or crystal cylinder in horizontal position surrounded by radiating strips of metal resembling sun's rays, on ornate stem and foot. Large examples, e.g. in Toledo cathedral, Spain, reach 14ft in height (*see custodia*). Some known to have been made in pewter in Middle Ages; earliest surviving examples 16th century. Not used in Reformed churches.

Monstrance. Silver and silver-gilt, made in Augsburg, 1730; set with semi-precious and paste jewels. Height 2ft4in.

Above:
*Monteith. English, 1709, by E. *Pearce. Indented rim for holding glasses lifts off. Solid hinged handles. Height 11in.*

Montelupo. Group of three maiolica plates, 17th century; painted with soldiers. Diameter of each 12¾in.

monstrance clock. Ornate clock, based on form of *monstrance. Made mainly in Augsburg, c1590–c1630. Gilt copper or brass, with case sometimes of rock-crystal. *Astronomical; yearly calendar dial indicating saints' days. Body of clock supported by pillar, worked as human figure in some examples, standing on base.

Montauban (Tarn-et-Garonne), France. Three faience factories established in late 18th century; closed by early 19th century (last in 1820). Early wares decorated in style of Moustiers, with blue and thick yellow.

monteith. Large silver bowl with notched or scalloped rim which appeared in late 17th century Britain and Europe. Initially used to cool wine glasses held in rim notches (10 or 12) with bowls lying in water or ice-filled bowl. Later examples with detachable rim used as punch bowls. Supposedly named after Scotsman who wore cloak with scalloped edge. Also made in glass, English delftware, porcelain, and creamware.

Montelupo (near Florence), Italy. Maiolica thought to have been made for use in Florence during 14th and 15th centuries. Workmen included *Fattorini family, who left to establish maiolica workshop at Cafaggiolo. Later dishes have soldiers sketchily painted in bright colours. In early 17th century, dishes painted with fr[illegible] and leaf designs, recalling Castel Duran[illegible] Venice, have blue dash edge (also [illegible] Dutch Delft and English delftware).

Montgolfier back. Type [illegible] named after Jacques and [illegible] following their balloon as[illegible]

Montre à tact *by A–L. *Breguet, no. 3877. Gold case with engine-turned decoration; edge has sharp points indicating hours.*

month mark. Sign of zodiac struck on Danish gold and silver indicating month of assay; in use from 1685.

Montpellier (Hérault). French faience made in 16th century includes pharmacy ware for city's medical school, and decorative ware in *istoriato* style; also *faïence blanche*. In 18th century, work difficult to distinguish from that of Marseille; *style Berain* and yellow enamel ground used from mid 18th century. Industry continued into 19th century.

montre à souscription. *See* subscription watch.

montre à tact or **tact.** Watch with front and back cover, devised by A-L. *Breguet for telling time by touch in dark. Less expensive than *repeating watch. Large hand attached to back cover of case is moved manually in clockwise direction until it stops; time then ascertained by feeling large knobs, set at each hour, on outside of case. Often also with ordinary dial at front. *See* blind man's watch.

Moody Salt. Silver spool-shaped *standing salt ($7\frac{3}{8}$in. high) with square base on cast shell feet. Circular well for salt hollowed in cornice which is smaller version of base. Bears London hallmark for 1664; property of Victoria & Albert Museum, London.

Mooleyser, Willem (fl mid to late 17th century). Dutch glass engraver. Specialized in *hatched technique. Worked mainly on goblets, [illegible]akers, and large *Römer*. Main subjects [illegible]dic, also elaborate figure motifs, e.g. [illegible] peasants, and flowers, birds, and fruit- [illegible] Glasses made 1685–97 signed WM

[illegible] English ceramics. Mottled [illegible]tion introduced *c*1810 by J. *Wedgwood II for use on white earthenware vessels in form of shells.

moons (in porcelain). *See* Chelsea.

Moore, James the Elder (d 1726). English cabinet maker to George I. Partner of J. *Gumley, 1714–26. Noted for gilt gesso furniture. Succeeded by son, James (fl 1726–34), cabinet maker to George, Prince of Wales, 1732.

Moorfields carpets. Factory producing hand-knotted pile carpets set up in Chiswell Street, Moorfields, London, by Thomas Moore in mid 18th century. In 1756, entered carpet for Royal Society of Arts award (for best 'Turkey carpet'); although Moore's judged finest, award went to rival, T. *Whitty, whose carpet was only one-third as expensive and of same size and similarly high quality. Moore apparently worked only for select clients; also often employed by R. *Adam to make carpets to his designs, a number of which survive in fine condition, e.g. example at Syon House (Isleworth, Middlesex) of typical neo-classical design, executed in brilliant colours by Moore in 1769, and others at Osterley Park (near London) bearing neo-classical and floral motifs; two probably made *c*1775 and *c*1778.

Mortar. English, bronze, dated 1669 and inscribed with initials. Height 5in.

moquette or **Brussels carpets.** European carpets, woven on narrow looms in manner of velvet, but with coarse wool and linen. *Tournai medieval centre of production. Peak period 16th to 18th centuries. Continental centres: Abbeville, Antwerp, Amsterdam, Leyden, and Utrecht. English centres: Bradford, Kidderminster, Norwich, and Wilton; also made in Ireland. Brussels carpet English term.

Morel-Ladeuil, Léonard (1820–88). French sculptor and silver designer; pupil of A. *Vechte. Worked as designer for *Elkington & Co of Birmingham (1859–88); from 1862 in firm's London premises. Favoured Renaissance motifs; designed mainly presentation pieces. Masterpiece, Milton Shield, won gold medal at Paris Exhibition of 1867 (now in Victoria & Albert Museum, London).

moresque ornament (in silver). Pattern of stylized intertwining scrolling and foliage; derived from Middle Eastern art. Popular on 16th century silver as engraved primary ornament. Revived in mid 19th century England.

Morrill, Benjamin (b 1794). American clock maker, working 1816–45. Made *New Hampshire mirror clocks; also example of Massachusetts shelf clock.

morris chair. Armchair with upholstered arms, cushioned back, and seat. Back hinged at base, allowing angle to be adjusted. Dates from *c*1860.

Morris, Henry (1799–1880). English porcelain painter. Employed at Swansea, *c*1815. Noted for painting of flowers and fruit. Signed plate exists.

Morris, William (1834–96). English artist, designer and medievalist: led return to craftsmanship in applied arts, and rejected growing use of machine-made objects. Also advocated simplicity of design and use of untreated woods. Formed furniture company, Morris, Marshall, Faulkner & Co (1861), which received medal in Exhibition of 1862. Firm later Morris & Co.

mortar. Vessel, usually of cast bronze (especially *bell-metal), used with pestle for grinding or pounding foodstuffs or chemicals. Common throughout Europe from 14th to 18th centuries.

Mortimer & Hunt. English firm of silversmiths; succeeded *Storr & Mortimer in 1839, and continued production of elaborate, sculptural domestic and display silver in tradition of P. *Storr. Partners J. Mortimer, J. S. Hunt, and son, J. Hunt, registered joint mark, but many pieces bear mark (ISH) of elder Hunt. In 1844 when Mortimer retired, the Hunts took Robert Roskell as partner and firm became *Hunt & Roskell.

Mortlake tapestry works. Royal Manufactory of Tapestry at Mortlake, Surrey, second English

*Mortlake Tapestry. c1665, after original design by F. *Cleyn; one of six depicting story of Hero and Leander, here swimming the Hellespont. Height 9ft6in.*

tapestry manufactory, established *c*1619 by Sir Francis Crane under instructions of James I; employed 50 Flemish weavers under direction of P. *de Maecht. From 1623, F. *Cleyn chief painter. Manufactory flourished under patronage of Charles I; peak period 1625–35, with tapestries rivalling Flemish and French works. Numerous tapestries woven from cartoons by P. P. *Rubens, Anthony van Dyck, and Cleyn. Also copies of contemporary Flemish tapestries. Most important work, eight-piece copy of Acts of the Apostles. Favourite subjects during first half of 17th century include History of Vulcan and Venus, The Five Senses, The Twelve Months, and Hero and Leander. Despite disruption of Civil War (1640–49), good quality tapestries produced. Deterioration during reign of Charles II: prosperity declined under combined effect of increasing competition from e.g. Gobelins, Beauvais, and Brussels, and domestic economic problems. Numerous weavers left to establish smaller workshops, e.g. F. *Poyntz, S. *Demay, and J. *Vanderbank. Latterly, subjects taken mainly from old designs, or copied from French models. Manufactory finally closed 1703. Mortlake identification mark: shield quartered by broad cross; often found also on tapestries by ex-Mortlake weavers.

mortuary wares. *See* ming-ch'i.

Mosaïk. German border ornament; dot and scale pattern, or diapered colour, used for porcelain border decoration after *c*1760, usually in monochrome purple, pink, green, etc. Attributed to K. J. C. *Klipfel. Appears notably on decorative and table wares from Ansbach, Berlin, and Meissen.

Mosan brass. *See Dinanderie.*

Mosbach (Baden). German faience factory founded 1770. Products bear some resemblance to Strasbourg faience. Glazed earthenware from end of 18th century unpainted, greyish or brownish white. Marks include MT (Mosbach-Tännich after J. S. F. Tännich, manager 1774–81), and CT (Carl Theodore, Elector Palatine).

Moser, George Michael (1706–83). Goldsmith and enameller born in Schaffhausen, Switzerland; began career, 1736, in London as chaser of bronze and gold. Made oval boxes set with portrait miniatures or plaques with classical scenes *en grisaille*. *Illustration at* J. Ellicott II.

mote-skimmer or **mote spoon.** *See* strainer-spoon.

mother-of-pearl. Hard, smooth, iridescent lining of certain shells, e.g., pearl oyster and abalone, polished to bring out colour, then cut and used for furniture inlay and marquetry, mainly in 17th century. Also refers to German porcelain on which purplish *Böttger lustre is used in combination with enamel colours, and gold-painted decoration; notably on Meissen porcelain under J. G. *Herold, *c*1720–40. Same colour used in lustre decoration of Hispano-Moresque ware, and at Deruta.

moth painter. Unidentified porcelain painter at Derby in 1750s and 1760s. Painted large moths; also other insects, landscapes with figures, birds, and, rarely, flowers.

motion work. In clock or watch, gearing between minute and hour hands, normally mounted immediately behind dial, producing usual 12:1 ratio.

mould-blown glass. Made by blowing *gather into mould; design cut in mould appears on outer surface of vessel. Method first used by Romans with clay or stone moulds. Earliest vessels, e.g. bottles, jugs, cups, and jars, usually straight-sided, followed by use of more elaborate patterns, e.g. net-work and ribbing. One-piece moulds used until 19th century, mainly for domestic hollow-ware. In 1802, glasshouse in Stourbridge, Worcestershire, invented two-piece mould, with hinge, allowing deep-cut work to be produced. From *c*1830, three-piece moulds with two hinged sections used, usually for intaglio baroque scrolls, fan and arch patterns. Known in America as *blown-three-mould. From 1835, mould-blown glass finished by fire-polishing in attempt to eliminate *mould mark: slight swelling on surface of glass, unlike thin line in pressed glass. *Illustration at* Islamic glass.

mould-cast glass. Made by pouring molten *metal into shaped mould. Said to have been used by Romans for making glass plates for windows. Application limited until development of *plate glass for windows and mirrors in 17th century France.

moulded pedestal or **Silesian stem.** Stem style in English glasses *c*1715–*c*1765. Stem moulded into pedestal narrowing at base, used mainly for *tazze* and sweetmeat glasses. Early examples (*c*1715–*c*1725) four-sided, then (from *c*1720) six-sided. Commonest is eight-sided form, made from late 1720s, usually accompanied by moulding on bowl and foot. *Illustration at* sweetmeat glasses.

mould mark. Mark caused by join between pieces of mould on *mould-blown glass. Also on pressed glass; especially noticeable in early American pressed glass, as not hand-finished.

mount. Decorative, protective, etc., metal support or other attachment to furniture, porcelain, etc. Extensively used on furniture from late 17th century, particularly in France. In ceramics, examples occur in Chinese *Ting-chou ware and in Isnik pottery. In Germany, mounts added to stoneware in 15th and 16th centuries. English silver mounts added in 16th and 17th centuries to imported German stoneware (*tigerware), home-produced imitations, and *ostrich-egg cups, *nautilus cups, etc. Silver also used in mounts for porcelain (e.g. tankards) made at Meissen and Saint-Cloud.

Peak of fashion for ormolu-mounted objects in late 18th century. French ormolu mounts added to porcelain made at Chantilly and imported Chinese porcelain; P-P. *Thomire made mounts for 18th and 19th century Sèvres pieces. In England, M. *Boulton main producer of ormolu, including mounts; also adapted marble or blue john vases with neo-classical ormolu mounts for use as candlesticks, *cassolettes*, etc. Wedgwood jasper ware medallions and plaques mounted by Boulton, often in cut steel. (For fan mounts, *see* leaf.)

Mount Vernon Glass Works. Founded 1810 in New York State by group of businessmen. Taken over by Granger family in 1833. Produced flint-glass tableware, bottles, historical flasks, and blown-three-mould glass. Premises moved in 1844 to Mount Pleasant, near Saratoga. *Illustration at* railroad flask.

Mount Washington Glass Works. Founded 1837 in Boston, Massachusetts, by D. *Jarves for son, George. Made blown, cut, and pressed glass. Specialized in soft, pastel colours (Burmese glass). Taken over by Pairpoint Manufacturing Company in 1894.

mourning fan. 18th century European fan decorated with memorial motifs, e.g. urns or willows; carried by mourners.

mourning jewellery. Rings, brooches, etc. worn in mourning. In 16th and 17th centuries, themes of jewellery directly related to death: coffins, skulls, skeletons, etc. After execution of

Mourning jewels. Mid-Victorian brooches, set in gold. Below: plait of hair encircled by motto and snake motif. Right: pearls and diamond with black and white enamelling.

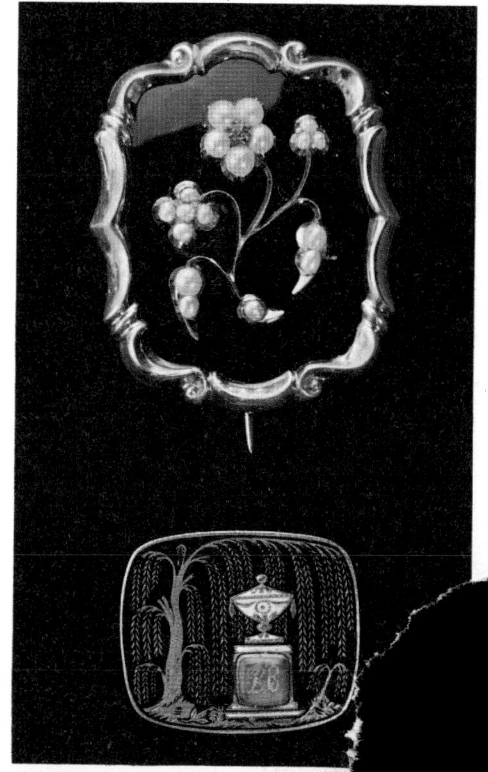

Moustiers. Faience dish, c1710, decorated in blue-and-white; central panel depicts The Rape of Helen, surrounded by arabesques in *style Berain. *Diameter 1ft11in.*

Charles I, rings or brooches with initials CR worn. From 18th century, crystal medallions or brooches containing locks of hair; some examples bear initials. Fashion for mourning jewellery reached height in 19th century for both national and private mourning. Wide range of materials included jet, ebony, tortoiseshell with *piqué* ornament, ivory, black enamel, and plastic; usually mounted in gold or substitutes, e.g. pinchbeck.

Moustiers (Basses-Alpes), France. Faience made at factory of J. *Clérissy from late 17th century, and other factories from early 18th century. Light body, thinly potted, covered with smooth white glaze. Early shapes and designs follow those of Clérissy factory until *c*1739; painting only in underglaze blue. **Style Berain* introduced *c*1710; forms soon adapted to echo angles and curves of painting. In 1740s, high-temperature polychrome decoration associated with factory of J. *Olerys closely resembles *Alcora, although pale buff body differs from reddish body of Alcora. Some enamel painting after *c*1770 imitated faience of e.g. Marseille and Strasbourg.

mouth wire. Wire sprung-in and soldered to mouth of e.g. silver vessel made by *raising. In general use for articles *turned up from cone from mid 18th century.

Muçur carpets. *See* Mudjur carpets.

mudéjar style. Spanish decorative style with fusion of Moslem and Gothic Christian elements (named after *mudéjares,* Moslems living in Christian Spain), combining geometrical, star-like, and flower motifs with heraldic patterns, and Gothic and Kufic lettering. Dates from 15th century and used throughout 16th century. [illegible]plied to *Hispano-Moresque ceramics (not-[illegible] *Manises), carpets, and furniture inlaid [illegible]e or ivory.

[illegible]homas (1715–94). English clock [illegible]aker; apprenticed to G. *Graham. [illegible]er escapement for pocket watches [illegible] worked on marine chronometers. From 1776, watch maker to George III. Regular supplier of watches to Ferdinand of Spain. Lived in Plymouth from 1771 until death.

Mudjur, Mujur, or **Muçur carpets.** East Anatolian prayer rugs with short, Turkish-knotted woollen pile on cotton or woollen foundation; nearly square. Richest coloured Turkish prayer rugs: 11–13 shades with bright red, pea-green, olive-yellow, and pale blue dominant. Mihrab usually solid red, edged with rows of tiny flower heads inside multi-fold outline; spandrels ornamented, often with ibriks; decorated panel above arch. Broad main border has distinctive tile-effect pattern of ornamented star-rosettes stylized into lozenges.

muffin cover. Slightly domed cylindrical lid (deeper than *bun cover), with slight waist; found on early 17th century pewter flagons.

muffineer. Small silver or Sheffield plate *caster used for sprinkling salt or sugar on muffins; made from late 18th century.

muffle colour. Enamel colour painted on glazed porcelain (or faience) after first hard firing (up to *c*1450°C), and fixed by lesser heat of *muffle kiln (*c*750°C).

muffle kiln. Covered kiln, in which contents kept out of contact with products of combustion; used to fix *enamel colours on glaze of faience or porcelain, from *c*1700, in Europe.

mug. Lidless drinking-vessel similar to *tankard. Made in silver from mid 17th century, commonly with baluster-shaped body. Made in pewter (tavern mug) from late 17th century to *c*1720 in tapering cylindrical form; decoration, if any, consists of band of gadrooning, moulded base, and hoops or bars round body. Some marked with names of tavern and often of innkeeper, and date. Few made from *c*1720 to late 18th century; these followed tankard styles, particularly tulip shape and later cylindrical type with in-curving base, moulded foot, and plain single or double-curved handle. In late 18th and 19th centuries Sheffield plate mounts applied to stoneware mugs. *See also* cann, christening mug.

Mughal carpets. *See* Mogul carpets.

Mujur carpets. *See* Mudjur carpets.

mukade. *See* Japanese sword-guards.

mulberry spoon. *See* strainer-spoon.

mule chest. Box-chest with one or more drawers below main storage area, making much-used items more accessible than objects stored in main chest. Forerunner of chest of drawers; dates from *c*1650.

mull. *See* Scottish snuff mull.

Müller, Gottfried (fl *c*1720–*c*1730). German sculptor. Carved wooden models for Meissen porcelain figures, *c*1725, e.g. Chinese god, and dragon.

Munden (Hanover). Small German faience factory founded *c*1737; associated with same family for 60 years. Typical are pierced, double-walled vases, plates with open basket-work rims painted with flowers, usually in pale high-temperature colours. Enamel colours seldom used. Mark (*c*1737–*c*1793): three crescents (from arms of C. F. von Hanstein, owner).

Munich tapestry. Little organized activity in Munich until workshop established 1604 by Flemish tapestry master-weaver, J. *van der Biest, under patronage of Elector Maximilian I. Until 1615, tapestries woven for decoration of palace. In 1684, colony established by Flemish Protestants, under patronage of Elector. Manufactory established *c*1718. Produced mainly mediocre quality tapestries in ambitious grand historical style or with mythological subjects. Works include History of House of Bavaria, Flora, Fauna, and Banquet of the Gods. Closed 1803.

muntin(g). In series of vertical members running between horizontals in framing or panelling, all but the two outside verticals. *cf* stile.

Muntz's metal. *See* patent metal.

Murano glass. *See* Venetian glass.

Muromachi period (1334–1573). Japanese period following Kamakura dominated by civil war in 15th century; short period of peace under Yoshimitsu (1358–1408) and Yoshimasa (1435–90) saw revival of arts, e.g. metal-work and lacquer-work. Increasing interest in tea ceremony provided impetus for ceramic production. Most pieces imported from China or Korea, e.g. Chinese *Chien ware, with *temmoku glaze, or Korean *Ido tea bowls. Followed by Momoyama period.

musical box. Developed from musical movements set in clocks and watches in mid 18th century. Music at first produced by nest of bronze bells and hammers. In late 18th century, musical movement combined with automata in Swiss *'singing-bird' box. Invention in Switzerland of brass revolving cylinder with projecting pins acting on tuned metal comb to produce musical notes (pin-barrel) resulted in development of musical box proper. This movement, perfected *c*1825, made possible more complicated tunes, including operatic overtures. Decoration of box useful for dating. Scenes from battles or mythology painted on lids of musical snuff-boxes before 1850; views of cities common later. Early cases of larger musical boxes made of elm, rosewood, or cherry; locks consist of hook-and-eye. After 1830 cases more elaborate with rosewood veneer and marquetry designs. Musical movements combined with automata, such as dolls, monkeys, orchestras, soldiers marching, etc., from *c*1850. *See* automata.

musical clocks. First popular in late 16th century with *carillon or miniature organ, as in *nef clock. Again fashionable in bracket and long-case forms in 18th century, many in conjunction with elaborate striking and chiming systems and automata; widely produced in England and Switzerland for export to *Turkish market. Musical movement, usually powered by separate train, has bells actuated by pin-barrel as in *musical box, sometimes with several tunes selected by lever on dial and set in motion at hourly or three-hourly intervals, or at will.

Musical watch. By Timothy Williamson, London, no. 3401, c1780–85. Two-tune musical train and six bells. White enamel dial with centre seconds hand and subsidiary hour, minute and lunar dials, small $\frac{1}{5}$ seconds dial and tune indicator. Hanging on contemporary watch-stand of ivory, ebony and tortoise-shell. Diameter of watch $4\frac{7}{8}$in.

Some types have organ in base. Fine musical clocks were produced by London makers, e.g. *Vulliamy family. Many French examples of ornate form made *c*1725–*c*1775 have musical box in base, e.g. by J-B. *Baillon, followed by similar types in Louis XVI style until *c*1790.

musical glasses. Sets of different-sized glasses, mounted in felt frame, 'played' by rubbing rim with wet finger. Popular in 17th century. Revived 19th century, when mounted in oak or mahogany case.

musical watches. Earliest examples from 18th century (few survive) of carillon type with tune played on bells or gong, a cumbersome arrangement replaced in late 18th century by 'comb' of steel reeds plucked by pins on revolving cylinder (pin-barrel) or, after 1800, on flat disc. Watches with this type of mechanism, set off every hour or at will, made mainly early 19th century in Switzerland, some also containing miniature singing-bird automata. Musical movements occasionally incorporated in seals attached to watch *fobs.

music bench. Rectangular bench with hinged lid opening to reveal shallow storage area for sheet music; made for keyboard instruments. Dates from *c*1850.

music stool. Round-topped stool, usually on pedestal and tripod base. Has swivel mechanism by which seat height can be altered. Designed for keyboard instruments; made from *c*1750.

*Mustard pots. All made in London. Back: left to right: 1) by C. *Fox, 1843. 2) 1798, height $3\frac{3}{4}$in. 3) 1798. Front left: by R. *Hennell, 1783. Front right: by Edward Aldridge, 1794. All except centre pot have blue glass liners.*

Mustafa (fl mid 16th century). Painter of Isnik pottery. Work includes mosque lamp, made to order of Suleiman the Magnificent for The Dome of the Rock, Jerusalem. Painted in blue, turquoise, and black, with arabesques and inscription identifying painter, date, 1549, and (unique in Isnik pottery) place of manufacture.

mustard barrel. 18th century British and European silver or silver-gilt barrel-shaped mustard container with lid and occasionally scroll handle. French examples with small boy wheeling barrel on wheelbarrow made.

mustard pot. Mustard not generally used in paste form before 18th century; dry powder earlier used in small silver or pewter pierced or *blind caster. From early 18th century, pots for paste in silver with cylindrical, ovoid, or octagonal body, scroll handle and domed lid with opening for *mustard spoon. From *c*1760 many with pierced silver or Sheffield plate body and blue glass liners.

mustard spoon. Small silver spoon resembling *teaspoon but with longer stem; fits notch in lid of mustard pot; in use mainly from mid 18th century.

mutchkin. Scottish $\frac{3}{4}$ (Imperial) pint measure; also a pewter pot of this capacity made from 17th century.

Myddleton Cup. English silver-gilt standing cup with egg-shaped bowl, baluster stem ornamented with three cast scroll brackets, and a high trumpet foot. Ornament is flat-chased scrollwork on matted ground. Cup was presented to Sir Hugh Myddleton by Goldsmiths' Company in 1613, but bears London hallmark for 1599. Property of Goldsmiths' Company since 1922. Fine example of late 16th century English standing cup.

Myer Myers. Milk jug with gadrooned rim and scrolled handle; made in New York, 1750–85. Height c5in.

Myers, Myer (1723–95). American silversmi[illegible] working in New York; son of Dutch J[illegible] immigrants. Domestic silver based on [illegible] styles, e.g. cake baskets, coasters[illegible] recorded American dish-ring. M[illegible] work, synagogue silver, includin[illegible] bells for Torah scrolls (*c*1765). M[illegible] rectangle.

Mystery clock. Dial with single hand stands on glass column with ormolu mounts. Striking mechanism in base. French, c1835–40. Height 19in.

mystery clock. Fashionable in early 19th century, mainly French. Dial is mounted separately from movement, e.g. on pillar or column, with no visible connection. Also in form of figure standing above clock, holding apparently free-swinging pendulum.

Nabeshima ware. Japanese ceramics, made for Prince Nabeshima at Okawachi (or Okochi), in Hizen province, near Arita. Factory started *c*1660, at first using materials supplied from Arita. Mature works have smooth flawless glaze over porcelain body. Enamel colours resemble Chinese *tou ts'ai from reign of Cheng Hua; soft underglaze blue used for outlines, with thin washes of bluish-green, clear, pale yellow, and orange, or vermilion. Usually decorated with flowers. Best period contemporary with reign of [illegible]hinese emperor, *Yung Cheng (1723–35). [illegible]ns drawn in charcoal on tissue paper, [illegible]on to biscuit-fired clay. Comb-waved [illegible]en decorates deep foot of bowls; [illegible]b-base'.

[illegible]Réné or **Nadal l'aîné** (1733–after [illegible]. Became *maître-menuisier* in 1756. Worked for crown under Louis XV and Comte d'Artois making neo-classical furniture. Stamp: J. NADAL. LAINE.

Nabeshima ware. Porcelain plate, early 18th century. Decorated in underglaze blue and overglaze enamels with toadflax flowers.

Nailsea glass. Mid 19th century objects from bottle glass: centre, inkwell; left and right, miniature 'dumpies' containing traditional flower in pot.

Nailsea. English glassware said to have originated at Nailsea glassworks (1788–1873), near Bristol, but widely copied, e.g. in England at Bristol, Newcastle-upon-Tyne, St Helens and Warrington (Lancashire), Stourbridge (Worcestershire), and in Yorkshire; also at Alloa in Scotland. As tax on bottle glass substantially less than on flint-glass (*see* Glass Excise Act), Nailsea and other glassworks specialized in domestic ware, e.g. jugs, two-handled vessels, long-necked bottles, and bowls, in dark brown, dark green, or smoky-green bottle glass. To increase attractiveness, pieces decorated with fused-on enamel flecks or splashes in various colours; also threads, loops, and stripes in white enamel. Another, more sophisticated, range of products (also termed Nailsea) includes ornamental vessels (*gimmel flasks, bellow flasks, covered jars) and novelty items (*rolling pins, canes, shoes, bells, pipes, and *witch balls). Made in clear flint or pale green glass, with *latticinio* or combed glass decoration, usually white or pale pink, occasionally red, blue or green, rarely yellow or dark red. Crimping sometimes added to body of vessels. Many novelty items made as love or friendship tokens, with inscriptions such as Be True to Me. Rarely possible to ascertain place of origin or date, though most existing examples are 19th century.

namban. *See* Japanese sword-guards.

Nancy tapestry. Manufactory established 1612 in Nancy by Duke of Lorraine, with weavers from Brussels. Active throughout century. Designs first copied Brussels tapestries, then Gobelins and Beauvais models.

Nankin or **Nankeen porcelain.** Blue-and-white Chinese porcelain made 1790–1850 at *Ching-tê-chên, for export to rest of world mainly from nearby port of Nankin, Kiangsi province. Underglaze blue ranges in tone from greyish to bright blue; early paste has grey, blue, or green tint, later dead white. Mainly comprises tableware in various shapes; also vases, candlesticks, inkwells, and basket-work *bonbonnières*; intended for everyday use. Borders usually geometrical patterns; decoration often from engravings or copies of e.g. *willow pattern.

Nan-tai (Fukien). Chinese ceramic kiln site near Fu-chou; important from Han to Six Dynasties periods for Yüeh ware. Few pieces known.

Nantgarw, Glamorgan. Porcelain made in 1813 by W. *Billingsley and partner; manufacture transferred to *Cambrian Pottery Works, Swansea in 1814, but proved too costly. Attempts made to adapt formula, but in 1817 business returned to Nantgarw. Paste very white and translucent, subject to high kiln loss. Produced tableware, mainly plates, often with borders of flowers in relief; much sent to London for decoration. Painting at Nantgarw includes sprigs of flowers, notably roses, and *chinoiseries*. Billingsley left to work at Coalport in 1820; some Coalport of this period resembles Nantgarw. Factory closed in 1822. Mark: NANT GARW/C.W. (i.e. China Works), impressed. Swansea products marked SWANSEA, sometimes with one or two tridents.

napkin press. Wooden device composed of two horizontal boards connected by one or two screws, for pressing table linen. Damp linen placed between boards; these screwed tightly together, thus removing creases in material. Dates from 16th century; in use until 19th century.

Naples. Italian ceramics. Porcelain made at *Capodimonte factory (1743–59) on outskirts of city. Royal porcelain factory established 1771 under patronage of Ferdinand IV. Early tableware in rococo style. From 1782, large services made for presentation to foreign courts, e.g. Spanish and English. Neo-classical style inspired by excavation of Pompeii and Herculaneum. Figures, both biscuit and glazed, include portrait busts and figures, sometimes very large; also groups of figures in contemporary dress. Factory closed in 1806. Marks include: crown with FRF (i.e. *Fabbrica reale Ferdinandea*) painted in purple, red, or blue, until 1787; N impressed, incised, or in underglaze blue in late 18th century.

Little known about maiolica made in city; large vases, dated 1684, decorated with biblical scenes in blue, probably been made. In 17th and 18th centuries, maiolica made at nearby *Castelli.

Naples tapestry. Naples manufactory established 1737 by Charles III, with weavers from defunct Arazzeria Medici (*see* Florentine tapestry). Low-warp and high-warp tapestries woven. Operated until French conquest in 1799. Numerous hangings, mainly based on Gobelins tapestry designs, include The Elements (almost exact copy of Gobelins's Don Quixote series), and History of Henri IV.

Napoleon watch. *See* half-hunter watch.

Nara period (646–794). In Japanese ceramics, noted for introduction of coloured glazes on pottery; mostly monochrome, streaked or spotted, sometimes in green, yellowish-brown, and white together. Resembles Chinese T'ang dynasty ware. Kilns supposedly located near Nara and Kyoto; manufacture primarily for court and Buddhist temple use, e.g. incense burners, urns, wine vessels. For contemporary domestic ware, *see* Sué.

narghile, hookah, qalian or **kende.** Tobacco pipe in which smoke passes from bowl, through water in bottle below, and is inhaled through long flexible tube, ending in mouthpiece. In Middle East, originally made from decorated coconut (Persian, 'nargil') shell. Examples occur in pottery, glass, or metal. Made in Chinese blue-and-white porcelain of Ming period for export. In reign of Wan-li, examples occur in form of elephant and frog.

Naskhi script. Cursive Arabic script, from which modern Arabic writing derived, used in ceramic and other decoration. Long curving strokes often connect end of word with initial letter. Decorative motif on *Islamic pottery, often used as background to bolder *Kufic script; also appears in Hispano-Moresque decoration.

Nassau-Saarbrücken. *See* Ottweiler.

nautilus cup. 16th and 17th century ceremonial drinking vessel with nautilus-shell bowl and silver or silver-gilt mounts. Foot and stem in various shapes, particularly associated with sea, e.g. mermaid or merman, Neptune, etc. Sometimes in fantasy shapes, e.g. bird. Made primarily in Italy, Germany, Austria, and Netherlands; few English examples survive.

navigating instruments. *See* astrolabe, backstaff, cross-staff, magnetic compass, octant, quadrant, sextant.

Neale & Co. Pottery at Hanley, Staffordshire, previously owned by H. *Palmer. J. Neale, partner from 1766, succeeded Palmer in 1778 and engaged R. Wilson as manager. Wilson became partner in 1786; firm Neale & Wilson, until his death, then David Wilson and Sons, until closure, 1918. Good quality creamware produced; also blue-painted and lustre-decorated tableware, jasper, and Egyptian black vases in neo-classical style. From *c*1790, small, neatly potted figures, including set of Seasons, characterized by bright colours, e.g. turquoise and dark brown; costumes often patterned with flower sprigs; square bases sometimes painted with red, brown, or gilt line and topped with mound on which figures stand. Large figures in pearlware from *c*1800, with bluish-tinted glaze. Marks: NEALE & CO, I. NEALE HANLEY on circular band (1778–86); NEALE & WILSON (1784–95); crown over crescent, WILSON (1795–1801); all impressed.

*Nantgarw porcelain. Left: ice-pail from *Mackintosh Service; painted and gilded decoration done in London. Right: locally decorated plate. Both early 19th century.*

Nautilus cup. Engraved nautilus shell mounted in silver-gilt. Cover, hinged at grotesque mask, is modelled as man riding dolphin. 17th century.

Narghile. Islamic pottery made at Meshed, early 17th century. Height 8½in.

nécessaire. Box for toilet and household equipment, such as scent bottles, knife and spoon, sewing equipment; larger counterpart of *étui* for use on dressing-table. Variety of materials and decoration as for snuff-boxes. Used in 18th century Britain and Europe. *Illustration at* shagreen.

nécessaire de voyage. *See* canteen.

necessary stool. *See* close stool.

necklace. Ornament made of metal (gold, silver, base metal), gems, glass, faience, etc. Necklaces rare in Middle Ages; more typical ornament was decoration of neckline and sleeves of robes with gems. Gold chain necklaces in great variety of shapes and sizes worn by both men and women in 15th and 16th centuries. Fashion spread from Italy to England and remainder of Europe. Chains sometimes combined with pearls. In 16th century single or double strings of pearls popular, sometimes interspersed with gems. Often worn with *pendant. Filigree and enamel bead necklaces popular in Venice. In early 17th century necklaces commonly made of linked pieces; gold scrolls, arabesques, flower-shaped links decorated with gems, pearls, and enamels.

Nef. German, parcel-gilt, made in Nuremberg by Caspar Beutmuller II, c1620. Height 12½in.

From mid 17th century faceted gems became dominant in necklace; use of enamel declined. Diamond most fashionable stone from late 17th century; much imitated in *paste. Silver most common setting, though diamonds usually backed with gold. Popular type of massed gem necklace was *rivière*, usually consisting of row of large stones (e.g. diamonds), bordered by smaller stones (e.g. rubies or emeralds). From late 18th century, linked cameo necklaces fashionable. 19th century necklace influenced by Gothic revival. Enamelling and *granulation reintroduced.

nef. Model ship in gold, silver, and other precious materials, made in Europe, particularly France, from Middle Ages, some used as ceremonial *salt, marking place of honour at table. Many examples made in Europe from mid 19th century for display. *See* Burghley Nef.

nef clock. Ornamental clock in form of ship, derived from *nef: typically German, late 16th century. Example in British Museum from Augsburg *c*1580 made for Emperor Rudolph II; has elaborate automaton figures, organ, gun at bow of ship, and mechanism to produce rolling movement across table, all actuated with striking at hourly intervals.

Neilson, James or **Jacques** (fl mid 18th century). Scottish tapestry master-weaver. Among most active Gobelins weavers, 1749–88. Main achievement, improvements to low-warp loom to meet demands of fashionable 'woven painting' tapestry designs of F. *Boucher and J-B. *Oudry; also experimented with dyeing processes to increase range of tones.

Nelme, Anthony (fl 1679–1722). English silversmith working in London. Apprenticed 1672, obtained freedom 1679. Earliest domestic silver derived from Dutch work; designs soon after show Huguenot influence, although in 1697, signed petition to William III attacking Huguenot silversmiths. Commissions for royalty (e.g. Queen Anne) and aristocracy. In 1697 and 1704 made sets of snuffers and candlesticks for Board of Ordnance. Son, Francis, continued in trade. Mark: AN in monogram, with e added in 1697. *Illustration also at* sconce.

Anthony Nelme. Beer jug made 1711. Baluster-shaped with domed cover, thumbpiece, scroll handle and lidded spout. Height 10¾in.

Below left:
Neo-classical (Pompeian) style. Armchair in carved and gilded wood, upholstered in ottoman silk. English, c1796–99. Derived via French sources from antique Roman models, and modified. Height 2ft9in.
Below right:
Nesting beakers. German, made in Augsburg by Johann Wagner, 1690. Set of five with cover.

Nelson chair. *Sheraton elbow chair, with rope, anchor, and dolphin motifs, commemorating victory at Trafalgar (1805). Also known as Trafalgar chair. *See* Trafalgar furniture.

neo-classical style or **classical revival.** Style derived from forms and decorative motifs of classical Greece and Rome, which emerged in mid 18th century France following excavations at Pompeii and Herculaneum (begun 1738), and spread through Europe, Britain, and America during 18th and early 19th centuries. Straight lines replaced rococo curves, and classical motifs were used, e.g. acanthus, cherubs, cloven hooves, draperies and swags, dolphins, fluting, *guilloches*, lyres, medallions, ram and lion masks, satyrs, tripods, urns, etc. Typified by light, delicate treatment. *See* Adam style, American Directoire style, Directoire style, Empire style, Etruscan style, Federal style, Hepplewhite style, Louis XVI style, Regency style, Second Empire style, Sheraton style.

neo-Gothic style. *See* Gothic revival.

Neri, Antonio (fl early 17th century). Italian. Wrote **Arte Vetraria* (published 1612), one of best-known books on glass making; based mainly on experience at Venetian glassworks in Antwerp. Became priest in Florence.

nesting beakers. European silver or silver-gilt beakers, made from the 16th century, shaped to fit inside each other; sets of 6 or 12 made. Ornament mainly engraved; rare 17th century examples have embossed floral and foliate designs. 19th century English examples fit completely inside each other made in decreasing sizes.

nest of drawers. Miniature case piece consisting of several drawers for holding small objects. Popular in 18th and 19th centuries. Also, cluster of drawers at back of *bureau.

nest of tables. Set of three or four portable tables graded in size to fit underneath each other for storage. Dates from 18th century. *See* quartetto tables.

netsuke. Japanese ornament attached to end of cord, from which originally (in 16th century) *inro was suspended; acted as toggle when pulled through sash or belt, preventing cord and attachments from slipping down. Made by decorators of *Japanese sword-guards, but majority carved by specialist craftsmen from 17th to 19th centuries. When tobacco became popular, pouches or pipe-cases added to articles carried on netsuke. Noted for ornate, miniature carving, in boxwood, ebony, cherry, or bamboo, ivory or horn. Sometimes different materials combined. Earliest and simplest form was manju ('bun', indicating doughnut shape), but most popular and varied shapes are figures of old men, drunkards, wrestlers, dancers, animals, fruit, birds, etc. Seal forms, shells, or masks favoured. Trick, toy examples also found, e.g. loose seeds in lotus pod, worm slipping in and out of rotten fruit, or mouse running under cloak. Died out as ornament with adoption of western clothing (with pockets) in 19th century.

Netzglas. *See vetro a reticelli.*

Neuber, Johann Christian (1736–1808). German box maker who worked in Dresden. Pupil of H. *Taddel. Made court jeweller in 1775. Used **Zellenmosaïk* technique. In some boxes, hardstones were numbered and identified in book concealed in base. No mark known; occasionally inscribed work Neuber à Dresde. *Illustration at* German snuff-boxes.

Neuchâtel. Centre for watch and clock production in Switzerland. Term 'Neuchâtel clock' often applied to bracket type with waisted case derived from *balloon clock, made from mid 18th century to present day.

Netsuke. Japanese, c1800; carved ivory depicting Baku, mythical animal who ate nightmares. Height 2in.

*Nevers faience. *Wig stand, painted with typical blue and white oriental design. Late 17th century.*

Neudeck or **Neudeck-Nymphenburg.** *See* Nymphenburg porcelain factory.

Neuillet, Guillaume (d 1724). French-born maker of red earthenware teapots in Delft, Holland. Previously woodcarver. Worked for L. *van Eenhoorn, 1691–1703. Also made small figures in red earthenware.

Neuzierat (German, 'new ornament'). Porcelain moulding introduced at Berlin factory in 1763; restrained rococo relief scrollwork on tableware borders. Later copied elsewhere.

Nevers (Nièvre), France. Faience workshops established by *Conrade family in 1603, P. *Custode *c*1633, and others from mid 17th century. Early faience, following maiolica models, resembles that of Lyon. From *c*1640, both imported Chinese porcelain and contemporary French silver influenced form and decoration. Colours include blue, pale yellow; also pure, bright copper-green, sometimes softened with antimony-yellow; soft outlines painted in manganese-purple. From *c*1630, coloured grounds used in **bleus de Nevers*. Designs, often taken from contemporary engravings, include hunting and pastoral scenes; oriental subjects include birds and foliage, or landscapes with figures. In 18th century, products included faience in style of Rouen and Moustiers; also **faïences parlantes*.

Glass makers brought to Nevers from Italy in mid 16th century by Ludovico Gonzaga (acquired duchy through marriage to Henrietta of Cleves). Glasshouse founded 1603 under patronage of Henry IV. All kinds of *façon de Venise* glassware made; town became famous for

Nevers. Enamelled glass figure of Louis XIV, late 17th century.

small glass figures and objects fashioned at lamp, known as *verre filé de Nevers*. Glass rods softened at lamp, and manipulated, often round copper wire core. Use of tin oxide gave many objects faience glaze. Base usually clear glass with added colour to represent rocks, grass, etc. Earliest known figures, small toy animals made for young Louis XIII in 1605. Increasing numbers made in 17th and 18th centuries. Main subjects: religious figures and elaborate scenes, miniature *commedia dell'arte* figures, and groups representing The Seasons. *Verre frisé* (curled glass) often applied for decorative effect, and *verre filé* (glass threads) used for draperies and small detail. Figures rarely taller than 6in. In 18th century, similar work produced by glass makers in Paris, Rouen, Bordeaux, and Marseille.

New Bremen Glass Manufactory. Founded 1784 in Frederick County, Maryland, by J. F.

New Bremen Glass Manufactory. Wine glass from set made for George Repold of Baltimore and engraved with his initials. Height 4in.

*New England Glass Company. Early 19th century glass, *blown-three-mould. Left: emerald decanter; height 10in. Right: *celery glass; height 6¼in.*

Newcastle. Baluster-stemmed glass with armorial engraving; arms of Anne, daughter of George II, and William IV, Prince of Orange. Engraved work is Dutch.

New Geneva Glass Works. Light green goblet, c1797–1800; enclosed in stem is Albert Gallatin's Prix de Diligence *medal from University of Geneva, Switzerland. Height 9¼in.*

*Amelung. Produced decanters, bottles, flasks, drinking glasses, and various white free-blown and mould-blown wares. Occasionally coloured. Quality lower than imported European glass, but with fine engraving. Closed 1796.

Newcastle-upon-Tyne. Important English glass making centre in 18th century. Immigrant craftsmen established glasshouses in wooded areas along River Tyne in 17th century, particularly members of Dagnia, *Henzey and Tyzack families. Glass making flourished under Sir R. *Mansell, who developed local coal-mining industry (coal replaced wood in furnaces). Several glass houses produced window and bottle glass; Dagnias, who specialized in table and domestic ware, perfected brilliant, clear flint-glass by 1725. Newcastle flint-glass achieved great distinction at home and abroad during 18th century; particularly prized in Holland for engraving (*see* D. *Wolff, F. *Greenwood, J. *Sang) and in Norway (some makers settled in *Nøstetangen). Majority of glasses made by stuck shank method (bowl, stem, and foot made separately) allowing more elaborate stem decoration, e.g. balusters, multiple knops, tears, and air twists. Feet often domed and terraced; bowls round or funnel-shaped. In mid 18th century, many *Jacobite glasses produced; 1720–1800 white enamelled glasses popular (*see* W. and M. *Beilby). Glass making declined in 19th century; after 1833, region noted mainly for pressed glass made to imitate cut glass.

New England Glass Company. Founded 1818 by D. *Jarves and associates. Under Jarves's management, leading American producer (in quality and quantity) of fine glassware including blown-three-mould, free-blown, cut, engraved, and pressed glass. Later noted for silver and cameo glass. Closed 1890.

New England Pottery Company. Established at Cambridge, Massachusetts in 1854 to make earthenware with yellow glaze or *Rockingham ware. Later made cream-coloured earthenware, ironstone china, and porcelain (all after 1875).

New Geneva Glassworks. Founded 1797 in Pennsylvania by the Swiss, Albert Gallatin, and associates, formerly employed by *New Bremen Glass Manufactory. Produced window glass, bottles, and small amount of free-blown and pattern-moulded tableware, mainly green or yellow. Moved to Greensboro, Pennsylvania, in 1807.

New Hall. English porcelain factory opened in 1782 at Shelton, Staffordshire by company including S. *Hollins, J. *Warburton, and J. *Turner, after purchasing patent for manufacture of hard-paste porcelain from R. *Champion (1781). Early hard-paste porcelain tableware in shapes derived from contemporary silver, often decorated with sprig designs and formal borders, or *chinoiseries*. By *c*1810, paste contained bone ash and had developed glassy look. Mark, New Hall, printed in red enclosed by double circle, sometimes used after 1810 on bone porcelain. Products usually bear simple numerals.

New Hampshire mirror clock. American wall clock, produced in New Hampshire, *c*1830. Rectangular shape, *c*33in. high, with door of case extending whole length of clock. Dial on upper section, sometimes surrounded by decorative tablet; long mirror beneath. Eight-day brass movement. Makers include J. *Collins and B. *Morill.

Newport school. Branch of American baroque cabinet making centered in Newport, Rhode Island in 18th century; main exponents J.

New Hall porcelain. Three cream jugs, all produced c1795.

*Goddard and *Townsend family. Style characterized by use of *block front, often decorated with shell motif; ogee-shaped Goddard block foot also typical.

Newsam, Bartholomew (fl late 16th century). English clock and watch maker; made watches and table clocks for Queen Elizabeth I.

New Standard. *See* Britannia Standard.

Newton, Sir William John (1785–1869). English miniaturist. Miniature-painter-in-ordinary to William IV (whose portrait he painted 13 times), Queen Adelaide, and Queen Victoria. Portraits in watercolours or chalk on paper; miniatures on ivory.

New York clocks. Clocks produced in New York State. Many shelf clocks. Version with torsion pendulum and one-year movement patented in 1829. Calendar clocks, wall or shelf, manufactured in Ithaca from 1866; two dials indicating, separately, time and date. Clocks, or clock movements manufactured in Connecticut also, distributed and sold in New York.

nickel silver. *See* argentine.

Nicole, François (1776–1849). Swiss maker of small musical boxes whose experiments extended range of mechanism by several octaves, increasing repertoire. Geneva firm of Nicole Frères, established 1815, continued until after 1880. Boxes stamped Nicole Frères à Genève; individual components also stamped Nicole Frères or NF; boxes numbered.

Niculoso, Francisco, or **Il Pisano** (d 1529). Italian tile painter working in Seville, Spain, by specialized in large-scale architectural work. Painted religious and decorative subjects in orange, yellow, brown, purple, and green, with dark blue or black outlines and conspicuous use of cross-hatching and stippling. Work includes altar and tile-panel, The Visitation, in the Alcázar of Seville; church portal of Santa Paula; altarpiece, Life of the Virgin (1518) in church of Nuestra Señora de Tentudía, Badajoz.

Niderviller (Moselle), France. Faience production encouraged from 1748 by Baron Jean-Louis de Beyerlé and wife. Artists from *Strasbourg produced ware similar to that made under P-A. *Hannong. Noted for elegance of forms derived from silverware. Flowers, landscapes, and bird patterns painted in delicate polychrome. *En camaïeu* painting in green or crimson. After 1770, **décor bois* popular. Figures made from models by P-L. *Cyfflé and C-G. *Sauvage. Output continued until French Revolution. Porcelain production by Baron de Beyerlé (from 1765) opposed by Sèvres; factory sold in 1770. Much porcelain in rococo style. Dishes and tureens made in naturalistic forms; other tableware decorated with flower sprig patterns or landscapes painted in colour or monochrome. Porcelain figures in biscuit, some very large, e.g. Shepherd Boy (24in. high), Bathing Shepherdess (25in.). Marks include: Beyerlé monogram in manganese-brown or black on faience and porcelain, or in blue, only on porcelain (1754–70); crossed C and reversed C with coronet in blue, brown, or black (1770–93); NIDERVILLER impressed, sometimes on applied label (late 18th century figures). N in black used from start of factory; Nider or Niderviller in black from late 18th century. *Illustration at décor bois.*

Niedermayer, Johann Josef (d 1784). Austrian sculptor, *Modellmeister* at Vienna porcelain factory (1747–84). Responsible for best-known Vienna figure models, e.g. musicians, shepherds, hawkers, biblical and neo-classical subjects. Softly enamelled yellow, mauve, and brown predominate. Bases at first high and scrolled, later domed or pancake-shaped; c1770, decorated with gilt crested border or scrollwork.

niello. Black compound of sulphur, lead, silver, and copper used to fill engraving on silver, etc., as decorative contrast. In use at least from 10th century, fashionable in 15th and 16th centuries. Widely used in Russia and Caucasus. Also known as Tula work after place of origin. *Illustrations at* matchbox, Russian snuff-boxes, reliquary.

nien hao or **reign mark.** Name given to reign of Chinese Emperor, chosen after accession and applied from start of first full year of reign. Reign and dynasty names both optimistic quotations from classical texts, e.g. K'ang Hsi, 'Joys of Peace'. Appear on ceramics as four or six character marks, sometimes as seal marks in archaic script (seal characters). May be accompanied by date on cyclical system, which repeats every 60 years.

Nien hsi-yao. Director-general (1726) of Imperial kilns at Ching-tê-chên during reign of Yung Chêng (1723–35). Blue and white porcelains manufactured, with silver-white paste; underglaze blue has slight lavender tint (blackish when used thickly, through addition of manganese oxide in small quantities to glaze composition). Smooth, even glaze sometimes contains fine bubbles. Credited with improvements in **famille rose* decoration, notably in quality of pink enamel. Tendency to imitate earlier (mostly Sung) wares developed under his direction; more apparent in work of *T'ang Ying, who succeeded to post in 1736.

*Night clock. By E. *East of London, c1620. Ebony case with plinth, and broken pediment surmounted with ormolu griffin séjant. Disc behind aperture in painted dial revolves; light shining from oil lamp behind shows up relevant perforated hour chapter. Height 2ft10in.*

night clock. Any device for telling time in dark. In 17th century, makers including Joseph *Knibb and E. *East produced clocks of bracket type with revolving dials; hour divisions pierced and illuminated by lamp placed behind movement. Also popular type with Italian makers in same period and later. *Illustration also at* Italian clocks.

night table, bedside cupboard, table à chevet. *Bedside table with cupboard for chamber pot, or storage cupboard and (in sliding cabinet below) a *close stool. Has solid or *tambour door on front. As *table à chevet,*

*Night table. George III. Satinwood, with *tambour-shuttered front; behind simulated drawer is bidet stand which slides out. Width 1ft9in.*

*Nipt-diamond-waies. Moulding above flared foot on base of *coin tankard which contains George II shilling dated 1750. Height 7¼in.*

popular Louis XVI piece, with tambour door, marble top (often with gallery), and elaborate decoration. Night table often has handles or hand-holds at sides for easy lifting, as stored out of sight in daytime.

Niglett, John (fl mid 18th century). Painter, probably freelance, of Bristol delftware by 1720. Credited with designs incorporating leaves painted with short brush strokes, and Chinese figures derived from K'ang Hsi *famille verte* style. Dish dated 1733 with initials N over JE (supposedly standing for John Niglett and wife, Esther) attributed to him.

Nilson, Johann Esaias (1721–88). German

Nonsuch chest. English, late 16th century. Oak with inlay of various woods in Rhenish style.

artist; published engravings, including *chinoiserie* subjects, widely copied in porcelain decoration at Ansbach, Kiel, and most German porcelain factories, *c*1755–80.

Ninsei (d after 1699). Studio name of Japanese potter, Seiemon Nonomura active from *c*1640. Came from Tamba area, which had long tradition in ceramic work. Studied Chinese Ming enamel work, and gold lacquer art, dyeing, and weaving. Decorated glazed stoneware in enamel colours. *Kenzan was pupil from 1689.

'nipt diamond waies'. 17th century glass ornamentation. Thick vertical ribs round vessel pincered together to form diamond pattern. Often used by G. *Ravenscroft on decanters, bottles, and glasses.

noble pewter. *See* Edelzinn.

nocturnal dial. Astronomical instrument used for finding time at night, using fixed star or group of stars as reference points.

noggin. Measure of (usually) 1 gill; also, Irish baluster measure, without handle or lid, made in pewter in varying capacities.

Nonsuch chest. Chest with inlay decoration representing building, wrongly associated with Henry VIII's palace, Nonsuch. Introduced to England from Germany and Flanders in 16th century. Some English examples possibly made by immigrant craftsmen.

Northern and Southern Dynasties. *See* Six Dynasties.

northern celadon ware. Chinese ceramics: brownish-grey stoneware with feldspathic glaze, and olive or brown tone caused by effects of oxidation on small iron content of glaze. Best examples made in Sung perioe, attributed to Honan province. Decoration resembles that of Yüeh ware : designs carved under glaze on foliate dishes include leaves and flowers, but moulded patterns common. Distinguishable from Yüeh ware by deeper brown foot-rim.

Northwood, John I (1837–1902). English glass engraver at Stourbridge, Worcestershire. Originally apprenticed to Stourbridge firm of Richardson & Webb; specialized in engraving *cameo glass after 1860. In 1873, completed first major success, Elgin Vase (in Leamington Spa Museum, Warwickshire), decorated with group of riders from Parthenon frieze. In 1876 won £1000 prize offered by Richardson & Webb for copy of *Portland Vase, most important piece of English cameo glass.

Norton, Captain John, son Lyman, and grandson Julius (fl late 18th to mid 19th centuries). Potters at Bennington, Vermont. John established pottery there in 1753. Succeeded by sons in 1823; Julius manager from 1841. 1844–47, Julius partner with brother-in-law C. W. *Fenton who then formed new pottery, at first in same premises, moving away in 1848.

Norwegian tapestry. Primarily folk art, developed from 13th century. Mainly small figure pieces used for furniture covers and panels. Geometrical decorative motifs dominate patterns; human and animal figures always extremely stylized. 16th and 17th century tapestries influenced by more sophisticated designs of imported German and Flemish examples; borrowed motifs and designs generally adopt rigidly geometrical forms.

Norwich glass. *See* Lynn glass.

Nøstetangen. Norwegian glasshouse established in 1741 near Drammen under patronage of Christian VI of Denmark and Norway; produced domestic ware, bottles, and window glass. Employed German glass blowers and

Left:
Norwegian tapestry. The Ten Virgins and their Parents, c1750. 6ft×4ft.
Centre:
Nuremberg glass. With solid multi-knopped stem; bowl engraved with landscape. Late 17th century. Height 11½in.
Right:
Nuremberg. Tin-glazed earthenware jug, c1700, painted with landscape and signed I O H Schaper; silver mounts with maker's mark and N. Height 8½in.

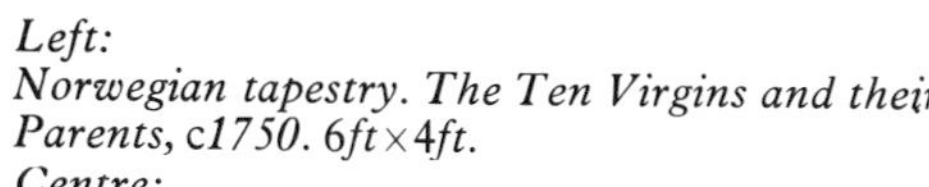

engravers for finer work for nobility. From 1755, specialized in fine tableware and ornamental glass. Two glass makers from *Newcastle-upon-Tyne joined factory, introducing flint-glass in Anglo-Venetian style. In 1760, factory was granted monopoly for table glass. Produced drinking glasses similar to Newcastle glasses in style, with baluster and air-twist stems, but with high domed foot and German-style engraving. Royal monogram popular motif. Goblets made with elaborate crown-shaped finial. *Nipt diamond waies popular decoration on vessels such as jugs, covered jars, and bowls. Simple, bulbous-shaped, stoppered decanters and fine chandeliers also made. After death of Christian VI, factory patronized by Frederick V. After his death (1766), standards declined. Factory closed 1777.

Nottingham ware. Brown salt-glaze stoneware developed in Nottingham, England, late 17th or early 18th century. Brown surface with metallic sheen produced by coating with iron oxide wash before glazing. Decoration usually incised: simple flower patterns and wide criss-cross bands; sometimes fretwork cut with knife or punch. Shapes include small double-walled cups decorated with pierced leaf patterns, puzzle jugs, and cups in form of bears.

Nove. *See* Le Nove.

Novyi factory. Russian porcelain and faience factory established in early 19th century at Kuziaevo, near Moscow (directed, in succession, by three brothers Novyi and widow and son of last). Good quality tableware decorated with foreign designs adapted to Russian provincial and olk tradition. In early 19th century, usual mark was Cyrillic N in underglaze blue or impressed; F.K.A. Novia used from 1852 until factory closed *c*1860.

nozzle. Socket of candlestick, sconce, etc., into which candle is fitted; usually detachable.

nulling. *See* knurling.

numerals (on clocks and watches). Roman numerals normally used for hours, with Arabic type appearing on painted dials in late 18th century and in wider use in 19th century. Exceptions include early continental dials with normal I–XII numerals ringed by Arabic 13–24 for use with Italian 24-hour system (*see* time measurement) and some *precision clocks in 18th century with 24-hour dials. Figure IIII used instead of IV for balanced appearance with VIII on normal 12-hour dials. Arabic numerals general for minutes, usually at five-minute intervals outside hour ring, and for seconds dials. Clocks and watches for Turkish market have distinctive numeral system, variant of original form from which so-called Arabic numbers derived.

Nuremberg (Bavaria). Centre of metal industry of Germany from 15th century and of Europe in 16th century when reached peak of production of arms, armour, bronze, brass, and silver. Famous for clocks, watches, mechanical devices, and scientific instruments. Bronze foundries, notably those of *Vischer family, founded 1453, and Pancraz Labenwolf (1492–1563), produced statuary bronzes, many after Italian Renaissance style. 15th and 16th century craftsmen produced numbers of elaborately embossed brass bowls for display and ecclesiastical use; these and other wares, particularly bronze or brass sets of *weights, were famous throughout Europe. Relief-cast pewter made from *c*1560, remained popular for over a century; main exponents were N. *Horchhaimer, Albrecht Preissensin, and Kaspar Enderlein, who copied work of F. *Briot. Pewter wares gained immediate popularity, disrupting long tradition of brass craft, which diminished in early 17th century. *See* German clocks, German watches, German gold and silver.

**Hafner*, already well established, started manufacture of tin-glazed earthenware in early 16th century. Examples attributed to Nuremberg, dated 1530–55, decorated with delicate plant-scrolls. In late 16th century, dishes decorated with portraits enclosed by border of scrolled leaves, e.g. Madonna in Glory. Secular and religious subjects appear on plates with wavy rims in early 17th century. Later, faience made e.g. at Hanau and Frankfurt, decorated by *Hausmaler* in styles they had used on glass.

Faience factory founded 1712, managed by J. C. *Ripp. During 18th century, baroque style evolved. Chinese and Dutch decorative influence less strong than in other German faience factories, perhaps because centre for stove-making and **Hafnerware* for previous 200 years. Most notable period *c*1720–*c*1740. Products include plain and reeded dishes; narrow-necked jugs (similar to Ansbach and Hanau); cylindrical tankards painted in vivid blues, yellows, and manganese high-temperature colours often on grey or grey-blue ground. Production declined after import restrictions lifted (1770); ceased in 1840. Marks: NB in monogram (after 1750), also some painters' initials. *Illustration at* weights.

Nuremberg egg. Name applied to early German watch, perhaps through misreading of *Eierlein* ('little egg') for *Uhrlein* ('little clock'), or from oval shape of some examples.

Nuremberg glasses. 17th century goblets made in Nuremberg, Germany. Stem simple baluster and bulb, joined by several **mereses*; further *mereses* join stem to small bowl and wide foot. Popular subjects for engraving.

nursing chair. Wooden or wicker side chair, with low seat and high back. Used when nursing infant. Dates from 19th century.

nutmeg grater. Tiny silver box large enough to contain nutmeg and steel grater. Hinged at top for use of grater and at bottom for removal of grated spice. Made in variety of shapes including heart, teardrop, cylinder, acorn, and

Nutmeg graters. English silver. Left: cylindrical box made by J. Willmore, 1840. Centre: upright grater, handle decorated with shell and gadrooned sides, made in London, 1828; length 4in. Right: box, by Phipps & Robinson, London 1804.

*Nymphenburg porcelain. Bust of girl from model by F. A. *Bustelli, c1761; marked with impressed shield from arms of Bavaria.*

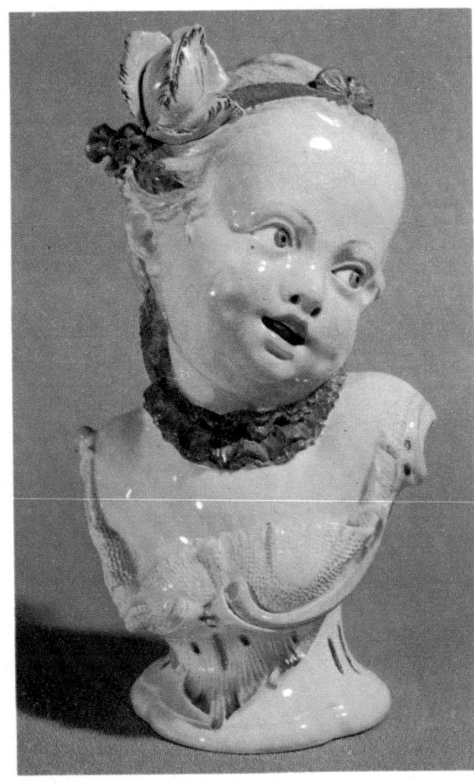

barrel. Decoration scratched in and later bright-cut or engine-turned. In use in England from mid 17th century to *c*1860.

Nymphenburg (Bavaria). Hard-paste porcelain first made successfully at Neudeck-ob-der-Au, near Munich in 1753, by arcanist J. J. *Ringler, with J. P. R. *Hartl, who became manager; under patronage of Elector of Bavaria, Maximilian Joseph. In 1761, moved to purpose-built factory at Nymphenburg Palace, where production still continues. High-quality porcelain paste, exceptionally white and almost flawless. Glaze gathered in hollows has green or greyish tinge. Figures by F. A. *Bustelli, *Modellmeister* 1754–63, include Crucifixion group, Chinese figures, *commedia dell'arte* characters, *putti*, and series of Trades and Seasons; *Galanterien*, walking stick handles, etc., also made. Few figures painted; colour, when used, occurs in touches or flat washes, with lavish gilding. J. P. *Melchior employed 1797–1822; most of figures then left in biscuit. Moulded work includes small articles, like snuff-boxes or, e.g. mirror frames, candlesticks and holy water stoups. Early decorative and table ware in rococo style. Decoration includes flowers, fruit, birds, and landscapes with figures; borders in pink, pale blue, and gold lacework. Low-relief modelling on tableware gilded; moulded rococo scrolls on *Galanterien* accentuated with enamel or gilding. Original forms include cylindrical foodwarmer. Later decoration *décor bois*, and chintz pattern, resembling shot silk. White porcelain cast from original moulds in late 19th century. Factory controlled by state of Bavaria until 1862; then leased to private company. Marks include variations of shield, impressed, or hexagram mark (1763–67), alchemist's sign for four elements, consisting of six-pointed star, with number or letter at each point, printed in underglaze blue.

Nyon, Switzerland. Porcelain factory founded *c*1780; made hard-paste tableware decorated with floral sprigs, festoons, and medallions; also paintings of figures in landscapes, in polychrome or *en camaïeu*. Factory closed in 1813. Mark: two small fish in blue.

oak-leaf chargers. *See* blue-dash chargers.

oak-leaf jars. Italian rounded maiolica drug-jars, made in or near Florence (1425–55). Heraldic beasts or portraits; characteristic background of oak leaves painted in *impasto blue, and purple.

obelisk cup. *See* steeple cup.

Obermaler (German, 'chief or master painter'). Chief decorator in porcelain (or faience) factory. Comparable to position of **Modellmeister*, e.g. J. G. *Herold *Obermaler* and J. J. *Kändler *Modellmeister* at Meissen porcelain factory.

objects of vertu, objets de vitrine, or **bibelots.** Generic term for carefully worked luxury articles in gold, silver, gems, enamel, lacquer, porcelain, glass, etc. Includes all types of small *boxes, e.g. étuis, *nécessaires*, patch-boxes, pomanders, snuff-boxes; also automata, buttons, chatelaines, fans, fob seals, quizzing glasses, scent bottles, spy-glasses, stick-handles, and wine labels.

Obrisset, John (*c*1666–after 1728). French Huguenot ivory carver who worked in London after 1685. Made horn and tortoiseshell boxes, 1690–1712, moulded with portraits of English monarchs, bacchic, or religious scenes. Boxes mainly of horn, oval, $2\frac{3}{4}$–$3\frac{1}{2}$in. wide. Often signed monogram OB.

obsidian or **volcanic glass.** Natural glass of cooled volcanic lava. Usually black, dark green or dark grey. Used by early man for weapons, bowls, and ornaments.

Ochsenkopf glasses (German, 'ox-head' glasses). **Humpen* made in Fichtelgebirge region, Bavaria, in 17th century. Enamelled with view of local mountain (called Ochsenkopf), and, superimposed, wild life and symbolic ox-head.

octagonal bottle. Chinese porcelain form of Ch'ing period. Four-sided bottle made by joining together flat 'bats' of clay with slip; sometimes four angles thus made are flattened, producing irregular eight sides to form. Decoration of both four and eight sided shapes often illustrates Seasons.

octagonal bowls. Eight-sided porcelain bowls, often with lip and raised foot, made at Meissen factory during Kakiemon vogue in late 1720s, early 1730s; decorated in polychrome enamels in Kakiemon patterns, copied directly from Japanese originals. Subsequently copied at Chelsea.

octant. Navigational instrument for measuring altitude of sun, etc., in form of one eighth circle, introduced 1731. Two mirrors, one fixed and silvered over half diameter, second on movable sighting arm, enabled user to view sun and horizon at same time. Elevation of sun read from graduated arc. Evolved into *sextant *c*1760.

Odiot, Jean-Baptiste-Claude (1763–1850). French silversmith working in Paris; master in 1795. Goldsmith to Napoleon; most important exponent of Empire style. Executed commissions for Russian and Austrian courts, also prominent English military figures. Made range of domestic silver. Before Revolution, mark a fleur-de-lis crowned, two pellets, JBCO, and a helmet; after, JBCO, and a bellows in a lozenge. *Illustration at* tea service.

Oeben, Jean-François (*c*1720–63). German-born *ébéniste*; lived in Paris. Worked for C-J. Boulle, son of A-C. *Boulle. Received commissions from Mme de Pompadour; in 1754 became *ébéniste* to Louis XV. Gained reputation for elaborate and original ideas and for fine marquetry. Began work on the *Bureau de Louis XV* (finished after his death by pupil, J. H. *Riesener). Widow carried on business, using his stamp, J-F. OEBEN, until 1767.

oeil de perdrix. French ceramic decoration. Diaper pattern with rings of gilt dots enclosing tiny white circles. Popular on blue and turquoise grounds; introduced at Sèvres in mid 18th century. *Illustration at* Sèvres.

Oettingen-Schrattenhofen (Bavaria). German faience factory founded 1735. Many cylindrical tankards painted in high-temperature colours, often with horizontally-striped lozenges on handle, and greenish-grey or ivory glaze. Production of white and cream-coloured earthenware continued until mid 19th century. Marks include Schrattenhofen, with owner's name (Kohler), or Schrattenhoffen im Riess.

OG clock. *See* ogee clock.

ogee. Double continuous curve in cross-section, concave below, convex above. Used as shape for mouldings on furniture and silver, and for furniture parts, e.g. chair arms, brackets, etc. In

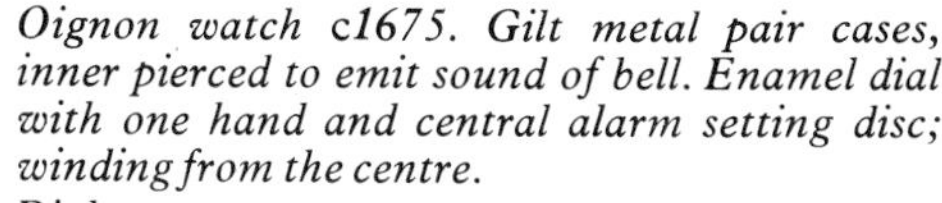

Oignon watch c1675. Gilt metal pair cases, inner pierced to emit sound of bell. Enamel dial with one hand and central alarm setting disc; winding from the centre.
Right:
Old English pattern. Table spoon, table fork, and dessert spoon, dated 1790.

antique trade also used to describe *baluster shape of silver vessel.

ogee or **OG clock.** Connecticut shelf clock, with curved moulding of S-shaped section on door and sides. Rectangular case. Made in several sizes, *c*16–*c*34in. high. Produced in bulk, 1825–1914, notably by C. *Jerome, who also exported them to England. Many makers, including J. C. *Brown, S. *Thomas, and *Ansonia factory.

oignon watch. Form of French watch, with thick movement, widespread in late 17th and 18th centuries; called *oignon* because of bulky shape, slightly resembling onion. Many examples with single hand only. Wound through centre of dial. Gilt brass or silver case; engraving on dial. *See* turnip watch (English equivalent).

oil and vinegar stand. *See* cruet frame.

oil gilding. *See* gilding.

oil-lamp. *See* lamp, crusie, Argand, Sinumbra, agitable.

Old English pattern. English silver flatware pattern: flat, rounded stem-end turns downwards. In use from mid 18th century.

Old Moor's Head, The ('t Oude Moriaenshooft). Delft factory, managed from 1761 by G. *Verstelle, who married owner in 1769. In 1772, united with *Young Moor's Head factory.

oleaginous style. *See* Dutch grotesque style.

Olerys, Joseph (1697–1749). French potter and faience painter, born in Marseille. Working for P. *Clérissy at Moustiers by 1721. In 1723, returned to Marseille. Director of Alcora factory in 1720s and 1730s. In 1738, established factory at Moustiers; introduced polychrome painting.

Made faience echoing styles developed at Alcora, e.g. *décor à guirlandes,* grotesques, *potato flower; painted in brown, purple, green, yellow, and blue. Production continued until 1793. Mark, 1738–*c*1790: monogram of OL, sometimes with painter's initials.

Oliver, Isaac (1556–1617) and son Peter (1594–1647). English miniaturist. Isaac probably of Huguenot French origin, pupil of N. *Hilliard, whose manner he followed until visit to Venice (1596) brought Italian influence. Later work sometimes with landscapes or room interiors; also classical and religious subjects. Portraits include Elizabeth I and Sir Philip Sydney. Peter painted miniature copies of old master paintings and portrait miniatures.

olive spoon. *See* strainer-spoon.

ollio pot or **Ollientopf.** Covered porcelain bowl on three feet with stand, intended to hold meat broth. Shape derived from ancient Chinese

*Ollio pot and cover. Du Paquier period, *Vie na, c1730.*

Isaac Oliver. Unknown member of the Dorset family. c1615.

ceremonial vessels. Made at Vienna in du Paquier period, decorated with *Laub- und-Bandelwerk,* and at Meissen. Also made e.g. in Dutch Delft. *cf pot-à-oille.*

Ollivier, François (1731–95) and son Jacques-Marie (1785–1871). French potters; made faience at Aprey: François 1769–92 (after working at Nevers), Jacques-Marie 1806–32.

ombre table. Triangular gaming table with money dishes on top; used for card game, *ombre,* for three players, introduced from Spain after mid 17th century. Tables made from late 17th to late 18th centuries.

omnium. *See* whatnot.

O'Neale, Jeffryes or Jeffrey Hamett (1734–

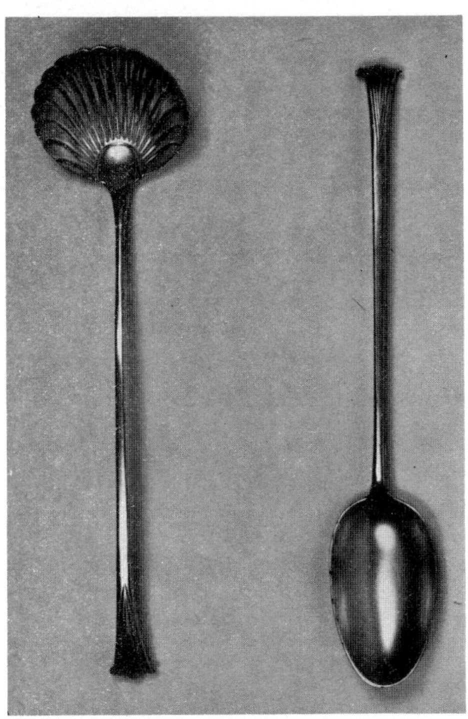

*Onslow pattern. Terminals to George III soup ladle with shell bowl (left) and George II *serving spoon (right).*

Opaline glass. French, c1820, decorated with enamelling and gilding; glass on left is painted with figure of Napoleon.

*Opaque-white glass. Tea-canister, probably from *South Staffordshire, with cap of painted enamel on copper. Painting attributed to M. *Edkins. Height 5¾in.*

1801). Irish-born artist and porcelain painter. Illustrated myths and Aesop's fables on porcelain made at Chelsea. Exhibited miniatures at Society of Artists, 1763–66. At Worcester, 1768–70, probably as outside decorator, painted landscapes with figures, animals, rocks, wind-blown trees, banks of cloud; also fable illustrations and classical subjects. Later, worked for W. *Duesbury, and J. *Wedgwood. Initials O.N.P. found on Worcester and Chelsea porcelain; also signed pieces of Worcester porcelain. *Illustration at* Chelsea.

onion pattern. *See Zwiebelmuster.*

Onolzbach. *See* Ansbach.

Onslow pattern. Mid 18th century British silver flatware pattern: stem-end turned back and curved forming rolled scroll. Face of stem moulded into series of ridges converging to a point mid-way along it. Plain or leaf drop reinforcement on back of spoon bowl. Named after Arthur Onslow (1691–1768), Speaker of House of Commons.

onyx. *See* chalcedony.

onyx marble or **oriental alabaster.** Hard, semi-translucent banded calcite, used from antiquity for small bottles, etc., and other decorative purposes. Takes high polish.

opal. Solidified gel of microscopic crystals of quartz mingled with minute droplets of water; rarely of gem quality. Opals range in colour from milky white to brightly coloured fire and black opal. Characteristic colour produced by varying refractive properties of thin layers of gel and water. Relatively soft stone, easily damaged; usually cut in *cabochon* form. Many superstitions (good and bad) centred on stone since first use by Romans. Infrequently used until 19th century when discovered in Australia; previously, Hungarian mines probably only source. Usually found in nodules and stalactites in volcanic rock, hot spring deposits, etc.

opaline. 19th century term for fine opal-like, translucent white, blue, green, or pink glass. Particularly popular in 19th century France and England for glassware made in imitation of porcelain. *cf* opaque-white glass.

opaque twist. Style of stem used in English glasses *c*1745–*c*1780, using Venetian **latticinio* technique: canes of opaque-white glass introduced into clear stem, then drawn and twisted. Also combined with *colour twists and *air twists. *Illustration at* English wine glasses.

opaque-white glass. In ancient Egypt, calcined bones used to produce watery white glass, later known as milk-and-water glass. Early 15th century Venetians revived technique, as *lattimo* glass, used e.g. for bowls and vases. Appearance varied from dull opaque-white to almost transparent opalescent glass; decorated with gilding, painting, and splashes of colour. Opaque-white canes embedded in clear glass first used as decorative device by Romans; later developed by Venetians in **filigree* and **vetro di trina* glass. Opaque-white glass produced throughout Europe by early 18th century, imitating Chinese and Meissen porcelain in Bohemia (*Beinglas*), Germany, France, and England. Decoration in transparent polychrome colours popular for rococo motifs, e.g. *chinoiseries,* scenes after J-A. *Watteau, mythological subjects, genre painting. Arsenic and tin oxides used as colouring agents, giving glass creamy porcelain-like appearance. In England, *Bristol opaque-white glass made from late 18th century; notable examples painted by M. *Edkins, who favoured *chinoiserie* motifs, particularly on tea-caddies and candlesticks. In Germany, known as *Milchglas* or *Porzellanglas* for resemblance to porcelain. In late 17th and early 18th centuries, framed sheets of *Milchglas* occasionally enamelled after contemporary paintings. Enamelled opaque-white glass continued in production until early 19th century in northern Germany and Bohemia. In 18th century, similar glass produced in Venice for tableware, decorated particularly in red monochrome.

open knot. *See* Persian knot.

open thumbpiece. Thumbpiece on European pewter vessels, similar in outline to *chair-back thumbpiece, but with centre cut out.

openware lantern. Chinese Ch'ing dynasty form. Ovoid lamp standing on base; for use on table. Sides decorated with fret patterns, cut out of firm porcelain body before firing. Often with overglaze enamel decoration, e.g. *famille verte* or *famille rose*.

Oppenheim, Meyer (fl 18th century). English glass maker, in London when granted patent in 1755 for making red glass; obtained by adding ½oz of gold solution to every pound of materials for flint-glass. Red glassware sometimes ornamented with gilding; examples rare, as gilding usually faded or disappeared with age. Set up glass furnace in Birmingham *c*1760; took out patent for flint ruby glass, 1764. In 1789 'Meyer Oppenheimer de Bermingham' granted patent in France for improved method of glass manufacture.

Oppenord, Gilles Marie (1672–1742). Dutch architect and designer; a leading exponent of rococo style. Studied in Italy, then worked in Paris; produced designs for Louis XV.

Ordos style. Name given to *animal style decoration found on bronzes of nomadic people of Ordos Desert area within loop of Yellow River, from *c*500B.C. Small objects include harness ornaments and finials. Motifs include animals fighting and serpent designs. *cf* Huai style.

organ. Most complex of wind instruments;

Organ. English chamber organ. c1750. Mahogany case with dummy gilded metal pipes. Keys of ivory and ebony.

consists basically of tuned pipes, wind supply system, and operating mechanism made up of one or more keyboards, *stops, pedalboard, etc. Earliest form, *hydraulos,* or water organ, probably invented by Ktesibios of Alexandria in 2nd century B.C.; also used by Romans. Water system stabilized air pressure which fed organ. One keyboard or manual. Large cathedrals of early Middle Ages required powerful organs, hence 'great' organs built in 13th and 14th centuries. Smaller, positive (non-portable) organs developed from 10th century; stood either on floor or on table or stand; continued to be made until 17th century. Small portable organ (slung round neck, leaving one hand free to operate bellows and other, keys) used from 12th to 16th centuries (most popular in 15th century) for processions and also for home use. Number of keyboards, type of stops, action etc. varied considerably. Pedalboard, found in German organs from as early as 14th century, adopted later in rest of Europe and much later in Britain. Stops in general use in 15th and 16th centuries. In Britain, many organs destroyed during Reformation. Reached height of popularity as church and artistic instrument c1650–c1750. Most important centres of production: France, Germany, and Holland. *Chamber organ developed at this period for home use. Organ pipes usually symmetrically arranged; whole may be lavishly ornamented (particularly baroque examples). *See* barrel organ, bird organ.

Oribe ware. Japanese ceramics of Momoyama and early Edo periods made near Seto. Earliest examples indistinguishable from Shino, with thick pottery body and white, feldspathic glaze, but later painted (E-Oribe) wares distinctive, with free, abstract decoration, in brown oxide; also versions of flowers, grasses, fruits, landscapes, etc. Later examples include figures of European visitors to Japan, e.g. in form of candlesticks. Incense burners, covered bowls shaped like fans, or cake-dishes shaped like baskets, often found. Black glaze sometimes used (Kuro-Oribe); bright copper-green (Ao Oribe), or red glazes (Aka-Oribe), sometimes with brown and white mixed clay body.

oriental alabaster. *See* onyx marble.

Oriental Lowestoft. Chinese porcelain manufactured in second half of 18th century at *Ching-tê-chên. Examples of Lowestoft or New Hall porcelain shipped to East for exact copying, to fill European orders. Usually painted with flowers, originally copied by English decorators from Chinese enamel colours. Plain white wares sometimes transported to nearby Canton for decoration before shipment.

Orloff Service. Large silver dinner service of *c*3000 pieces in neo-classical style ordered by Catherine the Great of Russia from J-N *Roettiers of Paris for her favourite, Prince Gregory Orloff; delivered 1771–75. Executed by Roettiers, helped by his father, and others including L-J. *Lenhendrick. Includes dinner plates, meat dishes or platters, dish covers, candelabra, candlesticks, wine coolers, tureens, teapots, chocolate pots, ollio pots. Most of service in Kremlin and Hermitage, Leningrad until 1930–31; now dispersed between Russia, the Louvre, Paris, Metropolitan Museum, New York and other collections.

Ormskirk watches. Made at Ormskirk, Lancashire in early 19th century. Escapements often variety of verge, some with two escape wheels on same arbor, others of individual design. Movements often with going *barrels, some with open mainsprings.

ormolu (French *or moulu,* 'ground gold'), **gilt bronze, bronze doré,** or **bronze gilding.** Brass or bronze objects or mounts gilded or covered with gold-coloured lacquer. Used mainly in France from 16th century; to lesser extent in England.

orrery. Instrument driven by clockwork and showing movements of planets, named after first planetarium made in England for Charles Boyle, 4th Earl of Orrery, by G. *Graham. Others driven by hand, and adjustable for demonstration of celestial system.

Orry de Fulvy, Jean-Louis-Henri (1703–51). French aristocrat and financier; engaged Gilles and Robert *Dubois (1738–41) to experiment on manufacture of porcelain in royal Château de Vincennes. Maintained experiments by F. *Gravant after departure of the Dubois until formation of C. *Adam's company (1745).

Orvieto (Umbria), Italy. Primitive green and purple ware made in 13th, 14th, and early 15th centuries. Later products similar to Faenza, although body darker; decoration sometimes includes masks or animals in relief surrounded by branched stems with fruit and foliage in outline, against background of purple cross-hatching. Other designs include portraits and figures, also against cross-hatched background.

os de mouton scroll. *See* ram's horn scroll.

ossekoppen (Dutch, 'ox heads'). Ceramic decoration: arabesque motifs resembling wide horns at corners of Dutch tin-glazed tiles, from early 17th century.

ostensory. *See* monstrance.

Osterspey, Jakob (1730–82). German porcelain painter. Worked at Frankenthal (1759–82). Signed pieces (J.O. pinxit) include vases and table service featuring mythological subjects, and snuff-boxes.

ostrich-egg cup. 15th and 16th century ceremonial standing cup with ostrich-egg bowl set in silver, silver-gilt, or gold mount; made principally in England and Germany. Most common stem was figure of ostrich. *See* gryphon's egg.

Ottoman or **Ottoman-Cairene carpets.** *See* Turkish Court Manufactory carpets.

ottoman or **ottomane.** Named after Turkish low, wide bench, covered with cushions. In 18th century France, as *ottomane,* a small *canapé, often with oval seat; curving back and arms upholstered as one piece; may have loose cushion at either end. British and American ottoman dates from late 18th century; initially upholstered bench, often with back, perhaps designed to fit into corner of room. Box ottoman has hinged seat, storage space inside. Also, circular or polygonal overstuffed seat, often with buttoned upholstery, and back-rest in centre resembling truncated cone; flat top of back section might hold e.g. potted plant.

Ottweiler or **Nassau-Saarbrücken** (Rhineland). German faience and porcelain factory founded 1763. Porcelain body variable in quality and colour. Tableware shapes in French style (e.g. pear-shaped jug with hinged lid), finely painted, sometimes in purple monochrome and underglaze blue with mythological scenes and restrained rococo borders. A plain white figure (after Vincennes) has been attributed to this factory. Mark: NS (Nassau-Säarbrücken) in

Ottoman. Louis XV, stamped by Tilliard; moulded and painted frame: crest-rail surmounted by heart-shaped cabochon. Width 6ft.

underglaze blue or gold. Faience tableware, pierced and fluted in neo-classical forms, is unmarked.

Oude Loosdrecht. Dutch porcelain factory, transferred from *Weesp, using same moulds and equipment. L-V. *Gerverot employed until 1782. Factory changed hands; transferred to *Amstel in 1784. Products include vases with pierced decoration; also oval tea and coffee pots and jugs. Painted e.g. with seascapes or hunting scenes. Figures in landscapes with buildings predominantly in brown.

Oudenaarde tapestry. Flemish tapestry weaving centre active from 15th century. In 16th century, large numbers of mediocre quality hangings produced, mainly *verdures* and figure tapestries, with mythological, biblical, and historical subjects, including History of Alexander the Great, Judgement of Paris, and History of Troy. Early 16th century tapestries characterized by quiet, cool colour schemes (often with much yellow), using no strong reds or crimson. From 1544, trademark was device resembling pair of spectacles (probably water bougets) on town shield. In early 17th century, nearly equalled *Brussels in importance. Subjects: landscapes and *verdures,* some figure tapestries with grand historical themes. Renowned for furniture tapestries. Numerous cartoon artists included D. *Teniers. From mid 17th century, industry crippled by Spanish wars. Mass emigration of finest weavers (mainly to France), including P. *Béhagle in 1684. Limited revival in 18th century when subjects mainly followed contemporary Brussels and particularly Gobelins designs. Last workshop closed 1787.

Oudry, Jean-Baptiste (1686–1755). French painter, noted for animal paintings, illustrator, and tapestry designer. Official painter to Beauvais tapestry manufactory from 1726, and credited with introduction of 'woven painting'; director from 1734. In 1736, also entrusted with supervision at Gobelins of Hunts of Louis XV, for which had prepared cartoons; thereafter chief director of Royal Manufactory's productions. Caused dissension among weavers by insisting on exact reproduction of painter's effects in tapestry, even to extent of creating illusion of oil painting. Required use of innumerable subtle and delicate nuances of colour, difficult to obtain and prone to fading; finer shades would begin to deteriorate within five years. French State factories maintained Oudry's approach – imitating painting in tapestry – into 20th century.

Oushak carpets. *See* Ushak carpets.

out-quenchers. *See* douters.

Outrebon, Jean-Louis-Dieudonné (d after 1789). French silversmith from family of silver craftsmen, working in Paris; master in 1772. Made domestic silver in neo-classical style. Mark: a fleur-de-lis crowned, two pellets, JLO, and a shell. Son, N. *Outrebon II, continued in trade.

Outrebon, Nicolas, II (d 1779). French silversmith working in Paris; master in 1735. Made range of domestic silver in rococo style, probably filling some commissions for F-T. *Germain: when latter bankrupted, appeared to request payment for merchandise supplied. Mark: a fleur-de-lis crowned, two pellets, NOB, and a rosette.

outside decorators. Painters using enamel colours and gilt to decorate wares, usually porcelain, bought in the white from French and English factories; equivalent to German *Hausmaler*. English outside decorators include W. *Duesbury (1751–53) and J. *Giles (by 1760) in London; W. *Absolon at Yarmouth from 1790; T. *Baxter working at Worcester from 1814. In early 19th century, white porcelain sold by Sèvres factory decorated in style of 18th century. T. M. *Randall decorated porcelain of Coalport, Nantgarw, Swansea, and Sèvres to order from dealers.

oval-back Windsor. *See* loop-back Windsor.

overglaze colours. *See* enamel.

overlay glass. *See* cameo glass.

overmantel mirror. Ornamental, usually, rectangular mirror designed to be placed above mantelpiece. Dates from 18th century. From mid 19th century, flanked by shelves for displaying small objects.

overstamping (in silver). Practice of silver retailer stamping own mark on piece already stamped with maker's mark.

overstuffing. Use of padding on seat furniture over or within framework and underneath upholstery, giving shape and comfort. Used from 19th century.

ovolo moulding. Classical moulding formed of repeated oval shapes; *cf* egg-and-dart. Much used in late 16th and 17th centuries, especially as stamped silver ornament. Revived in England in early 19th century.

Owari seiji. Japanese ceramics of 9th century Heian period. Feldspathic glaze introduced from China; used in Owari province (now Aichi prefecture). Imitations of Chinese celadon include, notably, Lung-ch'üan, Ch'ing pai, Ting, Chien, Yüeh. In 12th century, production centre moved to *Seto. No examples known.

owl jug or **Eulenkrug.** Earthenware jug in shape of owl, with detachable head for use as

*Ox-blood glazed vase. Glaze has run thin at neck and formed thickly at foot. *Ch'ien Lung period. Height 15in.*

*Overmantel mirror. Rococo gilt-wood frame in style of W. *Ince and J. Mayhew, mid 18th century. Length 6ft7in.*

cup. Made by *Hafner of Nuremberg, Germany in mid 16th century. Early specimens have feathers in applied relief, painted in underglaze blue; armorial shields, moulded in high relief on breast, painted in gold and oil colours. Later specimens have painted feathers only. Perhaps made as prizes for shooting contests, bearing arms of prize-givers. Also made at *Caltagirone in 17th century. Occur in 17th century English slipware and, rarely, salt-glaze, with dark brown detail.

ox-blood glaze or **sang-de-boeuf** or **lang yao.** Red glaze, associated with Ch'ing monochrome ware. Originated as underglaze red colour in Ming period, but technique lost in reign of Chia Ching. Usually finely crackled; copper based, fired in reducing atmosphere. Shine reputedly achieved by mysterious ingredients (e.g. cornelian, or amethystine quartz). Fine examples from reign of K'ang Hsi have deep cherry red colour, sometimes with streaked effect, and downward flowing movement, ending in uneven line at base. Colour sometimes drained away at lip, revealing bone-white or green rim. Some glazes have even, orange peel texture. Later 18th century potters lost art of controlling flow of glaze in firing: glaze ran over foot and was ground away. 19th century vases with characteristic heavy foot also have red glazes of this type.

ox-eye cup. *See* college cup.

Oxford chair. Two different styles of English mid 19th century chair. Either, light side chair with cane seat and slightly splayed legs (yoke-rail and back-slat extend beyond vertical back supports). Also, *easy chair with high back, deep seat, and open arms with upholstered tops.

*Oystering. Walnut on Queen Anne chest-on-stand, also decorated with concentric *stringing.*

oxidizing atmosphere. Kiln conditions in which fire burns brightly with excess of oxygen which passes over pots, allowing metallic pigments to remain as oxides. *cf* reducing atmosphere.

oystering, oyster veneer, or **oystershell.** Veneer made of decoratively-arranged cross-sections of root or small branch of some fruit trees, lignum vitae, olive, walnut, or laburnum. Pattern of grain resembles oyster shells. Used mainly on late 17th and early 18th century English furniture.

Ozier pattern. German ceramics. Moulded patterns resembling wicker-work (osier), probably designed by J. J. *Kändler, first used on borders of Meissen tableware during 1730s; sometimes in conjunction with painting in Kakiemon style. *Ordinär-Ozier* (*c*1735) involves zig-zag basket work moulding on rim; *alt-Ozier* (early 1730s) features basket weave spaced with radial ribs; in *neu-Ozier* (1742) ribs are S-shaped. *See* Sulkowski service.

pad foot. *Club foot resting on attached disc.

Padua (Veneto), Italy. Lead-glazed *sgraffiato* ware made from 15th century; plaque with Virgin and Child (*c*1500) has yellowish glaze splashed with blue and bright yellow. This and other examples have background entirely excised behind decoration of slip. In 16th century, maiolica has *berrettino* glaze painted with blue leaf patterns or fruit in polychrome, as at Faenza and notably Venice. Drug-pots with grey enamel over relief-moulded flowers made until 18th century.

pagoda motif. Lines and shapes used to create pagoda silhouette. Pagoda roof shape used in European and British case pieces, and later chair backs, from *c*1650; also in 18th century America.

pagoda-top. Top part of long-case clock, surmounted by finial, loosely resembling form of oriental pagoda. Introduced in late 18th century England. Sometimes with break-arch dial, and lacquered case.

pagod. *See* magot.

paillons (French, 'straws'). Thin rolls of gold, silver, or coloured foil shaped into pattern and fired between two layers of translucent enamel. Technique developed in 18th century France by J. *Coteau.

paintbrush or **tassel foot.** American form of *Spanish foot, scrolling inwards and tapering to resemble stylized paintbrush.

painted enamels. Image painted in enamel colours on *enamel blank, fired to set colours. Technique developed in 15th century Venice and improved at *Limoges. Technique employed in 18th century in *Birmingham, *Battersea and *South Staffordshire; in Europe, notably by A. *Fromery in Berlin.

painted tin. *See tôle peinte,* japanned metal ware.

pair case. Watch case almost universal in England, 1650–1800; also used in Europe. Inner case with glass front contains movement, surrounded by glass-less outer 'pair' case, often decorated with *repoussé* work, enamel, semi-precious stones, etc. Cases usually of similar metals, but outer may be brass, gilded, or covered with leather, horn, shagreen, etc.

pair plate. *See* marriage plate.

Pajou, Augustin (1730–1809). French sculptor. Modelled figures made in biscuit porcelain at Sèvres. Work includes Birth of the Dauphin, busts of Blaise Pascal, and Madame du Barry.

paktong (Chinese, 'white copper'). Alloy, mainly of copper and nickel (45% copper, 30% nickel, 24% zinc, 1% pure iron) used in Yunan province of China from early times for money and household utensils. Introduced in Europe in late 18th century. Used for grates, candlesticks, etc. Polishes to brightness of silver; does not tarnish.

pale celadon. Chinese ceramics; small group of celadon pieces, mostly in private collections in West. Pale grey body, with light-coloured glaze, and distinctive double-bevelled foot-rim. Dates from early Sung dynasty; origin unknown.

pale family. Porcelain figures made at Derby *c*1756–70. Body light in weight, with chalky texture; glaze bluish; colours pale.

Palermo (Sicily). Principal centre of maiolica manufacture in Sicily in late 16th and early 17th centuries. Products, including drug-pots and vases, decorated e.g. with trophies in style of

Palissy, Bernard. Oval dish decorated with snake, crayfish, lizard, frog, insects, shells, and leaves. Length 13*in.*

Castel Durante. Sometimes marked S.P.Q.P. (*Senatus populusque Palermitani*), or Fatto in Palermo, and date.

Palissy, Bernard (*c*1510–90). French potter. At first, maker of stained glass. In 1542, established as potter at Saintes (Charente-Maritime). Made earthenware dishes decorated with realistically modelled plants, fish, reptiles, molluscs, etc.; also figure subjects in relief set in interior or landscape. Polychrome glazes used to produce marbled grounds. In 1555, commissioned to make grotto for Italian garden. Established Paris workshop in 1566. Huguenot imprisoned for heresy. Moulds used for many years after death; many reproductions and forgeries made up to 19th century.

Palladian style. Architectural style defined by Andrea Palladio, 16th century Venetian architect, based on strict classical proportions and principles. Palladian architecture first introduced into England by Inigo Jones in 17th century; further encouraged by 3rd Earl of Burlington in early 18th century. Principal designer of interiors and furniture for English Palladian buildings was W. *Kent, whose furniture, designed to harmonize with specific buildings, combined architectural features (columns, pediments, etc.) with opulent carved baroque decoration and gilding; work noted for massive size, also for marble or other stone tops on console and pier tables, and gilding on chairs, tables and frames.

Palmer, Humphrey (fl *c*1747–*c*1786). Potter at Hanley, Staffordshire. In 1760 inherited Church Works, established *c*1680. Maker of decorative black basalt and jasper ware, contemporary with J. *Wedgwood. Firm became Neale & Palmer (1776), then *Neale & Co (1778). Marks (1760–78): H.P. and PALMER, impressed.

palmer's shell. *See* badge.

palmette. Decorative motif derived from branching palm tree; used on classical architecture, oriental carpets, and pottery from 14th century Persia and 15th century Turkey. Copied on maiolica of Faenza and Tuscany from mid 15th century. Popular on furniture, silver, etc., in late 18th century Europe. *Illustration at* Bijar carpets.

palm top motif. *See* boteh motif.

palm-tree thumbpiece. Thumbpiece with stem and spreading horizontal branches found on late 17th century tankards, etc.

pancake or **pannekoek plates.** Flat Dutch Delft plates, made in 18th century for home and export market. Reverse usually marked by struts used for support in kiln.

pan or **panel-back.** *Wainscot chair back in shape of panel, common in 16th and 17th centuries.

p'an. Ancient Chinese ritual bronze vessel, dating from late Shang and Chou periods; shallow, round basin, on ring foot, used for ritual washing of hands. Often decorated with fish and serpentine dragon motif at centre.

panelled furniture. *See* joined furniture.

panelling. Method of decorating glass by cutting or grinding on flat edge of wheel. Also known as flat-cutting, or sunken panel. Flattened, upright, oval, or round-topped arch pattern popular in 18th century; narrow, upright arch, often tapering at foot, popular in late 18th, early 19th centuries.

Pannemaker, François (d 1700) and André. Father and son, Brussels weavers; worked at Gobelins, then established royal manufactory at Lille. Produced mainly landscape tapestries.

pannikin. *See* saucepan.

Pantin, Simon (d *c*1729). Huguenot silversmith working in London; apprenticed to P. *Harache; received freedom in 1701. Made notable plate for royalty and aristocracy. A. *Courtauld II apprenticed to him in 1701. Son continued in trade. Marks: PA with a peacock above enclosed in a keyhole (1701); SP with a peacock above (1720).

papal or **golden rose.** Gold or silver-gilt bouquet of roses (or single rose) awarded annually by Pope to prince who had done outstanding service to Church. Earliest surviving example is early 14th century, but custom was older. Generally one central rose, with some secondary roses and rosebuds; stem complete with thorns and leaves. Sometimes set with gems. Dipped in spices and holy oils. Later examples have foot or stand. Practice continued into 20th century.

papal sword. Sword of precious metal, set with gems, awarded annually by Pope to a prince for services rendered to Church. Custom probably originated in 9th century, though earliest surviving example is sword of 1446 given by Pope Eugenius IV to John II of Castile. Scabbard and belt which accompanied sword also ornamented with gold or silver and gems; scabbard could be of leather or velvet. Many in Spanish royal armoury in Madrid.

Papal workshop. Tapestry workshop (San Michele Workshop) established in Rome 1710 by Pope Clement XI. Peak period 1717–70. Numerous subjects, with designs mainly copied from contemporary French models and ancient tapestries. Work discontinued 1791; revived on small scale in early 19th century; closed *c*1860.

pap boat. 18th and 19th century British silver container with low, boat-shaped body narrowing to spout at one end. Used for feeding semi-liquid food (pap) to infants. Might have ornamented rim. Many converted to cream containers by addition of handle and feet; these generally hallmarked beside handle.

Pap-boat, gold, made in London by John Lamb in 1816. Length $5\frac{1}{2}$*in.*

Paperweights. French, 19th century. Top: bouquet paperweight, *Cristallerie de Saint Louis; diameter $2\frac{1}{2}$in. Bottom: Crown Imperial paperweight, *Baccarat; very rare spray of flowers in clear glass; diameter 3in.

Papier mâché furniture. *Games table with folding top, inlaid with mother-of-pearl; painted and gilded. English, 1850–60. Height 2ft3in.

Parcel gilt. Beaker, made in Augsburg, c1685. Lower part chased with matted and plain fluting, engraved above with panoramic view of city of Frankfurt.

paperweights. Earliest glass paperweights, attributed to *Cristallerie de St Louis, Paris, mostly produced 1845–49. Few dated, except for years 1847 and 1848; some also have initials, SL (or initials and no date). Characterized by soft, delicate colours, particularly blue, pink, white, yellow, dark and light green. *Millefiori* weights usually arranged in bouquet form, with florets and green foliage; single flower, fruit, vegetable and reptile weights also made. Most prized form, overlay: cased in opaque coloured glass, cut as in *cameo glass to reveal decoration (usually bouquet) embedded in clear glass beneath; principal overlay colours, deep blue, emerald-green, and pink.

*Baccarat weights, 1846–49, often incorporate date in design; majority are *millefiori* designs, also flower weights, a few overlays, and reptile and butterfly subjects. Frequently distinguished by star-cut base. Usual size, 3in. in diameter, but Baccarat also produced magnum weights *c*4in. across, and miniatures slightly less than 2in. *Clichy weights also mainly brightly-coloured *millefiori* designs, with small group of overlays, bouquets, swirls, and miniatures; sometimes signed C, more rarely, CLICHY.

First English weights, made at *Stourbridge, show Clichy influence, but colours pastel; characteristic forms include yellow baskets with coloured florets on turquoise background, and heart-shaped tartan-ribbon designs. *Bacchus & Sons, Birmingham, made similar weights; brighter coloured examples made by Islington Glass Works, London, signed I G W. A. *Pellatt made fine *sulphide weights. Some also produced at Bristol, Nailsea, and *Whitefriars Glass Works, London.

In mid 19th century, American firms produced variety of weights, some using Pellatt's sulphide technique. Nicholas Lutz, formerly of Cristallerie de St Louis, worked with *Boston & Sandwich Glass Company making floral bouquets or miniature fruit resting on *latticinio* bed; *New England Glass Company produced almost life-size single fruit weights resting on clear glass cushion; mainly by François Pierre, formerly of Baccarat. In late 19th century, pressed glass weights made in shape of landmarks, e.g. Plymouth Rock, and books or animals.

papier mâché. Eastern technique of making small pieces of furniture and other articles from paper pulp composition (containing chalk, size, and sand). Brought to France in 17th century and to England in second half of 18th century. Also popular in 19th century America. Small boxes, trays, clock cases, chairs and chair backs, tables, etc., made from papier mâché alone; larger objects have wooden frame with papier mâché covering. H. *Clay of Birmingham patented (1772) technique of papier mâché construction: whole sheets of paper glued together, then moulded, pressed, and baked. First called Clay ware, technique adopted by Jennes & Betteridge of Birmingham, who used it especially in first half of 19th century. Surfaces of papier mâché objects often lacquered, inlayed with mother-of-pearl, or painted with flowers, landscapes, allegorical scenes, etc.

parachute (in watches). Device invented by A-L. *Breguet to protect balance if watch dropped or jolted; bearings of balance staff supported on springs and yield to excess pressure.

paraison. Gather or 'gob' of unformed glass metal partly shaped and hollowed with blowpipe.

parcel gilt. Medieval term denoting partly gilded, often referring to silver and occasionally to pieces of wood, with some gilt decoration. Technique used in silver for ornamental contrast, but also inside bowls of chalices (for liturgical reasons) and inside salts (to prevent corrosion) or any other silver object likely to be damaged by contents.

parchment panelling. *See* linenfold panelling.

Pardoe, Thomas (1770–1823). English flower painter. Decorated porcelain made at Derby and Worcester; also worked at Swansea (1790–1809) and Nantgarw. Independent enameller at Bristol (1809–21). Work includes studies copied from Botanical Magazine. Signed examples exist. *Illustration at* Cambrian Pottery.

parian ware. Fine-grained hard-paste porcelain, usually unglazed, sometimes with smear glaze, resembling marble in appearance; introduced commercially by W. T. *Copeland in 1846; used chiefly to make biscuit figures, often in imitation of marble figures, and tableware. By 1850, made by many firms; introduced in America in unglazed form (*Bennington

Parian porcelain. English jug, c1860. Painted and gilded with Renaissance-inspired ornament. Marked *COPELAND impressed. Height 8½in.

Paris porcelain. Plate, c1810, made at Rue de la Roquette in neo-classical style; matt ground and chiselled gilding.

parian) at United States Pottery. Until c1850, generally known as statuary porcelain. Coloured parian ware popular from c1870.

Paris. Faience made at *Saint-Cloud and other factories in Paris district during late 17th century includes *faïence blanche* made for use by servants in châteaux (examples from 1670s), and work in style of Rouen, painted in blue with outlines in black and lacking red characteristic of Rouen. Soft-paste porcelain made at major factories situated near Paris and at branch of Saint-Cloud actually in city. Hard-paste factories established after discovery of kaolin at Saint-Yrieix, encouraged by decrees of 1780s reducing Sèvres monopoly. Porcelain of late 18th and early 19th centuries usually good quality imitations of Empire-style Sèvres; later other styles adopted. Pierre-Antoine Hannong, son of Paul-Antoine *Hannong. after starting manufacture of hard-paste porcelain at Vincennes (1765), established factory in Faubourg Saint-Denis in 1771, using mark of crossed flags in blue (until 1776); from 1779 under patronage of Comte d'Artois, using mark C-P and ducal coronet, stencilled in red. La Courtille factory, also started in 1771, lasted until 1841. Clignancourt under royal protection from establishment (1771); also Rue Thiroux (from 1775), patronized by Marie Antoinette, marked with crown over A in blue. Rue de Bondy began in 1780 under patronage of Duc d'Angoulême; mark, monogram stencilled in blue, or under Rue de Bondy in red; also, (1780–93) MANUF^re/de M^or le Duc/d'Angouleme. Factory established in Rue Popincourt, 1782, making clock cases, biscuit figures, and imitations of jasper ware, became very prosperous; mark NAST/A/PARIS stencilled in red. Factory and decorating workshop at Rue de Charonne from c1795 later succeeded Saint-Cloud faience production at Rue de la Roquette (until 1840). Cream-coloured earthenware made at Pont au Choux from 1743.

Parisot, Peter (fl mid 18th century). French émigré working in London from 1748. Organized first major knotted-carpet weaving venture in England in 1750. *See* Fulham carpets.

Paris tapestry. First major European high-warp loom tapestry weaving centre, active from 13th century. First important period in 14th century, under successive patronage of Charles V of France; Louis I, Duke of Anjou; Philip the Bold, Duke of Burgundy; and Jean, Duke of Berry. Prominent merchant-weavers included N. *Bataille, whose main work, the *Angers Tapestry, is only surviving major 14th century French tapestry. Produced mainly vast, long narrow hangings with simple Gothic style compositions strongly influenced by book illuminations. Also smaller pieces for church and court furnishings. Subjects include allegorical, chivalric, pastoral, and hunting scenes, and armorial tapestries. Industry declined during Hundred Years' War, and collapsed when Paris fell to English in 1418. Weavers dispersed; centre shifted to Flemish town of *Arras. Paris regained importance in 16th century under patronage of increasingly powerful French monarchy. Numerous small workshops operated; manufactory established 1551 at Hôpital de la Trinité. By 17th century, Paris had ousted Brussels as European centre. In 1607, Henri IV instructed M. *de Comans and F. *de la Planche to establish first low-warp loom tapestry workshop (formed basis for *Gobelins manufactory); also re-housed (1608) Dubourg and Laurent's high-warp loom tapestry workshop in Louvre Palace. Fleur-de-lis and P adopted as Parisian trademark, with initials of master-weaver. In 1662, Parisian workshops combined into state-owned *Gobelins factory, which determined tapestry styles from then until decline of weaving art in 19th century.

Parker & Wakelin. *See* E. and J. *Wakelin.

parlour chair. Originally, light single chair with carved ornament on frame and pierced back; used also in sets as dining-room chairs. By mid 19th century, had become heavier side chair with upholstered seat. Term also used in 19th century to include most single chairs (excluding bedroom chairs).

Parquetry. Commode, probably Austrian. 18th century.

Parnassus service. German ceramics; porcelain table service made at Meissen by J. J. *Kändler c1745. Centre dishes in form of rocks, with decoration of modelled flowers and figures of Apollo and Muses.

parquetry. Geometrical designs of wood, at first made by sinking pieces of various woods into a ground to form design; later by affixing pieces in patterns to separate ground and attaching entire sheet of design to surface as a veneer. Used in England from c1660. Also popular in 18th century France and Italy. *Illustration also at bureau.*

partners' desk. Large writing table, usually on two pedestal bases, with drawers and storage areas on both sides; designed for two people sitting opposite each other. Many examples made c1750–1800.

partridge pattern. *See caille* pattern.

parure. Set of matching jewellery; usually necklace, brooch, earrings and bracelets. *Demi-parure* was smaller set, e.g. brooch and earrings or necklace and earrings.

Passau. *See* kaolin.

Passavant, Claude. Swiss-born Huguenot; master-weaver in England. Established early English knotted carpet manufactory in Exeter, 1753, operating with equipment and weavers from defunct *Fulham carpet manufactory. First carpet (woven 1755) won Royal Society of Arts prize for best 'Turkey Carpet'. *Exeter carpets woven until 1761, when Passavant went bankrupt. Designs copy Savonnerie or Turkish models.

passementerie button. 18th century fabric-covered button decorated with beads and braid.

Passglas. Narrow, cylindrical, beaker, generally with *kick in base, resembling **Stangenglas,* but ringed with glass threads for use in

Patch-box. Made by M. Philippe, Paris, 1758. Black lacquer and gold; inside gum brush, two compartments, and mirror. Length 2½in.

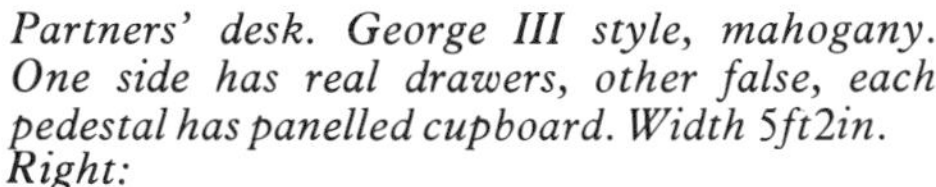

Partners' desk. George III style, mahogany. One side has real drawers, other false, each pedestal has panelled cupboard. Width 5ft2in.
Right:
Paste jewellery. French or English, 18th century. White paste hair ornament (top), white, yellow, and red paste brooch (middle), both set in silver; yellow paste brooch set in gilt-metal (bottom).

drinking contests. Participants attempted to drink exact amount of liquid between divisions; if unsuccessful, had to drink to next line. Made in Low Countries and Germany, late 16th to 18th centuries.

paste. Glass cut into gem-like forms. Used by Romans for seal *intaglios and *cameos. From 9th century, Venice exported coloured glass gemstones throughout Europe. In 15th century Venetians developed *cristallo* (*crystal glass), a clear, decolourized glass, used to imitate rock-crystal and diamond. Little medieval and Renaissance paste jewellery survives and most is of poor quality. Paste jewellery depends for attractiveness on underlying foil which, when tarnished or otherwise damaged, severely reduces beauty of piece. *c*1675 G. *Ravenscroft in England discovered *flint glass which provided hard, colourless, highly refractive glass taking a high polish ideal for paste gems. Best period for paste jewellery *c*1700–*c*1865; produced in England, France, Spain and Portugal. Chief exponent, Frenchman G. F. *Strass working in Paris. Fine paste jewellery often referred to as 'strass'. In 18th century worn in highest strata of society; not intended to counterfeit diamond. Designs French inspired. Stones facet-cut like diamond and set very close together in clusters; variety of sizes and shapes; backed with foil, as were all gems before early 18th century. Most 18th century paste silver-mounted; gold mounting usually late 18th or early 19th century. *c*1780–*c*1820 opaline paste made in France and England, from glass (mainly containing oxides of tin, arsenic, or phosphorus) which, after careful cooling, has milky appearance of opal.

Pink coloured examples backed with rose-coloured foil to produce jewels (many in floral or **girandole* styles). Paste jewellery of lower quality machine-produced in 19th century; rarely backed with foil; tinted by addition of metallic oxides; lacked brilliance of 18th century counterpart. Stones also standardized (e.g. round and oval). Many **parures* made. After *c*1840, colourless pastes permanently silvered, by method used by mirror manufacturers; made to appear as much like diamond as possible. In mid 19th century many brooches made in animal shapes, cornucopia, floral sprays, etc. *See* J. Tassie.

pastille-burner. *See* perfume-burner.

Patanazzi family (fl 1580–1620): Antonio, Alfonso, Francesco, and Vicenzio. Italian maiolica potters and painters at Urbino. Associated with introduction of applied relief decoration and figure modelling; much work painted with grotesques, often with dark orange predominating. Pair of vases (1580) first dated examples, although ewer painted with coat of arms may date from 1579.

patch-box or **boîte à mouches.** Circular or oblong container for taffeta patches worn as beauty spots by both sexes in 17th and 18th centuries. Shallower than snuff-box, but similarly decorated. In late 18th century, had mirror set into lid, and compartments for patches, rouge, and gum brush.

patch family. Porcelain figures made *c*1760–*c*1770 at Derby, with three or four dark unglazed patches left by pads of clay which supported them in glaze firing. Figures often rather stiff, with long noses and salmon-pink cheeks; setting often *bocage*. Colour includes *dirty turquoise; much flower painting on clothes, also lavish gilding; body is creamy-white with colourless glaze. Models include copies of Meissen, figures of Milton and Shakespeare, Britannia, gods and goddesses; also animals. Patches also occur rarely on figures made at Chelsea. *Illustration at* Derby.

patch-stand. Miniature glass **tazza* placed on lady's dressing-table to hold face patches or patch box. Stem follows contemporary wine glass forms. Made during 17th and 18th centuries; examples rare.

pâte de marbre. French biscuit hard-paste porcelain made from 1769 by P-L. *Cyfflé at Lunéville. Condition of authorization from Sèvres to continue porcelain manufacture was sale as *terre cuite*.

pâte dure. Hard-paste porcelain. Made in France from 1769 at Sèvres, after discovery of kaolin at Saint-Yrieix, near Limoges.

paten. Ecclesiastical gold, silver-gilt, or pewter plate or dish; circular, with rim and depression; fits into top of chalice bowl; held wafer for consecration. From *c*1000, used as chalice cover.

Paten. Made in London, 1654, by Arthur Manwaring. Engraved with contemporary crest plumed mantling. Diameter 6in.
Right:
Pâte-sur-pâte *decoration in white on black flask made by *Minton, c1870.*

Pavé *setting. Garnet, diamonds, and turquoises on head of English gold snake necklace, dated 1844.*

Medieval symbolism saw chalice as tomb of Christ and paten as stone blocking entrance. Central depression sometimes lobed; ornament usually engraved or embossed scenes or symbols, e.g. crucifix, Lamb of God, hand of God, crown of thorns, flames, etc. Generally ornate. Footed paten sometimes accompanied first British *communion cups in mid 16th century. From late 17th century, general use of bread in Church of England communion service made larger paten necessary. Flat silver dish on trumpet foot used; evolved into secular *salver design. Plain flat dish or bowl sometimes also used. *Illustration also at* communion cup.

patent metal, Muntz's metal, or **yellow metal.** Alloy of copper and zinc patented (1832) by G. F. Muntz; primarily used for sheathing ships (resisted corrosion by salt water); also as substitute for *ormolu.

patera. Flat, round, or oval motif in low relief, sometimes resembling flower. Embossed or cast applied ornament on neo-classical silver hollow-ware, and carved, inlaid, or painted on furniture of same period. In early 19th century furniture, brass *paterae* used.

Paterna (Valencia), Spain. Tin-glazed earthenware decorated in green and manganese-purple from 13th century. Figures and heraldic devices of European decoration combined with Kufic script, bands of geometrical ornament, and other designs of Moslem origin. Later tin-glazed ware indistinguishable from other Valencian wares.

pâte-sur-pâte. Decoration with porcelain slip developed at Sèvres, *c*1850–*c*1875. Decorative motif, usually on dark ground, built up with porcelain slip in varying thicknesses to give shaded effect. M. L. *Solon worked on development of technique from *c*1859.

pâte tendre. Soft-paste porcelain, probably first manufactured in France from *c*1673 at Rouen, and at Saint-Cloud by *c*1678. Later made, e.g. at Chantilly (from 1725), Mennecy (from *c*1735), and Vincennes, under royal monopoly until 1766, when competitors again allowed, under certain conditions, to make porcelain.

patina. Smooth surface of wood etc., or oxide layer on some metals, occurring as result of aging or chemical treatment. Commonly used to refer to sheen and satiny feel, especially of silver, acquired through long use and polishing. *See also* bronze patination.

pattern book (in silver). Book of engraved patterns circulated among European silversmiths. Originated in various countries, e.g. Germany in 16th century, Netherlands in mid 17th century.

*Pattern book. Engraved page from pattern book of J. E. *Heuglin, showing designs for candlesticks, snuffer and tray, spoon,* tazza, *and covered bowls.*

Paul, Nikolaus (fl mid 18th century). Itinerant German porcelain arcanist. Initiated in 1755 by E. H. *Reichard at Wegely's factory, Berlin. Helped to establish porcelain factories at Weesp, Holland (1764); Fulda (1764–65); Cassel (1767); and Kloster-Veilsdorf (1766–68).

Pauzié, Jérémie (1716–1779). Swiss goldsmith; worked in Russia, 1740–64. Made snuff-boxes of cartouche, circular, or oblong shape with relief work in scroll or floral pattern on engraved diaper ground. Some with monogram of Empress Elizabeth to whom he was court goldsmith. Work unsigned.

pavé. Method of gem setting with stones placed close together (in manner of paving stones) to hide backing metal. Classic *pavé* arrangement is cluster of seven stones set touching each other. Popular in late 18th and 19th centuries.

paw foot (in furniture). Archaic leg terminal in shape of paw of various animals. Known in ancient Egypt and China, classical Greece, and Rome. Generally popular from late 17th to end of 19th century.

pax. Small tablet or plaque, usually with figure of crucifixion, in general use from late 13th century for celebration of Mass; handed round and kissed by congregation at 'kiss of peace'. Wealthier churches and abbeys usually owned silver examples; others, base metal. Enamel frequently used to ornament central figure or frame.

Pazyryk or **Altai carpet.** Oldest known knotted carpet, measuring 6×6½ft; woven 6th century B.C. and discovered in 1949 preserved in ice of south Siberian Pazyryk valley. Woollen foundation and fairly fine Turkish-knotted woollen pile. Oblong red field infilled with rows of star-rosette decorated squares. Two main borders with friezes, outer of light-coloured horsemen on red ground; inner of red stags on light ground.

peach-bloom. Chinese ceramic glaze introduced during reign of *K'ang Hsi. Copper-based; pale red, sometimes mottled or shading to pink, over light green background (due to small iron content). Subdued colour favoured by Chinese for decorating writing equipment, e.g. *brush-rests.

Peacock, The (De Paeuw). Delft factory (1651–1779). Shares held from 1662 by L. *Cleffius and W. *van Eenhoorn, who handed share to L. *van Eenhoorn. From 1701, owned by family of G. *Kam; D. *Kam owner until 1719, succeeded by widow. Bought *c*1725 by J. *Verhagen. Mark registered 1764.

peacock feather motif. Ceramic decoration: traditional motif of eye from peacock's tail feathers. Used on Italian maiolica in late 15th century, notably at Faenza.

peacock plates. Dutch Delft plates, decorated in blue or polychrome, with flowers and foliage in vase, arranged in fan-shape at centre; border decoration of flowers, feather motifs, and scrolls. Produced from mid 18th century by many potters including J. *Brouwer and *Mesch family.

pea green. Green enamel ground colour introduced at Sèvres in 1756. Copied, e.g. at Chelsea from 1768, and at Worcester (*apple green).

Peale, Charles Wilson (1741–1827). Versatile American artist: portrait and miniature painter, engraver, wax modeller, taxidermist, museum proprietor, etc. First miniatures after meeting J. S. *Copley in Boston (1768). In 1776, raised company of foot and served with George Washington, of whom he painted earliest known portrait and several miniatures. Younger brother James (1749–1831) also miniature painter.

pear motif. *See* boteh motif.

pearl. Concretion formed by mollusc (e.g. marine oyster, freshwater mussel). Produced when foreign particle is covered by layers of pearl tissue (nacre) with which shell of mollusc is

Peach-bloom glaze. On water pot. Incised decoration. K'ang Hsi period. Diameter 5in.

lined (mother-of-pearl). Pearls are classified according to shape and lustre (iridescence and translucence). Most prized, spherical and drop shapes; other valued forms are *baroque pearl, minute seed pearl, blister pearl (grows attached to shell and has nacre on one side only). Pearls vary in colour depending on habitat of mollusc; range from cream, pale yellow, green, pink, etc. to black; colour changes over years with loss of lustre. Best pearls formed by marine oysters in Persian Gulf, Indian Ocean, off coast of Malaya and Australia. Worn in earrings and other jewellery from Roman times. During Renaissance, used in necklaces and pendants, and worn in hair. Remained popular for earrings, bracelets, necklaces, etc. In 19th century, seed pearls used to form floral brooches in Britain.

pearlware. Pale *creamware with lead glaze tinted with cobalt, introduced 1779 by J. *Wedgwood. Developed by refining and hardening body of bluish-glazed creamware which had been produced from 1740. Widely manufactured, 1790–1820, e.g. by *Neale & Co and *Leeds Pottery.

pear-shaped bottle. One of oldest Chinese ceramic forms; notable early examples in celadons of Sung dynasty. Globular body, rising to elongated, elegant neck, with narrow mouth. Also common in Ming and Ch'ing dynasties. Form probably derived from archaic *Persian ewer shape. *cf* garlic vase.

pedestal case. Upright, rectangular filing cabinet, composed of several leather-covered cardboard drawers which can be locked by device of similar design to lock on *Wellington chest. Dates from early 19th century.

pedestal clock. French mantel clock, set on tall pedestal, resembling long-case clock in appearance. Tapering, rather than rectangular, sides. Introduced during Louis XIV period. Often richly decorated, with Boulle-work and ormolu. Made e.g. by J. *Thuret.

pedestal desk. Writing table, often mahogany, with frieze drawers; supported by two pedestals also with drawers. Dates from 18th century.

Pedestal table clock. German, probably late 17th century; single hour hand. Drum-shaped water gilded case has baluster pillar support and circular domed base. Height 12in.
Pedestal desk. English, mahogany, c1730. decorated with architectural carving.

pedestal salt. 16th century silver or silver-gilt *standing salt shaped like pedestal of architectural column. Cylindrical or square body on ornamented foot; lid surmounted by figure finial in classical pose. Most surviving examples English.

pedestal sideboard. Sideboard consisting of two pedestal end sections flanking table-like central section with frieze drawer. Sideboard may have gallery at back for plate display. Sometimes has *cellaret, designed *en suite,* in space beneath centre section. Dates from late 18th, early 19th centuries.

pedestal table. General term for table supported by central column.

pedometer. Device for measuring distance walked; first recorded in southern Germany in 16th century. Earliest form is counter attached to belt with ratchet wheel actuated at each step by cord tied to foot. Row of dials indicates number of paces. Later type, made in late 18th and 19th centuries, in shape of watch, with mechanism operated by movement of weighted lever, and button at top of case to set hands to zero. *See* waywiser.

pedometer watch. *See* self-winding watch.

Pegg, William 'Quaker' (1775–1851). English porcelain painter from 1788. Noted for *botanical flowers painted at Derby (1796–1801); usually single blooms covering almost whole surface of plate. Ceased painting for religious reasons; worked at other jobs, but returned to Derby (1813–20). On retirement became shopkeeper in Derby.

peg tankard. Scandinavian tankard in silver, silver-gilt or base metal with vertical row of pegs or studs inside to measure amount of liquid contained. Originated in 17th century Denmark. A few examples made in England at York under Scandinavian trading influence.

Pellatt, Apsley (1791–1863). English glass maker in London. Studied *cristallo-ceramie* technique and patented improved form in 1819, known as *sulphides or cameo incrustation. In glasshouse in Falcon Street, Southwark, produced sulphides enclosed in flint-glass flasks, paperweights, and pendants. At Great Exhibition in London (1851), his exhibits included cut glass chandeliers in white, ruby, and blue glass; Anglo-Venetian tableware; and sulphides. In 1848, published Curiosities of Glassmaking. Retired in 1852, when elected Member of Parliament. *Illustration at* sulphides.

Peg tankard. Ball and claw feet; decoration of chased and engraved baroque sprays of foliage; lion and ball thumbpiece. Norwegian, 1709, made by Johannes Johannesen Reimers of Bergen. Height 7½in.

Pelletier, John or Jean (fl *c*1690–1710). French-born gilder and carver; worked in England for William III.

Pellevé, Etienne-Dominique (fl mid 18th century). French painter and potter. Worked with faience and porcelain, first at Rouen; mentioned as director of Sinceny (1737). At Ottweiler (1763–67); signature found on flower-painted porcelain jug. Also at Pfalz-Zweibrücken (*c*1767).

Pellipario, Nicola (fl *c*1510–*c*1550). Italian maiolica painter, associated with **istoriato* style. Worked at Castel Durante, *c*1510–1527. Earliest known work is *Correr Service. Also decorated dinner service for Isabella d'Este with coat of arms at centre of each item, surrounded *bianco sopra bianco* border of palmettes; rim with scenes from Ovid's Metamorphoses, painted in rich colours. Other work includes bowl, dated 1521, with painting of enthroned king, signed Nicolo; also two plates made at Fabriano in 1527. From 1528, worked at Urbino; decoration includes scenes painted *en grisaille,* heraldic devices, and grotesques, some painted at workshop of son, G. *Durantino. Plate with painting, The Presentation of the Virgin at the Temple, decorated with lustre by G. *Andreoli in 1532. *Illustration at* Castel Durante.

Pembroke table. Portable table, usually *c*2ft high; oval, or rectangular with rounded corners; drop leaves with bracket-supports at both ends. One or two frieze drawers beneath top. Named possibly after 9th Earl of Pembroke (who may have designed it) or Countess of Pembroke (who may have first ordered one). Dates from *c*1750. *See* harlequin table, sofa table.

Pembroke table. Top veneered in satinwood cross-banded with kingwood; chamfered edges. Legs solid satinwood. English, 1795.

Pendule d'officier. *Ormolu case with applied musical instrument motifs. Early 19th century.*

pencilled decoration. *See* Worcester.

pendant. Ornament in variety of materials (precious metals, gems, wood, glass), hung from necklace, bracelet, etc. During Middle Ages, pendants containing relics, e.g. in cross shape, worn. Important feature of Renaissance jewellery in France, Germany and England; often three-dimensional with figures. Many depict mythological or biblical scenes, marine monsters, ships, birds, reptiles, etc. From 16th century *cameo pendants fashionable; also *baroque pearl pendants, especially in Italy. Gold pendants with enamel decoration commonly set with rubies, diamonds, seed pearls, etc. Lavishly decorated on reverse, usually with enamel. In late 16th century architectural designs with fully modelled arches, pillars, volutes, figures; often set with square-cut gems. Use of this type of pendant waned in 17th century. Coins, medals, badges, crosses, miniature portraits in jewelled frames, all served as pendants. Floral or **girandole* form set with clusters of gems sometimes used in 18th century. In 19th century, medieval and Renaissance designs revived. So-called *ferronière* featured pendant worn on centre of forehead supported by heavy chain circling head. *See* Canning Jewel, locket.

pendant. Shaft on watch case carrying *bow, and (on *keyless watches) winding button.

pendule cage or **régulateur de cheminée.** French mantel clock introduced during Louis XVI period. Rectangular case of chased bronze, with glass panels, and pendulum. Often decorated with painted plaques, made from Sèvres porcelain. Makers include A. *Janvier, F. *Berthoud, etc. Later examples have plainer bronze or gilded cases with large glass panels on

*Pennsylvania-Dutch. Chair, c1820, with *balloon back and balloon seat. Wood painted with typical floral pattern and banding.*

all sides and mercury or gridiron pendulum. Made *c*1840–*c*1910; called French regulators.

pendule de voyage. *See* carriage clock.

pendule d'officier. Square French travelling clock in brass or gilt, introduced from *c*1770. Also, specifically, model devised by A-L. *Breguet, *c*1800; used by officers in Napoleon's army. Probably original from which *carriage clock derived.

pendule religieuse. Early French pendulum clock, made *c*1660–*c*1690. Mantel or wall clock, with rectangular case, in architectural style, with corner columns. Similar to English bracket clock but with less depth. Also Dutch influenced. Arched top, with finials at sides and centre; some examples with dome-shaped top. Dial with gilt hands and chapter-ring, set against velvet backing; decorative motifs, such as representation of Father Time, in ormolu below dial. Oak case veneered with ebony, and tortoiseshell; elaborate gilt and bronze ornamentation in later examples. Named because outline slightly resembles nun's habit. Makers include I. *Thuret.

pendule sympathique. Pair of timekeepers, devised by A-L. *Breguet, 1793–95. Accurate clock, resembling large carriage clock, surmounted by watch stand, containing ordinary-sized pocket watch. Watch wound and regulated by mechanism of 'parent' clock. Example with gold case, silver engraved dial, and gold hands.

pendulette. French clock in form of large watch, often contained in folding case.

pendulum. Rod, normally with heavy metal bob at bottom, oscillating at constant frequency and used to control timekeeping of clock: first applied by C. *Huygens in 1675. Bob pendulum for verge escapement usually not longer than 9·8in. (i.e. beating half-seconds), often less. With growing use of anchor escapement invented by R. *Hooke, pendulum beating seconds, 39·14in. long, became general for *long-case clocks. Longer forms sometimes found, e.g. $1\frac{1}{4}$ seconds, 6ft 1in.; clocks made for these have door in base for access to bob and four divisions between each 5-second interval on dial. Clocks adapted to longer pendulum to enhance value often identifiable by retention of seconds dial with five divisions. Pendulums longer than this for turret clocks only, except for early experimental use by T. *Tompion. In English clocks, pendulum usually suspended by flat spring, with time regulation by threaded nut to move bob up or down rod; with verge escapement, pendulum rod fixed directly to verge, back pivot formed as knife-edge; usually with threaded pear-shaped bob without separate nut. European suspension often by silk thread adjustable for regulation (*see* Brocot suspension). Variations from basic type include *conical pendulum and forms with *compensation.

Pénicaud, Nardon (*c*1470–*c*1543). French enamel artist working at Limoges. Work based on German or Flemish prints. Production continued by his family.

penner. Hollow silver tube (5–6in. long), generally wider at one end, with compartments for ink, quills; usually has seal finial. Used from 17th century in Britain.

Pennington, James (fl mid 18th century) and John (d 1786). English potters and decorators, brothers of S. *Pennington. James made delftware and cream-coloured earthenware at Liverpool from 1769; said to have worked factory at Copperas Hill, Liverpool, 1773–74; succeeded by John who moved business to Islington, Liverpool in 1779, making either delftware or porcelain until death, when James took over with John's son and widow. James left Liverpool for Worcester; his son believed to have worked at Worcester as painter.

Pennington, Seth (fl late 18th century). One of family of Liverpool potters. Partner in factory at Shaw's Brow, Liverpool, *c*1760–99, then sole owner until retirement in 1805. Delftware includes large punchbowl decorated with fleet of ships. Blue-and-white porcelain, has bluish glaze, and greenish translucency in transmitted light; decoration copied Chinese landscapes and figures; porcelain punchbowls decorated in Delft style.

Pennis, Johannes (d 1774), son Anthony (d 1770), and grandson Johannes II (d 1789). Dutch potters at Delft. 1723–63, Johannes I director of The Porcelain Plate factory. From 1750, with Anthony, also owned The Two Ships factory; succeeded by Johannes II and mother, Anthony's widow. Johannes I made plates in series depicting trades, e.g. smithing, with monogram IP. Anthony made figures; also made Delft ware replacements for damaged porcelain, e.g. lids or vases for matching sets; signed AP. Sauceboats with lids representing pike, initialled IP, made by Johannes II.

Pennsylvania-Dutch or **Pennsylvania-German style.** American folk-style decoration found in eastern Pennsylvania (particularly Lancaster County); evolved from native styles of south-west German immigrants who settled there in 18th century. Furniture, of simple rectilinear design, usually of fruit wood, maple, pine, or walnut, with distinctive decoration: wood or wax inlay or brightly-coloured painting. Motifs include stylized flowers, fruit, and geometrical patterns. Popular subject for decoration was Dower chest; three vertical panels across front painted or inlaid, and often bear initials of owner.

Earthenware made by German and Swiss immigrants in America in tradition of European ancestors; produced from first colonization in Pennsylvania in late 17th century. Local red clay used to make lead-glazed plates and vessels covered with yellow slip, often with *sgraffiato* decoration, including geometrical patterns, flowers (notably *tulipware), birds, animals, and frequently heart motif. Production greatest in early 18th century in Bucks and Montgomery counties. (Pennsylvania-Dutch derives from 'Pennsylvania-Deutsch', and has no connection with Holland.) *Illustrations also at* sawbuck table frame, toleware.

Pennsylvania tin ware. *See* toleware.

pennyweight or **dwt.** Measure of weight: 24 grains or $\frac{1}{20}$oz Troy. *See* Troy weight.

Penrose, George and William (fl late 18th, early 19th centuries). Irish businessmen (brothers); foresaw expansion of glass industry when freedom of trade granted in 1780 (*see* Glass Excise Act). No previous connection with glass-making, but invested £10,000 in new enterprise known as *Waterford Glass Works. Also granted subsidy by Irish Parliament to cover expense of building and equipment. Employed J. *Hill to manage factory and establish high standard of craftsmanship. Sold works to Ramsey, Gatchell & Barcroft in 1799. Under Penrose ownership, glassware signed Penrose Waterford.

penwork. Furniture-decorating technique imitating marquetry; design inked in black on pale wood background. *Chinoiserie* scenes common. Popular Regency technique.

Penwork (detail). On early 19th century cabinet.

Pepersack or **Peppersack,** Daniel. 17th century French tapestry master-weaver. From 1625, *tapissier* to Duke of Mantua. From 1633, owned main workshop at Reims, producing tapestries mainly on religious and classical themes.

pepper pot. Earliest pepper-casters were in form of small pierced balls attached as finials to 16th and 17th century bell salts. Later examples in form of *caster.

Percier, Charles (1764–1838). French; architect to Napoleon I; published, with P. *Fontaine, *Recueil des décorations intérieures* (1812), laying down principal tenets of *Empire style.

Perepedil carpets. *Kuba carpets often with typical 'ram's head' design, with horn-like stylized stem scrolls and ground infilled with scattered stylized flower and animal forms. Persian influence apparent in pieces with *herati pattern in central field or border. Ground usually in light shades. Edges overcast with white wool, or wool and cotton.

perfume-burner or **pastille-burner.** Small silver container with pierced cover for burning perfume pastilles; used at least from 16th century in Britain and Europe. Various shapes; single lateral handle or two handles like *porringer; sometimes also found with stand on three or four feet. From *c*1650, often known as **cassolette*. Also made in earthenware or porcelain. Examples in English slipware date from early 18th century; made in form of half-timbered cottage by T. *Whieldon in 1750s. Porcelain modelled as cottages, other buildings, or animals, at Bristol (1773–78), also at Coalport, Rockingham, Spode, and Minton factories in early 19th century. Burners in vase form with perforated cover made e.g. at Mennecy in mid 18th century, and at Derby under R. *Bloor. Examples made at Nymphenburg (*c*1760–65) and Berlin; cherubs on pedestal holding jar over flame made at Meissen; at Ludwigsburg, examples decorated with moulded garlands and rococo medallions with polychrome painting of birds. Also made at Le Nove in form of cylindrical pedestal with detachable base and conical cover. *Illustration at* G. M. Mason.

Perfume burner. In form of castle, probably made in Staffordshire, c1835.

Pergolesi, Michelangelo (fl 1760–1800). Italian-born engraver and designer. In England from 1760, working for J. and R. *Adam. Published Designs for Various Ornaments, 1777.

Peridon, Hendrick Janzon (d 1722). Dutch Delft painter. Apprentice at The Rose factory. Worked at The Fortune factory, and at The Metal Pot factory from 1702 probably until death. Decorated bowls and vases in **cachemire* style, with flower pattern in underglaze colours. Mark: HIP.

perpetual calendar. Date indicator in clock or watch automatically self-adjusting for short months and leap years. Full-time calendar, or semi-perpetual calendar, adjusts for months but not for leap years.

Perrin, Veuve (d 1793). French faience maker at Marseille. Born Pierrette Caudelot; married Claude Perrin (1696–1748) who established faience factory at Marseille *c*1740. After husband's death, produced faience painted in enamel colours, either polychrome or *en camaïeu*; sometimes in gold alone. Ground colours include yellow, aquamarine, and brown. Decoration includes naturalistic flowers painted from life against white ground, Mediterranean scenes, and still-lifes of fish. *Chinoiseries* taken from engravings of J. *Pillement. Succeeded by son, Joseph. Enamelled faience marked with initials VP, sometimes monogram or with asterisk; often copied on forgeries.

Persian carpets. Among most highly prized, fine oriental carpets (renown has made 'Persian' general term for oriental carpets). Art developed under court patronage and as peasant craft. Earliest recorded use of Court carpets in 6th and 7th centuries under Sassanian dynasty. Earliest documented carpet, legendary 6th century *Spring of Chosroes carpet. During Abbasid Caliphate at Baghdad (750–1258) carpets used in palaces and wealthy homes. Main centres, Armenia (with good quality wool, water, and dyes), and north-west Persia. Both knotted-pile and *kelim carpets woven in wool or silk. Some with inscriptions on monochrome fields; others with portraits of kings or animal figures. Palette limited; grounds often dark blue. Increased production in 14th and 15th centuries, with Turkish influence apparent in carpets of geometrical design. Field patterns with small crosses, stars, rosettes, arranged in rows or squares. Borders often with Kufic script. In 15th century, court industry developed under patronage of Timurids. Finest quality materials used. Best period under Safavid dynasty (1501–1736) with continuing royal patronage: huge carpets made, most with finely Persian-knotted pile of wool or wool and silk. Revolution in design *c*1500 gave new prominence to illuminators: carpet designs follow book illustrations. Range of colours extended, patterns varied, draftsmanship improved (e.g. designs by miniature painters). Innovations in design included medallion stressing centre of field; foliate and floral motifs, arabesques and trellises; forms from miniature-painting, e.g. animals, clouds, and cloud-bands. Also cotton introduced into foundation weaves, improving firmness and regularity. During rule of Shah Tahmasp (1524–76) numerous types of court carpet developed. Most important were *medallion carpets (finest surviving example, *Ardebil carpet); also *garden, *floral, *vase, and *animal carpets. Under patronage of Shah Abbas (1571–1629), elaborate types developed, e.g. *arabesque carpets. Centres of Persian court carpet industry included *Tabriz, *Kashan, *Isfahan, *Kirman and *Herat. With end of Safavid dynasty in 18th century, court industry largely collapsed; production of fine prayer rugs continued, with major manufactories in *Bijar, *Heriz, *Ferahan, *Melayer, *Meshed, Kirman, and *Hamadan. From 15th century, Persian carpets widely exported, influencing Caucasian and Turkish designs, and introducing carpet industry to India. Also extensively exported to Europe, first as royal gifts, later for individuals. By 19th century, European market major influence on carpet production, with several types (e.g. *Saruks and *Mahals) woven particularly for export. From 18th century, carpets usually have Persian-knotted woollen pile, on wool and/or cotton foundation. Knotting particularly fine, with up to 1200 knots per square inch on some silk pile examples.

'Persian' ewer. Chinese ceramic form, found in all periods of pottery manufacture from T'ang dynasty. Originally imitation of Persian bronze or silver vessels. Pear-shaped body, with elongated neck, sometimes surmounted by animal spout, e.g. phoenix or chicken head. Often with relief decoration, e.g. palmettes, rosettes, foliage.

Persian, Sehna, asymmetrical, or **open knot.** Knot used to form pile on hand-knotted carpets. Yarn strand wound first under warp thread then round next thread, so that one knot end protrudes from each space between adjacent warps. Allows for great density of pile, producing close, fine surface. Favoured for following types of carpet: *Mamluk, *Turkish Court Manufactory carpets, central and east *Persian court carpets, *Turkoman, *Chinese, and 18th and 19th century commercial *Turkish carpets. *cf* Turkish knot.

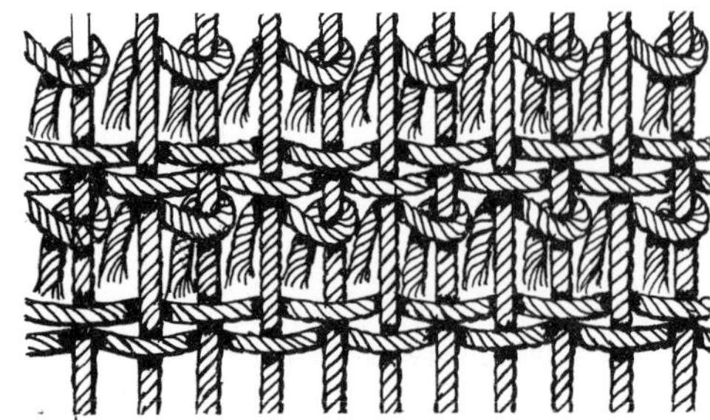

Pesaro (Marche), Italy. Documentary evidence suggests manufacture of maiolica from late 14th century; orders from family of Isabella d'Este for pottery and tiles recorded in 15th century. Maiolica made from 1540 with *istoriato* decoration, grotesques, and applied relief in style of Urbino. Privilege for gilding granted in 1567. A. *Casali and F. A. *Callegari established factory in 1763 to reproduce porcelain in tin-glazed earthenware.

petit feu. *See* enamel.

Petit, Jacob (b 1796). French porcelain maker. From 1815 associated with hard-paste porcelain factory at Fontainebleau (Seine-et-Marne). In 1820, bought factory at Belleville, near Paris. With brother, Mardochée, bought Fontainebleau factory in 1830; moved to Belleville (1834). Products, in revived rococo style, include clock cases, candlesticks, vases, and figures. Noted for **veilleuses,* particularly in form of figures, with lower part of body as base and upper part as container. In 1851, moved factory to Avon (Seine-et-Marne); later sold it to employee (1862). Opened new factory in Paris in 1863. Mark: J.P. in underglaze blue or incised.

Petit, Nicolas (1732–91). French; became *maître-ébéniste* in 1761. Early work in rococo style, using lacquer and floral marquetry; later pieces more restrained and classical. Stamp: N. PETIT. Another N. Petit, possibly cousin, used similar stamp. *Illustration at chiffonnier.*

Petitot, Jean, Senior (1607–91) and Jean-Louis, the Younger (1652–1702). Enamel painters. Jean Swiss-born; worked in Geneva, then with J. *Toutin, painting watch cases. In England from *c*1634; encouraged by Charles I to paint portraits; work includes miniature copies from paintings by Anthony van Dyck. During Civil War, went to Paris; court painter under Louis XIV from 1645. After revocation of Edict of Nantes (1685), imprisoned, forced to renounce Protestant faith before able to flee to Geneva. Most enamel paintings very small. Son, Jean-Louis, pupil; settled in London under patronage of Charles II, except for period in Paris (1682–95).

petuntse. Fusible rock of granitic origin but less advanced in decomposition than *kaolin. Used in hard-paste porcelain, melts at 1300°–1400°C, binding particles of kaolin into impermeable mass. Also used as glaze, ground and dusted over body with *flux, e.g. lime and potash; fused in single firing of body. English equivalent is *china stone.

Petzold, Hans (1551–1613). German silversmith working in Nuremberg; master in 1578; burgher in 1579. Made pieces for Nuremberg council as gifts for important visitors, including standing cups (pineapple, nautilus, etc.), and salt-cellars. Also worked for Rudolf II, Holy Roman Emperor in Prague.

pew groups. Salt-glaze groups of two or more simple, hand-modelled figures, sometimes playing musical instruments, sitting on high-backed bench. Features and costume details picked out in dark brown or black. Decoration of pew includes heart-shaped perforations, a tree shape inlaid in dark brown, or stamped motifs, sometimes leaves or flowers. Made in mid 18th century Staffordshire; many attributed to A. *Wood.

pewter. Alloy of tin and lead or copper, sometimes with antimony and/or bismuth as hardening agent. Cheap, tough, cast ware, greyish in colour, made in Europe from Roman times (a few early bowls, ewers, etc. survive) until largely replaced by ceramics or electroplated ware in 18th and 19th centuries. Pure tin proved unsuitable for most purposes, due to brittleness and cost; addition of copper or lead improved malleability and lowered price. Too much lead, however, made wares heavy and black. Pewterers' guilds set up in most European capitals during 13th and 14th centuries. Pewterers customarily marked their wares (*see* pewter marks). Charter of London guild (1348) designated *fine pewter for use for *sadware and square or ribbed pieces; and a tin/lead pewter, later known as *lay, for hollow-ware, rounded candlesticks, etc. *Black metal used for cheaper tavern pieces. Because pewter is soft, easily dented and scratched, many old pieces melted down and recast. Domestic items for everyday use cast in plain clay moulds constructed in more than one piece and therefore re-usable. Pieces with relief decoration cast in brass moulds with intaglio designs usually cut by specialists. Latter method much used from 16th to 18th centuries in Europe, where styles more elaborate, and much *repoussé* and engraved work done. English pewter generally left plain and highly burnished until 17th century when cast relief decoration grew in popularity and other kinds of ornament used, commonest being *wriggle-work. Some pieces bore engraving or punched work. Gilding of pewter articles for public sale prohibited in England (allowable on gifts, if proof of purpose available); in France, gilding occurred on church plate and, from late 17th century, on some domestic articles; in Germany, gilding sometimes applied to purely decorative objects, e.g. those made at Nuremberg.

Surviving early medieval wares include *pilgrims' badges, ecclesiastical pieces, and certain vessels, e.g. *Hanseatic tankards. From 14th century onwards, pewter increasingly used for all kinds of drinking vessel, e.g. beakers, tankards, mugs, also plates, dishes, bowls, flagons, measures, salts, candlesticks, spoons, etc.; shape and decoration often followed contemporary silver styles. Original standards of metal not constant; in early years penalties enforced on makers of sub-standard metal, but rules and control slackened, especially in provinces, and during 17th century.

pewter marks. Custom of marking pewter wares with personal *touch of maker made compulsory in England in 1503; known to have been practised earlier, for identification purposes. Devices incorporated initials or full name of maker and/or emblem, often rebus of name. Many dated. Majority round or oval, others shield-shaped. Guilds laid down strict standards of quality and appointed searchers to maintain them. Faulty wares seized, struck with Government 'broad arrow head' mark (mentioned in 15th century records) and presumably melted down; maker was fined, or, for serious or repeated offences, had letters 'ff' or knot-device added to touch to signify past malpractice.

From 1509, official strake of tin (portcullis shape) and lilypot marks used by guild to indicate quality. Mid 16th century pot-lids bear simplified lilypot mark in form of fleur-de-lis. Rose and crown mark allowed in second half of 16th century to certain makers of high quality metal; in 1671 same mark adopted for goods exclusively for export; by 1690, mark generally and officially used by pewterers in combination with own touches. Pewterers often stamped extra, unofficial, marks on wares, e.g. much-used four small shields (known from 1580), direct copies of silver *hallmarks. Practice frowned upon by Goldsmiths' Company, but shields enclosing variations of lion rampant, initials, rose device, etc., continued for many years despite bans. From 16th to 18th centuries, pieces often bore initials of client (housemark) in form resembling silver mark, e.g. in small shield.

Crowned X, found on many pieces from late 17th century, first used only on 'extraordinary' (i.e. finest quality) metal, e.g. hard plates and dishes; but also much used on poor quality 19th century tankards, etc.

Pieces frequently passed through hands of more than one pewterer, and bear marks of each. Unmarked pewter often slipped through; also marks sometimes rub off with constant use.

European pewter normally bore seal or coat of arms of city, and maker's individual emblem; practice sporadic from 14th century in most areas, becoming general in 16th century. Sometimes (e.g. in Nuremberg), two marks combined to form single touch. From late 16th century, dates appear on some pieces, referring to year in which e.g. official change of alloy declared, or maker became master. Pewter containing higher than normal amount of tin marked with 'triple touch' (repetition of one of normal marks, or additional district mark) or X mark, signifying alloy of 10 parts tin to 1 part lead. Copper content indicated by additional mark of angel, rose, or crown. Parisian pewterers obliged from 1643 to strike initials, crowned hammer, and letter P on ordinary wares, adding shield-shape and words *estain fin* on better quality pieces. Official marks for these wares: crowned C for ordinary pewter, crowned FF on best quality. Decline of guild system in 18th century led to omission of city marks, and makers often struck full name instead of emblem.

Pfalz-Zweibrücken or **Gutenbrunn** (Palatinate). Small German porcelain factory near Frankenthal, established 1767; directed initially by L. *Russinger. Until 1775, when earthenware production started, fine wares made from Passau clay, and domestic wares in underglaze blue and white. Some polychrome flower painting or landscapes in purple with gilded scroll-work. Also some unidentified figures. Mark: monogram of PfZ.

Pfau family (fl 1591–1738). Members of family manufacturers of tiled stoves at *Winterthür, Switzerland, late 16th to mid 18th century. Also produced dishes with bible scenes, landscapes, or coats of arms, enclosed in scrolled borders with plants and birds; also rounded jugs with plant-scrolls. In early 18th century, stove tiles painted with figures in colours including yellow, orange, green, and, notably, black. Examples often found, signed and dated, e.g. by Ludwig (d 1623), Hans Heinrich (work dated 1632), David (work dated 1636), David II (d 1702), Abraham (work dated 1660 and 1686), Ludwig II (d 1683) and David III (work dated 1738).

pharmacy jar. *See* drug pot.

Philadelphia Chippendale style. American interpretation of *Chippendale style, as expressed by Philadelphia cabinet makers, e.g. T. *Affleck, J. *Gostelowe, B. *Randolph, W. *Savery, and T. *Tufft, from mid 18th century. Mahogany chairs, high-boys, and low-boys

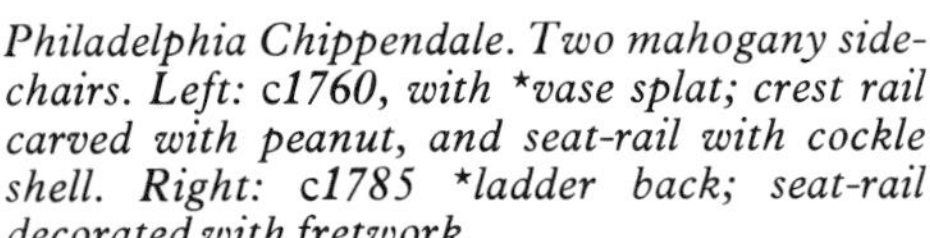

*Philadelphia Chippendale. Two mahogany side-chairs. Left: c1760, with *vase splat; crest rail carved with peanut, and seat-rail with cockle shell. Right: c1785 *ladder back; seat-rail decorated with fretwork.*

*Pianoforte. Upright cabinet piano by J. *Broadwood & Sons. English, 1834. Rosewood case inlaid with brass; natural keys of ivory, accidentals of ebony.*

noteworthy, with rich carving, and bonnet or scroll pediment. Best period, *c*1755–85.

Phipps & Robinson. London silversmiths who made boxes, wine-labels, vinaigrettes, and other objects of vertu, 1783–1816.

Phyfe or **Phyffe,** Duncan (1768–1854). Scottish-born cabinet and chair maker. Worked in New York City from 1783. Pieces in mahogany, seldom with metal mounts. Work at first influenced by English Sheraton and Regency styles, then by French Directoire and Empire. Furniture made in his New York shop, *c*1805–47, noted for good proportion, elegance, fine carving, and restrained ornament. Common motifs include lyre (particularly on table supports, chair backs), ribbons, reeding, swags, and acanthus.

pi. Chinese ritual jade shape. Flat disc with circular hole about one third of total diameter. Associated with worship of Heaven. Earliest examples, dating from Shang dynasty, undecorated, but later often covered with small nipple design (ku wên).

pianoforte or **piano.** Stringed keyboard instrument characterized by hammer action; damper (padded bar resting on upper surface of strings) used to mute or cut off sound; earliest examples worked by hand-stop – as in organ – later by pedal. Invented *c*1709 by B. *Cristofori in Florence, Italy; called *gravicembalo col piano e forte* (harpsichord with soft and loud), indicating intention of making improved harpsichord. Buckskin-covered hammers substituted for harpsichord quills, enabling sound volume to vary with force applied to keys. Development continued in Germany by G. *Silbermann *c*1745. Early shape same as *harpsichord (associated with grand piano); horizontal strings at right angles to keyboard. J. C. *Zumpe, pupil of Silbermann working in London *c*1760, made square or oblong piano with so-called English action; strings horizontal, at right angles to keyboard; often wrongly called spinet in England; remained popular until *c*1860. Upright model perfected by American, Dr John Hawkins, in Philadelphia, Pennsylvania, in 1800; strings vertical. Superseded square piano for home use by *c*1860. Development of so-called Viennese or German action by J. A. *Stein working in Vienna *c*1770, resulted in popularization of instrument (of grand piano form). First French piano made in 1777 by S. *Erard. Complete cast-iron framework for square piano perfected 1825 by American Alpheus Babcock in Boston, Massachusetts; J. *Broadwood's firm produced first iron-framed grand piano in England in 1851; American firm, Steinway, perfected metal frame for grand in 1855. In 1826, Frenchman, Henri Pape, introduced felt for hammers, though this did not become universal until after 1850. Piano had superseded clavichord and harpsichord as popular amateur and concert instrument by 1800. Wooden piano case sometimes with inlay (other woods, ivory, etc.), and/or painting.

Piccolpasso, Cipriano (1524–79). Italian maiolica painter at Castel Durante, later engineer. Wrote account of maiolica manufacture, *Li tre libri dell'arte del vasaio*, 1556–59.

pickle. Solution of various acids in water for cleaning metal surface, e.g. to remove oxide or sulphide film.

pickled finish or **lime whitening.** Pale, white-streaked surface on furniture; produced by residual paint and plaster after paint has been stripped with vinegar solution, or by exposure (by stripping) of lime bleach used under paint.

Pictorial flask. 'For Pike's Peak.' 19th century. Reverse shows hunter shooting deer. Height 8¼in.

pictorial flasks. American flasks blown in full-size two-piece moulds; usually olive-green, olive-amber, or amber glass, occasionally blue, emerald-green, or amethyst. Bear intaglio designs of figures, flora, and fauna. Widely made 1815–70.

picture-frame clock. French clock, made from late 18th century. Gilt picture-frame, encasing clock face set against ground of coloured velvet. Also examples with painted, animated scenes, e.g. sea with lighthouse containing clock face. Other versions (including windmill or church clock-tower, as main features), produced in Black Forest, *c*1830–*c*1870, also in Malta.

Pidoux, Protais (fl mid 18th century). Swiss painter. Worked at Mennecy in 1759. Credited with introduction of enamel painting on faience at Aprey in 1760.

Picture-frame clock. c1800, oil painting on wood panel, signed on reverse Saville, London. Three-train verge movement with hour strike on gong, quarter-hour strike on bell. Music box operated at will.

Pie-crust table. Carved mahogany with tripod legs and acanthus scroll feet. English, mid 18th century.

*Pier glass. Frame of carved and gilded wood, *Chippendale style. English, mid 18th century.*
Above right:
*Pier table. French *Régence; oak. Frieze and cabriole legs carved with shell medallions, foliage, and trellis ornament; *x-stretcher. Width 5ft4in.*
Below right:
Pietra dura. *Panels including marble, lapis-lazuli, malachite, cornelian, and agate. English, early 19th century.*

pie-crust, Chippendale, or **Bath border.** Scalloped or scrolled raised border on British 18th century furniture, e.g. round rim of tea table, and on silver, e.g. rim of salver.

pie-crust table. Mid 18th century *tea table, usually in mahogany with tripod support. Rim around top scalloped or otherwise decorated like edge of pie-crust.

pied-de-biche. *See* hoof foot.

pied-de-biche spoon. *See* trefid spoon.

pierced carving. Decorative open-work carving.

pierced-work. Ceramic open-work decoration, derived from metal-work; sides, edges, or lids of vessels and plates perforated either by cutting or by stamping; primarily ornamental, but serves useful purpose, e.g. in sugar sifters and pot-pourri vases. Pierced rim found on faience plates made by Perrin factory, Marseille. Delicate pierced shapes popular at Niderviller from mid 18th century to 1770s, in both faience and porcelain. Open-work decoration found on Wedgwood creamware and frequently on cream-coloured earthenware made at Leeds, and imitated; e.g. at Douai, Hubertusburg, Naples. Much used on porcelain made in late 1760s, e.g. at Meissen and Berlin.

piercing. Method of working metals in which background of design is cut away by hand or machine. Earliest technique used hammer and chisel; saw employed from 18th century. Sheffield plate manufacturers adopted punching and piercing machines in 1760s. Common from 16th century on perfume-burners, pomanders, etc. Much used in late 18th century for baskets, dish-rings, slices, etc.

pier glass. Tall mirror with frame, often ornate. Usually companion piece to *pier table or *commode, and hung above table, between two windows. Dates from late 17th century.

pier table. Architectural piece placed against wall between two windows; often of *console design. Frequently with *pier glass on wall above. Dates from late 17th century.

Pieterson, Jan (fl late 17th and early 18th centuries). Dutch potter and Delft ware painter. Worked for L. *Victorson; work includes **cachemire* vases with polychrome floral decoration, marked with initials IP.

pietra dura (Italian, 'hard stone'). Ornamental work with *hard stones. Much used in Italy from late 16th century for cabinets, table-tops, etc., and imitated in **scagliola*.

Pigalle, Jean-Baptiste (1714–85). French sculptor, elected to *Académie Royale des Beaux-arts* in 1744. Work includes Nymph Removing Thorn from her Foot, allegorical figures *l'Amour* and *l'Amitié*, statues of Louis XVI and Voltaire. Among sculptures reproduced in biscuit porcelain at Sèvres are Venus and Mercury (1744, reproduced 1770).

Piguet, Isaac-David (b 1775). Swiss musical box maker, 1811–29. Perfected musical snuff-box with fan-comb movement manufactured principally by his firm, Piguet et Meylan of Geneva. Boxes stamped with diamond containing initials PM.

Pijnacker, Jacobus (d 1701) and Adriaen (d 1707). Dutch potters at Delft. Sons-in-law of A. *Keyser. Worked at potteries including The Golden Flowerpot and The Two Ships from 1680.

pilaster. Architectural term for flattened column (generally of one of classical orders) attached to façade. Often used on furniture.

pilgrim bottle or **flask,** or **wine bottle.** Silver or silver-gilt bottle with flattened ovoid body, narrow neck, moulded foot, and chain stopper made from 16th century in Britain and Europe. Modelled on medieval bottle or costrel, of leather, earthenware, stoneware, or pewter, fitted with loops or rings through which cord or chain passed for slinging over shoulder or saddle. In 17th century, very large examples used as *sideboard plate. Also made in early 18th century with elaborately embossed ornament. Scent bottles made in same shape. *See* flagon.

pilgrim flask. Chinese ceramic shape, originating in Six Dynasties period. Flat vessel formed of two moulded pieces; has long neck, and loop handles on shoulders. Foot is flat: unique Chinese modification of common Near Eastern vessel.

Pilgrim furniture. Simple, utilitarian American furniture made in New England for Puritans ('Pilgrims') during 17th century. Reflecting contemporary English country furniture styles, pieces are simple, with turned or carved decoration. *See* Brewster chair, Carver chair, Hadley chest.

pilgrims' badge or **shell.** *See* badge.

pillar (in clocks). Distance piece separating plates of clock or watch movement. Elaborately decorated in many watches; earliest type of square section, often engraved; after *c*1660, tulip shape popular; tapering 'Egyptian' style used from *c*1680, followed by baluster from *c*1690 to early 19th century. Ornate pierced shapes found from mid 18th century. Plain, cylindrical pillar became general by early 19th century. Pillar decoration in clocks restrained, becoming plainer as factory production evolved.

pillar and scroll clock. American shelf clock, probably designed by E. *Terry, *c*1816. Made in large quantities until 1830s. *c*28–30in. high; 30-hour wooden movement. Top surmounted by three pillars (at each side, and in centre); upright twin scrolls, cut out in same wood as case, form decorative motif around central pillar. Dial on upper section of clock; painted tablet below, with opening through which pendulum can be seen. Pendulum off-centre in some examples. Other makers include S. *Thomas.

pillar carpet. Chinese Persian-knotted carpet; narrow, without borders, designed to drape or wind round pillar so that edges fit together giving continuous pattern, e.g. coiled dragon. Probably made from mid 18th century.

pillar clock. Style popular in mid 16th century Europe with movement in base and revolving hour band, globe, or similar device mounted on top of pillar: time indicated by pointer (or by hand of figure, etc.) fixed to base. One variety is *crucifix clock. Alternatively, type of *Japanese clock.

pillar plate. Plate of watch movement immediately behind dial, to which one end of each pillar is riveted, other end being fixed to back or top plate by pins or screws. In clock movements pillar plate position varies with age and national practice.

Pillement, Jean (1727–1808). French designer and engraver; associated with fantastic *chinoi-*

Pilgrim bottle. English, c1700, unmarked. Engraved with coat of arms of Underhill.

Pillar and scroll clock. Painted glass panel below dial. 1817.

Pillar carpet. Knotted in coloured wools on linen warps. Chinese, Kansu, c1800. 8ft3in.×3ft3in.

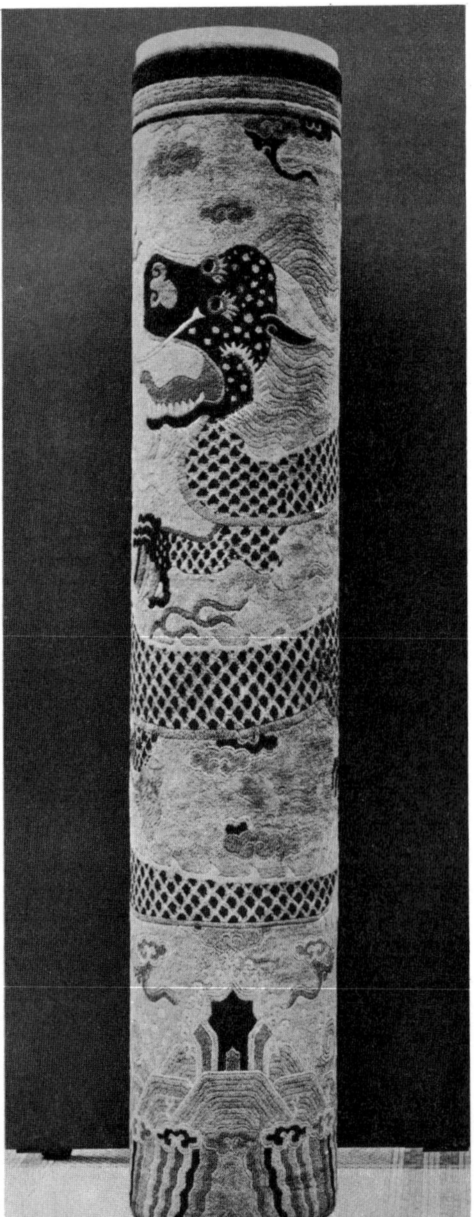

series, many published in Paris and London. Influenced English silver with *chinoiserie* decoration in mid 18th century. Style imitated, e.g. on faience made at Marseille, notably by Veuve *Perrin in 1760s, and on porcelain at Lowestoft *c*1775.

pill slabs. Flat slabs of English delftware in simple shapes, e.g. rectangle, octagon, shield, or heart, pierced with one or two holes for hanging. Often decorated with arms and motto of Apothecaries' Company or City of London, rarely dated. Made 1663–1700, many in London.

pinchbeck. Alloy of 10% zinc and 90% copper resembling gold, invented by Christopher Pinchbeck of London (watch and clock maker), in early 18th century. Much used for snuff-boxes, étuis, watch cases, seals, etc., throughout 18th century, and for jewellery in 19th century *See* Dutch metal.

Pineapple cup and cover. Silver-gilt, made in Nuremberg by Caspar Beutmuller, c1620.
Below:
Pinxton. Porcelain mug, c*1800. Painted with view of Chatsworth by W. *Billingsley. Marked on base with red P.*

pinched trailing. *See* quilling.

pincushion seat. *See* compass seat.

pineapple cup. 16th and 17th century German silver *standing cup with pineapple-shaped bowl. Stem either tree trunk (sometimes ornamented with woodman figures) or simple figure. Finial on cover in form of mythical figure or vase of flowers. Bowl decorated with bosses. Less common type has bowl made up of two to four pineapple shapes.

Pineau, Nicolas (1684–1754). French designer. Worked on palaces in Russia, then for rest of life in Paris, designing interiors. Early exponent of rococo style in France; introduced asymmetry into his decoration.

pine motif. *See* boteh motif.

pinion (in clocks and watches). One of smaller toothed wheels in *train, usually of cut or drawn steel, gearing with larger wheels of brass. Alternative type, lantern pinion, of open form with steel pins or 'trundles' fitted into end collars.

pink ground. Deep pink porcelain enamel ground used first by J. G. *Herold at Meissen factory *c*1725, with reserved panels on ornamental pieces and tableware, and periodically throughout 18th century. Imitated with varying success by other European factories.

pin pallet escapement. *See* escapement.

pin wheel escapement. *See* escapement.

pinwork. Gold or silver studded decoration on leather, e.g. on outer case of watch, particularly English, *c*1715–*c*1750. *Illustration at* clock watch.

Pinxton, Derbyshire. Porcelain factory established in 1796. Translucent soft-paste containing bone ash made by W. *Billingsley, until 1801. Tableware decorated with flowers or landscapes. After Billingsley's departure, near-opaque porcelain of inferior quality made until factory closed in 1813. Marks include P, painted in red, and star with crescent, painted in purple.

pipeclay or **terre de pipe.** Earthenware body used in Lorraine to make figures, from mid 18th century, e.g. at Lunéville, Niderviller, and Saint-Clément.

pipe-kiln. Cylindrical wrought-iron frame on four feet and with ring handle, to hold clay pipes during cleaning (achieved by putting pipe-laden kiln in oven). Also used as pipe-rack. Made in Britain and Europe from 17th century (following introduction of tobacco).

pipe-lighter. Type of *brazier in Sheffield plate; sometimes with pierced body and horizontal handle of turned wood; on feet, or with matching stand. Usually has copper lining to hold combustible material. Joints usually riveted. Made from late 18th century.

pipe-stopper or **tobacco-stopper.** Small, flat-ended tool for pressing tobacco into pipe-bowl, made from 17th century in silver, brass, pewter, porcelain, ivory, bone, wood, etc., in decorative or purely functional forms. Cast brass stoppers shaped as, e.g. hand, leg, animal head, usually date from late 19th century, though earlier examples exist. *Illustration at* smoker's tongs.

pipe tongs. *See* smoker's tongs.

pipkin. *See* saucepan.

piqué. Inlay of fine gold or silver strips (*piqué posé*) or points (*piqué point*) in tortoiseshell or ivory to form design. Popular decoration for outer case of watches, especially English, in late 17th century; applied to tortoiseshell base. Also used for various types of boxes.

pitch. Thick, dark, resinous, semi-liquid substance. Silver vessel filled with pitch to prevent buckling during chasing or placed in bowl of pitch or on pitch-block during embossing. Sometimes used for *loading candlesticks, knife handles, etc.

Piqué. *Pair of French Louis XIV candlesticks inlaid with gold and mother-of-pearl; two English 18th century* piqué point *boxes.*

pitcher. *See* jug.

Pitkin brothers. American watch makers. Henry (d 1846) and brother, James F. (1812–70), established partly mechanized factory in Hartford, Connecticut, in 1838, and produced first entirely American watch. Venture failed in 1841 after production of *c*800 pieces.

pitkin flasks. American glass flasks, finely ribbed and with swirled pattern moulding made by *German half-post method. Mainly green or amber. Associated with Pitkin Glass Works, though also made in other Connecticut and New Hampshire glasshouses. Some produced in mid West in more varied colours; shape more rounded. Made *c*1780–1830.

Pitkin Glass Works. Founded 1783 in East Manchester, Connecticut. Produced amber and olive-green bottles, flasks, and hollow-ware. Closed *c*1830. *See* pitkin flasks. *Illustration at* sunburst flask.

Pitts, William, the Elder (fl late 18th and early 19th centuries). English silversmith and chaser; made several pieces for *Rundell, Bridge & Rundell for royal collections (e.g. tankard of 1811 with figure subject after Cellini). Used inserted embossed and chased panels in cast work. Son, William the Younger, continued in trade.

Pitts, William, the Younger (d 1840). English sculptor, silversmith, and silver designer; apprenticed to father. Developed new techniques of embossing and chasing. Worked on T. *Stothard's Wellington shield for *Rundell, Bridge & Rundell, also on J. *Flaxman's *Shield of Achilles. In 1830s, worked for *Storr & Mortimer as designer and chaser.

Planché, Andrew (1728–1805). Huguenot porcelain maker and modeller; in 1740 apprenticed to London goldsmith. Worked at Derby *c*1750–*c*1756; some *dry-edge figures attributed to him; also credited with dancing figures, series depicting The Five Senses, The Four Seasons, classical and Chinese figures, and animals.

planetarium. Device to demonstrate orbits of planets around sun; made in hand or clock operated forms from early 18th century. *See* orrery.

planishing. Levelling of metal surface using broad, smooth-faced hammer and anvil.

plaque. Decorative tablet of porcelain, enamelled copper, or metal. *See also* wall-plaque.

plaquette. Bronze (occasionally lead or silver) one-sided medallion used to embellish furniture and household utensils. Made throughout Europe from 15th century; especially popular in Italy and Germany. Cast in square, rectangular, or oblong shapes with religious, historical, or mythological scenes. Much collected; reproductions abound.

plaster of Paris. Fine white calcined gypsum. When mixed with water, swells and rapidly sets. Used in pottery for making moulds. Introduced to Staffordshire from France, *c*1745.

Planetarium. English, c*1820, made by W. Jones of London. Engraved and hand-coloured paper face with scales of months, days, signs of zodiac, solstices, equinoxes, longest and shortest days of year in London, four seasons and planets. Below: brass Monthly Preceptor no 2.*

Plate pail. Slatted mahogany sides, bound with brass at base and rim, brass handle. English 18th century. Height 12*in.*

Plate clock. Cow's tail pendulum swinging in front of dial. Signed A. Borm, Nuremberg, c*1780.*

Plat de Ménage (French, 'condiment set'). Porcelain table set made at Meissen factory in 1737 to designs of J. J. *Kändler, for Count H. *von Brühl. Elaborately modelled, gilded, and subtly enamelled Chinese figures form oil ewer, salt cellar, mustard pot, and sugar casters; centrepiece, decorated with brightly coloured festoons, bird mask handles, and pierced shell panels, also has Chinese figures with umbrellas.

plate. Articles made of gold or silver for domestic or ceremonial use. Term incorrectly used to describe plated wares (*see* electro-plate, Sheffield plate). Also circular *dish for food, made in metals and ceramics from Middle Ages, in many sizes and variously named platter, *charger *trencher, dish, saucer (smallest size, used for sauce or spices). Many pewter examples made, with styles varying only slightly over 400 years, usually in decoration and width of rim. *See* broad-rimmed pewter ware, wavy-edged plate, cardinal's hat, reeding.

plateau. Late 18th and 19th century British silver, Sheffield plate, or electro-plated base or stand with glass or mirror top placed on table beneath épergne, candelabra, etc. for display purposes. Most important English examples made by *Rundell, Bridge & Rundell.

plate basket, carrier or **pail.** Bucket-shaped container in brass, brass-bound mahogany or wooden slats or lattice-work. Used in 18th century for carrying warmed plates to dining-room and dirty plates to kitchen. Open slot from top to bottom allowed easy removal of plates.

plate clock or **Telleruhr.** Popular in Europe throughout 17th century; made until *c*1750. Plate-shaped; later examples with silver or pewter chapter ring, highly decorated *repoussé* centre, and hand or hands often elaborately pierced; designed to hang or stand on small pedestal.

plate glass. *See* de Nehou, Louis-Lucas.

plate frame. Framework of flat parallel plates forming basis of clock or watch movement; originally horizontal in drum, hexagonal, and other table clocks, placed vertically in long-case and bracket clocks, etc.

Platel, Pierre (d 1719). Huguenot silversmith working in London; family settled in England *c*1688. Received freedom of Goldsmiths' Company in 1699. Made range of domestic silver; executed commissions for aristocracy, e.g. solid gold ewer and basin for Duke of Devonshire (1701). P. *de Lamerie apprenticed to him in 1703. Mark: Pl with a crown and star above.

plateresque style (in furniture). Small delicate, complex decorations on flat surfaces of 16th century Spanish furniture, resembling contemporary silversmith's (*platero*) work. Motifs include masks, wreaths, urns, birds, and cherubs.

plate-warmer. Wooden or metal (especially wrought-iron) device to stand before open fire, holding plates. Various shapes, usually on tripod, sometimes in *Dutch oven form, or revolving cage. Triple-X form, known as cat, common, made of three crossed rods. Used in 18th and 19th centuries.

plating. *See* electro-plating, Sheffield plate.

plectrum. Quill or blade used to sound strings of some musical instruments.

pliant. *See* stool.

Plimer, Nathaniel (b 1757) and Andrew (1763–1837). English miniaturists. Brought up as clock makers in Wellington, Somerset. In London, Nathaniel became assistant to H. *Bone; Andrew servant to R. *Cosway. Andrew more prolific; style influenced by Cosway, but draughtsmanship often indifferent; some large miniature group portraits.

plinth. In clocks, properly applies to base; now often used for skirting of case.

plique à jour enamelling. Unbacked metal cells filled with translucent enamel permitting light to pass through to give stained-glass window effect. Rare technique, used from 11th century in Russia and Scandinavia.

plumbago miniatures. Pencil drawings on vellum or paper, executed with fine graphite point, notably by British miniaturists from mid 17th to mid 18th centuries, e.g. D. *Loggan, R. *White, T. *Forster, J. *Ferguson.

Plymouth, Devon. Porcelain factory opened in 1768 at Plymouth, Devon, by W. *Cookworthy for manufacture of hard-paste porcelain; transferred to *Bristol in 1770. Porcelain body has glassy appearance, often slightly ridged or lop-sided because of uneven shrinkage in kiln. Glaze sometimes has pitted appearance and contains minute bubbles; colour stained brownish by smoke; firecracks common. Underglaze blue has blackish tint; blue-and-white decoration combines Chinese motifs with borders in classical style. Domestic ware and vases made in styles of Worcester and Sèvres; figures, inspired by Longton Hall and Derby, have scrolled bases picked out in brownish-red. Colours include yellow, red, and iridescent green. Cups and saucers, and large vases decorated with exotic birds by *Soqui; shell-shaped salts on base of coral and small shells attributed to *Tebo. In general, difficult to distinguish from later Bristol ware; sometimes marked with alchemists' sign for tin in underglaze blue, blue enamel, or gold.

Plumbago miniature. Charles I by Faber.

Plymouth porcelain. Bell-shaped, polychrome mug. Late 18th century. Marked in red enamel.

pochette. *See* kit.

pocket watch. First popularized in 17th century with English *Puritan watch: later became general, with watch attached to clothing by *fob-chain or chatelaine.

Podmore, Robert (fl mid 18th century). At Worcester porcelain factory, worked on manufacture of soapstone porcelain. Had taken formula to R. *Chaffers's Liverpool factory by 1756.

poinçon (French, 'mark'). *See* hallmarks, charge mark, discharge mark.

point cut. Form of diamond-cutting in which stone tapered to point (pyramid structure); involved cleaving along octahedron faces (natural form of diamond crystal). Sometimes called writing diamond because point was sharp enough to write on glass. Used during Middle Ages and Renaissance. Superseded by *rose cut.

poison tankard. 16th century German tankard with crystal body and silver mounts. Traditionally crystal thought to reveal presence of poison in drink.

poker work. Simple furniture decoration made by burning design into surface with red-hot poker or other hot metal object. Loose ash cleaned away, then roughnesses of design sanded smooth. Cottage craft technique; popular in late 19th century.

pole-head. *See* Friendly Society emblem.

pole screen. Adjustable fire or draught screen mounted on wooden or metal pole, usually on tripod base. Screen e.g. rectangular, circular, oval, or shield-shaped; solid wood or frame enclosing needlework; slides up and down pole. Popular in 18th century.

polish. Glossy finish on furniture achieved by application of oil and/or other substances, with lengthy and repeated friction rubbing. Nut, poppy, and linseed oils used from 16th century; beeswax (usually darkens wood) and turpentine (imparts golden colour) came into use later. Various staining agents used to obtain different colour effects. *See* French polish, varnish.

Polish carpets or **tapis polonais.** Very elaborate, silk and metal brocade Persian court carpets

Polish carpet (detail). Silk thread with gold and silver; period of Shah Abbas; probably woven on the court looms. Early 17th century.

Pomander. Gold with late Renaissance enamelled decoration, set with stones. French, c1600. Height 3⅞in.

woven mainly for export in early 17th century; many commissioned by Polish royalty and nobility, hence name. *See* arabesque carpets.

polychrome wares. General term for Chinese ceramics from T'ang dynasty decorated in two or more colours. T'ang polychromes usually on non-porcellanous biscuit; consist of lead glazes, allowed to run together. Common colours: green, amber, yellow, blue. Later, on some Ming dynasty porcelains, lead enamels used, separated by incised lines or threads of slip as in *cloisonné*. Alternatively, on Ming and Ch'ing porcelains, underglaze blue line design painted on biscuit, glazed, then coloured enamels applied to complete decoration. *See* wu ts'ai, san ts'ai, *famille verte, famille rose* (in Ch'ing dynasty).

pomander. Container for aromatic substances used in 16th and 17th century Europe; name perhaps derived from French *pomme d'ambre*, 'apple of ambergris', substance commonly used as prophylactic. Generally of spherical shape in gold or silver, 1–2in. in diameter, decorated with engraving, often divided into hinged segments or compartments for carrying 4–8 different spices and perfumes in paste form. Worn threaded on chain around neck. Precursor of *vinaigrette.

pome. Sphere of metal, 5–6in. in diameter, which can be opened to insert hot charcoal; or with small hole closed by screw for filling with hot water. Used by priests and wealthy laity to keep hands warm during services, primarily during Middle Ages, but also later. Examples in precious metals uncommon. Ornament engraved or pierced.

Pompadour fan. French 18th century fan with some **brins* broadened into ornamented medallion shape. Also matched on guards.

Pompeian scrolls. Ceramic decoration of scrolls in neo-classical style; accompanies grotesques and *putti* inspired by frescoes at Pompeii. Found on porcelain made at Sèvres from *c*1780; sometimes used in black or brown as diaper pattern on pale blue or yellow enamel ground. Similar decoration found on porcelain made in Paris, Vienna, Naples, and at Meissen.

Pompeian style. *See* Etruscan style.

pontil or **punty rod.** Solid iron rod (*c*5ft long) used by glassmaker to hold vessel, after removal from blow-pipe, by attaching it to small gather of hot glass at extremity. Scar (pontil or punty mark), usually on base of blown glass, caused by removal of pontil rod on completion of vessel. From *c*1780, mark ground smooth and polished.

Pontipool ware. Mass-produced *japanned metal-ware in imitation of *Pontypool ware, made in Wolverhampton, Staffordshire, from 1760s. Typical examples are trays decorated with bright colours. From *c*1812 bronze powder used as enrichment; designs block-printed, transfer-printed, or stencilled from mid 19th century.

Pontypool ware. *Japanned metal ware made 1680–1822 at Pontypool, Monmouthshire, by Allgood family. J. *Allgood's original process of 1680 improved by Edward Allgood (1681–1763), who founded Pontypool Japan Works *c*1725. First ground colour black; crimson developed *c*1741, and tortoiseshell in 1756. Early boxes circular (4in. diameter), black, decorated with *chinoiserie* or in gold with name of owner, date, and name of his house. English lacquered boxes unrivalled in Europe except by *Stobwasser family in Germany. From 1760s, decoration more varied, including colourful rustic and sporting scenes. Hand-painted work costly; mass-produced work, made elsewhere (e.g. *Pontipool ware), much cheaper. Quality of work declined from end of 18th century and factory closed 1822.

Popov, Alexei Gavrilovich (d 1750s). Russian porcelain manufacturer, previously merchant. From 1811, owner and director of porcelain factory near Moscow (established 1806), trading under name Popov. Produced both fine, costly tableware and profitable everyday porcelain. Established colour laboratory and invented glazes coloured green and deep blue. At first imitated figures of *Imperial porcelain factory; later produced brightly coloured Russian characters. Succeeded by children and grandchildren; factory then changed owners rapidly and closed in 1875. Mark usually AP in Cyrillic characters, in underglaze blue or black.

porcelain. *Ceramic material made from white refractory clay mixed with fusible substance (glass, soaprock, or feldspathic rock) to lower temperature of fusion; body non-porous, white and translucent unless heavily potted. *Soft-paste (artificial) porcelain can be marked with a file; glaze is glassy and sometimes uneven; enamel colours often sink in slightly. *Hard-paste (true) porcelain cannot be marked with a file; thin, glittering glaze; enamel colours lie on surface and can be felt with fingertips. *Bone ash added to both forms; with hard-paste porcelain makes *bone china.

Porcelain Axe, The (De Porceleyne Bijl). Delft factory (1657–1803) bought in 1739 from *Mesch family by J. *Brouwer, who was succeeded by son Hugo.

Pontypool tin ware. Tea caddy, late 18th or early 19th century; painted with flowers and strawberries, and gilded; brass handle.

*Alexei Popov porcelain factory. Figure of tartar archer after J. J. *Kandler, and P. *Reinicke of Meissen; c1810.*

Porcelain Bottle, The (De Porceleyne Fles). Delft factory (1653 to present day). W. *van Eenhoorn and Q. *van Cleynhoven partners from 1655. *Cape plates made *c*1700. Revival of blue painting with Chinese decoration in late 19th century. Only surviving Delft factory.

Porcelain Claw factory, The. *See* Sanderus, Lambertus.

Porcelaine de France. In 18th century France, trade name for soft-paste porcelain (*pâte tendre*).

Porcelaine royale. French hard-paste porcelain (*pâte dure*) manufactured at Sèvres from 1769. Large scale production also by other French factories from *c*1772.

Porcelain Plate, The (De Porceleyne Schotel). Delft factory (after 1612–1800) owned by J. *van Duyn, 1763–77.

porcelain rooms. Rooms containing vases, figures, mirror frames, and even fittings, e.g. cornices, made of porcelain; sometimes to house porcelain collections. Examples in German palaces from late 17th century, e.g. Charlottenburg palace (designed in 1703) and Japanese palace holding collection of Augustus the Strong. Porcelain made at Capodimonte used to furnish room in royal villa at Portici (1757–59) and moved in 1865 to palace of Capodimonte includes interlocking wall plaques, and Chinese figures set in moulded rococo frames. Larger room in same style constructed at palace of Aranjuez, near Madrid, with porcelain made at Buen Retiro (1760–67).

porceleyn. In mid 17th century Dutch Delft, finer tin-glazed ware, as distinct from tiles.

Porzellanglas. *See* opaque-white glass.

porringer or **eared dish.** Individual eating or drinking bowl, varying in width and depth, with one or two handles, with or without lid, made in pewter from 14th to 19th centuries, and silver in 17th and 18th centuries; some also made in Sheffield plate. Earliest known pewter examples from mid 16th century have two flat handles or 'ears' in form of fleur-de-lis. Later types sometimes have different ears: one plain, with pierced hole for hanging, other decorated with piercing or other ornament. From early 17th century, commonly made in pewter with one ear only; term also applied to silver and silver-gilt examples in *two-handled cup form, sometimes with cover and finial. Until *c*1650, sides straight, slanting inwards to flat base, sometimes with central boss; later, rounded sides and baluster shape became popular. Ears often strengthened by additional wedge or ring. In Germany, some examples have three feet and are slightly deeper than English versions; in France, sometimes with cast relief ornament; in Holland, often with rose decoration (much copied). Many American examples known, including simple style with solid handle, pierced for hanging, and style with elaborately pierced handle. Another type has initials of maker or owner cast in handle. Term also loosely applied to many bowl-shaped objects, e.g. *wine-taster and, in America, *bleeding-bowl.

Porringer. English, 1680; maker's mark IR. Flat chased chinoiserie *decoration; acanthus leaf finial on cover. Height 7in.*

Porrón. *Clear glass with* *latticinio *decoration. Spanish, 17th century. Height* c15*in.*

porrón. Spanish handleless drinking vessel with flat base and long spout for pouring wine into mouth. Often produced in *latticinio* glass, or decorated with tooled trailing. Originally from Valencia; also made in Catalonia during late 17th and 18th centuries.

portable altar. Oblong slab of semi-precious substance (agate, onyx, jasper, etc.) with gold or silver frame. Often inlaid with precious stones. Relic could also be placed in frame. Used on journeys; common at time of Crusades, but few made after 13th century when church virtually forbade use.

porter chair. Armchair upholstered in leather with wide 'wings' extending at top to form continuous arch, protecting user from draught. Designed for hall porter. Dates from 16th century; popular in Georgian period.

porter's badge. *See* badge.

Portland Vase. Most famous example of *cameo glass. Roman, *c*1st century. Two-handled urn (*c*10in. high) of dark blue glass cased with opaque-white glass, from which mythological figures carved in relief. Reproduced in jasper ware by J. *Wedgwood in 1790, in glass by J. *Northwood in 1870. Smashed in 1845, but restored; now in British Museum. Named after Duke of Portland, previous owner.

portrait box or **boîte à portrait.** Sixteenth century flat, oval, or rectangular gold box with miniature portrait on or inside lid; decorated with enamel and jewels. Sometimes with ring at top for use as pendant. During reign of Louis XIV in France developed into *tabatière à portrait.*

Type of porcelain snuff-box also called portrait box, made in considerable numbers in Germany at *Meissen factory during 1730s, sometimes with portrait of donor or recipient painted on inside of lid, e.g. one of *Augustus the Strong (*c*1730), attributed to J. G. *Herold, and pair depicting Count *von Brühl and wife (*c*1738). J. M. *Heinrici noted painter of miniatures on boxes. *Illustration at* French snuff-boxes.

portrait flask. 19th century American flask blown in full-size, two-piece mould, impressed on one side with bust of president or other famous person, e.g. George Washington, Benjamin Franklin, Henry Clay.

portrait watch. Fashionable in late 18th century, originally carrying actual portrait on case, later with purely decorative miniatures. Painting usually in enamel, often set in ring of pearls or *paillons* of gold or silver. Portraits also occur inside case, e.g. French royalist watch with concealed miniature of Louis XVI and family.

Portuguese carpets. Elaborate 17th century court carpets from south Persia or India, named for corner-piece designs of European ships manned by figures in Portuguese dress. Field has enormous central motif of superimposed medallions with large-scale, leafy outlines.

posnet. *See* skillet.

posset cup or **posset pot.** *See* caudle cup.

posset glasses. English glasses made *c*1600–1769. Usually squat and rounded, with two handles, spout, and cover. Earliest example of soda-glass, later lead-glass. For serving posset or syllabub. *cf* caudle cup.

post or **posted bed.** *See* fourposter.

post horn. Small brass or copper horn; crescent-shaped, straight, or coiled, without valves or other means of producing notes apart from those of harmonic series; name derives from use by mail-coach outriders to announce arrival (from 16th century in Britain and Europe). Larger variety with cup mouthpiece, straight conical tube, wide bore, and ending in funnel-shaped bell without flare, known as coach horn. Usually *c*36in. long; made in two sections.

posted or **bird cage frame.** Frame composed of four brass pillars, or posts, joined to corners of two plates, top and bottom; some with small turned feet, finials on top. Structure forms case of *lantern clock and *chamber clock, also frequently used in cheaper movements until 19th century, and to recent times in Holland and Black Forest.

postman's alarm clock. Weight-driven wall clock with long pendulum and alarm mechanism, housed in wooden case with circular dial; usually of German origin, especially from Black Forest.

posy ring or **brooch.** Ring or brooch with 'poesy' or rhyme engraved on inner side. Term not used before 16th century though such rings probably made before this period. In 17th century, rhymed couplets popular. Made in Britain and France.

pot. *See* kitchen utensil, tankard.

pot-à-oille. French silver *tureen used from 18th century; almost spherical in shape. Generally with salver or stand. *cf* ollio pot.

potash glass. Glass in which potassium carbonate used as fluxing agent. Potash produced before 19th century from boiling vegetable ash in pots. Quality of glass depended on type of ash. *See Waldglas, verre de fougère.*

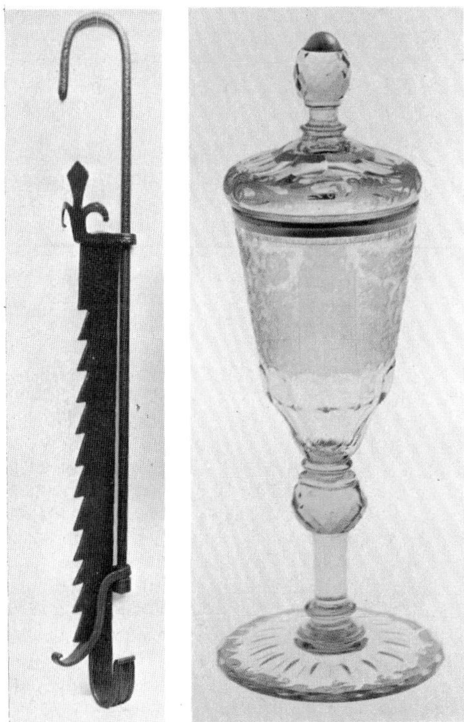

Pot-hook. English wrought-iron, made in Sussex, 18th century. Length 4ft2in.
Right:
Potsdam. Glass goblet and cover, 1740. Exported to Holland and engraved by German emigrant, Gottfried Schneider. Stem has two collars above faceted knop. Height 7¼in.

*Pot-lid. Mid 19th century, by F. & R. *Pratt & Co, designed by J. *Austin.*

potato flower or **fleur de solanée.** Ceramic motif included in polychrome decoration of faience in 1730s at Alcora, and from mid 18th century at Moustiers. Flower of potato or other solanaceous plant, alternating with flower sprays, or associated with fantastic figures or animals and plants in orange monochrome, green outlined in purple, or polychrome.

potato ring. *See* dish-ring.

pot-bellied measure. Earliest form of characteristically Scottish pewter measure. Thought to derive from European models. Made, *c*1680–*c*1740, with or without lid, basically in baluster form, but with exaggerated swelling curve above base.

pot board. In dresser or court cupboard, bottom shelf. Used to hold pots.

pot cupboard. 18th century term for *night table.

Poterat, Edmé (1612–87). French potter. Made faience at Rouen from 1647 under 50-year monopoly throughout Normandy (authorized 1648). Rare examples of *faience blanche* marked faict à Rouen 1647. Established factory in 1656 at Saint-Sever-lès-Rouen. Made tiles and vases for *Trianon de porcelaine* at Versailles in 1670. Granted barony; succeeded by younger son.

Poterat, Louis (1641–96). French potter, elder son of E. *Poterat. From 1673, authorized to produce porcelain and faience at Rouen; privilege renewed in 1694. No porcelain certainly identified; faience often painted in blue, *style rayonnant.*

pot-hook. Wrought-iron hook fixed to mantelpiece or ceiling of fireplace, for hanging cooking-pot over fire. Designs vary from simple S-shape to scrolling bracket and chain, and include methods of adjusting height by ratchet. Used from Middle Ages. In simplest form, often used in conjunction with *chimney-crane.

Poudreuse. *French, Louis XV period, in quarter veneered tulipwood.*

*Pounce pot (left) on stand with taperstick and ink pot, made by M. *Boulton, 1801. Height 3in.*

pot-lids. Decorative hard earthenware lids fitting wide, shallow pots containing bear-grease and, later, preserves. Initially printed with labels in black; then outline transfers coloured by hand. From 1845, decorated with underglaze engravings, notably by J. *Austin and made by F. *Pratt. Also pewter lids for earthenware tavern-pots from 16th century, forming large part of pewterers' output.

potpourri bowl. Small silver bowl to hold sweet-smelling herbs. Bowl has foot-ring and pierced cover surmounted by finial. Generally unornamented. Particularly popular in 18th century in Netherlands.

Potsdam. German glasshouse, founded 1674 by Elector Frederick William of Brandenburg. Directed by J. *Kunckel from 1679. Produced gold-ruby glass as well as green and blue cut and engraved glass. Engravers included G. *Spiller. In 1736, works moved to Zechlin. Flourished until 1890. Noted for large tankards and style of goblet with domed cover, heavy foot, and baluster stem. Most common motifs military and mythological. Potsdam glasses popular with engravers, especially in Bohemia. Produced *opaque-white glass under name *Porcelleinglas.*

pottery. All types of earthenware; formerly referred also to stoneware and porcelain.

pouch table. *See* work table.

poudreuse. 18th century French dressing-table, often veneered or inlayed. Usually has oval top in three sections; centre section hinged at back, opens to reveal mirror (on under-side of lid) and storage space. Outer sections hinged at side, providing extra surface and access to further storage space. False drawer fronts on frieze.

pouffe or **pouf.** Large stuffed cushion, often leather, used as footstool or seat. Popular from mid 19th century.

pounce. Fine ground pumice, powdered resin or other material sprinkled on parchment or writing-paper to prevent ink from spreading. *cf* sand.

pounce pot or **box.** Pot with pierced lid

used to sprinkle *pounce. Made from 18th century in silver, Sheffield plate, pewter, or cut glass with metal mounts as part of equipment of *inkstand, or to stand alone. Early form cylindrical; late 18th century examples in baluster shape resemble contemporary sugar *casters; from *c*1820, many made in shape of birds or animals: owl and pug dog particularly popular. Britannia metal used from *c*1820, also other metals, e.g. brass. Pounce pot used alternatively as *sand-caster.

pounces or **sponsen.** In ceramic decoration, cards pricked with outlines of drawings or engravings. Powdered charcoal or pumice forced through holes on unfired glaze of Dutch Delft. Patterns then rapidly painted over dots. Used in mass production of tiles from 17th century.

Poussierer. *See* Bossierer.

powder-blue. *See* Mazarin blue.

Poyntz, Francis. Most important 17th century English tapestry master-weaver. Among last technical directors at *Mortlake tapestry works; then (1679) established workshop at Grand Wardrobe, Hatton Garden, London, for restoration and storage of royal tapestries as well as manufacture of new pieces. Works include Playing Boys, Sea Battle of Soleby, and portrait series, Kings and Queens. Signed work with initials.

Pratt, Felix (1780–1859). Staffordshire potter. Worked in father's pottery at Lane Delph. In 1812, with brother established pottery, F. & R. Pratt at Fenton. Associated with *Pratt ware. Made Toby jugs, figures, and relief-decorated jugs in earthenware. Painted terracotta with classical scenes in bright polychrome enamel from early 1840s. From mid 19th century, firm noted for manufacture of decorated *pot-lids with polychrome engravings by J. *Austin. Rare mark, from 1818, F.&R.P. impressed; terracotta marked F&R PRATT FENTON. *Illustration at* pot-lids.

Pratt ware. British earthenware decorated with underglaze colours including blue, green, ochre, orange-brown, and purplish-brown, often sponged or stippled, sometimes over moulded relief, *c*1790. Associated with F. and R. *Pratt; made in Staffordshire, north of England, and (*c*1795–*c*1830) Scotland. Colours used e.g. for flower designs on tableware and decoration of Toby jugs and figures, also plaques.

prayer rug. Easily transportable mat on which Moslem kneels, facing Mecca, to perform devotions, when not in mosque (*cf* *saph). *Mihrab usually important feature of design; in manufactory-made examples, original significance of mihrab often lost; becomes merely decorative feature. As subjected to particularly hard wear, few old prayer rugs survive. *Illustrations at* Ladik carpets, Melas carpets.

precision clock. Timepiece intended for accurate performance rather than decoration; made from early 18th century in forms of *chronometer, and regulator clock, incorporating technical improvements of G. *Graham, J. *Harrison, P. *LeRoy, and others. Typical regulator is of undecorated long-case type with dead-beat *escapement and gridiron or mercury *compensation; dial is plain, of brass, silvered brass, or white enamel, often with centrally-mounted minute hand and minute ring on circumference enclosing subsidiary hour and seconds dials. In 19th century mantel regulators produced with half-second pendulum.

Preissler or **Preussler,** Daniel (1636–1733) and son, Ignatz (1676–*c*1741). German *Hausmaler*. Enamelled Bohemian and Silesian glass, and, after *c*1720, Chinese, Meissen, and Vienna porcelain. On Chinese pieces, mythological, hunting, battle, and travel scenes depicted (*c*1721) in **Schwarzlot* and gold. Later style involves light baroque scrollwork, C and S shaped foliate scrolls in combinations of black, gold, red, and **Laub-und-Bandelwerk*. Ignatz more prolific. No marks.

press cupboard. Two-tiered long, rectangular cupboard. Bottom unit contains drawers; upper unit has three small, recessed cupboards (outer two often canted) with narrow shelf in front. Dates from mid 16th century in Britain, mid 17th in America. May be so-named because drawers used to store clothes. *cf* clothes press.

pressed glass. Glass formed in mould under pressure. Molten glass is poured into mould forming exterior of vessel, and plunger forces mass into shape. Once glass has solidified, plunger is withdrawn, leaving dull, smooth interior surface. Manual pressing practised in antiquity before technique of glass blowing invented; also used in Holland, England, and Ireland from *c*1785 for decanter stoppers and feet for salts. Mechanical pressing developed in America; first patent, to make furniture knobs, granted to *Bakewell & Co in 1825. Glassworks particularly associated with perfecting mechanization of pressed glass are *Boston & Sandwich Glass Co. (due to efforts of D. *Jarves) and *New England Glass Co. Mechanical pressing allowed cheap mass-production of glass. Early American pressed glass imitated Anglo-Irish cut glass, but more suitable pattern for pressing was *lacy glass, made 1825–50. Most common early

Left:
Precision clock. Mahogany case. By S. Rentzsch. English c1805.

*Pressed glass. American, 19th century. Left: salt, probably from *Boston & Sandwich Glass Company; height $1\frac{3}{4}$in. Centre: *lacy glass bowl, probably from Pittsburgh, Pennsylvania. Length $7\frac{1}{2}$in. Right: opaline cup plate from Sandwich Glassworks. Diameter $3\frac{3}{4}$in.*

examples are cup-plates and salts, but by *c*1840 complete tableware services produced, mainly in plain glass; by mid 19th century *marble glassware popular. Machine pressed glass quickly adopted in Europe, particularly in France and England. By *c*1840, tableware, glasses, lamps, candlesticks, and vases made in imitation cut glass. Experiments with patterns, shapes and colours continued, mainly in late 19th century. Main features of pressed glass are regularity and smoothness of glass, and mould seam (after *c*1830 almost obliterated on better pieces by fire-polishing, which also gave extra brilliance).

press-moulding. Ceramic technique: moist clay beaten or rolled into flat 'bat', pressed into mould and trimmed. Used from early 18th century; moulds first of fired clay, later wood, alabaster, or plaster of Paris. Dishes shaped over convex moulds with ridged or incised patterns to be decorated with slip. Best known dishes attributed to S. *Malkin. By 1740s, figures frequently pressed into two-piece moulds and assembled when firm by uniting edges with slip. From 1750s, parts of figures moulded separately.

Prévost, Pierre (*c*1640–after 1716). French silversmith working in Paris; founder of family of silver craftsmen. First mark: crowned fleur-de-lis, two pellets, and sword between initials PP; second mark, in 1680: crowned fleur-de-lis, two pellets, and helmet between initials PP. Made most of pieces in *Chatsworth Toilet Service.

Prewitt, William (fl 1735–50). English enamel painter, pupil of C. F. *Zincke. Also worked in watercolours.

pricket candlestick. Earliest type of candle-holder with conical spike for impaling candle; probably first made for ecclesiastical use in gold, silver, silver-gilt or base metal. Surviving 16th century examples in silver with straight stem, wide grease-pan and domed base. Domestic use became rare in early 17th century; though production for altar use continued.

prie-dieu. Low kneeling-desk with slant top for prayer-book and sometimes shelves or cupboard below; slanted base for kneeling. Originally from 14th century Italy.

prie-dieu chair or **kneeling chair.** Single chair, upholstered, with low seat for kneeling; high back has wide top piece as prayer-book rest. Popular 19th century chair.

Prince Henri pattern. French ceramic decoration, adapted from Meissen *red dragon pattern, on porcelain at Chantilly from 1730. Named after Louis-Henri de Bourbon, Prince de Condé, founder of Chantilly porcelain factory, 1725.

Prince of Wales plumes. Ornamental device of three ostrich feathers, as in badge of Prince of Wales. In furniture, incorporated in chair back decoration in late 18th and early 19th centuries. Characteristic Hepplewhite motif.

prince's metal. Brass alloy invented in 1670s by Prince Rupert of Bavaria, resembling gold. Sometimes used for door furniture, buttons, snuff-boxes, etc. Does not tarnish.

privateer glasses. Rare English drinking glasses engraved with picture of, or reference to, a British privateer ship. Usually with bucket bowl and opaque-white twist stem. Made mainly in Bristol, *c*1756–70.

processional cross. *See* cross.

profiles. *See* silhouettes.

Left:
Pricket candlesticks. South German, brass, mid 18th century. Height c1ft9in.
Prie-dieu *chair. Upholstered in beadwork with carved beechwood frame. English, mid 19th century.*

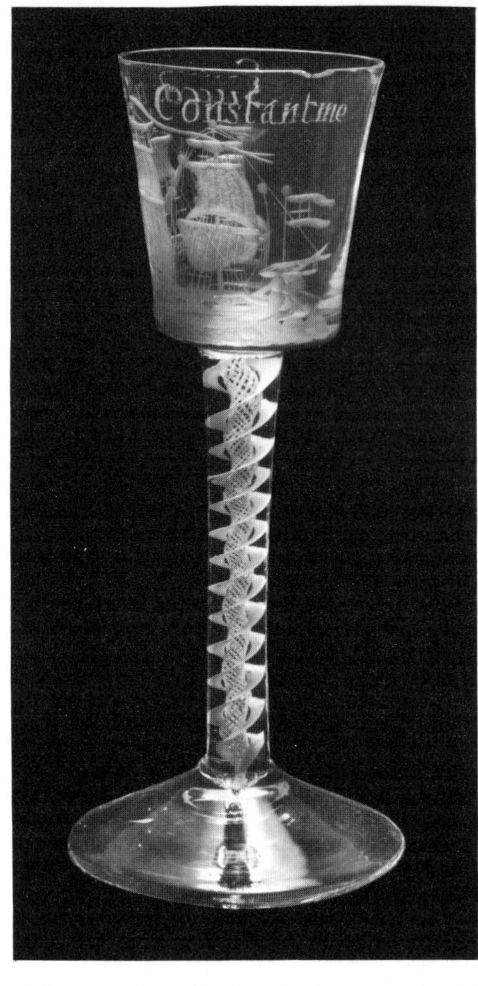

Privateer glass. Bucket bowl engraved with three-masted frigate and inscribed above in diamond etching: Success to the Constantine. Opaque twist stem. English, c*1757. Height* c*6in.*

Projection clock. Bronze case with gilt dial. Light can be put in the box at night; time projected on wall. French, c*1830. Height* $9\frac{1}{2}$*in.*

projection clock. Development of *night clock; produced in England and Europe in early 19th century, with lantern throwing image of translucent dial on to wall.

proto-porcelain. Term applied in West, among early 20th century scholars, to group of fine Chinese stoneware pieces with feldspathic glaze, probably originating in Han dynasty; termed proto-Yüeh by modern writers. Usually has combed or incised decoration; some features imitate bronze ware, e.g. loop handles. Precursor of celadon ware. *See* Yüeh ware.

province mark. Mark of one of Dutch provinces used as *hallmark. First instituted (1663) by Emperor Charles V in western Friesland where crowned provincial lion used.

prunt. Lump or blob of glass applied to glass vessels for decoration or to provide grip. Three main shapes are: thorn (plain and drawn out to a point as in *Igel); berry (resembling a raspberry); medallion (impressed with shape such as lion's head). *Illustration at Römer.*

Puente del Arzobispo, near Toledo. Spanish tin-glazed earthenware made from 17th century, resembles that of Talavera. Often decorated with heraldic motifs.

Pugin, Augustus Welby Northmore (1812–52). English architect, interior decorator, and furniture, ceramics and designer; also medievalist and leading exponent of *Gothic revival. Many publications include Gothic Furniture (1828), and Contrasts (1836), advocating Gothic as truly Christian style, and works on furniture design, stained glass, etc. First silver designs *c*1826 for *Rundell, Bridge & Rundell. Designed silver and jewellery from 1838 for J. *Hardman. Designed marriage jewellery in Gothic style for intended third wife (1847); shown at Great Exhibition, London, 1851 and established vogue for Gothic jewellery. Revived use of enamelling in jewellery. *Illustration also at* Minton, H.

pulley salt. *See* spool salt.

pull-up. American term for *wax-jack.

pulse watch. From *c*1700, watch with seconds hand and means for stopping it, used by doctors for taking pulse, etc. Also form of *repeating watch with striking hammer connected to pin projecting from case and indicating number of blows to deaf user.

punch. Tool for stamping or piercing design on metal. *See* chasing.

punch bowl. Large silver, silver-gilt, or Sheffield plate bowl (diameter *c*12–24in.) used to serve punch; used from late 17th century. Sometimes also has two handles (usually ring) and foot-ring. Only ornament on earliest examples was moulded rim and engraved arms. Short spool-shaped stem common from *c*1730; ornament then embossed fluting, foliate and floral designs. Also made in English delftware, e.g. at Bristol decorated by J. *Flower, and at Liverpool, often painted with nautical subjects. Hunting scenes also popular decorative theme; examples made in porcelain at Worcester with designs by R. *Hancock. In Chinese export porcelain, sometimes decorated with views of Chinese ports.

punched work. Relief decoration on metal made by grouping two or more blunt tools in geometrical or floral pattern and punching them, together or separately, on to object.

Puente del Arzobispo. Maiolica tazza, *late 17th to early 18th century.*

Punch bowl. Decorated only with band of engraving of lattice-work at rim, and cartouches of bacchanalian figures astride barrels. Made by Richard Bailey, 1717. Small size, diameter $8\frac{3}{4}$*in.*

*Proto-porcelain. Jar, *Han dynasty, decorated with series of incised lines and band of wavy combing; inside of rim and upper part covered with smear-glaze. Height* 10*in.*

A. W. N. Pugin. Table to his design made by Holland and Sons. Oak and burr-walnut veneer, c1850. Length 4*ft.*

Punched work ornamentation on Pennsylvania tin ware coffee-pot. American, early 19th century. Height 12½in.

Popular in 16th and 17th centuries, much used for border ornament. Revived in 19th century.

punch ladle. Silver, gold, or Sheffield plate ladle with deep bowl (with or without pouring lip) and long handle or stem; used for serving hot punch. Bowl of ladle circular or oval sometimes with everted rim; alternatively shell-shaped. In Britain from mid 18th century, bowls often hammered from silver coins. Handles frequently of wood, whalebone, or ivory. Similar pewter ladles known from 17th century in England, but more common in other parts of Europe.

Punch'ŏng or **mishima ware.** Korean ceramics of Yi period, produced in large quantities in central and southern regions. Stoneware, in bold, strong forms, typical. Early pieces similar to inlaid celadon ware: white slip applied to greyish clay under greenish or bluish glaze. Patterns simple and geometrical, small daisy-head motif or, notably, *rope curtain pattern. In 15th century, another variety appeared: hakeme ('brush-marked') ware, with white slip applied in streaks, using small 'broom' made of rice-straw. Sometimes with simple *sgraffiato* decoration, e.g. arabesques, flowers, birds, or fishes. Another variety, kohiki ('powdered') ware, covered in slip, including base, with dry finish to glaze. Many examples in Chinese ritual bronze shapes. Chinese characters sometimes incised among decoration, usually near, or at centre of, bowl or dish, occasionally on side of cup or vase, crudely-formed, and intended to form part of design. Precise dating of ware seldom possible, although marks indicating official use became widespread during Koryo period, departments in charge of banquets or cookery for palaces had names inscribed, often preceded by place-name. Prominent kiln-sites: Sangju and Koryong, north Kyongsang province, and Keryongsan, near Taejon, south Korea, which specialized in all-over white slip wares, with bold decoration in iron-brown or black. Best examples are large wine jars.

Punct, Carl Christoph (d 1765). Porcelain modeller at Meissen 1761–65. Noted for models of Diana and Actaeon made 1760 for Frederick the Great during Seven Years' War, and groups of children symbolizing The Elements (1764), on rococo scrolled bases. Style transitional between J. J. *Kändler's rococo and Louis XVI style.

punty. *See* pontil.

purchase. *See* thumbpiece.

purdonium. *See* coal-scuttle.

Puritan or **stump-top spoon.** Mid 17th century silver, pewter, or latten spoon with flat stem widening towards square-cut end. Derived from earlier *slip-top style. *Illustration at* knop.

Puritan style. *See* Commonwealth style.

Puritan tankard. *See* Commonwealth tankard.

Puritan watch. Plain undecorated oval watch common in mid 17th century England. Normally up to 2in. long, with silver case and dial, and simple engraved Roman numerals: probably carried in pocket. Movement still elaborately decorated.

Purman, Marcus (fl late 16th century). Maker of sundials in Munich, Germany. Noted for dials of unusual form, e.g. in shape of chalice or drinking-cup.

purple monochrome. Painting on faience and porcelain in manganese-purple; introduced to 18th century Germany by D. and I. *Preissler in 1720s for tankards, etc. Other examples in porcelain from Meissen and Höchst (*c*1750–60), Fürstenberg and Frankenthal (*c*1765–70), and Ludwigsburg (*c*1770–80). *See* red monochrome.

Puritan watch. English, with fusee movement, verge escapement, and unsprung balance silver pair case, made in London by Elias Volant, c1635.

purple Ting. *See* Ting-chou ware.

push-piece (in watches). Small projection on edge of case, used in key-winding watch to open case; in *keyless mechanism watches to engage hand setting action.

Pu-tai Ho-shang. In Chinese ceramics, apostle of Buddha; occurs in decoration of later porcelain pieces, or as figure. Smiling, corpulent monk, carrying bag, surrounded by children.

putti. Chubby, naked boys, often found as figures, or painted on pottery and porcelain, and embossed or engraved on silver, etc., from late 15th century.

puzzle cup. *See* wager cup.

puzzle fan. 18th century European *brisé* fan with overlapping sticks which can be manipulated to produce different scenes.

puzzle jug. English pottery drinking vessel, usually with pierced decoration around top. Liquid drunk through small opening at spout, connected to tube leading around top and through handle to inside of jug near base; sometimes other holes had to be covered by fingertips. Made from Middle Ages, particularly in late 17th and early 18th centuries.

Pyne, Benjamin (d *c*1732). English silversmith working in London; received freedom in 1676. Prime Warden of Goldsmiths' Company in 1725. Made range of domestic silver in Huguenot style; commissions for Queen Anne and aristocracy. Bankrupted in 1727. Marks (1697): PY in Gothic script enclosed in an oval, or PY with crown above.

pyx. Small box, sometimes with conical lid surmounted by cross, in which consecrated

*Puzzle jug. *Scratch-blue salt-glaze ware, Staffordshire, c1755.*

Pyxes. English silver. Top: Commonwealth pyx, c1635–49, engraved on lid with cross, IHS and Sacred Heart pierced with nails; diameter 2in. Bottom: Charles II oval pyx, c1660 (back shown), engraved with the Lamb. The sides decorated with twisted wire; diameter $1\frac{3}{8}$*in.*

wafers placed e.g. for carrying in procession, or by priest when visiting sick or dying; probably used from 8th century. Examples from *c*1400 often have foot resembling that of chalice. Made of various materials including gold, silver, crystal, ivory, beryl, enamel. Lavishly ornamented inside and out with inscriptions and scenes relating to Eucharist. Sometimes made in pewter or enamelled copper from Middle Ages; none survives from before 16th century.

qalian. *See* hookah.

quadrant. Instrument for measuring altitude, used from late 16th century; in form of quarter circle, graduated on rim, and sighting rule (alidade) pivoted at apex of radii. Astronomical quadrants fixed to wall; had up to 4ft radius in 17th century, over 6ft in mid 18th century. Size limited by problem of casting large sections of iron or brass without warping. Portable quadrants for surveying made of wood or iron in 17th century, of brass from *c*1700, with plumb-line for setting vertical and pair of fixed sights in line with 0° on scale. Metal horary quadrants used from early 14th century to *c*1800. Instrument is inclined until sun's rays pass through two fixed sights. Time is shown by intersection of weighted thread and engraved scale.

quadrant drawer. Three-sided (quarter circle) drawer beneath desk top for storing ink and

Quaiches. Left: made in Inverness by Thomas Baillie, c1740. Right: made in Edinburgh by John Rollo. Diameter of bowl 2in.

*sand. Attached to desk at apex; opens by swinging outwards. Dates from 18th century.

quadrillé. French ceramics. Diaper pattern with quatrefoil motifs forming ground of square shapes. Painted in blue enamel on soft-paste porcelain made at Chantilly in mid 18th century.

quaich or **quaigh.** 17th and 18th century Scottish silver or, rarely, pewter drinking vessel with large, circular bowl like *mazer but also two flat handles. Sometimes low, circular foot. Often engraved to represent wooden staves. Made in various sizes.

quail clock. Similar to *cuckoo clock but with bird-call simulating cry of quail. Often quail sounds quarters, and cuckoo hours. Made in Black Forest, Germany.

quail pattern. *See caille* pattern.

Quaker chair. Simple side chair, with upholstered circular seat, balloon-back, and turned front legs; made at High Wycombe, Buckinghamshire, in 19th century.

Quare, Daniel (1648–1724). English clock and watch maker; invented repeating watch *c*1680. Known also for work on equation clocks. Quaker religion prevented appointment as Royal Clockmaker. Became master, Clockmakers' Company, 1708. Made long-case and bracket clocks, and watches with unusual features. *Illustration at* back plate.

Queen Anne style. Serving table. Oak with three drawers cross-banded in walnut; original brass handles.

quartetto tables. T. *Sheraton's term for *nest of four tables.

quartz. Family of stones with crystalline and cryptocrystalline varieties (known as *chalcedony). Made up of crystalline silicon dioxide. Most common forms of crystalline variety used in jewellery and decorative purposes are *rock-crystal (colourless), amethyst (all shades of violet), *cairngorm (yellow or brown), and citrine (yellow) often wrongly called quartz-topaz or simply topaz, though gems are different. Rock-crystal used more or less continuously from classical period as gemstone; other members of family mainly from 19th century.

quatre-couleur gold. *See* four-colour gold.

quatrefoil. *See* trefoil.

Quattrocento (Italian, '15th century'). Term refers particularly to Italian art and literature of early *Renaissance period.

Queen Anne style. Furniture style in England during reign of Queen Anne (1702–20), though influence apparent until *c*1750. Decoration more restrained than in preceding *William and Mary style; more curving lines introduced, particularly in cresting and supports; cabriole legs developed and became most common form. Walnut or walnut veneers commonly used. Ornament included herring-bone banding, or cross-banding particularly on drawer fronts), carving (e.g. cabochon and acanthus motif on knee of cabriole leg), lacquered finish (especially on cabinets, chairs, chests, and frames). Scroll and hoof feet characteristic of early years of period, with simple claw and ball feet becoming increasingly popular (on cabriole legs). Side tables often have tops of marble, *scagliola*, etc.

Typical Queen Anne pieces are heavily-draped tester bed; tripod-based candlestand (often elaborately carved and gilded *en suite* with side table or mirror); china cabinet, cabinet-on-chest, and Welsh dresser; popular 'Queen Anne chair' (with back curved to fit spine, spoon-shaped splat, and cabriole legs), winged armchair, reading chair, hall chair, chest-on-frame, chest of drawers, tallboy, and dome-topped lacquered chest; wall mirrors (often with ornate carved and

Queen's pattern on dessert spoon and fork, table spoon and fork by George Adams, 1854.
Right:
*Queensware. *Wedgwood. Left: Victorian covered kitchen jug, c1850, made to early 19th century design. Right: teapot, c1780, transfer printed with The Death of Wolfe.*

gilt, or glass, frames, shaped at both bottom and top), swing toilet mirrors on drawer stands, and pier glasses with mirror area made of two pieces of glass; settees and sofas, with lower backs than William and Mary examples, and love seats in designs similar to settees (all contributed to declining popularity of day-bed); architect's table, circular, folding, square, or rectangular card tables (of *concertina construction), dressing-table, gate-leg table, lowboy, and toilet table; knee-hole writing table, gilt gesso pieces, and secretary-tallboys. Common upholstery fabrics included tapestry work, velvet, and silk. Handles brass, often pear-drop shaped or curving, and attached to solid brass backplate. *Illustrations at* bachelor chest, blanket chest, gesso, oystering, reading chair, tea table, toilet mirror, trunk.

Queen's pattern. 19th century British silver flatware pattern. Resembles *King's pattern, but has palmette reinforcement on back of bowl instead of shell; curlier stem edges; and rosette between anthemion motifs on face and back half-way down stem.

Queen Charlotte, whorl, or **Catherine wheel pattern.** Design in Chinese style used on porcelain at Worcester from *c*1760: alternating spiral stripes of underglaze blue and red enamel, with gilding. Later copied at Derby and Lowestoft. Probably derived from Meissen.

Queensware. Light, white earthenware with thin, brilliant glaze; refinement of *creamware, developed by J. *Wedgwood and named in honour of patroness, Queen Charlotte (1765). Production continues. Mark: WEDGWOOD impressed from 1769 to present day. Also made by *Stafford Pottery.

quilling or **pinched trailing.** Glass decoration of applied bands of glass pinched into wavy form, e.g. on small bottles produced at *Nailsea in 19th century.

*Race cup by W. *Cripps, made in 1751 for the Newton Hunt race; elaborately moulded and chased with scrolls, vines, and roses; cover terminates in acorn finial. Height 13¾in.*
Right:
Rack clock. Made by Mossbrucher of Saverna, c1780. Spring-driven; must be wound every day by pushing movement downwards.

quintal flower horn. *See* finger vase.

quizzing fan. 18th century European fan with peep-holes of transparent fabric in leaf.

quizzing glasses. Regency ladies' fashion *c*1814–30. Initially lens in gold circular frame with loop for ribbon. Evolved into female lorgnette and male monocle later in century.

rabeschi. Italian term for *arabesques.

race cup. Gold, silver, or silver-gilt cup presented to owner of winning horse at race meeting; shapes included two-handled cup, classical urn or vase. Custom dates from 17th century in Britain and Europe. In America silver punchbowls sometimes used as prizes. In England from mid 18th to early 19th centuries considered of utmost importance in silversmith's output; brought prestige to maker and retailer. Most important race cups made during heyday of *Rundell, Bridge & Rundell (*c*1800–30). Declined in popularity from *c*1830 and superseded by trophies of sculptured figures manufactured by *Hunt & Roskell, *Garrards, etc. Also called cups.

rack. *See* striking mechanism.

rack clock. Type deriving power from own weight, sliding down toothed vertical rack, which engages with pinion in movement; made from *c*1600. Also as trick form in 18th century, spring-driven, climbs up rack and is pushed down to wind.

Radeloff, Nicolas (fl *c*1650). Danish clock maker famous for weight-driven clock in Renaissance style similar to mid 17th century German spring-driven type, with wooden base on animal-shaped supports and highly-ornamented architectural case. Also made clock with cross-beat *escapement controlled by steel ball falling in spiral; cases gilded and engraved on ebony and tortoiseshell base.

Radford, Thomas (fl late 18th century). English engraver of plates for transfer-printing on cream-coloured earthenware. Worked at Cockpit Hill, Derby, probably until closure (1779); signed teapot with Russian arms and portrait of Catherine the Great in black, dated 1765. Then worked at Shelton, Staffordshire; mugs printed in black with signed engraving of The World in Planisphere. Sometimes marked work with signature, transfer-printed in black, e.g. Radford sculpsit DERBY Pot Works.

Raeren, Germany. Important centre of *Rhineland stoneware production in 16th century, notably *c*1560. Body at first brown, later grey with panels of clear blue lead-glaze (introduced by J. *Emens). Noted for large **Doppelfrieskrüge*. After 1590 relief decoration became highly ornate; best potters moved to *Westerwald.

Raes, Jan (fl 1593–1649). Most prominent tapestry master-weaver in early 17th century Brussels. Numerous tapestries woven, many from designs by *Rubens; worked with C. and J. *Geubels. Most famous piece, **Acts of the Apostles,* woven from cartoons *Raphaël.

Raffaelle ware. In 19th century ceramics, dealer's term for maiolica made e.g. at workshop of O. *Fontana and by *Patanazzi family, decorated with grotesques.

railroad flask. 19th century American glass flasks blown in full-size, two-piece moulds, featuring horse-drawn or steam-propelled railway coach or engine. Occasionally inscribed 'Success to the Railroad'. Coloured mainly amber or green.

railway watch. 19th century form of *mail guard's watch.

raised anchor period. *See* Chelsea.

*Railroad flask. American, mid 19th century. Blown and moulded glass, olive green; inscribed Success to the Railroad; of the type made at *Mount Vernon Glass Works, New York.*

raising (in silver). Hollow-ware made with stake and hammer. Silver sheet first roughly-shaped by *bossing up or beating into block, then raised on stake by hammering from base upwards in series of concentric circles. Work must be annealed repeatedly. Hammer marks removed from outside surface by *planishing; almost always visible inside finished object; thickness of shell variable.

raku. Japanese pottery, created by Raku-Chojiro (1515–92), and produced thereafter in Kyoto area. H. *Koyetsu notable among 14 generations of raku potters after Chojiro. Objects hand-modelled exclusively for tea ceremony use. Low-fired, pottery, with soft lead-glaze, usually black, red, or yellow, and applied in several thin layers, running down when fired to leave part of body exposed; sometimes top layer of glaze stops in wavy line half way down. Influenced by Korean Yi period bowls in style and feeling. Impressed with seal of raku (Japanese, 'enjoyment of freedom') and, in Edo period, also inscribed with name of potter. At that time influence of raku spread to many centres all over Japan, notably Chi, in Kanazawa province, where redder, denser-bodied ware made; and Horaku, near Nagoya, which specialized in lacquer-work on raku bodies. Early 19th century tea-bowls from this area notable.

Ramage, John (1748–1802). Irish-born American painter; executed life-sized portraits in crayons or pastels, and miniatures. Worked in Boston, Massachusetts, before American Revolution; then established in New York.

ram's head motif. Mask in shape of ram's head; used on 18th century French and English furniture. In silver, embossed, cast, or stamped as ornament on neo-classical hollow-ware (baskets, coffee-pots, tureens, two-handled cups, etc.). Sometimes with ring in mouth for use as handle. *See* lion mask.

ram's horn or **os de mouton scroll.** Scroll shape used mainly on legs, stretchers, and arms of chairs; resembles stylized elongated ram's horn. Found particularly on Louis XIII and American 18th century pieces.

ram's horn thumbpiece. Scrolling, horn-shaped thumbpiece on some English pewter vessels of late 17th and early 18th centuries.

Randall, Thomas Martin (1786–1859). English painter and porcelain maker. Apprentice at Coalport, then worked at Derby and Pinxton. In partnership with R. *Robins established enamelling workshop, Robins & Randall, at Spa Fields, London. *c*1825, started soft-paste porcelain factory at Madeley, Shropshire; at first operated as decorating workshop. Made imitations of Sèvres porcelain and painted hard-paste porcelain, bought in white in England and from elsewhere, with decoration in Sèvres style. Factory closed *c*1840. Work usually unmarked. Later, worked as potter at Shelton, Staffordshire (1841–56).

Randolph, Benjamin (fl *c*1750–90). Cabinet maker, chair maker, and carver in Philadelphia, Pennsylvania. Worked mainly in *Philadelphia Chippendale style. Set of heavily-carved sample chairs believed to be his work.

Ranftbecher. German glass beaker, wider at top than bottom, with protruding base, often faceted or fluted, usually engraved, painted or gilded. Very popular **Biedermeier* shape in 19th century. *Illustration at Biedermeier style.*

Raphaël (1483–1520). Raffaello Sanzio, Italian painter, master of high Renaissance. For Pope Leo X, drew cartoons (1515–16) for *Acts of the Apostles tapestry, intended for Sistine Chapel. From completion of weaving in Brussels in 1519, Italian school of painting dictated European tapestry design, ousting Bruges school. Raphaël's dramatic pictorial style gained lasting popularity. At Gobelins, under direction of C. *Lebrun, a number of tapestry designs taken from his paintings, notably Vatican frescoes (begun 1508 for Pope Julius II), e.g. eight-piece History of Constantine, woven 1660; in 1667, Acts of the Apostles rewoven. All Gobelins tapestries from manufactory's first period (1662–94) conspicuously Raphaëlesque.

Raphaelesque ware. *See* Worcester.

Raqqa. North Mesopotamian pottery centre, 9th to 14th centuries. Products have buff body with relief decoration covered in opaque turquoise or clear greenish glaze. In 12th and early 13th centuries, black or blue and black slip painted under clear glaze, sometimes stained with manganese-purple, resembling contemporary Egyptian pottery. Lustre decorated ware also made.

ratafia glasses. English glasses made *c*1740–70; long, narrow, funnel-shaped bowl, usually with drawn stems of similar length.

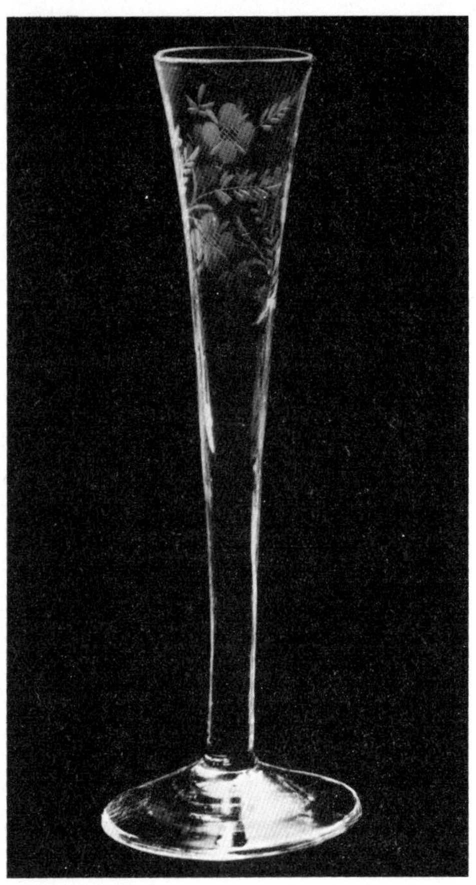

Ratafia glass. English. Plain stem; funnel bowl engraved with spray of flowers; conical foot. Height 7½in.

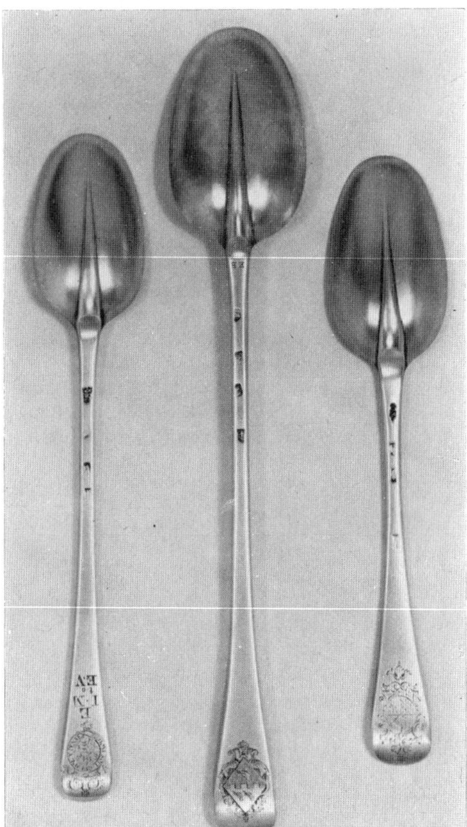

Bowl usually plain, clear glass, or engraved with floral spray. Stem plain, occasionally air or opaque twist after 1750. Foot always plain. Used for drinking brandy-flavoured fruit cordial.

Rato (near Lisbon). Portuguese faience factory established in 1767 by T. *Brunetto. Tableware, often in forms from contemporary silver, decorated in style of Savona and Turin. Also produced large figures and tureens in form of birds. Mark: FR with monogram TB, or SA (after 1771).

rat-tail spoon. Silver or pewter spoon with elongated V-shaped extension of stem on back of bowl for reinforcement. Found on late 17th and early 18th century spoons; later spoons have mainly single or double drop reinforcement (cast as part of spoon bowl, never applied separately). Usually found on *wavy-end spoon and *Hanoverian pattern.

Raven, Samuel (1775–1847). English lacquer painter who decorated Birmingham papier mâché boxes. Subjects included Sir Thomas Lawrence's portrait of George IV, landscapes, and genre scenes by Sir David Wilkie. Signed works in red inside lid.

Ravenet, Simon-François (1706–74). French designer and engraver working in London from *c*1746. Began working for William Hogarth; later chief designer and engraver of enamels at Battersea. Subjects included royal portraits, scenes from religion and mythology, and genre scenes.

ravensbill. Early 17th century *ewer.

Ravenscroft, George (1618–81). Trader and technologist; son of wealthy shipowner. Based researches on Merret's translation of *Arte Vetraria.* Set up glasshouse in Savoy in 1673 for experimental purposes. Produced clear white glass, but affected by crizzling due to imbalance of salt fluxes in relation to base mixture. First patent for crystal glass granted in 1674; encouraged and patronized by Glass Sellers' Company, established second glasshouse and laboratory at Henley-on-Thames, Oxfordshire. By 1675 had overcome crizzling by reducing salts and adding lead oxide. New type of crystal (flint) glass made of English raw materials, perfected by Ravenscroft's successor, paved way for English dominance of crystal glass market in 18th century. Retired 1678.

*George Ravenscroft. *Helmet-shaped jug, gadrooned and with twisted handle, at base of which is raven's head seal, c1676. Cloudy effect is due to *crizzle. Height 9in.*

Right:

*Rat-tail spoons. English. Left: P. *de Lamerie, 1721. Centre: Isaac Davenport, 1709. Right: D. *Willaume the Elder, 1710; engraved with arms of Queen Anne.*

Reading chair. Queen Anne, walnut. Leather-covered back with two hinged and swivelling compartments; outwards-splayed pad feet; H-shaped stretcher.

raven's head seal. Seal granted (1676) to G. *Ravenscroft by Glass Sellers' Company to mark success of new flint-glass. Small glass disc impressed with raven's head, taken from Ravenscroft arms.

Rayy, Persia. Main centre for production of *Seljuq ware. Pottery made by early 13th century; buff body covered with clear glaze, painted with gold lustre and, often, blue. *Minai ware with cream or turquoise glaze decorated e.g. in blue, purple, red, green, white, and gold. *Sgraffiato* decoration cut through black slip, covered with clear or turquoise glaze.

reading or **cock-fighting chair.** Chair with horizontally curving continuous yoke-rail and arms; book support can be attached to back of yoke-rail, allowing user to sit facing back of chair and read, with arms supported. Dates from early 18th century. In 19th century, term described armchair with book support attached to end of one arm. Candle-stand may be incorporated in either model.

reading seat or **Albany couch.** 19th century upholstered day-bed with one high end, shaped to fit user's back and give head support.

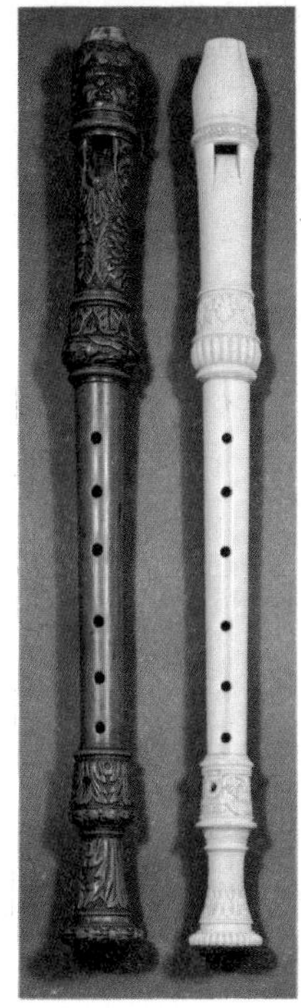

*Reading stand. *French provincial, Louis XV, walnut.*
Recorders. Left: late 17th century, probably German, carved ivory. Right: late 18th century, stamped J. W. Oberlender; carved boxwood.
*Red stoneware. Teapot made at Meissen under J. F. *Böttger, modelled by C. J. *Lücke; contemporary silver mounts, c1715. Width* $7\frac{1}{4}$*in.*

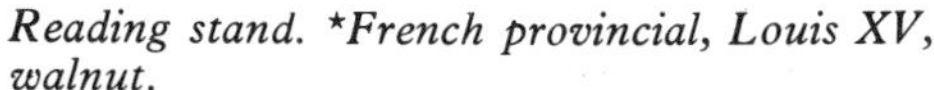

reading stand. Wooden stand, often mahogany, with slanting top resembling lectern, and tripod base; used to support book. May have candle-holders attached. Dates from *c*1750.

rebus button. French late 18th century button engraved or painted with coded motto or picture. Mottos mostly amatory.

récamier. Backless French day bed with ends of equal height, scrolling outwards at top. Associated with Mme Récamier (J-L. David's portrait shows her seated on one of these). Dates from Directoire period.

recessed carving. *See* sunk carving.

recoil or **anchor** escapement. *See* escapement.

recorder or **flûte à bec** (French, 'beaked flute'). End-blown *flute, usually of wood (particularly boxwood), or ivory; bore hole mainly conical, sometimes beaked mouthpiece inserted in block or plug. Used from antiquity; known as recorder in England from late 14th century. Until late 15th century, had six fingerholes and rear thumbhole; later another hole added, and sometimes duplicated, to facilitate playing with either hand (unused hole being stopped up with wax). Extremely popular in 16th and 17th centuries. By early 17th century, made in various sizes (*c*8in. to 6ft4in. long); sets would include treble, alto, bass, soprano, etc. forms. Remodelled in mid 17th century France, with three separate joints (previously in one piece). Unfashionable by mid 18th century; recently revived in popularity.

red anchor period. *See* Chelsea.

red dragon. German ceramic decoration. Kakiemon pattern of birds in circular arrangement at centre of plate, with two dragons on border, painted in red and gold on white ground; copied by J. G. *Herold at Meissen factory on dinner service ordered in 1734 for Saxon court. Many replacements and additions made during following ten years. Marked with crossed swords in underglaze blue enamel, also frequently with K.H.C. or K.H.C.W., royal marks.

red monochrome or **Eisenrotmalerei.** Painting in red enamel on faience and porcelain in 18th century Germany. Popular with *Hausmaler* including F. F. *Mayer, F. J. *Ferner. Notable porcelain examples from Meissen (*c*1720–25), Vienna (*c*1730), and Fürstenberg (*c*1765). *See* purple monochrome.

red 'porcelain' or **china.** In 17th and 18th centuries, unglazed *red stoneware body of Yi-hsing teapots exported after mid 17th century from China with tea. Copied in red earthenware at Delft (*c*1672–*c*1731). J. *Dwight patent refers to red 'porcelain' (i.e. red stoneware).

red stoneware. Unglazed red stoneware body of Yi-hsing teapots (originally wine-pots). Efforts to reproduce secret process of manufacture began with hard red earthenware (*red 'porcelain') made at Delft from *c*1672. In England, J. *Dwight accused other potters (1693–94) of infringing his stoneware patent by manufacturing red teapots. Among potters accused were J. P. and D. *Elers. Later made by most Staffordshire potters, notably J. *Wedgwood. In Germany, very hard red stoneware (*Böttgersteinzeug*) produced at Meissen by J. F. *Böttger in 1708 during search for hard-paste porcelain with E. W. *von Tschirnhaus; considered as semi-precious stone; could be polished and cut into facets, or engraved on lapidary wheel. Teapots shaped after *Yi-hsing ware; other designs inspired by contemporary fashions in silver. Colour ranged from bright red to dark brown and grey-black, according to firing heat; sometimes marbled effect resulted from clay composition. Painted decoration of thick, dry enamels and silver or gilt applied either to red body after firing or over black glaze. Occasionally mounted in gold or silver, or with e.g. garnets applied. Rare figures include copies of Chinese porcelain originals, German Renaissance ivory carvings, or religious sculptures; some *commedia dell'arte* figures coloured in enamel (*c*1715). Marks (1710–20): occasionally shield enclosing double or quadruple crucifix impressed, or B incised. *See* Brandenburg porcelain. *Illustration at* J. P. and D. Elers.

reducing atmosphere. Shortage of oxygen in kiln with smoky conditions. Any oxygen present in pottery combines with free carbon in atmosphere; colouring oxides reduced to metal (*cf* oxidizing atmosphere). Atmosphere in which firing takes place can affect colour: copper oxide is blue-green, whereas copper is red; iron produces orange-reds and browns in oxidizing atmosphere, blacks and greys in conditions with little or no oxygen; manganese oxidized gives blue, black, or purple, and black only, reduced; blue cobalt oxide becomes black when reduced. In firing where atmosphere alternates, underglaze colour can be fired in reducing atmosphere just before fusion point of glaze, which, in melting, seals over reduced metal allowing firing to be completed in oxidizing atmosphere.

reducing machine. Mechanical device invented by Achille Colas in 1839; used in production of small, inexpensive, but accurate bronze replicas of sculptures. Exploited in partnership with F. *Barbedienne.

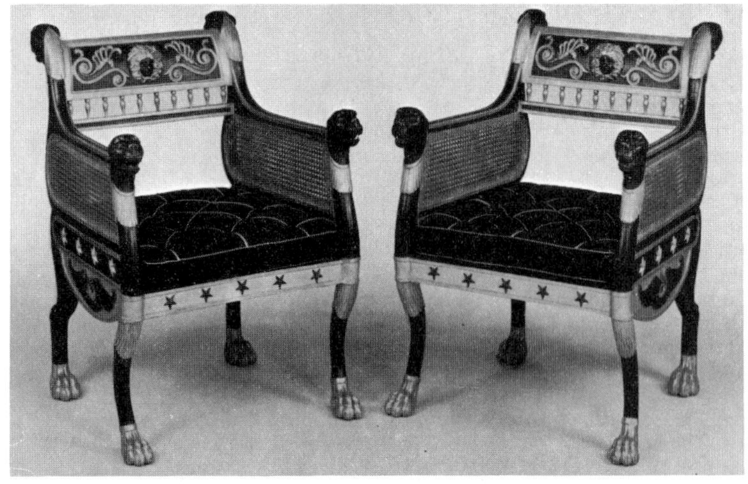

*Regency style. Armchairs, designed by G. *Smith. Ebonized and gilded wood, with cane-work sides; lion mask terminals to arms and backs; lion's paw feet.*
Regency style. Revolving bookcase. Mahogany. Cupboard in base; four tiers of shelves surrounded by metal grilles. Maximum height 5ft5in.

Top:
Redware. Early 19th century American earthenware. Oval dish with marbled glaze, length 14½in. Water-carrier, height 8½in.
*Reed-and-tie moulding. On two pairs of spoons and forks made by *Boulton & Fothergill in 1774. Length of spoon 8½in.*
Regency Music stand. c1810. Telescopic brass stand; pair of brass candle sconces; painting of laurel leaves and lyre on paper laid on wood.

redware. Red earthenware made in American colonies from late 17th century, for domestic use; manufacture continued well into 19th century. Lead-glazed and decorated with slip. *Pennsylvania-Dutch potters produced *sgraffiato* designs, sometimes with added colour.

reed-and-tie moulding (in silver). Border ornament of reeds bound with ribbon. Much used on neo-classical silver.

reeding. Series of thin, parallel convex ribs or reeds used to decorate stems, borders, furniture legs, etc., in late 18th century. Derived from classical column. Used also round rim of English and European pewter plates, *c*1675 to late 18th century; multiple or triple reeding used on broad and narrow-rimmed plates *c*1675–90; single-reeded design from *c*1690 to second half of 18th century.

refectory table. Generally, long table, usually oak, on trestle or frame base; originally used for communal dining, as in monastery refectory or great hall. Dates from Middle Ages.

regard ring or brooch. Ring or brooch set with row of small stones of different kinds initial letters of which spell word, e.g. 'regard' (stones could be ruby, emerald, garnet, amethyst, ruby, diamond). Popular from mid 18th century in Britain. *Illustration at* amatory jewellery.

Régence style. French transitional furniture style, *c*1700–20, combining baroque and rococo elements (Regency for Louis XV lasted only 1715–23). Classical motifs common in Louis XIV style used, e.g. shells, flowers, acanthus leaves, C and S scrolls, but given lighter, more elegant treatment. Romantic subjects from mythology began to replace earlier heroic ones, and oriental and *commedia dell'arte* figures appeared in decoration. Veneer and marquetry became more common, as did carving and gilding. *Illustration at* candlestand, pier table, x-frame stool.

Regency style. General term for several furniture styles found in Britain *c*1795–1820 (George IV's Regency lasted 1810–20); in America *c*1800–30. Styles include Directoire-influenced neo-classical and Egyptian styles, severe neo-classicism based on Empire style, and popular revival of Gothic and *chinoiserie* designs and motifs.

Mahogany, rosewood, and satinwood common woods, often decorated with banding, stringing, and brass mounts. Bamboo-turning used on *chinoiserie* pieces; monopodium base common neo-classical feature. Characteristic furniture includes boat bed, lismos, fancy chair, convex mirror, flower stand, pedestal furniture, sideboard tables, sofa tables, bureau book cases, and whatnots. Influential designers and cabinet makers: H. *Holland, T. *Sheraton, G. *Smith. *See* Abbotsford style. *Illustrations also at* Carlton House desk, chaise longue, roll-top desk, cheval glass, rolled paper work, sofa table, window seat.

Régnard, Pierre-Louis (d 1771). French silversmith working in Paris; master in 1759. Made range of domestic silver in rococo style. Some commissions for F-T. *Germain; after latter bankrupted, completed outstanding commissions. 1767–71, both marks found on pieces. Mark: fleur-de-lis crowned, two pellets, PLR, and fox.

régulateur or **horloge de parquet.** French long-case clock, introduced after *c*1700. First forms derived from *pedestal clock, with tapering sides, and bulge in case to allow for movement of pendulum. Case design follows period styles: highly curved during Louis XV era, then symmetrical, with straight sides. Example by F. *Berthoud.

régulateur de cheminée. *See pendule cage.*

regulator. *See* precision clocks.

Rehn Pattern. Ceramic decoration; central pattern of fruiting and flowering plant, on *bianco sopra bianco* ground with border of lines and leaf scrolls echoing wavy edge of plate; painted in blue or manganese on faience at Rörstrand in mid 18th century. Designed by Swedish artist and industrial designer Jean Erik or Eric Rehn who provided Rörstrand with examples of French faience for copying on return from business trips to France.

Reichard, Ernst Heinrich (d 1764). German porcelain *Modellmeister* and arcanist at *Wegely's factory, Berlin (1752–57). Arcanist also at Berlin (1761), and art director of porcelain factory until 1764.

Reichsadlerhumpen (German, 'Imperial eagle glass'). 16th and 17th century *Humpen* with enamelled decoration portraying double-headed eagle of Holy Roman Empire (with crucifix or Imperial orb on breast), with outstretched wings consisting of shields bearing coats of arms of Electors. Precise form and treatment of symbolic eagle varies.

Reid, William (fl mid 18th century). Liverpool porcelain maker. Established Reid & Co China Manufactory at Brownlow Hill by 1756. Sold blue-and-white bone china at Liverpool warehouse. Firm bankrupt *c*1759. *Illustration at* Liverpool porcelain.

reign mark. *See* nien hao.

Reims tapestry. 17th century tapestry-weaving centre. Chief workshop owned by D. *Pepersack.

Reichsadlerhumpen. *German, dated 1650, enamelled with arms of Electors.*

Reinicke, Peter (d 1768). German porcelain modeller; worked at Meissen 1743–68. Modelled in lighter style than J. J. *Kändler during 1740s. Figures usually (until *c*1750) stand on mound with applied flowers and leaves. Created figures from *commedia dell'arte* for Duke of Weissenfels (1744), series of *chinoiserie* groups and figures (1745–50), and *Cris de Paris* (1752). Helped Kändler model a series of Popes for Vatican (*c*1745), and the **Affenkapelle* group (*c*1750).

Reinmann, Paul (d 1609). Maker of *sundials in Nuremberg, Germany. Produced many folding diptych dials of metal and ivory.

relief. Moulded, carved, or stamped figures, etc., projecting to various degrees from plane or curved surface: high relief or low relief (bas-relief). In silver, relief ornament achieved by *casting, **repoussé* work, *embossing.

Reliefmosaïk. Design or scene carved in various precious and semi-precious stones cemented to hardstone boxes, etc. Technique employed by *Berlin school in mid 18th century.

religieuse clock. *See pendule religieuse.*

*Reliquary cross. Russian, 17th century. Gold and silver. Gold relief figure of Christ; reverse side of cross (right) engraved in *niello with portraits of saints whose relics it contains.*

reliquary. Elaborately-ornamented container for relics of martyr or saint; made in various materials (e.g. silver, silver-gilt, gilt-copper, enamel) and shapes (e.g. casket, statuette, architectural). Most unusual were those shaped like part of body of saint or martyr, containing e.g. heart, hand, head, shoulder blade, foot. Relic might be enclosed in glass or crystal inside reliquary.

Rembrandt flagon or **tankard.** Baluster-shaped pewter flagon or tankard, such as appear in several pictures by Rembrandt (1606–69).

Remmey, John (fl 1735–1820). German-born potter working in America; brother-in-law of W. *Crolius. In New York from 1735; established pottery, producing stoneware decorated e.g. with patriotic symbols, incised or stamped and coloured with blue slip. Examples have stamped mark J.REMMEY/MANHATTAN WELLS/ NEW-YORK.

remontoire. Device to supply constant force to escapement of clock or watch movement, regardless of variations in main power source. Rare. Used by J. *Harrison and other makers in 18th and 19th centuries in form of intermediary spring wound at frequent intervals by mainspring. Small weight also used, e.g. by J. *Burgi. Gravity escapement devised originally for Westminster clock constitutes form of remontoire: pendulum receives impulse from pair of weighted levers dropping through constant distance, thus is freed from influence of wind or snow on hands.

Renaissance. Revival of classical ideals in European art and literature, which grew in Italy from late 14th century, culminating in 16th century with period known as High Renaissance, when influence widely felt throughout Europe. Gothic style gradually ousted; classical proportions, shapes and ornament increasingly used. Renaissance style epitomized by symmetry of form, emphasis on horizontal, and use of classical draped figures, also medallions, grotesques, etc. Characteristically grandiose and luxurious; rich fabrics (velvet, brocade, damask, silk), oriental carpets, marble, bronzes, silver, gold and gold leaf, brilliant colours, and bold patterns. Furniture sparse and simply constructed, becoming more ornate (*cassoni*, beds, etc.), with painted and gilt gesso and intarsia panels. In 16th century, heavy and elaborate carved wooden (particularly walnut) *cassoni* fashionable; rich decoration also on some tables and chairs, cabinets, and frames of pictures and mirrors. Plainer pieces typically covered with rich cloths; beds had ornate hangings, carved posts, and head and foot boards.

Outside Italy, style first influential in France (from *c*1495): Renaissance features first applied to Gothic structures; Italian craftsmen working in France helped to establish Renaissance style and spread it throughout Europe. In late 16th century, reaction in Italy against classical standards resulted in *mannerist style.

Rendsburg (Holstein). Small German faience factory founded 1764 or 1765. Early work frequently painted in blue or manganese, e.g. tureens, cane-handles, snuff-boxes. After 1772, only cream-coloured earthenware produced. Mark: CR (Clar-Rendsburg, or Clar: joint founder, C. F. Clar).

rent table. Type of *library table, with polygonal or circular top (often revolving), on pedestal base. Drawers around frieze marked with letters of alphabet, days of week, etc., to form filing system; sometimes also has drawers in pedestal. Used for efficient filing of legal and business documents, or for collection of rents (when drawers marked with days of week). Made *c*1750–1800.

repairer. Workman who moulded and assembled parts of figure or vessel made in pottery or porcelain, usually from block made by another modeller. Marks of repairers often incised or impressed on porcelain.

repeating clock or **watch.** Timekeeper with mechanism to strike at will the hour, often the quarter, rarely the five or single minute most recently past; set off by pulling cord, moving lever, etc. Found in clocks and watch until *c*1825, then chiefly in watches.

repoussé. Type of *embossing in metal-work with design finished by surface *chasing to sharpen detail. Much used on late 16th and 17th century silver. Revival in 19th century in Britain and Europe led by A. *Vechte and L. *Morel-Ladeuil. *Illustration at* German gold and silver.

reredos. *See* fireback.

reserve. Ceramic decoration; panel left free of e.g. ground colour, diaper pattern. Usually defined by cartouche or border and enclosing painting. Characteristic element of much decoration at Sèvres.

resist lustre. *Lustre decoration fashionable in England, 1810–*c*1840; patterns of silver lustre stencilled on surface of glazed pearlware. J. *Davenport patented technique of waxing over stencils of design, removing stencil, and brushing over design with lustre; wax resist removed before firing. Later, design painted on glaze in resist material, e.g. honey, glycerine, or varnish; ware dipped or brushed to cover with metallic solution; resist then washed off or burned off in kiln.

Restoration style. Style in furniture in Britain and American colonies during latter half of 17th century, roughly from Restoration of Charles II (1660) to abdication of James II (1688). Less severe than Commonwealth style, partly as reaction against Puritan austerity, partly from influence of Dutch and French designs, brought to England by royalists returning from exile or by Dutch workmen who settled in England after 1660. Common Restoration pieces are heavily-draped beds; numerous cabinets, including glass-doored china cabinet; Dutch-style armchair, with caned rectangular or oval back, caned seat, scrolled and spiral-turned supports and perhaps a symbolic crown (representing Restoration) on yoke-rail; wing chair; chest of drawers; court, press, and hall and parlour cupboard; desk box and writing desk; chair-back and upholstered settees; oak refectory table; gate-leg table, draw-table, side table, and gaming table; joined stool, and stools matching chairs.

Walnut replaced oak as most common wood; severe rectangularity of Commonwealth furniture softened by introduction of C and S scroll supports, turned supports, and ball, bun, and scroll feet. Cane used on backs and seats of chairs, settees, and day-beds; geometrically-carved panelling decorated façades; marquetry and veneering became commoner. *Oyster marquetry characteristic of period. Gilt gesso furniture introduced. Iron replaced by brass for fittings; characteristic handles in drop shapes attached to square or round eyes. Dutch influence popularized lacquered pieces (particularly cabinets). Upholstered furniture became more common; popular coverings included leather, needlework fabrics (including crewel), velvet, brocade, and turkey work, finished with fringe.

Restoration furniture. Chair, Charles II period. Oak with drawer under seat for pipes and tobacco.

Paul Revere the Elder. Tankard, made in Boston, Massachusetts, 1730–50. Grotesque head terminal to end of handle. Mark PR within shield can be seen to right of top of handle. Height $8\frac{1}{4}$in.

reticello glass. *See vetro a reticelli.*

reticulated ware. *See Böttgerporzellan.*

Revere, Paul the Elder (fl early 18th century). American silversmith. Huguenot emigrant from Guernsey; name Americanized from Apollon de Revoire. Apprenticed to J. *Coney. Worked in Boston, Massachusetts, making domestic silver in Huguenot style.

Revere, Paul the Younger (1735–1818). American silversmith working in Boston; also accomplished copperplate engraver and maker of copper and brassware; trained by father. Made range of domestic silver in English styles. In 1765, estate attached for £10 debt, so turned to engraving prints. Much involved in politics of colony; made silver punch-bowl for Sons of Liberty (92 members of Massachusetts General Court who refused to pay new taxes imposed by England). After Declaration of Independence, returned to silversmithing and established workshop; also imported Sheffield plate from England. Much silver of period probably designed and made by his staff. Mark: REVERE in a rectangle.

Révérend, Claude and François (fl late 17th century). French faience makers, brothers. In 1664, granted patent for manufacture of faience. Recorded as employers of workmen from Rotterdam at Saint-Cloud in 1667. Products not positively identified; believed to have resembled blue-and-white Dutch Delft.

revived rococo. Version of rococo style used in

Paul Revere the Younger. Pair of sauce-boats made in Boston, c1785; oval shape with bombé sides, each on three scroll and shell feet with larger applied shell above; beaded rims and curved lips; rising double scroll handles capped by leaf.

*Rhinoceros vase. First version, made at *Rockingham works, 1826; Height 3ft9in.*

decoration of English porcelain from 1820s until *c*1850; possibly inspired by work in silver, e.g. by *Rundell, Bridge & Rundell. Wide, curving shapes decorated with asymmetrical motifs and relief moulding, particularly of flowers, stems, and leaves; gilding often lavish. Relief decoration more suitable than painting for quantity production to high standard. Style established by 1830, e.g. at *Rockingham, Derby and, notably, Coalport. In central Europe, rococo style of mid 19th century especially noticeable in modelling of figures, either from 18th century models, or with figures in contemporary dress, set on moulded scrollwork bases. Examples of ornamental ware from Russian *Imperial Porcelain Factory include vases with scrolled cartouches and encrustation of small flowers, dating from *c*1850.

Rewend, Christian F. (fl mid 18th century). German potter; founded faience factory *c*1739 at Potsdam, near Berlin. Produced red-bodied wares with decoration similar to Berlin and Delft. Sons, Friedrich and Johann, inherited factory; directors until 1775. Pear-shaped, reeded vases, waisted above spreading foot, have been identified. Mark: P over R; or P.Dam sometimes used.

Reydams, Henri (fl mid 17th to early 18th centuries). Prolific Flemish tapestry master-weaver. Much work in association with other weavers, especially U. *Leyniers.

Reymond, Pierre (d *c*1584). French enamel artist working with family at Limoges; work mainly *en grisaille* enamelling. *Illustration at* Limoges.

Rhineland or **Rhenish stoneware.** German ceramics: *stoneware with salt-glaze produced notably 1520–1600, sometimes inaccurately termed *grès de Flandres*. Jugs, bottles, tankards, usually have brown glaze, sometimes grey, grey-white, or grey-blue, usually with orange peel texture. Some shapes derived from leather bottles. Production grew to industrial scale *c*1525–50. Simple ornament incised and applied in Gothic tradition gradually gave way to more rounded, baroque designs through Italian influence. Three centres of production expanded concurrently: *Cologne, *Siegburg, and *Raeren. By late 16th century many of best potters had moved to *Westerwald; imitations of Rhineland stoneware made in France, Flanders, and later England. Jugs and tankards often reproduced with serial number on base. *See* tigerware jug. *Illustration at* bellarmine, Cologne, Siegburg.

Rhinoceros Vase. Porcelain perfume jar made at Rockingham works in 1826. 3ft9in. high, painted by J. W. *Brameld with scenes from *Don Quixote*. Stands on three lion's legs, resting on trefoil-shaped base. Neck, perforated with hexagonal openings, has three moulded bees. Moulded and gilded oak leaves surround three enamelled panels, separated by three knotted oak handles picked out in gold. Cover surmounted by gilded rhinoceros. In Clifton Park Museum, Rotherham, Yorkshire. Second, later, Rhinoceros vase (in Victoria & Albert Museum, London) has panels enamelled with flowers and grapes.

Rhodes, David (d 1777). English pottery painter. From 1760, in partnership with J. *Robinson at Leeds, enamelled creamware made at Leeds Pottery, notably in black and red; also decorated wares made in Derbyshire, Liverpool, and by J. *Wedgwood. In 1763, became sole proprietor of firm, employing Robinson. Left Leeds in 1768 to work in London decorating workshop; by 1770, head of Wedgwood enamelling workshop in Chelsea. Work on stoneware and cream-coloured earthenware includes figures, landscapes, flowers, and designs incorporating stripes or chevrons. Later introduced small, neat border patterns. *Illustration at* Leeds Pottery.

Rhodes carpets. *See* Megri carpets.

Rhodian ware. *See* Isnik.

ribband or **ribbon motif** (on furniture). Wooden ornament imitating decoratively-arranged silk ribbon. Late 18th century; used on French and German pieces and on English chairs. T. *Chippendale published designs for ribband-back chairs (in Director).

rice grain decoration. *See* Gombroon ware.

Richardson, Joseph (1711–85). American silversmith working in Philadelphia, Penn-

Joseph and Nathaniel Richardson. Sugar bowl and cover of inverted pear form; gadrooned borders, domed cover has wrythen finial. Made in Philadelphia c1772.

*William Ridgway. Earthenware jug, *smear glazed, c1848. Moulded decoration of scene from Tam o'Shanter.*

sylvania. Many surviving pieces include coffee and tea pots, salvers, jugs, salt-cellars, etc. Mark: IR in an oval. Sons, Joseph Jr and Nathaniel, continued in trade.

Richter, Christian (1678–1732). Stockholm-born miniaturist and oil painter; in England from 1702. Made miniature copies of paintings e.g. by Sir Godfrey Kneller and Sir Peter Lely.

Ridgway, Job (1759–1813). Staffordshire potter. Worked in Leeds as journeyman potter; Wesleyan preacher. Partner with brother at Bell Works, Shelton, from 1792, trading as Ridgway, Smith & Ridgway (1793–99) and Job and George Ridgway (1799–1802); then at Cauldon Place, Shelton. Produced earthenware, transfer-printed in blue; also stone china, notably dinner services. Made porcelain from 1808.

Ridgway, John (1785–1860) and William (1788-1864). Staffordshire potters. Took over Bell Works, Shelton, in 1802, when father, Job *Ridgway, broke partnership with his brother, George; continued manufacture of earthenware and stone china. Marks include J & W RIDGWAY, J & WR, or J.W.R. From 1830, John worked at Cauldon Place; made stone china and porcelain tableware; also large articles, e.g. fountains. Marks include J.R. in ribbon below royal arms.

Riedel, Gottlieb Friedrich (1724–84). German porcelain painter and designer. Painter at Meissen 1743–56. Designer at Höchst, *c*1756; possibly made models for unidentified groups, e.g. Minuet Dancers. Director of painting at Frankenthal (1757–59); director of painting and designer at Ludwigsburg (1759–79), thus confusing identification of figures from last three factories. Subsequently *Hausmaler* at Augsburg.

Riedel, Joseph (fl first half of 19th century). Bohemian glass manufacturer and wholesaler; developed two fluorescent yellow-green colours, *Annagrün* and *Annagelb* (named after wife, Anna).

Joseph Riedel. Annagelb *cup and saucer, c1835, with cut, enamelled, and gilded decoration.*

Riesener, Jean-Henri (1734–1806). German-born *ébéniste,* working in France; exponent of neo-classicism. Joined J-F. *Oeben's workshop *c*1754 and took over business on latter's death (1763). In 1768, married Mme Oeben and became *maître-ébéniste.* Succeeded G. *Joubert as *ébéniste ordinaire* to Louis XVI in 1774. After 1884, royal budget reduced; Riesener received fewer commissions, as prices too high. Style more classical than Oeben's. Used Oeben's stamp, J. F. OEBEN while working for Mme Oeben; then J.H. RIESENER.

Riesenpokal (German, 'giant cup'). Large 16th century silver standing cup with cover; some examples 3ft4in. high; meant for display rather than use.

Francesco Righetti. Pair of bronze figures, Actaeon (left) and Bacchus. Italian, 18th century.

ring. *See* episcopal ring, mourning jewellery, posy ring, regard ring.

ring-handled vase. Chinese ceramic form imitating bronze ware; originated in Han and T'ang periods. Often with moulded relief or carving of monster or animal head.

Ringler, Joseph Jakob (1730–1804). German porcelain arcanist. In Vienna (*c*1744) learned secrets, especially of kiln construction, with help of director's daughter. Took knowledge to Künersberg (1747–48), Höchst (1750–51), Strasbourg (*c*1751), Nymphenburg (1753–57), Schrezheim (1757), Ellwangen (1758–59), and Ludwigsburg (1759–1802). Associated indirectly with other factories through contact with arcanists J. *Benckgraff and C. D. *Busch.

ring watch. Miniature form made from *c*1725; rare. Revived late 19th century.

Ripp, Johann Caspar or Kaspar (1681-1726). A leading German faience painter and arcanist, apprenticed at Delft. Worked at Frankfurt (1702–08), painting only *chinoiseries,* at Hanau (1708–10), and Ansbach (1710–12). Started faience factories at Nuremberg (1712–13), and Bayreuth (1714). Also worked at Brunswick, Zerbst (1720), and Fulda (1724). Sometimes signed work KR.

riven wood. Wood cut into planks by splitting tree-trunk in quarters, radially, then cutting resulting wedges into smaller wedges, and trimming them into planks. Finely marked wood best shown by this method, but extremely wasteful. Used for early furniture, especially chests.

roasting-jack. *See* bottle-jack.

Roberts, Samuel the Younger (1763–1848). English inventor, designer, and manufacturer of

Sheffield plate working in Sheffield. Started in business in 1784 (with George Cadman) by father, Samuel the Elder, who had been involved with several firms manufacturing Sheffield plate. From 1785–1810, design and quality of works influenced other makers; took out many patents for improvements. Introduced silver edges, stamped silver-filled feet, handles, and mounts; used bright-cut engraving for border ornament; and perfected process of 'rubbing in' silver shields on Sheffield plate, also various folding and telescopic items. Last patent related to plating on nickel. Cadman died in 1823; in 1826 Roberts took nephew, Evan Smith, as partner and firm became Roberts, Smith & Co. Samuel retired in 1834 and son, Samuel III, took over interest in business with existing partners, Sidney Roberts and William Sissons. On death of father (1848), Samuel III left business which became Smith, Sissons & Co; firm's mark remained a bell, which also appears on electro-plated wares.

Roberts, Thomas (fl *c*1685–1714). English cabinet maker; supplied William and Mary and Queen Anne with beds, firescreens, and seats. Pieces decorated with carving and gilding.

Robertson, Andrew (1777–1845). Scottish miniaturist. Painted many miniatures before moving to London (1801) to study at Royal Academy. Miniatures frequently rectangular; features sketched in brown monochrome. Pupils included W. C. *Ross.

Robertson, Charles (1760–1820) and Walter (1750–1802). Irish miniaturists, sons of Dublin jeweller, who also produced pictures in hair; both worked first in this medium. Charles exhibited at Royal Academy 1790–1810; produced delicately-painted miniatures, often with facial shading in grey or blue; also small watercolour portraits and flower paintings. Walter went to United States in 1793; work includes miniatures from life of George Washington; backgrounds finely cross-hatched; facial modelling with long, fine brush strokes and blue shading, particularly around eyes.

Robertson, George (d 1835). English porcelain decorator; painted shipping scenes on porcelain made at Derby, *c*1796–*c*1820.

Robins, Richard (fl early 19th century). English porcelain painter. Worked at Pinxton, *c*1800. Independent decorator at Spa Fields, London with T. M. *Randall.

Robinson, Jasper (fl mid 18th century). English enameller of cream-coloured earthenware and salt-glazed stoneware at Leeds. Partner (1760–63), then employee, of D. *Rhodes.

rocaille (French, 'rockwork'). Ornament derived from rockwork; characteristic of rococo style.

Rochat, Frères. Swiss firm which manufactured automata in Geneva from 1810–25, e.g. 'singing-bird' box. Also placed singing birds in model cages, parasol handles, and in barrels of gold and enamel pistols (only three made). Movements signed FR.

rock-crystal. Colourless variety of quartz, crystalline silica. Popular, particularly in

Rocking chair. 18th century English Windsor type in yew wood.

Renaissance Europe, for drinking vessels, salts, caskets, jewellery etc., with gold, silver, or silver-gilt mounts. *See* poison tankard.

rock-crystal watch. Rock-crystal popular material for watch cases throughout Europe *c*1600–*c*1675; smoky variety rarer than clear. Case usually formed from two blocks, one hollowed to take movement, with metal frames to carry hinge and catch and riveted *pendant; crystal cut in facets or lobes, sometimes patterned with shallow cuts, very rarely left smooth. Watches sometimes striking, with bell below pierced edging, and movement attached to plate underneath.

rocking chair. Side chair or armchair with front legs joined to respective back legs by *bends, allowing gentle rocking motion. Introduced mid 18th century (although cradle on bends dates from Middle Ages). Early styles usually based on straight-backed stick chairs, often with cane seats; designs of *Boston and *Salem rockers gave user greater comfort. Bentwood or metal models appeared *c*1850; design based on raked S-shape, with bends incorporated in frame design. Well-known example of this style by M. *Thonet. Platform rocker (or swing rocking chair), dating from latter half of 19th century, has bends resting on solid base. *Illustration also at* bentwood furniture.

Rockingham glaze. English ceramic glaze stained brown with manganese oxide; developed *c*1806 at *Rockingham Works from brown glaze in use by 1785. Chocolate-brown, sometimes with purplish bloom, used to cover earthenware, e.g. *Cadogan teapots and moulded jugs. Glazed earthenware known from 1826 as Rockingham ware; also made at other factories until present day.

Rockingham or **brown ware.** English earthenware covered with brown *Rockingham glaze. In America, Rockingham ware has yellow earthenware body covered with mottled brown glaze; used for household wares, from *c*1840, e.g. at *Bennington.

Rockingham Works. Pottery established *c*1745 on estate of Marquis of Rockingham at Swinton, Yorkshire. Trading as The Swinton Pottery, produced earthenware and, later, high quality creamware. In 1785, *Leeds Pottery took controlling interest; creamware and earthenware with transfer-printing or coloured glazes closely resemble those made at Leeds. *Rockingham glaze developed from inferior brown glazes in general use. J. *Brameld regained control in 1806; family ran factory until closure (1842). From 1826, traded as Rockingham Works. Brown-glazed earthenware includes *Cadogan teapot and other tea ware, rarely marked. Transfer-printed creamware decorated, e.g. with pastoral scenes, landscapes, or *willow pattern; sometimes also enamelled or gilded; output small after *c*1826. Also produced creamware enamelled with labelled *botanical flowers, or moulded e.g. in pattern of cabbage leaves and covered with green glaze. Caneware jugs and mugs have applied relief decoration, usually in white or blue, occasionally green or brown. Soft-paste porcelain introduced *c*1826, using bone ash and Cornish stone and clay, has hard, translucent body, decorated in *revived rococo style; products include table services, baskets, figures, cottages, and vases, notably *Rhinoceros vase. Marks on earthenware include BRAMELD followed by cross and number or symbol, CADOGAN, ROCKINGHAM, or ROCKINGHAM BRAMELD, all impressed. Caneware marked BRAMELD within garland, embossed in colour of relief decoration. Porcelain marks include Rockingham Works Brameld, or Royal Rockingham Brameld in script with griffin from Rockingham arms, printed. *Illustration at* Rhinoceros Vase.

rococo style. Decorative, curvilinear style characterized by light, delicate, asymmetrical motifs based mainly on rock, shell, floral, and leaf

Rococo. Ormolu fire-dog. Louis XV period. Finish matt and burnished. Height $13\frac{1}{2}$*in.*

shapes. Name derived from synthesis of words *rocaille and *coquillage. Style evolved in France in early 18th century and rapidly spread throughout Europe, then to England where it reached its peak c1750–70, and America c1760–80. Style revived in England and America in early 19th century. (*See* J. Cobb, H. Copland, M. Lock, W. Vile, J. Belter, T. Chippendale, Louis XV style.)

Rococo porcelain made at many European factories c1745–75, notably at Nymphenburg; also at Chantilly, Chelsea, and Venice. Rococo faience e.g. from Rouen, Niderviller, Strasbourg, Alcora, and Höchst. In France, characterized by *chinoiserie* designs developed by F. *Boucher and J. *Pillement. Rococo style in ceramics continued longest in Germany and Scandinavia, with taste for toys (**Galanterien*), fanciful figures, and tableware in form of birds, fish, or vegetables. *Revived rococo ceramics made from 1820s.

rod-back Windsor. Windsor chair popular in America c1800–30. Neither bow nor arms continuous. Back rectangular with arms attached to terminal back spindles (may slant backwards). Ogee-shaped arms curved downwards at ends. Box stretcher. Side chairs also made.

Rodney decanter. *See* ship's decanter.

Rodney jug. *See* Derby. Also made by T. *Whieldon and at Leeds Pottery.

roe or **roey.** Variegated spots or flakes, reminiscent of fish roe, on East Indian satinwood, mahogany, and other hardwoods.

Roentgen, David (1743–1807). German-born *ébéniste*; took over family business at Neuwied in 1772. Began own business making clocks, mechanical toys, and musical boxes, and eventually furniture with secret drawers and elaborate locks. Became *ébéniste-méchanicien* to Louis XVI and Marie Antoinette in 1779, *maître-ébéniste* in 1780, court furnisher to Friedrich Wilhelm II in 1781. Work seized during French Revolution. Marquetry characterized by shading with individual small pieces of wood, rather than by burning; motifs influenced by J. J. R. *Zick's paintings. Stamp: DAVID, but seldom used.

David Roentgen. Detail of his marquetry from Louis XVI secrétaire.

Roettiers, Jacques (1707–84). French silversmith, medallist, and coin engraver; master in 1733 and royal goldsmith to Louis XV. In c1734, took over management of silver workshop of father-in-law, N. *Besnier. From 1735–38, executed *Berkeley Castle Service. In 1750s began to abandon rococo style for Greek architectural motifs, probably designed by son, J-N. *Roettiers, who succeeded him on retirement (1772). Mark: fleur-de-lis crowned, two pellets, IR or JR, and wheat-sheaf.

Roettiers, Jacques-Nicolas (1736–after 1784). French silversmith working in Paris; master in 1765; assisted father on royal commissions. Made royal goldsmith in 1772; retired 1777. Made various liturgical vessels (1769–70) for Dauphin's Chapel (now in Troyes Cathedral). All works for French crown destroyed. Most important surviving work, *Orloff Service. Mark: fleur-de-lis, two pellets, JNR, and a wheat-sheaf.

Rogers, John (1760–1816) and George (1763–1815). Staffordshire potters, brothers. Established pottery at Dale Hall, Longport, in 1780. Made good quality cream-coloured earthenware transfer-printed in blue. Patterns include zebras and elephants in oriental settings, classical views, and scenes from plays and operas. Much exported to America. From 1815, traded as J. Rogers & Son; pottery closed in 1836. Mark: ROGERS, impressed.

rolled paper work (in furniture). Decorative device applied to furniture. Shallow frame placed round area to be decorated, then filled with design composed of pieces of rolled card. Popular in 19th century England.

Rolled paper work decorating Regency tea-caddy.

*Rolltop-desk. English, Regency, mahogany. Design by *T. *Sheraton, illustrated in Cabinet Dictionary of 1803.*

rolling ball clock. *See* ball clock.

rolling clock. *See* inclined-plane clock.

rolling pin (in glass). Early examples taper slightly towards knopped ends. From early 19th century, made in coloured *Nailsea glass, particularly purple, blue, amber, green, and opaque-white, also mottled and striped. Popular as gift or love token. Often gilded, painted, or enamelled, and inscribed with initials, dates, verses, biblical quotations, and mottos, e.g. May the Eye of the Lord Watch over You, or, Be True to Me. Sea subjects, sporting and country scenes also popular.

Rollos, Philip the Younger (fl early 18th century). Huguenot silversmith working in London; served part of apprenticeship with father, who obtained freedom of Goldsmiths' Company in 1697. Granted freedom 1705. Made domestic plate for aristocracy, including huge wine coolers for 1st Duke of Kingston and Marquess of Exeter. Marks: RO with anchor between initials; or PR (1720).

roll-top or **cylinder-top desk,** or **bureau à cylindre.** Desk with writing area and upper storage space concealed, when not in use, by horizontally-slatted *tambour or solid cylindrical section, which slides back into body of desk when open. Dates from second half of 18th century. Style popularized by J-F. *Oeben and J-H. *Riesener's *Bureau du Roi* for Louis XV.

Romano, Giulio (1492–1546). Giulio Pippi, Italian architect and artist, pupil of *Raphaël. Numerous designs and sketches made for cartoons for 16th century Flemish tapestries. In 17th century, his designs among most popular Gobelins subjects, include The Subjects, History of Scipio, Fruits of War, Grotesque Months, and *Putti at Play.*

Romayne work. Profiles set within lozenges on front panel of 16th century English chest.

Rörstrand faience. Tray, mid 18th century, set into contemporary oak table frame.

Römer. Pale green tinted glass, cup-shaped bowl, hollow stem, with four rows of applied raspberry *prunts. 17th century. Height 11½in.

Roman spindle-back. *Windsor chair with back of five beaded, turned spindles.

Roman striking. *See* striking systems.

Romayne work. Italian Renaissance motif; carved profile head contained in medallion. Introduced to England in early 16th century and found on church panelling, furniture, etc.

Rombrich, Johann Christoph (d 1794). German porcelain modeller at Fürstenberg (1758–94). Used simple, rustic, style for peasant groups or Chinese figures; also attributed with dishes and boxes shaped like animals, fruit, etc., cane handles, and copies of **Affenkapelle*. After 1770, produced biscuit busts on conical pedestals with spiral gilt grooves and medallions of contemporary French and German personalities.

Rome. Italian ceramics. In 14th and 15th century, green and purple, or blue maiolica made in manner of Florence and Orvieto. Ware retrieved in research from mud of River Tiber includes small bowls with inward curving sides painted with arms of Pope Callixtus III (1455–58). Examples of tiles date from *c*1485. Work in 16th century by potters from other centres, e.g. Faenza. Vases and large vessels made with relief decoration in style of Urbino from *c*1600. Porcelain factory operating 1761–64 made figures marked FATTO. IN. ROMA./DA. GIO. PAULO./SAVINO. MDC. Another factory, established 1785, manufactured e.g. reliefs of saints in biscuit porcelain, and altar candlesticks in cream-coloured earthenware. Factory closed in 1831. Mark: G. VOLPATO/ROMA impressed.

Römer. Form of wine glass in **Waldglas* developed in 15th century and found from Low Countries to central Europe. Finest examples German, dating from 17th century. Cup-shaped or ovoid bowl on hollow stem with applied prunts, and usually hollow, coiled glass foot. Became standard German wine glass shape, used into 18th century; survives, in modified form, to present day.

rope curtain pattern. In Korean ceramics, stamped ground of white mesh or hatching, found on type of Punch'ŏng ware, known as mishima, made in Yi period. (Name mishima possibly derived from idea that pattern simulated effect of fine lettering, found in almanacs issued by Mishima Shrine, Izu province.)

rope moulding. Convex half or quarter round moulding turned to resemble rope. Popular in 18th century friezes, case pieces, etc.

Rörstrand. Swedish faience factory, established by company formed 1726, in production from 1727. Early faience painted in blue with design adapted from *style rayonnant*; also rare figure subjects. Other decoration includes *bianco sopra bianco* background patterns, introduced by 1745, and painting in high-temperature blue, purple, yellow, and green, outlined in black, possibly introduced by J. *Buchwald, employed *c*1757. Enamel painting in strong colours, predominantly yellow and green, also blue and purple, introduced in 1758. *Rehn pattern used from mid 18th century. Transfer-printing introduced in 1761. Forms, at first derived from Delft and German faience, later include e.g. trays and sauceboats moulded with curling leaves after silver shapes. Marked with Stockholm or contraction of Rörstrand, and system indicating date, painter, manager, and sometimes price. Cream-coloured earthenware, introduced in 1771, replaced manufacture of faience by late 18th century; transfer-printed with willow pattern from *c*1826, Swedish views by 1830s. Black basalt made e.g. into cameos and vases in Staffordshire style from late 18th century. After mid 19th century, produced majolica and imitations of Palissy ware; also ironstone and bone china.

rosary. Chaplet of beads for counting prayers used by Catholic church. Traditionally consisted of three chaplets, each with five decades made up of one Pater Noster bead and 10 Ave Maria beads (i.e. 15 Pater Nosters and 150 Aves). In Middle Ages number of beads varied. Earliest literary record of rosary is string of jewels used by Godiva and left by her to religious house founded in Coventry in 1043. Probably in more general use by 13th century. Variety of materials used, e.g. chalcedony, enamelled gold, rock crystal, filigree amber,

Rosary. 17th century Italian, with seven decades of carved boxwood beads. Cross and pendant are gold and enamel.

ivory, lapis lazuli, jet, coral, maple; Pater Noster beads usually different from Aves. In mid 15th century, sometimes worn by women as necklace in England and Spain; fashion continued in Spain in 16th century. Such rosaries usually had pendant cross or charm (holy figure, coral fist-shaped amulet against evil eye, etc.).

Rose, John (*c*1772–1841). English potter. Apprentice to T. *Turner at Caughley. In 1780, started pottery at Jackfield, Shropshire. Founded porcelain factory at *Coalport, *c*1796. In 1799, bought Caughley factory, almost opposite Coalport on bank of River Severn. Managed both factories until closure of Caughley (*c*1814). Hired W. *Billingsley to reproduce soft-paste body of Swansea and Nantgarw at Coalport. Bought moulds from Nantgarw in 1822 and from Swansea in 1823 or 1824. Succeeded in firm by nephew.

rose. Openwork ornament resembling rose found in soundhole of certain instruments; later versions incorporated device identifying maker. In 17th century England, referred to as knot; in 16th century Germany, as *Stern* ('star').

Rose, The (De Roos). Delft factory (1666–*c*1858). Owners (1662–1755) include D. *Hofdyck (1694–1712) and A. *van Dijk (from 1712). Specialized in religious subjects in blue painted ware. Produced tile pictures painted in polychrome (including *delft noir*), *cachemire* style vases, and domestic ware. Luminous green characteristic. *Illustration at* Delft.

rose and crown. London Pewterers' Company mark, used in 16th century only for high quality work; in 17th century used on goods for export; later on good quality pieces generally.

rose cut. Form of diamond cutting in which stone resembles hemisphere covered with triangular facets (flat base rising to point at top). Developed in mid 17th century in Holland and France (where sponsored by Cardinal Mazarin). Dutch rose has 24 facets, French *rose recoupé* has 36. In general use until end of 18th century. Superseded by *brilliant cut. Also used for other gems.

rose du Barry. *See rose Pompadour.*

Rosenberg, Carl Christian or Charles (1745–1844). English silhouettist. Born in Germany; arrived in England (1761) as page to Queen Charlotte. Many royal portraits, some full-length, usually in plain black on flat glass backed with pink paper. Also produced conversation pieces, and small profiles mounted in jewels or on snuff-boxes. Worked in Bath, Somerset, 1787–1816; then King's Messenger at Windsor until 1834.

rose-engine. Machine or lathe attachment producing eccentric movement of cutting point on rotating surface. Used in decoration of dry, unfired ceramics. M. *Boulton said to have supplied J. *Wedgwood with rose-engine for decoration of stoneware and jasper. *See* engine-turning.

rose Pompadour. Pink overglaze enamel ground colour introduced on porcelain at Sèvres in 1757. Little used after deaths of Marquise de Pompadour (1764) and J. *Hellot (1767). Claret ground colour based on *rose Pompadour* announced at Chelsea in 1760; sometimes called *rose du Barry* in England, although Madame du Barry did not appear at French court until 1769.

*Charles Rosenberg. Silhouette, c1793. Church, King and Constitution (Bishop of Winchester, George III and Lord Loughborough, the Lord Chancellor). Painted on flat glass with *églomisé decoration. 15in.×13in.*

Rose Pompadour. *Flower-pot, *Sèvres, 1757; mark two Ls enclosing an E, also crescent in blue enamel. Painting of birds in reserve panels possibly by J-P. *Ledoux.*

rosewater ewer and basin or **dish.** Before forks came into common use in 17th century, diners rinsed hands at table after meal with rosewater poured from *ewer into matching basin of gold, silver, silver-gilt, or occasionally pewter or brass. Basins of bowl or dish shape; large, diameter *c*18–24in.; ornament matched that on ewer. Some made in 18th century, but increasingly as ceremonial plate. Smaller versions made for *toilet service.

rose-water sprinkler. *See almorrata.*

Roskopf watch. Originally cheap, rugged watch with form of pin pallet *escapement from factory founded at La Chaux-de-Fonds, Switzerland, by George Roskopf, *c*1866. Later incorrectly applied to any watch of this type.

Roskopf. Pocket watch, mass-produced, with enamel dial and nickel case; inscribed 'Système Roskopf. Patent'. c1870. Keyless winding with push-piece for engaging hand-setting mechanism.

Ross, Sir William Charles (1794–1860). English miniaturist; pupil of A. *Robertson. Subjects include Queen Victoria; also Belgian and Portuguese royalty. In 1839, elected member of Royal Academy and knighted. Technique of flattening large shavings of ivory from tusks slowly in hydraulic press allowed unusually large ivory miniatures; most of these have tended to crack.

Rossetti, Giorgio Giacinto (fl *c*1820–*c*1850). Italian maiolica and porcelain maker. Thought to have painted faience at Marseille; at Lodi, signed work (1725–30) in *style Berain*. *c*1736, acquired maiolica factory established 1725 in *Turin. With financial help from King Carlo Emmanuele (1737), experimented in manufacture of porcelain; in 1742 employed painter J. *Helchis, and by 1743 had produced examples of hard-paste porcelain, e.g. teaware and vases.

Rossler, Wolf (*c*1650–1717). German *Hausmaler* working on faience at Nuremberg (*c*1680–90); also known as The Monogrammist W.R. Examples of fine painting include *Schwarzlot* decoration on faience jugs from Hanau or Frankfurt, and, later, effect of enamel colouring heightened by *kwaart* used on biblical or mythical subjects, sometimes covering whole surface.

rosso antico. Red stoneware first produced by J. *Wedgwood at Brick House works. Style inspired by ancient Greek and Roman red pottery; mainly engine-turned, but later decorated with applied figures in black or white. *Illustration at* canopic jar.

Rost, Rostel or **Rosto,** Jan (d 1560). Prolific tapestry master-weaver from Brussels, brought

Rouen faience. Early 18th century sugar caster of violet faience (painted blue and white in manner of Delft).

to Italy 1536 by Ercole II d'Este to establish and direct Ferrara manufactory with N. and J. *Karcher. With N. *Karcher, commissioned by Cosimo I de' Medici to establish and direct Arazzeria Medici in Florence in 1546 (*see* Florentine tapestry). Considered 'first master-weaver' of mid 16th century Italy.

Rouen (Normandy). French ceramics. Tiles made in 16th century, but production of faience lapsed until establishment of factory by E. *Poterat. **Style rayonnant* introduced by 1700, painted at first in blue monochrome, later with touches of red (characteristic of Rouen); from early 18th century, palette included full range of underglaze colours. Large dishes made, up to 24in. diameter; also table vessels including ice pails, salts, *sucriers,* and spice boxes; commemorative cider jugs provide guide to dates of decoration. Imitations of K'ang Hsi *famille verte* porcelain made *c*1720–*c*1750 at J-B. *Guillibaud's factory. Rococo style from *c*1740 includes pastoral subjects enclosed in borders of shells and garlands. Designs introduced in mid 18th century include *décors *à la corne* and **au carquois.* Enamel painting used in imitation of porcelain decoration from 1770s, e.g. by M-T-P. *Levavasseur. Painting of Rouen faience influenced faience decoration throughout France, particularly in northern area. Works of large size produced include celestial and terrestial globes 4ft11in. high (1725), and N. *Fouquay's busts of Apollo and The Seasons. L. *Poterat authorized (1673) to produce porcelain; none positively identified.

rouge box or **boîte à rouge.** Small box in variety of shapes, usually with lift-off lid, used to contain rouge in 18th century Europe. Sometimes with small mirror in lid and separate compartment holding kohl for eyes. Materials and decoration similar to snuff-boxes.

roundabout chair. *See* corner chair.

Rouquet, Jean or André (*c*1703–59). Swiss-born enamel painter, in Paris during youth, then in London for almost 30 years. Imitator of C. F. *Zincke.

Rouse, James (1802–88). English porcelain painter; flower painter at Derby factory (*c*1815–*c*1830). Later worked at Coalport, painting flowers in style of Nantgarw.

Roussel, Pierre (1723–82). French *maître-ébéniste* (1745); received commissions from Prince de Condé for Château de Chantilly and Palais Bourbon. Made many commodes and tables from mid to late 18th century, decorated with lacquer-work, marquetry, and mosaics. Business carried on by widow and two sons.

rout furniture. Simple painted *side chairs and benches, usually with cane seats, hired out by furniture makers for evening parties (routs) during 18th and beginning of 19th centuries. Glasses (rout-glasses) and refreshments (rout-biscuits) also available.

Royal Copenhagen Porcelain Manufactory. *See* Copenhagen.

royal portrait chargers. *See* blue-dash chargers.

royal portrait spoon. *See* spoon.

Rubati, Pasquale (fl mid 18th century). Italian maiolica potter. Worked at Clerici factory in Milan. Established rival pottery in 1756. Associated with services decorated in relief, painted in opaque-white and bright polychrome enamel; designs include roses and insects on plate with wavy rim. Succeeded by family. Mark: F over PR over Milon, sometimes within heart.

Rubens, Peter Paul (1577–1640). Flemish painter, draughtsman, and etcher. From 1618 produced numerous tapestry cartoons (for Spanish Archdukes in Brussels, for Louis XII of France, and Charles I of England), including History of Decius Mus, Triumph of the Eucharist, and History of Constantine. Designs of Rubens and his school major influence on Flemish tapestries throughout 16th century and into 17th. Besides development of central composition, borders varied with central scene; backgrounds minimized.

ruby and **sapphire.** Gemstones, two varieties of corundum (aluminium oxide), next hardest mineral after diamond (impure form, emery, is used as abrasive). Ruby coloured red by chromic oxide; sapphire, blue by mixture of chromium, iron, and titanium oxides. Ruby found notably around Mogok, Upper Burma. Sapphire less rare: deposits e.g. in Ceylon, Siam, Australia, and United States. Ruby used in jewellery mainly after 16th century; sapphire mainly after 18th century.

Ruckers family (fl *c*1597–*c*1670). Flemish firm of harpsichord makers working in Antwerp. Founded by Hans Ruckers (*c*1550–*c*1620). Produced many harpsichords with one or two manuals and oblong virginals; cases elaborately painted.

rudder (in furniture). Hinged member below level of top on drop-leaf table; swings out under leaf to support it when raised. In profile, resembles rudder or wing.

Rude, François (1784–1855). French sculptor. Won Prix de Rome in 1812. Works include Mercury Tying his Sandals, and relief group of Volunteers of 1792 (*Le Départ*) on Arc de Triomphe, Paris. Leading sculptor of romantic school; pupils included **Animaliers* E. *Frémiet and A-N. *Cain.

rug. Term generally applied to any *carpet designed for use on floor, usually rectangular (older examples tend to be long and narrow); occasionally, irregular shapes made to fit particular position; also, rarely, round: probably intended for use in tent.

Rumanian carpets. Peasant tapestry-weave carpets, woven from 17th century. Types range from broad all-over floral patterns with little differentiation between field and border, to more regular Turkish influenced lozenge and geometrical patterns. Colour schemes limited and bold. Many *kelims made, usually including birds in design. *Illustration at* kelim carpets.

rumblers. Set of up to five brass bells worn on horse's show harness. *See* horse-brass.

rummer. Heavy English drinking glass, made *c*1770–1850. 18th century examples usually have large, ovoid bowl mounted on short, plain stem and thick, circular foot. By 1800, bucket bowl common, occasionally cut or engraved; stem knopped, and foot often square, plain, or terraced. Common bowl forms: round, funnel-shaped, ogee, and double ogee.

Rundell, Philip (1743–1827). English jeweller and silver retailer working in London. In 1767, moved from Bath (where born and served apprenticeship as jeweller) to London; worked as shopman for Theed & Pickett, goldsmiths and jewellers. In 1772 became partner; 1785 bought Pickett out; in 1786 sole owner. In 1788 took John Bridge as partner and in 1805 nephew, E. W. Rundell (when firm became *Rundell, Bridge & Rundell). Rundell extremely shrewd businessman. Bought plate and jewellery cheaply from French *émigrés,* which Bridge then altered and sold at large profit. Own silver influenced by French design. Firm's plate superior to any other English work of period.

Rundell, Bridge & Rundell. London firm of silversmiths and jewellers founded by P. *Rundell. Appointed royal goldsmiths to George III, possibly through partner, J. Bridge's contacts. In 1808 sculptor W. *Theed became partner. Firm had two workshops managed by B. *Smith (1802–23) and P. *Storr (1807–19). When Smith left, production concentrated at Dean Street workshops. When he left, no attempt made to replace him; plate probably continued to be made by workers Storr trained. Firm had agencies worldwide, e.g. in Paris, Vienna, St Petersburg, Constantinople, Baghdad. Much patronized by Prince Regent, and later also involved in purchase of antique plate for him (as George IV). Artists who designed for firm included J. *Flaxman, T. *Stothard, and E. H. *Baily. Produced large range of domestic,

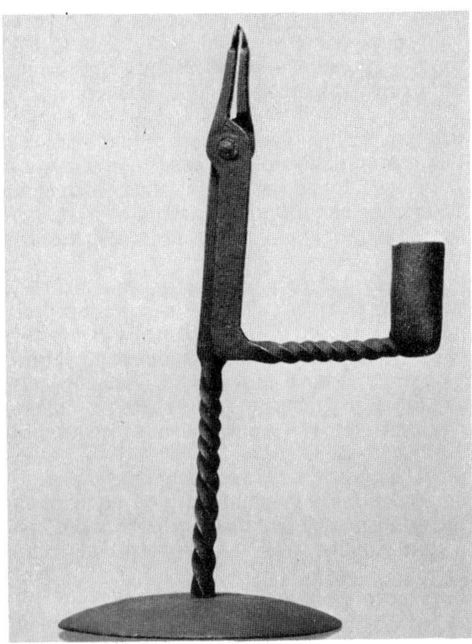

Rushlight holder. English wrought-iron. Height c9in.

presentation, and display silver. Design staff revived rococo motifs, probably inspired by dinner service made (*c*1740) by N. *Sprimont for Frederick, Prince of Wales. Also involved in Gothic revival: member of staff discovered A. W. N. *Pugin. After death of P. Rundell (1827) and Bridge (1834), firm's capital drastically depleted. Orders farmed out to several silversmiths. Attempts made to recoup fortunes, but firm dissolved in 1842; ledgers destroyed. For 33 years, as silversmiths to Prince Regent (later George IV), unchallenged arbiters of taste.

runner (in furniture). Strip of wood on which drawer runs. Also, *bend on rocking chair.

running dog motif. Oriental carpet border design of stem scroll or animal forms reduced to hook-like motif.

rushlight holder. Various sizes and shapes of holder made in 17th and early 18th centuries for rush-pith which, dipped in tallow and lit, gave weak but inexpensive light. Floor-standing type held rush with adjustable clip on iron stand *c*4ft high, driven into oak block, or with tripod or similar iron support; smaller size made for standing on table. Another version hung from ceiling on adjustable ratchet-type fitting. Some holders incorporated sockets for candles.

Russian glass. Until 19th century, Russian glass generally limited to court circles. Little made until establishment of two successful glasshouses in Moscow in 1760s. First founded by merchant, Thomas Maltzof, succeeded by brother Jacob who employed Subanov, considered greatest Russian glass engraver. Second glasshouse, founded by Bakhmetev family, produced fine European-style glassware until 1917. In late 18th century, rococo style enamelling and gilding used. After 1763, every piece marked. In 1777 Prince Potemkin founded Manufacture Impériale de Cristal at St Petersburg, producing domestic ware and fine glass for court, including chandeliers, vases, goblets, and some opaque-white glass similar to that made at *Bristol; pieces occasionally marked (in Cyrillic lettering) S.P. Burg; factory state-owned under Catherine the Great, ceased to make domestic ware. Most 18th century Russian glass almost indistinguishable from European forms imitated, apart from some distinctive engraving (popular subjects, portraits and monograms), stained black from *c*1743; style revived in 19th century by Bakhmetev factory, which specialized in ornamental glass; Maltzov glassworks turned to domestic ware.

Russian glass. Wine glass, either from Imperial Glass Factory or Bakhmetev Glass Factory, c1820, decorated with opaque-white glass plaque bearing portrait en grisaille *of Alexander I. Opaque-white glass Easter egg, c1840, painted, gilded, and with traditional inscription, Christ is Risen.*

Russian gold and silver. Medieval icon covers and other ecclesiastical wares (chalices, crosses, reliquaries, etc.) made or mounted in precious metal survive. Centres of production included Moscow, Kiev, and Novgorod. Silver copies of earlier wooden native Russian drinking vessels made for royalty and nobility in 16th century. In early 17th century, silver workshop established in Kremlin; in 1624 gold workshop detached from it. Besides native Russian vessels, also produced dishes, cups, goblets, book-bindings, crosses, chalices, icon covers, etc. Enamel, niello, and filigree ornament at height of development. Workshops closed in 1700 by Czar Peter the Great. Because of his enthusiasm for western European styles, French and English inspired domestic silver produced, and native forms neglected: tankards, beakers, etc., replaced *bratina, *charka, and *kovsch.

In 1700, Czar introduced hallmarking system: maker's mark in Cyrillic characters and town mark (e.g. double-headed Imperial eagle for Moscow) with city name beneath; replaced *c*1730 by St George and the Dragon. *See* Kremlin silver.

Russian porcelain. Porcelain made at *Imperial Porcelain Factory by 1750, as result of experimentation begun in 1744 by arcanists including C. K. *Hunger and D. *Vinogradov. Private factories, such as *Batenin, *Novyi, *Popov, *Iusupov and *Kudinov started after 1750, but only that of F. *Gardner lasted into 19th century, with state-owned Imperial Factory. Notable among later factories was *Kornilov, established 1835.

Russian snuff-boxes. Gold boxes mainly made by foreign craftsmen attracted to St Petersburg, Russia, from *c*1714. Copied French styles. Oval, circular, or oblong form lavishly decorated with diamonds and, from *c*1770, with miniatures. Foreign goldsmiths working in Russia included: J. *Pauzié (Swiss), and J-P. *Ador (French). Silver boxes produced from 1780 reaching peak of production after 1825. 18th century boxes varied in shape; predominantly circular. In 19th century virtually all rectangular. Niello decoration, with landscapes and/or views of buildings. Boxes gilded inside and often also outside.

Russian tapestry. Czar Peter the Great established tapestry manufactory at St Petersburg in 1716, with workers from Gobelins. First work, copy of Gobelins's Indies, woven from set presented to Czar in Paris. After 1720, weavers

*Russian snuff-box. Silver box, made in Moscow, 1855. Decorated with bright-cut engraving and *niello.*

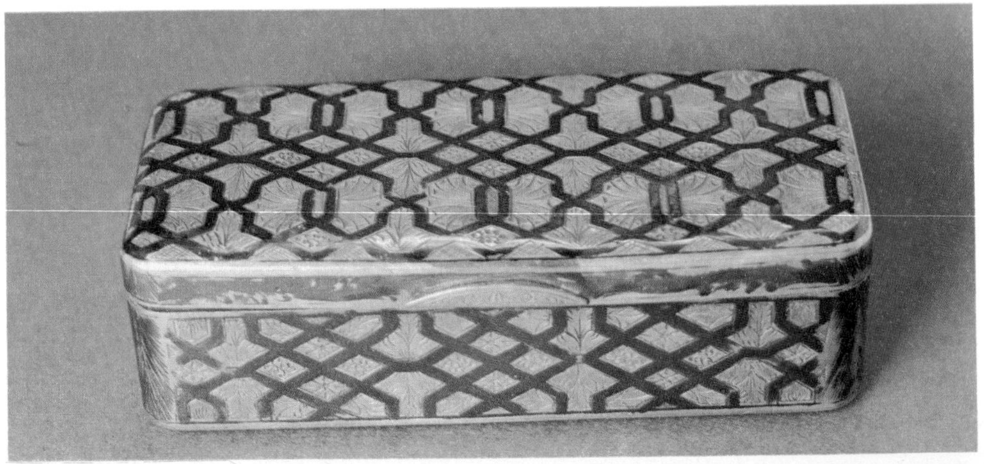

Rustic furniture. Triangular chair, English, mid 17th century. Ash with rush seat. Each upright has hole at top for candle.

mainly Russian; produced tapestry portraits and decorative panels, allegorical and mythological subjects, etc. French style dictated compositions. Folk tapestries also woven in small home-workshops from 15th century.

Russinger, Laurentius (fl late 18th century). German porcelain modeller; worked at Höchst as modeller from 1758; *Modellmeister*, 1762–66. Inspired by style of F. *Boucher for figures like Boy with Bird's Nest and Girl Running from a Snake. At Pfalz-Zweibrücken, 1767–68, then paused at Fulda en route for Paris (La Courtille) where he worked 1774–1810.

rustic furniture. Furniture with legs and other parts designed to resemble tree trunks, branches, leaves, etc. Made from 1740s, early example of rococo style; revived in 19th century England, mainly as garden furniture. Much used for chairs, also tables and benches. Term also describes simple English country or provincial furniture, e.g. trestle tables, chairs with rush seats, from Middle Ages onwards.

sabre or **Waterloo leg.** Concave chair leg, rectangular in section, curved like cavalry sabre; also called scimitar. Introduced during Greek revival; copied from *klismos. After 1815 called Waterloo leg. *Illustration at* Directoire furniture.

sack-back Windsor. *See* bow-back Windsor.

sacrificial cup. In Chinese ceramics, Buddhist ritual object; used, e.g. in marriage ceremonies for libations. Copied from bronze shapes of Han dynasty (also often imitate rhinoceros horn cup); beaker with flared rim, and relief decoration. Found in all later periods. *cf tsun.*

Sadang-ni. Important 12th century (Koryo period) kiln site, at Kangjin, south-west Korea. Produced celadons and black Koryo ware, also inlaid (*zogan) work. Roof-tiles with celadon glaze, discovered at site, provide earliest date for Korean celadon; in 1157, ornamental pavilion specially commissioned by King Uijong. Only known record of such use. Decorated with arabesques or medallions in relief.

*John Sadler and Guy Green. *Transfer-printed Liverpool pottery tile, late 18th century.*

saddle seat. Chair seat with two shallow indented areas separated by slight central ridge, similar to seat of English saddle. Common on *Windsor chairs.

sad iron. *See* flat-iron.

Sadler, John (1720–89). Engraver for transfer-printing at Liverpool Printed Ware Manufactory (1756–70); owner in partnership from 1763 with G. *Green; claimed to have invented transfer-printing *c*1750. Decorated ware made, e.g. in Liverpool and Staffordshire, notably by J. *Wedgwood, who initially sold him salt-glaze and Queensware and repurchased it transfer-printed. Also printed porcelain for Longton Hall; may have bought stock for decoration on closure of factory. Early work chiefly in black; later brick red also used.

sadware. Flat pewter ware, e.g. plates, dishes, chargers, trenchers, as opposed to *hollow-ware and *trifle. Made from *fine pewter, cast in moulds and finished by hammering, scraping away rough edges left by moulds, and burnishing.

Saint, Daniel (1778–1847). French miniaturist. Exhibited at Paris salon, 1804–39. Subjects include Napoleon I, Empress Josephine, Charles X, and Louis Philippe. Most fashionable after restoration of French monarchy (1814).

Saint-Amand-les-Eaux (Nord). French faience factory established in 1718. Early ware thought to be in style of Rouen; later imitations of Strasbourg made. From 1760, decoration in opaque white over pearl grey glaze with flowers or landscapes, sometimes with figures painted in manganese purple or blue; continued under J-B-J. *Fauquez, grandson of founder, from 1773. Rare work in Delft style has turquoise ground. Porcelain (made 1771–78) decorated in blue or purple. Also made white and cream-coloured earthenware in English style from late 18th century. From early 19th century, porcelain again manufactured by M-J. *de Bettignies in style of Tournai and Chantilly; later produced forgeries of soft-paste porcelain, e.g. of Sèvres. Marks include fs with flourishes on faience, cream-coloured, and white earthenware (in underglaze blue, 1718–1882). From 1771, similar mark with more angular fs between initials SA used on soft-paste porcelain.

Saint-Clément (Meurthe-et-Moselle). Faience factory established in 1758. P-L. *Cyfflé partner *c*1763. From 1770s, faience in style of Sceaux, gilded and decorated with enamel colours, notably orange-red. Also produced figures after models by Cyfflé in *terre de Lorraine* and enamelled faience. In early 19th century, stronger colours used, including green and brown. Much good quality *faîence fine* also produced. Marks include SC in blue (rare) on faience from 1758; in 19th century, St Clement stencilled in blue; St C^{t} impressed (on white figures with translucent glaze).

Saint-Cloud (Seine-et-Oise), France. Faience made by C. and F. *Réverend, under patent of 1664, not yet identified. Other faience possibly made by H-C. *Trou, recorded (1679) as *maître-faïencier*. Porcelain manufacture developed by *Chicaneau family. Soft-paste, with smooth texture, creamy in tone; pitted glaze often has appearance of satin. Forms, often influenced by silver, have much relief moulding. Motifs include prunus blossom, scattered fruit and flowers, reeding, and scaled surface. Tureen dating from 1725–50 has relief design of birds, flowers, and foliage, gadrooned edges and mask handles; snuff-boxes of same period sometimes modelled in form of animals, e.g. sheep, can be dated by silver mounts. Jugs and teapots often in form of birds and humans; others sometimes have dragon-head handles and spouts. Spice con-

Saint-Cloud. Coffee-pot, c1740; white porcelain with applied sprig decoration.

tainers have strawberry finial; plain knobs, widening towards top, also characteristic. Figures often left unpainted, never marked, usually made after 1730. Painting notably in blue, influenced by decoration of Rouen faience; occasionally in polychrome enamel. Marks, registered 1696, include face of sun in blue (until *c*1722), St C over T, incised or in blue (1722–66); crossed arrows probably mark of branch in Paris (1722–42). *Illustration at* knife and fork handles.

Saintes (Charente-Maritime), France. Faience factory established in 1731; lasted two years. *c*1738, workman from Montpellier opened new factory; products closely followed styles of Nevers.

Saint-Jean-du-Désert. *See* Marseille.

Saint Louis glass. *See* Cristallerie de St Louis.

Saint-Porchaire or **Henri II ware.** French fine-grained, soft, white earthenware covered with transparent lead glaze, made *c*1530–*c*1570; probably most produced after 1550. Attributed to area of Saint-Porchaire, near Poitou (Charente-Maritime). Decorated with impressed patterns filled in with coloured clays. Early pieces decorated with bands of small, repeating patterns in black, brown, or reddish clay; simple metal-work forms. Second group, in architectural shapes, have applied relief decoration, e.g. of masks, figures, shells, and intricate tracery, in red or yellow clay, sometimes with touches of blue, green, or purple glaze, and, rarely, gilding. Examples include salts, ewers, goblets, and candlesticks. Rare, late examples have reptiles in relief, resembling work of B. *Palissy. Decoration of all groups frequently includes coats of arms and heraldic devices.

Saint-Porchaire. Faience ewer, c*1550, decorated with bands of patterning and angel in relief under spout. Height 11½in.*

Salem secretary. Mahogany inlaid with satinwood and other woods, made in Salem, Massachusetts, 1795–98. Height 7ft3in.

Saint-Yrieix. *See* Limoges.

salad bowl. Large, circular, or boat-shaped bowl of elaborately cut glass made in late 18th and early 19th century England and Ireland. Earliest examples usually Irish, often supported by three feet. When circular, bowl usually has deep overhanging rim. Later examples often mounted on solid or hollow moulded stand, square, diamond shaped, round, or oval. Occasionally bowl and stand made as separate pieces.

salad servers. Silver utensil for serving salad used in Britain and Europe from late 18th century. Consisted of large spoon and fork with spoon-like bowl divided into prongs.

salamander. Thick circular or rectangular iron plate on long handle, used from 18th century. Put in fire and heated until red-hot, then held against bread or other food to brown or warm it. (Named after European salamander, attributed in antiquity with immunity to fire.)

Salem rocker. American rocking chair, made particularly in Salem, Massachusetts, from *c*1820. Similar to *Boston rocker, but with oval seat.

Salem secretary or **desk.** American desk surmounted by recessed bookcase with two or four glazed doors. Drawers and storage space below writing surface (sometimes provided by slant front), and in pedestal supports. Drawers for writing materials may be incorporated in bottom of bookcase. *See* butler's sideboard.

saler. *See* salt.

Salor rugs. Smooth-textured, very delicately patterned Turkoman rugs woven by Salor tribe. Short, finely-knotted wool and silk pile on woollen foundation; kelim panel often added at bottom. Meticulously drawn, all-over field pattern of medium-size stepped guls, ornamented with Tekke and Saryq guls. Minute diamond forms fill liver-red ground. Design in cold blues, pale yellows, and browns, with touches of strong reds, magenta, or lilac.

Salt, Charles (1810–64). Potter at Hanley, Staffordshire; son of R. *Salt. Maker of parian ware; also earthenware figures, similar to those of father, with inferior finish. Mark: SALT impressed.

Salt, Ralph (1782–1846). Potter at Hanley, Staffordshire; enameller and lustre painter (1812–43); maker of figures and toys in style of J. *Walton. Figures include gardeners, fops, Fire, Dr Syntax, and animals, notably dogs and sheep; title sometimes impressed with lettering in lustre. Mark: SALT on or above scroll.

salt. Container for salt, originally called saler (probably from French, *salière*). Made in gold, silver, silver-gilt, or pewter from Middle Ages, though few early examples survive. *Standing or master salt, most important article of table plate or pewter, stood in front of host; smaller salts placed centrally on lower tables for less important diners. From mid 16th century, pewter salts (sometimes referred to as chapnet or chopnut) probably small and shallow, circular, triangular, or polygonal, with hemispherical depression for salt; sometimes lidded, or in *bell form. 17th century styles in pewter include *spool or bobbin type, circular, rectangular, or octagonal shapes, solidly cast, with comparatively shallow depressions; some have small rounded protuberances on rim to prevent salt touching usual covering napkin. *Trencher

Salt. English gilt, c*1575, date letter and maker's mark indecipherable. Cylindrical body embossed with strapwork and bunches of fruit. Domed cover with baluster finial. Height 3½in.*

salt, antecedent of *salt-cellar, also made in glass from 17th century; followed metal shapes. By *c*1750, *cup salt in general use; glass examples often decorated with *mascarons. Salts also made in Sheffield plate, ceramic materials, and, in America, in pressed *lacy glass.

salt-cellar. Silver, silver-gilt, or Sheffield plate salt container made from early 18th century; usually small, descendant of *trencher salt. At first, plain circular bowl with gadrooned border, supported on three or four feet or low stem and moulded foot. Also cauldron-shaped bowl on three or four feet common in mid 18th century. In late 18th century made with pierced silver or Sheffield plate body and glass liner. Boat and shell shapes also popular at this time; copied in 19th century. *Illustration at* A-S. Durand.

salt-glaze. Hard transparent glaze with irregular orange-peel surface texture, achieved by throwing common salt into kiln at height of firing (1200–1300°C); salt reacts with silica and alumina of clay to form thin vitreous coating.

salt-glaze ware, Staffordshire salt-glaze, white stoneware, or **common white.** White salt-glazed stoneware made in Staffordshire and most English pottery centres from *c*1730, by adding powdered calcined flints and white Devon clay to buff stoneware body in effort to compete with porcelain. Greatest quantities produced 1740–60. Pieces include cups, mugs, and teapots with applied motifs stamped or sprigged, plates and dishes with moulded scroll-work, basket-work and trellis patterns, some with incised or open-work decoration. Figures include *pew groups and small animals press-moulded in *solid agate ware. Introduction of *slip-casting *c*1745 made possible more intricate designs, e.g. teapots in form of camels, ships, and houses, and other tableware with low-relief decoration. Colour applied to surface as touches of cobalt, also used in *scratch blue and *Littler's blue. Enamelling introduced *c*1740, sometimes confined to decoration of applied reliefs, later painting includes pastorals and landscapes on much plainer shapes, e.g. simply rounded teapots. Vessels moulded in vegetable forms, e.g. cabbage, possibly by W. *Littler (1750–60). Some transfer-printing *c*1760, e.g. by *Sadler & Green on dishes for J. *Wedgwood, with moulded rims enamelled in turquoise. Gradually superseded by creamware from *c*1760, but examples occur until late 1780's. *Illustration also at* scratch blue.

Salt-glaze. English. Left: house teapot, c1750. Centre: jug with polychrome enamel, c1760–65; height 7½in. Right: drab-ware coffee pot, c1745–50.

*Salver. English, 1743, made by R. *Abercrombie, engraved with arms of Robert Willimott, Esquire, who donated it to Coopers' Company. Diameter 15½in.*

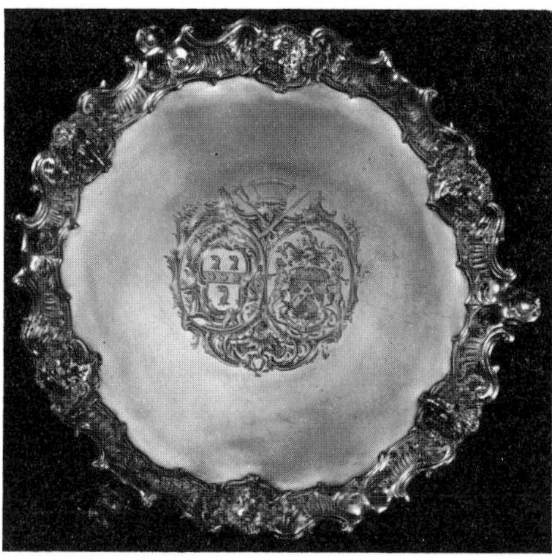

salt-spoon. Small silver spoon with shovel-shaped, circular or ovoid bowl in use from early 18th century. Stem design generally followed *spoons and forks.

salver or **waiter.** Silver or silver-gilt plate or tray used for offering food or drink; earliest surviving examples, from late 17th century, round and mounted on circular trumpet or pillar foot; later, three or four small feet common. 18th century examples include square and octagonal shapes with cast, chased, or pierced ornament; various sizes. Many formed part of *toilet service. Made in Sheffield plate from *c*1760. Centre of salver often engraved or chased. *See* seal salver, tea tray.

Samadet (Landes). French faience factory established in 1732. Products decorated in **style Berain*; also with *chinoiseries*, and naturalistic flowers and insects. Grotesques in green outlined in purple, though not exclusive to Samadet, regarded as characteristic. Factory continued until 1790s. Later, domestic ware made until mid 19th century.

Sambo clock. American, made in Connecticut, c1875. Thirty-hour clock in painted cast iron case; eyes, connected to balance, roll as clock ticks. Height 15in.

Sambin, Hugues (fl late 16th century). French architect and furniture designer from Dijon; exponent of Burgundian branch of *Henri II style furniture, characterized by rich, vital, carved decoration.

'Sambo' clock or minstrel clock. American type made in Connecticut, etc. *c*1850. Figure holds dial simulating banjo.

samovar. Russian silver tea urn with spherical, pyriform, or ovoid body, cylindrical neck, one or more taps, two handles, and domed lid with finial; made from 18th century. Designed to stand over spirit lamp; alternatively shaft down middle of urn held hot coals inserted through funnel-shaped opening on top; this type has ash-pan at bottom.

Samson, Edmé, et Cie. French ceramic firm, established 1845 in Paris. Manufactured reproductions of many types of porcelain including Chinese armorial porcelain and Meissen figures; also porcelain from Chelsea, Derby, and Sèvres. Imitated faience including Strasbourg and Dutch blue-and-white Delft. Most porcelain reproductions in hard-paste. Chinese and European imitations hard to distinguish from originals. All ware said to be marked S, often with mark resembling that of original maker, or on oriental wares, imitating seal mark.

San Bernardino rays. Italian ceramic decoration: rays of light radiating from sacred monogram, I.H.S. Device occurring in *Gothic floral style of 15th century maiolica.

Sanda (Settsu). Japanese kiln site in Arita district; produced celadon-glazed porcelains in 19th century, copying Chinese Sung wares, notably *Lung-ch'üan.

sand caster, dredger, or **box.** Sand container with pierced lid, used for blotting ink at least from 16th century, initially in pewter, brass etc., and almost indistinguishable from *pounce box. Made in silver and Sheffield plate from 17th to 19th centuries as fitting on inkstand. Sometimes of glass with silver mounts, decorated *en suite* with other fittings. 18th and 19th century examples often confused with sugar *caster. *Illustration at* inkstand.

sand-casting. Method of casting metal in moulds made of pounded and dried mixture of quartz and sand, with loam and binding agents (horsehair, manure, etc.), and contained in iron frame, prepared in position with channels and air-vents. Molten metal is poured into channels and left to cool, when sand can be broken away. Articles cast in this way need finishing, or chiselling smooth, to remove seams. Cheaper method than *lost-wax process, but applicable only to simple forms, usually for domestic use; also *bronzes d'édition* in mid 19th century.

Sanders, B. Danish button maker who worked in Birmingham, England. Patented cloth-covered button with metal shank early in 19th century.

Sanderson, Elijah (1751–1825) and Jacob (1757–1810) Cabinet makers in Salem, Massachusetts whose workshop produced furniture for export. Some pieces carved by S. *McIntyre.

Sanderus, Lambertus (d 1813). Dutch potter at Delft: owner of The Porcelain Claw factory from 1763. In 1764, registered stylized claw as factory mark. Products include peacock plates. In 1806, sold 75% of shares in factory; successors sold remaining shares in 1822. Factory changed hands in 1840.

sand-glass or **hour-glass.** Two pear-shaped bulbs with small connecting hole, held vertically in frame, usually wood or iron, occasionally silver, ivory, or bone. Quantity of fine sand takes fixed length of time to fall from one bulb to other. Invention attributed to 8th century monk in Chartres, France. Earliest examples of bottle glass in iron frame. Bulbs made separately and bound together over holed metal disc with putty and linen or leather. From *c*1720 also made of flint-glass. Units welded together over brass bead drilled with hole, often still leather-bound. From *c*1760, glass blown in one piece. Usually timed for one hour or half-an-hour, rarely three-quarters. Ships used several glasses in one frame set at different times, or one four-hour glass.

Sang, Jacob (fl mid 18th century). Dutch glass engraver of German origin. Worked in Amsterdam on English flint-glass from Newcastle-upon-Tyne using fine German-style wheel engraving. Pieces include baluster and facet stemmed wine glasses and *Hogarth glasses, commemorating bethrothals, weddings, and births. Covered goblet (in British Museum, London) depicts *Velzen*, one-hundredth ship built by Dutch East India Company. Popularized naval subjects among many followers. Glasses made 1752–62 signed J. Sang Inv:et:Fec:, with date. Unsigned work includes armorial and allegorical subjects.

*San ts'ai. Bowl, late 17th century; yellow, green, and pale aubergine enamels applied on biscuit. Around outside are drawn Buddhist worthies. Base has white feldspathic glaze on which is six character mark of *Chia Ching. Diameter $7\frac{1}{2}$in.*

sang-de-boeuf. *See* ox-blood glaze.

San Michele workshop. *See* Papal Workshops.

Santa Barbara tapestry manufactory. Spanish Royal Tapestry Manufactory established 1720 in Madrid by Philip V under direction of master-weaver from Antwerp, J. *van der Goten. Until 1729, only low-warp looms used. Early subjects include *'Teniers', hunting scenes, and Don Quixote series, designed by Andrea Procaccini. Most important works of manufactory, 45 tapestries, woven 1776–91, from cartoons by *Goya. Manufactory declined at end of 18th century; closed 1835.

san ts'ai (Chinese, 'three colour') **ware** or **Ming fa-hua.** Chinese ceramics, made from 16th century, decorated with traditional san ts'ai colours: chiefly yellow, purple, and green. Buff or grey stoneware, sometimes porcelain, with colour applied inside raised lines of clay, similar to Chinese *cloisonné* work; carved or incised decoration added. Styling possibly derived from earlier *T'zu-chou ware, though Ming colours applied to biscuit porcelain or stoneware. Jars, e.g. *tsun, boldly decorated. San ts'ai colours supplemented by darker green, brown-yellow, and whitish glazes. Rarely exported at the time. Notable in reign of Chêng Tê.

saphs. Communal prayer rugs, designed for family or mosque use, with field divided into one or two rows of *mihrabs.

sapphire. *See* ruby.

Saqui. *See* Soqui.

sarcophagus. *See* cellaret.

Sardinian green. Green enamel ground colour introduced by W. T. *Copeland in mid 19th century.

sardonyx. *See* chalcedony.

Sargon Vase. Pear-shaped Syrian vase, *c*4in. high. Carved from solid block of green soda-glass, although now appears white with green and silver iridescence. Engraved in cuneiform characters with name of Sargon II, King of Assyria (722–705 B.C.), and lion. In British Museum, London.

Saruk, Sarug, or **Sarouk carpets.** Leather-hard, central Persian medallion design carpets woven in Saruk from mid 19th century. Short, lustrous, finely Turkish-knotted or Persian-knotted pile on cotton or wool foundation. Field almost completely covered by large central medallion and broad corner-pieces; herati motif often used as background pattern. Strong colours, particularly rust-red, ivory, and blue-black. Also trade name for finest quality carpets from Arak and surrounding area.

Satsuma brocaded ware. Japanese porcelain, manufactured at numerous potteries in Kagoshima prefecture, Satsuma province, in 18th and 19th centuries. Early examples copied Korean Yi dynasty porcelain: monochrome glaze coloured with amber or black iron oxide, or white. One kiln, Tateno, produced copies of *Sawankalok ware. White pieces, sometimes heavily enamelled over glaze, and gilded, giving 'brocaded' effect.

sauce-boat or **gravy-boat.** Sauce container with boat-shaped body made from 18th century or before, e.g. in silver or Sheffield plate. Early examples with spout at each end and applied arch handle or two loop handles; moulded base or feet. In 1720s assumed final form with spout at one end and handle at the other; high, circular moulded foot or three or four individual feet. *See* argyle.

saucepan, pannikin, or **pipkin.** Silver vessel with bellied, pear-shaped, or cylindrical body; usually with straight handle (sometimes of turned wood) set at right-angles to pouring lip or spout, if present. Occasionally accompanied by spirit burner and stand. Smallest examples

*Sauce-boat. Made in London, 1780, by R. *Hennell. Handle formed as nymph; base as dolphin, shells, and rocks with frosted finish.*

often used to warm brandy. Larger examples generally made with covers, sometimes hinged. In use from 17th century, though most surviving examples 18th century. A few made in Sheffield plate. *See* skillet.

saucer-dish. In Chinese ceramics, round, flat shape with upward curve at edge. Found in Sung dynasty celadon wares, and porcelains of all subsequent periods.

Saucepan. English, c1685; maker's mark IS with cinquefoil below. Curved spout, angles to turned wood handle; rounded base; crested cover fitted to pan by slip-lock. Height 6¾in.
Sauce tureen. William IV silver, made by Thomas Wimbush and H. Hyde; applied decoration of oak sprays and acorns. Width 9¾in.

saucer-dish (in silver). *See* strawberry dish.

sauce tureen. Silver or Sheffield plate container for sauce. Modelled on soup *tureen but much smaller. In use from mid 18th century though adopted later than *sauce-boat. Late examples occasionally have stand attached to feet. Accompanied by small ladle.

Saunier, Claude Charles (1735–1807). French. Became *maître-ébéniste* in 1752. Noted for marquetry; early work in rococo style, later work neo-classical. Stamp: C.C. SAUNIER.

Sauvage, Charles-Gabriel, *dit* **Lemire** (1741–1827). French sculptor, modeller of figures made in biscuit porcelain at Niderviller from 1759. Early style influenced by P-L. *Cyfflé; later noted for modelling of nudes and figures in classical style. Work includes allegorical group to commemorate Marie-Antoinette's visit to Strasbourg on way to marry Louis XVI. Signature: LEMIRE PERE, incised.

Sava, Persia. Islamic pottery. Lustre ware produced from mid 12th to 13th century, characterized by chequer-patterned trees in decoration. *Minai ware also produced in 13th century.

Savery, William (1721–87). Cabinet maker in Philadelphia, Pennsylvania; noted for furniture in *Philadelphia Chippendale style.

Savona (Liguria), Italy. Maiolica made in district of Savona, at *Albisola, and in *Genoa, 16th to 18th centuries; little early ware identified. Interchange of workmen and styles makes distinction between Albisola and Savona work difficult. In 17th century, much ware painted in blue monochrome, influenced by early import of Chinese porcelain and by forms of contemporary silverware. Thinly potted plates and dishes with moulded relief and open-work or serrated rims characteristic. Decoration in *compendiario* style, e.g. by *Chiodo family and G. A. and D. *Guidobono. In early 18th century, figures in sketchy landscapes with buildings and spattered foliage painted in green, blue, and orange, or in blue monochrome. Later painting generally in polychrome.

savonette. Watch with dial protected by domed metal cover, equivalent of *hunter watch.

Savonnerie. Carpet factory set up in 1627 by S. *Lourdet in failed soap-works on Quai de Chaillot, Paris; associated with workshops of P. *Dupont in Louvre. Originally made carpets exclusively for royal use or presentation; early products small in size, with designs reflecting contemporary styles of decoration. Factory flourished under Louis XIV, after re-organization by Colbert and appointment of C. *Lebrun as director (as at *Gobelins tapestry works) in 1663. Many large carpets produced

Savonnerie. Tapestry screen panel, illustrating one of Aesop's fables, mid 18th century. Height 6ft.

*Sawbuck table. *Pennsylvania-Dutch, mid 18th century, oak. Height 2ft5½in.*
Scagliola. *Detail of top of early 19th century Italian table.*

for royal apartments, with classical motifs, landscapes, mythological subjects, and often royal emblems in central panel. Connection with Gobelins was close, with many artists producing designs for both concerns. Lighter, rococo patterns used from early 18th century, with floral garlands, etc., appearing on series of carpets made for palace of Versailles from 1712. Designs in mid 18th century include those from paintings of F. *Boucher. Royal monopoly of output ended in 1768, but high prices deterred most private buyers. Production continued on lesser scale through Revolution and Napoleonic period, but factory closed in 1825; business transferred to Gobelins.

Techniques used at Savonnerie derived from oriental practice, with close Turkish-knotted pile of wool or sometimes silk on hemp warp and weft. Term Savonnerie carpet widely applied to similar products of other European factories.

Savoy Glass House. Founded 1673 in London by G. *Ravenscroft who employed Italian glass blowers to work with experimental *metals. Granted seven year patent (1674) for crystal glass. *Raven's head seal used from 1677. Retired 1678, succeeded by Hawley Bishopp. Early glass subject to *crizzling and very fragile. Thicker flint-glass developed by Bishopp in 1682 (double flint). Variety of glassware produced, including posset pots, ewers, rummers, and flasks decorated with ribbing, gadrooning, and twisted handles. Rarely engraved (*cf* Buggin Bowls). Few extant examples.

Sawankalok celadon. Thai ceramics, manufactured 60 miles north of Bangkok, near Yom river. Kilns established at end of 13th century by Chinese Yüan dynasty potters. Closely resembles *Lung-ch'üan ware; large plates, pots, jars, bottles, vases, figures, etc., plain, or decorated with designs incised or stamped under glaze. Light grey stoneware body, sometimes whiter, approaching porcelain; burns red if unglazed. Translucent, watery-green glaze gathers in grey-flecked pools at bottom of bowls or dishes. Irregular crazing frequently found. Dating depends on comparison with Chinese pieces. Circular shadow on base, or marks inside pieces, left by supports used in firing. Used in south-east Asia, as ritual vessels. Industry probably ceased in late 15th century, with increased export of Chinese blue-and-white porcelain. Examples highly valued.

sawbuck table. American long table with top resting on X-shaped ('sawbuck') supports. Popular from end of 17th to mid 18th century.

saxe ombré. In German ceramics, naturalistic flowers painted on Meissen porcelain, from *c*1732. Flower specimens carefully shaded. Associated with J. G. *Klinger. *See deutsche Blumen.*

scagliola. Imitation marble, composed of marble chips, isinglass, plaster of Paris, and colouring substances. Used in late 18th century, e.g. for floors, columns, and table and chest tops.

scale-blue ground. Pattern used on porcelain made at Worcester from 1763. Overlapping scales painted in underglaze colours, usually blue, although pink also used. Early scale outline brushed in darker blue over powdered blue ground; later scale produced by wiping away highlights: yellow and brick-red scale achieved in this way.

scale pattern or **scaling.** Decoration resembling overlapping fish-scales. Found as border ornament on 15th century Venetian glass, as decoration in blue or green on 16th century Turkish pottery, and on Western ceramics, e.g. Worcester *scale-blue ground. Motif used on furniture and silver in first half of 18th century, often combined with shell and acanthus ornament; also for frets on clock cases; sometimes known as imbricated pattern. *Illustration at* Worcester.

scalloping. Edge or rim pattern of convex semi-circles or half ovals.

Scandinavian ceramics. In Denmark, principal manufacture of faience and porcelain was at *Copenhagen. At *Herrebøe, in Norway, faience made in rococo style from *c*1758 includes large pieces, such as *wall-fountains and *bishop bowls. Swedish faience made at *Rörstrand, near Stockholm, and *Marieberg. From late 18th century, cream-coloured earthenware (*flintporslin*) began to replace faience. Soft-paste porcelain made at Marieberg in 1760s resembles that of *Mennecy.

Scandinavian clocks and watches. Relatively few distinctive forms; most styles copied from French or German work of appropriate period. Long-case clocks derived from English examples.

Scandinavian glass. Glass used in 16th and 17th century Denmark and Norway, mainly imported from Italy and Germany, although a few local craftsmen supplied glass to court. Frederick III set up glasshouse (1652–58) within palace grounds in Copenhagen. First wholly successful venture was *Nøstetangen glassworks, established 1741 under patronage of Christian VI; produced fine lead crystal glass showing German and English influence, often with wheel engraving. When Nøstetangen closed (1777) most craftsmen transferred to Hurdals Verk, which opened *c*1757 to produce *crown glass. Some engravers, e.g. J. A. *Becker, worked independently, making many Norwegian engraved monogrammed glasses (during late 18th century) with distinctive cartouche enclosing initials, e.g. flower wreath, fine trellis-work, or open crown. Wide range of lead crystal glass produced at Hurdals Verk 1777–1809, included air and colour twist stemmed glasses, and German-style goblets. From 1780, coloured glass also made, particularly blue and purple, occasionally poorly enamelled and gilded; engraving austere and classical. After closure, craftsmen transferred to Gjorvik glasshouse (1809–47), which produced lead crystal, coloured glass, and cheaper soda-glass, e.g. distinctive long-necked carafes with bulbous body and handle (*zirat fladke*), decorated with prunts, trailing, and gadrooning. Deep blue glass also associated with Gjorvik.

First successful glasshouse in Sweden was Kungsholm Glasbruck, active 1676–1815. During 17th century, *façon de Venise* vessels of thin, often crizzled soda-glass made, mainly for court; distinguished by royal initials and crown on stems, handles, and finials, German and Bohemian influence predominated in 18th century; glass became thicker, stems shorter. Baroque engraving, e.g. royal coat of arms, monograms, the sun, and North Star. Products included stopperless, conical decanters and copies of contemporary silver beakers with three feet and lid. Skånska Glasbrucket, North Scania, made similar glass 1691–1762 as well as domestic ware; Kosta, founded 1742, made domestic ware and small chandeliers.

Scandinavian gold and silver. Little medieval plate survives in Denmark, Norway, or Sweden. Drinking vessels commonest article found in precious metal from 14th century. Earliest type was drinking horn; many survive from 14th and 15th centuries, a few mounted in silver, more commonly in gilt copper. Beakers and tankards made from 16th century. Early tankards tall, cylindrical, with engraved and *repoussé* ornament (scrolls, arabesques, figures, etc. in panels). In late 17th and 18th centuries, squatter tankards made, with three cast feet (e.g. pomegranates, lions, etc.); popular thumbpiece was two acorns. *Coin and *peg tankards also made. Tankards remained popular in Scandinavia longer than in Britain and Europe: continued to be made into 19th century. Beakers usually plain or with cast feet; followed tankard styles of decoration in 16th or early 17th century. Late 17th and 18th century examples frequently decorated with embossed flowers on a granulated ground. In late 17th century in Sweden some covered beakers made with three ball feet and ornamented with filigree work; sometimes also with enamel plaques. 18th century Scandinavian domestic silver modelled on that of England and France.

Marking of gold and silver in Denmark dates from late 15th century, when town mark and master's mark in use. From 1685, assay master's mark and month mark added. These four marks used in Norway only from mid 18th century. In Sweden, master's mark used from late 15th century; town mark added in 16th century, and date letter from 1689 (compulsory in 1758). State assaying system initiated in 1752, when triple-crown mark of state replaced assay master's mark.

Sceaux faience. Flower-holder; marked on base Me fecit Sceaux—Penthière, 1773; painted with exotic birds; simulated marble base.

*Scent bottle. *Chelsea porcelain *toy, 1760.*

Sceaux (Seine). French faience factory, established in 1735. Employed J. *Chapelle from *c*1750, (proprietor 1759–63); produced *faïence japonnée*. Leased (1763–72) to J. *Jullienand S. *Jacques; sold in 1772. In 1793, resold, and production of good quality ware ceased. Styles closely followed contemporary fashion of Sèvres, rococo shapes giving way to neoclassicism in 1770s and 1780s. Figures and groups stand on high bases resembling rocks. Soft-paste porcelain made despite Sèvres and Vincennes monopoly (privilege refused 1748), but probably only under management of Jullien and Jacques. Porcelain closely resembles *Mennecy; some has painting of cupids in pink monochrome, with flowers and birds, which also occurs on Sceaux faience.

scent bottles. From 13th century, Venetian and Murano glass makers produced scent bottles simulating semi-precious stones, e.g. agate, chalcedony, aventurine. Few surviving 15th and 16th century bottles have simple shapes in clear glass, trailed with coloured beads or *latticinio* glass. Venetian workers in Netherlands, Nuremberg, and Nevers made coloured scent bottles in elaborate shapes. In 17th and 18th century Germany, *Milchglas* scent bottles decorated with flowers or figures. In France, *verre églomisé* beads on an ivory ground used to simulate needlework on flat, pear-shaped bottles. Barrel-shaped bottles splashed with colour made at *Baccarat, *Clichy, and *St Louis. Opaque-white glass scent bottles with enamel decoration and blue glass bottles with gilded floral sprays, birds, etc., made in Bristol, 1750–1800.

Among porcelain *toys commonly made in 18th century Europe. French examples, made in soft-paste porcelain, notably at Chantilly, Mennecy, and Saint-Cloud, include bottles of flattened pear-shape with *chinoiserie* decoration. At Meissen in 1720s, pilgrim bottle form painted with harbour scenes, *chinoiseries*, etc.; in 1730s, bottles made in form of animal, bird, or human figure, with separately modelled head attached to body by metal mount; in 1740s, wavy rococo shapes have scrolled edges outlined in gilding. Other makers include Fürstenburg, Nymphenburg, Vienna, and Capodimonte. Large output at *Chelsea in 1750s seriously threatened marked for Meissen products. Scent bottles and other toys made by 18th century English potters in *solid agate ware. From *c*1845, forgeries of 18th century porcelain bottles made by E. *Samson in France.

Enamel scent bottles made in 17th and 18th centuries. A. *Fromery's workshop in Berlin produced gold-mounted scent bottles with *chinoiseries* or landscapes. Battersea, Birmingham, and South Staffordshire bottles decorated similarly to snuff-boxes and *étuis*. Copied porcelain shapes.

Gold and silver bottles popular from 16th century. Gold elaborately chased, scenes worked in relief or enamelled. Contained in case of mother-of-pearl with gold or silver *piqué*, or Japanese lacquer.

Schadow, Johann Gottfried (1764–1850). German sculptor and porcelain modeller; in late 18th century worked at Berlin; modelled delicate biscuit portrait figures (*c*1795), and épergne for 1st Duke of Wellington (1818).

Schaper or **Schapper,** Johann (1621–70). German *Hausmaler* at Nuremberg. Painted on glass and faience, typically in **Schwarzlot*, adding gilt and red and steel-point engraved details; also used transparent enamels. On pear-shaped Hanau faience jugs, painted landscapes with ruins, either encircling piece, or in panel enclosed by *Laub-und-Bandelwerk* border, sometimes in red. Base and lid of jug often painted with fruit, sometimes lightly gilded. Mark: monogram of IS. Style imitated by many *Hausmaler*, e.g. D. and I. *Preissler.

Scharff, Johann Gottlieb (d after 1808). Russian box maker who worked in St Petersburg for Catherine the Great. Became master 1772. Made circular gold boxes decorated with enamel and gems.

Schepers, Gaetano (d after 1764) and son Carlos (d 1783). Porcelain makers. Gaetano, son of arcanist at *Capodimonte factory, succeeded father (dismissed in 1744); successfully formulated soft-paste porcelain, used throughout life of factory. At *Buen Retiro, succeeded by G. *Gricci as acting director, *c*1764, and by Carlos Schepers in 1770.

Schissler, Christoph the Elder (*c*1530–1609). Instrument-maker in Augsburg, Germany. Directed workshop producing wide variety of instruments, many for export to England and Italy. Made form of *waywiser for use on foot or for attaching to horse or carriage. Succeeded by son of same name.

Schleswig, Germany. Faience made 1755–1814; best examples, before *c*1773, include *bishop bowls, rococo tureens, shallow dishes, large trays. Usually painted in high-temperature manganese-purple with greyish and yellowish green. Some enamel decoration. Rarely marked Schleswig, in full and contracted, or S over L (*c*1758).

Schlick, Benjamin (fl 1844–49). Danish-born architect and silver designer; employed (1844–50) by *Elkington & Co in Birmingham to make copies of antique pieces for *electrotyping. Made moulds; sometimes changed original to suit specific purpose (e.g. taperstick in shape of Roman sandalled foot). Some pieces exhibited at Great Exhibition (1851).

Schmelzglas. *See calcedonio.*

Schnell, Martin (fl early 18th century). German lacquer artist at Saxon court; painted lacquer in green, blue, red, and yellow on red stoneware made at Meissen under J. F. *Böttger (1712).

Schnelle. Tall, tapering German stoneware tankard with pewter or silver cover and thumb-piece, neck and foot with smooth, moulded bands. Examples made at *Siegburg (*c*1530–90) and Cologne in five sizes corresponding with standard measures.

Schofield, John (fl late 18th century). English silversmith working in London; not a freeman of Goldsmiths' Company. Made some of finest examples of domestic silver in neo-classical style. Registered mark with Robert Jones in 1776: RI above IS; in 1778 registered own mark, IS.

John Schofield. Hot water jug. George III, made in London, 1785; wooden handle.

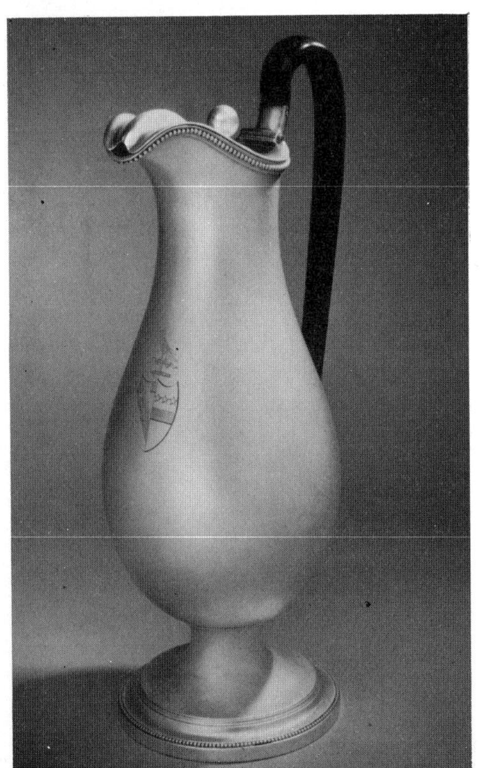

Schönau, Johann Elias Zeissig (b 1737). German painter and engraver. Known by name of birthplace (Gross Schönau). Studied in Paris, worked at Meissen porcelain factory as designer and art director (1773–96); developed French style characteristic of period under Count C. *Marcolini.

Schönheit, Johann Carl (1730–1805). German porcelain *repairer at Meissen 1745–65; modeller 1765–1805. Noted for figures in style of M-V. *Acier, including series, Five Senses (1772).

Schottenuhren. Miniature versions of Black Forest clocks, *c*3–4in. high; made in Germany and Austria from mid 18th century.

Schouman, Aert (1710–92). Dutch artist and amateur glass engraver from Dordrecht. Associate of F. *Greenwood. Stippled wine glasses made mainly as gifts for friends. Subjects of few known signed pieces usually own compositions, e.g. half-length figure of man drinking, and *Hogarth glass with faint stippling, depicting bust of Prince William (now in Victoria & Albert Museum, London). Unsigned wine glass with portrait of Greenwood, after Schouman print, also attributed to him.

Schrezheim (Württemberg). German faience factory established 1752 by J. B. *Bux; best work (1752–1800) includes candlesticks, holy water stoups, wall plaques, wine and beer barrels; also, smaller boxes and dishes in animal and vegetable shapes. Red-brown body covered with bluish tin-glaze. Colours usually high-temperature blue, manganese, green, and yellow; enamel colours also used. Rococo altarpiece of St Anthony made by L-V. *Gerverot (*c*1775). Work marked with arrowhead above various unidentified marks.

Schrödel, Friedrich Reinhard (d 1796). German silversmith working in Dresden; became master in 1755. Prolific maker of domestic silver. Mark: name in full.

Schultz, Anton (fl *c*1725–75). Austrian porcelain painter at Vienna factory (1726–41), worked as *Hausmaler* in Vienna (1741–43); moved to Fulda (1743). Work includes landscapes and *chinoiseries* after Meissen (in 1730s). Signature, A.S., appears in 1740 on coffee-pot, coffee cup and saucer.

*Friedrich Reinhard Schrödel. Soup tureen and stand of *baroque form, Dresden, c1750. Height 11in.*

Schwarzlot. *Beaker painted with figure of Pantaloon from* *commedia dell'arte. *18th century. Height 3⅛in.*

Schuppe, John (fl 1753–73). Silversmith working in London; probably of Dutch origin. Specialized in *cow creamers. *Illustration at cow creamer.*

Schwanhardt family (fl 17th century). Bavarian glass engravers working in Prague, Czechoslovakia, and Nuremberg, Germany. Georg the Elder (1601–67) pupil of C. *Lehmann in Prague. On latter's death (1622), inherited patent for glass engraving and returned to native Nuremberg, where school of glass engraving grew up around him and family. Specialized in wheel engraving of highest quality, combined with areas of diamond-point, e.g. tiny, delicately drawn landscapes with contrasting formal scrollwork. Some signed work exists. Sons, Georg the Younger (d 1676) and Heinrich (d 1693) also wheel engravers; latter credited with discovery of method of etching on glass using hydrofluoric acid. Three daughters, diamond-point engravers, specialized in floral subjects and fine calligraphy.

Schwarzlot painting. Painting in black on glass and ceramics with low-viscosity mixture of copper oxide and powdered glass, fused to surface by firing. May appear sepia if applied thinly. Sometimes used in combination with iron-red enamel or gilding. Developed by J. *Schaper before 1670; more generally used in Germany throughout 18th century, particularly on faience and imported porcelain decorated at Augsburg (1720–30). Also used on early Vienna porcelain by J. *Helchis in 1720s and for Meissen *harbour scenes (*c*1730–50).

sconce, candle-sconce, or **wall-sconce.** Wall bracket candleholder consisting of oval or oblong back-plate and one or two arms with nozzles for candles; made from wood, brass, ormolu, silver, etc. Back-plate at first embossed with foliate ornament in silver examples. Later back-plates heavier and more elaborate; less frequently silver-framed mirror used. Very

*Sconce. By A. *Nelme. Made in London, 1697; decorated with repoussé cartouche of* putti, *fruit, leaves and scale-work surrounding panel on which is engraved coat of arms.*

fashionable in late 17th century; few made after *c*1700. *See girandole. Illustration also at* A. van Vianen.

scorper. Small chisel with interchangeable blades of various shapes used in engraving.

scotia. Concave moulding, semi-circular in cross-section; reverse of *astragal.

Scottish glass. Scottish glass making industry established at Wemyss, Fife, by George Hay, later Earl of Kinnoull; granted 41-year monopoly in 1610. Clashed with Sir R. *Mansell, when Venetian craftsmen employed by latter went to Fife. Glasshouse failed, and monopoly passed to Mansell in 1627. In late 17th and 18th centuries, Leith, near Edinburgh, noted for wide variety of bottles. First bottle-making establishment opened in 1628 to produce black and green bottles; became Edinburgh & Leith Glass Company in early 18th century. In 1682, second glasshouse founded in Leith by Charles Hay; produced clear wine glasses, later, chemistry and apothecary wares. During 18th century several other bottle-houses established in Leith, also making beer and wine glasses. Some bottles, made by injecting pure spirit into *gather, which forced *metal to expand while evaporating, have capacity of over 100 gallons. In late 18th and 19th centuries, some Scottish glasshouses produced fine crystal glass. Verreville glass house in Glasgow (1770–1835) produced cut and engraved crystal glass, including goblets, decanters, lustres, and candlesticks; taken over in late 18th century by partnership, including two glass manufacturers from Newcastle-upon-Tyne. Undecorated wares of simple form sold by weight; cut and engraved glass sold by the piece. In 19th century, crystal glass produced notably by glasshouses at Leith and Perth. Edinburgh & Leith Flint Glass Works, founded 1864, changed ownership several times (becoming Webb's Crystal Glass Co. Ltd. in 1921). Fine, undecorated crystal glass tableware produced; most wine glasses with drawn stems. Competitor was *Moncrieff's Glass Works at Perth. Glasshouse at Alloa noted for distinctive work, founded 1750 to produce bottles; glass-maker from *Nailsea, Timothy Warren (also worked at Newcastle), settled at Alloa and widened scope of factory to include Nailsea wares, e.g. rolling pins and gimmel flasks, in streaked bottle glass and opaque-white glass. Fine Newcastle-style glasses also made, *stipple-engraved with seals, coats of arms, and country motifs.

Scottish gold and silver. Ornaments in precious metal, resembling those produced in Ireland, but fewer in number, survive from very early times. Attempted conversion of pagan Scotland, mainly by Irish Catholic monks in early 8th century, introduced ecclesiastical plate forms, e.g. chalice, reliquary, crozier. Little medieval Scottish silver survives; some pieces, found in Scandinavia, presumably looted by Viking raiders. Edward I of England (1272–1307) also looted Scottish abbeys and melted down their plate. In 16th century, Reformation and reign of Mary, Queen of Scots (1542–87) completed destruction of remaining Scottish silver: any available plate, private or ecclesiastical, was melted down to help royal, political, or religious causes.

Group of *mazers from second half of 16th century are first important surviving pieces of Scottish domestic silver. A few coconut cups and spoons survive from early 17th century. In late 17th century *quaiches (native Scots vessels) first made in silver; also *thistle cups. A few other items of domestic plate, e.g. candlesticks, casters, tankards, also made. From Union of Scottish Parliament with English in 1707, Scottish silver adopted predominantly English styles. Production of domestic silver increased greatly. Quaich continued to be produced until mid 18th century; *bullet teapot, with foot and stem, another favoured Scottish form.

Some post-Reformation plate exists. First type of communion cup for Scottish Reformed church was secular mazer with foot, or goblet. In 1617, Act of Scottish Parliament required each parish to have communion cup and laver and basin (*see* lavabo). Early shape for communion cup was deep, bell-shaped bowl with baluster stem and spreading foot; became heavier in mid 17th century. Covenanters opposed ornamental plate and many churches adopted plain beaker as communion cup.

In 1457 James II of Scotland set up controls for standard of gold and silver; *deacon's mark and maker's mark used at first in Edinburgh; town mark, a castle, added in 1485. Hallmarking dates from 16th century in Glasgow. In 1681, date letter introduced in Edinburgh and Glasgow; lapsed in Glasgow shortly afterwards, and not renewed until 1819. Silver also marked in Dundee, Aberdeen, Canongate (in Edinburgh), etc. making generalizations difficult. In 1759, thistle became standard *Sterling mark (replacing assay master's mark). In 1836 new law required silver to be marked in Edinburgh, Glasgow, or London.

Scottish measure. Originally (17th century) made in three sizes: *tappit hen, *chopin, and *mutchkin, all in shape of first. *See* measure, pot-bellied measure, thistle measure. *Illustration at* measure.

Scottish snuff mull, 1825; horn mounted with silver and set with pink quartz.

Scratch-blue. Salt-glaze ware. Mug, and jug dated 1757. Height of jug 6½in.

Scottish snuff-mull. Snuff-box made in Scotland in late 18th and early 19th centuries, of horn, ivory, shell, deer's hoof, etc., mounted with silver or pewter (hinged lid and tip); sometimes entirely of metal, sometimes set with semi-precious stone such as *cairngorm. Two makers who impressed name on wares were Constantine (late 18th century), and Durie of Inveraray (early 19th century).

scratch-blue. White salt-glaze stoneware with cobalt rubbed into simple outline designs of birds and flowers incised in firm clay before firing; made in England mid 18th century. Signed, dated examples made by Enoch *Booth. *Illustration also at* puzzle jug.

scratch carving. Method of incised carving used on 16th and 17th century country furniture. Simple outline scratched on surface of wood to form pattern. *cf* chip carving.

scratch cross group. English porcelain. Pear-shaped jugs and cylindrical mugs, marked with cross or nick incised in base or foot ring. Made at Worcester in 1750s, soon after transfer of

Screen. Carved giltwood firescreen by Guiseppe Maria Bonzanigo. Covered in contemporary silk. c1775.

*Lund's factory from Bristol. Vessels have strong rounded feet and handles with curled lower terminal ending in straight-cut edge. Scratch cross also found on mugs attributed to Bow, and on ware thought to have been made at Liverpool and Bristol.

scratched blue. Chinese ceramic decoration introduced in K'ang Hsi period; design, lightly incised in porcelain paste, had scratches filled with blue, rarely apple green, before application of glaze. Also popular in reigns of Yung Chêng and Ch'ien Lung. *cf* scratch-blue.

screen. Portable covered frame, used to shield user from excess light, heat, or draught. Folding screens date from Middle Ages, becoming increasingly elaborate in 16th and 17th centuries. Oriental lacquered folding screens also found in Europe and Britain at this period. *Cheval screens date from 17th century Europe; popular in 18th century Britain. *Pole screens date from early 18th century. Portable silk screens with tripod stand and travelling case made in mid 19th century. *See* back screen, library screen, slide screen.

screen fan. *See* fans.

scroddled ware or **lava ware.** American *solid agate ware, usually combination of brown and grey clays, with clear glaze. Produced in limited quantities at Bennington, Vermont (1853–58).

scroll-back. 19th century single-chair back with backward-curving scroll at top.

scrolled pediment. *See* swan-neck pediment.

scroll or **knurl foot.** Furniture foot curving inwards, creating scrolled effect. Found on late 17th and 18th century objects.

scroll leg. Furniture leg (particularly of cabinet or table, sometimes chair) in form of extended scroll. Used from *c*1650.

scroll salt. *See* spool salt.

sea-green ground. *See* turquoise ground.

sea-horse scent bottles. Small, free-blown smelling bottles with body drawn out thinly and curled under in form of sea-horse. In clear or coloured glass; decorated with trailing, *quilling, and sometimes ribbing, in same or contrasting colour. Made mainly during late 18th and early 19th centuries at Manheim Glass Works and Boston & Sandwich Glass Works in America, and at Bristol and Nailsea in England.

seal. Engraved stamp for making impression on sealing wax; mounted in various forms. Fob seal worn on chatelaine from early 18th century; small mount of low carat gold; seal matrix (surface which makes impression) of hardstone, steel, or glass. In early 19th century, with decline of chatelaine, matrix set in large mount of silver, gold, hardstone, or pinchbeck in various shapes, e.g. animal or human head, shell, or flower. Declined in use *c*1830; replaced by desk or hand seal with heavy ornamented handle in gold, silver, pinchbeck, ivory, or hardstones.

Glass seals made from *c*1740, with moulded monogram, initials, crest, or device; usually mounted in metal, e.g. gold, silver, brass, or steel. Made in colours imitating precious or semi-precious stones. From 1770s, opaque-white popular. In late 18th century, seal shaft sometimes made with coloured twist of glass similar to contemporary wine glass stems. After *c*1845, some shafts decorated with *millefiori* florettes.

Seals. Desk or hand seals. 1) Hardstone seal, gold mounted with eagle carved in obsidian; height $1\frac{1}{2}$*in. 2) In form of hand holding double seal, mother-of-pearl hand, agate sleeve, mounted in gold; height* $2\frac{1}{4}$*in. 3) Handle with alternate bands of engraved gold and lapis lazuli; length* $4\frac{1}{2}$*in.*

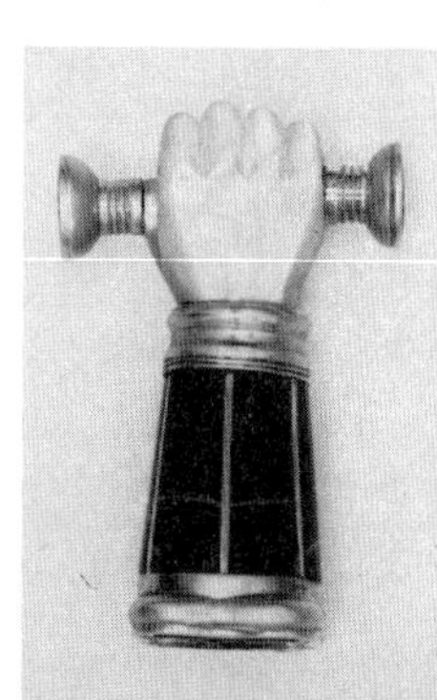

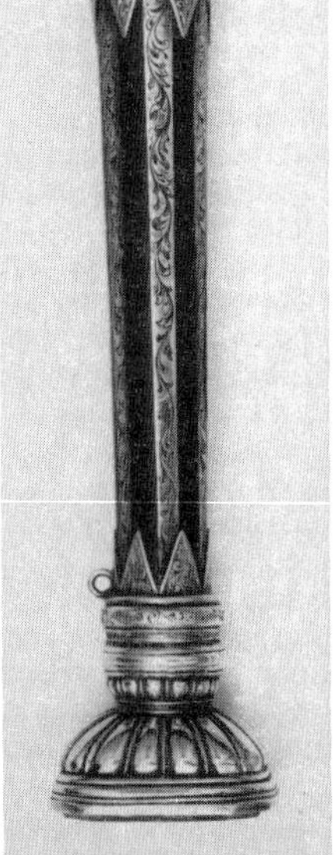

Sealing-wax red decoration. Isnik jug, 17th century.

seal box. *See* skippet box.

sealing-wax red. Ceramic decoration: rich vermilion or scarlet added to palette of *Isnik pottery, *c*1555. Achieved with slip of infusible ferruginous clay (Armenian bole), which remains raised under brilliant glaze.

seal salver. *See* seal cup.

seal-top spoon. Silver, pewter, or brass spoon made in Britain and Europe from mid 15th to 17th centuries with knop shaped as circular capital of column or as baluster. *Illustration at* knop.

seaweed marquetry. *See* endive marquetry.

Second Empire style. General term for several derivative styles in French furniture, *c*1850–70. Pieces generally show characteristics of Louis XIV, Louis XV, or Louis XVI styles, but with more elaborate ornamentation (bronze mounts, inlay, etc.). Upholstered furniture, often fringed, was popular; also e.g. cabinets, with French Renaissance features.

seconds hand. *See* hands.

secrétaire. French desk; architectural piece appearing in various forms. Dates from 18th century.

secrétaire à abattant. *See secrétaire en armoire.*

secrétaire à capucin or **secrétaire à Bourgogne.** French 18th century dual pupose writing desk and table. Table-top hinged at one side, opening to form writing surface, with desk storage compartment rising at back by spring or ratchet mechanism. May be named for supposed resemblance to Capuchin monk's hood or after Duc de Bourgogne, who owned mechanical furniture.

secrétaire en armoire or **à abattant.** French; tall writing and storage desk, dating from 18th century. Resembles **armoire* in shape with door or doors on front of base, often marble top, and flap-front on upper section, hinged to provide writing surface when open. Base may contain strongbox. Interior contains writing equipment, storage space, and secret compartments.

secrétaire en dos d'âne, secrétaire en pente, or **secrétaire en tombeau.** French; desk with slant front (giving profile of half of 'donkey's back'), hinged at base. Front folds down to form work surface. Drawers beneath writing surface; top contains drawers and pigeon-holes. Such desks occasionally made in pairs, backing each other, giving whole profile of 'donkey's back'. Popular Louis XV style.

secretary. American term for writing desk with slanting drop-front, or drawer front, hinged at base and opening to form writing surface. *See* bureau, *secrétaire.*

Secrétaire *en armoire. By René *Dubois; tulipwood with purple heart and kingwood frieze mounted with ormolu *Vitruvian scrolls. Height 4ft2in.*

Sedan chair. French, painted and gilded wood. Domed leather canopy with urn finials at corners; chinoiserie *scenes painted on leather sides; silk damask interior. Height 5ft8in.*

secretary cabinet. Piece of furniture in two sections. Upper section consists of compartments, cupboards, etc. enclosed by one or two doors. Single door type may have bevelled mirror on door. Lower section is bureau with sloping fall-front concealing pigeon holes, drawers, etc., and long drawers beneath. Many examples decorated with marquetry. Made throughout 18th century; especially popular in America. Also known as bureau cabinet.

'secret colour'. *See* Yüeh ware.

secret signature. On watches by A-L. *Breguet, form of authentication to combat widespread forgery. Consists of signature in cursive script combined with number of watch; only visible if dial turned slantwise to light. On enamel dials occurs below figure XII, on metal dials at either side of figure. Thought to have been executed with diamond stylus on pantograph after glazing.

sedan chair. Portable seat, with sides, or completely enclosed in box-like structure with doors and open window-like areas; horizontal pole extends at front and back on each side, allowing chair to be carried on shoulders of two men. Dates from 16th century Italy; use spread through Europe and to England by 17th century, where it remained in use until *c*1800.

sedan clock. Travelling clock, hung in *sedan chairs and coaches *c*1750–*c*1800. Like large watch, *c*6–7in. wide; often circular, but sometimes square or octagonal; wooden or metal case; 30-hour verge watch movement.

Seddon, George (1727–1801). English cabinet maker; established flourishing business in mid 18th century, which, under various names and partnerships, continued into 19th century, furnishing Somerset House in London, and Windsor Castle.

Seefried, Peter Antonius (d 1831). German porcelain modeller and repairer, at Ludwigsburg (1766), Kelsterbach (1767–69), and Nymphenburg (1756–76 and 1769–1810); has been erroneously credited with some figures by F. A. *Bustelli.

Sehna knot. *See* Persian knot.

Sehna, Senneh, Sinah or **Sinandaj** carpets. Small, narrow, west Persian carpets of granular texture woven from 17th century in Sehna (now Sinandaj), major weaving centre of Kurdistan. Extremely short, Turkish-knotted woollen pile on wool or silk foundation; warp often dyed silk. Meticulously executed intricate designs, particularly all-over boteh patterns: small or large botehs in rows with tops all pointing in same direction; or diagonal coloured bands with small vertical or horizontal botehs. Also herati motif pattern with central rhomboid medallion. Main colours reds, pale greens, and soft yellows. Also, very fine small *kelims made, often with herati pattern and light-coloured diamond medallion. Numerous prayer rugs.

Seichur, Sejur, or **Seyshur carpets.** Caucasian carpets from *Kuba area, with longish, finely-knotted pile (higher than other Kubas), and silky texture; blue and white edges on woollen foundation. Field pattern often has several vertical rows of large star medallions linked by thick diagonal bands; also found with all-over floral design. Ground colour commonly ivory, sometimes yellow. Main border typically has blue *running dog motif on white ground.

self-winding watch. Watch in which mainspring wound either through vibrations of

Self-winding watch – pedometer movement; oval weight moves with wearer and winds watch. c1780.

weighted lever with movements of wearer's body, transmitted through ratchet and train of gears to barrel (pedometer watch), or by action of opening and closing case via series of levers and ratchet wheel.

Seljuq carpets. *See* Konia carpets.

Seljuq ware. Ceramic tiles made in 12th and 13th centuries in empire of Seljuq Turks, who overran Persia, Iraq, Syria, and Asia Minor. Pottery made at *Isnik from late 15th century. In Persia, rare white semi-vitrified body resembling porcelain and containing frit and powdered quartz made at *Rayy and *Kashan. *Minai and *lajvardina wares decorated with enamel colours. Coloured glazes developed, notably rich turquoise-blue alkaline glaze, sometimes applied over thick black coating of slip with incised decoration, or over painting in black, blue, and turquoise. In Mesopotamia, underglaze painting or lustre used. Seljuq decoration, often moulded or carved in bands, includes Naskhi inscriptions and foliage; also animals, birds, and figures.

selvage. *See* edges.

semainier. Piece of upright rectangular French case furniture with seven shallow drawers for storing papers; may be *en suite* with *secrétaire*. Also, letter-rack with seven slots, or razor case for seven razors. Dates from 18th century, most popular in Louis XV and XVI periods.

Semainier. *Louis XVI. Veneered in tulipwood, with ormolu keyholes and mounts on chamfered corners and at feet. Marble top.*

Jean-Baptiste-Claude Séné. Ecran de cheminée. *Louis XVI, signed I-B. *Sené; lion paw trestle feet in giltwood; covered with contemporary *Beauvais tapestry. Height* 3ft10*in.*

Séné, Jean-Baptiste-Claude or **Séné l'aîné** (1748–1803). French. Became *maître-menuisier* in 1769. Made furniture in neoclassical style. From 1785 received commissions from Louis XVI; produced furniture for palace at Saint-Cloud. Stamp: I.B. SENE.

Senneh carpets. *See* Sehna carpets.

serinette. *See* bird organ.

serpent. Musical wind instrument; bass member of cornet family. Conical tube, usually wooden and bound with leather, shaped in series of sharp curves resembling snake or serpent (*c*7ft long). Hollow, cup-shaped mouthpiece at end of metal crook added later (making total length 8ft). Six fingerholes arranged in two groups of three. Invented *c*1590 in Auxerre, France, by Edmé Guillaume; used as church instrument. In late 17th or early 18th century, use spread to England, Germany, and Flanders. Adopted by military bands in mid 18th century. Keys (levers for covering holes out of reach of fingers) added at this time; three keys standard in early 19th century, but number increased to as many as 14.

serre bijoux (French, 'jewellery holder'). Cabinet resting on tall base, used to store jewellery. Some examples large and elaborate, heavily carved, inlaid, gilded, etc. Dates from Louis XIV period.

serre-papier. *See cartonnier.*

servante. *See* serving table.

serving, basting, or **hash spoon.** Large silver spoon with oval bowl (sometimes pierced) in use from late 17th century in Britain. Earliest stem was *Puritan. From *c*1690 made with tubular stem, domed finial, and rat-tail. From early 18th century followed stem patterns of smaller spoons. Sometimes known as basting spoon, but probably not confined to kitchen use. In Scotland and Ireland, referred to as hash spoon. *Illustration also at* Onslow pattern.

serving table, servante, or **table servante.** Small dining-room side table, often oval or round; used beside each diner to hold wine, plates, etc. May have sections to hold cutlery, wine bottles, and other items not actually in use. Dates from late 18th century; used for informal meals, eliminating need for servants.

Seto (Owari). Centre of Japanese pottery industry from Kamakura to early Muromachi periods, producing stoneware: bottles with turnip-shaped base, jars, pots, pitchers, incense burners, bowls, etc., covered with yellow or amber coloured glaze. Earliest attempt at celadon glaze, often uneven and streaky. Such examples, particularly tea ceremony utensils, often called Ko Seto (Old Seto). In early Muromachi period, more iron added to glaze produced smoother yellow, sometimes termed Ki Seto (Yellow Seto); lustreless, opaque yellow most prized. Simple incised designs, e.g. peonies, chrysanthemums, willows, pine twigs, or prunus blossom, sometimes coloured with brown iron oxide, or copper green. In 15th century, manu-

Serving spoons. English, William and Mary period; cylindrical handles and baluster finials.

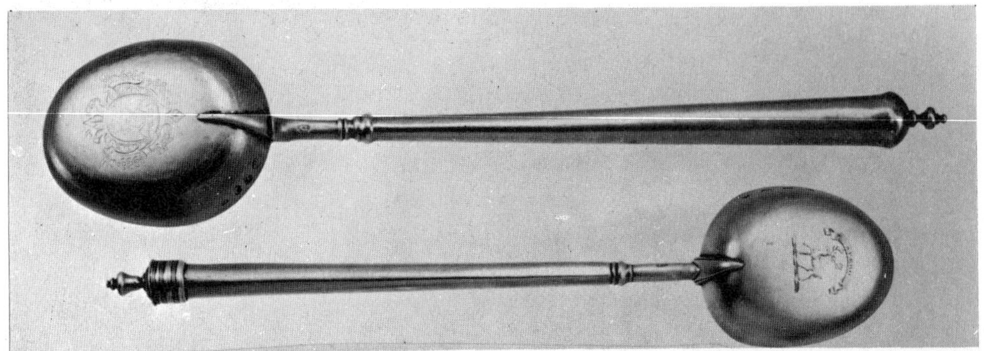

facture of celadon ware ceased, but similar glaze applied to white porcelain paste produced in Seto area in subsequent periods. In 18th and 19th centuries, Seto kilns also produced folk pottery. Coarse greyish body, covered with creamy glaze, painted with bold, free brush strokes. Crude, heavy stoneware plates also made, decorated with cobalt-blue or iron black.

settee. Wide seat, with arms, designed for two or more people. Evolved in 17th century Europe and Britain (particularly after 1660 in England); popular in England and America in 18th and 19th centuries. Two main designs are those with upholstered seat and back, and those with back formed by two or three joined chair backs with upholstered or caned seat. Some examples of former have vertical indentations in back upholstery, giving appearance of two or three connected chair backs. Made in fashionable style of period.

Seto. Stoneware jar with brown glaze, 13th to 14th century. Height 9¼in.

Settee. George II. Mahogany frame with carved ornament; fluted seat rail, scrolled feet, and cabriole legs. Original needlework cover in gros point and petit point. Width 4ft 11in.

settle. Long bench with high back and arms or sides at each end, designed to seat more than two people. Base often built as chest, with seat hinged at back, opening to give access to storage area. Dates from Middle Ages.

settle table or **bench table.** *Settle with back section, hinged to back of arms, which swings forward and down to rest on arms and form table. Dates from 17th century.

Seuter, Bartholomäus (1678–1754). German *Hausmaler* from well-known family of engravers in Augsburg. Until 1720, painted faience tankards and jugs with bunches of flowers, insects, birds (especially goldfinches from own coat of arms). After 1720, bought unpainted porcelain pieces from Meissen for enamelling and gilding in Augsburg workshop, silhouetted figures painted in black, red, and gold (*c*1730), also **deutsche Blumen*. Helped (*c*1730) to illustrate botany treatise. Initialled work B.S.

Sèvres (Hauts-de-Seine) and (until 1756) **Vincennes.** French national porcelain production; experimentation begun by Gilles and Robert *Dubois in 1738, continued by F. *Gravant at Vincennes, financed until 1745 by J-L-H. *Orry de Fulvy, then by C. *Adam, in whose name company formed. Privilege granted, giving exclusive right to manufacture painted and

Sèvres. Porcelain écuelle, *c1770, turquoise* *oeil de perdrix *ground.*

gilded porcelain for next 20 years. Second order, made in 1747, forbade other factories to make porcelain or to employ workmen from Vincennes. Appointments in 1745 include J. *Hellot as chemist and J-J. *Duplessis as modeller; J-W. *Bachelier, employed from 1748, art director by 1751. Earliest porcelain paste not yet positively identified; thought to have resembled that of Chantilly. Decoration, inspired initially by Meissen, includes version of *yellow tiger pattern, and **deutsche Blumen*; lobed shapes recall Chantilly. Modelled flowers achieved early success; by 1748 regarded as highly as Meissen flowers.

After repayment of executors of de Fulvy, new company formed with Louis XV contributing quarter of capital. In 1753, privilege confirmed with prohibition extended to manufacture of white pottery with polychrome decoration. Crossed letter Ls adopted as factory mark, and date letters introduced. Move to Sèvres, proposed in 1753, carried out in 1756.

Good quality, pure white paste developed by 1750, difficult and expensive to produce; in 1750s used for rococo style ware, e.g. vases, and sauce-boats with shell and scroll decoration; other tableware has wavy edges. Ornamental pieces include *toys, flowerpots, perfume burners, and potpourri vases with modelled flower decoration in **vaisseau à mât* form. Designs include seascapes or landscapes, Chinese groups after F. *Boucher, cupids, birds, and flowers; painting often **en camaïeu* in red, green, or, more often, blue with added flesh tints and gilding. Ground colours, **gros bleu*, **bleu céleste*, **jaune jonquille*, *pea-green, **rose Pompadour*, and **bleu de roi*, often softened with gilded diaper patterns, **oeil de perdrix*, **caillouté*, or **vermiculé*. Painted reserves in ground colour characteristic of Sèvres decoration. Thickly-modelled figures produced in 1740s tended to warp during firing; by 1750, small detailed figures could be successfully made. Subjects include children after Boucher, modelled e.g. by L. *Fournier and notably *Blondeau (including rare coloured examples). Porcelain at first glazed and usually left in white, superseded in early 1750s by biscuit. E-M. *Falconet appointed in 1757 to supervize modelling.

Few models produced in 1760s; sales of biscuit figures low. Louis XV bought factory out of debt in 1759; acquired company's privilege in 1760. Negotiations started with P-A. *Hannong in 1753 to obtain secret of hard-paste manufacture resulted in Hannong leaving Stras-

*Sèvres. Porcelain plaques on Louis XVI ormolu-mounted tulipwood cabinet stamped M. *Carlin JME. Plaques bear date-letters for 1774 and 1775; painted by Levé and Méréaud on *apple green ground. Cabinet height 2ft9in.*

bourg for Frankenthal in 1755 through enforcement of Sèvres-Vincennes monopoly; dealings followed with other members of Hannong family, and with owners of Weesp and of Nymphenburg factories. Ban on rival manufacture of porcelain lifted, providing products bore marks registered with police authorities, and were not gilded, painted with coloured flowers, with ground colours, or with miniatures, or moulded. Hard-paste produced only after source of kaolin at Saint-Yrieix came to attention of Sèvres in 1768; deposits bought in 1769. Resulting **Porcelaine royale* made concurrently with soft-paste (**Porcelaine de France*) before replacing it in 1804.

Attempts in 1778 and 1784 to control rival activities had little success; in 1787, concessions effectively ended Sèvres monopoly. In spite of financial difficulty (1790), Louis XVI refused to sell. In 1770s, range of ground colours enlarged to include brown, greyish blue (**bleu turc*), and tortoiseshell (**fond écaille*). Often painted with gilded or silvered patterns, e.g. *chinoiseries*. Yellow and blue ground colours paler, often patterned with black or brown Pompeian scrollwork by late 18th century. Painting became heavier and more mannered; flowers painted in festoons; reserve panels entirely filled with enamel painting. Medallions *en grisaille* imitated cameo portraits, against striped or patterned ground. Borders of scrollwork and *putti* in Pompeian style, introduced in 1770s, appeared until First Republic. Large elaborate vases often used as centrepieces in services produced for diplomatic presentation. Services made, e.g. for Madame du Barry (1770–71), decorated with festoons and monogram; for Cardinal Prince Louis de Rohan (1772), with medallions of exotic birds elaborately gilded against *bleu céleste* ground; for Catherine the Great of Russia (1778–79), in hard-paste with central monogram E made of flowers, crowned in reserve on uneven turquoise blue ground, bordered with portrait medallions and mythological scenes in brown and white; service date-marked 1788, made for dairy of Marie Antoinette at Rambouillet, decorated with plant forms and animals. *Jewelled decoration introduced *c*1780; rare examples include vases. L-S. *Boizot in charge of modelling department from 1774 (with Bachelier still art director), year of Louis XVI's accession; used hard-paste especially for larger figures. Sculptors whose models were used for figures include J-B. *Pigalle, *Clodion, A. *Pajou, and J-A. *Houdon. By 1780, pastoral subjects replaced by mythological, literary, and theatrical scenes. Busts of contemporary personalities made after bronze or marble sculptures. Large ornamental vases, more easily made in hard-paste, designed by Boizot and P-P. *Thomire. Clock cases combining marble, ormolu, and porcelain also work of Thomire. Plaques for inlaying in furniture, made from Vincennes period, were subject to damage in firing. In 1760s, wavy-edged panels sometimes set in trellis-patterned cabinet fronts. Later, larger regular-shaped plaques with flower painting fitted into writing desks (example date-marked 1768) or *secrétaires* (example dated *c*1790 has large floral panel of Sèvres porcelain and medallions of jasper ware made by Wedgwood factory). Unglazed relief plaques also made at Sèvres, resembling Wedgwood products.

At start of First Republic, factory nationalized; brought under jurisdiction of Napoleon's household. A. *Brongniart, appointed as technical administrator, reorganized factory, abandoning production of soft-paste; by 1815 sold-off accumulated stock of undecorated ware, much then painted elsewhere in earlier Sèvres styles. Improvements also made in paste, glaze, and colours. Much produced for personal use of Napoleon, also celebrating his exploits; table top made 1806–10 has circular central plaque portraying Napoleon surrounded by portrait medallions of his 13 favourite officers, painted by J-B. *Isabey. Empire style porcelain includes vases and some tableware in forms inspired by Etruscan vases. Gilding became even more lavish, sometimes used for entire lining of cups. Predominant ground colours green, derived from chromium (introduced 1802), and deep blue. Techniques developed under Brongniart made possible production of large plaques (4ft×2½ft) by 1830s. 19th century revivals of 18th century features include open-work decoration, but in such a way as to remove any use from object, e.g. perforated goblet; biscuit porcelain and soft-paste both reintroduced in mid 19th century. **Pâte-sur-pâte* technique developed after 1850. Other introductions include reproductions of Chinese *flambé, sang de boeuf*, and celadon glazes.

Very wide range of marks used. Factory marks on glazed porcelain only. Until 1793, royal cipher of two crossed letter Ls, usually in blue, sometimes with flourishes and containing date letters from 1753; with crown above cipher on hard-paste only. In First Republic, marks include versions of RF sèvres in blue (1793–1800); sèvres, usually in blue (1800–1802). First Empire: M Imple/de Sèvres, in red (1804–09); crowned imperial eagle surrounded by Manufacture Impériale SEVRES (1810–14). Later marks contain e.g. L cipher and fleur-de-lis (Louis XVIII), C cipher (Charles X), often Sèvres, S, or RF (i.e. République Française). From 1753, also workers' marks, usually initials: painters' and gilders' in colour or gold; sculptors' and potters' incised. Date letters A (1753) to Z (1777), AA (1778) to RR (1795). Also various date marks used 1801–16 including 7 (1807) to 10 (1810), oz (i.e. *onze*, 1811) to sz (i.e. *seize*, 1816). Many of these marks found on spurious or undecorated pieces. *Illustrations also at* biscuit porcelain, *rose Pompadour*.

Sèvres clock. Clock with case made of Sèvres porcelain.

sewing chair. 19th century side chair, with low seat for sewing in comfort. Seat and back often caned.

sewing-machine table. Table used to hold treadle sewing machine; has iron-work base, supporting wooden top. Also, table with iron pedestal and base, and wooden top to which hand-operated sewing-machine could be fixed. Dates from mid 19th century.

Sextant. Light-weight Troughton type, brass with silver scale, made by W. & T. Gilbert, London (instrument makers to the East India Company in 1820). Double frame c9in. radius secured by brass pillars. Index arm bearing magnifier. Two sets of coloured filters.

sewing table. *See* work table.

sextant. Navigational instrument developed from *octant with extent of graduated arc increased to 60°. Introduced by Captain John Campbell *c*1757, widely used by end of 18th century. Greater accuracy achieved by using telescopic eyepiece and screw device for fine adjustment. Early sextants of bulky construction, with brass, ivory, and ebony, but from *c*1775, makers favoured lighter, undecorated brass form.

Seymour, John (*c*1790–1810). Cabinet maker in Boston, Massachusetts. Pieces show influence of Sheraton and Hepplewhite styles; distinguished by ivory inlay (sometimes with *bellflower motif), with cupboard interiors painted light blue. Noted for *tambour doors; many pieces in satinwood.

Seymour Salt. English coverless *standing salt made *c*1662 and belonging to Goldsmiths' Company, London. Body of rock-crystal held by four vertical silver-gilt straps connecting base and cornice. Above, surrounding depressions for salt, are four large eagles perched on orbs alternating with four small hounds also on orbs. Ornate examples of *spool salt.

Seyshur carpets. *See* Seichur carpets.

sgraffiato or **sgraffito.** Pottery decoration: designs cut with pointed instrument through thin slip coating to reveal contrasting coloured clay. Used on Tz'ŭ-chou stoneware, Islamic lead-glazed ware, 10th century Byzantine pottery, and later European slipwares. *Illustrations at* Bologna, harvest jug.

shades. *See* silhouettes.

shagreen. Polished skin of shark or other fish of shark family, usually dyed green or black. Used in protective cases for valuable articles, such as objects of vertu.

Shah Abbas carpets. *See* arabesque carpets.

*Shagreen. *Nécessaire containing four gilded blue glass scent flagons and penknife. English, mid 18th century.*

Shaker furniture. Left: Sister's sewing rocker. Right: round stand, height 27in. both cherry wood. From New Lebanon, New York, c1815–20.

Shaker furniture. American furniture made in late 18th and 19th centuries by Shaker communities (religious sect), particularly in New York State. Pieces characterized by good proportion and extreme simplicity; undecorated, apart from simple turning and shaped knobs at top of uprights, end of arms, etc. Commonly used woods include fruitwood, maple, pine.

Shang dynasty. Traditionally dated 1766–1122 B.C.; probable actual dates, 1523–1028 B.C. Earliest known Chinese historical period with bronze culture. Feudal society centred in Honan province. First discovered, 1898; excavations at Anyang uncovered third and last Shang capital, sometimes called Yin (*c*1300–1028 B.C.), showing mature Bronze Age culture. Recent excavations at Cheng-Chou (Ao in Shang period) uncovered earlier capital (*c*1450–1300 B.C.), possibly proving theory of Chinese discovery and development of bronze casting techniques independently from western Asia. Most important cultural developments, ritual bronze vessels (*see* Chinese bronzes), and carved jade (*see* Chinese jade), stone carving, thrown pottery, and writings.

Shang yao Chên. *See* Shou-chou ware.

Shang-yü (Chekiang). Chinese town near sites of numerous Yüeh and other celadon kilns discovered in 20th century. Active under Six Dynasties, T'ang, and Five Dynasties. Fragments of ewers, bowls, basins, and ink-stones found, incised or impressed with e.g. waves, lotus petals, dragons, phoenixes, and other birds.

sharito. *See* Japanese metal-work.

shaving chair. Chair, often *corner or spindle-back type, with shaped head-rest attached to centre of yoke-rail. Forerunner of *barbers' chair; dates from 16th century.

shaving-dish. *See* barber's bowl.

shaving stand or **table.** Small dressing-table, usually on high legs, with hinged lid and drawers beneath. Fitted with folding or hinged mirror, divisions for shaving materials; top contains recesses for basin, soap dish, etc. Popular from *c*1750.

sheaf-back. Chair-back of gracefully splayed rods resembling stylized wheat-sheaf. French, late 18th and early 19th centuries.

Shearer, Thomas (fl *c*1788). English designer and cabinet maker; designs incorporated in The Cabinet-Maker's London Book of Prices, 1788. Washstands and dressing tables with ingenious fittings.

sheep's-head clock. English *lantern clock, where whole circumference of dial extends noticeably beyond frame of clock; made from *c*1650. Term probably corruption of Dutch term.

Sheffield or **fused plate.** Fused sheets of silver and copper; process discovered *c*1742 by T. *Boulsover in Sheffield. Copper ingot and sheet of Sterling Standard silver of same size beaten with hammer; silver surface covered for protection with copper sheet treated with chalk and water (to prevent it sticking to silver); whole bound with iron wire. Fired until silver seen to 'weep', or melt around edges; cleaned, and reduced to sheet, at first by hammering, later by rolling mill. Double plating (copper plated with silver on both sides) perfected in 1760s. Proportion of silver to copper initially very high (1 part to 10), decreased over period of production of Sheffield plate (*c*1750 to *c*1860), to e.g. 1 part to 60.

Plated wire perfected *c*1768: copper wire covered with thin strip of silver and then drawn. Applied silver edging used *c*1775 to cover tell-tale copper at edges of object: U-shaped silver wire soldered to edges. Variety of mounts increased from late 18th century, first by using cast silver mouldings, then stamped ones (e.g. beaded, gadrooned, egg-and-dart).

Sheffield plate made silver available to rising middle class. Makers in Sheffield and Birmingham at first copied older silver styles; rococo style still popular after decline in London. Neo-classical or Adam style soon found to lend itself particularly well to stamping in plated copper. Ornament often stamped and applied, etc. For bright-cut work, extra coating of silver necessary. Piercing done with special tools so that metals are squeezed together and silver coating pulled over copper. For engraved shields, piece cut out of body and replaced by one with thicker silver coating. Rubbed-in shield perfected *c*1810 by S. *Roberts the Younger: pure silver shield-shaped piece with tapering edges applied to body by heating and burnishing until two surfaces fused.

Marked tendency towards elaborate decoration in 19th century. Makers began to lag in production of new styles, due to expense of good dies for stamping. From *c*1845, silver-coloured *argentine used as base for plating (instead of copper), meant that makers no longer had problem of copper showing through.

Numerous household articles made in Sheffield plate; mainly hollow-ware, because problem of covering copper at edge of flatware never successfully solved; also, hard wear tended to erode silver coating. Among most popular items were tea trays, salvers, tea and coffee pots, candlesticks and candelabra, wine coolers, entrée dishes, etc. Certain items made predominantly, in Sheffield plate include cucumber slicer, argyle, pipe-lighter, and toasted-cheese dish. Among the most successful manufacturers were S. *Roberts the Younger of Sheffield, and M. *Boulton of Birmingham. Sheffield plate production much diminished with acceptance of cheaper *electro-plating after Great Exhibition of 1851, and discontinued by 1880.

Sheffield plate generally unmarked. In 1773, Act was passed forbidding striking of marks or letters on silver-plated ware, or on wares made of a silver substitute. In 1784, further Act specified that maker's surname with mark could be stamped on plated ware. Few makers bothered to do this; M. Boulton (mark: two suns) and S. Roberts the Younger (mark: a bell) among few who consistently marked products.

Sheldon Tapestry Works. First English tapestry manufactory, established mid 16th century by William Sheldon at country mansion in Barcheston, Warwickshire. Most important master-weaver, Flemish-trained R. *Hyckes. Tudor designs with strong Flemish influence, wide borders, largely floral backgrounds, or grounds with strapwork and flowers. Subjects include maps, armorial tapestries, biblical scenes. Mainly furniture covers, hangings, and panels. Production continued into 17th century.

Shelley, Samuel (1750–1808). English miniaturist. Self-taught; exhibited at Royal Academy 1773–1808. Miniatures often horizontally elliptical, pale green and greyish in tone. Work also includes watercolour figure subjects, often allegorical, oil paintings, and book illustrations.

shell motif. Ornament in shape of scallop shell, e.g. on silver. Classical motif popular in 16th century; towards 1600 spice-boxes made in shell shape. Common ornamental motif on baroque and rococo hollow-ware (tureens, jugs, épergnes, etc.). Form also used for small dishes, inkstands, sauce-boats, baskets, bowls of punch ladles, and many important early 19th century British *wine labels.

Shêng-erh and **Shêng-i.** *See* Chang family.

Sheraton, Thomas (1751–1806). English furniture designer; possibly never practised as cabinet maker. Published The Cabinet-maker and Upholsterer's Drawing Book, 1791, 1794, and The Cabinet Dictionary, 1803. Designs in neo-classical and Regency styles.

Sheraton style. Furniture style in England *c*1790–*c*1805, and in America *c*1795–*c*1820, based on drawings in T. *Sheraton's major design books. Noted for fine proportion and elegance, Sheraton furniture reflects influence of R. *Adam's neo-classicism (particularly in chair designs, and use of e.g. lyre, plume, ribbon, swag, urn, and vase motifs); also of Louis XVI and Directoire styles (in adoption of forms including *canapé, duchesse,* and *commode,* and use of elaborate inlay and metal mounts). Characteristic ingenuity is apparent in swivel cheval screen, and dual-purpose pieces, e.g. table-bed, chair bed, and harlequin table. Furniture basically rectilinear, with sharp, simple lines and slender appearance, emphasized by fluting, or, more often, reeding, on supports. Tapering legs, and strong perpendicular lines (e.g. on chair backs, with vertical tripartite division) also characteristic. Shield, oval, and round shapes uncommon in Sheraton designs, except for screens. Mahogany and satinwood veneers commonly used, sometimes inlaid with various contrasting hardwoods, or with brass stringing. Also popular were pine and beech furniture, often painted, and decorated with medallions and plaques, in manner of artists e.g. A. *Kauffmann and A. P. *Zucchi. Beech and pine chairs often gilded or painted black, white, or green, with contrasting painted or gilt ornamentation; also *fancy chairs based on these. Brass fitments used; typical Sheraton handles circular.

Tripod foot (with three or four toes) was popular table, screen, and stand base. Common or characteristic furniture of period includes *pedestal sideboard; upholstered or chair-back *settees; tall narrow bookcases (with arching or curved glazing bars on doors); elaborate, refined fire and draught *screens (some lacquered or painted, others filled with worked satin or glass-covered print); and numerous tables (*Pembroke, *sofa, *gaming, *work, *dressing, *drum, and *rent tables; also desks (e.g. *roll-top, *Carlton house, **bonheur du jour,* etc.).

Later Sheraton designs show influence of French Empire style; generally less light and lacking in harmony between line and decoration. *See* Phyfe style *Illustrations also at* backgammon table, *bonheur du jour,* canterbury, cylinder-top desk.

Sherratt, Obadiah (1775–*c*1846). Staffordshire potter, maker of earthenware figures and toys at Burslem from *c*1811. Figures in style of J. *Walton (though usually without *bocage), often large. From 1820s, bases have four or six feet. Work includes bull-baiting groups, Polito's Menagerie and The Death of Munrow. Succeeded by widow and son; business closed in 1850s. No known mark.

shield-back. Late 18th century chair-back, outlined as shield, filled with various open-work designs, e.g. *ribband motif, Prince of Wales plumes, etc.

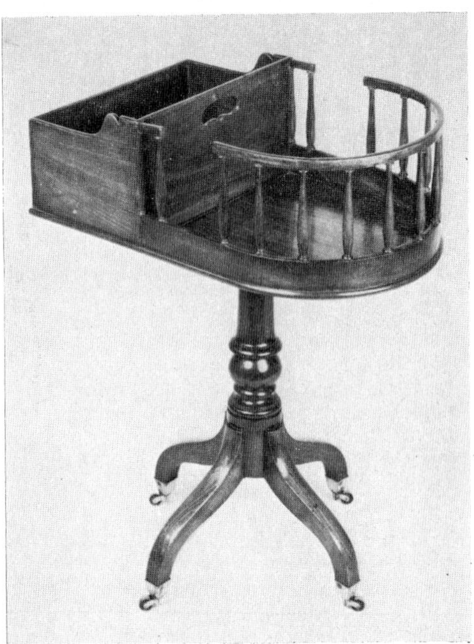

Sheraton style. Cutlery stand combined with plate rack. Mahogany, late 18th century.

*Sheraton. Breakfront *secretary cabinet in West Indian satinwood with original grille doors; scalloped cornice, neo-classical marquetry of urns and oval panel between pendant swags. Height 6ft9in.*

shield-end spoon. *See* wavy-end spoon.

Shield of Achilles. Ornamental silver-gilt shield designed in 1818 by J. *Flaxman, from description in 18th book of Homer's Iliad. Flaxman made plaster mould from which

Obadiah Sherratt. Earthenware figure of Neptune, enamelled in bright colours. Made in Burslem, c*1785.*

Shino. Stoneware bowl painted in underglaze blue. Late 16th century. Diameter 3⅝in.

Shirvan carpet. 19th century. 9ft5in.×3ft9in.

silversmiths worked. Executed mainly by W. *Pitts the Younger, for *Rundell, Bridge & Rundell in 1821; two shields made at this time (master copy for George IV, signed by firm and bearing king's cipher within Garter), and a third in 1823.

shih-tzŭ or **lion.** Chinese ceramic figure found as guardian of Buddhist shrine or temple. Mythological beast, sometimes spouting flames. *cf* dog of Fo.

shingen tsuba. *See* Japanese sword-guards.

shining black ware. *See* 'Jackfield' ware.

Shino wares. Several groups of Japanese pottery made at kiln site in present-day Gifu prefecture (Mino province), near Seto. Best periods, Momoyama and early Edo. Heavy, coarse body, unevenly overlaid with translucent, white feldspathic glaze, tinged red where thinly applied. Decorated in brown with iron oxide, or engraved under glaze. Glaze on painted pieces more transparent and smooth, with light shade of brown oxide. Green oxide decoration sometimes found; colouring added directly to glaze composition for monochrome work, producing bright, sea-green colour, found on *Oribe ware (Ao oribe). Abstract motifs derived from flowers, grasses, plants, or landscapes. In 17th century, European influence shows in designs. Primarily utensils for tea ceremony; elegant shallow dishes with bird-and-grass designs, on finely coloured glaze.

ship's or **Rodney decanter.** English glass. Designed for use onboard ship. Conical shape, straight-sided, with exceptionally wide, heavy base for stability. Body usually plain, with cut neck and base. Named after Admiral Rodney (following victory at battle of St Vincent in 1780). Made late in 18th century.

shirazi. Carpet edges strengthened by overcasting with coloured threads of wool, cotton, goat-hair, and occasionally silk.

Shirvan carpets. South-east Caucasian carpets woven in Shirvan district from 18th century. Low, finely-knotted pile with velvety touch, on white to brown woollen foundation; bottom ends cut and braided. Profusion of colours in geometrical field patterns, including vertical rows of stepped polygons and large star medallions on fine lozenging. Numerous stylized birds and animals as ground fillers. Stylized leaf-and-tendril borders. Until *c*1800, fine prayer rugs with all-over patterns of botehs or stylized flowers infilling mihrab and spandrel, and angular botehs in arch-band and border.

shoe piece (in furniture). Vertical projection attached to back of chair seat; used to secure base of *splat.

Shorthose, John (1768–1828). Potter at Hanley, Staffordshire. Made cream-coloured and blue transfer-printed earthenware, often enamel-painted for export; also three-piece tea-sets in black basalt, with engine-turned and moulded decoration. From *c*1800, made some transfer-printed porcelain. Marks include: SHORTHOSE, SHORTHOSE & HEATH (1795–*c*1815); Shorthose & Co, with two crescents, printed in blue, and S impressed (*c*1817–22).

Shou characters. Chinese archaic calligraphic form, standing for 'longevity'. Often used as decorative motif on porcelain pieces. Sound of shou homonym for peach tree; Ch'ing enamelled ware frequently bears fruiting stem twisted into form of character. Porcelain wine pots sometimes moulded in shape of shou with spout and handle added. Character often combined with fu and lu for Taoist Triad of Happiness, Preferment, and Longevity. Homonyms of e.g. fu, bat, combined with shou, peach in numerous rebuses. Seal characters used for impressing patterns on porcelain. More than 120 variants or geometrical patterning of shou known. *cf* Shou Lao. *Illustration at* double gourd vase.

Shou-chou ware. Chinese celadon manufactured at kiln sites near Huai-nan shih (Ma-chia-kang, Shang yao Chên) in Anhui province, during late T'ang, and early Sung periods; yellow glaze. Identified first from literary source, Tea Classic, by Lu Yü, also from recent excavations. Examples rare.

Shou Lao. Chinese god of longevity: disembodied spirit of Lao Tzŭ, founder of Taoism. Often appears in decoration of porcelain, or as figure. Represented as old man with high protuberant forehead, riding an ox or enthroned on Hills of Longevity. Sometimes accompanied by deer (another symbol of longevity). Found in Ming and Ch'ing periods.

Shou Lao, god of longevity. Holding peach in left hand and scroll in right. Painted in famille rose *enamels, Ch'ien Lung period. Robes decorated with Chinese characters for Shou. Height 11½in.*

shoulder (in furniture). *See* knee.

Shudi, Burkhardt (1702–73). Swiss harpsichord maker, working in London after *c*1718. Like German rival, Jacob Kirckman (arrived *c*1730), produced high quality instruments from *c*1750; many survive. J. *Broadwood was partner and son-in-law. Latest surviving Shudi and Broadwood harpsichord dated 1793.

Shu-fu ware. Chinese porcelain made at *Ching-tê-chên in late Sung, and Yüan periods. Relief decoration under thick, pale blue glaze; base left unglazed. Similar to Ying Ch'ing ware, though heavier; both foreshadow Ming white wares and blue-and-white porcelains. Typically bowls and dishes, incised with the characters shu-fu ('privy council' or 'central palace') sometimes concealed in floral pattern. Term indicates official use.

shuttle. Instrument used in weaving to pass weft thread between warps.

Sicardi, Louis or Luc (1746–1825). French miniaturist. Attached to ministry of Foreign Affairs to paint diplomatic gifts; notable work includes portraits of Louis XVI and Marie Antoinette for mounting on snuff-boxes.

Sicily. Italian maiolica, mainly in styles of Castel Durante, made at *Palermo, also e.g. at *Trapani and *Caltagirone in late 16th and early 17th centuries. Much maiolica also imported from mainland.

sideboard. Originally to hold side table plate, etc. From late 18th century dual-purpose side table and dresser, with drawers and cupboards beneath top for cutlery, wine, and dining equipment; may be solid down to floor, or set on high legs.

*Sideboard. English, mahogany, late 18th or early 19th century, *Hepplewhite design, *serpentine form.*

Siegburg. Salt-glazed stoneware salt cellar in form of lion. 17th century. Height 6¼in.

Siena maiolica. Dish decorated in *istoriato *style with mythological scene.* c*1740.*

sideboard case. Storage case for extra leaves of dining-room table; has hinged side, allowing leaves to be slotted into case along interior guide rails. Dates from 18th century.

sideboard plate or **cupboard plate.** Large, ornate silver or silver-gilt vessels (flagons, vases, rose-water ewers and basins, ginger-jars, beakers, dishes, etc.); intended for display on mantelpiece or sideboard; used in 17th century Britain and Europe. Ornament usually embossed (acanthus motif, ovolo moulding, etc.) or engraved (*chinoiseries*, etc.). *See garniture de cheminée.*

sideboard table. *See* sideboard.

side or **small chair.** Chair with no arms. *See* fancy chair.

side cords. *See* edges.

side table. Decorative, usually rectangular table designed to stand against wall: frieze along back therefore not decorated. May have e.g. hardstone or marquetry top. Most examples 18th century; particularly popular in England and France. *Illustration at* B. Goodison.

Siebenbürger carpets. *See* Transylvanian carpets.

Siegburg, Germany. Important production centre of *Rhineland stoneware, notably *c*1550–90. Vessels usually grey, occasionally almost white; sometimes marked FT. Noted particularly for **Schnellen* by A. *Knütgen.

Siena (Tuscany), Italy. Pottery made from mid 13th century. Maiolica industry, connected with Faenza, well established by 1500; *Maestro Benedetto started workshop in 1503. Products include dishes and drug-pots; also tile pavements of excellent quality.

sign. Wrought-iron device or painted wooden board erected by shopkeeper to declare business to illiterate public; used from Middle Ages. Examples include boot for cobbler, brush for chimney-sweep, tobacco-roll for tobacconist. By 18th century, increased size and weight considered hazard to passers-by, and such signs banned in 1760s. Inn-signs remained; elaborate wrought-iron, occasionally lead, examples still in use.

sign bracket. *See* bracket.

Silbermann, Gottfried (1683–1753). German organ-builder and clavichord-maker working in Freiburg, Saxony. In late 1720s began unsuccessful experiments to develop pianoforte from clavichord. *c*1745, adopted B. *Cristofori's mechanism, and further developed grand piano type.

sileh or **sille carpets.** Caucasian *sumak carpets made *c*1800 in two parts on narrow looms and sewn together. Design of S-shaped figures arranged in squares on blue and red grounds.

Silesian stem. *See* moulded pedestal stem.

silhouette, profile, or **shade.** Portrait in profile, with solid, plain colour replacing facial detail; hair and clothing treated similarly or depicted in varying detail; scope ranges from bust length to equestrian portraits and groups of figures in surroundings of furniture (conversation pieces). Named after Etienne de Silhouette (1709–69), Louis XV's minister of finance, and amateur profile cutter. His austerity measures led to name being used to denote meanness or cheapness; hence applied in derogatory way to profiles. Term probably introduced to English usage in book (1835) by A. *Edouart.

First identified English profile artist was *Joliffe (exhibited 1758). Vogue for profiles as cheap portraits lasted *c*1770–*c*1860, when supplanted by photography. Human profile attributed scientific significance in book by J. C. *Lavater, who, with Goethe, an amateur profilist, devised chair to take subject and paper; other apparatus used, e.g. by S. *Harrington, included *camera obscura* and form of pantograph for reducing size of picture. Techniques include cutting from paper (e.g. S. Harrington, A. Edouart), painting on paper or card (e.g. A. *Charles, F. *Torond), on plaster of Paris composition (e.g. J. *Miers) and on underside of glass (e.g. I. *Beetham, W. *Hamlet, C. *Rosenberg, I. *Thomason); sometimes embellished with bronzing (e.g. E. *Foster, J. *Field). Miniature silhouettes painted on ivory or glass for use in jewellery (rings – particularly mourning rings – and brooches, bracelets, lockets, etc.) or on objects of vertu (card cases, snuff-boxes, etc.), notably by Miers.

In late 18th and early 19th centuries, silhouettes in *verre églomisé* made mainly in Germany and Austria; silhouettes also used to decorate porcelain. Appear on gift and commemorative pieces, e.g. from Bristol, Worcester (George III on his Jubilee, 1809), Nyon, and Sèvres (Mirabeau, Benjamin Franklin). Silhouettes of Frederick the Great on German porcelain from Dresden, Fulda, Gotha, Höchst, and Nymphenburg.

Silla period (57 B.C.–A.D. 736). Korean period, contemporary with Chinese T'ang dynasty; covers Three Kingdoms: Silla (*c*57 B.C.–A.D. 668); Koguryo (*c*37 B.C.–A.D. 668); and Paekche (*c*18 B.C.–A.D. 660). Stoneware produced; some hand-modelled work, with surface marking but mainly ash-grey stoneware with accidental smear glaze. Covered bowls, vases, and stem cups characteristic; also, notably, circular boxes with slightly domed lid; foot often perforated, as if for use as chafing dish over hot charcoal. Later Silla wares bear stamped decoration like T'ang pieces, but with more geometrical character: trefoils, chevrons, circles, etc. Some animal forms found, anticipating later work of Koryo period. Crude olive-brown glazed ware with impressed decoration also ascribed to period.

sille carpets. *See* sileh carpets.

silver. Brilliant white precious metal, resistant to oxidation. Widely distributed throughout world, and known from earliest times, though comparatively scarce. Occurs mainly in native form (as alloy with other metals) usually associated with gold or copper; also in argentiferous ores, e.g. sulphides of lead, copper, zinc. Recovered by various refining processes; earliest was *cupellation. In pure state, second in *malleability and *ductility to gold, and half as dense. Used by ancient civilizations for religious objects, ornament, coinage, and domestic vessels. From late 15th century, much used in Britain and Europe for domestic vessels for display and, traditionally, for coinage. Sometimes gilded to achieve appearance of gold, and prevent tarnishing (e.g. in medieval and Renaissance drinking vessels). From late 17th century, particularly in England, domestic silver became status symbol for rising mercantile class; production increased greatly. Like gold, too soft to be used without *alloying; standards vary in different countries. *See* Britannia standard, Sterling standard.

silver cabinet. Domestic and ceremonial plate of a European royal or aristocratic family.

silver furniture. though occasional items of furniture in silver (e.g. footstools, cradles, etc.) date from before 17th century, more pieces made in reign of Louis XIV (1643–1715). These included tables, chairs, large mirrors, and fire-irons, fire-screens, **guéridons,* and large stands ornamented with mythological figures supporting bowl of fruit, vase, etc. (carried by two or more bearers). Most pieces had wood or iron base covered with sheet silver embossed with foliage, *putti,* floral swags, etc. Charles II brought fashion to England at Restoration (1660), but fashion confined to British and European courts and wealthy nobles. Little survives: most melted down and converted to coinage for economic reasons.

silver-gilt or **vermeil.** Silver covered with thin film of gold. Use widespread in Middle Ages and Renaissance period, especially for church plate; also for 18th and 19th century neo-classical plate made e.g. by J. *Schofield, A. *Fogelberg, and *Rundell, Bridge & Rundell. *See* gilding, parcel gilt.

silvering. Method of decorating glass and occasionally ceramics used as alternative to, or combined with, *gilding. Rare, because of tendency to tarnish. Silver leaf popular in first half of 18th century in Germany and Bohemia in **Zwischengoldglas* technique. Used alone or with gold-leaf, occasionally with green and pink transparent lacquer. In mid 19th century England, thinly blown double-walled vessels, e.g. goblets and vases, popular with silver filling. Exterior wall sometimes coated with colour, cut or engraved to reveal silver background. *Mirrors silvered from 16th century with tin and mercury. Silver leaf applied to surface of furniture on same principle as gold-leaf in gilding, but as less malleable than gold (often three times as thick), must be varnished or lacquered to prevent tarnishing. Sometimes covered with yellow lacquer to resemble gilding. Used mainly from late 17th century in England and Europe.

Silvering. Salts, clear glass bases. English, c1760. Height of tallest 3½in.

Singing-bird box. Swiss, early 19th century, gold and enamel. Length 3½in.

silversmithing. *See* annealing, boss up, burnishing, casting, fire mark, flat hammering, gilding, loading, metal spinning, planishing, raising, stamping, turning up, wire-work.

silver toy. *See* miniature silver.

Simpson, Ralph (fl late 17th century). Staffordshire potter decorating slipware; contemporary of T. *Toft. Frequently used roundel motifs and heads on borders of dishes. Possibly father and son of same name signed work Ralph:Simpson.

Sinah carpets. *See* Sehna carpets.

sinah knot. *See* Persian knot.

Sinceny (Aisne). French faience factory established *c*1733; produced plates painted in blue with borders of foliage. From *c*1737, workmen from Rouen introduced own styles of decoration; later ware distinguishable from Rouen only by tone of red, mark, and greenish tinge of glaze. Enamel colour introduced *c*1775; painting often in style of Strasbourg. Marks include S, reversed S, or Sincheny in blue (1733–75), then à Sinceny̆ in black, or s.c.y̆.

singeries. Pictorial decoration representing monkeys (*singes*) in human situations. Popular rococo motif. *See Affenkapelle. Illustration at* Boulle-work.

singing-bird box. Swiss gold and enamel snuff-box invented in late 18th century by P. *Jacquet-Droz's firm, La Chaux-de-Fonds. When medallion in lid is lifted, enamelled bird stands up, flutters wings, and sings. Motion produced by coiled spring and song by means of bellows forcing air into whistle tube. Produced in quantity by Jacquet-Droz, Frères *Rochat, C.

A. *Bruguier, and J. *Frisard; decline in quality after 1850.

singing-bird watch. Very rare form of *musical watch made in mid 18th century with miniature figure of bird, sometimes with moving wings, etc., appearing through panel in case while music plays.

single-loop pile. *See* weft loop pile.

single-reeded. Category of pewter plates with reeded rim made *c*1690 to late 18th century. *See* reeding.

single-warp knot. *See* Spanish knot.

sinumbra or **French lamp.** Developed *c*1820 from *Argand lamp; brass-stemmed lamp with burner beneath ring-shaped oil reservoir and mushroom-shaped shade.

Sir Hans Sloane's plants. *See* Hans Sloane plates.

Six Dynasties or **Northern and Southern Dynasties** (220–581). General but inaccurate term embracing whole Chinese period between fall of Han dynasty and reunification of China under Sui dynasty. Six Dynasties strictly at Nanking: Wu (220–280), Eastern Chin (317–420), Liu Sung (420–479), Southern Ch'i (479–502), Liang (502–557), Ch'en (557–581). Other contemporary kingdoms of importance: Northern Wei (386–535) and Northern Ch'i (550–557). Probably as result of fall of highly organized Han régime and following insecurity of period, Confucianism declined and Buddhism became firmly established, with profound effect on arts. Most important are cane sculptures at Yün-kang in Shansi and Lung-Mên in Honan. *Illustration at* *mingèch'i.*

skeleton clock. First widely made in France from *c*1750, later popular in England after 1851. Wheels of movement pivoted not in solid plate but in open framework, usually of brass, mounted on base of wood, marble, etc., and covered by glass dome. Dial often plain silvered ring fixed to front frame. Mid 19th century examples often show neo-Gothic influence, some with elaborate frame in shape of cathedral, etc.

skewer. Pin for holding meat together during cooking and for serving. Silver skewers in use from early 18th century; made in sets containing various lengths (6–15in.). Earliest had loop terminal for easy removal; shell terminal introduced in 1730s and became fashionable *c*1760. After 1770, terminal sometimes decorated to match pattern on flatware.

skillet. Bronze three or four footed cooking-vessel; until late 16th century, often in form of cauldron with handle (sometimes called posnet). In 17th century, shallower, with sloping sides. Handles decorated with names, dates, mottos. 17th century British silver examples generally with plain cylindrical bowl, rounded at base, and long straight handle of turned wood or *tankard handle. *See* saucepan.

skimmer. Long-handled, shallow, pierced ladle used for skimming cream or fat in 18th and 19th centuries. Made of brass, handle usually iron.

Skeleton clock. English, mid 19th century, made by James Condliffe of Liverpool. Circular silvered dial, quarter-chiming; verde antico *base. Height 2ft1in.*

*Skillets. English, probably of *bell-metal, inscribed along handles, C U B Loyal to his Magisty, and Pity the Poor, 1684. Length from tip of handles across diameter of bowl, 18¼in.*

skippet box. Engraved oval box, generally of silver, for carrying seal, used in Britain from 17th century. Slit at both ends for seal tassels.

skirting board. *See* apron.

skirt foot. Wide foot-ring, usually concave in profile, extending well beyond sides of body of vessel. Found on mid 17th century silver tankards.

skull watch. 17th century Swiss, French, or German *form watch, lower jaw of skull-shaped case opens to remove dial. Examples found in silver or ivory cases (rarely gold).

slat. Flat, horizontal strip across width of chair-back. *cf* splat.

slat-back. *See* ladder-back.

Sleath, Gabriel (fl first half of 18th century).

Skippet boxes. Pair, made in London c*1740. Seal is of a medieval Chancellor of Oxford University; two lids engraved with arms of Oxford University within rococo cartouche. Length 3in.*

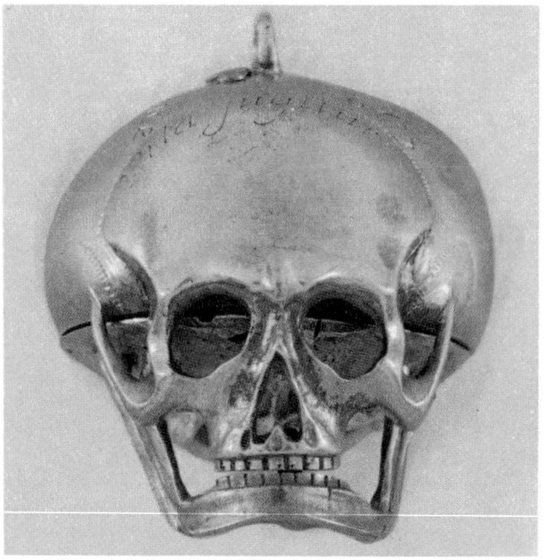

Skull watch with movement made by J. C. Wolf of Germany c*1620. Silver case.*

English silversmith working in London; granted freedom in 1701. Prolific maker of domestic silver in various styles. Mark registered 1706–07, SL; in 1739, GS in script. Francis Crump the Elder, apprenticed to him in 1726, became partner in 1753; mark: GS with F above and C below. *Illustration at* teapot.

sleigh bed. Bed, similar to French Empire *lit en bateau* or *boat bed, made in America in mid 19th century.

sliced fruit painter. *See* cut fruit painter.

slider. *See* coaster.

slide screen or **sliding fire screen.** Square or rectangular screen mounted on trestle feet; has overlapping panels which, extended, double or treble screen size. Dates from 18th century.

slip. Clay mixed with water to a creamy consistency.

slip-casting. Method of ceramic figure making. Slip poured into hollow plaster of Paris moulds. Plaster absorbs water, building up layer of clay on mould walls. Excess slip poured out; clay removed from mould when firm.

slipped-in-the-stalk spoon. *See* slip-top spoon.

slipper box stool. American stool incorporating storage box for slippers and shoes. Stool seat upholstered and hinged, opening to give access to storage area. Made from *c*1830 to end of century.

slipper chair. American side chair with short legs, low seat, and long back; possibly used while putting on footwear. Dates from 18th century.

slip-top, slipped-top or **slipped-in-the-stalk spoon.** Silver, brass, or pewter spoon with narrow hexagonal stem, and tip cut away leaving bevelled or sloped-off end. Made in late 15th and 16th century Britain and Europe.

slipware. Pottery decorated with slip. Use of slip decoration probably originated in Far East. Fragments of red slip-coated pottery thought to date from *c*3000 B.C. excavated in southern Japan. In Europe, Cretan pottery decorated with brush patterns and white slip *c*2000 B.C.; and *c*500 B.C., Greeks used iron-rich slip to make shining black designs on unglazed clay surfaces. Han dynasty Chinese developed *combed slip decoration, not seen in Britain until 18th century. Tang and Sung decoration included brush patterns incised through washes of white slip, and combed or marbled effects with coloured slips. Early 15th century Chinese made bowls of highly translucent porcelain with hidden design incised in semi-opaque white slip. In 17th century, relief floral sprays made by superimposing layers of white slip on bottles made in dull-coloured clay. In 16th century, **sgraffiato* dishes of red clay coated with white slip made at Florence and Faenza. Technique developed in France, Austria, and Germany, and by 18th century, Rumania, Poland, Portugal, and Scandinavia. Before Spanish conquest, brushed slip-decorated pottery made in Mexico and Peru. European settlers established production of slipware in America. Examples include Pennsylvania-Dutch slipware, both for domestic use, with flat decoration, and ornamental, with raised lines of decoration. In 17th century England, centres near London (*Wrotham, and *Metropolitan slipwares *c*1630–70), and in Staffordshire (*see* Staffordshire slipware), where work of *Toft family and R. *Simpson notable. Also, Buckinghamshire, Derbyshire, Yorkshire, the West Country, and Wales. New techniques of slip decoration introduced in reign of George I include combing and use of press-moulds incised with lines of decoration to produce ornamental dishes more efficiently. In 19th century England, slip decoration often applied by funnels with several spouts, each trailing stream of coloured slip on surface of vessel being turned on lathe. Bands of slip sometimes further decorated with brown feathery shapes in *mocha ware. Combed slip decoration found on jugs, mugs, and dishes from Staffordshire, Yorkshire and north-east England.

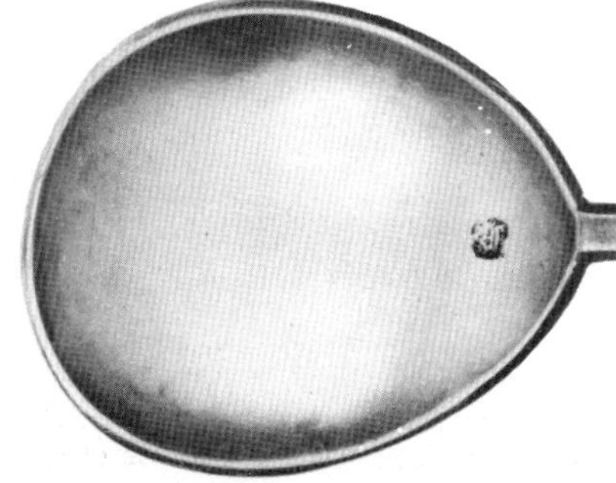

Slip-top spoon. Charles I, 1636. Length 7in.

Sloane, Sir Hans. *See* Hans Sloane plates.

Slodtz, Antoine-Sébastien (*c*1695–1754). French designer, eldest of five brothers who created designs for theatre and court of Louis XV. Appointed *Dessinateur de la Chambre* to Louis XV; succeeded by brother, Paul-Ambroise (1702–58).

Slodtz, Réné-Michel *dit* Michel-Ange (1705–64). French sculptor and designer. Employed by Louis XV; succeeded P-A. *Slodtz as *Dessinateur de la Chambre.* Produced sculpture for Mme de Pompadour.

slop basin. Bowl of silver or porcelain used to hold slops (tea rinsings); part of *tea service. Probably in use from early 18th century in Britain. *Illustration at guilloche.*

small chair. *See* side chair.

small-tall clock. *See* dwarf-tall clock.

Smart, John (1741–1811). English miniaturist. Exhibited at Royal Academy from 1784. Miniatures usually with plain coloured backgrounds. In India in 1780s and 1790s. Son John, also miniaturist, settled there (d 1809).

smear glaze (in ceramics). Slight glazing which occurs in firing when glaze material present on surfaces round objects being fired. Often unintentional, but sometimes used on parian ware. *Illustration at* W. Ridgway.

Smith, Benjamin the Elder (d 1823). English silversmith working in Birmingham and London. In early years, worked for M. *Boulton. Came to London in 1802 worked with Digby Scott for P. *Rundell; left in 1814, but continued to fill commissions for Rundell's and other retailers. In 1816 in partnership with son, Benjamin the Younger, who continued business after father's death. Mark with Scott in 1802: DS above BS; in 1807 registered own mark, BS, and in 1816 joint mark with son, BS above BS.

Smith, Benjamin the Younger (1793–1850). English silversmith working in London; apprenticed to father (1808); granted freedom (1821); took over father's business (1822). Son, Apsley, married daughter of G. R. *Elkington; supplied Elkington with models for electro-plating during 1840s. In 1840, placed in charge of Elkington's plating workshop in Moorgate, London; unsuccessful; relieved in 1849. Continued to work as silversmith, throughout this period, in organic naturalistic style favoured by contemporary intellectuals. Exhibition pieces include flower-shaped drinking cups, and dessert plates electrotyped from vine-leaves. Son, Stephen, succeeded to business.

Smith, George (fl *c*1805–30). Cabinet maker in London; Regency designer using Gothic and Chinese motifs. Received commissions from George IV. Influential published works include A Collection of Designs for Household Furniture and Interior Decoration in the most Approved and Elegant Taste (1808); A Collection of Ornamental Designs after the Manner of the Antique (1812); and The Cabinet-Maker's and Upholsterer's Guide, Drawing Book and Repository of New and Original Designs for Household Furniture (1826). *Illustration at* Regency style.

Smith, Sampson (1813–78). Potter at Longton, Staffordshire. Decorator of pottery from 1846. From 1851, made figures in white earthenware and porcelain, decorated in bright colours, often large, including dogs, cottages, Toby jugs, and topical figures. Work sometimes marked SS (1846–60) or SS Ltd (from 1860). Factory still operates.

Smith's blue. *See* Derby blue.

smoke-jack. *See* spit.

Sampson Smith. Flatback, made at Longton, c1850.

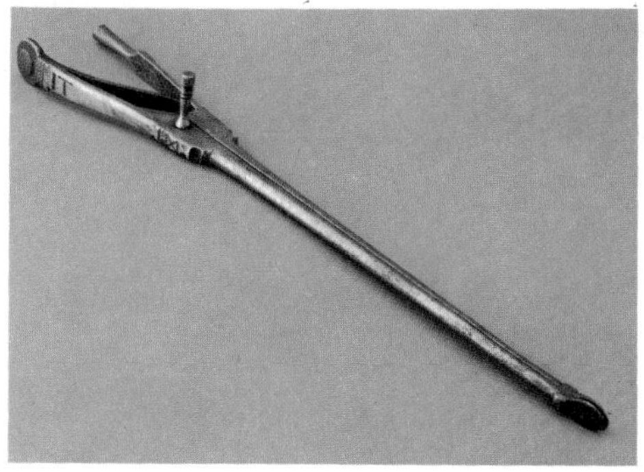

*Smoker's tongs. Peg at top of handles is *pipe-stopper. Steel, c1680. Length 18in.*

Snap top table. American, from the south, c1740–60. Cherry wood. Height 28½in.

smokers' bow. Variation on *low-back Windsor chair, made from *c*1825 in England. Has continuous yoke-rail and arms, with central back section higher than arms, or crested. May have saddle seat.

smoker's tongs, pipe-tongs, or **ember-tongs.** 18th century iron tongs, with sprung handle, for lifting glowing embers from hearth or brazier to light pipe.

Smyrna carpets. Trade name for thick, heavy west Anatolian carpets with broad distinctive designs, woven for export to Europe and America; distributed through port of Smyrna (Izmir). Exported in great numbers in 18th century.

snailing. Method of decorating flat surfaces in clock and watch movements by producing pattern of shallow eccentric curves.

snake-skin green. Chinese glaze colour derived from copper. Invention attributed to *Ts'ang Ying-Hsüan. Medium-fired glaze with low iron content; has iridescent sheen. Normally used without further decoration.

snap, tilt-top, or **tip-top table.** Pedestal table, usually on tripod base; top hinged to base (often with *birdcage fitting), tilts vertically when not in use, allowing table to be stored against wall. Of medieval origin, popular in 18th century. Tilt-top American term.

snarling iron. Long, shaped piece of iron with up-turned, domed end inserted in hollow-ware for embossing or *repoussé* work; when tapped with hammer produces boss.

snowman figures. Group of *c*40 primitive English porcelain figures covered with thick glaze full of minute bubbles. Produced by W. *Littler or associate *c*1750 at Longton Hall. Simple mound bases often decorated with applied flowers and leaves. Figures include birds, animals, *commedia dell'arte* characters, and Ceres.

snuff bottle (in Chinese ceramics). Form popular in porcelain from 18th century (tobacco probably imported to East by Spanish or Portuguese in 17th century). Small bottles, originally used for drugs or aromatics, then also for snuff. Favoured shape echoes prevalent taste of late Ch'ing period for elaborate miniature work: human figures, butterflies, fruit, etc. carved, relief-modelled, enamel painted, gilded. Fine examples bear mark of Chia Ch'ing or Tao Kuang. Opaque glass examples from same period also noteworthy.

snuff-box or **tabatière.** Tobacco introduced to Europe in 16th century. Habit of taking snuff (powdered tobacco for inhaling) by both sexes began in 17th century France, and reached peak in 18th century. First devotees used personal *snuff rasp rather than commercially rasped snuff. Louis XIV disliked habit and courtiers used *boîtes à portrait* as secret snuff containers. Use of snuff-boxes spread to England and other European countries. No 17th century boxes survive, though existence known from literary sources. Because tightly-closing box necessary to contain snuff-powder, hinged lids most common; stand-away hinge superseded by integral hinge after 1730. Boxes became prized gifts, often used for other purposes. By 1830 snuff-taking no longer fashionable; consequent decline in production. *See* American, Austrian, English, French, German, Russian, Swedish, and Swiss snuff-boxes, Iserlohn box, tobacco-box, Scottish snuff-mull.

snuffers. Silver implement for trimming candle-wicks, in use from 16th century. Earliest surviving example, dated 1512, in scissor form with blades terminating in two small boxes

Snuffers and stand. Made in 1703 in London by Andrew Raven. Coat of arms of Raymond family on stand and snuffers.

*Snuff bottles. Chinese. Left: *Canton enamel bottle, with blue Ch'ien mark, painted with European scene, 18th century, gilt metal stopper. Centre: brown and yellow amber bottle, early 19th century, carved as recumbent stag with vase on back; height 1⅞in. Right: coral bottle, early 19th century, carved in relief with Ho Hsien-Ku; height 3¼in.*

Snuff rasp. Carved ivory, reverse with steel grater and snuff compartment. French, made in Dieppe, c1690–1700. Length 7¾in.

Soap box. Part of set with ewer and basin. By François Riel, made in Paris; 1771.

which formed heart shape when closed and served to retain bits of charred wick; when not in use rested on matching tray. In early 17th century also made with only one box (semi-circular) attached to lower blade. From late 17th century, some made to fit into socket on upright stand similar to base of candlestick. From mid 18th century more often made in Sheffield plate, cast brass, cut steel, pewter, or iron (sometimes japanned). Many with three short legs. Use declined in mid 19th century with more efficient candle-wicks and adoption of oil and gas lighting.

snuff or **tobacco rasp.** Metal grater used from mid 17th century by snuff-takers. Early examples, iron, in plain wooden frame; later steel, sometimes brass or silver, with more decorative frames and covers of ivory, wood, or silver. Some with container for ground snuff. Smaller sizes (*c*3in. long with leather or embroidered cloth cover) for carrying in pocket; large, plainer types (7–12 in.) in wooden frames, sometimes painted, for use in tobacco shops. By mid 18th century, snuff generally sold ready-ground; individual rasps no longer required.

snuff spoon. Silver spoon (2in. long) with shallow oval or shovel-shaped bowl, used to carry powder from snuff-box to nose; used from 17th century in Europe. Not hallmarked because too light.

soap box. 18th century silver soap container with spherical body and round, moulded foot. Similar box with pierced cover thought to hold sponge. *See* toilet service.

soapstone or **soap-rock porcelain.** English soft-paste porcelain using *soapstone as fusible ingredient. Introduced at B. *Lund's Bristol factory, *c*1748; then characteristic of Worcester until *c*1823. Also made at *Liverpool (from *c*1755), Derby (*c*1765–*c*1770) and Caughley (from 1772).

soapstone, soap-rock, or **steatite.** Massive form of talc (magnesium silicate) used, ground, in *soapstone porcelain. Also added to soft-paste porcelain made at *Cambrian Pottery Works from *c*1815. Stone used for carving, notably in China.

sociable. *See confidante.*

social table. Table, usually horse-shoe shaped, kidney-shaped, or semi-circular, often with brass rail along concave side. Has frame to hold decanters and bottles, attached centrally on concave side of table, and swinging horizontally from one side of table to other. Dates from 18th century.

socle or **zocle.** Simple block base for case furniture or pedestal.

soda-glass. Glass in which sodium carbonate used as a flux. Produced in Mediterranean region until development of *soda-lime glass. Soda obtained from salt-water vegetation, *barilla. Glass cooled more quickly than potash or lead-glass, and had to be blown thinly to avoid brown, yellow, or grey tinge. Fragile, lacks resonance. *See cristallo.*

soda-lime or **lime-soda glass.** Glass using lime and soda as alkalis; Venetian glassmakers obtained both from **barilla. Cristallo* is soda-lime glass decolourized with manganese.

sofa. Originated in East, as raised section of floor or long bench, carpeted and cushioned (Arabic, suffah). In 18th century France, wide, upholstered armchair, like **canapé*, but with curved back continuing into rounded arms. In Britain and America, informal, upholstered *settee; rare before *c*1750.

sofa bed. Sofa which converts into canopy bed; bedstead folds into seat area of sofa when not in use. Popular during 18th and beginning of 19th centuries.

sofa table. Late 18th, early 19th century

Sofa table. English, Regency period. Rosewood with gilding and brass inlay; *X-frame supports mounted with ebonized lion masks; and with paw feet.

development of *Pembroke table; designed to be used by ladies seated on sofa. Usually rectangular, sometimes with two frieze drawers and hinged leaves at each end; pedestal base or supports at either end. Might have sliding panel in top revealing gaming board, or mechanism for inclining section of top to give reading or writing surface.

soft-paste or **artificial porcelain.** Imitation of *hard-paste porcelain produced with mixture of white clay and fusible substance, e.g. *frit or soapstone; firing takes place at *c*1200°C, with narrow margin for error. Few examples of Chinese hard-paste porcelain to reach medieval Europe admired for translucency. Many attempts to imitate it using glass opacified with tin oxide, but this lacked comparable handling properties. Hence experiments with mixture of clay and glass (as frit), e.g. by Venetian glass manufacturers in late 15th century. *Medici porcelain made in Florence *c*1575. Earliest French porcelain possibly made by L. *Poterat at Rouen *c*1673; production in quantity at Saint-Cloud before 1700. In England, patent granted to T. *Frye (1744) for manufacture of porcelain at Bow, but first known examples are *goat-and-bee jugs made at Chelsea in 1745; *soapstone porcelain made from *c*1748 in Bristol. Usually glazed with modified lead-glaze, sometimes whitened with tin oxide, in second firing at lower temperature.

In 18th century Chinese ceramics, paste with some of the kaolin in usual recipe for hard-paste porcelain replaced by hua shih (probably steatite or pegmatite) fired at lower temperature. Fine-grained, opaque, light in weight and harder than European soft-paste; has fine crackle. Use confined to small objects, e.g. snuff bottles, bowls, brush-holders, often painted in blue (very rarely with any enamel decoration). Alternatively, sometimes used as slip to cover hard-paste porcelain bodies; such items also termed 'soft porcelain'.

Soho Manufactory. *See* Boulton, Matthew.

Soho Tapestry Works. Most productive 18th century English tapestry manufactory, established *c*1691 by master-weaver J. *Vanderbank. After 1727, directed by master-weaver Paul Saunders (d 1772). Numerous tapestries woven for private clients. Subjects include allegorical scenes, landscapes with softly designed trees, classical buildings, ruins and waterfalls; also 'Eastern' tapestries (e.g. Pilgrimage to Mecca) and *arabesque tapestries, influenced by work of J. *Berain.

solder. Fusible alloy used to join edges of metals with higher melting point. For silver, modern solder is alloy of silver and zinc; previously silver and brass used, requiring greater heat (charcoal flame). Colour of solder may be helpful in detection of forgeries. Spout, handle sockets, feet, foot-ring, mouth wire, etc., soldered to body of vessel.

solid agate ware. English ceramics. Pottery variegated throughout body, made by wedging together and moulding differently coloured clays to produce marbled effect. In Chinese ceramics, technique dates from T'ang period, when contrasting clays covered with clear glaze. Known in 1st century Roman Britain. Reintroduced in Staffordshire, *c*1730; manufacture

Soho Tapestry Works. Tapestry in chinoiserie *style of J. *Vanderbank. Early 18th century.*

declined in early 1790s and ceased *c*1820. Solid agate earthenware combining white with brown (manganese), green (copper), or blue (cobalt), moulded e.g. into teapots, mugs, knife handles, scent bottles, and figures, notably cats. J. *Wedgwood produced vases closely resembling natural stone. Other makers include T. *Whieldon, Leeds Pottery, *Fishley family. Salt-glaze agate ware rarely used for vessels; figures, e.g. cats and rabbits, date from *c*1740.

solid casting. *See* lost-wax process, sand-casting.

Solis, Virgil (1514–62). German silversmith working in Nuremberg. Designs, published 1541, popularized gourd cup and nesting beakers.

Solon, Marc-Louis or **Miles** (1835–1913). French porcelain decorator, from *c*1859 among artists who helped perfect technique of **pâte-sur-pâte* decoration. Worked in Paris and (from 1870) at Minton factory. Author of books on English pottery and porcelain; also published account of *pâte-sur-pâte* technique.

Sondag, Rudolph (1726–1812). Dutch silversmith working in Rotterdam; master in 1746. Made mainly domestic silver in mixed French rococo and neo-classical styles. Also made plaquettes with religious scenes in relief, and funeral shields for guilds. Mark: a sun.

Soqui, Saqui, or **Lequoi** (fl late 18th century). Painter of English porcelain; said to have worked at Sèvres. Painted exotic birds in strong colours with thick stippling against pale landscape with faint trees; sometimes landscapes

Simeon Soumaine. Lidded tankard, made in New York 1720–30. Decorated with rib of beading along handle. Height 6¾in.

alone. Work includes vase and coffee cups painted *en camaïeu* in blue and red, with mark of Plymouth, large hexagonal vases, painted on white ground at Bristol, and many pieces with characteristic bird painting at Worcester, *c*1770–75.

Sorgenthal porcelain. *See* von Sorgenthal, Konrad.

soufflé dish. Silver or Sheffield plate vessel for making and serving soufflé; in two parts: inner liner goes in oven, decorative outer container with two handles and three or four feet, is placed on table. Made from *c*1820 in Britain.

Soumain, Simeon (1685–1750). London-born goldsmith working in New York. Surviving

Left:
*South Jersey glass. Possibly from glassworks of C. *Wistar. Centre: covered sugar bowl of olive-green glass, c1760–80. Right: candlestick of aquamarine glass, c1760–80. Height 6½in.*

Right:
*Spanish glass. Left: cruet, Catalan, late 16th century; straw-tint glass with white opaque combed bands; height 6in. Centre: wine jug, mid 18th century; blue-green glass, strap handle, body decorated with ribbing and spiral trail around rim; height 5⅜in. Right: covered jar, 18th century, from La *Granja de San Ildefonso. Engraved and gilded with flower sprays. Height 13in.*

work includes domestic silver tankards, coffee and tea pots, beakers, casters, etc. Mark: SS in a square.

soumak carpets. *See* sumak carpets.

southern Kuan ware. Chinese celadon ware of Sung period; originally manufactured in northern provinces, but transferred to Chekiang (after 1127) when court fled from Chin Tartar invaders. Manufactured first at kilns of *Hsiu-nei-ssu, then *Chiato-t'an. Carefully finished pieces, with *crackle glaze, and dark body. Covered in glaze except on foot-rim and ring of spur-marks. Colours vary from blue-green to grey, or white. Pale yellow colour known as mi se. Distinguished from northern *Kuan ware by high quality of crackled glaze; with red or black pigment rubbed into network of cracks. Delicate shapes include faceted cups, shallow bowls, and incense vases. Copied in porcelain at *Ching-tê-chên in Ming period. *See* brown mouth and iron foot.

South Jersey glass. Various small glasshouses established in southern area of New Jersey in late 18th century by ex-employees of C. *Wistar. Much tableware produced, including coloured glass. Also off-hand pieces free-blown from bottle or window glass for use of blowers. Ornament decoration includes lily-pads, prunts, neck threading, and crimping of feet and handles. Style first associated with *Wistarburg Glass Works. *cf* whimsey.

South Staffordshire enamels. Chief centres of production at *Bilston and *Wednesbury. Prolific production of boxes, plaques, candlesticks, tea canisters and caddies, mustard pots, salt cellars, trays, *étuis,* scent bottles, etc. Difficult to date. *c*1760–1800, boxes were oblong, with rounded corners, convex lids, straight or bombé sides, and gilt-metal mounts; painted on lids and sides in turquoise-blue, midnight-blue, green, or rose with reserved transfer-printed scenes from F. *Boucher, Nicolas Lancret, J-A. *Watteau, and the *Ladies' Amusement. Lids also decorated with gilded scroll-work in raised white enamel or box as a whole covered with a raised diaper pattern or crossed lines applied over solid ground colour. Same decorative devices applied to other objects. Quality declined after 1780 because of pressure of mass production: decoration became excessive; enamel, transfer-printing, painting, and gilding all of lower quality. Production virtually ceased after 1800, because foreign markets lost. *Illustration at* enamel.

Southwark delftware. Tin-glazed earthenware made in Southwark, London, from late 16th century; includes dishes, barrel-shaped jugs, posset cups, and wine bottles. In early 17th century, blue decoration imitated Wan-Li porcelain. Later ware hard to distinguish from Lambeth. Potters from Southwark established factory near Bristol in mid 17th century.

souvenir box. Small enamel box painted with local view, and sometimes inscription, e.g. 'A trifle from . . .'. Produced in late 18th century *Birmingham and *South Staffordshire.

souvenir watch. Viennese, *c*1780; typical form has small dial connected by thin metal tube to circular base housing movement; designed to be worn as pendant, normally without extensive decoration, but occasionally including elaborate *automaton figures and *repeating mechanism.

soy frame. Silver or Sheffield plate stand similar to *cruet frame with rings to hold glass bottles (usually with silver or Sheffield plate mounts) for soy and other sauces (East India Company imported soy sauce to Britain from *c*1725); central loop handle on vertical rod. Shapes varied; late 18th century examples pierced.

spandrel. Space between arch or circle and rectangle or square, e.g., on prayer rugs, area of central field above *mihrab. On clock dial, ornamental corner-piece, often gilded: earliest pattern on English clocks, *c*1670, cherub's head and wings. Then more elaborate, with scroll-work, foliage, crowns, and sceptres, etc. (*c*1720). By late 18th century, debased rococo patterns. Usually cast in brass, quality of finish declines with development; supplied to clock makers by specialist founders.

Spanish carpets. *See* Alcaraz, Cuenca, and Madrid carpets, Alpujarra rugs.

Spanish ceramics. *Hispano-Moresque ware made under Arab rule, notably at *Malaga. In 15th century, Valencia became pottery centre, with *Paterna and *Manises. Lustre decoration used; Moorish motifs gradually replaced by heraldic and floral designs. Tiles and pottery made at Seville in 16th century, and later at *Talavera; also *Toledo and *Puente del Arzobispo. At *Alcora, in 18th century, new styles developed in decoration of tin-glazed ware. Porcelain made at *Buen Retiro, after transfer of manufacture from *Capodimonte (Naples), by Charles III.

Spanish foot. Form of *club foot, ribbed, with enlarged base and folded foot. *Illustration at* low-boy.

Spanish glass. Glass making began before Roman occupation, but most fine and domestic glassware imported. In 11th and 12th centuries, Spain produced mainly window glass. 15th century Islamic glass makers in Almeria, Valencia, and Barcelona produced vessels with trails, trellis-work, and multiple handles. Venetian influence predominated in 16th century. Barcelona noted for green and white glass with enamelling and cold gilding, and Catalonia for *latticinio* glass. Indigenous forms of Spanish glassware, e.g. **almorrata*, **cántaro*, and **porrón*, widely produced in 17th and 18th centuries. Wheel engraving and oil gilding introduced in early 18th century by immigrant workers at royal factory of La *Granja de San Ildefonso, founded 1728; made window glass, mirrors, and chandeliers. Factory dominated Spanish glass industry until early 19th century. *Illustration at porrón.*

Spanish gold and silver. Centres of production at various periods included Barcelona, Valencia, Madrid, Saragossa and León. More plate survives in Spain, from so-called 'golden age' (15th to 17th centuries), than in any other European country, though restrictions on possession and use of silverware (1601), and wars, particularly Napoleonic campaigns, took heavy toll. Most surviving pieces ecclesiastical, either commissioned by clergy, or gifts from wealthy patrons. Objects include chalices and patens, altar cruets, ciboria, pyxes, reliquaries, monstrances, censers, candlesticks. Probably most important item of Spanish ecclesiastical plate was **custodia*; much older silver objects melted down to produce them. Decoration, usually extremely lavish, in Gothic, Renaissance, and mannerist styles. Surviving secular plate of period includes rose-water ewers and basins, salts, and caskets. 18th century secular plate shows mainly French influence, e.g. inkstands, dishes, cruet frames. Spanish royalty and nobility commissioned plate from foreign silversmiths as well as native craftsmen, but most was converted to coin during 19th century.

Goldsmiths and silversmiths were organized into guilds from Middle Ages. Marks on silver and gold: goldsmith's mark (name in full or abbreviated), assayer's mark, and town mark (abbreviated, e.g. BAR for Barcelona, town arms, or symbol of city, e.g. patron saint).

*Spanish silver. Silver-gilt *ciborium c1530; container in late Gothic style with lobed decoration; baluster stem in early Renaissance style. Crucifix, 17th century.*

Spanish knot or **single-warp knot.** Carpet pile knot, used only on Spanish carpets. Yarn wrapped around alternate single-warp threads; four or five thick weft threads between rows of knots; all knots cut at same time. Technique produces zig-zag textured pile, making use of straight lines in designs very difficult. Used exclusively on earliest carpets, later mixed with *Persian and *Turkish knots; finally almost completely replaced by latter.

Spanish tapestry. From 14th century, massive import of Flemish tapestries brought influx of Flemish weavers for their maintenance. In 1579 Anne of Austria appointed Pedro Guttierrez royal *tapissier*; in 1581 he established workshop in Madrid. In 1623, small Flemish colony of weavers established (under François Tons) at Pastrana, Guadalajara. First large tapestry manufactory, *Santa Barbara, established by Philip V in Madrid in 1720.

Spanish trencher. Narrow-rimmed pewter *trencher made in England from mid 16th to late 17th centuries in imitation of Spanish type.

sparrow-beaked jug. *See* bird-beaked jug.

spatter ware. *See* sponged ware.

speculum. Alloy of tin, copper, and other elements which, when polished, gives high, silvery shine; used for mirrors for centuries until method of *silvering glass became general in 17th century.

spelter. Zinc, often alloyed with lead. Much used in 19th century for cheap, decorative cast articles, e.g. candlesticks, clock cases.

spherical watch. Probably oldest watch shape; about six very early surviving examples include German piece, *c*1550 and earliest dated French watch, 1551. Typical movement of brass plates and iron wheels, going and striking trains with springs and *fusees. Ormolu case with dial opposite pendant. Designed for portability, but superseded by drum shape. Some cases engraved with map of world; probably made as centres of *armillary spheres and later adapted for personal use.

*Spice box. English, silver gilt, 1598; maker's mark, triangle intersected with a line. Scallop shell form and scallop feet, sides banded with *strapwork ornament. Height 4in.*

spice box. Small silver box with hinged cover to hold sweetmeats, spices, sugar, etc. In use from 16th century. Usually refers to 16th and 17th century silver box shaped like scallop shell with interior divided into compartments. Convex cover embossed like shell hinged and closed with hinged hasp. In early 18th century spice (or sugar) boxes in form of oval caskets.

spice dredger. *See* kitchen pepper.

spigot. Peg or pin turning through right angle controlling flow of liquid through tap. Silver spigots fitted to tea and coffee urns, wine fountains, etc. From late 18th century, detachable version for small kegs of ale or beer made in Britain.

Spiller, Gottfried (1663–after 1721). German glass engraver; pupil of M. *Winter. Worked independently, often using *Potsdam glasses as subjects for *Tiefschnitt* designs; subjects include naturalistic scenes and human figures. F. *Gondelach was pupil.

spindle (in furniture). Slim turned member, at times resembling spindle; much used in chair backs. May be of constant width or with tapering ends.

spinet. *See* harpsichord family.

Spinner, David (1758–1811). Potter in Bucks County, Pennsylvania. Made earthenware dishes decorated with slip trickled through quill. Worked in Pennsylvania-Dutch style; some dishes in pairs with e.g. hunting theme; many commemorative signed examples exist.

spinning. *See* metal spinning.

spirit-measure. *See* measure.

spit. Metal rod which pierced joint of meat; rotated before open fire by human, animal, or mechanical means. Until 16th century, boys (turnspits) used for this purpose, spit resting on *spit-dog; alternatively, trained dogs worked treadmill attached to wall, and system of chains or ropes turned spit. By 16th century, *spit-jack in use. Smoke-jack, worked by rising hot air, used, though not widely, *c*1690–*c*1750. Clockwork *bottle-jack, introduced 1760s, improved in 1790s and widely used. *Hastener also much used.

spit-dogs. Similar to *andirons, but also used to support spit with hooks; made in pairs; used in kitchens from Middle Ages to 16th century. Front stems terminate in cup shape, to hold container of basting liquid, or in flatter shape for warming plates. Discontinued when boy turnspits replaced by mechanical devices in 16th century.

spit-jack. Mechanical brass or iron device, worked by stone or iron weights, later clockwork, for turning *spit. Introduced late 15th century; used in various forms until late 18th century.

spittoon or **cuspidor.** Pottery or metal receptacle into which smokers could spit tobacco juice. Pan may be open and decorated, concealed, or disguised, e.g., in covered frame resembling footstool. Used mainly in 19th century. 'Cuspidor' American term.

splat or **splad.** In chair back, central flat support between seat-back and yoke-rail. Often decoratively shaped, carved, or pierced.

splint seat. American chair seat composed of long thin lengths of wood, e.g. oak or hickory, woven together. Dates from 17th century.

split-end spoon. *See* trefid spoon.

split turning. Any turned shape, split lengthwise, and applied as decoration to surface of piece of furniture, usually vertically on front of case piece. Common on late 16th and 17th century furniture; revived in 19th century. *Illustration at* Connecticut chest.

Spode, Josiah, I (1733–97). Staffordshire potter. In 1749, apprenticed to T. *Whieldon. Succeeded J. *Turner as manager of stoneware firm in Stoke-on-Trent in 1762. Made cane-coloured stoneware, including teapots with relief decoration of figures framed with cartouches picked out in green and blue enamel; finial in form of reclining woman. Engine-turned teapots in red, black, and cane-coloured stoneware. Pearlware transfer-printed in blue, covered with transparent glaze, made from *c*1782. Marks: Spode, impressed from 1770, printed in blue from 1784.

Josiah Spode II. Left: porcelain trio (saucer with coffee and tea cup), c1800, pattern 287, based on Japanese Imari pattern. Right: earthenware plate, c1820, transfer-printed with blue-and-white Girl at Well pattern.

Spode, Josiah, II (1754–1827). Staffordshire potter, son of J. *Spode I; managed factory from father's death. Continued production of blue transfer-printed ware. Designs include Italian patterns (from *c*1800), Indian sporting series (from *c*1810), Caramanian series of Middle Eastern views (by 1809), patterns showing oriental influence (e.g. Willow, India, Two Birds, Hundred Antiques), general designs (e.g. Milkmaid, Woodmen, Waterloo), and outline designs coloured by hand. Also made porcelain using natural feldspar. Credited with discovery of formula which became standard for English bone china, replacing some of china clay with bone ash. In 1805, introduced *stone china, later decorated with *famille rose* and Japan patterns, coats of arms, and designs incorporating birds and flowers, notably peacock and peony pattern (introduced *c*1814). Stone china used for tableware and huge vases with, in 1820s, ormolu pedestals. *Jardinières* and fish tanks often have flower-patterned rims and designs painted on reserves on dark blue ground, sometimes with ormolu mounts. In 1827, succeeded by son, Josiah III (d 1829). In 1833, business passed to W. T. *Copeland and partner T. *Garrett. Marks include Spode, painted in red with design number (*c*1790–*c*1820); Spode, over or across rectangle with Stone China printed in black (*c*1805–*c*1815) or blue (*c*1815–*c*1830); SPODE Felspar Porcelain printed in blue, or in puce with garland of flowers (1815–1827). *Illustration also at* transfer-printing.

sponged ware or **spatter ware.** Inexpensive domestic ceramic ware decorated in bright colours applied with sponge over thick glaze; often tea-sets made in thickly-potted *granite ware. Sponged decoration used either alone or with painting in enamel or occasionally underglaze blue. Made by Staffordshire potters, mainly for export to America in mid 19th century. Seldom marked.

Sponged ware. Plate, exported to America from England, early 19th century.

Spool salt. Octagonal. Charles II, with maker's mark, IS.

sponsen. *See* pounces.

spool, capstan, pulley, or **scroll salt.** Mid 17th century silver or silver-gilt salt container with spool-shaped body and scroll brackets at edge of top for supporting plate or napkin. Last form of *standing salt. *See* Moody Salt.

spool turning. Decorative turning on furniture legs, rails, etc., composed of a row of spool shapes. Popular in England during late 17th century; in America, mid 19th century.

spoon (in clocks). Device for locking rising hood on early *long-case clocks. Trigger inside trunk of case releases hood, which thus cannot be raised without unlocking door of clock.

spoon. Medieval British and European spoons usually of wood or horn; silver and gold examples probably adopted by nobility during 14th and 15th centuries; pewter and latten examples also survive. Early metal spoons had fig-shaped bowl, tapering end attached to

Spoons. Tablespoon, dessert spoon, and teaspoon; handles decorated with bright-cut engraving. Made in London in 1790 by Samuel Howland.

hexagonal stem, and terminal *knop. Bowl and stem made from one piece of metal; knop soldered on. Classified by type of knop: *ball or fir-cone (pineapple) form is earliest, followed by *diamond-point, *acorn knop, *wrythen-knop, *maidenhead, *apostle, and seal spoon, etc. Other types were *stump-end or *slipped-top spoons. Late 16th century pewter spoons sometimes have latten knops; in 17th century, some brass examples were tinned and burnished to resemble silver. By mid 17th century, knops less popular; ends of stems hammered flat and square (e.g. *Puritan spoon), soon becoming rounded (*trefid, *wavy-end with egg-shaped bowl. By late 17th century, bowls were longer and narrower, and stems also longer. Royal portrait spoons have finials cast as heads of William and Mary, later Queen Anne; fashion revived to commemorate marriage of George III in 1761. Accounts of complete evolution of European silver spoon based largely on British examples, as many survive. However, many British styles derived from continent, particularly France, e.g. *trefid and *wavy-end spoons. Flat stem and back of bowl in late 17th century spoons ornamented with foliate scrollwork in low relief. From late 17th century, junction of bowl and stem strengthened by addition of reinforcement in various shapes (e.g. *rat-tail); bowl became narrower and oval. 18th and 19th century spoons classified by stem pattern: *Hanoverian, *fiddle-head, *King's, *Old English, *Onslow, etc. From mid 19th century, many spoons electro-plated. Spoon handles in porcelain made e.g. at Meissen in 18th century.

spoon-back. Chair back with splat shaped to curves of human back. Common on Queen Anne chairs.

spoon rack. Wall rack for storing spoons, composed of back board with narrow shelf attached. Shelf pierced, and spoons slip, handle downwards, into holes. Sometimes has tiered shelves. Examples exist from first half of 17th century, but probably made earlier.

Spout cup. Beaker-shaped body with swan neck, tubular mouth-piece; hinged cover with baluster finial. By William Vere and John Lutwyche, 1765.

spoon tray. Small oval silver dish with plain or ornamented edge (fluted, scalloped, etc.) on which tea drinker laid spoon. Used in Britain from early to mid 18th century. Continued to be used even after saucer came into general use.

spout-cup or **feeding cup.** Silver one or two handled covered cup with curved spout attached at base; probably used for wine and other liquids in 17th and 18th century Britain and America. Sometimes single handle placed at right angles to spout. Many made in slightly bellied cylindrical tankard shape with stepped cover.

sprigging. Ceramic decoration of small pads of moulded clay attached to surface of vessel with slip; some details, e.g. flower or vine stems, modelled by hand. On *bellarmines, *jasper ware, etc. Method still in use.

Sprimont, Nicholas (1716–70). Belgian-born silversmith apprenticed in 1730, working in London from *c*1740; mark registered at Goldsmiths' Hall in 1742. Partner in *Chelsea porcelain factory until 1750, then manager; proprietor, 1756–69. In 1750s under secret patronage of Duke of Cumberland.

Silver pieces influenced by designs of J-A. *Meissonier; little made after 1746. Surviving works include tea kettle and stand (in Hermitage Museum, Leningrad), service made for Frederick, Prince of Wales in early 1740s (still in royal collections), épergne of 1747 (in Victoria & Albert Museum), and shell and dolphin sauce-boats (also made in porcelain).

spring (in clocks and watches). Coiled metal band, usually of steel, serving two functions. Mainspring, normally contained in barrel, supplies motive power to going and striking trains. Traditionally first applied by P. *Henlein, as substitute for weights. Balance spring or hair spring used to regulate motion of *balance in *escapement; very rarely made from other materials: glass occurs in a few chronometers, e.g. by E. J. *Dent.

spring detent escapement. *See* escapement.

Spring of Chosroes carpet. Sumptuous silk brocade Persian court carpet, inlaid with precious and semi-precious stones and measuring about 90sq. ft. First carpet mentioned in written records; woven in 6th century for palace of Chosroes I; destroyed during 7th century Arab invasions. Design copied layout of formal oriental garden with flowerbeds, trees, paths, and streams. Prototype for Persian *garden carpets of 16th and 17th centuries.

spring-tongs. *See* sugar tongs.

spun glass. Glass rods heated and drawn out to fine threads. Used by ancient Egyptian, Roman, and Islamic glass makers to make and decorate vessels and ornaments. Revived by 16th century Venetians; spread with *façon de Venise,* to become part of glass maker's art. Used for delicate rigging on glass ships in 16th and 17th century Italy and Holland. Widely used for decorating whimseys and ornamental glass from 17th century (*see* Nevers). Particularly popular in 19th century for ornamental animals, flowers, ships, and birds. Objects such as épergnes, vases, and tableware decorated with fine coloured threads spun by hand on revolving wheel. From *c*1840, used for weaving silk-like cloth. Blue and white glass tie shown at 1851 Great Exhibition

Spun glass. Deer and flower under glass dome. English, mid 19th century.

*Spyglasses. English. Left and right: early 19th century, gold and enamel. Centre: ivory, decorated with cut-steel; and Wedgwood *jasper ware stem,* c*1810.*

Stackfreed. Movement of pocket watch, c*1620, steel and gilded brass; also visible regulator numbered 1–6 and *foliot balance.*

in London. Richardsons of Stourbridge, Worcestershire, granted patent in 1860s for glass-threading machine used for applying finely-spun glass.

spur motif. *See alicate.*

spy-glass. Regency affectation; evolved into opera glasses and binoculars in mid 19th century.

square baluster vase. Chinese ceramic form, made of slabs of porcelain paste, press-moulded and cemented together with slip. Found in Ming and Ch'ing periods.

squirrel. *See* birdcage.

S-scroll (in silver). Decorative motif in form of letter S. Also handle, especially on tankards, ewers, two-handled cups, etc.; dates from 16th century.

staartklok. *See* Dutch clocks.

stackfreed. In 16th century German watches, device consisting of curved spring pressing against snail-shaped cam attached to mainspring; resultant varying friction roughly equalizes decrease in power of spring as it unwinds. Later superseded by more efficient *fusee.

Stadtler, Johann Ehrenfried (b *c*1701). German porcelain draughtsman and painter at faience factory in Dresden, afterwards at Meissen porcelain factory from *c*1723, listed as flower painter under J. G. *Herold. His signature is on small covered tureen decorated with richly coloured oriental flowers and birds. Probably painted *chinoiseries*, with figures outlined in black or iron-red.

Stafford Pottery. One of several potteries at Stockton-on-Tees, Yorkshire. Established in 1824 to produce brown earthenware. Also made cream-coloured earthenware, enamelled or transfer-printed in blue (from 1826) and pearlware (from *c*1835). Traded 1826–55 as William Smith & Co. Made Queensware marked WEDGEWOOD or WEDGWOOD & CO until injunction granted to Wedgwood firm in 1848. Produced mugs transfer-printed and enamelled with carriages and early locomotives. Marks include WS & CO, QUEEN'S WARE STOCKTON, and WS & Co STAFFORD POTTERY, usually impressed, sometimes printed.

Staffordshire portrait figures. White earthenware figures commemorating contemporary personalities and events, made in large numbers from *c*1840 by many Staffordshire potters; also made in Scotland. Usually unmarked, but marks, e.g. of S. *Smith, occasionally occur. Subjects include royal family, figures connected with Crimean War, Indian Mutiny, and Franco-Prussian War; also e.g. sportsmen, religious leaders, criminals, theatrical personalities, and characters from contemporary plays and literature. Characteristic colouring combines deep blue and sometimes black under glaze with enamel colours and gilding.

Staffordshire salt-glaze. *See* salt-glaze ware.

Staffordshire slipware. Produced in Staffordshire from late 17th century; includes *Toft ware and comparable work by R. *Simpson. Hollow-ware introduced *c*1710, e.g. posset cups often with crinkled vertical strips of clay, loving cups with several handles, small spherical jugs, owl jugs, and miniature cradles commemorating baptism. Decoration includes flowers, notably tulips, and circular impressed motifs, e.g. wheels, rosettes. Much *combed slip decoration. Dishes, posset cups and cylindrical mugs with sgraffiato decoration of animals and leaves incised in dark brown slip, covered with warm brown glaze date from early 18th century. Simple trailed designs in red or white slip continued at least until 1796; dishes often have notched edge. Moulded dishes dated *c*1725–55 have designs outlined in relief, containing patches of slip; makers include S. *Malkin. From 1747 to 1779, bowls and jugs decorated with *sgraffiato* designs of animals, birds, flowers, leaves, and rarely vertical stripes; or sometimes with moulded lines and check-patterned bands.

Stafhell, Gustaf (d 1761). Swedish silversmith working in Stockholm; master in 1714. Made domestic silver in French rococo style; mark: GS. Son, Anders (d before 1772), also worked in this style; mark: STAFHELL.

Staigg, Richard Morell (1817–81). English-born miniature, genre, and landscape painter; in America from 1831, settling in Newport, Rhode Island. Exhibited work from 1841. Painted miniatures on ivory, many large, until 1862.

stake. Small anvil-like tool fixed to bench-vice or block and used to shape hollow-ware. Object tilted over end of stake; hammered row by row to achieve desired shape.

Stampfer, Hans Jacob (1504–79). Swiss goldsmith, medallist, and coin engraver working in Zürich. Made ornate standing cups e.g. terrestrial globe cup (in Basel Historical Museum, Switzerland).

stamping or **die-stamping.** Shaping of small metal objects by pressing between male and female steel dies; from 16th century, used to ornament foot-ring of beakers, cups, etc., and for coins and medals. Improved process patented 1769 by J. Pickering of London. Cheaper than casting and/or engraving; use became widespread; adapted for production of buttons and mounts for coaches, furniture, coffins, etc. In 1769, R. Ford of Birmingham adapted process to produce dished shape from sheet metal in making saucepans, basins, warming pans, etc. In 1779, invention of rolling cylinders with dies attached developed process further. Used by M. Boulton for Sheffield plate.

stand. Metal structure to protect table from heat or damp from dishes. Earliest surviving examples in silver from early 18th century, as part of large dinner service. Varied shapes and sizes, with or without feet; might contain spirit-burner. Matching stands made for tea, coffee, and chocolate pots, kettles, tureens, *entrée* dishes, etc. From late 18th century, many made in Sheffield plate.

stand-away hinge. Hinge used on boxes before 1735. Projected prominently from body of box. Precursor of *integral hinge.

standing cup. Large ceremonial covered drinking vessel used in Britain and Europe from early Middle Ages. Surviving 14th to 17th century examples entirely of silver or with bowl made from an ostrich egg, etc., on silver or silver-gilt mount. Baluster or other architectural stem on spreading foot. Name of cup may derive from shape, e.g. *font, *gourd, *steeple; or material of bowl, e.g. *coconut, *nautilus shell. Also known as hanap.

standing salt. Large gold, silver, or silver-gilt salt container, often of architectural form. Used in Britain and Europe from Middle Ages to mid 17th century. Most surviving examples British (property of Oxford and Cambridge colleges). Probably placed before host or guest-of-honour at table. Forms include *bell, *hour-glass, *pedestal, *steeple, and *spool; generally had covers surmounted by finials. *See* Cellini Salt, Gibbon Salt, Monkey Salt, Moody Salt, Seymour Salt.

standing tray. *See* butler's tray.

standish. *See* inkstand.

Stangenglas (German, 'pole glass'). Tall, slim, cylindrical German beaker, often with spreading hollow foot. 17th century examples usually enamelled. *cf Passglas.*

star-Ushak carpets. Moderate size, vividly-coloured 16th and 17th century *Ushak carpets. Field dominated by dark-blue Persian-influenced medallion pattern of large, ornate star-medallions and smaller ornate diamond-shaped medallions alternating in staggered horizontal rows. Red ground strewn with multi-colour blossoms on angular boughs. Kufic borders on early carpets, later stylized to angular scroll motifs. Widely exported and copied.

statuary porcelain. *See* parian ware.

statuette. Small gold and silver figures of saints and other religious personages formed part of medieval church plate; also used as *reliquaries. Some spoon finials (*see* apostle spoons) may have been based on statuettes, as well as figures set in niches in architectural style *croziers, **custodiae*, etc. In late 17th and 18th centuries, figure stems used for candlesticks, but examples rare.

stays (in furniture). Two spindles extending from tongue to yoke-rail on *braced-back chair.

steatite. *See* soapstone.

steel. Iron, with addition of carbon. Hardest of common metals, known from *c*3000 B.C. Used

Stangenglas. *Enamelled decoration of arms of Bradstetter of Austria; set in silver-gilt mount. Probably south German, dated 1562.*

Star-Ushak carpet. 1578.

Steel. Scissors. English, c1840, engraved with arms and supporters of Cavendish; exhibited at Great Exhibition, 1851. Length $4\frac{1}{4}$in.

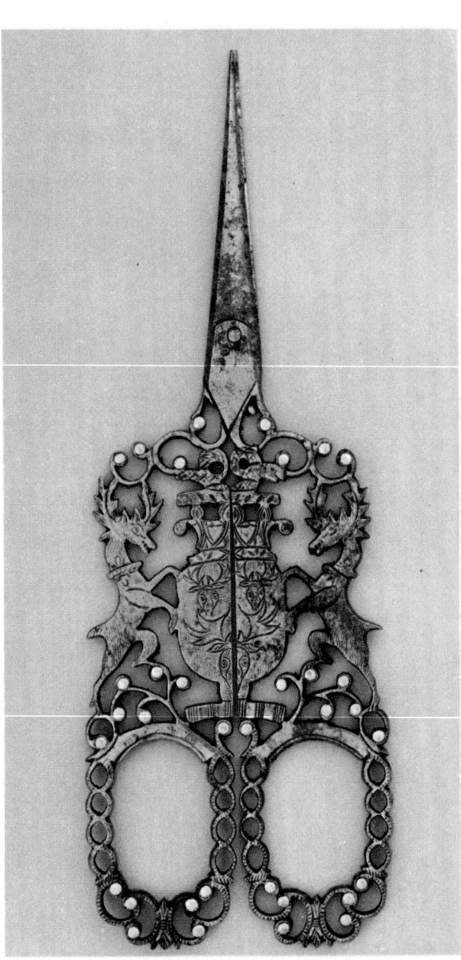

Steeple cup and cover. Silver-gilt, maker's mark T C date 1616–17. Bell-shaped bowl engraved with flowering plants between two plain bands; cast openwork steeple joining cover with caryatid brackets. Height c15in.

for armour, weapons, tools; for construction work and domestic objects subjected to hard wear, e.g. grates, fenders; also for sharp blades of knives, razors, scissors. Iron is hardened and sharpened by carbonization, then further hardened by rapid cooling (quenched) and heated again (tempered) to reduce brittleness. *See* cut steel, chiselled steel.

steel furniture. Although 16th century European examples exist (e.g. chair made for Rudolf II, Holy Roman Emperor) and are included on 18th century list of French royal furniture, a greater quantity was made in 18th century in Tula, central Russia. Shows English influence, reflecting *Adam style in design and techniques of M. *Boulton in faceted and polished steel bead-work decoration. Other examples overlaid with brass, copper, silver, pewter. No surviving 19th century examples.

Steel or **Steele,** Thomas (1772–1850). English porcelain painter, noted for naturalistic still-lifes of fruit, painted at Derby and later at Rockingham. Also worked for J. *Davenport and (1825–43) at *Minton factory. Signed examples exist.

steeple clock. American shelf clock, made from *c*1843; adaptation of Gothic style. Simple form has pointed top with single spire each side; glass front divided into two sections; dial on upper part, with painted design or decorative scene below. Coiled springs. Variations include twin steeple with two spires on each side, and steeple on steeple, with clock on decorated rectangular base, framed on either side by single spires, rising above level of dial. Height 10–24in.

steeple or **obelisk cup.** Late 16th to mid 17th century British silver *standing cup with trumpet-shaped base and stem, egg-shaped bowl, and cover with steeple or obelisk finial on scroll brackets. Embossed ornament of acanthus leaves, fruit, etc.

steeple salt. 16th century British salt with cylindrical body and cover with steeple finial supported on scroll brackets. Ball or ball-and-claw feet.

Stein, Johann Andreas (1728–92). Austrian piano maker working in Vienna; inventor of Viennese or German action (*see* pianoforte). Instruments noted for light touch. Dampers operated by knee-piece worked with either left or right knee. Replaced by pedal in 1789.

Steingut. German *cream-coloured earthenware, introduced in Schleswig-Holstein, notably at Rendsburg, by 1770s.

Steinkabinettstabatieren. Type of snuff-box made by J. C. *Neuber in Dresden, using *Zellenmosaïk* technique. Hardstones set in numbered gold cells; key to numbers inside box.

Steinzeug (German 'stoneware'). *See* stoneware.

stem cup. Chinese pottery form derived from ritual bronze shape; Shang and Chou dynasties. Flared, circular bowl mounted on small columnar pedestal (*c*5–6in. high). In Ming and Ch'ing periods, decorated in underglaze blue or *copper-red, or with enamel colours. Notable

*Stem cup. Early 15th century, reign of *Hsüan Tê; *copper-red dragons among underglaze blue waves. On inside are two running dragons in an hua slip technique. Diameter* 6*in.*

examples from reign of Hsüan Tê, decorated with fish motif.

stepped lid. Flat-topped dome cover with surrounding flange found on some tankards, from 16th to 18th centuries, e.g. *Commonwealth tankard.

Sterling mark. Lion passant mark instituted in by Goldsmiths' Company in 1544 as guarantee that silver in an article which bore it was of Sterling standard. Thistle used for this purpose in Scotland from 1759.

Sterling standard. Standard of purity of English silver in use at least since Anglo-Saxon period (except for period 1697–1720); standard for coinage established by statute in 1300. Troy pound to contain 11oz2dwt of pure silver and 18dwt of alloy, i.e. 925 parts per 1000 pure. *See* Britannia Standard.

stick-back. Chair back of wooden rods or spindles. Found on Windsor chairs.

stick-handle. Walking-stick or cane used from 16th century. 17th century handles commonly made of ivory *piqué*. In 18th century, gold, enamel, silver, or porcelain used; decoration similar to that on snuff-boxes; some contained vinaigrette or spirit-bottle. Among toys or *Galanterien* made at many European porcelain factories in 18th century.

sticks (in fan). Ivory, mother of pearl, or wood rods on which fan leaf mounted, held together at one end by rivet or pin; leafless *brisé* fan has ribbon threaded through slots at broad end. Outer sticks known as guards.

'sticky' blue. Characteristic bright blue used at Liverpool in painting of porcelain.

Stiegel glass. Engraved, enamelled, and pattern-moulded glass first made in America by H. W. *Stiegel. Engraving usually by copper-wheel, enamelling similar to German peasant glass. Mould-blown glass often incorporates diamond daisy design. Made in green, blue, or plain glass.

Stiegel, Henry William. German; in America from 1750. During 1760s, founded three glass-

*Stiegel glass. Decanter of Stiegel type glass, possibly made at *Manheim Glass House, c1770. Free-blown in leadless glass and engraved. Height* c10*in.*

houses in Pennsylvania; employed European craftsmen. Called 'Baron' because of luxurious life-style. Over-rapid expansion caused financial failure. Imprisoned for debt in 1774; factories closed. *See* Manheim Glass House, Stiegel-glass.

Stiehl, Christian Gottlieb (1708–92). German maker of hardstone boxes in Dresden. Used *Zellenmosaïk* technique; also mounted stones without backing for stained-glass window effect.

stile. In series of vertical members running between horizontals in framing or panelling, the two outside verticals. *cf* muntin.

stile bello (Italian, 'beautiful style'). Maiolica decoration with elaborate floral and classical motifs, often accompanying *istoriato* painting; developed at Faenza, Urbino, and other Italian maiolica centres in early 16th century.

stile severo (Italian 'severe style'). Maiolica decoration: simple style emphasizing form of vessel, in primary colours which, from 1430s, gradually supplanted predominant green and brownish-purple of early maiolica. Development apparently initiated in or near Florence.

stippling. Glass engraving technique in which design consists of tiny dots applied to surface by diamond point or steel needle embedded in hammer. Dutch 18th century development. *See* F. *Greenwood, D. *Wolff.

stirring rod or **molinet.** Rod projecting through aperture in lid of *chocolate pot.

Stirrup cup. Fox-head form made in London, 1806, by T. Phipps and E. Robinson. Length 4½in.

Stomacher. Gold, set with rose-cut diamonds and enamelled. Five flowers along top on gold springs; tremble when moved. Spanish, 18th century.

Usually of wood with knop or terminal of silver, ivory, etc. Chocolate pots complete with original stirring rod are rare.

stirrup-cup or **fox-head cup.** English late 18th and 19th century silver drinking vessel used at meet (before hunt began); bowl in form of a fox's mask or more rarely a hound's head. 18th century examples often engraved with hunting mottos on collar.

Stobwasser, Georg Siegmund (d 1776). German who founded family lacquer firm, only real competitor of Birmingham producers. Granted production monopoly by Karl I of Brunswick. Made trays, boxes, and furniture. Boxes resemble English products: small and round, with black sides, and brightly coloured lids decorated with copies of European paintings or topical portraits. Factory signature inside lid. Produced until 1830, when box production went into decline.

Stöckel, Joseph (d 1802). French *maître-ébéniste* (1775). Noted for marquetry, bronze mounts, and classical motifs.

Stockuhr or **Stutzuhr.** Austrian mantel clock, standing on base *c*10in. wide and high; supporting columns, often with mirror behind. Skeleton dial sometimes displaying automaton figures; one example set in Vulcan's forge. Dial with ornaments (frequently dolphins) on each side; surmounted by imperial eagle. Introduced mid 18th century; particularly popular 1815–30.

stoeltjeklok. *See* Dutch clocks.

Stölzel, Samuel (d 1737). German kiln-master for J. F. *Böttger at recently formed Meissen porcelain factory (1713–19). Deserted as arcanist, helping in establishment of rival factory at Vienna (1720). Returned to Meissen with permission of J. G. *Herold, as potter and colour-chemist (1720–37).

stomacher. Large jewelled ornament usually in floral, **girandole*, or foliate cross design worn over front piece of corset. Much used in Britain and Europe from early 18th century.

stone china. Hard, heavy English earthenware containing feldspar; strong, resonant body has bluish-grey tint. Developed by J. *Spode II; first marketed in 1805. Smoother, improved body introduced *c*1810, initially sold as New Stone China. Early decoration enamel; later, underglaze transfer-printed outlines painted with enamel and picked out in gilding; patterns often oriental. Used to make large dinner services; also e.g. octagonal jugs, and plates with open-work decoration. Other makers include J. *Davenport, *Mason family, J. & W. *Ridgway. Much exported to America.

stoneware, grès, or **Steinzeug.** Pottery using refractory clays which, fired at 1200–1400°C, vitrify without collapsing. Body impermeable to liquids; hardness allows engine-turned decoration. First produced in Shang dynasty, China (*c*1550–1025 B.C.); European manufacture began in Germany *c*1300. *Rhineland stoneware much exported to England in 16th and 17th centuries (*see* tigerware jug). First made in England by J. *Dwight and D. and J. P. *Elers. From *c*1720, white *salt-glaze produced in Staffordshire, sometimes decorated with enamel from *c*1750. Coloured stoneware includes Egyptian black, caneware, and red stoneware made, e.g. by S. *Hollins and refined by J. *Wedgwood.

Left:
Stoneware. German, made in Nassau, late 17th or early 18th century. Grey jug with blue glaze and incised ornament, moulded medallion; height 6in.

French provincial, Louis XV. Carved and waxed beechwood with contemporary needlework covering.

stool. Archaic form of seat with neither back nor arms; usually on three or four legs. Increased in sophistication as furniture became more common. At 16th and 17th century English and French courts, elaborate etiquette surrounded use of *fabouret. *Joined stools appeared in 16th century and were common until mid century; also a popular product of 19th century Gothic revival. Another recurring style is X-frame folding stool or *pliant,* also of antique origin; extremely popular Louis XIV and Regency style. By late 17th century, stools were often designed to match chairs in a room, when usually rectangular or oval. In 18th century, varied designs made for different purposes (e.g. round stool for dressing table, rectangular for window seat). Some 19th century low footstools conceal a *spittoon beneath hinged top. *See* back stool, gout stool, music stool.

stool table. Ample stool with drawer attached to underside of seat. Made in late 17th century.

stop. Set of organ pipes or harpsichord strings of one tone colour throughout compass of instrument, e.g. flute stop, oboe stop (organ), and lute stop (harpsichord); also, knob, lever, or other device for operating these. In relation to stringed instrument, pressing of string against fingerboard or fret; in wind instrument, closing of fingerhole.

stopper. Common from mid 18th century for plugging mouth of decanter or small bottle used at table, e.g. cruet. Loose fitting stoppers sometimes made in late 17th century for wide mouth of jug-shaped decanters. Blown in high hollow dome with small, solid finial. By 1700, made in solid form, also with finial, occasionally incorporating tear; ends flat, showing tool marks. From *c*1740, stoppers ground into neck to ensure perfect fit; conical 'spire' stoppers popular, at first smooth, later cut to match vessel. In 1760s vertical disc-shaped stoppers made with plain surface, encircled with diamond-cutting or scalloping; pear, heart, and clover-leaf shapes followed. Mushroom stoppers, separated from neck by short stem, favoured for later, heavily cut vessels; decoration, impressed with pincers, unassociated with body ornament. Remained popular until *c*1820, when more elaborate forms became popular, e.g. heavy pinnacle, globe, or hemispherical shape; usually solid, occasionally blown. Square decanters for spirits made with diamond-cut ball-shaped stopper. From *c*1840, stoppers usually machine pressed, except when made to match fine free-blown or cut-glass decanters of late 19th century.

Store Kongensgade. *See* Copenhagen.

Storr & Mortimer. English firm of silversmiths established 1822 by P. *Storr and J. Mortimer in London. Over-stocking (by Mortimer) brought firm to edge of bankruptcy in 1826, but Storr's nephew, John Samuel Hunt, became partner and contributed £5000, thus saving firm. In early 1830s, E. H. *Baily joined design staff, later headed it. On Storr's retirement (1839) firm became *Mortimer & Hunt, and *c*1843, Hunt & Roskell.

Storr, Paul (1771–1844). English silversmith working in London; father silver chaser, later victualler. Apprenticed to A. *Fogelberg (*c*1785). From 1792–95, in partnership with a W. Frisbee. From 1807 managed workshop in Dean Street, Soho, London, known as Storr & Co., for *Rundell, Bridge & Rundell; made partner in 1811. Left Rundell's in 1819. Made range of domestic silver for royal and aristocratic patrons; noted for silver on grand scale, e.g. christening font with figures of Faith, Hope, and Charity for Duke of Portland (1797–98). Worked in revived rococo style (had bought silver from French *emigrés* after Revolution), and classical Roman style. Worked alone until 1822, when John Mortimer became partner (firm called *Storr & Mortimer). Retired in 1839. Mark: PS (also used while with Rundell's). *Illustrations at* fish-slice, honeypot, soup tureen.

Stothard, Thomas (1755–1834). English painter, book illustrator, and silver designer. Elected to Royal Academy in 1777. Designer for *Rundell, Bridge & Rundell, but his *Wellington shield, designed in 1814, was made *c*1822 by B. *Smith the Elder (who employed W. *Pitts the Younger as chaser), for retailers Green, Ward & Green.

Stourbridge, Worcestershire. Important English glass making centre from 17th century. Immigrant glassmakers, particularly members of Tyzack, *Henzey and Tyttery families (*see* Lorraine glass makers) settled in Stourbridge area in early 17th century, attracted by local clay used for making furnace melting pots since mid 16th century. Under Sir R. *Mansell, local coal-mining developed to provide coal for firing furnaces. By 1696, 17 glasshouses established: seven for window glass, five for bottles, and five for flint, green, and potash glass. During 18th century, number of glasshouses increased. In late 18th century, improved annealing produced tougher lead-glass, particularly suited to cutting in German-style deep relief. During *Glass Excise Act period, many workers went to Ireland (e.g. J. *Hill), but 19th century gave new impetus to glass making, particularly Great Exhibition of 1851. Area noted for fine quality *metal, variety of colours, and individual styling and decoration. J. *Northwood inspired interest in *cameo glass. Ruby-red, blue, and opaque-white decoration popular, with classical or floral and foliare motifs. Paperweights made from mid 19th century, mainly in pastel *millefiori* designs; also weighted inkwells, scent-bottles, door-knobs, knife-rests, and seals. From early 19th century, moulds used for some cut glass; originally imitated handwork, later more elaborate, often with distinctive pointed fluting. Pressing introduced 1833. In mid 19th century, glass threading machine used for decorating tableware and vases, particularly with old-gold coloured glass.

*Tureen and stand. By P. *Storr, London, 1808. Decorated with gadrooning and beading. Tureen handles terminate in *lion masks; stand has *lion's paw feet. Length of stand $21\frac{1}{2}$in.*

Stourbridge glass. Miniature inkwell and stopper; base and stopper set with concentric rows of *millefiori *canes and including date, 1848.*

Strachan, A. J. (fl 1800–25). English box maker who worked in London. Chief maker of gold *freedom boxes and royal presentation boxes. Signed initials.

Stradivari, Antonio (*c*1644–1737). Italian violin-maker working in Cremona; pupil of N. *Amati. Greatest maker of Cremona school. Standardized length of violin body at 14in. Also made cellos and a few violas.

straight banding. Decorative use of thin strips of veneer, cut with the grain, on furniture or

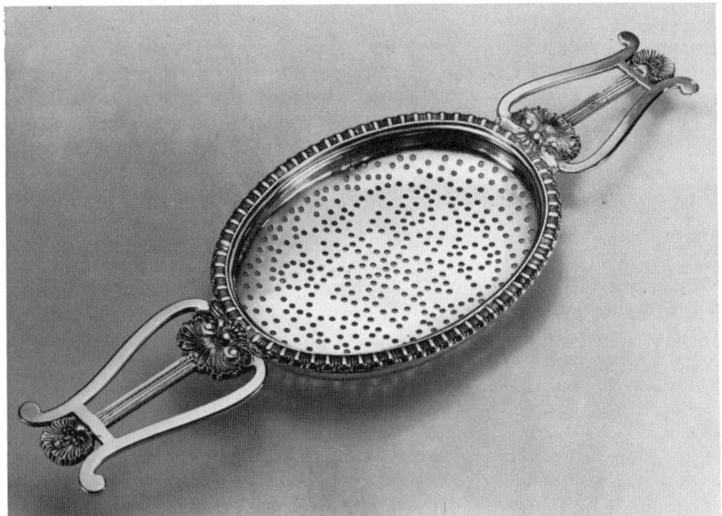

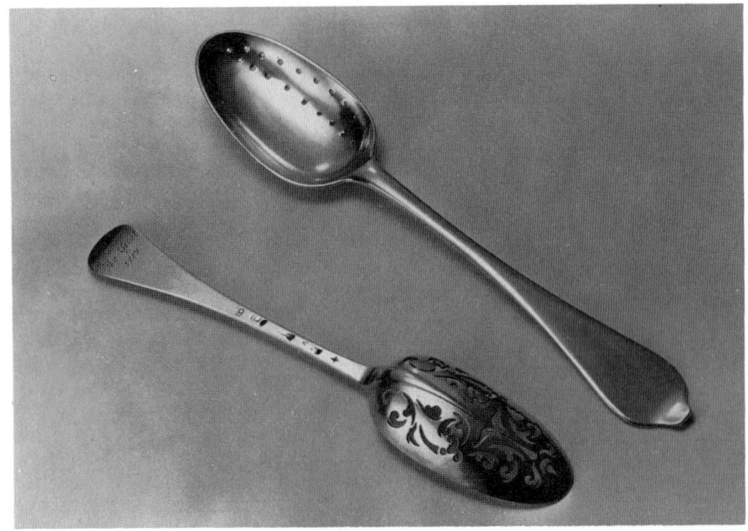

Strainer. Made in 1819 by Robert Gray of Glasgow. Holes pierced in geometrical design; gadrooned border and lyre handles. Length c12in.
Right:
Strainer spoons. English, early 18th century. Often used in churches for wine; spoon on left inscribed All Hallowes the Great, 1719.

panelling. *See* cross-banding, herring-bone banding.

strainer. Silver utensil with shallow, circular, pierced bowl; one or two handles, plain, of ornamental shape, or pierced. Used for straining particles (e.g. orange or lemon pips) from punch, mainly in late 17th and 18th centuries.

strainer spoon, mote-skimmer or **spoon, mulberry** or **olive spoon.** Small silver spoon with pierced bowl and circular tapering stem with spiked end. Made in Britain from end of 17th century and thought to belong to tea service: spike used to clear tea leaves from perforations inside bottom of spout. Early bowls punch-pierced; later pierced with elaborate designs. Stems occasionally varied, e.g. formed as eel. No evidence that spoon used for eating mulberries or olives.

Stralsund (Pomerania). Faience factory founded *c*1755 (when Stralsund belonged to Sweden). Leased by J. L. E. *Ehrenreich (1766), founder of Marieberg faience factory. Pieces produced from 1766–70 bear resemblance to Marieberg wares, notably rococo tureens, with small figures in applied relief and painted with birds, flowers, and foliage; open-work plates characterized by violet-blue colouring. Factory marks include date, initials of owner and painter, with three nails of Crucifixion in arrowhead formation, with initial E. Explosion interrupted production in 1770; after changes of ownership, factory finally closed in 1792.

strap work. Pattern of interlaced strap-like bands; originated in 16th century Netherlands. Extensively used on northern European furniture and metal-work during 16th and 17th centuries. On silver, engraved or flat-chased until early 17th century; often enclosed scrollwork, foliate ornament, etc. In early 18th century, cast and applied ornament on bodies of two-handled cups, tankards, etc. *Illustration at* spice box.

Strasbourg Alsace, France. Faience produced at existing clay-pipe factory from 1721, by father of P-A. *Hannong. In 1724, branch established at Haquenau; products possibly decorated at Strasbourg. Early work, painted in blue *style rayonnant,* includes large octagonal fluted dishes. From *c*1740, polychrome *chinoiserie* decoration. From 1748, workers from Höchst, including A. F. *von Löwenfinck (director of Haquenau from 1750 until death), with experience in porcelain painting, introduced enamel colours, including bright red derived from gold, used for edging tureens. J. W. *Lanze employed as modeller, 1745–54; work includes figures and vases. Rococo forms, gradually introduced (1749–60), include clock cases, sconces, and wall fountains; also tureens modelled as vegetables or fruit. Flower painting, from 1749, includes **indianische Blumen* introduced by von Löwenfinck, and naturalistic **deutsche Blumen.* In 1754, P-A. Hannong left to establish porcelain factory at *Frankenthal; in 1762, son Joseph-Adam returned as director, continuing rococo style.

Porcelain made from 1752 until transfer to

Strasbourg faience. Octagonal plate, early 18th century; blue and white colouring. Diameter 13in.

Strawberry dish. Swiss, made in Neuchâtel, c1730.
Straw marquetry. Detail of mirror frame, straw on silk base; English, c1670.

Frankenthal (1754); early ware resembles that made in Germany. Another attempt to establish hard-paste porcelain manufacture in 1766. Decoration skilfully painted on tableware in Louis XVI style. Figures include original work and copies, e.g. from Vincennes, Babet with a Birdcage, and The Little Stonemason. In 1781, factory failed and J-A. Hannong fled to Germany, heavily in debt.

Faience marked with monogram of P-A. Hannong (*c*1740–*c*1760) and J-A. Hannong (1762–81), sometimes accompanied by painter's mark. Porcelain marked with PH impressed, or monogram IH impressed, incised and in blue.

Strasbourg flowers. *See deutsche Blumen.*

Strass or **Stras,** Georges-Frédéric (1700–73). French goldsmith and jeweller working in Strasbourg and Paris. In 1724 joined Paris jeweller's firm. *c*1730 became famous for *paste jewellery. In 1734, appointed jeweller to Louis XV. Fine paste jewellery sometimes referred to as 'strass'. Employed lapidaries to cut, shape, and polish his paste gems.

strawberry-dish or **saucer-dish.** Shallow silver dessert or salad dish with fluted sides and scalloped rim; not necessarily used for strawberries. Sometimes found in sets with serving dish. Made in Britain and Europe in early 18th century.

straw marquetry or **work.** Decoration of wooden, metal, or papier mâché furniture by applying lengths of coloured straw in geometrical patterns or simple pictures. Originated in 16th century Italy; used in England at end of 17th century.

stretchers. Strengthening and stabilizing rails, running horizontally between legs of pieces of furniture. Various designs and shapes: plain, turned, or carved, and in X, H, and Y shapes, etc. *See* box stretcher, cowhorn-and-spur stretcher, H-shaped stretcher.

strike-a-light. Specially-prepared flint used in tinder-box. Also, 18th century pistol-shaped tinder-box. Pulling trigger caused spring-activated lever to strike piece of flint against pivoted steel, producing spark to light cotton rag, from which sulphur-dipped 'match' lit in turn.

striking mechanism. Part of clock designed to strike hours, and sometimes quarters, on bell or gong. Striking train usually powered by separate weight or spring, and set in motion by pin on wheel of minute hand of going train. Two forms. Locking-plate or count-wheel striking controlled by slotted wheel: space between slots determines number of blows struck; in this type, striking can become unsynchronized with time shown by hands. Rack striking system invented by E. *Barlow *c*1675 uses position of stepped cam (snail) connected to hour hand to control striking; quickly replaced locking plate in high quality clocks, but earlier method still used in e.g. provincial long-case clocks to end of 18th century. In quarter-hour striking, train may be let off by sprung lever known as 'flirt'. To counter tendency of train to speed up as it runs, 'fly' or small fan is attached with enough air resistance to produce steady running.

striking systems. Earliest form of striking remained most usual throughout development of clock: hours marked by number of blows from one to twelve on bell. Originally produced by locking-plate *striking mechanism, later largely superseded by rack type. Simplest variant is addition of single stroke on same bell for half-hours. 'Roman' striking, devised by J. *Knibb for economy of power in eight-day and month clocks, uses two bells of differing pitch representing Roman numerals I and V, two strokes of V bell serving for X: total number of strokes thus much reduced. Rarely found: recognizable by use of figure IV on dial instead of usual IIII. In 'Dutch' striking, hours are struck normally, half-hours by sounding next hour on smaller bell. Developed *c*1700 into *grande sonnerie,* with each quarter followed by preceding hour. French **Comtoise* clocks have unique system (Morbier striking), repeating hour strokes after interval of two minutes. *Japanese clocks strike six day and six night hours by sequence of 9, 8, 7, 6, 5, and 4 blows, 9 indicating midnight and noon. Half-hours are sometimes marked by two strokes following odd-numbered hour divisions, one stroke following even numbers. 'Ting-tang' quarters are struck on two bells, second of lower pitch; two strokes at first quarter, four at second, six at third and eight at hour, followed by normal hour strokes. Chiming clocks sounding tune or scale on four or more bells at quarters and hours became common in 18th and 19th centuries; most popular version, Cambridge chimes, adapted *c*1788 from 5th bar of 'I know that my Redeemer liveth' from Handel's Messiah, and later modified for *Westminster clock (hence also called Westminster chimes). *See* carillon, musical clocks, repeating clocks and watches.

stringing (in furniture). Inlay composed of very thin pieces of hardwood, e.g. ebony, holly, satinwood, used in border decoration on veneered objects. 'Strings', square in section, vary from $\frac{1}{8}$in. thickness to paper thin. *Illustration at* oystering.

strut clock. Small shallow-cased clock made from *c*1850 e.g. by *Cole brothers; stands on table, etc., supported by strut in manner of photograph frame.

Stuart tankard. *See* tankard.

stump-end spoon. Rare 15th and 16th century pewter or latten spoon; tapering stem, cut straight, with no knop, narrows towards bowl.

stump foot. Bottom end of furniture leg which has no shaped foot. Used in 18th century. Also, turned foot used on heavy case furniture.

stump-top spoon. *See* Puritan spoon.

Stutzuhr. *See Stockuhr.*

style Berain or **décor Berain.** Ceramic decoration associated with J. *Berain. Incorporates grotesque figures, animals, masks within framework of garlands, scrollwork, and architectural motifs; laterally symmetrical, usually around central classical scene; emphasis on delicacy and balance of design. From *c*1710, found on faience of Moustiers, at first in blue and white only, later with addition of orange, purple, and green. Much imitated, e.g. at Marseille and Lyon; also in Italy and Spain. Copied on porcelain at Rouen and Saint-Cloud. *Illustration at* Moustiers.

style rayonnant. French ceramic decoration, characterized by *lambrequins, lacy motifs, scrollwork, and flowers, pointing towards central reserve; simple symmetrical design or, after 1709, coat of arms at centre of dish. Introduced on faience at Rouen by 1700; popular on French porcelain and faience until mid 18th century. At first blue on white ground, or white on blue; later enriched with other high-temperature colours, notably red (characteristic of Rouen).

subscription or **souscription watch,** or **montre à souscription.** Large circular watch (*c*2in. diameter), made to order for subscribers by A-L. *Breguet. Designed to combine greatest accuracy in timekeeping with minimum cost (though still very expensive). Dial finely calibrated; single hour hand indicates hours and minutes. Case usually silver, with gold bezel and pendant-ring. *Illustration at* A-L. Breguet.

subsidiary dial. Indicator on clock or watch serving other than main timekeeping function, e.g. *calendar, *astronomical, *equation, *lunar, and *up-and-down dials.

sucket spoon. Silver implement with rat-tailed spoon at one end and two or three-pronged fork at other; stem flattish, usually scratch-engraved on both sides. Approximately 5–6in. long in thin gauge silver. Used in Britain for eating candied fruit. Earliest surviving examples 17th century, though made earlier. Fork later made separately.

Sué or **Iwaibe ware.** Japanese ceramics; hard grey stoneware, with greenish natural ash glaze, made *c*300–600. Brought to country by Korean

Sucket spoons. English, 1680–90.

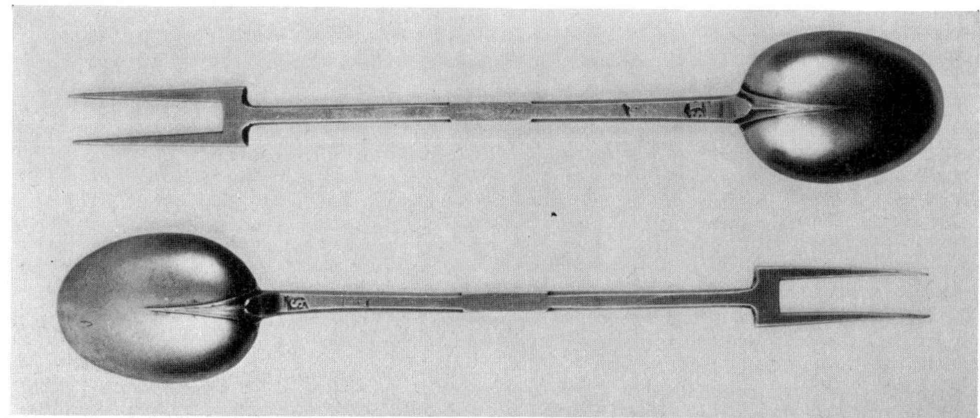

*Sugar bowls. Left: plain, circular bowl with spreading foot and moulded rim, made in Dublin by Edward Workman, 1717; diameter 4½in. Right: covered bowl with spreading foot and raised cover, made by W. *Fleming, 1718.*

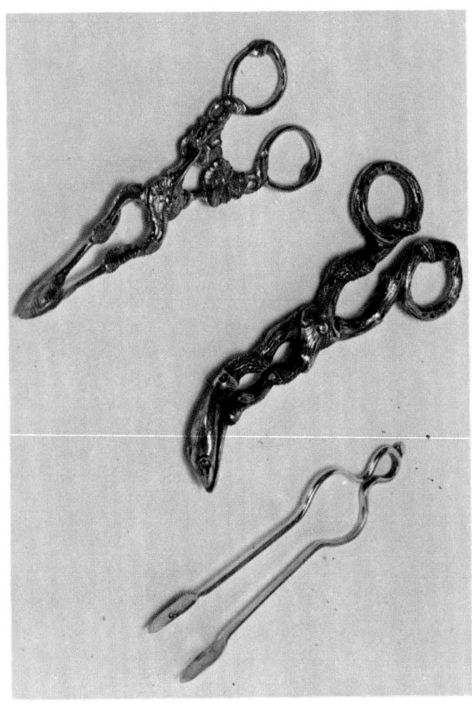

*Sugar tongs. Top: silver gilt, made by S. *Hennell, c1820. Centre: in form of serpent by Yapp and Woodward, 1847. Bottom: made by George Gillingham, c1715. All c5in. length.*

immigrants (*see* Silla period). Domestic objects include jars, bottles, dishes, cups, pots. Characterized by high, hollow foot, with triangular or rectangular cut openings. Figures of humans, animals, birds, ships, etc., decorate top of vessels.

sugar bowl. Silver sugar container used from early 18th century. Earliest examples had circular or polygonal bowl and slightly domed cover with finial. In mid 18th century, made in vase or box shape *en suite* with tea-caddy. From c1760, boat-shaped basket with swing handle and pedestal base common; pierced examples had glass liner; sometimes made with matching cream basket. Squat, basin shape with two handles formed part of tea service in late 18th century. Also made in Sheffield plate, later, electro-plate.

sugar crusher. Silver or Sheffield plate rod with disc at one end and ring at other; approximately 5in. long. Used to break lumps from sugar loaf in 19th century Britain. *cf* sugar nippers.

sugar nippers. Wrought-iron or steel (rarely, silver) pinchers used from 18th century for breaking up loaf sugar. Often set on wooden block for use at table. Up to 1ft long and strongly constructed. Term also used for *sugar tongs.

sugar sifter or **shifter.** Small silver ladle with pierced bowl for sprinkling sugar. Introduced mid 18th century. In 18th century England, common practice was to pierce and emboss sauce ladle of earlier period to produce rarer sugar-sifter.

sugar spoon. 18th and 19th century British and European silver spoon shaped like small shovel or with circular bowl pierced for sprinkling.

sugar tongs. Silver implement for handling lumps of sugar; used from late 17th century, originally same pivoted form as fire tongs. In early 18th century shell-shaped pans (sometimes oval, leaf-shaped, etc.) adopted, with scissor-type construction. Spring form with spoon-shaped pans introduced in 1760s; decorated e.g. with scroll or floral piercing or plain with bright-cut engraving. Both types continued to be made in 19th century.

Sui dynasty (589–618). Short Chinese period when country reunited under Yang Chien, follower of Buddhism: reconstructed country's administration, preparing way for subsequent renaissance under 'T'ang' dynasty. In addition to dated Buddhist stone sculptures, many cream-glazed pottery *'ming-ch'i' articles, often ascribed to 'T'ang' dynasty, should be attributed to Sui.

suite of carpets. Auctioneer's term for three carpets, one broad and two narrow, of same pattern.

Sulkowski Service. German porcelain table service modelled by J. J. *Kändler at Meissen (1735–38); commissioned by Count A. J. von Sulkowski, Prime Minister of Saxony and previously in charge of porcelain collection at Japanese Palace. Shapes, e.g. of tureens and candlesticks, inspired by contemporary silver. Rich gilding emphasizes modelling of scroll feet and gadrooned edges. Arms of Count and Countess painted in polychrome on every piece, also small sprays of flowers in Japanese style. Plates with wavy rims have borders of **Ozier* pattern. Tureens surmounted by lion holding scroll painted with Sulkowski arms. Candelabra in form of nymph holding four branches. Mark: crossed swords in underglaze blue.

Sully, Henry (1680–1728). English clock maker. After travelling settled in Paris; colleague of J. *LeRoy. Attempted unsuccessfully to set up factory at Versailles. Worked on marine timekeeping in 1721. Published *Règle Artificielle du Temps* in Vienna, 1714.

Sully, Thomas (1783–1872). English-born miniaturist, in America from childhood. Studied under J. W. *Jarvis and J. *Trumbull. Shared studio with B. *Trott. In later years abandoned miniatures for larger works.

sulphides, cristallo-ceramie, or **cameo incrustation.** Clear glass in which white, unglazed porcellanous cameo or medallion enclosed. Experiments made in late 18th century Bohemia and early 19th century France, producing crude, grey-tinted sulphides. Process perfected by A. *Pellatt, who found flint-glass best for displaying enclosed items. Used for glass balls, paperweights, door handles, portrait medallions, occasionally tableware, and jewellery. Best English examples made 1819–35, sometimes decorated with deep cutting. French glass houses at *Baccarat, *St Louis and *Clichy copied Pellatt's method, particularly for paperweights.

Sultanabad carpets. *See* Mahal carpets.

sultane. *See lit de repos.*

sumak or **soumak carpets.** Type of tapestry-weave carpets of Caucasian origin. Coloured weft threads passed over several warp threads and then drawn back through warp, leaving loose ends on reverse side. Early carpets favoured yellow and white in design on light ground; later, blue tones dominate patterns on red-brown ground. Standard design, vertical

*Sulphide medallions. Left: inset into wooden box; depicting Wellington, by A. *Pellatt, c1820. Right: in paperweight, French, c1840.*

Sun and moon dial watch. By Windmills, London, c1700; silver with champlevé *enamel numerals.*

rows of large, lozenge-medallions with outlines forming crosses. Also some unpatterned rugs with foundation overlaid and entirely concealed by needle-stitch embroidery.

sun and moon dial. On some watches *c*1700: minutes shown normally, but hours indicated by pointers in form of sun for day and moon for night on revolving plate visible through semi-circular aperture in upper half of dial; twelve hours starting and ending at VI marked at circumference. Similar in appearance to dial of *wandering-hour watch.

sunburst flask. American glass flasks blown in two-piece moulds. Sunburst motif popular in America and extensively used on both sides of early flasks, occasionally on reverse side of *American eagle flasks. Mainly produced by Keene and Mount Vernon glasshouses in early 19th century.

Sunderland ware. Ornamental and commemorative lustre-decorated earthenware made by several potteries in Sunderland, County Durham from early 19th century. Much exported *c*1820–*c*1860; production continued until 1880s. Pink *lustre obtained by application of gold oxide over light-coloured body or glaze. Mottled lustre effect achieved by use of sprayed oil resist. Figures include religious and pastoral subjects, topical personalities, and animals; dogs usually white, with splashes of pink or copper lustre. Similar ware also made at Liverpool, Bristol, and in Staffordshire.

sundial. Earliest device for showing time of day, using shadow cast by standing rod or straight-edge (gnomon). Known throughout world; fixed and portable forms, e.g. 10th century English silver pocket-type with gold and jewelled mounts

Sunburst flask. c1815–20, made in New England, possibly Pitkin, Connecticut. Pint capacity.

*Sunderland ware jug. Transfer-printed with view of The Iron Bridge over the Wear. *Lustre decoration. Early 19th century.*

from Canterbury Cathedral. For accuracy, gnomon must be at correct angle, dependent on latitude; portable sundials, often of ivory, have adjustable gnomon and compass for alignment. In 18th century, some dials marked to record minutes. Dial normally flat, sometimes two or more dials hinged together (diptych dial); variants include cylinder, hemisphere with hours marked internally (invented by Berossus of Babylon *c*300 B.C.) and adjustable ring dial, *c*1550, with hours indicated by sun's rays passing through small aperture on to scale.

Sung dynasty (960–1279). Chinese period following power struggle after fall of T'ang dynasty. Very high standard of craftsmanship in arts generally, but, apart from fields of painting and pottery, both of which achieve success from experimentation, work tends to suffer from nostalgia for Han and T'ang dynasties.

*Sundial. Cube dial by D. *Beringer, signed on north face, late 18th century. Hand-coloured printed paper scales each with gnomon for four points of compass. Pivots on wooden turned support, wooden base inset with paper compass rose. Base* 3×4*in.*

Illustrations at Chün ware, Hang-chou ware, hare's furglaze, Kuan ware, Lung Ch'uan.

sunken panel. Panel with main surface slightly recessed from frame. Shallower than *coffered panel.

sunk or **recessed carving.** Simple furniture decoration formed by carving out area around desired ornamental shape.

supper service or **set.** Large tray with variously shaped dishes fitting into recesses; sometimes designed to hold hot water to keep food warm. Perhaps intended to be adapted to desserts; used from late 18th century in Britain; usually of Sheffield plate, but also found in silver; rare.

Surrey enamel. **Champlevé* enamelling used in 17th century England and Europe for brass objects (e.g. andirons, candlesticks, powder flasks); shapes to be filled with enamel are cast at same time as object, instead of being hand-cut. Name derives from theory (unsubstantiated) that technique originated in county of Surrey.

surveying instruments. Used for map-making and establishing compass bearings, heights of geographical features etc. on land. Many also used in navigation, e.g. *cross-staff, *magnetic compass, *quadrant, *sextant. Early device for measuring horizontal angles was circumferentor, graduated circle with pivoted sighting rule (alidade). Theodolite, with scales at right-angles for measuring horizontal and vertical angles described by Thomas Digges in 1581; made with open sights in 17th and early 18th centuries. Became principal instrument in surveying after

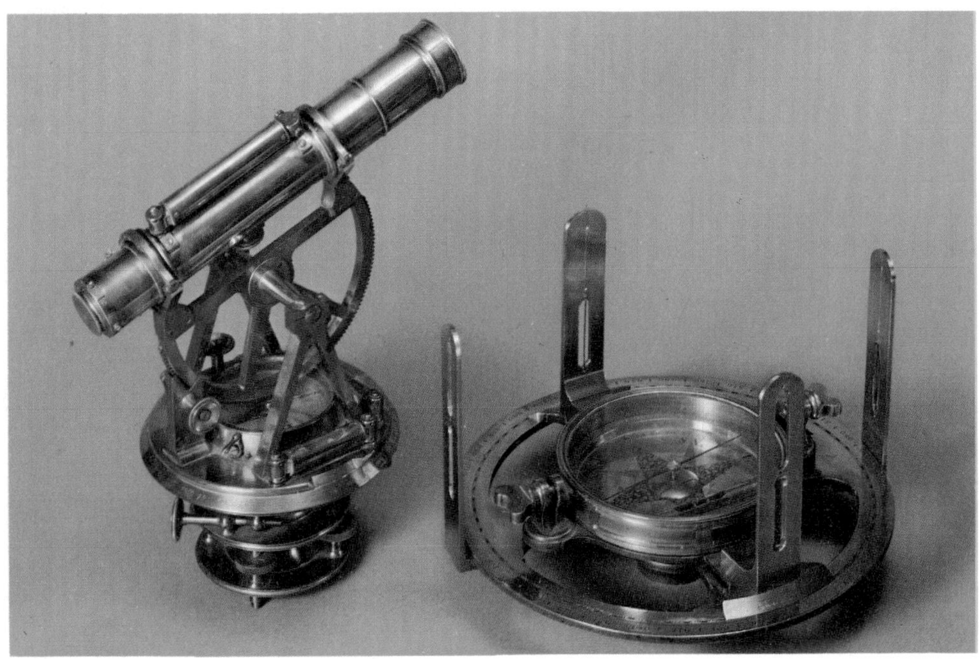

Surveying instruments. English. Left: early 19th century altazimuth theodolite for measuring angles of altitude or depression, signed Berge, London, late Ramsden. Brass telescope mounted on semi-circular arc above silvered compass; length of closed telescope with eyepiece 13in. Right: circumferentor, predecessor of the theodolite, signed T. Heath fecit; base plate with circle of degrees, four vertical sights; in centre, compass and spirit level.

addition of telescopic sights in late 18th century; also incorporated devices for levelling and orientation, and later, micrometer telescope for accurate reading of scale. Simplified exact measurement of angle between objects of different height.

suspension. In clocks, method of supporting pendulum, by spring, silk thread, knife-edge, etc.

suspension rod. Ornamental wrought-iron device, sometimes used in place of chain in 17th and early 18th centuries for suspending chandelier from ceiling. Surviving examples, decorated with scrolls, rosettes, and geometrical patterns, often painted or gilded, are *c*3–5ft long.

Sutherland Wine Cistern. Silver wine cistern with deep oval bowl (38in. long, 25in. wide, and 18in. high), with recurving scroll handles terminating in lion masks, and high oval foot. Bowl richly chased with masks and shells on matted ground. Made by P. *de Lamerie in 1719; weighs 700oz. Now in Minneapolis Institute of Art, Minnesota.

swag. Ornamental festoon of fruit, flowers, drapery, etc. Classical architectural decoration, commonly used on neo-classical furniture, and silver. *See* festoon.

swage. Shaped border on salver, tray, etc. Also metal-worker's tool for forming border or shaping up small articles from flat; consists of male and female blocks with metal placed between, hammered or held in screw-press. Article thus shaped in sections, not at one time as with dies used in *stamping.

Swan, Abraham (fl *c*1745–65). English cabinet maker; published architectural handbooks and design books showing furniture of classical form with rococo decoration.

swan-neck, bonnet-scroll, goose-neck, or **scrolled pediment.** Broken pediment with sides in form of sloping S-scrolls. Found on 18th century clocks, tall-boys, etc. Bonnet-scroll pediment American term.

Swansea. *See* Cambrian Pottery Works.

Swan Service. Elaborate porcelain table service made (1737–41) at Meissen factory from models, e.g. by J. J. *Kändler and J. F. *Eberlein; commissioned by Count H. *von Brühl. Every piece is variation on a water theme, including intricate dolphins, sea-nymphs, and swans. Swans modelled in low relief with storks on cups and plates; in the round on tureens. Emphasis on modelling rather than painting (which is sparse). Marks transition at Meissen between baroque and rococo periods.

'Swatow'. Chinese porcelain exported in quantity from Swatow in southern China, to Java, south-east Asia, Japan, and India, in late 16th, early 17th centuries. Probably manufactured in Fukien province. Coarser than late Ming porcelain of *Ching-tê-chên. Noteworthy for bold ornamentation. Large jars, dishes of all sizes, plates, bowls, and small covered boxes in white with incised patterns, or decorated with monochrome slip, underglaze blue, or red and green enamel.

sway or **swey.** *See* chimney-crane.

Swedish snuff-boxes. Gold and silver boxes made in Stockholm mostly modelled on Paris styles. Cartouche-shaped boxes made *c*1730: oval and oblong enamelled *en plein* *c*1759; vari-coloured gold *c*1770–75.

Swedish tapestry. Developed mainly as peasant craft. In mid 16th century, King Gustav I introduced Flemish weavers, and established small, short-lived manufactory after model of Fontainebleau workshop. 17th century tapestries mainly depict proverbs or simple tales; woven in coarse panels. In 18th century, small panels with flowers and birds popular.

sweep-seconds hand. *See* centre-seconds hand.

sweetmeat box. *See* spice box.

sweetmeat box, bonbonnière, comfit box, or **drageoire.** Very small 17th or 18th century box for sweets or cachous. Made in variety of materials and shapes; decoration similar to that on snuff-boxes.

sweetmeat or **dessert glass.** English glasses for serving sweetmeats at end of meal. Usually have saucer-shaped bowl with stem and circular foot. Made from late 17th century in flint-glass. Large numbers produced in 18th century.

Swatow dish. Decorated in red, green, turquoise, blue, and sepia overglaze enamels. Central character fu, within double ring. Ming dynasty, early 16th century. Diameter c16*in.*

*Sweetmeat box. In form of girl's head, porcelain mounted in gilt metal, *girl-in-a-swing family. c1750.*

*Sweetmeat glasses. English. Left to right: 1) Opaque twist glass with double ogee bowl, lip decorated with cog wheel formation, 1755; height 6½in. 2) Opaque twist glass with double ogee bowl flared at rim, set above triple collar and dumbell stem, 1770; height 7in. 3) Opaque twist glass with double ogee bowl with folded rim and hammered lower half, 1780; height 7in. 4) Cut glass with wide double ogee bowl cut with diamonds and lozenges; dentil rim; eight-sided star-studded *moulded-pedestal stem, 1790; height 6½in.*

Usually cut glass; earliest examples have hollow diamonds and edge flutes on bowl; later, deep cutting common. Scalloped rims, hollow diamonds cut in stem, and feet fluted in fan-shaped panels feature throughout 18th century.

swing-leg table. Drop-leaf table, similar to *gate-leg table in construction, but swinging support has no stretcher.

Swiss ceramics. **Hafnerware* made from early 16th century; from *c*1600, *Winterthur chief centre of manufacture. At *Zurich, rare examples of soft-paste porcelain made, and, from *c*1765, hard-paste; later, hard-paste porcelain made at *Nyon.

Swiss snuff-boxes. Mainly produced *c*1790–1850. Enamelled gold boxes produced in quantity for export trade with local scenes or popular paintings on lids. Many with scalloped edges or in *fantasy shapes, e.g. butterfly, flower, or book, bordered with pearls and painted in vivid enamel colours. Transparent colourless enamel, developed in Geneva *c*1780, fired over painting to prevent chipping. Musical snuff-boxes produced in quantity from *c*1810: oblong, decorated with enamelled scenes, containing musical mechanism in shallow, hinged compartment at bottom of box. Perfected by I. D. *Piguet.

Swiss watches. Watches made in 16th century Geneva, mainly following French styles; by late 17th century Swiss **oignon* rivalled best French product. After revocation of Edict of Nantes in 1685, many Huguenot makers moved to Switzerland. In 18th century, leading makers emigrated from Switzerland to England and France, e.g. J. *Vulliamy, J-A. *Lépine, F. *Berthoud, A-L. *Breguet. Swiss products then not of best quality; included cheap movements for export to England. After 1800, Turkish market captured from England; like English examples, Turkish market watches decorated; movements often with non-functional jewels. *Chinese watches also made. Early 19th century Swiss specialities include watches with *complicated work, repeaters with automata, thin watches, and types with annular enamel chapter rings surrounding visible movement or gilt ornament. In late 19th century, Swiss makers revived fashion for *form watch. Modern Swiss watch making industry based on work of F. *Japy and others with invention of machine tools as basis of mass production in late 18th century, first in Geneva, later in other cantons.

syllabub glass. English glasses for serving dessert of whipped cream, wine, and spices; most popular in late 17th and 18th centuries. In late 17th century, similar to *posset glasses, with two handles and spout. Gradually became like *jelly glasses, with wide lip, bell-shaped bowl, short, knopped stem (or none), and scalloped feet cut to match brim. Often larger than jelly glasses, occasionally with handles.

symmetrical knot. *See* Turkish knot.

Syng, Philip the Younger (1703–89). Irish-born silversmith; family settled in Philadelphia, Pennsylvania *c*1714, where he took over father's workshop, *c*1724. Amateur scientist; also very active in colonial affairs. Made silver inkstand used at signing of Declaration of Independence. Domestic silver, in English styles of early and mid 18th century, includes silver braziers, coffee-pots, salvers, tankards, sauce-boats. Mark: PS in heart, shaped shield, or rectangle.

tabatière. *See* snuff-box.

tabatière à cage. *See* cage-work box.

tabernacle clock. German domestic clock of *c*1570–*c*1680. 4–6in. square at base, 6–9in. high, with case varying from simple archi-

*Swiss snuff-boxes. Top: snuff-box including musical box and watch, enamel and gold, 1810. Left: enamel and gold snuff-box bordered with plaques showing regional costumes of 22 cantons. Right: musical snuff-box by J. L. *Richter, enamel and gold set with turquoises, 1800–10.*

Syllabub glasses. English, c1870. Height of tallest 3½in.

Tabernacle clock. German, late 16th century. Gilt metal; spring-driven iron movement. 24 hour dial. Inscribed Vas Posen. Lion séjant finial. Height 12*in.*

Table bell. Dutch, 18th century. Made in The Hague by Cornelis de Haan. Curved, fluted bell with moulding at rim, middle, and join with handle, which has swirling leaf finial. Height $5\frac{3}{4}$*in.*

Tabriz carpet. Silk, c1830. 5ft7in.×4ft2in.

tectural to highly elaborate. Going train in front of striking train; verge *escapement with layout similar to English *lantern clock but usually with mainsprings and gut-driven *fusees. Original all-steel movement modified during 17th century to include brass wheels, others entirely of brass, apart from arbors and pinions. Larger and more complicated examples often have dials on all four sides.

table. Primitive tables originally composed of loose planks laid across supporting trestles. Form with permanently fixed top dates from *c*15th century in Europe. *See* architect's table, artist's table, bachelor's table, bedside table, bed table, *bouillotte* table, breakfast table, butterfly table, card table, chair-table, claw table, console table, credence, deception table, draw table, dressing table, drop-leaf table, drum table, flower table, games table, gate-leg table, harlequin table, library table, loo table, Martha Washington sewing table, nest of tables, night table, ombre table, pedestal table, Pembroke table, pie-crust table, pier table, quartetto tables, refectory table, rent table, sawbuck table, serving table, settle table, sewing table, sewing machine table, shaving table, side table, snap table, social table, sofa table, stool table, swing-leg table, *table à déjeuner*, table bedstead, *table en guéridon*, tea table, work table.

table à chevet. *See* night table.

table à déjeuner (French, 'luncheon table'). Light table, circular, kidney-shaped, or oval, usually for serving meal for one person. Dates from 18th century.

table bedstead. Combined side table and bed; bed folds into body of table when not in use. Dates from end of 18th century.

table or **hand bell.** Used for summoning servants; known from 16th century or earlier in Europe; much used in 18th century; usually of silver or bronze with handle of ivory, bone, or wood, in variety of shapes. Many reproductions exist of rare and elaborate early bells.

table centrepiece. *See* épergne.

table-chair. *See* chair-table.

table clock. Small metal-cased clock with horizontal dial, mainly German, late 16th to early 18th centuries. *See* drum clock, hexagonal table clock. Also more correct description of many clocks termed *mantel or *bracket clocks, especially English *c*1675–1800.

table cut. Form of gem cutting in which stone has flat, horizontal 'mirror' facet on top. Used for diamond before invention of *rose cut in mid 17th century.

table en guéridon. French *tea table, evolved from **guéridon*; has circular top, usually surrounded by grille. Also, small table with top composed of two or three tiers of graded sizes (with largest tier at bottom).

table servante. *See* serving table.

table service. Set of matching silver dishes, tureens, sauceboats, candlesticks, flatware, etc., made for wealthy or princely British and European families from early 18th century. Might include tea and coffee service. Also made in electro-plate. Use declined from 1880s.

tablette. Leaf of ivory enclosed in decorative case for note-writing, in use in 18th century. Case in gold, silver, or enamel, often inscribed.

tablet-top (in furniture). Yoke-rail on chair made of basically rectangular panel (tablet) painted, carved, or otherwise ornamented. Popular in late 17th and early 18th centuries.

tabouret. French stool with rigid (non-folding) legs; at first drum (*tambour*) shaped, then usually rectangular. Used at Louis XIV's court: right to sit on *tabouret* was matter of court privilege and etiquette.

Tabriz carpets. Bold, elaborate, north-west Persian court carpets with short, finely-Persian-knotted wool pile on wool and or cotton foundation; woven in Tabriz during 16th and 17th centuries. Main border with arabesque scrolls, cartouches alternating with star-rosettes, or pairs of facing flowers. 12–15 tones used: deep red, blue, and sometimes white dominate pattern; ground often dark blue. Types continued in modified form through 18th and 19th centuries; widely copied.

tact. *See montre à tact.*

Taddel or **Dattel,** Heinrich (d *c*1794). German box maker, master goldsmith in 1739; inspector of repository of Saxon royal treasures, known as the Green Vaults. Creator of *Zellenmosaïk* technique of decorating hard-stone boxes commonly associated with pupil, J. C. *Neuber.

tailpiece (in furniture). Horizontal support extending behind seat on *braced-back chairs; forms lower terminal for *stays.

Talavera de la Reina (Castile), Spain. Production of pottery decorated in underglaze colours recorded in 1484. Colours include blue, bright green, yellow, and orange, against characteristic thick, milky glaze. Royal patronage (granted 1575) and decree (1601) restricting possession and use of silverware contributed to fast rise in trade throughout Spain. Religious orders, hospitals, and aristocratic households supplied with pharmaceutical and tableware, decorated e.g. with coats of arms, architectural designs, or hunting scenes. Tile panels decorated with battle scenes or religious subjects. *Illustration also at albarello.*

Talavera de la Reina. Pottery plate, 17th century, painted with helmeted head in characteristic figurative style.

*Tallboy. American, made in Salem, Massachusetts, 1796. Attributed to W. *Lemon; design and carving attributed to S. *McIntire.*

Talish carpets. Long, narrow south-east Caucasian carpets with medium Turkish-knotted pile, woven around Talish from 18th century. Woollen foundation usually undyed; weft often strengthened by threads inserted along edge; fringe at bottom only. Narrow field – dominated by border – either plain or filled with overall pattern of strongly-coloured stepped stars, star lozenges, or small flowers on blue or yellow ground. Broad, main border with white ground and brightly-coloured star rosettes alternating with groups of four stick-ray squares.

tallboy, chest-on-chest, or **double chest.** High chest of drawers, resembling two chests, one on top of other, with lower section slightly wider and deeper than upper one. Dates from late 17th century; called chest-on-chest or double chest until late 18th century. May have drawers to floor or rest on long legs, with lower section resembling *low-boy; popular during 18th century. *cf* high-boy.

tallboy-secrétaire. 18th century *tallboy with one desk-level drawer-front hinged at base, opening to form writing surface, and reveal nest of drawers and pigeon holes.

tall, floor, or **hall clock.** In America, *long-case clock.

Tamba ware. Japanese kiln site in Hyogo prefecture, active throughout Edo period. Produced domestic ware, used in Japan, mainly heavy brown-glazed bottles and pepper jars.

tambour. Flexible sheet composed of series of reed-like lengths of wood glued side by side on piece of canvas or similar fabric. Used as lid of roll-top desk, or on table or other piece of furniture to conceal storage space, work area, etc. Tambour slides in grooves into interior of object when not in use. Dates from late 17th century France; popular in 18th century English and American furniture. *Illustration at* night table.

tambour watch. Early form of German watch case in use *c*1540; of drum shape, pierced, and decorated. Iron movement, usually with striking or alarm mechanism, is latched to case. Also type of later French watch with movement secured to case by screws.

T'ang dynasty (618–906). Chinese rulers of powerful and far-reaching empire. Period of great prosperity lasted *c*150 years; Chinese domination stretched as far as Samarkand in west and influenced Korea and Japan in east. Chinese art in turn inspired by foreign influence in pottery, sculpture, and metal-work. From 755, dynasty weakened through corruption, rebellion, and border invasion. Although arts apparently continued to flourish, late T'ang pieces lack earlier vitality. *Illustration also at* amphora.

T'ang Ying. Chinese potter of Ch'ing dynasty. Assistant from 1728 to *Nien Hsi-yao, director-general of Kilns at Ching-tê-chên; succeeded him (1736–49). Produced highly-finished, translucent porcelain; imitations of Sung wares hardly distinguishable from originals. Recreated glazes of *Chün type, in varying shades of red and purple. Mastered new techniques in decoration of porcelain, e.g. **cloisonné* work, silver enamel, painting in sepia, etc. Perfected use of enamel colours to simulate natural or other substances, e.g. tarnished silver, red lacquer, grained wood, mother of pearl, bamboo. Styles imitated e.g. Japanese Imari, Venetian glass, Dutch Delft, and Limoges enamels. (After retirement in 1739, remained at factory until 1753, delegating work. In later years of Ch'ien Lung reign, style deteriorated, becoming mechanical and contrived; colours lost subtlety. Noted for writing, including list (1729) of all items produced during reign of Emperor Yung Chêng, and 'Instructions for the Manufacture of Porcelain', (1743).

tankard. Drinking vessel for beer, ale, or cider with single handle and usually hinged lid; form resembles wooden cask or tub used by water carriers in Middle Ages. Silver tankards in use in Britain and northern Europe from 16th century or perhaps earlier; English and European styles generally indistinguishable. Body shape, handle, lid, foot, thumbpiece varied; specific style not usually confined to particular period. Produced with minor variations in succeeding centuries. Shape of earliest surviving English examples possibly derived from earthenware vessel; had globular body with cylindrical neck widening at rim, domed lid, S-shaped handle, rectangular thumbpiece, and moulded foot. These went out of fashion with appearance of tapering concave body, moulded foot, S-scroll handle, and domed lid with rectangular thumbpiece. Decorated with flat-chased strapwork, foliage, birds, etc. In 16th century Germany, glass or crystal cylindrical body sometimes enclosed in silver filigree frame as in *poison tankard.

Early 17th century tankard much larger than 16th century counterpart (some hold four or five pints), with straight, tapering, cylindrical body, flat lid, and moulded foot; lid and foot sometimes elaborately embossed. Superseded in mid 17th century by squatter shape with plain, cylindrical body, deep, concave spreading foot, scroll handle, and flat lid. Often only ornament was narrow band of moulding at junction of body and foot and sometimes engraved coat of

T'ang dynasty. Jar with blue glaze from Honan province. Height 8in.

Tankard. American pewter. Left: 18th century tankard, attributed to John Skinner of Boston, unmarked, diameter $4\frac{1}{2}$in. Right: 18th century lidded tankard in traditional 17th century shape.

Tapersticks. English, 18th century. Left: moulded nozzle with everted rim, octagonal Silesian stem which terminates in star-studded domed foot. Centre: faceted nozzle, stem, and domed foot; height $6\frac{7}{8}$in. Right: stem of series of graduating rings; terminates in beaded base knop and beehive foot.

arms. Globular or jug-shaped tankard also made in 17th century. Moulded feet (three or four) and thumbpiece introduced later in 17th century; first used in Scandinavia on tankards with cylindrical body and low, domed lid. Shapes include pomegranate, lion, double scroll, etc. Engraved or embossed ornament. Coins sometimes set in lids of German and Scandinavian 17th and 18th century tankards. From late 17th century tankards in British styles made in America.

18th century styles include plain, cylindrical body with simple, tapering scroll handle and moulding at lip, base, and one-third of way up body; lid domed and thumbpiece scroll-shaped. Tankard with bulbous, baluster-shaped body, boldly-moulded foot, double scroll handle, and domed lid also made. Tankards out of fashion by mid 18th century in Britain; few made in Sheffield plate. Copied silver styles. In Britain in 19th century (especially from *c*1830–80) old tankards were heavily embossed and sometimes converted, though fraudulently, into jugs by addition of short spout. *See* bellied tankard, coin tankard, Commonwealth tankard, peg tankard, whistle tankard.

Pewter tankards were used in taverns and private houses from 13th century; earliest surviving English examples date from mid 17th century. Sometimes referred to as goddards. Early 17th century records refer to Ephraim pots, or pints, and Danske pots, both with and without lids. These are assumed to be tankards, the latter similar to tall, slim, straight-sided contemporary Danish types. Early English (Stuart) tankards similar in shape to contemporary silver examples, sometimes with slight convex curve and flat hinged lids, various thumbpieces and *wriggle-work decoration. Rims of lids are extended in front, often decorated with pierced or serrated designs, a feature taken from early Scandinavian tankards (which had no thumbpieces, so lid-opening device necessary). Domed and double-domed lids, introduced *c*1685, remained popular until *c*1750; few flat lids made after 1700. Handles were plain curve, with ball terminal to *c*1710, then 'fish-tail' terminal to *c*1750. Some tankards (*c*1675–*c*1730) bear capacity seals as on *measures. *c*1730–*c*1800, tulip-shaped tankards made, often with domed lids, until *c*1760 (few lidded tankards of any kind made later). In late 18th and 19th centuries handles often *double-curved or *broken; from *c*1770 lower ends of handles usually flush with body, and without terminal. 19th century examples have few decorative details; many glass-bottomed examples made. *Illustration also at* peg tankard.

Tännich or **Tönnich,** Johann Samuel Friedrich (b 1728). Itinerant German painter, potter, and kiln maker. Painted porcelain at Meissen (1750), and Frankenthal (1757–59); also faience at Strasbourg (1755). Director of faience factories at Jever (1760–63) and Kiel (1763–68); founder and director of Hubertusburg faience factory (1770–74), and Mosbach faience factory (1774–81).

Tanqueray, David (d *c*1726) and Ann (d *c*1737). David, Huguenot silversmith working in London; apprenticed to D. *Willaume in 1708; received freedom in 1722. Surviving works in Huguenot manner include spice box, and pair of teacup stands. Marks: TA (1713), entered before obtaining freedom, and DT (1720). On death, business continued by wife Ann, daughter of Willaume; surviving work in royal collection. Also worked on dinner service made by London silversmiths in 1734 for Empress of Russia. Her marks (in 1726): AT and TA.

tantalus. Wooden or metal case for holding spirit decanters; decanters visible, but locked into case by metal bar which fits around necks or over stoppers. Dates from *c*1850. Named after Tantalus of Greek legend, son of Zeus, condemned by gods to stand up to neck in water which receded if he attempted to drink. *Illustration at* Bristolglass.

T'an-tou. *See* Hsiao-pai-shih.

Tao Kuang (1821–50). Chinese Emperor, Ch'ing dynasty. In ceramics, reign marked by deterioration of both porcelain (became chalky and thin), and quality of glazes (became oily). Combined enamel colours of *famille rose* and *famille verte* palettes, unbalanced by dominant iron-red tone. Revivals of *tou ts'ai work (less often also *wu ts'ai) and imitation of K'ang Hsi underglaze blue work found. Interest developed in miniature work, e.g. snuff bottles. Some pieces identified by Mongolian script celebrating marriage of Emperor's daughter to Mongol prince, Baragon Tumed.

t'ao-t'ieh mask. One of most widely used motifs on Shang and early Chou bronzes, and used continuously in decoration down to modern times: monster's head, part bovine, part feline. When used as decoration on vessels, often formed by two geometrical dragons confronting each other; have bulging eyes, prominent eyebrows, horns and ears, and open mouth showing fangs. First named in 4th century B.C. as glutton mask, and as symbol of retribution.

taper box. *See* bougie box.

taper leg. Leg of table, chair, cabinet, etc., narrowing towards bottom; square in section throughout. Dates from *c*1750.

taper-stand. *See* wax-jack.

taperstick. Small candlestick (5–7in. high) for holding taper. Made from late 17th century; popular in second half of 18th and early 19th centuries. Follows larger metal, porcelain, and glass counterparts in style, though less ornate. Sockets deep and narrow. Glass examples usually with moulded pedestal shaft (sometimes shallow diamond-cut), with knops, tears, or *mereses.* Mounted on domed or terraced foot, sometimes decorated by cutting. Almost all 18th century silver examples follow designs for larger candlesticks (except for some shaped like Harlequin figure). During early 19th century in Britain various other designs made including rustic figure stems, miniature chamber candlesticks (made *c*1820–50 in Birmingham), and leaves supporting stem in form of small plant.

tapestry-weave carpets. Carpets without pile, woven in manner of tapestries. Oriental tapestry-weave carpet types include *kelims and *sumaks. In Europe, numerous folk types woven; main manufactory type, *Aubusson carpets.

tapis polonais. *See* Polish carpets.

tappit hen. Scottish pewter *measure, at first strictly of one Scottish pint (three Imperial pints); extended to cover any capacity in characteristically tall, slim, shape with cylindrical base, concave middle section, and shorter cylindrical neck. Earliest known example, 1669; most made mid 18th to mid 19th century. Lidless and dome-lidded examples followed in late 18th century by crested type with small finial on domed lid. *Illustration at* measure.

taquillon (Spanish). Chest-like base for **vargueño*. Similar size to latter, with two drawers at top and two cupboard doors below. Slides above drawers have shell or grotesque terminals and support *vargueño* front when extended. *Taquillon* less ornate, although decorated with carving, gilding, and inlay.

tassel foot. *See* paintbrush foot.

Tassie, James (1735–99). Scottish engraver and modeller of gems, cameos, etc. In Dublin from 1763, reproducing precious stones and antique cameos. Developed porcellanous material from finely ground glass; this could be softened by heating and pressed into moulds after wax casts of original. Set up workshop in London in late 1760s. Used opaque-white and coloured glass paste to reproduce engraved antique gems and cameos, mainly used for jewellery. Particularly noted for large profile portrait medallions. Used white paste on glass background, backed by coloured paper. Sold intaglio and cameo moulds to J. *Wedgwood from *c*1770. In 1775 published Descriptive Catalogue of a General Collection on Ancient and Modern Engraved Gems, Cameos as well as Intaglios, taken from the most celebrated Cabinets in Europe. Neo-classical silversmith, A. *Fogelberg, ornamented plate with silver medallions copied from Tassie's reproductions of gemstones. Succeeded by nephew, William Tassie (1777–1860), who specialized in reproducing engraved gems.

Tatham, Charles Heathcote (1772–1842). English opponent of Adam style, pupil of H. *Holland. In 1799 published Ancient Ornamental Architecture at Rome and in Italy and in 1806 Designs for Ornamental Plate. Advocated designs with massive effect; insisted on fine modelling and chasing. Inspired massive, sculptural presentation silver of early 19th century (e.g. J. *Flaxman's Trafalgar Vase and Shield of Achilles, T. *Stothard's Wellington Shield). Views also influenced domestic silver, which became more massive and sculptural.

Tatham, Thomas (1763–1818). Cabinet maker and upholsterer in London. Joined workshop of W. *Marsh in 1795; headed firm of Marsh & Tatham. Firm soon became Tatham & Bailey, upholsterers to Prince of Wales (later George IV).

tavern clock. *See* Act of Parliament clock.

tavern mug. *See* mug.

Ta-yao (Chekiang). Chinese kiln site active in Sung dynasty. Traditionally believed to be pottery of younger member of *Chang family, Shêng-erh. Shards unearthed have crackled glaze, similar to that used at important nearby centre, *Lung-ch'üan.

Taylor, John (1711–*c*1775). English japanner employing *Pontypool method. Worked in Birmingham from 1738. After 1750 turned to papier mâché as base for lacquer. Also made painted enamel ware, such as buttons and boxes, from *c*1740.

tax-farmer. Individual responsible in France for collecting tax or duty on gold and silver from late 17th century to Revolution. Practice of French monarchy to 'farm out' to financiers collection of tax on a particular commodity; lump sum was paid by these individuals for a stated period and they then tried to make up their investment. Offices were maintained where silversmiths brought work to have *charge and *discharge marks struck on pieces.

tazza. Vessel with wide, shallow, saucer-like bowl mounted on stem and foot, or directly on foot. May be flat topped, with or without rim. Popular Venetian form in 16th century in **cristallo* or coloured glass, often enamelled and gilded. In later 16th and early 17th centuries, often finely engraved in diamond-point. Form common throughout Europe with spread of *façon de Venise*. Also term used to describe gold, silver, or silver-gilt drinking vessel of similar shape; sometimes has cover with finial. Made in Britain and Europe from early 16th century. Dutch examples extremely elaborate: embossed with mythological, biblical, or genre scenes and interior set with embossed circular plaque. Early 17th century examples had baluster stem and plain bowl. Revived in Britain as form for *race cup and other presentation plate in mid 19th century.

tea and coffee machine. Sheffield plate tea and coffee server; three urns, with spigots and taps mounted on base. Larger central urn is sometimes mounted on swivel to allow refilling of smaller vessels. Rarest of Sheffield plate wares.

tea caddy or **canister** (caddy, from kati, Malay weight of $1\frac{1}{3}$lb). Container for storing tea. Tea-caddies made in silver date from end of 17th century. Known as canister until end of 18th century. Examples in sets of two or three, kept in locked *tea chest. Oblong or octagonal caddy with straight sides, flat top, and hole or short neck with domed lid. Sliding bottom made refilling simple. After 1725, vase-shaped caddies made in sets of three, one large, two small; often chased and embossed (e.g. with *chinoiseries*). Box-shaped caddy with curved sides bulging at top and concave lid with finial dates from mid 18th century; also cylindrical caddy with hinged cover and own lock. Caddies with own locks did not have accompanying case. Made in Sheffield plate from late 18th century. Glass canisters, also made during 18th century in various shapes, including square or flat bottle form, metal mounted. Produced in opaque-white glass at Stourbridge and Bristol, where enameller M. *Edkins also made tea labels, e.g. GREEN, HYSON, BLACK, BOHEA.

tea chest. Small chest or box with hinged, locking lid, to hold sets of *tea caddies, or with interior divided into sections for storage of tea and sugar. Many examples in hardwoods, or veneered; also covered in shagreen, tortoise-shell, mother-of-pearl, etc.; some of papier mâché. Mounts in silver or brass. Dates from 18th century. Also made in oval or long octagonal shape entirely of silver in late 18th century.

Tazza. *Elizabethan, maker's mark, a bunch of grapes, dated 1567. Silver-gilt; inside of bowl is chased with scene of meeting between Isaac and Rebecca; sides engraved with strapwork and arabesques, the foot with marine creatures. Height* $5\frac{3}{4}$*in.*

*Tea caddy. By P. *de Lamerie, 1747. Chased with* chinoiserie *scenes of tea growing. Height* $5\frac{5}{8}$*in.*

teacup. Small silver drinking vessel made in Europe in late 17th and early 18th centuries after introduction of tea. Circular, with two handles or none. Most examples from before 1715; superseded by porcelain cups, because silver unpractical. Some 18th and 19th century examples exist, but are rare.

Ceramic teacups at first not differentiated from cups for chocolate and coffee. Later, chocolate cups were two-handled with **trembleuse* saucers; coffee cups became straight-sided and single handled (coffee cans, made in porcelain, e.g. at Sèvres and Derby), teacups remained shallow and without handle (single handle present by mid 18th century).

teacup stand. *See trembleuse.*

tea fountain. *See* tea urn.

tea jar. Japanese ceramic form, used in tea ceremony. Tea leaves stored in oviform, or cylindrical, vessel, covered with lid. Sometimes small ceramic spoon made to accompany jar. As with other tea utensils, i.e. kettle, kettle-stand or mat, or tea-bowls, highly valued by owners, and imbued with ceremonial and spiritual significance.

tea kettle. Large silver, Sheffield plate, or electro-plated vessel for hot water, resembling teapot; used from early 18th century. Fixed or bail handle with ebony or wood inset. Matching tripod stand and spirit lamp. Common early form of *kettle of flattened, globular or octagonal shape embossed with rococo ornament; followed in mid 18th century by pear-shape (embossed with rococo ornament). Kettle superseded by tea urn *c*1760. Revived in early 19th century, but some examples have spigot and tap instead of spout.

tea kettle stand. Low *claw table for holding tea kettle and spirit lamp. Dates from 18th century.

teapot. Ceramic, silver, Sheffield plate or electro-plated container for brewing tea (rarely made in base metals, but examples known from *c*1850 in pewter, Britannia metal, japanned metal, etc.); usually modelled on Chinese wine or hot-water pot used in Britain and Europe from mid 17th century and slightly later in America. First European ceramic teapots made at Delft from *c*1672 in red earthenware imitating Yi-hsing red stoneware (also copied by J. F. *Böttger in red stoneware at Meissen). Short-spouted Delft form probably in turn model for Chinese white export porcelain teapot. Later ceramic teapots generally based on silver forms. Earliest silver teapot similar to coffee-pot with tapering cylindrical body, straight spout, handle at right angle to spout, and domed cover. Examples based on Chinese models have egg-shaped body, curved handle and spout at opposite ends, and domed lid with finial. Early 18th century teapot has rounded, polygonal or pear-shaped body, domed lid with finial, and moulded foot; handle and spout sometimes still set at right angles to each other, though placing at opposite sides became general. Inverted pear shape introduced *c*1730. Succeeded in 1760s and 1770s by flat-bottomed, drum-shaped teapot with straight spout and flat lid. In late 18th century, oval, rectangular, and faceted boat-shaped teapots common. Flat-bottomed types often had matching stand to protect surface of tea table. In some cases, stand is later addition by different maker. In early 19th century (*c*1815) pear shape revived; all examples lavishly ornamented. *See* bullet teapot, cauliflower ware, Frisian teapot, salt-glaze ware, tea service.

teapoy. Small pedestal or three-legged table

Right:
Teapoy. English, c*1830. Rosewood with beading decoration along edges of chest.*

Below:
*Teapot. Pear-shaped, on rim foot, with curved, octagonal spout; high domed cover with baluster finial and wooden handle. English, 1718, made by G. *Sleath.*

Tea kettle and stand. Ivory handle and knob to lid. Dutch, by Arnoldus Coolhaas; made in Utrecht, c*1640.*

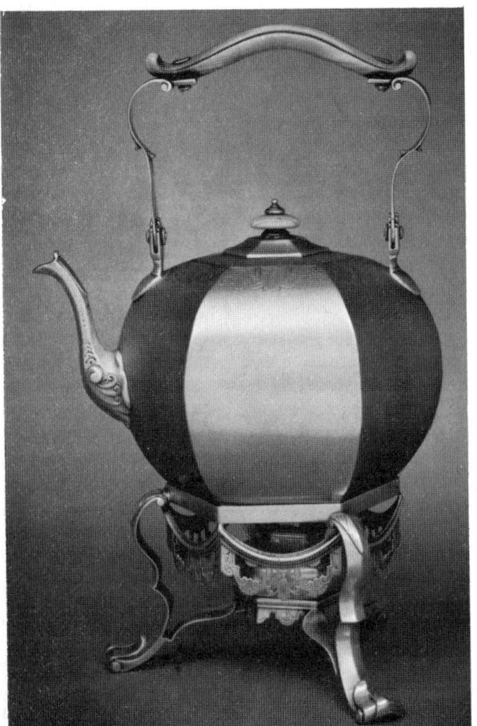

*Tea service. Silver gilt, made in Paris by *Odiot, early 19th century, in *Empire style. Left to right: tea caddy,* sucrier, *tea urn, hot water jug, and teapot. Height of urn* c17*in.*

Tea table. Made in New England, early 18th century, in Queen Anne style. Height 2ft4in.
Tea tray. Made in Sheffield, 1858, by W. & G. Sissons, engraved with leafage, foliate masks and flowering plants in cartouches. Width 2ft7in.

Below:
Tea urn. Made in Edinburgh by P. Robertson, 1780; neo-classical style with decoration of swags, ribbons, paterae, *and fluting.*

(from Indian and Persian meaning 'three feet'). By erroneous association with tea, came to mean small tea chest with fitted interior, standing on small tripod table with tray top or mounted on stand or legs; also small table for serving tea.

tear. Tear-shaped air-bubble enclosed in solid glass, first accidentally, then as ornament. Formed by pricking metal and covering with second gather, entrapped air inside being expanded by heat into bubble. Also made by inserting fine hollow pipe into hot metal and blowing into required shape, or by inserting drop of alcohol. Particularly popular in 18th century wine glass stems and as clusters in finials and knops.

tea service. Silver, Sheffield plate, or electroplated teapot, milk or cream jug, and sugar bowl made *en suite* from early 18th century in Britain, Europe, and America. (*See* Cabaret set.) Most examples date from late 18th century. Sometimes included tea kettle and spirit lamp, coffee-pot, and tea tray. 19th century British services massive; many different designs. In mid century some made with naturalistic decoration, but commonly with rococo-style ornament.

teaspoon. Small silver *spoon forming part of tea service. In use in Britain and Europe from late 17th century. Earliest had trefid stem and rat-tail reinforcement at back of bowl; development generally followed larger spoons.

tea table. Occasional table with raised rim (often of pierced design) to prevent tea cups from slipping off. Form dates from late 17th century England; term used from middle of 18th century. *See table en guéridon.*

tea tray. Silver, Sheffield plate or electro-plate tray or salver for serving tea, used in Britain and Europe from early 18th century. Size and shape vary greatly, but usually large (up to 20in. long); oval or oblong, with four feet. Earliest type has simple moulded edge; rococo examples have elaborate cast border. In Britain *c*1750, table sometimes made same size as tea tray with sockets into which feet fitted. Oval tray with vertical pierced gallery and hole at each end for hand-hold made during late 18th century. Many made in Sheffield plate; from *c*1800–*c*1840 more trays made than any other article in Sheffield plate. Elaborate silver rims, chased designs, and engraved shields.

tea urn or **fountain.** Large silver, Sheffield plate or *japanned metal hot-water urn used instead of tea kettle from mid 18th century in Britain and Europe. Earliest examples have pear-shaped body on four feet or on square base with four feet, a spigot and tap at bottom of body, two handles, and domed cover with finial. Classical vase-shape also made. Urn usually has compartment inside for red-hot iron to keep water hot.

Tebo (fl mid-late 18th century). Porcelain modeller and repairer in England; supposedly French (Thibaud). Work with impressed mark T^0, presumed his, appears on porcelain from Bow (*c*1750–*c*1765), Plymouth (1768–70), Bristol, and Worcester (*c*1770–75). Noted for pieces including salts and small dishes with shells and *rocaille* in applied relief; also rococo vases and many figures made at Worcester. In 1774, worked briefly for J. *Wedgwood. Later, went to Dublin.

*Tê-hua. Figure of *Kuan-yin. 17th century. Height* 10*in.*

Tê-ch'ing (Chekiang). Chinese kiln site, at Tê-ch'ing Hsien, discovered in 1930. Important from Han period to Six Dynasties. Produced *Yüeh and *temmoku ware. Glaze on former usually green in comparison with other contemporary celadons. *Illustration at* chicken-head ewer.

Tê Hua (Fukien). Chinese white porcelain made for export from 15th to 18th century, called in France *blanc-de-chine.* Prized in Europe for dense, luminous whiteness; glassy body and milky glaze (tinged with soft grey or pink, or pure white) perfectly fused. Variety of objects produced, unchanged, over long period makes dating difficult. Most examples in West imported from K'ang Hsi period onwards. Potters' seals found, but markings often obscured by glaze on base. Figures, coarsely modelled with detachable head; or elaborate, delicately finished, often with minute fingers and soft folds in fabric. Some items, e.g. cups, decorated in China with red and green enamels or underglaze blue. More often, plain white ware painted after shipment to Europe, e.g. in Holland. Porringers and tankards made in imitation of German and English 17th century stoneware. Some caricatures of foreigners. Objects made to European specifications also known. Vases decorated with moulded relief of prunus blossom or dragon; forms incised or with sunken panels. *An hua decoration also found.

Tekke carpets. Finely-knotted, south Turkoman carpets woven by Tekke tribe. Distinctive gul, a flattened octagon with inner coloured area, and contrasting outer band with leaf or bird-head motifs. Field has rows of guls linked by thick perpendicular lines dividing field into rectangular areas and often dwarfing guls. Predominantly rich red colour. Main border with stick-rayed stars, octagons and small stars, or toothed lozenge band.

telescope. Simplest form of refracting telescope with plano-concave eyepiece lens (flat on one side, concave on other) and biconvex objective lens (rounded on both sides) mounted at ends of card or parchment tube. Known from beginning of 17th century and applied to astronomy by Galileo, and Simon Mayer in 1609. Developed by many makers throughout 17th century, including R. *Hooke and C. *Huygens. Quality limited by problems of producing and grinding glass for lenses. Early examples often have sliding card tubes, covered with leather, etc., lenses mounted in wooden rings. Wood used for tubes from late 17th century; brass common from *c*1700. Improvements in glass making in 18th century led to development of telescopes with combination lenses giving greater magnification and reduced distortion. Reflecting telescopes using finely polished mirrors developed first by Sir Isaac Newton in late 17th century; improvements during 18th century, mainly by astronomers, culminated in work of William Herschel and production in 1788 of 40ft telescope with mirror of 48in. diameter.

Telleruhr. *See* plate clock.

tell-tale clock or **watchman's clock.** Forerunner of modern factory clocking-in machine, devised in late 18th century by J. *Whitehurst: rotating 12 or 24 hour dial, housed in oak case, carries projecting pins at half-hour intervals around circumference, depressed by push-piece outside case to leave record of visits by night-watchmen, etc. Pins automatically restored to alert position after examination by supervisor.

Tell-tale clock. English, c1875, by John Smith of Derby. Eight-day fusee movement with registration pins on dial; teak case.

temmoku glaze. In Japan, denotes black or brownish-black glaze, originating on Chinese *Chien ware, manufactured in Fukien province; used e.g. on Ting-chou ware in Sung dynasty. Has silvery iridescence, sometimes forming rings, like oil-spots, or with blue or grey streaks, known as 'hare's fur'. Copies made in Honan and Kiangsi provinces, where whiter clay bodies covered with dark slip under glaze. Exported items treasured in Japan. *Illustration at* hare's fur glaze.

temper. Term used to describe tin when alloyed with copper; alternatively copper or antimony content of tin alloy (*cf* tin and temper). Tempering also heat treatment of previously hardened steel, producing required degree of hardness and elasticity in knife blades, springs, etc.

Temperantia Dish. Masterpiece (1585–90) of F. *Briot. Pewter dish, diameter 18in., with moulded and embossed decoration including allegory of Temperance and other figures in mannerist style. Copies made Kaspar Enderlein and others throughout 17th century.

Tempestà, Antonio (1555–1630). Italian engraver. Hunting scenes by him copied on faience made at Talavera de la Reina in late 16th century, Nevers in mid 17th century, Moustiers (*c*1679–1710), and later Marseille (Saint-Jean-du-Désert).

temple clock. French architectural style clock, simulating ancient Greek or Roman temple. (Some, with small gilt cupids inside, known as *temples d'amour.*) Made *c*1770–1810. Horizontal dial band.

Teniers, David the Younger (1610–90). Flemish painter, son of artist. Court painter to Archduke Leopold Wilhelm in Brussels; also keeper of his art collection which inspired his painting and engraving. Most famous for peasant scenes and rustic landscapes, widely copied and imitated. Miniature versions often appear on snuff-boxes. 'Teniers' (or 'Tenières') tapestries woven to designs based on paintings, initially in Brussels; much copied in 17th and 18th century France and England. 'Teniers subjects' painted *c*1725–65 on porcelain at Meissen, Berlin, Frankenthal, and Höchst; also at some *Hausmaler* workshops.

terracotta (Italian, 'baked earth'). Lightly fired earthenware, often red or brownish in colour. Small figures of religious or magical significance date e.g. from neolithic Greece. Later examples include Chinese grave figures of Han and T'ang periods (*see* ming-ch'i). Harder terracotta, fired at higher temperature, used for architectural and ornamental purposes e.g. by L. *Della Robbia, F. *Pratt.

terre cuite. *See pâte de marbre.*

terre de Lorraine. Unglazed ceramic body varying in composition from pipeclay to hard material resembling biscuit porcelain; used to make figures in Lorraine, notably at Lunéville

David Teniers. The Village Fête, 'Teniers' tapestry, woven in Brussels by Jerome Le Clerc and Jacques van der Borght in wool and silk; late 17th century.

Thistle cup. Scottish, made by William Scott of Banff, c1680. Miniature size: height $1\frac{3}{4}$in.

from mid 18th century by P-L. *Cyfflé; also at Niderviller from moulds made by Cyfflé and C-G. *Sauvage.

terre de pipe. *See* pipeclay.

terrella. Small sphere of natural magnetic ore, claimed (erroneously) in 16th century to reproduce rotation of earth of own accord.

terrine. *See* tureen.

Terry, E. (1772–1852). American clock maker, inventor, and businessman, from Connecticut. Many patents; first was for equation clock in 1797. Produced large quantities of clocks, notably shelf clock, with wooden movement. Typical example *c*24in. high, with painted iron dial, and decorated tablet below. Pointed feet; scroll decoration at top and bottom of clock. Patented *box-case clock, 1816; probably designer of *pillar and scroll clock. Produced own tools for large-scale manufacture of clocks.

Terry, Silas Burnham (1807–76). American clock maker and inventor; son of E. *Terry. Maker of shelf, steeple, and wall clocks.

tester. Wooden canopy over bed, supported by bed posts or by foot posts and headboard.

test piece. *See* assay.

tête-à-tête (in ceramics). *See* cabaret.

tête-à-tête (in furniture). *See confidante.*

tête de poupée (French, 'doll's head'). French mantel clock, introduced *c*1680. Head-shaped dial, with arched top, and two symmetrical side-pieces, or ears (sometimes with pendants attached). Set on raised stand, supported by feet. Inlay decoration in brass and tortoiseshell.

Theed, William (1764–1817). English sculptor; studied at Royal Academy schools; visited Rome. Worked as designer for J. *Wedgwood; in 1808, joined *Rundell, Bridge & Rundell. Designed display and presentation silver.

The Hague (Holland). Decorating workshop established in mid 18th century. Hard-paste porcelain made in Germany marked with stork painted in blue over underglaze blue A, mark of Ansbach factory. Soft-paste porcelain made at Tournai decorated with birds and landscapes in polychrome, often with narrow, wavy blue borders picked out in gold. Hard-paste porcelain manufactured at The Hague (1776–90) painted with cupids in style of F. *Boucher, in purple monochrome; also polychrome flowers. Mark: stork holding eel, in underglaze blue or blue enamel. Delft ware made from mid 17th century. Factory established in 1680s by J. T. *Godtling, in partnership. No products identified.

theorbo. *See* lute.

thermometer. Instrument for measuring temperature; first made in form of glass bulb and tube containing liquid *c*1640 in Italy. Expansion of liquid in tube gives indication of temperature. Water and alcohol first liquids used; mercury became general from *c*1720. Makers used arbitrary graduations until Fahrenheit and Reamur established accepted scales in early 18th century.

thirdendale or **thurndell.** Pewter measure or tankard known from 16th century records; thought to contain either 3 pints or $\frac{1}{3}$ gallon.

thistle cup. Scottish mug made from late 17th century. Has slightly bulging body, decorated round base with applied spoon-handle decoration, and everted rim: shape suggestive of thistle. Handle usually of scroll form. Alternatively, 16th century British or European gold, silver, or silver-gilt standing cup with thistle-shaped bowl; generally on bracketed baluster stem (scroll brackets link bottom of bowl with upper part of baluster knop); slightly domed cover with finial. Originated in Germany. *See* Bowes Cup.

thistle mark. On Scottish pewter from 17th century, mark equivalent to English *rose and crown.

thistle measure. Scottish pewter measure in thistle shape made *c*1800–*c*1830; banned for tavern use by weights and measures authorities because when tipped, some liquid remains in bowl. Many destroyed for this reason, and examples rare.

Thomas, Seth (1785–1859). American clock maker from Connecticut. Skilled carpenter and joiner. Worked with E. *Terry from *c*1808. Made tall clocks; also *pillar and scroll clocks. In business from 1813; firm formally established as Seth Thomas Clock Company, 1853.

Thomason, I. or J. (fl late 18th and early 19th centuries). English silhouettist. Assistant to J. *Miers in Leeds. In Dublin, 1790–92, then in north of England before moving to London. Painting on card or plaster of Paris composition follows style of Miers; characterized by knot of ribbon at front of bustline in female profiles. In early 19th century, painted on glass, using touches of colour; wax backings. Produced likeness of George Washington.

Thomason, Sir Edward (1769–1835). English manufacturer of Sheffield plate and silver in Birmingham; trained with M. *Boulton; founded firm in 1793. In 1810, experimented with plating steel or iron with silver using tin as solder. Credited with invention of *wine wagon.

Responsible for bronze reproductions of *Warwick vase (1820). Firm taken over in 1835 by G. R. *Collis.

Thomire, Pierre-Philippe (1751–1843). French *fondeur-ciseleur,* working in both neo-classical and Empire styles. Started career as sculptor. Learned bronze-casting from P. *Gouthière and cast sculptures for Houdon and Patjou. Made bronze mounts for porcelain at Sèvres from 1783, and from 1784 received commissions from the *Garde Meuble de la Couronne.* Made mounts for J-G. *Beneman. Received commissions from Napoleon; appointed his Maker of Bronzes in 1813. Retired in 1823. Work frequently marked. Firm first known as Thomire-Dutherme et Cie, later as Thomire et Cie. *Illustration at* Empire style.

Thonet, Michael (1796–1871). Prussian joiner, carpenter, and furniture maker, whose *bentwood was among earliest mass-produced furniture. Began experiments in bentwood shapes *c*1830; granted patents 1841–42. Furniture popular in England after showing at Great Exhibition, 1851. *Illustration at* bentwood furniture.

thread-and-shell pattern. Pattern used to decorate spoons and forks in *fiddle pattern. Stem edged with moulded thread line; relief shell pattern on face of stem end and forming reinforcement on back of bowl.

threaded edge. Moulded thread or line on edges or rims of silver, particularly flatware; common in late 18th and 19th century British silver. *Illustration at* fiddle pattern.

threading. *See* trailing.

Three Friends. In Chinese ceramics, motifs of bamboo, pine, and prunus blossom, symbolizing respectively the founders of three dominant eastern religions: Confucius, Lao Tzŭ (Taoism) and Buddha. Used in most periods.

Three Golden Ash-barrels, The (De 3 Vergulde Astonnekens). Delft factory (1655–1803) owned by W. *van Eenhoorn, from 1668 with G. *Kam, then sole owner (1679–1805), succeeded by family. Zacharias Dextra manager from 1712, owner-director 1721–57; introduced enamel colours. A. *van Rijsselberg employed early 18th century. From 1730, produced many animal figures, and dishes in form of animals.

Three Porcelain Bottles, The (De Drye Porceleyne Flesschen). Delft factory (1661–1777), property of J. *Brouwer, bought for son, Hugo, manager and, from 1767, co-owner.

three-train clock. Clock with separate *trains for going, striking, and chiming.

thumbpiece, billet, or **purchase.** Small lever attached to hinged lid of silver or pewter tankard, flagon, or measure above handle, for opening lid with thumb. Used throughout Europe from 17th century. Cast in decorative shapes; main varieties are *wedge, *ball-and-wedge, *ball, *hammerhead, *bud-and-wedge, *double volute, *chair-back, *open, *ball-and-bar, *embryo shell, *twin acorn, *corkscrew, *ram's horn. Also small grip on snuff-box, etc., for opening lid.

Thuret or **Turet,** Isaac (d 1700). French clock and watch maker. Clock maker to Louis XIV from 1686. Maker of *oignon* watch (*c*1680) and mantel clocks, including *pendule religieuse.* Succeeded by son, Jacques (d *c*1738).

thurible. *See* censer.

thurndell. *See* thirdendale.

tiara. Ornamental coronet of classical origin, circular or crescent-shaped, worn by women from 19th century. Early forms often extremely elaborate; popular design consisted of open scrolls *pavé*-set with gems (usually diamonds) and with pearl drops or emerald **briolettes* hanging in intervening spaces; often with focal stone at centre. Popular style in Napoleonic France included cameos linked by fine chains. Gothic style tiara popular in mid 19th century, with gold tracery and enamel or gems.

Tiefschnitt (German, 'deep cut'). Intaglio engraving on glass; technique perfected by 18th century Bohemian and Silesian engravers; popular throughout Germany. Sometimes used in conjunction with **Hochschnitt.* *Potsdam glasses popular subjects for technique.

T'ien Ch'i (1621–27). Chinese emperor, Ming period. Porcelain surviving from unsettled reign mostly primitive dishes, roughly painted in greyish underglaze blue, with imperfect enamel colours. Style of enamel work (in green, red, aubergine, and yellow) popular in Japan, providing origin of *kutani palette. Pieces, especially bearing *nien hao, rare.

tigerware jug. Big-bellied jug in salt-glazed stoneware with mottled surface resembling tiger or leopard markings. Originated in Germany; imported to England in 16th century, where mounted with e.g. embossed and engraved silver or silver-gilt cover, neckband, and foot-ring. Various examples with foot-ring, *c*8–10in. high.

Tijou, Jean (fl *c*1689–1712). Huguenot designer and artist in *wrought iron. Arrived in England from Holland *c*1689; worked at many great houses, e.g. Hampton Court, Castle Howard, Chatsworth, Burghley House. Greatest work considered to be sanctuary screen in St Paul's Cathedral, London. Publication in 1693 of A New Booke of Drawings Invented and Desined by John Tijou disseminated his style throughout England.

tile pictures. Ceramic decoration, painted over number of ceramic tiles. Thought to have been introduced in Europe by Italian maiolica painters; first signed example (1503) by F. *Niculoso, influenced by maiolica style of Faenza. Manufacture notably at Talavera de la Reina (late 16th and early 17th centuries), Valencia (17th century); also, rarely, at Alcora in 18th century. Tile pictures made in 16th century Portugal, influenced by both Italian maiolica and Flemish tiles; in 17th century, decoration mainly in blue. Many exported to Brazil. In Antwerp, work of Italian potters, including G. *Andries, influenced by Flemish engravings, decorated with grotesques and strapwork; earliest example dated 1547; tile panel depicting The Return of the Prodigal, by J. *van den Bogaert, dated 1570. In late 16th

Tigerware jug. Elizabethan silver-gilt mounts; band at neck chased with strapwork; upstanding hinge with two acorn finials. Maker's mark IC, made in London, 1566.

*Tile picture. Twelve tin-glazed tiles from factory of J. *Aelmis, Rotterdam, depicting Christ on the Cross with St Mary Magdalene. Painted in manganese-purple,* c*1760. Height 1ft10in.*

century, Dutch cities, notably Rotterdam, established as centres of production; pictures frequently large, e.g. allegorical scene of Love, Justice, Unity, Fidelity, and Steadfastness, painted in purple with touches of blue over 357 tiles. Subjects include flowers, landscapes, seascapes, harbour scenes, and religious subjects, e.g. Hagar and Ishmael painted after engraving by J. *Aelmis (1691). Polychrome tile pictures of flower vases used to decorate backs of fireplaces; usually 13 tiles high and 8 across. Scenes from Chinese life painted in *delft noir*.

tiles. Thin slabs, usually of earthenware, for surfacing floors or roofs, and for decoration of walls, fireplaces, etc. Floor tiles decorated with impressed designs filled with contrasting coloured clay (notably in France and England). In Germany, impressed decoration in relief formed basis of *Hafner* tiles. Tin-enamelled paving tiles decorated by Italian maiolica painters; first examples date from early 15th century. Designs include foliage, portraits, and frequently, heraldic devices; later trophies, grotesques, strapwork, and festoons. Technique developed by Italians, e.g. G. *Andries, in Flanders. French paving tiles dated 1535 to after 1564 made at Rouen and by *Conrade family at Nevers from 1578.

Walls decorated with tiles by 9th century in Near East. By 14th century, mosaics made of tin-glazed tiles cut in geometrical shapes, notably at Seville (e.g. decoration of Alhambra Palace), and Valencia (in late 14th and early 15th centuries); mosaic paving made at Manises and Paterna. **Cuerda seca* technique introduced in mid 15th century; **cuenca*, introduced later, used in 16th century to decorate ceiling tiles. In 17th and 18th centuries, blue painting gradually replaced polychrome decoration at Seville and Talavera de la Reina. 17th and 18th century Dutch tiles developed from *Antwerp-style maiolica tiles of 15th century; Rotterdam became centre of production; manufacture also at e.g. Delft and Haarlem. *Pounces used to mass-produce lines of decoration including ripe pomegranates, bunches of grapes, other plant forms, and geometrical patterns; corners patterned, e.g. with fleurs-de-lis, scrolls, or **ossekoppen*. From *c*1625, use of corner motifs gradually ceased, and blue or manganese-purple monochrome more often used for increasingly pictorial painting. Stove tiles with blue painting made at Hamburg, wall tiles at Ansbach, Augsburg, and Nuremberg.

English delftware tiles made at Bristol (e.g. with landscapes painted in blue by J. *Bowen) and Lambeth; at Liverpool, transfer-printed by J. *Sadler G. *Green. Cream-coloured earthenware superseded delftware in late 18th century. German, French, Spanish, and Portuguese tile makers also influenced by Dutch tiles in 17th and 18th centuries. Tiles occasionally made in porcelain (at Meissen and Fürstenberg), or in German or English stoneware.

Early American tiles made at Philadelphia, Pennsylvania, mid 19th century.

tilt-top table. *See* snap table.

time measurement. Solar time as shown by *sundials is governed by daily rotation of earth with respect to sun, varying slightly in length through year: clocks normally show mean time, i.e. with days averaged to equal duration. *Equation clocks have dial to show difference between solar and mean time on any day. Sidereal time used by astronomers depends on rotation of earth regardless of orbit around sun: sidereal day is 3 minutes 56 seconds less than mean solar day, thus sidereal clocks must run slightly faster than normal.

Different methods of dividing day into hours were evolved throughout world, some with hours of varying length, e.g. Japanese time measurement, or with day officially starting at different points, as sunrise or sunset. Italian hour system in use in parts of Europe to 19th century has hours 1–24 starting at sunset, while German system, later generally adopted, has two 12 hour cycles starting at midnight and midday. *See* clock, fire clock, nocturnal dial, sundial, watch, water clock.

timepiece. Strictly, clock or watch with time-keeping mechanism only, i.e. without striking or alarm work.

tin. Soft, brittle, white metal normally used in alloy, e.g. bronze and pewter, or combined with other metals to give rust-resistant finish or protective covering, e.g. on interiors of brass or copper, or Sheffield plate cooking vessels.

tin and temper. Hard, close-textured pewter alloy of tin and small quantity of antimony.

tinder-box. Box made of latten, iron, wood or Sheffield plate, containing fire-making equipment of flint, steel, and tinder; used from 15th to 19th centuries in various forms. To produce flame, piece of specially prepared flint struck on steel blade often decoratively shaped, until spark appears; this falls on tinder – usually charred linen and corkwood fungus, or oil-soaked rag – which burns or smoulders. Sulphur-dipped splinter of wood held against this used as match to light candles, etc. Wheel-lock tinder-box (16th century improvement) has trigger and wound spring mechanism; steel wheel revolves against piece of iron disulphide, or pyrites, producing sparks which, with gunpowder, ignite tinder. Many variations and improvements made on basic form (*see* strike-a-light), and small examples designed for carrying in pocket.

ting. Originally, pottery cooking vessel of neolithic cultures, e.g. Lung Shan and Yang Shao; made also in bronze from Shang period. Rounded bowl, set on three legs, with loop handles on rim. Late Shang types sometimes have four legs and rectangular body. Earliest examples, 12th to 11th century B.C.

Ting-chou ware. Chinese ceramics of northern *Sung dynasty. First Imperial palace ware of period; made in Hopei province. White glaze, of ivory tint, covers thinly potted white porcelain body. Glaze collects in characteristic teardrop pattern. Small foot also typical. Fired resting on rim; edge sometimes sheathed with metal band. Sometimes has *temmoku glaze (black Ting), and some brownish celadon (purple Ting). White glazed ware copied in all later periods.

Ting glaze. Chinese ceramics. Dense, ivory-white glaze originally used on Sung porcellanous ware; also, imitations of glaze in subsequent periods.

tin-glass. *See* bismuth.

Ting shape. Bronze ritual cauldron decorated with frieze of hooked dragon motifs arranged in confronted pairs; double upright loop handles. 11th–10th century B.C., from An-Yang. Height 5¾in.

*Ting glaze. Vase of *mei-p'ing form with incised decoration. Greyish white porcelain with ivory glaze. Vase thrown in three parts and joined horizontally. Height 14½in.*

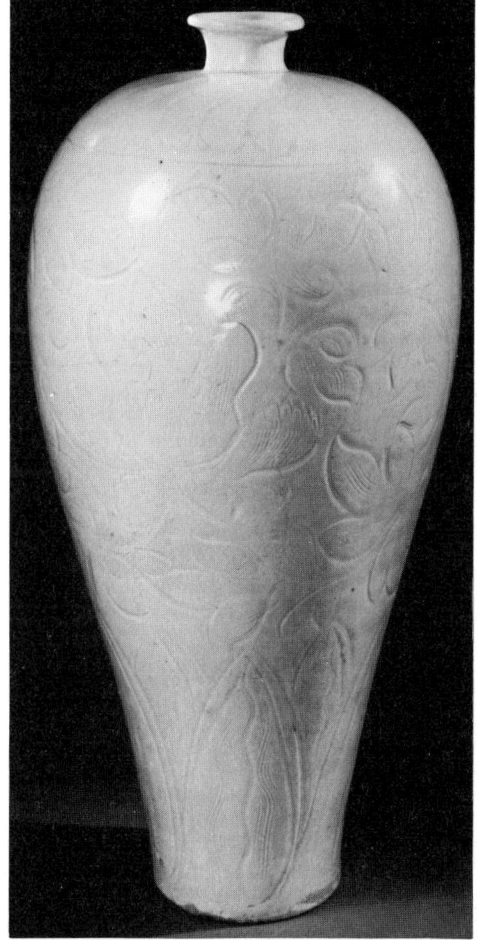

*Tin-glazed earthenware. One of pair of Brussels faience *bird tureens, in form of duck,* c*1780.*

tin-glaze or **tin-enamel glaze.** *Lead-glaze made opaque by addition of tin oxide; sometimes coloured with metallic oxide, e.g. cobalt in *berrettino* glaze. Used in *tin-glazed earthenware. Introduced, e.g. in Assyria, by 8th century B.C., for glazing building bricks; apparently died out until 9th century when used in Mesopotamia. Spread to Spain in 13th century: used on Hispano-Moresque wares; also in Italy from 13th century, reaching height in 15th and 16th centuries; then in rest of Europe.

tin-glazed earthenware. Earthenware covered with *tin-glaze. The material of *maiolica, *faience, Dutch *Delft and *English delftware. Made by dipping *biscuit in liquid glaze; water absorbed, leaving even deposit of glaze over surface. Decoration in high-temperature colours developed by second firing, which also fuses glaze. Largely superseded by cream-coloured earthenware in late 18th century.

ting-tang. *See* striking systems.

tinning. Coating of tin on base metal surface; object is dipped in, or sprinkled with, sal ammoniac and heated; molten tin then poured over surface. Sal ammoniac promotes fusion of metals. Extensively used in production of Sheffield plate domestic ware for use in preparation or consumption of food. Inside and underside of single-plated articles, e.g. teapots, cream jugs, waiters, trays, etc., are tinned.

tin-plated iron. Earlier method of covering iron plate with layer of tin superseded *c*1730 by method whereby tin completely fused with iron, giving whitish colour and uniform texture. First made at Pontypool, Monmouthshire, and sold for manufacture of kitchen utensils (bowls, basins, pans, funnels) and used as base for *japanned metal; overcame problem of peeling, which had proved insurmountable with surface-tinned iron. Large tureens and serving-dishes sometimes made of tin-plated iron and highly burnished, before introduction of *Sheffield plate.

Toasted cheese dish. English, Sheffield plate, c*1805. Length* 8*in.*

Toast rack. George III period, made in Edinburgh. Length 10*in.*

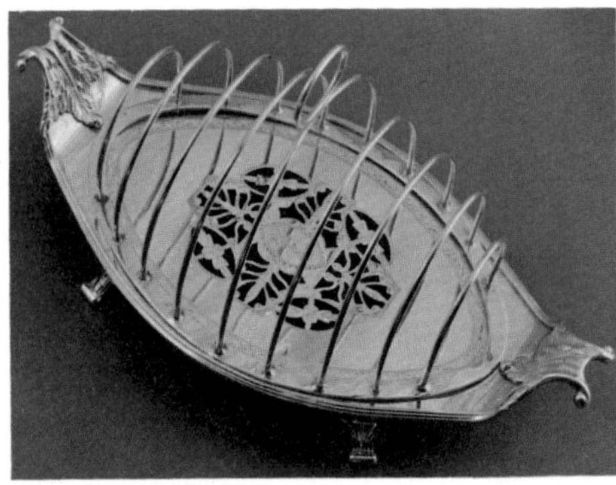

Right:
Toasters. English, dated 1794, 1798, and 1804.

tipsy key. *See* key.

tip-top table. *See* snap table.

toasted cheese dish. Silver or Sheffield plate oblong or oval dish with hinged cover, resembling entrée dish; usually with projecting handle of turned wood. Sometimes has compartment for hot water and/or small dishes for individual servings. In use in Britain in 18th and early 19th centuries.

toaster. Long-handled forks commonly used as toasters from 16th century, sometimes with fitment for resting on bars of grate or fender. Various devices used in 18th and 19th centuries. Wrought-iron tripod type holds pole with adjustable fitment of prongs, sometimes on bell-shaped frame with ring beneath to hold greasepan for toasting small birds. Trivet type has brass or steel sliding prongs.

toast-master glass. English drinking glass

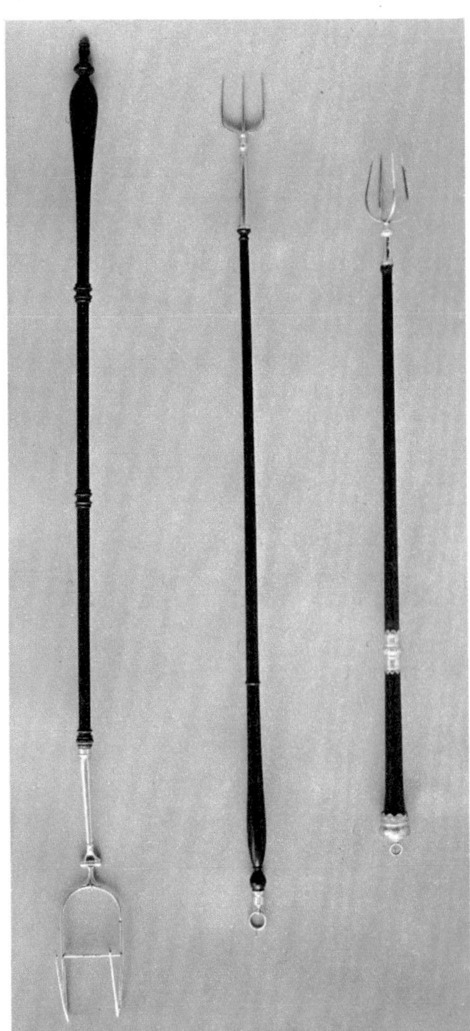

Tobacco boxes. English silver. Left: Charles II, made in London, 1677; slip-over cover engraved with contemporary coat of arms. Centre: box probably made in Devonshire, c1690, maker's mark, IE; corded edge to base and cover, contemporary coat of arms. Right: very early Commonwealth box, made in London, 1655, maker's mark, GS, with spear between initials. Slip-on cover engraved with name Hugh Gould and date July 13th 1655.

*Toby jug (right) with *Martha Gunn jug. Stoneware, made by R. *Wood I, c1770.*

*Charles Toft. Ewer in *Henri II ware, shown at exhibition of 1862, London. Based on 16th century patterns. Height 15in.*

with tall stem, solid conical foot, and straight sided, deceptively thick-walled, bowl. Holds $c\frac{1}{2}$oz liquid, to ensure sobriety of toast-master who drank long succession of toasts. Occasionally found as commemorative presentation glass. Made from *c*1740. Always fine quality.

toast rack. Silver, Sheffield plate, or electroplated wire rack, sometimes detachable, fitting into oval tray base. Used from late 18th century in Britain. Later shapes of base include oblong and boat-shaped. Generally has seven wires or bars to hold six slices of toast. Sometimes has central vertical rod with ring handle.

tobacco box. Small metal box with tightly-fitting hinged lid for tobacco. Earliest are Dutch examples, made from early 17th century in brass and/or copper, and much copied elsewhere: long, rectangular boxes (occasionally square or oval) engraved, later embossed, with smoking, military, rustic or sporting themes, landscapes, figures, biblical scenes. Common 18th century Dutch type incorporates perpetual calendar and bust of Julius Caesar or Pope Gregory; others have bust, probably of Cabot or Vespucci, date 1497, and globe, relating to discovery of America. Typical 18th century English type is plain, engraved with coat of arms, name, or monogram. Steel boxes, plain or engraved, made in late 18th and early 19th centuries. M. *Boulton made some in Bath metal. Many also made in silver, Sheffield plate, lead, sometimes pewter, in similar style. *See* Iserlohn boxes.

tobacco cutter. Wooden-handled steel blade hinged to wooden block, used for cutting tobacco from compressed roll, from 18th century. Brass and mahogany used in early 19th century. More complicated type, made from *c*1870, equipped with self-propelling mechanism and sliding tray.

tobacco jar. Lidded container for tobacco, widely made in lead from early 17th to late 19th centuries. Earliest are cylindrical; from late 18th century, rectangular shape, with deeply chamfered corners and decorated sides on moulded base. Lids usually domed, with ornamental knop, often incorporating lead weight inside to press down tobacco and keep lid tightly closed. During 19th century, many examples brightly painted, but few remain in original state. Decorative devices include smoking or sporting themes, commemoration of military events, agricultural or masonic symbols, or, on jar belonging to inn, emblem of ownership, e.g. fox, crown, spread eagle, wheat-sheaf, etc. Brass and cast iron examples in similar shapes and styles, particularly Gothic revival style, made in early 19th century. Pewter also popular, usually in similar styles and following silver designs.

tobacco rasp. *See* snuff rasp.

tobacco-stopper. *See* pipe-stopper.

Tobi seiji (Japanese, 'spotted celadon'). Ceramics of Kamakura period, when Chinese celadons widely admired and imitated. *Lung-ch'üan especially popular, and *iron-brown spotted variety often copied, mainly at Kyoto potteries.

Toby jugs. Earthenware jugs representing man, usually wearing tricorne hat, holding jug of beer and pipe or glass. Early Toby jugs made by R. *Wood I from *c*1760; those made by R. *Wood II in brighter colours, including orange, black, green, and blue, more thickly potted and raised on higher bases. Rarer variations depict other personalities, e.g. *Martha Gunn, The Thin Man, Prince Hal, The Planter, The Sailor, The Squire, Lord Vernon, and later religious figures inspired by preaching of John Wesley. Other Makers include E. *Wood, *Neale & Co, S. *Hollins, and J. *Spode I. Many imitations, occasionally in porcelain, produced to present day.

toddy lifter. English glass vessel used to convey hot toddy or punch from bowl to glass. Long neck sometimes decorated with one or two wide rings, or groups of three closely spaced rings, ending in bulbous container of *c*3oz capacity with hole in flat base. Held by first and second fingers, plunged into bowl until full. Thumb placed over mouth to create vacuum and removed to release liquid into glass. Most examples resemble small decanter. Scottish examples usually club-shaped. In Regency period, often elaborately diamond-cut or engraved. Made from late 18th century.

Toft, Charles (1832–1909). English ceramic modeller at H. *Minton's factory, Stoke-

Thomas Toft I. Slipware dish, c1675, decorated with royal coat of arms.

Toilet service. English, dated 1683 with maker's mark, W F; silver-gilt. Service consists of pair of

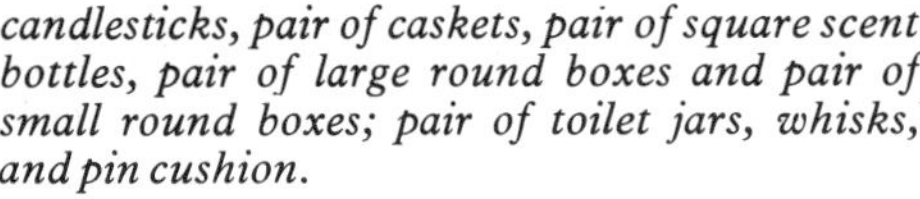

candlesticks, pair of caskets, pair of square scent bottles, pair of large round boxes and pair of small round boxes; pair of toilet jars, whisks, and pin cushion.

Toilet mirror. Queen Anne period, early 18th century. Lacquered in olive green; two small drawers at base, and writing flap; mirror swings; cresting of carved giltwood.

on-Trent. In 1854, took out patent for inlay decoration on earthenware; grooves turned in surface of pottery and filled in with coloured slip. Made close copies of Saint-Porchaire ware marketed as Henri II ware.

Toft family, notably Thomas I (d 1689), his brother Ralph (b *c*1638) and son Thomas II (*c*1670–1703). Makers of large Staffordshire slipware dishes and rarely posset cups (*Toft ware). Dishes inscribed Thomas Toft, rarely with date, made from *c*1660; Ralph Toft dishes dated 1676, 1677, 1683; posset cup dated 1683.

Toft ware. Slip-decorated earthenware produced in Staffordshire *c*1660–83; associated with *Toft family. Usually dishes, although loving cup and jug exist. White slip designs on dark grounds; also brown clay on white slip ground with large areas of design filled in with red; occasionally greyish-green slip marked with mesh pattern. Designs, emphasized with dots of white, include portraits of Charles II, coats of arms, heraldic animals (e.g. lion, eagle), The Pelican in Her Piety, and mermaid combing her hair. Dishes normally 17–22in. diameter and 3in. deep. Rims often decorated with trellis formed by slanting lines of contrasting coloured slips; usually bear inscription, sometimes date.

toilet-and-writing table. Dual-purpose table with mirror and compartments for toilet articles, as well as writing surface and storage space for writing equipment. May have mirror on underside of lifting top with toilet compartments beneath, and writing surface and storage areas incorporated in top drawer. Some examples have baize-covered top for writing. Dates from 18th century France.

toilet or **dressing mirror** or **dressing-glass.**

Small bedroom or dressing-table mirror designed to stand on table or chest of drawers. Adjustable mirror attached half-way down each side to two vertical supports either on trestle base or attached to small box base containing drawers. Dates from 18th century; dressing-glass 19th century term. Alternatively, mirror attached to underside of *dressing-box lid. *Illustration at* J-F. Leleu.

toilet service. Set of toilet articles in gold, silver, or silver-gilt; made from 16th century for aristocratic British and European ladies. Largest, most elaborate sets made in 17th century; silver or silver-mounted. Included numerous items, e.g. mirror, brushes and combs, covered bowls, boxes, salvers, scent bottles, pin-cushions, candlesticks, comb boxes, and sometimes bodkins, tongue-scrapers, toothpicks, etc. *See* Cadaval Toilet Set, Chatsworth Toilet Service, Treby Toilet Service.

toilet table. *See* dressing table.

tokens. Trade tokens (unofficial coins of copper or bronze) used by tradesmen and others from Middle Ages to supplement inadequate production of small official coinage. Used within limited areas and exchangeable for goods or, in number, for official coinage of higher denomination. Officially recognized in 1613; largely replaced by issue of official farthings and halfpennies (1672). Returned to popularity in 18th century, until M. *Boulton improved mechanical coin-presses in late 18th century; production made illegal in 1817. Examples bear tradesmen's names, portraits of current political figures, slogans, etc. Small circular porcelain tokens issued by Worcester Porcelain Company, possibly to employees. One face bears company's moulded initials (WPC); other has inscription, printed over glaze, promising to pay bearer on demand one shilling (small token) or two shillings (larger token). Rare examples date from 1770s. Similar tokens issued at Pinxton; example dated 1801. Tokens of moulded or stamped pewter and lead used in England by church during 18th and 19th centuries; issued in advance to those wishing to attend Holy Communion and collected at service.

Tokyemon, Toshima (fl mid 17th century). Japanese pottery merchant, dealing mostly in *Imari or *Arita ware. Traditionally believed to have learnt art of enamel-painting on porcelain from Chinese at Nagasaki. Possibly also taught painting. S. *Kakiemon assistant-collaborator.

tôle or **tôle peinte** (French, 'painted tin'). Originally, objects (e.g. *jardinières*, potpourris, candlesticks), made in France from 1740s, of sheet-iron, coated with varnish and decorated in floral patterns, etc., also with many-coloured varnishes, sometimes gilt borders. Mass-produced from 1768. Also made in Holland. Term now often applied to all objects of painted tin made in Birmingham and elsewhere in 18th and 19th centuries. Articles include many kinds of boxes, trays, coffee-mills, ornamented with rustic scenes, flowers, etc. *cf* japanned metal ware.

Toledo (Castile), Spain. Produced sturdy ceramic ware in 15th and 16th centuries. Examples include storage jars for grain, oil, and water, well-heads, and baptismal fonts, generally decorated with *mudéjar* designs. During early 16th century, *cuerda seca* method of glazing tiles quickly replaced by *cuenca*. From 1560s, tile panels of high quality painted with strapwork, masks, and fruit, surrounding sacred and heraldic medallions.

*Toleware. Made by *Pennsylvania-Dutch craftsmen, early 19th century. Left to right: covered molasses jug, document box, mug.*

toleware or **tolerware.** American *japanned metal made in New York, New England, and elsewhere from sheets of tin-plate imported from England to Boston in late 18th and 19th centuries. Examples include lampshades, vases, *jardinières*, tea-caddies. Discovery of many such articles in Pennsylvania led to adoption of term Pennsylvania tin ware. *See* tôle.

tomato red. Islamic pottery colour: red used in touches, resembling *sealing-wax red, used in polychrome decoration of pottery made at *Kirman from late 16th century.

tombac. Reddish alloy of copper and zinc; used in 18th century for small articles, e.g. buttons.

Tompion, Thomas (1638–1713). English clock and watch maker, known for mechanical skill and craftsmanship. Manufactured mechanisms invented by E. *Barlow, R. *Hooke, etc. Set up business, 1674, producing large quantities of accurate timepieces. Made watches with balance-springs, and applied first version of cylinder *escapement for watches in 1695. Among types of clocks produced are: long-case, bracket, lantern, *sheep's-head, and travelling clocks. Cases of ebony, oak, etc. Some clocks with elaborate astronomical or calendar work, also scientific instruments.

tongs. *See* asparagus tongs, cake tongs, sugar tongs.

Tönnich, Johann Samuel Friedrich. *See* Tännich, J. S. F.

topaz. Mineral popular as gemstone, formed of crystals of fluosilicate of aluminium; has perfect cleavage and is harder than quartz. Found in various colours due to presence of trace elements. Best-known variety is sherry-coloured (sometimes confused with quartz gemstone citrine). Found in various areas of world; chief regions in Brazil, and Urals and Siberia in Russia. Widely used in jewellery from 18th century.

Topino, Charles (fl *c*1773). French *maître-ébéniste* (1773). Noted particularly for small tables and desks in Louis XVI style.

Charles Topino. Commode en demilune. *Louis XVI. Marquetry with moulded Carrara marble top. Width 3ft2in.*

Toppan, Abner (1764–1836). Cabinet maker at Newbury, Massachusetts. Worked in rococo and classical styles.

top-rail. *See* yoke-rail.

torchère. *See* candle-stand.

Torond, Francis (1742–1812). Pseudonym of French Huguenot silhouettist working in England. Worked in Bath, Somerset, and from 1780 in London. Painted coloured miniatures, religious pictures, and bust-like silhouettes. Noted for conversation or family pieces: group silhouettes in Indian ink on card.

tortoiseshell. Brown, mottled shell plates of certain species of sea-turtle used in marquetry, inlay, and veneering, after being heated and pressed into flat sheets. Used from early 17th century in Germany and Low Countries, and in 17th and early 18th centuries in France and England. Technique most highly developed by A-C. *Boulle in latter half of 17th century. Also used for objects of vertu (e.g. snuff-boxes), toilet articles, etc., often with *piqué ornament.

tortoiseshell ware. English cream-coloured earthenware, unevenly covered with powdered oxides of cobalt (blue), manganese (brown), and copper (green), or sometimes manganese alone, which mingled with lead glaze during firing to produce tortoiseshell effect. Made by T.

*Tortoise-shell ware. Earthenware plate, made by T. *Whieldon, c1755.*

*Whieldon and others in mid 18th century. Mainly tableware, some pieces moulded with branches in relief and topped with bird finials; also animal figures, predominantly coloured with manganese.

torus. Large classical moulding, semi-circular in cross-section; usually at base of column.

Toshiro (possibly fl 13th century). Legendary Japanese potter, known as founder of porcelain industry. Tentatively identified as Kato Shirozaemon Kagemasa, who visited China (1222–23), working at potteries making e.g. *T'zŭ-chou, and *Chien ware, then returned to Japan. Established potteries at Seto, where kaolin readily available locally. Noted for high quality tea jars or caddies. However, as celadons with body approaching porcelain appeared first in Japan in earlier Heian period, Toshiro may have been potter working in Seto area, associated with foundation of potteries. Name continued in family of potters for 27 generations.

tou. Chinese ancient ritual bronze food vessel; same shape made in neolithic pottery. Bowl mounted on high columnar stem. Earliest example dated 9th century B.C. Originally had vertical sides, but by 500B.C., hemispherical lidded, bowl shape with ring handles became standard form. Made until 3rd century B.C. *cf* stem cup.

touch. Maker's mark stamped on pewter wares. Equivalent of hallmarks on gold and silver, but less authoritative.

touchplate. Pewter panel, held by Worshipful Company of Pewterers, London, on which are struck *touches of members. Earliest known mention 1540, earliest surviving example, 1668. Previous plates are assumed to have been destroyed with Pewterers' Hall in Great Fire of London, 1666. Earliest touchplate includes some re-struck touches, i.e. those of members whose touches had appeared on previous plate; these date from 1640 or earlier (undated). Touches subsequently appear in chronological order, until end of 18th century. Five touchplates exist, bearing 1090 touches in all. Also elsewhere in Britain and Europe for different guilds or companies, but few survive.

touchstone. Piece of dark flint or similar hard, fine-grained stone used in simplest method of *assaying gold or silver. Streaks made by metal under test and by 'touch-needles' of various known qualities are compared for colour after treatment with nitric acid. J. *Wedgwood supplied pottery blocks for same purpose in late 18th century.

tourbillon or **tourbillion** (in watches). Device invented by A-L. *Breguet: carriage holding *escapement of watch or chronometer which revolves in course of one minute, reducing timekeeping error due to position. Similar system, introduced *c*1895, called 'karrusel' rotates in longer periods, usually 52½ minutes.

Tournai (Belgium). Soft-paste porcelain factory established in 1751 under patronage of Empress Maria Theresa. Robert *Dubois became director, 1753. From *c*1755, produced fine quality porcelain with creamy tone; early work in imitation of Meissen and Sèvres. Ribbed forms characteristic; generally rococo style treated with restraint. J-G-J. *Mayer, painter from 1754, succeeded H-J. *Duvivier as chief painter, 1774. Much painting in blue includes *Zweibelmuster* and *décor aux cinq bouquets*. Painting in Sèvres style includes exotic birds and monochrome landscapes of Duvivier. Armorial services produced from *c*1780. Service with birds painted after Buffon; bowls often have Pompeian scrolls in gold, portraits *en grisaille*, or birds, painted in rectangular reserve panels on wide *bleu-de-roi* band. Modellers include N-F. *Gauron, N. *Lecreux, and J. *Willems; figures usually glazed and white, though biscuit or enamelled figures occur. Much porcelain sent for decoration at The Hague and later at Arras. Marks include tower, or, from 1756, crossed swords with small crosses, painted e.g. in blue, gold, or crimson. From 1783, managed by de Bettignies family; bought by H. *de Bettignies in 1818. Until 1850, like Saint-Amand-les-Eaux, produced copies of porcelain made at Sèvres, Worcester, and other factories. Recent copies of old Tournai porcelain made in Tournai.

Tou bronze. Sung dynasty. Inlaid with malachite and silver in geometrical strapwork designs and formal scroll motifs. Height 10¾in.

Tou ts'ai jar. Underglaze blue outlines and washes, overglaze enamel washes of green, red, and ochre yellow. Ming dynasty, late 15th century. Height 3¾in.

Tournai tapestry. Tapestries woven in Tournai from 14th century, with designs similar to contemporary *Arras tapestries. From mid 15th century, Tournai replaced Arras as high-warp loom tapestry-weaving centre for Burgundian court. Subjects included chivalric, religious and mythological tales, also histories of ruling house; bright colours used, with prominent figures in foreground, often heavily outlined. Unchronological eposodic format with various episodes superimposed. Field infilled with appropriate motifs. No borders. Production declined late 15th century, with loss of royal patronage, but activity continued through first half of 16th century, with designs following *Brussels tapestries. Official trademark from 1544, a tower. From mid 16th century, industry largely destroyed by effects of religious persecution and political upheavals; weavers emigrated and quality deteriorated. Unsuccessful attempt to revive industry made in 17th century by P. *Béhagle, when production largely confined to armorial pieces and *verdures*.

Tours tapestry. Tours equal in importance to Paris as tapestry weaving centre in 16th century; main workshop established by Alexander Motheron the Younger, with grant from Henry IV. Good quality tapestries woven, following design and technique of larger Parisian workshops. Industry declined in late 17th century.

Toutin, Jean (1578–1644). French goldsmith. Discovered technique for painting on enamel, *c*1630.

tou ts'ai (Chinese, 'fighting or contrasting colour'). Chinese ceramic decoration; red, yellow, apple-green, and other enamel colours applied in thin, translucent washes over underglaze blue outlines, on porcelain from reign of *Ch'êng Hua.

towel or **clothes horse.** Wooden frame used to air clothes, and to hold or dry towels; made of well-spaced horizontal turned bars attached at each end to vertical supports. Form known from Middle Ages.

Tower weight. System of measure based on 'standard pound' kept in Tower of London: 5400 grains or $11\frac{1}{4}$oz *Troy weight. Legal mint pound in England until 1527, when superseded by Troy pound.

town mark. Towns arms, initials, or symbol struck on gold or silver wares by wardens of guild after *assay, e.g. crowned fleur-de-lis for Paris, crowned harp for Dublin, anchor for Birmingham, etc.

Townsend, Christopher (1701–73). Cabinet maker at Newport, Rhode Island. Father of John *Townsend, brother of Job *Townsend. Member of *Newport school.

Townsend, Edmund (1736–1811). Cabinet maker at Newport, Rhode Island. Son of Job *Townsend. Member of *Newport school.

Townsend, Job (1699–1765). Cabinet maker at Newport, Rhode Island. Credited, with J. *Goddard (son-in-law), with creation of *block front structure and block-and-shell motif. He and family formed nucleus of *Newport school.

Townsend, John (1721–1809). Cabinet maker at Newport, Rhode Island. Son of C. *Townsend. Member of *Newport school.

Townsend, Stephen (fl 1760–71). Cabinet maker of Charleston, South Carolina; partner of W. *Axson Jr, 1763–68. Furniture in Georgian style.

toy. Small 17th and 18th century object intended as curiosity or trinket for adult rather than child's plaything. Examples in metal, tortoiseshell, etc. include snuff-boxes, beads, miniature furniture, models of animals; also seals, tobacco-stoppers. In porcelain, wide range includes scent bottles, *étuis,* snuff-boxes, *bonbonnières,* made in form of e.g. figures, animals, or fruit, equivalent of Meissen **Galanterien*; many examples ascribed to Mennecy in mid 18th century. In England, associated with Chelsea; often made in form of figures, particularly cupids; introduced in raised anchor period. *See* miniature silver. *Illustrations at* bodkin case, Caughley, scent bottle, sweetmeat box.

trade tokens. *See* tokens.

Trafalgar furniture. Regency sideboards and chairs decorated with nautical motifs (rope moulding, anchors, etc.) to commemorate Nelson's victory at Trafalgar (1805). *See* Nelson chair.

Trafalgar vase. Silver two-handled cup or vase of *krater form designed by J. *Flaxman for presentation to senior officers who fought at Battle of Trafalgar (1805); 66 made. Supplied by *Rundell, Bridge & Rundell. Made by P. *Storr or B. *Smith the Elder.

trailing or **threading.** Method of decorating glass since antiquity: molten glass can be drawn into threads of varying thickness, which are then applied to surface of heated vessel. Much used for decorating rims and bases (e.g. *Römer,* decanter) and body of vessel (e.g. *quilling, *nipt diamond waies). Most sophisticated form is Venetian *latticinio* glass.

train (in clock or watch). Series of wheels and *pinions transmitting source of power to *escapement (or striking and chiming mechanism, where present). Number of teeth in wheels and pinions of going train is determined by number of vibrations made by *balance or *pendulum in one hourly rotation of *centre wheel: often known as 'count' of train.

trammel. *See* chimney-crane.

Daumenglas. *17th century, made in Low Countries. Recessed holes around sides; applied milled, trailed decoration. Height* $12\frac{1}{2}$*in.*

transfer-printing. Process of transferring engraved print to enamel or porcelain surface. Print first made on paper, which is then laid on surface and baked in muffle kiln until design fuses to surface and paper burns away. Process invented in England by J. *Brooks in 18th century. Patterns applied to pottery or porcelain from engraved copper plates by means of bats (*bat printing), or, from early 19th century, paper. Technique developed at Liverpool in mid 18th century, e.g. by Z. *Barnes and, notably, J. *Sadler and G. *Green. Overglaze red, purple, or black used on porcelain at Bow (1756) and Worcester (from 1757) by R. *Hancock; underglaze blue by 1759. First earthenwares printed in underglaze blue made by T. *Turner at Caughley in 1780; similar wares produced in Staffordshire, Lancashire, Yorkshire, South Wales, and in Europe, before 1800; process especially fashionable after *c*1820. Gold transfer-printing patented 1810. Printed wares mainly cheap; decoration usually monochrome, often blue. By *c*1825 other underglaze colours possible, e.g. black, green, red, purple, brown, and yellow. Polychrome printing developed in Staffordshire by F. and R. *Pratt in 1840s. First successful American transfer-printing in New Jersey, 1840. *Illustrations also at* Grainger Lee & Co, Sadler & Green.

transition clock. Connecticut shelf clock, produced late 1820s. Stencilled decoration on top, door, and side columns; designed by E. *Terry.

Transylvanian or **Siebenbürger carpets.** Late 17th and early 18th century Turkish prayer rugs, first found in small Protestant churches of Transylvania, Hungary. Woollen, with short, coarsely Turkish-knotted pile. Design, structure, and size modelled on *Ushak prayer rugs of *c*1600. Differences include: more

*Transfer printing. Left to right: 1) black transfer-printed plate from *Cambrian Pottery, c1830. 2) bat-printed design in light black on *Spode porcelain coffee can, early 19th century. 3) *Lowestoft porcelain saucer with underglaze transfer print of Woman and Squirrel pattern, c1785. (All other examples overglaze printed.) 4) *Worcester porcelain coffee cup transfer-printed in jet enamel black by R. *Hancock with his design,* Les garçons chinois; *colour painted in by hand; 1760.*

variable colour-scheme with yellow, natural, or white grounds as well as usual Ushak red; borders with distinctive motif of alternating cartouches and star-medallions. Double-ended prayer rugs common.

transverse flute. *See* flute.

Trapani (Sicily). Coarse Italian maiolica, notably *albarelli*, made in 17th century.

travelling clock. Describes wide range of portable timekeepers. Those in watch form too large to be worn, made 16th to early 17th century, particularly by English makers, e.g. E. *East. Originally with protective outer case, some with striking mechanism. (*See also* sedan clock.) In 18th century developed into form of *carriage clock, mainly French, often with elaborate striking and chiming, later *repeating. Production continued into 20th century.

*Travelling clock. By A-L. *Breguet, c1800. Silver case; alarm; repeats hours and quarters. Left-hand dial tells age and phase of moon; right-hand dial is for setting alarm. Knob below, for setting hands, is chained to dummy knob for safety; date indicators below dials.*

*Travelling service. Made in Augsburg, c1730. Fits into leather case (not shown). Knife, fork, spoon, and *egg spoon made by Andreus Wickhardt; bowl by Philip Stenglin, length 5in. Double-ended *egg cup with maker's mark I L.*

travelling service. Service of table silver packed in special cases or caskets and used by European royalty and nobility while travelling; particularly popular in 18th century. Sometimes porcelain dishes instead of silver are included. Service may also contain tea, coffee, and/or chocolate services. *See* canteen.

tray table or **voider stand.** X-shaped folding support for tray, with webbed fabric bands forming top. Dates from 18th century.

tray-top table. General term from mid 18th century for table with raised rim or *gallery.

Treasury inkstand. British silver or Sheffield plate inkstand consisting of box with double lid, central handle, and four claw feet. Made from 17th century. Derived form and name from inkstands issued to Treasury in 1686.

Treby Toilet Service. Most famous English silver toilet service; 29 pieces; made by P. *de Lamerie in 1724. Ornamented with chased strapwork, medallions, and rococo motifs. Now at Ashmolean Museum, Oxford.

treen. Small simple household articles made of wood, often turned, including bowls, plates, spoons, mugs, etc. Term (meaning 'wooden') in use from 15th century.

trefid, trifid, split-end, or **pied-de-biche spoon** (French, 'doe's foot'). Silver, pewter, occasionally brass spoon with rounded stem end divided into three sections by two small cuts, in manner of cloven hoof, and hammered until wide and flat. Shape also made by casting, generally with rat-tail reinforcement at back of bowl. Known from *c*1650. Later examples stamped or engraved with foliage. *Illustration also at* Garthorne, F.

Treen. Wassail, English, c1660. Turned from lignum vitae wood. Consists of bowl, cover with three finials, central covered cup for holding spices, and three turned cups.

Trefid terminals. On set of six two-pronged forks; maker's mark W over S for William Scarlett. Two made in 1694, remainder 1695.

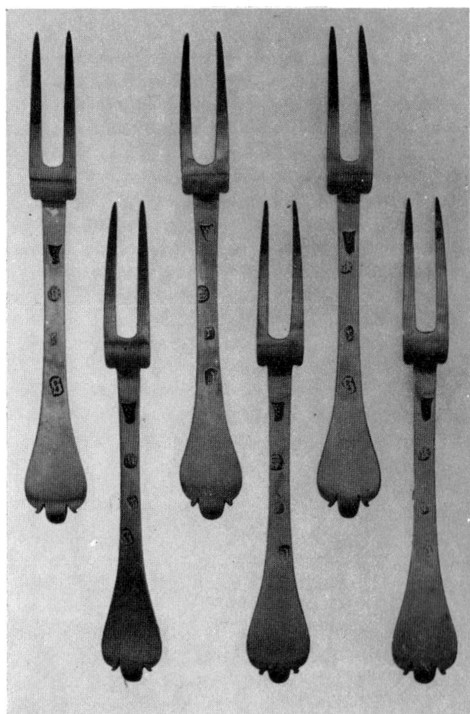

trefoil (in silver). Gothic ornament in form of three symmetrical leaves; similarly quatrefoil ('four leaves'), and cinquefoil ('five leaves'). Shapes used for *trencher salts, salvers, etc. Motif much used in Gothic revival silver and jewellery of 19th century.

trek. Outline used in painting on Dutch Delft and, rarely, other tin-glazed earthenwares; usually in dark blue, manganese-purple, or black. Introduced in late 17th century, possibly by S. *van Eenhorn.

Trembleuse. *Saucer and two-handled cup. *Derby porcelain, c1758.*

Trencher salts. Left: made in Paris, 1745, by Claude Dargent, oval form with shell lid and scroll base. Centre: made in London by Mary Rood, 1723, plain form. Right: made in Lyon, France, 1758, by Mathieu Bouvier. Each 3$\frac{1}{4}$in. long.

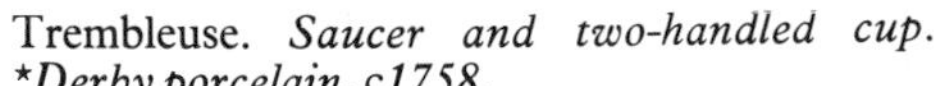

Trestle table. Henry VII, oak, rounded ends raised on broad X-shaped supports forming pierced Gothic ogee arches, moulded stretcher. Length 5ft7in.

trembleuse. Saucer with deep recess or raised ring (some porcelain examples with openwork decoration) to keep cup from sliding. In silver, made mainly in Europe with detachable ring-stand to hold silver or porcelain tea or chocolate cup. Sometimes known as teacup stand. Made in French porcelain in early to mid 18th century, notably at Saint-Cloud; copied e.g. at Vienna in *Du Paquier period, Derby, and Nyon. Also in maiolica at Castelli.

trembly rose painter. English ceramics. Unknown decorator working at Longton Hall porcelain factory in 1750s. Painted flower sprays characterized by thread-like stems and crumpled petals. *Illustration at* Longton Hall.

trencher. Originally, wooden plate, sometimes dished on both sides, allowing use for two courses. (Antecedent, of same name, was thick slice of bread.) Dates from 16th century. Pewter examples made from late Middle Ages; by 17th century, rim often reinforced with beading round. Mid 17th century examples often tinned copper for richer appearance and greater resistance to scratching. Also made in silver.

trencher salt. Small, low, individual or shared salt consisting of slab or block-like form (e.g. triangular, quatrefoil, octagonal, etc.) with shallow circular or elliptical depression or bowl; introduced *c*1630. Made in pewter to early 18th century, surviving silver examples date from mid 17th to mid 18th centuries. Also made of crystal with silver mounts.

trespolo (Italian, 'trestle'). Small bedroom stand for mirror, on high tripod base. Dates from 18th century.

trestle foot (in furniture). Foot formed by attaching horizontal piece at right-angles to vertical support of object. Used on screens, mirrors, etc.

trestle table. Form developed from earliest tables: long boards laid parallel over horse or trestle supports. After 15th century, supports evolved into sturdy frame, attached to underside of top, and strengthened with stretchers. Particularly common in 16th and 17th centuries.

triangle period. *See* Chelsea.

Trianon de Porcelaine. Building near Versailles, with exterior and floors entirely covered in faience tiles supplied by makers in e.g. Rouen, Nevers, and Holland; also decorated with large faience vases. Colours predominantly blue and white. Erected in 1670 by Louis XIV for Madame de Montespan; demolished in 1687 because faience failed to withstand weathering.

Trivet. Brass. English, mid to late 18th century. Height 11$\frac{1}{4}$in.

tricoteuse (French, 'knitter'). Form of *work table, originating in 18th century; top oblong with curved ends and raised rim hinged at bottom along one side. Lower shelf between legs.

trifid spoon. *See* trefid spoon.

trifle. Small pewter article of little value, e.g. toys, buckles, buttons, spoons, forks, small bowls. Makers known as triflers. *cf* toyman.

triple-reeded. Category of pewter plates with reeded rim made *c*1675–90. *See* reeding.

tripod table. *See* claw table.

trivet. Three-legged stand, placed before fire, for cooking vessels, utensils, etc. Widely, any such stand (*cf* footman). Made from 17th century. Early examples of wrought iron, later brass, several with iron frame, and decorative pierced brass top. From 1750s, type introduced with one standing leg and two hooks resting on fire bars; leg later changed to diagonal support. Most have projecting wooden handles.

trompe l'oeil (in ceramic decoration). Usually tin-glazed earthenware vessels, e.g. tureens, moulded and coloured to represent vegetables, fruit, etc., or plates containing naturalistically modelled vegetables, fruit, or nuts. Popular in 18th century. Generally thought to derive from moulded decoration of L. *Della Robbia. Found, notably, on Strasbourg faience, also e.g. at Nevers and Brussels. Tureens made in Meissen porcelain. Term also applied to effect of **décor bois* and to imitations of pastry and cooked poultry made in *can-coloured stoneware, e.g. by Wedgwood.

trophies. Originally arms of vanquished enemy displayed by victor. Later motif of grouped

Trunk. *Queen Anne travelling trunk with two drawers in bottom; wood covered with leather and bronze studs.*

Tsun. Bronze vessel, decorated with stylized dragons; c*780 B.C. Height* $10\frac{1}{2}$*in.*

Tub chair. George III. Mahogany frame, carved with guilloche *pattern seat rail and snarling dog's head handles; cabriole front legs.*

weapons, extended to include decorative arrangements of musical instruments or tools of trade. Decoration *a trofei,* described by C. *Piccolpasso, in use on maiolica at Castel Durante until 17th century, also e.g. at Castelli and Faenza, and Palermo. In 18th century France, examples include bow and arrows of *décor* **au carquois.*

Trott, Benjamin (1770–1843). American miniaturist and portrait painter. Made miniature copies of many portraits by Gilbert Stuart. In Philadelphia, 1808, shared studio with T. *Sully.

Trotter, Daniel (fl late 18th, early 19th centuries). Cabinet maker in Philadelphia, Pennsylvania, working in Philadelphia Chippendale, American Directoire, and Sheraton styles.

Trou, Henri-Charles (fl late 17th century), sons Henri II (1680–1746) and Gabriel, and grandson Henri-François (1711–78). French makers of soft-paste porcelain at Saint-Cloud. In 1679, Henri-Charles married widow of P. *Chicaneau, proprietor of Saint-Cloud factory; secured patronage of Duc d'Orléans. Patent renewed, 1722, in favour of Henri II and Gabriel. From *c*1742, Henri II sole proprietor of Saint-Cloud and Paris factories. Succeeded by son, Henri-François; from 1764 in partnership until factory closed in 1766.

Troy weight. Standard weight system in English-speaking countries for gold, silver, and precious stones; 5760 grains or 12oz to Troy pound. In practice only ounces and *pennyweights used. Thought to be derived from weight used at fair in Troyes, France, in Middle Ages. Adopted in England in 1527, though in use for at least a century before. Abolished as general measure in 1878 in favour of avoirdupois system, except for precious metals and stones.

truckle or **trundle bed.** Low wooden bed, dating from Middle Ages; designed to slide under higher bed when not in use. Used to save space. Common until 19th century.

true porcelain. *See* hard-paste porcelain.

Trumbull, John (1756–1843). American painter. During American Revolution, aide-de-camp to George Washington. After war, painted many large-scale historical paintings of Revolution. Miniatures all in oil on wood.

trumpeter clock. Made on principle similar to *cuckoo clock, sounding hour on trumpet operated by bellows: some also sound quarters. Variant also with mechanically-played drums.

trumpet turning. Turning on leg of chair, table, etc., flaring outwards like up-turned trumpet. Used on late 17th century English and American furniture.

trundle bed. *See* truckle bed.

trunk. Box-like portable container, with hinged lid, used to hold possessions when travelling; early form possibly a hollowed out tree trunk. Leather-covered models with close-nailing date from 15th century; lid often vaulted so that rain would run off. By *c*1600, some with fitted interiors, drawers in base, and brass mounts and fittings.

trunk (in clocks). Thin portion of *long-case clock between hood and base or plinth. Also lower part of *drop-dial and *Act of Parliament clocks, housing weights and pendulum.

Ts'ang Ying-hsüan. First director-general (1683–1726) of Chinese Imperial porcelain factory at *Ching-tê-chên after rebuilding. Period noted for thin porcelain paste, with brilliant glazes. Credited with invention of many glaze colours, e.g. spotted yellow, *snake-skin green, turquoise blue. Decoration in *cloisonné* enamel style first appears in this period. Same enamels used for monochrome and polychrome pieces, e.g. **famille verte* work and peacock green monochrome. Further innovations: *peach-bloom, *Mazarin blue, *soft-paste porcelain. Copies of earlier Sung wares, especially crackle-glazed celadons found, often with Sung marks. *San ts'ai and *wu ts'ai work continued.

tsuba. *See* Japanese sword-guards.

Tucker Porcelain Factory. Jug made in 1828 by William Ellis Tucker, hand painted and gilded. Height 9in.

Tumblers. English, Left: London, 1665, height 2¼in. Centre: Leeds, c1690. Right: London, 1690.

tsun. General term for ancient Chinese ritual bronze vessels, mostly wide-bodied vases with flaring mouth, and high foot rim (*cf ku* shape). Mainly made during Shang dynasty, but some 10th century examples of square section with heavy ornamentation found. Zoomorphic variations, produced from 12th century B.C., include rams and elephants, shaped as containers. Term also applied later (Sung dynasty onwards) to porcelain forms, modelled to resemble animals, mainly rhinoceros and elephant. During Ming and Ch'ing periods, term applied to further adaptations of shape, e.g. potiche, or covered wine jar, with swelling, curved sides.

tsung. Chinese ritual jade shape. Hollow tube carved within rectangular cube. Associated with worship of Earth. Earliest examples, dating from Shang dynasty, usually only a few inches long; later, during Chou dynasty, up to 20 in. long, and probably used as astronomer's sighting tube.

tub chair. *Easy chair with incurved back, and wide wings designed to protect user from draughts. Made in late 18th century by T. *Sheraton; popular late Victorian style.

tuckaway table. *See* gate-leg table.

Tucker, William Ellis (d 1832). Maker of first American porcelain produced in commercial quantities for home market. In partnership, established factory at Philadelphia, Pennsylvania, in 1826, for manufacture of hard-paste domestic and ornamental porcelain. First decoration in sepia monochrome; polychrome enamel and gilding in Sèvres style introduced in 1828. Decorative wares painted with flowers, American views, or portraits.

Tudor green ware. Relief-decorated pottery; whitish body covered with green glaze. Made in Surrey, late 16th century. Rare examples include stove tiles, dishes, cisterns, and wall sconces.

Tudor & Leader. Earliest large-scale manufacturers of Sheffield plate; firm active from *c*1760; introduced horse-power for rolling metal. Produced wide range of domestic articles, e.g. coffee and tea pots, salt-cellars, candlesticks, etc. Also produced silver wares for which Henry Tudor registered mark in London before Assay Office established in Sheffield in 1773. Sheffield silver mark: HT over TL; Sheffield plate mark: HT & Co in cursive script, or HT in Gothic letters. S. Nicholson taken into partnership 1783, and name of firm changed to Tudor, Leader & Nicholson (Sheffield plate mark: TUDOR & Co in rectangle). Firm split up in 1797 when Thomas Leader retired.

Tudor rose motif. Stylized rose, adopted as badge by Henry VII (reigned 1485–1509) and used as ornament on furniture, silver, etc. throughout Tudor period.

Tudor style. Furniture style in England from accession of Henry VII (1485) to that of Elizabeth I (1558). Pieces usually of solid oak construction, although some joined furniture made. Late medieval motifs prevailed in decoration (predominantly carved) and included *linen fold panelling and architectural tracery, heads, roses, vines, and grotesques. Chip carving sometimes used to decorate flat surfaces. Renaissance motifs introduced, e.g. profile heads in roundels, and **putti*. Trestle stools, benches, and tables often have wide, flat, shaped supports set at right-angles to seat board. Other common pieces were *aumbry, *chest, and *settle.

Tufft, Thomas (fl *c*1760–80). Cabinet maker in Philadelphia, Pennsylvania. Worked in *Philadelphia Chippendale style.

tui. Ancient Chinese bronze bell made from late Chou dynasty, during period of Warring States. Oval in section, with wide bulbous shoulder narrowing to base. Suspended from loop, often in form of tiger, mounted on flat top with everted rim. *cf* chêng, chung.

Tula. Town in central Russia where Czar Peter the Great established factory (1705) for production of small-arms; also made furniture (e.g. chairs, beds, tables) entirely of steel, with silver, gilt, brass, and cut-steel enrichment; and smaller articles, e.g. candlesticks, caskets, inkstands. Early 19th century work largely discontinued on orders of Alexander I, in effort to further production of arms; small number of articles made since. Tula also particularly associated with viello decoration on silver.

tulip chargers. *See* blue-dash chargers.

tulip Ladik carpets. *See* Ladik carpets.

tulip ornament. Popular motif in early 17th century silver ornament, especially Dutch. Embossed and chased on silver; cup bowls made in tulip shape. Fashion at height in Europe and Britain in mid 17th century, coinciding with spread of 'tulipomania' from Holland.

tulip-shaped tankard. *See* tankard.

tulip ware. *Pennsylvania Dutch pottery with symmetrical designs of tulips and leaves.

tumbler. Small, cylindrical, silver drinking cup with thick, hemispherical base which prevents it from tipping over. Made in Britain and Europe in 17th and 18th centuries. Majority plain, some engraved. Earliest probably formed part of canteen or travelling set. Sometimes used as race or cock-fighting prize.

Tunbridge ware. Wood mosaic objects made at

Tunbridge ware. Writing box of rosewood with marquetry of various woods showing view of Eridge Castle surrounded by roses. Mid 19th century.

Tung ware. Bottle-shaped vase with string-lined body; slender neck with three raised rings and expanded dish-shaped mouth. Buff ware with thick translucent greyish-green crackled glaze. Sung dynasty. Height 8*in.*

Tunbridge Wells, Kent, from 17th century. Many types of boxes, tea-caddies, tables etc. made with diamond, star, or square mosaic patterns. After 1840, more elaborate designs (birds, animals, flowers), and foreign woods used to increase range. Designs made by glueing together slim shafts of wood, in various colours, so that required picture or pattern appears at end of cluster of sticks. Cluster then sliced thinly, across design, to form veneer, which is attached to surface of object.

Tung ware. Chinese celadon ware, made in Sung period, with greyish body and soft, fine celadon glaze. Mentioned in literary sources as product of north Honan province. Items tentatively identified.

turbelik carpets. *See* graveyard carpets.

Turcman carpets. *See* Turkoman carpets.

tureen, soup tureen, or **terrine.** Large silver serving-dish in use from early 18th century. Oval body supported on four cast feet or on spreading base with two handles and domed cover with handle or finial. Generally up to 17in. long and 11in. high. Neo-classical style tureens *c*1760–90 had oval tray or stand with raised central plateau to steady feet of tureen. Smaller *sauce tureen made from mid 18th century. Also made in ceramics and Sheffield plate. *See* bird tureens.

Turet, Isaac. *See* Thuret, Isaac.

Turin (Piedmont). Italian maiolica made from 16th century; a number of factories in operation, 17th and 18th centuries. Decoration in blue or polychrome includes designs in oriental style of animals and birds with plants and rocks. Hard-paste porcelain factory established under patronage of Charles Emmanuel III in 1737; produced examples of teaware and ornamental vases by 1743, but production ceased soon after. Only known pieces, two small busts, marked with cross of Savoy and monogram GR incised, with TORINO in underglaze blue.

Also among most prolific 18th century Italian tapestry-weaving centres. Major low-warp loom tapestry manufactory established 1737 by V. *Demigot under royal patronage. High-warp looms, under direction of Antonio Dini, also operated 1737–54. Numerous classical and historical subjects used. French Revolution caused decline of industry.

Turkbaff carpets. *See* Meshed carpets.

Turkestan carpets. *See* Turkoman carpets.

Turkey work. Small panels of Turkish-knotted carpet woven in England during late 16th and 17th centuries as furniture coverings. Early designs copied from Turkish carpet patterns and worked in simple colours. In late 17th century, new design of large floral patterns, often with central heraldic device worked on black ground. By 18th century, superseded by needlework upholstery.

Turkish carpets. *See* Anatolian animal carpets, Brussa, Ghiordes, graveyard, Hereke, Konia, Kula, Ladik, 'Lotto', Medjid, Megri, Melas, Mudjur, Smyrna, and Ushak carpets, and Turkish Court Manufactory.

Turkish Court Manufactory, Ottoman, Cairene, or **Ottoman-Cairene carpets.** Meticulously executed mid 16th to 18th century Turkish court carpets with Persian-knotted wool pile on silk foundation. Probably first made by Egyptian weavers. Persian-influenced, naturalistic floral patterns based on textile and ceramic designs; worked in seven or eight basic tones, particularly warm red, strong green, and yellow. Field motifs include curled leafy fronds, palmettes, rosettes, and arabesques. Small ogival or round medallions and decorated corner-pieces common. Borders have floral meanders with rosettes, palmettes, and arabesque stems. Large numbers exported to Europe.

Turkish, Ghiordes, symmetrical or **closed knot.** Knot used to form pile on hand-knotted carpets. Yarn strand laid across two (or more) warp threads, then drawn round them, reappearing between threads so that knot ends protrude between adjacent pairs of warp threads. Favoured for following types of carpet: some *Turkish, *Caucasian, north-west

*Persian, some *Turkoman, and European carpets (excepting Spanish carpets).

Turkish market clocks and watches. Made in England; with few exceptions, not by leading makers. Made mainly from *c*1740, following late 17th century development of trade with Turkey. Clocks of bracket type with ebony, ebonized pear, or occasionally, walnut and lacquer cases; many long-case clocks also exported from England to Turkey, but very few have returned. Watches with lacquer or tortoiseshell decoration, and brass or silver mounts, often with hemispherical dome tops. Both clocks and watches highly elaborate, with Turkish *numerals on dial and striking, chiming or musical movements. Market in watches later lost to *Swiss watches.

Turkoman, Turkman, Turcman, Turkestan, or **Bokhara carpets.** Hard-wearing, utilitarian carpets woven by nomadic and semi-nomadic tribes of western Turkestan (steppe country extending from Caspian Sea *c*1000 miles across Asia). Craft practised for centuries, but oldest surviving carpets 19th century. Great numbers woven for domestic use. Few exported

Turkish market watch. Made in 1837 by Edward Prior, London, no. 54188; white enamel dial with Turkish numerals. Diameter of dial $1\frac{1}{2}$*in.*

to West until late 19th century, when distributed through oasis towns, mainly Bokhara. Classified by tribal origin, e.g. *Ersaris, *Salors, *Saruks, *Tekkes, and *Yomuds; also, from border area, *Afghans and *Baluchis. Constructed of heavy-textured wool and/or camel-hair Turkish of Persian knotted pile (400–600 knots per sq in.), on sheep or goat-hair foundation; broad *kelim ends in various colours, sometimes striped or embroidered. Bold, geometrical designs, distinguished by octagonal or diamond shaped tribal guls, differing from tribe to tribe, quartered by colour change and arranged on field in regular horizontal or vertical rows, with smaller secondary guls in spaces. Backgrounds infilled with stylized animal, bird, and floral motifs. Borders narrow, separated from field by colour (rather than design change), often composed of narrow stripes with tiny geometrical figures. Predominant design and ground colour, warm red, ranging in tone from chestnut, through mahogany, to liver. Minor colours: cold dark blues, blue-greens, natural browns and greys, light yellow and flame-orange, and ivory. Border patterns often dissimilar, some with only two sides alike, some with all four different. Also numerous prayer rugs.

Turner, John (1738–87). Staffordshire potter; apprenticed to T. *Whieldon. From *c*1755, maker of salt-glaze at Stoke-on-Trent; cane-coloured stoneware includes dishes with lids imitating pie crust; jugs with spherical body decorated with scenes in relief, cylindrical neck, and part of handles covered with brown, black, and blue. At Lane End, from 1762, products include jasper, basalts, blue transfer-printed ware, and creamware similar in body and yellowish glaze to that of Leeds pottery; much exported to Holland. Some creamware enamelled by *Absolon and in Holland. Partner at New Hall China Manufactory, 1781–82. Lane End factory inherited by sons; closed early 19th century. Marks: TURNER, TURNER & Co, impressed.

John Turner. Flower holder in chocolate and cream stoneware, late 18th century.

Turning. Baluster-turned wheelspokes and legs on 17th century English spinning wheel. Height c3ft.
Turning. Spiral turning on legs and stretchers of French Louis XIII walnut chair.

Turner, Thomas (1749–1809). English potter; pupil of R. *Hancock at Worcester. In 1772, took over earthenware factory at Caughley, Shropshire; began porcelain manufacture. From 1775, mainly produced blue-and-white transfer-printed porcelain, e.g. *willow pattern. Sold factory in 1799.

turning (in furniture). Ancient method of shaping members by revolving piece of wood on lathe and shaping with cutting tools. Forms include baluster, bobbin, spiral, split, spool, and trumpet turning.

turning up (in silver). Sheet metal made into cylinder or cone by soldering, hammered to produce desired hollow shape. Method used from 17th century to make tankards, tea and coffee pots, etc. Mark of soldered seam sometimes detectable inside body on handle side.

turnip watch. English term sometimes used for watches with thick movement, developed in 17th century and popular until 19th century, particularly in provincial areas. Similar to French **oignon* watch.

turquoise. Cryptocrystalline mineral valued as gemstone, with blue or bluish-green colour. Formed of hydrous aluminium phosphate; colour sometimes deteriorates if stone becomes dry from exposure to sunlight. Name probably derived from Turkey (best turquoise came from Persia and travelled to Europe via Turkey). Relatively soft stone but takes good polish; waxy lustre.

turquoise. French sofa or settee with ornament or carving reflecting Eastern (Turkish) design, crescent moon, etc. Popular in latter half of 18th century.

turquoise or **sea-green ground.** Porcelain enamel ground colour invented by J. G. *Herold *c*1725. Used on decorative pieces and tableware at Meissen periodically during 18th century (particularly 1727–45). **Bleu céleste*, used at Sèvres, nearest European equivalent.

turret clock. Timekeeper with large movement,

Turret clock movement. Probably 14th century. Length $21\frac{1}{2}$in.

often of iron, mounted in church tower or public building. Type includes earliest known mechanical clocks, some with striking mechanism only and no dial, others with elaborate *automaton figures. First examples have verge *escapement and *foliot, later anchor and gravity escapements used. Reached peak of development with *Westminster clock.

tutania. Alloy of copper, calamine, antimony, and tin patented (1770) by William Tutin; his firm, Tutin & Haycraft of Birmingham, produced small articles in tutania, e.g. spoons, buckles.

twig handles. Ceramic decoration; handles modelled like twisted stems, painted green. Found on 18th century German porcelain tableware, e.g. a Meissen teapot (*c*1720–25), and *Volkstedt cups and soup bowls (*c*1770–80). Imitated at Venice by G. *Cozzi, and in England.

twin-acorn thumbpiece. Thumbpiece in form of wedge surmounted by two acorns; found on English pewter tankards from 17th century.

twin-cusped thumbpiece. Thumbpiece in form of two half-moons; found on English pewter tankards from 17th century.

two-handled cup. Gold, silver, or silver-gilt drinking or display vessel with straight or bulbous sides, moulded foot, domed cover with finial, and ring, scroll, caryatid, etc., handles; size varied. Sometimes with salver. Made in Britain and Europe from late 16th century, though earliest surviving examples are 17th century. Distinction among smaller examples e.g. as caudle cup, posset cup, porringer, purely arbitrary. *See* loving cup, race cup.

Two Little Ships, The (De Twee Scheepjes). Delft factory (1653–*c*1796). Tiles produced under ownership of A. *Keyser. A. *Pijnacker owner 1693–1707. From 1750, owned by J. *Pennis; succeeded by family.

tyg. Large pottery drinking vessel with three or more handles, intended to provide each of a number of drinkers with clean portion of rim. Common in 17th and 18th century England.

t'zu chin. *See* café au lait glaze.

Tyg. Nine handles. Iron glazed. c*1660.*

Tz'u-chou. Grey stoneware vase, Sung or Yüan dynasty, decorated with cream and black slip with clear glaze. Height 11*in.*

Tz'u-chou stoneware. Chinese ceramics, made notably on borders of Honan and Hopei provinces in Sung and Yüan periods. Greyish stoneware covered with white or brownish slips; *sgraffiato* designs usually plants or animals; human figures occasionally used. Glazes tinted green, brown or polychrome. Some painting in brownish black, e.g. with peony and butterflies; later decoration sometimes in enamel. Products normally large, e.g. wine jars, vases, brush pots, and pillows.

ultra violet light. In ceramic research, examination of porcelain under ultra violet light reveals restoration: new substances introduced show different fluorescent effects from original paste or glaze. Also useful guide to age if porcelain formula known to have changed at certain date, e.g. Chelsea porcelain made before 1755 shows peach coloured fluorescence against violet for later pieces. Comparison with fluorescence of definitely identified example may expose otherwise undetectable fake.

umbrella stand. Piece of hall furniture, in various forms, often whimsical, e.g. elephant's foot, used to hold folded umbrellas upright. Dates from 19th century.

unaker. China clay introduced to England from Virginia *c*1744, and used, e.g. in early manufacture of English porcelain. Also used as ingredient of *jasper ware in late 18th century.

underglaze colours. *See* high-temperature colours.

United States Pottery Company. *See* Bennington.

up-and-down dial. Subsidiary indicator on high-grade watches and chronometers to show state of winding of mainspring.

Urbino (Marche), Italy. Maiolica made by 1477. *c*1520, G. *Durantino established workshop, and with O. *Fontana continued *istoriato*

Urbino. Maiolica plate with broad flat rim, painted story of Calamus and Alexander. Base inscribed with date 1532, Urbino, and name of story.

style of father, N. *Pellipario, who also worked in Urbino from 1528. F. X. *Avelli, also painting in *istoriato* style, signed pieces dated *c*1530–42. Style made increasing use (1530–80) of grotesques on white ground and much relief moulding, e.g. snake-handled jugs, salts with birds' or lions' heads, and huge wine coolers, vases, holy water stoups, and fountains, with elaborate relief; associated in 16th and 17th centuries with *Patanazzi workshop.

urn. Classical pottery vessel or vase of oval form, often with shoulder. Shape copied in neo-classical silver and Sheffield plate hollow-ware and finials; also ornamental motif. (*See* amphora, Borghese urn, krater, Trafalgar vase.) From *c*1760 to 19th century term also applied to *japanned metal (iron or copper) hot-water container, used for making tea or coffee. At first contents kept hot by charcoal in base; type fitted with case to contain iron slab, heated until red-hot in fire, introduced in late 18th century. Spirit-lamps also used. Originally made in quart, 3 pint, and 1 gallon sizes; from early 19th century, larger sizes made. Hot water drawn off by turning tap or spigot in base. Also in silver and Sheffield plate (*see* coffee urn, tea urn).

urn or **vase clock.** French mantel clock in form of urn or vase, standing on base; introduced during Louis XVI period. Marble or gilt-bronze; sometimes whole vase made of porcelain, or base decorated with Sèvres plaques. Horizontal hour and minute band revolves at top of urn, with decorative arrow or snake's head, indicating time. Some examples with calendar dial on base. Style may have evolved from clock in form of covered cup, as example in silver, probably English *c*1580, now in Victoria & Albert Museum, London.

urn stand. Small four-legged table; top has raised rim and drawer beneath. Used to hold tea urn. Dates from *c*1750.

Ushak or **Oushak carpets.** West Anatolian wool carpets with Turkish-knotted pile, woven from 15th century in Ushak. In 16th and 17th

*Urn clock. By B. *Vulliamy, no 228, ormolu. Mounts attributed to M. *Boulton; decorated with Wedgwood *jasper ware plaques, which conceal winding, and rise and fall apertures. *Derby biscuit figure of woman after model by Jean-Jacques Spengler. Veneered satinwood plinth with oval painting in manner of G. B. *Cipriani. Height 5ft8in.*

centuries, Ushak principal Anatolian carpet production centre. Numerous types of vividly coloured court carpets include: geometrically stylized floral, *Holbein, and *Lotto carpets; Persian influenced, medallion-scheme *star-Ushaks and *medallion-Ushaks; bird, and badge of Tamerlane design *white Ushaks. Large numbers exported, and designs widely copied. Industry declined in 18th century; patterns revived 19th century in coarse, poor quality carpets. Also fine *prayer rugs, especially enormous 17th century *saphs designed for mosques. Red or blue mihrabs with either single arabesque indicating position for worshipper's feet, or naturalistic flower and/or leaf scrolls overlaid by curved medallion; curved arch above hanging lamp; spandrels infilled with stylized flower and cloud-band scrolls. *Illustration at* star-Ushak.

Usk ware. *Japanned metal ware made at factory at Usk, Monmouthshire, started in 1763 by two sons of Edward Allgood of *Pontypool. Produced wares stylistically similar to those of Pontypool; decorative features included flower sprays, military scenes. In early 19th century, commissions undertaken to depict clients' houses, grounds, coats of arms, etc. Factory closed *c*1862.

Utzmemmingen. *See* Ellwangen.

Vachette, Adrien-Joseph-Maximilien (d 1839). French box maker and jeweller. Pre-Revolutionary boxes were *tabatières à cage* incorporating plaques of porcelain, enamel, tortoiseshell, oriental lacquer, or gouache miniatures. For Napoleon, made mainly portrait boxes. Signed initials A.V. and cock device.

vaisseau à mât. French porcelain potpourri vase introduced in period 1756–63 at Sèvres. Boat-shaped, with pierced cover extended like mast at centre. Example designed by C-T. *Duplessis (*c*1757) decorated in deep blue and green with elaborate relief moulding and gilding.

Valadier, Luigi (1726–85). Italian silversmith working in Rome; apprenticed to father. Went to study in Paris (1754); returned to Rome (1756); took over father's business (1759); became master (1760). Fourth consul of guild (1766–69). In 1779, made *cavaliere* of Pope Pius VI: official silversmith to Sacred Apostolic Palace. Commissions varied, e.g. shrines for relics and other church plate; mounted antique cameos for Vatican Museum, and domestic silver for Pope. Also domestic silver, e.g. dinner services, in English and French styles for Italian nobles and foreign visitors. Specialized in épergnes (some in architectural forms, e.g. Trajan arch). After his suicide, large workshop maintained by son, Giuseppe (b 1762), who used same mark: three fleurs-de-lis and LV.

valance. Length of fabric, pleated or gathered, covering frame or open area of furniture. Also synonym for *apron.

Valenschwerck (Dutch, 'Flemish work'). Early Flemish tin-glazed earthenware; manufacture started before 16th century. Influenced by maiolica from Spain, Portugal, and Italy. Made for everyday use.

van Aelst or **van d'Alost,** Pieter. Most important early 16th century tapestry master-weaver in Brussels. *Tapissier* to Philip I and Charles V, also Pope Leo X and Pope Clement VIII. Most famous work, *Acts of the Apostles tapestry. Numerous other subjects include The Passion, History of David, and History of Troy.

van Blarenberghe, Louis (1716–94) and son Henri-Joseph (1741–1826). French miniaturists. Louis military and marine painter; gouache miniatures mounted under glass in lids of *bonbonnières,* gold boxes and occasionally in earlier *tabatières à cage.* Subjects included *fêtes champêtres,* and Boucher-like pastoral scenes. Son, Henri-Joseph, worked in same style; later drawing-master to children of Louis XVI.

van Cleynhoven, Quirinus (d 1695). Dutch potter at Delft; in 1655, with W. *van Eenhoorn, bought The Porcelain Bottle factory; manager until death. Member of trade delegation sent to England in 1684.

van Dalen, Lieven (fl late 17th and early 18th centuries). Member of family of Dutch potters; worked in Delft, 1667–1730. Bought The Young Moor's Head factory from widow of R. *Hoppesteyn in 1692. Made domestic ware, e.g. teapots, with flowered branches, birds, or insects, carefully drawn on dark brown or olive-green ground; border designs of spirals, scrolls, or herring-bone bands.

van den Bogaert, Jan (fl 1552–71). Potter at Antwerp. Credited with large maiolica jug (dated 1562) painted with scenes from Apocrypha (story of Tobit) in panels on yellow ground decorated with **ferronnerie*; marked F (i.e. *fecit*) over initials IAB; tiled panel has same initials. Another tiled panel, depicting The Return of The Prodigal, dated 1570 and initialled IB. Son with same name worked in 1570s.

Vanderbank, Vanderbanque, or **Vandrebanc,** John. Belgian émigré tapestry master-weaver, active in England 1689–1727. Chief *tapissier* to English court. Established *Soho Tapestry Works, *c*1691, which became most important English tapestry workshop, after Mortlake tapestry works closed in 1703. *Illustration at* Soho Tapestry works.

van der Biest, Hans or Jans (fl late 16th, early 17th centuries). Tapestry master-weaver, commissioned 1604 by Maximilian I, Duke of Bavaria, to establish and direct manufactory at Munich. Remained until 1615, executing tapestries for palace. Chief works: History of House of Bavaria, Grotesques, Night and Day and The Four Seasons.

van der Burgh, Cornelis (1653–99). American

Cornelis van der Burgh. Beaker made in New York, c1685, engraved with sprays of flowers and birds; strapwork under rim. Height $5\frac{7}{8}$in.

silversmith of Dutch descent working in New York. Made domestic silver; little survives. One of earliest pieces, a beaker, made *c*1685 in Dutch manner engraved with strapwork and floral motifs.

van der Ceel, Abraham (d 1741), son Maarten (d 1756), and grandson Abraham II (d 1810). Dutch potters at Delft. From 1723, Abraham owner and manager of The Porcelain Ewer factory (established 1637). Succeeded by Maarten, whose widow remarried; her husband became owner of factory in 1756. Abraham II manager from 1778. Products include decorative tableware; some vases and beakers decorated with *trompe-l'oeil*, landscapes or flowers in border. Marks include Lpkan (1723–78) and LPK (1778–1811).

Vandercruse-Lacroix, Roger (1728–99). French. Became *maître-ébéniste* in 1755. Commissions from the crown under Louis XV and XVI, Mme du Barry, and the Duc d'Orléans. Work characterized by marquetry, mosaic, and oriental design. Retired during the Revolution. Stamp: R.V.L.C.

van der Goten, Jacob (d 1725). Prominent Flemish tapestry master-weaver. In 1720, commissioned by Philip V of Spain to establish and direct *Santa Barbara tapestry manufactory in Madrid. Brought *'Teniers' tapestry tradition to Spain.

van der Hecke, François or Frans. Tapestry master-weaver in Brussels. Court *tapissier*. Works included Triumph of the Church, after cartoons by *Rubens and C. *Lebrun, and History of Achilles, from designs by J. *Jordaens.

van der Hecke, Jean-François (fl mid 17th century). Tapestry master-weaver in Brussels; son of F. *van der Hecke. Worked in close association with *Rubens. Tapestries include History of Achilles (in collaboration with father), from designs by J. *Jordaens.

van der Hecke, Pierre (d 1752). Master tapestry-weaver in Brussels; son of J-F. *van der Hecke. Most important works: History of Psyche, after cartoons by Jan van Orley; The Four Seasons, and The Elements, from designs by L. van Schoor; Peasants Carousing, after D. *Teniers.

van der Laarn, Jan (fl late 17th century). Dutch potter at Delft; in 1690s, master potter at The Heart factory. Plates with heart pattern initialled IVL attributed to him.

van der Lely or **Lely,** Gabynus (d 1754). Dutch silversmith working in Leeuwarden, Friesland; master in 1731. Son of J. *van der Lely. Work mainly domestic, though some church plate. Specialized in embossed ornament of flowers and strap work on matt ground. Mark: crowned lily in foliate panel.

van der Lely or **Lely,** Johannes (fl 1695–1749). Dutch silversmith working in Leeuwarden, Friesland; grandson of J. *Gerrits. Influenced by designs of D. *Marot. Produced domestic and church silver; much survives, including brandy bowls, spoons, tea kettles, teapots and caddies, censers, reliquaries, pyxes, plaquettes, etc. Preferred embossed and chased foliate ornament on matt ground; embossed work in minute detail. Mark: crowned lily. Son, G. *van der Lely, continued in trade.

van der Planken, Frans. *See* de la Planche, François.

van Dijk, Abraham (d 1727). Dutch potter at Delft. Owner of The Rose factory from 1712; succeeded by family. Products include lidded jars, and vases, some in **cachemire* style; tableware and sets of dishes decorated in enamel colours.

van Duyn, Johannes (d 1777). Potter at Delft, owner of The Porcelain Plate factory from 1763 until death. Signed work includes candlestick on leaf-shaped base painted with Kakiemon design in blue; also perforated fruit dish with stand, painted with flowers in polychrome on yellow ground. Mark: VDuyn.

van Dyck, Peter (1684–1751). American silversmith working in New York. Made domestic silver in English styles. Surviving work includes canns, tankards, chafing dish, casters, etc. Also noted for snuff-boxes using tortoiseshell with *piqué* decoration in silver. Mark: PVD in trefoil.

van Eenhoorn, Lambert (d 1721). Dutch potter at Delft from *c*1689. Son of W. *van Eenhoorn. Bought The Metal Pot factory after death of L. *Cleffius in 1691. Monogram mark LVE objected to by V. and L. *Victorson; hardly distinguishable from their LVF monogram. Ware includes large vases decorated in polychrome colours. Also made red stoneware teapots. Mark registered *c*1680: rearing unicorn surrounded by LAMB. VAN EENHOORN in oval line.

van Eenhoorn, Samuel (fl late 17th century). Dutch potter at Delft. Son of W. *van Eenhoorn. From 1674, manager of The Greek A factory; received factory as wedding present in 1678. Credited with bowls, etc., marked SVE, decorated with detailed figure groups, outlined in blue-black or purple; glaze shaded from light blue to greenish-grey. In 1684, member of trade delegation to England.

van Eenhoorn, Wouter (d 1679). Dutch potter at Delft. Involved with five potteries; exported Delft ware to Germany, England, and France. 1658–78, owner of The Greek A factory, in partnership until 1663. Partner with G. *Kam in The Three Golden Ash-Barrels factory from 1668.

vane, weathercock, or **weather-vane.** Wrought iron or copper flag, usually triangular, erected on building or in exposed area to show wind direction; used in Britain since before Norman conquest. On private house, also used to display owner's coat of arms. By 16th century, often square, fretted banner; developed into various shapes, e.g. cock or other bird or animal or human (often saint) figure, surmounting fixed direction pointers.

van Frijtom, Frederik (d before 1702). Dutch potter, painter, and landscape artist. Decorated plates and small plaques, and sometimes metal-mounted wine jugs, with freehand painting of Dutch landscapes, using different shades of blue to create perspective and create cloud effects. Signed examples dated 1659 and 1692.

van Gelder, Marinus Hendriksz (fl 17th century). Dutch flax merchant and amateur glass engraver. Worked in *hatched technique. *Façon de Venise* drinking glasses signed M.v.G., or name in full.

van Heemskerk, Willem (1613–92). Dutch cloth merchant, poet, dramatist, and amateur glass engraver of Leyden. Worked in diamond-point, occasionally with added wheel engraving. 259 examples of work known, mainly long-necked green bottles; also *façon de Venise* baluster-stemmed glasses and goblets and *winged glasses. Specialized in flourished calligraphy using couplets and quotations, many biblical, often adding full name and date.

van Orley, Bernard (1490–1541). Flemish artist, student of Raphaël; adviser on *Acts of the Apostles tapestry. Court painter to Marguerite of Austria (1480–1530). Numerous tapestry designs; attempted to reconcile new Italian style with formal art of tapestry. Cartoons for tapestries include Last Supper, Le Chemin d'Honneur, Hunts of Maximilian, Battle of Pavia, and History of Jacob.

van Rijsselberg, Ary (d 1735). Dutch ceramic painter at Delft. Worked at The Greek A factory in early 18th century as painter in enamel colours, including gold. Decorated e.g. plates with medallions enclosing hedges, birds, and vines, in Kakiemon style; also with prunus branches and parrot, predominantly in red and green, in *famille verte* style. Later work, mainly narrative, includes scenes with horsemen. Also made figures, e.g. of cows, decorated in polychrome, and some tableware in blue. Work initialled AR.

van Risenburgh, Bernard or **B.V.R.B.** (d *c*1767). French *ébéniste* of Dutch origin; worked in Paris, mainly in rococo style with some neo-classical elements in later work. Noted for pieces with floral marquetry and lacquer-work. Stamp: B.V.R.B.

van Roome, Jan (fl late 15th, early 16th centuries). Court painter to Marguerite of Austria (1480–1530). Major influence on early 16th century Brussels tapestry design and style. Surviving works include Communion of Herkenbald.

van Schurman, Anna Maria (1607–78). Dutch glass engraver of Amsterdam. Younger contemporary of A. R. *Visscher. Adopted same style. Work always signed.

van Vianen, Adam (*c*1565–1627). Dutch silversmith working in Utrecht; developed aspects of *Dutch grotesque style, derived from brother, P. *van Vianen. Became master *c*1593; assayer of Utrecht guild in 1606, 1607, 1610, and 1611; dean of guild, 1615. Earliest work in Renaissance style, *c*1613–19, featuring motifs such as scrollwork, grotesques, and molluscs. Later style characterized by controlled irregularity. Pieces hammered from sheet silver (not cast) with embossed and chased ornament. Few works survive, but influence on contemporary European silversmiths considerable. Made

Adam van Vianen. Wall sconce, made in 1622; wall plaque chased with mythological scene, surrounded by pierced border of auricular scrolls. Height 1ft11½in.

tazze, plaquettes, ewers and basins, candlesticks, salts, etc. Mark: AV in monogram. Son, C. *van Vianen, continued in trade. *Illustration also at* Dutch grotesque style.

van Vianen, Christian (b 1598). Dutch silversmith working in Utrecht and London; son of A. *van Vianen; master in 1628. In England *c*1630–47 and *c*1660–66; in service of Charles I. Most important work in England, set of altar plate for St George's Chapel, Windsor (1637), looted during Civil War (1642). In 1650, published volume of own and father's designs, *Modelles artificiels de divers vaisseaux d'argent.* Credited with introducing *Dutch grotesque style to English silversmiths. Used same mark as father: AV in monogram. Work in England usually bears full signature, otherwise unmarked.

van Vianen, Paul (*c*1558–1613). Dutch silversmith working in Munich and Prague; brother of A. *van Vianen. Probably trained by father; visited Rome, then settled in Munich in 1596. Became master in 1599. Made silver armour and small objects for Duke of Bavaria. Appointed court goldsmith to Archbishop of Salzburg (1601). Became royal goldsmith to Rudolf II in Prague (1603); made mainly silver plaquettes with religious or mythological relief figures in landscape. In *c*1607, began to develop lobate or *Dutch grotesque style for border ornament; style further developed by brother, Adam, from *c*1613. Also made *tazze,* ewers and basins, etc.

*Vargueño. Walnut; fall-front with pierced and gilt-metal lockplates and hinges. Interior of drawers and cupboards faced with ebony and bone. Supported on *barley sugar twist columns and fluted columns. Spanish, 17th century. Height of cabinet 2ft5in.*

Vase carpet (detail). Persian, 16th–17th century.

Vardy, John (d 1765). English architect; designed furniture in Palladian and rococo styles.

vargueño or **bargueño.** Spanish writing and storage desk; dates from 16th century. Square or rectangular, with flap front concealing architecturally designed interior of drawers. Flap, supported when open by lopers, forms writing surface. *Vargueño* rests on open or cupboard-like stand. By 17th century, elaborately decorated with inlay, carving, gilded, and iron mounts backed with velvet.

varnish. Solution of resinous substance in spirit or oil; used to protect and give shiny appearance to surface of wood, etc., as alternative to *polish. Refinement, **vernis Martin,* introduced *c*1730, much used to imitate oriental lacquer during vogue for *chinoiserie. c*1820, varnish superseded by French polish.

vase baluster (in furniture). Baluster turned to give shaft shape of vase; found particularly on late 16th and 17th century furniture.

vase carpets. Richly-coloured 16th and 17th century Persian court carpets made in north-west Persia. Ascending design of blossom and foliage lattices emerging from vases; or system of ascending flower scrolls. Ground usually blue. Extensively copied.

vase clock. *See* urn clock.

vase splat. *Splat shaped at sides to give silhouette of vase; common on *bended-back and Windsor chairs. *Illustrations at* corner chair, Philadelphia Chippendale.

Vase splat. On early 18th century English walnut chair; original upholstery. Height 3ft4in.

Vechte, Antoine (1799–1868). French silversmith and designer working in Paris and London. First made arms and armour in Italian Renaissance style. Commissioned by *Hunt & Roskell to make Titan vase, completed in 1847; after revolution of 1848 (and abdication of Louis-Philippe I), persuaded to live in England; became permanent employee. Vase contributed to medal won by firm at 1851 Great Exhibition. Produced extravagant exhibition pieces, elaborately chased and embossed.

vegetable dish. Covered serving dish made in Britain in silver or Sheffield plate from *c*1800; similar in shape to *entrée dish but with domed cover with fixed handle. Often found with stand, usually of Sheffield plate, with spirit lamp or hot iron for keeping food hot.

veilleuse. French *sofa with back higher at one end than other; arms of correspondingly different heights. Often made in pairs, placed opposite each other at either side of fireplace. Dates from Louis XV period.

veilleuse. Pottery or porcelain warmer for food or drink. Consists of hollow base containing burner (usually small vessel for oil and floating wick) on which covered bowl or, later, teapot stood. Made by many potters between 1750s and 1860s. English delftware *veilleuses,* made 1750–55, among earliest examples; made in soft-paste porcelain at Sèvres (1758–59). In mid 18th century, examples made in porcelain, e.g. at Höchst, Nymphenburg, Frankenthal, and Fulda; in faience at Durlach, Kelsterbach, Stralsund, etc. From *c*1830, often made in form of figure, notably by J. *Petit.

veneering. Thinly-sliced sheets of wood, notable for colour and grain, glued to surfaces of furniture made of less fine wood. Suitable woods for veneer include mahogany, rosewood, satinwood. Veneer may be halved, quartered, etc., then glued in symmetrical patterns on object. Thin sheets of other materials, e.g. ivory and tortoiseshell, may also be used. Technique introduced into England from Holland in mid 17th century; very popular in 18th century Britain, Europe, and America.

Venetian fair groups. Porcelain figures first modelled at Ludwigsburg factory, after fairs instituted by Duke Carl Eugen on return from visit to Venice (1767). Include variety of fair booths, stalls, peddlers, etc. Originals modelled by J-J. *Louis.

Venetian glass. Earliest recorded Venetian glass making in 11th century; industry already established, particularly bead making and Byzantine style mosaic work. In 13th century, Venetian glass makers formed guild which controlled all aspects of glass making; strict regulations guarded manufacturing techniques and forbade workers to abscond. In 1291, Grand Council of Venice ordered all glass workers except bead makers to move to island of Murano, partly to avoid fire risk from furnaces, partly to make absconding more difficult. Glass makers were divided into *cristallai,* optical glass makers; *fioleri,* makers of vessels and window glass; *specchiai,* mirror makers. Earliest surviving examples of Venetian glass are 15th century coloured, enamelled, and gilded vessels,

*Venetian glass. 16th century wine glass, bell bowl set on squat hollow baluster and *folded foot; decorated with* *lattimo; *height* $5\frac{1}{8}$*in.* Tazza *with ribbed foot and gadrooned bowl, folded rim with blue edge and blue trail; traces of gilding;* c*1500; diameter* $10\frac{1}{2}$*in.*

e.g. beakers and goblets, using Islamic techniques. Coloured glass, particularly dark blue, red, green, and opaque-white, used for e.g. portraits, mythological and allegorical subjects. Coloured beads and fish-scale motifs popular border patterns. In 16th century, armorial subjects and simple decorative motifs common. Diamond-point engraving gradually superseded enamelling, but examples rare. Clear *cristallo* also developed in 16th century; colourless when thinly blown; manipulated into intricate, delicate shapes, e.g. jugs in form of ships, and vessels with elaborate stems, handles and finials, e.g. *winged glasses. Venetians excelled in decorative techniques, mainly revived from Egyptian and Roman times. Opaque-white glass (**lattimo*) popular during 16th and 17th centuries; opaque-white canes also used, alone or combined with coloured canes, to produce **latticinio* and **vetro di trina* glass in lace-like and combed patterns. *Aventurine, **millefiori, *calcedonio, *fondi d'oro* and ice glass used for elegant forms, e.g. *tazze,* jugs, vases, wine glasses, covered goblets, bowls, beakers, and large plates, many with applied gadrooning, trailing, pinching, prunts, and *mascarons. From early 16th to late 18th century, Venice produced mirrors and chandeliers, later examples festooned with flowers and fruit. From late 17th century, glass making declined, as lead-glass superseded *cristallo* in popularity. In 18th century, *Miotti Glasshouse produced enamelled opaque-white glass, G. *Briati produced Bohemian-style mirrors, and many glasshouses made fragile novelty glass. From mid 19th century, Renaissance styles and techniques revived. *Illustration also at* aventurine glass.

Venetian maiolica. Italian maiolica identifiable from 1520s; most importance during mid 16th century. Decoration on *berrettino* glaze, possibly inspired by Ming porcelain via Isnik blue-and-white pottery. From *c*1550, *istoriato* subjects, covering whole surface of plate, or surrounding portrait medallions or coats of arms (sometimes of German families). Reverse of dishes usually plain, sometimes ringed with concentric yellow circles.

Venetian porcelain. First porcelain factory in Venice established by F. *Vezzi in 1720; closed 1727. German refugees from Dresden made porcelain at Udine (1758–61) and Venice (1761–63). P. *Antonibon permitted by Senate to make porcelain at *Le Nove from 1763, but production lapsed because of his illness (1763–65). Some workmen from Antonibon factory left to join G. *Cozzi, manufacturer from 1765. Figures and unidentified useful wares made at Este from 1781, also by workmen from Le Nove. Porcelain said to have been made at Treviso, 1759–77; no examples known. Treviso porcelain, made from late 18th century to 1840 in paste resembling that of Le Nove and Cozzi factory, includes cylindrical mugs painted with figure subjects. Porcelain believed to have been made at Vicenza (1793–1800) and *Angarano (1777–80) indistinguishable from that of Le Nove.

Venetian tapestry. Though Venice was important trade centre, no major tapestry industry existed until manufactory established 1760 by Antonio Dini with grant from magistrates. Operated until *c*1789. Works copy early Italian tapestries and contemporary Gobelins designs.

venison dish. Large oval silver or Sheffield plate meat dish (usually 18–20in. long) with ribbed base (forming cross) and well at one end to collect gravy; not exclusively for venison. Often on two stud feet, gravy-well forming third foot. Sometimes with hot-water compartment for keeping meat hot. Used in Britain in early 19th century. *Illustration at* meat dish.

venturine. *See* aventurine.

verdure tapestry. Rustic landscape tapestry design, developed from medieval *mille-fleurs* pattern; used primarily for bedroom hangings, screens, or furniture covers. Style developed in 15th century; immensely popular in 18th century.

verge escapement. *See* escapement.

Vernis Martin. Book rest detachable from Louis XV bedside table.

Verhaer, Nicolas (*c*1685–1750). Dutch silversmith working in Utrecht; master in 1710. Held post of assayer and treasurer of guild. Made silver plaques with scenes in relief; guild shields. Also church plate. Mark: three lozenges beneath coronet.

Verhagen, Johannes (d 1740). Dutch potter at Delft. Owner of The Peacock factory from *c*1725. Made ornamental and tableware decorated in blue, with biblical subjects, landscapes, and country scenes, including plates dated 1725–30.

vermeil. *See* silver-gilt.

vermiculé. French ceramic decoration; trailing pattern breaking up ground colour into irregular patches, introduced at Sèvres in second half of 18th century. Usually gilded, sometimes painted in blue on pink ground, giving marbled effect.

Vermont Glass Factory. Founded 1813 in Salisbury, Vermont, by a stock company, for production of window glass. Branch factory also built at East Middlebury to produce bottles and hollow-ware. Both closed in 1817.

verneh rugs. South Caucasian tapestry-weave rugs usually made in two parts and sewn together. Field pattern of squares and/or lozenges and realistically-drawn animals; worked in sombre colours, particularly deep reds and blues.

vernis Martin. Technique reproducing effect of Chinese lacquer, invented by G. *Martin in France. Mixture of tree resin, linseed oil, and turpentine; dried by heat. Used on boxes and other objects of vertu, and household articles, including furniture and clock cases. Most famous European lacquered ware; height of popularity in mid 18th century Paris. *Illustration at* French snuff-boxes.

*Giacomo Verzelini. Goblet, bowl decorated by A. *de Lysle with gilt coats of arms, inscriptions, date 1590, and name Wenyfrid Geares. Hollow-blown inverted baluster stem with moulding terminating in thick collar and folded conical foot. Height 7¼in.*

'vernis Martin' fan. Mid 18th century French *brisé* fan covered with lacquer and thus associated with Martin firm; no proof that Martin brothers made fans.

verre de fougère. French glass, similar to **Waldglas*, but using fern or beechwood ash for alkali. Green or pale amber colour. Probably produced in limited quantities since Roman times. Widely produced by 14th century, particularly in Dauphiné in south-eastern France, Normandy, and Lorraine. Used for simple domestic ware, e.g. small bottles, bowls, jugs, and beakers. Style very plain, main decoration applied prunts.

verre églomisé. Type of **fondi d'oro* glass decoration named after French picture and mirror framer, Glomy (d 1786), who used it extensively in 18th century. Gold or silver foil applied to reverse side of glass and engraved with needle. Backed with black or contrasting colour and enclosed by second layer of glass or coating of varnish. Used for decorating mirror borders, etc., in late 17th and 18th centuries. *Illustrations at* W. Hamlet, C. Rosenberg.

verre filé de Nevers. *See* Nevers.

Verstelle, Geertruy (fl mid to late 18th century). Dutch potter at Delft. Manager of The Old Moor's Head factory from 1761; married owner in 1769. Work includes chocolate-pot and stand in rococo silver form, decorated in blue, and spice-box with pastoral scenes in polychrome, initialled G:V:S:.

Verzelini, Giacomo (1522–1606). Venetian glass maker. At *Crutched Friars, London, from 1571; assumed control when J. *Carré died (1572). Set up new factory in Broad Street when Crutched Friars burnt down (1575). Granted 21-year monopoly by Elizabeth I to produce *façon de Venise* glass. Specialized in table glass and goblets, usually elaborately engraved in diamond-point. In 1592, sold business and monopoly to Sir J. *Bowes.

Vestier, Antoine (1740–1824). French painter. In Paris from 1860, copied paintings in enamel. Later painted miniatures and portraits in oils and pastels.

vetro a reticelli, reticello glass, or **Netzglas.** Venetian glass, variant of **vetro di trina* with two layers of *latticinio* glass fused together to form net pattern with small bubble of air in each cell of network. Reproduced in 19th century.

vetro di trina (Italian, 'glass [made] of lace'). Venetian glass made from late 16th century; elaborate form of **latticinio* technique, with layers of opaque threads and bands forming interlacing patterns. Reproductions made in 19th century. *See vetro a reticelli.*

Veuve Perrin. *See* Perrin, Veuve.

Vezzi, Francesco (1651–1740). Italian porcelain maker, originally goldsmith. Believed to have made hard-paste porcelain in Venice from *c*1720 with help of C. C. *Hunger. Porcelain very translucent; white, creamy, or greyish. Products include tableware, notably octagonal teapots, and vases. Decoration, often in relief with enamel painting, includes *chinoiseries,* garlands of flowers, and coats of arms. Underglaze blue used in *chinoiserie* and bird designs; occasionally gilding and enamel colours added. Some figures and foliage painted in iron-red enamel with cross-hatched shading. Factory closed in 1727. About 150 specimens identified.

Francesco Vezzi. Porcelain cup and saucer, c1725.

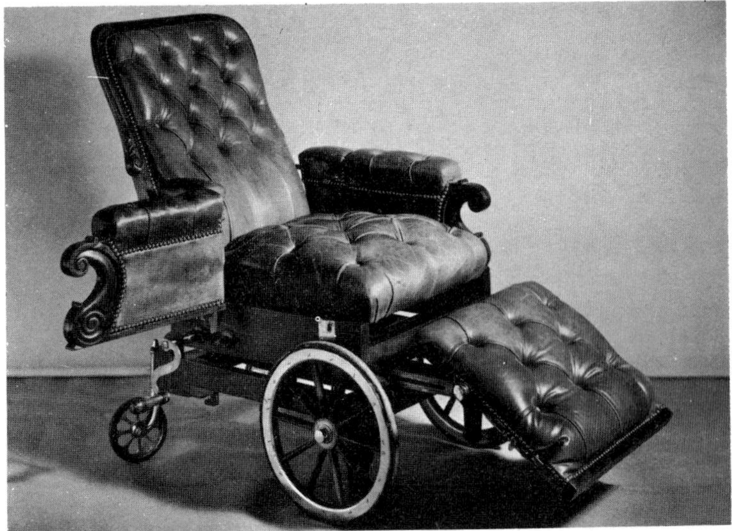

Victorian period. Mechanical chair. Mahogany with leather upholstery and brass fittings. English, mid 19th century.

Marks include Venezia, Vena in underglaze blue, blue, red, or gold enamel, or incised.

Vickers, John. Metal worker in Sheffield, Yorkshire, in 1769. Introduced a tin alloy (Vickers' White Ware) which could be polished to resemble silver. Wares advertized in 1780s included teapots, cream-jugs, tobacco boxes. Mark: I. Vickers.

Victorian style. Loosely describes various eclectic styles fashionable in England during reign of Queen Victoria (1837–1901). Early furniture (*c*1837–50) showed simple classicism; mid Victorian (1850–75), return to rococo curves and ornateness; late Victorian (1875–1901) medieval Gothic and Renaissance features. Some pieces combined features from several different periods. Many pieces in mahogany or rosewood; from *c*1850 black walnut also used.

Victorson, Victor (d 1713) and son, Louwijs (fl *c*1688–1735). Dutch potters at Delft. Owners (1668–1735) of The Double Jug factory, established 1661. Products decorated in K'ang Hsi style; often white designs on blue background alternate with flourishes in blue on white. In 1713, Louwijs succeeded father as head of factory until 1735. Marks include monogram of LVF (easily confused with mark of L. *van Eenhoorn).

Vienna, Austria. Hard-paste porcelain factory established in 1719, with help of workmen from Meissen, S. *Stölzel and C. C. *Hunger, under directorship of C. I. *Du Paquier. Greenish-white paste exceptionally thin and translucent; early production noted for high quality, but unprofitable. Two-handled, fluted chocolate cups with *trembleuse* saucers typical of early period; forms of tableware inspired by contemporary silver fashions. Painting by e.g. A. *Schultz and J. P. *Dannhöfer characterized by formal baroque scrollwork and trellis-like panels in *Schwarzlot,* red monochrome or polychrome. Moulded decoration occurs, e.g. on tureens. Produced small number of snuff-boxes in *fantasy shapes painted with gaming motifs *c*1725–35. Scent bottles made in silver and glass shapes with flowers, *chinoiseries,* and formal borders. Some bottles moulded in relief and painted. Figures made after purchase of factory by Austrian state (1744) include dwarfs in style of Meissen and *commedia dell'arte* characters. J. J. *Niedermayer (*Modellmeister,* 1747–84), and L. *Dannhauser credited with everyday, contemporary figures and mythological or biblical characters, noted for vivacity and bright, pale colouring, particularly brown, mauve, and yellow. From 1778, style echoed in figures of contemporary fashion modelled by A. *Grassi. In 1784, K. *von Sorgenthal provided financial help in crisis, after which factory prospered. Decoration includes use of coloured grounds in style of Sèvres; J. *Leithner painter and chemist from 1770. Production declined from 1805. After closure in 1864, some forgeries made of work from von Sorgenthal period, with fake signatures. Mark, on work in Chinese style (*c*1720–30), double cross enclosed in square, in blue; from 1744, variations of shield impressed, incised, or (from 1750) in blue, sometimes with A in red or green. Products also decorated (*c*1720–70) by *Hausmaler,* possibly including D. and I. *Preissler and I. *Bottengruber. Financial problems of Du Paquier period may have encouraged sale of outdated wares in the white. *Illustration also at* ollio pot.

Vienna Porcelain Factory. Wine cooler, c1740, realistically painted with a mouse among *deutsche Blumen. *Height 6½in.*

Right:
Vienna regulator. Early 19th century. Mahogany and glass case. Height 5ft.

*Vinaigrette. English, made in Birmingham, 1805, by M. *Linwood to commemorate Battle of Trafalgar. Lid decorated with Nelson's portrait, grille (shown) with H.M.S. Victory.*
Vincennes. Porcelain sugar box and cover, 1753; *jaune jonquille *ground with* putti *painted in blue by Vieillard.*

Vienna regulator. Austrian wall clock with long pendulum and glass-fronted door in trunk; dial often enamel. Later examples of same type (after 1840) made in Black Forest, Germany, usually with pendulum beating $\frac{2}{3}$ second.

Vile, William (d 1767). English cabinet maker. Partner of J. *Cobb, cabinet makers to George III. Work distinguished by superb quality and fine carving.

vinaigrette. A container of aromatic substances in use in Europe from *c*1800, consisting of small gold or silver case containing sponge soaked in aromatic vinegar held behind pull-out grille. Initial shape was rectangular with closely fitting hinged lid; later made in *fantasy shapes with engraved and *repoussé* ornament and pierced grilles. Late Victorian versions of silver-mounted glass and ivory.

Vincennes (Val-de-Marne), France. Soft-paste porcelain manufacture (1738–56) moved to *Sèvres. Member of *Hannong family established faience factory in 1765, produced hard-paste porcelain until 1770, then moved to Paris (Faubourg Saint-Denis). *Illustration at* Sèvres.

vine dish. In Chinese ceramics, round porcelain dish (15–30in. in diameter), with vine motif or sometimes bunch of lotus flowers, tied with ribbon, at centre; foliate edge, with formal scroll or wave patterned border. Popular in late 14th and 15th centuries, for both Imperial and export ware. Notable examples from reign of *Hsüan Tê.

vine leaf or **ivy leaf decoration** (in ceramics). Vine or ivy shaped leaves trailed in gold lustre, blue, or both, on Hispano-Moresque pottery made in Valencia *c*1427 to late 15th century. Often combined with *acacia leaf design.

Vinogradov, Dmitri (d by 1758). Russian arcanist. In 1748, followed C. C. *Hunger in attempt to start porcelain factory at St Petersburg, initiated by Empress Elizabeth. Successful only in producing some small pieces of hard-paste porcelain.

Vinovo (Piedmont). Italian porcelain factory established near Turin in 1776 under royal patronage. Figures and groups, tableware, ink-stands, and knife handles made in creamy hard-paste with brilliant glaze. Decoration includes *barbeau* sprigs, crimson roses in style of Strasbourg, landscapes in purple, blue, or black and green enamel; also portraits, cupids, or landscapes enclosed in medallions, and festoons. Pierre-Antoine Hannong director from 1778, but unsuccessful: factory closed in 1780. Re-opened same year; French invasion (1796) halted production. Resumed 1815–20. Mark: cross of Savoy, usually over V, incised or in underglaze blue, sometimes with initials of director or painter.

viola. *See* violin family.

viola d'amore. Stringed musical instrument played with bow; hybrid of *viol and *violin families. Developed *c*1700 in Germany; popularity confined almost exclusively to Germany, though Italian composer, Antonio Vivaldi (1678–1741) composed some pieces using it. Body shaped like viol, but played at shoulder like violin. Six or seven gut strings (more often seven) with six or seven brass or steel sympathetic strings below (not touched by fingers or bow but intended to vibrate in sympathy). Out of fashion by late 18th century. Wooden body sometimes ornamented with carving, inlay, etc.

viol family. Family of stringed instruments played with bow; origin obscure; immediate ancestor probably 13th to 15th century *vihuela da mano* (six or seven stringed guitar) which, when played with bow, *vihuela da arco*, became viol. In early 16th century viol assumed characteristic appearance, discarding hour-glass shape of *vihuela*. Back of viol usually flat (shoulders slope to neck); usually six-stringed; fretted; C-shaped soundholes; bridge less arched than in violin; often with carved rather than scroll head. Bow used is older, out-curved type; hand held under bow. Made of thin wood, and lightly constructed. Members of family, developed by mid 16th century, vary greatly in size; all were played upright, smaller types on or between knees of seated player, and larger between legs. Chief viols were treble, alto, tenor, bass (usually called *viola da gamba*), and double bass (*violone*). Popularized in England *c*1520 by players from Spanish-ruled Flanders, and Venice. Extremely popular until early 17th century; superseded throughout Europe by violin in late 17th century. By 1680, only bass viol still used in England and Italy. Wooden body sometimes ornamented with inlay of ivory, various woods, etc.

violin family. Stringed musical instruments played with bow; origin obscure; emerged in Europe in early 16th century and existed beside *viol family until late 17th century, when former became dominant. Earliest member was violin; some examples probably three-stringed, but by *c*1550 traditional form had four gut strings. Most important centres of production (for violin family) from late 16th to 18th centuries were Brescia and Cremona, Italy, country of renowned families of makers, e.g. *Amati, *Guarneri, *Stradivari. Only non-Italian maker with international reputation at this time was Stainer working near Innsbruck, Austria. Quality of instruments depended on choice of woods for body, special varnish, and excellent craftsmanship. Extremely complex instrument with numerous parts: basically waisted body, with convex belly and back, attached at right-angles to neck, terminating in pegbox and scroll; strings attached to tailpiece; bridge set between F-shaped soundholes in mid-body (waist). Until 18th century, made in larger and smaller size (body length $13\frac{1}{2}$–$14\frac{1}{2}$in.); standardized by A. Stradivari. Violin achieved modern shape *c*1800, due to modifications necessitated by shift of instrumental music from private chamber to public concert hall. Family also includes larger viola, violoncello (or cello), and double-bass. Violin and viola played at shoulder; cello and double-bass stand on floor, former between legs of sitting player. Double-bass differs from other members of family in number of strings, initially three, later four or five, and tuning string. Bow given modern standard form by François Tourte (1747–1835) working in Paris. Original bow shaped like early weapon (also for viol); Tourte bow has concave curve rather than convex, also slightly longer and heavier than original. Bow held below hand for playing instruments of violin family. Violins made in variety of materials other than wood, e.g. copper, brass, silver, glass, papier mâché, etc. Other members of family also inlaid with ivory, mother-of-pearl, etc. Ornament made appearance more attractive, but probably detracted from tone.

violin flask. Free-blown or mould-blown violin-shaped flasks made in 19th century America. Often vividly coloured in blue, purple, yellow, and opaque-white. Usually decorated with commemorative emblems.

violoncello, *See* violin family.

virginal. *See* harpsichord family.

virgule escapement. *See* escapement.

Visscher, Anna Roemers (1583–1651). Dutch scholar, poet, and glass engraver. Worked in linear diamond-point, introducing original note in occasional use of *stippling, anticipating mid

18th century Dutch glass decoration. Used large *Römer* of thin greenish glass, and tall fluted covered goblets, mainly engraved as gifts for friends. First and finest exponent of calligraphic decoration on glass; bowl surface covered with intricate motto or proverb, inscriptions in Roman capital letters or in Greek letters, usually with signature and date, into which realistically-treated flowers, insects, and fruit interwoven.

Visscher, Maria Tesselschade (1595–1649). Dutch glass engraver of Amsterdam. Younger sister of A. R. *Visscher. Adopted same style.

Vitrearius. *See* Laurence Vitrearius.

vitrine. Glass or glass-fronted cabinet, standing either independently or on stand-base; for display of curios, china, etc. Dates from mid 18th century.

Vitruvian scroll or **wave pattern.** Convoluted scroll-pattern resembling series of C-forms or waves; classical origin. Used in 18th century architecture, and as border ornament on silver, etc. *Illustration at secrétaire à abattant.*

V-loop pile. *See* weft-loop pile.

Vögelesdekor. German ceramic decoration: scattered pattern of flowers, leaves, exotic birds and small clusters of dots; characteristic of faience painting at Hanau from late 17th century. Often found in blue, on grey ground, on tall jugs with rope-like handles. Used in 18th century on faience made at Nuremberg and, particularly, Ansbach.

Vitrine. *French, 18th century. One of pair decorated in style of A-C. *Boulle.*

voider, voiding dish, or **voyder.** From middle Ages, tray in silver, pewter, wood, etc., used for clearing scraps from table. Surviving examples very rare. Superseded in early 18th century by brass or copper voiding pail; by *c*1750, often produced with outside in brass-bound mahogany.

voider stand. Stand, usually with x-frame, used from 18th century to support voider or butler's tray.

Volkmer, Tobias (*c*1560–1629). German goldsmith and instrument-maker; worked at Bavarian court from 1594. Produced fine gilt-brass surveying instruments, etc.

Volkstedt (Thuringia). German factory founded 1760, making soft-paste porcelain; later used hard-paste formula. Most early wares have imperfect greyish body covered with extensive relief decoration in imitation of contemporary Meissen. Large potpourri vases notable. Under control of *Greiner family from 1799, when produced glazed and biscuit portrait reliefs, painted plaques in rococo-moulded frames, etc. Marks include, 1760–99, crossed hay-forks of Schwarzburg (deliberately resembled Meissen mark, until objections made in 1787); 1799–1817 or later, R (Rudolstadt, name of local prince); and many 19th century marks. Production continues.

volute. Spiral scroll on capital of Ionic column. Ornamental form, e.g. in silver, dating from Renaissance.

von Brühl, Count Heinrich (1700–63). Minister of *Augustus III and director of *Meissen porcelain factory at height of achievement, 1733–63. Commissioned various works, including *Swan Service, and **Plat de Ménage.*

von dem Busch, Ernst Augustus Otto (fl *c*1748–*c*1775). Canon of Hildesheim, Germany. Outside decorator, comparable with *Hausmaler*; engraved designs in porcelain glaze with diamond, then rubbed black pigment into incisions. Result impermanent, because black colour not fixed. Obtained wares in the white from Meissen and, rarely, Fürstenberg. Decoration includes landscapes, birds, flowers, etc.

von Jünger, Christoph (d 1777). Austrian producer of enamel wares in Vienna from *c*1764; brother Johann continued workshop to 1780. Under royal protection, made *toys and large household objects based on Sèvres porcelain models.

von Löwenfinck, Adam Friedrich (1714–54). Pottery director and ceramic painter. Apprenticed Meissen 1726–34, worked at Bayreuth (1736), Ansbach (1737–40), Fulda, as 'Court-Enameller' (1741–44), Hochst, as founder and director (1746–49), and Strasbourg, as director (1750–54). At Strasbourg, introduced painting of *deutsche Blumen* (Strasbourg flowers). Most signed work on Meissen porcelain, where probably responsible also for much unsigned flower painting. Best known for *chinoiseries.* First European to paint large Chinese figures; sometimes placed oriental and western figures in same landscape. Harbour scenes, birds, and fabulous beasts also feature. Used much gold and bright enamel colours. Faces usually drawn in black with touches of blue. After 1736, most painting on faience; some pictorial plaques ascribed to him may be work of wife, painter Maria Schick (married 1747). Mark: F v L.

von Lücke, Johann Christoph Ludwig (d 1780). German sculptor, ivory carver, modeller at Meissen 1728–29. Figure of Augustus the Strong in red stoneware (later repeated in white porcelain) attributed to him, also life-sized bust of court jester. Made snuff-boxes and *Galanterien* based on originals elsewhere. Worked at Vienna (*c*1750), Fürstenberg (1751), founded Schleswig faience factory (1754–55). Visited Copenhagen (*c*1752–57) as arcanist, and England (in 1760) to exhibit ivory portrait of George II.

von Münnich service. Porcelain table service made in Germany at Meissen factory by J. J. *Kändler in 1738 for Field-Marshal von Münnich. Elaborately modelled in style of *Sulkowski service.

von Sorgenthal, Konrad (d 1805). Austrian wool manufacturer; became director (1784) of Vienna porcelain factory; achieved 20 years of success in spite of factory's initial financial failure. Products of period sometimes known as Sorgenthal porcelain. Typical is tableware, with *gold ground and elaborate miniature painting in medallions; also cylindrical, neo-classical style coffee cups with angular handles, painted all over, using raised enamels to achieve jewelled effect. Biscuit figures and busts made by A. *Grassi. Blue ground and other colours by J. *Leithner.

von Tschirnhaus, Ehrenfried Walter (1651–1708). German nobleman from Saxony; chemist, and much-travelled student of mathematics and physics. By 1675 had begun experiments to find formula of hard-paste porcelain; had succeeded in producing small sample in 1694. Director of experiments by J. F. *Böttger at Meissen from 1703.

voyder. *See* voider.

voyeuse. French side chair with low seat and padded yoke-rail. Sitter faced back with arms resting on rail. Designed for watching card games, *c*1740.

voyeuse à genoux. *Voyeuse* with low seat and higher back, allowing user to kneel rather than sit.

Voyez, Jean (*c*1768–*c*1800). French-born modeller: worked in Staffordshire from mid 18th century. Joined J. *Wedgwood in 1768, but dismissed in 1769 went to work for H. *Palmer; helped to make good copies of Wedgwood basalt. Also worked for the *Wood family. Signed pieces include jug moulded as tree trunk with figures and inscription 'Fair Hebe'. Marks include I. Voyez and date impressed.

Vulliamy family (fl 18th to mid 19th centuries).

Noted family of clock makers: Justin (1712–97) emigrated from Switzerland to London, *c*1730. Son, Benjamin (1747–1811), mechanical adviser to George III; made regulator for Kew Observatory and other long-case clocks with grasshopper *escapement; also bracket clocks and ornamental types with ormolu and porcelain mounts made e.g. at Derby, influenced by French styles. Son, Benjamin Lewis (1780–1854) became leading maker of his day, carrying on father's business, also producing carriage clocks and other French types, e.g. elephant clock. Noted for high quality work and attention to detail, but refused commission for Westminster clock, believing terms impossible. *Illustrations at* temple clock, urn clock.

Wa-cha-p'ing (Honan). Chinese kiln site, near Ch'ang-sha. Centre of pottery manufacture from T'ang dynasty onwards, although some remains of Han bronze-style pottery and domestic stoneware also unearthed at site. Most products resembled Yo-chou ware, some domestic pieces with earthenware body covered in pale buff slip; usually thinly potted, greyish stoneware coated with mauve or grey slip. Some work lacks slip covering. Glazes varying in colour from yellow to green, have tendency to flake, and sometimes show fine crackle. Carving or incised decoration with foliate patterns predominant.

Wadsworth, John (fl *c*1796). Chair maker in Hartford, Connecticut. Specialized in *Windsor chairs.

wafer box. Silver or Sheffield plate box for thin adhesive discs or wafers; *inkstand fitting, matching inkpot, sandbox, pounce box, etc. Used from 16th to mid 19th centuries.

wager cup or **puzzle cup.** 16th or 17th century trick cup. Common type had two bowls, one inverted forming base of cup and other swivelling between two up-stretched arms. Contents of larger cup had to be consumed first; cup then inverted to drink from smaller swivel cup. First made in Germany and Holland; few made in England. *See* Jack-in-the-Cellar, *Jungfrauenbecher,* windmill cup.

Wagner, J. G. (fl mid 18th century). German porcelain painter who worked at Meissen from 1739. Work includes presentation snuff-box for Frederick II with scenes of Silesian War (1741).

wagon-spring clock. *Connecticut shelf clock with laminated flat-leaf spring for power instead of normal coil form; invented by J. *Ives. Adopted by other makers *c*1825–*c*1855. *Illustration (of movement) at* double and triple decker clocks.

wag-on-wall clock. Early form of American wall clock, made *c*1767. Hooded top, in manner of tall clocks, but with unenclosed weight and pendulum hanging below. Popular term describing any European wall clock, particularly from Black Forest, in which pendulum is clearly visible.

wainscot (in furniture). Literally, wagon boarding. From 14th to late 17th century, oak imported to England from northern Europe for panelling and furniture; later, any wood usable for joinery. Split and *quartered wainscoting suitable for chairs, chests, beds, etc. By 17th century, general term used in England and America for solid wooden panelling, or furniture (chairs, tables, etc.) built of solid wood.

Wager cup. Silver-gilt, Jungfrauenbecher *type, made by John Angell, 1827. Top, decorated with acanthus leaves, swings when cup is tilted. Height 7in.*

waiter. Small *salver or tray in precious or japanned metal used during 18th and 19th centuries, usually for handing letters, wine glasses, sweetmeats, etc.; in silver often forms part of set, e.g. two small, one large.

Wakelin, Edward (d 1784) and John (d *c*1802). English silversmiths working in London; Edward apprenticed to Huguenot silversmith in 1730. In 1747 joined firm owned by G. *Wickes, probably taking over silver side of business. In *c*1759, J. Parker became partner in firm (Parker & Wakelin); mark: IP above EW, with Prince of Wales plumes above. From 1776–92, Edward's son, John, and another partner, William Tayler, ran firm (Wakelin & Taylor); mark: IW above WT, with Prince of Wales plumes above. In 1792 Parker died and Tayler disappeared from records; J. Wakelin took R. *Garrard the Elder as partner (firm became Wakelin & Garrard). On retirement or death of Wakelin in 1802, Garrard left in charge of firm, selling mainly work of various manufacturing silversmiths. Accounts indicate that, from 1766, firm supplied by some 70 plate-workers, each specializing in manufacture of particular objects. Also sold Sheffield plate wares supplied by M. *Boulton and S. *Roberts the Younger.

Wakelin ledgers. Business accounts of firm founded by G. *Wickes, which was subsequently run by E. *Wakelin and his son before descending to R. *Garrard the Elder. Ledgers contain information regarding management of successful firm of London silversmiths and silver and jewellery retailers in 18th and 19th centuries. First two volumes (1735–47) in possession of successors of *Garrard & Co.; remaining volumes (1747–1820) in Victoria & Albert Museum Library.

Waldglas (German, 'forest glass'). Glass made in wooded areas of Germany, etc. Tradition, probably surviving from late Roman times, revived in Middle Ages. Usually green glass, also amber or brownish; potash obtained by burning forest vegetation used as flux (*cf verre de fougère*). Specifically German forms made in *Waldglas* include 15th century **Igel*, **Kuttrolf*, **Maigelein*, and 17th century **Krautstrunk* and **Römer*. *See* Wealden glass.

Wall, Dr John (1708–76). Among original shareholders in Worcester porcelain factory. Studied medicine in Oxford and London; practised in Worcester, 1740–74; investigated problem of poisoning from use of lead-glazed vessels; also amateur painter. Credited with founding of porcelain factory in 1751 to produce soapstone porcelain. Name associated with first period of work at factory. Retired in 1774. Thought to have painted some porcelain, including enamelled mug with scenes of Conquest and Gratitude commemorating 1747 Worcester parliamentary election, probably dated after 1751.

Wallbaum, Matthäus. *See* Wallpaum, M.

wall clock. Category includes many forms of clock intended for wall-mounting, especially

Wall clock. American, by Seth Thomas, c1860. Rosewood case with ringed gilt columns, and panels of flowers and game birds.

Wallendorf porcelain. Group of farmer and wife fleeing from burning house, c1775. Height 8in.

John Walton. Lion and the Unicorn figures, with impressed mark Walton, c1830.
Wandering-hour watch. Silver pair cases; outer case engraved with crest of William III. By Joseph Windmills, London, c1695.

variant of English 30-hour *lantern clock with square dial plate and case similar to top of *long-case clock, *c*1660–*c*1800.

Wallendorf (Thuringia). German porcelain factory founded 1764 by arcanist in partnership with two members of *Greiner family. Porcelain paste indifferent white. Decoration of tableware copied from Meissen **Zwiebelmuster* and **Blaublümchenmuster* underglaze patterns; also some enamel painting. Until 1778, marked with W adapted to resemble Meissen marks; after objections, classical double V used.

wall fountain. Earthenware water container with low tap, and often large matching basin. Examples occur in **Hafnerware* from 16th century. Part of dining room furniture in Spain and France in 17th and 18th centuries. Made e.g. at Alcora, from early to mid 18th century, Marseille and Strasbourg in mid 18th century. *cf* lavabo.

Wallpaum or **Wallbaum,** Matthäus (1554–*c*1632). German silversmith working in Augsburg. Made silver and silver-mounted religious and secular objects, e.g. triptychs, caskets, standing cups, etc. Pieces include cup in shape of Diana on stag, with clockwork mechanism in base to propel it along table.

wall-plaque. Ornamental plate, e.g. of stamped brass or cast iron (often painted), hung on interior wall for decoration; particularly popular in 19th century. Main subjects: rustic or marine scenes, animals, children.

wall pocket or **wall vase.** Earthenware or porcelain vase, flattened and pierced on one side for hanging against wall. Examples made in English delftware, notably at Liverpool, also at Lambeth. In salt-glaze, made by W *Greatbatch. Porcelain examples made at Worcester moulded in cornucopia form with flowered twigs painted under glaze, or modelled landscapes (*c*1755).

wall-sconce. *See* sconce.

Walpole Salver. Salver made by P. *de Lamerie from George I's Exchequer seal for Sir Robert Walpole. Engraving attributed to W. *Hogarth.

Walton, John (before 1780–after 1835). Potter at Burslem, Staffordshire. By 1818, owner of colour works in Burslem, and earthenware factory. Made variety of earthenware figures, after contemporary porcelain originals, characterized by streaky opaque colouring, usually with tree and bocage background. Early pieces often stand on mound coloured dark green with patches of brown, or on square base painted to represent marble; some later figures have blue-framed oval panel at front of base. Figures include classical and religious subjects, rustic groups, soldiers, sportsmen, and animals; also made Toby jugs and brightly enamelled toys. Regarded as leading potter of Walton school, makers of similar figures, e.g. C. and R. *Salt, O. *Sherratt. Mark: WALTON, impressed on scroll.

wandering-hour watch or **chronoscope.** Shows time by dial with semi-circular opening through which hour numeral moves; at each hour, numeral disappears from opening and next appears at other end. Minute scale on circumfeerence of semi-circle. Introduced *c*1700.

Wan-li porcelain. Named after Chinese emperor, Ming dynasty (1573–1619). Noted for overglaze *wu ts'ai decoration. Imperial blue-and-white pieces distinguished by violet shade in underglaze blue; large quantities exported to West. *Chia Ching styles and techniques continued. *Illustration at* wu ts'ai.

Warburton, Anne (d 1798). Staffordshire enameller; member of family manufacturing early cream-coloured earthenware at Hot Lane, Cobridge in late 18th century. Enamelled Queensware for J. *Wedgwood.

Warburton, Jacob (1740–1826). Staffordshire potter. Son of A. *Warburton. Manufacturer of cream-coloured and white earthenware. Member of *New Hall China Manufactory. Mark: WARBURTON, impressed.

Wardian case. Metal-framed, glass-enclosed dome, to hold house plants. Named after N. B. Ward, early exponent of cultivating plants under glass; used from *c*1850.

wardrobe. Originally, small room next to bedroom, or recess, where clothes were stored. In 17th and 18th centuries, term interchangeable with *clothes press. From *c*1750, in England, wing wardrobe became increasingly popular: tri-partite front, with base and central upper section fitted with drawers and two side sections providing hanging space. By 19th century, term described tall architectural cupboard for storing clothes, often with long mirror in central front panel, or attached to inside of door.

warming-pan or **bed-warmer.** Metal pan containing hot embers used for warming bed. Known in Europe in different forms from 15th century or earlier, apparently not in England until 16th century, when usually in brass, occasionally copper. Long iron handle had ring at end for hanging when not in use. After *c*1650, handles wooden (oak, beech, ash), sometimes

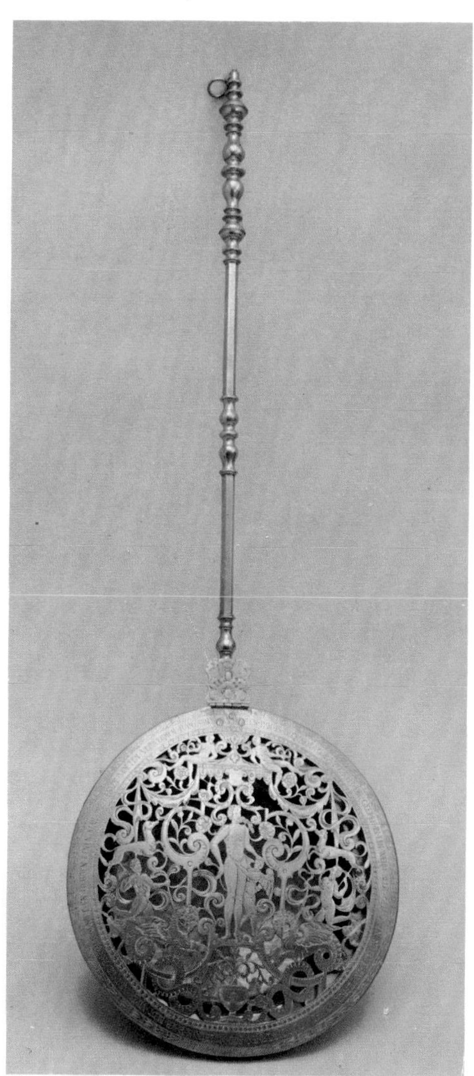

Warming pan. Brass. Dutch, dated 1602.

carved or ebonized and knopped. Hinged lid, pierced to allow heat to escape and to keep embers red-hot, decorated with variety of punched or embossed ornament; sophisticated examples have engraved coat of arms or similar decoration. Inscriptions common. Pans straight-sided and flat-lidded until *c*1780, when curved sides became general and low-domed lids produced by stamping process. By this time handles often japanned, and detachable, so that pan could be left in bed. Used from 18th century in America. Warming pans occasionally made in silver. Hot-water pans, made from 1770s in brass or pewter in similar shapes, with screw opening, replaced ember pans entirely by *c*1810; these in turn gradually replaced during 19th century by plain copper or earthenware bottles.

warp. *See* weft.

Warring States period (481 B.C.–221 B.C.). Chinese sub-period of Chou dynasty, during which feudal states fought for supremacy. Ended in establishment of Ch'in dynasty by Shih Huang Ti, who succeeded in uniting country under single rule. Iron casting apparently introduced during this period. *See* Chinese bronzes, Chinese lacquer, Huai style, Ordos style.

Warsaw. Polish faience factory established in 1774; traded as Belvedere factory. Work usually in style of Chinese-inspired Meissen porcelain. Service decorated in Imari style with enamel and gold, bearing Turkish inscription, made 1776, possibly as gift to Sultan of Turkey. Marks include B, and Varsovie.

Warwick frame. British silver *cruet frame with cinquefoil or quatrefoil base (generally five leaves, for two cruets, three casters); each leaf has guard rign of moulded wire shaped to cruet or caster. Usually has central, vertical ring handle; may also have feet. Introduced *c*1715 and popular until mid 18th century.

Warwick vase. Shape derived from classical Roman vase found in grounds of Warwick Castle, England. Reduced copies in silver made by P. *Storr from 1812 as wine coolers. Also made in Sheffield plate.

Washington inaugural buttons. Hand-stamped copper, brass, or Sheffield plate buttons made for delegates to Washington inaugurations (1789 and 1793); 22 designs including eagle and star, initials G. W., and sun surrounded by rays and clouds.

washstand, washing stand, or **wash hand stand.** *See* basin stand.

wassail bowl. Large two-handled bowl, often in pewter, passed round table on festive occasions for each diner to drink toast; drinker holds one handle while previous drinker holds other. Sometimes inscribed with word 'wassail'.

waste mould. *See* investment.

waster. Pottery discarded because of breakage or faults. Comparison with wasters sometimes provides guide to origin in cases of uncertain attribution.

watch. Timekeeper for personal use, carried or worn, probably first produced in form distinct from *clock by P. *Henlein, *c*1510, in Nuremberg, Germany, which remained centre of production in early part of 16th century, with French makers following lead *c*1550. *Drum, *spherical, and *globe watches typical of period, usually with *striking mechanism, developing into decorative types, e.g. *rock-crystal and *form watches.

In early 17th century, oval and octagonal shapes common; English makers became active, first copying continental patterns, then evolving *Puritan watch. Large French industry was based at Blois, producing enamelled watches, with **oignon* form becoming general in late 17th century. Introduction of *balance spring, *c*1675, applied first to verge *escapement, later to improved forms, led to decrease in importance of case decoration with greater accuracy of movement. Concentric hour and minute hands became standard, with occasional variants e.g. *wandering-hour and *sun and moon dials. Movements with verge escapement remained common throughout 18th century, usually mounted in *pair-case, but other types also favoured, e.g. cylinder and duplex, together with innovations including *repeating and *calendar work and use of seconds hand. In 19th century, lever escapement became almost universal in English and continental watches,

Watch case made at Lyon, c1650. Movement by Jean Vallier; pierced and engraved silver case.

but England lost lead in world market through mechanization of watch industry in France, Switzerland, and America. *See* American, Dutch, English, French, German, Swiss watches.

watch case. Before introduction of *balance spring *c*1675 and resulting improvement in performance, watches worn to large extent for ornament or as jewellery. Case thus of prime importance except in e.g. English *Puritan watch. Main styles of case elaboration include: engraving with landscapes, allegorical scenes, patterns, etc., on covers and dial, piercing of case and sometimes dial, often combined with chiselling and engraving; chasing and repoussé work; inlay and (more rarely) niello work; lapidary work as in *rock-crystal watch and agate or other hardstone cases, some set with pearls and gems, enamelling of various forms, including *Blois enamel. *See* form watch, pinwork, *piqué*.

After 1675, case styles became less exuberant with more attention to movement; standard round shape adopted; piercing and engraving continued with mainly floral motifs but enamel usually limited to dial; *repoussé* work more common, but cast and chiselled cases gradually discontinued. Rococo style general after *c*1725, particularly in France with asymmetrical *repoussé* decoration, followed in mid 18th century by use of *four-colour gold often set with ruby and turquoise; *engine-turned cases common from 1790, with plain gold or silver usual in 19th century.

watch-chain. *See* fob chain.

watch glass. Glass cover for watch dial, introduced *c*1630: dials previously left uncovered or occasionally enclosed in cases of rock-crystal. Early dome or shaped glass formed from sections cut out of blown spheres. Rock crystal also used *c*1630–*c*1700; rarely used later, e.g. by A-L. *Breguet.

watch jewels. *See* jewelling.

watch key. *See* key.

watchman's clock. *See* tell-tale clock.

watch paper. Disc of paper printed with name of maker or repairer and engraved decoration, sometimes placed at back of watch case for protection and used for advertisement. In England used from late 18th century; in America, printed papers from *c*1800 preceded by cloth, sometimes silk with design or message.

water clock. Device known in antiquity as clepsydra. Used to measure time by regular flow of water from container, etc.; time often indicated by float connected to pointer. Revived in 17th and 18th centuries, sometimes in elaborate form, e.g. slowly falling drum caused to rotate by gradual flow of water from one internal division to another. (Many spurious examples with false inscriptions made in England *c*1920 to designs without any precedent in antiquity.)

Waterford Glass Works. Established 1783 in Waterford, Ireland, by *Penrose brothers who advertised 'all kinds of plain and flint glass, useful and ornamental'. Employed J. *Hill as manager and *c*70 craftsmen, majority brought by Hill from Stourbridge, Worcestershire. Hill succeeded by former clerk, Jonathan Gatchell, who became partner when firm taken over in 1799. By 1811, Gatchell sole proprietor. Main product fine, clear, cut glass tableware and decorative pieces, occasionally coloured. Before *c*1800, decanters, jugs, and finger-bowls often marked Penrose Waterford. Factory noted in 19th century for cut glass lustres. Gatchell sold business in 1851.

Water clock. Signed and dated 'Arnold Finchett, Cheapside, 1735'. Water contained in partitioned drum below, which slowly revolves and turns hour hand. Light can be placed inside main case for illumination at night.

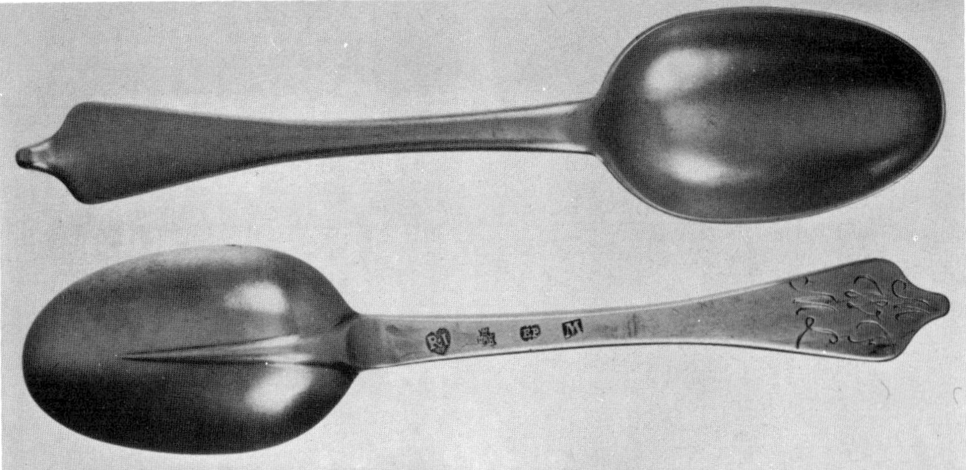

Wavy-end spoons. Queen Anne, rat-tailed table spoons by Robert Inglis of Edinburgh, 1707.

water gilding. *See* gilding.

water-jug. *See* jug.

water-leaf ornament. Stylized water-lily leaf: large, unribbed, rounded or tapering leaf. Used e.g. on neo-classical silver.

Waterloo leg. *See* sabre leg.

Watteau, Jean-Antoine (1684–1721). French painter and designer. From *c*1707, worked with court painter, Claude Audran, on decorations for royal chateaux; probably involved with him on design of Gobelins tapestries. Mature paintings are early expression of rococo style. Work widely copied on porcelain, (e.g. at Meissen), enamels, etc., probably from engravings.

Watteau service. *See* green Watteau service.

wave pattern. *See* Vitruvian scroll.

wave-patterned border. Chinese ceramic decoration, found at all periods from Sung, e.g. as incised naturalistic motif round rim or interior of celadon cups and bowls. Decoration of flowers, clouds, or floating fish often added over glaze. More stylized diaper of spiral coils, narrow borders of zig-zags used on Ming and Ch'ing porcelains. Naturalistic crested wave border also common.

wavy-edged plate. Pewter plate common in Europe, copied in England *c*1750–75; basically circular, with undulating edge. Larger oval dishes also made for serving; rim usually moulded, sometimes with reeded pattern.

wavy-end, shield-end, or **dog-nose spoon.** Silver, pewter, or latten spoon made in Britain and Europe *c*1690–*c*1710; has long, narrow bowl, generally with rat-tail, and long stem with flattened, undulating end (resembling modified *trefid spoon handle), usually with central section curved upwards. Sometimes referred to as dog-nose spoon in auction catalogues.

wax-jack, wax-winder, taper-stand or **pull-up** (American). Silver, Sheffield plate, or brass stand for wound sealing-wax taper, in use from 18th century. Various types; in some, reel holding taper mounted vertically on circular base or horizontally between two uprights. Taper end held between flattened blades or scissor-like grips attached to reel, or projecting through small nozzle above horizontally placed reel. *c*1775, open wire-work frame, sometimes globular, holding horizontal spindle inside; often includes conical extinguisher. *See* taper-stick.

waywiser. Device for measuring distances, used by surveyors from late 17th century. Wooden

*Wax-jack. English silver, by *Emes & Barnard, 1810.*

Waywiser. English, mid 18th century, made by Heath and Wing. Brass with iron-bound wheel. Glass-covered dial shows measurements in yards, poles, furlongs, and miles; brass tube above this, connected to the hub, would once have had wooden steering handle. Radius of wheel 6in.

wheel, usually *c*3ft diameter, with handle for pushing in front of user; drives dial mechanism to record number of revolutions (hence distance covered). Some examples have two wheels joined by axle with dial mounted above.

Wealden glass. Earliest recorded glass making in England was in wooded Weald of Surrey, Sussex and Kent, from 13th century until introduction of *façon de Venise* in 16th century. Potash glass, similar to German **Waldglas*, made mainly for window glass, but also for domestic ware, e.g. beakers, with low foot decorated with trailed threading at neck, and small mould-blown bottles. Notable craftsmen: *Laurence Vitrearius (13th century window glass); John le Alemayne (14th century window glass, semi-opaque bottles, and domestic ware); J. *Carré and other Lorrainers (16th century window glass and blown drinking vessels).

weathercock or **weather-vane.** *See* vane.

Weber, Franz Joseph (fl mid 18th century). German painter and pottery chemist; worked at several German porcelain factories including Ludwigsburg, Frankenthal, Höchst, and Ilmenau. Author of The Art of Making True Porcelain, published 1798.

web foot (in furniture). *Ball-and-claw foot, with webbed foot. Found on Irish and northern English pieces.

Webster, Moses (1792–1870). Flower painter on porcelain made at Derby and Worcester. Later worked at R. *Robins and T. M. *Randall's decorating workshop in Islington, London. Also painter at Nantgarw and Swansea.

wedding casket. *See* marriage casket.

wedge thumbpiece. Thumbpiece on 16th and 17th century English pewter vessels; thick end of wedge is over handle, thin end at centre of lid.

Wedgwood, Josiah I (1730–1795). English potter and industrialist, born in Burslem, Staffordshire. From 1739, worked for brother, becoming apprentice from 1745. Attack of smallpox *c*1742 interrupted work as potter then, and by causing knee infection *c*1745, led to amputation of leg in 1768. Partner in firm at Stoke-on-Trent, producing agate ware, Egyptian black, salt-glaze, and tortoiseshell ware. From 1754, partner of T. *Whieldon at Fenton; produced salt-glaze and tortoiseshell ware; also experimented on improvement of earthenware body and coloured glazes. In 1759, established own firm at Ivy House Works, Burslem; used green glaze to cover tableware moulded in leaf shapes. Moved to Brick House Pottery, later known as Bell Works, also at Burslem; manufactured domestic ware (1762–63); by 1763, developed *cream-coloured earthenware, later refined into *Queensware. Transfer-printing of domestic ware by J. *Sadler and G. *Green; early painting by A. *Warburton, J. *Robinson and D. *Rhodes; later, decorators employed in London. Products include *'Frog' service. Introduced ornamental vases decorated with coloured slips or glazes in imitation of granite or other stone. By *c*1767 developed *black basalt, used for reproductions of ancient Greek vases from 1769. In course of trade at Liverpool, whence goods exported to America, met T. *Bentley, partner from 1768; firm traded as Wedgwood & Bentley. New premises at Etruria in use from 1769, at first for production of ornamental ware, until manufacture of domestic ware gradually transferred (1771–73). Work included **rosso antico* (introduced at Brick House, 1763), *cane-coloured and other stoneware, rarely with enamel decoration. Introduced *jasper ware *c*1774 and *pearlware *c*1779. In 1783, elected Fellow of Royal Society after developing pyrometer. From Bentley's death, sole proprietor until 1790, when took into partnership three sons and nephew, T. *Byerley, trading as Wedgwood, Sons & Byerley until 1793, when Josiah *Wedgwood II took over shares from brothers. Firm traded as Wedgwood & Son & Byerley until 1795.

Workmen at Wedgwood factories not encouraged to sign pieces; therefore most are difficult to identify. J. *Tassie employed from 1769 for design of medallions. Artists employed to reproduce and adapt models from original works in Rome under direction e.g. of J. *Flaxman, who also modelled medallions. W. *Hackwood chief modeller 1782–1832. Other modellers include *Tebo and J. *Voyez.

Marks (1769–80) include: WEDGWOOD & BENTLEY. ETRURIA in circle between concentric lines, stamped around screw on vases other than jasper; WEDGWOOD & BENTLEY, or W & B. From 1771 on useful wares, and from 1780 on all types: WEDGWOOD, or Wedgwood (other marks containing name Wedgwood used by *Stafford Pottery on Queensware). Also *Wedgwood date-letters. *Illustrations at* black basalt, canopic jar, J. Flaxman, jasper ware, Queensware, T. Whieldon.

Wedgwood, Josiah II (1769–1843). Staffordshire potter, son of J. *Wedgwood I. Partner of father from 1790. Retired 1795; factory managed by cousin, T. *Byerley. Resumed management in 1804. Manufactured porcelain (*bone china) 1812–22, running down production from 1816 in favour of jasper ware and Queensware (production resumed in late 19th century). In 1832, Whig member of parliament for Stoke-on-Trent. Successors were sons, Josiah III (1795–1880), until 1842, then Francis (1800–88), a partner from 1827. Firm remained a partnership until 1895, then limited company. From 1840, manufacturing modernized; solid jasper reintroduced; coloured earthenware bodies developed; *parian ware also made.

Wedgwoodarbeit (German, 'Wedgwood work'). Imitations of Wedgwood porcelain, including *jasper ware, made in Germany *c*1775–1810, notably at Meissen under C. *Marcolini.

Wedgwood date letters. System of marks in addition to usual name mark on earthenware; introduced at Wedgwood factory in 1860. Three capital letters denote month, potter, and year respectively. Months January to December represented by letters J, F, M, A, Y, T, V, W, S, O, N, D (1860–64) and by J, F, R, A, M, T, L, W, S, O, N, D. Year marks in alphabetical cycles O (1860) to Z (1871), A (1872) to Z (1897), etc.

Wedgwood jewellery. *Black basalt and *jasper ware cameos produced by J. *Wedgwood in late 18th and early 19th centuries; used in England as brooches, bracelets, belts, parts of diadems, etc. Mounted in gold or cut steel; some made at M. *Boulton's Soho Manufactory from 1787 onwards. Subjects of cameos (oval, round, or octagonal) were classical scenes, portraits, etc. Some modelled by J. *Tassie and J. *Flaxman.

Wednesbury, Staffordshire. Produced enamelled wares; industry started by S. *Yardley in 1776. *See* South Staffordshire enamels.

Weesp. Dutch porcelain factory established in 1757. Hard-paste porcelain manufactured from 1759 with help of German workmen including N. *Paul. Tableware made from very white porcelain paste in contemporary German styles, decorated with figures and landscapes after J-A. *Watteau; also birds and naturalistic flowers. Figures made, e.g. by N. F. *Gauron *c*1775. Factory transferred to *Oude Loosdrecht in 1771. Mark in underglaze blue resembles Meissen crossed swords, with dots.

weft or **woof**. In weaving, threads woven into and across warp threads, which extend lengthwise in loom. In tapestries, and tapestry-weave carpets, coloured weft threads produce design. In pile carpets, used primarily to secure knots.

weft-loop, single loop, or **V-loop pile.** Most primitive form of knotted carpet pile. Knots formed by single or double-strand pattern threads pulled through alternate warp threads to form V-shaped loops. Several weft threads between rows of knots. Notable examples: Egyptian *Fostat carpets and Spanish *Alpujarra rugs.

Wegely's factory, Berlin. German porcelain factory founded 1752 by W. K. Wegely and J. *Benckgraff, producing white porcelain with thin glaze. Decorative wares include large covered vases with brightly coloured applied flowers, stems, leaves, and *putti*. Some figures copied from Meissen, e.g. *commedia dell'arte* characters; original models of artisans etc. ascribed to *Modellmeister*, E. H. *Reichard; later founder of *Berlin Porcelain Factory. Many figures left unpainted because of difficulties with chemistry of enamel colours, but black, lilac, and red used. Tablewares feature Watteau figures in monochrome (by I. J. *Clauce), or simply-coloured flowers. Factory closed 1757. Marks: W in underglaze blue and impressed.

weights. Standard bronze weights in graded sizes made from 15th century or earlier. Two main types exist: bell-form with ring handle; and flat cylindrical shapes with slight central depression, fitting into each other to form pyramid or nest. Both continued in use into 20th century. Wool weights, changed with each monarch, vary in shape and bear royal arms and official stamps. Reproductions abound.

Weisweiler, Adam (*c*1750–after 1810). German-born *ébéniste*; studied under D. *Roentgen. In Paris before 1777; *maître-ébéniste* in 1778. Supplied furniture to royal palaces including Saint-Cloud. Features of work include caryatids and columns. Stamp: A. WEISWEILER.

welcome cup. *See Willkomm.*

Wellington chest. Early 19th century English cabinet designed to hold coins, medals, etc. About 24in. high, with 6 to 12 shallow drawers. Vertical flap, hinged to front of one side of cabinet, can be bolted to upper and lower frame of chest front, thus locking drawers. Among pieces of furniture named after 1st Duke of Wellington after English victory at Waterloo (1815).

Wellington Shield. Ornamental silver shield designed by T. *Stothard and made by B. *Smith the Elder for Green, Ward & Green, London. Presented to 1st Duke of Wellington by merchants and bankers of City of London *c*1822.

Weights. Bronze nest of weights by Paulus Ritter, stamped with his initials. Made in Nuremberg, 1752. Height 8in.

Adam Weisweiler. Pedestal cupboard. Cupboard door veneered with ebony, framed in ormolu and mounted with figure of Bacchus; side panels of contre-partie *Boulle marquetry; marble top. French, late 18th century. Height 3ft7in.*

Welsh dresser. Architectural storage and display piece; low cupboard with series of open shelves above. Made in Wales and other parts of rural Britain from late 17th to early 19th century.

Welsh harp. Used in Wales from *c*10th century; horsehair strings; derived from Irish harp. In 15th century, given additional gut strings, becoming first chromatic harp in Europe. In 17th century, three rows of strings.

Westerwald stoneware. Westerwald area became important centre of German stoneware production in 1590s. Potters from Rhineland, including J. *Emens and sons of A. *Knütgen, settled in Höhr, Grenzau, and Grenzhausen. Main products were tankards and jugs in grey, at first decorated with stamped and incised designs, notably vertical and horizontal lines of beading. Gothic influence less strong and baroque style more pronounced than in Rhineland, especially in late 17th century. Clear manganese lead-glaze introduced early 17th century. Manufacture of peasant pottery continued until 18th century; revived in 19th and 20th centuries. Modern reproductions have serial number on base.

Westminster clock. Timekeeper in tower of Houses of Parliament, London, often called 'Big Ben' (strictly, name given to bell on which hours are struck); constructed and fitted in 1859 by firm of *Dent from design by E. Denison (Lord Grimthorpe), with gravity *escapement and pendulum beating two seconds. Tune used for chimes became popular for late 19th century chiming clocks.

whale's tail decoration. Decorative motif on tall clocks with break-arch hood, introduced in America, *c*1790. Curved edge of top ornamented at front by band of wavy, scroll-like shapes, known locally as whale's tails. Principal maker, T. *Harland.

whatnot, omnium or **étagère.** Portable stand with several open tiers, to hold or display small objects, curios, etc.; sometimes with shallow drawers. Triangular models in 19th century. Form dates from 18th century, popular in 19th.

wheel-back. *Windsor chair back with pierced wheel design in splat. Also, late 18th century chair back, oval or circular, with back area containing radiating spindles resembling wheel spokes.

wheel engraving. *See* engraved glass.

wheel-lock tinder-box. *See* tinder-box.

Whieldon, Thomas (1719–95). English master-potter at Fenton, Staffordshire *c*1740–*c*1780. Financially successful; became High Sheriff of Staffordshire in 1786. Made lead-glazed earthenware and stoneware. Employees included W. *Greatbatch, A. *Wood, J. *Spode I, and J. *Wedgwood I. Produced teaware, knife and fork handles, and salad bowls of solid agate ware in mixtures of brown, cream, and blue or green. Noted for *tortoiseshell ware. During partnership with J. Wedgwood (1754–59) made light slip-cast figures inspired by Far Eastern and Meissen porcelain, decorated with coloured oxides. No mark. *Illustration also at* tortoiseshell ware, agate ware.

whimsey. Oddment made by glass-blowers from left-over metal, e.g. toys, rolling-pins, button-hooks, bells, ships, and oddly shaped hats. Particularly popular in 18th and 19th

Thomas Whieldon. Group of wares produced 1755–58 by Whieldon and Wedgwood. Top, left to right: marbled mug, Egyptian black glazed teapot, Egyptian black tea-caddy and teapot. Bottom, left to right: marbled cream jug, marbled glazed teapot, marbled knife handle and creamware biscuit teapot with marbled glazed lid.

century England and America, but also made in glasshouses throughout Europe. *cf South Jersey glass.*

whistle tankard. Silver tankard with hole in lower part of hollow handle. Hole prevents hot air becoming trapped inside handle (causing bubbles or depressions) during soldering to body. Theory that handle was used to whistle for another drink probably unfounded.

White, Robert (1645–1704) and son George (*c*1671–*c*1731). English plumbago miniaturists. Robert pupil of D. *Loggan; portraits include Charles II and James II; many works engraved. George pupil of father; at first portrait painter in oils, and plumbago miniaturist; more notable as engraver.

Whitefriars Glassworks. English glasshouse founded *c*1680 on site of old Carmelite friary near London docks, which provided access for shipments of coal and glass-making materials from Newcastle-upon-Tyne. Produced fine flint table glass and domestic ware. From 18th century, only two heavily cut chandeliers dated 1788 known. At 1851 Exhibition, showed cut and engraved table glass in Anglo-Irish tradition; also simpler pieces with deeply cut leaf motifs. Although table glass remained basic product, experiments with colour and ancient techniques carried out in mid 19th century. *Millefiori* and mosaic glass produced, also stained-glass windows from medieval recipes. Artists employed included Edward Burne-Jones, Ford Maddox-Brown and W. *Morris. In 1860s, produced clear, softly tinted soda-lime glasses based on Venetian and ancient Roman specimens. Ownership changed frequently. Bought by James Powell & Sons in 1833. Firm continues, but moved from original site in 1922 to Wealdstone, Middlesex.

Whitehurst, John (1713–88). English clock maker in Derby, then in Fleet Street, London. Maker of turret clocks, etc.; inventor of *tell-tale clock. Descendants carried on work at Derby.

white metal. *See* Britannia metal.

whiteness. Guide to purity of silver; fine silver turns white during firing, distinguishing it from alloys. *See* touchstone.

White Star, The (De Witte Star). Delft factory (1660–1804). Owned by D. *Hofdyck after 1705. Work in late 18th century includes figures, sometimes adapted for use e.g. as candle-holders.

white stoneware. *See* salt-glaze ware.

white Ushak carpets. 16th and 17th century *Ushak court carpets. First Turkish rugs woven with undyed weft. Distinctive white ground for both field and border. Two types: bird carpets with all-over muted colour or monochrome brown-black pattern of leaves stylized to bird-like forms radiating in fours from rosette, and spaces infilled with small palmettes and rosettes; badge of Tamerlane carpets with diaper pattern of three circles arranged in triangle above two waves, sometimes overlaid with central armorial device.

Whitty, Thomas (1716–92). English carpet-weaver and manufacturer. First knotted-carpet woven 1755 at his newly established *Axminster Carpet Manufactory modelled on P. *Parisot's *Fulham carpet manufactory. Reputation secured by three awards from Royal Society of Arts for best 'Turkey carpet'. Whitty's innovations in weaving and dying techniques established Axminster among most prominent English manufactories.

whorl foot (in furniture). *Scroll foot which turns outwards; 18th century form.

whorl pattern. *See* Queen Charlotte pattern.

Wickes, George (d *c*1770). English silversmith working in London. Registered first mark in 1721–22. Appointed 'goldsmith, jeweller and silversmith' to Frederick, Prince of Wales, son of George II; also worked for other aristocratic patrons. Marks: WI, or G enclosing W (1721–22); GW, with crown above (1735), and GW in Gothic script with Prince of Wales plumes above (1739). For history of firm from 1747, *see* E. and J. Wakelin; Garrard & Co; Wakelin ledgers.

wig stand. Device for holding wig or wigs when not in use. Often has turned wooden pedestal with wider base and knob top; examples with arms projecting from pedestal base held several wigs. Used from mid 17th until late 18th centuries. Also made e.g. in Dutch Delft in late 17th century. Usually decorated with oriental-inspired designs in blue monochrome. *Illustration at* Nevers.

Willard, Aaron (1757–1844). Massachusetts clock maker from Grafton. Worked in Roxbury from 1780; set up factory in Boston, *c*1792. Succeeded in business by son, Aaron Jr, in 1823. Made tall and wall clocks; also banjo clock, with eagle finials, and long curved scrolls on each side of trunk, between dial and base. Developed production of *Massachusetts shelf clock. *Illustration at* banjo clock.

Willard, Simon (1753–1848). Massachusetts clock maker and inventor; brother of A. *Willard. Worked in Grafton, *c*1766–80, then in Roxbury. Work includes tall, wall, and Massachusetts clock in late 1790s; patented, 1802. Made lighthouse clocks, 1822. Also invented clockwork roasting jack.

Willaume, David, the Elder (*c*1658–1741). Huguenot silversmith working in London; trained in France; most prolific and successful of refugee silversmiths. Probably arrived *c*1686; granted freedom in 1693. Many commissions for aristocracy. Apparently specialized in wine cisterns; three survive. Range of domestic silver includes ewers and basins, salvers, flatware, knives, etc. Marks: WI with two stars above and fleur-de-lis below (1697 and again in 1718–19); DW with two stars above and fleur-de-lis below (1720). From 1716 son, David the Younger, in charge of workshop; apprenticed to father 1706; obtained freedom 1723. *Illustrations at* caster, rat-tail spoon.

Willems, Joseph (d 1766). Flemish-born sculptor, modeller of porcelain at Tournai and Chelsea (*c*1750–66). Many models copied from Meissen; others adapted from engravings. Allegorical figures include Sciences, Seasons, Continents, Senses, and Arts; also figures from everyday life, e.g. workmen, and *commedia*

William and Mary style. Spice chest, made in Philadelphia, c*1690–1720. Walnut with drop handles to the three drawers.*

dell'arte characters. Tableware in form of birds, fruit, or vegetables.

William and Mary style. English and American colonial furniture style during reign of William III (1689–1702). Like preceding Restoration style, reflected Louis XIV style in carved and gilded decoration, and Dutch influence in use of hood tops on case furniture and mirrors, scroll legs, marquetry, etc. Influences partly came from continuing influx of Dutch and French craftsmen, e.g. G. *Jensen and D. *Marot, and circulation of designs by J. *Berain. Furniture continued mainly rectilinear; straight lines broken by curved cresting, hooded domes, scroll legs, and curved stretchers.

Walnut remained predominant wood (although cottage furniture continued to be oak); much matched veneer and *endive marquetry, and less carved decoration. Lacquer-work popular for cabinets, frames, etc. Cabriole leg became more common, and straight pillar-leg (Louis XIV style) also used. Ball, bun, and Spanish feet characteristic. Upholstered pieces often covered in silks, brocades, velvet, or needlework fabrics. Common decorative motifs include acanthus, drapes, husks, masks, vases. *Illustration at* chest of drawers.

Williston, Samuel (d 1874). Founder of first American factory making cloth-covered buttons, Easthampton, Massachusetts, 1833. Buttons marked on back S. Williston.

Willkomm (German, 'welcome' cup). Gold, silver-gilt, etc., standing cup used in Germany from 16th century by Guilds, presumably to toast important visitors, or new members. Ornament often related to craft of guild. *See* guild cup.

Willkomm glasses (German, 'welcome' glasses). **Humpen* bearing welcoming inscription, offered to guests on arrival.

willow pattern. Pseudo-Chinese design incorporating pagoda, willow tree, two flying birds, and bridge, usually with figures, used by many English pottery and porcelain makers from *c*1780 to decorate blue transfer-printed ware. Design attributed to T. *Minton, first used by T. *Turner. Legend attached to scene appears to be English in origin. *Illustration at* Grainger, Lee & Co.

Wilson, Robert (fl late 18th century). Staffordshire potter. In 1778 became manager of *Neale & Co; partner from *c*1785. Succeeded in 1802 by son David.

Wilton carpets. Modest *ingrain carpets (without pile and made by tapestry-weave method) probably produced in England at Wilton, Wiltshire, from late 17th century. Charter granted to clothiers of Wilton by William III in 1699 often considered starting-point of English loom-woven carpet manufacture. Though carpet-weavers not specifically mentioned in charter, existence of strong, protected guild of woollen manufacturers in district would make Wilton natural centre for carpet manufacture. From available evidence, *Kidderminster in fact more probable cradle of industry. First horizontal Brussels looms in England set up at Wilton in 1740 by two ex-Savonnerie master-weavers, Anthony Duffossee and Peter Jemaule, manufacturing looped pile *moquette (or Brussels) carpets instead of ingrain. Kidderminster followed in 1749, and thereafter beneficial rivalry existed between two centres. Method of cutting loops of moquette pile to produce cut or velvet pile carpet probably initiated at Wilton; patented by Duffossee in 1741, and became known as 'Wilton' cut pile carpet from then onwards, regardless of place of manufacture. Fire in 1769 interrupted production of Great Factory; of new firms founded in Wilton at that time only two survived its rebuilding. Records indicate that designs followed Persian or Turkish models, but no early surviving examples known. Carpets typically woven in long, narrow strips which could be joined together to form large piece. Despite strong competition from imported hand-knotted carpets, Wilton factories' comparatively cheap but high quality products gained favour, reaching peak of production at turn of century, when carpet manufacture formed bulk of town's business. Decline of industry followed after war with France (culminating in battle of Waterloo in 1815). By 1833, only two small factories remained. In 1835 Blackmore & Son purchased premises in Wilton (since known as Wilton Royal Carpet Factory), and absorbed *Axminster Carpet Manufactory, complete with looms and activities, e.g. hand-knotted carpet production, not previously practised at Wilton. In 1840s, industry revived once more, and factory soon won reputation for making luxury carpets. Hand-knotted carpets continued in production, financed by successful trade in machine-made pieces.

Wincanton delftware. Tin-glazed earthenware

Wincanton delftware. Plate, c*1745. Powdered manganese ground with iron-red decoration in reserve panels. Diameter 9in.*

Windmill cup. Detachable windmill with two figures on ladder; bowl engraved with medallions containing ships and figure of Fortune; later inscription along rim of bowl. Dutch, 17th century. Height 11½in.

made at Wincanton, Somerset, c1737–c1748, by potters from Bristol. Early pieces include posset cups painted with figures in Chinese style. Designs include flower patterns of small circles with central dots. Splashed pinkish-manganese-purple often used as ground, surrounding white reserve panels. Pink-tinged body covered in bluish glaze with numerous pinholes.

Winchester measures. Measures for which standards are still kept at Winchester, Hampshire; term also used for pewter measures of those standard capacities.

*Windmill watch. Gilt metal case, bezel set with *pastes; enamel dial incorporating sweep seconds and windmill, driven by wheel inside watch. Verge escapement. By Barraud of London.*
*Window seat. Regency, c1805, in manner of Thomas Hope. Ebonized and gilded; seat banded in *key pattern. Length 5ft4in.*

windmill cup. Late 16th and 17th century Dutch silver *wager cup in shape of windmill; body acted as bowl. Sails set in motion by blowing down a tube and contents had to be drunk before they stopped. Sometimes cup made of glass and sails of silver.

windmill watch. Style fashionable c1800; painted landscape scene on dial contains windmill with sails automatically turning with action of watch movement.

window seat. Long bench-like seat placed at window-sill level and fitting into window alcove. Originally architectural feature, built into wall; developed into independent piece in 18th century (as windows became larger and extended to floor): long upholstered seat, sometimes with end pieces (often scrolled or rolled), and low back. Common in England, Europe, and America after c1750.

Windsor furniture. Most common piece, Windsor chair, is spindle or stick-back chair; various models based on English Gothic prototype made in Britain and America. Contemporary Windsor benches, stools, tables, high chairs, etc., have spindle-backs, stretchers, and legs. Source of name uncertain, possibly derives from Windsor, Berkshire: spindles on English Windsors made from beech-wood grown locally.

In Britain, Windsor chairs in general use by end of 17th century: made in many parts of rural England, Wales, and Scotland; centre of production by 19th century was High Wycombe, Buckinghamshire. Each part of chair made from most suitable wood (beech, elm, fruitwoods, oak); town models, made in London, sometimes in mahogany. Country Windsors made by primitive assembly-line production, with different worker making each part.

By second half of 18th century, common English models included *bow-back, *comb-back, combined bow-and-comb back, *fan-back, *loop-back, and *rod-back. By late 18th century some bow, fan, and comb back models had central splat pierced with urn motif or Prince of Wales plumes; after c1820, wheel-pierced splat used. Some English Windsors have cabriole legs; *cowhorn-and-spur stretcher also of English origin.

American Windsor chairs made mainly from c1725–1870; predominant styles include *arch-back, *arrow-back, bow-back, comb-back, fan-back, *fire house, loop-back, *low-back, and *rod-back. Writing Windsor indigenous to America.

American Windsors first made in Philadelphia; by late 18th century made in Connecticut, Massachusetts, and Rhode Island. Like English counterparts, each section of chair made from most suitable wood (ash, chestnut, hickory, maple, pine, oak, etc.), but American Windsor made entirely by one craftsman. American Windsor chairs characterized by splayed legs; on English Windsors, legs set nearer edge of seat and straighter. *Illustrations at* comb-back chair, fan-back chair, rocking chair.

wine bottle (in pottery). Globular English delftware bottle with handle, made at Lambeth; labelled in blue with name of wine, e.g. Sack, White, Claret, or Rhenish, above a date (1629–72). Sometimes other decoration including flourish, crown, or coat of arms, with touches of yellow. Perhaps contained sample of wine, or intended as gift at Christmas or New Year. *Illustration at* Lambeth delftware.

wine bottle (in silver). Late 16th century bottle resembling *pilgrim bottle; used as *sideboard plate. Large, weighed as much as 483oz. Often made in pairs.

wine cistern. Large oval or urn-shaped silver or silver-gilt vessel for cooling wine bottles; on feet or base; generally two handles. Filled with cold water or pieces of ice. Vary from 200oz to 8000oz. Used in Britain and Europe from late Middle Ages; surviving examples date from late 17th and 18th centuries; occasionally made in early 19th century. Larger cisterns sometimes accompanied by matching wine fountain. In 18th century may have been used to rinse glasses. Also made in copper, pewter, brass, and wood with lead or tin liners.

wine cooler, ice bucket, or **ice pail.** Two-handled gold, silver, silver-gilt, or Sheffield

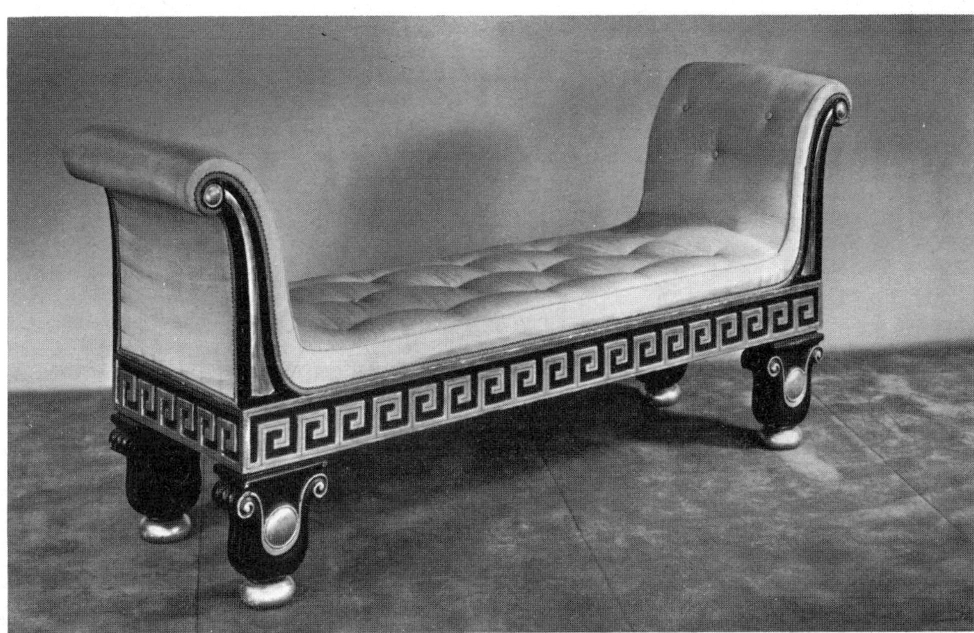

*Wine cooler. English one of pair made by Richard Cooke, 1809. Lower half is *gadrooned. Height 10¼in.*

*Wine funnels. English. Left: George III, silver, c1800. Right: electro-plate by *Elkington & Co, dated 1852.*

plate vessel on low foot or feet, used to cool single bottle of wine. Vase, urn, or tub shaped; usually with detachable liner; sometimes with stand. Used in Britain and Europe from end of 17th century until *c*1850 (though most popular at end of 18th when *wine cistern lost favour). Usually found in pairs. *See* Borghese urn, Warwick vase.

wine cup. *See* goblet.

wine flagon. *See* flagon.

wine fountain or **wine vase.** Large, covered silver, brass, or tin-lined copper vessel, of vase or urn shape with lid; spigot and tap at bottom of body; two or more handles; sometimes with ice chamber. Used from late 17th to mid 18th centuries in Britain and Europe to hold large quantities of wine. Sometimes found *en suite* with *wine cistern.

wine funnel. Cone-shaped silver funnel fitted with removable strainer for decanting wine; sometimes accompanied by domed saucer-like dish on which it rested inverted. Rim sometimes gadrooned or beaded. Made in silver from 17th century, though largest number made from mid 18th to mid 19th century.

wine glass cooler. Wide based bowl, sometimes with short knopped stem and foot, with one or two lips in brim for wine glass stem. Filled with cold water, then wine glass placed upside down in bowl for cooling. Popular 1750–1860. Made in gilded *Bristol blue glass in late 18th century, with matching plate and finger bowl. Simple cutting on earlier examples, more elaborate later. From *c*1820, also in ruby and green glass. Large wine glass cooler known as *Monteith.

wine glass stand. 17th century Dutch silver-gilt stand for wine glass resembling stem of standing cup with three or four scroll brackets at top to hold glass. Baluster and cast mythological figure stems both common.

Wine jar. Underglaze red and blue, decorated with four carved-out quatrefoil panels with applied moulding of flowering branches surrounded with beading. Yüan dynasty, c1350. Height 13½in.

*Wine labels. All for Madeira. Left: 1811, by M. *Linwood. Centre: silver-gilt, made in 1827 by Charles Rawlings. Right: 1818, by *Emes & Barnard.*

wine jar. Chinese ceramic shape. Earliest examples ritual vessels of Chou and Han periods (*see* tsun). Usual shape, round, curving pot with short neck and wide lip, 12–24in. high. Form influenced by Persian metalware. During Ming and Ch'ing periods, often found in fanciful shapes resembling fruit (e.g. peaches), animals, etc.

wine labels. Made from *c*1725 in England to identify contents of glass decanters. Earliest labels of silver; 18th century labels difficult to identify: did not have to be hallmarked until 1790. Earliest shapes were rectangular, escutcheon, and crescent. Prominent makers: H. *Bateman, *Phipps & Robinson. Labels hand-worked before *c*1800, then die-stamped. Process developed by M. *Linwood in Birmingham. Die-stamped labels lighter than hand-worked ones, ornamented with fauns, cupids, intricate foliage. From 1810, labels cast or made in mould; larger and heavily decorated with masks, foliage, and scenery in relief. After 1840, design and workmanship deteriorated. Production ceased in 1860 when law called for individual paper labels on bottles.

From *c*1750 enamel labels made in Battersea, Birmingham, and south Staffordshire. Battersea labels designed by S-F. *Ravenet; white enamel with transfer-prints of cupids, fauns, satyrs, and Negro boys in wine-making scenes. Wavy escutcheon shape, $2\frac{1}{2} \times 2\frac{1}{4}$in. South Staffordshire same shape, slightly smaller, with names of wines in English or French in black lettering, decorated with flower spray and bunch of grapes. Probably exported in large numbers. Labels also made in Sheffield plate; identification of makers difficult because hallmarking forbidden by law. A few also made in mother-of-pearl and porcelain.

wine measure. *See* measure.

wine taster. Small, plain or embossed silver or pewter vessel with shallow bowl used by vintners to test wine. One, two, or no handles, usually slightly domed bottom. Made in Britain and Europe from Middle Ages though earliest surviving examples from 17th century. Term now often used to describe any small metal bowl.

wine vase. *See* wine fountain.

wine wagon. 19th century English silver or Sheffield plate *coaster raised on wheels like wagon, usually holding two bottles.

wine waiter. 18th century trolley with top divided into sections to hold wine bottles and decanters.

wing chair. Armchair with side pieces or 'wings' extending upwards from arms to top of high back, set roughly at right-angles to back; intended to shield occupant from draughts. Dates from end of 17th century; popular in 18th century.

Wine taster. French silver, made in Rouen, c1735. Circular, with kidney-shaped thumb-piece engraved Je Luy Seray Fidele *above seated cherub holding dog on lead; domed base. Diameter 3½in.*

Wine wagon. English, Sheffield plate, c1810.

Wing chair. William and Mary, covered in contemporary needlework; overscroll cresting; overscrolled arms; squab cushion; cabriole legs; double pad feet.

winged glass. Wine glass with tooled decoration on stem representing wings, though often more like sea-horse or snake. Wings usually of blue glass, often with added clear trailing. Made by Venetians from mid 16th century. In 17th century, stem disappeared in elaborate wing pattern. Later, heavier examples made throughout Europe, particularly in Holland, Belgium, and Germany (known as Flügelglas). *Illustration at façon de Venise.*

wing-lantern clock. English *lantern clock, with wide-swinging pendulum between going and striking train. Case extended either side by two 'wings' with glass front through which movement of pendulum is visible. Upper edges decorated with fretwork, resembling that on top of case. Late 17th century.

wing wardrobe. *See* wardrobe.

Winslow, Edward (1669–1753). American silversmith working in Boston, Massachusetts. Range of domestic silver includes two-handled cups, sweetmeat boxes, salvers, tankards, etc. Mark: EW with fleur-de-lis below, in a shield.

Winter, Martin (d 1702). Bohemian glass engraver; worked in *Hochschnitt* and *Tiefschnitt*. Until 1680, patronized by Friedrich Wilhelm, Elector of Brandenburg; in 1687 established engraving workshop in Berlin, affiliated to *Potsdam Glass Works. G. *Spiller pupil.

Winterstein (fl *c*1750–85). German porcelain figure painter. Worked at Höchst factory, and Frankenthal (1758–81), where signed pieces include table service dated 1764, painted with subjects after D. *Teniers.

Winterthur (Switzerland). **Hafnerware* made in 16th century include tankards with decoration of applied relief, or splashes of manganese-purple against yellowish ground. In late 16th century, produced painted tile stoves, and rounded jugs with leaf scrolls; also dishes painted with heraldic motifs or figures in landscapes with borders of fruit or scrollwork. *Pfau family principal makers. Signed and dated examples often found.

wire-work (in silver). Rod of metal reduced to thin wire by using *draw-plate. Repeatedly annealed to retain malleability. Silver, gold, or Sheffield plate wires used to make baskets, toast racks, etc., or as ornament, e.g. *filigree.

Wistar, Caspar (1695–1752). German; in America from 1717. Established first American factory making buttons in Philadelphia. Learned glass blowing from German immigrants and founded *Wistarburg Glass Works (1739). Succeeded by son, Richard, who produced buttons guaranteed for seven years. *Illustration at* south Jersey glass.

Wistarburg Glass Works. Founded 1739 by C. *Wistar in Salem, New Jersey, employing German glass blowers. Produced window glass, bottles, and opaque and coloured glass hollow-ware. Initiated *South Jersey glass tradition. Sold in 1780 during Civil War.

witch ball. Hollow spheres of coloured or multi-coloured glass, often with hole in top for string. Earliest examples may have small neck. Made in England from 18th century. Said to have been hung in homes of glass blowers to ward off evil eye. Several 18th century examples exist, but most date from early 19th century, particularly silvered and unusually coloured balls made as novelties, also green balls used for floating fish nets. Made in America from early 19th century.

wit goet (Dutch, 'white earthenware'). White Delft ware without decoration, made in 17th and 18th centuries for domestic or ornamental use; includes bowls with fluted rims, pitchers, plates, snuff-boxes, and toy kitchenware. Pharmacy ware often with description of contents inscribed in cartouche. Figures, made from *c*1750, include cows, horses, and groups.

wodewose spoon. 15th century English silver spoon with knop in shape of wild man of the woods with club. Club either brandished or dropping from right hand at side.

Wohlfahrt, Freidrich Karl (fl mid 18th century). German porcelain painter from Ellwangen. Worked at Frankenthal (1766), Pfalz-Zweibrücken (1767–68), Ottweiler, where some work signed (1769–70), and Höchst (1771–73).

Wolff, David (1732–98). Dutch glass *stipple engraver. Signed work dates from 1784–95. Earliest examples show allegorical figures of naked or clothed children. Later, favoured commemorative and portrait subjects. Mainly worked on English flint-glass from Newcastle-upon-Tyne.

Wood, Aaron (1717–85). Potter in Burslem, Staffordshire, brother of R. *Wood I. In 1746, joined T. *Whieldon as modeller. Cutter of alabaster intaglio moulds for salt-glaze teapots in form of camels, houses, Admiral Vernon's flag-ship, etc. Many *pew-groups attributed to him.

Wood, Enoch (1759–1840). Son of A. *Wood; apprentice to H. *Palmer; partner of R. *Wood II. Master-potter in Burslem, Staffordshire from 1783. Partner in Wood & Caldwell until 1819, when founded Enoch Wood & Sons (closed 1846). Made enamel-painted figures, including

Enoch Wood. Earthenware night watchman jug, decorated with enamelled colours, c1810. Ralph Wood I. Group of shepherd and shepherdess, c1760. Impressed mould number 86. Height 9½in.

large-sized groups, busts of e.g. John Wesley, Voltaire, and small lions, in brown and ochre. Also produced basalt reliefs, domestic creamware, and some porcelain. Marks include: W(***) (mainly found on porcelain), E.WOOD, ENOCH WOOD, WOOD & CALDWELL (1790–1819), *c*1819–*c*1846 shield motif surrounded by words, ENOCH WOOD & SONS BURSLEM.

Wood, Ralph I (1716–72). Potter in Burslem, Staffordshire; brother of A. *Wood. Noted for figures of animals, *Toby jugs, and groups, e.g. The Vicar and Moses, thinly potted in greyish creamware, usually lightly splashed with brown, purple, and green, glazed only on outside and often standing on open bases resembling rocks. Some figures marked with four trees in relief. Made salt-glaze tableware; blocks for moulds dated 1749–70, initialled RW. *Illustration also at* Toby jug.

Wood, Ralph II (1748–97). Potter in Burslem, Staffordshire; continued to specialize in figures like those by father, R. *Wood I, on paler creamware body; base closed, sometimes marked Ra. Wood/Burslem. From *c*1780, added bright enamel colours. Also made domestic wares and low-relief wall plaques.

Wood, Samuel (fl mid 18th century). English silversmith working in London; apprenticed 1721; granted freedom 1730. Became Prime Warden of Goldsmiths' Company in 1763. Prolific maker of domestic silver. Mark registered in 1733, SW in oval shield; in 1739, SW in script.

Wood, William (*c*1760–1809). English miniaturist and watercolour painter. Exhibited at Royal Academy, 1788–1808. Painted miniatures from 1790.

Woodstock, Oxfordshire. Cottage industry producing small articles of chiselled and cut steel from 17th to early 19th century; ousted by M. *Boulton's Soho Manufactory, Birmingham, which did similar work.

woof. *See* weft.

Worcester. English porcelain manufacturing centre. In 1751, R. *Holdship leased Warmstry House, which became site of soapstone porcelain manufacture by Worcester Porcelain Company, founded 1751 by 15 partners including Holdship, his brother, and J. *Wall. Among employees was R. *Podmore, who had worked on preliminary experiments with Wall, and defected in 1756 to R. *Chaffers's factory in Liverpool. In 1752, firm bought business of B. *Lund's factory in Bristol, including moulds for use at Warmstry House. Continued as partnership until 1783, when bought by T. *Flight and managed by sons; then with M. *Barr and family traded as Flight & Barr (from 1793), Barr, Flight & Barr (from 1807), Flight, Barr & Barr (1813–40).

Paste and glaze with cobalt oxide added producing greyish appearance, greenish by transmitted light. Could be made thinner than contemporary English porcelains. Resistant to hot water. Glaze even, thin, and hard, free from crazing. Paste formula remained constant from 1755 until late 18th century. From 1755, Worcester characterized by line without glaze around inside of foot-ring, which rarely shows evidence of grinding-down after firing.

First wares almost identical with Lund products, from same moulds, sometimes with green leaf painted over raised Bristol mark. Other early wares also moulded in silver shapes; some thrown, often in forms from Chinese porcelain, including *scratch cross groups; also fluted or faceted shapes, e.g. teapots and hexagonal vases. Characteristic jugs with body of moulded overlapping cabbage leaves and mask spout (later copied at Caughley and Lowestoft), produced from late 1750s. Much blue and white painted ware, decorated with *chinoiseries* and flower painting.

Transfer printing introduced by R. *Hancock *c*1757; overglaze black perfected and used, notably, in portrait prints, e.g. of royalty, known as jet enamels; also scenes with figures, and hunting scenes (on punchbowls). Many overglaze prints coloured by hand with washes of enamel colour. Some printing in lilac or purple. Underglaze printing in blue by 1759. R. Holdship also involved in transfer printing until departure, *c*1759.

From *c*1755, Meissen influence evident in painting of *deutsche Blumen* and landscapes with figures. Silver shapes with much moulding of leaves continued (e.g. *blind Earl pattern from *c*1760), but simpler forms introduced, including bell-shaped mugs and globular teapots. *c*1760–65, monochrome black enamelling with fine brush known as pencilled decoration. By *c*1760, wares sent to J. *Giles in London for decoration. From 1765, artists from Chelsea brought Sèvres influence; some Sèvres patterns copied. Ground colours from Chelsea include claret and version of Mazarin blue; others introduced by 1769 include **bleu céleste* and *pea-green (later *apple-green). **Mosaïk* pattern probably suggested *scale blue ground (from 1763). Much honey-gilding of high quality. In late 1760s and early 1770s, painting includes exotic birds by Giles workshop and *Soqui (*c*1770–75); also mythological subjects by J. *O'Neale, probably working as outside painter; a few pieces painted by F. *Duvivier. Oriental wares include some close copies of *famille verte* and *famille rose.* Worcester Japans produced from *c*1760; adaptations of Kakiemon (e.g. **caille*, stock pattern until 19th century), Imari, and Arita wares; also *Queen Charlotte pattern and hexagonal vases elaborately decorated with free adaptations of Chinese and Kakiemon designs. *c*1770, elaborately moulded wares, including shell-shaped sweetmeat dishes, open-work baskets, and large vases with applied flowers, bear mark of *Tebo, also probably responsible for rare figures, produced 1769–71.

In 1772, partnership reconstituted, including Hancock until 1774; left to work for ex-pupil T. *Turner at Caughley. From *c*1770, painted blue-and-white ware gradually dropped in favour of underglaze blue printing, to compete with Caughley and cheap Chinese imports. From *c*1780, transfer-printed willow pattern in violet-blue introduced; porcelain body with greyish-brown tinge and straw or orange translucency. Earlier patterns continued, including painted blue *Chantilly sprig.

Rococo styles of 1770s replaced in Flight period by neo-classical styles, with whiter body, fluted shape, and sparse decoration with mercury gilding. During Flight & Barr period, bone ash introduced into paste. In 1810s and 1820s, lavish gilding and decoration in Empire style. Early 19th century painters include T. *Baxter.

Other factories in Worcester during 19th century were *Grainger, Lee & Co and R. *Chamberlain's firm, which amalgamated with Flight, Barr & Barr in 1840. Warmstry House used only for tile manufacture; sold in 1847. Cheaper wares produced 1840–51, including door furniture, buttons, even false teeth. In 1852, company became Kerr & Binns, then Worcester Royal Porcelain Company (1862 to present). Late wares include porcelain with *jewelled decoration; reproductions of Limoges enamels (from 1753); parian ware figures and busts; Raphaelesque ware, including nautilus vases, after 18th century Doccia porcelain from

Above left:
*Worcester porcelain in underglaze blue. Left to right: 1) Cream boat by B. *Lund of Bristol, c1750, unmarked; length 4¼in. 2) Cream jug with rococo handle; 1755; height 3½in; painter's mark. 3) Mustard spoon, 1765–70; length 3¾in. 4) Egg cup, with painter's mark; height 2½in.*

Above right:
*Worcester porcelain. Scale pattern in pink on borders of cup and saucer, c1770, decorated in London by J. *Giles.*

*Worcester porcelain. Tea-cup and saucer painted with hop-trellis pattern (derived from Sèvres), c1770; diameter of saucer 5in.; unmarked. *Scale-blue plate, c1768; crescent mark. Diameter 7¼in. Right: Worcester porcelain. Pair of vases. Flight, Barr & Barr, c1820. Painted with roses and stocks. Height 8¾in.*

15th and 16th century maiolica originals (from *c*1870); imitations of Japanese ivory and lacquer (from 1871); and earthenware copies of Henri II ware. 18th century Worcester imitated in 19th century, e.g. at Tournai.

No regular mark on early work; some with script W, or crescent in blue or red. Other marks include: spurious Japanese lettering on Japans (*c*1760–75); version of Meissen crossed swords; Flight (1783–93), with crown in blue or red from 1788; Flight & Barr with crown, in red (1793–1807), also with DB incised on paste containing bone ash; B.F.B. with crown, impressed (1807–13); F.B.B. with crown, impressed (1813–40); Chamberlain Worcester (*c*1840); flower-like shape in circle (1852–62); WORCESTER ROYAL PORCELAIN WORKS or ROYAL WORCESTER with date letters or numbers (from 1862). *Illustrations also at* bocage, knife and fork handles, transfer-printing.

work or **sewing table.** Small, light table designed to hold materials for needlework, knitting, etc. Many designs, usually with raised rim round top. Angle of top may be mechanically adjusted. May have drawers or storage areas beneath top. Alternative version, often known as pouch table, has bag or pouch, usually of pleated silk, hanging from underside of top; top can be raised to give access to storage pouch. Work tables date from 18th century; popular in 19th. *See* Martha Washington table, *tricoteuse.*

Worshipful Company of Goldsmiths. *See* Goldsmiths' Company.

Below:
Work table. Rosewood with two drop-leaves. English, c1830.

Worshipful Company of Pewterers, London. Recognized guild of pewterers existed before 1348, gained in size and scope and in 1473 became Worshipful Company of Pewterers with master and two wardens responsible for maintaining quality. Further officers appointed later. Members took livery after several years' apprenticeship and further work; then eligible for various offices. Forfeits imposed on those refusing office; heavy penalties on producers of sub-standard metal or poor workmanship.

wreathing. Faint spiral ridges on surface of porcelain which has shrunk unequally in kiln because wetted or worked unevenly when thrown; e.g. on early porcelain of Plymouth and Bristol in 1770s.

wriggle-work. Most common form of decoration on English pewter, from early 17th to mid 18th centuries; produced by pushing engraving tool over surface of object at angle of *c*45°, at the same time rocking or turning it from side to side. Variations obtained by using wider or narrower tool, changing angle, number of turns, etc. *Illustration at* marriage plate.

wrist watch. Devices for attaching small pocket watches to wrist-bands or bracelets known from early 17th century. Wrist watches of modern type not in use before early 20th century.

writing chair. *See* corner chair.

writing desk. From Middle Ages, portable or fixed writing box, with sloping lid; light enough to rest on knee. From 16th century, larger, heavier forms, often placed on stand or frame, or, especially in Germany, combined with cabinet containing drawers and compartments. Subsequently many different styles developed, *see* bureau, Carlton House desk, desk box, partner's desk, pedestal desk, roll-top desk, *secrétaire*, etc.

writing Windsor. American Windsor chair with writing surface attached to left or right arm. Often has drawer below writing area; another beneath seat. Dates from 18th century.

Writing desk. Maple wood. Slant top and with one drawer below; baluster-turned frame; wrought-iron hinges. American, c*1700–25*

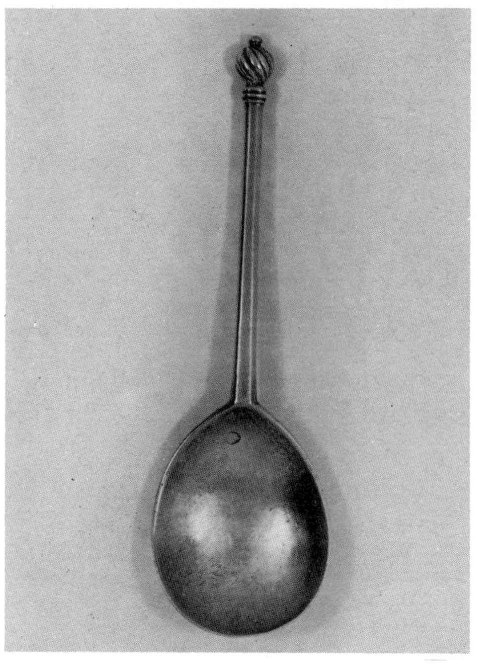

Wrotham slipware. Jug, dated 1693, decorated overall with applied figures and patterns.
Wrythen-knop spoon. Henry VIII period, probably 1526; maker's mark, fringed S. Length 5⅞in.

Below:
Wrought-iron. Parcel gilt side table of serpentine outline with moulded marble top; armorial cartouche in centre supported by two eagles. French, mid 18th century.

Wrotham, Kent. Source of earliest notable English slipware from *c*1612 to early 18th century. Characterized by stamped decoration of e.g. flowers, stars, rosettes, and devices possibly derived from German stoneware. Mugs and cups with ground often divided into panels with white slip 'stitching' reminiscent of sewn leather. Tygs and candlesticks have handles capped with white clay and incorporating twists of dark red and white clay, and small balls of red pressed into outer edges.

wrought iron. Iron worked into shapes; technique in general use in Europe from Iron Age for both functional and decorative purposes. Used as strengthening device for wooden doors, then for doors themselves, and gates, screens, grilles in churches. Became more decorative as spaces between strips filled with scrolls, rosettes, etc. Use finally extended through iron-bound chests to smaller items, e.g. brackets, candlesticks, lanterns, locks, other church fittings, and domestic articles, e.g. pot hooks, andirons. Craft developed in technique and artistry to become, by 17th century, necessary adjunct to interiors (staircases, etc.) and exteriors (gates, etc.) of fashionable town and country houses. (*See* J. Tijou.) From mid 18th century, craft declined throughout most of Europe, many articles previously wrought being produced by casting; only isolated revivals kept craft alive. For small domestic items, e.g. door-handles, knockers, method of producing cheap, malleable cast iron, invented in 1804, superseded use of wrought iron.

wrought plate. Gold or silver objects made from sheet or block worked with hammer; may be single piece, or several pieces soldered together.

wrythen or **writhen.** Twisted or coiled decoration, sometimes found on pewter ware, in which cast ribs spiral round object.

wrythen-knop spoon. 15th and 16th century English silver, pewter, or brass spoon with knop in shape of spirally-fluted sphere.

Wu-chou ware. Chinese porcellanous ware of T'ang period, identified solely from Tea Classic by Lu Yü. Green glazed, similar to *Yüeh ware;

*Wu ts'ai. Pen tray. Underglaze blue and overglaze red, green, yellow, and sepia. *Wan-li porcelain, Ming dynasty. Length 11½in.*

X-frame stool. French Régence. Giltwood with upholstered seat. Folding X-frames have carved leaves and flame motifs, intersections with sunflowers.

manufactured at Chin-hua Fu, Chekiang province.

Würth, Ignaz Joseph (fl 1775–1800). Austrian silversmith working in Vienna for court and nobility. Made domestic silver in French neoclassical style. Member of family of silversmiths active in Vienna for three generations. Mark: IIW. (Also working at this time was Johann Sebastian Würth; mark: IS above W).

Würzburg (Bavaria). German porcelain factory founded by J. C. *Geyger, flourished 1775–80. Tableware features landscapes, with gilt rococo scrolls, garlands, and sprays. Borders sometimes have moulded basket-work *Mosaïk* pattern painted crimson. Mark: CGW in triangular formation.

wu ts'ai (Chinese, 'five colour'). Porcelain decoration principally found in reign of Wan-li, though introduced under Chia Ching. Range of colours makes use of underglaze blue, and enamels in red, green, yellow, and black. Powerful designs, precisely executed.

Wycombe chair. Windsor or other simple wooden chair made in or near High Wycombe, Buckinghamshire, from *c*1800.

X frame or **curule frame.** Support (often folding) for chair, stool, or stand, based on X-shaped structure. Archaic origin (known in ancient Egypt, Greece, and Rome); used particularly in Middle Ages, and 18th and 19th centuries.

Yamout carpets. *See* Yomud carpets.

Yang Chêng (Shansi). Chinese kiln site supposedly manufacturing black-painted wares in Sung period. Known only from literary sources; no examples identified.

yang ts'ai. *See famille rose.*

Yao-chou (Shensi). Chinese kiln site active in Sung period. Products known only from literary references: in 13th century, ware compared with that of *Yüeh. 14th century source mentions inferior wares of *Jü type. Fragments of yellowish-glazed *grey ware unearthed at site.

Yardley, Samuel (fl 1776). Founder of enamelling industry in Wednesbury, south Staffordshire. Probably started by buying up stocks of Bickley factory in Bilston. Produced enamel toy watch with no movement popular with miners and ironworkers.

yard-of-ale. English drinking glass, *c*36in. long, with trumpet mouth and bulbous end. Made from 17th century, when also had foot. Few examples exist from before 1860. Popular, because of trick involved in drinking: liquid splashes on drinker's face, unless drunk slowly because of inrush of air into bulb when vessel tilted. Half-yards also made.

Yayoi period (200B.C.–A.D.200). Japanese period when people migrating from Korea introduced new ceramic techniques, e.g. throwing pottery on wheel. Yellow or light-brown earthenware produced includes pots, plates, and jars, with distinctive foot, much smaller in diameter than rim, giving top-heavy look. Incised decoration found, in form of broken, dotted lines, and zig-zags. Generally plain, simple ware, relying on form for effect.

yellow ground. German ceramic decoration, ground colour introduced at Meissen by J. G. *Herold *c*1726; ranged from clear straw to canary-yellow colour. Used in ornamental and table ware at intervals throughout 18th century, notably in late 1720s and 1730s. Imitated at Worcester.

yellow metal. *See* patent metal.

yellow tiger. German ceramic decoration. Kakiemon style pattern of tiger, bamboo, and plum tree against white ground, adopted by J. G. *Herold of Meissen for large table service commissioned (*c*1728), for display in Japanese Palace; marked with crossed swords in underglaze blue enamel. *cf* red dragon.

yen yen vase. Chinese shape found in Ming and Ch'ing periods; has baluster body with long trumpet-shaped neck. (Name means 'beautiful'.)

Yi (1392–1910). Korean period initially under overlordship of Chinese Ming dynasty; Confucianism dominant religion, leading to bureaucratic organization, and peaceful prosperity under Chinese protection in trade. Most arts influenced by China; landscape painting and floral or animal depiction resembled Sung style; by 18th century more characteristic Korean style emerged. In 16th century, with Japanese invasion, many artists deported to Japan to encourage arts, especially ceramics. Official industry brought to stop, but rustic, native arts continued to flourish, e.g. Ido bowls. Simple handicrafts best works of period; rough blue-and-white porcelain, more sparsely decorated than Chinese, was developed, also coarse form of lacquer-work, in red or black, inlaid with mother-of-pearl.

Yi-Hsing (Kiangsi). Chinese ceramics. Unglazed red or brown stoneware of Ming dynasty manufactured at T'ai Hu Lake, near Shanghai. Used chiefly to make teapots of deep or light red, brown, buff, or blackish-brown clays, sometimes mingled colours. Natural gloss from kiln heightened by rubbing in use. Often engraved with poetic inscriptions, stamped with key fret or diaper pattern, or with pierced designs. Some pieces ornamented with naturalistic details: fruits, nuts, snails; or formed into shapes such as pumpkin, lotus pod, tortoise, bundle of bamboos. Exported with tea, initially to Holland by Dutch East India Company; imitations made at Delft, e.g. by A. *de Milde and J. *de Caluwe, in hard red earthenware; other European copies made e.g. by J. F. *Böttger and D. and J. P. *Elers in red stoneware.

Ying-ch'ing ware. *See* Ching pai ware.

Yo-chou ware. Chinese celadon manufactured near Yo-yang, Hunan province, in late T'ang and early Sung periods. Decoration sometimes applied or painted; glazes sometimes mottled, often liable to flaking; body brittle. Identified from literary source, *Tea Classic,* by Lu Yü. Pieces rare.

yoke-rail, crest-rail, or **top-rail.** On chair back, the uppermost horizontal rail.

Yomud or **Yamout carpets.** Most gaily-coloured Turkoman carpets, with longish, coarsely-knotted pile, woven by Yomud tribe around eastern shores of Caspian Sea. Extensive adaptation of Caucasian designs and colours. Typical pattern has rows of large, diamond-shaped guls, often with latch-hook projections, worked in contrasting colours to form diagonal bands on red or purple-brown ground.

York flagon. *See* acorn flagon.

Young Moor's Head, The (Het Jonge Moriaenshoofft). Delft factory (1654–92) owned by J. W. *Hoppesteyn, 1664–71; succeeded by widow and (1680–92) son Rochus.

yu. Ancient, Chinese bronze ritual vessel for storing wine. Made during Shang period. Similar to bronze *kuei in form, i.e. bowl mounted on ring foot, but with expanding curved sides; has lid and loop handle.

yüan. Archaic Chinese jade shape similar to *pi and *huan but with very much larger hole concentric with outer edge. Also general name given to jade rings without ritualistic function.

Yüan dynasty (1260–1368). Chinese period under rule of Mongol conquerors. Mongols not interested in arts; little new creative work produced, apart from introduction of cobalt-blue decoration on porcelain. Much Lung-Ch'üan celadon; large dishes, wine jars, etc. for India and Middle East; wares more heavily potted or with more moulded and carved decoration. *Illustrations at* brush-rest, Ching pai, iron-brown spots, wine jar.

*Yüeh ware. *Celadon box with incised decoration. Sung dynasty. Diameter 5¾in.*

Zanesville Glass Manufacturing Company. Flask with swivelled ribbing, 19th century. Height 6¾in.

Yuch'on-ni. Kiln site of Koryo period at Puan, on west coast of Korea. Produced high quality celadon wares, with incised, carved, and *zogan designs. Some white porcelain also found at site (earliest known Korean manufacture). Decoration on both types includes flying cranes, lotus petals, peonies, chrysanthemums. Porcelains more thinly potted than celadons, like Chinese Ting pieces.

Yüeh ware. Earliest known type of Chinese pottery with brownish or greyish-green celadon glaze and grey porcellanous body. Manufactured in provinces of Chekiang and Fukien from late Han period. Early shapes imitate bronze metal objects; engraved or stamped decoration under glaze. Concave base characteristic. Important kiln sites at Chiu-yen and Tê-ch'ing. Some mortuary ware (*see* ming-ch'i), other items for domestic use. Later ware of T'ang and Five Dynasties periods prized for resemblance to jade; flowing shapes and smooth green glazes recorded as reserved for use by princes. T'ang Yüeh widely exported to India, Japan, Persian Gulf. Type known as *grey ware also produced.

Yü-huang-kuan. *See* Ku-i.

Yung Chêng (1723–35). Chinese Emperor of Ch'ing dynasty; developed more direct imperial control of factories at *Ching-tê-chên, under directorship of *Nien Hsi-yao, *Tang Ying employed from 1728. Actively encouraged archaistic copying of earlier wares, especially Sung celadons, and Ming blue-and-white porcelain. Styles and *nien hao of K'ang Hsi, and Chêng Hua most often copied; some Hsüan Tê pieces also simulated. Monochromes notable, particularly in K'ang Hsi styles. Nien hao often obliterated from pieces, either when stolen or in order to pass them off as earlier period wares. Influence of western art also increased (e.g. *Jesuit porcelain), as did export trade. **Famille rose* work notable for emergence of Chinese influence in designs, rather than use of European inspired motifs, e.g. birds, butterflies, flowers. Tints range from ruby red to pale pink, against white background. Some dishes with ruby monochrome on reverse made chiefly for export. *Illustrations at famille rose,* Ku Yüeh Hsüan.

Yung-ho Chên (Kiangsi). Chinese kiln site at Chi-Chou, Kiangsi province; active in Sung period. Produced ware resembling purple Ting-chou ware, though coarser. Mentioned in literary works as centre of production of large flower vases, small decorated vases, and crackled pieces with pigment rubbed into fissures, giving 'cracked ice' effect. Other references to 'painted blue decoration'. If correct, earliest attempt at this form, predominant in Yüan and later dynasties. At close of Sung period, potters fled from site (for unknown reasons) to *Ching-tê-chên.

Yung Lo (1403–24). Chinese Emperor of Ming dynasty. Founded capital, Peking, in 1421. Ardent Buddhist. Built porcelain pagoda, 1413–32. Ching-tê-chên ceramic factories well-organized by end of reign. Porcelain of period rarely marked; Imperial quality pieces unknown. Blue-and-white bowls with landscape scenes and sometimes poetic inscription typical. Unmarked blue-and-white with distinctive heavily constructed foot usually ascribed to reign. Copper-red underglaze work highly valued at time, according to literary sources.

Yü-yao (Chekiang). Chinese kiln site near capital of southern Sung court, Hangchou. Continued production in Yüan period. Produced Imperial palace ware, greyish-green celadon pieces, often mentioned in literary sources. Wares dated by discovery of celadon tablet, with epitaph from third year of Ch'ang-ch'ing (823), placing earliest pieces in T'ang dynasty. Covered boxes, bowls, dishes, thinly potted, with hard, porcellanous body and moss-green glaze unearthed at nearby kiln site of Huang yen. Sometimes confused with similar Kuan ware.

Zaandam clock. *See* Dutch clocks.

zaffer or **zaffre.** In 18th century English pottery, roasted mixture of cobalt ore and sand, used as blue underglaze colouring.

Zanesville Glass Manufacturing Company. Founded 1815 in Zanesville, Ohio, for production of white hollow-ware, and physicians' and apothecaries' ware. Window glass and green hollow-ware department added in 1816. Main output remained window glass, bottles, and hollow-ware. Noted for historical flasks. Closed 1851.

Zappler clock. Miniature clock, *c*2½in. high, made in Austria from *c*1800. Notable for rapid movement of pendulum or double pendulums, in front of dial. Made in many shapes; cases in embossed brass, mother-of-pearl, etc.

Zellenmosaïk (German, 'cell-mosaic'). Mosaic decoration of hardstones set in gold cells. Employed in boxes made in Dresden from 1760 e.g.

by C. G. *Stiehl, H. *Taddel and J. C. *Neuber.

Zerbst (Saxony-Anhalt). German faience factory founded 1720 with help of J. C. *Ripp (left 1724). Produced mainly blue-and-white wares, and high-temperature polychrome pieces with slightly flawed glaze. Marks: Z or Zerbst, but painters' marks predominate. Faience production ceased in 1806; glazed earthenware made until 1861.

Zeschinger, Johannes (fl mid 18th century). German painter, worked at Höchst faience factory from *c*1750. As painter, signed or initialled tureens modelled in form of animals. Went with father-in-law, J. *Benckgraff, to Fürstenberg factory in 1753; painted scroll-shaped porcelain scent-bottles with *commedia dell'arte* characters, fashionable gallants and ladies; names of perfume inscribed on bottles.

Zethelius, Pehr (d 1810). Swedish silversmith working in Stockholm; master in 1766. Produced domestic silver in neo-classical style.

Zick, Janarius Johann Rasso (1730–97). German painter of frescoes, portraits, and genre scenes. D. *Roentgen based designs for marquetry on Zick subjects.

zinc. Though known in East as pure metal, used in alloys in calamine form until method of extraction discovered in Europe in late 17th century. Pure zinc first used in brass in 1780; by 19th century, important ingredient of many alloys, and used in rust-proofing iron (galvanization). *See* spelter.

Zincke, Christian Friedrich (1684–1767). German-born enamel painter, son of goldsmith, pupil of C. *Boit. In England from 1706, produced many small, brilliantly coloured enamel portraits, until retirement in 1746.

Giacomo Zoffoli. Plaque of Perseus and Andromeda in relief, signed G.Z.F., c*1770,* $9\frac{1}{2}$×*7in.*

Zwischengoldglas. *18th century goblet. Decoration around funnel bowl shows the Five Senses. Height 7in.*

zither. Stringed musical instrument played by plucking; popular folk instrument in Austrian Tyrol and southern Germany, known from mid 17th century in Austria. Early examples have rectangular, shallow, wooden box resonator with number of metal strings strung over surface. Two modern types developed *c*1830. Shallow box-shape retained, but Salzburg type rounded on one side and Mittenwald type rounded on both sides. Large central soundhole. Front edge, which lies flat in front of player, has *c*29 frets over which are stretched four of five melody strings; remaining strings (27–40) used for accompaniment. Player's left hand stops melody strings and right hand holds ring-shaped plectrum for plucking.

Zoan Maria or **Giovanni Maria** (fl *c*1500–*c*1520). Italian maiolica painter at Castel Durante. Painted scenes with *putti*, centaurs, or groups of figures, on dishes, sometimes with borders of foliage, trophies, masks, or grotesques and scrollwork, in blue, green, and brownish-orange. Reverse decorated with concentric patterned bands, and rings in blue. Signed work Zovan Maria.

zocle. *See* socle.

Zoffoli, Giacomo (1731–85) and Giovanni (*c*1745–1805). Italian brothers, possibly trained as goldsmiths or silversmiths; made small bronze replicas of classical statues.

zogan or **inlaid ware.** Ceramic decoration; technique well developed by Korean potters in Koryo period. Design cut out of clay body with sharp implement before firing; incisions filled with contrasting clay or slip, usually white, or reddish-brown. Surface carefully cleaned or trimmed down evenly, then glazed, e.g. with celadon glaze or, on porcelain, with transparent glaze. Brown clay turned black under celadon glaze, while white areas became even more pure and lustrous. Sparkle sometimes found round edges of inlay, due to varying tensions of different clays during firing process; known as hoseki zogan or 'jewelled inlay'.

zotjes (Dutch, 'sillies'). Ceramic decoration: motif of dancing children derived from K'ang Hsi style, found on blue-and-white Delft from late 17th century.

Zucchi, Antonio Pietro (1726–95). Venetian painter; travelled with R. *Adam in Italy. Executed ornamental painting in Adam-style interiors in England *c*1776. Noted for mythological subjects. Married A. *Kauffmann.

Zumpe, Johann Cristoph (fl late 18th century). German piano-maker working in London; pupil of G. *Silbermann. Worked for B. *Shudi, then *c*1760, began manufacture of square pianos.

Zunftbecher (German, 'guild beaker'). Late 17th century glass beaker decorated in enamel with symbols associated with particular guild.

Zurich, Switzerland. Porcelain and faience factory established as democratic foundation in 1763. Soft-paste porcelain containing soaprock replaced *c*1765 by hard-paste with yellow tinge. From *c*1790 concentrated on output of faience and lead-glazed cream-coloured earthenware (sometimes with transfer-printing). Richly decorated tableware includes épergnes; snuff-boxes, toys, walking-stick handles, etc., also made. Some decoration in brown monochrome. Figures include townspeople in contemporary dress; series of Seasons, Continents, and Elements; also mythological subjects and *commedia dell'arte* characters, mainly from models of Ludwigsburg. Mark usually Z in blue or Greek letter zeta incised.

Zwiebelmuster (German, 'onion pattern'). Porcelain decoration painted in underglaze blue or purple; of Chinese origin; introduced at Meissen in 1739 for use on functional wares. Formalized flowers and fruits misnamed onions. Subsequently copied by several European factories. 18th century examples very rare.

Zwischengoldgläser (German, 'gold sandwich glasses'). Beakers, occasionally goblets, made by ancient technique revived in 18th century Bohemia. Gold (sometimes silver) leaf, etched with steel-point design, sandwiched between two layers of glass precisely fitting one over other. Earliest examples anonymous; first successful maker identified, Austrian J. J. *Mildner.

APPENDICES

CERAMIC MARKS

In a brief appendix, it is not possible to provide a usefully comprehensive selection of ceramic marks. The illustrations below are therefore limited to marks mentioned in the text but containing elements that cannot be conveyed adequately in a brief description. Many of the marks shown exist in various forms, of which only one example is given in each case. The marks are listed in the order of the entries to which they are linked. More extensive coverage of marks may be found in the various works devoted to them, including *Handbook of Pottery and Porcelain Marks* by J. B. Cushion and W. B. Honey (Faber and Faber), from which the illustrations below are reproduced.

Ansbach (from *c* 1765)

Antonibon, Giovanni Battista (Le Nove)

Augustus Rex mark (Meissen)

Berlin (1835–44)

Bow

Bristol porcelain

Brunswick

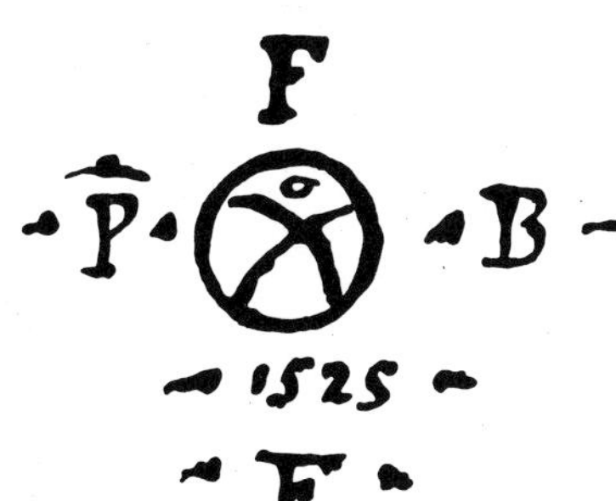

Casa Pirota (Faenza)

Caughley (from 1780)

Chantilly

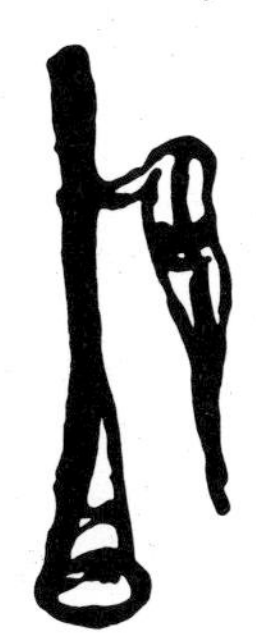

Chiodo family (Savona)

Coalport (1830–50)

Copenhagen

de Caluwe, Jacobus (Delft)

de Milde, Ary (Delft)

Frankenthal (*c* 1755–59)

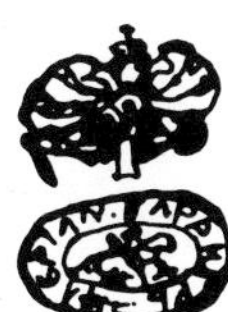

Francis Gardner Porcelain Factory

Furstenburg

Groszbreitenbach (from 1788)

Guidobono, Gian Antonio, ascribed to (Savona)

Herculaneum Pottery (Liverpool, 1833–36)

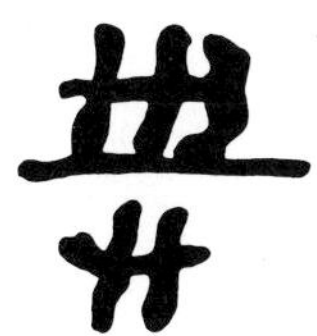

Herreboe (Norway)

Hochst (1747–51)

Holitsch

Hoppesteyn, Rochus (Delft)

Kiel

Kloster-Veilsdorf

Limbach (1772–88)

Limoges (from 1784)

Longton Hall

Ludwigsburg

Marieberg (1769–88)

Medici porcelain (Florence)

Meissen (caduceus mark)

Meissen (*c* 1724–25)

Munden

Niderviller (1770–93)

Nymphenburg (1754–65)

Nymphenburg (hexagram mark)

Nyon

Paris (Faubourg Saint-Denis, 1771–76)

Paris (Rue de Bondy, from 1781)

Pinxton

Plymouth

Rockingham

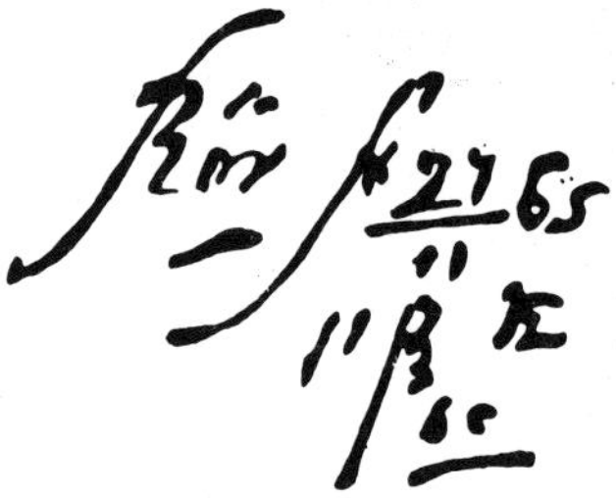

Rorstrand

Saint-Amand-les-Eaux

Saint-Cloud

Schrezheim

Sevres (with date letter for 1753)

Sevres (1851)

Spode (1815–27)

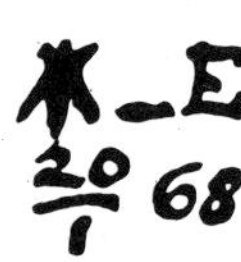

Stralsund

The Hague

Tournai (1756–81)

Vienna (on Chinese style, *c* 1720–30)

Vienna (1744–49)

Vinovo

Volkstedt

Wallendorf (before 1778)

Wood, Enoch (Burslem)

Wood, Ralph I (Burslem)

Worcester (1755–90)

Worcester (1852–62)

Zurich

SILVER DATE LETTERS

London

1678 a
1679 b
1680 c
1681 d
1682 e
1683 f
1684 g
1685 h
1686 i
1687 k
1688 l
1689 m
1690 n
1691 o
1692 p
1693 q
1694 r
1695 s
1696 t
1697 a b
1698 c
1699 d
1700 e
1701 f
1702 g
1703 h
1704 i
1705 k
1706 l
1707 m
1708 n
1709 o
1710 p
1711 q
1712 r
1713 s
1714 t
1715 v
1716 A
1717 B
1718 C
1719 D
1720 E
1721 F
1722 G
1723 H
1724 I
1725 K
1726 L
1727 M
1728 N
1729 O
1730 P
1731 Q
1732 R
1733 S
1734 T
1735 V
1736 a
1737 b
1738 c
1739 d
1739 d
1740 e
1741 f
1742 g
1743 h
1744 i
1745 k
1746 l
1747 m
1748 n
1749 o
1750 p
1751 q
1752 r
1753 s
1754 t
1755 u
1756 A
1757 B
1758 C
1759 D
1760 E
1761 F
1762 G
1763 H
1764 I
1765 K
1766 L
1767 M
1768 N
1769 O
1770 P
1771 Q
1772 R
1773 S
1774 T
1775 U
1776 a
1777 b
1778 c
1779 d
1780 e
1781 f
1782 g
1783 h
1784 i
1785 k
1786 l
1787 m
1788 n
1789 o
1790 p
1791 q
1792 r
1793 s
1794 t
1795 u
1796 A
1797 B
1798 C
1799 D
1800 E
1801 F
1802 G
1803 H
1804 I
1805 K
1806 L
1807 M
1808 N
1809 O
1810 P
1811 Q
1812 R
1813 S
1814 T
1815 U
1816 a
1817 b
1818 c
1819 d
1820 e
1821 f
1822 g
1823 h
1824 i
1825 k
1826 l
1827 m
1828 n
1829 o
1830 p
1831 q
1832 r
1833 s
1834 t
1835 u
1836 A
1837 B
1838 C
1839 D
1840 E
1841 F
1842 G
1843 H
1844 I
1845 K
1846 L
1847 M
1848 N
1849 O
1850 P
1851 Q
1852 R
1853 S
1854 T
1855 U
1856 a
1857 b
1858 c
1859 d
1860 e
1861 f
1862 g
1863 h
1864 i
1865 k
1866 l
1867 m
1868 n
1869 o
1870 p
1871 q
1872 r
1873 s
1874 t
1875 u
1876 A
1877 B
1878 C
1879 D
1880 E
1881 F
1882 G
1883 H
1884 I
1885 K
1886 L
1887 M
1888 N
1889 O
1890 P
1891 Q
1892 R
1893 S
1894 T
1895 U
1896 a
1897 b
1898 c
1899 d
1900 e

Birmingham

Year	Letter
1773	A
1774	B
1775	C
1776	D
1777	E
1778	F
1779	G
1780	H
1781	I
1782	K
1783	L
1784	M
1785	N
1786	O
1787	P
1788	Q
1789	R
1790	S
1791	T
1792	U
1793	V
1794	W
1795	X
1796	Y
1797	Z
1798	a
1799	b
1800	c
1801	d
1802	e
1803	f
1804	h
1805	g
1806	i
1807	j
1808	k
1809	l
1810	m
1811	n
1812	o
1813	p
1814	q
1815	r
1816	s
1817	t
1818	u
1819	v
1820	w
1821	x
1822	y
1823	z
1824	A
1825	B
1826	C
1827	D
1828	E
1829	F
1830	G
1831	H
1832	J
1833	K
1834	L
1835	M
1836	N
1837	O
1838	P
1839	Q
1840	R
1841	S
1842	T
1843	U
1844	V
1845	W
1846	X
1847	Y
1848	Z
1849	A
1850	B
1851	C
1852	D
1853	E
1854	F
1855	G
1856	H
1857	I
1858	J
1859	K
1860	L
1861	M
1862	N
1863	O
1864	P
1865	Q
1866	R
1867	S
1868	T
1869	U
1870	V
1871	W
1872	X
1873	Y
1874	Z
1875	a
1876	b
1877	c
1878	d
1879	e
1880	f
1881	g
1882	h
1883	i
1884	k
1885	l
1886	m
1887	n
1888	o
1889	p
1890	q
1891	r
1892	s
1893	t
1894	u
1895	v
1896	w
1897	x
1898	y
1899	z
1900	a

Sheffield

Year	Letter
1773	E
1774	F
1775	N
1776	R
1777	H
1778	S
1779	A
1780	T
1781	D
1782	G
1783	B
1784	I
1785	Y
1786	k
1787	T
1788	E
1789	A
1790	L
1791	P
1792	U
1793	N
1794	m
1795	q
1796	Z
1797	X
1798	V
1799	E
1800	N
1801	H
1802	M
1803	F
1804	G
1805	B
1806	A
1807	S
1808	P
1809	K
1810	L
1811	C
1812	D
1813	R
1814	W
1815	O
1816	T
1817	X
1818	I
1819	V
1820	Q
1821	Y
1822	Z
1823	U
1824	a
1825	b
1826	c
1827	d
1828	e
1829	f
1830	g
1831	h
1832	k
1833	l
1834	m
1835	p
1836	q
1837	r
1838	s
1839	t
1840	u
1841	v
1842	X
1843	Z
1844	A
1845	B
1846	C
1847	D
1848	E
1849	F
1850	G
1851	H
1852	I
1853	K
1854	L
1855	M
1856	N
1857	O
1858	P
1859	R
1860	S
1861	T
1862	U
1863	V
1864	W
1865	X
1866	Y
1867	Z
1868	A
1869	B
1870	C
1871	D
1872	E
1873	F
1874	G
1875	H
1876	J
1877	K
1878	L
1879	M
1880	N
1881	O
1882	P
1883	Q
1884	R
1885	S
1886	T
1887	U
1888	V
1889	W
1890	X
1891	Y
1892	Z
1893	a
1894	b
1895	c
1896	d
1897	e
1898	f
1899	g
1900	h

Edinburgh

Year	Letter
1705	A
1706	B
1707	C
1708	D
1709	E
1710	F
1711	G
1712	H
1713	I
1714	K
1715	L
1716	M
1717	N
1718	O
1719	P
1720	Q
1721	R
1722	S
1723	T
1724	U
1725	V
1726	W
1727	X
1728	Y
1729	Z
1730	A
1731	B
1732	C
1733	D
1734	E
1735	F
1736	G
1737	H
1738	I
1739	K
1740	L
1741	M
1742	N
1743	O
1744	P
1745	Q
1746	R
1747	S
1748	T
1749	U
1750	V
1751	W
1752	X
1753	Y
1754	Z
1755	A
1756	B
1757	C
1758	D
1759	E
1760	F
1761	G
1762	H
1763	I
1764	[illegible]
1765	[illegible]
1766	[illegible]
1767	K
1768	L
1769	M
1770	N
1771	O
1772	P
1773	Q
1774	R
1775	S
1776	T
1777	Y
1778	Z
1779	U
1780	A
1781	B
1782	C
1783	D
1784	E
1785	F
1786	G
1787	G
1788	H
1789	I J
1790	K
1791	L
1792	M
1793	N
1794	O
1795	P
1796	Q
1797	R
1798	S
1799	T
1800	U
1801	V
1802	W
1803	X
1804	Y
1805	Z
1806	a
1807	b
1808	c
1809	d
1810	e
1811	f
1812	g
1813	h
1814	i
1815	j
1816	k
1817	l
1818	m
1819	n
1820	o
1821	p
1822	q
1823	r
1824	s
1825	t
1826	u
1827	v
1828	w
1829	x
1830	y
1831	z
1832	A
1833	B
1834	C
1835	D
1836	E
1837	F
1838	G
1839	H
1840	I
1841	K
1842	L
1843	M
1844	N
1845	O
1846	P
1847	Q
1848	R
1849	S
1850	T
1851	U
1852	V
1853	W
1854	X
1855	Y
1856	Z
1857	A
1858	B
1859	C
1860	D
1861	E
1862	F
1863	G
1864	H
1865	I
1866	K
1867	L
1868	M
1869	N
1870	O
1871	P
1872	Q
1873	R
1874	S
1875	T
1876	U
1877	V
1878	W
1879	X
1880	Y
1881	Z
1882	a
1883	b
1884	c
1885	d
1886	e
1887	f
1888	g
1889	h
1890	i
1891	k
1892	l
1893	m
1894	n
1895	o
1896	p
1897	q
1898	r
1899	s
1900	t

BIBLIOGRAPHY

Adam, Robert
The Furniture of Robert Adam, Eileen Harris (Alec Tiranti, London, 1963)

Adam style
Adam Silver, Robert Rowe (Faber & Faber, London, 1965)

Adams family
A History of the Adams family, P. W. L. Adams (London, 1914)
William Adams, an Old English Potter, W. Turner (Chapman & Hall, London, 1904)

albarello
The Albarello: a Study in Early Renaissance Maiolica, H. Wallis (London, 1904)

amatory jewellery
Victorian Sentimental Jewellery, Diana Cooper and Norman Battershill (David & Charles, Newton Abbot, Devon, 1972)

American ceramics
American Potters and Pottery, John Ramsay (Hale, Cushman & Flint, Boston, 1939)
Book of Pottery and Porcelain, Warren Cox (Crown Publishers, New York, 1944)
Early American Folk Pottery, Harold F. Guilland (Chilton Book Company, Philadelphia, 1971)
Early American Pottery and China, John Spargo (Century, New York, 1926)
Early New England Potters and Their Wares, Lura Woodside Watkins (Harvard University Press, Cambridge, Massachusetts, 1950)
Our Pioneer Potters, A. W. Clement (published by the author, New York, 1947)

American clocks
Antique American Clocks and Watches, Richard Thomson (Van Nostrand Reinhold, New York, 1968)
A Book of American Clocks, Brook Palmer (Collier-Macmillan, New York, 1950)
A Treasury of American Clocks, Brook Palmer (Collier-Macmillan, New York, 1967)
The Contributions of Joseph Ives to Connecticut Clock Technology, Kenneth D. Roberts (American Clock and Watch Museum, Bristol, Connecticut, 1970)

American Federal style
American Furniture: The Federal Period (1788–1825), Charles F. Montgomery (Viking Press, New York, 1966)

American furniture
American Furniture, 1650–1850, Charles Nagel (New York, 1949)
American Furniture: Queen Anne and Chippendale Periods, Joseph Downs (Macmillan, New York, 1952; revised edition, Viking Press, New York, 1967)
The American Heritage History of Antiques, Marshall B. Davidson (American Heritage Publishing Co, New York, 1969)
Country Furniture of Early America, Henry Lionel Williams (A. S. Barnes & Co, New York, 1963 and Thomas Yoseloff, London, 1963)
A Dictionary of American Antiques, Carl W. Drepperd (Charles T. Branford Company, Boston, 1952)
English and American Furniture, Herbert Cescinsky and George Leland Hunter (Garden City Publishing Co, New York, 1929)
Furniture Treasury, Wallace Nutting (Macmillan, New York, limited edition 1928, reprinted 1968)

American glass
American Historical Glass, Bessie M. Lindsey (Tuttle, Rutland, Vermont – Prentice-Hall, London, new edition 1967)

American silver
American Church Silver of the 17th and 18th Centuries (Museum of Fine Arts, Boston, Massachusetts, 1911)
American Silver: A History of Style, 1650–1900, Graham Hood (Praeger Publishers, New York, 1971)
American Silver, John Marshall Phillips (Chanticleer Press, New York, 1949)
American Silversmiths and their Marks, Stephen G. C. Ensko (privately printed, New York, 3 volumes, 1927–48)
The Collector's Dictionary of the Silver and Gold of Great Britain and North America, Michael Clayton (Country Life, London, 1971)
A Directory of American Silver, Pewter and Silver Plate, Ralph M. and Terry H. Kovel (Crown Publishers, New York, 1961)
Historic Silver of the Colonies and its Makers, Francis Hill Bigelow (Macmillan, New York, 1917)
The Old Silver of American Churches, E. A. Jones (privately printed by Arden Press, Letchworth, Hertfordshire, 1913)
The Practical Book of American Silver, Edward Wenham (J. B. Lippincott Co, Philadelphia, Pennsylvannia, 1949)

American watches
Almost Everything you Wanted to Know About American Watches and Didn't Know Who to Ask, George E. Townsend (Published by the author, Vienna, Virginia, 1970)

apostle spoon
Apostle Spoons, C. G. Rupert (Oxford University Press, London, 1929)

Ardebil shrine
Chinese Porcelains from the Ardebil Shrine, J. A. Pope (Kegan Paul, London, 1956)

Arnold, John
John Arnold & Son, V. Mercer (Antiquarian Horological Society, London, 1972)

assay
Ancient Trial Plates, J. H. Watson (H.M. Stationery Office, London, 1962)
English Goldsmiths and Their Marks, Sir Charles Jackson (Macmillan, 2nd edition 1921, reprinted by Constable, London, 1965)

astrolabe
The Astrolabes of the World (2 Vols.), Robert T. Gunther (Oxford University Press, Oxford, 1932)
The Principles and Use of the Astrolabe, W. Hartner, contained in Vol. III of *A Survey of Persian Art from Prehistoric Times to the Present,* edited by A. U. Pope (Oxford University Press, Oxford, 1939)

barometer
English Barometers, 1680–1860, N. Goodison (Cassell & Co, London, 1969)
The History of the Barometer, W. E. Knowles Middleton (Johns Hopkins, Baltimore, 1964)

base metals
Iron and Brass Implements of the English House, J. Seymour Lindsay (Medici Society, London and Boston, 1927)
Metalwork, Hanns-Ulrich Haedeke, translated by V. Menkes (Weidenfeld & Nicolson, London, 1970)

Bateman, Hester
Hester Bateman, David S. Shure (W. H. Allen, London, 1959)

Battersea
Battersea Enamels, E. Mew (Medici Society, London, 1926)

Bennington
ABC of Bennington Pottery Wares, John Spargo (Bennington Historical Museum, Bennington, 1948)
Bennington Pottery and Porcelain, R. C. Barrett (New York, 1958)
Color Guide to Bennington Pottery, Richard Carter Barret (Crown Publishers, New York, 1966)
Potters and Potteries of Bennington, John Spargo (Houghton Mifflin and Antiques, Boston, 1926)

Berlin iron jewellery
Cut-Steel and Berlin Iron Jewellery, Anne Clifford (Adams & Dart, Bath, 1971)

black basalt
The Makers of Black Basaltes, Maurice H. Grant (1910, reprinted by Holland Press, London, 1967)

blanc de chine
Blanc de Chine: The Porcelain of Têhua in Fukien, P. J. Donnelly (Faber & Faber, London, 1969)

blue-and-white transfer-printed ware
Blue and White Transfer Ware 1780–1840, A. W. Coysh (David & Charles, Newton Abbot, Devon, 1970)
Staffordshire Blue, W. L. Little (B. T. Batsford, London, 1969)
The Blue-China Book, A. W. Camehl (Dutton, New York, 1916)
Pictures of Early New York on Dark Blue Staffordshire Pottery, R. T. Haines Halsey (Dodd, Mead, New York, 1924)

bottle
English Bottles and Decanters, 1650–1900, Derek C. Davis (Charles Letts & Co, London, 1972)

Boulton, Matthew
The Great Silver Manufactory: Matthew Boulton and the Birmingham Silversmiths 1760–90, Eric Delieb and Michael Roberts (Studio Vista, London, 1971)
Matthew Boulton, H. W. Dickinson (Cambridge University Press, 1937)

Breguet, Abraham-Louis
A-L. Breguet, Horloger, C. Breguet, translated by W. A. H. Brown (E. L. Lee, Enfield, Middlesex, 1963)
Breguet, Sir David Salomons (J. & H. Bumpus, London, 1921)

buttons
Buttons, Diana Epstein (Walker & Co, New York, 1968)
The Collectors' Encyclopedia of Buttons, Sally C. Luscomb (Crown Publishers, New York, 1967)

buttons—*continued*
The Complete Button Book, Lilian Smith Albert and Cathryn Kent (World's Work, London, 1952)

cameo glass
Nineteenth Century Cameo Glass, Geoffrey W. Beard (Ceramic Book Co, Newport, Monmouthshire, 1956)

Capodimonte
Capodimonte and Buen Retiro Porcelains, Period of Charles III, Alice W. Frothingham (Hispanic Society of America, New York, 1955)

carpets and rugs
Antique Rugs from the Near East, Wilhelm von Bode and Ernst Kühnel, translated by C. G. Ellis (G. Bell & Sons, London, 4th revised edition 1970)
The Book of Carpets, Reinhard G. Hubel, translated by K. Watson (Barrie & Jenkins, London, 1971)
Carpets from the Orient, Jesaya Meyer Con, translated by M. Clarke (Merlin Press, London, 1966)
Carpets of the Orient, Ludmila Kybalová, translated by T. Gottheiner (Paul Hamlyn, London, 1969)
Central Asian Rugs, Ulrich Schürmann, translated by A. Grainge (Verlag Osterrieth, Frankfurt-am-Main, 1969 - George Allen & Unwin, London, 1970)
European and Oriental Rugs and Carpets, Ignaz Schlosser (B. T. Batsford, London, 1963)
A History of British Carpets, C. E. C. Tattersall and Stanley Reed (F. Lewis, Leigh-on-Sea, Essex, revised edition 1966)
Islamic Rugs, Kudret H. Turkhan (Arthur Barker, London, 1968)
Oriental Carpets, Michele Campana (translated by A. Hartcup (Paul Hamlyn, London, 1969)
Oriental Carpets: an Account of Their History, Kurt Erdmann, translated by C. G. Ellis (A. Zwemmer, London, 1961)
Oriental Carpets and Rugs, Albrecht Hopf, translated by D. Woodward (Thames & Hudson, London, 1962)
Oriental Rugs: a Complete Guide, Charles W. Jacobsen (Tuttle, Rutland, Vermont and Prentice-Hall, London, 1962)
Oriental Rugs: an Illustrated Guide, Hermann Haack, translated by G. and C. Wingfield Digby (Faber & Faber, London, 1960)
Oriental Rugs in Colour, Preben Liebetrau, translated by K. John (Macmillan Company, New York and Collier-Macmillan, London, 1963)
Oriental Rugs and Carpets, Arthur U. Dilley (Charles Scribner's Sons, New York, 1931)
Oriental Rugs and Carpets, Fabio Formenton, translated by P. L. Phillips (Hamlyn Publishing Group, London, 1972)
Rugs and Carpets of the Orient, Knut Larson (Frederick Warne & Co, London, 1966)
Seven Hundred Years of Oriental Carpets, Kurt Erdmann, translated by M. H. Beattie and H. Herzog (Faber & Faber, London, 1970)
The Techniques of Rug Weaving, Peter Collingwood Faber & Faber, London, 1968)

cartoon
The Raphael Cartoons, Victoria & Albert Museum (H.M. Stationery Office, London, 1950)

Caucasian carpets
Caucasian Rugs, Ulrich Schurmann, translated by A. Grainge (Klinkhardt & Biermann, Braunschweig - George Allen & Unwin, London, 1967)

Caughley (Shropshire)
Caughley and Worcester Porcelains 1775–1800, Geoffrey A. Godden (Barrie & Jenkins, London, 1969)

celadon
Celadon Wares, G. St-G. M. Gompertz (Faber & Faber, London, 1969)

ceramics
The Book of Pottery and Porcelain, Warren E. Cox (Crown Publishers, New York, 1946)
Concise Encyclopaedia of Continental Pottery and Porcelain, R. G. Hagger (André Deutsch, London, 1960)
Dictionary of Ceramics, A. E. Dodd (George Newnes, London, revised edition 1947)
The Dictionary of World Pottery and Porcelain, Louise Ade Boger (A. & C. Black, London, 1971)
European Ceramic Art, Vol. 1: *Introduction and* Illustrations; Vol. 2: *Dictionary of factories, artists, terms and general information,* W. B. Honey (Faber & Faber, London, 1949–52)
From Gold to Porcelain: Art of Porcelain and Faience, Ruth Berges (Thomas Yoseloff, New York, 1963
Porcelain and Pottery, Frank Giffin (Frederick Muller, London, 1967)
Porcelain and Stoneware, Daniel Rhodes (Pitman, London, 1960)
Pottery and Ceramics, E. Rosenthal (Penguin Books, Harmondsworth, 1949)
Pottery and Porcelain, A. Butterworth (Collins, London, 1964)
Pottery and Porcelain, J. P. Cushion (Ebury Press, London, 1972)
Pottery and Porcelain, a Handbook for Collectors, Emil Hannover, edited by Bernard Rackham (Ernest Benn, London, 1923)
Pottery and Porcelain, a Guide to Collectors, Frederick Litchfield, revised by Frank Tilley (A. & C. Black, London, 1953)
Pottery and Porcelain 1700–1914, England, Europe and North America (Weidenfeld & Nicolson, London, 1968)
A Reader's Guide; Pottery and Porcelain, W. B. Honey (National Book League, London, 1950)
World Ceramics, edited by R. J. Charleston (Hamlyn, Feltham, 1968)

chair
The Englishman's Chair, John Gloag (George Allen & Unwin, London, 1964)

chamber clock
The Almanus Manuscript, John H. Leopold (Hutchinson, London, 1971)
Weight-driven Chamber Clocks of the Middle Ages and Renaissance, E. L. Edwardes (Sheratt & Sons, Altrincham, Cheshire, 1965)

Champion, Richard
Champion's Bristol Porcelain, F. Severne Mackenna (F. Lewis, Leigh-on-Sea, Essex, 1947)

Chelsea
Chelsea and other English Porcelain, Pottery and Enamel in Irwin Untermyer Collection, Yvonne Hackenbroch (Thames & Hudson, London, 1957)
Chelsea, Bow and Derby Porcelain Figures, Frank Stoner (Ceramic Book Company, Newport, Monmouthshire, 1955)
Chelsea Porcelain: The Gold Anchor Wares, F. Severne Mackenna (F. Lewis, Leigh-on-Sea, Essex, 1952)
Chelsea Porcelain: The Red Anchor Wares, F. Severne Mackenna (F. Lewis, Leigh-on-Sea 1951)
Chelsea Porcelain: The Triangle and Raised Anchor Wares, F. Severne Mackenna (F. Lewis, Leigh-on-Sea, 1948)

Chelsea-Derby
Chelsea and Derby China, John Bedford (Cassell & Co, London, 1967)

Chinese carpets
Antique Chinese Rugs, Tiffany Studios (Tuttle, Rutland, Vermont and Prentice-Hall, London, 1969)

Chinese celadon
Chinese Celadon Wares, G. St-G. M. Gompertz (Faber & Faber, London, 1958)

Chinese clocks
Heavenly Clockwork, J. Needham, Wang Ling and D. J. Price (Cambridge University Press, Cambridge, 1960)

Chinese export porcelain
China-Trade Porcelain, J. G. Phillips (Metropolitan Museum, New York, 1956)
The Book of Porcelain, Walter Staehelin, translated by M. Bullock (Lund Humphries, London, 1966)
Chinese Export Art in the Eighteenth Century, M. Jourdain and Soame Jenyns (Country Life, London, 1950)
Porcelain of the East India Companies, M. Beurdeley (Barrie & Rockliff, London, 1962)

Chinese pottery and porcelain
Ceramic Art of China and other Countries of the Far East, W. B. Honey (Faber & Faber, London, 1945)
Chinese Blue and White, Ann Frank (Studio Vista, London, 1970)
Chinese Ceramics Vol. 1: T'ang and Sung Periods, with Korean and Thai Wares, John Ayers (Collections Baur, Geneva, 1968)
Chinese Ceramics, Bronzes and Jades in the Collection of Sir Alan and Lady Barlow, Michael Sullivan (Faber & Faber, London, 1963)
Chinese Porcelain, Anthony de Boulay (Weidenfeld & Nicolson, London, 1967)
Chinese Pottery and Porcelain, R. L. Hobson, Cassell & Co, London, 1950)
Later Chinese Porcelain, Soame Jenyns (Faber & Faber, London, 1965)
Oriental Blue and White, Sir Harry Garner (Faber & Faber, London, 1964)

chinoiseries
Chinoiserie, Hugh Honour (John Murray, London, 1961)

Chippendale style
Chippendale, Edward T. Joy (Hamlyn Publishing Group, Feltham, Middlesex, 1971)
Chippendale Furniture, Anthony Coleridge (Faber & Faber, London, 1968)

chronometer
The Marine Chronometer, R. T. Gould (Potter, London, 1923, reissued by Holland Press, London, 1960)
see also Arnold, John

Clockmakers' Company of London
Catalogue of the Library of the Clockmakers' Company, G. H. Baillie (A. R. Mowbray & Co, London and Oxford, 3rd edition 1951)
Catalogue of the Museum of the Clockmakers' Company, G. H. Baillie (A. R. Mowbray & Co., London and Oxford, 3rd edition 1949)
Some Account of the Worshipful Company of Clockmakers of the City of London, S. E. Atkins and W. H. Overall (London, 1881)

clocks
Clocks and Watches, Eric Bruton (Paul Hamlyn, London, 1968)
Clocks and Watches, 1400–1900, Eric Bruton (Arthur Barker, London, 1967)
Clocks in the British Museum, H. Tait (British Museum, London, 1968)
Clocks, Watches and Chronometers, reprint of sections from Rees' *Cyclopaedia* (1819–20), Abraham Rees (David & Charles, Newton Abbot, Devon, 1970)
Clocks and Watches, an Historical Bibliography, G. H. Baillie, (N. A. G. Press, London, 1951)
The Collector's Dictionary of Clocks, H. Alan Lloyd (Country Life, London, 1969)
European Clocks, E. J. Tyler (Ward Lock & Co, London, 1968)
The Evolution of Clockwork, J. Drummond Robertson (Cassell & Co, London 1931, reprinted by S. R. Publishers, 1972)
In Quest of Clocks, Kenneth Ullyett (Spring Books, London, 1969)
Investing in Clocks and Watches, P. W. Cumhaill, (Barrie & Rockliff, London, 1967)
Old Clocks, H. Alan Lloyd (Ernest Benn, 1970)
Old Clocks and Watches and their Makers, F. J. Britten (first published 1899, revised edition by G. H. Baillie and others, Eyre & Spottiswoode, 1969)
The Orpheus Clocks, P. G. Coole & E. Neumann (Hutchinson, London, 1972)
The Science of Clocks and Watches, A. L. Rawlings (New York, 1944, 2nd edition, Sir Isaac Pitman, London 1948)
Watch and Clockmaker's Handbook, Dictionary and Guide, F. J. Britten (Spon, London, 1884, 15th edition 1955)
Watchmakers and Clockmakers of the World, G. H. Baillie (first published 1929, N. A. G. Press, London, 1951)

Coalport or Coalbrookdale, Shropshire
Caughley and Coalport Porcelain, F. A. Barrett (F. Lewis, Leigh-on-Sea, Essex, 1951)
Coalport and Coalbrookdale Porcelains, Geoffrey A. Godden (Barrie & Jenkins, London, 1969)

commedia dell' arte
The Commedia dell'Arte, G. Oreglia, translated by L. F. Edwards (Methuen, London, 1968)

Coney, John
John Coney, Silversmith, Hermann Frederick Clarke (Houghton Mifflin Co, Boston, Massachusetts, 1932)

Cookworthy, William
Cookworthy's Plymouth and Bristol Porcelain, F. Severne Mackenna (F. Lewis, Leigh-on-Sea, Essex, 1946)

copper and brass
The Book of Copper and Brass, Geoffrey Wills (Country Life, Feltham, Middlesex, 1969)
Chats on Old Copper and Brass, F. W. Burgess (Benn, London, 1954)
Collecting Copper and Brass, Geoffrey Wills (Arco Publications, London, 1962)

Courtauld family
Silver Wrought by the Courtauld Family of London Goldsmiths in the Eighteenth Century, S. A. Courtauld and E. A. Jones (privately printed, Oxford, 1940)

cream-coloured earthenware
English Cream-coloured Earthenware, Donald C. Towner (Faber & Faber, London, 1957)

cup
How to Identify English Silver Drinking Vessels 600–1830, Douglas Ash (G. Bell & Sons, 1964)

cut glass
English and Irish Cut Glass, E. M. Elville (Country Life, London, 1953)

cutlery
A Chronology of Cutlery, H. Raymond Singleton (Sheffield City Museum, Sheffield, Yorkshire, 1966)

cut-steel jewellery
Cut-Steel and Berlin Iron Jewellery, Anne Clifford (Adams & Dart, Bath, 1971)

decanter
How to Identify English Drinking Glasses and Decanters, Douglas Ash (G. Bell & Sons, London, 1962)

de Lamerie, Paul
Paul de Lamerie: Citizen and Goldsmith of London, Philip A. S. Phillips (B. T. Batsford, London, 1935, reprinted by Holland Press, London, 1968)

Delft
Delft Ceramics, C. H. de Jonge (Pall Mall Press, London, 1970)
Dutch Tiles, C. H. de Jonge (B. T. Batsford, London, 1970)

Derby
Derby Porcelain, F. Brayshaw Gilhespy (McGibbon & Kee, London, 1961)
Derby Porcelain 1750–1848, Franklin A. Barrett and Arthur L. Thorpe (Faber & Faber, London, 1971)
Old Derby Porcelain and its Artist-Workmen, Frank Hurlbutt (Laurie, London, 1925)
Royal Crown Derby China, F. Brayshaw Gilhespy and D. M. Budd (Skilton, London, 1964)

Doulton pottery
Royal Doulton 1815–1965, Desmond Eyles (Hutchinson, London, 1965)

Dummer, Jeremiah
Jeremiah Dummer: Colonial Craftsman and Merchant, Hermann Frederick Clarke and Henry Wilder Foote (Houghton Mifflin Co, Boston, Massachusetts, 1935)

Dutch gold and silver
Dutch Silver, Douglas Ash (The Golden Head Press, Cambridge, 1965)
Dutch Silver, J. W. Frederiks (Martinus Nijhoff, The Hague, 1952)
Dutch Silver, M. H. Gans and Th. M. Duyvené de Wit-Klinkhamer, translated by Oliver van Oss (Faber & Faber, London, 1961)

electro-plating
Victorian Electroplate, Shirley Bury (Country Life, London, 1971)
Victorian Silver and Silver-Plate, Patricia Wardle (Herbert Jenkins, London, 1963)

Empire style
Empire Furniture, Serge Grandjean (Faber & Faber, London, 1966)

enamelling
The Enamelist, Kenneth F. Bates (World Publishing Co, New York, 1951)
English Painted Enamels, Therle and Bernard Hughes (Country Life, London, 1951)
European Enamels, Isa Belli Barsali, translated by Raymond Rudorff (Paul Hamlyn, London, 1969)

English ceramics
British Pottery and Porcelain, Stanley Fisher (Arco, London, 1962)
British Pottery and Porcelain 1780–1850, Geoffrey A. Godden (Arthur Barker, London, 1963)
The Collector's Encyclopaedia of English Ceramics, G. Bernard and Therle Hughes (Lutterworth, London, 1956)
A Collector's History of English Pottery, Griselda Lewis (Studio Vista, London, 1969)
Concise Encyclopaedia of English Pottery and Porcelain, Wolf Mankowitz and Reginald Haggar (Andre Deutsch, London, 1957)
The Decoration of English Porcelain, Stanley Fisher (Derek Verschoyle, 1954)
English and Scottish Earthenware, G. Bernard Hughes (Lutterworth, London, 1961)
English Blue and White Porcelain of the Eighteenth Century, Bernard Watney (Faber & Faber, London, 1963)
English Ceramics, Stanley Fisher (Ward Lock, London, 1966)
English China Collecting for Amateurs, J. P. Cushion (Frederick Muller, London, 1967)
The English Country Pottery, P. C. D. Brears (David & Charles, Newton Abbot, Devon, 1971)
English Porcelain, Eighteenth Century, F. Severne Mackenna (F. Lewis, Leigh-on-Sea, Essex, 1970)
English Porcelain (1745–1850), edited by R. J. Charleston (Benn, London, 1965)
English Porcelain and Bone China, G. Bernard and Therle Hughes (Lutterworth, London, 1955)
English Porcelain Figures of the Eighteenth Century, Arthur Lane (Faber & Faber, London, 1961)
English Pottery and Porcelain, W. B. Honey, 6th edition revised by R. J. Charleston (A. & C. Black, London, 1969)
An Illustrated Encyclopaedia of British Pottery and Porcelain, Geoffrey A. Godden (Barrie & Jenkins, London, 1966)
Investing in Pottery and Porcelain, Hugo Morley-Fletcher (Barrie & Jenkins, London, 1968)
Jewitt's Ceramic Art of Great Britain: 1800–1900, edited by Geoffrey A. Godden (Barrie & Jenkins, London, 1972)
Medieval English Pottery, Bernard Rackham (Faber & Faber, London, 1947)
Pottery Trade and North Staffordshire 1660–1760, Lorna Weatherill (Manchester University Press, 1971)
Victorian Pottery, Hugh Wakefield (Barrie & Jenkins, London, 1962)

English clocks
A Book of English Clocks, R. W. Symonds (Penguin Books, London, 1947)
Clock & Watchmaking in Colchester, England, Bernard Mason O.B.E (Country Life, London 1969)
Clockmaking in Oxfordshire, 1400–1850, C. F. C. Beeson (Antiquarian Horological Society, London, 1962)
Devonshire Clockmakers, J. K. Bellchambers (Antiquarian Horological Society, London, 1962)
English Church Clocks, 1280–1850, C. F. C. Beeson (Antiquarian Horological Society and Phillimore, Chichester, 1971)
English Clocks, Muriel Goaman (Connoisseur and Michael Joseph, London, 1967)
English Domestic Clocks, H. Cescinsky and M. R. Webster (Spring Books, London, 1969)

English clocks—*continued*

The Making of Clocks and Watches in Leicestershire and Rutland, J. A. Daniell (Leicestershire Archaeological Society, 1952)
The Old Clockmakers of Yorkshire, Rev. N. V. Dinsdale (Dalesman Publishing Co, Lancaster, 1946)
Somerset Clockmakers, J. K. Bellchambers (Antiquarian Horological Society, London, 1968)

English delftware

English Delftware, F. H. Garner, revised by Michael Archer (Faber & Faber, London 1972)
English Delftware Pottery in the Robert Hall Warren Collection, Anthony Ray (Faber & Faber, London, 1968)

English furniture

Dictionary of English Antique Furniture, Douglas Ash (Frederick Muller, London, 1970)
The Dictionary of English Furniture, Ralph Edwards (Country Life, London, revised edition 1954)
English Eighteenth Century Furniture, David Nickerson (Weidenfeld & Nicolson, London, 1963)
English Furniture, 1550–1760, Geoffrey Wills (Guinness Superlatives, Enfield, 1971)
English Furniture Designs of the 18th Century, Peter Ward-Jackson (H.M. Stationery Office, London, 1958)
English Furniture Styles from 1500 to 1830, Ralph Fastnedge (Penguin Books, London, 1955)
The London Furniture Makers, 1660–1840, Sir Ambrose Heal (B. T. Batsford, London, 1935)
Nineteenth Century English Furniture, Elizabeth Aslin (Faber & Faber, London, 1962)
The Shorter Dictionary of English Furniture, Ralph Edwards (Country Life, London, 1964)

English glass

English Glass, W. A. Thorpe (A. & C. Black, London, 3rd edition 1961)
English Glass, edited by Sidney Crompton (Ward Lock, London, 1967)
English Tableglass, E. M. Elville (Country Life, London and Charles Scribner's Sons, New York, 1951)
A History of Old English Glass, Francis Buckley, (Ernest Benn, London, 1925)
An Illustrated Guide to Eighteenth Century English Drinking Glasses, L. M. Bickerton (Barrie & Jenkins, London, 1971)
English and Irish Antique Glass, Derek C. Davis (Arthur Barker, London, 1965)
English and Irish Glass, W. A. Thorpe (The Medici Society, London and Boston, 1927)
English, Scottish and Irish Table Glass, G. Bernard Hughes (B. T. Batsford, London, 1956)
19th Century British Glass, Hugh Wakefield (Faber & Faber, London, 1961)

English gold and silver

Anglican Church Plate, J. Gilchrist (Conoisseur–Michael Joseph, London, 1967)
British and Irish Silver Assay Office Marks (1544–1968), Frederick Bradbury (J. W. Northend Ltd, Sheffield, Yorkshire, 12th edition, 1969)
Caroline Silver, 1625–1688, Charles Oman (Faber & Faber, London, 1970)
The Collector's Dictionary of the Silver and Gold of Great Britain and North America, Michael Clayton (Country Life, London, 1971)
English Church Plate, Charles Oman (Oxford University Press, 1957)
English Domestic Silver, Charles Oman (A. & C. Black, London, 4th edition, revised, 1959)
English Goldsmiths and their Marks, Sir Charles Jackson (Macmillan, London, 2nd edition 1921, reprinted by Constable, London, 1965)
English Silver, Jessie McNab Dennis (Collector's Blue Book series, Walker & Co, New York, 1970)
English Silversmith's Work, Civil and Domestic: An Introduction, Charles Oman (H.M. Stationery Office, London, 1965)
Goldsmiths and Silversmiths, Hugh Honour (Weidenfeld & Nicolson, London, 1971)
An Illustrated History of English Plate, Sir Charles Jackson (Country Life, London, 1911)
An Introduction to Old English Silver, Judith Banister (Evans Brothers, London, 1965)
Investing in Silver, Eric Delieb (Barrie & Rockliff, London, 1967)
The Marks of the London Goldsmiths and Silversmiths–Georgian Period (c1697–1837): A Guide, John P. Fallon (David & Charles, Newton Abbot, Devon, 1972)
Silver, Gerald Taylor (Penguin Books, London, 2nd edition, revised, 1963)
Victorian Silver and Silver-plate, Patricia Wardle (Herbert Jenkins, London, 1963)

English tapestry

English Tapestries of the Eighteenth Century, H. C. Marillier (The Medici Society, London, 1930)
Tapestry Weaving in England, W. G. Thomson (B. T. Batsford, London, 1914)

English snuff-boxes

English Snuff-boxes, G. Bernard Hughes (MacGibbon & Kee, London, 1971)

English watches

English Watches, J. F. Hayward (Victoria & Albert Museum, H.M. Stationery Office, London, 1969)

escapement

Clock and Watch Escapements, W. J. Gazeley (Heywood & Co, London, 1956)
It's About Time, Paul Chamberlain (New York, 1941, Holland Press, London, 1964)
Watch Escapements, J. C. Pellaton (London, not dated)

fan

Fan Leaves, Fan Guild (privately printed, Boston, Massachusetts, 1961)

Flemish tapestry

Flemish Tapestries, Roger-A. D'Hulst, translated by F. J. Stillman (Editions Arcade, Brussels – W. Heffer & Sons, Cambridge, 1967)

French ceramics

French Faience, Arthur Lane (Faber & Faber, London, revised edition, 1970)
French Porcelain, Hubert Landais (Weidenfeld & Nicolson, London, 1961)
French Porcelain of the 18th Century, W. B. Honey (Faber & Faber, London, 1950)
Seventeenth and Eighteenth Century French Porcelain, George Savage (Spring Books, London, 1960)

French clocks

French Clocks, Winthrop Edey (Studio Vista, London 1967)

French furniture

French Furniture, André Saglio (George Newnes, London, 1907)
French Furniture and Interior Decoration of the 18th Century, Pierre Verlet, translated by G. Savage (Barrie & Rockliff, London 1967)
French Royal Furniture, Pierre Verlet (Barrie & Rockliff, London, 1963)
Wallace Collection: Catalogue of Furniture, Francis J. B. Watson (London, 1956)
The Wrightsman Collection, Francis J. B. Watson (The Metropolitan Museum of Art, New York, 1966)

French gold and silver

A Guide to Old French Plate, Louis Carré (Chapman & Hall, London, 1931, reprinted by Eyre & Spottiswoode, London, 1971)
Three Centuries of French Domestic Silver: Its Makers and its Marks, Faith Dennis (The Metropolitan Museum of Art, New York, 1960)
Treasures of the Churches of France, Jean Taralon, translated by Mira Intrator (Thames & Hudson, London, 1966)

French tapestry

French Tapestry, edited by André Lejard (Paul Elek, London, 1946)
French Tapestry, Roger-Armand Weigert, translated by D. and M. King (Faber & Faber, London, 1962)

furniture

Cabinet Makers and Furniture Designers, Hugh Honour (Weidenfeld & Nicolson, London, 1969)
The Complete Guide to Furniture Styles, Louise Ade Boger (George Allen & Unwin, London, 1961)
The Connoisseur's Guide to Antique Furniture, edited by L. G. G. Ramsay and Helen Comstock (The Connoisseur, London, 1969)
The Connoisseur Period Guides, edited by Ralph Edwards and L. G. G. Ramsay (The Connoisseur, London, 1956–58)
Decoration and Furniture, Bruce Allsopp (Sir Isaac Pitman & Sons, London, 1952–53)
The Encyclopedia of Furniture, Joseph Aronson (B. T. Batsford, London, 1970)
Furniture 700 to 1700, Eric Mercer (Weidenfeld & Nicolson, London, 1969)
Period Furniture Design, Charles H. Hayward (Evans Brothers, London, 1956)
A Short Dictionary of Furniture, edited by John Gloag (George Allen & Unwin, London, 2nd revised edition 1969)
A Social History of Furniture Design from B.C. 1300 to A.D. 1960, John Gloag (Cassell & Co, London, 1966)
World Furniture, edited by Helena Hayward (Paul Hamlyn, London, 1965)

gemmology

Practical Gemmology, Robert Webster (N. A. G. Press, London, 4th edition 1966)
The Retail Jewellers' Guide, Kenneth Blakemore (Iliffe Books Ltd, London, 1969)

Georgian style

English Furniture: The Georgian Period (1750–1830), Margaret and Rose F. Jourdain (B. T. Batsford, London, 1953)
Georgian Cabinet-makers, c1700–1800, Ralph Edwards and Margaret Jourdain (Country Life, London, 3rd revised edition 1955)

German ceramics

Bohemian Porcelain, E. Poche, translated by R. K. White (Artia, Prague, no date)
Eighteenth Century German Porcelain, George Savage (Spring Books, London, 1968)
German Porcelain, W. B. Honey (Faber & Faber, London, 1947)
German Porcelain of the 18th Century: The Pauls

Collection, Vol. 2: *Höchst, Frankenthal and Ludwigsburg,* Erika Pauls-Eisenbeiss (Barrie & Jenkins, London, forthcoming 1973)
Meissen and Other Continental Porcelain in the Collection of Irwin Untermeyer, Yvonne Hackenbroch (Thames & Hudson, London, 1956)

German gold and silver
Old Table Silver, Herbert Brunner, translated by Janet Seligman (Faber & Faber, London, 1967)
Royal Treasures, edited by Erich Steingräber, translated by Stefan de Haan (Weidenfeld & Nicolson, London, 1968)

glass
The Art of Glass, Wilfred Buckley (The Phaidon Press, London, 1939)
The Book of Glass, Gustav Weiss, translated by J. Seligman (Barrie & Jenkins, London, 1971)
Chats on Old Glass, R. A. Robertson (Dover Publications, New York and Constable and Co, London, revised edition 1969)
The Collector's Dictionary of Glass, E. M. Elville (Country Life, London, 1961)
Coloured Glass, Derek Davis and Keith Middlemas (Barrie & Jenkins, London, 1968)
Continental Coloured Glass, Keith Middlemas (Barrie & Jenkins, London, 1971)
The Country Life Book of Glass, Frank Davis (Country Life, London, 1966)
5000 Years of Glass-Making, Jaroslav R. Vávra, translated by I. R. Gottheiner (Artia, Prague, 1954—W. Heffer & Sons, Cambridge, 1955)
Glass, George Savage (Weidenfeld & Nicolson, London, 1965)
Glass–A World History, Fritz Kämpfer, translated by E. Launert (Studio Vista, London, 1966)
Glass and Crystal (Vol. I), Elka Schrijver (Merlin Press, London, 1963)
Glass Through the Ages, E. Barrington Haynes (Penguin Books, Harmondsworth, revised edition 1959)
The Hallmarks of Antique Glass, R. Wilkinson (Richard Madley, London, 1968)
Masterpieces of Glass (The British Museum, London, 1968)

gold
The Book of Gold, Kenneth Blakemore (November Books, London, 1971)
Gold, C. H. V. Sutherland (Thames & Hudson, London, 1959)
Medieval Goldsmiths' Work, Isa Belli Barsali, translated by Margaret Crosland (Hamlyn, London, 1969)

hallmarks
The Book of Old Silver: English, American, Foreign, with available marks including Sheffield Plate marks, Seymour B. Wyler (Crown Publishers, New York, 1937)

Hancock, Robert
The Life and Work of Robert Hancock, Cyril Cook (Chapman & Hall, London, 1948)

Han dynasty
Chinese Pottery of the Han Dynasty, Berthold Laufer (Tuttle, Rutland, Vermont, 2nd edition 1962)

Harrison, John
John Harrison and his Timekeepers, R. T. Gould (National Maritime Museum, Greenwich, 1958, reprinted from The Mariner's Mirror, 1935)
John Harrison, the Man who Found Longitude, Humphrey Quill (John Baker, London, 1966)

Hispano-Moresque ware
Hispano Moresque Ware of the Fifteenth Century, A. Van de Put (London, 1951)
Lusterware of Spain, Alice W. Frothingham (Hispanic Society of America, New York, 1951)

Hooke, Robert
The Diary of Robert Hooke, edited by H. W. Robinson and W. Adams (Wykeham Publications, London, 1968)
The Life and Work of Robert Hooke, vols 6, 7, 8, 10 & 13 of *Early Science in Oxford,* R. T. Gunther (first published 1923–45, facsimile edition, Dawsons of Pall Mall, Folkestone, 1968)

Huguenot silver
Huguenot Silver in England, John Hayward (Faber & Faber, London, 1959)

Hull, John
John Hull: a Builder of the Bay Colony, Hermann Frederick Clarke (The Southworth-Anthoensen Press, Portland, Maine, 1940)

Hurd, Jacob
Jacob Hurd and his Sons Nathaniel and Benjamin, Silversmiths 1702–81, Hollis French (privately printed by Riverside Press, Cambridge, Massachusetts, 1939)

Huygens, Christiaan
Horologium Oscillatorium, Christiaan Huygens (facsimile of 1673 edition, Dawsons of Pall Mall, Folkestone, 1966)

Irish silver
British and Irish Silver Assay Office Marks (1544–1968), Frederick Bradbury (J. W. Northend, Sheffield, Yorkshire, 12th edition 1969)
Irish Georgian Silver, Douglas Bennett (Cassell & Co, London, 1972)
Irish Silver in the Rococo Period, Kurt Ticher (Irish University Press, Shannon, Ireland, 1972)

iron
The Craftsman in Metal, Raymond Lister (G. Bell & Sons, London, 1966)
Decorative Cast Ironwork in Great Britain, R. Lister (G. Bell & Sons, London, 1960)
Decorative Wrought Ironwork in Great Britain, R. Lister (G. Bell & Sons, London, 1957)
English Ironwork of the XVII and XVIII Centuries, J. Starkie Gardner (B. T. Batsford, London and New York, 1911)

Islamic pottery
Later Islamic Pottery, Arthur Lane (Faber & Faber, London, 1957)
Turkish Art and Architecture, Oktay Aslanapa (Faber & Faber, London, no date)
Iranian Ceramics, Charles K. Wilkinson (New York, 1963)
Islamic Pottery from the 9th–14th Centuries, Arthur Lane (Faber & Faber, London, 1956)
Islamic Pottery and Italian Maiolica, Bernard Rockham (Faber & Faber, London, 1959)

Italian furniture
A History of Italian Furniture from the Fourteenth to the Early Nineteenth Century, William M. Odom (The Archive Press, New York, 1966–67)

Italian gold and silver
Art Treasures of the Medici, Antonio Morassi, translated by Paul Colaciechi (Oldbourne Press, London, 1964)
The Goldsmiths of Italy, Sidney J. A. Churchill and Cyril G. E. Bunt (Martin Hopkinson & Co, London, 1926)
Italian Jewelled Arts, Filippo Rossi, translated by Elisabeth Mann Borgese (Thames & Hudson, London, 1957)

Italian porcelain
Italian Porcelain, Arthur Lane (Faber & Faber, London, 1954)
Italian Porcelain, Francesco Stazzi (Weidenfeld & Nicolson, London, 1967)

Japanese clocks
Japanese Clocks, N. H. N. Mody (Kegan Paul, London, 1968)
The Clocks of Japan, R. Yamaguchi, with summary of text in English (Nippon Hyoron-Sha Publishing Co Ltd, Tokyo, 1950)

Japanese pottery and porcelain
The Ceramic Art of Japan, Hugo Munsterberg (Tuttle, Rutland, Vermont, 1964)
Japanese Ceramics, Roy A. Miller (Toto Shuppan, Tokyo, 1960)
Japanese Porcelain, Soame Jenyns (Faber & Faber, London, 1965)
Japanese Pottery, Soame Jenyns (Faber & Faber, London, 1971)
World of Japanese Ceramics, Herbert H. Sanders (Kodansha International, Tokyo, 1967)

japanned metal ware
Pontypool and Usk Japanned Wares, W. D. John (Ceramic Book Co, Newport, Monmouthshire, 1953)

jasper ware
Wedgwood Jasper, Robin Reilly (Charles Letts & Co, London, 1972)
Wedgwood Jasper Ware, John Bedford (Cassell & Co, London, 1964)

jet
Victorian Sentimental Jewellery, Diana Cooper and Norman Battershill (David & Charles, Newton Abbot, Devon, 1972)

jewellery
Antique Jewellery: its History in Europe from 800–1900, Erich Steingräber (Thames & Hudson, London, 1957)
Collecting Victorian Jewellery, Mary Peter (MacGibbon & Kee, London, 1970)
Four Centuries of European Jewellery, Ernle Bradford (Country Life, London, 1953)
A History of Jewellery, 1100–1870, Joan Evans (Faber & Faber, London, 2nd edition 1970)
Jewellery 1837–1901, Margaret Flower (Cassell & Co, London, 1968)
Jewellery, Peter Hinks (Paul Hamlyn, London, 1969)
Jewelry, Graham Hughes (Studio Vista, London, 1966)
Jewelry through the Ages, Guido Gregorietti, translated by Helen Lawrence (Paul Hamlyn, London, 1970)
Victorian Jewellery Design, Charlotte Gere (William Kimber, London, 1972)

Kenzan
Kenzan and His Tradition, Bernard Leach (Faber & Faber, London, 1966)

Knibb, John and Joseph
The Knibb Family, Clockmakers, Ronald A. Lee (Manor House Press, Byfleet, 1964)

Korean pottery
The Arts of Korea, Chewon Kim and Won-Yong Kim (Thames & Hudson, London, 1966)
The Ceramic Art of Korea, Chewon Kim and G. St-G. M. Compertz (Faber & Faber, London, 1961)
Corean Pottery, W. B. Honey (Faber & Faber, London, 1947)

Koryo period
Korean Celadon: and other wares of the Koryo Period, G. St-G. M. Gompertz (Faber & Faber, London, 1963)

Kremlin silver
The English Silver in the Kremlin, 1557–1663, Charles Oman (Methuen & Co, London, 1961)

Leeds
Historical Notices of the Leeds Old Pottery, J. and F. Kidson (1892, reprinted by S. R. Publishers and Connoisseur, London, 1971)
The Leeds Pottery, D. Towner (Cory, Adams & Mackay, London, 1963)

Liverpool
Illustrated Guide to Liverpool Herculaneum Pottery 1796–1840, Alan Smith (Barrie & Jenkins, London, 1970)

long-case clock
The Grandfather Clock, E. L. Edwardes, (J. Sheratt & Sons, Altrincham, 1952, 3rd edition 1971)
The Long-case Clock, Eric Bruton (Arco Publications, London, 1964)

Longton Hall
Longton Hall Porcelain, Bernard Watney (Faber & Faber, London, 1957)

Louis XVI style
Louis XVI Furniture, Francis J. B. Watson (Alec Tiranti, London, 1960)

Lowestoft porcelain factory
The Illustrated Guide to Lowestoft Porcelain, Geoffrey A. Godden (Barrie & Jenkins, London, 1969)

Lund, Benjamin
Worcester Porcelain and Lund's Bristol, Franklin A. Barrett (Faber & Faber, London, 1966)

lustre decoration
Old English Lustre Pottery, W. D. John and Warren Baker (Ceramic Book Company, Newport, Monmouthshire, 1951)
Old English Lustre Ware, John Bedford (Cassell & Co, London, 1965)

maiolica
Five Centuries of Italian Maiolica, G. Liverani (London, 1960)
Italian Maiolica, Bernard Rackham (Faber & Faber, London, 1964)

marks
Collectors' Handbook of Marks and Monograms on Pottery and Porcelain, William Chaffers; revised by Frederick Litchfield Reeves, London, 1968)
Dictionary of Marks – Pottery and Porcelain, Ralph M. and Terry H. Kovel (Crown Publishers, New York, 1953)
Dictionary of Marks and Monograms on Delft Pottery, Jean Justice (Herbert Jenkins, London, 1930)
Encyclopaedia of British Pottery and Porcelain Marks, G. A. Godden (Herbert Jenkins, London, 1964)
The Handbook of British Pottery and Porcelain Marks, G. A. Godden (Herbert Jenkins, London, 1968)
Handbook of Pottery and Porcelain Marks, J. P. Cushion and W. B. Honey (Faber & Faber, London, 1956)
Pocket Book of English Ceramic Marks, J. P. Cushion (Faber & Faber, London, 1965)
Pocket Book of French and Italian Ceramic Marks, J. P. Cushion (Faber & Faber, London, 1965)
Pocket Book of German Ceramic Marks, J. P. Cushion (Faber & Faber, London, 1961)

Mason, G. M. and C. J.
Illustrated Guide: Mason's Patent Ironstone China and the related ware, Geoffrey A. Godden (Barrie & Jenkins, London, 1971)

Meissen
Dresden China, W. B. Honey (A. & C. Black, London, 1934)
German Porcelain of the 18th Century: the Pauls Collection, Vol. 1: *Meissen from the beginning until 1760,* Erika Pauls-Eisenbeiss (Barrie & Jenkins, London, forthcoming 1973)
Meissen, Hugo Morley-Fletcher (Barrie & Jenkins, London, 1971)

microscope
The Evolution of the Microscope, S. Bradbury (Pergamon Press, Oxford, 1967)
History of the Microscope, R. S. Clay and T. H. Court (Chas. Griffin & Co, London, 1932)
Micrographia, Robert Hooke (facsimile of 1665 edition, Wheldon and Wesley, Hitchin, 1961)
Micrographia, Robert Hooke (extracts, Alembic Club Reprints, E. & S. Livingstone, Edinburgh)

Ming
Ming Porcelains, their Origins and Development, Adrian M. Joseph (Bibelot Publishers, London, 1971)
Ming Pottery and Porcelain, Soame Jenyns (Faber & Faber, London, 1953)
The Wares of the Ming Dynasty, R. L. Hobson (Tuttle, Rutland, Vermont)

ming ch'i
Chinese Pottery Burial Objects of the Sui and T'ang Dynasties, H. M. Moss (Hugh M. Moss, London, 1970)

miniatures and silhouettes
Aspects of Miniature Painting, T. H. Colding (Ejnar Munksgaard, Copenhagen, 1953)
British Portrait Miniatures, Daphne Foskett (Spring Books, London, 1969)
British Profile Miniaturists, Arthur Mayne (Faber & Faber, London, 1970)
British Silhouettes, John Woodiwiss (Country Life, London, 1965)
A Dictionary of Miniature Painters, J. J. Foster (Philip Allan & Co, London, 1926)
Early American Portrait Painters in Miniature, Theodore Bolton (Frederic Fairchild Sherman, New York, 1921)
Miniatures and Silhouettes, Max von Böhn, translated by E. K. Walker (J. M. Dent & Sons, London, 1926)

Minton, Thomas
Minton Pottery and Porcelain of the First Period, 1793–1850, Geoffrey A. Godden (Barrie & Jenkins, London, 1968)

musical box
Collecting Musical Boxes, Arthur W. J. Ord-Hume (George Allen & Unwin, London, 1967)
Musical Boxes, David Tallis (Frederick Muller, London, 1971)

musical instruments
Musical Instruments: a comprehensive dictionary, Sybil Marcuse (Country Life, London, 1966)
Musical Instruments in Art and History, Roger Bragard, translated by B. Hopkins (Barrie & Rockliff, London, 1968)
Musical Instruments of the Western World, Emanuel Winternitz (Thames & Hudson, London, 1966)
Musical Instruments through the Ages, edited by Anthony Baines (Penguin, Harmondsworth, Middlesex, 1961)

Myers, Myer
Myer Myers, Goldsmith, J. W. Rosenbaum (The Jewish Publication Society of America, 1954)

Nantgarw
Nantgarw Porcelain, W. D. John (Ceramic Book Company, Newport, Monmouthshire, 1948)

navigating instruments
The Art of Navigation in England in Elizabethan and early Stuart Times, D. W. Waters (Hollis & Carter, London, 1958)
History of Nautical Astronomy, C. H. Cotter (Hollis & Carter, London, 1969)
Instruments of Navigation, H. O. Hill and E. W. Paget-Tomlinson (National Maritime Museum, Greenwich, 1958)

neo-classical style
Adam, Hepplewhite and other Neo-Classical Furniture, Clifford W. Musgrave (Faber & Faber, London, 1966)
On Neoclassicism, Mario Praz, translated by A. Davidson (Thames & Hudson, London, 1969)

New Hall
New Hall and its Imitators, David Holgate (Faber & Faber, London, 1971)

objects of vertu
Objects of Vertu, Howard Ricketts (Barrie & Jenkins, London, 1971)

oriental Lowestoft
Oriental Lowestoft, J. A. Lloyd Hyde (Ceramic Book Company, Newport, Monmouthshire, 1954)

paktong
Tutenag and Paktong, A. Bonnin (Oxford University Press, Oxford and New York, 1924)

paperweights
Antique Glass Paperweights from France, Patricia K. McCawley (Spink & Son, London, 1968)
The Encyclopedia of Glass Paperweights, Paul Hollister, Jr (Clarkson N. Potter, New York, 1969)
Glass Paperweights, Evelyn Campbell Cloak (Studio Vista, London, 1969)
Paperweights and Other Glass Curiosities, E. M. Elville (Country Life, London, 1954)

parian ware
Victorian Parian China, Charles and Dorrie Shinn (Barrie & Jenkins, London, 1971)

Paris
Paris Porcelain 1770–1850, Régine de Plinval de Guillebon (Barrie & Jenkins, London)

paste
Antique Paste Jewellery, M. D. S. Lewis (Faber & Faber, London, 1970)

pewter
Antique Pewter of the British Isles, R. F. Michaelis (G. Bell & Sons, London, 1955 and Dover Publications, New York, 1971)
British Pewter, R. F. Michaelis (Ward Lock, London, 1969)
British Pewter and Britannia Metal, Christopher A. Peal (John Gifford, London, 1971)
Chats on Old Pewter, H. J. L. J. Massé (Benn, London, revised edition 1949, and Dover Publications, New York, 1969)
Old Pewter: Its Makers and Marks, Howard H. Cotterell (B. T. Batsford, London, 1929, and Tuttle, Rutland, Vermont, 1963)

Piccolpasso, Cipriano
The Three Books of the Potter's Art: Li tre libri dell'arte del vasaio, Cipriano Piccolpasso, translated by Bernard Rackham and Albert Van de Put (London, 1934)

piqué
Piqué: A Beautiful Minor Art, Herbert C. Dent (Connoisseur, London, 1923)

porcelain
Antique Porcelain Digest, G. Ryland and Cleo M. Scott (Ceramic Book Company, Newport, Monmouthshire, 1961)
European Porcelain, Mina Bacci, translated by A. Hartcup (Hamlyn, London, 1969)
Continental China Collecting for Amateurs, J. P. Cushion (Frederick Muller, London, 1970)
Continental Porcelain of the 18th Century, Rollo Charles (Ernest Benn, London, 1964)
Porcelain, Eileen Aldridge (Hamlyn, London, 1969)
Porcelain, H. Tait (Hamlyn, London, 1962)
Porcelain through the Ages, George Savage (Cassell & Co, London, 1961)

pot lids
Staffordshire Pot Lids and their Potters, Cyril Williams-Wood (Faber & Faber, London, 1972)
Underglaze Colour Picture Prints on Staffordshire Pottery (the Pictorial Pot Lid Book), Harold George Clark (London, 1955)

pottery
The Art of the Potter, W. B. Honey (Faber & Faber, London, 1946)
European Pottery, Maria Penkala (Tuttle, Rutland, Vermont, 1968)
History of Pottery, Emmanuel Cooper (Longman Group, London, 1972)
A Potter's Book, Bernard Leach (Faber & Faber, London, 1945)
Pottery, Henry Hodges (Hamlyn, Feltham, Middlesex, 1972)
A Pottery Bibliography, M. L. Solon (London, 1910)
Pottery through the Ages, R. G. Haggar (Methuen & Co, London, 1958)
Pottery through the Ages, George Savage (Cassell & Co, London, 1963)

prayer rug
Oriental Prayer Rugs, Roy E. Macey (F. Lewis, Leigh-on-Sea, Essex, 1961)

pressed glass
American Pressed Glass and Figure Bottles, Albert Christian Revi (Thomas Nelson & Sons, London and New York, 1964)

Regency style
Regency Furniture, Margaret Jourdain (Country Life, London, 1949)
Regency Furniture 1800–30, Clifford W. Musgrave (Faber & Faber, London, revised edition 1970)

Ridgway, Job
Ridgway Porcelains, Geoffrey A. Godden (Barrie & Jenkins, London, 1972)

ring
Rings for the Finger, G. F. Kunz (J. B. Lippincott, Philadelphia, Pennsylvania, 1917)

Rockingham, Swinton, Yorkshire
Rockingham Ornamental Porcelain, D. G. Rice (The Ceramic Book Company, Newport, Monmouthshire, 1966)
The Rockingham Pottery, Arthur A. Eaglestone and Terence A. Lockett (Rotherham Municipal Museum and Art Gallery, 1967, new edition, David & Charles, Newton Abbot, Devon 1973)
Rockingham Pottery and Porcelain, D. G. Rice (Barrie & Jenkins, London, 1971)

Russian porcelain
The Art and Artists of Russia, R. Hare (Methuen & Co, London, 1965)
Russian Porcelains, Marvin C. Ross (University of Oklahoma Press, Norman, 1968)

scent bottle
Scent Bottles, Kate Foster (Connoisseur, London, 1966)

scientific instruments
The Mathematical Practitioners of Tudor & Stuart England, E. G. R. Taylor (Cambridge University Press, Cambridge, 1954)
The Mathematical Practitioners of Hanoverian England, 1714–1840, E. G. R. Taylor (Cambridge University Press, Cambridge, 1966)
Scientific Instruments of the 17th and 18th Centuries and their Makers, M. Daumas, translated by M. Holbrook (B. T. Batsford, London, 1972)

Scottish gold and silver
Old Scottish Communion Plate, Thomas Burns (R. & R. Clark, Edinburgh, 1892)
Scottish Gold and Silver Work, Ian Finlay (Chatto & Windus, London, 1956)

self-winding watch
The History of the Self-Winding Watch, 1770–1931, Afred Chapuis and Eugene Jaquet (Rolex Watch Co, Geneva, English edition 1956)

Sèvres porcelain factory
Sèvres, Carl Christian Dauterman (Studio Vista, London, 1970)
Sèvres Porcelain, James A. de Rothschild at Waddesdon Manor Collection, Svend Eriksen (National Trust, Aylesbury, 1968)

Sheffield plate
The Book of Sheffield Plate, Seymour B. Wyler (Bonanza Books, New York, 1949)
History of Old Sheffield Plate, Frederick Bradbury (Macmillan, London, 1912)
Old Sheffield Plate, Edward Wenham (G. Bell & Sons, London, 1955)
Sheffield Plate, Henry Newton Veitch (G. Bell & Sons, London, 1908)

Sheraton style
Sheraton Furniture, Ralph Fastnedge (Faber & Faber, London, 1962)

silversmithing
Metal Techniques for Craftsmen: A basic manual for craftsmen on the methods of forming and decorating metals, Oppi Untracht (Robert Hale, London, 1968)
Metalwork and Enamelling: A Practical Treatise on Gold and Silversmiths' Work and their Allied Crafts, Herbert Maryon (Chapman & Hall, London, 4th edition 1959)
Metalworking for Schools, Colleges and Home Craftsmen, Oscar Almeida (Mills & Boon, London, 1967)
A Silversmith's Manual, Bernard Cuzner (N. A. G. Press, London, 1949)
Silversmithing, Robert Goodden and Philip Popham (Oxford University Press, London, 1971)

skeleton clock
Skeleton Clocks, F. B. Royer-Collard (N. A. G. Press, London, 1969)

slipware
English Slipware Dishes 1650–1850, Ronald G. Cooper (Alec Tiranti, London, 1968)

snuff-box
All Kinds of Small Boxes, John Bedford (Cassell & Co, London, 1964)
Antique Gold Boxes, Henry and Sidney Berry-Hill (Abelard Press, New York, 1953)
Eighteenth Century Gold Boxes of Europe, Kenneth Snowman (Faber & Faber, London, 1966)
European and American Snuff-Boxes, Clare le Corbeiller (B. T. Batsford, London, 1966)
Silver Boxes, Eric Delieb (Herbert Jenkins, London, 1968)

Spanish furniture
Antique Spanish Furniture, Rafael Doménech (Galissá) and Luis Pérez Bueno, translated by G. H. Burr (The Archive Press, New York, 1965)
Hispanic Furniture, Grace Hardendorff Burr (The Archive Press, New York, 1964)

Spanish glass
Spanish Glass, Alice Wilson Frothingham (Faber & Faber, London, 1964)

Spanish silver
The Golden Age of Hispanic Silver 1400–1665, Charles Oman (H.M. Stationery Office, London, 1968)

Spode
Antique Blue and White Spode, S. B. Williams (B. T. Batsford, London, 1947)
Old Spode China, John Bedford (Cassell & Co, London, 1969)
Spode, a History of the Family, Factory, and Wares from 1733–1833, Leonard Whiter (Barrie & Jenkins, London, 1970)

spoons
English and Scottish Silver Spoons, G. E. P. and J. P. How (privately printed, London, 1952)
Old Base Metal Spoons, F. G. Hilton Price (B. T. Batsford, London, 1908)
Old Silver Spoons of England, Norman Gask (Herbert Jenkins, London, 1926)

Staffordshire portrait figures
Staffordshire Portrait Figures of the Victorian Age, Thomas Balston (Faber & Faber, London, 1958)
Staffordshire Portrait Figures and Allied Subjects of the Victorian Era, P. D. Gordon Pugh (Barrie & Jenkins, London, 1971)

Staffordshire portrait figures—*continued*
The Victorian Staffordshire Figures, a Guide for Collectors, Anthony Oliver (Heinemann, London, 1971)

Staffordshire salt-glaze
Staffordshire Salt-Glazed Stoneware, Arnold R. Mountford (Barrie & Jenkins, London, 1971)

Storr, Paul
Paul Storr, the Last of the Goldsmiths, N. M. Penzer (B. T. Batsford, London, 1954)

sundial
Sundials, F. W. Cousins (John Baker, London, 1969)
Sundials Old and New, A. P. Herbert (Methuen & Co, London, 1967)

surveying instruments
Catalogue of the Collection of the Science Museum of South Kensington, Geodesy and Surveying, E. Lancaster Jones (Science Museum, London, 1925)
Surveying Instruments, their History and Classroom Use, E. R. Kiely (Teachers College, Columbia University, New York, 1947)

Swansea
Swansea Porcelain, W. D. John (Ceramic Book Company, Newport, Monmouthshire, 1958)

Swiss watches
The Swiss Watch, Alfred Chapuis and Eugene Jaquet (Boston Book and Art Shop, 1953, Paul Hamlyn, London, 1970)

Talavera
Talavera Pottery, Alice W. Frothingham (Hispanic Society of America, New York, 1944)

tapestry
The Art of Tapestry, edited by Joseph Jobe, translated by P. Rowell Oberson (Thames & Hudson, London, 1965)
A History of Tapestry, W. G. Thomson (Hodder & Stoughton, London, revised edition 1930)
Medieval Tapestries, Dora Heinz, translated by J. R. Foster (Methuen & Co, London, 1967)

teapot
Talking About Teapots, John Bedford (Parrish, London, 1964)
Teapots and Tea, Frank Tilley (Ceramic Book Company, Newport, Monmounthshire, 1957)

telescope
History of the Telescope, H. C. King (Griffin, London, 1955)

thermometer
History of the Thermometer and its Use in Meteorology, W. E. Knowles Middleton (Johns Hopkins, Baltimore, 1964)

tiles
Guide to the Collection of Tiles: Victoria and Albert Museum, Arthur Lane (H.M. Stationery Office, London, 1960)
Tiles, a General History, Anne Berendson and others (Faber & Faber, London, 1967)
Victorian Ceramic Tiles, Julian Barnard (Studio Vista, London, 1972)

time measurement
The Discovery of Time, S. Toulmin & J. Goodfield (Hutchinson, London and Penguin Books, Harmondsworth, 1967)
How Time is Measured, Peter Hood (Oxford University Press, Oxford, 1955)
Time Measurement, F. A. B. Ward (Science Museum, London, H.M. Stationery Office, London, 1966)

tin-glazed earthenware
Collecting Delft, Diana Imber (Arco, London, 1968)
Maiolica, Delft and Faience, Giuseppe Scavizzi (1966), translated by Peter Locke (Hamlyn, London, 1970)

Toby jugs
Toby Jugs, John Bedford (Cassell & Co, London, 1968)

Tompion, Thomas
Thomas Tompion: His Life and Works, R. W. Symonds (B. T. Batsford, London, 1951, Spring Books, London, 1969)

tulip ware
Tulip Ware of the Pennsylvania-German Potters, E. A. Barber (Pennsylvania Museum, 1903)

veilleuses
Veilleuses 1750–1860, Harold Newman (Thomas Yoseloff, New York, 1967)

Venetian glass
Italian Blown Glass, Giovanni Mariacher, translated by M. Bullock and J. Capra (Thames & Hudson, London, 1961)
Old Venetian Glass, Karel Hettes, translated by Ota Vojtisek (Spring Books, London, 1960)

Vienna
Vienna Porcelain of the Du Paquier Period, J. F. Hayward (Barrie & Rockliff, London, 1952)

vinaigrette
English Vinaigrettes, E. Ellenbogen (Golden Head Press, Cambridge, 1956)

watches
The Country Life Book of Watches, T. P. Camerer Cuss (Country Life, London, 1967)
English and American Watches, George Daniels (Abelard-Schuman, London, 1967)
The Mechanism of the Watch, Sir James Swinburne (N. A. G. Press, London, 1950)
The Story of Watches, T. P. Camerer Cuss (MacGibbon & Kee, London, and Philosophical Library, New York, 1952)
Watches, G. H. Baillie (Connoisseur's Library, London, 1929)
Watches, C. Clutton & G. Daniels (B. T. Batsford, London, 1965)
The Watchmaker's Handbook, Claudius Saunier, translated by Tripplin & Rigg (9th impression, The Technical Press, London, 1945)
see also clock for titles covering both subjects

Wedgwood, Josiah
Decorative Wedgwood in Architecture and Furniture, Alison Kelly (Country Life, London, 1965)
Story of Wedgwood, Alison Kelly (Faber & Faber, London, 1962)
Wedgwood Ware, W. B. Honey (Faber & Faber, London, 1948)
Wedgwood Ware, Alison Kelly (Ward Lock, London, 1970)
The Collector's Book of Wedgwood, Marian Klamkin (David & Charles, Newton Abbot, Devon, 1972)

Windsor chair
The Windsor Chair, Thomas H. Ormsbee (Deerfield Books, New York, 1962)

wine label
The Book of the Wine Label, N. M. Penzer (Home & Van Thal, London, 1947)
Wine Labels, E. W. Whitworth (Cassell & Co, London, 1966)

Worcester
Coloured Worcester Porcelain of the First Period, H. Rissik Marshall (Ceramic Book Company, Newport, Monmouthshire, 1954)
Old Worcester China, John Bedford (Cassell & Co, London, 1966)
Illustrated Guide to Worcester Porcelain 1751–1793, Henry Sandon (Barrie & Jenkins, London, 1969)
Worcester Porcelain, Franklin A. Barrett (Faber & Faber, London, 1953)
Worcester Porcelain, Stanley W. Fisher (Ward Lock, London, 1968)
Worcester Porcelain, F. Severne Mackenna (F. Lewis, Leigh-on-Sea, Essex, 1950)

Yi period
Korean Pottery and Porcelain of the Yi Period, G. St-G. M. Gompertz (Faber & Faber, London, 1968)

ACKNOWLEDGMENTS

Illustrations for this book appear by courtesy of the people, collections, and organisations listed below. Many of the illustrations for which no photographer's name is given in parentheses were taken by Angelo Hornak and Karin Hoddle. The letters indicating the positions of illustrations on the page give the order, running down column by column, in which the left hand edges of the pictures appear.

American Museum in Bath, 44c, 53a, 53b, 82c, 99e, 101b, 103b, 141c, 175b, 178, 219d, 226d, 246a (on loan from the Corning Museum of Glass), 246c, 263a, 266a, 266c, 266d (on loan from the Corning Museum of Glass), 275b (on loan from the Corning Museum of Glass), 278a, 309c, 336a, 347a, 353a, 381b.
Asprey & Co., London, (A. C. Cooper and R. A. Fortt) 55b, 90a, 154c, 262b, 357a, 373b.
Baltimore Museum of Art, U.S.A. (Cooper Bridgeman Library) 23d.
Barrie & Jenkins Ltd., 56c, 56e, 62c, 114a, 230, 246b, 259c, 279a (by courtesy of Monsignor R. J. Foster, Rector of St. Mary's College, Oscott), 283c, 314c, 317a, 323a.
R. Bayne-Powell Collection, 103d, 105d, 106a, 139a, 179e, 234b, 251d.
Bethnal Green Museum, (Cooper Bridgeman Library) 215a.
Birmingham Assay Office, 109b, 168, 274e, 284b.
N. Bloom Ltd., London (A. C. Cooper), 228a, 250a, 280c, 330b, 346b, 365a, 375a.
British Museum, (Museum photos), 20a, 20b, 33b, 55a, 62a, 70b, 76b, 83b, 89b, 93d, 96c, 100b, 114b, 117b, 123a, 123b, 148a, 148b, 149b, 162b, 169c, 172b, 186b, 191b, 193a, 195a, 206c, 226c, 238a, 240, 245c, 249c, 251a, 256a, 270c, 276d, 278d, 280d, 292c, 296a, 297c, 305c, 312c, 314d, 323b, 326c, 328b, 342b, 350a, 355d, 356c, 366c, 367b, 368a, 373a.
Bristol City Art Gallery, 63b, 139d.
Brooklyn Museum, U.S.A., 46a (Dick S. Ramsay Fund).
Duke of Buccleuch Collection (Cooper Bridgeman Library) 324b.
Borough of Bury St. Edmunds (J. Gershom Parkington Memorial Collection) 25b, 32c, 91a, 99a, 159a, 241a, 261b, 355c.
Cameo Corner, London, 22a, 49b, 72a, 160b, 239a, 239b, 259b, 260d, 291d, 326b.
Cecil Higgins Art Gallery, Bedfordshire, 282c.
China Choice, London, 271b, 377b.
Christie, Manson & Woods, (A. C. Cooper & Michael Plomer) 27b, 26b, 30d, 33a, 34b, 37c, 39a, 43b, 47b, 54e, 59a, 63c, 65c, 67b, 73d, 74a, 77a, 94b, 97b, 108c, 118, 123d, 124a, 125b, 140a, 156c, 160c, 173a, 181b, 187b, 189a, 195c, 205, 218, 219b, 235a, 242a, 247b, 248a, 254a, 255, 259a, 267d, 271a, 282b, 287a, 287c, 289b, 290c, 305a, 306c, 315a, 316c, 330a, 334a, 334c, 338b, 347b, 352c, 357b, 368b, 372c, 373b, 378c, 378d.
Church of St. Katharine Cree, Leadenhall Street, 21.
Cinzano Collection, 192b (centre).
L. Coen Collection, Rome (Arte Fotografica), 175a.
Cooper Bridgeman Library, 24, 46b, 49a, 186a, 186e, 257a, 257b, 269b, 272c, 274b, 318a, 331a, 338c, 351a, 365b, 386c.
Corning Museum of Glass, U.S.A., 23b, 36, 38a, 101a, 200c, 214b, 224b, 227c, 319a, 325b, 331b.
Delomosne & Sons, London, (R. A. Fortt) 66a, 73a, 83c, 96b, 98a, 105a, 112a, 116, 128c, 180b, 188a, 220b, 366a, 376b, 377d.
Richard Dennis, London, 72b, 185a, 252b, 330c.
Exeter City Museum, 56f, 145a.
Fine Art Society, London, 87c.
Franses of Piccadilly, 27a, 65b, 249a.
Mrs T. Frith Collection (Rodney Todd-White), 69a.
Garrard, London, 37a, 77c.
Worshipful Company of Goldsmiths, (Peter Parkinson), 61b, 70c, 79d, 79e, 80b, 83a, 100a, 102b, 163b, 166a, 204c, 237b, 244b, 273a, 296c, 297b, 299a, 328c, 337b, 373c.
Eila Grahame Antiques, London, 350c.
Gabriela Gros Collection, 49d, 288b.
Hakim & Sons, London, (Rodney Todd-White), 49c, 54f, 77b, 132b, 139b, 152, 158b, 269c, 309b, 332c, 333b.
Hanley Museum & Art Gallery, Staffordshire, (Museum photos), 25a, 31, 42, 54a, 74b, 84f, 84g, 99c, 101c, 108a, 113b, 127b, 134, 145d, 153b, 166b, 173b, 174b, 176b, 190b, 206a, 215b, 221b, 223b, 227a, 227b, 236a, 247a, 260b, 264, 278c, 288a, 295b, 304c, 311a, 312d, 315b, 331c, 345b, 346a, 348a, 355a, 356a, 366b, 376a, 378b.
Haslam & Whiteway Ltd., London, 235b, 258a, 277b.
Peggy Hickman Collection, 44b (National Portrait Gallery photo), 84c (Cooper Bridgeman Library), 129b, 171b (Cooper Bridgeman Library), 234b (National Portrait Gallery photo), 292a (Cooper Bridgeman Library).
Henry Ford Museum & Greenfield Village Collection, Michigan, U.S.A., 38b, 56d, 120c, 121c, 153, 180a, 202b, 227d, 268b, 286b, 296b.
Henry Francis Dupont Winterthur Museum, Delaware, U.S.A., 68, 125a, 153c, 184a, 241c, 318b.
Angelo Hornak Library, 23a, 23c, 68b, 74d, 77a, 86a, 261c, 377e.
Earl of Iveagh Collection, (Cooper Bridgeman Library), 341a.
Anthony James & Son, London, 82b.
Jellinek & Sampson, London, 19c, 32a, 61a, 84b, 123c, 209d, 215c, 226a, 297a, 314b, 316a, 351d, 372b.
Jeremy Ltd., London, 310b.
Alexander Juran, London, 200b.
A. F. Kersting, 2.
Kunstmuseum, Düsseldorf, 208a, 222c.
Leonard Lassalle, Tonbridge Wells, 30b, 54c, 82a, 99d, 105c, 108b, 120a, 156a, 161c, 164a, 197d, 276a, 279b, 286a, 289a, 291a, 295a, 352a, 355c.
Peter Lazarus Collection, 67a, 132c, 136a, 146, 192b (left & right), 242c, 278c, 333a.
R. A. Lee, London, (R. A. Fortt), 29a, 109a, 128b, 203b, 675a.
Leeds City Art Gallery (Gilchrist Photography), 204d, 356b.
Lady Lever Art Gallery, Port Sunlight, (Museum photos), 27d, 30c, 51a, 69c, 89a, 91b, 140b, 140c, 141a, 165b, 185b, 199, 238c, 245b, 312a.
London Museum, 84d.
Thomas Lumley Ltd., London, (A. C. Cooper), 43a, 111c, 129a, 130b, 138, 149c, 154e, 166c, 179b, 217c, 244d, 257c, 268a, 298b, 316c, 320a, 328d, 338a, 342a, 345a.
Mallett & Son, London, (Richard Irwin), 37b, 40a, 52b, 54b, 61d, 86b, 111b, 174a, 216e, 258c, 263b, 267b, 267e, 270b, 272b, 284e, 317c, 326d.
Mallett at Bourdon House, London, 74c, 81b, 144a, 283a, 284d, 290b, 291c.
Mercers' Company, (Peter Parkinson), 321c.
Honourable Society of the Middle Temple, (Peter Parkinson), 320b.
Mobilier National, Paris, (Cooper Bridgeman Library), 163a.
Lennox Money, London, 67d, 170b.
Mount Vernon Ladies' Association of the Union, U.S.A., 41a.
Musée des Arts Decoratifs, Paris, (Cooper Bridgeman Library) 231a.
Museum of Applied Arts, Prague, 212b.
Museum of Fine Art, Boston, U.S.A. (M. & M. Karolik Collection) 335b.
Museum of National Antiquities, Stockholm, 143b.
National Museum of Wales, (Museum Photo), 243a.
New York Historical Society, U.S.A., 156b, 321b.
Old Sturbridge Village, U.S.A. 378a.
Osterley Park, Middlesex, 19b.
Palazzo Reale, Turin (Angelo Hornak Library), 304a.
Parke Bernet Galleries Inc., New York, 76a, 122c, 125c, 272a, 339b, 372a.
Frank Partridge & Son, London, (A. C. Cooper and R. A. Fortt), 48b, 79a, 84e, 89c, 103c, 105b, 124d, 128a, 132a, 133a, 142, 159b, 201c, 202a, 204b, 210a, 213b, 219c, 262c, 274d, 284c, 290a, 306a, 310a, 312b, 344c, 346c, 359d, 362, 364.
Percival David Foundation, London, (Museum photo), 94a, 172a, 188b, 198a, 207a, 213a, 261a, 298a, 325a, 332b, 340a, 343b, 348c, 354b, 379a; 380a.
Perez, London, 88b, 137b, 159c, 177c, 189b, 200a, 231b, 311c.
Phillips Auctioneers, London, (A. C. Cooper) 30a, 35b, 66c, 75, 78c, 81a, 91c, 102a, 103a, 113a, 122b, 137a, 199b, 252a, 305b.
Phillips of Hitchen Antiques, Ltd., (R. A. Fortt), 60b.
S. J. Phillips, London, (A. C. Cooper), 40b, 41b, 61c, 73b, 99b, 114d, 124e, 135a, 197b, 228d, 241b, 244a, 256b, 260c, 269a, 317b, 326a, 339a, 350b, 351b, 353b, 363a.
Pilgrim Society, Massachusetts, U.S.A., 62b.
Pilkington Museum of Glass, Lancashire, (Museum photos), 126c, 151, 161a, 161b, 190a, 207c, 319b, 360a.
Pratt & Burgess Ltd., London, 143c, 144b, 166d, 210b.
Private Collections, 46b, 51c, 191c, 228c.
P. D. Pryce Collection, 71b, 71c, 59b, 80c, 220a, 321a, 349b.
Rotherham Museum & Art Gallery, Yorkshire, 287b.
Royal College of Music Museum of Instruments, (A. C. Cooper) 169b, 182a, 184, 224a, 283b.
Leslie Scott, London, 172d, 237a, 249b, 322c.
Sheffield City Museum, (Cooper Bridgeman Library) 344b.
Shelburne Museum, Vermont, U.S.A., 24, 281.
S. J. Shrubsole Ltd., London, 27c, 50a, 70a, 92b, 106c, 107b, 135b, 143a, 202c, 226b, 229c, 251b, 280a, 322a, 327a, 329, 373a, 374c.
Sotheby & Co., (Sotheby photos) 47a, 50b, 50c, 51b, 56a, 58b, 66b, 72d, 87b, 95a, 110a, 121a, 123e, 130a, 145c, 154b, 172c, 173c, 177b, 186c, 186d, 194a, 194b, 209a, 209b, 209c, 210c, 216b, 221a, 233c, 236b, 262a, 271c, 277a, 304b, 308a, 322b, 324d, 334b, 335c, 337a, 348b, 350d, 359a, 374d, 375b, 381c. (A. C. Cooper) 22b, 34a, 35a, 41c, 54c, 56c, 76c, 95b, 122a, 124b, 124c, 126b, 127a, 139e, 148c, 165a, 171a, 175c, 176a, 197f, 214a, 217b, 225a, 233a, 253b, 277d, 282d, 306b, 307b, 314a, 351c, 355c, 359b.
(Sperryn's), 63a, 65a, 71a, 79b, 88a, 89e, 93c, 97a, 107a, 136b, 171c, 206d, 207b, 212a, 237c, 248b,

276c, 282a, 291b, 313b, 343a, 361c, 368a. (Norman Jones) 44a, 185c, 187a, 193b, 214c, 288c, 361b, 379b, 381d.
Sotheby's Belgravia, (Sotheby photos), 26a, 68c, 77d, 80a, 98b, 112c, 122d, 130c, 144c, 195b, 228b, 231c, 276b, 299b, 339c.
Simon Spero Collection, 59b, 80c, 204a, 219a, 220a, 250c, 349b, 377a.
Spink & Son, London (R. A. Fortt), 77e, 147, 177a, 267c, 362c.
Jerome Strauss Collection, Pennsylvania, U.S.A., 246d.
Strike One, London, 19a, 267a, 340b.
John Stuart Collection, 285b, 294b, 294c.
Talavera Antiques, London, 20c, 72c, 94c, 110c, 179a, 179d, 224c, 277c.
Temple Newsam House, Leeds, (Gilchrist Photography) 113c, 148d, 160a, 164b, 197e.
The Clock Shop, London, 126a.
Alan Tillman Antiques, London, 96a, 157, 233d, 273b, 313a, 327b, 333c, 349a.
University of Edinburgh, Russell Collection, (Tom Scott), 253a, 266b.
Usher Art Gallery, Lincoln, 222.
Joseph and Earle Vanderkar, 79c, 89d, 104, 149a, 197c.
Victoria & Albert Museum, London, (Museum photos), 29b, 39b, 60a, 87a, 93a, 131a, 143d, 145b, 179c, 183, 200d, 201b, 217a, 225c, 234a, 248c, 268c, 274a, 294a, 307a, 311b, 352b. (Sally Chappell), 28, 93b, 111a, 153a, 169a, 189c, 206b, 208b, 216c, 216d, 229a, 285a, 324c, 344d, 367a. (Cooper Bridgeman Library), 70d, 78b, 93c, 131b, 164c, 198b, 223a, 225b, 229b, 242b, 245a, 250b, 258b, 345c, 359c. (Angelo Hornak & Karin Hoddle), 34c, 112b, 114c, 114e, 117a, 119a, 139c, 141b, 158a, 191, 192a, 201a, 243c, 245b, 252c, 292b, 293a, 307a, 307c, 324a, 328e, 335a, 354a, 362b, 363b.
Vigo-Sternberg Galleries, London, 133b.
Wadsworth Atheneum, Connecticut, U.S.A., 48a.
James Walker Collection, (Peter Parkinson), 29c, 119b, 120b, 203a, 260a, 279c, 328c, 339d, 341b.
By Courtesy of the Trustees of the Wallace Collection, 58, 67c, 72e, 101d, 105c, 181a, 212c, 370b.
Josiah Wedgwood & Sons Ltd., 52a, 197a, 280b, 371.
Colonel Samuel Whitbread Collection, Southill Park, (Cooper Bridgeman Lbirary), 244c.
Winifred Williams Ltd., London & Eastbourne, 74d, 84a, 119c, 154d, 162c, 232, 251c, 295c, 344a, 362a, 377c.
Harriet Wynter, Arts & Sciences, London, 32b, 121b, 162a, 222b, 270a, 309a, 331d, 332a, 369.
Yale University Art Gallery, U.S.A., (Gift of C. Sanford Bull, B.A.) 107a.